SIMON REYNOLDS

RIP IT UP AND START AGAIN

Post-punk 1978-84

faber and faber

First published in 2005
by Faber and Faber Limited
3 Queen Square London WC1N 3AU
This paperback edition published in 2006

Typeset by Faber and Faber Limited
Printed in England by Mackays of Chatham, plc

A CIP record for this book
is available from the British Library

ISBN 978-0-571-21570-6
ISBN 0-571-21570-X

10 9 8 7 6 5 4 3

To my brother Tim, who turned me on to punk in the first place,
my son Kieran,
and
in memory of Rebecca Press
and Burhan Tufail

CONTENTS

PART TWO: NEW POP AND NEW ROCK

For Discography and Discography Part 2: Post-punk Esoterica (the latter featuring extensive commentary) go to the Faber website www.faber.co.uk

For footnotes, transcripts, links and other post-punk material go to the *Rip It Up and Start Again* site at www.simonreynolds.net

ILLUSTRATIONS

AUTHOR'S NOTE

Grappling with a period as extended – seven years, 1978–1984 – and teeming with simultaneous activity as post-punk presented some problems in terms of organising the material. With so many things happening in parallel, straight chronology obviously wasn't an option. My solution was to break up the period into micro-narratives, most of them determined by geography: city-based scenes (New York's No Wave and mutant disco eras, for instance), regions (Ohio's Cleveland–Akron scene), or whole countries (Scotland). Other chapters are based on genre or sensibility: industrial, synthpop, New Pop, and so forth. Some are oriented around particular clusters of artists: the milieux of Rough Trade and 2-Tone, along with kindred-spirit groups not on either label. In other cases, two artists are paired because of direct links and/or an affinity: The Pop Group and The Slits shared common members and were on the same label at one point; Wire and Talking Heads had no such links but still seemed to belong together. Because each micro-narrative is followed from its earliest beginnings to its conclusion (or what felt like the best cut-off point), *Rip It Up and Start Again* proceeds in a sort of three steps forward, two steps back fashion. But, by and large, each new chapter starts a little bit further along the historical timeline than the previous one, and by the end of the book the events are taking place in 1983–4. For a sense of fully integrated chronological flow, consult the Timeline near the end of the book, and marvel at the sheer density of simultaneous post-punk action.

INTRODUCTION

Punk bypassed me almost completely. Thirteen going on fourteen at the time, growing up in a Hertfordshire commuter town, I have only the faintest memories of 1977-and-all-that. I vaguely recall photo spreads of spiky-haired punks in a Sunday colour supplement, but that's it really. The Pistols swearing on television, 'God Save the Queen' versus the Silver Jubilee, an entire culture convulsed and quaking – I simply *did not notice*. As for what I *was* into and up to instead – well, it's a bit of a haze. Was 1977 the year I wanted to be a cartoonist? Or, having moved on to science fiction, did I spend my time systematically working through the local library's cache of Ballard, Pohl, Dick? All I know for sure is that pop music scarcely impinged on my consciousness.

My younger brother Tim got into punk first, a godawful racket coming through the bedroom wall. On one of the many occasions I went in there to complain, I must have lingered. The profanity hooked me first (I *was* fourteen, after all): Johnny Rotten's 'Fuck this and fuck that/Fuck it all and fuck her fucking brat'. More than the naughty words themselves, though, it was the vehemence and virulence of Rotten's delivery – those percussive 'fucks', the demon-glee of the rolled 'r's in 'brrrrrrat'. There's been a thousand carefully reasoned theses validating the movement's sociocultural import, but if anyone's really honest, the sheer monstrous *evil* of punk was a huge part of its appeal. The sickness of Devo, for instance – I'd never heard anything so creepy and debased as their early Stiff single 'Jocko Homo' b/w 'Mongoloid', brought round to our house by a far more advanced friend.

When I got into the Pistols and the rest, around the middle of 1978, I'd no idea that this was all officially 'dead'. The Pistols were long split; Rotten had already formed Public Image Ltd. Because I'd been otherwise occupied and missed the entire birth, life and death of punk, I also cannily skipped the mourning after – that sickening '78 crash experienced by almost everybody who was 'there' and aware during the exhilarating '77 rush. My belated discovery of the movement coincided with when things began to pick up again, with what soon became known as 'post-punk' – the subject of this book. So I was listening to X-Ray Spex's *Germ Free Adolescents*, but also the first PiL album, Talking Heads' *Fear of Music*, and *Cut* by The Slits. It was all one bright, bursting surge of excitement.

Music historians celebrate being in the right place at the right time: those critical moments and locations when and where revolutions are spawned. Which is tough on the rest of us, stuck in suburbia or the provinces. This book is for – and about – the people who were not there at the right time and place (in punk's case, London and New York *circa* 1976), but who nevertheless refused to believe it was all over and done with before they'd had a chance to join in.

Young people have a biological right to be excited about the times in which they're living. If you are very lucky, that hormonal urgency is matched by the insurgency of the era – your innate adolescent need for amazement and belief coincides with a period of objective abundance. The prime years of post-punk – the half-decade from 1978 to 1982 – were like that: a *fortune*. I've come pretty close since, but I've never been quite as exhilarated as I was back then. Certainly, I've never been so utterly focused on the present.

As I recall it now, I *never* bought any old records. Why would you? There were so many new records that you had to have that there was simply no earthly reason to investigate the past. I had cassettes of the best of The Beatles and the Stones taped off friends, a copy of The Doors' anthology *Weird Scenes Inside the Goldmine*, but that was it. Partly this was because the reissue culture that inundates us today didn't exist then; record companies even *deleted* albums. As a result, huge swaths of the recent past were virtually inaccessible. But mainly it was because there was no time to look back wistfully to something through which you'd never lived. There was too much happening right now.

I didn't think of it in this way at the time, but, in retrospect, as a distinct pop cultural epoch, 1978–82 rivals those fabled years between 1963 and 1967 commonly known as the 'sixties'. The post-punk era certainly rivals the sixties in terms of the sheer amount of great music created, the spirit of adventure and idealism that infused it, and the way that the music seemed inextricably connected to the political and social turbulence of the times. There was a similar mood-blend of anticipation and anxiety, a mania for all things new and futuristic coupled with fear of what the future had in store.

Not that I'm especially patriotic or anything, but it's also striking how both the sixties and post-punk were periods during which Britannia ruled the pop waves. Which is why this book focuses on the UK, plus those American cities where punk happened in any major way: the twin bohemian capitals of New York and San Francisco; Ohio's post-industrial dreadzones Cleveland and Akron; college towns like Boston, Massachusetts, and Athens, Georgia. (For reasons of sanity and space, I have regretfully decided not to grapple with European post-punk or Australia's fascinating but deep underground scene, except for certain key groups such as DAF, Einstürzende Neubauten and The Birthday Party, all of whom significantly impacted on Anglo-American rock culture.) In America, punk and post-punk were much less mainstream than in the UK, where you could hear The Fall and Joy Division on national radio, and where groups as extreme as PiL had Top 20 hits which, via *Top of the Pops*, were beamed into ten million households.

I have subjective and objective reasons for writing this book. Foremost among the latter is that post-punk is a period that's been severely neglected by historians. There are scores of books on punk rock and the events of 1976–7, but virtually nothing on what happened next. Conventional histories of punk generally end with its 'death' in 1978, when the Sex Pistols auto-destructed. In the more extreme or sloppy accounts – TV histories of rock are particularly culpable – it is implied that nothing of real consequence happened between *Never Mind the Bollocks* and *Nevermind*, between punk and grunge. Even after the boom in eighties nostalgia, that decade still tends to be regarded as a wasteland redeemed only by mavericks like Prince or Pet Shop Boys, and such worthies as REM and Springsteen. The early eighties especially are still viewed as a campy comedy zone – an era characterized by clumsily pretentious stabs at video-as-artform, by English eyeliner-and-synth fops with silly haircuts. Fragments of the post-punk story have emerged here and there, usually in biographies of specific bands, but nobody has attempted to go for the big picture and capture post-punk as what it was: a counter-culture that was fragmented yet shared a common belief that music could and should change the world.

Being as impartial and detached as I can manage here, it seems to me that the long 'aftermath' of punk up to 1984 was musically *way* more interesting than what happened in 1976–7 itself, when punk staged its back-to-basics rock 'n' roll revival. Even in terms of its broader cultural influence, it's arguable that punk had its most provocative repercussions long after its supposed demise. That's part of this book's argument: the notion that revolutionary movements in pop culture have their widest impact after the 'moment' has allegedly passed, when ideas spread from the metropolitan bohemian elites and hipster cliques that originally 'own' them, and reach the suburbs and the regions. For instance, the counter-culture and radical ideas of the sixties had far more currency in the mainstream during the first half of the seventies, when long hair and drug-taking became common, when feminism filtered through to popular culture with 'independent women' movies and TV shows.

Another objective reason for writing this book is that there's been a huge resurgence of interest in the period of late, with compilations and reissues of archival post-punk, and a crop of new bands who've modelled themselves on such post-punk subgenres as No Wave, punk-funk, mutant disco and industrial. A young generation has finally emerged who have no memory of this era – some weren't even born in 1984, when this book ends – and find the period massively intriguing. Through being neglected for so long, post-punk has become one of the few untapped resources for the retro industry, inspiring a gold-rush frenzy.

Subjective reason #1 for the book is my memory of this period as superabundant, a golden age of newness and nowness that made you feel like you were moving at high speed into the future. Subjective reason #2 relates more to the present. As a rock critic, when you reach a certain age, you begin to wonder if all the mental and emotional energy you've invested in this music thing was such a shrewd move. Not exactly a crisis of confidence, but a creasing of certainty. In my case, this prompted me to wonder when, exactly, it was that I made the decision to embark upon a life of taking music seriously. What made me believe music could matter this much? Of course, it was growing up in the post-punk era. That nearsimultaneous double whammy of the Sex Pistols' *Bollocks* and PiL's *Metal Box* set me on my present course. But it was also the writing in the British music press around the time of these records, and records like them, that formed me – writing that, week by thrilling week, explored and tested just how seriously you could take music (a debate that continues to this day in different forms and other places).

So this book is in part a reckoning with my younger self. And the answer I came up with is . . .

PROLOGUE: The Unfinished Revolution

'The Sex Pistols sang "No Future", but there *is* a future and we're trying to build one.'
Allen Ravenstine, Pere Ubu, 1978

By summer 1977, punk had become a parody of itself. Many of the movement's original participants felt that something open-ended and full of possibilities had degenerated into a commercial formula. Worse, it had proved a rejuvenating shot in the arm to the established record industry that the punks had hoped to overthrow. Where to now?

It was at this point that punk's fragile unity between working-class kids and arty, middle-class bohemians began to fracture. On one side, you had the populist 'real punks' (later to evolve into the Oi! movement) who believed that the music needed to stay accessible and unpretentious, the angry voice of the streets. On the other side was the vanguard that came to be known as 'post-punk', who saw 1977 not as a return to raw rock 'n' roll but the chance to make a break with tradition, and who defined punk as an imperative to constant change.

Oi! and its approximate American counterpart 'hardcore' deserve their own books (indeed, they already have some: Stewart Home's *Cranked Up Really High* and various oral histories of hardcore). This book, though, is a celebration of post-punk: bands like PiL, Joy Division, Talking Heads, Throbbing Gristle, Contortions and Scritti Politti, who dedicated themselves to fulfilling punk's uncompleted musical revolution, and explored new sonic possibilities through their embrace of electronics, noise, reggae's dub techniques, disco production, jazz and the classical avant-garde.

Some diehards accused these experimentalists of merely lapsing back into what punk had originally aimed to destroy: art-rock elitism. And it's

xvii

true that a high proportion of post-punk musicians had art-school backgrounds. The No Wave scene in New York, for instance, was virtually wall-to-wall painters, film-makers, poets and performance artists. Gang of Four, Cabaret Voltaire, Devo, Wire, The Raincoats, DAF . . . these are just a handful of the bands started by fine art or design graduates. Especially in Britain, art schools have long functioned as a state-subsidized bohemia, where working-class youth too unruly for a life of labour mingle with slumming middle-class kids too wayward for a career in middle management. After graduation, many turn to pop music as a way to sustain the 'experimental lifestyle' they'd enjoyed at college, while maybe, just maybe, making a living.

Of course, not everybody in post-punk attended art school or even university. Many of the key figures in British post-punk come from the socially indeterminate grey area where upper working class bleeds into lower middle class. Self-educated in a scattered, omnivorous fashion, figures like John Lydon and The Fall's Mark E. Smith fit the syndrome of the anti-intellectual intellectual, ravenously well read but scornful of academia and suspicious of 'art' in all its institutionalized forms. But, really, what could be more arty than wanting to destroy art by smashing the boundaries that keep it sealed off from everyday life?

Those seven post-punk years from the beginning of 1978 to the end of 1984 saw the systematic ransacking of twentieth-century modernist art and literature. The entire period looks like an attempt to replay virtually every major modernist theme and technique via the medium of pop music. Cabaret Voltaire borrowed their name from Dada; Pere Ubu took theirs from Alfred Jarry. Talking Heads turned a Hugo Ball sound-poem into a tribal-disco dance track. Gang of Four, inspired by Brecht and Godard's alienation effects, tried to deconstruct rock even as they rocked hard. Lyricists absorbed the radical science fiction of William S. Burroughs, J. G. Ballard and Philip K. Dick, and techniques of collage and cut-up were transplanted into the music. Marcel Duchamp, mediated by 1960s Fluxus, was the patron saint of No Wave. The record-cover artwork of the period matched the neo-modernist aspirations of the words and music, with such graphic designers as Malcolm Garrett and Peter Saville, and labels like Factory and Fast Product, drawing from Constructivism, De Stijl, Bauhaus, John Heartfield and Die Neue Typographie. This frenzied looting of the archives of modernism culminated with the renegade pop label ZTT – short for Zang Tuum Tumb, a snatch of Italian Futurist prose-poetry – and their conceptual group

xviii

The Art of Noise, named in homage to Luigi Russolo's manifesto for a Futurist music.

Taking the word 'modernist' in a less specific sense, the post-punk bands were firmly committed to the idea of making modern music. They were totally confident that there were still places to go with rock, a whole new future to invent. For the post-punk vanguard, punk had failed because it attempted to overthrow rock's Old Wave using conventional music (fifties rock 'n' roll, garage punk, mod) that *predated* the dinosaur megabands like Pink Floyd and Led Zeppelin. The post-punks set forth in the belief that 'radical content demands radical form'.

One curious byproduct of this conviction that rock 'n' roll had outlived its usefulness was the mountainous abuse heaped on Chuck Berry. A key source for punk rock, via the guitar playing of Johnny Thunders and Steve Jones, Berry became a negative touchstone, endlessly namechecked as a must-avoid. Perhaps the first example of Berry-phobia occurs as early as the Sex Pistols demos exhumed on *The Great Rock 'n' Roll Swindle*. The band begins jamming on 'Johnny B. Goode'. Then Johnny Rotten – the group's closet aesthete, who'd go on to form the archetypal post-punk outfit Public Image Ltd – half-heartedly jabbers the tune before groaning: 'Oh fuck, it's *awful* . . . Stop it, I fucking hate it . . . AAARRRGH'. Lydon's howl of disgusted exhaustion – he sounds like he's choking, suffocated by dead sound – was echoed by scores of post-punk groups: Cabaret Voltaire, for instance, complained, 'rock 'n' roll is not about regurgitating Chuck Berry riffs'.

Rather than rama-lama riffing or bluesy chords, the post-punk pantheon of guitar innovators favoured angularity, a clean and brittle spikiness. For the most part, they shunned solos, apart from brief bursts of lead integrated with more rhythm-oriented playing. Instead of a 'fat' sound, players like Talking Heads' David Byrne, The Fall's Martin Bramah and The Slits' Viv Albertine preferred 'skinny rhythm guitar', often inspired by reggae or post-James Brown funk. This more compact, scrawny style of playing didn't fill every corner of the soundscape. Bands tried to do innovative things with structure, too. Drawing on Brian Eno's solo albums or Captain Beefheart's jagged Cubist R&B, groups such as Devo, XTC and Wire broke up the flow with a stop–start anti-groove approach – a nervous, twitchy style dubbed 'geometric jerky quickstep' by *New Musical Express* writer Miles.

It wasn't just the guitar that was radicalized: every instrument responded to the challenge of renewing rock music. Drummers Hugo

Burnham of Gang of Four, Steve Morris of Joy Division, Budgie of The Banshees, and The Raincoats' Palmolive avoided the clichés of heavy rock and developed new rhythm patterns that were starker and often 'inverted' in feel. Tom-toms were typically used to create a kind of tumbling 'tribal' propulsion. The bass abandoned its hitherto inconspicuous supportive role and stepped forward as the lead instrumental voice, fulfilling a melodic function even as it pushed the groove. In this respect, post-punk bassists were playing catch-up with the innovations of Sly Stone and James Brown, and learning from contemporary roots reggae and dub. Pursuing a militant and aggressively monolithic sound, punk had mostly purged 'blackness' from rock, severing the music's links to R&B while simultaneously rejecting disco as escapist and vapid. By 1978, though, the concept of a dangerous dance music began to circulate in post-punk circles, expressed in such terms as 'perverted disco' and 'avant-funk'.

Along with dance music's sensuality and swing, punk had also rejected all those hyphenated compound sounds (jazz-rock, country-rock, folk-rock, classical-rock, etc.) that proliferated in the early seventies. To punks, this kind of thing smacked of virtuoso showing off, meandering jam sessions, pious hippy platitudes about how 'it's all music, man'. Defining itself against this limp, 'all gates open' eclecticism, punk proposed a strident purism. While 'fusion' remained a discredited notion, post-punk ushered in a new phase of looking outside rock's narrow parameters – to Black America and Jamaica, obviously, but also to Africa and other zones of what would later be called 'world music'.

Post-punk also rebuilt bridges with rock's own past, vast swaths of which had been placed off limits when punk declared 1976 to be Year Zero. In the process, a myth was installed that still persists to this day in some quarters: the notion of the pre-punk early seventies as a wasteland. Actually, it was one of the richest, most diverse periods in rock history. The post-punk groups, tentatively at first (after all, no one wanted to be accused of being a crypto-hippie or progressive rocker in disguise), rediscovered those riches, drawing inspiration from the arty end of glam rock (Bowie and Roxy Music), or from out-rock eccentrics such as Beefheart, and in some cases the more acute end of prog (Soft Machine, King Crimson, even Zappa). There's a sense in which post-punk *was* 'progressive rock', only drastically streamlined and reinvigorated, with better haircuts and a more austere sensibility (no ostentatious virtuosity). In hindsight, it's punk rock that seems the historical aberration – a clear-the-decks return to basic rock 'n' roll that ultimately turned out to be a brief blip in an otherwise unbroken continuum of art-rock spanning the seventies from start to finish.

If truth be known, some of the definitive post-punk groups – Devo, Throbbing Gristle, Cabaret Voltaire, This Heat – were pre-punk entities, existing in some form or other for several years before The Ramones' 1976 debut album. Punk threw the record industry into confusion, making the majors vulnerable to suggestion, and fluxing up all the aesthetic rules so that anything abnormal or extreme suddenly had a chance. Through this breach in the wall of business-as-usual, all sorts of obscure freaks broke through and grabbed an opportunity for a wider audience.

It was a particular kind of 'art rock' to which post-punk pledged allegiance, though. Not prog's attempt to merge amplified electric guitars with nineteenth-century classical instrumentation and extended compositions, but the minimal-is-maximal lineage that runs from The Velvet Underground to Krautrock and the more intellectual end of glam. For a certain kind of hipster, the music that sustained them through the 'wasteland' of the seventies was made by a cluster of kindred spirits – Lou Reed, John Cale, Nico, Iggy Pop, David Bowie, Brian Eno – who were united by their descent from or debts to The Velvet Underground, and who collaborated with one another in various combinations throughout this period. Bowie, for instance, had associations with almost all of these people at various points, either producing their records or collaborating with them. He was the connector, rock's greatest dilettante: always chasing the next edge, always moving on. More than anyone, it was he who was the inspiration for post-punk's ethos of perpetual change.

1977 might have been the year of The Clash's debut and the Pistols' *Never Mind the Bollocks*, but in truth post-punk music was far more deeply affected by the four Bowie-related albums of that year: his own *Low* and *'Heroes'*; and Iggy Pop's *The Idiot* and *Lust for Life*, both produced by Bowie. All recorded in Berlin, this astonishing series of albums hugely impacted listeners who already suspected that punk rock was turning out to be just more of the same-old-same-old. The Bowie and Iggy albums proposed a shift away from American rock 'n' roll towards Europe and a cool, controlled sound modelled on the Teutonic 'motorik' rhythms of Kraftwerk and Neu!; a sound where synthesizers had as big a role as guitars. In interviews, Bowie talked of his move to Berlin as an attempt to extricate himself from America both musically (in terms of the soul and funk that shaped *Young Americans*) and spiritually (an escape from the quicksand decadence of rock 'n' roll Los Angeles). Informed by this deliberate feat of dislocation and self-alienation, *Low* lived up to the album's original working title, '*New Music Night and Day*', most thoroughly on its astonishing second side, a suite of twilight-gloomy instrumental atmospheres and yearning, wordless plainsong. *Low*, said Bowie, was a response to 'seeing the Eastern Bloc, how East Berlin survives in the midst of it, which was something that I couldn't express in words. Rather it required *textures*.' Which is why he leaned on Eno, texturologist par excellence, as his mentor and right-hand man during the making of *Low* and '*Heroes*'. Already a post-punk icon for his synth-noise in Roxy Music and his proto-New Wave solo albums, Eno, in the wake of the Berlin/Bowie albums, became one of the great producers of the era. He documented the New York No Wave scene and worked with Devo, Talking Heads, Ultravox and, much later, U2 (Bono quipped, 'Some bands went to art school; we went to Brian Eno').

Bowie and Eno's New Europeanism chimed with the post-punk feeling that America – or, at least, *white* America – was politically and musically the enemy. When it came to contemporary inspiration, post-punk looked beyond the rock 'n' roll heartland: to urban black America, to Jamaica and to Europe. For many of the post-punk persuasion, 1977's most significant singles weren't 'White Riot' or 'God Save the Queen', but Kraftwerk's 'Trans-Europe Express', a metronomic, metal-on-metal threnody for the industrial era, and Donna Summer's Giorgio Moroder-produced porno-Eurodisco smash 'I Feel Love', a track made almost entirely from synthetic sounds. Moroder's electronic disco and Kraftwerk's serene synthpop conjured glistening visions of the Neu Europa – modern, forward-looking, and pristinely post-rock in the sense of having absolutely no debts to American music. The idea that synths, sequencers and machine rhythms offered the possibility of an authentically un-American sonic identity proved enormously seductive to such fledgling bands as The Human League and Soft Cell.

Black rhythm, European electronics, Jamaican production wizardry: these were the coordinates for post-punk's radicalization of form. But what of the radical *content*? Punk's approach to politics – raw rage or agit-prop protest – seemed too blunt or too preachy to the post-punk vanguard, so they tried to develop more sophisticated and oblique techniques. Gang of Four and Scritti Politti abandoned tell-it-like-it-is denunciation for songs that exposed and dramatized the mechanisms of

xxii

power in everyday life: consumerism, sexual relationships, common-sense notions of what's natural or 'obvious', the ways in which seemingly spontaneous, innermost feelings are actually scripted by larger forces. 'Question everything' was the catchphrase of the day, closely followed by 'the personal is political'. But at the same time, the most acute of these groups captured the way in which 'the political is personal' – how current events and the actions of governments invade everyday life and haunt each individual's private dreams and nightmares.

When it came to politics in the conventionally understood sense – the world of demonstrations, grass-roots activism, organized struggle – post-punk was more ambivalent. Art students and autodidacts alike tended to prize individuality. As bohemian nonconformists, they were usually made uncomfortable by calls to solidarity or toeing the party line. They saw the plain-speaking demagoguery of overtly politicized groups like The Tom Robinson Band and Crass as far too literal and non-aesthetic, and regarded their soapbox sermonizing as either condescending to the listener or a pointless exercise in preaching to the converted. So, while most British post-punk groups participated in the Rock Against Racism tours and festivals of the era, they were wary of both RAR itself and its sister organization, the Anti-Nazi League, suspecting them of being thinly disguised fronts for the militant, left-wing Socialist Workers Party (who valued music purely as a tool for radicalizing and mobilizing youth). At the same time, post-punk inherited punk's dreams of resuscitating rock music as a force to change if not the world, then at least the consciousness of individual listeners. Crucially, though, this radicalism was manifested through words and sound equally, rather than the music serving as a mere platform for agit-prop. As for the words, their subversive potential pertained to their formal aesthetic properties (how innovative they were in terms of language or narrative) rather than simply to the 'message' or critique they delivered.

Post-punk was a period of astonishing experimentation with lyrical and vocal technique. The Fall's Mark E. Smith invented a kind of North of England magic realism that mixed industrial grime with the unearthly and uncanny, voiced through a unique one-note delivery somewhere between amphetamine-spiked rant and alcohol-addled yarn. David Byrne's flustered, neurotic mannerisms perfectly suited his wry, dry examination of such non-rock subjects as animals, bureaucracy, 'buildings and food'. The Pop Group's Mark Stewart yowled imagistic incantations like a cross between Antonin Artaud and James Brown. This was a boom period for idiosyncratic female expression, too, with the previously unheard perspectives and dissonant tones of The Slits, Lydia Lunch, Ludus and The Raincoats. Other singer-lyricists – Joy Division's Ian Curtis, Magazine's Howard Devoto, Paul Haig of Josef K – were steeped in the shadowy unease and crippling anxiety of Dostoevksy, Kafka, Conrad and Beckett. Three-minute mini-novels, their songs grappled with the classic existentialist quandaries: the struggle and agony of having a 'self'; love versus isolation; the absurdity of existence; the human capacity for perversity and spite; the perennial 'suicide – why the hell *not?*'

It's no coincidence that Manchester and Sheffield, both declining industrial cities in the North of England, formed the bleak heartland of British post-punk. Bands with similar lyrical preoccupations and approaches to sound emerged in Cleveland, Ohio (the once formidable but now ailing heart of America's Rust Belt), and Düsseldorf (regional capital of Germany's densely industrialized Ruhr). In parallel but distinct ways, Cleveland's Pere Ubu, Sheffield's The Human League and Cabaret Voltaire, Manchester's Joy Division and Düsseldorf's DAF all used synthesizers. To varying degrees, they all grappled with both the problems and the possibilities of human existence in an increasingly technological world. Growing up in cities physically and mentally scarred by the violent nineteenth-century transition from rural folkways to the unnatural rhythms of industrial life, these groups had a privileged vantage point from which to ponder the dilemma of alienation versus adaptation in a machine age.

And yet, as colour-depleted and crumbling as these now *post*-industrial cities were, it was possible – perhaps *essential* – to aestheticize their panoramas of decay. The post-punk groups found two writers especially inspiring in this regard. Anthony Burgess's 1962 novel *A Clockwork Orange*, set in a near-future Britain, features roving gangs of marauding youths midway between skinheads and punks, vicious dandies who live for gratuitous ultraviolence. Both the book and the 1970 Stanley Kubrick film version capture the desolate psychogeography of the new Britain created by the 'visionary' town planners and fashionably Brutalist architects of the 1960s – all high-rise blocks, shadowy underpasses, concrete pedestrian bridges and walkways. This same traumatized urban landscape served as the backdrop – but also, in a sense, the main *character* – in J. G. Ballard's classic seventies trilogy of *Crash*,

Concrete Island and *High-Rise*. Likewise, Ballard's earlier short stories and cataclysm novels obsessively conjure an eerie, inhuman beauty from vistas of dereliction – abandoned airfields, disused weapons ranges, drained reservoirs, deserted cities. In interviews, Ballard waxed lyrical about the 'magic and poetry one feels when looking at a junkyard filled with old washing machines, or wrecked cars, or old ships rotting in some disused harbour . . . An enormous mystery and magic surrounds these objects.' Pere Ubu and Joy Division made music that captured the bereft Ballardian beauty of their home towns. Shaped by Cleveland and Manchester in the seventies but not wholly reducible to time and place, their music existed in the borderland between historical and geographic specifics and timeless, universal fears and longings.

The post-punk era overlaps two distinct phases in British and American politics: the centre-left governments of Labour prime minister Jim Callaghan and Democratic president Jimmy Carter, who were then near-simultaneously displaced by the ascent of Margaret Thatcher and Ronald Reagan, respectively – a swing to the right that ushered in twelve years of conservative politics in America, and a full eighteen in Britain. The post-punk period begins with the paralysis and stagnation of left-liberal politics, seen as fatally compromised and failed, and ends with monetarist economic policy in the ascendant, mass unemployment and widening social divisions.

Especially in the early years, 1978–80, these dislocations produced a tremendous sense of dread and tension. Britain saw a resurgence of far right and neo-fascist parties, both in electoral politics and in the bloody form of street violence. The Cold War reached a new depth of frigidity. Britain's leading music magazine, *New Musical Express*, ran a regular column called 'Plutonium Blondes' about the deployment of American Cruise missiles in Britain. Singles like Kate Bush's 'Breathing' and UB40's 'The Earth Dies Screaming' brought nuclear dread into the Top 20, and countless groups – from This Heat on their concept album *Deceit* to Young Marble Giants with their classic single 'Final Day' – sang about Armageddon as a real and imminent prospect.

Part of the poignancy of this period of dissident music is its increasingly out of synch relationship with the broader culture, which was veering towards the right. Thatcher and Reagan represented a massive backlash against both the counter-cultural sixties and the permissive seventies. Stranded in a kind of internal cultural exile, post-punk tried to build an alternative culture with its own independent infrastructure of labels, distribution and record stores. The need for 'complete control' (which The Clash could sing about only bitterly in the song of that title, having ceded it to CBS) led to the birth of pioneering independent labels Rough Trade, Mute, Factory, SST, Cherry Red and Subterranean. The concept of do-it-yourself proliferated like a virus, spawning a pandemic of samizdat culture – bands releasing their own records, local promoters organizing gigs, musicians' collectives creating spaces where bands could play, small magazines and fanzines taking on the role of an alternative media. Independent labels represented a sort of anti-corporate micro-capitalism based less on left-wing ideology than the conviction that major labels were too sluggish, unimaginative and commercially minded to nurture the most crucial music of the day.

Post-punk was concerned as much with the politics of music as with anything in the 'real world'. It aimed to sidestep or sabotage rock's dream factory, this leisure industry that channelled youth's energy and idealism into a cultural cul-de-sac, while generating huge amounts of revenue for corporate capitalism. Coined by the Liverpool group Wah! Heat, the term 'rockism' spread as a shorthand for a set of stale routines that restricted creativity and suppressed surprise: conventions of production (like the use of reverb to give records a 'live', auditorium sound); the predictable rituals of touring and performing (some post-punk bands refused to do encores; others experimented with multimedia and performance art). Aiming to break the trance of rock-business-as-usual and jolt the listener into awareness, post-punk teemed with meta-music critiques and mini-manifestos: songs like Television Personalities' 'Part Time Punks' and Subway Sect's 'A Different Story' addressed punk's failure or speculated about the future.

Some of post-punk's acute self-consciousness came from the radically self-critical sensibility of 1970s conceptual art, in which the discourse around the work was as important as the art objects themselves. The meta-music nature of much post-punk helps to explain the extraordinary power of the rock press during this period, with some critics playing major roles in shaping and directing the culture itself.

This new role for the music papers began with punk. Because radio and TV largely spurned that movement, because the mainstream print media was largely hostile, because for a while it was even hard for punk bands to play gigs, the UK's weekly music papers assumed huge importance. From 1978 to 1981, market leader *New Musical Express* had a circulation hovering between 200,000 and 270,000, while the combined sales of it, *Sounds*, *Melody Maker* and *Record Mirror* were over 600,000. Factor in the unusually high 'pass-on' rate – each copy was generally read by several people – and you probably have a combined readership of two million.

Punk mobilized a huge audience who were looking for the way forward and were ready to be guided. The music press had virtually no rivals for this function – monthly general-interest magazines such as *Q* or style magazines like *The Face* didn't yet exist, while pop coverage in quality newspapers was meagre. As a result, the weekly music papers had enormous influence, and individual writers – the driven ones, those with a messianic complex – enjoyed a prestige and power barely imaginable today. By identifying (and exaggerating) the connections between groups and articulating the unwritten manifestos of the resulting movements or city-based scenes, the critics could intensify and accelerate the development of post-punk music. In *Sounds* from late 1977 onwards, Jon Savage championed 'New Musick', the industrial/dystopian sci-fi side of post-punk. Paul Morley at the *NME* progressed from mythologizing Manchester and Joy Division to dreaming up the concept of New Pop. *Sounds*' Garry Bushell was the demagogue/ideologue of Oi! and Real Punk. The combination of 'activist critics' and meta-minded musicians whose work was a form of 'active criticism' fuelled a syndrome of runaway evolution: trend competed with trend and each new development was swiftly followed by a backlash or a swerve. All of this contributed to the surging-into-the-future feeling of the era, while simultaneously accelerating the disintegration of punk into squabbling factions.

Musicians and journalists fraternized a lot during this period – their kinship related perhaps to a sense of solidarity, comrades in the culture war of post-punk versus Old Wave, but also in the era's political struggles. Roles shifted: some journalists made records; musicians – Pere Ubu's David Thomas (under the pen-name Crocus Behemoth), Joy Division's Steven Morris, Manicured Noise's Steve Walsh – wrote record reviews and features. Because so many people involved in post-punk were non-musicians initially, or came from other artistic fields, the gap between those who 'did' and those who commented on what they were doing wasn't nearly as wide as in the pre-punk era. Throbbing Gristle's Genesis P-Orridge, for instance, described himself as a writer and thinker first and foremost, and not really a musician at all. He even used the word 'journalist' as a *positive* descriptive term for TG's documentarian approach to harsh post-industrial realities.

Changes in the style and methods of rock writing heightened the post-punk sensation of moving at speed into a bold new era. Music journalists in the early seventies typically blended traditional critical virtues (objectivity, solid reporting, authoritative knowledge) with a New Journalism-influenced 'rock 'n' roll' looseness and informality. This jammed-out, chatty style, juiced with 'ain't's, hep slang and sly, winking references to drugs and chicks, didn't suit post-punk. And the intellectual underpinnings of this older rock criticism – notions of rebellion as male misbehaviour, genius-as-madness, the cult of street credibility and authenticity – were among the very things being scrutinized and challenged by the anti-rockist vanguard. The writing of the new generation of music journalists who took over – Morley, Savage, Ian Penman, Jane Suck, Dave McCullough, Chris Bohn, to name only the most influential – seemed to be made of the same *stuff* as the music they championed. The stark urgency and clean lines of their prose mirrored the light-metal severity of groups like Wire, The Banshees and Gang of Four, just as the record-design aesthetic of the time emphasized a bold, bracing geometry of hard angles and primary colour blocks. The new school of music writing merged puritanism and playfulness in a way that simultaneously undercut the casual tone of the old rock journalism while puncturing its stodgy core of certainty – hidden assumptions and taken-for-granted notions about what rock was all about.

What bands and journalists talked *about* also contributed to the sense of entering a new era. An interview with a rock band today tends to become a laundry list of influences and reference points, such that the story of a band's life typically is reduced to a journey through taste. This sort of 'record collection rock' didn't exist in the post-punk era. Bands referred to their inspirations, of course, but they had so many other things on their minds – politics, cinema, art, books. Some of the politically committed bands felt it was self-indulgent or trivial to talk about *music*; they felt duty-bound to discuss serious issues. At the time, this reinforced the concept that pop wasn't a segmented category insulated from the rest of reality. This lack of interest in discussing influences also created a sense of post-punk as an absolute break with tradition. It felt like the culture's eyes and ears were trained on the future, not the past, with bands engaged in a furious competition to reach the eighties a few years ahead of schedule.

On a mission, and fully in the now, post-punk created a thrilling sense of urgency. The new records came thick and fast, classic after classic. And even the incomplete experiments and 'interesting failures' carried a powerful utopian charge, were part of an exhilarating collective conversation. Certain groups existed more on the level of an idea than a fully realized proposition, but nevertheless contributed simply by existing, by talking a good game in the press.

Many groups born in the post-punk period went on to enjoy huge mainstream fame: New Order, Depeche Mode, The Human League, U2, Talking Heads, Scritti Politti, Simple Minds. Other 'minor' or 'background' figures at the time went on to achieve success in a different guise: Björk, The KLF, The Beastie Boys, Jane's Addiction. But this book is definitely not a history written according to the victors. There are dozens of bands who made landmark albums but never got further than achieving an abiding cult status, earning the dubious consolation prize of being an 'influence' and 'reference point' for nineties alt-rock megabands (Gang of Four beget Red Hot Chili Peppers; Throbbing Gristle sired Nine Inch Nails; and Talking Heads even supplied Radiohead with their name). There are scores more who made just one or two amazing singles, then disappeared with barely a trace.

Beyond the musicians, there's a cadre of catalysts and culture warriors, enablers and ideologues, who started labels, managed bands, became innovative producers, published fanzines, promoted gigs and organized festivals. One recurring motif in this book is the crucial role of the hip record store – Rough Trade in London; Drome in mid-seventies Cleveland; 99 Records in New York. From 1950s 'race' music through to nineties rave culture, record stores have long operated as crucial nodes in the informal networks of music culture. They provide jobs and inspiration for struggling musicians, function as information exchanges where bands stick up ads and fans pick up flyers about shows. The store even operates as a small-radius radio station, with staff 'playlisting' certain favourite records and pushing them on the customers. Many post-punk record stores eventually evolved into record labels, transforming their retail awareness of what's hot into a potent A&R instinct.

The prosaic work of creating and maintaining an alternative culture lacks the glamour of punk's public gestures of outrage and cultural terrorism. Destroying is always more dramatic than building. Post-punk was constructive and forward-looking, its very prefix implying faith in a future that punk had said didn't exist.

Punk briefly united a motley array of malcontents as a force *against*. But when the question shifted to 'What are we *for*?', the moment/ movement disintegrated and dispersed, each strand nurturing its own creation-myth of what punk meant and its own vision of where to go next. Yet, even as the arguments raged, the very disagreements affirmed what was still held in common: punk's revival of belief in the power of music, and the responsibility that came with this conviction. It made the question 'Where to now?' worth fighting over. The byproduct of all this division and disagreement was diversity, a fabulous wealth of sounds and ideas that rivals the sixties as a golden age for music.

1: POST-PUNK

1

PUBLIC IMAGE BELONGS TO ME: John Lydon and PiL

Public Image Ltd

'Ever get the feeling you've been cheated?'

Johnny Rotten's infamous parting shot to the audience at Winterland, San Francisco, on 14 January 1978, was not a question so much as a confession. Despite being the frontman of the most dangerous band in the world, Johnny was *bored* – sick of The Sex Pistols' music, tired of his own 'Rotten' persona, disappointed with how punk as a whole had panned out. Winterland was the last date of the Pistols' turbulent debut tour of America, and a few days later the band disintegrated in acrimonious confusion.

Rotten's disillusionment had been brewing for months. The first public sign occurred during 'The Punk and His Music', a 16 July 1977 show on London's Capital Radio, during which Rotten voiced his frustration with the predictability of most punk bands: 'You do feel cheated. There should be loads of different things.' Spliced together from interview chat and records selected by Rotten, the show also revealed that the singer had far more diverse and sophisticated taste in music than his public image suggested. If you tuned in anticipating nothing but punk, you were immediately thrown for a loop by the first selection, Tim Buckley's 'Sweet Surrender' – a lush, sensual R&B song swathed with orchestral strings. Over the next ninety minutes Rotten further tweaked expectations, playing languid roots reggae, solo efforts by former Velvet Underground members Lou Reed, John Cale and Nico, a surprising amount of hippie-tinged music by Can, Captain Beefheart and Third Ear Band, and two tracks by his hero Peter Hammill, a full-blown progressive rocker.

3

Just about everything Lydon played on Capital gave the lie to Punk Myth #1: the early seventies as cultural wasteland. And, if this were not treasonous enough, he also broke with his Malcolm McLaren-scripted role as cultural terrorist by effectively outing himself as an aesthete. Along with his hipster music choices, the interview revealed a sensitive, thoughtful individual rather than the thug-monster of tabloid legend.

For Rotten, this image makeover was a matter of survival. A month before his radio appearance, the Pistols' anti-Jubilee single 'God Save the Queen' had defied airwave bans and record-store embargoes to become the best-selling single in the country. Demonized by the tabloids, Rotten was repeatedly attacked by enraged royalist thugs. Scared, scarred, in practical terms almost under house arrest, he decided to take control of his destiny. His anarchist/Antichrist persona – originally Rotten's own creation, but hyped by Pistols manager McLaren and distorted by a media eager to believe the worst – had spiralled out of control. Agreeing to do the Capital Radio interview without consulting his management, Lydon embarked on the process of persona demolition that would soon result in 'Public Image' (the song) and Public Image Ltd (the group).

During 'The Punk and His Music', Lydon sounded frail and vulnerable as he discussed the street attacks: 'It's very easy for a gang to pick on . . . one person and smash his head in – it's a big laugh for them, and it's very easy for them to say, "What a wanker, look at him run away!" . . . I mean, what's he meant to do?' Positioning himself as victim and revealing his feelings of humiliation, Rotten deliberately rehumanized himself.

This naturally incensed McLaren, who accused Rotten of dissipating 'the band's threat' by revealing himself as a 'man of taste'. McLaren saw the Pistols as anti-music, but here was the group's frontman waxing lyrical about his eclectic record collection and gushing, 'I just like *all* music . . . I *love* my music,' like a fucking hippie! From that point onwards, McLaren decided that Rotten was at heart 'a constructive sissy rather than a destructive lunatic', and he focused his energy on moulding the more suggestible Sid Vicious into the Pistols' true star, a cartoon psychopath, wanton and self-destructive.

In the latter months of 1977, a chasm grew between Rotten and the other Sex Pistols that mirrored the polarization of punk as a whole into arty bohemians versus working-class street toughs. Rotten came from an impeccably deprived background, but his sensibility was much closer to that of the art-school contingent. He wasn't the unemployed guttersnipe mythologized by The Clash, but earned decent money alongside his construction-worker dad at a sewage plant, and worked at a playschool during the summer. And, although he often professed to hate art and despise intellectuals, he was well read (Oscar Wilde was a favourite) with fierce opinions (Joyce was not). Where Steve Jones and Paul Cook were early school-leavers, Rotten had even made a brief foray into further education, studying English literature and art at Kingsway College. Above all, Rotten was a music connoisseur. He couldn't play an instrument or write melodies, but he had a real sonic sensibility and a sense of possibilities much more expansive than those of his fellow-Pistols.

The reggae and art-rock that Rotten played on 'The Punk and His Music' sketched out the emotional and sonic template for Public Image Ltd. When he talked about identifying with Dr Alimantado's 'Born for a Purpose', a song about being persecuted as a Rasta, you got an advance glimpse of PiL's aura of paranoia and prophecy: Rotten as visionary outcast, an internal exile in Babylon UK. Musically, what he loved about Beefheart and the dub producers was their experimental playfulness: 'They just love *sound*; they like using any sound.' Effectively, 'The Punk and His Music' offered a listening list for a post-punk movement yet to be born; hints and clues for where next to take the music.

Punk seemed to be 'over' almost before it had really begun. For many early participants, the death knell came on 28 October 1977 with the release of *Never Mind the Bollocks*. Had the revolution come to this, something as prosaic and conventional as an album? *Bollocks* was product, eminently consumable. Rotten's lyrics and vocals were incendiary, but Steve Jones's fat guitar sound and Chris Thomas's superb production – thickly layered, glossy, well organized – added up to a disconcertingly orthodox hard rock that gave the lie to the group's reputation for chaos and ineptitude. Lydon later blamed McLaren for steering the rest of the band towards 'a regressive mod vibe', while admitting that his own ideas for how the record should have sounded would have rendered it 'unlistenable for most people because they wouldn't have had a point of reference'.

Journalist Jon Savage reviewed *Bollocks* for *Sounds* and recalls it feeling 'like a tombstone . . . airless, no spaces in the music' – a comment that pinpoints the record's failure as a deficiency of dub. Compared to the mirage-like unreality of reggae production, all glimmering reverb haze, disorienting FX and flickering ectoplasmic wisps, most punk records sounded retarded: stuck in the mid-sixties; before 24-track psychedelia; before *stereo*. The sharper bands coming out of punk knew they had some serious catching up to do. Some, like The Clash and The Ruts, picked up mostly on the protest aspect of roots reggae – the blunt sloganeering and sermonizing of The Wailers' 'Get Up Stand Up', the radical chic of Peter Tosh's Rasta guerrilla persona. At the other extreme from this 'roots rock rebel' version of reggae, the more experimental post-punk bands responded to reggae as a purely sonic revolution: an Africanized psychedelia, shape-shifting and perception-altering. During the half-decade from 1977 to 1981, reggae's spatialized production and sophisticated-yet-elemental rhythms provided *the* template for sonically radical post-punk – a privileged status rivalled only by funk.

In Jamaica itself, though, roots militancy and dub ethereality were two sides of the same cultural coin, indivisible. The glue that held them together, Rasta, is a millenarian creed – 'part journalism, part prophecy' in the words of James A. Winders, ultimately anti-political and theocratic. Rasta spirituality was something most white Britons couldn't buy into easily, partly because of its illiberal traits (it possesses a nasty streak of anti-feminism) but mostly because the absolutism of its blood-and-fire visions was temperamentally alien to a secular British youth whose idea of religion generally derives from Anglicanism: non-committal, wishy-washy, as close to being agnostic as you can get without pissing off God. Out of the cadres of post-punk, perhaps only one person really tapped into a spiritual ferocity to rival Rasta: Johnny Rotten.

Raised in London as the child of Irish Catholic immigrants, he had his own window into the postcolonial dislocation of the former British Empire's neglected subjects. It's no coincidence that his autobiography bears the subtitle *No Irish, No Blacks, No Dogs* – what many English landlords put in 'room vacant' ads before the Race Relations Act outlawed the practice. Rotten's identification with the black British experience of 'sufferation' and 'downpression' and his passion for Jamaican riddim and bass-pressure suffused his post-Pistols music, desolating PiL's sound with eerie space and heavy dread.

The ex-Pistol Rotten arrived back in Britain after the band's disastrous American tour only to be immediately invited to board another jet by Virgin Records supremo Richard Branson – this one heading to Jamaica. Rotten, renowned for his reggae expertise, would accompany Branson as an A&R consultant for Virgin's new roots 'n' dub imprint, The Front Line. This 'working holiday' would give Rotten time in which to consider his future. Nice work if you can get it: he spent most his time lounging poolside at the Kingston Sheraton Hotel, gorging on lobster and hanging with the cream of Jamaican reggae – personal heroes like Big Youth, U Roy, Burning Spear and Prince Far I.

A few days after the Pistols' break-up, Rotten had announced his intention to form a new band that would be 'anti-music of any kind'. On his return from the Caribbean, he started recruiting. He invited his friend John Wardle, an East Ender with piercing blue eyes who'd reinvented himself as Jah Wobble, to play bass despite his being barely acquainted with the instrument. 'John wanted to play in a band where the bass was prominent,' recalls Wobble. 'We used to fuck about with graphic equalizers and customized bass bins, and experiment with putting rock records through the system to see how far you could take the low end.'

Reggae was the crucial point of intersection for PiL's three core members – Rotten, Wobble and guitarist Keith Levene – otherwise a motley crew both musically and personally. 'The whole reason PiL worked at all was that we were just total dub fanatics,' says Levene. 'We were always going to "blues".' The latter were illegal reggae parties, somewhere between a shebeen and a full-on sound system, usually held in someone's house or flat, with money made through selling alcohol and cannabis. Long a fanatical reggae collector, Rotten had been introduced to sound systems by his black friend Don Letts, a DJ who played at legendary punk venue the Roxy, and is often credited with turning the punk audience on to reggae. With Letts as his escort, Rotten frequently found himself the only white person inside ultra-heavy clubs like the Four Aces in Dalston, east London. 'You'd feel a bit dodgy sneaking into those blues,' says Wobble, 'but it was fine on the whole. Black people were just cool about it. It'd be like "What's these white kids doing here?" but no one would hassle you. In fact, as a punk rocker, you were safer in those days at the black dances than you were going down the local white-boy pub. For me, hearing the bass that loud was a huge thing. The physical nature of it just left me gobsmacked.'

Wobble had grown up on Whitechapel's Clichy Estate, located at the junction of Jamaica Street and Stepney Way – neatly symbolizing the collision of East End and West Indies that would define him. He met Rotten at Kingsway College and the two became part of a misfit crew known as the Four Johns – the others being John Ritchie (a.k.a. Sid Vicious) and John Grey. At this point, Wobble had a reputation for being something of a thug. 'I think we were all emotional cripples, back then,' he says, with a hint of regret. But when he picked up Vicious's bass guitar, something was released in him: 'I immediately felt bonded to the instrument.

It was very therapeutic, although I didn't understand that at the time.' Drawing on his knowledge of Jamaican music and fuelled by tons of speed, he taught himself to play reggae bass – the simple, recurring phrase that worked simultaneously as melodic motif and steady rhythmic pulse. Picking up reggae tricks like using old strings (they have no twang) and taking off all the tone with the instrument's tone knob, he learned how to 'play soft, not in a percussive way. You caress the string. Pure vibration.' Wobble's basslines became the human heartbeat in PiL's music, the rollercoaster carriage that simultaneously cocooned you and transported you through the terror ride. And, because Wobble's bass carried the melody, Keith Levene's guitar was given licence to freak out.

One of PiL's most curious features is that, for an avowedly anti-rock band, they had a guitar hero at their core – the Jimi Hendrix of postpunk. Unlike most of his peers, Levene had serious skills. Before punk, he'd done what guitarists were supposed to do in the days of prog-rock virtuosity: practice, practice, practice. As a teenager growing up in north London, he'd spend days on end jamming at a friend's house; eight-hour sessions. And his guitar-hero was Steve Howe of Yes, for whom he worked as a roadie aged fifteen.

Punks were supposed to purge their collections of King Crimson and Mahavishnu Orchestra albums, though; or at least hide them in a cupboard. 'A lot of people in punk could play guitar much better than they made out,' claims Levene. 'But I never pretended I couldn't play lead.' However, despite all his prog skeletons in the closet, Levene hurled himself into the early punk fray and became one of the founding members of The Clash. But his harsh, discordant style became increasingly at odds with that group's anthemic rock 'n' roll. Even then he was developing the style that would become his PiL trademark: the deliberate incorporation of mistakes. When Levene hit a wrong note, he'd immediately repeat the error to see if the wrongness could become a new kind of rightness. 'The idea was to break through conditioning, take yourself out of one channel, and into another space.' It wasn't 'musical differences' that led to his exit from The Clash, though: Levene was expelled because of his negative attitude towards the band, which his colleagues attributed to amphetamine moodswings.

Levene and Rotten first bonded during the aftermath of a shared Clash/Pistols gig at a Sheffield pub in July 1976. The singer and the guitarist were both sitting apart from their respective groups, and looking miserable. Levene approached Rotten, and during their conversation suggested they work together if their bands ever disintegrated. Eighteen months later, PiL was shaped by Levene's and Rotten's disgust with what happened to their previous bands: the relapse into the American hard-rock tradition. 'To me, the Pistols were the *last* rock 'n' roll band. They weren't the beginning of anything,' says Levene. 'Whereas PiL really felt like the start of something new.'

The name Public Image Ltd was ripe with meaning. The phrase first caught Rotten's imagination when he read Muriel Spark's *The Public Image*, a novel about an unbearably egotistical actress. 'Limited' initially signified keeping his persona under a tight leash, 'not being as "out there" as I was with the Sex Pistols'. Seemingly symbolizing this jettisoning of the swollen alter-ego, Rotten reverted to his real name, John Lydon. (In fact, McLaren had claimed ownership of 'Johnny Rotten' and put an injunction on the singer using the stage name. At the time, almost nobody knew about this legal subtext, though, so the Rotten/Lydon shift seemed like a powerful statement: the singer symbolically reclaiming his true identity and making a fresh start as part of a collective, Public Image Ltd.)

The idea of 'Ltd' soon escalated to take on its business meaning: the limited company. PiL, proclaimed Lydon, was not a band in the tradi-tional sense but a communications company for whom records were just one front of activity. Enthused, he and Levene talked about diversifying into movie soundtracks, graphics, making 'video albums', even design-ing music technology. To show they were serious, PiL recruited two non-musician members: Dave Crowe, an old schoolfriend of Lydon, acted as the band's accountant; while Jeanette Lee (an old girlfriend of Don Letts, with whom she'd managed the clothing store Acme Attractions) would be the group's videomaker. Lee also now happened to be going out with Levene. 'Jeanette was telling me how she'd had a lot to do with the edit-ing of Don's punk-rock documentary, and the script for his next movie, *Dread at the Controls*, which never got made,' says Levene. 'I was into the idea of PiL not doing straightforward videos, and she basically talked me into her joining. Wobble was dead against it.'

Part of the impetus behind PiL posing as a corporation was to continue punk's project of demystifying the record business. While The Clash lamented the industry's knack for 'turning rebellion into money', PiL reversed that syndrome, and suggested that money-making could be sub-versive: working from within, a stealth campaign, less spectacular than the Pistols' revolt but more insidious. It was also more honest and less starry-eyed to present rock bands as they were: capitalist enterprises, as opposed to a gang of guitar-wielding guerrillas. Accordingly, Lydon and his colleagues overhauled their image, ditching anything redolent of punk clichés and wearing tailored suits. This anti-rock 'n' roll image culminated with Dennis Morris's artwork for PiL's debut album – fashion magazine-style portraits of each member of the group, immaculately coutured and coiffed. Lydon appeared on the front under Italian *Vogue* lettering, while the reverse saw Wobble sporting a debonair 1920s lounge-lizard moustache.

Stridently opposed to all the stale, standard rock routines and procedures, PiL had no manager and declared they would never tour. Above all, this was not the Johnny Rotten Band, a star vehicle: PiL was a genuine collective. A noble idea, but in reality the group's privileged status – an experimental outfit funded by a major label – depended on Virgin's belief in Lydon as their hottest property: the most charismatic and significant British frontman to emerge since Bowie; a potential superstar seemingly set to dominate the next decade of music. Thanks to the peculiarly indeterminate feel of 1978 – punk in its death throes, the future wide open – PiL were in an unprecedented position of strength. Virgin were prepared to indulge Lydon's artistic whims in the belief that he would either come up with the goods or come round eventually and embrace a more accessible sound.

That's a cynical way of looking at it, though: in truth, Virgin's co-founder and main music man Simon Draper paid more than lipservice to experimentation and innovation. During the early seventies, Virgin was one of the key 'progressive' labels, home to Henry Cow, Faust, Gong, Tangerine Dream and Robert Wyatt. By 1978 the company had trimmed its roster, shifted focus from albums to singles, and repositioned itself as the leading major label for 'modern music', with a New Wave portfolio that included XTC, Devo, Magazine and The Human League. 'They weren't such a big label in those days, still living off the luck of Mike Oldfield's *Tubular Bells*,' recalls Levene. 'Branson was like a superhippy – a hippy with no qualms about making money. He didn't mind trying a few crazy things. We were lucky we were on Virgin.' Although Lydon would publicly lambast Branson & Co. as mere 'Hampstead hippies', Virgin did subsidize three of the most extreme albums ever released by a major label: *Public Image, Metal Box* and *Flowers of Romance*.

Given Lydon's initial talk of PiL as anti-music and anti-melody, the group's debut single, 'Public Image', was a massive relief for all concerned – record company, Pistols fans, critics. It's a searing, soaring statement of intent: the glorious chiming minimalism of Wobble's bassline and Levene's plangent ringing chords mirror Lydon's quest for purity as he sheds not just the Rotten alter-ego ('Somebody had to stop me . . . I will not be treated as property') but rock 'n' roll itself. 'That song was the first proper bassline I ever came up with,' says Wobble. 'Very simple – a beautiful interval from E to B. Just the joy of vibration. And incredible guitar from Keith, this great burst of energy.' Wrapped in a fake newspaper with tabloid shock-horror headlines, the single shot to Number 9 in the UK charts in October 1978.

The fake tabloid newspaper sleeve of PiL's debut single 'Public Image', 1978

While the single was greeted with rapture, *Public Image* the album received a mixed reception. *Sounds* gave it a derisory 2½ stars out of 5 and voiced the widespread sense held by punk diehards that Lydon had lost it, abandoning the opportunities and responsibilities inherent in being *the* punk figurehead and instead wallowing in arty self-indulgence.

The album *was* uncompromising, throwing the listener in at the deep end with the nine-minute death-wish dirge 'Theme', a near-cacophony of suicidal despair and Catholic guilt (Lydon howling about masturbation as mortal sin). Next up was the anti-clerical doggerel of 'Religion I'/'Religion II' (a blasphemous ditty written for the Pistols and originally titled 'Sod in Heaven'), followed by the hacking thrash-funk of 'Annalisa' (the true story of a German girl who starved to death because her parents believed she was possessed by the devil and turned to the Church rather than psychiatrists for help). If side one was loosely themed around religion, the more accessible second side largely concerned the tribulations of punk Messiah-hood. 'Public Image' reasserted Lydon's rights over 'Johnny Rotten' – 'Public image belongs to me/It's my entrance, my own creation, my grand finale' – only to end with him shedding the persona with an echo-chamber yell of 'GOODBYE'. 'Low Life' fingered McLaren as the 'egomaniac trainer/traitor' who 'never did understand', while the foaming paranoia of 'Attack' showed that the mental scars from summer 1977 – when Lydon was UK Public Enemy #1 – were still livid.

What's most striking about PiL's debut is that, for such a vociferously anti-rock group, a surprisingly large proportion of *Public Image* rocks *hard*. The single is like a blueprint for a reborn, purified rock for the 1980s: you can hear U2's The Edge in its radiant surge. 'It's so clean, so tingly, like a cold shower,' says Levene. 'It could be really thin glass penetrating you but you don't know until you start bleeding internally.' Combining raw power and uncanny dubspace, 'Low Life' and 'Attack' sound like *Never Mind the Bollocks* would have if Lydon's reggae-and-Krautrock sensibility had prevailed. 'Theme' is nothing if not an orgy of twisted guitar virtuosity. Eschewing overdubs and multi-tracking, Levene generated an astonishing amount of sound from a single guitar: 'In the beginning, it was just my onstage sound, no effects, just whacking things off in one take. Sometimes not even knowing what I was going to play, writing the tune on the spot. The first album is the one time when we were a *band*. I remember worrying a little at the time: Does this do too much what we publicly say we're not going to do? – meaning, *rock out*. But what we were doing really was showing everybody that we were intimately acquainted with what we ultimately intended to break down. And we started that dismantling process with the album's last track, "Fodderstompf".'

As often happens with bands committed to progression, the most extreme track on the preceding album is the springboard for the next – in PiL's case, 1979's *Metal Box*. On one level, 'Fodderstompf' was a throwaway: an extended disco spoof, almost a parody of Donna Summer's 'Love to Love You Baby', with Lydon the anti-sentimentalist taking the piss out of romance, affection and commitment. 'I hate love. There isn't a love song in us . . . It's bullshit,' he told Sex Pistols biographers Fred and Judy Vermorel. On 'Fodderstompf', Rotten and Wobble yowl, 'We only wanted to be loved' into an echo-chamber using shrill Monty Python-style housewife voices, adlib insults at the studio engineer behind the glass, blast the fire extinguisher at the mike, and generally goof off. 'Me and John, I think we'd had a bit of wine or whatever that night,' chuckles Wobble. The track runs for almost eight minutes because its *raison d'être* was to stretch the album to the bare minimum length of thirty minutes as stipulated by their contract. In a pointed fuck-you to Virgin, and arguably to the listener too, Wobble at one point warbles, 'We are now trying to finish the album with a minimum amount of effort, which we are now doing very suc-cess-ful-leeee'. He says now, 'It was this confrontational thing, a real mickey take on the record company.' Yet, musically, the track is the most compelling cut on the debut. Its hypnotic dub-funk bassline, subliminal synth-burbles and monstrous snare sound (drastically processed and absurdly prominent in the mix) look ahead to *Metal Box*, when the group fully embraced the studio-as-instrument methodology of disco and dub. 'People loved that track; it's got quite a sense of anarchy,' says Wobble. 'In its own way, it's as mental as Funkadelic. And it had the perfect funk bassline.'

Around this time, Lydon started telling the press that the only contemporary music he really cared for was disco – a striking rhetorical move, given the standard punk line was that disco sucked. PiL, he stressed, were a *dance* band. Disco was functional music, useful. It dispensed with all the bollocks – the false hopes and unwise investments in rock-as-counter-culture – that punk had ultimately perpetuated. All this was part of Lydon's continued rhetorical campaign against rock – which, if not dead, certainly ought to be killed off. PiL were the men for the job. Chiming in with his anticlericalism and his 'Anarchy in the UK' self-description as Antichrist, Lydon compared rock to 'a church . . . a religion . . . a farce.'

But the reluctant saviour still had to deal with the expectations of his devout congregation of punk believers. Making their UK live debut on

Christmas Day 1978, PiL played the Rainbow: as traditionally rockbiz a venue as could then be imagined. Slightly less conventional was the fact that Wobble played the entire show sitting on a chair (he couldn't physically play the bass any other way). Lydon sauntered onstage carrying two plastic shopping bags stuffed with lager cans. After a year's absence from live performance in the UK, he greeted the audience with a cheery, 'So what you fuckers been doing since I've been away, eh? I hope you ain't been spending time and money down the King's Road.' The audience hollered for Pistols tunes, but Lydon was adamant: 'If you wanna hear that, fuck off! That's history.' Although the music was intermittently powerful, PiL's performance suffered from first-night nerves and equipment problems. Lydon pontificated, upbraided the audience, but ultimately failed to connect. One of the cans he handed out to the audience was hurled back, unopened, glancing off his face and drawing blood. As a result, Lydon and Levene spent portions of the show with their backs turned to the crowd. There was no encore and the gig ended sourly, energy blocked, like bad sex.

So 1978 limped to a close for PiL, the group's future unclear. Many wondered whether Lydon had blown it, all that awesome power at his disposal, effectively abandoning the audience he'd mobilized and who were looking to him for leadership. But 1979 lay wide open, and Lydon's greatest *musical* triumphs actually lay ahead of him.

2

OUTSIDE OF EVERYTHING: Howard Devoto and Vic Godard

Buzzcocks. Magazine. Subway Sect.

Howard Devoto gets the prize for clairvoyance: he abandoned the ship of punk long before it started to sink – almost immediately after it left harbour, in fact. In February 1977, the Buzzcocks singer quit the Manchester band he'd co-founded just as their first release, the *Spiral Scratch* EP, hit the stores. Buzzcocks were already one of the four or five leading bands of what was clearly Rock's Next Big Thing, and the group were dismayed by what seemed like a bizarrely self-sabotaging decision. But Devoto had seen the way punk was going and wanted to distance himself. 'I just don't like movements,' he explained to the *NME* a year later. 'I'm just perverse.'

Devoto exemplified the secret truth of punk: it was a movement based in the rebellion of middle-class misfits as much as those mythical 'kids on the streets'. He was studying philosophy and literature when he met Pete Shelley at the Bolton Institute of Technology and formed Buzzcocks. Punk's own rhetoric, though, suppressed the art school and university undergraduate contribution, and amplified the imagery of tower blocks, urban deprivation and youth unemployment. This was taken as gospel by the music press and newspapers, such that by early 1977 a media feedback loop had spawned a second wave of punk bands narrowly based on The Clash's 'the truth is only known by guttersnipes' creed. The resultant self-parodying yobbishness Devoto found both 'silly' and 'quite unpleasant'. Punk, he says, 'felt like a cult thing originally, and in a way you could say that what went wrong is that it *caught on*'.

'Once the tabloids picked up on punk with the Bill Grundy incident and the whole Anarchy tour, you started to see all these totally Xeroxed bands coming through,' says Richard Boon, Buzzcocks' manager and Devoto's best friend since their days at Leeds Grammar School. 'And it became clear punk was going to get constrained rather than be about opening up things. Originally we'd incited people to do something of their own. They *were* doing something of their own, except it was actually a slavish copy – and a copy of something that hadn't really been there in the first place.'

Devoto's looser conception of punk was based on the diet of mavericks he'd consumed during the mid-seventies: Iggy & The Stooges, John Cale, and the first stirrings of the New York scene around CBGB and Max's Kansas City. Like Lower East Side poet-rockers Richard Hell and Tom Verlaine, he reinvented himself, swapping his stodgy all-too-English surname Trafford for the sleek and enigmatic Devoto. Shelley, originally Peter McNeish, did the same thing, renaming himself after the Romantic poet. The pair originally met when Devoto, looking for someone to soundtrack an art video he'd made, turned up at the college's Electronic Music Society. Having built his own oscillator, engineering student Shelley had already made a whole album of experimental synth music, inspired by his love of Kraftwerk and other German bands.

'To me, Buzzcocks came from the better side of punk, the bands who were aware of things like Faust and Can,' recalls Paul Morley, creator of local fanzine *Out There* and Manchester correspondent for the *NME* – in whose pages he would champion Devoto as 'The Most Important Man Alive'. 'I remember delightedly screaming, "This is like fucking Ornette Coleman!" when I went to see Buzzcocks play very early on. The guitars and bass were skidding, the drums just seemed to be completely polyrhythmical, the voice was flailing away. If you stood back a couple of inches, you thought: This is like free jazz.'

Spiral Scratch, the group's first recording, sounded less chaotic and more conventionally rock 'n' roll, but by way of compensation you could hear the stiletto wit of Devoto's words. 'Boredom', the immortal punk classic, was actually an exercise in meta-punk: it expressed real ennui ('I'm living in this movie/but it doesn't move me') but it also commented on 'boredom' as a prescribed subject for punk songs and punk-related media discourse – a topic that was predictable to the point of being, well, a bit *boring*. Shelley's deliberately inane two-note guitar solo sealed the conceptual deal: a 'boring' solo that was thrillingly tension-inducing in its fixated refusal to go anywhere melodically.

buzzcocks

spiral scratch

Buzzcocks' *Spiral Scratch* EP, 1977. L to R: John Maher, Steve Diggle, Pete Shelley, Howard Devoto

Boredom was why Devoto decided to quit on the eve of *Spiral Scratch*'s release. He was fed up with the 'unrelenting nature' of punk music, including Buzzcocks' ultra-fast thrash. He told the press he was 'tired of noise and short of breath'. The onslaught of distorted guitars was drowning out his words, which, he felt, warranted close attention. The perversity of quitting so prematurely also appealed. 'A key factor to the way I function . . . is that I thrive on what I'd term "negative drive",' he told the *NME*. 'I get bored very easily and that boredom can act as a catalyst for me to suddenly conceive and execute a new vocation . . . In fact "negative drive" was always what I believed the punk ethic . . .

should have been about: constant change, avoidance of stale conceits, doing the unacceptable.'

Devoto's 'constant change' ethos recalls David Bowie and his ever-shifting serial personae. In 1977 Bowie returned to the British scene in a big way, with the release of two albums of his own, *Low* and *'Heroes'*, plus two Iggy Pop albums he'd produced. *Low*, especially, revealed most UK punk to be sonically and intellectually staid. Intriguingly, it was released just a few weeks before Devoto announced he was quitting Buzzcocks in February 1977. Had he seen the writing on the (Berlin) wall? Devoto admits the Bowie and Iggy albums had 'a huge impact on me. Just the *sound* of *Low* was extraordinary: the drum sound, the minimalistic nature of the production, all the electronic stuff Eno did on side two.'

With Iggy's *The Idiot*, also released in early 1977, Devoto loved the sonorous Sinatra-esque croon Pop had developed. 'You really started to hear the richness of his voice, and when I later tried singing in a low register on Magazine songs like "Motorcade", that was definitely me trying to emulate Iggy a little.' More than anything, for Devoto the rabid Stooges fan, it was just great to have an Iggy record *at all*, four years after *Raw Power*. 'And then to learn he was going to go on tour! I think I was the first person at the box office at the Manchester Apollo, and we ended up with tickets in the front row. Then it was announced Bowie was going to be onstage playing with him and the tickets sold out within a few days. Those people were *giants* in my psyche at that time.'

The European feel of *Low* and *The Idiot*, the music's rich textural palette and its often downbeat aura were all extremely influential on Devoto's vision for his post-Buzzcocks band. While the idea gestated, he helped Richard Boon manage Buzzcocks, accompanying him on trips to London for talks with major labels, and subsisted on money from *Spiral Scratch* (which had unexpectedly sold like hot cakes). Boon and Devoto lived together in a house on Lower Broughton Road, along with Devoto's girlfriend Linda Sterling a.k.a. Linder – a graphic design student and collage artist who'd soon front her own post-punk feminist band, Ludus. Pete Shelley lived a few doors up the road and was a constant presence. A hive of artistic activity and idea-swapping, the Lower Broughton household 'was a bit like a small version of Warhol's Factory,' says Paul Morley. 'We were all voracious readers,' recalls Linder. 'We would bring in books and exchange them continuously. I'd be exploring sexual politics and religion, and Howard was into philosophy, the Symbolist poets, Huysmans' *Against Nature*.'

In the summer of 1977 Devoto pinned up a notice in Manchester's Virgin record store, appealing for 'musicians to perform and record fast and slow music. Punk mentality not essential.' The implication that a punk mindset could be a straitjacket on creativity was a heretical gesture so early in 'the year of punk'. The players Devoto pulled together to form Magazine were all *un*-punk in their undisguised accomplishment: Barry Adamson's bass was agile and glossily textured; John McGeoch's chromatic guitar was thickly textured and not the least bit shy of epic riffs or swashbuckling solo flourishes; replacing the group's first keyboard player (an avant-garde music student who didn't quite gel), Dave Formula was a seasoned musician whose CV included playing at the Ritz Hotel in a cabaret trio. Formula's keyboard playing provided Magazine's music with a rich sense of drama and ornament. It's hard to imagine today, but the mere presence of keyboards seemed controversial in the immediate aftermath of punk – the instrument, still associated with prog rock, seemed decadent in its decorative excess.

Flyer for joint gig by Magazine and Buzzcocks, with artwork by Howard Devoto's live-in lover Linder, 1978

In the first Magazine interviews, Devoto firmly defined himself against what punk had become: yob rock or agit-prop. 'I'm not stupid and I refuse to pretend to be,' he told the *NME* in October 1977. 'Somebody said I'm smart: well read and well groomed. What e.e. cummings called an intelligentleman . . . I don't deal in messages . . . I deal in ideas, and the effects of ideas.' Elsewhere he described his songs as being 'as complete a picture of confusion as I can put together', an interior soundtrack for 'people who might sit in the corner of a café very quietly going out of their minds'.

Critics raved about the enigmatic Northerner with the nice line in cryptic profundities. Morley compared him to Samuel Beckett and identified his major preoccupation as 'the absurdity of existence'. This was in part auto-suggestion, triggered by Devoto's own literary name-drops: Camus, Plath, Gerard Manley Hopkins. Describing *Spiral Scratch*'s 'Breakdown', the singer archly compared the paranoid protagonist with 'Dostoevsky's underground man or any of them existentialists'. A few years later he'd condense *Notes from Underground* into the pop single 'A Song from under the Floorboards'. Devoto responded to Dostoevsky's idea of man's essential perversity – the ways in which spite and self-sabotage impel him towards negative things. *Notes from Underground*, in particular, was written as a riposte to the progressive ideologies of its era, with their notions of human perfectibility and benign social engineering. This mid-nineteenth-century battle between 'negative drive' and utopian socialism was at root the same as the 1978 struggle between angsty, arty post-punkers and the politicized contingent who saw punk as a form of agit-prop or Social Realism.

Magazine signed to Virgin and expectations escalated. A *Melody Maker* front-cover headline screamed, 'Devoto – The Man For 78'. The singer simultaneously courted and recoiled from the attention, cultivating an image of aloofness and inscrutability. Emulating Dylan, he ran rings around interviewers, leaving them convinced he knew something they didn't. 'Glam mysterioso' was the cliché on every hostile hack's lips. The 'glam' referred to Devoto's image – a combination of eyeliner, elfin features and widow's peak that made him resemble Eno in Roxy Music, but stopping just short of full-blown feather-boa'd androgyny.

Everything was building towards a crescendo, and 'Shot by Both Sides', Magazine's debut single, rose to the occasion. The riff, originally written by Pete Shelley, had the ringing grandeur of Springsteen's 'Born to Run'. 'Shot' sounded like an anthem, but its emotional core was the opposite of everything anthems stood for: battle-shy and non-committal, it was a clarion for all those who refused calls to solidarity or partisanship.

Without specifically referring to any of the great divisive issues of late seventies Britain (Rock Against Racism and the Anti-Nazi League versus the resurgent far right; the collectivist left that was taking over the Labour Party versus the pro-entrepreneur right wing that dominated the Conservative Party), 'Shot' captures the era's sense of dreadful polarization, and the vacillation of those caught in the cross-fire with the centre ground disappearing beneath their feet. It is about a non-combatant, an *in*activist. It's a defence of the bourgeois art-rock notion that the individual's struggle to be different is what really matters.

It's tempting to read 'Shot' as an answer record to Tom Robinson Band's 'Better Decide Which Side You're On'. Constantly playing benefit gigs, providing info and contacts for various worthy causes on their record sleeves, TRB were icons of radical chic for all who'd hoped something constructive would emerge out of punk. The genesis of the lyrics for 'Shot', though, came from a heated political argument between Devoto and a socialist girlfriend a few years earlier. 'I was playing my devil's advocate role, saying, "Yes, but . . .",' recalls Devoto. In the end, exasperated, the girl declared, 'Oh, you'll end up shot by both sides.' The phrase stuck in Devoto's head and came to encapsulate his emerging ideal: the truly heroic life based on not making your mind up. 'The idea that the true enlightenment involves somehow making the paradoxical and contradictory the focal point of your life, just holding on to them and making them dance,' he says. 'In some ways it can seem like a cop-out place to be, but it can also be one of the most difficult places to live.'

In 'Shot by Both Sides' you also get a sense of Devoto recoiling from the rabble-rousing vulgarity that typified most punk gigs by the middle of 1977. The song's key lines are 'I wormed my way into the heart of the crowd/I was shocked by what was allowed/I didn't lose myself in the crowd'. Mob rule and mobilized mass movements alike can seem scary because of their de-individualizing effect. In this respect, 'Shot' could also be seen as a riposte in advance to Sham 69's 'If the Kids Are United', a massive mid-1978 hit. Spearheaded by Sham and similar groups like Cock Sparrer, the non-arty side of punk was devolving into 'real' punk, a.k.a. Oi!: crude, macho, always up for a ruck, a sound stunted by inverted snobbery. Caught between this hooligan punk on one side and TRB-style dogmatism on the other, Devoto saw himself as the dissident aesthete 'on the run to the outside of everything'.

Of course, in the context of early 1978 – six months after the street battles of Lewisham, where Anti-Nazi League protesters had battled the police who were guarding a National Front march that provocatively passed through a black neighbourhood – you could argue that Devoto's refusal to stand up and be counted was questionable. 'I've always found political commitment very difficult,' he admits. Still, 'Shot by Both Sides' conveys the honour of art-rock's individualistic ethos, the glory attainable if you can somehow turn the affliction of being different, a freak, into a life of creativity. 'Shot' was Devoto's best shot at making that art-rock dream come true.

In early 1978 the majesty and sheer momentum of the single seemed irresistible. 'It was travelling the world; even Greil Marcus was writing about it in *Rolling Stone*,' says Paul Morley. 'It was huge, the ultimate rock riff.' On the brink of the Top 40, Magazine were invited to appear on *Top of the Pops*. At first Devoto refused. Asked again the following week, he buckled to pressure from Virgin and agreed. But he remained extremely uncomfortable about miming to the song on television. 'It was very artificial. The whole thing seemed absurd . . . and scary.' At the last minute he decided to make a gesture that would indicate his disdain for the corny charade. 'I didn't want to jump around in an obedient, "here's your entertainment" way. I wanted to be bloody-minded, but in a fairly understated way.' He got the BBC make-up girl to do him up in white-face, but instead of a striking glam alien, 'he looked like Marcel Marceau', recalls Morley (who was glued to the TV because seeing a band like Magazine on *Top of the Pops* was 'so rare' in those days). 'And then Devoto decided, because his mind was racing so quick, that he was far ahead of the game and he'd just be still. Very, very still. And this great song was playing, but Devoto stood stock-still. And the next week the record went *down* the charts – possibly the first time that's ever happened in the history of pop, that you get on *Top of the Pops* and the single goes down the next week. And from then on, everything shut down. Killed stone dead.'

Despite rave reviews for the debut album, *Real Life*, Magazine's career never quite recovered. Negative drive in full effect, Devoto had shot himself in the foot. At the close of 1978, he rationalized the anticlimactic *TOTP* performance, arguing that 'the only way I could bring any significance to it was by taking everything away'. That's a flattering spin. It was as much a combination of squeamishness and stage nerves; someone failing to seize the moment, frozen in the headlights of oncoming fame.

Following the unexpected failure of their most singular single, Magazine fell back on the prog-rock approach of slow-and-steady career building through albums and touring. 'Prog' was the invidious reference point brandished in the inevitable critical backlash that greeted 1979's *Secondhand Daylight*. Magazine had tried to get Bowie's producer Tony Visconti, but settled for Colin Thurston, the young engineer who'd worked with Visconti on *'Heroes'* and helped record Iggy's *Lust for Life*. But, instead of Bowie and Iggy, the album was compared to Genesis and Pink Floyd. *Sounds'* Garry Bushell – a member of the Socialist Workers Party and champion of Sham 69-style real punk – put on his steel-capped Doc Martens and stomped seven shades of shit out of the album, ridiculing everything from its gatefold sleeve to Devoto's mannered vocals. Densely produced and overwrought, *Secondhand Daylight* still contained at least one masterpiece in 'Permafrost', a deliberately sluggish tune whose highlights include Adamson's glutinous bassline, an angular McGeoch solo worthy of Bowie's *Lodger*, and Devoto's most quoted couplet: 'I will drug you and fuck you/On the permafrost'.

Magazine's third album, 1980's *The Correct Use of Soap* received a warmer greeting: it was hailed, correctly, as the band's masterpiece. Devoto's lyrics drew inspiration from an idea he'd found in a book of essays on love and lust by Theodor Reik – the notion that you are particularly vulnerable to falling in love after you've experienced some kind of trauma or life crisis. 'I may love you out of weakness/Is that what I was afraid of?' he wonders on the superb 'Stuck', a strange track loping somewhere unclassifiable between art-funk and jazz-metal. Enhanced by the crisp edges and eerie hollows of Martin Hannett's production, Magazine's music finally matched the lofty themes, while Devoto penned some of his most darkly witty and literate lines: 'I know the meaning of life/It doesn't help me a bit'; 'I could have been Raskolnikov/But Mother Nature ripped me off' (a reference to the anti-hero of Dostoevsky's *Crime and Punishment*). But on this particular front – existentialist doubt with arena-ready riffs – Magazine had already been eclipsed by fellow-Mancunians Joy Division, whose 1979 debut *Unknown Pleasures* had also been produced by Hannett. Realizing that Magazine's momentum had stalled, Virgin preceded *The Correct Use of Soap* with a desperate flurry of profile-raising singles taken from the record and released in monthly succession. But to no avail: the hit never came. Magazine limped on through a live record and a fourth album, then thankfully heeded Devoto's advice from 'Stuck': 'stop when you cease to amaze me'.

Vic Godard of Subway Sect. Photo by Kevin Cummins

Subway Sect were one of the original punk bands, making their live debut at the 100 Club's 'Punk Fest' in September 1976, alongside The Banshees, the Pistols and The Clash. Taken on by the latter's manager Bernie Rhodes, they joined Buzzcocks and The Slits on The Clash's legendary May 1977 White Riot tour. Subway Sect made a big impression in the North of England and Scotland, where their dressed-down image struck a chord with the local punks, who were much less fashion oriented than those on the London scene. There were no punky postures or stage theatrics, but instead a diffidence and oddness that was utterly un-rock 'n' roll. Singer Vic Godard, for instance, often held his guitar at a strange, jutting angle. 'I loved Vic's gestural things,' recalls Richard Boon, an admirer. 'On one tour he'd sing the lyrics off a notebook and tear off the pages.' The music, too, was arrestingly different. 'The very early Subway Sect was great; their concerts were just pure distortion,' recalls Mark Stewart, then fronting a nascent outfit called The Pop Group. 'They really kickstarted that whole post-punk wall-of-noise thing.'

Of all the groups to emerge out of punk but not exactly *be* punk, Subway Sect remain the most shrouded in mystique. Partly this is because they hardly released any records in their own lifetime. Mostly it's due to the peculiar anti-charisma of Vic Godard. Where Howard Devoto deliberately cultivated intrigue with his oblique comments and evasions, Godard seemed simply to exude a haze of indeterminacy, a mousy vagueness that felt shifty and slightly seedy. Slovenly and nasal, his voice suggested a dulled mind, but this was just a cover for wits as sharp as a fox. His face similarly blended striking and commonplace: angular, almost Cubist, with a massive bridge of aquiline nose-bone, and piercing, beady-black eyes that didn't miss a thing.

A hefty portion of Subway Sect's initial impact came from their appearance – neither punk nor rock 'n' roll, 'an oasis of undersell', as Jon Savage put it. They looked 'regular' yet slightly out of time. Instead of wide collars, straggly perms, flares and kipper ties (the uniform of ordinary young men in 1976), they wore old school pullovers and Oxfam clothes, suggesting the not-quite-kempt, not-exactly-scruffy look of a 1960s clerical worker.

Sonically, too, Subway Sect stood out from the pack. Their roots were sixties mod – The Who, along with more obscure bands like The Sorrows and The Eyes (guitarist Rob Simmons was a sixties Brit-beat fiend). In the early days, the group favoured the brittle bite of the Fender Mustang, the tone knob tweaked to sound 'as trebly as possible': the itchy sound of cerebral unrest. Godard wanted the band to sound scrawny and wiry, never 'heavy' (that thickly layered, muscular menace perfected on *Never Mind the Bollocks*). Following the trails blazed by the Richard Hell's guitarist Robert Quine and by Television's Tom Verlaine, this was guitar playing that owed nothing to rhythm & blues or Chuck Berry: no note-bending, raunchy licks or solos. Rhythm guitar was the lead instrument. 'The music's based on trying to do anything that doesn't sound quite right,' Godard told *ZigZag*. 'If the chords to a song sound anything like a normal "ROCK SONG" then we don't use it.'

The singer's approach to lyrics was equally refreshed and askew. Intensely literate, Godard and his comrades were classic post-punk autodidacts. 'We were really into libraries . . . We used to go round the borough of Richmond in west London in this little Transit van, checking out every library. Looking through all these records. That's how we got into things like medieval music. And books, too.' Songs were often distilled from Godard essays. 'I like to use words that seem *out of place* in a "ROCK SONG",' he told *ZigZag*, talking about how he consciously purged Americanisms in favour of English idiom.

Godard was no jingoist, though: his real passion was European culture. He changed his lowly and prosaic Anglo-Saxon surname, Napper, to something infinitely more glamorous, Gallic and avant-garde. Enrolled in a European studies course at Ealing College, Godard specialized in French art and literature. 'I used to get the other people in the band to take parts in Molière plays and tape 'em,' he chuckles. Before Subway Sect gigs, the group would play Debussy over the PA. Along with France, he developed a crush on the Eastern Bloc, after a school trip to the Soviet Union. 'My room was covered in communist posters. We used to dye our clothes grey!' This infatuation with communism was fundamentally aesthetic rather than political. 'Parallel Lines', one of Godard's greatest songs, comes from a similarly 'rigorously apolitical' (Howard Devoto's words) place as 'Shot by Both Sides', declaring, 'Class war will never change history . . . we've got no belief in your truth'. Like Devoto, Godard seemed non-aligned: the outsider as acute, unforgiving observer. He wasn't scared to tackle weighty subjects: predestination, in the awesomely clangorous 'Chain Smoking'; media mind-control and the corruption of language in 'Nobody's Scared', which starts with the salvo 'Everyone is a prostitute/Singing the song in prison'. But he scrupulously avoided conclusions: questions were more important than answers. 'Double Negative' was his passive-aggressive anthem, close in spirit to Devoto's concept of 'negative drive'. Then there were the meta-rock anthems, critique with a beat, like 'Don't Split It', which famously proclaimed, 'Don't want to play rock 'n' roll'.

Godard rivalled John Lydon's caustic eloquence when it came to the subject of punk's failure and the urgent necessity for rock's decease. In a *Sounds* interview, he trumped Devoto by claiming that punk was starting to go awry as early as September 1976: 'even by the time of [the 100 Club's Punk Fest] all the energy was gone. The Pistols and Clash had already reached their peaks.' Subway Sect envisaged rock not as a safety valve for 'releasing people's tension so that they can go back to work the following morning', he told *Melody Maker*, but as potentially 'a really good secondary education system . . . Teaching [people] to educate themselves.' All this was crystallized in the meta-musical rallying cry 'A Different Story', a blistering critique of rock as the opiate of the (young) people. 'We've just been waiting for it to fall/We oppose all rock 'n' roll,' sings Godard. Only cowardice, the song argues, prevents us all from stepping off the beaten track of rock's twenty-year-old narrative and entering some kind of new cultural space. Ironically, by the time 'A Different Story' was recorded as the flipside of their second single 'Ambition', it had become their most traditional rock-sounding song.

Godard cultists regard 'Ambition' as one of the greatest singles of all time. Strangely, though, manager Bernie Rhodes delayed putting it out for a long time. According to Richard Boon, 'Ambition' was only released at all because he made it a condition of Subway Sect getting the support slot on Buzzcocks' big national tour of late 1978. Instead of Rhodes having to 'buy on to' the tour – the standard industry practice – all he had to do, remembers Boon, was 'just put out a Subway Sect record, Bernie'. Dissatisfied with the recording of 'Ambition', just one of many Subway Sect songs languishing in the can, Rhodes – in the band's absence – sped it up and added a clumsy synth-line, making an already Who-like anthem sound even more like 'Baba O'Riley' or 'Won't Get Fooled Again'. The single was finally released in November 1978. 'Every week of that three-week Buzzcocks/Sect tour,' recalls Boon, 'it was Single of the Week in a different music paper – the *NME*, *Melody Maker*, *Sounds*.'

Despite the hosannas – the *NME* called Godard one of the 'Important People', alongside Lydon, Devoto, Shelley and Alternative TV's Mark Perry – Rhodes continued to sit on the Subway Sect's debut album, which remains unreleased to this day. 'Just circumstance, nothing sinister,' is Godard's explanation. 'Bernie was too busy with The Clash, they'd just taken off, and he was in America a lot. We always lagged behind 'cos we were his number-two band. Maybe he just didn't think the album was good enough. We never really found out why.' Bizarrely, Rhodes's next bright idea was to instruct Godard to sack his group. 'He said, "Your band are useless but you're a great songwriter. I just want your songs."' Brill Building style, Godard was placed on a retainer to write five songs a week at twenty quid per song. Some were performed live by another group managed by Rhodes, The Black Arabs, but were never recorded.

A later, shortlived incarnation of Subway Sect abandoned rock altogether for Northern Soul. Up-tempo sixties soul in the Motown mould, this music had inspired a cult scene in the Midlands and North of England during the early seventies, and was essentially the continuation of mod's love of amphetamine-fuelled all-night dancing to fast black music. Thereafter, Godard's disdain for rock 'n' roll deepened. His next swerve looked back to pre-rock showbiz, swing, and easy listening: the good old days 'when they wrote the songs with pride and they were Song songs,' he told *Sounds*. Godard had always been a fan of crooners like Sinatra, Bennett and Mathis. Now he formed a new line-up of Subway Sect, dressed in demob suits and bow ties, and cited songwriters like Billy Strayhorn and Cole Porter as his role models. Godard informed interviewers that he had no interest in having a trendy audience, but would rather play to middle-aged people and get his records on Radio 2. Instead of infiltrating the world of real MOR, though, Subway Sect became the focus of a short-lived, pseudo-cabaret retro scene centred on Soho's Club Left. The songs were great, but Godard, with his scrawny voice, couldn't quite cut the mustard as a crooner.

Still in his twenties, Godard settled into a young-fogey image, telling *Sounds*, 'I wish I'd lived fifty years ago or something. I wish I had been born in the aristocracy.' Everything was studiously un-rock 'n' roll. Interviews took place in ice-cream parlours rather than pubs. He'd talk about his hobbies: golf, birdwatching, horseracing (he liked a flutter on the gee-gees, and even worked as a bookie). He became the kind of cult figure around whom outlandish stories accreted. There was one rumour that he had a pet otter. Another that he'd performed a gig in Paris dressed as a dolphin. At the same time, he cultivated a René Magritte-style façade of conventionality. As his lyric for 'Be Your Age' put it: 'She always says she dislikes the abnormal, it is so obvious/She says the normal is so much more simply complicated and interesting'. He got a job in an East Sheen hamburger joint and eventually married the manageress. Most famously, he became a postman.

Records appeared sporadically through the eighties, typically hampered in some way or released after a long interval. The mystique of Godard as the nearly man of punk grew, enhanced by the release in 1984 of a brilliant, blistering compilation of early recordings and John Peel radio sessions. Critics and hipsters love nothing more than the lost cause, and Godard was about as lost a cause as you could get. There's always a certain glory to the notion of genius thwarted and possibilities squandered, the hint of what might have been. And, in the end, the *idea* of Subway Sect proved more potent and influential than the few records they released in their own, all-too-brief and underachieving lifetime.

3

UNCONTROLLABLE URGE: The Industrial Grotesquerie of Pere Ubu and Devo

Pere Ubu. Devo.

In July 1978, Stiff Records and *Sounds* magazine jointly announced a competition to win a trip to Akron, Ohio. Highlight of a weekend spent in the 'rubber capital of the world' was a guided tour of the Firestone tyre company. The runner-up would win some Firestone tyres and Stiff's *Akron* compilation, a sampler of local New Wave talent with a scratch 'n' sniff sleeve – the odour, naturally, being rubber.

It's hard to believe now, but there was a brief period – about eighteen months – in which Akron and its neighbour Cleveland, forty miles north, were considered the most exciting cities on earth when it came to rock music. Akron, undistinguished and barely known outside America, and Cleveland, declining capital of the steel industry, seemed *exotic*, albeit in a harsh, appropriately post-punk way. 'Marvel at the desecration of the earth's crust,' exhorted Stiff's music-paper adverts, hailing Akron as the place 'where the American dream ends'. Radar Records enticed the punters to buy Pere Ubu's *Datapanik in the Year Zero* using pictures of poisoned fish in the pollutant-rich Cuyahoga River and the slogan 'The beauty of Cleveland pressed into vinyl'. Journalists hyped the crud-choked Cuyahoga as a new Mersey running through two cities, Akron and Cleveland, surely destined to be as important to late seventies rock as Liverpool had been in the sixties. There was just one catch. The cities each had only one band of true greatness: Devo and Pere Ubu. But in the hype storm, such lesser local lights as Tin Huey, The Bizarros and Rubber City Rebels garnered media coverage and record deals.

The concept of 'industrial music' is usually attributed to Throbbing

Gristle. But the Ohio bands built that buzzword, too. In 1977, as TG's Death Factory began churning out grisly product, Pere Ubu talked about their music as 'industrial folk', while Devo described themselves as an 'eighties industrial band'.

Synonymous with US steel, Cleveland was the engine-room of America's industrial revolution. But after the steel-hungry Second World War, the city began to ail. 'The mills didn't modernize themselves after the war, so they weren't as cost-efficient as foreign rivals,' says Scott Krauss, Pere Ubu's drummer. Then the seventies oil crunch hit north-east Ohio hard: the region had fed Michigan's automobile industry for decades, but people now wanted little Japanese cars that didn't guzzle gas.

There's something about cities that were once prosperous – the residues of wealth and pride make a rich loam in which bohemia can flourish. There's the material legacy of former prosperity: handsomely endowed colleges, art schools, museums, galleries; grand houses grown shabby and cheap to rent; derelict warehouses and empty factories, easily repurposed as rehearsal or performance spaces. A husk from Cleveland's heyday provided Ubu with their first regular opportunity to play live: a scuzzy bikers' bar called the Pirates' Cove that had once been John D. Rockefeller's first warehouse in the heavily industrialized riverside zone known as the Flats. Ubu waxed lyrical about the area in their first interviews: ore-loaded barges floating down the Cuyahoga; steel foundries pounding flat out night and day; the glare from blast furnaces bruising the night in hues of green and purple; belching chimneys and lattices of piping silhouetted against the sky. 'We thought it was magnificent . . . like going to an art museum or something,' singer David Thomas recollected some twenty years later.

You could find similar oddly picturesque industrial zones in Northern English cities like Sheffield and Manchester, whose hipster youth felt a powerful connection with the synth-enhanced music of Ubu and Devo, and were already making their own bleakly futurist music. Teetering into the *post*-industrial era, those cities shared a common attitude with Cleveland, too: a self-belief and swagger only slightly dented by having fallen on hard times. 'We used to be great . . . and we'll show you yet.'

It seems somehow symbolic that Pere Ubu owed their existence partly to inherited wealth. Synth-player Allen Ravenstine used trust-fund money to buy an entire apartment building called the Plaza in downtown Cleveland and rented out its thirty-six rooms cheaply to artistically minded friends, including every member of Ubu: guitarist Tom Herman, bassist Tony Maimone, the group's original co-founder Peter Laughner, drummer Krauss, and singer David Thomas. An imposing Gothic building, the Plaza was just one block south of Euclid Avenue, known in the nineteenth century as 'Millionaires' Row' because the steel barons built houses for their mistresses there. Now Cleveland's red-light district, it wasn't somewhere most people would willingly reside, but Ubu loved its ghost-town ambience and saw themselves as urban pioneers reclaiming the de-industrialized wilderness.

Early Pere Ubu flyer

Another byproduct of Ravenstine's inherited fortune was his expensive EML 200 synth, and the fact that he could take two years out to learn to play it. Living in his house in the country, he clocked in for eight hours' practice a day, just as if it were a job. The EML resembled an 'old-fashioned telephone-operator switchboard, full of jacks to plug in,' recalls Krauss. Because it had a touch-tone dial instead of a keyboard, Ravenstine immediately bypassed the prog-rock style of synth playing – twirling arpeggios and Bach-like folderol – and got stuck right into the messy business of moulding raw sound using frequency envelopes. 'He'd make a noise like a five-pound can with a whole bunch of bumble bees inside,' says Krauss. 'Then he'd change the sine-wave and it'd sound like a beach with a whole bunch of people on it. Ten seconds later, it'd flip to a freight-car noise. The imagination-activating level was absolutely amazing.'

Pere Ubu punningly described their sound as 'avant-garage'. Like Ravenstine's smeary blurts of electronic abstraction, David Thomas's high-pitched bleat immediately marked out the group as more than your average bar band. Whinnying like some peculiar asexual monster, Thomas sounded like Beefheart if his balls had never dropped. Unlike Beefheart, though, there was no blues in Thomas's throat. 'I had all sorts of rules I would follow because I was obsessed with not ripping off black music,' he says. 'So I had rules where I would refuse to bend a note or extend a syllable past one beat.' Often he favoured a kind of dyslexic vocalese. 'I was totally obsessed with the abstract. That's why early on you can't understand anything I'm singing.'

If Thomas and Ravenstine were the quirk-out elements in Ubu's sound, drummer Krauss and bassist Maimone created a solid but inventive foundation for the freaky stuff. Guitarist Herman, alternating between heavy riffing and sculpted arabesques of twisted metal, shifted around somewhere between 'avant' and 'garage'. 'David at one point drew a line across the stage and said, "This is the intellectual side of the band and that is the tank side" – "tank", as in warfare,' recalls Krauss. The rhythm section were designated as the military muscle; Ravenstine and Thomas himself as the scrambled brainiacs. Tom Herman stood dead centre, in no man's land.

In the 1970s, Cleveland prided itself as the first musically sophisticated city west of New York. According to Thomas, it was 'a real hothouse' of connoisseur cliques defining themselves through unusual taste. 'Everybody in bands worked at record stores and each store competed to have the most complete catalogues,' he says. As well as ultra-hip record shops like Drome, the city was blessed with one of the most progressive radio stations in America, WMMS. Its early seventies playlist reads like John Lydon's Capital Radio show: Velvet Underground, Roxy Music, Soft Machine, even Peter Hammill's band Van Der Graaf Generator.

At high school, Thomas's tastes leaned towards the progressive: he was a massive Zappa fan, especially the tape-splicing studio collages of *Uncle Meat*, and regarded Beefheart's *Trout Mask Replica* as a sacred audiotext. The Stooges and The Velvets were common ground across the Cleveland pre-punk scene, as much for the attitude as for the music's raw power pummel. 'We were two or three years post-hippy, and those two or three years were pretty significant,' says Thomas. 'We felt the hippies were pretty useless as any sort of social happening.' This was the generation that treated *Creem*'s Lester Bangs as the prophet, bought marked-down LPs by Velvets and Stooges, and closely studied Lenny Kaye's *Nuggets* anthology of sixties garage punk. In Cleveland, a whole proto-punk scene developed around these sounds. Like Ubu, though, the primitivism was studied – artistic gesture rather than lumpen impulse. The Electric Eels wore safety-pins, rat-traps and swastikas years before the UK punks did, and called what they did 'art terrorism'; The Styrenes' performances featured modern dance and spoken-word elements.

Pere Ubu were also something of an art project. The name came from the monstrously cruel and scatologically crude despot in Alfred Jarry's play *Ubu-Roi*, in its day (the 1890s) as scandalous as punk. Thomas explained the choice by saying, 'I am in a lot of ways a grotesque character' – a reference to his corpulence and gnarly features – 'and the band has a grotesque character. What we are is not pretty.' Thomas also admired Jarry's 'theatrical ideas and narrative devices' – his use of placards with words to set scenes, as opposed to stage props and backdrops, which forced the audience to use its imagination. Thomas developed similar alienation effects for Ubu's performances. Between-song patter might entail him thinking aloud: 'Maybe I should get into some sort of audience rapport here.' At one point, the live shows included 'Reality Dub' – not a song but the simulation of a highly realistic-looking accident.

Pere Ubu formed from the ashes of Thomas's and Laughner's previous band, Rocket from the Tombs, a less obviously art-warped proposition modelled on the raw powerblast of The Stooges and MC5. The new group's inaugural act was recording one of Rocket from the Tombs' least

The baleful bulk of Pere Ubu's David Thomas, *circa* 1979. Photo by Janette Beckman

characteristic tunes as a single. In Ubu's rendition, '30 Seconds over Tokyo' – an attempt to create the 'total sonic environment' inside American bombers as they set off on their Second World War mission to flatten Japan's capital – became even more eccentric. It starts out like some loping, rhythmically sprained hybrid of Black Sabbath and reggae, speeds up a bit, dissolves into freeform splinters, flips back to avant-skank mode, lurches into a sort of doomladen canter, then expires in a spasm of blistered feedback. Over six minutes long, scrofulous with twisted virtuosity, almost prog in its structural strangeness, it sounded about as far removed from The Ramones as, say, The Eagles did. Nevertheless, when the single – self-released on their own Hearthan label – began to circulate in early 1976, Pere Ubu found themselves recruited to 'punk', then gathering momentum as journalists continued to talk up the New York CBGB scene while monitoring the early stirrings of insurrection in London.

While they felt kinship with Television (the New York scene's most psychedelic, least punkish band) and other American eccentrics like The Residents that were coming through the door opened by punk, Pere Ubu were suspicious of the English scene. 'Our ambitions were considerably different from the Sex Pistols',' sniffs Thomas, who regards that band's brand of rebellion as puerile and destructive. The Brits, he believes, attached fashion and politics to something that was purely about music and artistic experimentation. Pere Ubu didn't want to piss on rock music; they wanted to contribute, help it mature as an artform. 'Our ambitions were to move it forward into ever more expressive fields, create something worthy of Faulkner and Melville, the true language of human consciousness,' he says loftily. UK punk's class-war rhetoric didn't compute: Ubu were proudly bourgeois: 'My father was a professor. I had an academic upbringing and certainly an academic path was indicated. This was the strength of our middle-class upbringing.' Having lost friend and founder-member Peter Laughner to drugs, they had no time for Vicious-style death tripping. 'Things are rough, things are weird, there's no sense in ignoring that – which is why Ubu music isn't all sweetness and light,' said Ravenstine in one interview. 'But you gotta *confront* the problems.'

Pere Ubu may have disdained the UK's alternately politicized and nihilistic versions of punk, but it was British audiences who most fervently embraced Ubu's music. After '30 Seconds', two more Hearthan singles followed in 1976: 'Final Solution' b/w 'Cloud 149' and 'Street Waves' b/w 'My Dark Ages'. Most of the copies were shipped to the UK and Europe, where they sold very well. Touring the UK for the first time in the spring of 1978, the band were greeted as the Second Coming. Such emerging bands as Joy Division and Josef K were in the audiences, assimilating Herman's fractured guitar and the ominous atmosphere of songs like 'Real World' and 'Chinese Radiation'. In 1978, decades before he developed the only-Americans-can-rock theories he touts today, Thomas appreciated the intense ardour and seriousness of the British response: 'The people seem more politically aware, spiritually aware. It's all on a higher level – significantly higher. They study the music.'

Meanwhile, back in America, 'Street Waves' had fallen into the hands of Mercury Records' A&R man Cliff Burnstein, who decided Ubu would be the ideal signing to launch his new subsidiary label Blank. Inspired by New Wave's pared-down, no-frills aesthetic, Burnstein had developed a fresh approach to breaking bands: recording them cheap, so that only 25,000 sales were required before label and band started earning. This was a break with the standard seventies major-label tactic of extravagant recording budgets and promotion. These costs, recoupable against royalties, saddled the artists with debt, which left them vulnerable to corporate pressure along the lines of 'Dilute your sound; we want a return on our investment *now*'.

In 1978, Cleveland and Akron reigned as the fulcrum of the post-punk universe. In March, Blank released Ubu's debut album *The Modern Dance* to massive acclaim. In April came Radar's *Datapanik in the Year Zero* EP, which contained the best tracks from the three Hearthan singles. At the height of their powers, Pere Ubu sealed the impression of creative floodgates hurled open wide when they unleashed a second, even more impressive album only seven months after the debut. *Dub Housing* got its evocative name not from any reggae leanings but a stoned eye's view of Baltimore as the band drove through the city in their tour van. 'In Baltimore they had these row houses, and somebody said, "Oh, look, dub housing,"' says Krauss. The vistas echoed endlessly, paralleling the way that drum hits, guitar chords and horn-licks were turned into reverb-trails by dub producers. Underlining the band's difference from the rock norm, the UK release of *Dub Housing* was celebrated with a unique performance: a 'Ubu Mystery Trip' that transported the audience by coach to a secret destination. Unfortunately, the gig's location – the chalk-walled Chiselhurst Caves – suffered from terrible acoustics, and was so cold that Tom Herman had to wear gloves with the fingers snipped off in order to get his fingers on the frets.

But after their 1978 triumphs – two hugely acclaimed albums, two tours of the UK and one each for Europe and America – Pere Ubu reached a crossroads. They now had a big-time rock manager and he advised the band effectively to formularize their sound, then beat the public over the head with it. Remake *Dub Housing* two or three more times, he said, and you'll be stars. Thomas recalls asking him, 'What if we *can't* repeat it? What if we don't *want to* repeat it?' The manager told Ubu they'd always get signed to deals and be able to release records, but they'd never transcend cult status. It was meant to be a dire warning, but, laughs Thomas, 'Our eyes lit up. "*That* sounds pretty good!"'

Pere Ubu's art-rock integrity and belief in constant progression came into play, along with a certain wilfulness. *The Modern Dance* and *Dub Housing* both contained absurdist sound collages and exercises in pure Dada such as 'The Book is on the Table' and 'Thriller'; these now became the blueprint for the third album, *New Picnic Time*. 'Our problem is that we never wanted to repeat *Dub Housing*,' Thomas once said. 'That desire never to repeat became as much of a trap as trying to repeat formulas the way some bands do.' Although he likes to argue that 'all adventurous art is done by middle-class people' because they always have other career options and don't need to worry about making money, the corollary is that bourgeois bohemians don't possess that vital hunger to succeed that drives those from less privileged backgrounds. 'We were on the edge of being popular but we were fundamentally incapable of being popular,' admits Thomas, 'because we were fundamentally perverse.'

'Devo, it's like the *Titanic* going down or something,' Allen Ravenstine once said of their Akron allies, who early on often shared stages with Pere Ubu. 'The impression I've got from their songs and from talking with them is that they're really much more into making a mockery of everything, not really giving a damn.'

Actually, Devo's 'cynicism' was borne of having once cared too much. Unlike Ubu, Devo had been hippies, of a sort. Gerald V. Casale and Mark Mothersbaugh, the group's conceptual core, were among the anti-war students protesting at Kent State University, Ohio, on 4 May 1970 when the National Guard opened fire. Two of the four slain students – Alison Krauss and Jeffrey Miller – were friends of Casale. 'They were just really smart liberal kids, eighteen and nineteen, doing what we all did back then,' he says. 'They weren't crazy sociopaths.' He recalls the dazed, slow-motion sensation when the guns started firing, 'like being in a car accident'; the blood streaming down the sidewalk; the eerie sound of moaning from the crowd, 'like a kennel of hurt puppies'. At first, 'even the National Guard was frozen, freaked out. Then they marched us off campus and the university was shut down for three months.'

That date in May 1970 is one of several contenders for 'the day the sixties died'. 'For me, it was the turning point,' says Casale bitterly. 'Suddenly I saw it all clearly: all these kids with their idealism, it was very naïve.' Participants in SDS – Students for a Democratic Society – like Casale reached a crossroads. 'After Kent, it seemed like you could either join a guerrilla group like The Weather Underground, actually try assassinating some of these evil people, the way they'd murdered anybody in the sixties who'd tried to make a difference. Or you could just make some kind of whacked-out creative Dada art response. Which is what Devo did.'

Devo was born in those three months that Kent was closed down. 'Gerry would come round to my house and we started writing music,' says Mothersbaugh. He'd first noticed Casale because of a prankster performance-art piece he'd done during Fine Art Faculty shows. 'I'd be this character Gorge who wore an enema-bag bandoleer,' says Casale. 'My sidekick Poot Man dressed in black wrestling shorts and a black full-face mask like those Mexican wrestlers. He walked around like a monkey, knuckles trailing on the ground. The art was always bad, derivative stuff – endless mindless landscapes and still lifes. I'd point at a picture and go, "Poot Man!" and he'd rub his ass on the artwork, or hold his nose like it stunk. Every time Poot Man took a pretend shit on the graduate student art, I'd reward him with milk, which he'd suck through the enema tube. People would be disgusted and move out the way, and somebody would get security. After a few of these events, they'd be waiting for us.' Says Mothersbaugh, 'I saw him do the Poot Man thing, and I was like "Who's this guy?" Everybody hated Gerry so I *knew* I was going to like him.' Casale, meanwhile, had already admiringly noted Mothersbaugh's artwork – decals of puking heads in profile.

For a band that later defined New Wave music, Casale's and Mothersbaugh's roots were unpromising. 'Mark was playing in a band that did Yes and ELP covers,' says Casale. 'He had long hair down to his waist and a stack of keyboards.' An accomplished bassist, Casale had played in numerous blues bands and was steeped in everything from the original Delta blues to the electric Chicago sound. Prog and blues collided in a mutual passion for Captain Beefheart and the Magic Band. But everything that was primal and earthy about Beefheart became deliberately sterile and stilted in Devo's hands. Their quest, says Casale, was to discover 'what devolved music would sound like. We wanted to make outer-space caveman music.'

Devo's other big inspiration was the glam grotesquerie of early Roxy Music. You can hear Bryan Ferry's android vibrato in Mothersbaugh's edge-of-hysteria bleat, while his synth spurts owe a lot to Eno. 'I loved his asymmetric, atonal synth solos in Roxy. He brought a whole new way to think about the instrument – as opposed to Rick Wakeman and Keith Emerson, who just sounded like glorified organists. I used to write synth parts I could play with a fist instead of fingers. We were looking for sounds like V2 rockets and mortar blasts; things that weren't on the settings when you bought a synth.' Rather than a keyboard, Devo treated the synth as a noise-generator: 'The more technology you have, the more primitive you can be,' Mothersbaugh told one interviewer. 'You can express guttural sounds, bird noises, brain waves, blood flow.'

In Devo's earliest days, the group experimented with machine rhythm. 'Our first drummer was my youngest brother Jim, who left to be an inventor,' says Mothersbaugh. 'He created a home-made electronic drum kit, using acoustic drums with guitar pick-ups attached to their heads, which he'd feed into wah-wah pedals, fuzztones and echoplexes. It sounded really amazing, like a walking, broken-down robot.' Ultimately, Devo found Alan Myers, 'this incredible, metronomic drummer', and the group started to explore disconcertingly disjointed time signatures like 7/8 and 11/8. 'Those timings make you feel rigid right away,' says Casale.

In the early-to-mid seventies, with punk barely a glimmer on the horizon, Devo defined themselves against the ruling American mainstream rock of the day: chugging feelgood boogie and slick, slack country-rock. Just as their music's twitchy angularity was the antithesis of FM radio's soft rock, likewise Devo's attitude – neurotic, uptight, stiff-necked – revolted against the chilled-out babyboomers. 'We were anything but hippies – loose, natural,' Casale recalled years later. Devo rejected all those 'flabby leftover ideas from the sixties' that by 1972 had degenerated into self-absorbed and complacent hedonism. Back then, their ungroovy rhythms – midway between spasm and stricture – were as appealing to Akron audiences as a cup of cold puke. Because no one wanted to hear original music, Devo pretended to be a cover band to get gigs. 'We'd say, "Here's another one by Foghat," and then play one of our tunes, like "Mongoloid",' chuckles Mothersbaugh. 'Angry hippy factory workers charged the stage trying to stop us. Often we'd get paid just to quit. Sometimes the police would be called.'

The group's first two singles, 'Satisfaction' and 'Jocko Homo' – like Ubu's, self-released, on Devo's own Booji Boy label – were relatively torpid compared with their later frantic sound. This was partly because 'Jocko Homo' and its B-side 'Mongoloid' were recorded in a garage with no heating during a freezing winter, with the band wearing gloves. After five wilderness years in Akron, playing only a handful of gigs and funding the band through a series of grim jobs (Casale's CV includes projectionist in a porno cinema, methadone-clinic counsellor, and graphic artist at a janitorial supply firm), the singles were Devo's calling card to the wider world. 'No one will ever know the effort it took for us to get out of Akron,' says Casale. 'Driving down to Cincinnati with just enough cash to get two thousand copies pressed at Queen City Records. Mark and me sitting up endless nights gluing together the covers that we'd printed. Akron was like boot camp. We practised day and night, at weekends, when other people were out getting loaded and getting laid, over and over until we got good.'

It worked. Devo evolved into a tightly drilled package of sound-and-visuals, sharing as much with the shock-rock theatre of Alice Cooper and The Tubes as with the no-frills punk rockers. Whenever feasible, Devo gigs began with *The Beginning Was the End: The Truth about De-Evolution*, a ten-minute film directed by their friend Chuck Statler, whom they'd originally met in an experimental art class at Kent State. The short generated the enduringly famous images of Devo: Mothersbaugh as the mad professor in bow tie and white coat giving a lecture on 'de-evolution'; the rest of the band wearing plastic sunglasses and coloured tights pulled tightly over their heads to squash their features, bankrobber style. And it was Statler who in 1975 showed Devo a popular science magazine with a feature on laser discs, then on the verge of being introduced to the market. 'We read that it was the same size as an LP but had moving pictures on it,' says Mothersbaugh. 'And we thought: Oh my God, that's what we want to do!' Originally an aspiring film director more than a musician, Casale fantasized about making 'an anti-capitalist science-fiction movie' and always saw Devo as a visual entity: 'The theatrics and the ideas and the staging were as important as the music.'

Champing at the bit to kickstart the Videodisc Revolution, Devo were impatient to reach the future. The seventies had been a write-off, merely the sixties sagging into decadence – supine and sour. Devo yearned to be the first band on the block making eighties music. Like Pere Ubu, they went beyond punk, really the last gasp of seventies rock 'n' roll, before punk even properly existed; not just sonically, with their synths and industrial rhythms, but conceptually, too. They shared punk's never-trust-a-hippy attitude, but, says Mothersbaugh, 'We thought the punks never learned from the failure of the hippies. Rebellion always gets co-opted into another marketing device.' Selling out, using the system to spread the virus, seemed like the most insidious strategy for Devo, who saw themselves as a 'postmodernist protest band'. Putting out the Booji Boy singles independently was just a step on the ladder, a way of attracting attention. The game plan was to join rock's ruling class. 'We figured we'd mimic the structure of those who get the greatest rewards out of the upside-down business and become a corporation,' Casale told *Soho Weekly News*. 'Most rock musicians, they're no more than clerks or auto mechanics.'

D.E.V.O.

DEVO

THE RAZZ BAND

& READY MADES

Sunday October 9

10pm

443 BROADWAY
SAN FRANCISCO

MABUHAY GARDENS

TELEPHONE
(415) 956-3315

Flyer for Devo show at the Mabuhay, San Francisco's legendary punk club. L to R: Mark Mothersbaugh, Gerald V. Casale, Bob Mothersbaugh, Alan Myers, Bob Casale

So Devo gigs started with a bombastic synth jingle, the Devo Corporate Anthem, during which the group lined up solemnly to give a salute. Because 'individuality and rebellion were obsolete', Devo 'dressed identical so you couldn't tell who was who,' says Mothersbaugh.

'We wanted to look like a machine or an army onstage. We felt that the real mindless uniform was rock's blue jeans.' Instead, the group 'dressed like maintenance worker geeks', says Casale, wearing outfits he'd acquired during his stint at the janitorial supply company. They built up a mix-and-mismatch wardrobe that blended the regimental (boy scouts, servicemen, football teams) and the technocratic (hazardous-waste protection suits, rubber gloves). This they spiced with kitsch flamboyance – cheesy alien masks, peculiar plastic helmets styled to look like extremely bad hairpieces. Devo also developed a tautly choreographed repertoire of jerky stage moves inspired, says Casale, by seeing a Russian Constructivist ballet. 'And then we played this very precise music like James Brown turned into a robot. And it really pissed everybody off!'

Well, not *everybody*. In 1977 things got confusing as first Iggy Pop and David Bowie, then Brian Eno and Robert Fripp, jostled to produce Devo's album debut. Thrilling to the sensations of dislocation and menace their music induced, Eno raved about Devo as 'the best live show I have ever seen'. Neil Young, of all people – 'the grandfather of Granola Rock', as Casale nicknamed him – invited Devo to appear in his feature-length movie *Human Highway* as a squad of disgruntled and radioactively glowing nuclear-waste workers. Iggy Pop was so enamoured he wanted to fill his next album with Devo songs. At the group's first New York show in July 1977, Bowie came onstage to introduce the second set and announced, 'This is the band of the future. I'm going to produce them in Tokyo this winter.' Finally, it was settled that the record would be produced by Eno in Germany, with Bowie contributing only at weekends (he was busy making the movie *Just a Gigolo*). 'We didn't even have a record deal, but Eno said he'd pay for the flights, the studio costs, everything,' says Mothersbaugh. 'Eno was just certain we would get a record contract.'

Sure enough, Warner Bros, Island and Bowie's production company Bewlay Brothers began competing for the group. 'Sick' was hot, and Devo looked like the next gang of marketable monsters after The Sex Pistols. Then Virgin entered the fray. In early 1978 Richard Branson invited Mothersbaugh and guitarist Bob Casale to fly to Jamaica. When the boys were very stoned, Branson popped the question: what did they think about inviting Johnny Rotten, freshly fired from the Pistols, to become Devo's singer? 'He said, "Johnny's in the next room; there are journalists from the *NME* and *Melody Maker* here,"' recalls Mothersbaugh.

'"It's a perfect time to go down the beach, take some photos together, and announce he's joined Devo. What do you think?" I was too stoned to make the correct answer, which was "Sure!" 'Cos we could have done the picture session, got the publicity, and then gone back to Akron and just said, "No way! Forget it."'

Still embroiled in negotiations with record labels, Devo recorded their debut, *Q: Are We Not Men? A: We Are Devo!*, in Conny Plank's studio, a converted farm twenty miles outside of Cologne. It's their masterpiece, but suffers slightly from a neither-one-thing-nor-the-other quality: it lacks some of the frenzy of their live shows yet is not a full-on foray into Eno's post-*Low* soundworld. 'In retrospect, we were overly resistant to Eno's ideas,' says Mothersbaugh. 'He made up synth parts and really cool sounds for almost every song on the album, but we used them on only three or four songs. Some we did, like the loop of monkey chanters that's on "Jocko Homo". I'd kind of like to hear what the album would have sounded like if we'd been more open to Eno's suggestions. But in those days we thought we knew everything.'

You can still hear the Eno imprint, though. Tinted and textured, Casale's bass glistens wetly. 'Shrivel Up' is dank with synth slime, an abject feel that fits the lyrics about decay and mortality. 'Gut Feeling' takes garage punk's woman-done-me-wrong rage and gives it a perverse twist: 'You took your tongs of love and stripped away my garment'. 'Uncontrollable Urge' makes rock's 'wild sexuality' seem as absurd and humiliating as an involuntary nervous tic. 'Come Back Jonee' likewise turns Chuck Berry's 'Johnny B. Goode' inside out: the heartbreaker bad-boy 'jumps into his Datsun', the OPEC 1970s fuel-economy version of a 'real' rock 'n' roll automobile like a T-Bird.

While the band toiled away on their debut, Devo-mania escalated. Stiff Records licensed the original Booji Boy singles and re-released them in quick succession. In April 1978, their cover of the Rolling Stones' 'Satisfaction' was a big hit in several European countries and stopped just short of the UK Top 40. Devo's disco-punk version sounded like 'a stupid perpetual-motion machine clanking around the room', as Mothersbaugh put it. After defiling this iconic sixties classic by reducing it to a desiccated theorem, Devo then riled the 100,000-strong army of Old Wave fans at that summer's Knebworth Festival. Sandwiched on the bill between Jefferson Starship and Genesis, Devo aggravated the audience with their uniform appearance (yellow chemical-protection body-suits, fluorescent orange skateboard helmets), manic stage moves, and the sheer palsied attack of their music. 'Everybody started throwing stuff, having fights,' recalls Mothersbaugh. 'A lot of people got pissed off.'

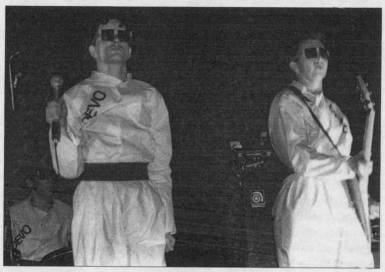

Devo at Max's Kansas City, New York, 1979. L to R: Alan Myers, Mark Mothersbaugh, Gerald V. Casale.
Photo by Marcia Resnick

By the time *Q: Are We Not Men?* hit the record stores at the end of August, the hype and marketing overkill were beginning to raise hackles. The UK press shifted into premature backlash mode. What were Devo *about*, anyway? Their interviews were full of opaque pseudo-scientific jargon and references to a menagerie of bizarre characters (like the ninny naïf Booji Boy, a grown man with a baby's face), all of which sceptics found both contrived and silly. It was fatally unclear if the group's de-evolution theories represented a critique or a cynical celebration of cultural atrophy, corporatized rock and the recline and fall of the West.

Hatched by Mothersbaugh and Casale in the early days, de-evolution was a patchwork parody of religion and quack science woven together from motley sources: the Second Law of Thermodynamics, sociobiology, genetics, the paranoid science fiction of Burroughs and Philip K. Dick, anthropology. An especially key source was a series of dubious nineteenth-century eugenic theories involving notions of degeneration and the decline of civilization (often attributed to racial interbreeding).

Virgin's press release for the album claimed the band 'devolved from a long line of brain-eating apes, some of which settled in north-eastern Ohio'. Casale sampled this absurdist notion from a 300-page treatise by a deranged Bavarian pseudo-scientist. The tract argued that humans descended from cannibalistic monkeys whose diet of ape brain had resulted in bizarre mutations and the loss of their ability to live in nature. Devo also pillaged evangelical crank literature and pamphlets from such Christian sects as the Jehovah's Witnesses. 'Two of the biggest televangelists, Rex Humbard and the Reverend Ernest Ainsley, broadcast out of Akron,' says Mothersbaugh. 'We saw how disgusting and evil these people were, so we took delight in turning their cosmology upside down.' The album's most physically galvanizing song, 'Praying Hands', was a stab at imagining a Christian fundamentalist dance craze.

In Devo's music, a puritanical streak of revulsion jostled with an urge to revel in the mire. Talking of American pop culture, Casale describes being 'raised in mindless electric filth'. Devo seemed to be starting from the same place – a sense of impotence and suffocation – as those great misanthropes of modernist literature, Louis-Ferdinand Céline and Wyndham Lewis, whose quest for purity in a tarnished world made them sympathetic to Nazism. In the first three decades of the twentieth century, abhorrence of capitalism led almost as many intellectuals to fascism as it did to communism. And some were quick to accuse Devo of being 'fascist' themselves, most notably *Rolling Stone* magazine (who clearly recognized on some level that everything they stood for was 'the enemy' in Devo's worldview). Actually, it's more the case that Devo managed to include both the abjection and 'fascist' response to it within their art simultaneously, in their pantomime of disgust and discipline. Without their uniforms, Casale said, they'd be 'just like a horrible maggot with no crustacean shell . . . You'd be like a pinchy little blackhead.'

Properly attired, Devo went forth as the 'clean-up squad', on a mission into the goo-goo muck of mainstream American culture. Interviews teemed with imagery of purulence, decay, obesity, excretion, flaccidity, infestation, tumours, putrefaction and bulimia. Progress was a belief system that had gone 'absolutely rancid', while one sequence during *The Truth about De-Evolution* saw the group, sealed inside latex bags, writhing 'like maggots, paramecium, foetal things'. But Devo's favourite set of metaphors revolved around constipation, with the band themselves variously figuring as the laxative, the enema nozzle, the enema bag and 'the fluid in the bag'. 'Gerry and I both had parents who'd read in

Dr Spock that it was a good idea to give your kids enemas once or twice a month,' says Mothersbaugh. 'We lived in fear of the next enema, the warm soapy water. When we were in our twenties we finally said, "Dad, that's enough!"'

This squeamishness contaminated Devo's sex songs, from their earliest efforts like 'Buttered Beauties' (in which Mothersbaugh imagines female secretions smeared all over him like 'glossy tallow') to the chorus 'I think I missed the hole' in the debut album's 'Sloppy (I Saw My Baby Getting)'. They loved pornography, whether Bataille's avant-garde version or *Hustler*'s mass-market hardcore. The latter was the first news-stand porn mag to show gynaecologically explicit photographs. 'I wrote a song called "Penetration in the Centerfold" about the first *Hustler* I ever saw,' says Mothersbaugh. 'Porn is important to the lower economic levels, simply because you can't afford real sex.'

What emerged from these impulses and inputs were songs that, beneath the Dada quirky surface, were often plain misogynistic in the most conventional sense. On the debut album, 'Gut Feeling' segues straight into 'Slap Your Mammy'. 'Triumph of the Will' on the second album, *Duty Now for the Future*, reads like a Nietzschean justification for rape: 'It was a thing I had to/It was a message from below/It was a messy situation . . . It is a thing females ask for/When they convey the opposite'. Much of *Duty* sounds like a robotic version of The Knack's sexually pent-up 'My Sharona' – choppy New Wave guitar, frantically pelvic beat-off rhythms.

Unlike Pere Ubu, who happily remained a cult band, Devo's project – subvert from within – could only really make sense if it was massively successful. They moved to Los Angeles, capital of the entertainment business, and with 1980's *Freedom of Choice* made a record even more calculatedly commercial than the clinical-sounding *Duty*. The concept was 'electro R&B' but the results were more like a fusion of New Wave and Eurodisco. Everything was played by the band in the studio, but it sounded like it was programmed using sequencers; the electronic textures felt standard issue, like the pre-set sounds you get on a synth. Still, *Freedom of Choice* achieved a New Wave-inflected dance-rock sound that Billy Idol would later ride to stardom. And it gave Devo their own platinum album, spurred on by the Top 20 success of 'Whip It'.

Written during the ailing twilight of the Carter presidency, 'Whip It' offered Dale '*How to Win Friends and Influence People*' Carnegie-style advice to the embattled leader: 'Come on, Jimmy, get your shit together,'

Devo at the height of their success, on the cover of American New Wave magazine *Trouser Press*,
February 1982

says Mothersbaugh. By the time Warners allowed them to make a promo video for it, it was clear that Reagan was heading for a landslide victory, so Devo made the video into a surreal commentary on America's shift to the right. The result was a promo that nearly twenty-five years later has not dated in the least and is still a huge hoot: Devo's one moment of mass-cultural triumph. Pitched somewhere between John Ford and David Lynch (*Eraserhead* was a favourite for the Ubu–Devo set), this genuinely creepy video perfectly crystallizes Devo's 'freakshow aesthetic'. As a bunch of Texan stud-muffins and blonde bimbos gawk and giggle, Mothersbaugh wields a whip and one by one lashes away the garments of a strange Grace Jones-like Amazon of a woman; her legs start trembling in an indescribably abject way as she waits for the final whipcrack to strip off her last shred of modesty. Meanwhile, the rest of Devo perform the song cooped inside a cattle pen – pasty-faced spud-boys wearing shorts that show off their scrawny knees and the famous 'flowerpot hats' (actually meant to look like Aztec temples or ziggurats). 'We were horrified by Reagan's ascent,' says Casale. 'So we were just making fun of myths of cowboys in the West. It was based on a magazine I'd found, one of those fifties gentlemen's magazines with softcore nudies. It had an article about a dude ranch owned by an ex-stripper and her husband. As part of the entertainment, he'd whip her clothes off in the corral for all the guests to watch. I showed the piece to Mark and he was agog, so I said, "Let's do it!"'

As the new decade proceeded, the original 'eighties industrial band' was devoured by the industry. Even as they railed against Reaganism with songs like 'Freedom of Choice' and 'Through Being Cool', Devo slowly but steadily capitulated to the record-biz way of doing things. They'd sold two million albums by 1981, but this only made Warners increase the pressure in the hope of harvesting an even bigger return on their investment. 'They wanted us to be at The Cars' level,' sighs Casale. They struggled on for years, wrangling for the 'Whip It'-scale radio hit that never came, stuck at a middling-level success just a notch above cult. In a savage irony, they succumbed to their own unique form of de-evolution, winding up as a kind of semi-popular Kiss, peddling costume rock for their fanbase of nerdish diehards. Obsessed with flashy hi-tech projections, they resorted to playing gigs to a click-track fed through headphones, in order to stay in sync with the visuals. Instead of a parody of regimentation, they became the real thing – slaves to slickness, peons in the 'corporate feudal state'.

49

4

CONTORT YOURSELF: No Wave New York

James Chance & The Contortions. Suicide. Lydia Lunch. DNA. Mars. Lounge Lizards.

By 1977, the New York punk scene had run out of steam. Signed to big labels, the major bands – Television, The Ramones, Talking Heads, Blondie, Patti Smith – were increasingly drawn away from the city by touring. Meanwhile, the upstart Brits had stolen New York's thunder, ratcheting up punk's outrage element with anarchist rhetoric and a subversive anti-fashion look light years beyond CBGB's scruffy retro-rock. Photogenic, foul-mouthed and with a political edge the bohemians of New York lacked, the UK punks commandeered the headlines on both sides of the Atlantic, to the point where most mainstream media seemed convinced punk was a British invention.

New York punk also suffered from not being sufficiently forward-looking. One of the first articles to discuss CBGB, written in 1975 by James Wolcott, pinpointed the way the scene couched itself as a *return* to something lost. Headlined 'A Conservative Impulse in the New Rock Underground', the *Village Voice* feature celebrated the downtown punk bands for creating a feeling of local community in opposition to a mainstream rock culture now degenerated into just another branch of showbiz, with its own aristocracy of untouchably remote stars.

But the musical translation of this egalitarian impulse involved jettisoning the entirety of the 1970s thus far and going *back*. 'Punk is just real good basic rock & roll . . . real basic fifties and early sixties rock,' declared no less an authority than Nancy Spungen. When you looked at The Ramones' leather jackets and cult of all things teenage, how different was it really from the fifties revivalism in America's pop mainstream

– *Grease* and *Happy Days*? The Ramones' bracing blast of speed and minimalism served its purpose, showing up the flabby, flaccid indulgence of mid-70s rock. But within two albums the band exhausted their point. Elsewhere, The Heartbreakers' stodge of refried Chuck Berry was barely more advanced than British pub rock – Dr Feelgood on an IV drip of smack rather than lager. And even the scene's most adventurous band, Television, drew heavily on late sixties music, their quicksilver twin guitars interplay steeped in the West Coast acid rock of The Byrds, Country Joe & The Fish and Grateful Dead.

Into this vacuum of innovation charged a second generation of New York bands who came to be called 'No Wave'. They were determined to sever all connections with rock tradition. 'I hated almost the entirety of punk rock,' Lydia Lunch, ravenhaired queen of the new scene, recalled. 'I don't think No Wave had anything to do with it.' Lunch's group, Teenage Jesus & The Jerks, and their comrade bands, Mars, Contortions and DNA, defined radicalism not as a return to roots but as deracination. Scour the history of rock and you'll find only a handful of precedents for No Wave: Velvet Underground at their least songful and most white-noise punishing; Yoko Ono's primal screech and John Lennon's guitar gougings for The Plastic Ono Band; the convulsions and discords of Beefheart's *Trout Mask Replica*. But, crucially, the No Wave groups *acted* as if they had no ancestors at all.

No Wave was defined less by a sound than by this Year Zero approach. Musically, they ranged from Teenage Jesus' stentorian dirges to Contortions' jazz-scarred thrash-funk, from Mars' guitar-flagellating clangour to DNA's dislocated grooves. Curiously, the No Wave groups staged their revolt against rock tradition using the standard rock format of guitar, bass, and drums. Occasionally, they leavened this restricted arsenal with horns or keyboards – always basic, sixties-style organs, though, rather than synthesizers. It was as if they felt the easy electronic route to making a post-rock noise was *too* easy. Instead, they used rock's tools against itself. Which is why No Wave music irresistibly invites metaphors of dismemberment, desecration, 'defiling rock's corpse'.

Ironically, a traditional blues and country technique, slide guitar, provided No Wave with some of its most disconcertingly novel noises. As used by three female guitarists – Conny Burg in Mars, Lydia Lunch in Teenage Jesus, Pat Place in Contortions – slide offered musical novices the quickest way to generate startling sounds. You didn't even

51

need to learn how to hold down chord shapes on the guitar strings. 'Who wanted chords, all these progressions that have been used to death in rock?' jeers Lunch. 'I'd use a knife, a beer bottle . . . Glass gave the best sound. To this day, I still don't know a single chord on the guitar.'

As well as shunning electronics, the No Wave bands never really embraced the sound-warping possibilities of the recording studio. Playing in a small club at overwhelming volume: that's where No Wave really worked. The handful of recordings that survive the scene are like footnotes to the live experience. Along with the sheer sonic assault, No Wave shows often had a performance-art aspect. James Chance, bandleader and singer/saxophonist in Contortions, turned gigs into happenings by attacking the audience: jostling, slapping, legendarily grabbing a girl by the hair at one show and biting another woman 'on the tit' (or so he claimed in an interview). 'James was like a Jackson Pollock painting, such an explosive personality,' says Adele Bertei, Contortions' keyboard player. 'And he had a strong masochistic streak. So he'd jump into the crowd and start kissing some girl. The boyfriend would push him off and a fist-fight would ensue. Our bassist George Scott and me would leap offstage and get into the mêlée. Then we'd all get back on to the stage with blood running down our faces – James being the worse for wear always because he'd get the brunt of it; plus he's so tiny.'

Partly sensationalist, calculated to procure the band notoriety and press attention, these tactics were also impelled by the perennial avant-garde urge to shatter physically the performer/audience barrier: to turn a spectacle into a situation, spectators into participants. And it worked. The shows started to sell out. 'A big part of it was the art crowd,' says Pat Place. 'The violence plus the noise element made our shows something like performance art combined with music.'

Place was a typical No Waver: an artist who'd come to New York looking to have a career in the downtown art world, only to be drawn towards the underground rock scene. Fresh out of art school in Chicago, where she'd studied painting and sculpture, she arrived in New York hoping to become some kind of conceptual artist. 'Performance art was the hot thing at that point,' she recalls. And it was also a breeding ground for No Wavers: DNA's Arto Lindsay and Robin Crutchfield, and Mark Cunningham of Mars came from experimental theatre or performance-art backgrounds. Along with several other future No Wave luminaries, Cunningham and Lindsay attended Eckerd College in St

Petersburg, Florida. 'Like other small, progressive colleges of the early seventies, it was putting into practice sixties ideas like freeform studies, so it was perfect for self-expression and a magnet for freaks and misfits from around the country,' recalls Cunningham. 'I met Arto the first day I was there and we ditched our assigned roommates and moved in together.'

New York beckoned as the home of all things conceptual and multi-media, the world capital of aesthetic border-crossing and 'total art'. All the avant-garde ideas of the sixties, from Fluxus to the Vienna Aktionists, 'had filtered down to us kids in the early seventies,' says Lindsay. 'There was a youthful thing of seeing how far you could push anything.' Lindsay's hero was the poet turned performance artist Vito Acconci. 'Especially his piece *Seed Bed*, where he built a false floor under a gallery. He lay under that floor for a few hours every day and there was a sign on the wall saying, "The artist is under the floor listening to you, fantasizing and masturbating while you're in the gallery"!' Lindsay also admired extremists like Chris Burden and Hermann Nitsch, who staged ritualistic, blood-soaked feats of endurance and abjection.

Artists gravitated to New York's underground rock scene partly because there seemed to be more possibilities for making something happen there. The art market was depressed, the gallery circuit tough to break into for young painters. But even successful artists like Robert Longo played in bands. Punk had restored rock's status as the heat-generating power spot of modern culture. It made the downtown milieu of SoHo's art spaces, home to concerts by minimalist com-posers, multimedia installations and performance pieces, seem pallid and genteel. Although some 'real' musicians participated in No Wave – Chance was conservatory-educated – most had no previous involve-ment with rock beyond being a listener. Typically, their primary voca-tion was film, poetry or the visual arts. Coming to music from other directions, they had a slightly distanced approach, which enabled them to grapple with their instruments (often chosen arbitrarily) as foreign objects, tools to be misused or reinvented.

Although they pre-dated both No Wave and punk by several years, Suicide were in many ways the archetypal New York collision of art and rock. Singer Alan Vega was a sculptor who used electric lights and ready-mades (Catholic kitsch trinkets, plastic toys, porno cards, celebrity photos) to create trash-culture shrines from some post-cataclysmic America of the near future. In the late sixties, he joined the Art Workers

Coalition, a militant socialist group that once barricaded the Museum of Modern Art. Then he became a lynchpin of the Project of Living Artists, an anarchic workshop/performance space in SoHo, funded by the New York State Council of the Arts. Vega worked at the Project by day and lived there, illegally, by night. It was here that he met free-jazz musician Martin Rev and formed Suicide. The band emerged out of endless freeform jamming. 'Suicide was like the Big Bang of the universe,' says Vega. 'Chaos, then after a while the gases began to form little balls that became the galaxies. Same with us, except the gases began to form little songs – first "Cheree", then "Ghostrider".' A unique sound developed: Vega's half-spoken/half-sung incantations resembled a cross between rockabilly and method acting; Rev generated pittering pulses from a beaten-up electronic keyboard and crude but hypnotic beats using a cruddy drum machine originally designed for weddings and bar mitzvahs.

As infamous as they were infrequent, Suicide's live performances worked as supercolliders in which ideas from minimalism, auto-destructive art, living theatre and Pop Art clashed. Vega's lyrics reveal a Warhol/Lichtenstein-like attraction to the two-dimensional myths, pulp fictions and larger-than-real-life icons of American mass culture. Suicide's name itself came from 'Satan Suicide', an issue of Vega's favourite comic book, *Ghost Rider*. Like a sci-fi Elvis, Vega's voice was swathed in eerie reverb and delay FX that harked back to the echo on Presley's voice *circa* the Sun sessions while simultaneously evoking the vapour-trails of a rocketship. Deliberately simple, his lyrics risked corn and trusted in the timeless power of cliché.

You could see Suicide's confrontational shows and physical altercations with the audience (who sometimes responded in kind – 'knives, axes, I got hit one time in the eye with a wrench!' says Vega) as performance art, but in truth Vega got the idea from Iggy Pop. In 1970, he went to see The Stooges at the New York State Pavilion. 'Iggy's flying into the audience, then he's back onstage, cutting himself up with drumsticks, bleeding. The whole set lasted, like, twenty minutes. And whoever was in the sound booth put on one of Bach's Brandenburg Concertos immediately afterwards, instead of the usual rock 'n' roll, and that was perfect, because what we had just seen was great art. For the first time in my life, the audience and the stage merged into one. It became this environmental thing. And that showed me you didn't have to do static artworks; you could create situations.'

Suicide, New York, 1978. L to R: Alan Vega, Martin Rev. Photo by Marcia Resnick

Suicide were the godfathers of No Wave. Almost literally: Lydia Lunch, arriving in Manhattan as a sixteen-year-old runaway from upstate, was 'kind of adopted by Martin Rev, who had a son who was older than me. Marty looked after me, gave me vitamins. What better parents could you have than Suicide! They were my first friends in New York. Oh, the early Suicide shows, what fucking beauty!' James Chance likewise felt filial towards Suicide. 'First day in New York, straight outta Milwaukee, James approached us,' says Vega. Chance recognized a kinship in their audience-assaulting urge to smash the fourth wall. And Vega loved Chance's Sinatra-esque cool onstage: 'I thought he was going to be a superstar.'

By the time the No Wavers started arriving in New York, the heartland of bohemia had shifted from SoHo to the even cheaper Lower East Side, a.k.a. L·E·S·. Today, traces of its former scuzz peek out here and there amid the gentrification, but in the mid-seventies, there was not a bou-tique or a trendy restaurant in sight. A patchwork of burned-out build-ings and vacant, garbage-strewn lots, the L·E·S· looked like a warzone. Most 'regular' folk had fled to the suburbs, leaving the area to bums, bohos, junkies and the ethnic poor. Unable to rent out all their rooms and unwilling to sell because property values had plummeted, landlords turned increasingly to insurance scams: resorting to arson themselves, or letting services deteriorate to the point when the tenants burned down their own tenements in order to get rehoused by the city authorities. In 1978 alone there were 354 suspicious fires in the L·E·S·.

If you were prepared to live somewhere that looked like Beirut, and where heroin was easier to buy than groceries, the L·E·S· was paradise. 'I had a place on 2nd Street between Avenues A and B that cost about $110 a month,' says James Chance. A homeless Lydia Lunch came by one night and ended up staying at the fifth-floor walk-up apartment for almost a year. Conny Burg, Mark Cunningham and Arto Lindsay all lived on 10th and B, across from the only substantial patch of greenery in the whole L·E·S·, Tompkins Square Park. 'It was really dangerous,' recalls Burg. 'I saw someone shot almost every day; dead bodies just left in the park.'

The cheap rents allowed the No Wavers to work sporadically, if at all, and dedicate themselves to their art. And to hedonism. Downtown was almost unpoliced: the city let the neighbourhood fester. 'People were running around free; after-hours clubs were everywhere,' says Pat Place. Along with the clubs, the No Wavers frequented artist bars like Barnabus Rex and the Ocean Club, where the drinks were very cheap. 'I think there was one winter where I didn't see daylight!' laughs Place. 'You'd see the sunrise as you were going home and you'd go to sleep, then get up about four in the afternoon and start all over again.' Fuelling this freak scene of night creatures were drugs of every kind – speed, pot, downers. 'But heroin was the most appealing,' says Place. 'And the most deadly.' Between A and B, 3rd Street was home to artists, No Wave musicians, and the notorious drug den the Toilet. As with other L·E·S· cop spots, lines of customers waiting to score stretched down the sidewalk. 'I almost feel like drugs were pushed down here to anaesthetize us, and we all succumbed,' says Adele Bertei. 'I remember a time when almost every woman I knew had a copy of William Burroughs' *Junky* next to her bed and was shooting up.' The flood of pure Iranian heroin on to the market claimed many lives, including The Contortions' bassist George Scott III.

Pre-AIDS and pre-Reaganism, downtown New York existed in a peculiar bubble of Weimar-like decadence: drugs, drink, polymorphously perverse sex. The city as a whole might have been teetering on the edge of bankruptcy, but the artists of the L·E·S· found ways to have a wild time in the midst of collapse. Although it shared the apocalyptic Cold War mindset of the late seventies, No Wave was weirdly insulated from the political urgencies of the time. 'It was much more about personal insanity than political insanity,' says Lunch. 'We didn't have someone like Mayor Giuliani breathing down our necks. It was a very loose time. There wasn't much to fight against, except tradition: where you came from, what your parents were. It was like you'd been thrown into this adolescent adult funfair and left to figure it out.'

In classic bohemian fashion, art replaced politics as the way to change reality. Simply living a nonconformist lifestyle was itself an artform. Says Bertei, 'We all lived by walking into art openings, stealing all the food. Everyone gawked at us because we were almost like an exhibition of our own. My head was shorn down to about an inch, my eyebrows were shaved, I used to wear these flea-bitten Buster Keaton suits. The art scene was very conservative: in the galleries everyone would be wearing suits. In a way we were more exciting than the art that was on the walls.'

No Wave existed on the slippery cusp between art and 'anti-art'. Lydia Lunch scorned the a-word, preferring to see herself as journalist, writer, conceptualist: 'Music was just a particular tool to get across the emotional impact. If spoken word had been more readily available in the late seventies, I'd have done that.' James Chance once declared: 'I hate art. It makes me sick . . . SoHo . . . should be blown off the fucking map, along with all its artsy assholes.' In the cultural geography of downtown New York, No Wave's mixed feelings about art translated into a hostile, jostling rivalry between the Lower East Side and SoHo, which only a few years earlier had been *the* area for artists to live and work, but was now becoming gentrified, speckled with galleries. So DNA deliberately shunned SoHo performance spaces like the Kitchen for as long as possible, preferring the sweat and rowdiness of proper rock 'n' roll joints like CBGB and Max's. 'The Kitchen was for people who'd read about events in the *New York Times*,' says Lindsay. 'The audience would be sitting down and they'd accept anything you presented them with. It was more exciting for us to play to a crowd that were drinking and trying to pick somebody up, and try to wrest their attention away from that.'

The two worlds collided at Artists Space, a non-profit gallery/performance space in Tribeca (a then-desolate area to the south of SoHo) that hosted a five-day festival of New York underground rock in May 1978. The first nights featured long-forgotten No Wave fellow-traveller groups ('They were failed painters; now they're failed musicians,' someone in the audience quipped) but the festival climaxed at the weekend with two double bills: DNA and Contortions on Friday; Mars and Teenage Jesus on Saturday. The Contortions' set was interrupted by a fight between Chance and *Village Voice*'s chief rock critic Robert Christgau. Eyewitness accounts vary wildly, with some maintaining that Chance punched Christgau's pregnant girlfriend or smashed her over the head with a mike stand; the venerable critic supposedly pummelled the diminutive singer into a bloody pulp. According to Christgau himself, Chance left the stage and began 'playfully or pseudo-playfully' to hit a female friend of his. The woman's husband waded in but was pulled off, 'at which point I intervened and basically sat on Chance. Maybe I held him down, too. He's a little guy.'

In the audience stood a fascinated Brian Eno. He'd arrived in New York on 23 April, planning to stay for only three weeks while he worked on various projects, including the mastering of Talking Heads' second album, which he'd produced. But, Eno told *Melody Maker* in 1980, 'it turned out that I happened to be in New York during one of the most exciting months of the decade, I should think, in terms of music – it seemed like there were 500 new bands who all started that [May]'. He ended up staying for another seven months, totally absorbed in the cross-town traffic between music and art.

Outwardly, Eno had little in common with No Wave's fanatical extremists. A dilettante sensualist, English to the core, Eno's brand of decadence was much gentler. According to Bertei, who briefly worked as his personal assistant in New York, 'He'd send me out on these insane errands, give me an envelope of hundred-dollar bills and a list of what he needed that day: an Olivetti typewriter, French voile socks, magazines of bald-headed black women with huge tits.' In another sense, though, No Wave could hardly have been more in tune with Eno – an art-school grad who came to music with a weird mixture of technical naïvety and conceptual sophistication. This combination enabled him to approach rock from an oblique angle, reinventing instruments and dismantling structures. The No Wave scene was chock-full of mini-Enos. Talking to *Creem* magazine in late 1978, Eno celebrated No Wave in terms that could equally be applied to applaud his own role as pop vanguardist. The city was packed with 'research bands', he said, who took 'deliberately extreme stances that are very interesting because they define the edges of a piece of territory'. Other bands might not choose to go that far, but 'having that territory staked out is very important . . . It makes things easier for everyone else.'

Convinced that this experimental-but-ephemeral scene urgently required documentation before the moment passed, Eno proposed the idea of a No Wave compilation, with himself as producer. The sessions for *No New York* bore barely a trace of the studio treatments and textural colorations for which Eno was famous. James Chance recalls the Contortions tracks being 'done totally live in the studio, no separation between the instruments, no overdubs. Just like a document.' Only Mars saw any of Eno's legendary studio magic. 'He was totally hands on, using the board as an instrument,' says Mark Cunningham. 'We were actually more conservative than Eno, feeling that the music's radicalism didn't need to be saturated in special effects.' Some of the bands voiced unhappiness with the results. But the most controversial aspect of *No New York* was the decision to limit the line-up to the four major No Wave bands – Contortions, Teenage Jesus, DNA and Mars – who each contributed four tracks, rather than reflect the full scope of the scene.

Two highly regarded bands – Theoretical Girls and The Gynecologists, who'd shared the Wednesday night of the Artists Space festival – had been pointedly excluded, because of their associations with the SoHo art scene. The Gynecologists included Rhys Chatham, music director of the Kitchen and an avant-classical composer, while Theoretical Girls boasted *two* composers in its line-up, Glenn Branca and Jeffrey Lohn. After Theoretical Girls disintegrated, Branca started composing symphonies for electric guitar, performed by large ensembles of players and amplified so that they stunned the audience into rapt submission. As well as taking several leafs out of Chatham's book (there's some dispute over who invented the 'guitar army' idea), he drew some inspiration from Mars, who generated a metallic cacophony by percussively pounding their guitars.

The first No Wave group to form, Mars started as 'a quirky rock group', says Conny Burg, then systematically shed 'all the conventions of rock 'n' roll music'. Unified tempo was first to go, followed swiftly by tonality. Mars explored detuning the guitar, retuning within songs, having the tuning be mobile. 'Insects in upstate New York' inspired the chittering soundswarm of 'Helen Forsdale', says Burg. 'We were trying to get the guitars to buzz.' Towards the end of Mars' brief lifespan, second guitarist Sumner Crane – a skilled blues player – generated noise by playing the guitar jack and using the mouthpiece of a trumpet. Despite the post-Velvets whiteness of Mars' torrential noise and the total absence of groove or funk, there were subliminal 'African elements', says Mark Cunningham: 'When I started detuning my bass it became very primitive and percussive.' On arriving in New York, he and roommate Arto Lindsay had ransacked the city's records stores of ethnomusicological albums. Long before the eighties world-music craze, there had been 'the great boom of field recordings of native music . . . all kinds of African stuff and trance music were easy to find and very inspiring'.

What Cunningham calls 'ecstatic trance music' would be a good tag for Mars, with one qualification: think 'the agony is the ecstasy' rather than mystic bliss. Burg's and Crane's vocals sounded like torture victims or people undergoing extreme states of dissociation or mania. Voice as weapon or wound, their singing sounds deeply disturbed and is genuinely perturbing – at the extreme (say, in 'Hairwaves') resembling the debris of a shattered psyche. 'Most of the falsetto is Sumner, and most of the low singing is me,' says Burg. 'That juxtaposition, that gender switch, was interesting to us.' This dovetailed with one of the most striking – in 1978 – aspects of Mars: the two women–two men line-up, with Nancy Arlen taking on the traditional masculine job of drumming.

Mars polarized audiences. 'We had our fans and we definitely had our detractors,' laughs Burg. 'The girlfriend of Stiv Bators from The Dead Boys threw a chair at me at one show. We were always accused of being "arty and empty". A critic wrote that about us, which we turned into the song "RTMT".' Mars were the No Waver's No Wave band. 'I saw Mars before Teenage Jesus existed,' Lydia Lunch recalled. 'I was very encouraged. They were so dissonant, so obviously insane. There were no compromises or concessions to anything that had existed previously. They were truly creating from their own torture.'

A poet who turned to music as the most readily available means of expression, Lunch was a bit like the anti-Patti Smith. Where the Rimbaud-and-Dylan-worshipping Smith exalted oceanic feelings, Lunch detested music that 'flows and weaves', telling *Melody Maker*: 'it's like drinking a glass of water . . . I'd rather drink razor blades'. Lunch conceived Teenage Jesus & The Jerks as an act of cultural patricide (or matricide, in Patti's case). 'The whole goal was to kill your idols, as Sonic Youth later put it. Everything that had influenced me up to that point I found too traditional – whether it was Patti Smith, The Stooges, Lou Reed's *Berlin*. It was fine and good for its moment, but I felt there had to be something more radical. It's got to be *disembowelled*.'

Lydia Lunch, New York, 1979. Photo by Marcia Resnick

Teenage Jesus' music matched Lunch's personality. Her self-description is 'Coarse, harsh, bitter – I was such a frightening person!' Drummer Bradley Fields couldn't play drums and didn't even have a proper kit, just a single cymbal and a dysfunctional snare. 'I couldn't play guitar, but that wasn't the point,' says Lunch. 'I developed my own style, which suited the primal urgency I needed to evacuate from my system before I exploded like a miniature nuclear-power plant.' Lunch's singing was equally minimal, a piercing and piteous one-note wail. 'I like my own note,' she once quipped. 'What's wrong with the note I have?' With some songs as brief as forty-one seconds, a typical Teenage Jesus performance lasted about ten minutes.

'Orphans' is probably their most famous song (largely for its couplet 'No more ankles and no more toes/Little orphans running through the bloody snow'), but the group's archetypal 'short fast soundstab' is 'The Closet'. Fields' hammer-blow snare and Lunch's harrowed shriek merge into a tolling death-knell rhythm midway between spasm and dirge. The whole vibe runs the gamut of vaguely Teutonic s-words: stark, severe, strict. Lunch was a disciplinarian: 'In rehearsals I would literally beat them with coat hangers if they made any mistakes at a gig. We rehearsed ad nauseam and were pretty fucking tight. It's pretty fascist sounding, and I was the fucking dictator.' Onstage, Lunch remained rigid, disdaining to engage with the audience through eye contact or banter, maintaining an unbridgeable moat of alienation between performer and spectators. James Chance was an early member of Teenage Jesus, but Lunch kicked him out for having too much contact with the audience: 'I didn't think TJ should mingle with the audience, even if to attack them. Don't touch those bastards, let 'em just sit there in horror!'

Simultaneous with her leadership of Teenage Jesus, Lunch played in Beirut Slump, a more atmospheric outfit whose reeling malaise of noise she compared to 'The Blob – it oozes under doors and people either run away fast to avoid it or they like to let this gooey junk surround them'. Like Teenage Jesus, Beirut Slump was composed largely of people who'd never played music – film-maker Vivienne Dick, for instance, contributed keyboards. Dick was a prime mover in the No Wave-affiliated 'New Cinema' scene. Co-founded by one-time Contortions guitarist James Nares and fellow-film-makers Becky Johnston and Eric Mitchell, the New Cinema was a movie theatre as well as a movement. A fifty-seat space on St Marks Place, it showed Super-8 movies that had been transferred to video – works like Nares's *Rome 78*, Scott and Beth B's *Black Box*, and Mitchell's *Red Italy*. The New Cinema directors drew on a pool of actors that included downtown scenesters like Patti Astor and Tina L'Hotsky, along with just about every musician in No Wave. Lunch, for instance, co-starred with Pat Place in Dick's *She Had Her Gun All Ready*. 'Vivienne's films were very primitive and psychological,' says Place. 'We made this trip out to Coney Island, where I ended up murdering Lydia's character on the Cyclone, after a long series of these weird, vague, psychotic interactions!'

Lo-fi and low budget, New Cinema flicks were made at astonishing speed – in some cases, they were scripted, filmed and premiered within a week. Breaking with the ruling avant-garde cinema aesthetic of Stan Brakhage-style abstraction, the New Cinema directors preferred narrative, harking back to the earlier sixties underground of Warhol and Jack Smith, along with B-movie genre films from the 1950s, all pulp plots and ultra-violent thrills. No Wave and New Cinema alike felt a mixture of appalled fascination and envious admiration towards all exponents of antisocial or pathological behaviour: murderers, terrorists, cult leaders like Jim Jones. All possessed ruthless will-to-power and an unflinching capacity to translate thought into deed. James Chance crystallized the attitude when he told *Sounds*: 'I can't stand liberals. They're so stupid and wishy-washy and their whole philosophy is so half-assed. They're not extreme and I only like people who are extreme.'

Chance himself fused three great American musical extremists – Iggy Pop, James Brown and Albert Ayler – into his short, scrawny frame. Before coming to New York, he'd done a three-year stint at the Wisconsin Conservatory of Music and played in a Stooges-influenced rock band called Death. Arriving in Manhattan, he'd tried to make a name for himself in the loft-jazz scene, but wasn't exactly warmly embraced: his punk attitude chafed against the late sixties mindset of the predominantly black milieu. One ensemble he played in, called Flaming Youth, had a gig at Environ, a space that was a dance studio by day. When it was his turn to solo, he leaped in mid-air, skidded across the polished wood floor and blasted his alto sax in a girl's face. 'I totally freaked out the audience,' he recalls. The critic Robert Palmer wrote a scathing review, mentioning a certain saxophonist who was closer to a 'contortionist act' than a musician. Unwittingly, Palmer had christened Chance's next project.

As for the James Brown influence, Chance pinpoints a single track as the founding musical text for Contortions: 1970's 'Super Bad, Pts 1 and 2'. 'What really got me into JB was the sax solos on that single – real out-there playing like you'd get on an Ayler or Sun Ra record.' Combining Brown's regal showmanship with Iggy's kamikaze theatrics, Chance invented punk-funk. Hopped up on death-drive and artificial energy, Contortions' music was riddled with tics and jerks – a prickly, irritable sound, like a speed-freak scratching at hallucinatory bugs under the skin. Imagine funk's low-down, life-affirming energy trapped and turned against itself; soul, denied an outlet, become cyst-like. Rhythmically and lyrically, James Brown songs like 'Sex Machine' and 'I Got Ants in My Pants' pointed towards a racked ecstasy of painful pleasure that was almost dehumanizing. Picking up on these hints, Chance imagined funk as voodoo possession and cold-fever delirium – the perfect vehicle for exploring themes of addiction, sexual bondage and morbid obsession.

As JB-style band-leader, Chance exerted total control over Contortions. 'When it first started, no one else had ever played their instruments before,' he told one magazine. 'People who can't play have more fresh ideas. I looked for people I could teach to play.' The tv

James Chance, New York, 1978. Photo by Marcia Resnick

women were recruited simply because they looked cool: Place, tall and androgynous with cropped blond hair; Bertei, 'this pint-size girl who came on like some kind of lesbian pimp', according to Chance. A Clevelander who'd lived in a reformatory for troubled teenage girls, Bertei 'approached the keyboards like I play a conga drum, which was real percussive, slapping the keys in clusters', she told *East Village Eye*. 'Sometimes I'd beat them with my fists or elbows . . . Once I jumped up on the keyboards at a particularly frenzied gig and I kinda danced on them, which fucked the keyboard up.' Place remembers the 'complete cacophony' of the first Contortions gig: 'At the end I had two strings left on my guitar and it was completely blood-splattered. I didn't know how to strum the guitar and it just ripped the skin right off my fingers.'

Contortions played fast early on, such that their funk could pass for punk. Ultimately, this would be one reason for the band combusting. 'Live, James would insist on counting everything, and he'd always double the time,' drummer Don Christensen told *Melody Maker* in 1980. 'One time he counted it out so fast we couldn't play it,' added second guitarist Jody Harris. 'He couldn't just relax and let the music get into any kind of groove – he had to have absolute control over the sound.' But this paroxysmic intensity went down well with the CBGB and Max's Kansas City audience, along with the vicarious thrills of ultra-violence. And musically, Contortions were more accessible than the other No Wave bands: 'My songs were always in a key, they had some kind of tonal centre,' says Chance. 'But I didn't have chord structures; I constructed the songs out of interlocking parts played by each instrument, an idea I more or less got from James Brown.' Chance's ulcerous alto-sax could be heard 'levitating above the fray' of tightly meshed rhythmic cogs, 'like snake charming gone terribly wrong', as Glenn O'Brien, one of No Wave's journalistic supporters, put it.

DNA had a similar approach, except the parts slotted together like some faultily designed 3D jigsaw. 'Skeletal, stop–start, lots of silences', the songs often seemed to disassemble themselves in front of the listener's ears. Arto Lindsay had a twelve-string Danelectro guitar, but instead of using it in the obvious way – for melodic, folky arpeggios and finger picking – he played it as a rhythm instrument, chipping out a scrabble of texture shards, like scrambled Chic. 'It was sculptural as opposed to painterly, shapes that poked out at you, rather than a surface.'

DNA were a trio of rootless cosmopolitans: Lindsay grew up in Brazil with his missionary parents; keyboard player Robin Crutchfield was a gay misfit who performed surreal street-theatre pieces; drummer Ikue Mori was Japanese and a complete novice at her instrument. She could also barely speak English. 'Communicating with Ikue, a lot of it was diagram and gesture,' says Crutchfield. 'Arto might have to act out in charade what he wanted to do, shuffling and shaking his arms to a certain beat or gesturing for a pause or tempo change.' Lindsay gave her a record of Brazilian drum beats, which she tried to imitate, while bringing in elements of Japanese court music: 'the kind of thing that has real rhythmic authority,' he says, 'but you can't exactly work out what the rhythm *is*'. As a result, Mori developed a totally idiosyncratic approach to drumming. Lindsay's singing was no less disorienting: animalistic barks and growls, flubbed vocal smears and shamanic grunts. 'Sometimes it was an extension of the sheer feeling aspect of the blues,' he says. 'Or like singing in languages you don't understand, like Indian. In Florida, I'd been in this student-directed theatre group, and we done exercises in using the voice in nine different ways, like "OK let's improvise for half an hour, don't make it human but don't make it mechanical either".'

Early DNA is incredibly abstruse, but when Crutchfield (who'd been playing keyboards sculpturally, according to visual patterns of clustered keys) quit in 1978, the band acquired more of a groove with the arrival of bassist Tim Wright. 'DNA doesn't get much credit for this, but we were very funky,' says Lindsay. In some ways the group's closest kin weren't the other No Wavers but black New York musicians like Prime Time (Ornette Coleman's band) and James 'Blood' Ulmer, who translated Coleman's theories into scorching, tempestuous punk-funk that wowed the mostly white audiences at such New Wave discos as Hurrah's. At the same time, there was nothing really jazzy about DNA. Because it came across so abstract and self-deconstructing, people assumed their music was totally improvised, but DNA actually rehearsed everything down to the smallest gear change. It was all intensely premeditated and discussed, from the overall band style (early on, they theorized about DNA sounding like 'one giant instrument' or 'if a rat got loose inside a computer') to the internal mechanisms of a specific piece, to the lyrics. Lindsay approached the words as language exercises rather than stories or emotional expression: he'd set himself the task, say, of depicting 'a sex act observed from the bridge of a nose'.

Overlapping with DNA, Lindsay played in The Lounge Lizards, an ensemble explicitly based on the idea of punk-jazz. Formed by his friend John Lurie, a New Cinema film-maker and actor in performance pieces at the Squat Theater, The Lounge Lizards owed a lot to James Chance's image – the retro-panache of sharp suits and pompadour quiffs. 'Lurie used to more or less follow me around in the street,' says Chance with a snigger. 'When I first met him he didn't look so dapper at all.' Originally called The Power Tools, Lurie's group played its first gig dressed in suits. 'The girls went nuts for it,' says Lindsay. 'We were instant sex symbols.' Not bad going for Arto, considering his normal apparel – 'lived-in pants and second-hand-looking sweaters, simple button-down shirts and horn-rimmed glasses', according to Robin Crutchfield – 'made the guys from Devo look stylin''. Having changed their name, the group developed a sound and shtick that Lurie flippantly described as 'fake jazz' in an early interview. The quip stuck and became a millstone, infuriating the earnest custodians of the loft-jazz scene and making the whole exercise seem like a trivial pastiche. 'John spent many years trying to overcome that term, but it was actually apropos,' says Lindsay. 'We were playing jazz-like rhythms and melody lines, but none of the musicians were then capable of soloing over the changes, which is the essence of real jazz.' But The Lounge Lizards did get to make their debut album with Miles Davis's producer Teo Macero at Black Rock, a CBS studio on 57th Street where many jazz greats had recorded. Still, most jazz aficionados continued to believe 'they were punks taking the piss out of jazz', says Glenn O'Brien, 'which wasn't true'.

In 'The White Noise Supremacists', a controversial *Village Voice* essay published in April 1979, Lester Bangs pointed out the uncomfortable connections between the near-total absence of black musicians on the CBGB/Max's scene, punk's fashion for using racist language (all part of its anti-liberal, we-hate-everybody attitude), and the perilous ambiguity of punk's flirtations with Nazi imagery. Factor in the sheer whiteness of New Wave music, and you had a situation where, for the first time since before the 1920s hot jazz era, white bohemians were disengaged from black culture. Not only that, but some of them were *proud* of this disengagement. Just a week before Bangs' essay, *Village Voice* profiled Legs McNeil of *Punk* magazine. Writer Marc Jacobson discussed how McNeil and his cohorts consciously rejected the whole notion of the hipster as 'white Negro' and dedicated themselves to celebrating all things white, teenage and suburban. Years later, McNeil candidly discussed this segregationist aspect of punk in an interview with Jon Savage: 'We were all white: there were no black people involved with this. In the sixties hippies always wanted to be black. We were going: "Fuck the Blues; fuck the black experience."' McNeil believed that disco was the loathsome musical child of an unholy union of blacks and gays. *Punk*'s debut issue, in January 1976, began with a rabid mission statement: 'Death to Disco Shit. Long live the Rock! ... I've seen the canned crap take real live people and turn them into dogs! ... The epitome of all that's wrong with Western civilization is disco.'

Unaware of its gay underground origins, most punks saw disco as the mass-produced, mechanistic sound of escapism and complacency, uptown muzak-with-a-beat for the moneyed and glamour-struck. 'There was the disco culture up at Studio 54 and then there was us,' says Adele Bertei. 'When it came to disco, we were like these vicious little misanthropes with Tourette's syndrome. You'd get a torrent of expletives.' In the context of 1978, with CBGB types treating disco as both pariah and tyrant (it dominated the radio, ultimately taking over the only station in the city that played New Wave), just about the vilest act of cultural treason imaginable was for a punk band to go disco. Which is precisely what James Chance did.

The idea originated with Michael Zilkha, a young entrepreneur who co-founded the New York record label ZE. Zilkha came from an extremely genteel background (his family was very wealthy, he'd grown up in England where he attended a top public school) but he was totally infatuated with No Wave's extremism and saw real star potential in Chance and Lydia Lunch. He approached the Contortions singer with a proposition: ZE would release a 'proper' Contortions album simultaneously with a disco version of the James Chance experience. 'Michael said, "It doesn't have to be a *commercial* disco record. Just do whatever *your* idea of disco is,"' says Chance. '"Here's ten thousand dollars."'

The sheer conceptual shock value of becoming a disco turncoat and fucking with everybody's heads grabbed Chance's imagination. By January 1979 he was telling *Soho Weekly News*, 'I've always been interested in disco. I mean, disco is *disgusting*, but there's something in it that's always interested me – *monotony*. It's sort of jungle music, but whitened and perverted. On this album I'm trying to restore it to what it *could* be. Really primitive.' Suddenly the idea of going commercial and sounding 'slick' appealed to him. 'I'm not interested in being a starving artist,' he told *Sounds*. Fuck art: he was first and foremost 'a businessman'. For an infamous feature published in *East Village Eye*, Chance and lover/manager Anya Philips each penned a short but fulsome celebration of selling out. 'Anyone with any semblance of a brain should know by now that it's time to forget about all this outdated, cornball "new/no wave" drivel,' sneered Chance. 'Anyone who stays on the Lower East Side will become the inevitable victim of provincial mindrot . . . So dislocate yourself. Get slick, move uptown and get trancin' with some super-radioactive disco voodoo funk.' Philips boasted about how she'd groomed and styled Chance and set him on the road to fame and fortune: 'Money bought us a first-class ticket out of the Lower East Side pisshole. It's not my problem you're all waiting to leave on standby.'

A major downtown scenester/catalyst until she contracted cancer in 1979, Philips was a formidable character. Chance says, 'Anya was the one who more or less put my whole image together. She made clothes but most of the stuff we found in thrift stores – tuxedos, white dinner jackets, sharkskin jackets like sixties soul singers wore.' The look reinforced No Wave's break with punk's rock 'n' rollness, resurrecting the elegance and razzle of pre-rock showbiz.

To the other Contortions, though, this manipulative Chinese-American beauty was a Yoko Ono-like figure. 'She began to cause a rift between James and the band, make him the star,' says Bertei. 'Not that he wasn't already the leader, but it became the James Chance Show after she became manager.' For the disco album *Off White*, the members of Contortions were hired as session musicians and the project was credited to James White and The Blacks. (Philips had wanted to call it 'and His Blacks' but Zilkha baulked at that). Live, they added a horn section and two teenage dancing girls called the Disco Lolitas, making the experience more like a traditional soul revue. For *Off White*'s launch party, ZE rented Irving Plaza and the group did a disco-style appearance, miming to the songs, with no live instruments. They staged a boudoir scene for 'Stained Sheets', the voluptuous Lydia Lunch duplicating her cameo vocals while reclining on a couch. The song resembles a sordid S&M twist on Donna Summer's 'Love to Love You Baby': it's a phone-sex duet between Chance and Lunch, juxtaposing his blasé sneer with her orgasmic whimpers and non-verbal desperation.

Off White and its sister album *Buy* probed the darker corners of sexuality. *Buy*'s cover featured Terry Sellers, author of *The Correct Sadist*, scantily clad in panties and a strange, deconstructed bra designed by Philips. Inside, 'I Don't Want to Be Happy' confessed that Chance's 'idea of fun' was 'being whipped on the back of the thighs', while in 'Bedroom Athlete' he yelps, 'I won't be your slave unless you will be *mine*'. *Off White*, meanwhile, verged on a musical essay about racial tourism, with the track 'Almost Black' representing the most dubious homage to blackness as sexy sociopathology/virile primitivism since Norman Mailer's 1957 essay 'The White Negro'. The track features a white girl and a black girl bitterly disputing the attributes and defects of 'James White': 'Well, he's *almost* black', 'That nigger's *white*', 'Well, he's got some *moves*', 'But they *ain't right*'.

Inverting James Brown's pride and dignity to white bohemian self-abasement and cynicism, the Chance worldview stripped life of sentimentality, tenderness and all values. In a nutshell: life's cheap, love's a lie, narcotics numb the pain. The lyrics hammered the same idea over and over again: 'I only live on the surface/I don't think people are very pretty inside'; 'Reduce yourself to a zero'. Appearing on both *Buy* and *Off White* in different versions, the anthem 'Contort Yourself' evoked a sort of jaded Dionysian frenzy, the joyless flailing of empty souls trying to evacuate even more of their consciousness: 'Take out all the garbage that's in your brain . . . Why don't you try being stupid instead of smart?' In interviews, Chance maintained an impregnable façade of nihilism. 'It's ridiculous to believe in things,' he told one interviewer; 'it's the height of absurdity.' This shtick – Chance as voidoid – sometimes became comically overstated. 'I DO NOT relate to people!' he insisted to *New York Rocker*'s Roy Trakin. 'I have no respect for a fan. A fan is the lowest creature on earth.' Today, Trakin says, 'James Chance and Lydia Lunch, they both kept up a front. I found them kind of sweet in a way. There was pain underneath too; they were calling out. What was interesting was that they needed you to be part of the equation. It's a classic syndrome: you need an audience and you can't stand your audience.'

The cover of *Buy* featuring Terry Sellers modelling underwear designed by Anya Philips

Taken together, Chance's double debut represents No Wave's strongest and most enduring recorded statement: *Buy* captures the unsustainable intensity of the early scene, while the chic, sleek *Off White* points ahead towards 'mutant disco', the next phase of New York post-punk. But Zilkha's attempt to make Chance into a star failed. And he didn't do much better with Lydia Lunch's solo debut, *Queen of Siam*.

'The idea was to take these characters and make them attractive,' Zilkha says now, wistfully. 'Treat them like they were normal entertainers. For instance, I thought Lydia was a very attractive personality, but Teenage Jesus was a very tough listen. I thought she should be sex kittenish.' For *Queen of Siam*, Lunch temporarily dropped her banshee howl for a baby-doll voice, innocent yet coquettish, sweetness with an edge. 'It was letting the sick little girl out to play,' she says. Slightly less than half the album featured orchestral arrangements by Billy Ver Planck, a composer/bandleader who'd penned music for *The Flintstones*. 'I'd been watching a lot of afternoon cartoons like *Courageous Cat*, where the music was always so fantastic,' recalls Lunch. 'I told Billy my ideas and he translated them, but he hated the end result 'cos we massacred his compositions. At seventeen thousand dollars, that's the most expensive album I've ever done.' It might also be her best record – it's certainly the easiest on the ear – but it didn't make her into the pop star Zilkha envisaged.

No Wave was a cultural spasm, an extremist gesture, that could only exhaust itself. 'For Mars, the scene ended just a couple of months after *No New York* came out at the end of 1978,' says Mark Cunningham. 'Max's closed and CB's was becoming more of a mega-rock club. We didn't feel we had a place any more.' New spaces like Hurrah's and Mudd Club, oriented as much around DJs as live bands, started to take over, and New York's music scene veered towards fun and dance. The James White project had anticipated disco-punk, but Chance would not reap the benefits. After the original Contortions split, Chance played on with endlessly shifting backing bands, but problems with record companies, drugs and Philips' terminal cancer thwarted his career.

Lydia Lunch bounced between extremes – from the schmaltz *noir* of *Queen of Siam* to 8 Eyed Spy, an honest-to-goodness rock 'n' roll band. Grinding out snake-hipped boogie steeped in Americana and Faulkneresque Southern Gothic, 8 Eyed Spy covered Creedence Clearwater Revival and Bo Diddley; Lydia even wore a denim jacket at one show to complete her white-trash image. 'More than anything, I consider myself a conceptualist,' she says now. 'I feel more akin to Marcel Duchamp than any musician ever. I wanted to contradict not just everything that preceded me but my own previous music.' Lunch describes her self-confounding musical trajectory as 'purposeful and schizophrenic . . . contradictory, contrarian, conceptual' – words that distil the essence of No Wave itself.

5

TRIBAL REVIVAL: The Pop Group and The Slits

The Pop Group. Alternative TV. The Slits. New Age Steppers. Rip Rig & Panic.

The Pop Group wouldn't have existed without punk. They were on their way to the Roxy club when they came up with the band's name, during the train journey from Bristol to London. But punk for The Pop Group meant something more expansive and ambitious than it did for their Bristol contemporaries, such as The Cortinas. 'When I first heard the Pistols and The Clash you really thought they were questioning the value of everything,' says singer Mark Stewart. The genius of The Pop Group lay in the way they were pulled every which way by their passion for black music. They couldn't settle on just reggae, or just funk, or just jazz – so they went full throttle for all three simultaneously. This identity crisis caused their ultimate downfall, but along the way The Pop Group's chaotic gigs and flawed but compelling records served as an inspirational model for countless other bands looking for the way forward.

Funk sustained the future members of The Pop Group during the mid-seventies pre-punk doldrums. 'We were the Bristol Funk Army,' says Stewart. 'We'd go to clubs and dance to heavy bassline imports from America, tracks by T-Connection, B.T. Express, Fatback Band, Ultrafunk. I was fourteen in 1975 but could get into clubs because I was six foot seven.' In the West Country, funkateers called themselves 'kit chaps' because clothes were as crucial as the music. 'We wore things like brothel creepers, zoot suits, plastic sandals, mohair jumpers,' recalls Stewart. 'Later I discovered that in cities all over the UK before punk there'd been similar kids into funk and fifties clothes. And most of them got into punk when it arrived.'

As for reggae, The Pop Group assimilated that almost like breathing in the Bristol air; it was an environmental thing. The city had a substantial black population, some of whom long predated the 1950s immigration of Caribbeans – going back as far as the eighteenth century, when the city was one of England's leading ports in the slave trade. 'When I lived in Bristol there were still street names like Blackboy Hill,' says Pop Group drummer Bruce Smith. Mostly concentrated in the St Paul's area, Bristol's West Indian population made the city one of the UK's great zones of punk/reggae intermingling. A shabby neighbourhood of terraced houses and low-rise blocks, St Paul's didn't really look like a ghetto, but in April 1980 it unleashed one of the most destructive anti-police riots in British history. A few years before, Stewart, Smith and future Pop Group bassist Simon Underwood regularly ventured into the area to check out the blues parties. 'Generally we'd be the only white guys there, but we'd never get any hassle,' says Smith. 'Well, maybe I'd get ripped off trying to buy weed, before I got wise!' They also devoured reggae vinyl. 'Every Friday when we were, like, fourteen or fifteen, we'd go to this record store Revolver to check out the new reggae prereleases that had just arrived from London by van,' recalls Stewart.

Discovering jazz, the young friends thrilled to the ferocity of its abstract emotional expressionism, its lofty intellectual edge and cosmic ambition. Undeterred by lack of technique or formal grounding in the music, The Pop Group hurled themselves into improvisation, with Stewart's howled vocals and Gareth Sager's sax-blasts being the most obviously 'free' elements in the maelstrom. 'My remembrance of us playing was that it was either really extraordinary or pretty awful,' laughs Smith. 'There wasn't much in between!' The Pop Group worshipped the beat culture surrounding jazz, too: poets and writers like Ginsberg, Kerouac and Burroughs. Stewart's original fantasy version of the group was called The Wild Boys, after Burroughs' novel.

Blue-eyed funkateers, white Rasta ranters, 'beatniks of tomorrow' – The Pop Group refused to choose a single identity. 'In the early days of the band, the only peers I felt we had were Contortions,' says Stewart. But James Chance had just the punk-funk and jazz-punk things going on; The Pop Group threw dub delirium into the mix, too. Bearing impeccably hip references, exhibiting vaulting ambition, they arrived on the post-punk scene with perfect timing, just when everyone was scratching their heads and wondering: Where next?

Their impact on the music press was immediate. The Pop Group

The Pop Group's Mark Stewart, 1978. Photo by Janette Beckman

appeared on the front cover of the *NME* in September 1978, before they had even released a record. Their very amorphousness made them a Rorschach blot for critical fantasy – a colour-saturated canvas for exploring ideas about 'after-punk'. 'Older journalists dug us, 'cos they could use us to talk about the stuff they secretly preferred to punk rock – dub, Captain Beefheart, Miles Davis's early seventies records,' says Stewart. It also didn't hurt that the band looked great – their suits evoked both a timeless, un-rock stylishness and a bracing sobriety and seriousness. In interviews, they came across as intellectual firebrands. Early features on The Pop Group typically start with the journalist marvelling at the band's erudition and argumentativeness, while noting their impressive book and record collections. 'We were sixteen, seventeen, staying up all night talking, smoking weed,' recalls Smith. Sparks flew as systems of thought collided: Wilhelm Reich's libidinal liberation, Antonin Artaud's theatre of cruelty, Situationism's revolt against boredom. Drunk on ideas, the group dedicated itself to breaking down systematically all assumptions and received ideas. 'We started challenging everything right down to the core of personal relationships, the things between the audience and the band,' says Stewart. According to Vivien Goldman, a journalist friend of the band who dated Stewart for a while, 'The Pop Group had this obsession with finding a new way of doing everything.'

Out of this turmoil of inspirational input and self-questioning emerged a kind of Dionysian protest music, a maelstrom of writhing noise and imagistic words that dissolved the artificial divisions between politics and poetry, lust and spirituality. Stewart saw The Pop Group as part of a grand tradition of politically engaged avant-garde artists, a continuum stretching from the radical salons of the French Revolution, through Dadaists and Surrealists who were also committed communists, to 1960s movements like Fluxus and Situationism who saw radical art and political revolution as inseparable. Just as the Situationists railed against 'the poverty of everyday life' in the consumerist West, Pop Group songs like 'We Are Time' blazed with a rage to live. 'Not wanting to just be alive,' says Stewart, 'but to rid yourself of all constrictions. We had this romantic idea of going through nihilism, this intense deconditioning process, and emerging the other side with something really positive.' Comparing The Pop Group to the then little-known syndrome of spontaneous human combustion, Stewart told *ZigZag*: 'Our creating music is the result of acute internal pressure.' Fire figured in The Pop Group's imagination as an ideal state of being, evoking inner-city riots, pagan rituals, the 1960s free jazz of Archie Shepp's Fire Music. One of the band's best songs, 'Thief of Fire', used the Prometheus myth to exalt the quest for 'prohibited knowledge, going into unknown areas'.

The Pop Group's rise had a wildfire quality. Within a few shows, they became the epicentre of the Bristol post-punk scene. Soon they were opening for major artists like Patti Smith, Elvis Costello and The Stranglers, whose singer Hugh Cornwell was so infatuated he produced and financed their demos. In the late spring of 1978, they accompanied Pere Ubu – then at the height of their critical stature – on the latter's debut tour of the UK. The Pop Group began talking to Andrew Lauder, the founder of Radar Records, which released Ubu's *Datapanik* EP. A veteran A&R man who had previously signed Buzzcocks and The Stranglers to United Artists, Lauder had deftly survived the transition from pre-punk progressive music to the New Wave and was looking to recruit more cutting-edge groups.

Released by Radar in March 1979, The Pop Group's debut single, 'She Is Beyond Good and Evil', was an exhilarating splurge of disco-funk bass, slashing punk-funk rhythm guitar, and deranged dub noise, with Stewart caterwauling lines like 'Our only defence is together as an army/I'll hold you like a gun'. Lyrically, says Stewart, the song was 'a very young attempt to mix up poetic, existentialist stuff with political yearnings. The idea of unconditional love as a revolutionary force – the way it kind of switches on a light, makes you hope for a better world, gives you this idealism and energy.'

To record 'Beyond Good and Evil', The Pop Group hooked up with Dennis Bovell – at that point the only British reggae producer brilliant enough to bear any comparison with Jamaican greats like Lee Perry and King Tubby. A key figure in the UK reggae scene, Bovell had operated the Jah Sufferer Hi-fi Sound System, formed the popular British roots band Matumbi, and pioneered the hugely successful genre of lovers' rock (a UK fusion of reggae and soft American soul that appealed largely to women). If that wasn't enough, he wrote and produced the musical backing for militant poet Linton Kwesi Johnson's albums while releasing his own LPs, such as *Strictly Dub Wize*, under the name Blackbeard. Bovell's musical scope stretched way beyond reggae, though: he believed the first dub track ever was Hendrix's 1967 song 'Third Stone from the Sun', and he'd played lead guitar in a Jimi-influenced band called Stonehenge.

Bovell's mix of acid-rock wildness and dub wisdom made him the perfect foil for The Pop Group. For '3-38', the B-side to 'Beyond Good and Evil', he took the A-side's music and ran it backwards, psychedelia-style, then built a new rhythm track for it with Bruce Smith. 'That really blew the band away,' says Bovell. Necessity was the mother of invention here. 'We'd almost run out of studio time. That's why I reused the A-side.' Creative *and* cost-efficient? Bovell was the ideal candidate for the not hugely enviable task of giving The Pop Group's unruly sound some semblance of cohesion. Working on the debut album, *Y*, Bovell quickly grasped that the rhythm section held together the whole band. 'Simon Underwood and Bruce Smith, they were the Sly & Robbie of the post-punk period – *tight*,' says Bovell. 'The thing that was *not* together about The Pop Group was Gareth Sager's and John Waddington's guitars, and Mark's singing, which would be drifting all across the frame.' Although the sheer funk force of Underwood and Smith made the uptempo songs like 'We Are Time' physically compelling, elsewhere *Y* veers into texture-saturated abstraction with sound-paintings like 'Savage Sea' and 'Don't Sell Your Dreams'. Distended with effects and positively varicose with creativity, *Y* garnered a mixed reception. Typically, the faint praise went something along the lines of the *NME*'s verdict: 'a brave failure. Exciting but exasperating.' Today, it seems a notch more admirable and impressive – a heroic mess, glorious in its overreach.

John   Mark   Gareth   Dan   Bruce
Waddington   Stewart   Sager   Catsis   Smith

Radar Records' publicity photo of The Pop Group, 19?

To coincide with the album's release in April 1979, The Pop Group launched the Animal Instincts tour, a post-punk package including Linton Kwesi Johnson, Manchester's avant-funk outfit Manicured

Noise, and Alternative TV, the group led by punk icon Mark Perry. Founder of the original do-it-yourself fanzine *Sniffin' Glue*, Mark P was second only to Johnny Rotten as a punk ideologue. 'For the first few months of the movement's existence, I felt it was important that punk identify itself, musically, fashion-wise, the way the posters looked, the punk graphics,' he recalls. 'But it quickly became a straitjacket. The DIY thing was great, up to a point, but I was disappointed by the lack of musical progress.' After a dozen issues of *Sniffin' Glue*, Perry left to make an active contribution to opening up things musically, in the form of Alternative TV. The group's debut LP, *The Image Has Cracked*, featured punky anthems but also noise experiments, reggae rhythms, synths, studio-as-instrument malarkey, and a cover of an obscure Frank Zappa B-side. Perry's most striking statement was to open the album with 'Alternatives', a thirteen-minute live recording of an audience-participation segment that regularly occurred during Alternative TV gigs: Perry handed the microphone to members of the crowd and encouraged them to say whatever was on their mind. Inevitably, these idealistic experiments in cultural democracy and smashing the performer/audience barrier would degenerate into a farrago of abuse and squabbling. Still, this set up Perry to upbraid the crowd for their failure to live up to punk's challenges.

After *The Image Has Cracked*, Alternative TV pushed out even further. Recorded in the last months of 1978, *Vibing up the Senile Man* encompassed tribal percussion, spoken-word recitation, gongs, clarinet, detuned piano, shortwave radio, but, pointedly, almost no guitar. 'There are free-jazz influences – I'd got into Art Ensemble of Chicago, Sun Ra,' says Perry. 'I'd moved into this house with an amazing music room – pianos, clarinet, you name it – and we'd always be picking up stuff from junk shops.' Every song was a first take, Perry refusing to perfect or fine tune. On its release in early 1979, the album provoked a uniformly hostile response from reviewers perplexed by Perry's metamorphosis from working-class hero into bourgeois art-wanker. 'ATV had become a bloody good rock band, but here I was, chucking away my career for this weird twang-crash-bang-wallop. People thought I'd flipped my lid!'

The Pop Group, though, liked Perry's talk of 'total freedom' and invited him to join the Animal Instincts tour. Determined to practise onstage what *Vibing* had preached on vinyl, Perry decided there would be no rehearsals, 'just this spontaneous improv thing'. Rock conventions got turned on their heads whenever possible: a guitarist was given the job of playing drums; Perry sawed away discordantly on a violin; and Anno, the singer from hippy festival band Here and Now, joined the group onstage, despite being pregnant. But Alternative TV still had a hardcore of punk fans, and they reacted violently. 'In Portsmouth, the crowd wanted to kill us! I can laugh now, but back then I was so passionate about it, I got furious with them. I was yelling, "You thick bastards! That's not what the punk spirit is about, just giving you what you want!"' Everything came to a head – Perry's head, to be precise – in Derby when a hurled bottle knocked him unconscious. 'When I came to behind the amps, I was very upset, in tears,' he recalls. He decided the only way out of the deadlock was the 'truth in advertising' manoeuvre of changing the band's name to The Good Missionaries, so audiences would know they weren't going to get ATV's greatest hits. 'After we changed the name, the rest of that tour was fantastic; the crowds were totally with us. The Pop Group would come onstage and jam with us. The encore would be a total Ornette Coleman-style freakout, and the audience response wasn't "Fuck off!"; it was "*Yeah!*"'

The Slits started where Alternative TV and The Pop Group ended up – total chaos. Other punk bands talked about not being able to play, but were secretly competent. Genuinely inept, The Slits really sounded cacophonous, with only the faintest subliminal skank indicating their punky-reggae intentions. Some people reckon the 'true' Slits is this early naïve sound of girls struggling with their instruments and vocal chords, impelled forward by sheer glee and gall. Personally, I think The Slits got better when they, ah, got *better* – picking up some rudimentary instrumental skills and establishing a firmer rhythmic foundation (something helped when original drummer Palmolive, unable to provide the reggae-inflected groove the rest of the band wanted, moved on and was replaced by a guy who called himself Budgie). The Slits also established a studio relationship with Dennis Bovell, who helped them transform their rampaging racket into a more shapely disorder.

The Slits were a feral girl gang. Aged just fifteen in 1977, singer Ari Up recalls being 'wild and crazy, like an animal let loose – but an innocent little girl with it, too'. From her striking image (tangled dreadlocks, knickers worn on the outside of her clothes) to her seemingly pre-social antics, Ari inspired fear and fascination in equal measure. On one infamous occasion, she urinated onstage. 'It wasn't to shock anyone,' she insists. 'I needed to pee, there wasn't a toilet near, so I pissed onstage – on the side, but everyone in the audience saw it. I just didn't care.'

Ari's background was German and wealthy, but her heiress mother Nora was a bohemian and rock scenester. The family home served as open house for all kinds of stars, from Yes singer Jon Anderson to Joe Strummer. The Slits' guitarist Viv Albertine also came from a genteel background and went to art school, where she met The Clash's Mick Jones. Blonde, charismatic and trailing a host of male punk admirers, Albertine shared a squat with Keith Levene and played in a short-lived band with him and Sid Vicious called Flowers of Romance. Balefully dark haired and laconic, bassist Tessa Pollitt came from another all-girl punk group who trumped The Slits with a name – The Castrators – worthy of radical feminist Valerie Solanas, founder of the Society for Cutting Up Men.

A fan of Solanas's *SCUM Manifesto*, Malcolm McLaren attempted to manage The Slits, seeing them as the female Pistols. Legend has it his managerial come-on was: 'I want to work with you because you're girls and you play music. I hate music and I hate girls. I thrive on hate.' But instead of thinking up outrageous ideas worthy of Solanas or Sid Vicious, McLaren's masterplan was wildly sexist and degrading. After attacking the rock industry, he wanted to infiltrate the disco movement. At first, he tried to get The Slits to sign to the cheesy German disco label Hansa. Then, when Island moved to sign the band and invited McLaren to make a movie around them, he came up with a screenplay that envisioned The Slits as an all-girl rock band who go to Mexico only to find themselves effectively sold into slavery and ultimately turned into pornodisco stars. The Slits shrewdly extricated themselves from McLaren's grasp, but they did sign to Island and started working on their debut album, *Cut*, with Dennis Bovell in the summer of 1979.

Bovell was an obvious choice. The Slits, especially Ari, were reggae fiends. 'We used to find the blues parties just following the bass,' she says. 'We would be streets away and listen for the vibrations. In 1976–8, there were zero white people. And I was not just the only white girl but the only one with dreads. In fact, I was the first person to have the tree – I had my locks up in a tree-type shape. But I got away with it because I was dancing the hell out of their blues parties. Back then the style of dancing was called "steppers" and I was such a good stepper.' As she developed beyond the basic punk screech into plaintive, reedy singing, her Bavaria-meets-Jamaica accent made her sound like Nico on spliff rather than smack.

Punk diehards sometimes claim that Dennis Bovell dulled The Slits' edges, domesticated them. The band were ambitious, though: they wanted to be pop stars. Island boss Chris Blackwell thought that they had potential in spades and he gave Bovell as much studio time as required. 'The Slits had so much input that it was more a case of sorting out what should go,' says Bovell. 'They were just bulging with material and I had the task of sorting it out and saying, "This goes here." It was like an enormous jigsaw puzzle all dumped in your lap.' *Cut*'s songs do often sound like polyrhythmic cogs and jutting mechanical parts cobbled together to form slightly wonky but captivating contraptions. Albertine's itchy-and-scratchy rhythm guitar darts between Pollitt's sinuous basslines and Budgie's clackety clockwork drums. According to Bovell, Albertine 'was no Jimi Hendrixette . . . She'd do the occasional bit of single-note lead guitar, but mostly she was more like a female Steve Cropper from Booker T and the MGs, doing all these great rhythm things. She was always very conscious of not wanting to play the guitar like a man, but actually trying to create a style of her own.'

Probably the most delightful element in The Slits' sound is the strange geometry of the clashing and overlapping vocals: Albertine and Pollitt weave around Ari's shrill, slightly sour warble. On the opener, 'Instant Hit', the girls form a roundelay of haphazard harmonies that Ari describes as 'a kind of "Frère Jacques" thing'. Albertine's lyrics to 'Instant Hit' depict an unhealthily thin boy who 'don't like himself very much/'cos he has set his self to self-destruct' – a barbed portrait that applied equally to Sid Vicious and Keith Levene, her junkie bandmates in Flowers of Romance. 'So Tough', a frenetic piss-take of macho posturing, gives way to the doleful skank of 'Spend, Spend, Spend', its sidling bass and brittle-nerved percussion perfectly complementing the lyric's sketch of a shopaholic vainly trying to 'satisfy this empty feeling' with impulse purchases. 'Shoplifting' turns 'Spend, Spend, Spend' inside out: woman-as-consumerist-dupe becomes petty-thief-as-feminist-rebel. Frantic punk-reggae, the song surges into adrenaline overdrive as Ari, caught red-handed, yells, 'Do a runner!' The song climaxes with a shattering scream that mingles terror, glee and relief at escaping the supermarket detective, a yowl that collapses into the giggled gasp, 'I've pissed in my knickers.'

The fast songs on *Cut* are exhilarating: 'Shoplifting'; the romance-as-braindeath parody 'Love Und Romance'; and the single, 'Typical Girls', a diatribe against un-Slitty females who 'don't create, don't rebel' and whose heads are addled with women's magazine-induced anxieties about 'spots, fat, unnatural smells'. But the most haunting songs on *Cut* are the clutch of downtempo, despondent tracks: 'FM', 'Ping Pong Affair', and 'Newtown', which takes its title from the urban centres that sprang up after the Second World War. All these towns started life as an architect's and urban planner's utopian vision before swiftly degenerating into characterless gridzones of anomie and despair. The song draws a disconcerting parallel between the conformists hooked on cultural tranquillizers such as 'televisiono' and 'footballino', and The Slits' own bohemian peers zonked on illegal narcotics; Albertine's jittery scrape mimics the flesh-crawling ache of cold turkey. Withdrawal of an emotional kind inspired 'Ping Pong Affair' – Ari measuring out the empty post-break-up evenings with masturbation ('Same old thing yeah I know/Everybody does it') and cigarettes. Dub-inflected and desolate, *Cut*'s slow songs impart a sense of atomized individuals numbing their pain with pop culture's illusions; romance junkies and glamourholics adrift in a haze of cheap dreams. Underneath it all you could sense The Slits' yearning for a simpler, natural life. *Cut*'s famous cover photograph of the group as mud-smeared Amazons combined *nostalgie de la boue* with she-warrior defiance to jab the casual record-shop browser right in the eye. Naked but for loin-cloths and warpaint, The Slits stand proudly bare-breasted, staring out the camera. Behind them you can see the wall of a picturesque cottage, brambles and roses clambering up the side, as if to underline the 'we're no delicate English roses and this is no come-hither look' message. The cottage was Ridge Farm, the studio where Bovell produced *Cut*. Says Ari, 'We got so into the countryside when we were doing the album, to the point of rolling around in the earth. So we decided to cover ourselves in mud and show that women could be sexy without dressing in a prescribed way. Sexy, in a natural way, and naked, without being pornographic.'

Cut's cover echoes the photo of the Mud People of Papua New Guinea on the front of *Y*. Like The Slits, The Pop Group pined for a lost wholeness they imagined existed before civilization's debilitating effect. On 'She Is Beyond Good and Evil', Mark Stewart had yowled, 'Western values mean nothing to her.' A tape of African drumming preceded The Pop Group's arrival onstage during the Animal Instincts tour, and via a *Melody Maker* interview they appealed to their fans to bring drums and whistles, and transform gigs into tribal ceremonies. In an *NME* feature, Gareth Sager argued that Western civilizations, being 'based on cities', were

The Slits get raw on the cover of *Cut*, 1979. L to R: Ari Up, Viv Albertine, Tessa Pollitt

sick because they were cut off from 'natural cycles', unlike African tribes where repression simply didn't exist. He proposed abolishing conventional education and spending the money helping people to de-indoctrinate themselves. Language itself might be the enemy: 'Words Disobey Me' proposed stripping away layers of conditioning and recovering a pure, naïve speech of the heart. 'Speak the unspoken/First words of a child . . . We don't need words/Throw them away', beseeched Stewart.

The Slits shared The Pop Group's naïve idealization of noble savagery and pure instinct, a cult of innocence and intuition that sometimes took on an anti-intellectual tinge. The two groups got 'so close we were like one tribe', says Ari Up. Bruce Smith took over from Budgie as The Slits' drummer, and played both sets when the two groups did a joint tour of Europe. There was even tribal endogamy: Sager went out with Albertine;

Cover of The Pop Group's 1979 debut album, *Y*, featuring the Mud People of Papua New Guinea

Sean Oliver (the last of The Pop Group's several bassists) fathered a child with Pollitt; Bruce Smith dated and eventually married Neneh Cherry, a friend of Ari who eventually joined The Slits as stage dancer and backing vocalist. Full merger as a single tribe was formally anointed when the groups founded their own independent label, Y, in 1980, administered by Pop Group manager Dick O'Dell. The Slits had parted company with Island, while The Pop Group severed their links with Radar after learning to their horror about the parent company WEA's links to the Kinney conglomerate, which was involved in arms dealing.

Out of all these conflicted emotions emerged the single 'We Are All Prostitutes', The Pop Group's first post-Radar release. Musically, it's their most powerful recording. The lyrics, though, abandoned *Y*'s imagistic delirium in favour of a histrionic rant against 'the most barbaric of all religions' – consumerism. 'Our children shall rise up against us,' warned Stewart. The Pop Group seemed to be changing – from lusty poet-warriors to puritanical doom-mongers. In interviews of the time, Sager declared it was frivolous to be 'talking about music' when they should discuss 'external things' – politics, current affairs, famine, war. 'I don't see the point in entertaining just now, it's pure escapism,' he told the *NME*. 'Rock and roll is taking your mind off reality.'

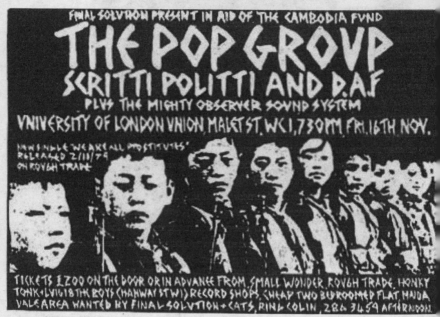

Flyer for Benefit in Aid of the Cambodia Fund, headlined by The Pop Group, 1979

The Pop Group weren't alone. Many post-punk musicians were fighting back with protest songs and benefit gigs galore. Rock Against Racism became the template for a host of issues, including Rock Against Sexism, Rock Against Thatcher and Scrap the Sus (a campaign against nineteenth-century anti-vagrancy laws that enabled police to harass black youth at will on the grounds of 'suspicious behaviour'). The Pop Group did benefits for Scrap the Sus and Cambodia, among many others. 'We gave away virtually all our money from concerts through doing so many benefits,' says Stewart. At one point, The Pop Group had to do a benefit for *themselves* because they'd gone into debt.

Still, something about The Pop Group's stridency began to rub their former supporters up the wrong way. The backlash came in March 1980, triggered by a split single that paired The Slits' 'In the Beginning There Was Rhythm' with The Pop Group's 'Where There's a Will'. The *NME*'s Ian Penman mocked the 'Bristol Baezes' (as in sanctimonious folkie Joan Baez). The second Pop Group album, *For How Much Longer Do We Tolerate Mass Murder?*, was panned as self-righteous soapbox agit-prop. The music was still fiery, and actually more focused than on *Y*, but it was hard to stomach the crude finger-pointing of songs like 'Blind Faith'. The band seemed to proceed methodically through a checklist of issues ('Justice' dealt with police brutality, 'How Much Longer' with Nixon and Kissinger's war crimes). And the self-flagellating guilt-trip vibe was off-putting. 'There Are No Spectators' chided the politically disengaged and passive: 'There is no neutral/No one is innocent'. From the sleeve, with its collage of news cuttings about such outrages as East Timor, to 'Feed The Hungry', all blurted statistics and strident denunciation, the album was relentlessly pinned to the specifics. Hectoring and lecturing, *How Much Longer* was as unpoetic as a fringe leftist pamphlet.

For The Pop Group, and above all Mark Stewart – always the intellectual engine of the band, its autodidact bookworm – the shift to plain speaking and speaking out was simply the right response to the urgencies of the era. Thatcher had surged to power in May 1979, carried by a massive swing to the right. 'It was a fiery time; you felt something was about to kick off,' says Stewart of 1980's apocalyptic atmosphere. 'See, I never felt that politics was this dreary thing. When we were ranting, it was all from the heart. It came out in a mad rush.' Stewart had been absorbing the music of The Last Poets, black Muslim radicals sometimes credited with inventing rap, who'd lashed 'white devils' and black counter-revolutionaries alike on albums like *This Is Madness* and *Chastisement*. And he'd been hanging with Linton Kwesi Johnson and such organizations as Race Today and the Radical Alliance of Black Poets and Players. Johnson didn't exactly mince his words: the anti-fascist anthem 'Fite Dem Back' vows, 'We gonna smash their brains in/'Cos they ain't got nuffink in 'em'. He wasn't a Rasta (indeed, he upset many Jamaicans when he mocked Rastafarianism as an ostrich religion), but his patois-thick voice and baleful cadences gave his words, seemingly simplistic on the printed page, a power and authority to which Stewart aspired.

For many white British bohemians, though, it was precisely roots reggae's millenarianism – Rasta's imagery of 'Armagideon' and 'crisus

dp

```
BEATEN IN THE FACE
STOMACH HEAD AND GENITALS
CHOKED UNTIL UNCONSCIOUS
COLD WATER POURED IN EARS
PLASTIC BAG HELD OVER HEAD
THROWN AGAINST THE WALLS    HIT WITH KARATE CHOPS
BENDING OF THE WRISTS    LIFTED UP BY THE EARS
BURNT WITH CIGARETTES
TEETH KNOCKED OUT
SPREADEAGLED AGAINST THE WALL
SPREADEAGLED ACROSS THE FLOOR
AND THEN JUMPED UPON
WITH THREATS OF DEATH
LIGHT SWITCHED OFF
THREATS OF RAPE

words taken from
AMNESTY INTERNATIONAL REPORT on
BRITISH ARMY TORTURE OF IRISH PRISONERS
```

john   mark   gareth   dan   bruce

THE POP GROUP

ROUGH TRADE RT023

'Amnesty International Report on British Army Torture of Irish Prisoners', the B-side of The Pop Group's 'We Are All Prostitutes', 1979

time', retribution and redemption – that resonated with their own sense of internal exile. 'We did feel like we were on the frontline of Babylon,' recalls Vivien Goldman. 'Rasta provided this mesh of the political, the spiritual, and the apocalyptic, and it helped you define your enemies.' There was friction, naturally, between trendy-lefty liberal ideas and Rasta's Old Testament morals and sexual chauvinism. But the sheer inspirational force of the music swept aside reservations. 'With the roots worldview, the logic was often questionable, but the feeling of spiritual uplift was undeniable,' says Stewart. 'Going to sound systems with black mates, they were like huge evangelical meetings, and you didn't get that kind of energy with rock gigs. That kind of yearning for a better world, that questioning of the system – it just made my hairs stand on end.'

As Stewart felt the pull of reggae, admiring the way it could shout down Babylon without lapsing into sloganeering, the other members of The Pop Group were being tugged in the opposite direction: they wanted to explore deeper their free-jazz side. 'It wasn't that I disagreed with the things Mark said; I was just concerned about it getting so dogmatic,' says Bruce Smith. 'It was like Mark saw the music as just a vehicle, a platform for messages.' Stewart, in turn, found it increasingly 'difficult to sing on the abstract stuff'.

He was also becoming increasingly involved in organized protest, spending three months working in the Campaign for Nuclear Disarmament's offices, helping to coordinate a massive anti-nuclear rally to be held in Trafalgar Square. After almost withering away in the early seventies, CND's membership resurged as Cold War fears intensified in the wake of the Iranian revolution and the Soviet invasion of Afghanistan. NATO's December 1979 decision to install American-controlled Cruise missiles convinced many that Britain was degenerating into little more than a US launching pad. The Trafalgar Square rally on 26 October 1980 was the last time The Pop Group performed together. 'We did a version of William Blake's "Jerusalem", 'cos I'd wanted to do a rallying cry for all the different age groups there,' recalls Stewart. 'That song is a real socialist anthem, but visionary and idealistic too, Blake being this real prophet.' But after this high point – playing to 250,000 people – The Pop Group fell apart. 'An organic disintegration,' says Stewart. 'There was no ill will.'

Meanwhile, The Slits drifted along, with Ari succumbing to a Rasta-infused mystic pantheism. 'I just see the Creator in everything,' she told one interviewer. Proposing a kind of cosmology of rhythm, 'In the Beginning There Was Rhythm' hymned all the pulsating patterns that structure reality: 'If we only would have known God is riddim . . . Riddim is roots and roots is riddim . . . SILENCE!!!! Silence is a riddim too!' She explained in another interview, 'Every sound that you hear is rhythm. Fucking is rhythm and so is the earth going round and every footstep and every heartbeat. The way you go about your music is the way you go about your life . . . Rhythm and life go together.' Hearing early rap records on a recent trip to New York inspired her percussive, chanted delivery.

As a sideline to The Slits, Ari formed New Age Steppers, a collaboration with dub producer Adrian Sherwood and his session musicians Creation Rebel. Another white-reggae fiend, Sherwood shared a squat :

Battersea with Ari and Neneh Cherry. 'Adrian was a hustler in a true sense,' says Ari. 'He managed various reggae artists and toasters, distributed reggae records and sold them out of the back of his van, taught himself how to do studio engineering. We partnershipped and I came up with the name New Age Steppers – stepper as in dancing to reggae, and New Age as in representing the new millennium.' The group's debut single, 'Fade Away', released in the first week of 1981, boasted one of Ari's finest vocal performances, but its trust-in-Jah fatalism (the power-hungry and money-minded will all 'fade away', leaving the righteous meek to inherit the earth) seemed disconcertingly passive, suggesting a retreat into hippy-like serenity.

One more Slits album, *Return of the Giant Slits*, appeared on CBS, an even bigger major label than Island. Influenced by African music, Sun Ra and Don Cherry (Neneh's father and a pioneer of ethnodelic jazz), the record's diffuse low-key experimentalism fell into a hostile marketplace. In songs like 'Animal Space', Ari's pantheism took an eco-mystical turn. 'Earthbeat', for instance, was a lament for a sorely mistreated Mother Earth: 'Even the leaves are wheezing/Even the clouds are coughing'.

After the band finally fell apart, she fled the Babylonian West in search of any remaining havens of unspoiled nature, flitting from rural Jamaica to the jungles of Belize and Borneo (where she lived with tribal Indians). Finally, she became a real earth mother with a family. For others in the Slits/Pop Group tribe, getting into world music sufficed: Africa's 'rhythms of resistance' became the new roots reggae for a certain breed of post-punk. WOMAD, for instance, was the brainchild of a group of people from the same Bristol milieu that spawned The Pop Group.

The Pop Group splintered into multiple groups. Glaxo Babies, Maximum Joy and Pigbag pursued slightly different versions of funk. Pigbag, helmed by Simon Underwood and still associated with Dick O'Dell's Y label, became a *real* pop group, scoring a massive UK hit with 'Papa's Got a Brand New Pigbag'. Bruce Smith and Gareth Sager, The Pop Group's most fervent free-jazzers, formed Rip Rig & Panic, taking the name from an old Roland Kirk album. They peppered their interviews with beatnik patter like 'cat', 'dig' and 'out there'; the music capered and cavorted in antic whimsy. Rip Rig & Panic was basically The Pop Group minus the reggae input and the politics. 'Yeah, it was *only* the music,' says Smith. 'We didn't even have a singer. Sager and our pianist Mark Springer would warble a bit into the microphone now and hen, but we didn't really have vocals until Neneh joined later.' In one early music-paper feature, Sager obliquely disses erstwhile comrade Mark Stewart: 'It's definitely time to give the moaners the elbow. I like the cats who are . . . they're complaining but they're saying "yeah" at the same time.'

Stewart, meanwhile, developed a relationship with Adrian Sherwood and the musicians surrounding the latter's On U label. He sang on the first New Age Steppers album, then made his solo debut in October 1982 with a fully realized version of the English hymn The Pop Group had massacred at Trafalgar Square. Produced by Sherwood and marrying churchy organ swells to dub's thunderquake bass, 'Jerusalem' unites Blake's vision of Albion as Promised Land with the Zion of Rasta's dreaming. And its declaration – 'I shall not cease from mental fight nor shall my sword sleep at my side/'Til we have built Jerusalem in England's green and pleasant land' – served as mission statement for Stewart's ongoing career as culture warrior. Amazingly, almost thirty years later, he's still shouting down Babylon.

6

AUTONOMY IN THE UK: Independent Labels and the DIY Movement

New Hormones. Fast Product. Factory. Rough Trade. Cherry Red. Desperate Bicycles. Thomas Leer. The Normal. Mute. Swell Maps.

Some people say, in all earnestness, that *Spiral Scratch* was a more important record than 'Anarchy in the UK'. Released in January 1977 on Buzzcocks' own label New Hormones, the EP wasn't the first independently released record (not by a long stretch), but it *was* the first to make a real polemical point about independence. In the process, *Spiral Scratch* inspired thousands of people to join the do-it-yourself/release-it-yourself game.

Spiral Scratch was simultaneously a regionalist blow against the capital (Manchester versus London) and a conceptual exercise in demystification (*spiral scratch*, because that's what a record materially is – a groove scraped into vinyl). The back cover itemized details of the recording process – which take of the song they'd used, the number of overdubs. Even the EP's catalogue number ORG-1 was a left-leaning bookworm's wisecrack: ORG-1 = ORG ONE = orgone = Wilhelm Reich's neuro-libidinous life-force. '*Spiral Scratch* was *playful*,' says Buzzcocks manager Richard Boon. 'Play was very important.'

For reasons hard to reconstruct fully in hindsight, the notion of independently releasing your own music felt fantastically novel at that particular time. *Spiral Scratch*'s initial pressing of 1,000 copies, funded by loans from friends and family, sold out with staggering speed. The single's first edition (it was reissued a few years later) ultimately chalked up sales of 16,000, an astonishing achievement given that a distribution network for independent records didn't even exist. 'Mail order was very important,' says Boon. 'Rough Trade was just a shop with a mail-order service in those days. And we knew the manager of Manchester's Virgin shop and he persuaded some of his regional colleagues to stock it.' People were buying *Spiral Scratch* for the music, but also for the sheer fact of its existence, its status as cultural landmark and portent of revolution.

Why was the idea of independently recording and releasing music so surprising? In late fifties America, around 50 per cent of rock 'n' roll and R&B hits went through independent labels, such as Sun and Hi. Throughout the sixties and seventies, independents flourished in regional markets and niche genres, like jazz (Sun Ra's Saturn; the UK free-improv imprint Incus), British folk (Topic) and Jamaican imports (Bluebeat). Even during the commercial boom of 'serious', album-oriented rock, when major labels dominated the market, you still had crucial 'progressive' independents like Virgin, Island and Chrysalis. One critical distinction between those labels and the post-punk independents, though, was that 'they all had financing and distribution from major labels', says Iain McNay, founder of leading post-punk indie Cherry Red. 'The people who started Virgin and Island were enterprising, sure, and "independent" in terms of what they did creatively. But they had the support of major record-company distribution, finance and marketing.'

Just before punk, a couple of labels formed who were independent both financially and in distribution terms: Chiswick and Stiff. Both emerged from the pub-rock scene: Chiswick debuted with the amped-up R&B of the Count Bishops in November 1975, Stiff with a Nick Lowe single the following year. Unlike the amateur-hour neophytes of New Hormones, though, the figures behind the pub-rock indies were seasoned veterans of the record business, entrepreneurially sussed *insiders*. And neither Chiswick nor Stiff made an ideological meal out of being independent. Both soon eagerly hooked up with major-label distribution, with Stiff becoming a leading New Wave hit-maker through Ian Dury and Elvis Costello.

When punk came along, the top bands without exception followed the traditional rock route and looked for the best major label deal they could get. 'The disappointing thing for me historically was The Clash and Sex Pistols signing to majors,' says Geoff Travis, co-founder of Rough Trade. Even Buzzcocks rapidly buckled. 'After Devoto had quit, we thought we'd do another New Hormones EP, *Love Bites*,' says Boon. 'But then the drummer's dad came to see me, saying his son had just left school and had an offer of a job as an insurance clerk and "What are you going to do with the band?" So that was when we had to decide, "God, we're in this for real!" Which meant finding other resources. Which meant signing to a major. Because doing it independently wasn't supportable at that point; you just couldn't get enough revenue selling through mail order and a few sympathetic retailers.'

As the band's manager, Boon got Buzzcocks a deal with United Artists, but he continued New Hormones as a back-burner operation for several years, sporadically releasing esoteric post-punk like Linda Sterling's band Ludus and the Pete Shelley side-project The Tiller Boys. Released at the very end of 1977, almost a full year after *Spiral Scratch*, ORG-2 wasn't even a record, but an A3 booklet of collages by Sterling and Jon Savage. 'It didn't have a cover price, so it didn't sell very well – nobody knew what to sell it for!' laughs Boon. 'But it did its job. The title, *The Secret Public*, was all about that other side of the DIY thing – trying to locate kindred spirits who would get it and respond.'

In 1977, many people did 'get' *Spiral Scratch* and responded to it as a signal, catalyst, call to action. 'My girlfriend Hilary gave me a copy and that was the key moment,' says Bob Last, founder of the Edinburgh indie Fast Product. The idea of Fast Product already existed in his mind as a brand, but Last had no specific ideas about what the actual merchandise would ultimately be. 'I had a logo and an idea of the attitude the company would embody, but it was *Spiral Scratch* that gave me the idea of music as the product. I popped into the Bank of Scotland and said, "I'm going to put a record out. Can I borrow some money?" And, bizarrely, they gave me a few hundred quid! I had absolutely no idea there'd been a history of independent labels before that. *Spiral Scratch* turned my head around.'

A former architecture student and technician/designer for a travelling theatre club, Last conceived Fast Product as a hybrid of art project and renegade commerce. The company's first press release trumpeted the slogan 'Interventions in any media' as a sort of all-purpose promise/threat. Starting with The Mekons' 'Never Been in a Riot' single in January 1978, Fast's products were strikingly designed and highly collectable. At a time when 'business' – big or small – was still regarded with suspicion as the Man, and consumerism was something to be guilty about, Fast provocatively highlighted the notion of the commodity-as-fetish. This became the label's signature balancing act: celebrating consumer desire while simultaneously exposing the manipulative mechanisms of capitalism. You could see a new kind of left-wing sensibility emerging that would flourish in the eighties: a 'designer socialism' purged of its puritanical austerity and pleasure-fear, attracted to stylishly made things but determined not to be hoodwinked or exploited.

Like New Hormones had done with *The Secret Public*, Fast Product moved quickly to show that it was more than just a record label. FAST 3, *The Quality of Life*, comprised a plastic bag filled with nine photocopied collages (including pictures of German terrorists, taken from a Sunday colour supplement but relabelled 'entertainment'), along with various items of consumer detritus. 'We had someone carefully peeling oranges and putting a bit of peel in each bag, to guarantee that each package would be unique, with a different pattern of rotting on each strip of peel.' A later non-musical release, *SeXex* – another plastic bag, this time containing a dozen photocopied sheets, a badge and an empty soup carton – was conceived as a promotional campaign for an imaginary corporation. 'Both *Quality of Life* and *SeXex* used the cut-up photocopied aesthetic of the time,' says Last. 'But what drove them was this sense that they were a perverse advertising campaign for a product that didn't actually exist. And they sold quite well, got debated and referred to quite extensively.'

'The first really arty, clever label was Fast Product,' says Tony Wilson, co-founder of Manchester independent Factory Records. 'A damn sight artier than us. If I could have put orange peel in a plastic bag and released it with a catalogue number, I would have been very proud.' Local TV presenter Wilson was a Cambridge-educated aesthete-provocateur who loved record packaging and wanted his label to have a clear design identity. He recruited young design student Peter Saville to give Factory its own visual signature, influenced by the starkness and severity of early twentieth-century modernist design: Bauhaus, De Stijl, Constructivism and Die Neue Typographie. Saville's record sleeves and label typography made Factory and its groups – Joy Division, Durutti Column, A Certain Ratio – stand out from the post-punk pack. The austere elegance was a breath of fresh air in rock packaging, a cleansing break both with pre-punk romanticism and the New Wave's own clichés. The label's first release, *A Factory Sample*, was a double EP packaged in glistening gatefold silver. 'It just seemed so *special*,' says Paul Morley. 'The fact that it was so beautiful looking showed the possibilities of what could be done, and it showed up the London record industry for being so boring.'

Soon Factory were outdoing Fast Product's collectable *Earcom* samplers and peculiar packages like *Quality of Life* by bringing a Duchamp-like absurdism to their catalogue. Numbers were assigned to anything and everything: pipe dreams, whims, unrealized projects, movies that were never finished or never started. Fac 8 was a menstrual egg-timer proposed by Linder Sterling but never constructed. Fac 61 was a lawsuit

FAC-2

A FACTORY SAMPLE

Factory's first record: the gatefold seven-inch double EP *A Factory Sample*, released December 1978

from the label's former house producer Martin Hannett. Fac 99 was a dentist's bill for Factory co-director Rob Gretton, who'd had his molars reconstructed. For Wilson, this brand of mischief was in the spirit of the Situationists the French anarcho-Dada movement of the sixties whose ideas he admired. The Situationists believed that rediscovering play was the remedy for 'the poverty of everyday life', the feelings of alienation amid abundance generated by Western consumer society. Above all, they wanted to smash 'the spectacle', all those mass-media forms of entertainment that enforce passivity rather than participation. The Situationists were also stern critics of commodity fetishism, however, so it's not all that likely they would have approved of Factory's sumptuously designed records.

In truth, the only remotely Situationist-like aspect to Factory was what Wilson described as the label's 'continual denial of profit'. No contracts were signed with the groups, who were free to leave whenever they liked and who retained ownership of their music. 'I sometimes flatter myself that the way we behaved, which was not about wanting to be rich, and the way we lived that every day, was maybe what might've been suggested by the Situationist philosophy,' says Wilson. Weirdly combining a sometimes ruinous aesthetic perfectionism (covers so expensive that the records were sometimes sold at a loss, most famously in the case of New Order's 'Blue Monday') with lackadaisical unprofessionalism, Factory didn't act like a business at all.

Far from Fast Product's and Factory's sly, postmodernist games, The Desperate Bicycles had a more earnest, but probably more faithful, take on the Situationist antagonism to 'the spectacle'. The Desps were DIY's most fervent evangelists. At the end of their early 1977 debut, 'Smokescreen', they chant, 'It was easy, it was cheap – go and do it'. That slogan then became the chorus of 'The Medium Was Tedium', the follow-up released later that same year. On the single's flipside, the anti-fascist battle-cry 'Don't Back the Front' declared, 'No more time for spectating' and incited the listener to 'Cut it, press it, distribute it/Xerox music's here at last'. A sleevenote revealed that 'Smokescreen' had cost only £153 and and said the band 'would really like to know why you haven't made your single yet'. Do-it-yourself/release-it-yourself, for Desperate Bicycles, spelled the overthrow of the establishment music industry because it was the people seizing the means of (record) production, making their own entertainment, and selling it to other creative and autonomous likeminds.

The Desps' actual music was almost puritanical in its unadorned simplicity. Frugal to the point of anorexia, the production spurned the 'fat' guitar sound of conventional punk production. For The Desperate Bicycles, it was as though sloppiness and scrawniness became signs of membership in the true punk elect. The very deficiency of traditional rock virtues – tightness, feel – stood as tokens of the group's authenticity and purity of intent.

Their 1977 singles had an even bigger impact than *Spiral Scratch*. The demystify-the-process data on the back of 'The Medium Was Tedium' and the group's fervent exhortation, 'Now it's your turn!' catalysed a scrappy legion of DIY bands, including many of the key figures of the post-punk era: Swell Maps, Scritti Politti, Young Marble Giants, The Television Personalities, Thomas Leer, and Daniel Miller, a.k.a. The

Normal. 'I don't know if I ever *heard* their records. I just got infected by the energy and inspiration The Bicycles put across in this *Melody Maker* article about how easy it was to make a record,' says Miller, who in 1977 was a twenty-six-year-old fan of German electronic music and a thwarted musician. After reading the *Melody Maker* feature, he rushed out and bought a second-hand Korg synth for £150 and then worked overtime at his film-editing job until he could afford a four-track ministudio. Working in his north London bedroom, he created 'T.V.O.D.' and 'Warm Leatherette', the two sides of his self-released debut single as The Normal. 'I never thought of approaching a "major" label,' he told the *NME* in 1981. 'I didn't like them because they'd ruined quite a few of my favourite bands – like Virgin did with Can, Faust and Klaus Schulze.'

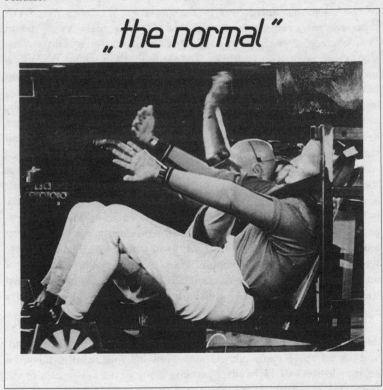

Mute Records' debut release – The Normal's 'T.V.O.D.' b/w 'Warm Leatherette', 1978

The Normal's sound was electro-punk. 'Warm Leatherette' especially, all harsh stabs of analogue-synth distortion and dispassionately perverse lyrics (about the eroticism of motor accidents, via J. G. Ballard's *Crash*), could hardly have been further from the floridly Romantic keyboard synths of prog-rock. The single did unexpectedly well, selling 30,000 copies, and inadvertently turned Miller into the CEO of his own record label. Mute Records was the name he'd put on the back of the single, along with his home address. Many people assumed Mute was a proper record label specializing in weird electropop. Within a week of 'Warm Leatherette' being released, all kinds of odd demo tapes started arriving through the letterbox. 'Fad Gadget was the first one I liked enough to want to put out,' recalls Miller. 'Before I knew it, I was running a record company – working from home, with no staff or anything like that, but a record label nonetheless.'

In mid-1978, a curious spate of cultural synchrony meant that 'Warm Leatherette' appeared around the same time as several other lo-fi electronic singles, all released on indie labels: Throbbing Gristle's 'United', Cabaret Voltaire's *Extended Play* EP, The Human League's 'Being Boiled', Robert Rental's 'Paralysis' and Thomas Leer's 'Private Plane'. 'There was this period when they all came out, one after the other,' recalls Leer. 'And it was, like, "Where are all these weird records coming from?" None of us knew each other. There was obviously something brewing.'

Actually, Leer and Robert Rental *did* know each other. Two Scottish friends who'd moved down to London *circa* punk, the pair decided to put out their own records – once again, prompted by The Desperate Bicycles' example. Renting a multitrack recorder and other equipment for five days, they took the gear round to Leer's flat in Finsbury Park to record his songs, then moved it across the river to Rental's Battersea pad. 'The singles came out at the same time and they sounded similar, because we actually made them together,' says Leer. They looked alike, too – the covers were photocopied, the labels hand-stamped. Leer and Rental were so captivated with the DIY ethos that they decided to operate their own labels – Oblique and Regular, respectively – rather than jointly release via the same imprint. Leer pressed only 650 copies of 'Private Plane' b/w 'International', but one of them made it to the office of the *NME*, where it was made Single of the Week.

'Private Plane' sounded electronic, but Leer didn't own a synth. Instead, he processed his guitar and bass using various devices and gadgets, and played Rental's Stylophone (a gimmicky electronic keyboard played with a pen) through an echo effect. All these gauzy, silver-swirl textures gave 'Private Plane' an ethereal feel perfect for its mood of remote serenity tinged with wistfulness, which was loosely inspired by a recent TV programme about the reclusive multi-millionaire Howard Hughes. Leer's fey voice is equally perfect, but owed something to contingency: he had to whisper the vocal because the recording took place at night in his one-room bedsit and he didn't want to wake his girlfriend.

Thomas Leer's debut single, 'Private Plane' b/w 'International', 1978

More than the electronic squad, though, The Desperate Bicycles' biggest impact was on the noisy guitar brigade. Teenagers growing up in Solihull, a middle-class suburb six miles from the centre of Birmingham, Swell Maps were a gang of friends centred on two brothers who hated their given surname (Godfrey) so much they renamed themselves Nikki Sudden and Epic Soundtracks. When 'Smokescreen' came out, Swell Maps had already existed for five years – as a sort of imaginary rock band, getting together to record albums on reel-to-reel tape-recorders, and turning them into cassettes complete with cover art and even inner-sleeve booklets. 'We would set up recording studios in the house when our parents went on holiday,' says Sudden. 'But it wasn't until Desperate Bicycles did their first single that we realized you could actually book a studio and make a record. We thought only major labels could hire them, which seems ridiculous now! As soon as we grasped that anyone could do it, we immediately booked this place in Cambridge called Spaceward, which used to advertise in the back of *Melody Maker* and cost a hundred and fifty quid for a ten-hour day session.'

Pooling their savings and borrowing more from the Godfrey parents, Swell Maps pressed up 2,000 copies of their debut 'Read about Seymour'. Released on the group's own label Rather, 'Read about Seymour' was widely thought to be about Seymour Stein, founder of America's New Wave-friendly label Sire. Actually, says Sudden, it's about a totally different Seymour Stein – 'this guy who was "King of the Mods" in the mid-sixties. I read about him in this column Marc Bolan used to write for *Record Mirror*."' The rest of the lyrics, though, were composed in cut-up fashion. Another song spliced its lyric together by combining text from an Enid Blyton story with words from a book about fighter pilots. Swell Maps were obsessed with war, but in a whimsical and boyishly innocuous way. 'Then Poland', 'Midget Submarines' and 'Ammunition Train' drew on military history (especially the eighteenth-century War of the Spanish Succession) and the *Boy's Own* adventures of fighter-pilot Biggles (Swell Maps member Richard Earle called himself 'Biggles Book'). The Maps also loved the Gerry Anderson puppet adventure TV shows of the sixties, *Thunderbirds* and *Stingray*, an episode of the latter providing the title for Swell Maps' debut album, *A Trip to Marineville*. 'I'd say our biggest influences were T Rex, Can and Gerry Anderson,' says Sudden. 'Which isn't a bad combination. We always wished we could use Barry Gray, the guy who did all the *Thunderbirds* themes, to do orchestrations of our tracks.'

Along with their pals The Television Personalities, Swell Maps invented a strand of post-punk that made a fetish of naïvety. Weak vocals and shaky rhythms, rudimentary droning basslines and fast-strummed discords: the DIY bands revelled in the noise-generating potential of the guitar, but they didn't exactly *rock* and they certainly didn't *roll*. For believers, much more than the 'sped-up heavy metal' that was first-wave punk, this was the true realization of the here's-three-chords, now-start-a-band ethos – except some of the groups didn't have even three chords. 'It took me two years to learn two chords,' Sudden told the *NME*. 'I can't ever see ourselves becoming polished, note perfect and all that. We hardly ever rehearse – about once every six months.'

Fervent amateurists, Swell Maps believed bands were ruined when they depended on playing gigs and releasing records in order to make a living. One of the reasons why the group split, shortly before the release of their second album, *Jane from Occupied Europe*, was that they were becoming too successful, with a tour of America looming. Many of the groups who followed in their wake, though, went a step further, equating amateur*ism* with amateur*ishness*: the deliberate avoidance of anything that smacked of professionalism or slickness. From the liberating declaration that 'Anyone can do it', DIY became a confining injunction to *sound* like anyone can do it. Swell Maps themselves were always more expansive and experimental than this: for every frantic racket like 'Let's Build a Car', there were glinting metallic instrumentals full of eerie, cavernous hollows and clangorous sonorities, the missing link between Neu! and Sonic Youth.

Back at the beginnings of their recording career, Swell Maps initially had some problems shifting 'Read about Seymour'. After nine months, sales had stalled at around 750 copies, despite an initial boost of support from Radio One DJ John Peel, who played it over a dozen times in three weeks on his late-night show. The day after recording a Peel session in London, though, Sudden happened to walk past Rough Trade's record shop, which also doubled as the HQ of the fledgling Rough Trade distribution company. 'One of the guys asked, "Have you got any of your single left?" I said, "Oh, about a thousand," and he said, "We'll take the lot."'

The alliance that subsequently developed between Rough Trade and Swell Maps was a prime example of the role the London label rapidly assumed as enabler-in-chief for the UK independent scene. Initially just one of the first wave of post-punk indie labels – alongside Small Wonder, Cherry Red, Rabid, Industrial and Step Forward – Rough Trade rapidly assumed a central role. Not so much the leader of the independent movement as its chief coordinator and connector, it freely dispensed information and encouragement. Even more crucially, it fronted money to bands to enable them to start their own labels or press up more copies of a release. Often it formed a partnership with small, one-band labels (like

Swell Map's own Rather), in which Rough Trade paid for the pressing of the record and received in return distribution rights for the release. On one level, this was entrepreneurially canny (Rough Trade made much of its money from distributing independent records), but these 'P&D' (pressing and distribution) deals were also freighted with intense idealism. Rough Trade was ideologically committed to support people in their attempts to achieve creative autonomy and self-realization. Daniel Miller, for instance, was given £300 to press up an extra 2,000 copies of 'Warm Leatherette', which Rough Trade then distributed. They also provided a base for his fledgling Mute label. Says Miller, 'I didn't have an office, so they let me get the records delivered there from the pressing plant, and do my mail-outs from their HQ.'

Like many independents in this era and later, Rough Trade was a record store before it was a record label. A music-obsessed Cambridge graduate, Geoff Travis hitch-hiked across America in his mid-twenties, where he picked up 'literally hundreds of records by the time I got to San Francisco', then shipped them back to London. A fantasy was forming in his head: 'Opening a shop where you could listen to records all day without anyone bothering you too much.' Acquiring more vinyl stock from a bankrupt Cambridge record store, Travis eventually settled on scuzzy, low-rent Ladbroke Grove as a London location that offered sufficient passing trade thanks to its mix of bohemians and reggae-loving Rastafarians from the local West Indian population.

Opening in February 1976, Rough Trade 'became a magnet for the local community', says Travis. 'It was somewhere you could hang out and browse without anyone harassing you; this place where you could listen to music really loud all day long. We had comfy chairs, huge speakers pumping out music, and all the reggae pre-releases, which I'd buy every week from a warehouse in Harlesden.' Because Joe Strummer's 101'ers played near by at the Elgin pub, and Mick Jones lived by the Westway flyover, 'Rough Trade made the connection with punk really early', says Travis. 'And Steve Jones from the Sex Pistols would come in to sell records he'd nicked!' Rough Trade was the only place in London where you could buy US imports such as *Punk* magazine or the Pere Ubu/Hearthan and Devo/Booji Boy singles.

In many ways, though, Rough Trade provided a crucial bridge between the new punk movement and its spurned precursor, the hippy counter-culture. Although it was a privately owned company, it was run as if it were collectively owned by the workers: everyone had equal say and equal pay. 'They actually had a rota, with everyone taking turns to make the tea or doing the sweeping up,' says Tony Fletcher, teenage editor of *Jamming* fanzine, who used to hang out at Rough Trade after school, still wearing his uniform. Constant meetings took place, discussing weighty ideological issues and mundane operational details with equal fervour. This kind of communal ethos was easily mocked as a hippy throwback, but Travis stresses that 'although people have this anti-leftist view of co-ops as disorganized, with people sitting around talking all day and nothing ever getting done, Rough Trade wasn't like that at all. It worked for a number of years and we got *a lot* done. But the lines of responsibility were quite clear – people looked after different areas.'

Collectivist values of this kind were very much part of the radical culture of the mid-seventies. Both *Liberation*, the French left-wing newspaper, and *Time Out*, London's trendy-lefty/hippy-hipster listings magazine, were run as co-operatives, with no hierarchy or pay differentials. By the late seventies, there were around 300 co-ops in the UK – half of them wholefood shops, the rest ranging from radical bookshops to crafts stores. In some ways, it was during the seventies that the counter-culture ideas of the previous decade were most widely disseminated and implemented. 'Squatting was huge,' recalls Travis. 'I lived in squats all over London – Mile End, Camden, Bloomsbury.' But it wasn't just about grubby commune-dwelling hippies and anarchists: collectivist ideas had currency in the political mainstream. In 1974, the Labour government's resident hard-left cabinet member, Tony Benn, had grand plans for state-subsidized workers' co-ops that would take over failed companies – something that actually happened with the *Scottish Daily News* and the motorcycle company Norton Villiers Triumph.

Travis could also draw on his first-hand experience of kibbutz life in Israel. 'I'm Jewish, and my parents sent me one summer to visit my distant relatives, and I spent some time on a kibbutz. There was a lot of idealism in the early days of the movement, the impetus was quite pure. I liked the way they were organized – people having breakfast together, living communally, making decisions in a relatively rational way. Everyone knows what's going on. It seemed a more sensible way to organize yourself – semi-utopian, but not impossible.'

As with other record shops-turned-labels, the Rough Trade staff's day-to-day activity of sifting through releases and judging which ones were good, the endless small decisions about how many to stock of a particular record and whether to reorder, soon evolved into an A&R-like intuition about what was hot musically and where post-punk as a whole was heading. Still, there were two full years between the opening of the store and the label's debut release in February 1978: Metal Urbain's 'Paris Maquis'. 'We thought they were the French Sex Pistols,' says Travis. Next came an Augustus Pablo single. But it was ROUGH 3 that really tapped the emergent post-punk gestalt: the *Extended Play* EP by Sheffield experimental trio Cabaret Voltaire.

The same egalitarian idealism that informed the day-to-day operations of Rough Trade governed the deals with artists: contracts were for one record at a time and based on a fifty/fifty split between band and label of the profits, after costs were recouped. 'We fronted all the money for recording, promotion, whatever,' says Travis. 'The artists provided their labour, inspiration and genius. The fifty/fifty split has since been adopted by countless indie labels – Joy Division at Factory, Depeche Mode at Mute, they were on that arrangement. And it's been proven that if the band sells a lot of records, it's much more generous to the artist than a conventional royalty.' Another advantage to these one-off deals, typically based on verbal agreement and personal trust rather than lawyers and contracts, was their rapid-response nature, so much more suited to the speedy stylistic fluctuations of the post-punk universe. 'It meant you could see an amazing band and say, "Let's make a record" that very night; and in four weeks, the record's out. You could get on with it.'

Travis believes the fifty/fifty, one-record-at-a-time deals helped create a nurturing environment for the bands: 'It creates the psychological conditions for musicians to do their best work, if they are in control but they have a partner who is not weak, that can help them.' In contrast, the major-label system rewarded bands with large advances in return for signing away their lives and then put them under immense pressure to achieve sales. 'It doesn't matter how much "creative control" a band is given,' Travis told *Rolling Stone*. 'You're still indentured. Long-term contracts will put a band in debt from recording and touring costs. Then you have to produce when you're not ready. You have to write songs when you have nothing to say.' Few bands survive to the sixth album often designated in their contracts.

There was a downside to the fifty/fifty split, though. According to Nikki Sudden, 'You make a lot of money if you sell lots of records. But if you don't sell many or any, you don't get *anything*.' With no advance to cover living expenses, bands were unable to give up the day job. Still, you could always work at Rough Trade, as many of the label's artists did. 'Me and Epic both worked in the shop for about a year,' says Sudden. 'I got sacked for being rude to the Rasta customers. They would come in and want to hear all the reggae pre-releases, six minutes long, all the way through, and you knew they were never going to buy anything. After a while I got fed up and put everything on for half a second.'

Having the musicians get their hands dirty as sales assistants or packing records for distribution seems to fit the Rough Trade philosophy. It has a faintly Maoist air, getting the intelligentsia to labour in the paddy fields. Certainly, Travis liked to think of the musicians less as artists or stars than as cultural workers. He talked of how Rough Trade was neither 'the record business' nor 'art' but a space of cultural production, involving collaboration and mutual support. It was this pragmatic, slightly dowdy vision that gave the company something of a 'brown rice', hippy image.

But Rough Trade weren't into romanticizing things, or preserving the mystique of rock 'n' roll. They believed in demystification. 'People exert control through mystification,' says Travis. 'They like to make you think it's all over your head. Recording engineers can be like that in the studio. I had no studio background at all, but I produced "Nag Nag Nag" by Cabaret Voltaire and co-produced records by The Raincoats, Stiff Little Fingers, The Fall. We didn't really know what we were doing, but at that point in history, you had the confidence just to go ahead and do it.'

Without effective distribution, the do-it-yourself ethos was just shouting into the void. Rough Trade's greatest achievement was organizing the Cartel, an independent distribution network built around the alliance of London-based Rough Trade and Small Wonder with its regional counterparts Probe, Revolver and Red Rhino. Nationwide distribution for small labels and self-released records held out the possibility for real communication: reaching a scattered audience of like-minded individuals, recouping your costs, carrying on. Unglamorous but absolutely crucial, the Cartel network provided the infrastructure for a genuinely alternative culture. Travis adamantly opposed notions of infiltrating the mainstream: 'Changing things from the inside is nonsense,' he told *Rolling Stone* – where were the historical examples of anyone who'd succeeded in doing this? Today he talks about independent distribution as being 'based on a sound political principle – if you control the means of distribution, you have a great deal of power. It was obvious that the channels of culture were being controlled: it made me angry you couldn't buy decent left-wing literature or the feminist magazine *Spare Rib* in retail chains like W. H. Smith. So there was a very clear political imperative to build a network of outlets for things we liked.'

These 'things we liked' included not just records but fanzines, the print media version of DIY. '*Sniffin' Glue* was so important,' says Travis. 'We bought loads off Mark Perry, and let him use the place as somewhere to staple it together.' By 1980, Rough Trade received an average of twelve new 'zines each *week*, and it distributed nationwide those that passed its quite rigorous scrutiny for ideological soundness. 'Rough Trade would actually tell fanzine editors, "We will read your 'zine and if there's anything racist or sexist in it, we'll return it,"' recalls Tony Fletcher. There were also unofficial interventions: 'I remember getting some returned copies of *Jamming*,' says Fletcher, 'and someone from Swell Maps had scrawled on it, 'cos they disagreed with my review of them! It was a very argumentative culture.'

A few blocks from Rough Trade's Ladbroke Grove base, a company called Better Badges started to offer fanzines something similar to the P&D deals: a print-now, pay-later service to help nascent 'zines get off the ground. Run by an idealistic hippy-turned-post-punker called Joly, Better Badges was the market leader in New Wave badges (a crucial way of emblazoning your allegiances on your lapels in those heady days). Now the company 'became the clearing house for 'zines,' says Fletcher. 'Joly gave *Jamming* a fantastic deal where the mag got printed at cost and in colour – which was really unusual back then. I don't think Joly ever made a penny out of the whole print-now, pay-later thing.' Rough Trade, meanwhile, was becoming increasingly businesslike and ambitious: diversifying into music publishing, organizing Rough Trade tour packages, and even talking about starting its own alternative culture magazine.

The idea of the independent label and DIY movement was so new and exciting then, says Travis, 'that people would rush out and buy anything that was part of it. This is what people forget: back then, the records used to *sell*. Nowadays, you'd shift maybe two thousand if you were lucky. Back then, anything halfway decent sold from six to ten thousand.' And certain epochal singles – such as 'Warm Leatherette' – could shift three times that amount, or more. But what really put the label on the map and made the majors sit up and take apprehensive notice was when *Inflammable Material*, the Rough Trade album by Belfast punk band Stiff Little Fingers, went straight in the national pop charts at Number 14 in February 1979.

By then, 'alternative' groups had their own target to aim for as well – the independent singles and albums charts, conceived by Cherry Red boss Iain McNay at the end of 1979 and published by the trade magazine *Record Business*. 'Independent' was defined as independently produced, manufactured, marketed, distributed and retailed. The weekly music papers had published indie charts before, but they'd been based on what was selling in a single shop, whereas the *Record Business* chart used sales data from small record stores across the country.

But, although the independent charts hugely strengthened the scene's sense of its own identity, some critiqued them for encouraging bands and labels to aim low, in the process creating a sort of neo-hippy ghetto. 'I don't believe in dropping out or alternative cultures or any of this nonsense,' Bob Last told the *NME*. 'I think the New Wave is . . . about dropping in, fighting your way in . . . You've got to get in there and struggle.' Accordingly, Last encouraged Fast Product's four major bands – The Mekons, Gang of Four, The Scars and The Human League – to sign to the London-based majors at the earliest opportunity. Eventually, he sold the entire Fast Product back catalogue to EMI and closed down the label, feeling its 'intervention' had been completed.

This question of independence versus infiltration, regionalism versus centralization, was one area where Fast Product and Factory strongly disagreed. Tony Wilson had watched how the first indies in Manchester – New Hormones and Rabid – had capitulated to the capital. He recalls asking Rabid's Tosh Ryan in the autumn of 1977 why they'd let London's majors take their biggest artists, Jilted John and John Cooper Clarke. 'I can remember him saying, "Oh, being independent was just a little period we went through of idealism." It was as if the only point of indie labels was to exist for a few months so that managers could get their bands signed to majors.' Wilson was determined to resist the centripetal pull of London and build up a power base in Manchester, the city he loved. His fervent pro-provinces stance was echoed by indie labels throughout Britain, especially others in the North and in Scotland. For a period, the independent album chart invariably featured a couple of region- or city-based compilations each week: Cardiff's *Is The War Over?*, Sheffield's *Bouquet of Steel* . . .

From style-conscious conceptualists like Fast Product and Factory to the more earnest, businesslike operations like Rough Trade and Cherry Red, the UK's post-punk independents often disagreed about music, packaging, politics, you name it. But for a brief golden age, a five-year stretch from 1977 to 1981, they were all in the same boat. 'The thing that united us', says Daniel Miller, 'was that none of us knew what we were doing! We were huge music enthusiasts, though, with a strong idea of what we liked and what we wanted. I had no business grounding whatsoever. But all of a sudden you realized you could have access to this industry that had always seemed very mysterious. The record industry went from being pretty closed, which it was even during the first wave of punk, to totally open. And that encouraged a lot of people like me and Tony Wilson – not obvious record-company people by any means – to get involved and make our dreams come true.'

7

MILITANT ENTERTAINMENT: Gang of Four and The Leeds Scene

Gang of Four. The Mekons. Delta 5. Au Pairs.

In Britain, the 1970s felt like one long crisis. Endless strikes, power cuts, runs on the supermarkets by hoarding housewives, rising crime, student protest, race riots, fascism resurgent on the streets, the IRA's terror campaign extending beyond Ulster to the mainland of Britain . . . The kingdom was disunited, simmering with resentments. Some mourned the nation's lost imperial role and recoiled from the multicultural reality of modern Britain. Others pushed for revolution, seeing every successful industrial action as a workers' victory bringing the Glorious Day a little closer.

In the mid-seventies, the trade unions were at their peak of power. Their rank and file understandably demanded pay rises to keep pace with runaway inflation – but this, of course, made prices rise faster and the country feel even more out of control. Using their full arsenal of weapons – sympathy strikes, secondary picketing – the unions effectively brought down the Conservative government in 1974. During the period of Labour rule that followed, many felt that the TUC was effectively co-regent with Prime Minister Jim Callaghan. An inevitable right-wing backlash gathered momentum. People speculated about coups being plotted by the military and whispered of private armies led by retired brigadiers training in English meadows under cover of darkness. Legitimate pressure groups – the Middle Class Association and the National Association for Freedom – emerged, dedicated to taming the unions, resisting 'declining standards', and restoring the word 'Great' to its proper place in front of 'Britain'.

In this polarized context, the decision by a bunch of students at Leeds University to call their band Gang of Four was a provocative gesture. 'Gang of Four' was originally the derogatory nickname for the leaders of China's Cultural Revolution Group, who'd been running that country until shortly after Mao's death in September 1976, when they were arrested by the new premier. The 1965–8 Cultural Revolution – Maoism at its most radical and uncompromisingly anti-bourgeois – was still fresh in the public memory. In 1977, you could still find Maoist groups active on many UK campuses.

The band weren't Maoists, or even card-carrying Leninist–Marxists, but they were definitely products of the left-wing university culture of the seventies, which even more than the previous decade was characterized by student militancy. Sociology was the hip course to study: its consciousness of class and implicit commitment to social justice made it attractive to radicals of all stripes. Students swelled the ranks of Trotskyite groups like the International Marxist Group and the International Socialists (later renamed the Socialist Workers Party) and joined picket lines alongside striking miners and dockers.

While the committed activists spouted the textbook party line, a more diffuse left-wing academic culture existed based on a sort of ideological pick 'n' mix – a trendy-lefty autodidactism fuelled by second-hand paperbacks and beginner's guides to key thinkers of the twentieth century. Chunks of Gramsci, Lukacs and Althusser, in a rich gravy of Benjamin and Brecht, garnished with Situationism (*Leaving the 20th Century*, a slim, green, attractively packaged anthology of texts and graphics by the Situationist International, was *the* radical-chic fetish object of its era). Blending often incompatible systems of thought, the resulting hodge-podge lacked rigour from the stern standpoint of academics and ideologues alike. But in rock music, a little rigour is rather bracing and galvanizing. Too much is plain *rigid*, but Gang of Four hit just the right balance. In the grand tradition of British art-rock, theory helped them achieve the sort of conceptual breakthroughs that more organically evolving groups never reach.

Leeds University's Fine Art Department, which spawned Gang of Four and its sister-groups The Mekons and Delta 5, encouraged a conceptual approach. Theory was considered inseparably intertwined with artistic practice. T. J. Clark, the department's head, had been a member of the short-lived British chapter of the Situationist International. Terry Atkinson, the studio-painting tutor who wandered around discussing the students' work, once belonged to Art & Language. Drawing on

Marxism and hardcore aesthetic theory, A&L created works that combined visual material with text (political posters, philosophy, even musical scores). For a while, they abandoned art production altogether in favour of criticism. The Mekons' Tom Greenhalgh enjoyed A&L's sarcastic, combative approach – the way they ripped into other critics for being 'woolly-minded and promoting the mystique of art'. Absorbing this sensibility, The Mekons and Gang of Four created a kind of meta-rock, radically self-critical and vigilant.

Leeds had an unusual density of art students: as well as the university, says Greenhalgh, 'Leeds Polytechnic had its own excellent art department, where a lot of work with performance and video was going on. And there was Leeds College of Art.' Factor in all the other students doing courses at the uni or poly, and you had the recipe for town-versus-gown tension. 'It was a Northern working-class city with a bunch of students dumped in the middle, most of them not from Yorkshire,' says Hugo Burnham, Gang of Four's drummer. '"Fookin' stooodents" was an expression you heard rather frequently!'

The tension was heightened by the not entirely unfounded perception that the students dossed around doing 'fook all' courtesy of the government's undergraduate grants, while ordinary people toiled. Or, increasingly, didn't toil but languished on the dole. In the industrial parts of Yorkshire, unemployment more than doubled between 1973 and 1978 (when it reached 6 per cent) as the traditional heavy industries declined. As prospects for youth narrowed, the far right prospered. Leeds became the Northern stronghold for the crypto-fascist National Front, while explicitly neo-Nazi organizations like the British Movement and the League of St George were also active in the area. 'Our very first gig, skinheads came looking for a fight,' recalls Burnham. 'There was real tension. The skins were taunting Andy Gill and then he smacked one of them in the face with his guitar.' Ironically, the crop-headed Burnham was often mistaken for a bootboy himself. 'They'd see me with my short hair, Doc Martens, braces and black Herrington jacket, and approach me and ask if I was a fan of Skrewdriver, the Oi! group.'

Burnham was actually studying drama at Leeds, oscillating between trying to set up a radical theatre group and playing rugby, a game that suited his stocky physique. 'I gravitated towards this fine arts drinking crowd; they seemed like the most interesting people around. At Leeds, there were two drinking groups really: the art students and the anarchists.' The centre of the scene was a pub called the Fenton, strategically placed midway between the university and the polytechnic. A long-established lefty-liberal hangout, its patrons mixed several generations of radicals and nonconformists: bearded sixties relics, gays, anarchists and 'the new breed' in their leather coats and Doc Martens. 'It was totally crowded, people squashed together and just raving it up,' recalls Greenhalgh. As much as Leeds Fine Art Department, it was the Fenton's ferment of alcohol-fuelled argument that shaped Gang of Four and The Mekons.

Gang of Four thrived on friction. 'Andy had really mastered the art of the put-down,' says Burnham. 'He would bait you. You get that sense from his guitar playing; it's very prickly.' Drawing on the jagged, choppy rhythm-as-lead style developed by Wilko Johnson of pub-rock trailblazers Dr Feelgood, Gill chipped out flinty harmonics and splintered funk, making the listener flinch from the shards and swarf shooting out of the speakers.

Love of Dr Feelgood – the stripped-down sound, the aura of barely contained violence – united Gill, Burnham and singer Jon King. But somewhere between their first gig in May 1977 and their first record, October 1978's *Damaged Goods* EP, a drastic transformation occurred. Recruited via an advert that described the group in Feelgood-like terms as a 'fast rivvum & blues band', bassist Dave Allen pushed the group firmly into the punk-funk zone. An accomplished player who'd done session work, Allen had been looking to make music 'like Stevie Wonder but heavy' before he met Gang of Four. In turn, the Gang trained their bassist to play more sparsely – 'a quarter of the number of notes he was actually capable of playing', according to Burnham. Gang of Four kept their music stark and severe. Andy Gill shunned sound-thickening effects like fuzz and distortion, while Burnham eschewed splashy cymbals. The band defined their sound as much by avoiding things as through positive choices. 'Instead of guitar solos, we had anti-solos, where you stopped playing, just left a hole,' says Gill. The very fabric of the band's sound was abrasively different. Valve amplifiers were *verboten*, says Gill. 'Valves is what every guitarist today wants – they're the prerequisite for a "fat" rock tone, that "warmth" that people talk about. I had transistorized amps – a more brittle, cleaner sound, and colder. Gang of Four were *against* warmth.'

Gang of Four had no truck with the heat of rock spontaneity either, the intuitive looseness of letting songs emerge organically out of jams. 'No jamming – that was the J-word,' says Gill. 'Everything was thought out in advance.' Burnham devised unusual drum parts that inverted or frustrated the usual rock modes of rhythmic motion – the 'continuous falling down the stairs flow' of 'Guns before Butter', the mechanistic drum loop of 'Love Like Anthrax'. Instead of stacking the instruments for a layered wall of sound, Gang of Four gave all the instruments room to breathe. Guitar, bass and drums existed on more or less equal footing. And in their most thrilling songs – the taut geometrical paroxysm of 'Natural's Not in It', for instance – everything worked as rhythm.

This egalitarian balance between instruments embodied the group's collectivist ideals. 'It's democratic music, where we don't have a star thing,' Jon King told *Sounds* in 1978. In an interview with the *NME*, Dave Allen declared: 'Gang of Four doesn't believe in the individual, and we believe that whatever you do is "political" with a small "p".' These ideals permeated every aspect of the group's existence, from the way the music was jointly composed to the four-way split of publishing rights to the constant, fiery debates about internal affairs and external issues. And every member of the group and its entourage was paid the same wage (thirty pounds), except for the roadies, who got *double* during tours.

In their early days, The Mekons were an extension of this sprawling collective. 'Without actually having headed notepaper to prove it, Gang of Four and Mekons were virtually a cooperative, sharing equipment and a rehearsal space,' says Burnham. 'We did gigs together, taking turns to headline.' The Mekons' version of democratized rock differed from Gang of Four's, though – less disciplined and clenched, more shambolic and sloppy. The group's founding principles, guitarist Kevin Lycett told the *NME*, were 'that anybody could do it; that we didn't want to be stars; that there was no set group as such, anybody could get up and join in and instruments would be swapped around; that there'd be no distance between the audience and the band; that we were nobody special'. Founding member Mark White had never played bass before and at their first jam used a door key to pick the strings; Lycett played a battered second-hand guitar that cost ten pounds. Exuberantly mixing informality with ineptitude, early Mekons gigs were 'complete art-noise chaos', recalls Burnham. 'They opened for Gang of Four at our second show ever and they had a sofa onstage representing a spaceship – it had the word "SPACESHIP" painted on it. It was genius and hilarious.' Lyrics, read off a piece of paper, devolved into improvised gabble; friends wandered on- and offstage. At another gig, the set disintegrated because the running order for songs had mistakenly been written out in a completely different order for every band member.

Taking the punk ideal of 'anyone can do it' even more seriously than Swell Maps, The Mekons ought to have gone nowhere. Amazingly, they had a record deal by their second show, supporting Scottish pop-punk outfit The Rezillos at the F-Club, Leeds' leading New Wave club. Bob Last was in the audience and decided The Mekons would be the perfect group to kickstart his still productless Fast Product. Slightly put-out at being so swiftly overtaken by their seemingly less serious brethren, Gang of Four were mollified when soon they too were signed to Fast.

A stumbling juggernaut of crude guitar and caveman drums, 'Never Been in a Riot', The Mekons' debut, was a sonic argument in support of the proposition that rock 'is the only form of music which can actually be done *better* by people who can't play their instruments than by people who can', as *Melody Maker*'s Mary Harron put it. Not everybody bought that argument initially. Rough Trade literally didn't buy it, refusing to take any copies of the single, saying it was just too incompetent. 'Shortly thereafter, though, it was made Single of the Week in the *NME*,' recalls Last. 'And everybody wanted it, including Rough Trade.'

NME's seal of approval was all the more significant because it came courtesy of the paper's resident punk rocker Tony Parsons, who took the lyrics of 'Never Been in a Riot' as an inspired piss-take of The Clash's streetfighting machismo ('White Riot', the allusion to 'sten guns in Knightsbridge' in '1977', etc). According to Tom Greenhalgh, the song is more about an admission of vulnerability: 'That you might be in a riot and be scared. Being open about that kind of weakness rather than trying to put on a front.' This was all part of The Mekons' self-effacing and humanizing project – a refusal to be larger than life. Later in 1978, Parsons interviewed the group for an *NME* special feature that celebrated Leeds as 'the new Akron'. In keeping with their ideals, The Mekons insisted on 'no photographs, no surnames . . . we don't want to push ourselves as INDIVIDUAL PERSONALITIES!' Says Greenhalgh now, 'We didn't want to be photographed for the *NME*, so we made this puppet creature and put a guitar around it.' Photographer Steve Dixon sneaked a snap of them anyway.

While The Mekons upturned both traditional rock-male personality cult and its punk successor (Strummer/Jones-style guitar-guerrilla heroics), Gang of Four gradually acquired a reputation as a sort of 'new, improved Clash': agit-punk with a proper grounding in theory. 'Damaged Goods', title track of their debut EP, showed the group had done its Marxist homework and knew about things like 'commodity

Publicity photo of The Mekons, 1979. L to R: Mary Jenner, Tom Greenhalgh, Andy Corrigan, Kevin Lycett, Jon Langford, Mark White

fetishism' and 'reification' (a term deployed by Lukacs and referring to the feeling of depersonalized objectification experienced by individuals caught up in the processes of mass production and the free market). 'Damaged Goods' uses the language of commerce and industry as a prism to offer disconcerting insights into affairs of the heart. With grim wit, the song represents a break-up in terms of refunds and emotional costs: 'Open the till/Give me the change/You said would do me good . . . You said you're cheap but you're too much'.

The EP's other stand-out track, 'Love Like Anthrax', took an even more cold, heartless view of romance. The music was estrangement enough by itself: 'this bizarre, totally robotic drum beat matched with a strange two-bar loop bassline, so that the emphasis in both drums and bass falls entirely in the unexpected place,' says Gill. 'And then my guitar coming in with random freeform noise.' In 1978, feedback hadn't been heard in rock for a long while, and Gill's howling cacophony was nothing like Hendrix's controlled-yet-orgiastic use of it to smear melody lines, or Velvet Underground's tidal waves of white noise. In rock's Romantic tradition, feedback typically signified the engulfingly oceanic, a swooning rush of Dionysian oblivion. In Gill's hand, it just sounded like migraine. Which totally suited the theme of 'Anthrax': love as a debilitating brain fever, something any rational person would avoid like the plague. King bemoans feeling like 'a beetle on its back': he's paralysed, literally drained – his lovesick thoughts trickle 'like piss' down the gutter.

'Love Like Anthrax' is constructed as a sort of Brechtian stereophonic duet: King wails the stricken lover's lament in one speaker; Gill recites dry-as-dust details about the recording process in the other. Burnham once compared 'Anthrax' to the split-screen techniques in Godard's 1975 movie *Numéro Deux*, where everyday life in a working-class French family is counterpointed with more dissonant, private scenes of the same characters. Gill and King ran Leeds University's student film society, so would have been familiar with Godard's work: the deliberately exposed means of production (like the clapperboard that flashes into view every so often in *La Chinoise*), the disjointedness (continuity lapses, incorrect eyeline matches, jump cuts, non-congruence between images and soundtrack), characters breaking down the fourth wall to address the audience, and all the other stylistic tics designed to make the viewer conscious of film as artefact and contrivance. Gang of Four and Godard both had a wary attitude towards the seductions of their chosen artforms: the latter described cinema as 'the most beautiful fraud in the world'. There's also a similar meta-knowingness: Godard, a veteran of the journal *Cahiers du Cinéma*, wrote, 'I'm still as much of a critic as I ever was . . . The only difference is that instead of writing criticism, I now film it.' And both inevitably faced accusations from traditionalists: too much concept and theory, not enough emotion, sensuousness and warmth.

Behind the experimental director and the agit-funk group lay a common source: Bertolt Brecht's anti-naturalistic, unabashedly didactic theatre. What Brecht called 'epic theatre' confronted the spectator with an arbitrary and absurd reality. Instead of feeling that the protagonist's woes were in accord with the ordained nature of reality (and therefore, as in tragedy, somehow noble), you were meant to feel that 'the sufferings of this man appal me, because they are unnecessary'. Brecht's 'alienation effects' dislocated the viewer from his 'natural responses', cutting through so-called realism to offer a glimpse of the deep structures that organize our lives. Brecht's imperative – 'what is "natural" must have the force of what is startling' – dovetailed with another Marxist thinker, Antonio Gramsci, whose work was being rediscovered in the 1970s. The ruling class exert 'hegemony' (Gramsci's most famous concept) by making the ways of the world seem like simple 'common sense'. Radical critique, for Gramsci, should unmask everything that appears 'obvious' as a man-made construct, a 'truth' that serves somebody's interest.

A Brecht fan to the point of having a picture of him on the walls of his Edinburgh flat, Bob Last incorporated alienation effects into the artwork of *Damaged Goods*. 'The group sent me a letter that was very precise about what they wanted on the cover,' he says. Enclosed was a newspaper clip with a photograph of a female matador and a bull, along with a caption of dialogue: the Matador explains, 'You know, we're both in the entertainment business, we have to give the audience what they want. I don't like to do this but I earn double the amount I'd get if I were in a 9-to-5 job', while the bull grumbles, 'I think that at some point we have to take responsibility for our actions'. In the event, Last ignored the Gang's wishes and designed a different cover, but reproduced the letter and the untidily snipped-out newspaper article on the back sleeve. 'This didn't exactly mollify the group, but I'm sure they recognized that, to the extent they were interested in deconstruction, this was an unassailable gesture!'

Released in the autumn of 1978, *Damaged Goods* received massive acclaim: here was a group who'd found a totally new way of negotiating that thorny danger zone known as 'politics-in-rock'. Abrasive but accessible, Gang of Four avoided both Tom Robinson-style preachy protest and the forbidding didacticism of avant-gardists like Henry Cow. Radical form, radical content; yet you could dance to it.

After *Damaged Goods*, Gang of Four made a controversial decision, encouraged by Last, to abandon the independent sector and sign to a major label. The idea of reaching the largest number of people possible made sense, given the group's propagandizing imperative. It also chimed with one of their main preoccupations: entertainment. It was much more provocative to intensify the contradictions and operate right at the heart of the rock-leisure industry. Where other politicized bands agonized over being connected to multinational conglomerates, Andy Gill says he and his comrades felt The Pop Group's and The Slits' dream of 'escaping Babylon was bollocks hand-wringing, as much as we loved both those groups. The point for us was *not* to be "pure" – Gang of Four songs were so often about the inability to have clean hands. It just wouldn't be on our agenda to be on a truly independent label, as if such a thing could even exist.' Several majors courted them, but EMI emerged as a favourite, precisely for its sheer monolithic size and bland image. Along with its globe-spanning muscle, the label offered them a surprising

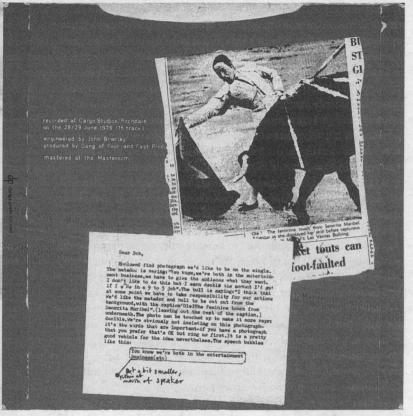

Brechtian mischief on the back cover of Gang of Four's *Damaged Goods* EP, 1978

degree of creative control. According to Gill, it was almost a production and licensing deal, with Gang of Four handing over the finished album tapes, produced by themselves. The group also designed their own album sleeves, posters, press ads and badges.

The Mekons made a second single for Fast Product towards the end of 1978 – the indie smash 'Where Were You?', which sold out its 27,500 pressing. But they too were eventually persuaded to step up to the major league – an album deal with Virgin. 'Bob Last convinced us there was nothing morally superior about signing to an indie label,' says Tom Greenhalgh. Ambushed by success, The Mekons had inadvertently ended up with a career on their hands, arriving at a level of gigging activity that needed the sort of funding only a major could provide. The group's irresistible rise probably peaked in March 1979, when they featured on the bill of what was only semi-jokingly dubbed the 'Gig of the Century' by the music papers: a Lyceum showcase of 'new music' that included Gang of Four and another Fast Product band, The Human League, along with The Fall and Stiff Little Fingers. But, not long after this, The Mekons' attempt to infiltrate the mainstream went awry.

The big time didn't really suit a group whose whole point was amateurish charm. All the life was kicked out of their debut LP, *The Quality of Mercy Is Not Strnen*, by being recorded in Virgin's top-flight studio, the Manor. By the end of 1979 the group seemed hopelessly confused, denying in interviews that they'd ever made a virtue out of ineptitude ('we were always desperately trying to play well', Greenhalgh told *Melody Maker*). They'd gradually reneged on their early impractical principles (no photographs, no personality cult) yet were too self-effacing to seize the possibilities of fame. 'When we first started, our only reason for existing was that we'd made this appalling record that should never have been a record but was,' said Greenhalgh. 'And we were a group that never should have been a group but were. Now we're at the stage where those sort of reasons for existing are irrelevant . . . so it's a question of what actually are we?' It would be five years – long after being dropped by Virgin following that lacklustre debut LP – before The Mekons discovered a new and brilliant purpose for themselves, after a painful, fitful process of self-reinvention.

While The Mekons struggled to promote *Quality of Mercy*, Gang of Four released their debut major-label single, 'At Home He Feels Like a Tourist', which obliquely critiqued leisure and entertainment as surrogates for real satisfaction and stimulation. While lyrically opaque, the song was sonically Gang of Four's starkest and most compelling track yet. Gill's backfiring guitar slashed across the robotic–hypnotic mesh of drums and bass, which sounded like 'perverted disco', in Jon King's words. Boosted by frequent evening play on Radio One, the single rose rapidly to number 64, at which point the group were invited to appear on *Top of the Pops*: a golden opportunity to penetrate the heart of mass cult, because exposure to an audience of eight million would almost certainly propel the single into the Top 30 the next week. But on the day of the show, the producers objected to the line 'the rubbers you hide in your top-left pocket', part of a verse about discos making their profits through selling sex, or the promise of it. Gang of Four offered to change the coarse slang term for condoms to the more neutral and ambiguous 'packets'. *Top of the Pops* insisted the word be changed to 'rubbish' because 'packets' sounded too obviously altered and they didn't want anyone to know there'd been censorship. After agonized debate, with minutes to go before recording was due to start, Gang of Four refused.

'At Home He Feels Like a Tourist' continued its rise anyway, and *TOTP* extended the invitation again, but on the same terms. 'We stuck to our guns,' says Burnham. 'We were all as one on that decision, and it felt great. But in retrospect, walking off *TOTP* essentially killed our career.' Burnham is convinced that the single would have shot into the Top 30 after the group's performance. 'Plus we would not have lost the support of a large number of people at EMI like we did. The exasperation on the promotions man's face when we announced we wouldn't do *TOTP* . . .'

Entertainment!, the debut album, did reasonably well critically and commercially, but by Gang of Four's own standards it fell short, given their mass-cultural ambition. Taken as an art object in itself (and considering its long-term impact), though, the album was anything but a failure. One of post-punk's defining masterworks, every aspect of the record – the lyrics, the music, the artwork (the famous cover image of the fooled Indian shaking hands with the cowboy eager to exploit him) – is perfectly aligned. The sheer sound of the record stood out: sober, flat, at once in your face and remote. *Entertainment!* broke with rock recording conventions by being extremely 'dry', in the technical sound-engineer sense of 'no reverb, drums that didn't ring', says Burnham. There was no attempt to capture what the group sounded like live, no gesture at simulating music being played in a real acoustic space. 'In retrospect, it would have been nice to hear those songs recorded in a way that was truer to how we sounded onstage.' But this was part of *Entertainment!*'s achievement, its alienation effect: this was obviously a studio artefact, a cold-blooded construction.

Entertainment! was dry in the emotional sense, too, using the scalpel of Marxist analysis to dissect the mystifications of love, 'capitalist democracy' and rock itself. The songs depicted relationships and situations in a diagrammatic fashion: even though Jon King often sang in the first person, there was an element of depersonalization, a sense of the song's human actors being buffeted by impersonal social forces. As Greil Marcus (an early champion of the group) suggested, the characters in their songs often seem to be on the brink of seeing through 'false con-

Colonialism and exploitation dissected on the cover of Gang of Four's *Entertainment!*, 1979

sciousness' and understanding the structural realities that govern their existence. But they never quite make it. So 'Contract', one of *Entertainment!*'s most unnerving songs, recasts matrimony in terms of a business arrangement, 'a contract in our mutual interest'. It quickly moves from the concrete specifics of an unhappy partnership – disagreements, disappointing sex – to the bigger picture: 'These social dreams/Put in practice in the bedroom/Is this so private?/Our struggle in the bedroom'. Recoiling from consumerism's 'coercion of the senses', 'Natural's Not in It' similarly insists there's 'no escape from society'. On a more meta-critical level, 'Not Great Men' challenged history written from the standpoint of heroic individuals like kings and generals while ignoring the little people who build palaces and fight wars. In *Sounds*, Garry Bushell sourced the song in Brecht's famous poem 'A Worker Reads History', which concludes: 'Every page a victory/Who cooked the feast for the victors?/Every ten years a great man/Who paid the bill?'

Then and now, political pop generally issues from a position of 'purity' – whether it's fingerpointing protest or wry social comment, the problem is *over there*. But Gang of Four's songs implicated listeners in the very processes being critiqued, rather than cosily dividing the world into a righteous 'us' versus a corrupt 'them'. That didn't mean there weren't enemies worth fighting, though. In spring 1979, Gang of Four participated in Rock Against Racism's month-long Militant Entertainment tour, a series of gigs across the country involving some thirty bands in rotating line-ups. The main target of this immense campaign was the National Front, who were fielding candidates in every single parliamentary seat in the impending May 1979 general election, thus earning the right to air party-political broadcasts on television. The backdrop, though, was the seemingly inevitable downfall of Callaghan's Labour government and its replacement by the Conservatives under the leadership of Margaret Thatcher.

In a January 1978 TV interview, Thatcher had expressed concerns about immigration, using the metaphor of 'swamping' to describe the impact of multiculturalism on the British 'character' and way of life. In response to a question about the National Front, she said that while most people didn't agree with that organization's stance on immigration and repatriation, 'at least it's talking about some of the problems'. In contrast, David Widgery, a key spokesperson for RAR and the Anti-Nazi League, imagined a rainbow coalition of workers and minorities uniting to build a hybrid British culture: 'She thinks we're being "swamped" by it,' he told *NME*, 'but I want it to swamp her.'

Leeds was on the frontline of this culture war. In part because of the large student population, it was one of the first cities in Britain to found a local branch of Rock Against Racism. But some of its working-class youth felt the pull of extremist right-wing groups. The National Front launched what it called the Punk Front in Leeds, attempting to recruit members at the F-Club. Such was the mutual paranoia of the time that one Marxist newspaper, *The Leveller*, claimed the F in F-Club stood for 'fascist' – a claim that incensed promoter John Keenan, a socialist who'd helped organize a few RAR gigs. Leeds was also the birthplace of Rock Against Communism, involving local right-wing punk bands like The Dentists, whose songs included 'Kill the Reds', 'Master Race' and 'White

Power'. Fascist bootboys attacked racial minorities, homosexuals and leftwing students. 'Our pub, the Fenton, was known as the place where all the commies and artists and fags hung out,' recalls Gill. 'One night about twenty National Front thugs burst in and smashed the place up. It was like a Wild West saloon, chairs flying everywhere, people getting hit, glasses going everywhere.' Gangs of skins would roam around the university campus, too: 'There'd be the occasional pitched battle – people lobbing stuff at each other.'

Fascist skinheads also regularly materialized at gigs by Gang of Four, The Mekons and their allies, starting fights in the audience, throwing abuse and projectiles at the bands. Delta 5's line-up – two guys and three women, dressed in the unisex feminist style of the day – particularly seemed to offend the goon squad: Ros Allen was denounced as a 'communist witch' at one gig. The girls gave as good as they got, though: at another show, Bethan Peters grabbed a *Sieg Heil*-ing youth and slammed his head against the stage.

Although the movement against 'political correctness' hadn't quite blossomed, Malcolm Bradbury's 1975 satire of British academia *The History Man* had helped fuel the increasingly widespread view of higher education as a hotbed of trendy radicalism. Fogeys fulminated about theory-mongers running rampant over traditional liberal shibboleths of objectivity and balance, 'truth and beauty', with their repugnant rabble of '-isms' – racism, sexism, classism, ageism. And it's true that in the seventies political culture that shaped Gang of Four, The Mekons and Delta 5, people were wont to use expressions like 'ideologically sound' without the slightest whiff of irony. 'When I write I try so hard to make sure the words are sound, that there's nothing sexist in them,' The Mekons' Mark White told *Sounds* earnestly. 'So a lot of the early songs were written wimpy on purpose.'

The women in Delta 5, meanwhile, often wrote from standpoints of defiance, aloofness, self-assertion and unapproachable autonomy. 'Mind Your Own Business', their debut single, was hilariously cold-hearted and stand-offish, resolutely barring entrance to someone craving intimacy and involvement: 'Can I interfere in your crisis?/No! Mind your own business!'. 'You', the second single, was funnier still, a series of accusations and recriminations: 'Who left me behind at the baker's/YOU, YOU, YOU, YOU! . . . Who likes sex only on Sundays/YOU, YOU, YOU, YOU!' Like Gang of Four, Delta 5 built distancing effects into the songs: as hostile as these songs about soured relationships were, they didn't feel confessional (something accentuated by the lack of gender specificity in the lyrics and the fact that many of the vocals were doubled). Delta 5 firmly believed in the personal-is-political approach: 'Personal songs can be just as relevant,' Bethan Peters told the *NME*. 'Personal relationships are like a microcosm of the whole world and in that way we are commenting on things in general.'

Genealogically, Delta 5 formed as an offshoot of The Mekons: Ros Allen had been the latter's original bassist; Bethan Peters and Julz Sale were both 'Mekons girlfriends'; Mekons drummer Jon Langford did the great artwork for the first two singles; even the name obliquely stemmed from The Mekons, via the Mekong Delta. But sonically and lyrically Delta 5 were closer to Gang of Four: punk-funk, with funk rather narrowly understood as clipped, scratchy rhythm guitar and hard, driving bass riffs assuming the melodic role. Delta 5 went one better than Gang of Four, though, and featured two bass guitars (Peters' more trebly; Allen's a low growl). Lyrically, they mostly stuck to love songs, something Gang of Four deemed ideologically suspect, but the Delta 5 treatment chucked the rose-tinted spectacles in the wastebasket.

Another mixed-gender agit-funk band scrutinizing sexuality with an unforgiving eye was The Au Pairs. 'They were in a different city, Birmingham, but they were definitely part of our thing,' says Hugo Burnham. 'We played a lot of gigs with The Au Pairs; they came on a Gang of Four tour.' Their most famous song, 'Come Again', depicts an egalitarian, non-sexist couple who are trying to achieve orgasmic parity. Sung as a duet, it's a micro-drama in which Paul Foad plays the eager-to-please man earnestly frigging his long-suffering partner, Lesley Woods. 'Is your finger aching?/I can feel you hesitating', she wonders, as the likelihood of orgasm fades to zero. By the end, despite everyone's best progressive intentions, she's simply discovered 'a new way to fake'. 'It's Obvious' sees Woods parrot the chauvinist platitude 'you're equal but different' in her trademark rasp of dour derision, wearing away its condescension and inanity through sheer repetition.

'Everything is political, everything you do in life, the way you relate to people around you is political,' Woods told *East Village Eye*. Feminism's focus on attitudes, language, the thousands of micro-political interactions that make up day-to-day behaviour, meant that being 'aware' involved being constantly *self*-aware. 'There was definitely a politicization element to relationships,' recalls Burnham. 'The women among our social circle were much healthier in terms of the male–female power dynamic. We were all into re-examining how you conducted your life, the things you took for granted. On our second tour of America, I wore an ERA T-shirt in support of the Equal Rights Amendment. At the same time, though, it didn't mean we didn't try to get laid at every opportunity. There was *nothing* puritanical about Gang of Four! There was a very hedonistic attitude with alcohol, but it wasn't in a way that was destructive of other people's dignity or space. The only dignity that suffered was our own!'

Gang of Four certainly liked a beer or two . . . or twenty. Hard drinkers who enjoyed nothing more than a chance to flex their powers of reason in a good discursive punch-up, the band – for all their anti-sexist rhetoric – were a rather masculine bunch, and repressed in ways that were at once typically English and characteristic of the hard Marxist left, which tended to fetishize rationality while disdaining emotionalism. Andy Gill, in particular, was your classic bottle-it-all-up Brit. 'Of all the people I worked with, he was the only one I never saw cry,' says Burnham. 'Unless he was so fucking drunk he'd hurt himself!' You saw glimpses of fragility now and then: the restless desolation of 'Glass', the supine despondency of 'Paralysed'. The spoken lyric to the latter, the opening track of the second album *Solid Gold*, was taken by most reviewers as the words of a man laid low by being laid off. According to Gill, who wrote and recited it, though, it's much closer to the blues in the original sense of the word.

Mostly, though, Gang of Four extolled hardness and unyielding reason. Re-recorded for *Entertainment!*, 'Love Like Anthrax' now featured a Gill dissertation on the love song as a staple of pop music issuing from one speaker, while the romance-ravaged Jon King wailed out of the other. Gill ponders why all these pop groups sing about love constantly, expresses doubt that everyone is capable of this allegedly universal emotion, and concludes, 'I don't think we're saying there's anything wrong with love; we just don't think that what goes on between two people should be shrouded in mystery'. The polemic is spot on: propagated by Hollywood and popular song throughout the twentieth century, the myths of romantic love gradually replaced religion as the opiate of the people. But the aridity of the world that Gang of Four implicitly propose – something you can *taste* in the gruff neutrality of Gill's classless voice – would make most people run back to the arms of that most cherished and consoling illusion: love as seemingly achievable heaven on earth.

The trouble with demystification is that it takes the mystery out of everything. It strips the world of superstition and sentimentality, but also eliminates intuition and other non-rational forms of perception and awareness. The 'unisex' brand of feminism in vogue on the Leeds scene meant that women became tough, assertive and 'dry'. The men, however, didn't become any 'moister' or more androgynous. Jon King rejected the notion that men needed to develop their feminine side: 'That sort of resort to the emotions is part of the oppression,' he told *Melody Maker*. 'If all the time you react to things on an emotional level, you'll never get anywhere.'

Was there even a sense in which Gang of Four feared music (sweet music) itself – its seductive power and primal energy, its invitation to cast logic aside and surrender to mindless bliss? Perhaps all the distancing devices were self-protective as much as anything else, making two selves – one involved, 'inside' the music, the other detached, standing slightly outside. Gill describes how Gang of Four loved the seventies hard-rock band Free 'because it was very rhythmic and stripped down. But then you had Paul Rodgers singing about his car and his woman. So you had to have a bit of suspended belief: you could love Free and yet be completely aware of the idiocy of the lyrics. You could say Free influenced Gang of Four, but our approach was "take that bit but leave that other *ridiculous* bit out", or "take that cliché and turn it inside out".' In post-punk terms, this approach was equivalent to a sort of checked and inhibited hard rock: cock rock castrated, the cock lopped off. Onstage, the group avoided the stereotypical phallic rock 'n' roll poses, but, as Burnham concedes, 'We did have a very quasi-violent stage presence – all the running around and bashing into each other that Jon, Andy and Dave did. Theatrically it was very intense, flirting with a violent undertone.' And because Gang of Four's music 'brought together the groove of black music with the hardness of guitar rock', as Gill puts it, some journalists critiqued it as a postgraduate version of heavy-metal funk: Hendrix-meets-Marx.

The band's rampaging balls-out rock side was captured on *Solid Gold*, released in early 1981. Sporadically exciting, the album's live-sounding production was more conventional than *Entertainment!*'s dessicated starkness. And lyrically Gill and King seemed to have lost their touch: the songs veered from crude third-person typology (the proto-fascist caricatures of 'Outside the Trains Don't Run on Time' and 'He'd Send in the Army') to clumsy satire (the anti-American 'Cheeseburger'). The better songs like 'Paralysed' and 'What We All Want' struck a note of sadness that tapped into the apprehensive mood at the start of the eighties, as the implications of the Thatcher–Reagan victories began to sink in.

Deemed a disappointment and an irrelevance in the UK – where pop trends had already moved on – *Solid Gold* is considered just one notch below *Entertainment!*'s classic status in America. During 1980 the Gang of Four had virtually disappeared from the British scene, touring America twice. 'Countless times in the States, people would come up to me after gigs and say, "I read the *NME* interviews and I thought you'd be really boring,"' says Burnham with a laugh. 'They were taken aback because we fucking *rocked*, rather than standing around in long macs looking miserable, like your typical post-punk band. That's why we did so well in the US. The propensity to *rock out* is more ingrained in the young American psyche than in Europe. It's the same reason The Clash were so successful in America. And we were The Clash without the cowboy outfits.'

Gang of Four inspired many groups in the UK to embrace hard funk as the 'sonically correct' format for politically conscious post-punk. But their greatest long-term legacy lay in America. Over the last twenty-five years, countless bands – including Pylon, B-52s, Romeo Void, Red Hot Chili Peppers (who enlisted Gill to produce their debut album), The Minutemen, Fugazi, Big Black, Helmet, Rage Against the Machine, Girls Against Boys, The Rapture – have seized on aspects of the Gang of Four template for a rock that's aggressive and violent without being oppressively macho. But none has rivalled the stunning originality of their total sound-and-vision.

8

ART ATTACK: Talking Heads and Wire

Talking Heads. David Byrne and Brian Eno. Wire. Dome.

Rock has never really made up its mind when it comes to the a-word. For some, 'art' is the antithesis of rock 'n' roll – genteel, gutless, elitist. Punk was partially a revolt against the art-rock pretensions of post-*Sgt Pepper's* 'progressive' music. Perhaps that's why Talking Heads, despite being products of art school, felt squeamish about the word. 'I object to us being called "artists who have chosen the medium of music",' sniffed the band's keyboard player Jerry Harrison. 'I find that distasteful and very unfunky. And we don't perform in galleries.' Singer David Byrne disliked 'art rock' as a label because of its connotation of dispassionate dabbling: the implication that Talking Heads didn't 'have sincere feelings about our music or we're just flirting with rock and roll and we're too reserved and detached . . . to rock out onstage'. And yet, as Colin Newman from Wire – another group composed of fine arts and design students – put it, their music 'wasn't "arty", we were doing fucking *art*. Punk *was* art. It was all art.'

Despite their disquiet about the a-word, Talking Heads wore their art-college background on their sleeves (including their record sleeves, usually designed by themselves). The earliest version of the group was even called The Artistics. It was formed by Byrne and drummer Chris Frantz at Rhode Island School of Design, where they studied alongside Frantz' girlfriend Tina Weymouth (at this point cheering from the sidelines but later bassist in Talking Heads). Conceptualism and performance art were at their height in the early seventies and the nascent Heads assimilated a sensibility of 'serious play' that would later inform their approach to making music. Byrne, for instance, once did a performance that involved him shaving off a long beard he'd grown, while a friend played accordion and his girlfriend held up cue-cards with Russian words on them. Because he didn't have a mirror, his face ended up a bloody mess. This sort of shenanigans, along with the 'photo-conceptual' work he was also doing, were a bit *outré* for RISD, and the college advised him to go to New York where performance and text-based art was all the rage.

By Christmas 1974, Byrne was living in a communal loft on the Lower East Side with Frantz and Weymouth. Its Chrystie Street location was only a few blocks from CBGB. Initially, though, Byrne was captivated as much by New York's cinema and experimental theatre as by the evolving punk scene. 'Seeing performances by Wooster Group, Mabou Mines, Richard Foreman, all this non-narrative theatrical stuff that was a collage of music, text, stylized movement: things you never thought possible to sit there and enjoy – boom, they did it! None of it was logical or linear, and it had that attitude of mixing together high and low culture.'

When Talking Heads began to play CBGB and Max's, they stood out from the punk pack immediately with their clean-cut, non-rock 'n' roll image and anorexic sound. Byrne preferred a 'thin, clean and clanky' guitar rather than the distortion-thickened chords found in most punk. 'I wanted it to sound like a little well-oiled machine where everything was transparent, all the working parts visible,' says Byrne. 'Nothing hidden in the murk of a big sound. Somehow that seemed more honest. And probably more arty as well.' Because he mostly played rhythm guitar and no solos, Weymouth's bass became the band's second melodic voice, after Byrne's singing. 'It's an enormous temptation to play lead parts and melodies, especially as I play in approximately the same range as the human voice,' Weymouth told *Melody Maker* in 1977. 'I always tend to fill in the middle tones, because if I played very low bass there'd be this huge gap like the Grand Canyon between my bass and David's guitar.'

In the early days, Talking Heads' 'skinny' sound seemed to slot right into the 'skinny tie' mould of New Wave bands like XTC and The Cars. The New Wave template consisted of choppy rhythm guitar (with hardly any lead playing), fast, ungroovy tempos and often keyboards. The vocals tended to be high pitched, geeky and very 'white'; the songs often had stop–start structures and melodies that were angular and jumpy rather than gently curving. Talking Heads' early stage fave 'Psycho

Killer' virtually patented that twitchy New Wave feel of abruptness and agitation. 'I always liked slightly herky-jerky spastic rhythms. I gravitated toward those,' says Byrne.

As part of its revolt against the Old Wave, the New purged many of the black-music-derived properties that innately juiced rock music in the sixties and early seventies: a relaxed jamming 'feel', swing, bluesy note-bending. Punk and New Wave constituted a near-total white-out, severing rock's links to sixties R&B while steadfastly ignoring the new directions taken by black music since – Sly Stone, Parliament–Funkadelic, James Brown, disco, reggae. Unlike most of their peers, though, Talking Heads always had a subtle funk pulse. Not in the 'passing for black' sense of, say, Scottish funksters Average White Band, but a more 'authentic', middle-class, Caucasian take. You could hear the urge to get down, but checked and frustrated by an uptight WASPishness – a square and stilted quality Byrne physically embodied onstage (what Barney Hoskyns called his 'everything-is-so-normal-it's-crazy!' persona).

Talking Heads' rhythm section – Weymouth and Frantz – steeped themselves in funk and disco. Weymouth told *Sounds* that the couple jostled over the hi-fi controls – she boosting the bass, Frantz turning up the treble to hear the high-hat patterns. She developed a style of playing bass using her thumb, roughly equivalent to Larry Graham's slap-bass technique. 'It gives an incredible piston action, like fuel-injection-fed,' she told *Melody Maker*. Byrne, meanwhile, had started to believe that the production techniques in black dance music (disco's extended remixes, the sumptuous layering and thick textures of everyone from The Jacksons to Funkadelic) constituted a bigger *musical* revolution than punk. 'When you started getting people doing the early remixes – stretching the song out, chopping it up – it was great,' he recalls. 'And it was all happening in the dance world; it wasn't happening in the rock world at all.'

'Art' was problematic enough, but 'disco' was anathema to the CBGB crowd. This doubtless explains why Talking Heads are totally excluded from *Please Kill Me*, the 'definitive' oral history of the New York scene assembled by *Punk* magazine's resident discophobe Legs McNeil. Talking Heads' image also made them black sheep among the black leather fraternity of CBGB. In the context of 1978 – the soft-rock mainstream still dominated by perms and facial fuzz; punk hidebound by its scuzzy style codes – Talking Heads' no-nonsense, 'regular' image was both refreshing and a statement. 'Some of those CB groups were really just continuing those rock 'n' roll Romantic archetypes, the rebellious attitudes and stage postures and all those inherited gestures,' says Byrne. 'I thought it wasn't saying anything new; it was just a sloppier version of the Stones. The same clothes and the same pose. I thought: Let's see if we can just throw all that out, start from square one. Walk onstage in your street clothes and sing with no affectation in a kind of unromantic but passionate way.'

Byrne had started dressing 'straight' – short hair, suits, double-knit pants – back at RISD, a dissident gesture against the let-it-all-hang-out mood of the early seventies. The only real precedent for this anti-rock 'n' roll neatness was Jonathan Richman and The Modern Lovers, whose Jerry Harrison was recruited to fill out Talking Heads' scrawny sound with his keyboards. Also crucial to the Heads' visual difference was the matter-of-fact presence of Weymouth, gamine and androgynous with her Jean Seberg crop. 'I think we were the first band that had a woman as a journeyman, not the front-person/singer/sex symbol of the band, but just a working musician,' Harrison has said, forgetting Mo Tucker in the Velvets but being more or less on the money.

Talking Heads, New York, 1978. L to R: Chris Frantz, Tina Weymouth, Jerry Harrison, David Byrne
Photo by Marcia Resnick

If Talking Heads had a polar opposite it was The Ramones, overgrown teenagers in black leather and torn denim, whose rock 'n' roll classicism led them to working with the relic Phil Spector, whereas the Heads teamed up with the future-minded Brian Eno. Both groups signed to America's leading New Wave label, Sire, and they embarked on a chalk-and-cheese tour of Europe in late spring 1977. (The Ramones were thoroughly freaked by the way the Heads *read books* on the road rather than raised hell.) During their stint in London, the Heads met Eno and immediately founded a mutual-admiration society.

In a 1978 interview with *Search & Destroy*, Weymouth gushed about the Englishman's sensitivity, courtesy, intellect and even his physical attractiveness: 'You know what he reminded us of? A young Jesuit monk. And he was very handsome in person . . . Beautiful hands, very long, slender fingers. Very idealistic hands, I would say.' Eno was equally captivated by the band and recorded the tribute song 'King's Lead Hat' (an anagram of Talking Heads) on his solo album *Before and After Science*. 'I think they're about the nicest four people I could ever hope to meet,' he told *Melody Maker*. He admired their music for being clearly 'the product of some very active brains . . . constructing music in a kind of conceptual way'. As should be evident, the Eno/Talking Heads relationship was freighted from the start with a sort of mirror-image narcissism. Eno embodied the very cerebral, well-raised qualities that made Talking Heads misfits in CBGB; the Englishman in turn saw the Heads as junior versions of himself, brilliant but still in need of a little avuncular guidance and nurturing.

In David Byrne especially, Eno found a soul-brother. He gushed to *Musician* magazine, 'It's like David . . . said to me the other day: "Sometimes I write something that I really can't understand, and that's what excites me." I felt such a sympathy with that position.' Words had always been a problem for Eno, 'in that I didn't have anything to say', he confessed to the *NME* in 1977 (a blasphemous comment in the year rock's meaning and relevance returned with a vengeance). 'I didn't have a message and I didn't have experiences that I felt strongly enough to want to write about . . . All my favourite songs had lyrics which I didn't quite understand . . . I decided I wanted these picture-lyrics.' Instead of straightforward emotions like sorrow, anger and joy, Eno preferred ambiguous mood-tones you couldn't quite finger. And he rejected rock's expressionist fallacy: the idea that emotive songwriting can come only from the personal depths. 'There are some bands who want to give the illusion . . . that the music itself is the . . . result of incredible, seething passions and turmoil from within,' he told *Creem*. 'The way I work . . . is to create music that creates a feeling in *you*.' Instead of unbridled subjectivity, the songs on his post-Roxy solo albums came out of a literally *object*ive approach – musically, they were sonic sculptures fashioned out of various materials, while the lyrics were 'syllable-rhythm' nonsense or methodically generated through language games.

Byrne approached songwriting with exactly the same playful spirit. 'I felt the challenge was to take something that was lyrically purely structural, had no emotional content whatsoever, but then invest the performance with leaps of emotion,' he says. In some Talking Heads songs, Byrne plays a character, as if the song were a mini-movie; in others, he plays with language itself. But however fragmented the narrative, the language in Talking Heads was always plain-spoken rather than poeticized – the sound of conversation or inner monologue. When it came to subject matter, Byrne's songs swerved past the things that occupy 96 per cent of rock's attention (love, sex, various forms of rebellion and misbehaviour) and instead explored the vast realm of other stuff that makes up the world – bureaucracy, TV, animals, electrical appliances, cities. Graced with a melody that shimmers like a hummingbird dipping for nectar, 'Don't Worry about the Government' (from the debut *Talking Heads 77*) broke with rock's tired tradition of 'Mr Jones' songs and instead empathized with office drones everywhere. Inspired by Maoist ideas and management theory, Byrne was playing with the notion – sacrilegious, in the rock mindset – that 'uniformity and restriction don't have to be debilitating and degrading'.

More Songs about Buildings and Food, the second album, was the first with Eno. It turned out be the first instalment in an Eno-produced trilogy of classic albums that were hugely diverse but unified by a loose concept: psychedelic funk. Both band and producer had been listening closely to the recent output of Parliament–Funkadelic, with its ultra-vivid palette of heavily treated instruments. This colour-saturated quality was especially ear-catching with the bass, an instrument normally played without much processing. Bootsy Collins' glossy, elasticated sound made him the Hendrix of the bass guitar. Parliament also pioneered synth-bass on tracks like 'Flashlight' (a massive US hit in 1978), with keyboardist Bernie Worrell stacking multiple Moog low-end tones to create the most gloopily lubricious bassline ever heard.

The songs on *Talking Heads 77* had all been written before Jerry Harrison joined, but now – with his keyboards integrated into the writing process – the group's music grew ever more thickly textured on *Buildings and Food*. And Eno loved creating strange new sound-colours using effects and the studio-as-instrument. You can hear this chromatic quality at its most intense with the splashy reverbed drums at the start of 'Warning Sign' and the famous 'underwater' sound of 'Take Me to the River'. Released as a single, this Al Green cover gave the band their first *Billboard* Top 30 hit and made a striking gesture of racial border-crossing at a time when New Wave was at its most starchy white.

With 1979's *Fear of Music*, Talking Heads plunged deeper into white funkadelia, but the feel is decidedly late seventies – psychedelia as media-overloaded disorientation, not trippy serenity. The title was inspired by a real (if rather rare) phobia that had come to Byrne's attention, but the phrase 'fear of music' obliquely distills the ominous mood of 1979: a year of geopolitical instability (the Iranian hostage crisis, the Soviet invasion of Afghanistan) and near catastrophe (nuclear meltdown at Three-Mile Island). Germany's Red Army Faction and the Symbionese Liberation Army (Patty Hearst's kidnappers) inspired 'Life during Wartime', the album's only overtly topical tune. Byrne goes beyond the obvious excitements of being an undercover terrorist (always on the move, switching identities, carrying several passports) by imagining the character's secret regrets: no time for 'fooling around', romance or night-clubbing. Elsewhere, the symptoms of disquiet and malaise are more quirky. 'Air' is the lament of someone so vulnerable that even contact with the atmosphere hurts ('some people don't know shit about the air', he whinges), while 'Animals' features an Alf Garnett-like grouch gruffly ranting about the wildlife being irresponsible and generally 'making a fool of us'. Its subliminal undertow of unease makes *Fear of Music* a sister album to 1979's other post-punk landmarks: Joy Division's *Unknown Pleasures* and PiL's *Metal Box*. But, unlike John Lydon or Ian Curtis, Byrne approached the subject in a less personal, more oblique manner.

Fear of Music represented the Eno/Talking Heads collaboration at its most mutually fruitful and equitable. By this point, Eno felt he and the four Heads had developed a group identity. His role encompassed being a kind of fifth player ('listening to what they were doing and picking out sounds and making new sounds from them . . . using delays to create new rhythms within their own') and being an editor who spotted 'little playing ideas that may have been accidents, or accidents of interaction' that the band might otherwise have missed. In a way, he'd become the group's George Martin. Indeed, the trilogy of records Eno and Talking Heads made together recalls the runaway evolution of The Beatles across *Rubber Soul, Revolver* and *Sgt Pepper's* – notably in the way each album's most radical tracks became the starting point for the next record.

In *Fear*'s case, the most advanced pieces, in terms of their structure and methodology, were the opening 'I Zimbra' and the closing 'Drugs'. The former combined Africa-influenced percussion, propulsive disco bass, and Byrne chanting nonsense syllables originally written and performed by Hugo Ball as Dadaist sound poetry. 'Drugs', a slow, faltering groove riddled with hallucinatory after-images and light-streaks, evoked altered states. In order to nail the panic-attack vibe he wanted, Byrne tried to make himself hyperventilate: 'I'd run around in circles until I was completely out of breath and then gasp, "OK, I'm ready to sing the next verse!"' The most radical aspect of 'Drugs' was its discombobulated gait and gap-riddled structure, full of lapses and phase shifts. 'Brian and I tore the song down to its basic elements and then built it up again with new stuff, replaying certain parts and replacing certain instruments.' The resulting mosaic of live band playing and sound collage was something almost impossible to reproduce onstage. 'Drugs' was the germ of the next album, *Remain in Light*, on which the band would generate a mass of rhythms and riffs that were then sifted through and stitched together at the mixing desk.

In the hiatus between these albums, Byrne and Eno launched a side project also intended to expand on the ideas of 'Drugs' and 'I Zimbra'. Byrne had long been a devotee of field recordings but now was also reading books by anthropologists and ethnomusicologists, such as Robert Farris Thompson and John Miller Chernoff, experts on African civilisation and the role of music in tribal societies. The project was initially conceived as a collaboration between Eno, Byrne and Jon Hassell, originator of the concept of 'Fourth World': the merger of hi-tech Western music and archaic ethnic musics from all corners of the globe. The original idea for what became *My Life in the Bush of Ghosts* was a fake field recording of a non-existent tribe. 'We'd invent a whole culture to go with it,' recalls Byrne. 'There would be ethnographic sleevenotes and everything.'

Speaking to *Musician* in 1979, Eno talked about the three areas he and Byrne planned to weave together: disco-funk, Arabic music from North Africa, and West African polyrhythms. 'Things sound really messy, and it's a kind of mess I've never had on anything before,' he enthused. 'It's a sort of jungle sound.' Soon a fourth element entered the picture: found voices. Eno and Byrne became fascinated with American radio's menagerie of evangelist preachers, right-wing pundits, and live callers to talk-radio shows. Radio, it seemed to Eno, was America's seething id, its political unconscious. 'In Britain or Europe the presenters are picked for their qualities of calmness and obvious rationality,' he told the *Guardian*. 'Here you get the nuttiest people in charge of the airwaves.' Tuning in to the born-again fundamentalists, they soon noticed 'a contradiction' at the heart of the ranting and raving. 'Some of it was declamatory finger-waving,' says Byrne, 'but with a lot of the preaching there was this ecstatic element: the performance was saying the opposite of what the text was saying. The words were all "thou shalt not" but the delivery itself was completely sexual. I thought, Great, the conflict is embodied right there.' Similarly, the fervour of Baptist and Pentecostal congregations struck Byrne as 'very similar to wild rock concerts or discos, the communal feeling where everyone gets swept up.'

Collecting radio voices for their polyrhythmic collages, Eno and Byrne found themselves especially attracted to the born-again Christian preachers because of their rocking-and-a-rolling speech patterns, midway between conversation and incantation. 'When people speak passionately they speak in melodies,' Eno told *East Village Eye*. Eventually, they asked themselves why the fundamentalists sounded *better* than the regular announcers, and concluded it was because they transmitted 'a sense of energy and commitment to some belief or other' – a fervour that was weirdly alluring against the bland backdrop of anomie and drift that was Carter's America. Byrne and Eno's diverse preoccupations were coalescing: themes of tribalism, ecstatic communal trance, the rival fundamentalisms of East and West versus the spiritual void of faithless liberalism. Reading about African culture, Byrne marvelled at the fact that the tribes made no distinction between dance music and religious music: dancing *was* worship. He and Eno imagined creating a ritual music for the postmodern West – a physically grounded transcendence connecting Funkadelic's 'dance your way out of your constrictions' with the holy-roller madness of born-again Protestantism.

Musically, *Bush of Ghosts* took the ideas of 'Drugs' and 'I Zimbra' to the next level. Rampant texturology: Eno and Byrne drastically extended the sonic range of conventional instruments through processing and effects. And the technique of interlocking: each instrument played very simple parts, which they then meshed into complex, ever-shifting webs of texture-rhythm. Two new approaches also informed the album: a 'Fourth World' mix of acoustic and hi-tech, so that hand percussion and the noise of wood mingled with state-of-the-art digital delays and synths; and a sensurround ambience that Eno called a 'psychedelic wash'.

Byrne's head was buzzing with all these ideas when he joined the rest of Talking Heads at Compass Point studios in the Bahamas in spring 1980 to begin work on *Remain in Light*. Rather than start from his melodies, the group decided to jam out tons of raw material – riffs, vamps, rhythmic pulses – and allow the songs to emerge later. The tracks were built out of layers of percussion, tics of rhythm guitar, synth daubs, and multiple bass riffs (on 'Born under Punches', there were at least five basses, each doing simple one- or two-note pulses). Glyphs of keyboard coloration darted through the drum foliage like tropical birds. When it came to the vocal melodies, Byrne had to find new modes of delivery in order to weave his voice into this teeming, gleaming rain forest. He'd assimilated the radio preachers' hypnotic cadences and commanding tones, but also picked up some tricks from early hip hop and even attempted a stiff-necked form of rapping on 'Crosseyed and Painless'.

Remain in Light has 'dry' and 'wet' sides that together make up a loose concept album: the restless panoramas of side one's triptych 'Born', 'Crosseyed' and 'The Great Curve' versus the flipside's 'Once in a Lifetime', a rapt aquatic swirl, and the glistening dreamscapes of 'Seen and Not Seen' and 'Listening Wind'. In 'Born' and 'Crosseyed' Byrne's protagonists are caged inside the clockwork grid of the industrial West, its hamster-wheel of schedules and time-is-money. In 'Once in a Lifetime' a suburban man wonders how he ended up here with all his beautiful property (house, car, wife). He's 'not upset or tormented', Byrne has said, 'just bewildered. And then in contrast the chorus is meant to convey a feeling of ecstatic surrender.' This shattering epiphany punctures the ordered absurdity of workaday life and brings the possibility of rebirth and renewed wonder. Or perhaps not: 'Once in a Lifetime' is immediately followed by the spooky 'Houses in Motion', in which we observe a man 'digging his own grave' in daily instalments of empty industriousness. *Remain in Light*'s concept wasn't especially original: in *The Waste Land* T. S. Eliot diagnosed Western soul sickness as a biorhythmic disconnection from natural cycles and there was a tang too of the sixties (Dylan's 'he not busy being born is busy dying'). Still, Talking Heads' fourth album brilliantly evoked both the illness (the itchy, rhythmic unrest) and its cure (deep trance, timeless flow).

If *Fear of Music* was about neurosis, *Remain in Light* reached for psychic wholeness, life newly reintegrated with nature and the body. Much of the album had a 'Western values *suck*; they're *sick*' subtext. 'The Great Curve' was an ecofeminist rhythm hymn to Gaia, its chorus 'the world moves on a woman's hips' inspired by the Yoruba's Great Mother cosmology. 'Listening Wind' makes us empathize with a North African man fighting Coca-Colonization by sending letter bombs and planting devices. Says Byrne, 'It's the point of view of someone being swamped by the West, their lives and culture destroyed. His retaliation is so limited compared to the might of the global powers, it's pretty easy to identify with – especially for someone who fancied himself an underdog in the music world.' At the end of the album, though, modernity's malaise reasserts itself with 'The Overload', a droning dirge inspired by Joy Division in uniquely oblique fashion – Talking Heads had never heard Joy Division's records, but had been intrigued by the record reviews. The whitest-sounding music on the album, the song is appropriately the most angst-racked, with Byrne numbly intoning lyrics about missing centres, terrible signals, 'a gentle collapsing'. It's as if the African dream has dissolved and we're back in the psychic hollow lands of *Fear of Music*.

A masterpiece, then – but *Remain in Light* shook Talking Heads to the core. Making the record had involved deconstructing the band. Assigned roles had been thrown into flux. For instance, everybody contributed keyboards and almost everybody played some bass. Recreating such multi-layered music onstage required the expansion of Talking Heads into a nine-piece ensemble modelled on Funkadelic (whose keyboard player Bernie Worrell was recruited, along with two other African-Americans – backing vocalist Nona Hendryx and second bassist Busta Jones). Before it even played a note, the racially and sexually mixed line-up of the Expanded Heads made a quiet multiculturalist statement, its onstage presence embodying the all-gates-open, communal uplift feeling that *Remain in Light* precariously grasped for.

Within the core quartet, though, tensions had emerged during the recording sessions. Weymouth, Frantz and Harrison were coming up with material but had 'no idea where it would end up', says Byrne. 'Everyone was pretty enthusiastic about cutting the tracks at the start. But the process of taking all the parts and forming them into songs – less people became involved. They probably felt a little bit left out. Their playing was still there but the vibe at the end might be completely different.' A rift opened up between Weymouth, Frantz and Harrison – effectively demoted to the level of session musicians – and Byrne and Eno, who were now incredibly tight. Emotions and loyalties were at stake, as well as questions of control. 'By the time they finished working together for three months [on *Bush of Ghosts*] they were dressing like one another,' Weymouth sniped in one interview. 'They're like two fourteen-year-old boys making an impression on each other.'

The conflict extended to the fraught question of writing credits and royalties. Song publishing traditionally assigns copyright to the composer of the topline melody and lyrics, but this was obviously inadequate for the radically decentred music the band was now producing. Eno understandably wanted appropriate credit for his role and pressed for double billing: 'Talking Heads and Brian Eno'. The band refused, but when the artwork came back they were horrified to find the songs credited to Byrne and Eno. In the end, the back cover declared, 'All Songs by David Byrne, Brian Eno, Talking Heads' – a compromise that satisfied nobody. Weymouth, Frantz, Harrison and eventually even Byrne began to suspect that Eno was trying, consciously or unconsciously, to turn Talking Heads into his backing band – a new Roxy Music, but with Byrne far more amenable to Eno's ideas than Bryan Ferry had been. 'It wasn't really a problem while we were making *Remain*, but when we were considering what to do next,' says Byrne. 'By this point the others were fed up with me and Brian and our ideas. And I probably thought: OK, I won't push it down their throats any more.'

For his part, Eno felt the album could have gone so much further if he'd had carte blanche. He was also irritated that the album had effectively stolen *Bush of Ghosts*' thunder. The Byrne and Eno album was originally meant to come out before *Remain in Light*, but it was delayed – partly because of legal wrangles over the use of one evangelist's voice, partly because the Talking Heads sessions gave the duo loads of new ideas for where to take *Bush of Ghosts*. Eventually released in January 1981 – four months after the massively acclaimed *Remain in Light* – *Bush of Ghosts* felt like an afterthought, not the ambush of new ideas Eno had planned. It also caught a critical backlash: some characterized Byrne and Eno as bloodless eggheads working in sterile laboratory conditions; others chastised them as sonic neo-colonialists appropriating Third World exotica – Lebanese mountain singer Dunya Yusin, Algerian Muslims chanting the Qu'ran, Egyptian pop star Samira Tewfik.

Despite the doubters, though, *Bush of Ghosts* was a career peak for both men. Even more than *Remain in Light*, the record's panoply of tactile rhythms, disjointed pulse grooves and eerily pitch-smeared arabesques of melody looked ahead to the innovations of sample-heavy genres like hip hop, house and jungle. It both pre-empted and influenced albums as diverse as Public Enemy's *Fear of a Black Planet*, DJ Shadow's *Endtroducing*, A Guy Called Gerald's *Black Secret Technology*, and Moby's *Play*. According to Byrne, the record was obliquely affected by hip hop – not so much rap music, though, as breakdancing! While working on the record in Los Angeles, the duo met dancer Toni Basil (later to do the choreography in the video for 'Once in a Lifetime'), who was working with bodypopping troupes like The Electric Boogaloos and The Lockers. 'She was going to do a whole programme of choreography based on these street dancers. Brian and I thought it was the most amazing dancing we'd ever seen and in some way the music we were doing was intended for her to use in some television programme with these dancers. But it never panned out.'

Remain in Light did well in Britain, where 'Once in a Lifetime' was a hit single, but in America the album was Talking Heads' worst seller. According to Byrne, 'It was perceived as too funky for the rock stations, while the R&B stations, of course, didn't want to know either. Sire never released "Once in a Lifetime" as a single.' The success of Tina Weymouth and Chris Frantz's delightfully poppy side project The Tom Tom Club – another big UK hit with 'Wordy Rappinghood'; the Stateside popularity of 'Genius of Love' on black radio stations, whose listeners assumed the group was African-American because the track was so damn funky – added further impetus to the idea of ending the relationship with Eno. For the sake of unity, Byrne went along with the general feeling that the band needed to rediscover the 'charm and tightness' of its earliest music. Call it vanguard fatigue: Weymouth talked of how the group 'spent so many years trying to be original that we don't know what original is any more'. Byrne strategically decided to divide his energies, channelling his experimental impulses into a plethora of side projects (like *The Catherine Wheel* album, music he composed for a ballet by avant-garde choreographer Twyla Tharp) while making Talking Heads the outlet for his pure pop instincts. After dissolving rock into an oceanic swirl of ethnofunkadelia, Talking Heads did the least expected thing and enjoyed a second act as a hugely successful pop group.

*

Back in the early seventies, long before his fateful meeting with the Talking Heads in London, Brian Eno was a regular visitor to Watford Art College. In those days Watford exemplified the anything-goes, mixed-media playfulness of the more progressive sort of British art school – what Eno later hailed as 'one of the most highly evolved forms of liberal education available on the planet . . . really something quite extraordinary'. At Watford, Eno hooked up with his friend Peter Schmidt, one of the foundation tutors. Schmidt did the watercolour artwork for several Eno albums and the pair created Oblique Strategies together. Fluxus in a box, this was an I-Ching-like set of cards with instructions and suggestions designed to help artists through creative impasses. Oblique Strategies' subtitle is 'Over one hundred worthwhile dilemmas' and its most famous maxim is 'Honour thy error as a hidden intention'. Other Oblique advice included 'Don't be afraid of things because they're easy to do', 'Retrace your steps', 'Turn it upside down', 'Is it finished?'

When Eno came to Watford to help with projects for the foundation course, he and Schmidt would often get a lift back to London from another tutor, Hansjorg Mayer. Sometimes there would be another passenger in the car, a young student of Mayer's named Colin Newman, who in a few years would become a founding member of Wire. 'In my view humans are inherently creative,' says Newman, 'but there is a process by which a particular individual becomes an artist, meaning that they can say they are an artist without being pretentious. If that happened at any given point to me it was during those car journeys. As soon as I stepped in that car I was no longer just a rather poor student but a friend and an equal – an artist sitting in a car with other artists. I could babble on about my ideas.'

Apart from drummer Robert Gotobed, Wire all came with an art-school pedigree. Bassist Graham Lewis was a fashion graduate doing freelance design for London boutiques. Guitarist Bruce Gilbert, old for a punk at thirty-one in 1977, was an abstract painter who worked as an audio-visual technician at Watford Art School. Singer Colin Newman, seven years his junior, studied illustration at Watford, where he'd gravitated towards the sound studio's facilities for experimenting with tape. 'Bruce and me specifically always brought a fine arts mentality to Wire,' says Newman.

Wire had a meteoric rise. Within six months of forming, Wire made their live debut in February 1977 at the Roxy, London's CBGB; four months later, they made their vinyl debut on the live compilation *The Roxy London WC2*; by year's end, they had released their debut album,

Pink Flag. Like Talking Heads, Wire were right at the heart of the punk scene, yet didn't quite belong. They were misfits whose distanced artiness made them distinctive but rubbed a lot of people up the wrong way.

Two words crystallize what Wire derived from art school: 'method' and 'design'. They approached making their music with a *method*ical objectivity, thinking of songs as 'pieces' – sonic material to be chiselled, like a sculpture, rather than an outpouring from their hearts and souls. Like Eno, they approached creation with a what if?/why not? curiosity – setting up processes and embracing constraints, just to see what would transpire.

Wire's design sensibility encompassed the striking cover art on their records (the concept invariably devised, if not executed, by Gilbert and Lewis) and their highly contoured and geometric music. Even at its most punk-like, there was a brutal elegance to the power chords and riffs: this was music you could practically visualize as clean lines, deliberate spacings, and blocs of texture. The name Wire itself was chosen as much for 'its graphic quality', says Lewis, as for its connotations (thin and metallic; electrical power lines). 'It was short and stark and would look big on a poster even if we were low on the bill!' Onstage, Wire looked equally styled and monochrome, sporting clothes in shades of black, grey and white, and using lighting that dispensed with rock 'n' roll clichés in favour of harsh, glaring white spots. The band projected a glacial aloofness: Newman stood stock still, eyes staring straight ahead, or struck stylized and frozen 'rock star' poses.

What made Wire 'punk' was their minimalism, their reductionist disdain for extraneous decoration. They arrived at their sound initially through removals and refusals. 'It was a process of elimination – all the things we don't do,' recalls Newman. 'At the end of the process, the list of things we actually *did* do was quite short!' Solos were shed first. In their earliest days, Wire included another Watford student on lead guitar, but when he was hospitalized for six weeks, the group noticed that the music dramatically improved in the absence of his solos. 'All the fat, all the meander, suddenly disappeared,' says Newman. 'Everything was edited drastically: the songs came down to one and a half minutes long.'

Brevity and severity became Wire's hallmarks, as heard on *Pink Flag*, which crams twenty-one compressed bursts of abstract fury into just thirty-five minutes. On an idle listen, Newman's uncouthly enunciated Mockney could pass for standard-issue punk singing. But, for all their aggression, the songs are as exquisitely etched as a finely honed haiku, and the absurdist titles – 'Ex-Lion Tamer', 'Three Girl Rhumba' – suggest this isn't mere ruckus for the Roxy rabble, but a conceptual enterprise. Many of the songs were written as acts of speculation: what would happen if you rewrote 'Johnny B. Goode' using only one chord? (The answer: *Pink Flag's* title track.) Newman composed '106 Beats That' on an agonizingly delayed train journey between Watford and London, during which he devised a complicated system of correspondences between the names of railway stations and guitar chords.

Wire's lyrics, mostly written by Graham Lewis, were no less process-oriented. His words for '106 Beats That' came out of a failed attempt to write a lyric that contained only a hundred syllables: 'It turns out it's got one hundred and six, but that doesn't matter, because you've created a process.' He and Bruce Gilbert would play absurdist games with sense and nonsense, narrative and fragmentation. Because making statements or self-expression weren't the point, nobody was precious about the words; they were material to be manipulated. For instance, Newman wrote a lyric about a lion tamer that Lewis mostly didn't care for, so he deleted all the bits he didn't like and replaced them – hence the song's eventual title, 'Ex-Lion Tamer'. Dismembering sequential narrative was a favourite Lewis tactic. But the kaleidoscopic perceptions in Wire songs often managed to be closer to the fractured way in which we experience reality.

Lewis once talked of Wire's quest for what he called 'the X Factor' – 'a kind of fear . . . something that you don't understand'. The idea is close to Eno's belief that art's biological function is exposing the listener to disorientation. 'What art does for you is that it constantly rehearses you for uncertainty,' he told *Melody Maker*. Most reviewers, though, compared Wire's enigmatic lyrics and non-linear dream logic to Syd Barrett-era Pink Floyd rather than Eno's solo albums – an easy link to make since Wire were signed to Harvest, EMI's psychedelic/progressive imprint, whose founder Nick Mobbs had originally signed Floyd. According to Newman 'EMI thought Wire were gonna be part of a new psychedelia, the next Pink Floyd. EMI saw us as the progressive element coming out of punk, with longevity and a more artistic approach – slower pieces, more depth and space in the sound, different noises that weren't just thrash thrash thrash.'

Wire started living up to these expectations with their second album, *Chairs Missing*. This record saw the band's relationship with producer Mike Thorne (the EMI A&R man who'd originally recommended them to Harvest) deepen to the point where he became their personal Eno, shaping the overall sound by helping the group create ear-catching textures and effects. *Chairs Missing* reinvents psychedelia while preserving the group's signature quality of monochromatic minimalism. The guitars have an ultra-vivid gloss; 'French Film Blurred' is a vitreous shimmer; on 'Being Sucked in Again' even the bass emits an unnatural glow, like fluorescent marble. Thorne had brought back state-of-the-art effects units from America: MX-R distortion, flanges, and new sound effects operating in what Thorne calls 'the time domain, like delays and chorus pedals. The combination of delays with distortion sounded very exciting and different, so we just went full tilt into that.' Says Newman, 'The MX-R unit provided this very clean and un-heavy metal distortion. "I Am the Fly" is literally that sound – like glass. On *Chairs Missing* we were just streets ahead when it came to guitar sounds.'

Practically a fifth member of the group, Thorne also played keyboards on *Chairs Missing*. In 1978, keyboards were still widely regarded with suspicion, as somehow anti-punk, but Wire got into the idea when they realized their guitars were so heavily treated they might as well be synths. Soon it was vice versa, says Thorne: 'We put synths through distortion pedals and got this electric sound that wasn't a guitar or a keyboard but somewhere in between.' This disorienting uncertainty about the instrumental provenance of particular sounds added to the album's hallucinatory feel.

For a towering post-punk masterpiece, though, *Chairs Missing* received a surprisingly mixed reception in 1978. Praised to the marmalade skies by some reviewers, it was lambasted by others for those keyboards, for the lyrics' trippy whimsy, and for having longer songs (the opener 'Practice Makes Perfect' made a statement by going on for four minutes, while 'Mercy' reached almost six). The *NME*'s Monty Smith accused the group of degenerating from *Pink Flag* to Pink Floyd in less than a year. But, apart from the odd Electric Prunes-like guitar sound, the only true sixties throwback on the album was the beguiling, Byrds-like 'Outdoor Miner' – the closest Wire ever got to a hit single – with its honeyed harmonies and idyllic, chiming chords.

Dense with assonance and internal rhyme, the lyric to 'Outdoor Miner' sounds like sensuous nonsense, a typical example of Wire revelling in language for its melt-in-your-mouth musicality rather than meaning. (Typical line: 'face worker, serpentine miner, a roof falls, an underliner, of leaf structure the egg timer'.) In fact, it was obliquely inspired by a Radio Four wildlife programme, from which Lewis learned about a bug called the serpentine miner, which lives inside holly leaves and eats chlorophyll. 'When I listen to my singing on that I just crease up,' Newman told *NME*. 'I should be singing "she loves me" . . . but what I'm singing about is insects.' The genesis of other songs was equally whimsical: 'French Film (Blurred)' came from Newman's attempt to watch a foreign movie on a TV with reception so poor he couldn't read the subtitles, forcing him to make up the dialogue; 'Marooned' was a fantasy vignette about an Arctic castaway resigned to his fate – 'as the water gets warmer my iceberg gets smaller'.

By their third album, *154*, Wire's music was becoming almost oppressively textured. The glaze of overdubs and guitar treatments produced a ceramic opacity, forbidding and impenetrable. The sessions were fraught: the pop-minded Newman and Thorne jostled with the abstractionist Gilbert and Lewis, who'd been making pieces at home on tape-recorder and venturing into the ambient zones later explored in their post-Wire project Dome. 'The vessel we were in just started getting a little small for all of us,' recalls Thorne, 'because it was starting to cramp the ways in which we wanted to develop.' The tension seemed to infuse the songs, which were unusually cold-blooded, even for Wire. The opener, 'I Should Have Known Better', sung by Lewis in a doomy baritone, expressed animosity with steely precision: 'I haven't found a measure yet/To calibrate my displeasure yet'. Newman's 'Two People in a Room' depicted emotional conflict as stratagem and manoeuvre ('Positions are shifted/The cease-fire unlifted') and elliptically evoked the disintegration of Wire itself into rival aesthetic camps. Ideas relating to number, measurement and cartography ran through the album, from songs like 'The 15th' and 'Map Ref. 41° N 93° W' to the title, *154*, itself.

Released in September 1979, *154* garnered universal acclaim. It possessed a sheer size of sound that suggested Wire could become a major band, but the group's first real brush with the big time – a sixteen-date tour as support to the reformed Roxy Music, a group they'd once admired greatly – turned them off the rock-biz way of doing things. Their relationship with EMI soured, too: the company had been caught chart-hyping 'Outdoor Miner', effectively sabotaging Wire's best shot at a hit. All densely overdubbed guitars and stacked vocals, 'Map Ref. 41° N 93° W', the single off *154*, was majestic but its beauty was oddly remote, just like the cartographer's eye-view lyric, inspired by a flight over Iowa. As pop choruses go, 'Lines of longitude and latitude/Define and refine my altitude' doesn't exactly scream, 'chart potential'.

To promote the single, Wire decided to bypass the standard option (a short tour of the UK) and opted for something unexpected: a show called *People in a Room* that ran for four nights at the Jeanette Cochrane Theatre in London, part of the Central School of Art and Design. Each member of Wire did a solo turn: Gilbert's performance-art piece involved a black trolley, a glass and a series of people pouring water into it; Newman's Glenn Branca-style guitar-drone symphony featured five people playing E, five playing A, and five playing D. When Wire finally took the stage, they played a new fifteen-minute composition called 'Crazy about Love'. Their gigs generally featured a high proportion of new material (once a song was recorded, the group lost interest in it) but at the Jeannette Cochrane they played only a couple of songs from *154*, destroying any promotional aspect to the event and pissing off EMI.

People in a Room was effectively a career suicide note, and on 9 February 1980 a terse announcement appeared in the music papers, accompanied by a scowling shot of Wire. The group and EMI had parted company, it declared, because of 'a breakdown of communication' and the label's 'reticence to consolidate future plans and projects'. Wire were impatient to move forward, to shake up the predictable industry way of doing things. They'd conceived an ambitious advertising campaign for *154* – enigmatic posters on buses, ten-second adverts on TV, all featuring just the cryptic number 154 – but EMI rejected the idea as too expensive.

Wire part company with EMI, from the *NME*, 9 February 1980. L to R: Bruce Gilbert, Graham Lewis, Robert Gotobed, Colin Newman

● Wire have left EMI Records, claiming that they are no longer under any contractual obligation to the label. They say that " the internal and corporate problems currently besetting EMI have led to a breakdown of communication between the company and the band". They are at present rehearsing new material.

Most of the more open-minded people at EMI had left, says Thorne, as the company took a turn at the end of the seventies towards play-it-safe and bottom-line oriented. But Wire, says Newman, felt like they 'were engaged in a creative project and had this very rich record company that we assumed would be excited by new ideas. We *wanted* to sell records. We were talking about video – this was before MTV but I'd seen from watching children's TV on Saturday mornings that videos were becoming very important. We had an idea for "Map Ref.", hugely expensive, but we could probably have been persuaded to do something a bit cheaper if there had been a budget. But EMI said, "You can't sell music on television – we've tried." Hilarious, considering what happened a year later. In hindsight, I can see how Wire really suffered from being ahead of our time. By 1980, if we'd been on a label that was willing to put money into a video, we would have been among the first generation of MTV bands, alongside Talking Heads.'

Unwilling to spend what it would take to make Wire happen as a pop group, EMI was equally disinclined to fund their more esoteric side – their proposal of a sub-label similar to Eno's Obscure imprint through Island, an outlet for a steady stream of experimental side-project releases, limited in appeal to hardcore Wire aficionados but cheap to produce and plentiful. 'The head of EMI put it quite succinctly,' recalls Thorne. 'Something like: "A record company is not an Arts Council." And, to be fair, Wire had lost touch with the fact that a large record company has to show a return on their investment.'

The press release about the Wire/EMI split also announced an upcoming show at the Electric Ballroom in late February 1980. But in a final, impressive feat of perversity, instead of using this as a showcase to secure another record deal, Wire staged an absurdist extravaganza redolent of the Dadaist cabaret revues of 1916–19. Each song in the virtually all-new set was accompanied by a daft spectacle. For 'Everything's Going to be Nice', two men tethered to an inflatable jet were dragged across the stage by a woman. Newman sang 'We Meet under Tables' dressed in a black knee-length veil. Lewis growled 'Eels Sang Lino' accompanied and lit by an illuminated goose. During 'Piano Tuner (Keep Strumming Those Guitars)', someone attacked a gas-stove, while 'Zegk Hoqp' featured twelve people with newspaper head-dresses playing percussion. The audience, which contained a sizeable contingent of people who still pined for *Pink Flag*-era punk ditties like '12XU' and 'Dot Dash', were either baffled or chucked bottles at the stage. It was Wire's last gig for five years.

Without ever formally disbanding, the group dispersed. Newman pursued the melodic side of Wire with his debut solo album, *A–Z* (produced by Thorne) and 1982's *Not To*. Meanwhile, Lewis and Gilbert virtually erupted with full-on experimentalism: a rash of albums and EPs released under the names Dome, Cupol, Gilbert/Lewis and Duet Emmo, and a series of installations and performances in collaboration with artist Russell Mills. These records paralleled Eno's ambient series for EG, especially *On Land*, with its amorphous dronescapes built out of unpitched timbres and found sounds like stones and rooks. In similar fashion, Gilbert and Lewis used makeshift improvised instruments and *musique concrete* – footsteps in an art gallery, the clattering noises of themselves stumbling around the studio in the dark and bumping into equipment and junk. Increasingly, they would enter the studio with absolutely nothing prepared, pursuing tangents and looking for sonic serendipity.

The percussive, vaguely tribal-sounding *Dome 3* could almost be seen as a radically estranged cousin to *Remain in Light* and *My Life in the Bush of Ghosts*, except that the music was relentlessly opposed to the idea of 'groove' and dismantled the propulsive function of rhythm altogether. Wire and Talking Heads had a huge amount in common, but one area they diverged was da funk. Robert Gotobed stayed true to punk's anti-dance stance by steadfastly shunning syncopation or swing in his drumming. Graham Lewis liked James Brown but in a curiously disembodied way: 'this brilliantly designed, pared-down, almost mechanical dance music'. He describes *Pink Flag*'s 'Lowdown' as 'an experiment in deconstructed funk, almost a critique of funk – very dark and slowed down, to the point of non-funkiness. The thing about Wire, we never wanted to make dance music – unlike lots of other post-punk groups, like The Pop Group, who were overtly influenced by funk.'

As Wire's sound evolved, it seemed to grow colder and whiter in both the racial/musical and snowy Alpine senses. When the four reunited in 1985 to have a second crack at being Wire, they rededicated themselves to the monolithic, funkless force rhythm they nicknamed 'dugga'. The first song they wrote after five years apart was called 'Drill'. And it sounded like one.

9

LIVING FOR THE FUTURE: Cabaret Voltaire, The Human League and the Sheffield Scene

Cabaret Voltaire. The Future/The Human League.

In most British cities, punk inspired kids to grab guitars and make sub-Clash two-chord thrash. In Sheffield, though, 'there were no punk bands *at all*', claims Phil Oakey of The Human League. The city's resident aesthetes dug the London bands' clothes and punk's shock value, but the idea of back-to-basics garageland rock seemed dated from the start. In Sheffield's garages – and bedsits and living rooms – you'd find youths grappling with synths, tape-recorders and crude rhythm-boxes.

Partly this stemmed from a bloody-minded Northern disinclination to follow London's lead. '"London's burning" they all shout/But I wouldn't even piss on it to put the fire out,' local post-punk band 2.3 declared on their Clash-mocking anthem '(I Don't Care About) London'. Sheffield's preference for electronic sounds also related to a local spirit of futurism and technophilia shaped by the city's role as one of the engines of the Industrial Revolution. World famous for its steel, Sheffield was the home of innovations such as stainless steel and Bessemer's converter (which made mass production of low-cost steel possible in the late nineteenth century). Although Sheffield is just ten minutes' drive from the picturesque Peak District and the vales of Derbyshire, its enduring popular image is grim and grey, based on the inner city and the industrialized East End. 'That's where I lived with my parents,' says Richard H. Kirk of Cabaret Voltaire. 'You looked down into the valley and all you could see was blackened buildings. At night in bed you could hear the big drop forges crunching away.' The Human League's Martyn Ware likewise talks of growing up in a kind of science-fiction noisescape – all the strange machine sounds and clangour generated by Sheffield's heavy industry.

One of the first British cities to become industrialized, Sheffield rapidly acquired a proletariat in the classic Marxist sense: human beings reduced to appendages of flesh attached to machinery, acutely conscious of both their exploitation and their common interest in struggling for better conditions. Until recently, the city was a bastion of Old Labour, the pre-Tony Blair party that was closely linked to the trade union movement and whose members took seriously the Labour charter's commitment to state ownership of major industries; like steel – 90 per cent of which was combined into the publicly owned British Steel Corporation in 1967. The People's Republic of South Yorkshire is what they used to call the Sheffield region. In its heyday, Sheffield's council flew the red flag from the town hall.

If you grew up in the suburban South of England, becoming a left-wing militant was rebellious, a way of defining yourself against your parents. But in Sheffield, where hard-left politics was an everyday backdrop, being an artist was much more of a dissident gesture. For the teenage Richard H. Kirk, being a member of the Young Communist League was almost akin to attending Sunday school. 'My dad was a member of the Party at one point, and I wore the badge when I went to school. But I never took it really seriously.' Instead, he was drawn to Dada's unconstructive revolt and intoxicating irrationalism.

Although much of Britain suffered from steadily rising unemployment and factory closures as the seventies progressed, Sheffield remained relatively prosperous through most of that decade. If there was deprivation, it was cultural. Nonconformist Sheffield youth grabbed on to whatever sources of aberrant stimulation they could find: pop music, art, glam clothes, science fiction, or, better still, a combination of all of them. That's why *A Clockwork Orange* – Burgess's book, Kubrick's film, *and* Walter Carlos's electronic movie score – had such an impact in Sheffield. The Human League titled their second EP *The Dignity of Labour* after a mural in the high-rise block where the book's teenage anti-hero Alex visits his parents. Martyn Ware and Ian Craig Marsh later named their post-Human League outfit Heaven 17 after an imaginary pop group in the book. Adi Newton, a former associate of Ware and Marsh, named his band Clock DVA – 'dva' meaning two in the pidgin-Russian slang that Alex and his thug minions speak in this near-future England. As for Carlos's score, this was simply the first time most Sheffield kids had heard full-on electronic music. There'd been tantalizing glimpses of synthesized sound here and there in progressive rock, from groups like Emerson Lake and Palmer. 'ELP were awful rubbish apart from when Keith Emerson was playing the Moog, and then it was sublime,' says Phil Oakey. 'We would just stand there at the student disco with our mouths open.' Otherwise, just about the hardest hit of electronic sound you could get from pop in the early seventies was Roxy Music, which featured Eno's abstract blurts of synth noise.

Roxy were massive in Sheffield. The group's flamboyant future-retro image inspired the post-hippy generation to glam up and dance at Sheffield clubs like the Crazy Daisy and Penthouse. And Roxy performed regularly in the city. 'When you went to see them you'd wait until you were on the bus before applying the glitter, so your mum and dad didn't see,' recalls Oakey. 'Martyn was more daring than me: he'd be going through the toughest areas of town in green fur jackets and high-heel shoes.' At parties, people used to greet Ware and Oakey with 'Oh, look, it's Mackay and Eno' – Andy Mackay being Roxy's fruity-looking saxophonist. Ambiguously pitched between irony and Romanticism, Roxy signified sophistication – the sax and the synth transcended 'mere' rock. They were the aesthete's option. 'Near where I lived there was a fantastic second-hand record store called Rare & Racy,' says Ware. 'Often I'd pick things out because of how the record looked. I remember buying the first Roxy album and listening to it with the gatefold sleeve open. The entire atmosphere around the record was as important as the music – it all came together as a piece of art, as far as I was concerned.'

The early seventies was the great era of rock theatre – both theatrical rock performers (Bowie, Alice Cooper, Peter Gabriel-era Genesis) and rock musicals (*The Rocky Horror Music Show, Rock Follies*). So it's only right that in glam-city Sheffield a future generation of local pop stars would be nurtured in a youth theatre project called Meatwhistle. Founded in 1972 and funded by the city council, Meatwhistle evolved into a kind of experimental performance space for bright teenagers. Among its participants were a good proportion of the future prime movers in Sheffield's post-punk scene: Marsh and Ware of The Future/The Human League/Heaven 17; Newton of The Future and Clock DVA; Paul Bowers, founder of punkzine *Gun Rubber* and leader of 2.3; Glenn Gregory, later the singer in Heaven 17.

'Meatwhistle started in the summer of '72 when I was about sixteen, as a city-wide project based out of the Crucible Theatre,' says Marsh.

'They came up with this idea of opening it up to secondary-school kids for the summer.' After a wildly successful production of *Marat-Sade*, Meatwhistle's organizers – arty bohemian playwright/actor Chris Wilkinson and his wife Veronica – were given an entire disused grammar school. 'It was a big old Victorian building, on Hollis Street, three or four floors, huge ceilings,' recalls Ware. The Wilkinsons lobbied successfully for funding for lights, video cameras and musical instruments. 'From '72 onwards, Meatwhistle got a lot more experimental and creative, as all the disaffected juveniles in Sheffield started congregating there,' says Marsh. 'Bands were rehearsing at Meatwhistle because there were loads of spare rooms. Generally speaking, everyone was free to do what the fuck they wanted. If the council had kept a close eye on the place, seen some of the stuff going on – like people smoking dope – it'd have been shut down instantly.' There was a strong element of everybody colluding, says Marsh, to pull the wool over the authorities' eyes, get away with as much as possible. The name itself, Meatwhistle, was irreverent. The Wilkinsons claimed it was Chaucerian; of course, it's slang for the male member.

Each Sunday, the Meatwhistle crew put on a show. 'Everyone who wanted to get up and do a half-hour slot would get the chance, whether it was a band or a comedy sketch or a play,' recalls Marsh. 'There'd be a big meal which everyone would cook together. There was that communal vibe – sort of semi-hippy but with an edge.' It was for one of these Sunday revues that Marsh formed his first band, the shock-rock duo Musical Vomit. 'I got the name from a *Melody Maker* live review of Suicide. To *MM*, with its prog-rock attitude, Suicide were a sheer insult to the audience's ears, so the reviewer described them as "musical vomit". I thought, What a great name for a band. This guy Mark Civico sang and I'd go onstage with a guitar I could barely play, making percussive noise and feedback.'

After a while, Marsh left and Musical Vomit became closer to a proper band, albeit with a spoof-rock edge and an ever-shifting, expanding-and-contracting line-up that included Glenn Gregory, Paul Bowers, and later Martyn Ware. The latter had been all set to apply for Oxford but then decided to skip higher education and instead bring some money into his working-class family home. While training to become a manager at the Co-op supermarket, he met Bowers. 'Paul said, "You must come to Meatwhistle, it's a riot," and dragged me down there,' says Ware. 'Paul was the catalyst who brought everybody together.' By this point,

Meatwhistle was 'a sort of intellectual youth club'-cum-arts lab. 'You could do arty Warhol-type stuff, 'cos they had professional video gear at a time when domestic video equipment wasn't even on the market. We were the luckiest people on earth, I thought.' But Meatwhistle had also evolved into a kind of experimental pop laboratory. There was an endless stream of imaginary bands, existing for one night only, with names like The Underpants, The Dead Daughters and Androids Don't Bleed. 'The vibe was very New York Dolls: everyone dressing up madly and adopting fake names like Eddie Brando and Dick Velcro,' recalls Marsh. Musical Vomit, meanwhile, had graduated to performing intermittently to real audiences – at Sheffield University's Drama Studio, at the Bath Arts Festival, and legendarily at the 1976 Reading Rock Festival. With sick-humorous songs about masturbation and necrophilia, and stunts like the lead singer puking up vegetable soup, the band operated somewhere between Alice Cooper-style shock-rock and the satirical-theatrical comedy-rock of The Tubes. Poly Styrene of X Ray Spex later declared Musical Vomit, whom she'd seen in the mid-seventies, to be the very first punk group in Britain.

Although they didn't participate in Meatwhistle, Cabaret Voltaire sank many a pint with the Musical Vomit crew. One thing they had in common was a passion for Roxy Music. 'That era, in '73 when Roxy were really at the cutting edge, that's what really got us going,' says Richard H. Kirk. 'Just reading Eno in interviews talking about how anyone can make music because you don't need to learn an instrument, you can use a tape-recorder or a synth.' The group were such fans that Kirk and fellow-Cab Chris Watson even went to hear Eno speak at Bradford Art College, clutching a reel-to-reel tape of their early recordings. Unable to buttonhole him after the lecture, they cornered the great man in the gents' toilet and pressed the demo reel into his apprehensive hands.

Prog-hating Eno defiantly described himself as 'non-musician', and 'We are not musicians' became Cabaret Voltaire's mantra, too. Initially the band saw themselves less as a musical entity than as a 'sound group', says Kirk, doing a sort of garage-band version of *musique concrete*. 'We started in late 1973, and initially there was a whole group of people involved. We were knocking about with some older people, and it was a weird, informal thing: a gang of mates interested in a bit of art and some films and a few strange books.' Most prominent among those 'strange books' was the work of William S. Burroughs. By the early seventies Burroughs was esoteric knowledge: his sixties notoriety had waned, he'd disappeared into reclusion, and his novels weren't that easy to find. Cabaret Voltaire were especially taken with the cut-up techniques the author had developed in tandem with Brion Gysin: chopping up text or sound and recombining them in order to disrupt the linearity of thought, each snip/splice a fissure through which 'the future leaks'. You can hear another influence from Burroughs – the flat, matter-of-fact depiction of extreme and grotesque acts of sex or violence – in the spoken-word voice-overs that accompany some early Cabaret Voltaire pieces, incongruously delivered in a dry Yorkshire accent. A prime example is the fetid imagery of 'Bed Time Stories': 'With dogs that are trained to sniff out corpses/Eat my remains but leave my feet/I'll hold a séance with Moroccan rapists/ Masturbating end over end.'

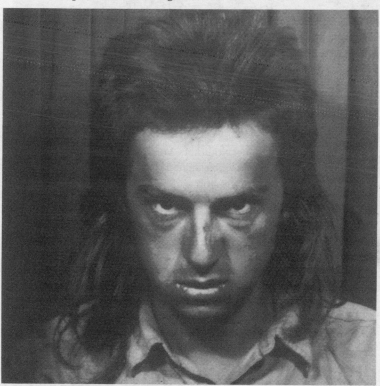

Photo-booth self-portrait of Richard H. Kirk in 1974, looking like Ziggy-era Bowie gone feral. From the cover of *Earlier/Later*, a CD anthology of Kirk's solo 'attic tapes'

Kirk had been to art school, completing a one-year foundation course in sculpture but then deciding not to take it any further. All the band were fans of the original anti-art movement, Dada. The name Cabaret Voltaire itself came from the Zurich nightclub/salon where Tristan Tzara, Hugo Ball *et al*. declaimed their sound poetry while the First World War raged across Europe. Outwardly the most 'normal' member of the group – his day job was as a telephone engineer – Chris Watson was a Dada fiend who'd stumbled on a book about the movement as a teenager in 1970, an experience that 'just hit me so hard it changed the way I've thought ever since'. Dada's assault on meaning and taste, along with its techniques of collage and photomontage, fired the group's imagination. 'To us, it *was* Dada to call ourselves Cabaret Voltaire, 'cos we were ripping them off,' Watson told *NME*.

By 1974, the gang had whittled down to Kirk, Stephen Mallinder and Watson, whose attic became their sound lab. 'We studiously went there Tuesdays and Thursdays every week and experimented for two hours or so, during which time we'd lay down maybe three or four compositions,' recalls Kirk. The trio recorded their abstract sound collages straight to tape, resulting in a massive archive, some of which was dug up for *Methodology '74/'78· Attic Tapes;*, a boxed set released in 2002. Creaky and homespun, the Cabs' early stabs at *musique concrete* – such as 'Dream Sequence Number Two Ethel's Voice' – have an alien-yet-quaint quality. The more ferocious tracks, like 'Henderson Reversed Piece Two' – all rattling synthetic percussion and soiled sheets of sound – recall avant-classical composers like Morton Subotnik.

At this point, Cabaret Voltaire didn't resemble a rock band in any respect. For a start, there was no drummer. 'We didn't want a rock guy showing off and doing drum solos,' says Kirk. 'We wanted steady, mechanical repetition.' At a Sheffield music shop, 'a dodgy-looking chap with a toupee' approached them and sold them a Farfisa drum machine he had at home – 'relatively advanced for 1974, it had these little buttons on the top for individual drum sounds'. Guitar didn't enter the picture until quite late. For a while, they didn't even have a proper synth. Instead, they used tape loops and an oscillator built by Watson. Kirk's primary instrument was the clarinet, fed through effects to sound harshly processed and eerie – the psychotic-bucolic 'Fuse Mountain' makes you imagine a crosslegged circle of hippies playing flutes and recorders on a slag heap outside a steel mill. 'No sound shalt go untreated' was another Cab motto. Almost every sound source – their voices, Mallinder's bass, Watson's organ, found sounds – was sent through ring modulators or a chain of effects devices, emerging on the other side warped and contaminated.

During these first couple of years before punk, Cabaret Voltaire 'never had any notion that we could ever make records or anything', says Kirk. 'It was all done for our own amusement. We'd do mad stuff – drive around in a van with tape loops playing out the back, or go into pubs with a tape-machine and play weird stuff. Just trying to wind people up, really. That's what we started out trying to do more than anything.' The Cabs drew hard stares for the way they looked, too. They were fashion crazy, starting with the skinhead look in their early teens, progressing to glam, and finally developing a kind of do-it-yourself eclectic style based on old clothes from Army and Navy Stores or Oxfam, which they'd customize with paint. 'I used to get white fabric and make screen prints or just paint it and make it into a shirt,' recalls Kirk. Mallinder was the group's ace stylist. 'He had two rooms in his flat, one in which he lived and the other which served as his wardrobe,' recalls NME's Sheffield correspondent Andy Gill (no relation to Gang of Four's guitarist). 'Mal was the most consummately stylish person I'd ever met.' As documented in the Sheffield 'zine Gun Rubber, a typical outfit for Mallinder might be: grey pleated flannels, snake-skin shoes, a Red Hawaiian shirt with the collar turned up, and a US Air Force suede jacket.

Anything to get noticed, to puncture the workaday routine. Fortunately, Sheffield was a surprisingly compatible environment for the bohemian lifestyle. You didn't need much money – thanks to the cheap council-subsidized buses (five pence a ride in the mid-seventies) and the plethora of disused factories and warehouses that could be squatted or cheaply rented as rehearsal spaces. There were plenty of resources connected to the art colleges and the University of Sheffield: student bars with dirt-cheap, subsidized beer and students' societies who put on gigs. Cabaret Voltaire conned one of these organizations, Science for the People, into letting them play during their Tuesday-night disco, reassuring the booker that 'oh yes, we play rock'.

So, on 13 May 1975, the Cabs played their debut gig to a room full of bemused students. Tristan Tzara would have been proud of the boys: they managed to trigger their own Dada-redux audience riot, worthy of the May 1920 chaos at the Salle Gaveau in Paris. 'We had . . . a tape loop of a recording of a steamhammer as percussion, and Richard was playing a clarinet with a rubberized jacket on it covered with flashing fairy-lights, and it just ended with the audience invading the stage and beating us up,' Watson told the *NME* five years later. In the mêlée, Mallinder fell offstage, chipped a bone in his back and had to be taken to hospital. Kirk wielded his clarinet like a club to beat off the attackers, then hurled his home-made guitar into the audience. According to Kirk, 'The people who attacked us ended up with the nastier injuries, 'cos a lot of people who came to see us, including some very dodgy people, took it upon themselves to take our side of the argument. Everyone was very drunk and everything just went mad.'

Cabaret Voltaire's next bout of *épater la bourgeoisie* also took place at the university. 'One of the guys in the Music Department got us to do a performance interpreting a piece called *Exhaust* by this bona-fide classical composer, Jean-Yves Bosseur,' recalls Kirk. 'We just played a tape loop of someone saying the word "exhaust" overlaid with some music, and we had film loops running that started melting. They were freaked out and we didn't get invited to the after-party.' This was 1976, the same year that Musical Vomit triggered an equally negative, if considerably more lumpen, response from the audience at the Bath Arts Festival: a hailstorm of beer cans driving them offstage.

When punk came along, Cabaret Voltaire and the Meatwhistle/Musical Vomit crew thrilled to its shock effects and sartorial provocations. 'It just seemed a natural progression, from glam to punk,' recalls Phil Oakey. 'The same kids that had been wearing fake animal prints were suddenly wearing vinyl with safety pins through it. I *did* have the first zip T-shirt in Sheffield –'cos I made it myself.' The first time Oakey met Ian Craig Marsh, the latter was dressed to distress. 'I had really tight drainpipe jeans, stitched at the crotch with leather, and instead of a T-shirt I had a pair of women's tights with the crotch ripped out pulled over my head and stretched really tight over my torso. And I'd got a cigarette and burned holes in it, so it was split everywhere. The finishing touch was the bracelets – two small, individual-portion baked-bean cans, cut out at both ends and then slipped over my wrists.'

In June 1977, all three members of Cabaret Voltaire joined Marsh, Adi Newton, Glenn Gregory, Martyn Ware and 2.3's drummer Hayden Boyes-Weston for one gig only as the punk-spoof supergroup The Studs. 'It was an anarchic raw event,' recalls Newton. 'One of our helpers had a bag of pigs' ears which were liberally thrown at the audience.' After chaotic improvised versions of The Kingsmen's 'Louie Louie', Lou Reed's 'Vicious' and Iggy Pop's 'Cock in my Pocket', plus a bizarre version of the

Dr Who theme, the band left the stage to howls of abuse.

Yet punk seemed to have outlived its usefulness by the end of that summer. 'Initially, we saw it as maybe a rebirth, and then we came to see it as the end of the cycle,' says Marsh. 'It was obvious that punk wasn't leading to anything interesting or new. When we started The Future, we were definitely on a mission to destroy rock 'n' roll.' Martyn Ware, who co-founded The Future with Marsh and Newton, didn't even bother to see The Sex Pistols and The Clash when they played in Sheffield. He'd *tried* to play guitar, but gave up in disgust when he learned that you had to soak your fingers in alcohol to stop them bleeding. 'We're not into things like that,' he sniffed in an interview with *The Face* a couple of years later, during which Ian Craig Marsh recalled their bemused grapplings with rock's favourite weapon: 'You can't make much sense of guitars. They seem a fairly strange instrument. I mean, the idea of six strings, four fingers, one thumb – it makes no sense. You have to *strain* to get a note.'

Luckily, in the summer of 1977, two epochal records arrived to show them the shining synth-paved path to tomorrow: Kraftwerk's *Trans-Europe Express* and Donna Summer's chart-topping 'I Feel Love'. Ware heard the former for the first time at a party in Richard Kirk's house. 'I'd never heard anything like it in my life,' he said. 'I was transfixed.' Ware and Marsh were instantly convinced that synths and machine rhythm were the way to go. 'We were dead against doing anything with guitars, full stop,' says Marsh. 'It became our manifesto: no standard instrumentation.'

Having dropped out of the Meatwhistle scene to work as a well-paid computer operator, Marsh now had money to burn. After messing around for a while with ring modulators and oscillators, he bought a build-your-own synth kit he'd seen advertised in *Practical Electronics* magazine. 'There were no real commercial synths available at the time – the early Moogs were custom made and cost a fortune, a hundred grand or something like that: strictly prog-rock supergroup territory. The synth kit I bought, you needed a degree of technical nous to be able to solder it together.'

He started hanging out at Meatwhistle again, sometimes dragging the machine down there and tinkering with it. Intrigued, Ware suggested an arrangement where he'd help Marsh pay for the synth in return for access to it. 'But it was virtually unplayable, and generally took about half an hour to tune up,' says Marsh. 'It was only really good for motorbike sounds and weird noises.' Between the two of them, they acquired two superior machines: the Korg 700S, a simple monophonic keyboard synth ('monophonic' meaning you could play only one note at a time, no chords) and the Roland System 100. The latter cost £800 – a small fortune in 1977 – but had almost infinitely more creative potential. Instead of a keyboard and pre-set sounds, the Roland was a 'patch-player' machine: the operator created his own sounds, 'synth-patches', by adjusting all kinds of variables. Its innards in plain view, the machine was a tangle of wires, sockets and knobs. In order to remember how you made a specific sound, you sketched out where all the cables went, the levels at which various 'potentiometers' were set, and so forth. 'It came with all these A4 sheets,' says Marsh. 'But however carefully you noted stuff down, there were so many critical variables you'd never quite get the same sound back. So there was a random element you just had to give yourself up to.'

In The Future, Marsh used the Roland to generate weird noises and textures, while Ware played melody lines on the Korg. The music was minimalist by default – 'an imposed minimalism', says Marsh, 'unlike Philip Glass or Steve Reich, say'. Melody was limited to one-finger motifs. Producing coherent rhythm proved even more challenging. In the days before drum machines, you could buy rudimentary rhythm generators and keyboards featuring pre-set beats (tango, disco, rumba, 'rock', etc.), but you couldn't program your own rhythms. To get round this, Marsh created percussion sounds from scratch using the Roland: he'd take a noise, filter it, then sculpt the 'envelope' of the sound so that it had the right attack and decay of a particular drum. White noise was good for ersatz high hats and cymbals; the duller-sounding pink noise could be made to resemble the woody thud of bass drums and snares. Gathering these pseudo-percussive noises, Marsh painstakingly sequenced them to resemble a full-kit drum track. Inevitably, the results were a bit stilted.

The Future's third member, Adi Newton, was the one most interested in abstract sound experiments using tape-recorders. 'Adi had been to art school and he introduced me to a lot of modern art stuff – Man Ray, Duchamp, Dada,' says Marsh. Newton had rented some rooms in a disused factory to use as studio workshops for painting and music. He also lived there, and 21b Devonshire Lane 'became a social focus, a location of many wild parties and a drug experimentation zone', recalls Newton. It also served as The Future's studio base.

Initially, The Future came up with the 'rather radical idea that we'd have shared vocals', says Marsh. 'We dispensed with our names and called ourselves A, B and C. It was all very computer orientated and linked to this lyric-composition program we created called CARLOS: Cyclic And Random Lyric Organization System.' A cybernetic version of Burroughs and Gysin's cut-ups or Surrealist automatic writing, CAR-LOS, says Ware, was a bit like 'a fruit machine. You'd pump in, like, a hundred nouns, verbs, adjectives, prepositions, whatever, and it would pump out random lyrics.' Specific lines or words were assigned to individual voices – A, B or C. 'In the end, we abandoned the system for more straightforward vocals, which Adi tended to do,' says Marsh wistfully. 'Blank Clocks', one of the few successful and surviving CARLOS tracks, shuffles a restricted number of nouns and modifiers in endless, slightly different combinations: 'Your heart the thigh my pain blank time your face the clock my mind/Blank heart your thigh the pain/My time blank face your clock/The mind my heart blank thigh your pain the time my face' etc.

At this point, The Future had a decidedly prog rather than pop slant: you can hear Tangerine Dream in the doomy techno-Gothic mindscapes of 'Future Religion', while the desolate electronic vistas of 'Last Man on Earth' are just ten minutes excerpted from a piece that was originally *ninety-seven* minutes long. Nothing could have been further from 1977's new punk norms – two chords and two minutes. But in August of that year The Future approached the London major labels in search of a record deal. They sent an eye-catching, computer-graphic-laden brochure to fifteen companies. 'Not many people in those days had access to computers, and we did all these bizarre dot-matrix designs on computer printout paper with perforated edges,' says Marsh. 'We sent out our manifesto and said we wouldn't be sending demo tapes, but would be in London on certain dates and would play them the tapes if they wanted to make an appointment. Surprisingly, we got nine replies: big names like EMI, Island, CBS.'

With punk at its height, the labels were looking for New Wave acts. 'The A&R guys were all forty and looked ridiculous in these rubber tops with zips they'd bought down the King's Road,' says Marsh, laughing. Most of the companies showed them the door after hearing the tapes, but Island Records expressed some enthusiasm. 'They said they were really interested but thought we should go away, work the music up into more song-like forms, and return in six months,' says Ware. 'This wasn't like a "Dear John" letter; it was constructive advice. So we did.' Shortly thereafter, Marsh and Ware realized that 'Adi couldn't actually sing a note, and, more to the point, didn't really *want* to sing. He was more into voice-as-weapon.' They decided to cut him loose. Surreptitiously, they moved all the equipment from Devonshire Lane to Marsh's flat and left Newton a note. 'We broke contact for a while, until he cooled off,' says Marsh.

Singerless, The Future made instrumentals for a while – like the beautiful 'Dancevision', a blueprint for Detroit techno with its neon-lights glimmer and strings-like sounds evoking some ambiguous alloy of euphoria and grief. But a vocalist was clearly required. In November 1977, Ware had a brainstorm: 'I told Ian I knew this guy from my schooldays who could sing and who looked fantastic. He was the coolest guy in Sheffield, rode big fuck-off Norton motorbikes and had this lop-sided hairstyle. He looked totally androgynous and the girls just thought he was gorgeous.' The guy was Phil Oakey, and the hairstyle was something he'd originally spotted on a girl on a bus. (She was a hair model sporting a version of a famous Vidal Sassoon cut from the sixties.)

Oakey was the youngest of four sons in a working-class-made-good family. 'My dad was a top postmaster and by the time I came along, we were quite well off – we lived in a posh suburb.' As a youth, his great passions were motorbikes, glam style, pop music and science fiction. 'I ended up working two years in a university bookshop and I had every science-fiction paperback you could get. I got really into Philip K. Dick and Ballard.' Dick's influence is all over early Human League: 'Circus of Death', the B-side of their debut single, was partly inspired by *Ubik*, while 'Almost Medieval' from the first album *Reproduction* is based on *Counter-Clock World*, a novel in which time goes backwards.

Oakey had no real ambitions to be a pop singer. He was a hospital porter when Ware suggested he try out as The Future's frontman. 'We gave him the backing track to "Being Boiled" and two days later he came back and said, "I don't know if you'll like this . . ."' He'd come up with a bizarre lyric blending stuff about the senseless slaughter of silkworms with confused, ill-digested notions of Eastern religion. Nonsense, but, delivered in Oakey's commanding baritone, it sounded wonderfully baleful. 'We heard the first lines – "Listen to the voice of Buddha/Saying stop your sericulture" – and it was a turning point.' Oakey joined the group, but he wasn't keen on The Future as the name, so they looked for an alternative. They found it in a science-fiction game called Star Force, one of whose scenarios involved the struggle between two intergalactic empires – the Pansantient Hegemony and the Human League.

With Oakey on board, the group shifted decisively in a pop direction with songs like 'Dance Like a Star' – a lo-fi, cobbled-together counterpart to Summer/Moroder's 'I Feel Love'. At the start of the song, Oakey taunts: 'This is a song for all you big heads out there who think disco music is lower than the irrelevant musical gibberish and tired platitudes that you try to impress your parents with. We're The Human League, we're much cleverer than you, and this is called "Dance Like a Star".' Shedding their prog past, The Human League began to develop a new aesthetic: not art-rock so much as art-pop. Highbrows aligning themselves with commercial dance pop (Abba, Eurodisco, Chic), they now sneered at middlebrow studenty notions of deep 'n' meaningful (the Pink Floyd/Cure/Radiohead continuum). As part of their new-found appreciation for conveyor-belt pop and epic schmaltz, The Human League started to work up all-synthetic cover versions of sixties classics like The Four Tops' 'Reach Out (I'll Be There)' and The Righteous Brothers' 'You've Lost That Lovin' Feeling'.

The next turning point for The Human League occurred courtesy of scenester and perennial catalyst Paul Bowers. His band 2.3 were set to release their debut single, 'Where To Now?', on Fast Product. Bowers loved The Human League's material, especially 'Being Boiled', so he gave a demo tape of the song to Bob Last, who liked it so much he wanted to release it in raw form, without any rerecording. Ian Craig Marsh, responsible for the song's formidable groove of programmed beats and synth-bass, was a huge Funkadelic fan, as was Last. 'When I heard this phenomenal, fat bass riff in the middle of "Being Boiled", it was like a mutant Bootsy Collins riff. I was like, "God, we've got to put this out."' Last's design sensibility also delighted in the League's presentation skills. 'The demo tape came with this cool computer printout manifesto, sort of absurd-futurist.' And he dug the way the band 'played with this whole cultural landscape of kitsch', embracing it while ridiculing it. This aspect came to the fore on 'Circus of Death', the companion track to 'Being Boiled', which Ware once described as 'a subliminal trip through all the very trashiest films'. The story involves an evil clown who runs a nightmare circus and uses the sinister mind-control drug Dominion to pacify the population, with Steve McGarrett from *Hawaii Five-O* flying in to the rescue.

'Being Boiled' b/w 'Circus of Death' was released in June 1978 with the slogan 'Electronically Yours' on its cover. That same month, The Human League made their live debut at the Psalter Lane Art College in Sheffield. To reproduce the tracks, they came up with a solution that was both a pragmatic fix and artistically appealing. 'We went onstage with a

Electronically yours: the cover of The Human League's debut single, 'Being Boiled', 1978

tape-recorder, with the rhythm and bass on tape,' says Marsh. 'We liked the idea of putting the machine where the drummer ought to be, with a spotlight on it. Then we'd come onstage, take our positions by the keyboards, and then very pointedly I'd walk over and press PLAY. We knew this would be a big wind-up to the rock 'n' roll fraternity, the keep-music-live crew. At that time the only people using backing tapes were disco artists doing PAs in nightclubs.'

The first show went well because some art students had erected a wall of badly tuned TV sets behind the band, but subsequent gigs suffered because The Human League weren't much of a spectacle. 'Me and Martyn were static behind the synths,' says Marsh, while Oakey was rigid with stage fright and not fond of dancing. Then a Psalter Lane art student called Adrian Wright approached them and offered to rectify their image deficit with slide projections. 'Adrian had access to professional Kodak slide machines: he could hire or scam them off the college,' says Marsh. So The Human League acquired its fourth member, giving him the title 'Director of Visuals'. 'How insane is that, a group that has a member who's on equal status but doesn't play any music?' marvels Ware.

Wright was an obsessive collector of pulp ephemera: *Man from U.N.C.L.E.* cards, toy Daleks, Rin Tin Tin books, memorabilia from Gerry Anderson's marionette series *Thunderbirds* and *Stingray*. 'If you went round to Adrian's bedsit, every single square inch of wall space, from floor to ceiling, was full of comics and toys,' says Ware. But Wright also had a fascination with celebrity culture, says Oakey: 'people who manipulated the media to their own advantage. He was absolutely fascinated by the Kennedys and Hitler, to the point where some people thought he was fascist. But, in fact, he was just interested in their use of image and propaganda.' For The Human League, Wright developed an increasingly complex set of slide projections, juxtaposing imagery from science and technology (rockets, graphs, diagrams, oil rigs), nature (flora and fauna) and popular culture (erotica, celebrities, landmarks like the Statue of Liberty, advertisements). 'The first time we had the slides, this free gig at the Limit in Sheffield, was our first really successful show,' says Marsh. 'The set was quite polished by that point too, and maybe we'd begun to incorporate covers like "You've Lost That Loving Feeling".' That song was both a crowd-pleaser and a striking gesture, almost transgressive. 'No one did covers really. During punk, you were supposed to do original material.'

Following 'Being Boiled' and their first gigs outside Sheffield, The Human League started to garner celebrity endorsements. David Bowie hailed them as a glimpse of pop's future; they played in Europe on the same bill as Devo and Iggy Pop; they were invited to support Siouxsie & The Banshees on tour, for which they made their own fibreglass 'riot shields' to protect the synths from lobbed beer. The partnership with Fast Product blossomed, with Bob Last functioning creatively almost as a fifth member of the band. Eventually, he became their manager. 'Bob had this fantastic sensibility where everything was an art event,' says Ware. 'Fast Product was disseminating the idea of art and music being combined; something I'd always been obsessed with.'

Along with a passion for concept and presentation, the League and Last also shared the same anti-hippy, anti-slacker stance, a sensibility later crystallized in the title of the Fast Product compilation *Rigour Discipline and Disgust*. 'The whole idea of hippies sitting around smoking dope all day was anathema to us,' says Ware. 'We were into action, this super-Protestant must-work-all-day outlook that is very much part of Sheffield.' The Human League's second release for Fast Product was a tribute to 'the worker'. *The Dignity of Labour* consisted of four electronic instrumentals inspired by the Soviet space programme. Each offered a different slant on a central concept: the extent to which 'modern technology depends almost entirely upon the worker'. In this case Russian miners toiled deep beneath the earth's crust, excavating the coal needed to make steel, the steel in turn being turned into gantries for Yuri Gagarin's spaceship. Gagarin appears on the EP's front cover as a splendidly isolated figure walking across a Moscow square to receive a medal for being the first human in outer space. The EP came with a free flexidisc, which documented – in true Brechtian fashion – the band and Last debating the sleeve's image. At the end Oakey makes a brief statement about the concept EP's theme: individualism versus collectivism.

The Dignity of Labour was released in April 1979, on the eve of the General Election – a massive defeat for the Labour government, heralding an era in which individualism would be championed at the expense of collective values. 'You couldn't live in Sheffield and not be aware that the industrial era was crumbling,' says Last. 'So, on one level, the record was a totally serious hymn to the dignity of workers, but at the same time it was imbued with many levels of irony, doubt, and alienation.' Despite its timely resonances and atmospheric, ahead-of-its-time electronica, however, the EP's pensive instrumentals confused most 'Being Boiled' fans.

Last believed there was no point in putting out a third League single on Fast and decided to secure a major-label deal for the group. Approaching the big companies again, The Human League pitched themselves as the Next Big Thing in music: a wave of positivity after punk's nihilism and outrage. 'Blind Youth', the first song on their demo tape, ridiculed fashionable doom-and-gloom mongers, especially people who depict modern urban life as some kind of dystopian nightmare. 'High-rise living's not so bad,' sings Oakey, a dig aimed equally at J. G. Ballard and The Clash. 'Dehumanization is such a big word/It's been around since Richard III'. Firmly rejecting punk's 'no future' posturing, The Human League exhorted the blind youth of Britain to 'Take hope . . . your time is due/Big fun come soon . . . *Now* is calling'.

*

THE HUMAN LEAGUE

THE DIGNITY OF LABOUR
PTS.1–4

Cover of The Human League's second release, *The Dignity of Labour* EP, featuring cosmonaut Yuri Gagarin and the Soviet masses

Cabaret Voltaire's response to punk was different. To some extent, they went along for the ride. Kirk began to push guitar to the fore; where once all three voices had been used, Mallinder settled into the role of singer, his vocals menacing and low in the mix. The Cabs started playing live regularly, renting rooms above pubs and self-promoting their gigs. And they wangled their way into the punk world, sending off tapes to New Hormones' Richard Boon, who didn't have the cash to release a record but gave them a support slot with Buzzcocks in March 1978. 'It was at the Lyceum. John Cooper Clarke and The Slits were on the same bill. A complete fucking nightmare,' recalls Kirk. 'Full of crazed punk rockers. We got covered in spit. It wasn't just us, though – someone threw an iron bar at the Buzzcocks.'

167

Shortly after the Lyceum gig, Cabaret Voltaire moved their operational base from Chris Watson's attic to a building called Western Works. The Cabs' new HQ had formerly been the office of the Sheffield Federation of Young Socialists. 'If you look at old photos of us rehearsing at Western Works, you'll see this wall behind us covered with all these old socialist posters from the sixties and seventies. We left them there 'cos we thought it made a nice backdrop.' Having a space to hang out and work at any hour of the day was a breakthrough, says Kirk. 'It made a big difference having somewhere to meet – sometimes just to have a spliff or listen to music, sometimes to make our music or get other bands in there and produce them. I used to describe Western Works as being like Andy Warhol's Factory on a fifty-pence budget!'

The critical threshold for the group, though, came with the acquisition of their own multitrack tape-machine and mixing desk. Now they could make recordings of good enough sound quality to release. This was the logical fulfilment of the do-it-yourself impulse – you didn't even need to hire a studio and deal with the resident recalcitrant engineer; you could record-it-yourself and spend as much time fine-tuning as you liked. Through the eighties and into the techno nineties, this kind of self-sufficient entrepreneurial collective would become widespread. In 1978, Cabaret Voltaire were developing the model for a kind of post-socialist micro-capitalism, an autonomy that represented – if not exactly resistance – then certainly grass-roots resilience in the face of top-down corporate culture. 'When you have your own studio, you don't have to be beholden to some record company that's paying the bills,' says Kirk. 'Western Works gave us the freedom to do what we wanted.'

Yet Cabaret Voltaire couldn't entirely do-it-themselves at first. Which is where the avuncular generosity of Geoff Travis came into play. 'Rough Trade advanced us enough money to buy the four-track and mixing desk,' says Kirk. Actually recorded before they set up the new studio, the group's debut record, *Extended Play*, was released by Rough Trade in October 1978. The four-song EP kicked off a remarkable run of releases via the label that lasted until 1982 and included six classic singles and four landmark long-players, plus numerous live albums and the odd mini-LP.

Somewhere between 1977 and 1979, the classic Cabaret Voltaire sound took shape: the hissing high hats and squelchy snares of the rhythm-generator; Watson's smears of synth slime; Mallinder's dankly pulsing bass; and Kirk's spikes of shattered-glass guitar. Everything coalesces on singles like 'Silent Command' and 'Seconds Too Late' to

CABARET VOLTAIRE

'EXTENDED PLAY.'

Cover of Cabaret Voltaire's first record, *Extended Play*, 1978. L to R: Chris Watson, Richard H. Kirk, Stephen Mallinder

create a stalking hypno-groove feel somewhere between death disco and Eastern Bloc skank. On other singles – 'Nag Nag Nag', 'Jazz the Glass' – there's an almost charming sixties garage-punk feel, the fuzz-tone guitar and Farfisa organ vamps recalling ? & The Mysterians or The Seeds.

Having originally played clarinet, an instrument redolent of Jethro Tull more than PiL, Kirk swiftly joined post-punk's pantheon of guitar innovators. You can hear the chill wind, the icy silver-machine whoosh of his guitar sound emerging on 'The Set Up' on the debut EP. Elsewhere, there's a choppy rhythm style, equal parts reggae's scratchy afterbeat and the itchy funk of Can's Michael Karoli. What really grabs your attention is Kirk's trademark timbre: a sensuous, brittle distortion like blistered metal or burning chrome, needling its way deep into your ear canal. Typically fed through delay units and heavy with sustain, Kirk's guitar arcs and recedes through reverberant yet claustrophobic soundscapes, like the dead chambers of bunkers or underground missile silos. 'Being a telephone engineer and good with electronics, Chris Watson was able to custom-build me a fuzzbox using this circuit he'd got from a magazine,' says Kirk. 'So no one else had this sound.' Another Cabaret Voltaire hallmark was dehumanizing Mallinder's vocal via creepy treatments that made him sound reptilian, alien or, at the extreme, like some kind of metallic or mineralized being. On 'Silent Command', for instance, Mal's vocal bubbles like molten glass being blown into distended shapes.

As committed to multimedia as The Human League but oriented more towards sensory overload, at their live shows Cabaret Voltaire used slide and cine projectors to create a backdrop of unsynchronized, cut-up imagery: French porn, TV news, images from movies. Bombarding the audience with data related to Cabaret Voltaire's conception of themselves as reporters. 'We were more like: "Let's just present the facts and let people make up their own minds,"' says Kirk. 'We got some grief through that approach.' He says the first EP's 'Do the Mussolini (Headkick)' – a song loosely inspired by the death of the Fascist dictator at the hands, and feet, of an avenging Italian mob – got misunderstood as somehow pro-fascist. 'We'd get National Front people coming to gigs 'cos they'd got the wrong idea. But, at the same time, we kinda liked the ambiguity.'

Although Cabaret Voltaire never propagandized or took an explicitly judgemental stance, their music was inseparable from the current events of the late seventies and early eighties. Visiting the USA for the first time in November 1979 inspired *The Voice of America*: they caught wind of the impending shift to the right with Reagan and his born-again Christian constituency. 'We were fascinated by America but aware of its darker side,' says Kirk. 'A big novelty for a bunch of kids from England, where TV finished at eleven o'clock and there were only three channels, was the fact that that America had all-night TV and loads of stations. We just locked into this televangelist Eugene Scott, who had a low-rent show that was all about raising money. And the only reason he wanted the money was to stay on the air.'

Scott's voice ended up on the Cabs' classic single 'Sluggin for Jesus', but before that came 1980's mini-album *Three Mantras*, an oblique response to events in the Middle East. Its two tracks, 'Eastern Mantra' and 'Western Mantra', contrasted the evil twins of fundamentalist Islam and born-again Christian America, beloved enemies locked in a clinch of clashing civilizations. 'The whole Afghanistan situation was kicking off, Iran had the American hostages . . . We were taking notice,' recalls Kirk. 'It kind of culminated with *Red Mecca*. It's not called that by coincidence. We weren't referencing the fucking Mecca Ballroom in Nottingham!' Purely through its sonic turbulence and tense rhythms, *Red Mecca* also seemed to tap into closer-to-home issues: the urban riots of summer 1981, unrest stoked by mounting unemployment as Thatcher's deflationary policies kicked in, then ignited by insensitive policing in inner-city areas.

If Cabaret Voltaire had any politics, they were of the anarcho-paranoid kind. They blended a Yorkshire-bred bloody-minded intransigence in the face of badge-holders and bureaucrats with the sort of pot-fuelled 'never met a conspiracy theory I didn't like' attitude you found throughout squatland. This almost superstitious attitude to power as a demonic, omnipresent force was boosted by reading Burroughs and absorbing his notion of 'Control' – a multi-tentacled yet eerily sourceless network of domination and mind-coercion. 'Being in a state of paranoia is a very healthy state to be in,' Mallinder once said. 'It gives you a permanently questioning and searching non-acceptance of situations.'

Along with paranoia, Cabaret Voltaire's other big p-word was 'pornography'. This was something else Burroughs obsessively explored in his fiction. For the Cabs and other Sheffield groups, though, J. G. Ballard was more important in this area – especially his hardcore experimental fiction of the late sixties, such short 'stories' (or 'condensed novels') as 'Plan for the Assassination of Jacqueline Kennedy' and 'Why I Want to Fuck Ronald Reagan', which were both later incorporated into the book-length anti-narrative *The Atrocity Exhibition*. Fusing amoral and clinically described avant-porn with Marshall McLuhan-like insights into the mass media, Ballard probed with forensic precision the grotesque (de)formations of desire stimulated by media overload and celebrity worship: a new psychomythology in which the gods and titanic figures were movie idols like Elizabeth Taylor, politicians like Reagan, and cult leaders like Manson. Tapping into this Ballardian vision of 'the communications landscape we inhabit' as a collective unconsciousness out of which the 'myths of the near-future' were emerging, Cabaret Voltaire pioneered what would eventually become an industrial music hallmark, the use of vocal snippets stolen from movies and TV.

If Cabaret Voltaire were like darkside Pop Art, mass culture dimly perceived through the murky prism of weed and speed, their friends The Human League were the poptimistic version of Warhol. You could imagine the Cabs watching the TV news with the sound off and a spliff burning, marinading their minds in an ambient broth of catastrophe and conflict. Meanwhile, on the other side of Sheffield, The Human League were tuning in to the cartoons, soaps, popular science programmes like James Burke's *Connections* and *Tomorrow's World*, and, naturally, *Top of the Pops*. The convoluted route by which they themselves appeared on *TOTP* is another story, to which we'll return.

10

JUST STEP SIDEWAYS: The Fall, Joy Division and the Manchester Scene

The Fall. Joy Division. Martin Hannett. The Passage. Factory Records. A Certain Ratio. Durutti Column.

In the late seventies, The Fall's singer Mark E. Smith rode his moped past an industrial estate called Trafford Park en route to his job in Manchester's docks. Legend has it he often passed a young man, dressed in the same donkey jacket, on *his* way to work: Ian Curtis, future frontman of Joy Division. 'It was a bit spooky. They looked quite like each other,' recalls Una Baines, Smith's girlfriend at the time and keyboard player in The Fall.

Joy Division and The Fall had much else in common: similar backgrounds (upper working class verging on the petit bourgeois), similar education (grammar school) and similar jobs (Smith was a shipping clerk; Curtis and Joy Division's guitarist Barney Sumner and bassist Peter Hook all did clerical work for the local council). They loved the same bands, too: The Doors, Velvet Underground, The Stooges, Can. Yet, despite rehearsing in the same building and even playing on some bills together, Joy Division and The Fall never acknowledged each other's existence. As if by tacit agreement, they engaged in a taciturn struggle to be *the* definitive Manchester band of the post-punk era. 'We never spoke to each other!' laughs Martin Bramah, The Fall's guitarist. 'I think they're great now, but at the time The Fall and Joy Division were definitely contending.'

Fronted by singers who exuded a shamanic aura, Joy Division and The Fall conveyed a sense of strangeness and estrangement that travels far beyond the specifics of time and place. But it's hard to imagine them coming from anywhere other than 1970s Manchester. Something about

173

the city's gloom and decay seemed to seep deep into the fabric of their very different sounds. Although he didn't identify the place by name, Smith immortalized the pollution-belching Trafford Park on 'Industrial Estate', an early Fall classic. 'The crap in the air will fuck up your face,' he jeers. 'That song is a very funny take on Manchester's history of having been the cradle of capitalism and then, by the 1970s, its grave,' says Richard Boon, who funded the recording of The Fall's first EP but then couldn't afford to release it on New Hormones.

'Grim beyond belief' is how Jon Savage describes his first impressions of Manchester as a Londoner relocating there in 1978. Even today, after a redevelopment boom, the bleakness endures in pockets. A partial facelift has dotted the city centre with flashy designer wine bars and slick corporate offices, but the old nineteenth-century architecture abides: sombre, imposing edifices testifying to the pride and deep pockets of Manchester's self-made industrial barons. The dark-red brickwork seems to soak up what scant daylight emanates from the typically slate-grey skies. Venture outside the town centre and the city's past as the world capital of mechanized cotton manufacture becomes more evident: railway viaducts, canals the colour of lead, converted warehouses and factories, and cleared lots littered with masonry shards and refuse.

By the 1970s, the world's first industrial city had become one of the first to enter the post-industrial era. The wealth had evaporated but the desolate, denatured environment persisted. Attempts to renovate only made matters worse. As in other cities across the UK, urban planners demolished the old Victorian terraced housing. Long-established working-class communities were broken up and the 'slum' residents forcibly rehoused in what soon turned out to be laboratories of social atomization: high-rise blocks and council estates. For Una Baines, this redevelopment figures as a kind of primal trauma: she remembers 'my mum crying on the corner of the street when they knocked down our row of houses in Collyhurst'. Frank Owen of the Manchester post-punk outfit Manicured Noise fulminates: 'Those planners should be hung for what they did. They did more damage to Manchester than the German bombers did in World War Two – and all under this guise of benevolent social democracy.'

In the pre-punk seventies Manchester seemed to have all the bad aspects of urban life – pollution, eyesore architecture, all-enveloping dreariness – with barely any of its subcultural compensations. 'There really was nothing going on until punk,' recalls Boon. 'The industry was

174

dying, the clothes were dreadful, the hair was awful.' Manchester's starved souls grabbed for whatever stimulus or sparkle they could find: fashion, books, esoteric music, drugs.

The Fall didn't go in much for style. Scrawny, lank-haired and typically wearing a scruffy pullover of indeterminate hue, Smith looked like a grown-up version of the runty schoolkid in *Kes*, Ken Loach's 1969 film. But The Fall were mad for the other three escape routes – literature, music and illegal substances. In its earliest incarnation, The Fall resembled a poetry group more than a rock band. They'd hang out at Baines's flat and read their scribblings to one another. 'We all wrote words then, not just Mark,' recalls Bramah. Although they would have spurned the word 'intellectual' – too close to the despised world of students and higher education – that's what the four original members of The Fall were: working-class intellectuals; bookworms, really, making good use of their library cards, devouring everything from Burroughs and Dick to Yeats and Camus. Their name came from the latter's novel *The Fall*, which bassist Tony Friel happened to be reading.

The Fall, Manchester, 1977. L to R: Una Baines, Martin Bramah, Karl Burns, Mark E. Smith, Tony Friel
Photo by Kevin Cummir

As for music, The Fall preferred what Smith called the 'real heavy stuff': drug music, mostly, but not blissed-out pastoralism or cosmic buffoonery. Instead, The Fall tranced out to the primal monotony of Can, the methedrine-scorched white noise of Velvet Underground, and sixties 'punkadelic' bands like The Seeds (who had just one keyboard riff, which they endlessly recycled). 'This is the three "R"s . . . Repetition repetition repetition,' quipped Smith on The Fall's mission statement 'Repetition'. Scorning 'fancy music' – the overproduced mainstream rock of the day – 'Repetition' fulfilled Smith's early goal of 'raw music with really weird vocals on top'. The rawness was supplied by Bramah's thin, wheedling guitar lines, Baines's wonky organ jabs (played on the cheap 'n' nasty Snoopy keyboard, rated by *Sounds* as the absolute worst on the market), Friel's capering bass, and Karl Burns' ramshackle drums. The freak vocal element came from Smith's half-sung, half-spoken drawl and wizened insolence.

In an early interview, Smith described The Fall as 'head music with energy' – 'head' meaning not cerebral or anti-dance but the sixties idea of a 'head': someone into turning on and tripping out. Manchester had a strong underground drug culture, not so much a 1960s hangover, says Bramah, as the true, if slightly belated, arrival of the sixties in the early seventies. 'We learned from people older than us, like John Cooper Clarke, the Manchester poet who lived in the same area as us, Prestwich. He was ten years older, from the sixties really. We were the next generation. We saw all the hippies who'd blown their brains out, and we felt we were wiser than that, but still attracted to the drug experience.'

Circa 1973, a few years before the group existed as a musical entity, sixteen-year-old Mark E. Smith used to take acid and go round clubs wearing swastika armbands (a proto-punk gesture of pure provocation rather than an indication of fascist sympathies). Bramah recalls being given 'microdots' and the next day going to Heaton Park, 'this stately home that is the nearest thing Manchester has to a common, where we dropped the acid and spent the whole day tripping'. Later, they discovered that Heaton Park was renowned among local 'heads' for its psilocybin mushrooms. 'There were just *fields* of them you could pick, and it was a totally free source of entertainment,' says Bramah. 'From then on, we were kind of pickled in mushrooms and LSD, really exploring music, and discovering ourselves.'

Amphetamines also made their mark on The Fall. Speed stoked the group's attitude – Smith's searing, see-through-you gaze, the icy arrogance. And it shaped the sound: the white lightning rush of discords. Smith sounds like someone speed-rapping, the words spat out with an oracular urgency, encrypted but mesmerizing. High doses of speed create a kind of eureka sensation: the user feels he's accessed a truth invisible to others, can see occult connections. On *Live at the Witch Trials*, the group's 1979 debut, 'Underground Medecin' and 'Frightened' evoke the positive and negative sides of amphetamine abuse: the rush that lights up your nervous system ('I found a reason not to die,' Smith exults, 'the spark inside.') versus the hyper-tense twitchiness of stimulant-induced paranoia. In 1981 Smith talked about the downside of 'taking a lot of speed' over a long period: 'you start looking in mirrors and getting ulcers'. But The Fall carried on writing songs like 'Totally Wired' and covering sixties amphetamine hymns like 'Mr Pharmacist'.

The 'pharmacist' in that song is a drug dealer, a street punk peddling 'energy'. The Fall were obsessed with the double standards surrounding drugs – the way some chemicals are proscribed while others are prescribed. Training as a psychiatric nurse at Prestwich Hospital, Baines came back every day from work and disgorged stories about the mistreatment and neglect she'd witnessed – including the use of downers to pacify the inmates. Her talk filtered into Smith's lyrics: 'Repetition' refers to electro-shock therapy (after you've had some, alleges Smith, you *lose* your love of repetition), while The Fall's 1979 single 'Rowche Rumble' got its title from Hoffman La Roche, the pharmaceutical multinational who dominated the market for antidepressants.

Drugs of the socially sanctioned kind flooded Manchester in the seventies. 'And if you get a bit of depression/Ask the doctor for some Valium,' Smith taunts on 'Industrial Estate'. Numbing and often incapacitating tranquillizers were massively over-prescribed to 'help' ordinary people – menopausal housewives, troubled teenagers, wage slaves cracked by stress and boredom – not so much manage as *be manageable*. In an area like Hulme – whose infamous Crescents were a paradigm of the 1960s housing project gone wrong – antidepressants were dispensed so freely (some quarter of a million tablets in 1977 alone) that they verged on a form of social control. At the same time, Hulme illustrated the double standards concerning drugs that Smith captured in the title 'Underground Medecin': the Crescents were also where most of Manchester's bathtub speed was manufactured.

Pills feature in 'Bingo-Master's Break-out', the title track of The Fall's debut EP not as a way of coping with soul-crushing mundanity but of escaping it permanently. A guy whose job is organizing other people's recreation – the bingo master – looks into his future and, seeing only encroaching baldness and years 'wasting time in numbers and rhyme', opts to end his life with a handful of pills washed down with booze. Smith had visited a bingo hall with his parents and been stunned by how regimented and mechanical the 'fun' was. The evening's mind-dulling entertainment formed a grim mirror image to the daytime's soul-destroying labour. 'It wasn't like a place you'd go for your leisure; it was a glorified works canteen,' Smith told *Sounds*. 'And people were going there straight from work.'

Macabre and hilarious, 'Bingo-Master's Break-out' typified The Fall's peculiar brand of social surrealism. Bramah described the band's songs as '*Coronation Street* on acid': 'It was us sitting in pubs, munching magic mushrooms and observing the daft things people did.' In the grand tradition of British misanthropic satire, Smith's invective seems to come from somewhere outside the class system: a vantage point from which everything seems equally absurd – the privileged upper class and middle-management bourgeoisie with their pretensions and illusions, for sure, but also the proles with their inverted snobbery, escapist pleasures, and grumbling acquiescence to the way things are and ever shall be. As unsparing towards 'his own' people as to everybody else, Smith's withering gaze scanned the whole of society, and found only grotesquerie. In many ways he resembled the 'judge penitent' of Camus's *The Fall*, who weighs up everybody's failings and hypocrisies, his own included. In the song 'New Puritan' Smith declared 'Our decadent sins/Will reap discipline'.

In the early days The Fall were regarded as heavy-duty politicos. Songs like 'Hey! Fascist' and 'Race Hatred' got them briefly tagged as New Wave commies, a misunderstanding partly based on the fact that bassist Friel had once been a member of the Young Communist League. But Baines says she and Smith did attend 'loads of political meetings – things like the International Marxists. We were never members, just interested in checking out the range of opinions.' Baines was also a forthright feminist who'd rejected her Catholic upbringing while still at her all-girls school, because the Bible was so anti-woman. 'There was a lot going on in Manchester with feminism then – the first rape crisis centres and women's refuges, abortion rights were hotly fought for – and we were right in the middle of that.'

In 1977–8 The Fall played numerous Rock Against Racism benefits, but, like many post-punk groups, they became disenchanted with RAR's treatment of music as a mere vehicle for politicizing youth. Soon, they distanced themselves from anything remotely resembling agit-prop or right-on trendy leftyism. Instead, Smith developed a way of writing about 'the real world' that was increasingly elliptical and non-linear. Equally important as subject matter was rock culture. Song after song skewered the platitudes and pieties of hipsters: 'It's the New Thing', 'Music Scene', 'Mere Pseud Mag Ed', 'Look Know', 'Printhead' (the last about an obsessive music-press reader who gets 'dirty fingers' every week perusing the 'inkies'). In interview and song alike, Smith took on the role of meta-pop spectre, stalking the periphery of the post-punk scene and maintaining a scathing running commentary on the failings of The Fall's peer groups.

One of his most famous pronouncements was his description of The Fall themselves as 'Northern white crap that talks back' (in 'Crap Rap 2', from *Witch Trials*). It captured the basic Fall stance of surly intransigence. 'I don't fully understand it myself,' Smith admitted to *Sounds*. 'It's meant to be, like, mystical.' The Fall assumed the mantle of perpetual outsiders, resisting being assimilated, pigeonholed or explained. In a way, Smith just added a kind of shamanic edge to what's simply standard-issue Mancunian cockiness – itself a sort of folk-memory survival from the city's industrial heyday, when Manchester 'kept all the machinery going for the rest of the country', as Baines puts it. Being proud of the city's industrial might, though, didn't mean you sided with the factory boss; quite the opposite. Throughout the nineteenth century, Manchester was a stronghold for working-class radicalism, from the machinery-wrecking Luddites to the vote-demanding Chartists. The co-author of *The Communist Manifesto*, Friedrich Engels, lived in Manchester for a time and wrote *The Condition of the Working Class in England* after observing the textile industry.

Punishing work in hostile conditions forged a kind of spiritual mettle – indomitable, tough as new nails. 'Fiery Jack', the Fall's fourth single, offered a coruscating portrait of one of Manchester's finest sons, the hard-bitten product of five generations of industrial life. Fiery Jack is a forty-five-year-old pub stalwart who's spent three decades on the piss, ignoring the pain from his long-suffering kidneys. Surviving on meat pies and other revolting bar snacks, Jack is an inexhaustible font of anecdotes and rants. The music sounds stubborn, incorrigible – a white-line rush of rockabilly drums and rhythm guitar like sparks shooting out of a severed cable. Speed might just be another of Jack's poisons, judging by his refusal to go 'back to the slow life' and lines like 'Too fast to write/I just burn burn burn'. Based on older blokes Smith had met in Manchester pubs, Jack was 'the sort of guy I can see myself as in twenty years', he told *Sounds*. 'These old guys ... have more guts than these kids will ever have.' Jack was the lad who grew old, battered by hard work and harder pleasure, but who never gave up and never gave in.

Joy Division began life as Warsaw – to most contemporary ears, a fairly undistinguished, punk-inflected hard-rock band. But if you listen to the early demos and strain your ears, you can hear a metallic gleam of difference – 'metal' in both the serrated and the Black Sabbath senses of the word. 'Digital', the group's first recording as Joy Division, sounds not a million miles from Sabbath's 'Paranoid': a dark, fast pummel, a full-tilt dirge fusing pace and ponderousness. Sabbath's Bill Ward claimed that 'Most people live on a permanent down but just aren't aware of it. We're trying to express it for people.' Ian Curtis's harrowed voice and words offered an equally 'heavy' vision of life. Look at his lyrics and certain words and images appear repeatedly: coldness, pressure, darkness, crisis, failure, collapse, loss of control. There are numberless scenarios of futile exertion, purposes 'turned sour' and doom 'closing in'. Above all, there are terminal words: endless 'end's and 'final's. But Joy Division's reference points were less lumpen than heavy metal's – not pulp super-hero comics or bastardized blues, but J. G. Ballard and Bowie's *Low*. Rather than the invulnerable 'Iron Man', Barney Sumner's guitar evokes the wounded, penetrable metal of *Crash* – twisted, buckled, splayed, torn.

Joy Division's originality really became apparent once they slowed down. Shedding punk's fast, distortion-thickened sound, the music grew stark and sparse. Hook's bass carries the melody, Sumner's guitar leaves gaps rather than fills the mix with dense riffage, and Steve Morris's drums seem to circle the rim of a crater. Curtis intones from 'a lonely place' at the centre of this empty expanse. All that space in Joy Division's music was something critics immediately noticed: it would have been hard to miss, even if Curtis hadn't put up signposts in the form of titles like 'Interzone' or lyrical references to 'no man's land'.

The group's original name was inspired by 'Warszawa', a haunting instrumental on side two of *Low*. Like the word 'Berlin', 'Warsaw' also appealed because of its World War Two and Cold War connotations: the uprising of the Jewish ghetto, the razing of the Old City, and the fabulous desolation of a city rebuilt rapidly after the war – all spartan tower-blocks, government ministries straight out of Orwell's *1984*, and disquietingly wide streets designed to allow Soviet tanks to roll down them should the need arise. The band's new name had even more dismal resonance. It came from *House of Dolls*, a 1965 novel written by a concentration-camp survivor who took the pen-name Ka-Tzetnik 135633 from the prisoner number branded on his arm. The novel is written from the point of view of a fourteen-year-old girl sent to Auschwitz's 'Camp Labour Via Joy', the 'joy division' where females were kept as sex slaves for German troops on leave from the Russian front.

You can argue, as Steve Morris does, that the name indicated identification with the victims rather than their tormentors: 'It was the flipside of it, rather than being the master race – the oppressed rather than the oppressor.' You can also talk, as Barney Sumner has, about the group being preoccupied with keeping alive memories of World War Two, the sacrifices of their parents' and grandparents' generations in the struggle of Good against Evil. Still, Joy Division's use of Nazi imagery stemmed at least as much from morbid fascination; and, as such, was often in questionable taste. On the mini-album *Short Circuit: Live at the Electric Circus* – a document of the Manchester punk scene – Curtis can be heard screaming at the crowd, 'Do you all remember Rudolf Hess?' In June 1978 the group self-released their first record, the Warsaw EP *An Ideal for Living*. The sleeve featured a drawing of a blond-haired Hitler Youth drummer boy and a photograph of a German stormtrooper pointing a gun at a small Polish Jewish boy. In the early days Sumner used the Germanic-sounding stage name Albrecht, and the group's image – grey shirts, very short hair, thin ties – had a monochrome austerity and discipline redolent of totalitarianism.

At a time when neo-Nazis were marching through the streets of Britain's major cities, when racial attacks were on the rise, some believed that *any* ambiguity in one's allegiances was irresponsible. Morris says the flak the group received – 'We knew we weren't Nazis but we kept on getting letters in the *NME* slating us for harbouring Eichmann in the coal cellar!' – just 'encouraged us to keep on doing it, 'cos that's the kind of people we are'. But the flirtations went a little further than just a 'perverse joke'. Years later, Hook and Sumner talked candidly about the fascination of fascism. Sumner enthused about how, out of 'all that hate and all that dominance', shone forth the beauty of the art, the architecture, the design, even the uniforms. Hook admitted the dark allure of 'a certain physical sensation you get from flirting with something like that . . . We thought it was a very, very strong feeling.'

Ian Curtis. Photo by Kevin Cummins

Curtis's obsession with Germany – according to his wife Deborah, their wedding featured a hymn sung to the tune of the German national anthem – stemmed partly from the Berlin chic of his glam heroes, Reed, Pop and Bowie. He was also intrigued by the mass psychology of fascism – the way a charismatic leader could bewitch an entire population into doing, or accepting, irrational and monstrous things. The early song 'Walked in Line' is about those who just did what they were told, committing crimes in a 'hypnotic trance'. An explorer of literature's darker precincts, such as Conrad and Kafka, Curtis simply enjoyed contemplating humanity's bottomless capacity for inhumanity. He also shared Una Baines's obsession with psychiatric disorders: one of his relatives worked in a mental home and brought back grim stories, while Curtis himself briefly worked in a rehabilitation centre for people with mental and physical disabilities. As Deborah Curtis mordantly observes in her memoir, 'It struck me that all Ian's spare time was spent reading and thinking about human suffering.'

Curtis' doomy baritone and obsession with the dark side often got him compared to Jim Morrison. Indeed, The Doors were one of the singer's favourite bands. Joy Division's 'Shadowplay' is like 'LA Woman' turned inside out, the latter's rolling, virile propulsion reduced to a bleak transit across a city that could hardly be less like sun-baked southern California. Gaping yet claustrophobic, Joy Division's space is the opposite of the utopian kind you find in sixties rock – the freeway-as-frontier imagery and 'explode into space' euphoria of Steppenwolf's 'Born to be Wild', the outward-bound cosmic surge of Pink Floyd and Hendrix.

All of that space in Joy Division's music needed room to breathe. Playing small clubs, they were 'a bit of a racket', says John Keenan, the Leeds promoter behind the Futurama festivals of post-punk music. 'But the next time I saw them, in a big hall, with a bit of echo, it suddenly made sense. They weren't a club band; they were meant to play stadiums.'

As Factory Records' house producer, Martin Hannett dedicated himself to capturing and intensifying Joy Division's eerie spatiality. Punk records typically simulated the boxy, in-your-face sound of the small club gig. The fast tempos and fuzzed-out guitars suited the tinny, two-dimensional sound reproduction of the seven-inch single – music for teenagers with their transistor radios and cheap record-players, as opposed to adults with proper stereo systems. But Hannett believed punk was sonically conservative precisely because of its refusal to exploit the recording studio's capacity to create space.

Factory's Tony Wilson talked of Hannett's genius in terms of synaesthesia: 'He could *see* sound, shape it, rebuild it.' This 'really visual sense that most people just don't have' was enhanced by Hannett's being a major spliffhead. Hash, he told one interviewer, is 'good for the ears'. Like John Cooper Clarke, with whom he worked, Hannett was a sixties character, a fan of psychedelia and dub. He also adored the psychogeography of urban space, talking about how 'deserted public places, empty office blocks . . . give me a rush'.

'Digital', Hannett's first Joy Division production, was titled after his favourite sonic toy, the AMS digital delay line. Hannett used the AMS and other digital effects coming on to the market in the late seventies to achieve 'ambience control'. He could wrap a song, or individual instruments within a track, inside a particular spatial 'aura', as if they came from imaginary rooms with real-seeming dimensions and sound reflections. Hannett talked of creating 'sonic holograms' through layering 'sounds and reverbs'. His most distinctive use of the AMS digital delay was subtle, though: he applied a micro-second delay to the drums that was barely audible but which created a sense of enclosed space – a vaulted sound, like the music was recorded in a mausoleum. Hannett also wove subliminal shimmers deep into the recesses of Joy Division's records. And he loved the occasional extreme effect: on the debut *Unknown Pleasures*, he miked up the clanking of an antique lift for 'Insight' and incorporated smashing glass on 'I Remember Nothing'.

In a reversal of the super-slick seventies mega-rock way of doing things (overdubs galore, musicians recorded separately and then reunited at the mixing desk, etc.), punk bands were often recorded playing together in real time. Hannett took it back the other way to an extreme degree: he demanded totally clean and clear 'sound separation' not just for individual instruments, but for each element of the drum kit. 'Typically on tracks he considered to be potential singles, he'd get me to play each drum on its own to avoid any bleed-through of sound,' sighs Morris. 'First the bass-drum part. Then the snare part. Then the high hats.' Not only was this tediously protracted; it created a mechanistic, disjointed effect. 'The natural way to play drums is all at the same time. So I'd end up with my legs black and blue 'cos I'd be tapping on them quietly to do the other bits of the kit that he wasn't recording.' This dehumanizing treatment – essentially turning Morris into a drum machine – was typical of Hannett's rather high-handed attitude to musicians. But the disjointedness certainly added to the music's alienated feel.

You can hear it on one of the high points of the Hannett–Joy Division partnership, 'She's Lost Control', with its mechano-disco drum loop, tom-toms like ball-bearings, a bassline like steel cable undulating in strict time, and a guitar like a contained explosion – as if the track's only real rock-out element has been cordoned off.

Hannett loved to play mind games with musicians to create tension. On one occasion, he forced Morris to dismantle his entire drum kit because of an unwanted rattling sound (which Hannett may have imagined or simply invented). 'Sometimes he'd go to sleep under the desk to create a state of panic,' Chris Nagle, the studio engineer on *Unknown Pleasures* and the singles 'Transmission' and 'Atmosphere', has said. 'Then he'd just impose his will on people and they'd go back into the studio really wound up.' Nagle's diabetes became another weapon for Hannett: he'd turn the studio air conditioning to its coldest setting, supposedly for the engineer's benefit. 'We'd literally be shivering at the back,' says Morris. Hannett wanted to discourage the musicians from sticking around after they'd laid down their parts, so he could have free rein with the material. But the Arctic temperature in Strawberry Studios seems to have seeped into Joy Division's music – you can almost see Curtis's breath forming condensation in the cold air.

At the time, Joy Division hated what Hannett did to their music. *Unknown Pleasures* sounded drained and emaciated to their ears; they'd rather have had something closer to the full-on assault of their live performances. But on the album Hannett used one of his favourite devices – the Marshall Time Modulator – to suppress the guitars and other instruments. 'It just made things sound smaller,' says Morris. 'A big tom-tom riff of mine would come out sounding like coconuts being hit with matchsticks!' Yet, without this denuded production, *Unknown Pleasures* would not have been such a strikingly wintry soundscape.

Released at the height of British summertime – June 1979 – the album caught the eye as well as the ear: the cover, designed by Factory's art director Peter Saville, was a matt-black void apart from a small scientific diagram of rippling lines whose crinkled crests and sharp slopes resemble the outlines of a mountain range. Barney Sumner had found the diagram in the *Cambridge Encyclopaedia of Science*: it's a Fourier analysis of 100 consecutive light spasms emitted by the pulsar CP 1919. Left behind when a massive sun exhausts its fuel and collapses in on itself, a pulsar is highly electromagnetic and emits regular flashes of intense energy, like a lighthouse in the pitch-black night. Perhaps that's how Ian Curtis was beginning to see himself – as a magnetic star sending out a signal, a beacon in the darkness. And could he have known that pulsars belong to a distinct class of heavenly bodies known as 'misanthropic' or 'isolated' neutron stars?

People gradually started to tune in to the signal. The slow-burning success of *Unknown Pleasures* and the hypnotic single 'Transmission' gave Joy Division an increasingly obsessive following, nicknamed the 'Cult With No Name' and, according to stereotype, consisting of intense young men dressed in grey overcoats. Joy Division understood the power and attraction of mystique from the start (some text on *An Ideal for Living* declared, 'this is not a concept EP, it is an enigma'). The band's refusal to do interviews (after some early bad experiences) only enhanced their aura. The cult expanded through the second half of 1979, as Joy Division played steadily more prestigious gigs. In August they headlined the Leigh Festival, a collaboration between Factory and its Liverpool counterpart Zoo; in September they performed near the top of the bill at John Keenan's Futurama Festival; in the last months of the year they supported (and upstaged) Buzzcocks on the latter's UK tour.

'Atmosphere', Joy Division's breathtaking next single, would surely have given the group their first hit in March 1980 if it had come out on Factory. Instead, they gave it to the obscure, ultra-arty French label Sordide Sentimental, who released it as a tiny limited edition under the title *Licht und Blindheit*. With its vast drumscape, permafrost synths and cascading chimes, 'Atmosphere' sounds like nothing else in rock, except maybe some dream collaboration between Nico and Phil Spector. The image on the original Sordide Sentimental release – a hooded monk, his back turned to the viewer, stalking a snow-covered Alpine peak – captures the moment when a certain religiosity began to gather around Joy Division. 'Possessed' is how the normally dry and sardonic Hannett described Curtis in an interview with Jon Savage. 'It was me who said "touched by the hand of God", to a Dutch magazine. He was one of those channels for the Gestalt: the only one I bumped into in that period. A lightning conductor.' You don't need to wax mystical, though, to see Curtis as a seer-like figure whose private pain somehow worked as a prism for the wider culture, refracting the malaise and anguish of Britain in the dying days of the seventies.

That private pain was mundanely specific, though – grown-up problems like a failing marriage, adultery and illness. Curtis had fallen out of love with his wife just as they were having their first child. He'd also become embroiled in an affair with a glamorous, demanding Belgian woman called Annik Honore. And, as if that were not enough, he also had to deal with epilepsy. Strangely, he'd been dancing onstage in a twitchy, convulsive style that resembled an epileptic fit for some time before he suffered his first attack in December 1978. Was he somehow able to channel a latent form of this electrical disorder of the nervous system and transform it into his performance signature? Or did the dance precipitate the condition? Both Deborah Curtis and Barney Sumner recall Curtis becoming friendly with an epileptic girl at the rehabilitation centre where he worked. The inspiration for 'She's Lost Control', she later died during a fit.

No one knows for sure why Curtis became epileptic. But it's clear that the heavy-duty tranquillizers prescribed to control the condition – downers like phenobarbitone and carbamazepine – clouded his mind, sapped his spirits, and made him even more vulnerable to the guilt and confusion caused by his infidelity. Hardly surprising, then, with such a pall hanging over the lead singer, that a 'strange social climate' (as Hannett put it) surrounded the March 1980 sessions for *Closer*, Joy Division's second album. Hannett described the record as 'kabbalistic, locked in its own mysterious world'. Sumner recalled staying up all night, sometimes sleeping in the control room, because 'At night you got a weirder atmosphere.' Compared with *Unknown Pleasures*, the textures of *Closer* are more ethereal and experimental: Peter Hook often used a six-string bass, for more melody, while Sumner built a couple of synthesizers from kits. Morris had acquired a drum synth and fed it through 'the shittiest fuzz pedal you can imagine' to generate the slaughterhouse of hacking and shearing, metal-on-bone noise in the background of 'Atrocity Exhibition', *Closer*'s opener.

In typically repressed British manner, neither Hannett nor Curtis's own bandmates were able to talk to the singer about his problems. Yet, eerily, they appear to have absorbed his pain and recreated it sonically. Listening, it's like you are inside his head, feeling the awful down-swirling drag of terminal depression. Side one is all agony: the swarming knives of 'Atrocity'; the ice-shroud glaze of 'Isolation' – Curtis swathed in a barbiturate haze, his voice mineralized by Hannett's effects. The treadmill motion of 'Passover' sounds like the group's batteries are running down. It's followed by the tough, punitive rock of 'Colony' and 'A Means to an End', on which the drums finally decelerate like a dying machine.

Closer's second side is even more disturbing, but this time on account of its serenity. It's as though Curtis has stopped struggling altogether: the numb trance and narcotic glide of 'Heart and Soul'; the alternately desperate and resigned 'Twenty Four Hours', its beautiful bass like the pulse of a heavy heart, Curtis's voice disconcertingly deep, like the microphone is right inside his chest; the epic colonnades of 'The Eternal', seen through misty eyes, as if Curtis is watching his own funeral procession; finally the listless, clip-clop beat of 'Decades', its synths eroded and washed out, like aged Super-8 home movies of happy childhood memories.

Curtis wrote his lyrics in a trance-like state, with no editing or rewriting. There are allusions to the dead marriage ('a valueless collection of hopes and past desires', 'the sound from broken homes') and to dislocations and the crushing sense of failure ('I'm ashamed of the things I've been put through/I'm ashamed of the person I am'). Most of all, there's fatigue. According to Sumner, Curtis blatantly told him: 'I feel like there's a big whirlpool and I'm being sucked down into it and there's nothing I can do.' The barbiturates Curtis was taking for his epilepsy were like little doses of death, freezing him from the inside. 'The barbs change people's personalities,' said fellow-Factory artist Vini Reilly, who had his own psychological problems and bonded with Curtis in this period. 'You lose sense of reality. That's what happened and he got further and further out, and so far out he couldn't get back.' Songs like 'Isolation' and 'The Eternal' come from the same lifeless emotional landscapes as Nico's *Desertshore* and *The Marble Index*, cut off from the warm-blooded mainland of human contact and fellowship. The last lyric Curtis ever finished, 'In a Lonely Place', featured a death-wish reference to 'caressing the marble and stone'. Reviewers of *Closer* picked up on this sense of the singer as already interred, buried alive in the blues: *Sounds*' Dave McCullough praised Hannett's production as 'the aural equivalent of a rich marble slab'.

In the gap between finishing *Closer* and its release in July 1980, Curtis had already attempted suicide with an overdose of pills. On top of everything else, he was depressed by his worsening epilepsy, which interfered with his ability to fulfil his role in the band. On one occasion, he had to leave the stage after suffering an attack. (Simon Topping, frontman of Factory band A Certain Ratio, took his place, but there was still an audience riot.) 'The doctor was telling him the only way to control epilepsy is to live a really quiet life,' says Hook. 'No drink, no drugs, no excitement. And here he was the singer in a band that was getting really big.'

Despite Curtis's overdose and his illness, no real attempts were made to reduce the band's workload: Joy Division's first American tour was in the pipeline. Curtis told some people he wanted to take time off, but in front of his bandmates he feigned excitement. He didn't want to disappoint his comrades or Factory (by this point the label was essentially carried by the band). At Factory's big London showcase at the Moonlight in April 1980, Joy Division played all three nights – they were the big pull that would get people in to see the label's roster of lesser lights. Yet he must have had severe doubts about being an icon. In 'The Atrocity Exhibition' he alternates between being the ringmaster of the horror show and the freak entertainment itself, prostituting his own neurosis and twisting his body onstage.

The crisis came on 18 May 1980. After visiting his estranged wife and asking, unsuccessfully, for her to drop the divorce, he stayed up all night, watching a movie by his favourite director Werner Herzog and listening to Iggy's *The Idiot*. Finally, he hung himself as 'that awful daylight' ('In a Lonely Place') approached.

Curtis's suicide at the age of twenty-three made for instant myth. The sheer commitment of the act confirmed the authenticity of Joy Division's words and music in a way that was quite problematic, entirely logical and ultimately inevitable. As Curtis always intended, he joined the pantheon of those who lived too intensely and felt too deeply to make it for long in this world of half measures and settling for less. Brushing away the tears, Factory threw itself enthusiastically into building and burnishing the legend. Saville gave the posthumous single 'Love Will Tear Us Apart' an exquisite abstract cover that looked like the lustrous stone interior of a cenotaph. *Closer*'s sleeve actually featured a photograph taken in a Genoa cemetry, a sculpted tableau of the dead Christ surrounded by grief-striken mourners.

'Love Will Tear Us Apart' became Joy Division's first chart hit. Curtis's crooning vocal, Hook's bass and Sumner's keyboard trace in unison the same shy, crestfallen melody, while Morris's drumming skitters with feathery unrest. On 'Love Will Tear Us Apart' and its savage B-side, 'These Days', the singer and the music both sound raw and exposed, like they've got no skin. The words are laceratingly candid glimpses into a dying relationship, snapshots of bad sex and broken trust. Although the marriage break-up was only one factor, 'Love Will Tear Us Apart' was taken as Curtis's suicide note to the public: the official explanation.

Mark E. Smith once suggested there were two kinds of factory in Manchester: the kind that makes dead men, and the kind that lives off a dead man. An unfair jibe, but it's true in the sense that Curtis's death sealed Factory's stature for ever. It also condemned the label to struggle for years to find a group as weighty and epochal as Joy Division. The two closest contenders on Factory's early roster, A Certain Ratio and Durutti Column, weren't close to being in the same league.

Tony Wilson came up with the name Durutti Column on behalf of guitarist Vini Reilly. Buenaventura Durrutti had led a nomadic brigade of revolutionaries during the Spanish Civil War, and Wilson was fond of a Situationist comic strip called 'The Return of the Durutti Column', which invoked the Catalonian anarchist's guerrilla spirit. The military allusion could hardly have been more incongruous for Reilly's fragile music – intricate skeins of guitar fed through an echoplex and always played with the fingertips, delicate and prismatic, like Jack Frost on a window pane. Far from being a soldier, Reilly had gone AWOL from normal life. He suffered from anorexia nervosa, and his music sounded as translucent as you'd expect from someone with almost no flesh. On the second Durutti album, 1981's *LC*, Reilly recorded a tribute to Ian Curtis, but the song, 'Missing Boy', could just as easily have been about himself.

A Certain Ratio played funk *noir*. Strongly influenced by The Pop Group, whom they'd seen supporting Pere Ubu in 1978, ACR received a big boost when they recruited a drummer who was just as talented as Bruce Smith. Donald Johnson's fatback drumming almost single-handedly prevented the group's nebulous sound from wafting off into the void. Heard best on the early single 'Flight' and the live side of *The Graveyard & The Ballroom*, ACR's music worked through the tension between dry funk (rimshot cracks and feverish snares, neurotic bass, itchy rhythm guitar) and dank atmospherics (trumpet that seems to drift through fog, diffuse smears of guitar so heavily processed it sounds more like synth). At times ACR sounded like Joy Division getting on the good foot: singer Simon Topping more or less cloned Curtis's baritone drone, while the lyrics hinted at dark drives and shadowy states of consciousness. 'ACR had a bizarre sense of fashion – close-cropped hair, baggy khaki shorts,' recalls Manchester pop historian Dave Haslam. This look, vaguely redolent of colonialism or the Afrika Korps, led to accusations of flirting-with-fascism (a morbid preoccupation that Topping also shared with Curtis). Still, the presence of a black man behind the drum kit helped to counteract A Certain Ratio's faintly dubious aura.

For a while, they were Factory's best hope of matching Joy Division's impact. Under the new name New Order, Hook, Sumner and Morris

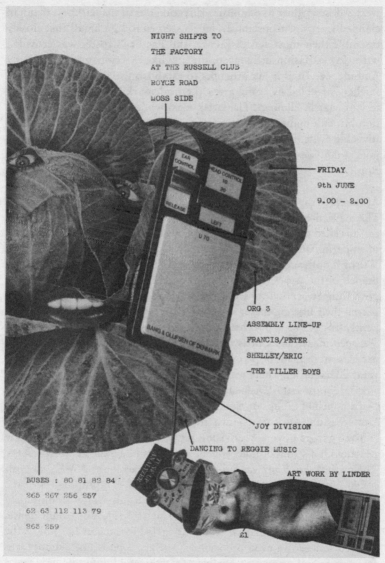

NIGHT SHIFTS TO
THE FACTORY
AT THE RUSSELL CLUB
ROYCE ROAD
MOSS SIDE

FRIDAY
9th JUNE
9.00 - 2.00

ORG 3
ASSEMBLY LINE-UP
FRANCIS/PETER
SHELLEY/ERIC
-THE TILLER BOYS

JOY DIVISION

DANCING TO REGGIE MUSIC

BUSES : 80 81 82 84
265 267 256 257
62 63 112 113 79
268 259

ART WORK BY LINDER

£1

Flyer for the Factory nights at the Russell Club, Manchester. This June 1978 show has Joy Division playing support to The Tiller Boys, the experimental side project of Buzzcock Pete Shelley

were still struggling to establish a direction out of the darkness that had claimed Curtis. Unconsciously, labels seemed to sign bands that closely resemble their most successful act, and Factory's roster was crowded with Joy Division-influenced outfits like Section 25 and Crispy Ambulance. Their weak attempts to establish their own identity were further enfeebled by being given the trademark 'Factory sound' courtesy of Martin Hannett. The latter, meanwhile, sank into heroin addiction but still managed to do some of his best work as one-half of The Invisible Girls, supplying the music for the genius Mancunian 'punk-poet' John Cooper Clarke on albums like the classic *Snap Crackle [&] Bop*.

As the city's top indie, Factory dominated Manchester's post-punk scene. The main alternative came from a cluster of activity around an organization called the Manchester Music Collective, which was the brainchild of experimental musicians Trevor Wishart and Dick Witts (one of Wilson's colleagues at Granada TV). Using a grant from a regional branch of the Arts Council, Wishart and Witts hired a basement in the posh King Street and turned it into a Monday-night showcase. The Fall played their first gig there, and Joy Division were regular MMC participants. 'It gave us somewhere to play, we met other musicians, talked, swapped ideas,' Ian Curtis told the *NME*. 'Also it gave us a chance to experiment in front of people.' Richard Boon recalls, 'The MMC was a great intervention. There was a whole stream of funny little groups who shared equipment – Dislocation Dance, Gay Animals, The Hamsters, and a bunch of groups on the Object Music label, like Spherical Objects, Grow-Up, and Dick Witts' own group, The Passage.'

The Passage gave Joy Division a close run for their money at one point, with a string of independent chart hits like their LP *Degenerates*. Their debut, *Pindrop*, was hailed by Paul Morley in the *NME* as a post-punk classic comparable to *Unknown Pleasures*, grappling with the grand themes of 'love, power and fear' in atmospheric, doom-laden music. Formerly a classically trained percussionist, Witts built dense, dramatic arrangements that were stirringly rhythmical but not in the least rock-like. 'We used bell sounds, military sounds like trumpet fanfares, brass and trumpets – anything that suggested things outside rock,' he says. Matching the epic sound was a thematic loftiness verging on the didactic: 'Devils and Angels' railed against organized religion, while 'XOYO' obliquely explored gender politics.

Witts had originally formed The Passage as a collaboration with Tony Friel, the first member of The Fall to defect from the band. By 1980, every single member of the original group had been replaced, except for Mark E. Smith. Kay Carroll, a psychiatric nurse who befriended Una Baines, started going out with Smith, then took on the job of managing the band. The power dynamics shifted. 'It became a bit of a Yoko and Lennon scenario,' says Martin Bramah. 'The girlfriend affirming his genius. Tony left first: he felt he'd invested a lot in The Fall – he'd come up with the name, and he was the only proper musician in the band.' Baines went next, for a very different reason: a mental breakdown triggered in part by the druggy lifestyle she was leading. 'I was twenty and had this serious illness. It took me twelve months before I could even speak to people again.' Drummer Karl Burns lasted until the end of 1978, and Bramah stuck it out to April 1979. 'What initially started out as a collective became a dictatorship,' he says. 'Mark's a genius, but he made it very hard for me to work with him. The break-up wasn't so much about the music, though; it was more how we were being treated as people on a daily basis.'

According to Baines, Smith recruited his new Fall from the group's roadies, who already had a band of their own and were more pliable. 'A word from Mark could decimate them,' says Rough Trade's Geoff Travis, who produced The Fall's third studio album, *Grotesque (After the Gramme)*. 'They loved him, but were a little bit awed. I remember sitting in a café with him and saying, "Don't you think it's really weird, Mark, that none of the band speak to you?" One of his sayings was: "Musicians are the lowest form of life."'

With Smith literally calling the tune, The Fall embarked upon their most intensely creative period, recording a series of visionary albums and numerous brilliant singles, first for Rough Trade and then for Kamera. As 1980 progressed, they drew level with Joy Division in the race to be Manchester's leading post-punk band, scoring two indie number 1 albums (*Totale's Turns*, a sort of live greatest hits, and *Grotesque*) and two indie number 2 singles, 'How I Wrote "Elastic Man"' and 'Totally Wired'. *Grotesque* offered a modern-day hallucinatory equivalent to Hogarth's caricatures of the English lower classes taking their pleasures, an idea pursued further on such singles as 'Lie Dream of the Casino Soul', a critique of the Northern Soul scene. On 'I'm into CB', for instance, Smith method-acts the role of a hapless radio ham (codename Happy Harry) who still lives with his parents: 'My father's not bad

The Fall in its second incarnation, *circa* 1981. L to R: Mark E. Smith, Steve Hanley. Photo by Janette Beckman

really/He got me these wires and bits/Apart from that he talks to me hardly'.

For the *NME*'s Barney Hoskyns, this era of Fallmusic – bookended by *Grotesque* and the mini-LP *Slates* – threw the listener into deranging 'wastelands of sound without themes, messages, or politics. These records *were* politics, living conjurations of the crass and the grotesque in Northern prole life . . . What [The Fall's music] implied was that the whole bastion of comfortable working-class traditions – the institutions of barbiturates, boozing, and bingo – could be transformed, could even transform themselves, into a deep cultural revolution.' Smith had broached this notion in the sleevenotes to *Totale's Turns*. Alluding to the Northern circuit of working men's clubs where The Fall played early on for lack of other opportunities, he speculated wildly: 'Maybe one day a Northern sound will emerge not tied to that death-circuit attitude or merely reiterating movements based in the capital.' This fantasy scenario inspired *Grotesque*'s epic closing track 'The N.W.R.A.', which stands for 'North Will Rise Again'. 'It's just like a sort of document of a revolution that could happen – like somebody writing a book about what would have happened if the Nazis had invaded Britain,' Smith told the *NME*.

Around this time, Smith coined the imaginary genre Country 'n' Northern to distance The Fall from self-consciously innovative groups like The Pop Group. 'We are a very retrogressive band in a lot of ways,' he declared. But even as The Fall's music seemed to become more hillbilly primitive and raw, Smith's lyrics became ever more intractably abstract – a frankly avant-garde torrent of found text (the British tabloids were a favourite source of inanities) spliced with his own encrypted utterances. The logorrhoea spilled on to The Fall's record sleeves, daubed with handwritten mini-rants and gnomic slogans, cartoons and doodles. Through the sleeve scribblings and songs like '2nd Dark Age' you could follow a fractured running narrative concerning ex-cabaret artist Roman Totale and his secret agent son Joe. Totale, said Smith, was an 'underground being . . . cursed with mystical insight'. He also had tentacles, which was why he had to go underground. 'It's like his face started *leaking*,' Smith explained. The singer cultivated this magical element to counter the prevailing but outmoded image of The Fall as being all about industrial decay and dole queues: 'I am a dreamer sort of person and I . . . resent being associated with realist bands.'

Along with the speed and 'shrooms, tales of cosmic horror fuelled Smith's dreams. This short-story genre was pioneered by nineteenth-century gentleman occultists like M. R. James, Arthur Machen, Algernon Blackwood and H. P. Lovecraft, all Smith favourites. For a band dedicated to stripping away rock's romantic mystifications, The Fall possessed a surprisingly strong streak of superstition. Smith believed he was attuned to the strange vibrations of certain places and that his writing was clairvoyant. 'I used to be psychic but I drank my way out of it,' he quipped in 1996. Reading speedfreak science-fiction writer Philip K. Dick gave him concepts like 'pre-cog' and 'psychic time travel'. The latter informed the song 'Wings', during which he recruits gremlins and goes back through a 'timelock' into the 1860s. A teenage phase of bumping into ghosts while out walking inspired songs like 'Spectre Vs. Rector' and 'Elves', in which Smith shrieks, 'The fantastic is in league against me!'

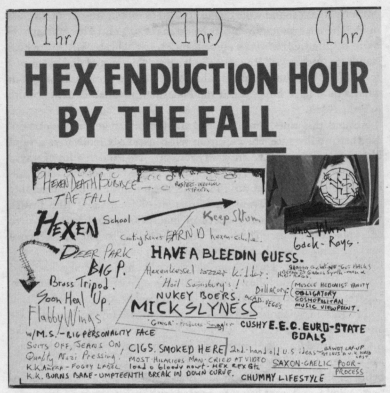

Gnomic Smith scrawlings scurry across the sleeve of *Hex Enduction Hour*, The Fall's 1982 masterpiece

The culmination of The Fall's fascination with the supernatural came with 1982's *Hex Enduction Hour*, half of which was recorded in Iceland, a country where most of the population still believes in elves. The track 'Iceland' was improvised in a Reykjavik studio with lava walls, the band oozing out a drone of two-note piano cycles and banjo that sounded like sitar, topped with incantations from Smith about casting 'runes against your self-soul'. *Hex* is The Fall at their most forbidding and primordial. On 'Just Step S'Ways', the group's two-drummer line-up brings a new polyrhythmic tumultuousness to the band's juggernaut rumble. 'Hip Priest' has an almost jazz-like swing, while the guitars on 'Who Makes the Nazis?' sound like flint shards hewn from a mountain face. And in case you are wondering who makes those Nazis, it's 'intellectual halfwits'. Ouch!

Hex was 'a huge sort of kiss-off to, like, everything', said Smith, and they've never topped it. But The Fall continued, alternating between relatively lacklustre phases and periods of renewed inspiration (1985's *The Wonderful and Frightening World of . . .* resembled a pop *Hex Enduction Hour*: dreamlike and almost lovely). By then, Smith had honed the media persona that made him a perennial favourite with interviewers: the classic British contrarian suspicious of do-gooders and improvers, a curmudgeon who scorns trendy humbug and political cant whether it comes from left or right.

His force of personality is matched only by the force of nature that is Fallmusic. Still going after almost thirty years, they've accumulated a body of work whose sheer size and density rivals Dylan's. A body of work like a body of water – never ending and ever shifting, its 'changing same' ceaselessly churns up scintillating new patterns. You never step in the same river twice, they say, and so it goes with The Fall. 'Repetition in the music' and they *still* haven't lost it.

11

MESSTHETICS: The London Vanguard

Scritti Politti. LMC. Flying Lizards. This Heat. Rough Trade. The Raincoats. The Red Crayola. Young Marble Giants. John Peel.

I step into the room and immediately stumble against a typewriter lurking on the dingy brown carpet. A small tower of books perches precariously on top of the machine. Next to it lies a half-drunk mug of coffee, its thick meniscus greeny-grey with mould. Jutting stacks of pamphlets, broadsheets,and academic paperbacks sprawl across every available surface – TV, mantelpiece, even the top of the gas fire – while the bookshelves look close to collapsing. On the wall above the fireplace, poking through an overlapping foliage of gig flyers and activist leaflets, there's a seven-inch single and a framed Hammer & Sickle, with a used teabag dangling irreverently off the latter's blade. And there's . . . Hang on a second . . . *Jesus* – what's that dreadful smell?

I never visited Scritti Politti's squat, located in a nondescript side street in Camden, north London. But I *feel* like I did. As a sixteen-year-old, I stared endlessly at the black-and-white photo of Scritti's living room on the front of their *4 A Sides* EP. It's a snapshot of a lifestyle: theory-addled, speed-stoked conversations raging until the crack of dawn; fevered debates about the radical potentials and counter-revolutionary pitfalls of popular music punctuated by visits to illegal reggae parties and post-punk gigs at Acklam Hall or the Cryptic One Club.

Scritti's squatted HQ and home at 1 Carol Street was the site of an outlandish experiment in rock. The group conceived of itself as an anonymous collective involving not just the three band members but a clan of non-musicians, whose participation might be 'all talk' but nonetheless counted as a vital contribution. The core band consisted of singer/guitarist Green (in those days, he never used his surname, Gartside), drummer Tom Morley and bassist Niall Jinks, but over the years Scritti's total membership fluctuated between six and twenty. 'The idea is that substantial decisions about what the group is doing are made by a larger number of people than actually pick up instruments at present,' Green told *After Hours* fanzine. Scritti aren't the only example of band-as-commune in rock history: Faust and Amon Düül, both products of Germany's post-1968 radical counter-culture, lived and worked together, while Crass, hippy veterans turned anarcho-punks, shared a farmhouse near Epping Forest. Nevertheless, the idea of a group in which players were outnumbered by non-musicians was unique.

Growing up in Wales, fifteen-year-old Green and his schoolfriend Jinks had tried to form a branch of the Young Communist League, but they succeeded in recruiting only one member. A few years later, Green studied art at Leeds Polytechnic at a time when conceptualist approaches were in the ascendant. Soon he stopped painting altogether and generated only writing. Like his contemporaries Gang of Four and The Mekons, Green assimilated Art & Language's sensibility, specifically the guiding conviction that the discourse around art was inseparable from the work itself; that every artwork was a form of 'active criticism', positioning itself in relation to other artists or movements. To choose one path implicitly entailed repudiating others, so why not be explicit and (self-)conscious about the process?

This kind of awareness infused the whole Scritti project. Originally inspired to pick up instruments after seeing 1977's Anarchy tour when it reached Leeds, but rapidly disillusioned by what they saw as the failure of the first-wave punks, Scritti latched on to theory as a crucial tool for navigating the quandaries of 'after-punk'. What is the 'correct' path to follow? Which 'ways of going on' (as Green liked to phrase it) are misguided or counter-productive? This is where the non-musician members, coalescing around the group after they moved to London, played their role: a buzzing theory-hive subjecting 'rock discourse' to rigorous scrutiny, 'interrogating' all its assumptions.

In Scritti's debut single, 'Skank Bloc Bologna', there's a brief, sardonic allusion to The Clash's idea of themselves as 'The Magnificent Seven'. (Green had read an *NME* interview in which the band compared themselves to the posse of vigilante heroes.) 'They said they felt like . . . a bunch of outlaws that would come into town to put everything to rights,' Green told one fanzine. The song's last verse, he explained, punc-

The living room of 1 Carol Street, Camden – Scritti Politti's HQ and home. From the cover of *4 A Sides*, 1979

tured this 'silly over-romanticized notion' of the rock group as 'macho gunslingers, the Robin Hoods of today'.

As a teenager, I found the title 'Skank Bloc Bologna' wonderfully mysterious and evocative. The 'skank' is easy to place: the loping white-reggae groove of the bass and drums, which Green overlays with plangent rhythm guitar closer to folk-rock than punk. The 'bloc' is a buried allusion to Gramsci (one of Scritti's favourite neo-Marxist theorists) and his concept of the 'historic bloc': an alliance of oppressed classes uniting to overturn the existing order and overhaul the dominant 'common-sense' worldview of what's natural, ordained, possible – revolution as the creation of a *new reality*. The 'Bologna' of the title is another story. It's often said that, in Italy, 1968 never ended. Unlike other countries, that year's civil unrest didn't subside but continued right through to the end of the seventies, with wildcat strikes, factory occupations and go-slows, acts of industrial sabotage. Students seized control of universities; occupations of housing by squatters groups occurred; an anarcho-surrealist tribe called Metropolitan Indians staged mass shoplifting incursions at luxury stores. All of this insurgency was aimed as much at Italy's established political left as it was against the conservatives. At its peak, Italy's Communist Party commanded the support of 37 per cent of the electorate and controlled many major cities in the industrial North. But, as far as Italy's radical fringe was concerned, the Communist Party – authoritarian and culturally staid – was actively *delaying* the revolution, not hastening it.

In early 1977 Bologna's Communist mayor lost control of the city to a riotous coalition of 'autonomists' and counter-culture radicals. This 'bloc' – squatters, feminists, gays, students, non-unionized workers and the semi-employed – developed an ad hoc form of 'post-political politics'. Self-organized and carnivalesque, *il Movimento* – as it was nick-named – aimed not to seize power but to smash it altogether, leaving everybody and nobody in charge. The Bologna riots of 1977 were as much a form of cultural revolt as a political uprising; what Italy had in lieu of punk, some claim. Artists' collectives proliferated. Pirate station Radio Alice filled the airwaves with uncensored rants, poetry and rallying cries. But Mayor Zangheri denounced the rioters as bohemian nihilists and enemies of the proletariat, and after several weeks called in armoured cars to crush the rebellion. Radio Alice was suppressed and its perpetrators jailed.

The title 'Skank Bloc Bologna' seems to imagine the Scritti squat as the germ of a future *Movimento Inglesi*. Yet the tone of the song is desolate. The verses zoom in on a girl adrift: the hapless, *hope*less product of bad education and stifled imagination, she's got no sense that change is even possible. Green sounds like he's fighting his own despair – in sleepy London town, revolution seems a long way off. But even if the girl doesn't know it, 'Something in Italy/Is keeping us all alive'. And closer to home there's 'the magnificent six' (the number in the Scritti collective at that point), with their schemes and dreams: 'They're working on a notion and they're working on a hope/A Euro vision and a skanking scope'.

Inspired by The Desperate Bicycles, Scritti grubbed together the money to record 'Skank' and two B-sides, and, with financial help from Rough Trade, released it on their own St Pancras label. On the photo-copied sleeve, they went one better than The Desps in the demystifica-tion stakes, itemizing the complete costs of recording, mastering, press-ing, printing the labels and so on, along with contact numbers for com-panies who provided these services. Released in autumn 1978, 'Skank' sold out its first 2,500 pressing quickly, thanks partly to the support of Radio One's John Peel, and eventually shifted around 15,000 copies. The melody's off-kilter beauty and the plaintive melancholy of Green's singing (indebted to the 'English soul' of Robert Wyatt), along with the intrigue of the lyrics and that cryptic title, captured the imagination. Even the group's name, a corruption of the title of a book by Gramsci, stood out: the sheer sound of it, *scritt-ee po-lit-tee*, brittle and chiming, just like the upwards-spiralling peals of lead guitar that pierce 'Skank Bloc Bologna'.

Scritti played their debut gig on 18 November 1978 at Acklam Hall in Ladbroke Grove, on a bill that included pragVEC and Rough Trade bands Cabaret Voltaire and The Red Crayola. Highly strung at the best of times, Green was almost crippled with stage fright, recalls pragVEC singer Sue Gogan: 'He was in hysterics and needed to have a substantial ego massage before he could be persuaded to go on and do a stunning fifteen-minute set.' The set was so short because the group had only four songs. Despite Green's caveat that the performance be taken as merely 'an open rehearsal', it was rapturously received, with the audience insist-ing Scritti play the quartet of songs again. At the end of the night, they were offered support slots on two different tours.

'Mark E. Smith said Scritti had the best rhythm section in the country,' recalls Rough Trade's Geoff Travis, whose label put out the group's second EP, *4 A Sides*. Scritti gigs were edgy, combustible affairs, with songs often being made up on the spot – a practice Green found hor-ribly draining, but which he pursued out of some perverse ideological commitment to deconstructing the process, tampering with rock's routines. Adding to the turbulence and cacophony – blades scratched along bass strings, tons of echo on the vocals and reverb on the tom-toms – the group were often joined onstage by as many as twelve asso-ciate members of the collective.

Detail of photocopied fold-out sleeve of Scritti Politti's 'Skank Bloc Bologna', 1978

Journalist Ian Penman was a member of Scritti's 'odd conglomerate' – hanging out at the squat, composing a Scritti communiqué, participating in some of the group's interviews, acting as a sort of fifth columnist by sneaking Scritti jargon and buzzphrases into his *NME* reviews. Sometimes he'd go onstage with the group and blow freeform saxophone. 'Or I would get up and, well, rap, I guess you would have to call it these days! Cut up a Lenin text and cross-reference it with Lee Perry's "Bafflin' Smoke Signals".' He adds a wry disclaimer: 'You have to understand, we took a *lot* of speed back then.' Penman recalls his time *chez* Scritti as an amphetamine blur of book swapping and cerebral frenzy: 'New records would be seized upon and reviewed en masse, gigs attended and feverishly discussed for days and days afterwards.' The soundtrack to all this 'speed talk' would be anything but straight-down-the-line rock: '*Lots* of Robert Wyatt', dub, warped jazz chanteuse Annette Peacock, British folk-rock like Martin Carthy and The Albion Band.

Overtaking The Desperate Bicycles, Scritti became icons of DIY, supreme exponents-cum-theorists of a wilfully fractured style of music-making: 'messthetics', as Green christened it in the manifesto-song of the same title. In one fanzine interview, he enthused about the new crop of 'scratchy-collapsy groups', such as The Raincoats, saying, 'we enjoy very much the enthusiastic, stop–start mistakes, falling-over sound they

'A Socialist Rockers Production': detail of inner sleeve of 'Skank Bloc Bologna' with demystifying data about self-releasing your own records

have'. 'We were anti-rock, it was too strong, too sure, too solid, a sound,' Green says now. 'We wanted music that *wasn't*, because *we* weren't strong, sure or solid.'

Interviews at the time created an intriguing image of Scritti as a shadowy collective skulking on the periphery of the music scene and exploring some fabulously uncompromised and far-reaching outer limit of politics-and-pop. Listening to songs like 'Is and Ought the Western World', whose lyrics oscillated line by line between the prosaic details of every-day oppression and the abstract contours of deep political structure, it was clear that Scritti had moved as far beyond Gang of Four's schematic case studies as that band had advanced upon Tom Robinson's tell-it-like-it-is protest songs. It didn't hurt that Scritti looked good, too: Tom the drummer had blond dreadlocks (at that time an extreme fashion statement), while pretty-boy Green was the incarnation of intellectual glamour – thin and frail in an oversize sweater, kohl etched around his blazing eyes.

Green became a kind of theory guru to many in the post-punk scene. 'Some of the people in the Manchester Music Collective scrutinized magazine interviews with Green in the same way Dylanologists pondered Bob's latest cryptic statements,' says Richard Boon. Green's eloquence and the fastidious complexity of his thought were attractive at a time when punk was fragmenting and entropy loomed. In the chorus of 'Messthetics' Green declares, 'We know *what* we're doing', by which he meant that the music was fractured on purpose. But in a larger sense Scritti managed to convince many people that they *did* – or at least were thinking more rigorously about the crucial quandaries than anybody else.

Prominent among the ideas whizzing about was Gramsci's concept of 'hegemony' – a catch-all term that covers the official ideology of state, Church and other institutions, along with the more diffuse and subliminal 'commonsense' assumptions that hold together a social system. In Scritti's brittle ditty of the same name Green personifies Hegemony as 'the foulest creature that set upon a race'. He sounds racked, as if he's desperately struggling to free himself from Hegemony's mental tentacles: 'How do you *do* this?/How can you do it to me?' At the chorus, the group derisively recite the sort of platitudes that seem pre-political in their 'obviousness' but actually work as hegemony's glue: 'an honest day's pay for an honest day's work'; 'you can't change human nature'; 'some are born to lead and others born to follow'. At song's end, Scritti mock the clichés that preserve rock's own stasis quo: 'rock 'n' roll is here to stay' 'but can you dance to it?'; 'walk it like you talk it'.

Influenced by the post-structuralist theories circulating at the end of the 1970s, Scritti increasingly focused on language itself as the mechanism of oppression. On the sleeve of the group's third release, the *Peel Sessions* EP, a page from the imaginary book *Scritto's Republic* proposes the idea of language as a sort of conductive fluid for power – permeating our consciousness and constructing 'reality'. In 'P·A·s' – the last track on *4 A Sides* – Green sings about Italy in 1920 and Germany in 1933 as moments when 'the language shuts down'. In his most honeyed, airy tones, he ponders the mystery of popular support for totalitarianism – 'How/Did they all *decide*? . . . What was irrational/Is national!' – then imagines mass unemployment making the same thing happen in eighties Britain.

Wittgenstein, another of Green's theory-gods, argued that all of humanity's problems stem from our bewitchment by language. The problem, then, was how do you think your way out of the cage, when your only tools are made of language? In these conditions, despair is

Scritto's Republic 180

predicates and is predicated of, a simple unit. When problems in handling the contradictions, inconsistencies and drives as 'I' get critical the heterogenous drives are exploded and language interrupted – ensuring the incommunicability of the repressed drives, desires, needs, contradictions of the subject.

Language pre-exists our entry into it and defines what is normal and represses that which will not or cannot be covered or developed by its framework. Drives meet the external organization of language and either structure accordingly or get repressed. To leave speech and language uninterrupted is to submit to the cultural order by which sexuality, thought etc. is regulated. There is a difficulty for productive language in beat music where semiotic instability is a norm, is style, but... and it was a big but

Table 4

Determiner	Noun	Adverb	Verb	Adverb
These	boys		walk	home
Some	men			away
		generally		
This	boy		walks	
A	man			out

COUNTING-OUT RHYME

Vizzery, vazzery, vozery vem,
Tizzery, tazzery, tozery tem,
Hiram, Jiram, cockrem, spirem,
Poplar, rollin, gem.

Warwickshire Folk-rhyme.

A fragment from *Scritto's Republic*, on the inner sleeve of the *Peel Sessions* EP, 1979

always just a heartbeat away. The fraught energy of *4 A Sides*' 'Bibbly-O'Tek' fades with the bleak aside, 'Which reminds me, there's no escape', before rallying itself for the struggle. Throughout *4 A Sides*, the sheer joy and fervour of music-making itself triumphs: 'Doubt Beat' sounds resolute, with Morley's driving drums and Jinks' wriggly, melodic, funk bass conjuring what Gramsci called 'optimism of the will' sufficient to counter the lyrics' 'pessimism of the intellect'. On the *Peel Sessions* EP, though, you can hear a group foundering. The music feels like it's shaking itself apart; Green sounds harrowed by thought. 'That's a genuinely ill record,' Green said of the EP some years later. 'As some kind of index to my state of mind at the time, I find it frightening and I can't understand it now at all.'

The group's hardcore lifestyle of self-neglect and self-abuse – not sleeping, eating infrequently, gobbling stimulants, the squalor of the

Carol Street squat, which had no bathroom – took its toll. But the stern regime of questioning everything and constant ideological wariness wore down Scritti, too. An abortive recording session, intended to produce a couple of EPs, went terribly wrong as the group's formidable powers of critique turned upon themselves and nothing they produced seemed valid. At the extreme, Scritti's impulse to challenge every aspect of 'the rock process' (even the word 'rock' was suspect; Green preferred 'beat music') could resemble Maoist self-criticism tribunals, where party members rebuked themselves for counter-revolutionary and crypto-bourgeois tendencies. 'It was all tunnelled through Green's absolutely monomaniacal insistence on what was CORRECT,' observes Ian Penman. 'He spent most of his time disapproving of things, like an unwashed Pope.'

Scritti's mindset started to grow distinctly paranoid. One minute Green proposed dismantling the entire capitalist structure of competition between bands ('Why can't Western rock bands work like jazz musicians – sharing equipment and ideas, helping each other at just that basic level of cooperation?' he asked in one interview); the next he was describing a battle to 'win space' that translated as barging rivals like The Pop Group out of the way by discrediting them ideologically. 'There must be *harder* than this,' Green pleads in 'Scritlocks Door', meaning harder than the flabby thinking and 'ill-sorted' ideas of rock culture. At the same time, there was a hefty component of pure ego involved in his intellectual combativeness. Typical of Scritti's interactions with 'opponents' was their encounter with the genial improvisers of the London Musicians' Collective, also based in Camden. Its headquarters were over the road from the Engineer, a pub whose back room had become 'the court of Scritti', says Steve Beresford, co-founder of LMC. One evening the entire Scritti collective attended an LMC performance. Afterwards everybody retired to the Engineer, where, says Penman, there was a 'big ideological Rob Roy squaring off between the two sides'. Beresford recalls Green 'denouncing the bourgeois imperialist improvisers . . . and claiming that *he* was playing "*people*'s music"'.

Founded just before punk, in 1975, the London Musicians' Collective was conceived as an open-ended alternative to the existing Musicians' Co-op (more of an invitation-only guild). British improvisational music culture had definite affinities with punk. Being such a small scene, it pioneered a do-it-yourself approach from the early seventies onwards: independent labels like Incus; samizdat publications like the 'squabblezine' *Musics*. 'There were anarchist ideas floating around,' says David Toop, another LMC co-founder. Proto-punk ideas of incompetence as liberating and musical training as a shackle on creativity also circulated, filtering down from Fluxus and John Cage to inform outfits like the Portsmouth Sinfonia – an orchestra in which everybody played an instrument at which they weren't fully proficient. Sinfonia participants included Steve Beresford, Brian Eno, and David Cunningham, who later formed the LMC-affiliated pop group The Flying Lizards.

One of LMC's articles of faith was the idea that a true heaven-made musical marriage would consist of ultra-virtuoso improvisers and non-skilled naïfs getting together and getting it on. Hence LMC's Jazz Punk Bonanza festival. 'At the time I was more interested in playing a sort of electric noise music, so I really liked the chaotic side of punk,' says Toop. He and Beresford especially loved the sheer exuberant racket of The Slits. Says Beresford, 'It was hilarious the way they chanted, "One, two, three, four," at the start of each song – not to count in the beat, but 'cos they thought that's what punk bands *did*, as a ritual. And Palmolive's drumming was amazing, like speech rhythms – she didn't think in terms of bar lines.' Beresford ended up *in* a later incarnation of The Slits, providing 'daft noises' on flugelhorn, keyboard and toy instruments during their American tour and contributing to the group's final album.

By 1979, post-punk's scope had widened so far that its activities overlapped with the pre-punk experimental fringe, and musicians like The Slits' Viv Albertine began to gravitate towards LMC, a place where absolutely anybody could play. 'We were in Camden, this punk centre,' says Toop. 'It just felt in some way you were in the right place.' A rival bohemian stronghold to Ladbroke Grove, Camden had cool record stores, a street market and the great independent bookshop Compendium. The LMC space, in a building formerly owned by British Rail, 'was filthy and had terrible acoustics', says Beresford. The facilities were rudimentary – usually no PA system, rarely any seats – and a fair proportion of the four or five gigs per week were 'hopeless, no redeeming qualities at all,' says Toop. Nevertheless, LMC became a creative vortex: 'The monthly meetings were hugely well attended, and quite fractious.'

One post-punk luminary drawn towards LMC was Mark Perry. After Alternative TV disintegrated, he participated in two different experimental outfits: The Door and the Window and The Lemon Kittens. 'The

Door and the Window had some great nights at LMC,' he recalls. 'Sometimes we did solo sets. Bendell from The Door and the Window, his set was playing the radiators. The whole idea was "to make music you don't need to have a musical instrument. Let's fuck the rules."' Led by Danielle Dax and Karl Blake, The Lemon Kittens made aggressively absurdist records like *Spoonfed and Writhing* and *We Buy a Hammer for Daddy*. Live, they had a confrontational performance-art aspect that Perry found hard to handle: 'At one gig, Danielle insisted the band all play in the nude. I walked into the dressing room, and Danielle's starkers and Karl and the guys are in their underpants and are all painted brown.' Primitivism and the fantasy of recovering some presocialized, childlike state of pure creativity and imagination were signature obsessions of the LMC scene. One expression of this was a collective fetish for toy instruments. Dutch improviser Han Bennink, a pioneer of this kind of play-power naïvety, was *the* LMC icon.

All this polymorphously perverse shifting and drifting, the fluid line-ups and one-off collaborations, represented an attempt to deconstruct the conventional rock band. Speaking to *Melody Maker*, Toop enthused about the 'flexibility and unpredictability' of new forms of organization that were 'opposed to hierarchical writing set-ups and the "eternal marriages" of groups'. These 'loose conglomerates' operating on the boundary between music and noise seem a world away from pop's melodic sweetness, brand recognition and long-term careers. Yet the LMC would outdo the entire post-punk world when The Flying Lizards – a Dada-pop outfit featuring contributions from Toop and Beresford, among others – scored a bigger chart hit than anything achieved by PiL, Joy Division *et al.*

In the autumn of 1979 The Flying Lizards' cover of 'Money (That's What I Want)' took the avant-classical sound of 'prepared instruments' into the UK Top 5. The record's bass drum isn't a drum but a bass guitar being hit with a stick. The banjo-like piano sound was created by throwing an assortment of objects – rubber toys, a glass ashtray, a telephone directory, a cassette-recorder, sheet music – inside the piano. Originally co-written by Berry Gordy Jr, 'Money' is probably most famous in its Beatles version. The Flying Lizards' cover sounds like the Fab Four decided to rerecord it *circa* 'I Am the Walrus'. The distortion-overloaded guitar solo gesticulates wildly, like an overexcited man, and the backing vocals sound like tribesfolk chanting in the rain forest. In the Beatles version, John Lennon's prole-on-the-make insolence thrills because the 'cynicism' (valuing material wealth over love) feels bracingly unsentimental and the song shakes with a working-class hunger and confidence that won't be contained. The Lizards' remake subverts The Beatles' subversion. All icily enunciated hauteur and blue-blooded sang-froid, singer Deborah Evans replaces Lennon's lusty rasp with the dead-eyed disdain of the ruling class. It's no coincidence that 'Money' was released a few months after the election of Margaret Thatcher, who spoke in a fake-posh voice not a million miles from Evans' exaggeratedly aristocratic tones and who championed a callous economic theory known as monetarism.

This unlikely fusion of avant-garde tomfoolery and subtle political satire became a massive novelty hit in the UK and a New Wave dance-floor cult smash in America. The mastermind behind The Flying Lizards was David Cunningham, whom Toop had met while teaching at Maidstone College of Art. Although Cunningham had already recorded and self-released an album of minimalist compositions, he wasn't really a musician so much as a self-taught producer – a scholar of record production, in fact, who listened closely to auteurs like Joe Meek, Phil Spector and Lee Perry. In a strong bargaining position after the success of 'Money', he negotiated a deal with Virgin that defined The Flying Lizards as a production company and allowed Cunningham to work with a range of musicians – some of whom received royalties while others were paid as session players. Over two albums, he drew on the talents of The Pop Group's Bruce Smith, NYC punk singer Patti Palladin, composer Michael Nyman (his mentor at Maidstone) and Robert Fripp, among others.

The Flying Lizards was an exercise in pop absurdism. The debut album featured a Brecht–Weill cover, Sanskrit chants, found sounds and unlikely instrumental textures. Cunningham's penchant for excessive studio processing and daft effects intensified the spirit of whimsical artifice that infused the whole project. The music press mostly heaped contempt on the project, suspicious that Cunningham was a disengaged dilettante. But Cunningham insisted that there was 'a kind of punk element to The Flying Lizards', if punk meant simply that you could 'do what you felt like doing'. Like Beresford and Toop, he found most punk too conventionally rock 'n' roll. His idea of punk in 1977 had been the 'distorted guitars and relentless rhythms' of This Heat, a group whose attempts to fuse sonic radicalism and political rage rivalled the infernal intensity of The Pop Group. Cunningham ended up managing This Heat and co-producing their debut album, convinced that they had the potential to be as big as King Crimson had been in their day.

Formed a few years before punk, This Heat originated from the same 'progressive' milieu as Crimson. There were still audible after-traces of the Canterbury Scene (Soft Machine, Hatfield and The North) in This Heat's music, especially the plaintive Robert Wyatt-like vocals. But Canterbury's mellow meanders of bucolic whimsy were replaced with late seventies dread and urgency, harsher textures, and a head-fuck extremism inspired by dub, *musique concrete* and sixties free jazz. This Heat's slogan was: 'All possible processes. All channels open. Twenty-four-hour alert.' Like the LMC crew, This Heat believed 'anything was potentially a source of music', says drummer Charles Hayward. So they collected piles of 'broken instruments, damaged toy pianos, half-functioning speaking dolls'. Non-musician Gareth Williams played a vital role: 'Sometimes it would just be down to him playing one note on a keyboard for twelve minutes and slowly manipulating all these effects pedals, making music out of that one note,' recalls Hayward. 'It was a refocusing of what "technique" was – instead of *andante* or *legato* it would be "angry" or "stumbling over".' The band's attitude to performance was confrontational. At one gig, Williams used a primitive sampling device repeatedly to trigger the phrase 'I think I'm going out of my head', as sung by Greek falsetto love-god Demis Roussos, attacking the audience with a fifteen-minute assault of helium-shrill histrionics.

Like Scritti, This Heat began in squatland. Hayward subsisted on five quid a week and a diet of porridge. Punk initially left him unimpressed, until he saw Alternative TV. 'They had this song called "An Alternative to Nato" – little more than a title, really, but it was expecting the world to change overnight, and even if it didn't really make sense, its sheer fuck-offness was so compelling.' After a couple of years in the wilderness, 1977 suddenly provided This Heat with a climate in which their 'desire to commit violence to accepted notions of music' made perfect sense. 'There was a wellspring of punk possibility that accepted and nurtured us, even though we weren't part of it,' says Hayward. They quickly garnered a reputation as an intimidatingly intense live experience. After one of these early shows, David Cunningham approached them and, according to Hayward, 'said it was the most aggressive, violent thing he'd ever seen in his life'.

Through Cunningham, This Heat gained access to a studio called Cold Storage, a former meat fridge in a disused pie factory in Brixton. 'We transformed Cold Storage into an incredible power base, somewhere we could develop ideas over a really long period, in much more detail,' says Hayward. This Heat plunged into intense experiments with tape-editing, splicing together lo-fi live recordings with twenty-four track stereo material recorded at another, more hi-tech studio. This meshing of different ambiences and feels made the music even more unsettling. On '24 Track Loop' – one of the highlights of their self-titled 1979 debut LP – they fed Hayward's frantically funky drums through a device called the Harmonizer to create chiming and creaking tuned-percussion timbres that prophesy nineties jungle.

This Heat's music wasn't experiment for experiment's sake, though – more like abstract protest music. *Deceit*, from 1981, was almost a concept album about nuclear Armageddon. 'There was a policy by our elders and betters called MAD, "mutually assured destruction",' says Hayward. 'They were so crazy they couldn't see they had identified their own policy as "mad"!' *Deceit*'s opener, 'Sleep', imagines power lulling people into apathy with consumerism and entertainment: 'a life cocooned in a routine of food'. Like so many of their post-punk peers, This Heat wanted to awaken listeners to an acutely discomforting awareness of the world's evils. The music itself, through its fractures and internal clashes, instilled a painful alertness. 'That's why our music wasn't psychedelic and drifty, why it was so hard-edged and angular. We had no interest in making people *stoned* with our sounds.' The band also projected this ferocious sobriety via their image. *Deceit*'s back cover shows the band – Hayward, Williams and multi-instrumentalist Charles Bullen – dressed in ties and jackets, with short, neat haircuts and stern frowns on their faces. 'We liked going to jumble sales. I had a lot of bus-conductor jackets, and I bought handfuls of ties for twenty pence,' says Hayward. 'It was a look related to the idea of pulling yourself together, so that you could fight back against these bastards who were ruining the world. The music bred a sort of pride, and you wanted to manifest as much of its essence on the surface of your skin as possible.'

Deceit was released on Rough Trade towards the end of a three-year period that saw the label at the height of its power and influence. Between 1979 and 1981, Rough Trade was the epicentre of London's post-punk vanguard. The label's roster included a hefty proportion of the city's most adventurous bands – Scritti, This Heat, The Raincoats, Essential Logic, The Red Crayola – along with non-London luminaries like Young Marble Giants, Pere Ubu, Swell Maps and many more.

Musicians worked on one another's projects, a cooperative ethos fostered by Geoff Travis, who thought the jazz model of fluid line-ups and temporary collaborations was preferable to rock's star system and competitiveness between bands. So Charles Hayward drummed on The Raincoats' off-kilter classic *Odyshape*, while Mayo Thompson's The Red Crayola evolved into a Rough Trade supergroup featuring Swell Maps' Epic Soundtracks, Essential Logic's Lora Logic and The Raincoats' Gina Birch.

Rough Trade's location in Ladbroke Grove contributed to its literally central role. 'It really was a scene where you'd run into everybody on Portobello Road on a Saturday afternoon without fail, whether you wanted to or not,' says Vivien Goldman, who owned a house on Ladbroke Grove itself. Geoff Travis was her flatmate for a while, and countless Rough Trade bands from outside London stayed there when visiting the capital to gig or record. 'The Grove was a real bohemia then: lots of squats, but the rents were very cheap, too. And within walking distance there were at least half a dozen places you could go rave all night – blues dances where you'd pay a quid on the door, get a Red Stripe and a spliff, and dance to dub and lovers' rock.'

The Raincoats' bassist, Gina Birch, lived in Ladbroke's immediate neighbour, Westbourne Grove, sharing a house in the squat-infested Monmouth Road. 'Some of the houses had been burned out; some were literally uninhabitable,' she recalls. 'The squat we lived in was not pretty. People would say, "We're making a post-holocaust film. Can we shoot in your house?" We had mushrooms growing out of the toilet wall. But there was a room in the basement we could use as a rehearsal space.'

A fan of conceptual art, Birch moved down from Nottingham to attend Hornsey Art College, arriving in London just in time to get swept up in punk's 'wild, unfocused energy'. The initial trigger for The Raincoats was seeing The Slits. 'I was absolutely sick and jealous – but it was that sort of motivating jealousy: "I would *love* to have done that."' Birch formed the group with Ana da Silva, a poetic Portuguese woman who, at twenty-seven, was eight years older than Birch and had a doctorate in languages and a thesis on Dylan under her belt. After various members male and female passed through the ranks, they settled on an all-girl line-up, with Palmolive (recently departed from The Slits) on drums, and Vicky Aspinall, a classically trained violinist who'd been playing in a feminist all-women collective called Jam Today.

'Being a woman is both feeling female, expressing female and also (for the time being at least) reacting against what a woman is told she "should" be like,' wrote Ana da Silva in a Rough Trade information booklet on The Raincoats. 'This contradiction creates chaos in our lives and if we want to be real, we have to neglect what has been imposed on us, we have to create our lives in a new way. It is important to try and avoid as much as possible playing the games constantly proposed to you.' The Raincoats' way of bypassing those pressures was to project ordinariness: unlike The Slits, who turned unkemptness into style, The Raincoats just looked slightly scruffy in a way that would have been unremarked-upon in an all-male band during this era. Coming from women, though, it took on the quality of a radical gesture, a strident abstention from glamour and showbiz.

'We were quite shy, really,' Birch admitted. Raincoats shows were less performances than 'like watching a process, which the audience kind of felt they were privileged to kind of spy in on'. Kurt Cobain, a passionate fan, used the same eavesdropping metaphor in his sleevenote for a Raincoats reissue: listening to the records felt like 'we're together in the same old house and I have to be completely still or they will hear me spying from above and, if I get caught – everything will be ruined because it's their thing'.

Although feminism was pervasive in universities, art colleges and squatland, the music industry was still in the Dark Ages when it came to awareness about sexism. It was common for advertisements for albums to use cheesily chauvinist copy or imagery suggestive of rape scenarios. In this context, the post-punk groups' obsession with 'ideological correctness' had moral force. Rough Trade, for instance, refused to distribute the first Nurse with Wound album because they felt the S&M imagery on the cover was degrading. The Raincoats sometimes addressed the 'big issues' – 'Off Duty Trip', for instance, concerned a notorious rape trial of the day, in which the perpetrator was treated leniently by a judge to avoid damaging his military career. But most Raincoats songs were more oblique, generally leaning towards the personal side of the-personal-is-political. And the music – an exuberant near shambles of folk-tinged punk – was far from didactic. 'We rehearsed for hours. You probably couldn't find a band that rehearsed more than we did, but we always fell apart,' says Birch. 'We always pushed ourselves a little bit beyond where we were capable of going.' Unlike many punk-inspired musicians who paid lip service to the ideas of non-technique and

The Raincoats playing in the upstairs room at the Chippenham pub, Westbourne Grove, London, 1979.
L to R: Gina Birch, Ana da Silva. Photo by Shirley O'Loughlin

anyone-can-do-it but were in reality skilled players, The Raincoats really did learn to play in public.

After the gloriously ragged eponymous debut, a whole world of exotic influences seeped into the group's music, from ethnic field recordings (inspired by a squatmate's collection) to Ornette Coleman and Miles Davis. The band started to pick up 'odd instruments from junk shops and markets', says Birch – 'like the balophone, this Mali instrument that's got gourds underneath it and beautiful bits of wood and mis-shapen holes'. The result of all these non-rock inputs was 'the strange, winding, splodgy journeys' of *Odyshape*.

The Raincoats' second album is post-punk that's been totally unrocked. 'My basslines started to get more and more sprawling and all over the place,' says Birch. The Raincoats' rhythms had always been loosely tethered: Palmolive had 'lots of tiny little toms, so it was always quite tribal. She wasn't so much driving the music as we were all clattering along together.' By *Odyshape*, though, Palmolive had quit and many of the songs were written without a drummer in mind. Percussion parts were added afterwards, courtesy of a series of guest drummers, including Charles Hayward and Robert Wyatt. A pre-punk cult figure for his Soft Machine work and solo albums, Wyatt had retired in the mid-seventies, until Geoff Travis coaxed the wheelchair-bound, card-carrying communist to record a brilliant series of politically charged singles for Rough Trade. *Odyshape*'s melancholy Englishness and fluid structures occasionally recall Wyatt's masterpiece, *Rock Bottom*. 'Only Loved at Night', the album's stand-out track, is like a gamelan music-box, the different patterns interlocking like intricate cogs. On this song, as with much of *Odyshape*, the group swapped instrumental roles (a common post-punk ruse to keep things fresh), with Aspinall playing bass and Birch contributing drone guitar, while da Silva produces wistful chimes from her kalimba, an African thumb-piano. Charles Hayward's clockwork percussion, added after the fact, is decorative, just one of many parallel pulses.

Throughout this period, Birch was moonlighting in The Red Crayola, having developed a rapport with Mayo Thompson, who'd co-produced the first Raincoats album. 'From my point of view, the stuff we did in The Red Crayola was a continuation of what I was doing in The Raincoats – take something quite normal and twist it out of alignment.' The original Red Krayola – reluctantly spelled with a 'K' to avoid trademark-infringement in the US – emerged out of the same mid-sixties Texas psychedelic scene as Thirteenth Floor Elevators. Krayola simultaneously partook of the era's freak-out spirit while standing slightly outside the grain of the times – a 'dissident among the dissidents' stance that became Mayo Thompson's signature. He imbued the group with a certain dry conceptualism at odds with late sixties let-it-all-hang-out mysticism. The group's second album, *Coconut Hotel*, recorded in 1967 and initially rejected by their record company for being too experimental, featured songs with titles like 'Vocal', 'Free Guitar' and 'Piano', along with a sequence of thirty-five one-second pieces – gestures towards deconstruction or Brecht-like distancing effects that anticipate post-punk.

In the early seventies, Thompson moved to New York and fell in with Art & Language, attracted by the sheer combative nature of their stance.

'They were looking for trouble, and I've always been looking for trouble,' he chuckles. 'Looking for some kind of action and an edge.' He made an album with A&L, *Corrected Slogans*. A good example of its trenchant lyrical style is 'the misery of being exploited is nothing compared to the misery of not being exploited at all'. Then he moved to England in time for punk – just the sort of 'action and edge' he craved. In the UK, Thompson befriended Pere Ubu, using them as his backing band on a new Red Crayola album, *Soldier-Talk*, then joining Ubu as replacement guitarist for the departing Tom Herman. He also became an increasingly pivotal figure in the Rough Trade collective. As well as producing or co-producing (with Geoff Travis) a staggering number of the best post-punk bands of the era, Thompson took on the role of public spokesperson for the label. He also acted as a sort of in-house ideologue – in the process often colliding with Green, a rival theory-guru figure in the Rough Trade milieu.

Unlike the tortured Green, though, Thompson found a certain bone-dry humour in the grotesque ironies of capitalist reality. Explaining his penchant for fractured musical structures, he once observed: 'I didn't fragment the world – I just happened to notice that it is fragmented.' Released on Rough Trade in 1981, The Red Crayola's *Kangaroo?* featured lyrics from Art & Language that addressed various 'monstrosities' produced by the internal contradictions of bourgeois culture. There were also whimsically ornate exercises in Soviet suprarealist rock like 'The Tractor Driver' and 'The Milkmaid' – humorous attempts, Thompson says, to imagine what 'a socialist song [would] sound like'.

Simultaneous with the revived Red Crayola, Thompson remained busy with Pere Ubu, now one of Rough Trade's prestige acts. Some commentators blamed Thompson for the un-rock direction Pere Ubu pursued at the label, but that process was already under way by the third album, *New Picnic Time* – partly motivated by an ornery impulse not to repeat, but also conditioned by David Thomas's religious beliefs (he'd been raised a Jehovah's Witness). At some point, the singer decided rock 'n' roll was incorrigibly reprobate. In interviews he railed against rock's immersion in fantasy and machismo, its 'wallowing in sexuality' and selfish emotions: 'It's very bad, because it's not real and it's not . . . nice!' He also jibed at the post-Ubu wave of 'gloomy-gusses' and 'misery goats', like Joy Division. Dread and decay, all the signifiers of 'industrial', were jettisoned on 1980's *The Art of Walking*, Ubu's first Rough Trade album, in favour of bucolic imagery, ecologically motivated anthropomorphism, and songs about fish and dinosaurs. 'The birds are saying what I want to say,' trilled Thomas on one song, while 'Go' counselled attentiveness to 'the small things that give pleasure'. Curiously, the attempt to move beyond rock's juvenile egomania led not to maturity but regression – the child's wide-eyed curiosity and gurgling delight. Mayo Thompson enjoyed deconstructing rock form, but soon he too pined for the old hard-riffing Ubu of 'Final Solution'. His nickname for Ubu's next album, *Song of the Bailing Man* – even more rustic and quirked-out than *Walking* – is '*Song of the Boring Man*'.

Ubu remained one of Rough Trade's biggest bands, but the jewel in their roster, sonically and in sales terms, was Young Marble Giants, a trio from Wales who did the post-rock pastoral thing so much better. Young Marble Giants' music had a spareness and stillness that felt startlingly fresh in 1980. The group's founder and main songwriter, Stuart Moxham, conceived the sound as a revolt against punk. YMG's music was a peculiar mélange: Duane Eddy's twangy tremolo riffs, Steve Cropper's crisp rhythm guitar, Devo's New Wave jerkiness. The group also loved mood music: the kind of light classical and MOR played on Radio Two, fairground music, 'cheesy organ sounds' like the Wurlitzers at the old picture palaces, and the kind of Testcard muzak you heard when British TV programming went off air in the afternoon.

Moxham developed a dry, choppy, suppressed-sounding style of rhythm guitar using an ultra-trebly Rickenbacker and a technique called 'muting' (resting his strumming hand on the strings to damp the vibrations). His brother Phil's bass – high, melodic, often mistaken for another guitar – was a beetling, scurrying presence. The interplay between the two instruments was 'almost like knitting', says Stuart – a strikingly unmanly metaphor that beautifully captures the quiet radicalism of YMG's music. The rhythms, generated from a rudimentary drum machine, were played live on a tatty mono cassette-player. Augmenting this sparse sonic palette were occasional keyboards and subliminal wisps of weirdness produced using a ring modulator or devices cobbled together by a tech-whiz cousin of the Moxhams.

But what made the Young Marble Giants unique was the low-key, almost-spoken singing of Alison Statton (Phil's girlfriend; Stuart never really wanted her in the band). When *NME* readers voted her the eighth best singer of 1980, Stuart spluttered, 'But Alison's not a singer! She's someone who sings. Alison sings as if she was at the bus-stop or something. A real singer sings with more control.' Inadvertently, he captured precisely what was so perfect about Statton's undemonstrative vocals – a seductive ordinariness, a cool pallor of tone. Her image, too – print dresses, white plimsolls, ankle-socks – fit the music's aura of fresh-faced provincial naïvety.

Cover of Young Marble Giants' debut LP, *Colossal Youth*, 1980

Young Marble Giants felt like music by introverts, for introverts. In one interview, Moxham talked about wanting to get a sound 'like a radio that's between stations, listening to it under the bedclothes at 4 a.m., and you get these fantastic shortwave sounds and snatches of modulated sounds'. Without knowing it, a lot of people had been waiting for a sound as subdued and insidious as this, and the group's first (and last) album, *Colossal Youth*, became Rough Trade's second-biggest seller of the period. YMG were practically adopted by the Rough Trade family – Moxham likens Geoff Travis to a father figure, and describes The Raincoats as 'feisty aunties who took us under their wing. On one level, they were kind of frighteningly feminist in a way that was new to us – they didn't shave their legs, for instance – but on the other, they were very kind to us.' YMG's un-rock 'n' roll behaviour – they often brought their dog with them to gigs – fitted perfectly with the Rough Trade style.

Sadly, internal tensions split the band only ten months after the March 1980 release of *Colossal Youth*. In the interim, they had released the *Final Day* EP. Its title track is perhaps their best and certainly their best-known song. 'That song just came out perfectly formed – it took as long to write as it does to listen to,' says Moxham. To get the single-note whine that runs through the whole track and evokes what Moxham calls 'the low-level dread' of living with the possibility of nuclear annihilation, he stuck a matchstick in one of the organ keys. But what's most chilling about 'Final Day' is its brevity (just 1 minute and 39 seconds) and Statton's fatalistic tone as she sings 'When the light goes out on the final day/We will all be gone having had our say'. 'Final Day' was a night-time Radio One smash throughout the second half of 1980, receiving especially heavy rotation on John Peel's show.

In the early seventies, John Peel was the BBC's resident hippy, playing a mix of folk-rock, prog, reggae and cult weirdos. But he was quick to embrace punk, and by 1979 had become a massively important figure for the post-punk do-it-yourself culture. 'If you knew that one of your favourite bands was doing a Peel Session, that was as important as going to one of their gigs,' says Tony Fletcher. 'If you had to be out for some reason, you'd get one of your mates to tape it.' Records Peel had discovered would sometimes trickle down into other Radio One DJs' shows, resulting in some unlikely UK chart hits. Downtown New York performance artist Laurie Anderson reached number 2 in the winter of 1981 with 'O Superman', an eerie eight-minute piece built largely around her electronically-processed vocals; and Pop Group offshoot Pigbag made the Top 3 in the spring of 1982 with 'Papa's Got a Brand New Pigbag', re-released a year after Peel had originally made it a late night radio hit.

Peel's support of the marginal and maverick was all the more crucial because Radio One, before deregulation of the airwaves, enjoyed a near monopoly over pop music in the UK. Yet it was precisely this centralized, nationwide nature of British radio that created the possibility of cultural decentralization. Peel received strange self-released records from every corner of Britain and beyond. He was not only conscientious about sifting through them, but an ardent regionalist inclined to give provincial outfits preferential treatment. And if Peel liked your record, you were instantly granted a national audience. 'You'd get records sent in by these stroppy lads from tiny towns in Lincolnshire, places you had to look up on the map,' he said. 'And I'm a great sucker for cheerful amateurism. Another thing I liked was that a lot of these bands were almost entirely without ambition. Their goal was often just to put out a single, or do one session with us.'

On the furthest edges of the Peel universe, the do-it-yourself principle proliferated like weeds in the form of the cassette underground: groups who thought that vinyl was too costly or too careerist and instead released their music in tape form – sometimes selling it for a nominal sum (£1.50), sometimes giving it away for free if you mailed them a blank C60. There were hundreds of cassette bands across the land, typically with absurdist/puerile names like God & The Turds, The Night the Goldfish Died, Anthrax for the People, The Scrotum Poles. And there were even a handful of cassette-only labels, like Smellytapes and Deleted Records.

But the kingpin of this micro-scene, its Rough Trade, was Fuck Off Records. Run by Kif Kif, formerly of the hippy band Here and Now but now playing noisepunk in his own group The 012 (motto: 'bad music is soul music'), Fuck Off's catalogue boasted over thirty cassettes. The label's star act was Danny & The Dressmakers, creators of such deathless classics as 'Come on Baby Lite My Shite' and 'Going Down the Sperm Bank Four Quid a Wank'. But the label's strongest conceptual statement was releasing the cacophonous C60 by The Teen Vampires, much of which consisted of an argument between singer and bassist. Kif described it as 'the worst tape I've ever heard' but felt compelled to release it 'just because it was so awful'.

Peel himself never went quite *that* far into the messthetics zone, but 'Peel band' did become practically the name of a genre of music during the 1979–81 period. A legion of eccentrics with four-track tape-recorders in their bedsits sent off singles, and if the track caught Peel's ear they'd enjoy a brief taste of glory on the national airwaves.

In tribute to both the DIYers and the late, great man himself, here's a Top 10 countdown of Peel Hits – my favourites, not necessarily his.

10 Prefects, 'Going Through the Motions', 1980

Taken from one of the two sessions this Birmingham band did for Peel, 'Going Through the Motions' takes the piss out of professionalized-to-living-death rock bands by fully enacting the title: the beat limps like it's sprained In both ankles, the guitars dirge gruesomely, Robert Lloyd's voice is a listless, tuneless wail.

9 The Cravats, 'Precinct' (1980)

Sax-squawking art-punk with significant Beefheart-damage. Originally recorded for a Peel Session, 'Precinct' was inspired by Redditch, the dreary Midlands 'new town' the band called home. Peel: 'The singer was called The Shend and one of the reasons I liked the band, to be honest, was because he was a really nice bloke. In fact, that's what he put on his business card – "The Shend: A Decent Bloke".'

8 Furious Pig, 'I Don't Like Your Face', 1980

Just vocals and percussion, Furious Pig's yowling zoo-music resembles a pygmy barbershop quartet. 'I Don't Like Your Face', their sole single for Rough Trade, was based on the sort of mean things children say in the playground, they told the *NME*: 'Kids are really nasty.'

7 Notsensibles, '(I'm in Love with) Margaret Thatcher', 1979

From its fluster-flurry of buzzsaw guitar chords to the gormless jabbered harmonies and lines like 'Margaret Thatcher is so sexy/She's the girl for you and me/I go red when she's on the telly/'Cos I think she fancies me', the Notsensibles' most famous ditty taps into the side of punk all about not taking *anything* seriously. This Lancashire group pioneered the 'movement' christened '*la punk pathetique*' by *Sounds* journalist Garry Bushell. Peel: 'Post-punk's thought of as something rather po-faced and sombre, but a lot of it was *funny*. We used to go to gigs and laugh like a drain.'

6 Spizzenergi, 'Where's Captain Kirk?', 1979

Leaning more towards the New Wave/early evening Radio One end of things, but a definite Peel fave, this hectic, panic-stricken hurtle enjoyed seven weeks at number 1 in the independent chart. Mainman Spizz changed the group's name to some new Spizz-variant – Spizzoil, Athletico Spizz '80 – on an annual basis: a brand-recognition-weakening gambit that doubtless sabotaged his later stab at mainstream success.

5 Family Fodder, 'Playing Golf (with My Flesh Crawling)', 1979

Sung by mainman Alig Fodder from the point of view of a man who's in a state of arrested putrefaction ('There's times I feel fungus growing on me') and wishes he could get it over with and be dead, this macabre yet chirpy ditty is a phantasmago-ria of wobbly processed vocals, jaunty organ and No Wave-like screech-guitar.

4 Killing Joke, 'Pssyche', 1980

Before these millenarian misanthropes established their Gothic reign as an eighties Black Sabbath, they were PiLheads producing thug-funk like 'Pssyche'. Ammonia-caustic guitar, jabs of atonal synth, and Jaz Coleman growling about sinister 'con-trollers' and nuns getting fucked – it's simultaneously silly and scary.

3 The Tiller Boys, 'Big Noise from the Jungle', 1979

Buzzcock Pete Shelley explores his Krautrock/Fripp & Eno avant-rocky side in tan-dem with a Manchester teenager called Eric Random to produce a blitzkrieg of pounding drums and Neu!-like guitar clangour.

2 Fatal Microbes, 'Violence Grows', 1979

The baleful pop tones of fifteen-year-old punk starlet Honey Bane survey London's frayed social fabric in a banner year for street violence. Gloatingly noting how bus conductors have learned to keep their traps shut when thugs refuse to pay, Bane then taunts the listener: 'While you're getting kicked to death in a London pedes-trian subway/Don't think passers-by will help/They'll just look the other way'. Slow-drone psychedelia midway between The Doors' 'The End' and the Velvets' 'Venus in Furs' swirls behind her. An astonishing one-off.

1 (And The) Native Hipsters, 'There Goes Concorde Again', 1980

Cloying whimsy collides with genuine psychedelic strangeness on this brainchild of two Wimbledon School of Art graduates, William Wilding and Nanette Greenblatt. Buoyed by moonwalking bass and keyboards that caper like tipsy aliens, Greenblatt plays the batty housewife peering through net curtains and cooing, 'Oooooooh, *look* – there goes Concorde again!' Peel: 'That was one of those records where you put it on and thought: This will be fantastically irritating in a fortnight, but until then let's play it to death.'

12

INDUSTRIAL DEVOLUTION: Throbbing Gristle and Music from the Death Factory

Throbbing Gristle. Whitehouse. Nurse with Wound. Clock DVA. 23 Skidoo

Thesis: Late seventies industrial music was the second flowering of an authentic psychedelia. Now, on first glance, the music of Throbbing Gristle and their comrades seems impossibly remote from 1967's blissed-out mystics frolicking through English meadows, from Syd Barrett with his nursery-rhyme melodies and children's storybook imagery. Industrial music is unremittingly urban, a sonic mirror to a world of dehumanizing brutality. Innocence figures only as something to be defiled. As for pastoralism, suffice to say, when Throbbing Gristle posed on an idyllic grassy cliffside overlooking the English Channel for their album 20 *Jazz Funk Greats*, it was a sick joke – Beachy Head being a favourite leaping-point for suicides.

Yet industrial music shared many things with psychedelia. The impulse to blow minds through multimedia sensory overload: almost every industrial band featured back-projected cut-up movies and extreme lighting redolent of 1960s happenings and acid tests. And an obsession with sonic treatments and extreme effects: psychedelia and industrial both abandoned the rock model of 'naturalistic' recording in favour of heavy processing, tape loops and electronic noise. The big difference (and what makes industrial an 'authentic' psychedelia rather than a mere revival) is that industrial replaces kissing the sky with staring into the cosmic abyss. Industrial is psychedelia inverted: one long bummer trip.

There were also direct historical links between the acid-dazed freaks of the late sixties and the autopsy aesthetes of the late seventies. The flyer for Throbbing Gristle's 1976 debut show – or 'disconcert', as they pun-

Throbbing Gristle's *20 Jazz Funk Greats*, 1979. L to R: Cosey Fanni Tutti, Genesis P-Orridge, Peter Christopherson, Chris Carter

ningly dubbed it – described the group as 'post-psychedelic trash'. This was plain truth: TG evolved out of COUM Transmissions, a taboo-smashing performance-art ensemble, but COUM had originally started as an absurdist cosmic rock group. In 1971, they supported Hawkwind, the leading band in Britain's 'post-psychedelic' underground. In pictures of singer Genesis P-Orridge *circa* 1969 he resembles no one so much as Neil the Hippy from *The Young Ones*: same droopy, sad-sack expression and long, lank locks. As it happens, his real name *is* Neil (Neil *Megson*, for added gormlessness). As late as 1979, the list of his favourite music fitted the classic profile of a 'head': The Doors, Pearls before Swine, The Fugs, Beefheart, Zappa.

In 1966, aged sixteen, P-Orridge organized a 'happening' at his

Solihull public school after reading newspaper stories on London's early acid freakouts. A few years later, he joined the art commune Transmedia Explorations, an offshoot of Exploding Galaxy, renowned for its 'Kinetic Theatre' performances at psychedelic raves like UFO.

'Transmedia' referred to the in-vogue notion of a new form of 'total art' involving the creation of 'experiences' through synergizing different artforms and smashing down barriers between performer and spectator. More striking, though, was Transmedia's communal lifestyle. Routines and habits were deliberately disrupted: members slept in a different bed each night and selected clothing out of a communal chest every morning; meals were eaten at odd times; and games were constantly played with roles, identity and language.

This quest for some kind of authentic 'pure' self, via a gruelling regime of deconditioning, became the hallmark of everything P-Orridge did in art and life. 'We need to search for methods to break the preconceptions, modes of unthinking acceptance and expectations that make us, within our constructed behaviour patterns, so vulnerable to Control,' he wrote years later, borrowing Burroughs' near-mystical concept of Control as an all-pervasive power that penetrates the fibres of consciousness itself. COUM and Throbbing Gristle both aimed to set off 'psychic detonations that negate Control'.

After his Transmedia adventures, P-Orridge returned to Hull (where he'd been an undergraduate studying social administration and philosophy) and formed his own arts lab/collective, COUM Transmissions. He fell for a flower child, Christine Carol Newby, who moved into COUM's communal HQ in a warehouse and soon renamed herself Cosey Fanni Tutti. COUM started as a rock band of sorts – making up music on the spot, undeterred by lack of grounding in improvisational technique, using broken violins and prepared piano as well as conventional rock instruments like drums and electric bass. Inspired by John Cage's writing and by primitivists like The Fugs and The Velvet Underground, P-Orridge believed that 'the future of music lies in non-musicians'. Gradually, the chaotic gigs became more theatrical and 'environmental', as first costumes and props, then full-blown installations, were added. P-Orridge and Tutti realized they could get grants from the Arts Council if they described what they did as 'performance art' rather than rock music.

Starting in July 1972 with an event called *The Alien Brain*, COUM staged a series of increasingly outlandish and shocking performances at art galleries and mixed-media festivals across Britain and Europe. An important predecessor for COUM was Fluxus, the international art movement of the 1960s whose work combined elements of Dada, Zen and pranksterism, often with a confrontational performance art aspect. P-Orridge admired Fluxus' 'running battle and commentary with art itself'. Another sixties touchstone for COUM was the Vienna Aktionists and their feats of abjection and self-mutilation. Typical components of a COUM performance included P-Orridge placing severed chicken heads on top of his penis and masturbating, or P-Orridge and Tutti engaging in simultaneous anal and vaginal sex using a double-pronged dildo. Various combinations of soiled tampons, maggots, black eggs, feathers, and syringes full of milk, blood and urine figured as props. For instance, P-Orridge might stick a hypodermic into his testicle and then inject the blood into a black egg. Or, for a pièce de résistance, he might give himself a blood and milk enema and then fart out the liquid, splattering the gallery floor.

By the end of 1973, COUM had moved to London. Their new HQ was the basement of a disused factory in the East End. Early the following year, they acquired a new member, Peter Christopherson, nicknamed 'Sleazy' because he was most interested in COUM's 'fab and kinky' sexual extremism. Sleazy worked as an assistant designer for Hipgnosis, famed creators of lavish artwork for prog-rock groups like Pink Floyd – another indication of industrial's connections to post-psychedelic music. As was the arrival in 1975 of Chris Carter, the fourth member of what would soon become Throbbing Gristle. Carter's road-to-Damascus experience was seeing Pink Floyd in 1968 while tripping on LSD. Rather than pick up an instrument, though, he started a light-show business. Later, as a fan of cosmic Krautrockers Tangerine Dream, he got into synthesizers.

Increasingly worried that COUM were being stifled by acceptance (they'd received coverage in art journals and invitations to perform all over Europe), P-Orridge decided it was time for a strategic shift into the world of pop culture. He wanted to find an audience more likely to be both genuinely challenged and galvanized to action by COUM's shock effects and radical ideas. P-Orridge was also captivated by the Warhol-like notion of using fame, hype and controversy as an artistic medium in itself.

Founded in September 1975, Throbbing Gristle threw themselves into the project of conceptualization and sonic research. They also assiduously cultivated a kind of group-mind. (According to P-Orridge, they slept together every weekend for a whole year.) During the week, Carter, a technical whizz, built speakers, effects units and synthesizer modules, and adapted conventional instruments like the bass and guitar.

Everything was fed through relays of multiple effects. All these multiplied-through-overlay treatments transformed the guitar and bass into sound-synthesizing machines, although extracting noise from them involved a hands-on physicality that gave the noises a uniquely pummelled and percussive feel. Vocals were often heavily processed, too, fed through a chorus echo that allowed Carter to speed them up and slow them down, make them sound slimy or wobbly. He cobbled together a unique gizmo, nicknamed the Gristle-izer, for Sleazy to play – a sort of *musique concrete* mechanism or primitive sampler. Its one-octave keyboard triggered an array of cassette machines, each loaded with found sounds – TV and movie dialogue, or everyday conversations surreptitiously recorded by a roving Sleazy.

TG's Hackney basement became a 'chaotic research lab', with P-Orridge and Carter exploring the perceptual and physical effects of high and low frequencies, distortion and extreme volume, using themselves as guinea pigs. 'We had moments when we had tunnel vision, couldn't walk or stand up straight and so on from certain frequencies we hit,' P-Orridge recalled in 1999. It seems no coincidence that TG formed the same year that Lou Reed released *Metal Machine Music*, his infamous suite of white-noise compositions. But where Reed saw *MMM* as a form of modern classical music, TG's goal was more visceral – a total body music, immersive and assaultive. They jettisoned songs, melody and groove in favour of the pure, overwhelming *force* of sound itself.

P-Orridge told *Voltage* magazine, 'It was very literally an experiment . . . Let's set up a band. Let's give it a really inappropriate name ['throbbing gristle' is Yorkshire slang for an erect penis]. Let's not have a drummer because rock bands have drummers. Let's not learn how to play music. Let's put in a lot of *content* – in terms of the words and the ideas. So normally a band would be music, skill, style and all those other things – we threw away all the usual parameters for a band and said, "Let's have content, authenticity and energy. Let's refuse to look like or play like anything that's acceptable as a band and see what happens."'

Throbbing Gristle's official public launch took place in October 1976 at the opening party for *Prostitution* – a COUM exhibition at the Institute of Contemporary Arts that the group saw as their swan-song. COUM's last gasp turned out to be their finest hour, in terms of grabbing media attention. Located in the heart of London, a short stroll from Buckingham Palace, the House of Commons and the National Gallery, the ICA represented a threshold: the place where art's radical fringe collided with high culture. The centrepiece of *Prostitution* was photo documentation of Cosey's work as a model in some forty porn magazines. This, plus the exhibition of used tampons, made *Prostitution* a perfect flashpoint for growing public concern about the subsidized avant-garde – what the Arts Council was doing with taxpayers' money at a time of recession and public spending cuts. Conservative MP Nicholas Fairbairn denounced *Prostitution* as 'a sickening outrage . . . Public money is being wasted here to destroy the morality of our society. These people are wreckers of civilisation!' Taken aback, COUM found themselves Public Enemy Number 1 in the tabloids (there were apoplectic headlines, smear stories, dirt-digging reporters) and a much-discussed symbol of declining standards for the more sober quality papers and broadcast media. Questions were even asked in Parliament.

Throbbing Gristle's montage of tabloid shock-horror concerning COUM's *Prostitution* show, 1976. The two punk rockers checking out the ICA exhibition are Steve Severin and Siouxsie Sioux of The Banshees

The *Prostitution* furore rivalled the December 1976 folk-devil panic about The Sex Pistols' swearing on TV. Some soon-to-be-famous punks attended Throbbing Gristle's ICA gig, but P-Orridge and crew were sceptical about punk's credentials as radical music – it was too rock, too *musical*. Speaking in the famous 'New Musick' November 1977 issue of *Sounds*, P-Orridge declared that *Sniffin' Glue*'s exhortation 'Here's three chords, now start a band' conceded far too much to traditional musicality. 'It starts with chords. They're saying "Be like everyone else, you gotta learn to play". You can start with *no chords*. Why not just say, "Form a band and it doesn't matter what it sounds like or whether you even make a noise, if you just stand there silent for an hour, just do what you want."' TG, he underlined frequently, was 'anti-music'. At one early gig – the Nag's Head, High Wycombe, February 1977 – P-Orridge poured scorn on the jeering punks in the audience: 'You can't have anarchy and have *music*.' During the cacophonous performance, Cosey bared her tits and P-Orridge poured fake blood over his head. Then he invited half a dozen kids from the audience onstage and handed them instruments.

TG believed that 'you should approach any instrument the way a child will', P-Orridge declared. He picked the bass because it was the instrument he was least qualified to play; Tutti, likewise, chose the guitar because it was the one to which she was least attracted. She never learned to play chords, but, like the female No Wave guitarists, used a slide to generate hair-raising glissandi, or just bashed the strings, using it as a rhythm instrument and – via a battery of effects – a source of abstract noise.

Apart from the rhythm tracks built by Chris Carter, TG songs were written live, from scratch, with only the vaguest musical guidelines discussed in advance. P-Orridge generally improvised his words too, after briefly consulting with the band about possible lyrical topics. The song 'Persuasion', for instance, was composed during a gig at Notting Hill's squat venue Centro Iberico. Just before going onstage, P-Orridge asked Christopherson what he should sing about today and received the reply 'persuasion' (people being cajoled into doing things – sexual things – against their will being one of Sleazy's obsessions). P-Orridge ad libbed lyrics about a guy pressurizing his partner to be photographed for the 'Readers' Wives' section of a porn mag.

There were upsides and downsides to TG's fixation on spontaneous composition/combustion. Check the live recordings (and, in a hangover from their performance-art days, TG exhaustively documented every show, eventually releasing all of them) and you'll encounter passages of astonishing intensity: molten, distended soundscapes like solar gas festooning off the surface of a star, strafing streaks and zaps from some audio battlezone. But, inevitably, TG developed an arsenal of riffs and tricks as predictable as any musical language: gouging bass blasts, pounding surges, upward careening arcs. As with free improvisation, for all the commotion and turmoil, the palette of sound-colours could start to feel somewhat samey.

Sixties free-music outfits like AMM (a big influence on Pink Floyd) were implicitly spiritual, yearning to recover the lost 'totality'. Stripped of Romanticism, TG's music simulated the soul-destroying rhythms of Fordist mass production. Carter compared the group to a 'sound assembly line', while P-Orridge coined the phrase 'Tesco Disco' to evoke 'rhythms based on conveyor belts, alienating work'. TG named their label Industrial Records to signal both the production-line quality of the way they churned out noise and the group's 'journalistic' ethos: records in the sense of files or information, a series of documentary reports on 'the savage realities of fading capitalism'.

P-Orridge saw TG as science-fiction music: 'we're writing about the future by looking at today,' he told *Melody Maker*. Although he cut off his hair in 1977 as a symbolic act of severance with the hippy era, the 'classic' TG of 'Slug Bait' and 'Hamburger Lady' sounds like a corroded, ailing Tangerine Dream: cosmic rock for a universe in the process of winding down. TG also made some pure, unabashed space music, like 'After Cease to Exist', which took up the whole second side of the debut album *Second Annual Report* with its diffuse wafts of wavery-toned, early Floyd/Syd Barrett guitar.

After finishing the debut, P-Orridge wandered outside, heard the sounds of a train clattering over a grubby Victorian viaduct and the grating of a local saw mill, and decided that the group hadn't 'invented' anything, merely absorbed their environment and reproduced it. In the late seventies, the East London borough of Hackney was one of the most deprived inner-city areas in the UK, with bad housing, rising unemployment, terrible street crime, and a strong National Front presence. TG called their Martello Street studio the 'Death Factory', partly as a nod to nearby London Fields, where victims of the plague had been buried. It was also, of course, a reference to the Nazi concentration camps. Industrial Records' logo was a deceptively benign-looking leafy lane with what looked like a factory at the end of it. In fact, it was a photo of

"INDUSTRIAL MUSIC......
FOR INDUSTRIAL PEOPLE"

ANOTHER DEVELOPMENT FOR

TESCO

SILVER

R.G.CARTER L?
BUILDERS

NORWICH

THROBBING GRISTLE

'Tesco Disco'. L to R: Chris Carter, Cosey Fanni Tutti, Genesis P-Orridge, Peter Christopherson

Auschwitz taken by P-Orridge during a trip to Poland. 'We called our album "Music from the Death Factory" as a metaphor for society and the way life is,' he told the *NME*. 'Everybody lives in their own concentration camp . . . What we're saying is: be careful, because it's not far from one to the other. The human race is the biggest masochist in the world.'

Yet, even as they made wildly melodramatic and insensitive generalizations, Throbbing Gristle also flirted with fascist imagery. The group's logo was based on the 'England Awake' lightning-flash insignia of Sir Oswald Mosley's British Union of Fascists. On the flipside of TG's first single, 'United', was 'Zyklon B Zombie', a parody of 'blockhead punk' that imagined the ultimate punk act as sniffing Zyklon B poison gas rather than glue. Two later singles featured Holocaust cover imagery – a towering mound of human skulls (on 'Subhuman'), and walking frames taken from the elderly and infirm before they were shunted into the death chamber (on 'Distant Dreams (Part Two)'). TG's investigations into twentieth-century atrocity were studiously dispassionate, presenting the information without moral judgement. But there's a fuzzy line

Advertisement for Throbbing Gristle's first single, the double A-sided 'United'/'Zyklon B Zombie', 1978

between anguished awareness of horror and morbid fascination – bordering on identification – with evil. TG constantly teetered on the edge.

This ambiguity became even more pronounced with TG's fixation on paedophilia and the abduction, rape and murder of children. 'After Cease to Exist', the long, spacey track on *Second Annual Report*, features some found speech – a pathologist discussing the murder of a teenager, a victim of a 1970s ring of homosexual paedophiles who operated in hostels for runaway boys. The first thousand copies of *D.o.A.: The Third and Final Report of Throbbing Gristle* (their second album, released at the end of 1978) came with a gift: a parody of a girlie calendar for 1979, but with a genuine little girl as the pin-up – blonde-haired Kama Brandyk, who looks about seven and is pictured on a bed wearing nothing but underwear. On the record's cover, another pre-pubescent girl is photographed next to a hi-fi unit, and there's an inset smaller picture of Brandyk reclined on a fur rug with her knickers showing. Five months after *D.o.A.*, TG released the single 'We Hate You (Little Girls)', with P-Orridge practically foaming at the mouth as he shrieked lines like 'I hate you little girls/With your little curls/And your pretty dress/And your little breasts'.

Psychopathology fascinated TG from the start. One of their earliest pieces, 'Very Friendly', concerns the mid-sixties exploits of Manchester's Ian Brady and Myra Hindley, the infamous 'Moors Murderers', who sexually tortured and murdered children. P-Orridge's lyrics focus on the killing of a non-minor, the young homosexual Edward Evans. His attention to both the grisly details and macabre incongruities of the murder salvage 'Very Friendly' from mere muck rolling – the 'German wine' with which Brady plies the hapless victim; the way blood spatters the Church of England prayer book and the TV screen image of broadcaster Eamonn Andrews; the 'bits of bone and white brain' that plop on to 'the hearth just near the brush they used to sweep the chimney, and there was lino on the floor, which was lucky'. Other songs, though – like 'Slug Bait', with its psycho cutting open a pregnant woman's belly and biting off the baby's head – seem just gratuitously gross.

Today, after the schlock-horror tactics of death metal and third-wave industrial (TG's grandchildren), 'Slug Bait' seems almost tame. At the time, though, nothing like it had been encountered in rock, with the possible exception of Alice Cooper's Grand Guignol theatrics. P-Orridge saw his words as continuing The Velvet Underground's expansion of rock lyrics into taboo areas such as sadomasochism and heroin. Ideas of the criminal-as-artist also had a long pedigree: de Quincey, de Sade, Dostoevsky, Bataille. In *Bomb Culture*, his classic 1968 account of the emergence of the British counter-culture, Jeff Nuttall pinpointed the Moors Murders as a pivotal moment. The demon lovers' 'beyond belief' crimes convinced many bohemians that society was going insane, the madness caged behind the prim English façade bubbling to the surface. Others recognized that Brady, a de Sade fan, put into gruesome practice the maxims of radical art: 'take your desires for reality', 'everything is possible and nothing is forbidden'.

Appropriately enough, TG's gigs were sadistic assaults on the audience. TG pursued a 'metabolic music' that directly impacted on the nervous system. They were fascinated by military research into the use of infrasound as a non-lethal weapon, with certain frequencies triggering vomiting, epileptic seizures, and even involuntary defecation. 'People . . . think music's just for the ears, they forget it goes into every surface of the body, the pores, the cells, it affects the blood vessels,' declared P-Orridge. The effects of volume, ultra-high and sub-bass frequencies and sheer repetition induced altered states in the band, too. P-Orridge recalled his whole body shaking and trembling; sometimes he'd reach the point where he was talking in tongues, a mere vessel for forces from 'beyond'. TG also used lighting as a retinal barrage – convulsive strobes, high-power halogen lamps aimed into the audience's faces.

Once audiences start to expect an extreme experience, though, it's time to flip the script. TG's first major swerve came shortly after *Second Annual Report*, an ultra-lo-fi affair recorded using a Sony tape-recorder, a single condenser microphone and an ordinary blank cassette. In contrast, the single 'United' was almost glossy enough to pass for pop: this disco-inspired song designed 'for people to fall in love to' (according to the Industrial press release) might have been chart material if not for its slightly defective groove and P-Orridge's runny vocals. 'United' was the first in a series of danceable electropop tracks somewhere between Giorgio Moroder and Cabaret Voltaire: the pulsating porno-disco of 'Hot on the Heels of Love', featuring Cosey's breathy whisper; the eerie, shimmering propulsion of 'Adrenaline' and its flipside 'Distant Dreams (Part Two)'.

In a typical TG twist, 'United' reappeared on *D.o.A.* speeded up so fast that its four minutes were reduced to sixteen seconds of bat-squeaky treble. *D.o.A.* confounded expectations in other ways, too. It contained archetypal TG songs like 'Hamburger Lady' (a nauseous churn of whim-

Flyer for Throbbing Gristle gig, 1978

pering, agonized sound inspired by the true story of a burns victim unrecognizably charred from the waist up) but also 'solo' tracks like the Abba-meets-Kraftwerk rhapsody of Chris Carter's 'AB/7A' and P-Orridge's unexpectedly plaintive and personal 'Weeping', made using four different types of violin sound. In his most piteously crumpled voice, P-Orridge mumbles accusatory lines like 'You didn't see me weeping on the floor/You didn't see me swallowing my tablets' – a reference to his suicide attempt of November 1978, when he downed a huge quantity of antidepressants and steroids before going onstage at the Cryptic One Club, and woke up in intensive care. The target of his jabs was Cosey Fanni Tutti, who'd left him for Chris Carter, which makes 'Weeping' industrial music's equivalent to Fleetwood Mac's intraband break-up anthem 'Go Your Own Way'.

As this giant rift in TG's group-mind widened, P-Orridge spent more time with Monte Cazazza, an extremist performance artist from San Francisco who had become a sort of unofficial fifth member of the band, and a real soul-mate/mentor to P-Orridge. They'd first made contact through the mail-art circuit, which involved sending people handcrafted, intricately designed works through the postal system (P-Orridge liked to mail Cazazza dead animals). Early in TG's existence, Cazazza had helped the group with conceptualization and strategy. He even coined the term 'industrial music' – 'sort of as a wisecrack originally: "industrial music for industrial people",' he recalls. 'I didn't mean for people to take it so seriously!' And the first non-TG release on Industrial Records was Cazazza's 1979 single 'To Mom on Mother's Day' b/w 'Candyman', the latter concerning a murderer of boys called Dean Corll who ran a sweet factory in Texas.

In 1979 Cazazza spent much of the year in England, bolstering P-Orridge's damaged morale. 'I always have more fun when Monte's here – he makes me more extreme,' P-Orridge said. An avid reader of survivalist literature and books about weaponry, Cazazza turned TG on to military imagery. Their April 1979 shows in Derby and Sheffield began with a sequence sampled from a US Army training tape featuring the distinctive firing sounds of various hi-tech weapons – grenade launchers, recoil-less rifles, anti-tank guided missiles, the flame-thrower of an armoured personnel carrier. The group started wearing camouflage gear. TG had always attracted a certain kind of fan that was genuinely *fanatical*, and P-Orridge saw the potential for creating a quasi-paramilitary cult. Through Industrial Records' newsletter, he invited fans to become TG agents: 'Do you want to be a fully equipped Terror Guard? Ready for action? Assume Power Focus. NOTHING SHORT OF A TOTAL WAR. NUCLEAR WAR NOW! Then send for a catalogue of available weaponry and regalia, survival kits and clothes.'

Around this time, TG embarked upon an experiment in totalitarian psychology that got a little out of hand. Hopped up on survivalist reading matter, the group turned their Beck Road home into a fortress, with black-painted windows, barbed wire on the garden wall, and a burglar-alarm system. A ragged tribe of itinerants had set up camp in the wasteland behind Beck Road and a neighbourhood crime wave appeared to coincide with their arrival. 'The police wouldn't do anything for us, so we just decided we had to get these people out of there,' says Cazazza. 'They were sort of making our lives hell and we fought back in an interesting manner.' So TG waged sound-war on the unsavoury nomads, beaming infrasonic frequencies at the encampment and causing the travellers considerable distress: headaches, anxiety, disrupted sleep patterns, nightmares. Eventually, they packed up their caravans and moved out, convinced the area was cursed.

P-Orridge was fully aware that these 'gypsies' (as they were popularly, if inaccurately, called by hostile townspeople throughout the UK) were uncomfortably close to the Romany wanderers rounded up by the Nazis and exterminated as 'vermin'. The entire episode seems like a deliberate journey into the darkside of paranoid psychology, the proto-fascist mindset of scapegoating and persecution. Recoiling from the squalid lifestyle of the itinerants, TG nicknamed them 'subhumans'. Two singles emerged from this playing-with-fire phase. 'Subhuman' featured a caravan image on its cover and lyrics like 'You make me dizzy with your disease/I want to smash you and be at ease'. 'Discipline' came in two different versions. The first, recorded live at Berlin's So36 club, effectively documents the song being written onstage. Given the theme-of-the-day by Cosey a few minutes before going onstage, P-Orridge improvised a series of barked commands: 'I want some discipline in here'. Eleven minutes long, the track starts shakily, then gathers cohesion, as if undergoing the very regimentation process it proposes. The beat sounds like a jackboot moistly pulping the infirm and lowly underfoot, while gruesome shearing sounds conjure an abattoir atmosphere. The later version, recorded in Manchester, is much tighter: P-Orridge declaims, 'Are you ready boys? Are you ready girls?/We need some discipline in here' like a cross between scout leader and Führer. On the single's front cover, TG pose in front of the building that once served as the Third Reich's Ministry of Propaganda, while the flipside features the slogan 'Marching music for psychic youth'.

How did TG, creatures of the sixties and its various liberation movements, succumb to this fascination with fascism? In truth, there's a slippery zone where anarchism (or at least that libertine and libertarian brand of anarchism less about workers' councils than a near-solipsistic individualism, in which we're each despots pursuing our every desire) flips into a curious appreciation and affinity for certain aspects of Nazism. The meeting-point is that whole Gnostic side of Nazism that concerned the pagan and primordial. P-Orridge's investigations into cults and secret societies had led to books that dealt with the Nazi inner circle's obsessions with occultism, alchemy and the quest for the Holy Grail.

TG were also 'fans' of Charles Manson, just one of several charismatic sociopaths who preyed on the drug-damaged children of the counterculture, inducting them into surrogate families where the group-mind was essentially identical to the father figure's warped worldview. (Journalists Robin Green, David Dalton and David Felton tagged the phenomenon 'Acid Fascism' in their book *Mindfuckers*.) P-Orridge's preoccupations were leading him towards the concept of Thee Temple of Psychick Youth, the cult-like organization he would build around his post-TG band, Psychic TV. A Throbbing Gristle gig in Manchester at the end of 1980 was the first to be described as a 'Psychic Youth Rally'. Earlier that year, P-Orridge had signalled his new sense of himself as a shaman with TG's fourth album, *Heathen Earth*, improvised live in the studio with a small audience of friends and associates. Recording a single performance in front of 'initiates' was an attempt to create an atmosphere of ritual and ceremony where magic – 'aural and philosophical', stressed P-Orridge – could take place. On the cover, a line from a Charles Manson song – 'can the world be as sad as it seems?' – was juxtaposed with an eerie-looking veterinarian's diagram of a dog's teeth.

By the spring of 1981, the tensions within TG caused by Cosey's break-up with P-Orridge made the situation unworkable. P-Orridge also felt the group had outlived its usefulness. Throbbing Gristle, he believed, had moved beyond the agrarian blues roots of rock and created a new kind of music (or anti-music) appropriate to post-industrial society. Now, he told a radio interviewer, 'we have to go beyond into where man meets space. I don't mean cosmic like Tangerine Dream; I mean inside the head.' The very fact that TG had built a substantial audience who accepted what they did (by *Heathen Earth*, Industrial Records' turnover had reached the point where they were one of the largest independents in the UK) was a sign it was time to move on.

Virtually from scratch, TG had constructed a new genre, an entire sub-cultural field: partly composed of peer groups (like-minds already pursuing a similar path, like Cabaret Voltaire, Non, SPK, Z'ev, Clock DVA, some of whom released records on Industrial) and partly of outfits directly catalysed by TG's example (not just in the UK but as far afield as Yugoslavia, Australia and Japan). Remarkably, Throbbing Gristle almost single-handedly created one of the most enduring and densely populated fields of post-punk music, despite having a rather disdainful attitude to music *per se*. Their music, in a sense, was best understood as a delivery system for their ideas – a hangover from COUM's previous existence in the world of conceptual art. TG knew exactly what they were doing and told the listeners in meticulous, hyper-articulate detail. Indeed, you could almost skip the records and read the eloquent interviews with Genesis P-Orridge, a disarmingly pleasant fellow.

By the time TG announced 'the mission is terminated', P-Orridge had come to feel that industrial was turning into a distinctly unwholesome scene. If that was the case, though, it could be reasonably blamed on TG themselves and their motivating idea that the extremes of existence are somehow more real or more valid than the middling areas. The most blatant example of a group who'd 'misunderstood' TG was Whitehouse, an outfit P-Orridge abhorred. In the sleevenote to the debut album *Birthdeath Experience*, leader William Bennett promised, 'this is the most brutal and extreme music of all time'. Using a Wasp synth to generate noxious noise and recording everything in the red zone for maximum distortion, Bennett remorselessly pursued his 'vision of . . . a bludgeoning, tyrannical sound'. Disregarding beat, melody and structure, severing all ties to any previous musical genres, Whitehouse spawned an 'ears are wounds' micro-genre of industrial later called 'power electronics'.

The goal was to 'cut to pure human states', which in Bennett's mind meant violence and sexual violation, conveyed in songs like 'I'm Coming up Your Ass' and 'Cock Dominant'. At their live 'aktions' (a nod to the Vienna Aktionists), Bennett screamed lines like 'It's your right to kill; it's your fucking nature!' and, after roughly fifteen minutes of skull-splitting noise, crowd ruckus, flying bottles and bloodshed, the police would usually arrive and pull the plugs. 'Bludgeoning, tyrannical' caught the flavour of Bennett's worldview, too. An expert on the Marquis de Sade, he'd probably have concurred with the virulent anti-humanism of Minister Saint-Fond from *Juliette*, who dreamed of establishing a neo-feudal system that treated an entire class of humanity as animals. 'I affirm that the fundamental, profoundest, and keenest penchant in man is incontestably to enchain his fellow creatures and to tyrannize them with all his might,' declared de Sade via Saint-Fond. 'The suckling babe that bites his nurse's nipple, the infant constantly smashing his rattle, reveal to us that a bent for destruction, cruelty, and oppression is the first which Nature graves in our heart.'

Although named after the porn mag *Whitehouse* (itself cheekily titled after the matronly anti-porn crusader), Bennett's group preferred ultra-hardcore 'specialist' publications like *Tit Pulp* and *Shitfun*, each of which inspired a song of the same name. Fascism was another fave: the title of *Für Ilse Koch*, a compilation released on Whitehouse's Come label, honoured the sadistic wife of Buchenwald's commandant. Not content with paying tribute to a genocidal she-monster, Whitehouse commemorated famous British serial killers with the albums *Dedicated to Dennis Andrew Nielsen* and *Bradford Red Light District*.

If you can judge a band by its fans, the biggest indictment of Whitehouse is Peter Sotos, who proved to be such a kindred spirit that he joined the group in 1983. The creator of *PURE* fanzine, Sotos is a connoisseur of paedophiliac rapists and the 'artists' of the Third Reich. One typical issue offered a feature on a Chicago gang who ceremonially mutilate women; 'Kiddie Torture', an essay on the 'sublime pleasure' of child-slaughter; and 'Nazi Triumphs', a photo-article about Mengele-style medical experiments in Nazi concentration camps.

Another of Bennett's early collaborators, Steve Stapleton, wasn't a full-time member but moonlighted from his musical day job at the helm of Nurse with Wound. Whitehouse's de Sade-inspired 1981 album *The 150 Murderous Passions* was a joint project with NwW, and Stapleton played some of the early live aktions. 'I have great respect for Whitehouse, whose unfaltering chasm of noise goes deeper and deeper into the realms of the atonal,' he declared in the early eighties, while dissing TG as 'weak music for weak minds'.

Stapleton rejects the term 'industrial', claiming Nurse with Wound were lumped in that category only because their first album's cover featured bondage-and-fetish imagery from the magazine *Latex and Leather*

Special. But they *do* belong in that pigeonhole because of their post-rock approach to abstract noise sculptures and found-sound collages. If NwW had a spiritual avatar, it wasn't de Sade but another French writer, Lautreamont, author of the 1868 Gothic prose poem *Maldoror.* The group's 1979 debut, *Chance Meeting on a Dissecting Table of a Sewing Machine and an Umbrella,* took its title from one of Lautreamont's deliberately absurd similes, whose dream-logic incongruity led to him being hailed by the Surrealists as an illustrious ancestor. *Chance Meeting* gleaned a five-question-mark rating in *Sounds* (????? as opposed to the usual *****) because reviewer John Gill wasn't totally sure if its seemingly arbitrary concatenations of noise constituted pure genius or sheer nonsense.

Musically, Stapleton's prime crush was Krautrock. He had lived in Germany for a while, roadying for minor *kosmische* bands like Guru Guru and Kraan. A massive and legendarily eclectic list of 'electric experimental music', ranging from free improv through Euro-prog to *musique concrete,* was included on *Chance Meeting's* sleeve. In some ways Nurse with Wound are the world's longest-running Faust tribute band, their aesthetic based on the same principles of jarring audio-montage as that group's most celebrated album, *The Faust Tapes.* If *Chance Meeting* sounded shapeless (it was recorded in six hours by a bunch of semi-musicians who'd never previously played together), by 1982's *Homotopy to Marie* Stapleton had developed a genuinely idiosyncratic way of organizing noise, using the studio-as-instrument to create bizarre sound-worlds as gorgeously grotesque as a Quay Bros animation.

One thing most post-TG industrialists shared was a resolutely Nordic approach to rhythm. At best, this meant metronomic pulse grooves in the Moroder mould; at worst, it meant clunky and portentous march beats. A few industrial bands embraced contemporary black dance music, though, and two of the best, Sheffield's Clock DVA and London's 23 Skidoo, were TG protégés.

Clock DVA was what Adi Newton did after he was kicked out of The Future. Initially, he explored abstract sound experiments – tape loops, cut-ups, filtered frequencies and other psycho-sonic effects. 'The very first DVA was just so screwed up – junk and violence and tape recorders, big kicks,' Newton recalled. 'Sex and magic in an industrial setting.' Forging a relationship with TG, DVA released *White Souls Black Suits* through Industrial. Culled from fifteen hours of improvisation, no overdubs or retakes, the album was an attempt, says Newton, 'to record that moment when intuitive magic occurs – what the Surrealists describe as pure psychic automatism'. With DVA's second album, *Thirst*, the funk influence – James Brown, The Pop Group – kicked in. 'That's what we're after – more edgy, nervous energy sort of funk stuff, body music that flinches you and makes you move,' Newton declared. Laced with moody, sick-inside saxophone and driven by a ruminative scowl of a bassline, '4 Hours' comes closest to achieving that funk *noir* goal. *Thirst* was released in 1981 on Fetish, a label set up by Rod Pearce, a TG fan who put out Gristle's final single.

Fetish also released records by 23 Skidoo, P-Orridge acolytes who took the industrial-meets-funk idea much further than Clock DVA. Drawing on a handful of black precursors (the cocaine-spiked voodoo-funk of Miles Davis's *On the Corner*, The Last Poets' fire-and-brimstone street oratory, Fela Kuti's hard-trance polyrhythms) 23 Skidoo conceived of funk as a sinister energy, an active metaphor for Control. Groove as trap and treadmill. Their 1981 mini-LP *Seven Songs* topped the independent chart and still sounds blood-curdlingly intense. It opens with 'Kundalini', a malevolent tumble of hand percussion, guitar feedback and guttural chants. On 'Vegas el Bandito', seething slap bass and brittle-nerved rhythm jostle with lost-in-endless-fog trumpet (an industrial motif invented by Cosey Fanni Tutti, who played cornet on several TG tracks). Best of all is 'Porno Bass', in which industrial finally makes a *long*-overdue explicitly anti-fascist statement. Bass drones reverberate in cavernous murk, through which drifts the aristocratic voice of the loathsome Hitler groupie Unity Mitford, taken from a radio interview. Dropped in the middle of an album that's thrillingly steeped in trance rhythms and black funk, Mitford's railing against pop music's 'senseless reiteration' as 'the sign of a degenerating race' is implicitly exposed as Aryan paranoia.

Alex Turnbull of 23 Skidoo says that, although they owed a lot to TG practically (P-Orridge let them rehearse at the Death Factory) and intellectually, they were more inspired by intensely rhythmic groups like This Heat and A Certain Ratio. Throbbing Gristle severed itself completely from the music of the African diaspora: jazz, R&B, funk, reggae. Skidoo allowed black America back in. And they let the rest of the world get a look in, too. Fans of Can's 'Ethnological Forgeries' series and Holger Czukay's pan-global borrowings, 23 Skidoo played the first WOMAD Festival in July 1982, composing a special set that combined ethnic polyrhythms with urban *musique concrete*. 'Instead of using pleasant "world music" sounds, we used city noises, gas canisters, explosions,' says Turnbull. 'It was just this barrage of noise. A third of the crowd fled immediately, but of the ones that stayed, most of them were like, "Wow, that was absolutely unexpected!"'

Part of the WOMAD set comprised side one of their next album, *The Culling Is Coming*. Side two's chime-fest of tuned gongs indicated a drift eastwards, towards the music of Bali. After an expedition to Indonesia, they recorded 1984's *Urban Gamelan*. The vibe is a sort of humid disquiet – imagine *Apocalypse Now: The Day After*. The track 'GIFU' – a different version of Skidoo's dance-floor smash 'Coup' – even featured the Vietcong war-cry 'GI, fuck you', for extra anti-imperialist edge. By this point Skidoo were interested less in Gristle-style extreme noise terror, says Turnbull, and more in the idea of using repetition and polyrhythms gently to induce 'a kind of trance, that idea of reaching ecstasy through the music'. (Coincidentally, around this time, a drug called Ecstasy was making its first incursions into the industrial scene, but that's a whole different story . . .)

Black(-sounding) sheep of the industrial family, 23 Skidoo and Clock DVA were atypical TG offspring. The vast majority of second-wave industrialists favoured either abstract noisescapes or metronomic Teutonica. Deeper into the eighties, Gristle's spawn became ever more legion: Lustmord, Nocturnal Emissions, Death in June, In the Nursery, a:grumh, Controlled Bleeding, Laibach, Skinny Puppy, Severed Heads, Front 242, Last Few Days, :zoviet*france:, Merzbow . . . Most shared their progenitor's anti-rock (even anti-*music*) bias and content-laden, concept-driven slant. As with The Velvet Underground (one of the very few groups TG acknowledged as a precursor), it sometimes seems that almost everybody who heard Throbbing Gristle started their own band.

13

FREAK SCENE: Cabaret Noir and Theatre of Cruelty in Post-punk San Francisco

The Residents. Tuxedomoon. Factrix. Chrome. The Sleepers. Flipper.

'San Francisco's the kook capital of the world,' The Residents' spokesman Jay Clem once observed. It has long rivalled New York as a bohemian capital, a centre for artistic experiment and non-conformist living. 'What this city means to me is the last stand on American ground,' Damon Edge of Chrome declared in 1979. 'People who don't fit in anywhere else come here . . . There's no place else to go in America.'

Everyone knows about the 1950s beat poets and writers clustered around City Lights bookstore, and about Haight Street and the Fillmore in the late sixties, the acid tests and be-ins. But San Francisco also enjoyed a third golden age with punk rock and industrial culture in the late seventies and early eighties – bands like Chrome, Tuxedomoon, The Residents, Factrix and Flipper, to name just a handful. Tuxedomoon's Blaine L. Reininger wrote of this era as 'our own "Belle Epoque" . . . San Francisco seemed to be full of geniuses then, and the scene which arose around places like the Mabuhay Gardens and the Deaf Club felt like Paris must have felt when people like Toulouse-Lautrec and Gauguin were meeting in the cafés in Montmartre . . . We felt possessed by some demon or god, and we went about our business in what I can only call a state of grace.'

Like New York, San Francisco in those days was somewhere you could live on virtually nothing, allowing artists to avoid full-time jobs and concentrate on their creative work. The downtown area south of Market Street was full of inexpensive, run-down apartments and lofts formerly used for light manufacturing. 'That "industrial" element was a big part of San Francisco culture,' says Joseph Jacobs, bassist of the city's

245

premier 'industrial' band, Factrix. All over the city there were faded-looking 'Victorians', large houses that could be rented dirt cheap. 'I had a fourteen-room Victorian for six hundred dollars a month which I shared with four other people,' says Tuxedomoon's bassist Peter Principle. 'You could get by because things were inexpensive and the community was supportive.'

San Francisco audiences had a high tolerance for pretentiousness. 'Sure, there was a lot of bad performance art!' confirms Factrix guitarist Bond Bergland. 'But that's OK – better that it was allowed. And people were *very* allowing!' When it came to the city's rock scene, though, the years immediately prior to punk had the feel of an aftermath – washed-up hippies wondering what the fuck *happened*, man. Live music almost disappeared as disco took over. Rock clubs were converted into discotheques, where only records were played; disco bands rarely performed live. 'If you were in a band at that time, the only way you could get work was by playing other people's songs,' says Jacobs.

When punk arrived, San Francisco was one of the first cities in America to embrace it. The scene centred on a handful of hang-outs – Café Flor, the Deaf Club, the Mabuhay and Temple Beautiful. Flor was the nerve centre for a host of artists, musicians and performers. Located in the sleazy Mission District, the Deaf Club was 'an authentic club for the deaf where you ordered beer in sign language and where presumably the patrons didn't mind the music because they couldn't hear it,' says Tuxedomoon's Steve Brown. 'I guess they liked the vibrating floorboards!' Surrounded by strip clubs, the Filipino restaurant Mabuhay held punk-rock gigs every night, while Temple Beautiful was an abandoned synagogue next door to cult leader Jim Jones's temple. 'They'd put a generator outside Temple Beautiful and just wire the electricity in for the night of the show,' recalls Principle.

Along with classic punk bands like The Avengers and The Dead Kennedys, the San Francisco scene was a hospitable environment for experimental outfits, who might have been inspired by punk's confrontational attitude but quickly moved into more expansive or esoteric musical terrain. It became America's second post-punk city after New York. But even more than No Wave Manhattan, San Francisco's scene explored the possibilities of mixed-media spectacle – a tendency shaped partly by the living legacy of the city's gay radical theatre groups (like the Angels of Light) and partly by the 'total art' ideas circulating in the milieu surrounding the city's Art Institute.

Tuxedomoon's Steve Brown, for instance, came out of sixties underground theatre. Blaine L. Reininger, the other co-founder of Tuxedomoon, had been exploring the idea of fusing music, writing and theatre into 'unified field art'. Factrix weren't so much art-damaged as Artaud-damaged. 'We were trying to bring the Theatre of Cruelty to the rock stage,' says Bergland. 'It was really about confrontation, pushing people over the edge – something you'd seen at full steam with the Living Theater in the 1960s. The hippy thing was culturally played down during punk, but it was still the clear revolutionary predecessor.' This post-sixties radical-theatre sensibility was shared by Factrix's contemporaries and collaborators: extreme performance artists like Monte Cazazza and Joanna Went; Mark Pauline, who staged spectacles under the name Survival Research Laboratories; and Z'ev, a late sixties veteran (his band Ariel briefly negotiated with Zappa's Bizarre label) renowned for ritualistic performances involving metal-bashing percussion.

Cinema was an equally crucial source of inspiration. Repertory theatres like the Strand and the Embassy played a mix of classic movies, obscure foreign films and cheap horror flicks. *Eraserhead* was *the* midnight movie in San Francisco for a couple of years. Inspired by Buñuel's *Un Chien Andalou*, Factrix talked of wanting to take 'a razor to the mind's eye'. 'Surrealism was a huge influence on Factrix, but mostly the films – the painting was a little too *nice*,' says Bergland. 'But everybody in San Francisco during that period was *heavily* inspired by film.' The Residents even tried to make their own modern surrealist movie, the ill-starred *Vileness Fats* – allegedly a fourteen-hour musical–comedy– romance set in a world of one-armed midgets! – which was eventually abandoned. But they did pioneer the promo video, while their live performances involved elaborate stage sets and costumes, including the famous giant masks that transformed each Resident's head into a monstrous eyeball.

The Residents *feel* like a post-punk band. That's definitely the era when they had their biggest impact. In 1978, when they first started to become widely known, they were often mentioned in the same breath as Pere Ubu and Devo – partly because of a shared vibe of grotesquerie, and partly because Devo and The Residents both released sacrilegious covers of The Rolling Stones' 'Satisfaction' as singles within a few months of each other. In the aftermath of punk, freaks like The Residents reached an audience they'd otherwise never have found. But the group had been around for nearly a decade before punk. Originally from Louisiana, they migrated to California in the late sixties, hoping to catch the high tide of psychedelia but arriving only in time to witness its ebbing. 'The Residents sprang . . . from the fact that Psychedelia dead-ended,' declared Hardy Fox of Cryptic Corporation, the organization that looked after the band's affairs. 'The people who were doing experiments in that direction stopped when they had barely scratched the surface.'

The Residents wanted to take psychedelia further. Being non-musicians, they felt, was the only way to guarantee truly free creativity. 'Before they started doing The Residents, they had never played,' Homer Flynn, also of Cryptic Corp, said. 'By teaching themselves, they felt it was a good path towards originality.' The music's wonderfully angular melodies and jerky rhythms seemed unprecedented but the band *did* have musical influences; it's just that they were unrecognizable because 'The Residents weren't *capable* of rendering them that faithfully', as Flynn put it.

Perhaps that's why Warner Bros rejected them. In 1971 the group (then nameless) sent off demo tapes to the label's Harve Halverstadt, who'd worked with their hero Captain Beefheart. Because they'd provided only a return address, the tapes came back addressed to 'Residents, 20 Sycamore St., San Francisco'. Now christened, but lacking an outlet for their music, The Residents set up their own independent label, Ralph Records. The band's do-it-yourself impulse went much further than even Rough Trade in England, aiming for complete cultural autonomy. Their warehouse HQ in San Francisco's Grove Street contained a recording studio, offices for the Cryptic Corporation and Ralph Records, a darkroom, a graphics studio for designing their own sleeve artwork, and a huge sound stage for making films and videos.

A couple of years ahead of Public Image Ltd, The Residents trailblazed the pop-group-posing-as-a-corporation strategy. With a twist: the group remained completely anonymous and faceless, and all dealings with the outside world were mediated via the Cryptic Corporation. The question 'Who *are* the Residents?' stirred much speculation. One persistent rumour maintained that they were the post-break-up Beatles rejoining in secret for neo-Dadaist mischief-making. This probably stems from the fact that early on the group toyed with calling themselves The New Beatles, while their 1974 debut, *Meet the Residents*, featured on its front cover defaced portraits of Lennon, McCartney, Harrison and Starr from *Meet the Beatles*. To the Residents, the Fab Four symbolized everything bad and everything good about pop: its tyrannical mind-controlling ubiquity (Lennon's 'we're bigger than Jesus' comment) but also the experimental potential of psychedelia.

MEET THE RESIDENTS

The First Album by North Louisiana's Phenomenal Pop Combo

The Residents' debut album, *Meet the Residents*, 1974

All these conflicted feelings came together on their 1977 single 'Beyond the Valley of a Day in the Life' – a piece also known as 'The Beatles Play the Residents and the Residents Play the Beatles' – which featured 'samples' of The Beatles' wilder moments woven into an eerie audio collage. At various points you hear Lennon singing, 'Don't believe in Beatles' (from his first solo album) and issuing this wan apology to their global audience: 'Please, everybody, if we haven't done what we could have done, we've tried.' The Residents had already released *The Third Reich N Roll* in 1976: a darkly comic satire of post-Beatles pop as totalitarianism, with *American Bandstand* presenter Dick Clark dressed as Hitler on the front. The sidelong 'Swastikas on Parade' is a medley of defiled sixties hits overlaid with blitzkrieg sound effects – air-raid sirens, dive-bombing Stukas, machine-gun fire. In its sleevenote the Cryptic Corporation describes the record as a 'tribute to the thousands of little power-mad minds of the music industry who have helped to make us what we are'.

After a flurry of releases in 1977–8, Cryptic Corp announced the imminent release of the grand masterwork that The Residents had been building up to – *Eskimo*. A sonic recreation of the world of the Inuit, the record would also serve as a tribute-cum-elegy to their vanishing folkways: bathing in urine, slaughtering superfluous newborn girls, putting the old folks out to die of hypothermia, that sort of thing . . . After six weeks of small ads in the music press that steadily whipped up your intrigue, Cryptic Corp abruptly announced the record's suspension from the Ralph release schedule. The Residents, it seemed, had gone AWOL and run off with the master tapes.

In a separate statement The Residents declared they'd split from Cryptic Corp and would never let 'those bloodsuckers' have *Eskimo*. Their managers responded with the claim that the group had gone mad through being 'cooped up' in the studio for too long making the album. 'Towards the end they were already being difficult and acting oddly – working all night and communicating only with strange cries when we – the Cryptic officers – were around,' Jay Clem told *Sounds* in September 1978. 'Then they locked us out altogether when they were working, and when I tried to reason with them they filled the reception area three mornings running with wicker baskets full of ice and sometimes fish from the Bay wharf.' This whole 'falling out' between Cryptic Corporation and The Residents was, of course, totally staged – a miniature masterpiece of disinformation and hype. Although to this day the pretence is studiously maintained that Cryptic Corporation and The Residents are separate entities, at some point the truth seeped out: The Residents and their 'representatives' were one and the same.

When the 'rift' was healed and *Eskimo* was finally released in the autumn of 1979, the record was deservedly hailed as a masterpiece, even if the *NME*'s verdict – 'without doubt one of the most important albums ever made' – is possibly a little over the top. It did sell 100,000 copies worldwide, though, a staggering achievement for so unsettling a record. Evoking the alien experiences of life on the polar ice cap – walrus hunts conducted in conditions of disorientating white-out, 'arctic hysteria' induced by the sensory deprivation of the long winter darkness – *Eskimo* seemed to make the temperature in your room plummet.

Eye to eye – The Residents, disguised, on the cover of the classic *Eskimo*, 1979

The Residents then swerved from *Eskimo*'s listener-challenging experimentalism to the surprising accessibility of *The Commercial Album*. It wasn't called that through any crossover ambition but because each piece was only one minute long – closer to the duration of a TV commercial than a pop song. The Residents' rationale for this condensed approach was persuasive: since most pop songs contain a verse and chorus repeated three times within three minutes, condensing that down to sixty seconds automatically trims away all the redundant material. *The Commercial Album* distils the quintessence of exquisite weirdness and macabre whimsy that is Residents music into forty jingles as intricate and succinct as Japanese calligraphy.

*

Ralph's other great release of 1980 was Tuxedomoon's debut album, *Half-Mute*, a lost masterpiece of synthpop *noir*. The group began as an offshoot of The Angels of Light, 'a "family" of dedicated artists who sang, danced, painted and sewed for the Free Theater', says Steve Brown. 'I was lucky to be part of the Angels – I fell for a bearded transvestite in the show and moved in with him at the Angels' commune. Gay or bi men and women who were themselves works of art, extravagant in dress and behaviour, disciples of Artaud and Wilde and Julian Beck [of the Living Theater] . . . we lived together in a big Victorian house . . . pooled all our disability cheques each month, ate communally . . . and used the rest of the funds to produce lavish theatrical productions – never charging a dime to the public. *This* is what theatre was meant to be: a Dionysian rite of lights and music and chaos and Eros.'

Despite these sixties roots, Tuxedomoon's music looked ahead to the electronic eighties. Blaine Reininger and Steve Brown originally met after enrolling in an electronic music class at San Francisco's City College, and each was blown away by the other's end-of-term performance. 'Blaine's effort was a full-blown "total art" spectacle,' says Brown. 'He sang and danced in a white smock, with a balloon head-dress, backdropped by projected Super-8 films.' For his piece, Brown set up a tape-loop system as diagrammed on the back of Brian Eno's *Discreet Music*, into which he played washes of string sounds using a Polymoog synth.

To help him with the piece, Brown called on the technical skill of a fellow Angel of Light called Tommy Tadlock, who was heavily involved in the Angels' music scores. Tadlock was the great lost catalyst figure of San Francisco post-punk. He became Tuxedomoon's mentor/guru/technician/manager and later worked with Factrix building bizarre sound-generating gizmos. When Reininger and Brown joined forces, they started rehearsing *chez* Tadlock. 'There in the house on Upper Market Street, we all cranked out our weirdness together into something called Tuxedomoon,' recalls Brown. 'To say Tommy was a pivotal, all-important first member of Tuxedomoon would be an understatement.' Tadlock played a crucial role as a 'audio systems designer . . . Blaine played both electronic violin and guitar on stage, and Tommy designed "Treatment Mountain" for him – a plywood pyramid displaying junction boxes or compressors or effects he had designed and built, as well as an Echoplex.'

Tuxedomoon developed a style based partly on what instruments were handy (Reininger's violin, Brown's saxophone, Tadlock's Polymoog) and partly on prohibition ('the only rule was the tacit understanding that anything that sounded like anyone else was taboo'). They were just starting when punk arrived, and although hearing 'God Save the Queen' initially encouraged them, Tuxedomoon soon felt that punk had 'ossified into a puritan dogma of guitars bass and drums and screaming vocalist', says Brown. 'When Blaine and I first started performing in public – a violin, a sax, a synth and a tape-recorder – the crowd threw beer bottles and screamed: "Where's the drummer?!"'

Gradually, Tuxedomoon expanded – not to incorporate a drummer, but recruiting underground radio activist Peter Principle as bassist, then performance-artist Winston Tong and movie-maker Bruce Geduldig. Principle recalls an unstoppable flow of creativity: 'Every three or four weeks we'd have a gig booked and say, "Let's write a new show – a whole new show." We wrote albums' worth of material that we later mined over our career. We all had other areas to draw on and feed us . . . Blaine had been trained as a classical musician and played in an orchestra; Steven was a kind of film-maker who was fascinated with soundtrack music; I had tried to do radio theatre – avant-garde psycho-dramas. I've also always been involved with foleys – the guy in the movies who collects the noise of, say, car horns on a bridge. So we all had experience with sound design and sounds used out of the context of pop music.'

Tong was a figure of some renown on the San Francisco scene. 'First time I saw him was on Upper Castro Street in a salon/party in a very nice Victorian apartment,' recalls Brown. 'The buzz of the party hushed and there in the centre of the room was Winston in a black tux with two dolls, for lack of a better word . . . They were really *alive* . . . these *creatures*, these homunculi he had created.' Tuxedomoon's concerts grew ever more multi-levelled and visually arresting. 'I can think of shows we did using tapes, live instruments, professional painted sets hanging onstage, a female chorus, Winston and his wondrous homunculi, Bruce Geduldig's film projections,' marvels Brown.

Around 1980, many people started talking up 'cabaret' as an alternative model to the rock gig, with its shabby setting, low production values and tired rituals (support groups, encores, etc.). Organizations like Cabaret Futura in London, groups like Kid Creole & The Coconuts and Pink Military Stands Alone, synthpop idol Gary Numan – all cast their eyes back to pre-rock ideas of showbiz, 'variety' and Broadway, while simultaneously glancing sideways to the contemporary margins (performance art, multimedia). Entertainment that was costumed, scripted and choreographed, that didn't hide its artifice but revelled in it, began to seem more honest than rock's faux-spontaneity. Tuxedomoon arrived at just the right moment to tap into this shift. 'Other San Francisco performers like Joanna Went used props and audience interaction but in a shock-oriented way, whereas we had a feeling for the cabaret thing,' says Principle. 'That's why we wore tuxedos in punk-rock clubs like the Mabuhay, like it was a dinner theatre. And we had this concept of loungezak – muzak made for existentially angsted New Wave people.'

Tuxedomoon even called their publishing company Angst Music. On songs like 'What Use?' and '7 Years', cold electronics, shudders of violin, and lugubrious saxophone conjured an atmosphere of languid melancholy. From the *Scream with a View* EP to the second album, *Desire*, themes of anomie and modernity recurred. 'Holiday for Plywood', for instance, is about consumer paranoia and dream-home heartache: 'You daren't sit on the sofa/The plastic makes you sweat/The bathroom's done in mirror tiles/The toaster wants your blood'.

Tuxedomoon's aura of jaded elegance always seemed somehow 'European', so it was hardly surprising that the group made their greatest impact overseas. Apart from New York – that most un-American city-state full of rootless cosmopolitans, where Tuxedomoon went down a storm at arty bohemian nightspots like the Mudd Club – the group didn't receive a warm reception on their rare forays outside San Francisco. 'In the American music scene at that time there was an attitude about authenticity,' says Principle. 'We had that problem even in San Francisco, so you can imagine how it went down in the middle of America. We also had a lot of trouble finding studio situations with engineers who could work with drum machines. Programmed rhythm was a foreign concept in America back then and there was a lot of hostility towards drum machines.'

'Tuxedomoon were kind of mentors to us,' says Joseph Jacobs of Factrix. 'Not musically, but in the sense of "You can actually *do this* – be in a band with no drummer and have audiences." When we started Factrix, we didn't even talk about having a drummer. We knew we wanted to do something different, so we removed one of the key components of rhythm and blues.'

Although the group talk of being more inspired by films and literature than music, Factrix were really excited by PiL's 'death to rock' rhetoric and Throbbing Gristle's commitment to sonic mutation. Tommy

Tadlock served as their Chris Carter figure, helping them build their own modified instruments – 'glaxobass', 'radioguitar', 'amputated bass' – and letting them use these bizarre proto-synths he'd acquired called Optigans. 'It stood for "optical organs",' says Bond Bergland. 'They were instruments for the family to play songs on, with the songs stored on these clear plastic acetates, which the Optigan read through some kind of light-reading device. Messing around with them, we realized right away that you could put the acetates in upside down and backwards – play them the wrong way. That was what was really inspiring to us at the time – "Let's see what happens if we do this *wrong*."'

Factrix tried anything and everything that wasn't standard rock instrumentation – whistling tea kettles, cheap gadgets from Toys R Us, an inexpensive early sequencer called the Mutron. 'But really the main instrument was Joseph's tape-recorder,' says Bergland. 'We did a lot of experiments with tape. We'd record the drum machine fast and slow it down to quarter speed, so it just made the drum sound much bigger.' Along with the latest technology, Factrix were equally interested in pre-modern and non-Western sounds: ethnic instruments with names like the doumbek and the saz. 'Even the drum-machine rhythms were trying to mimic African drumming in a very loose way, inspired by field recordings. This was years before "world music" existed,' says Bergland. 'My thinking was: If something sticks around for thousands of years, it probably has some meaning, something real about it. My guitar playing was really influenced by the human voice – I was listening to a lot of Bulgarian vocal music.' In this respect – a fascination for ecstatic ritual music – Factrix were a couple of steps ahead of Throbbing Gristle.

With its picturesque hills and quaint trams, its foggy bay and idyllic Golden Gate Park, San Francisco doesn't immediately seem like an 'industrial' city. Yet it ranked alongside Sheffield and London as a bastion of industrial music. Cabaret Voltaire and Throbbing Gristle performed to huge crowds in San Francisco; TG even played their last gig at the Kezar Pavilion in 1981. The city was also home to the unofficial fifth member of TG, Monte Cazazza, a renegade researcher into all things aberrant who describes himself as an 'outcast historian, a cultural mortician'. Cazazza, Factrix and Mark Pauline from Survival Research Laboratories formed what Bergland calls 'a little scene'. Together they staged a series of mixed-media extravaganzas that left audiences reeling. 'Most bands were playing the punk clubs like Mabuhay, but Factrix had a rule: we don't want to play there,' says Bergland. 'We wanted to make spectacles, so people were aware this was an unusual event. The first one we did together was at the Kezar Pavilion – Monte made a big stainless-steel swastika spinning on an axis, handcuffed himself to it, and hung upside down.'

Mark Pauline wasn't a musician but a sort of crackpot inventor who staged apocalyptic battles between robots he'd constructed. An alumnus of Eckerd College in Florida alongside No Wavers Arto Lindsay and Mark Cunningham, Pauline participated in San Francisco's first Punk Art Show in 1978 and made his solo debut performance with *Machine Sex* the following year. 'When Survival Research Laboratories threw an event, it really was a spectacle,' says Jacobs. 'It was like seeing a live movie. There was always this edgy element of danger because these machines were crude. Things would explode when they shouldn't, or wouldn't explode when they should!'

The most infamous multimedia shockfest staged by SRL, Cazazza and Factrix – *Night of the Succubus*, June 1981 – involved Pauline making automatons like the 'rabot', fashioned from metal, electrical wire and a rotting rabbit carcass. 'We got all these meat parts and sewed them on to this robot,' Pauline has said of another of his grisly creations. 'We used pig feet, pig hide and a cow's head and bolted it on to this little feller – it had a motor on it, and when you turned the motor on, it would just vibrate and shake like he was sick, like he maybe had a fever.' Christened Piggly Wiggly, the grotesque chimera could also turn its head and move its arms.

'The last song of the night we did a twenty-minute version of "Helter Skelter" from *The White Album*, and it sounded like the soundtrack to World War Three,' recalls Bergland. 'Mark had made these pneumatic airguns out of eight-foot pipes, and he'd taken all these eighteen-inch steel bolts and sharpened them to a razor point. And they were shooting these darts at incredible velocity over the heads of the audience into Piggly Wiggly, who was being pulled over the audience's head on a tether. After Piggly was full of darts, Joseph drilled out all his teeth, so the whole place was filled with cow-teeth dust. A few people got freaked out. Some "surrealist" friends of ours got disgusted with Piggly Wiggly, and one tried to break him with a chair. But everybody else was really turned on by this experience; their eyes were huge. For us, it was just super-deep, darkest-black humour.'

Factrix were engrossed by all things morbid and extreme. But there was also an otherworldly impulse in their music, a psychedelic yearning to jettison language and escape time. 'Scramble thought patterns, break up the syntax,' is how singer and lyricist Cole Palme characterized their intent. Bergland's guitar was blatantly trippy, billowing up in gaseous arabesques that placed him in the tradition of West Coast acid-rock and Krautrockers like Manuel Gottsching. 'I don't so much recall that we were tripping when we were making the music so much as we were tripping when we were performing,' chuckles Jacobs. Friends who 'wanted to ensure an interesting musical experience for themselves' would ply the band with magic mushrooms. 'Drugs weren't really informing our sonic experiments on a daily basis, though,' says Bergland, citing both poverty and 'a strong work ethic' as reasons for the abstinence. 'The mystical part of Factrix was the same as Coltrane or any musician who's trying to get to the place where the music is free. The sounds, they really did have a life of their own. We were really just following the sounds. We were disciples of feedback.'

'Disciples of feedback' would be a good description of Chrome, who were tagged 'industrial' but really were much closer to Throbbing Gristle's original self-description: 'post-psychedelic trash'. The band's musical genius, Helios Creed – an LSD-gobbling Hendrix fiend who'd migrated from his native Hawaii to San Francisco just a little too late for psychedelia's golden age – developed a guitar sound that was 'acid' in both the 'Aaaaagh, my face, my face!' and *Are You Experienced?* senses. It also sounds metallic, not in the sense of heavy metal as genre so much as conjuring visions of twisted and torn car-flesh.

The band was actually started by Damon Edge, a graduate of Cal Arts in Los Angeles, where he'd studied with Allan Kaprow, the guy who invented 'happenings'. At Cal Arts, Edge also dabbled in avant-garde music: tape experiments and '"not quite right" music' (as he dubbed it in one interview), some of which ended up soundtracking porn movies. The first incarnation of Chrome didn't feature Creed's guitar, and their 1976 debut, *The Visitation*, sounded like a belated West Coast trip band somewhere in the vicinity of Santana and Quicksilver Messenger Service. When Creed arrived to add his harshly treated guitar to Edge's synth and science-fiction lyrics, Chrome's sound made a quantum leap forward: they went from psychedelic johnny-come-latelys to 'making music for 1995', as Edge put it.

A turning point in the band's evolution occurred when Creed went round to Edge's house and heard *Never Mind the Bollocks* for the first time. 'I didn't know what to think, but the more we listened to it, the more we got behind it. So we decided "Wow, let's be a *punk* band. Let's cut our hair!" Then Damon played me these whacked-out tape loops he'd made in art school and I was, like, "Man, this is the best shit you've done. Let's mix our punk shit with your weird acid shit. And let's call ourselves 'acid punk'."'

In punk DIY style, Chrome released their own records – but only out of necessity. After being rejected by local indie label Beserkley, Edge borrowed money off his wealthy parents and started his own label, Siren, in order to release *Alien Soundtracks* (the first Chrome album to feature Creed). 'All the early copies, the first three hundred or so, were pressed up by hand with a crank,' recalls Creed. 'That was the cheapest way you could get records manufactured. And we glued the covers together ourselves.' *Alien Soundtracks* and its 1979 sequel, *Half Machine Lip Moves*, made them cult figures, especially in Germany and the UK (where they were eventually signed to Beggar's Banquet).

Chrome's own description, 'acid punk', fits but 'cyberpunk' would do just as nicely. One of the band members went by the name John L. Cyborg, and you could imagine Chrome classics like 'Chromosone Damage', 'All Data Lost' and 'Abstract Nympho' as a cold-rush soundtrack for *Neuromancer*, the 1985 genre-defining novel by William Gibson. (Who, a few years earlier, wrote a short story entitled 'Burning Chrome'.) Edge and Creed were both science-fiction fanatics, although the latter says their inspirations came more from movies than books. 'When I was in Hawaii I saw a UFO hovering right over my head – that really influenced me. Me and Damon had all these theories about how you could be channelled by aliens. They could make music through you that wasn't normal.'

Whether it was of extraterrestial origin or not, Chrome's music certainly sounded mindbending. As Creed puts it, 'the reality of the psychedelic experience isn't love and peace; it's *insanity*. One of the first things people noticed was Chrome sounds like a paranoid trip. If you actually took LSD and listened to our records, the trip would get so whacked-out you'd start laughing. Funny–scary, we called it. The bad trip would turn into a good trip, 'cos you'd already been to the most negative part of the universe.'

Flipper set their controls for precisely this pitch-black void core of the cosmos. Surfing the music's tidal wave of rubble and dregs, singers Bruce

Lose and Will Shatter delivered lines like 'Ever wish the human race didn't exist?' and 'Feel so empty feel so old/Just waiting to feel the death like cold' with a strange exuberance. Flipper stared into the abyss only to hawk some phlegm into it.

Of all San Francisco's post-punk groups, Flipper were the punkest, to the point of almost belonging to the hardcore scene. But their music leaned a little too far towards dirges to fit comfortably with that movement's 'loud-fast rules' dogma. Musically, they had more in common with Public Image Ltd's abstraction than The Dead Kennedys' anthems. PiL and Flipper both aimed for a kind of visceral vanguard music, sonically radical but not rarefied or pretentious. 'We want to experiment with the music without being an art band,' Shatter told punkzine *MaximumRockNRoll*. Like PiL, Flipper loved disco and funkateers like Rick James. The saxophone-boosted juggernaut 'Sex Bomb', Flipper's big crowd-pleaser, was steeped in funk. As in PiL, the bass (played alternately by Lose and Shatter) adopted the melodic role, allowing the guitarist to rain corrosive noise on the listener's head. Like Keith Levene, guitarist Ted Falconi rarely played riffs or distinct power chords, but instead just churned up distorted drone tones and writhing weals of feedback.

'I saw Bruce Lose at the PiL press conference in San Francisco in 1980,' says Joe Carducci, who co-produced the band's debut single. 'When they threw it open to questions from the audience, Bruce kept yelling, "What do you think of Flipper?" The question was ignored! Bruce was just pranking it, but he was obsessed with Johnny Rotten – he really wanted to meet him. And Flipper did actually get to open for PiL at their San Francisco show.' Flipper, though, weren't nearly as precious about what they did as Lydon's lot. Their attitude is captured in the slogan 'Flipper suffered for their art; now it's your turn' and in Falconi's immortal quip: 'Flipper doesn't want audiences with good taste; Flipper wants audiences that taste good.'

Live, Flipper managed to combine frat-party riotousness and audience confrontation. Carducci recalls one show where Shatter and Falconi engaged the crowd in a beer-can-throwing contest while Lose and drummer Steve DePace played a dirge groove for forty minutes. Lose remembers another occasion shortly after the birth of his son when he lugged three weeks' worth of soiled nappies to a gig and pelted the audience. 'The audience tended to throw them right back at the band. Steve got a dirty diaper in the face. The band thanked me *a lot* for that bright idea!'

'We tried to convey the irreverence and silliness Flipper projected onstage when we pulled together the live album *Public Flipper Limited*,' says Steve Tupper, who released the group's records on his SF-based indie, Subterranean. Humour permeated even the most nihilistic Flipper songs like 'Nothing' and 'Life Is Cheap'. 'It was kind of extremely optimistic and extremely bleak at the same time.' Tupper points out the ambiguity of Shatter's line 'Life is the only thing worth living for', delivered in a voice pitched exactly midway between cynical derision (at the sentiment's fatuity) and desperate belief.

Flipper may have evolved into a sort of *National Lampoon* PiL, but they had been founded by Ricky Williams, in between stints as the singer of a band some regard as America's version of Joy Division – The Sleepers. In his book *Rock and the Pop Narcotic*, Carducci described them as 'what Joy Division might have developed into had they the balls'. Today he waxes fondly about The Sleepers' 'slow, minor-chord Gothic songs' and the 'narcotic spectral jaw-dropping beauty' of guitarist Michael Belfer's playing. Williams was a mentally volatile, dysfunctional character, though. He had coined the name Flipper, inspired by finding a shark-ravaged dolphin on the beach while tripping on acid, but soon the rest of the band – hardly models of stability themselves – had kicked him out and replaced him with Lose.

'In the early days Flipper's music was so abstract, a lot of people thought they were just improvising,' says Carducci. 'Gradually it coalesced into something that was more groove-oriented and formulaic – a good formula, though. But Flipper's the reason I bought a tape-recorder – I taped all their early gigs because they were so evanescent at the start. You'd go, "Wow, that was a great gig but I can't even remember any of it." And I don't do any drugs!'

This same impulse to document something vital but fleeting inspired Steve Tupper to found Subterranean. 'There were all these bands in the San Francisco area and they weren't getting recorded. There was just one label really, 415, and they were doing New Wave pop stuff. The first Subterranean release was the *SF Underground* seven-inch EP with four different bands, including Flipper. The other three were all more conventional, straight-ahead punk. Flipper really stood out because they were totally different from anybody else in town.'

Tupper was an underground-culture veteran with a pedigree in late sixties protest and community activism – anti-Vietnam War campaigns, the Diggers, the People's Park in Berkeley, tenants' unions and a 1970 city-wide rent strike, food co-ops. But, apart from helping with one rock festival, he was never particularly involved in the musical side of the counter-culture – until punk took off in San Francisco. He participated in New Youth, an 'alternative non-profit production company' designed to create places for bands to play that weren't dependent on commercial club promoters, and helped to set up a local chapter of Rock Against Racism. Subterranean documented many local punk bands, as well as San Francisco's experimental fringe (Tupper put out the Factrix/Monte Cazazza album *California Babylon* and records by Z'ev). Flipper, Factrix, Z'ev and local synth-punk outfit Nervous Gender all appeared on *Live at Target* – a four-way split live compilation that is the West Coast counterpart to *No New York*.

Of all Subterranean's groups, Flipper had the greatest impact. *Album-Generic Flipper*, from 1981, rocked like a wild party on the rim of the void. Three years later, *Gone Fishin'* pushed the band's bass-grind dirge-punk into more experimental zones: stark and hypnotic, 'The Lights, The Sound, The Rhythm, The Noise' is a kissing cousin to Joy Division's 'Transmission', while the celestial maelstrom of 'You Nought Me' swirls with Sun Ra keyboards, multitracked vocals, and pitch-bent sounds, like a demonic kaleidoscope where all the colours are black. 'When we were making *Gone Fishin'*, one evening nobody showed up but me,' recalls Lose. 'So I laid down a huge number of extra tracks of sounds – fifty vocal tracks, piano work, percussion, clavinet, phasing effects. The next day, the guys flipped out and they were, like, "We've got to take twenty-five of these voices out" . . . But it was a lot of fun making that record.' By the closing 'One by One', Flipper sound like they're smashing their way through the planet's crust. 'Will's beating up his bass and trying to sound like the low-rumbling surf, Ted is playing the psalm of the ocean, Steve's drums are the waves crashing, and me, I'm singing the body of water,' says Lose, misty-eyed and mystical.

By 1985, though, the pace of Flipper's hedonism was wearing down the band. Some members favoured speed; others preferred downers and prescription drugs. Lose describes himself and Shatter as 'polymorphic drug users, doing anything and everything'. Within a few years of *Gone Fishin'*, Shatter died from a heroin overdose and Flipper disintegrated. 'Drugs did in most of the San Francisco bands quickly,' says Carducci. According to Helios Creed, this was one factor in the break-up of Chrome. 'Damon got introduced to heroin and I got introduced to speed. He became more introverted and agoraphobic, and I got the opposite. I was like, "This ain't no good. I've got to put a band together and go tour."'

San Francisco changed in the early eighties as the 'belle epoque' Blaine L. Reineger wrote about began to fade. The dual assassinations of Mayor George Moscone and City Supervisor Harvey Milk tolled the death-knell for an era of liberalism. 'Moscone was a Kennedy-like figure and Milk was the country's first openly gay elected representative,' says Steve Brown. 'It was a heavy blow. There was a very dark period after those killings: the energy was very heavy and negative. When the killer, this ex-cop Dan White, got off with such a light sentence based on his defence as being a family man under a lot of stress . . . there was an incredible outburst from the normally reserved gay community: a huge riot, dozens of burning police cars.' In the eighties, under new mayor Dianne Feinstein, the city's boho-friendly downtown was torn up for redevelopment: speculators moved in and brand-new office buildings went up. By this point, Tuxedomoon were feeling the pull of Europe, where they found themselves treated like artists, playing professional theatres with proper dressing rooms. 'We were touring Europe during the 1980 elections,' says Brown, 'and Blaine joked to interviewers that if Reagan was elected we weren't going back to America. And essentially this is what happened.'

Those who stayed in San Francisco found the scene contracting, becoming less receptive to experimentation. The energy that came out of punk split in two directions: the avant-garde/industrial fringe and hardcore punk, the latter based more in the suburbs. 'San Francisco doesn't really have an equivalent to Orange Country or Long Beach, the strongholds of hardcore in Southern California,' says Steve Tupper. 'But as you go down the peninsula towards San Jose, or over the Berkeley Hills to places like Walnut Creek, the sensibility does get more hardcore. And when hardcore took over, it was mostly a deterioration – less about people trying to do something different; more just trying to fit into a trend.' Says Lose, 'In the early days, it wasn't necessary for bands to play fast and loud. One night, you might see Factrix, Nervous Gender and The Avengers on the same bill – three extremely different acts. But by the early eighties you'd go to a hardcore show and you'd see three hardcore bands.' According to Bond Bergland, 'The really serious experimental people moved to New York' – including himself, after Factrix ground to a halt.

Joe Carducci, soon to move to Los Angeles to help run SST – a label that managed to be both hardcore *and* progressive – fondly remembers the late seventies San Francisco scene as 'real vital . . . a place people could get an audience, right up to the end of 1981'. The downside was a certain dilettantism: 'There's something about San Francisco that encourages you to fold your band up and do a side project or dabble around with somebody else.' Another problem with bohemian paradises is that they can breed their own odd brand of parochialism, Carducci argues. 'Except for Dead Kennedys and Flipper, those bands didn't take it out on the road. A lot of them felt, I think, that they were *way* ahead of the rest of the country.'

14

CAREERING: PiL and Post-punk's Peak and Fall

Public Image Ltd.

Public Image Ltd's big year was 1979. Virgin, still convinced John Lydon was their hottest property, allowed the group to treat expensive top-of-the-line studios as their sound laboratory and playpen. And, after the shaky debut, the music was starting to come together. PiL even lived together as one happy family *chez* Lydon. Just before embarking on the ill-fated Sex Pistols tour of America, Lydon had shrewdly used his slim earnings to buy a home. 45 Gunter Grove was a Victorian terrace at the scuzzy end of Chelsea. 'John had the top part of the house,' says Keith Levene. 'I had the bottom, and Dave Crowe lived in this bit you had to walk through to get upstairs.' Only Jah Wobble kept his distance, preferring to stay with his parents in Whitechapel.

Gunter Grove became a major hang-out for post-punk luminaries like The Slits and Don Letts. The fridge was always well stocked with lager, various other substances floated around, and Lydon's massive speakers in the communal upstairs living room pounded out a bass-booming reggae soundtrack. Still partially in the mindset of summer 1977 – when he was Public Enemy Number 1 – Lydon holed up and held court to a retinue of hangers-on and cronies. 'I love visitors,' he once said. 'They are here for my amusement.'

It wasn't all cosy laughs in the House of Lydon, though. Cannabis and speed were the main drugs, but heroin was creeping in with some of the coterie. Justifying Lydon's persecution complex, Gunter Grove was regularly raided by the local drugs squad. One visit in February 1979 took place at 6 a.m. – ironically, one of the few occasions when the amphetamine-fuelled PiL had gone to bed before dawn. The police smashed down the front door, ripped open Lydon's mattress, and pulled up the bedroom floorboards, but found nothing. Nevertheless, Lydon was taken to the local police station and had to walk home in his pyjamas.

Another shadow was death: in 1979, Lydon lost both his mother (to cancer) and his estranged best friend Sid Vicious (to heroin). Witnessing his mum, the great source of strength and encouragement in his life, slowly slipping away inspired Lydon's lyrics to 'Death Disco', the first PiL release after the debut album. Wobble's hard-funk bassline pushes forward like fear rising in your gorge. Levene generates a staggering amount of sound using a single guitar – simultaneously torturing the classical-kitsch melody of 'Swan Lake', hacking out rhythm chords that feel like blade touching bone, and scattering a microtonal scree of harmonics. Searing through this swarm of anguish, Lydon exorcizes his grief like Yoko Ono at her most primal-scream harrowing: 'Seeing in your eyes . . . Silence in your eyes . . . Final in a fade . . . Flowers rotting *dead*'.

PiL at Gunter Grove, 1979. L to R: Keith Levene, Jah Wobble, John Lydon. Behind Lydon's head is a poster based on the cover of 'Death Disco'. Photo by Janette Beckman

Released in June 1979, 'Death Disco' is arguably the most radical single ever to penetrate the UK's Top 20. I remember the *Top of the Pops* presenter (whose name escapes me) looking ashen-faced as he reluctantly uttered the song title when introducing the group. Wobble sat in a dentist's chair through the whole performance. 'Everyone else lined up to get made beautiful, but I just asked the BBC make-up people to have my teeth blacked out, so I could do a big smile at the camera with my front teeth missing.'

Inviting the Grim Reaper to the pop party was one kind of subversion. In its own way, just as radical was pairing the word 'death' with 'disco' – a form of music still despised by most of PiL's audience. The twelve-inch came with two disco-style versions, the '1/2 Mix' and the 'Megga Mix'. Lydon declared that disco was just about the only contemporary music he liked, while Wobble enthused to *ZigZag* that disco was 'very *useful*, practical music'.

PiL's next single, 'Memories', pursued the dance direction even more intently with its brisk groove of hissing high hat and crisp snares, and its disco-style breakdowns, where the sound strips down and the intensity rises several notches. Only Levene's glassy shrouds of Arabic-sounding guitar felt at odds with the dance-floor imperative. Well, that and Lydon's anti-nostalgia invective, which was not exactly an invitation to get down and boogie. Baying like a cross between a banshee and a mountain goat, he railed against some nameless fool still living in the past. Some speculated that Lydon was attacking 1979's burst of nostalgia (the mod and ska revivals), but when he sneered, 'This person's had enough of useless memories,' it felt like he was talking about his own need to sever ties to the past, whether memories of his loved ones or tangled regrets about his years in the Pistols.

'Memories' failed to make the Top 40 on its October 1979 release, but it whipped up fierce anticipation for PiL's second album. A big chunk of *Metal Box* had been recorded back in May, with the rest completed in sporadic fashion. Drummer Richard Dudanski departed halfway through the process, so Levene and Wobble supplied the beats on several tracks. Martin Atkins, who went on to become PiL's longest-enduring drummer, was recruited when the album was virtually finished. He received a summons to the studio in the form of an inconsiderate 3 a.m. phone call. 'When I got to Townhouse, someone says, "There's the drum kit, make something up,"' Atkins recalls. 'Wobble and I wrote "Bad Baby" off the top of our heads – what you hear on *Metal Box* is literally that first five minutes of us playing together for the first time. Within half an hour of meeting everybody, I was on the record.' As you might imagine, this isn't the best way for a band to operate. Indeed, 'Bad Baby' is the only real blemish on what otherwise stands as not only PiL's masterpiece but post-punk's pinnacle.

Metal Box is a peculiar blend of real-time spontaneity and obsessive post-production. Many songs were recorded in first or second takes, and a few were written as they were being played. But it all came together at the mix, informed by PiL's fondness for dub and disco. *Metal Box*, Levene has said, was an exercise in 'finding out what mixing was . . . a crash-course in production'. What's striking about the record is how PiL assimilated both the dread feel of roots reggae and the dub aesthetic of subtraction (stripping out instruments, using empty space), without ever resorting to obviously dubby production effects like reverb and echo.

The album starts with 'Albatross', ten minutes of pitiless bass pressure from Wobble, over which Levene scythes the air and Lydon sings like he's being crushed between two giant slabs of rock. 'Albatross' is 'Public Image' turned inside out: Lydon's confidence that he can outrun his past curdling into despair. 'Memories' and 'Death Disco' follow, the latter retitled 'Swan Lake' and now ending in a locked groove, Lydon's grief and horror frozen for eternity, like Munch's *Scream*.

After the surging urgency of the two singles comes the slow suspension and numb trance of 'Poptones'. Gyrating around Wobble's deep, probing bassline, Levene's guitar scatters a wake of harmonic sparks that merge with the lustrous halo of cymbal spray. Talking about his 'circular, jangly', almost psychedelic playing on 'Poptones', Levene once compared its repetitiveness to staring at a white wall: 'If you look at it for a second, you'll see a white wall . . . If you keep looking at it for five minutes, you'll see different colours, different patterns, in front of your eyes – especially if you don't blink. And your ears don't blink.'

Rising to the occasion, Lydon matches the music's sinister grace with one of his most quietly unsettling lyrics: sketched in oblique, fractured images, it's an account of someone who's been abducted, driven into the woods, and raped. 'Hindsight does me no good/Standing naked in this back of the woods', intones the victim, bitterly recalling the reassuring 'poptones' playing on the car's cassette player. It's not clear if the song is being sung by a corpse, or if the person got away and is now cowering and shivering in the wet foliage. 'John's lyric was so evocative and partly it came from us recording at the Manor and driving through the forest near the studio,' says Wobble. On 'Poptones' and other *Metal Box* songs, Lydon's delivery meshes with Levene's guitar in a weird modal place somewhere between Celtic and Arabic. 'When someone can't sing you get these natural voice tones,' explains Wobble. 'So PiL's music was based more around overtones and subharmonics, rather than harmony *per se*. The Beach Boys we were not! PiL actually had more in common with music from Lapland or China.'

'Poptones' whooshes straight into the Northern Ireland-inspired terror ride of 'Careering', during which Levene abandoned guitar for ominously hovering and swooping electronic sound-shapes created on the Prophet 5 – an early and expensive form of polyphonic synth. Then came 'No Birds Do Sing' – PiL's zenith, as far as Levene is concerned. Wobble and Dudanski set up a foundation-shaking groove, over which Lydon intones another scalpel-sharp lyric, dissecting suburbia's 'layered mass of subtle props', the serene narcosis of its 'bland, planned idle luxury'. Levene's guitar emits a strange metallic foam that's simultaneously entrancing and insidious. The instrumental 'Graveyard' is disco music for a skeletons' ball: it really sounds like dem bones doing the shake, rattle 'n' roll. After this, *Metal Box* loses its way with the underdeveloped 'The Suit' and 'Bad Baby', but then recovers dramatically with the last three songs: the psycho-disco of 'Socialist', all dry, processed drums and synth blips; the thug-funk stampede of 'Chant', with Lydon ranting about street violence and wet-liberal *Guardian* readers; and the unexpected Satie-like poignancy of 'Radio 4', with its sighing synths and gently sobbing bass.

In honour of reggae and disco's twelve-inch aesthetic and to ensure the highest possible sound quality, PiL insisted on releasing the album as three 45 r.p.m. records, rather than a single 33 r.p.m. disc. 'We were celebrating the idea of twelve-inch singles, pre-releases, slates,' says Levene. 'With that format, you got a better bass sound.' The idea of putting the three discs inside a matt-grey film canister came from Lydon's friend Dennis Morris, rock photographer and member of the all-black post-PiL band Basement 5. *Metal Box*'s striking packaging was possibly PiL's most impressive feat in terms of breaking with standard rock procedures. It effectively deconstructed 'The Album', encouraging the audience to listen to the tracks in any order. 'The idea is that you definitely don't play it from side one to side six,' Wobble told the *NME*. 'You just put on one song or two and leave it at that.'

The unusual packaging also appealed for reasons of sheer malicious perversity. Three unsleeved discs, snugly crammed into the circular canister and separated only by round paper sheets, were hard to remove without scratching the vinyl. 'We were turned on by the idea that it

PiL's innovative *Metal Box*, 1979

would be difficult to open the can and get the records out,' admits Levene. This prank cost PiL dear, though. 'Virgin called us out for a meeting on their boat and said, 'Look, if you want to do it in a tin, it's going to cost sixty-six thousand pounds extra. We can only do this if you give us a third of your advance back.' Which PiL did.

Released shortly before Christmas 1979, *Metal Box* was almost universally garlanded with praise. One measure of its colossal stature is that the *NME* made John Lydon its cover star on 24 November. But there was no interview with him inside; just a full-page review of the album. The timing was perfect, too: the second half of 1979 saw post-punk reaching its peak of popularity. There were epoch-defining festivals like September's Futurama, organized by Leeds promoter John Keenan, one night of which was headlined by PiL. Lydon infamously turned his back on the audience, the official reason being that someone had hurled a full can of lager at Wobble.

Post-punk was cresting creatively, and accordingly enjoyed as well a glorious if short-lived consensus of admiration among critics and fans alike. In the *NME*'s Christmas issue, the writers' Top 5 Albums of 1979 comprised Talking Heads' *Fear of Music* at 1, *Metal Box* at 2, Joy Division's *Unknown Pleasures* at 3, The Jam's *Setting Sons* at 4 and Gang of Four's *Entertainment!* at 5. The Slits' *Cut*, The Raincoats' debut, and albums by This Heat, Swell Maps, The Fall, Pere Ubu and Wire all featured lower down. In his end-of-year oration, Paul Morley hailed PiL as 'truly . . . what Miles Davis had in mind when he claimed he could put together the greatest rock 'n' roll group in the world. With such a restless ghost, and such incisive activity, rock will have to be appallingly negative to ever disappear into the desert again. Look at the growth.'

By definition, though, peaks precede troughs. Indeed, there's a sense in which musical golden ages engineer their own demise. Records like *Metal Box* and *Unknown Pleasures*, by dint of their very originality, ensure they'll be copied by lesser groups whose imaginations have been overpowered. In pop, every wave of innovation (psychedelia is a good example) inevitably heralds a host of new clichés and conventions. In the wake of PiL and Joy Division, a new underground of gloomy groups like The Sound and Killing Joke emerged. By the time of its second incarnation in 1980, Futurama was mocked as a sort of Castle Donington for the angst-rock brigade, its grim flocks of overcoat-clad boys as uniform as the denim hordes who followed Iron Maiden. Reviewing the festival, the *NME*'s Adrian Thrills wondered whether 'things really have come full circle and . . . the post-punks are the new hippies'. His colleague Morley complained that Futurama and similar events – the ICA Rock Week, the Lyceum post-punk multi-band specials organized by promoters Straight – signalled 'the unwelcome rise of a new underground . . . playing to fans who are not so much the converted as the contained'.

The clone army also put huge pressure on the pioneers to keep moving to new frontier zones. PiL started 1980 with two huge advantages. They still had Virgin's support. And, despite its experimentalism and high retail price, *Metal Box* had done well commercially, selling out the 50,000 limited-edition canister format by February 1980 and going into re-press as *Second Edition* (a conventional double album). But, as the year proceeded, the challenge of surpassing their own landmark record seemed to paralyse the band.

At first, PiL basked in the acclaim. An idle idol addicted to TV, Lydon told *Sounds*: 'if I could get away with it I wouldn't even walk. I'd love a mobile bed. One thing I've never understood is people complaining about bed sores. That's a luxury, isn't it?' In April 1980, PiL deigned to tour America, but only on the least strenuous, most stress-free basis: ten dates spread across three and a half weeks. Martin Atkins recalls spending three whole nights in Boston for just one gig and a radio interview, and having his own hotel suite. As the tour progressed, Lydon encouraged kids to come onstage and sing in his place (you have to wonder if this was just a ploy to shirk some work, rather than a noble egalitarian gesture). Despite its easy-going pace, though, the short traipse across America turned PiL off the idea of touring for good. Playing live had never been a passion for Lydon or Levene. The latter once declared, 'I'd rather send out a video of us than do a thirty-date tour.' Wobble, however, enjoyed connecting with the audience – an attitude Lydon mocked as 'this whole condescending attitude of playing for the kids'.

PiL playing 'Poptones' on the BBC rock show *The Old Grey Whistle Test*, 5 February 1980. On the music stand, a copy of *Second Edition*, the conventional double-album version of *Metal Box*.
L to R: Keith Levene, John Lydon, Jah Wobble. Photo by Kevin Cummins

Twenty years old, bursting with energy (not all of it natural), Wobble felt increasingly frustrated by PiL's inactivity on all fronts. He squirmed with embarrassment at the yawning gap between what PiL professed to be (not a band but a communications corporation) and what they achieved (fuck all, really). Levene still talked grandly in interviews about doing movie soundtracks, making video albums, even designing musical equipment (a drum synthesizer, a portable recording studio the size of a briefcase). But these were pipe dreams at best; pure bullshit at worst. 'That whole idea of the umbrella corporation – even at the time I thought, Fuck, what are we gonna do? We're going to make a *film*?' laughs Wobble. 'We're going to do *nothing*! And that irritated certain people, 'cos I'd take the piss a bit.'

More seriously frustrating for Wobble was PiL's workshy inactivity on the recording front. He'd already made a few solo singles and in May 1980 released his first album, the wonderfully goofy *The Legend Lives on . . . Jah Wobble in 'Betrayal'*. His gesture of independence triggered the first major crack in PiL's regal façade, and in August he left the group in a cloud of acrimony. Officially the dispute concerned Wobble's reuse of some PiL backing tracks *on The Legend*, but as part of its 'umbrella company' concept, PiL had always intended to diversify with solo releases as well as various non-musical projects. 'Versioning' reggae riddims was also a widespread practice in Lydon's beloved Jamaica, so what exactly was the problem with Wobble's thrifty recycling? In truth, the tension within PiL had been building since the later stages of recording *Metal Box*. 'The feeling got quite bad,' says Wobble, 'so I'd go off and do the rhythm tracks by myself in Gooseberry Studios in Chinatown.' Wobble felt especially frustrated because during the mixing of *Metal Box* Levene hogged the studio desk and hardly allowed him any creative input.

Another grievance was the irregularity and paucity of Wobble's PiL pay packets: 'I was on sixty quid a week and even struggling to get that.' PiL Corp's employment practices generally left a lot to be desired. After the American tour, Atkins was summarily fired – purely and simply, he claims, so PiL could avoid paying him a weekly wage when the band were doing nothing. Later in 1980 he was rehired when PiL started recording their third album. 'PiL wasn't run like a business,' he says. 'It would take me five attempts of going across London from Willesden Green to Chelsea before I could get anyone at Gunter Grove to open the door and give me my sixty quid. And I'd spend half of it on speed before

I'd got home. If it was a Thursday, I'd probably stay at Gunter Grove until Sunday. We'd all be up watching *Apocalypse Now*, speeding.'

In his last months as a member of PiL's dysfunctional family, Wobble told *Sounds*, 'I think sometimes we border on psychosis. I'm not using that word lightly. I really mean psychosis. In other words we lose touch with reality.' Throughout the second half of 1980, rumours circulated of ugly vibes at Gunter Grove: hard drugs, Lydon degenerating into a paranoid recluse. The regular police raids didn't help, and Lydon had recently been traumatized by a brief sojourn in Mountjoy, an infamous Irish prison, following an altercation with two off-duty cops in a Dublin pub. Factor in the amphetamine intake and you can see why a poster on the wall at Gunter Grove declared: 'Just because you're paranoid doesn't mean they're not out to get you'.

'It was a Hitler's bunker vibe – all the paranoia,' says Wobble. 'It added to the edge. It was a bit like that Nic Roeg film *Performance*.' In that movie Mick Jagger plays a burned-out sixties rock superstar holed up in his dilapidated Georgian terraced house in Powis Square, Ladbroke Grove. 'I don't think John ever regarded himself as a rock god as such; that would be unfair,' says Wobble. 'But there was that kind of general atmosphere of withdrawing from the world a bit – sort of, in *here*, this drama, is where it's at, rather than going out there into the world.'

Wobble sees PiL as a literally *wasted* opportunity, ruined by drugs and lethargy. The situation was worsened by the fact that the protagonists weren't even in the same chemical head-space. In 1996 Wobble described PiL as 'four emotional cripples on four different drugs'. Today he quips, 'If we had been on the same drugs, we might have kept it together a bit longer! Some people were on heroin, some on speed, some on very strong cannabis, and some on combinations thereof. Me, I was a speedfreak. I was into powders in a big way – drinking and powders.'

Nowadays Levene is cagey about discussing his heroin years in any detail, but in a 1983 interview for the *NME* he was candid about its effects on PiL: 'I was dabbling with it when we formed the band; then I was doing it constantly for about three years.' *Flowers of Romance*, the troubled follow-up to *Metal Box*, coincided with the worst stage of Levene's addiction. 'When you have to do something creative, it's very hard. When we did *Flowers*, I tried to make the session coincide with the part of the day where I really had the least amount in my system.'

Yet in the 1983 interview Levene also insisted that he 'used to run PiL when I was on junk'. Despite PiL having a full-time member, Dave Crowe, who'd been recruited to organize and keep accounts, Levene claimed that *he* ended up micro-managing every aspect of the band: 'I used to make all the music, get the money out of Virgin, make sure the record was promoted, find out if we were on *Top of the Pops* that week . . . [The heroin use] was because basically I was very lonely, and very scared, and under a lot of pressure.'

One side-effect of heroin is constipation. Creatively, if not literally, Levene had a chronic case during the sessions for the third album, which began in October 1980 at Virgin's Manor studio. 'It was like this horrible mental block,' he has said. Several days passed with PiL playing video games and watching movies, while being waited on hand and foot. 'There was a lot of avoiding the studio going on!' says Levene. 'I'd set up all the equipment, lots of funny little synth toys, and I'd be twiddling, getting sounds, but not necessarily making a record.' With Wobble gone, the old alchemy had disappeared – the way the bassist's untrained, intuitive approach would catalyse Levene's warped virtuosity. 'It would have been better if Wobble had stuck around,' says Levene. 'But for some reason I never thought of replacing him.'

Finally, a breakthrough of sorts occurred several days into the session. Instructing the engineer to keep the tape rolling no matter what, Levene tapped out some percussion patterns on a strange bamboo instrument that Virgin boss Richard Branson had brought back from Bali, then added synth sounds ('the animals' inside the percussive jungle, as he puts it). The result, entitled 'Hymie's Him', was the weakest track on *Flowers of Romance*, but it broke the deadlock and gave the group a direction. Making a virtue of Wobble's absence and Levene's aversion to the guitar (which, according to Atkins, was partly due to his arms being too swollen to play the instrument), PiL decided to orient the new album around drum sounds – a percussive, tribal feel Levene later described to *ZigZag* as 'very acoustic, human . . . but very fuckin' heavy'.

Moving to another costly Virgin studio, West London's Townhouse, PiL procured a bunch of second-hand acoustic instruments – ukulele, saxophone, banjo, violin – and generated raw sonic material for sculpting on the mixing desk. *Flowers* is the PiL album on which Lydon the non-musician contributes most – he actually *plays instruments*, like the three-stringed banjo on 'Phenagen' (a track named after a heavy-duty sleeping pill). In interviews, Levene talked later about deliberately using 'John's total ineptitude to an artistic advantage' while also putting himself in the position of childlike novice grappling with unfamiliar instruments. 'It was like two kids let loose in the studio, all restrictions lifted.'

Where *Metal Box* pushed rock's envelope to its fullest extent, *Flowers* tried to burst through into a totally post-rock space. 'Levene had this thing: "I'm not going to play anything that's ever been played before." Talk about hubris!' recalls Vivien Goldman, a regular visitor to Gunter Grove. On *Flowers*, Levene's guitar appeared only on 'Go Back' (self-parodically) and 'Phenagen' (psychedelically reversed). But the synth dabblings he'd first pursued on *Metal Box* weren't taken much further. *Flowers* really was all about using the studio itself as the primary instrument.

The album came together in a bizarrely disjointed fashion. Summoned to the studio to lay down beats, Atkins found Lydon and Levene weren't there. So he worked closely with engineer Nick Launay to create striking rhythm tracks. 'I'd fallen asleep with my Mickey Mouse watch against my ear and then woken up to that sound. So we put the watch on a floor-tom skin so it would resonate, and then Nick harmonized, looped and delayed that sound, and I drummed to it, and that became "Four Enclosed Walls".' Atkins was also heavily involved in the album's stand-out track, 'Under the House' – a stampeding herd of tribal tom-toms with string sounds shrieking across the stereo field. Lydon's processed vocals seem to emanate from his throat like malignant gas or ectoplasm. The lyrics allude to a supernatural experience – some accounts claim it's about a ghost that haunted the Manor studio, although Levene believes it refers more to an abstract sense of evil to which Lydon was unusually attuned.

Flowers was completed by the end of November 1980, but Virgin, who hated the record, delayed its release until the following April. In the meantime, as a stocking-filler for PiL fans, they rushed out that most rockist of stop-gap measures, the live album. Reviewing *Paris au Printemps* in the *NME*, Vivien Goldman alluded to *Flowers*' 'severe birth pangs' but, with her insider's knowledge, confidently pronounced that PiL had 'broken another sound-barrier'.

The title track on the album lived up to Goldman's hype about PiL inventing 'a new kind of rhythm'. Released as a single in March 1981, 'Flowers of Romance' reached number 24 and resulted in another deranged *Top of the Pops* performance: Levene pounding the drums in a lab technician's white coat, Jeanette Lee dwarfed by her double bass, and Lydon, dressed as a white-collared vicar, sawing dementedly on a fiddle. Such was PiL's eminence that when the album finally arrived the next month, it was automatically hailed as another paradigm-shattering masterwork. More sceptical commentators, though, noted the distinct lack of *work* involved – from the paltry length (thirty-two minutes) to its desultory packaging (a Polaroid of Jeanette Lee with a rose between her teeth). Tracks like 'Four Enclosed Walls' and 'Phenagen' startled on first listen with their extreme sonic treatments, stereo-panning sounds, and Lydon's prayer-wail ululations, but they didn't linger in the memory.

Essentially, what you got on *Flowers* was a reprise of the more outré antics of Europe's pre-punk vanguard – Faust, Cluster, White Noise, even Pink Floyd (from the wackier bits of *Ummagumma* to their abandoned project of recording an album using household objects). Today, *Flowers* sounds a braver mess than it did upon its release. More than aesthetic fearlessness, though, the record was shaped by an unattractive blend of indolence, negativity ('All it amounts to is that we don't like any music at the moment,' Levene told *Rolling Stone*) and gall. Where the record finally fails is in its emotional range. Lydon's palette of derision and disgust had curdled into self-parody. Of the leave-me-alone whinge 'Banging the Door,' Lydon later said, 'It's horrible to listen back to that kind of paranoia.' A creepy account of being seduced by a female journalist, 'Track 8' is particularly repellent, its vindictive imagery of fleshy tunnels 'erupting in fat' and naked, bulbous bodies betraying Lydon's Catholic fear of the flesh. In *Sounds* the self-confessed 'sexless little beast' decreed that sex was 'definitely over-rated. I think the human body's vile and I wish everybody would appreciate that. Look at people's faces: they're vile, big spotty blotches.'

Lydon's misanthropy reached its dismal nadir with the infamous PiL show at New York's Ritz club on 15 May 1981. Intended as a sort of performance-art/video spectacle, the show was hastily cobbled together, with Levene's genuine excitement about multimedia dragging along the unenthused Lydon and Lee. Unfortunately, the Ritz was not an art space like downtown Manhattan's the Kitchen: it drew a rock 'n' roll crowd, who were certainly not happy about paying twelve dollars to see the band only in 'live video' form. Skulking behind the venue's gigantic video screen, Levene and Lee made an amorphous cacophony, while Lydon taunted the audience with 'Aren't you getting your money's worth?' and direct incitements like 'I'm safe . . . you're not throwing enough. You're what I call a passive audience.' After twelve minutes, the crowd erupted into a full-blown riot. Levene, darting from behind the screen, got struck on the head by a flying bottle.

*

During the year of silence that followed *Flowers of Romance*, PiL relocated to New York. Staying at first in hotels, and then, as Virgin's advance on the next album ran out, moving to a large loft apartment, the band sank into a quagmire of apathy. Lydon spent whole days in bed watching TV, getting fat on lager and torpor. There was no shortage of sycophantic yes-men who'd eagerly troop out to replenish the beer supply. 'What was good about PiL when it worked was that he had a few *no*-men around,' says Levene. 'Like me and Wobble.'

By this point, Levene had quit heroin, but his relationship with Lydon was crumbling. What had been unique about the PiL set-up – a world-famous rock star working with an avant-garde virtuoso in a well-funded context of do what the hell you like – slowly unravelled. Lydon the non-musician began to resent his dependence on Levene's musical ability; Levene, dependent on the Lydon brand name, bristled because all the media attention was on Lydon. Early in PiL's career, the singer *had* made strenuous and sincere attempts to present the group as a real collective, not just Johnny Rotten's new backing band. But by 1982, says Levene, 'It was like John had decided to take that line in our first single literally – "Public Image belongs to me".'

Another source of confusion and conflict was the question of where to go after *Flowers*, which had sold poorly. That kind of untrammelled avant-gardism was clearly not going to keep PiL Corp solvent. In the short term, the group resorted to 'hit and runs' – one-off gigs done cynically for the fat fees they could demand on the back of the Johnny Rotten legend. But when it came to PiL recordings, a strategic shift towards accessibility seemed the best course. This was signposted by the working title of the fourth album, *You Are Now Entering a Commercial Zone*, and the oddly radio-friendly sound of its first side – sort of 'death disco' with most of the death deleted. At a press conference in Hollywood, Lydon adamantly stressed that PiL were not arty and wanted to be accessible.

Tensions reached a head in mid-1983 over the single 'This Is Not a Love Song'. When Levene entered the studio to salvage what he deemed a disastrous mix, he found himself under close surveillance from Martin Atkins, now Lydon's right-hand man. After a fraught all-night session, Levene received a phone call from Lydon, who was in Los Angeles, ordering him to 'get out of my fucking studio'. Following the departure of PiL's de facto musical director, Lydon hired a bunch of session musicians as his new backing band (Atkins doggedly hanging in there as drummer), did a lucrative tour of Japan, and rerecorded the album.

Towards the end of his PiL tenure, Levene had noticed a weird development: 'John Lydon sort of became Johnny Rotten again.' In truth, of course, the singer had never voluntarily relinquished 'Rotten'. For a while, McLaren managed to prevent Lydon from using the stage-name, a blow the singer turned around into a grand 'this is the real me' gesture. Living in America, Lydon found himself fêted by awe-struck fans and courted by big-shot managers who encouraged him to exploit his legend to the hilt. Eventually he decided, or realized, that the Sex Pistols adventure was where his rock-myth bread was buttered. After Levene left, the ex-Pistol started to do something during PiL gigs he'd once sworn he'd *never* do again: sing 'Anarchy in the UK' and 'God Save the Queen'. A decade and a half later, he reformed the Sex Pistols as a touring nostalgia revue, reneging on absolutely everything PiL represented.

II: NEW POP AND NEW ROCK

15

GHOST DANCE: 2-Tone and the Ska Resurrection

The Specials. Madness. The Beat. The Selecter. Dexys Midnight Runners.

Just as 'Death Disco' started sliding down the UK charts in July 1979, another single shot in like a rocket: 'Gangsters'. The Specials' debut shares a surprising amount with PiL's single: a bassline that pounds against your ribcage like a heart full of fear, baleful vocals (singer Terry Hall modelled his glowering persona on Johnny Rotten), and a sinuous, snake-charmer melody that's almost like a cartoon version of Lydon's muezzin wail. 'Cartoon' is the key word, though. For all the lyrics' conjuring of menace and corruption ('we're living in real gangster times'), the Specials' manic exuberance made 'Gangsters' pure pop. It reached number 6.

The Specials and their comrades – The Beat, Madness and The Selecter, all of whom started out on The Specials' 2-Tone label – dived into a chasm in the market that had emerged by 1979: the consumer demand for a sound that came out of punk but was instant, accessible, full of teen appeal and, above all, danceable. The post-punk vanguard, for all their experiments with funk, really made music for 'heads' at home, not bodies on the floor: PiL's 'Memories' and Gang of Four's 'At Home He Feels Like a Tourist', those groups' most blatantly 'disco' singles, hadn't exactly set discotheques on fire. Crucially, 2-Tone was dance music played by live bands (The Specials' first number 1 single would be a *live* EP). The movement reclaimed dance music from disco, which was based on DJs playing records, not live performance. Ignoring the innovations of seventies black music, with its intricate production and arrangement, the 2-Tone bands returned to the rawer, high-energy black sounds of the sixties – early soul and Jamaican ska – when a record was barely more than a document of the band playing in the studio.

Cover of The Specials' debut LP, 1979. L to R: Horace Panter, a.k.a. Sir Horace Gentleman, Terry Hall, Neville Staple, Jerry Dammers, Roddy Radiation, Lynval Golding, John Bradbury. They are staring up at the original rude boy: 'Walt Jabsco', 2-Tone's logo/mascot

The Specials' selftitled debut album makes a striking compare-and-contrast with *Metal Box* (they were released within a few weeks of each other in the winter of 1979). Where *Metal Box* was a studio concoction, *The Specials* was sparsely produced by Elvis Costello to capture the band's live energy. Where *Metal Box*'s featureless packaging *refused* image, *The Specials* revelled in it – the cover shows the seven members of the band looking super cool in pork-pie hats, thin ties and sharp sixties suits. PiL's matt-grey canister was starkly functional, a pointed exercise in demystification. But *The Specials'* black-and-white sleeve harked back to an older glamour: the monochrome period feel of the early sixties – British pop shows like *Ready Steady Go* (from before the introduction of colour television), early rock 'n' roll films like *A Hard Day's Night*, Northern social-realist movies like *Saturday Night, Sunday Morning* and *Billy Liar*.

And yet the social reality The Specials' songs depicted was bang up to date and essentially identical to that addressed by PiL, Gang of Four and the rest of the post-punk vanguard: Britain in 1979, on the cusp between failed socialism in retreat and re-energized Conservatism on the warpath. Despite The Specials' outward appearance of boisterous fun, their songs' worldview is strikingly *cheerless*. In 'Nite Klub', the wage slaves piss away their pay packets with beer that already tastes like piss. 'Too Much Too Young' starts as a taunting diatribe against an ex-girlfriend who's lost her youth to premature motherhood ('Try wearing a cap,' jeers Hall), then turns rueful and almost compassionate for the lives they've both lost: 'You done too much, much too young/Now you're married with a son when you should be having fun with me'. 'Stupid Marriage' is a marginally more jaunty take on the same scenario: Hall as the jilted boyfriend spying on his ex and her husband, then lobbing a brick through the bedroom window. This grim vision of matrimony as death trap – 'She's got him where she wanted and forgot to take her pill/And he thinks that she'll be happy when she's hanging out the nappies/If that's a happy marriage I'd prefer to be *unhappy*' – recalls The Who's 'A Legal Matter' and kitchen-sink dramas like *Up the Junction*.

The Specials eerily manages to *sound* like those sixties social-realist films *look*: monochrome. Its blend of the lively and the bleak dramatized the basic 2-Tone *mise en scène*: a dance floor hemmed in by desperation on every side. The minute you step out of the Mecca Ballroom and head home, fuzzy with drink, you're back in the 'Concrete Jungle'. The Specials song of that name, like PiL's 'Chant' and Fatal Microbes' 'Violence Grows', takes a snapshot of street life in 1979: a record year for racial attacks and muggings. Embellished with sound effects of breaking glass, 'Concrete Jungle' is driven by a disco-style walking bassline that periodically accelerates to a panicked sprint, the protagonist gibbering, 'Animals are after me' and, 'Leave me alone, leave me alone'.

Few urban jungles are as wall-to-wall concrete as The Specials' home town, Coventry. Located in the West Midlands, Britain's heartland for engineering and vehicle manufacture, the city was pounded relentlessly by the Luftwaffe during World War Two. Like its neighbours Birmingham and Wolverhampton, the city was rebuilt at speed according to the modernist architectural principles that prevailed post-war – all tower blocks, functional shopping centres and complicated motorway fly-overs. In one of the first music-press features on The Specials, *Sounds*' Dave McCullough describes 2-Tone's birthplace with brutal precision: 'Huge monoliths of planning diarrhoea stretch mercilessly to the blue sky above like they own the very souls of the few beings that totter out from their concrete cocoons, faceless and drained . . . [The Specials' neighbourhood] is dissected with subways that seem to throb with an invisible tension and deserted "play spaces", swings and trickling streams that poke fun at the surrounding slabs of gloom.'

No one would describe Coventry as pretty, then – indeed, guidebooks to England usually struggle to summon up *anything* to entice tourists to visit the place. But Coventry was a vibrant place . . . until the late seventies. The West Midlands was the success story of the post-war British economy, thanks to pent-up consumer demand for cars. Like that other motor city, Detroit, the compensations for living somewhere so harsh were plentiful jobs and good pay. But massive oil inflation in the early seventies began to affect the West Midlands car industry, causing the unemployment rates (for most of the postwar period, half the national average) to rise steadily. When Thatcher's monetarist policies mauled British industry at the end of the seventies, the boom towns of Coventry and Birmingham became ghost towns almost overnight.

In the fifties and sixties, Caribbean immigrants had moved to the area because of the work opportunities, so there was a long-established tradition of black and white musicians intermingling. Before punk, most of The Specials' five white and two black members had apprenticed in soul bands of one kind or another. Jerry Dammers, the band's founder, chief songwriter and keyboard player, had tried to persuade the groups in which he'd played, like The Cissy Stone Soul Band, to perform his songs. 'Before the New Wave happened it was just unthinkable to do original songs,' he told *Melody Maker*. 'It wasn't until The Sex Pistols came along that you realized that you could get away with doing your own songs.' Terry Hall was equally galvanized by the Pistols, especially Johnny Rotten: 'It was just the way he stood on stage and gazed for half an hour,' he recalled. 'I'd never seen anything like it. His stance was like an extension of standing still.' Hall developed his own 'meaningful glare', an unblinking scowl accented by his heavy eyebrows.

The Specials were socially as well as racially mixed. The rebellious son of a clergyman, Dammers had been a (very young) mod in the sixties, then a hippy, and then a skinhead. After school he studied art at Lanchester Polytechnic in Coventry, where he specialized in animated films and met fellow art student Horace Panter, who became The Specials' bassist. Another former mod, drummer John Bradbury, was also a fine arts graduate. Guitarist Roddy Radiation had paintbrush experience of a different sort, as a decorator for the local council, while second guitarist Lynval Golding supported his wife and daughter working as an engineer. Skilled working class – his pre-Specials job was as a clerk at a coin dealer's – Terry Hall was the perfect mouthpiece for Dammers' lyrics, lending them an authenticity they might otherwise not have possessed. Hall knew proletarian life from the inside but – in the tradition of Mark E. Smith and John Lydon – was too piercingly intelligent not to see right through its treadmills and traps.

Neville Staple – the seventh Special and, alongside Golding, its second West Indian member – was the group's resident rude boy. 'Compared to the rest of the band, I came from a rough-and-tumble part of the world,' he says. Staple's crime sheet included burglary and affray (he'd participated in a revenge attack on some National Front skins), and he stole timber to build the speakers for a sound system he helped operate. It was through his know-how of sound equipment that he ended up working as a roadie for The Specials. At gigs he would hang out by the mixing desk, and during the group's support stint on a Clash tour, he grabbed the mike and started 'toasting' over the music. He'd grown up around blues dances and sound systems, absorbing the 'DJ talkover' chatting of Big Youth, U-Roy and Prince Jazzbo. In The Specials he added a patois-gruff, rowdy-yet-baleful presence that contrasted superbly with Hall's utterly English intonation, alternately wry and sour.

Initially, Dammers' concept for The Specials was 'punky reggae'. But for a long while the group struggled to integrate the two styles even to the limited extent The Clash had managed on 'White Man in Hammersmith Palais'. 'We had songs where part of [them] were reggae, then they'd go into a rock section, then perhaps into reggae,' he recalled. 'And it would throw people off.' Eventually, the band fastened on ska as the solution: they would wind back pop history to a time when Jamaican music and the early forms of mid-sixties British rock (basically speeded-up R&B) were much closer. Dammers also felt that contemporary roots reggae was 'religious music'. He told the *NME*: 'When we've played with some black bands, these dreads have come up to me and said we should leave Jah-Jah music alone. So we do leave Jah-Jah music alone and go back to when reggae was more just straight dance music.' The Specials took the choppy rhythms of sixties ska and amped them up with punk's frenetic energy. The difference is most audible if you play one of The Specials' many cover versions next to the ska original: the sixties source invariably sounds sluggish in comparison, less aggressive, but also simpler in arrangement compared to the remake.

The Specials live onstage, 1979. Photo by Kevin Cummins

Ska began at the end of the fifties as a Jamaican twist on black American dance music – 'upside-down R&B', as guitarist Ernest Ranglin put it. The term is probably derived from the characteristic 'ska-ska-ska-ska' of the rhythm guitar stressing the 'afterbeat', which intensifies the music's choppy, chugging feel. Generally credited with inventing the 'afterbeat', singer/producer Prince Buster was even bigger in Britain than he was in Jamaica: he released more than *six hundred* singles in the UK between 1962 and 1967, and toured frequently, often escorted between gigs by a phalanx of scooter-riding mods. The Specials upheld the mod tradition of worshipping Buster. 'Gangsters' was loosely based on his 'Al Capone', replacing the original lyrics with all-new words about the record business's sharks and shysters, but 'sampling' the skidding car-chase tyres from the original. 'Stupid Marriage' stole its courtroom scenario – Staple as Judge Roughneck meting out harsh sentences to rude boys – from Buster's 'Judge Dread' hit of 1967.

In Jamaica the rude boys were ska's hardcore following. Disaffected, unemployed youths who dressed slick and got into trouble with the law, they were like the pre-conscious Malcolm X when he was just a street hoodlum. They were 'rude' because they had insubordinate spirit and a raw sense of injustice, but they hadn't matured to the self-discipline and ideological focus of militants like the Nation of Islam (a movement Prince Buster joined, unlike most of his contemporaries, who tended to choose Rastafarianism). 'Message to You Rudy', the Dandy Livingstone classic covered by The Specials, wasn't written from a 'conscious' standpoint, but it did counsel the rude boy to mend his ways: 'better think of your future'.

Love of Prince Buster's music united the UK ska revivalists, but Madness outdid everyone with their debut single – their sole release for 2-Tone. On one side, a version of Buster's 'Madness Is Gladness' made for an instant manifesto. On the other, 'The Prince' paid luminous tribute. 'A ghost dance is preparing,' announces singer Suggs McPherson, a nod to 'Ghost Dance', Buster's own homage to the sound system operators of his youth. 'This may not be uptown Jamaica,' sings Suggs, conceding that, 'although I'll keep on running, I'll never get to Orange Street' – a reference to the boulevard that was both Buster's birthplace and the centre of Kingston's music biz. 'The Prince' sounds joyous, but its lyrics capture the poignant pathos of the mod dream – escaping the impasses of England through a massive projection towards black music and black style.

When the ska revival bands appeared in 1979, they initially seemed like just one element of a larger mod revival. 'We're just continuing the line . . . from the mods and the skinheads,' Dammers told the *NME*. The 'line' was the British working-class passion for uptempo black music, sharp clothes, short hair and amphetamines. 'Looking good's the answer/And living by night', sang Ian Page of Secret Affair, the leading nouveau mod group. In 1979 a host of tribal revivals sprang up, based on high-energy dance sounds: music that was good for 'looking good' to – sixties soul, rockabilly, ska. The least impressive contingent in this renaissance of mod sensibility were the straightforward mod resurrection squad – Secret Affair, The Purple Hearts, Squire, The Merton Parkas – around whom clustered a literal-minded Xerox of the original sixties subculture: a swarm of dapper-dressed, small-faced boys riding Vespas and wearing Parkas with target symbols and Union Jacks on the back.

Partly triggered by the release of *Quadrophenia*, the movie based on The Who's 1973 concept album, the new mod owed more to The Jam, a group whose massive following constituted a mini-subculture in its own right. Singer/guitarist/leader Paul Weller, the original modfather, defined the movement's ethos as essentially anti-rock: 'I believe in . . . *clean culture, real culture*. Not all this bullshit . . . *rock fuckin' image* and . . . elegantly wasted wankers, like Keith Richards.' At core, mod sensibility is neurotic and neat-freak – meticulously groomed, detail-oriented, not in the least Dionysian or psychedelic. As articulated by Weller and doppelgängers like Ian Page, the mod resurgence was anti-hippy, freezing pop time in a perpetual 1966. In the late sixties those mods who hadn't followed the psychedelic path turned into ska-loving skinheads; by the early seventies, many had become Motown-fetishist Northern Soul fans. For Weller, and for Dammers, this was the true path. What the skins and Northern Soulies loathed was 'progressive' or 'heavy' music – the album-oriented, non-danceable rock made after *Sgt Pepper's*. In one 1975 feature, Northern Soul fans scorned 'progressive' music as nonsense noise for stoned weirdos: 'You talk to someone who likes progressive music and they'll say they listen to it just to *listen* to it . . . I like music to *dance* to, not to listen to.' You can imagine 2-Tone fans and neo-mods having the same baffled and derisive response to PiL and Cabaret Voltaire. Postpunk was dub-spacious, heard at its best on twelve inch (hence *Metal Box* and the Cabs' 2X45 album) and hi-fis. In contrast, the 2-Tone bands and the new mod groups made seven-inch music: brisk and punchy, near mono, and designed for transistor radios, it flashed back to the golden age of the single in the mid-sixties.

One element the mod resurgence – including 2-Tone – did share with the post-punk bands, though, was a sniffy attitude to rock as passé,

who conjured a mass movement virtually from scratch; Secret Affair's
Ian Page with his private army of 'glory boys' and cold-eyed disdain for
the dowdy straights; Paul 'I Was on a Mission' Weller. It's sheer mod, this
amphetamined obsession with 'purity' and the minutiae of style and
taste; this polarized vision ardour that divides the world into the righteous and the square. Weller captures the attitude best in The Jam's
'Start!' when he rejoices at meeting a soul-brother who, just like himself,
'loves with a passion called hate'.

Nobody exemplified this 'new puritan' spirit more than Kevin
Rowland, the singer and leader of Dexys Midnight Runners – a
Birmingham group who at one point were set to sign to 2-Tone but then
decided they'd rather start their own 'young soul rebel' movement. All
scowling fervour and mirthless dedication, Rowland was physically
unprepossessing but oozed a weird charisma. His voice was neither
strong nor pleasing, but by sheer will-to-be-soulful he overcame its deficiencies, sounding a bit like Strummer goes Stax.

Rowland had been a punk, fronting a band called The Killjoys, but as
the energy of 1977 dissipated he sank into disillusionment. Vintage soul
music pulled him out of the slough. 'I was totally fed up with everything
else at that time and so I started listening to all of Geno [Washington]'s
old records and any other soul singles I could pick up for 10p around the
markets,' he recalled. Convinced that rock was 'a spent force', Rowland
began to recruit musicians to form his ideal band. At first they played
mostly covers of soul classics, but gradually phased them out for new
songs written by Rowland and Dexys other main creative force, Al
Archer, all couched in a toughened version of the high-energy, horn-
driven Atlantic-Stax/Volt-style soul of the mid-sixties.

After a year of rehearsing, Dexys had the sound to match Rowland's
'new soul vision'. They also had the look. What sold Archer on the band
was Rowland's concept of 'a soul group with a brass section and all
looking good', he told *Tangents*. 'At the time, everyone was looking the
same. It was a bit post-punk.' Rowland added, 'We wanted to be a group
that would look like something . . . A formed group, a project, not just
random.' *Circa* their debut single, 'Dance Stance', Dexys early image
might be mistaken for an ultra-stylized version of council workmen:
woolly hats, donkey jackets, leather coats. Actually, the inspirations
were *The Deer Hunter* and *Mean Streets*. 'It was a very spiffy look, very
Italian with the little 'taches . . . [It fitted] that hot sweaty thing that
surrounded the music at that time,' Rowland explained. Then Dexys

switched to an athletic look: hooded tops, boxing boots, pony tails. With their staccato brass blasts and jabbing, jousting fanfares, Dexys songs actually *sounded* pugilistic. Rowland also liked the vaguely monastic quality of the boxer's hoods, which fitted the music's 'religious fervour, the real proud sort of staunchness of it'.

Projected passion, intense emotions – Dexys Midnight Runners live, 1980. L to R: Al Archer, Kevin Rowland, J. B. Blyte, Steve 'Babyface' Spooner. Photo by Janette Beckman

Dexys took mod's sexlessness to a new dimension: separating the intensity of their beloved sixties soul from its object (carnal desire), their passion was for passion itself. There was something decidedly ascetic about Dexys. In one song, Rowland declares: 'I'm going to punish my body until I believe in my soul.' After an early phase of using amphetamines (which suppress sexual drive and can create messianic self-belief), Dexys took up natural methods to forge a collective sense of mission, intense physical exercise. They worked out together and went running as a team. 'It definitely helped the spirit of the group,' Rowland recalled. 'The togetherness of running along together just gets . . . that fighting spirit going. We used to come into the rehearsal rooms in Birmingham still sweating from running, and there was all these other groups there and it just put us a million miles away from them. You realize you have absolutely nothing in common with them. It isolated us a bit more, which is what we wanted at that point.' Before gigs, the group would limber up with exercises in the dressing room, Rowland chanting phrases from James Brown's 'Sex Machine'. Pre-show drinking was strictly forbidden.

When Dexys hit the scene with 'Dance Stance', they polarized opinion. For a certain breed of young man, Rowland became an instant icon: like a Mark E. Smith who'd grown up on Northern Soul rather than Krautrock, here was a working-class hero with chips on both shoulders. He was 'searching for the young soul rebels' and these idealistic boys stepped forward as eager converts. Those of less fanatical disposition found Dexys ludicrous . . . or repugnant. The NME's Mark Cordery critiqued the band's self-conception as 'an elite of Pure and Dedicated men' in terms of 'Emotional Fascism' and lambasted their music as a perversion of soul that, unlike its black sources, had 'no tenderness, no sex, no wit, no laughter'.

Dexys sternly dismissed pop as trivial and plastic. In one communiqué, they castigated the entirety of popular music as 'shallow, conceited, foul tasting, non lasting, bubblegum'. Yet, in other respects, Dexys were totally pop savvy, as can be seen from their complete command of image (which they serially reinvented, à la Bowie and, later, Madonna) and video. There was also something characteristically Pop Art and postmodern about the way they used meta-musical references. Searching for the Young Soul Rebels, the debut album, starts with the sound of a radio dial being turned, someone scouring the airwaves for the next working-class-saviour band. There's a burst of the Pistols' 'Holidays in the Sun' and a blare of The Specials' 'Rat Race' before Rowland blurts, 'For God's sake, burn it down!' and Dexys launch into their first song.

'Geno', Dexys first number 1 single, was pure meta-pop: a homage to sixties mod hero Geno Washington. In his native America, Washington would have been a second-division R&B talent, but in the UK he carved out a cult: his high-octane performances fronting the Ram Jam Band appealed to the Dexedrine-gobbling mods. Rowland's older brother had taken him to see Washington when he was only eleven. In 'Geno' Rowland reminisces about the inspirational force of this first gig of his life, comparing Washington to the mod's pills of choice: 'That man was my bombers, my Dexys, my high'. The follow-up single 'There, There My Dear' went even further into the land of meta-pop: it's a vitriolic riposte to a sceptic (seemingly a real person, and most likely either a trend-hopping music journalist or a pretentious musician) who had the temerity *not* to 'welcome the new soul vision'.

Dexys did have some real 'content' amid all the self-reflexive bluster. 'There, There' also contains the classic class-war couplet, 'The only way to change things/Is to shoot men who arrange things'. 'I Couldn't Help It If I Tried' recounts Rowland's attempt to organize a strike only to be let down by his workmates. 'Dance Stance' savaged people who tell jokes about stupid Irishmen but don't know about Oscar Wilde, Samuel Beckett, Brendan Behan and the rest. The cover of *Searching* showed a photo of a Belfast Catholic boy carrying his belongings after being driven from his neighbourhood during the sectarian clearances of 1969. Half-Irish, Rowland explained, 'I wanted a picture of unrest. It could have been from anywhere but I was secretly glad that it was from Ireland.'

Still, there was a suspicious vagueness to Rowland's rhetoric. Calling their fan club Intense Emotions Ltd and titling one tour the Projected Passion Revue suggested both imminent self-parody and a certain hollowness at the heart of it all. The mission statement seemed to be 'We have a mission' or even 'We believe in the *idea* of having a mission'. Asked what the album title *Searching for the Young Soul Rebels* meant, Rowland admitted: 'I don't know . . . I just liked the sound of it, really.'

Prickly at the best of times, Dexys interviews became fraught affairs as journalists probed for something tangible and Rowland became increasingly defensive. In July 1980, with 'There, There My Dear' high in the charts, Dexys declared a press embargo, announcing that they'd no longer be doing interviews but would instead pay for their own essays to be printed in the music papers as adverts: 'We won't compromise ourselves by talking to the dishonest, hippy press. We are worth much more than that.' A series of pompous (if occasionally funny) communiqués followed, usually timed around the release of a single. Unfortunately, the new, embattled mood in the Dexys camp seemed to curdle the music: 'Plan B' was a small hit, but both 'Keep It Part Two' and 'Liars A to E' failed to make the charts. In early 1981, most of the band abandoned their leader to form a surrogate-Dexys band named The Bureau. Only a year after topping the charts with 'Geno', Rowland and his 'new soul vision' looked all washed up.

Too much (success) too young also had a calamitous effect on 2-Tone. Talking to *Melody Maker* in June 1980, Jerry Dammers sounded despondent: '2-Tone has become a monster.' Constant touring – including an exhausting traipse across America – put a huge, intolerable strain on relations within the group. Running the label pushed Dammers, who didn't find it easy to delegate, to the point of collapse. While mixing the soundtrack for the 2-Tone live performance movie *Dance Craze*, he cracked: 'I just went to pieces. I haven't had a week off in the past two years. I've been living out of a suitcase like some sort of tramp.' Meanwhile, a vast exploitation industry sprang up, churning out shoddy merchandise. The back pages of the music press teemed with ads for checked ties and badges, black-and-white modette suits, pork-pie hats, and T-shirts featuring the band and label logos. Not a penny of the proceeds reached 2-Tone's coffers.

One of numerous Dexy's communiqués to their fans printed as adverts in the music papers during the group's two-year embargo on interviews with the press. This one, from the *NME*, 7 March 1981, displays more than a hint of paranoia

Ska-revival clone bands swarmed across the nation. Most were unsuccessful (the exception being chart regulars Bad Manners, a comedy-ska troupe with a fat frontman called Buster Bloodvessel) but Dammers felt pressured to keep pushing things forward. 'It's time for the 2-Tone bands to begin getting experimental,' he declared. 'Some of the home-grown ska has started to become a cliché. We've got to start all over again.' For Dammers, this meant pursuing his fascination with mood music and easy listening – background sounds not designed for active listening, but which, if you paid attention, turned out to be weird, even creepy. According to Neville Staple, the obsession with Muzak occurred because The Specials were playing abroad all the time. 'We were in aeroplanes too much, man, and hotels! We were hearing that kind of elevator music, those drum-machine beats, everywhere we went. You soak up what surrounds you.'

In September 1980 the new post-ska Specials sound was unveiled with the double A-sided single 'Stereotypes' and 'International Jet Set'. The former whisked together a kitschedelic meringue of movie-score and lounge-music motifs: balalaikas and Cossack choirs, mariachi trumpets and milky-sounding organ pulses, all gently propelled by the pitter of programmed drum beats. The lyric revisited the leisure grindstone of 'Nite Klub' but in a more wry and distanced fashion, caricaturing a young piss-head who 'drinks his age in pints', drives while inebriated, and ends up 'wrapped round a lamp-post on Saturday night'. 'International Jet Set' was even more eerie and evocative. Laced with Casio-rumba rhythms and swirling Wurlitzer organs, it's a tale of frequent-flyer paranoia, sung by Terry Hall in a high-pitched, highly strung whinny. To Hall, barely able to keep his panic in check, a group of jovial businessmen 'Seem so absurd to me/Like well-dressed chimpanzees'. His fear of flying turns out to be justified: the plane has to make an emergency landing and the captain's voice is revealed as just a recording. 'What's going on in that song nearly happened when we were flying to Europe for a show,' says Staple. 'This twelve-seater plane almost crashed over the Channel.'

Brilliantly arranged, densely layered, and bursting with witty embellishments, 'Stereotypes' and 'International Jet Set' were impossible to recreate onstage. Where the first album documented songs that had been honed through two years of playing live, More Specials, the second album, was largely composed in the studio, and it showed. Dammers had fallen in love with the studio and its possibilities for endless overdubs and fine tuning in pursuit of absolute perfection (a passion that would ultimately be ruinous). But not everyone in the band cared for this new producer-dominated direction: John Bradbury and Roddy

Radiation both preferred high-energy sounds (Northern Soul and rocka-billy, respectively). As a result, *More Specials* was ultimately something of a motley compromise, a ragbag of revivalisms. Only the nuclear doomsday fantasy 'Man at C&A' approached the full-blown film-sound-track/Muzak fusion Dammers achieved on both sides of the single.

More Specials announced the end of the black-and-white 2-Tone aes-thetic with its full-colour cover: a blurry snapshot of the band relaxing (astonishingly, some of them were even *smiling*). The music's sudden drop in energy left their pork-pie-hatted audience bewildered. In truth, The Specials themselves seemed confused and dejected. 'Do Nothing', the next single off the album, was oddly subdued and fatalistic, a down-tempo rock-steady number about a stylish layabout who mooches down the High Street, 'trying to find a future'. The only ray of sunshine comes from the pair of new shoes on his feet. Yet the song seems to see right through the mod fantasy – dressing well as the best revenge over your social superiors, style as a magical solution. In a land where 'nothing ever changes', Hall sings, 'Fashion is my only culture.' But what happens when you stop believing in style, too?

Tensions had emerged that divided the band along class lines. 'The thing about the working-class image that The Specials had when they started . . . well, I'm not working class, and neither is Horace,' Dammers told the *NME* in 1983. 'We were trying to fit into something and eventually it became really tense.' In the early months of 1981, rumours of a split circulated. But their finest hour was yet to come: in June they released the *Ghost Town* EP. Inspired equally by a trip to Kingston, Jamaica, and by witnessing the effect of Thatcher's policies on Coventry's economy and nightlife, the title track sketched a sonic portrait of de-industrialization. The song starts with the desolate whis-tle of wind rustling through a deserted town. A wraith-like woodwind instrument drifts into earshot, soon joined by what sounds like a Wurlitzer playing in a long-derelict cinema. The lyrics contrast the gai-ety of the good-old days (the roaring nightlife back when workers had money to burn) with the present of idle factories and boarded-up night-clubs. 'All the places we used to rehearse in and play our early gigs, they were shutting down,' says Staple. Near the end, 'Ghost Town' cuts from Hall's exhausted sigh, 'Can't go on no more' to Staple's baleful 'People gettin' angry'. Finally, the song strips down to just bass and drums and the return of that whistling wind – so chillingly cinematic you can almost see the tumbleweeds.

Ghost Town turned out to be the most politically timely and momentous release since The Sex Pistols' 'God Save the Queen'. During its three weeks at number 1, Brixton, Moss Side, Toxteth, Wolverhampton, Birmingham and, poignantly, Coventry all erupted into bloody riots. Police used CS gas to quell the disorder, the first time it had been deployed outside Northern Ireland.

Two superb tracks on the flipside made the whole record a kind of concept EP: three angles on the British way of living death. Lynval Golding's 'Why' addressed the racist thugs who'd attacked him outside the Moonlight Club the previous year, asking plaintively, 'Did you really want to kill me?' Then the more belligerent Staple steps forward to shout down the fascist British Movement: 'You follow like sheep inna wolf's clothes'. Wonderfully wan and listless, Terry Hall's 'Friday Night, Saturday Morning' subverts The Easybeats mod classic 'Friday on My Mind' with its depiction of a wage slave's dismal idea of big fun: sinking pints at the Locarno while watching other people pick each other up, then waiting at the taxi-rank in the small hours (a meat pie in his hand, one foot planted in someone else's spew), wishing 'I had lipstick on my collar instead of piss stains on my shoes'.

Discussing the *Ghost Town* EP a year later, Terry Hall said, 'The thing about that was that it showed the two sides of Coventry. On one hand you have unemployment, the youths getting angry and fighting, and on the other you have the typical Friday night scene in the taxi queue, the vomiting and pissing . . . "Friday Night" is about me. I was saying, "What's the point in *me* going out and doing all that?" . . . That's what I used to do every weekend.' The EP makes you wonder just how potent and unstoppable The Specials could have been if Dammers had allowed the other songwriting talent in the band to blossom. But it was too late: Golding, Hall and Staple had been planning their departure for months before the EP's release. In late 1981 they announced the formation of a new group, Fun Boy Three – the name bitterly ironic, says Staple, 'because when we came from The Specials, we were burned out. It wasn't fun any more.'

With the defection of the trio, a crucial portion of The Specials' spirit seemed to have absconded. After the brilliant but commercially suicidal single 'The Boiler' (a harrowing rape account recited by Rhoda Dakar of The Bodysnatchers, 2-Tone's all-girl group) Dammers produced a trilogy of protest singles – 'Racist Friend', 'War Crimes' and 'Nelson Mandela' – whose sentiments were admirable but whose sonic execution lacked almost everything that had made The Specials special. *In the Studio*, the wryly titled third album, was enervated by its two-year gestation period. A sepia-toned soundtrack for a non-existent movie, its songs felt sedate and sedative. Fun Boy Three, meanwhile scored a series of hits that were alternately glum (the Reagan/Thatcher-inspired 'The Lunatics Have Taken Over the Asylum'; the world (affairs) weary 'The More I See the Less I Believe') and jolly (two Top 5 singles in partnership with all-girl trio Bananarama). Soon after, they too disintegrated.

The original 2-Tone bands were all fading: The Beat released an energy-sapped second album (aptly titled *Wh'appen?*), while The Selecter disappeared off the face of the earth. Only Madness seemed to prosper. Gradually they shed their nutty-boys image and started to seem more like a modern-day Kinks, singing wistful songs about the dead ends and fleeting glories of life in England – or, more specifically, London. The only major ska-revival group not spawned in the West Midlands, Madness all hailed from the Camden/Chalk Farm/Primrose Hill area of north London. A sense of place, always present in their music (the cover of *Absolutely*, their second album, showed them outside Chalk Farm tube station), gradually intensified, climaxing with 1982's *The Rise and Fall*. Here Madness shouldered past the 'new Kinks' tag and lunged for 'new Beatles' status. The front cover of the gatefold sleeve was a *Magical Mystery Tour*-like tableau of the band atop Parliament Hill and garbed in semi-surreal attire. Inside, 'Our House' (another massive hit) was Madness's 'Penny Lane', bittersweet nostalgia for the familiar surroundings of childhood. The group's McCartney figure, keyboard player Mike Barson, co-wrote the majority of the songs and fulfilled a Dammers-like role as musical director. Like Dammers, Barson had gone to art college, where he specialized in cartoons and commercial art. Instead of exhibiting in galleries, he quite fancied a career in TV ads.

'Commercial art' is a good tag for Madness's genius pop, but, if anything, *Rise and Fall* saw the group overreaching themselves a little, retracing the historical path from mod into 'progressive' art-pop. On 'Primrose Hill' – Madness's 'Strawberry Fields' – they even hired prog arranger David Bedford to write brass-brand orchestration. After several more Top 5 hits, the group seemed to lose their Midas touch, along with their sense of fun, and Barson suddenly quit. Then they took one step too far along the Beatles path, by leaving Stiff to start Zarjazz, their own foredoomed equivalent to Apple.

*

As for Kevin Rowland and Dexys, in 1982 they did something almost unprecedented, they reinvented themselves and became pop stars for a second time, and on an even bigger scale than before. Rowland's *new* 'new soul vision' was heralded in March with 'The Celtic Soul Brothers', which replaced the old Dexys horn fanfares with the jaunty jangle of mandolins and boisterous folksy violins (supplied by the Emerald Express Fiddlers). There was a new Dexys image as well: a raggle-taggle mixture of gypsy, rural Irish and Steinbeck Okie – dungarees, necker-chiefs, leather waistcoats, shawls, faded 'n' frayed jeans, hessian sweaters with big holes. 'Celtic Soul Brothers' faltered on the edge of the Top 40, but the follow-up, 'Come on Eileen', was a massive number 1 in the summer of 1982 – in Britain, America and around the world. Accompanied by an unexpectedly playful video, 'Eileen' was an honest-to-goodness love song. Rowland archly admitted to having impure thoughts: 'You in that dress/My thoughts I confess/Verge on dirty'. Another massive hit, a cover of Van Morrison's 'Jackie Wilson Said', acknowledged the heavy debts the new Dexys owed to the latter's 'Caledonian Soul' sound of Irish folk-infused R&B.

The success of these singles, and the album *Too-Rye-Ay*, brought Dexys a new MOR audience . . . which fucked with Rowland's head even more than his first encounter with fame *circa* 'Geno'. He felt like a sell-out, a fraud. Guilt about having a couple of nose jobs tormented him. Rowland's response was the calculated career-suicide move of 1985's *Don't Stand Me Down*, which featured no singles, just eleven-minute songs including bizarre comic dialogues like 'This Is What She's Like', rants against the English upper classes and meta-soul exercises like 'The Occasional Flicker'. On the front cover, Dexys made a final confounding image shift: they appeared wearing ties, pin-stripe suits and neatly combed hair, looking for all the world like investment bankers in a photo for a corporate prospectus. 'So clean and simple; it's a much more adult approach now,' said Rowland, rationalizing what in some senses was mod logic taken to the extreme: dressing like the ruling class.

2-Tone was cusp music, a transitional moment between post-punk and the New Pop movement that followed. Politically, it had more in common with the post-punk groups: from its goal of independent-label autonomy (albeit buttressed by major-label support) to its anti-racist and anti-Thatcher politics to the grim social realism of so many of its songs. But 2-Tone's emphasis on livening up the radio with dance energy and catchy accessibility, and its awareness of the importance of image and style, looked ahead to the New Pop bands – Adam Ant, The Human League, ABC. Like those groups, The Specials, Dexys and above all Madness were early masters of the pop video.

Where post-punk was resolutely modernist and obsessed with innovation, 2-Tone shared the postmodern sensibility of New Pop. Rather than a straightforward revival, 2-Tone sifted through pop's archives and mixed-and-matched elements of different period styles – ska, Northern Soul, easy listening, rockabilly – along with flavours from contemporary music like disco and dub. Post-punk bands rarely did cover versions, but 2-Tone signposted its sources and reference points with countless remakes, tribute songs and interpolations (like the 'no gimme no more pickneys' vocal lick from Lloyd Charmers' 'Birth Control', borrowed on The Specials' 'Too Much Too Young'). Even the 2-Tone logo – a black-and-white figure representing the imaginary rude boy Walt Jabsco – was modelled on a photo of the young Peter Tosh from The Wailers.

'We are reviving something that never existed in the first place,' Jerry Dammers declared – a comment that highlights the creativity that was integral to 2-Tone's 'second-hand culture' (Dammers' term). Somewhere between a movement and a fad, the ska resurgence lasted only two or three years, it's true. But the 2-Tone adventure stands as one of the few examples in pop history of a revival that is not inferior to the thing it's reviving. It may even be *better* than the original sixties ska – more musically expansive, more resonant, ultimately more defining of its own epoch.

16

SEX GANG CHILDREN: Malcolm McLaren, the Pied Piper of Pantomime Pop

Bow Wow Wow. Adam & The Ants.

In the spring of 1979, Malcolm McLaren looked finished. His hopes of turning Sid Vicious into a global superstar were dashed when the latter died of an overdose on 1 February. A week later, John Lydon's court case against McLaren – to extricate himself from the latter's managerial clutches and recover the Pistols' earnings – resulted in the worst possible outcome. The other Sex Pistols defected to the singer's side and McLaren lost control of the band that had made him infamous. With his company Glitterbest now administered by the receiver, McLaren had to walk away from *The Great Rock 'n' Roll Swindle*, his beloved Pistols movie, leaving director Julien Temple in charge.

Swindle was McLaren's self-aggrandizing rewrite of recent history. The Pistols figured only as puppets, with McLaren tugging the strings. Punk was portrayed not as a movement of working-class kids discovering their own power, but as a *tour de force* of cultural terrorism perpetrated by the arch-strategist McLaren according to a step-by-step masterplan. But off-screen, the kids – Lydon, Steve Jones and Paul Cook – finally wised up and kicked McLaren out of the picture. Exiling himself to Paris, he licked his wounds and wondered what to do next. To tide him over, his friends at Barclay Records gave him the opportunity to soundtrack some softcore porn films, using their vast library of African music as a resource.

The idea appealed to McLaren, not a feminist by any stretch of the imagination. His original choice of director for *The Great Rock 'n' Roll Swindle* had been porn auteur Russ Meyer, the Bresson of the breast, whose surreal softcore movies had a cult following of trash aesthetes.

304

McLaren teamed up with a pair of French screenwriters to write a 'soft-core rock 'n' roll costume musical for kids' called *The Adventures of Melody, Lyric, and Tune*, which involved three fifteen-year-old girls and their sexual exploits with adults against the backdrop of various Parisian tourist landmarks. The blatantly paedophilic material scared away any potential backers, so McLaren and his collaborators penned another script, *The Mile High Club*, and this time limited the under-age nookie to kids shagging other kids. A cross between *Lord of the Flies* and *Emmanuelle*, the screenplay concerned a tribe of teenage primitives who discover an abandoned jet formerly used by the Mile High Club (those who have sex in the cramped toilets of airplanes) and transform it into 'a children's club for sex-gang babies to make love'.

While McLaren struggled to break into the porn world, The Sex Pistols posthumously enjoyed a seemingly interminable run of chart success. Virgin released single after single from the *Swindle* soundtrack, which was released in February 1979 long before the movie was even completed. Cadaverous Sid Vicious got to number 3 twice in short succession with covers of Eddie Cochran's 'Something Else' and 'C'mon Everybody'.

In his more paranoid moments, McLaren was convinced that Virgin boss Richard Branson had 'out-swindled' him, nullifying the Pistols' threat through hippie-liberal tolerance. To his dismay, the record mogul had been prepared to go along with even the most offensive escapades McLaren proposed – like the desperate gambit of replacing Rotten as lead singer with escaped convict Ronnie Biggs of Great Train Robbery notoriety. After McLaren lost control of the band, Virgin surpassed even his cash-from-chaos cynicism. In the summer of 1979, they released *Some Product: Carri On*, a hastily assembled album of Pistols radio interviews, complete with a cover depicting imaginary Pistols spin-off merchandise – 'Fatty Jones' chocolate bars, a 'Vicious Burger', a Sid action doll complete with coffin. Later came the sick joke of *Flogging a Dead Horse*, a Pistols 'greatest hits' album.

Virgin had turned McLaren's punk critique of commodification into a *commodity*. As a good Situationist, McLaren should really have known all along that 'the spectacle' (mass media, the leisure/entertainment industry) could absorb any disruption, no matter how noxious, and convert it into profit. But this didn't stop him from trying to pull off exactly the same stunts and scandals with his next group, Bow Wow Wow. This time, though, he was determined to do it *right*. Others might have learned something from being sued by one's own clients (the simple lesson:

people don't like being manipulated) but not Malcolm. The experience of losing control over the Pistols just intensified his search to find some truly pliable human material to work with next time.

After failing to get his porn musical off the ground, McLaren ended up half-heartedly managing a London band called Adam & The Antz. Adam was an ex-art-school punk who'd built up a devoted cult following with mildly kinky songs like 'Whip in my Valise' and 'Beat My Guest'. Despite scoring a number 1 independent chart hit with 'Zerox' and appearing in Derek Jarman's punk movie *Jubilee*, Adam felt that his career had stalled. Impatient to become a real star, he eventually coaxed McLaren, whom he revered, to provide some guidance. For a flat fee of £1,000, McLaren shared the ideas percolating in his head about pop's 'next big thing', and developed a whole new image and lyrical approach for Adam.

McLaren astutely perceived that after punk there would be a return to swashbuckling glamour and heroic imagery – the inevitable backlash against punk's 'no more heroes'. Returning from Parisian exile, he'd found that his partner-in-couture Vivienne Westwood had been spending time down the Victoria & Albert Museum researching eighteenth-century fashions. Emboldened by McLaren's absence, she'd truly found her own independent identity as a designer. 'When Malcolm came back I think he got a bit of a shock,' says Fred Vermorel, co-author of the first biography of The Sex Pistols and an old art-school comrade of McLaren. 'But seeing all the stuff that Vivienne had already done, he said, "Why don't we hitch a band on to this look?" Because that's how it worked last time with the Pistols. Then Malcolm added his own touches – the pirates element came from him.'

The other key components of McLaren's new pop vision were tribal rhythms and taboo-tweaking lyrics about teenage sexuality (as rehearsed in the abortive porn musicals). In Paris, McLaren heard African music for the first time – the city teemed with immigrants from former French colonies, and another old art-school pal, Richard Scott (soon to score a worldwide number 1 with M's 'Pop Muzik') was dabbling with Burundi rhythms. McLaren hired Simon Jeffes, the classically trained musician who'd arranged the strings on Sid Vicious's 'My Way', to teach the Antz the rudiments of African polyrhythm.

During the few weeks of his involvement with Adam & The Antz, McLaren detected the germ of something special. Drummer Dave

Barbarossa and bassist Lee Gorman developed a fresh, distinctive sound, all tumbling tom-toms and frisky slap-bass. Adam seemed like a star in waiting. But the singer also had a mind of his own, and McLaren flinched from the prospect of dealing with another Rotten. Sensing that the band would be far more malleable, he connived with the Antz to sack their leader, and at the end of 1979 he gave Adam the bad news at a rehearsal. He apparently ran after the tearful singer and with a final spiteful flourish offered him the consolation prize of being the band's hair stylist.

The Adam-less Antz had developed a sultry, exotic sound, and the fashion side of McLaren's would-be 'subculture' was also in place, courtesy of Westwood. All he needed now was a subversive angle – something to goad the music industry and the media. After getting involved in a TV series called *Insider's Guide to the Music Business*, McLaren became interested in home taping, the industry's scapegoat for a sharp decline in record sales. Hard to imagine in today's era of peer-to-peer file-sharing, but back in 1980 the big worry for the music business was teenagers taping music off the radio. McLaren, naturally, thought the ruination of the record industry was cause for celebration. He penned lyrics praising cassette piracy and got the ex-Antz to write Burundi-rumbling backing music. The plan was to use the song 'C-30, C-60, C-90 Go!' as the TV series' theme tune, and end the programme with the slogan, 'MUSIC FOR LIFE FOR FREE' – a poke in each eye for the record biz.

But *Insider's Guide to the Music Business* died in the development stages, and, feeling guilty for getting the band all fired up, McLaren finally committed himself to managing them. But he still had to find a new singer. One of his friends discovered a fourteen-year-old Anglo-Burmese girl, Annabella Lwin, working part-time in a West Hampstead dry-cleaner's and singing along to Stevie Wonder on the radio. She eagerly agreed to join the band. Her mother, understandably concerned, was to prove a constant thorn in McLaren's side.

Meanwhile, McLaren threw himself into 'training' the three male members of the group, now called Bow Wow Wow, with a nocturnal regime of whoring in Soho's red-light district. McLaren stumped up the cash for the boys as part of his plan systematically to deprave them. Although reluctant (Barbarossa had a wife and baby), the hapless lads complied. Because the fourteen-year-old Annabella initially had problems fitting in with a bunch of much older lads, McLaren even persuaded the guys that the problem was her virginity. To get her out from under her mother's sway and make her commit to the group, one of them had to do the dirty and deflower the underage singer. Reluctantly, the band drew lots, and guitarist Matthew Ashman was dispatched to perform the task. He failed.

Bow Wow Wow singer Annabella Lwin, looking a bit fed up – with a feller called Malcolm, by any chance?
Photo by Kevin Cummins

Gradually, though, everything came together for McLaren. He was convinced that British youth, starved of ideas, would embrace his vision as an antidote to the grey post-punk and 2-Tone music that reigned, or *rained*, over 1980. Like punk, Bow Wow Wow was a patchwork of ideas plucked from history, topical issues of the day, and ahead-of-the-game elements – McLaren sniffing an approaching trend on the cultural breeze. For instance, his 'discovery' of African rhythm anticipated the vogue for world music by a good few years. When McLaren hailed Africa as the cradle of rock 'n' roll, his rhetoric prefigured the way ethnic music would be celebrated as a 'raw' alternative to the overcooked, slickly synthetic pop of the eighties.

The other idea McLaren touted, a return to heroic glamour, was already happening at nightclubs like Blitz, with an emerging scene called New Romanticism. Making a kind of conceptual pun, McLaren wittily connected pirate clothes with cassette piracy. But where he was truly far sighted was in predicting a massive transformation in the way people consumed music: rather than reverently listening to albums at home, they'd use music as a functional soundtrack to other activities. In one interview, he described being rapt by the sight of 'a tall elegant black man' sauntering down the street, a ghettoblaster on his shoulder (just like a pirate with a parrot), seemingly 'oblivious to everybody else'. The Walkman had also just arrived on the market. Sooner than most everybody, McLaren grasped that the rise of portable playback technology would make music omnipresent in people's lives but *less important*: mere disposable software for sleekly designed, highly fetishized pleasure-tech devices – just like today's MP3 players and iPods.

Bow Wow Wow served as McLaren's retaliation against post-punk. He found angst-racked groups like Joy Division drab and sexless – music for students, all atmosphere and mystique. He loathed the lack of a style element to post-punk, the sombre uniformity of the overcoats and black clothes. As a fan of fifties rock 'n' roll, he felt post-punk was progressive rock resurrected: albums solemnly treated as works of art and that *looked* like works of art, wrapped in lavish, pretentious packaging. Above all, McLaren scorned the path taken by the former Johnny Rotten: 'I don't find [PiL] musical. And, if they're not musical, I don't care how experimental they are . . . He's asking you to take a course in music before you understand it.'

Despite his own seven-year stint in art college, McLaren hated the new art-school groups. The middle class had taken over rock again, he complained. 'They didn't like punk because it was too hard and nasty, so they cleaned it up. They've used synthesizers because they think it's smart and new: "let's experiment with music" . . . Why do they take their lives so seriously? They're so hung up.' McLaren despaired of the eighteen-year-olds, school-leavers too close to real-world economic pressures to cut loose. He put his faith in thirteen-year-olds instead. This younger generation, unrestrained by any reality principle, would rise up and 'kick out that eighteen-year-old ex-comprehensive, university-graduate, art-school generation'.

McLaren also despised the independent labels, like Rough Trade. He saw them as a new crypto-hippy aristocracy, politically correct but 'poverty stricken in terms of imagination, street suss, and feeling'. By contrast, the old record biz giants like EMI, who signed Bow Wow Wow, despite the company's troubled past relationship with the Pistols, seemed more trustworthy precisely because they had no counter-cultural pretensions. Conglomerates like EMI also had the gigantic machinery of marketing and distribution to make pop sensations happen on a massive global level. By comparison, the indie labels resembled small merchants – mere 'grocers', as McLaren put it witheringly. This cunning sleight of rhetoric magically connected Margaret Thatcher ('only a grocer's daughter', her opponents jeered) to post-punk tradesmen like Geoff Travis: both were products of the same dreary English provincialism, Napoleon's 'nation of shopkeepers'. McLaren saw himself as a different kind of entrepreneur to these petty-bourgeois bean-counters and ledger-fillers – a dandy spendthrift, a cunning con man, a buccaneer in the grand British tradition of ransacking other cultures.

McLaren proposed Bow Wow Wow as a victory over Thatcherism. Rather than take the obvious post-punk path and bemoan mass unemployment, though, he mischievously framed the absence of work as liberation rather than affliction. Bow Wow Wow's 'W.O.R.K. (N.O. Nah NO! NO! My Daddy Don't)' declared, 'Demolition of the work ethic takes us to the age of the primitive'. Going to school was pointless because its function (socializing youth for a life of labour) had been outmoded. 'T.E.K. technology is DEMOLITION of DADDY/Is A.U.T. Autonomy', goes the chorus chant, taking the Situationist fantasy of automation enabling a utopian future of perpetual play and updating it for the microchip era.

When asked by one interviewer about the plight of the unemployed, McLaren declared: 'So what if you don't have a job? . . . I came back to England and everybody looks like bank clerks to me . . . They look like they're very, very worried, about their future, about money . . . There's a greyness in the culture that's beating everyone down to a pulp. I think Thatcher really likes it that people are worried.' McLaren's advice to the jobless was 'Be a pirate. Wear gold and look like you don't *need* a job.' Gold and sunshine were linked in his mind as un-English – the quintessence of spiritual extravagance. He fantasized, with endearing daftness, about importing sunshine, making the British Isles Mediterranean. 'Just pretend it's the tropics' was his remedy for the Thatcherite blues. Against the doom 'n' gloom of politicized post-punk, he imagined a kind of unshackled pleasure principle triumphing over economic reality, through style and sheer insouciance. Over endless coffee sessions in Soho greasy spoons, he brainwashed Bow Wow Wow: 'Don't be a grocer – a grocer's a money-grabber, and he don't spend his money when he have it.' If you had money, he believed, you should squander it. *Feeling* rich was the best way to beat Thatcher. Again, this attitude put McLaren ahead of the curve: Wham! rode exactly this carefree/careless attitude to fame a few years later, with the pro-dole 'Wham Rap!' (a rewrite of 'W.O.R.K.', essentially) and the sunshine anthem 'Club Tropicana'.

McLaren felt certain Bow Wow Wow would become the most important band since The Sex Pistols and consign dreary post-punk to history's garbage heap. But in July 1980, despite getting acres of press and hours of radio play, the debut single 'C-30, C-60, C-90 Go!' stalled just outside the Top 30. Ever the conspiracy theorist, McLaren believed EMI had bowed to covert pressure from the BPI, the organization that represented the record industry and was campaigning for a levy on blank cassettes as compensation for revenues lost to home taping. EMI, he believed, had sabotaged the single, falsifying its sales figures to ensure a low chart placing. Whipping up Bow Wow Wow into a fury, McLaren shepherded the group to EMI's headquarters, where they trashed a top executive's office, ripping gold discs from the wall and throwing a clock out of the window.

After getting kicked out of his own band, Adam Ant wiped his eyes, decided success was the best revenge, and set to extracting his full money's worth from McLaren's image makeover. As a pop package, Bow Wow Wow was crammed with ideas to the point of incoherence. Basically apolitical, Adam distilled it to three key elements: heroic imagery, sexmusic and tribalism. All had been part of his shtick already – the glam image, the kinky songs, the idea of his audience as 'antpeople' – but McLaren had given him a striking new look that mixed dashing pirate and Apache brave with a white stripe across the nose. As for the Burundi beat, Adam upped the ante on Bow Wow Wow by recruiting two drummers for maximum polyrhythmic impact. Working with guitarist Marco Pirroni, formerly of post-punk outfit Rema Rema, Adam wrote a bunch of sharp, catchy tunes. Remarkably similar to the tremolo-heavy playing of Bow Wow Wow's Matthew Ashman, Pirroni's twangy guitar evoked Duane Eddy, surf music and Morricone's spaghetti Western soundtracks.

In the winter of 1980, the singles 'Dog Eat Dog', 'Ant Music' and 'Kings of the Wild Frontier' smashed their way one by one into the UK Top 10. For a moment, there was a frisson of danger about Adam & The Ants. For sure, this was bubblegum pop – a teen craze perfect for kids, harder for adults to take seriously. Yet Adam's sheer self-belief lent a weird sort of conviction to ludicrous lines like 'Don't tread on an ant/He's done nothing to you/Might come a time/When he's treading on you'. On the cusp between culthood and stardom, the live Ants were an awesome experience. In some respects, Adam's whole tribal/heroic image was like a teenybop version of heavy metal's warrior-male fantasies. It also recalled glam gangleader Gary Glitter (another pop idol backed by two drummers stomping out a primal beat). And, like Glitter, Adam's peacock swagger was oddly asexual – more narcissistic display than real seduction.

During his early cult years, Adam had been endlessly mocked by the music press; now he revelled in creating an army of lookalike followers in his own mirror image. Even more delicious was the way Adam had managed to use McLaren's ideas more effectively than the man himself had. That winter, when Adam told *Sounds*, 'I think "cult" is just a safe word meaning "loser" . . . I don't want it any more,' he was partly expounding the New Pop ethos of ambition and mainstream infiltration. But he was also sticking the knife into McLaren and the turncoat Antz who'd become Bow Wow Wow. For all their manager's strenuous efforts, Bow Wow Wow remained a cult, languishing in a hit-less wilderness, whereas Adam and his new Ants were the pop sensation of 1980.

Adam's zenith came with 'Prince Charming', his September 1981 UK chart topper, and one of the strangest hit singles ever. Its keening coyote-yowl melody resembled a Native American battle cry; the beat lurched disconcertingly, a waltz turning into an aboriginal courtship dance. For the video, Adam glides between a series of arrested poses, frozen tableaux of defiance and hauteur that weirdly anticipate 'vogueing', the New York gay underground's form of competitive dancing inspired by photo spreads in fashion mags. At the end of the video, Adam impersonates a gallery of icons – Rudolph Valentino, Alice Cooper, Clint Eastwood, Marlon Brando. Song and video both expose a certain empty circularity to Adam's neo-glam idea of reinventing yourself: imitate me as I've imitated *my* heroes. The chorus is oddly brittle and defensive ('Ridicule is nothing to be scared of') while the ultimate message – dressing up in fancy finery as a way of flaunting self-respect – feels distinctly trite.

'Prince Charming' ultimately suggested that Adam's destiny was to run through history's wardrobe until he ran out of heroic archetypes. He'd already done highwaymen with the previous number 1 single, 'Stand and Deliver'. In the video for 'Ant Rap', the next big hit from the *Prince Charming* album, he dressed up as a knight in shining armour. He ended 1981 with a spectacular, no-expense-spared tour, the Prince Charming Revue. The word 'revue' signalled that he'd moved into the realm of pure showbiz.

In interviews, Adam talked in vague terms about providing kids with hope, a positive alternative to 'the rock rebellion rubbish'. He claimed he was perfectly happy offering escapist swashbuckling entertainment *à la Star Wars*. And he defended his squeaky-clean image: 'I'm sick and tired of being told that because I don't drink or smoke or take drugs that I'm a goody-two shoes . . . I don't like drugs and that is a threat to the rock 'n' roll establishment.' The art-school student who had hung around McLaren and Westwood's SEX and Seditionaries stores, thrilled by the fetish clothing and images of the Queen with a safety pin through her nose, now proudly performed at the Royal Variety Show, an annual charity event featuring Britain's top family entertainers. 'It would have been exactly the negative, inward-looking rock thing to have turned it down. If people think I'm clean and boring for shaking hands with the Queen then that's up to them . . . What would be outrageous? To spit at her? Drop me trousers? That's rock and roll rebellion and, like I say, I want nothing to do with that.'

While Adam transformed his faux-deviant cult charisma into defanged mainstream fame, McLaren seemed to imagine he could single-handedly conjure an entire subculture into being. Music alone was not enough. He and Westwood opened their latest King's Road boutique, called World's End and featuring her new line of flouncy romantic clothes. He also dreamed of making a movie around Bow Wow Wow, a second *Swindle* featuring his new clutch of concepts. And in the winter of 1980 he even attempted to start a magazine to promote the subversive sunshine-and-gold spirit embodied in Bow Wow Wow's music.

McLaren invited his old cohort Fred Vermorel to be editor of the EMI-funded project. 'The idea as he first broached it was something like *Schoolkids OZ*, a magazine written from the kids' point of view and a bit outrageous,' recalls Vermorel, referring to the special edition of the sixties underground paper that resulted in a high-profile obscenity case against the editors. *Playkids* was McLaren's original working title. He talked it up to the music press as 'a junior *Playboy* for kids getting used to the idea that they needn't have careers . . . a magazine about pleasure technology for the primitive boy and girl'. Proposed articles included a piece by celebrity ex-convict John McVicar on crime as a career option in an age of rising unemployment, and an article by Bow Wow Wow's Lee Gorman about prostitutes – where to go, prices and so forth.

But Vermorel started to grow anxious about some of McLaren's other ideas. Researching pop fandom for a book (later published as *Starlust*), he and his wife Judy unearthed lots of kinky fan letters, like one from a boy who worshipped Clem Burke from Blondie and dreamed of licking whipped cream from between the drummer's buttocks. McLaren wanted to publish the letter in *Playkids*. Except that now the magazine wasn't going to be *Playkids* – McLaren wanted to name it *Chicken*. 'Call us naïve, but nobody, not me and not the people at EMI, knew what "chicken" meant,' says Vermorel. 'So we said OK. But, of course, it's paedophile slang for young kids.'

Then there were the photo sessions. At one, Annabella was asked to pose nude (she refused). Another session was an all-day affair at a series of real people's homes, hired via an agency. 'The photographer told me Malcolm got increasingly heavy-handed during the day, and generated a kind of hysteria,' says Vermorel. The climax came with McLaren badgering a thirteen-year-old girl into removing her clothes: he succeeded, but only after reducing her to tears.

Vermorel believes McLaren's master-scheme was 'to create a child-porn scandal implicating as many people as he could': not just EMI, who were financing *Chicken*, but the BBC. A documentary crew headed by Alan Yentob had been following McLaren around for a programme on the marketing of Bow Wow Wow. Partly impelled by his usual lust for maximum media mayhem, McLaren also wanted to make a serious polemical point: the twin ideas of pop music as porn *for* children (hypersexual material that stimulated them precociously) and pop as porn *using* children (fresh-faced boy-men, cusp-of-jailbait-age girls) to titillate adults.

With typical ruthlessness, McLaren, in his eagerness to embarrass the music and media establishments, showed no concern whatsoever for the youngsters (like Annabella and the other teenage models) or old friends (like Vermorel) who would be embroiled in the scandal. When he went round to remonstrate with McLaren, says Vermorel, 'Malcolm just laughed and said, "You should be telling all this to the judge! When the shit hits the fan, *I'll* be in South America." So I told EMI what was going on, and they told Yentob, and he freaked out, and those tapes have been in the BBC vault ever since.' Vermorel also alerted the music press, telling *NME* that the magazine he'd thought was supposed to be 'the anti-*Smash Hits*' aimed at sex-positive, underage youth was turning into 'a magazine for adults that features kids as objects'.

McLaren accused Vermorel of being a closet puritan. Over the next few years photos seeped out here and there, on single sleeves and 'greatest hits' compilations, suggesting that the photo sessions had been decidedly dodgy. In one picture, Matthew Ashman wears just a 'Radio G-String' (a transistor-as-loincloth affair too small to conceal his genitals) and perches a scantily clad Indian boy (who looks about eight years old) atop his shoulders. In another photo, Annabella, naked underneath a loosely wrapped blanket, lies on top of a studio mixing board with a microphone jutting at her mouth at a suggestive angle. 'I wasn't nude,' she insisted later to *Sounds*, adding, with delicious ingenuousness: 'I was lying on a control panel . . . with all these knobs sticking in me.'

Chicken never hatched. According to Vermorel, 'the only physical evidence of *Chicken*'s existence was the rate card for advertising in the magazine.' But Bow Wow Wow's second release, *Your Cassette Pet*, continued to exploit the underage-sex angle. Most of McLaren's lyrics were reworked from the scripts for *The Adventures of Melody, Lyric, and Tune* and *The Mile High Club*. In 'Sexy Eiffel Tower', Annabella plays a suicidal girl about to leap from the top of Paris's most famous landmark. She gets implausibly horny in the proximity of death: 'Feel my treasure chest/Let's have sex before I die/Be my special guest'. Plunging through the air ('Falling legs around your spire') she enjoys a *petit mort* or two before the *grand mort* of hitting the ground. Annabella claimed, with apparent sincerity, that the panting sounds she expertly imitated weren't meant to be orgasm but the sound of panic. 'Louis Quatorze' concerns a pervy bandit-of-love who surprises Annabella with unannounced visits and ravishment at gunpoint. The music, though, almost vanquished any moral reservations: Bow Wow Wow had developed an exhilarating and unique sound, all frolicking polyrhythms, twangabilly guitar and frantic-but-funky bass. Add Annabella's girlish, euphoric vocals – especially charming on a cover of the Johnny Mercer standard 'Fools Rush In' – and the results were irresistible.

More striking than its contents, though, was *Your Cassette Pet*'s radical format: a cassette-only release midway in length between an EP and an album, it retailed at only £1.99 (half the price of a traditional vinyl album) and came in a 'flip-pack' carton similar to a cigarette packet. McLaren wanted music to become much more disposable, something kids casually picked up at their local cornershop as they breezed through on roller-skates – mere software to pop into their portable cassette players and boomboxes. Traditional record shops, already ailing because of falling sales, would disappear. EMI liked the idea of the cassette-only release for a different reason, one that subverted McLaren's own subversive intentions: cassettes were harder to copy than vinyl records (this was some years before tape-to-tape dubbing became widely available). But a couple of fatal flaws ruined the marketing plan. The tape's sound quality was too poor for radio DJs to play it. And the 'Is this an EP or an album?' ambiguity confused many record stores, resulting in *Your Cassette Pet*'s failure to penetrate the Top 40.

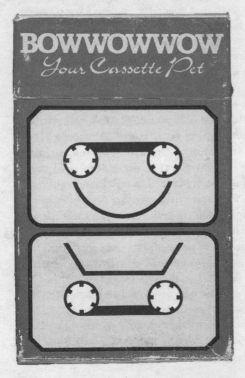

The flip-top cigarette-packet-style packaging of Bow Wow Wow's *Your Cassette Pet*, 1980.

Further singles, like 'W.O.R.K.' and 'Prince of Darkness', fared equally badly, and McLaren started to grow despondent. In the early Bow Wow Wow interviews, he'd argued that kids were desperate for new ideas, but clearly they weren't taking the bait. Gradually, it became apparent to everybody but McLaren that the one thing holding Bow Wow Wow back from success was the overbearing presence of their manager. Punters recoiled from the pungent odour of hype, the endless publicity stunts. The fact that *The Great Rock 'n' Roll Swindle* finally reached cinema screens around this time only exacerbated this impression of McLaren as an über-Svengali.

McLaren had conned himself into believing his own retroactive myth of punk as a meticulously planned swindle. He imagined that all he had to do was dream up a subculture, and the kids would simply fall in line. He often pontificated in interviews about how punk had liberated kids' energy, but any flesh-and-blood youngsters who fell into his clutches were deceived and dominated. If they showed any signs of independent thought or unwillingness to sacrifice themselves on the altar of the Idea, they were discarded.

McLaren firmly believed in the Great Man theory of history, the idea that through sheer will the visionary genius can transform everything. This conception of change as a top-down process, with revolutionary ideas dispensed from above, was profoundly anti-democratic and opposed to some of punk's core impulses – such as the do-it-yourself ethos. But, during the whole Pistols adventure, McLaren actually operated as an improviser rather than someone who had everything premeditated down to the last detail. He even boasted that his forte was being a *mis*-manager, someone who, at crucial moments, simply wasn't there.

Nor were The Sex Pistols mere cannon fodder for General McLaren's stratagems. As individuals, they had substance, character and their own ideas. Rotten, obviously, but also Steve Jones – an ex-villain whose ability to not give a fuck (or give several 'fuck's when required, as on Bill Grundy's TV show) contributed to the Pistols' volatile aura of chaos. In contrast, Bow Wow Wow were clearly marionettes who twitched at McLaren's beck. The early interviews featured McLaren doing most of the talking, but when you did hear from the group, they parroted the managerial line: 'We're not synthetic and grey'; 'Don't grocer it up'. They couldn't lend McLaren's script any conviction or life. 'Malcolm once said to me, *lamented* to me really, "This lot don't seem to know what to do,"' recalls Vermorel. 'Meaning that the Pistols always did – they were naturally delinquent.'

Anybody with a genuine spark was sharp enough to wriggle out of McLaren's clutches. Boy George, for instance, briefly joined Bow Wow Wow, after McLaren convinced him he should be a performer. (Until then, he'd been a sort of It Boy on the New Romantic scene, a widely photographed poseur in clubs.) Given the name Lieutenant Lush – a character from the *Mile High Club* script – George appeared with the band at a famous gig at the Rainbow, a venue McLaren filled with carousels and carnival rides to enhance the band's playpower image. But, although he could see George's star quality, McLaren's main aim was short term: making Annabella feel threatened and disposable, in order to keep her in line. Eventually, George was kicked out. 'I got really pissed off and first of all I just wanted revenge,' he told the *NME*. Initially, his plan had been to rip off Bow Wow Wow and 'be exactly like them but better'. Then he decided to build something of his own, resulting in Culture Club.

McLaren's contrived controversies kept backfiring. Desperate to stir up some buzz for Bow Wow Wow's debut album proper, he designed its cover as a simulation of *Dejeuner sur l'Herbe*, Manet's 1863 painting denounced as 'indecent' by Napoleon III for its image of a naked woman surrounded by fully clothed men. Annabella posed nude (under duress, she later revealed) but because she was still just under sixteen, her mother managed to stop the cover from being used. Another blow for McLaren came with the commercial failure of 'Chihuahua' – simultaneously Bow Wow Wow's most seductive single to date and their manager's most blatantly cynical gambit. Mouthing McLaren's words to a wistful, Blondie-like melody, Annabella sang about being a 'rock 'n' roll puppet', confessing, 'I can't dance and I can't sing/I can't do anything' and warning, 'I'm a horrible idiot/So don't fall in love with me'. You could mount a defence of 'Chihuahua' as a sly deconstruction of the pop industry's machinery of star-lust and fantasy. But if you consider McLaren's genuine anti-feminism, his real-world treatment of Annabella as meat (chicken, in fact), and the way he ventriloquized those humiliating words through Annabella's own lips, 'Chihuahua' leaves a bad taste.

Finally, Bow Wow Wow scored their UK pop breakthrough in early 1982 with 'Go Wild in the Country', an anti-urban fantasy featuring risqué lines about swinging naked from the trees and romping in fields 'where snakes in the grass are absolutely free'. With cassette piracy long discarded, the band's new concept was back-to-nature, as in the album title: *See Jungle! See Jungle! Go Join Your Gang Yeah! City All Over, Go*

Ape Crazy. 'Go Wild' exhorted youth to spurn KFC and McDonalds and go 'hunting and fishing'. On the sultry, bossa nova-inflected 'Hello Hello Daddy, I'll Sacrifice You', Annabella played the role of devouring earth-mother goddess as a coquette with a knife behind her back. The sweetly crooned lines about woman being 'more body than soul and more soul than mind' were vintage McLaren misogyny cobbled together from Lévi-Strauss, Jung and *The Golden Bough*.

Despite McLaren's often questionable lyrics, *See Jungle* was a pop masterpiece: charming, witty and altogether captivating. Musically, the group had achieved a uniquely ravishing sonic identity. And this was *precisely* the moment when McLaren finally lost all interest in them. According to Vermorel, the sixties art-school milieu from which he and McLaren came regarded music as a lesser artform and held pop in especially low esteem, seeing it, at best, as a mere backdrop to other activities. McLaren always insisted, and still does – despite all evidence to the contrary – that the Pistols couldn't play and punk had never been about the music. 'Christ, if people bought the records for the music, this thing would have died a death long ago,' he quipped to *The Sunday Times* in 1977.

By the time Bow Wow Wow scored their second UK Top 10 hit and American breakthrough with 'I Want Candy' – an exciting but vacuous remake of a sixties bubblegum tune – McLaren had pretty much ceased managing the band. Instead, he was seriously contemplating fronting his own project. Bow Wow Wow, he finally understood, never became popular in a mass-culture sense because of the authenticity gap – the fact that his ideas were being ventriloquised through a teenage girl. 'Annabella wasn't me, so when it came to singing a song like "W.O.R.K.", it was very difficult for her to hold that up,' he observed ruefully.

When Bow Wow Wow played New York, McLaren was exposed to hip hop and inspired by witnessing scratching and rapping in its native Bronx habitat. We'll return to the story of how Malcolm McLaren – a Jewish-Scottish ex-Svengali with absolutely no sense of rhythm – seized the mike and rapped his way into the charts at the end of the book.

17

ELECTRIC DREAMS: Synthpop

The Human League. Gary Numan. Ultravox. John Foxx. Visage. Spandau Ballet.
Martin Rushent. Soft Cell. Japan. DAF.

The Human League arrived with as much fanfare as any new group could desire. Signed to Virgin, they were touted as the 'next big thing'. David Bowie proclaimed that 'watching them is like watching 1980'. Admittedly, he said this in 1979, but still, an endorsement from the glamdaddy of all things cutting edge was not to be sniffed at.

When 1980 actually rolled around, though, The Human League seemed stuck. They'd been among the very first post-punk outfits to talk up 'pop' as something to aspire to – and yet they'd failed to become pop. Their first two albums, 1979's *Reproduction* and 1980's *Travelogue*, sold modestly. Compared to Giorgio Moroder's Eurodisco production of Donna Summer and Sparks, *Reproduction*'s version of electrofuturism sounded creaky and strangely *quaint*. And the League knew it. 'We were disappointed with the production; it sounded weak next to Moroder and Kraftwerk,' says Ian Craig Marsh. 'We wanted our records to be more brutal on the rhythmic level, but at that point the engineers and producers available in Britain weren't up to it.'

Travelogue sounded more forceful and glossy, but a hit single continued to elude the group. As if to rub salt in their wounds, on the eve of its release, pop-punkers The Undertones took the piss out of The Human League in their Top 10 hit 'My Perfect Cousin'. Kevin, the song's goody-two-shoes subject (he's got a degree 'in economics, maths, physics and bionics') starts an electronic band with some art-school boys. 'His mother bought him a *synthesizer*,' spits singer Feargal Sharkey with disgust, 'Got The Human League in to advise her'. Now that he's in a band,

Kevin has girls chasing him, 'But what a shame/It's in vain . . . Kevin, he's in love with himself'. This pretty much crystallized the early Human League's public image – music for narcissistic art-school poseurs and science geeks.

The group's cold, off-putting aura was exacerbated by the science-fiction subject matter of many early songs. *Reproduction*'s big single, 'Empire State Human', concerned a man who keeps on growing. *Travelogue*'s 'The Black Hit of Space' imagines a record so monstrously bland it turns into a kind of predatory cultural void sucking up everything in its path. As it climbs the charts, the rest of the Top 40 disappears, 'until there was nothing but it left to buy'. But all the clever astrophysical details (gravity being so multiplied in proximity to the disc that your record player's tone arm weighs 'more than Saturn', etc.) only confirmed the band's nerdy image. These were the sort of people who read *New Scientist* and watched *Tomorrow's World*.

In a bid to stake their claim to being 'tomorrow's pop today', The Human League came up with the crackpot idea of doing fully automated shows. 'Talking Heads asked us to be the support group on their 1980 UK tour and we said, "We'll do the gigs but we want to be in the audience and watch the show,"' says Marsh, still enthused by the idea over twenty years later. 'We'd got these new synchronization units that operated the slide show in sync with the music. We guaranteed that while we wouldn't be onstage we'd be at every gig: talking to the audience, shaking hands and signing autographs.' Martyn Ware adds, 'We'd gone a long way down the line: all the programming was done, it was going to be this big multimedia show, almost Exploding Plastic Inevitable level. But Talking Heads changed their minds; it was too much for them. Maybe they thought they were going to be upstaged.'

Almost in an act of charity, *Top of the Pops* invited the luckless League to appear on the show when the group's *Holiday 80* double single grazed the lower end of the Top 75. The band mimed along to their cover of Gary Glitter's 'Rock 'n' Roll, Part One', but even after this fabulous exposure to the Great British record-buying public, the group couldn't reach the true hit parade. What really hurt was that by mid-1980 it seemed like virtually *anybody* wielding a synth could become a pop star. One year earlier, Tubeway Army's 'Are "Friends" Electric?' had reached number 1. It proved to be the first in a string of huge hits for Gary Numan. *Après Gaz, le déluge*: throughout 1980, synth-laced chart incursions came from John Foxx, Orchestral Manoeuvres in the Dark,

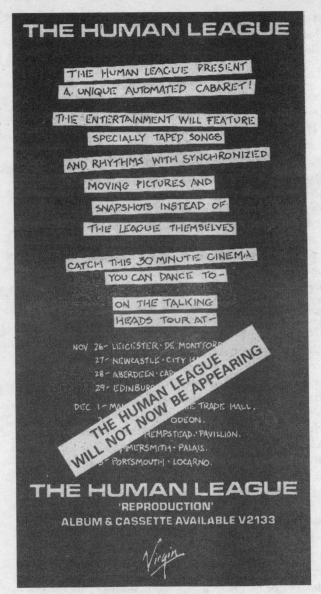

Advert announcing The Human League's being dropped from Talking Heads' 1980 UK tour, shattering the group's plan to put on a fully automated show

Ultravox, Visage and Spandau Ballet. In other words, everybody but The Human League. In the year since Bowie had heralded them as the sound of the new decade, the group had gone from ahead of their time to past their sell-by date.

Gary Numan became a synthpop pioneer almost by accident. Making the first Tubeway Army album in Spaceward Studio in the summer of 1978, he stumbled across a Mini-Moog left behind by another band. 'Although I liked some electronic music, I still associated it mainly with pompous supergroups,' he said. 'They conjured up visions of disgusting, self-indulgent solos that went on for half a hour.' Before the rental company reclaimed the synth, Numan messed around with it. 'Luckily for me, the synth had been left on a heavy setting, which produced the most powerful, ground-shaking sound I had ever heard.'

Tubeway Army's debut album abruptly swerved from its guitars-only conception to an electronically turbo-charged New Wave. This was a transitional sound – hard rock with a futuristic sheen, rooted in the clean, punchy riffs of glam. 'I was just a guitarist that played keyboards,' Numan recalled. 'I just turned punk songs into electronic songs.' The Moog sound was fat and doomy, not a million miles from the down-tuned bombast of Black Sabbath. And the way Numan's music *moved* had nothing to do with the sequenced pulse-beat of Moroder. On *Replicas*, Tubeway Army's breakthrough album, the rhythm section was human and potent; Numan continued to play guitar as well as keyboards. *The Pleasure Principle*, his next album – which was released under the Gary Numan name – upped the futurism and abandoned guitars completely in favour of synths. But Numan still avoided programmed rhythm, working with a real bassist and flesh-and-blood drummer. His music *rocked*, and even when it didn't, it possessed an almost symphonic grandeur – just listen to his most chillingly beautiful song, 'Down in the Park', a sort of dystopian power ballad.

Critics, possibly disconcerted by the way Numan had bypassed the music press en route to the top of the charts, unjustly pegged him as a Bowie Xerox. They sourced Numan's image in Bowie's aristocratic alien from *The Man Who Fell to Earth* and his sound in *Low*. But his debt to Bowie was actually less specific: the art of creative synthesis, or, as Numan put it with characteristic and admirable frankness, 'plagiarism' – weaving together an original identity out of pilfered bits and bobs. He also inherited glam rock's penchant for theatre and spectacle. Punk's 'anti-hero thing' and back-to-basics simplicity were 'against everything I've ever wanted to do', he told *NME*. He didn't believe in 'being the same as the audience'. And he liked distance, a literally physical gulf between the stage and the crowd. His tours featured stunning lighting, set design and even robots. 'Showbiz for showbiz's sake more than anything,' he told *Melody Maker*. 'I think I'm just taking it back to cabaret.'

Numan had no time for social realism or everyday subjects, instead adapting his lyrics from a science-fiction novel he'd tried to write. The saga concerned a city of the near future administered by a 'wise' mega-computer originally created by humans to bring their society back from the brink of anarchy. The machine decides that humans are actually the problem and embarks on a secret programme of elimination. Numan's lyrics featured a menagerie of 'types': the 'friends' of 'Are "Friends" Electric' are cyborg buddies or sexpals; the 'Grey Men' perform the IQ tests that determine who is culled first; the 'Crazies' are resistance guerrillas hip to the machine's master-scheme.

Lost to all but the most hardcore Numanoids, these details of this dystopian metropolis aren't as important as the atmospheres conjured by the song scenarios: moods of isolation, paranoia, emotional disconnection, and hints of sexual confusion. In his autobiography, *Praying to the Aliens*, Numan discussed the way in which *Replicas* teems 'with images of decay, seediness, drug addicts, fragile people and the abandonment of morals. The bisexual allusions are partly based on encounters I had with gay men, most of whom were much older than me, who had attempted to persuade me to try things. I was never interested in gay sex . . . but the seediness of those situations left an impression which I used in *Replicas*.'

Beyond the futuristic sound and imagery, what really hooked Numan's legion of fans was the vulnerability and sexual ambiguity. Gary's sullen pout and wounded eyes made for a perfect pin-up in the classic teenybop tradition, with transgender appeal: girls dreamed of thawing the iceman, bringing him back to life; boys identified with his loneliness, allegorized in songs like 'M.E.'. Here Numan sang from the point of view of 'the last living machine' on an earth where all the people have died. 'Its own power source is running down. I used to have a picture in my mind of this sad and desperately alone machine standing in a desert-like wasteland, just waiting to die,' he said.

Teen dreams of tech*noir* alienation, *Replicas* and *The Pleasure Principle* were like cartoon versions of Joy Division's *Unknown*

Pleasures and *Closer*. But Numan's primary contemporary parallel and inspiration was a far less revered band: Ultravox. Despite having a fairly fierce sound, Ultravox's mannered artifice sat uneasily with punk, and critics generally wrote them off as a glam johnny-come-lately. Guitars dominated their sound at first, but by 1978's synth-laden *Systems of Romance*, they verged on a kind of electropunk. Numan was listening and taking notes.

What made Ultravox crucial precursors of 1980's synthpop explosion was their European aura and singer/lyricist John Foxx's frigid imagery of dehumanization and decadence. The group's style was based on rejecting rock's standard 'Americanisms'; Billy Currie, their key-boardist, was a classically trained viola player and determinedly avoided blues scales. 'We feel European,' said Foxx, when *NME* asked why they'd recorded *Systems* with Kraftwerk producer Conny Plank at his studio near Köln. 'The sort of background and melodies we tend to come out with just seemed to be . . . Germanic even before we came here.' As for the atmosphere of numb anomie and alienated sexuality, Ultravox laid it all on the table with the debut's manifesto-like 'I Want to be a Machine' and Ballard-damaged 'MySex'. 'MySex is a spark of electro flesh,' sings Foxx. 'A neon outline on a high-rise overspill . . . skyscraper shadows on a car-crash overpass . . . It wears no future faces, owns just random gender.'

But after three unsuccessful major-label albums, Ultravox were in an even worse place than The Human League, and at the end of 1978, their label, Island, dropped them. Foxx went solo and totally synthetic (abandoning not just guitars but 'real' drums, too). On his debut album *Metamatic*, he developed the cinematic (and cinephilic) quality already glimpsed in such Ultravox songs as 'Hiroshima Mon Amour'. The imagistic lyrics resembled fragments torn from an avant-garde screenplay: 'A flicker of flashback, background dissolves', 'Underneath the green arcade/A blurred girl'. His unveiling as a solo artist coincided with Numan-mania and benefited from it. In the first half of 1980 Foxx brushed the edge of the Top 30 repeatedly with the singles 'Underpass', 'No-One Driving' and 'Burning Car.' But he didn't achieve anything comparable to the success of his young admirer Numan.

Meanwhile, two other ex-members of Ultravox, Billy Currie and guitarist Robin Simon, had stumbled on a developing scene based on electronic music and the romance of all things European and cinematic. After being ditched by Island and left by Foxx, Currie and Simon drowned their sorrows at a Soho nightspot called Billy's, where Rusty Egan was the DJ at a weekly event called 'A Club for Heroes'. Bowie was the patron saint – his 'Heroes' defined the musical mood of grandeur and decay, while his wardrobe of images and personae set the fashion tone somewhere at the intersection of aristocracy, androgyny and alien. Egan's playlist mixed the Berlin sound of Bowie and Iggy with Moroder, Kraftwerk, early UK electropop like 'Being Boiled' and 'Warm Leatherette', and new synthpop outfits such as Belgium's Telex and Japan's Yellow Magic Orchestra. When the club moved to a larger venue, the Blitz, its crowd became known as Blitz Kids.

At the core of this scene was Egan's flatmate, Steve Strange. He was the club's doorman, weeding out the riff-raff and preserving the atmosphere of in-crowd elitism, while his ever-changing image defined the Blitz Kid style: a blend of futuristic and retro elements that jumbled bolero hats, gold braid, toy-soldier coats, Russian cummerbunds, geometric haircuts and pill-box hats, along with stylized make-up that turned the face into an abstract canvas. Strange soon became the frontman of Visage, a confederacy of punk failures looking for a second shot at stardom. Founder-member Egan had drummed in The Rich Kids, the much hyped but unsuccessful group formed by Glen Matlock after he had left The Sex Pistols. Another Rich Kid, Midge Ure, played guitar in Visage, alongside Ultravox's Billy Currie and no fewer than *three* members of Magazine (keyboardist Dave Formula, guitarist John McGeoch and bassist Barry Adamson), another band who had failed to deliver on high expectations. Strange had the least impressive CV of the lot: his sole musical exploit to date had been a brief involvement with a punk outfit tastelessly named The Moors Murderers who had garnered a few outraged tabloid headlines.

Visage's timing was perfect: the Blitz scene was the vanguard of a general shift in pop culture back to fantasy and escapism. According to Strange, the new breed – now confusingly known as New Romantics *and* Futurists *and* Blitz Kids – were 'people who work nine to five and then go out and live their fantasies. They're glad to be dressed up and escaping work and all the greyness and depression.' And yet, weirdly, for all its brisk electrodisco rhythms, Visage's music was sepia-toned and at times almost funereal, with Strange's vocals exuding a fey sadness. Songs like 'Fade to Grey' and 'The Damned Don't Cry' conjured what Mark Fisher called 'the Euro-aesthete's "exhaustion from life"', especially in tandem with the videos, which evoked a pre-war desolation derived from *Cabaret* and Fritz

Lang. With impeccable timing, the late summer of 1980 saw Bowie staging his comeback with a number 1 hit, 'Ashes to Ashes', which tapped into the same effete, melancholy mood and European electronic sound, as if to remind everybody that he'd done it first with side two of *Low*. Steve Strange, dressed as a pierrot, made an appearance in the 'Ashes' video.

Instead of looking westwards (to America, the heartland of rock 'n' roll) for inspiration, the New Romantics pointedly turned their gaze to the east – Germany, obviously, but also Russia. Visage recorded a song titled 'Moon over Moscow', while Spandau Ballet, the other major group on the Blitz scene, plunged into Cossack/Constructivist kitsch with their single 'Musclebound'. Singer Tony Hadley's operatic vocals bore scant relation to black music. Picking up on the reference to Spandau – site of a purpose-built prison in western Berlin, where Nazi leaders such as Rudolf Hess and Albert Speer were incarcerated – and the neo-classical marble torso on the cover of their debut album *Journeys to Glory*, neo-fascist magazine *Bulldog* hailed Spandau as fine exponents of 'musclebound, Nordic' art. *Journeys* also featured a brief sleevenote that struck a Nietzschean tone of beauty-as-cruelty: 'Picture angular glimpses of sharp youth cutting strident shapes through the curling grey of 3 a.m. Hear the soaring joy of immaculate rhythms, the sublime glow of music for heroes driving straight to the heart of dance. Follow the stirring vision and the rousing sound on the path towards journeys to glory.' The Spandau ethos was openly elitist – their gigs were word-of-mouth only. New Romanticism, for them, represented a natural aristocracy: the collective narcissism of a self-chosen few. 'I am beautiful and clean and so very, very young,' as Hadley crooned on their first hit, 'To Cut a Long Story Short'.

Spandau Ballet's dalliance with the Eurosynth sound was short lived, though, and the group quickly reverted to their soul-boy roots, venerating black American music above all others and producing by way of tribute a series of stilted funk records. Meanwhile, Ultravox – reformed by Currie when he sensed that the pop weather had finally changed in their favour, and with Midge Ure as its new singer – plunged into full-blown Teutonica with the quasi-classical 'Vienna'. Wreathed in the sonic equivalent of dry ice, this ludicrously portentous ballad, inspired by a vague notion of a past-its-prime Habsburg Empire sliding into decadence, reached number 2 in the charts in the first weeks of 1981 and hovered there for what seemed like an eternity.

At one point a single man had almost the whole New Romantic scene locked up tight: Martin Rushent, who had produced New Wave groups like The Stranglers and Buzzcocks for United Artists. Rushent was in the process of forming his own label, Genetic, and its London office happened to be directly above Blitz. Despite zero fashion sense and a thoroughly untrendy beard, he regularly hung out at the club. 'It became just the hippest place on earth,' he recalls. 'I remember seeing Spandau down there for the first time, and they just blew me away – they were all wearing tartan kilts, odd clothes and hair, but the music was brilliant.' Soon Spandau, Visage and the reformed Ultravox were all lined up to sign to Rushent's fledgling label. But turmoil at Genetic's parent company, Radar, put the label in limbo, so Rushent urged the groups to seek separate deals of their own. In the meantime, he threw himself into building a £250,000 studio in the grounds of his home in the Berkshire countryside, complete with state-of-the-art equipment for making electronic music.

Between 1978 and 1980, synthesizers had become much more affordable and sophisticated. Dirt cheap (around £200) and light enough to be easily transported (unlike the prog-era synths), the Wasp was the great democratizer when it came to electronic music. Equally significant was the arrival at the end of the 1970s of instruments that hugely expanded the potential of machine rhythm, like the Linn drum computer: the first programmable drum machine to feature sampled percussive textures – realistic-sounding toms, kicks, snares, cymbals and so forth. If you preferred a more hands-on, drummerly feel, you could use syn-drum pads like Simmons. Played manually in real time rather than programmed, they were touch-responsive – the harder you hit, the louder they sounded. Each pad connected to its own module, allowing the user to switch between different drum timbres or feed the beat through effects to make it sound jarringly futuristic. The gimmicky, pinging syn-drum sound was smeared all over the early New Romantic records. Even at the time, it had a curious, ultramodern-yet-already-dated quality – a pre-echo of its status today as a period piece, a sonic signifier for 'early eighties'.

Rushent's first stab at electropop using these new tools was with former Buzzcock frontman Pete Shelley. The sound they developed was a transitional hybrid of guitar-based New Wave and electropop, heard at its best on the superb single 'Homo Sapien'. Released in August 1981, 'Homo Sapien' was a coded coming-out for Shelley, but the single's innuendoes (the fruity way Shelley enunciates '*homo* sapien', plus couplets like 'homo superior/my interior') provoked an unofficial ban from Radio

prospects. Shelley's solo debut
early 1982, by which time another group –
– had taken the Rushent electropop sound into the
Shelley's thunder.

Rushent had originally been called in for a last-ditch effort at salvaging The Human League's career in early 1981, when it was at its lowest ebb. After *Travelogue*, the group had become deadlocked by their inability to agree on a direction for the next album. Phil Oakey instigated the split, telling Martyn Ware, 'We're kicking you out of the group,' only to be thrown for a loop when Ian Craig Marsh decided to leave with Ware to form a new venture, British Electric Foundation. Worse, the music press reacted to the split by deciding that Ware and Marsh were the real musical brains, writing off singer Oakey and visual projectionist Adrian Wright as the talentless rump.

The decision for Oakey and Wright to retain the name The Human League made sense – there was an imminent European tour that had to be honoured (or risk huge debts), and the strikingly coiffured singer and Wright's slide images were the group's most recognizable elements. In a sense, Oakey's lopsided haircut had become the League's logo. It took some effort from manager Bob Last, though, to convince Oakey (who never liked the name) to keep operating as The Human League, and to convince Ware and Marsh (who *did* like it) to accept a pay-off for loss of the brand. The deal was 1 per cent of the take on the next album – which seemed merely symbolic. It was likely to be 1 per cent of next to nothing, given the parlous state of the band. Nobody could have predicted that the next Human League LP would be a megahit called *Dare*.

When they hooked up with Rushent in early 1981, The Human League were demoralized and directionless. 'They had no real material, just bits of ideas,' says Rushent, who had been invited by Virgin to produce a potential single called 'The Sound of the Crowd'. 'I listened to the demo and said, "Well, that's going in the bin; we're starting again." Their spirits picked up hugely when we'd completed "Sound of the Crowd", 'cos it did sound a hundred times better.'

'Sound of the Crowd' was the first fruit of Oakey's songwriting partnership with Ian Burden, formerly the bassist in Graph, an experimental Sheffield band. 'I still reckon that song is one of the maddest records that's ever got in the Top 20,' says Oakey. 'The whole thing runs on tom-toms, but they're synth toms, and it's got very odd screaming sounds.'

There's also a foreboding dub reco̶r̶ ̶o̶ ̶
space (Burden was a reggae fiend). 'I don't t̶
particularly impressed with the record. It was only wi̶
ful that Martin said, "I wanna do more."'

'Sound of the Crowd' also featured backing vocals from two oth̶
new recruits, Joanne Catherall and Susanne Sulley. Oakey had spotted
the teenage pair dancing during a 'Futurist night' at Crazy Daisy, the
club that had been the focus for Sheffield's glam youth since Roxy days.
'I was really into Michael Jackson's *Off the Wall* at that point, and
thought high voices were the way pop was going to go', he recalls.
'Martyn could do quite a nice high backing vocal in the old League, so
with him out of the picture, I was thinking: Do I know anyone who
sings falsetto? No. Get a girl then. We auditioned four people, but
Joanne and Susanne, being friends, were ideal 'cos they could look after
each other when the band was on tour.' That Catherall was darkly
handsome and Sulley blondely pretty didn't hurt in terms of the band's
visual chemistry, either. Although they loved New Romantic music,
Catherall and Sulley didn't especially care for The Human League –
they were hardcore Numan fans who dressed in black with red ties and
black trainers, just like their idol.

Oakey's decision to recruit 'the girls', as they universally became
known, was a stroke of genius. As Jon Savage points out, when they
plucked Joanne and Susanne off the dance floor at Crazy Daisy, The
Human League literally let the crowd into their sound. Overnight, the
League's music opened up, became populist, and then popular. 'That was
a totally conscious thing on Philip's part, he understood what he was
doing when he got the girls to join,' says Bob Last, who was extremely
dubious about the idea at first. Shining through their provincial attempts
at glamour, Catherall and Sulley's ordinary-girl charm banished the old
League's cold-fish image and visually matched a shift in Oakey's songwriting towards stories of everyday romance. Their sheer amateurish-
ness – 'I can't dance,' Sulley admitted in 2001, twenty years into her
career with the League, 'I've got no rhythm. We're not particularly great
singers' – made the League *lovable* for the first time.

'Love Action' and 'Open Your Heart', the rejuvenated League's next
two chartbusting singles, were practically manifestos for this new
humanized-not-Numanized direction in electropop. In a weird way,
'Love Action' sounds like its title: pulsing and glistening, an iridescent
affirmation. Yet, for all its warmth and wetness, 'Love Action' still

retains something of the aberrant quality of 'Sound of the Crowd', making it an unlikely candidate for a number 3 hit. 'It's not got a proper chorus,' admits Oakey. It's basically two different songs bolted together: the verses, from a song called 'I Believe in Love' are 'confessional nonsense, what I was feeling at the time', says Oakey, while the angular not-quite-a-chorus section is from another song about watching Sylvia Kristel in the softcore erotic movie *Emmanuelle*.

The new-look Human League, just before megafame, Sheffield, 1981. L to R: Susanne Sulley, Adrian Wright, Phil Oakey, Joanne Catherall, Ian Burden. Photo by Kevin Cummins

Rushent and The Human League had become a hitmaking dream team. 'To a large extent, I was their band,' says Rushent. 'I was certainly their drummer, because I programmed all the rhythms and made all the decisions about the grooves.' He worked closely with Burden on the bass sound and with another new League member, Jo Callis, on the song's chord patterns. 'One of the key things was that for the first time we had a proper band,' says Oakey. 'In the old League we had four people who fiddled with a lot of things. But suddenly we had Martin, who'd been a drummer, Ian Burden, who played bass, and Jo Callis, who'd been guitarist in The Rezillos and knew about chords.' Rushent's varied background in the recording industry – working with everybody from Shirley Bassey to Yes – was vital. 'Martin really knew what pop was,' says Oakey. 'He could take your mad sounds and they'd still be mad sounds but he could put them in places that made them pop. Really horrible things come out of synthesizers and that's what I like about them. But somehow Martin could make them work within a pop context, and I don't know how he did it.'

Released in October 1981, *Dare* represented a perfect meld of tradition and innovation. 'I'd learned a lot through working with the arranger Johnny Harris,' says Rushent. 'He used to conduct Lulu's orchestra and was band leader for all the big show singers like Petula Clark, Tom Jones, Shirley Bassey. Through watching him work, I learned about voicing instruments and how the most important element of music is silence. Don't clutter your arrangements, keep every instrumental part simple and "vocal", as if someone was singing it. If you listen to *Dare*, there's lots of space in the songs and there's loads of little parts, and you can sing them all. There's so many bloody little singalong bits and every one sticks in your head.'

Instead of an orchestra, though, Rushent, in tandem with Burden, Callis and Oakey, was working with machines. One particular 'magic machine' was especially crucial: the Roland Microcomposer, a combined synthesizer and sequencer that allowed the user to program complicated and extended note patterns, and that came with a labour-saving 'copy/insert' function that enabled the pasting of whole passages of music from one location in the piece to another. 'Today, the Microcomposer would be regarded as very primitive, and when you first grappled with it, the results sounded shitty,' recalls Rushent. 'But if you really read the manual and studied what it was capable of doing and spent days mastering it, then applied your engineering and production skills, well, you could end up with a style of playing that no one else had: stuff that was impossible to duplicate in the live environment, all the little inflections, bends and tonal changes. That was what was novel about The Human League at the time, the ultimate precision – no one had heard that before. When it hit the dance floor, it was like this massive machine – the thing was right up people's backsides. But there's enough feeling in it so it doesn't sound like Kraftwerk; it actually sounds like humans playing it.' Getting things to run 'like fucking clockwork' was a technical triumph in itself, given that in the pre-MIDI early eighties, electronic instruments all ran on different time codes.

From being an electropop band who made 'no standard rock 'n' roll instrumentation' their manifesto, The Human League mutated into a pop group who just happened to use synths. Abba became the group's new reference point – their ideal of quality pop with universal appeal. For *NME*'s Paul Morley, The Human League represented a new middle of the road that was simultaneously post-punk and post-Abba: *Dare* could have been made only by a group who knew about Roxy, Iggy and Kraftwerk, but their music was inviting and accessible enough to win over the great unhip masses – mums and dads, teenage girls, children, grannies. The avant-MOR tag made sense because *Dare*'s worldview and sentiments were positive, wholesome, in some ways just a notch away from conservative (with a small 'c'). 'The Things that Dreams are Made of' saw Oakey reeling off a list of life-enhancing stuff over electronicized Glitterbeat: 'Everybody needs love and adventure/Everybody needs cash to spend . . . Everybody needs two or three friends'. 'I Am the Law' turned The Clash's 'I Fought the Law' inside out – it was a sympathetic song about authority and the police inspired by Oakey's encounter with an injured bouncer back when he was working as a hospital porter. In interviews, Oakey rejected bohemian values (he was pro-marriage and anti-drugs), and exalted a new spirit of professionalism and commitment to entertainment – 'This new pride that I'm always talking about in pop music, *that* was destroyed by punk, the garage band ideal.'

'Don't You Want Me', the fourth single off *Dare* and the Christmas number 1 for 1981, was their most sonically conventional single yet, from its perky groove to its trim verse/chorus structure. 'Don't You Want Me' further underlined the importance of Joanne Catherall and Susanne Sulley to The Human League: their biggest hit was the one that gave the greatest prominence to their modest vocals. A duet between Oakey and Sulley, it deliciously rewrites the story of how 'the girls' were discovered and projects five years into the future. Oakey sings as the Svengali who plucks a girl from obscurity ('You were working as a waitress in a cocktail bar') and turns her into 'someone new', only to be abandoned by his protégé–lover now she has the world at her feet. Defiant (if ever so slightly off key), Sulley sings the part of the provincial dreamer who always knew deep down she was destined for better things, and is now determined to make her own path in life. (In reality, it was Catherall who became Oakey's girlfriend.)

The 'Don't You Want Me' video added further layers of artifice. A Brechtian conundrum, it depicted the band making a promo, cutting between scenes from the video-within-a-video and action off-set or in the editing suite (the band watching their own rushes). 'I don't know where that idea came from originally, whether it was Phil's or the director Steve Barron's,' says Bob Last. 'But from the band's point of view, a great deal of the appeal was that it was a film, shot on 35mm – something that was extremely unusual in those very early days of the video industry. And that was a straightforwardly aspirational thing: the idea of doing a video with high production values. If you look at the promo, there's a big film camera very prominent in it. And from a marketing standpoint, it was very smart, because here were these girls in the band who really were "regular girls" now appearing in a *movie*. It just made perfect sense.' A worldwide smash (it topped the charts in America as well as the UK), 'Don't You Want Me' propelled *Dare* to global sales of over five million. The Human League *were* Abba, to all intents and purposes.

The peak of synthpop occurred during the winter of 1981–2. Close behind The Human League in the warm-blooded electropop stakes was Soft Cell, scoring a number 1 with their torrid cover of Northern Soul classic 'Tainted Love', swiftly followed by the number 4 'Bedsitter' and number 3 'Say Hello Wave Goodbye'. Orchestral Manoeuvres in the Dark, a highly melodic, slightly wet, and increasingly pretentious synth duo from the Liverpool area, scored three Top 5 hits in a row between September '81 and February '82 – *two* of them, bizarrely, about Joan of Arc! The Top 10 was also haunted by Japan's electronic torch song 'Ghosts', Ultravox's interminable 'Vienna' and a couple of deceptively lightweight-seeming ditties by Depeche Mode. Two synthpop classics also staged a surprise return in early '82. With 'Don't You Want Me' still high in the charts, EMI reissued the League's original 'Being Boiled' single, and it broke into the Top 10. A few weeks later, another song from 1978 – Kraftwerk's 'The Model', the catchiest song on *The Man-Machine* – was released as a single and, as if to proclaim the Düsseldorf group's ancestral centrality for synthpop, promptly soared to number 1.

By the spring of 1982, electronic pop was so dominant that the Musicians Union made an attempt to limit the use of synthesizers. 'They seriously proposed the idea of rationing synthesizers, restricting them to certain recommended studios where they could be used to duplicate string parts,' says Ian Craig Marsh. 'Which sounds ludicrous, almost Stalin-esque. But they wanted to protect the jobs of orchestras.'

Synthpop was treated with equal suspicion in certain quarters of the rock scene. 'It's not experimenting at all, it's just using synthesizers to play pretty ordinary songs a lot of the time,' jeered Pete DeFreitas of Liverpudlian post-punkers Echo & The Bunnymen. 'A lot of these kids just don't have talent,' added bassist Les Pattinson. 'Any farmyard horse can kick a synth.' Perhaps he meant to say 'any clothes horse' – as per The Undertones' 'My Perfect Cousin', synthesizers were associated with effete poseurs. Conversely, it was precisely the instrument's symbolic coding as effeminate and un-rock that appealed to synth users and synthpop fans. Compared to the phallic guitar, the synth was for gender-benders: Oakey with his lipstick, eyeliner and asymmetric hair hanging long down one side of his face; Soft Cell's Marc Almond in his pervy black leather; skirt-wearing Martin Gore from Depeche Mode; the crop-haired, dominatrix image of Eurythmics singer Annie Lennox.

In America, attitudes to synths were even more polarized. For many metal fans, keyboards were innately queer, their presence immediately signifying the ruination of 'real' metal. For other Americans, being into 'English haircut bands' and 'art-fag' music served as an empowering act of cultural treason. If you grew up feeling different in a US high school during the eighties, surrounded by Mötley Crüe fans, and with the only home-grown underground consisting of hardcore punk muscularity, the sole alternative was to look towards England – to become a fan of groups like Depeche Mode. Since Bowie, if not earlier, there's a real sense in which England has connoted 'gay' in the American rock imagination. Which explains both Anglophobia *and* Anglophilia: for those alienated from the overbearing heterosexism of mainstream American rock, 'England' beckons as an imaginary haven, a utopia of androgyny. In the early eighties, gay or sexually ambiguous boys, plus a good number of smart girls, were attracted to British electropop – not least because the bands were generally full of pretty boys wearing make-up. (I should know: I married one of those brainy Anglophile girls!)

Japan, my wife's teenage favourites, could have been the ultimate Anglo art-fag nightmare as far as heartland rockers were concerned. Yet, far from living in some paradise for dandy aesthetes and members of the third gender, Japan were rebelling against the mundane realities of urban Britain, which is just as hostile to the artistically minded androgynous as any blue-collar town in America. The son of a rat catcher, singer David Sylvian grew up in dreary Catford in south-east London. 'It was disguise, a mask to hide behind,' Sylvian has said of his white face make-up and platinum-blond wedge-cut hair. 'The music was a mask as well. It says nothing about how I was, other than I was hiding, trying desperately to be anything but myself. Just because I thought that was the only way I could survive.' Even the singer's assumed name was masquerade, inspired by Syl Sylvain of the cross-dressing New York Dolls.

Japan arrived on the UK music scene just as punk started to explode, and it transformed everything to their disadvantage. The music press ridiculed them as behind-the-curve glamsters and mocked Sylvian's croon as second-rate Bryan Ferry. But after a debut album that sounded like The New York Dolls raunching out at Studio 54 – disco-rock dazzled by a cocaine glitterball – Japan developed an arresting post-Roxy sound built around exotic synth textures and Mick Karn's languid fretless bass. Japan's records sounded as exquisite as Sylvian and his band looked. In performance, the singer mesmerized listeners with his excessive poise and composure – a statuesque quality that carried through to his ultra-stylized vocals (almost a frieze of emotion) and the immaculately made-up blank-white façade of his face. Simon Frith could have been talking about Sylvian when he wrote about Bowie's 'art of posing': he 'wasn't sexy like most pop idols. His voice and body were aesthetic not sensual objects; he expressed semi-detached bedroom fantasies, boys' arty dreams . . . an individual grace that showed up everyone else as clods.'

The art-rock dream is achieving an aristocratic existence, dedicated to beauty: collecting and cherishing antiques and objets d'art, visiting exotic places, feasting your eyes. There's a hierarchic impulse underlying art-rock's obsession with distinction and perfection, and this often takes on an unnerving right-wing flavour. In Japan's case, it came out in the group's odd fascination with the former Axis powers – 'Suburban Berlin', 'Nightporter' (inspired by the Dirk Bogarde movie), Japan itself – and with other well-ordered societies. They wrote a song called 'Communist China' and another titled 'Rhodesia' – surely the only pop tune ever about this white-power postcolonial pariah of the civilized world!

Too refined for the crass self-mythologization of New Romanticism (they made Spandau Ballet and Visage look clumsy and garish) Japan nevertheless benefited as pop culture began to shift in a neo-glam direction.

Almost overnight, they became incredibly hip. Critical praise began to accumulate around 'The Art of Parties' single, turning into an avalanche for *Tin Drum*, a loose concept album about Mao's China. 'Ghosts', an electronic ballad eerily shaded with flittering synths but devoid of a beat or bassline, went Top 10 – the cue for a compelling *Top of the Pops* appearance, with the pale, still David Sylvian drawing the world into his hush. Paul Morley described Sylvian as 'too fragile to fuck'.

Soft Cell's Marc Almond was fragile too, but in a different way: wonderfully uncool and hyper-emotional. His vocal pitch wavered, the intonation was often excessive, but Almond's all-too-human passion burst through. Like The Human League, Soft Cell had no truck with the we-are-robots posturing of first-wave electropop: their songs nestled in the gap between glitzy dreams and squalid English reality. 'I like to mix personal experiences with film images and then exaggerate them,' Almond explained. Almond was studying art at Leeds Polytechnic when he met fellow student David Ball, initially enlisting Ball to provide the soundtrack for his cabaret-like art performances. Although Ball played Soft Cell's synths, Almond was the real scholar of electronic music. He particularly loved Suicide, especially the neon-twinkling textures of the duo's second album, which was more lushly textured and synthetic than the classic lo-fi debut. Almond played electronic dance pop when he DJ-ed at the Leeds Warehouse nightclub, and often penned Soft Cell songs in the cloak room. The Warehouse was the epicentre of the Leeds branch of the Futurist/New Romantic scene. 'When exhibitionism hit Leeds, it hit hard,' Almond recalled. 'It was a battle for who could wear the most make-up and most acres of material.'

Soft Cell's music emerged from the collision of Almond's electronic tastes and Ball's background as a fan of Northern Soul and the orchestrated sixties pop of Petula Clark and Burt Bacharach. Soft Cell essentially transposed Suicide's 'glamorous and dirty' New York vibe to provincial England – the red-light district of Leeds where Almond lived. 'Bedsitter', the group's second Top 5 hit, documented his lifestyle, alternating between a cramped flat and the hollow glitz of the New Romantic scene-dream. According to Almond the song came from 'living in really grotty bedsitters . . . [then] going out at night to clubs looking glamorous . . . Sort of mixing . . . the glitter with squalor . . . I used to wonder about these really glamorous people: what do they look like doing the dishes?' For the debut album, *Non-Stop Erotic Cabaret*, Soft Cell voyaged to New York to soak up the scuzz, recording songs like 'Seedy Films' and

Soft Cell's Marc Almond. Photo by Janette Beckman

'Sex Dwarf' in a studio near Times Square. If this first album played up the sleaze to an almost cartoon degree, the 1983 follow-up, *The Art of Falling Apart*, deepened Almond's obsession with beautiful losers into a harrowed empathy for the broken and discarded of this world.

Although they later blossomed into explorers of the dark side, Depeche Mode initially seemed to be the antithesis of Soft Cell: innocuous and innocent. Their jaunty singles 'New Life' and 'Just Can't Get Enough' raced up the charts and won them a teenybop following. Originally a guitar group and fans of punk, they'd bought synths, built up a songbook of winsome electropop ditties, and shunned major-label offers in favour of a fifty–fifty profit-splitting deal with Mute Records. Daniel Miller's label was home to bands Depeche admired, like synth pioneer Fad Gadget and Miller's own electronic projects The Normal and Silicon Teens, along with the ultra-intense German band Deutsch Amerikanische Freundschaft.

DAF came from a similar place, sonically and spiritually, to Soft Cell: art-school boys with a kinky, homoerotic image and a post-Moroder pulse-disco sound. Miller loved the fact that 'they weren't relying on past rock traditions at all – which is the criterion of what goes on Mute'. Renegades against what singer Gabi Delgado called 'Anglo-American pop imperialism', DAF's early sound was jagged and chaotic, a real electro-punk assault. 'They were part of a small but active Düsseldorf scene, little clubs and performance-art things,' recalls Miller. 'Robert Gorl was an electronic musician's dream of a drummer, 'cos he was so minimal. The guttural way Gabi sang sounded very threatening.' Early DAF featured a guitar, 'played with a vibrator, spurts of pure white noise'. The group moved to London and recorded their second album for Mute, *Die Kleinen und Die Bosen* – one side taped live (supporting their friends Wire at their Electric Ballroom Dadaist romp), the other recorded with Conny Plank. Then DAF honed the group to just Delgado and Gorl and stripped their music to a brutalist Eurodisco, signed to Virgin, and released a staggering trilogy of albums that made them critical darlings in the UK and genuine pop stars in Germany.

DAF espoused techno-primitivism. 'Most bands get a synthesizer and their first idea is to tune it!' Gorl told *Melody Maker*. 'They want a clean normal sound. They don't work with the POWER you get from a synthesizer . . . We want to bring together this high technique with body power so you have the past time mixed with the future.' Delgado exalted disco as 'body music' and rejected rock rhythms as 'too boring and static

. . . [DAF's] music is very mighty, you could say.' DAF's cult of muscularity strayed into that ambiguous zone where fascist-leaning Futurism and communist-leaning Constructivism collide – the aestheticization of physical perfection and physical force. 'They were influenced by a group of artists known as Die Junge Wilden,' says Chris Bohn, the *NME* journalist who championed DAF and other early eighties German art-punk groups. 'They were into deliberately taunting the German media by tackling Nazi and sex taboos head on – part of the confrontation being in the seemingly ambiguous use of Nazi imagery/references.' DAF broached this dodgy terrain with songs like 'Der Mussolini' – its chorus: 'Dance der Mussolini/Dance der Adolf Hitler'.

'Der Mussolini' and their first Virgin album, *Alles Is Gut*, sold hundreds of thousands of copies in Germany in 1981, making DAF the fifth-biggest German-speaking pop group in the country, and the focus of much media controversy. Even Delgado's sinister vocal style seemed too evocative of Germany's recent past, as he himself acknowledged: 'The singing . . . isn't like rock 'n' roll or pop singing. It's sometimes like in a Hitler speech, not a Nazi thing, but it's in the German character, that CRACK! CRACK! CRACK! way of speaking.' For DAF, the German language's precise speech rhythms fitted better with their strict rhythmic regime of sequenced synth-pulses.

Far from being fascists, though, DAF were erotic renegades in the tradition of Genet, de Sade and Bataille. They flirted with forbidden imagery only because they refused to recognize *any* taboos. Delgado was fascinated with sadomasochism and other forms of fetishistic sexuality deemed 'perverse' because unconnected to reproduction. 'Lust is always non-productive,' he declared. 'If you go over the top in lovemaking it gets too much and you are no more able to work. And criminals are obviously anti-social . . . I'm really interested in these things that are not fulfilling economic functions.' *Gold und Liebe*, the second Virgin album, touched on an alchemical theme: instead of chasing the profane gold of material wealth, the true quest is for gold of the spirit. It was DAF, not Spandau Ballet, who were the real New Romantics – from their un-American sound (they inspired a whole European genre of industrial disco called Electronic Body Music) to their cult of youth, evident in lyrics like 'You are beautiful and young and strong/Run to waste your youth'.

The irony of Anglo-Euro synthpop is that, for all its whiteness (DAF loved disco but prided themselves on not sounding black), it had a huge impact on black America. DAF and their offshoot group Liaisons Dangereuses influenced the embryonic black electronic sounds of Chicago house and Detroit techno, while Kraftwerk almost single-handedly inspired New York electro. 'Whenever we did anything that moved towards mainstream American success, it was notable that it had close connections with the black music market,' says Bob Last. 'Like The Human League's success with *Dare* in America – a crucial part of that was black radio stations in New York picking up on the record.'

Dare's fat synth bass and crisp Linn drum beats paralleled the electro-funk music played on New York stations like Kiss, where tracks were undergoing radical remixing and being montaged into seamless segues that lasted half an hour or more. Already aware of remixing's potential, Rushent introduced a dub-like spaciousness to records by The Human League and his other protégés Altered Images, moments when instruments drop out. Now he suggested making an instrumental version of *Dare*, hoping to showcase his production skills to the hilt and establish a new benchmark for electronic dance pop. 'I had to fight terrible opposition from both the band and Virgin, 'cos they didn't want to put it out, didn't want to pay for it. The band thought it was unfair to the fans and wanted to sell it cheap, which is what happened.'

Credited to The League Unlimited Orchestra – a cute nod to Barry White's instrumental project, The Love Unlimited Orchestra – *Love and Dancing* was released in June 1982: the back cover pointedly depicted the entire team behind the making of *Dare*, with photos of Rushent, studio engineer Dave Allen and even sleeve designer Ken Ansell, as well as the band. 'They *had* to have a picture of me. I did the whole thing on my own!' laughs Rushent. 'But I never got any writing royalties on it. In retrospect, I should have.' A masterpiece of editing and mixing-board wizardry, *Love and Dancing* took thousands of man-hours of intensive sonic surgery. Rushent created complicated vocal effects by hand, cutting up tiny bits of tape and then 'gluing them together until you'd got that stuttering "t-t-t-t-t" effect'. By the end of the process, the mastertape of *Love and Dancing* contained so many splices – 2,200 main edits and about 400 further small edits for repetition effects – that it was dangerously close to disintegration. 'You couldn't fast-forward it or fast-rewind it, so the first thing I did was copy the album on to another tape, before the original master fell apart.'

Making *Love and Dancing*, says Rushent, 'was the most creative experience I've ever had in my life, and something that's been very difficult to top. That may be why I gave up record production not so long afterwards. It's like those astronauts who go to the moon and come back and go a bit loopy. You've walked on the moon; what you gonna do now?' Rushent also confronted the other tragic irony that afflicts the superstar producer: he was showered with awards, named 'Producer of 1981' and besieged with offers of work – but only with mediocre artists. Bands with a strong aesthetic identity generally don't want to be stamped with a name producer's signature sound. The Human League, too, were on top of the world, and disconcerted by it. 'Almost the worst days of our lives have been when we've been told we're number 1,' says Oakey. 'I remember smashing the phone after I was told "Don't You Want Me" was number 1 in America. It's so much to live up to. And when you're number 1, nobody really *cares* about you any more. Everyone and their grandma knows about you, so no one wants to wear your badges any more.'

By the end of 1982, the deluge of synthpop artists – Thomas Dolby, The Eurythmics, Blancmange, Tears for Fears *et al.* – had diluted the impact of electronics. Soft Cell's David Ball correctly predicted an anti-synth backlash in response to the surplus of weak electropop. In a weird twist, the only way forward for pioneers like Soft Cell and The Human League was to start incorporating traditional instruments into their sound. At the end of 1982, Oakey raved about ABC, a Sheffield group who had started out as the sub-League electronic outfit Vice Versa but switched to making symphonic disco and scored monstrous chart success. 'They've changed my opinions enough to say I don't even think we'll be doing all-synthesizer records any more . . . We can't just do it with the gimmicks of synthesizers. We've got to compete in the areas of great string sections [and] great horn sounds – like they're doing.' The Human League's next single '(Keep Feeling) Fascination' had no violins or trumpets, but it did feature some electric guitar, signalling the abandonment of the band's 'synths only' policy. It was the end of an era.

18

FUN 'N' FRENZY: Postcard and the Sound of Young Scotland

Orange Juice. Josef K. The Fire Engines. The Associates.

In 1980, when post-punk seemed locked in a gloom-laden death trip, everything about Orange Juice felt different. The Glasgow group's very name was refreshing – sweet, wholesome, sunshine in a glass. 'None of us drank alcohol at the time,' singer/guitarist Edwyn Collins recalled. 'Orange Juice . . . seemed perfect because it was what we drank at rehearsals.' The music, a spring-heeled shambles of Byrds and Velvets, felt like a tonic, too. Above all, their debut single, 'Falling and Laughing', released in the spring of 1980, signalled the return of unabashed romance. Renouncing post-punk's demystification, Collins proclaimed the sacred singularity of his sweetheart: 'You say there's a thousand like you/Well maybe that's true/I fell for you and nobody else'.

You could trace Collins' fey, bashful voice – 'the sound of lovesick schoolboys', as one journalist put it – back to the glorious, lump-in-throat *wetness* of Pete Shelley. When Buzzcocks played their first dates in Scotland as part of the White Riot tour in 1977, they had more impact on the local scene than headliners The Clash. Buzzcocks 'subverted people's ideas about what a punk group should be like', said Collins. 'I thought they were very witty, very camp.' Another White Riot tour group also enjoyed a disproportionate influence in Scotland – Subway Sect. Collins thrilled to the sparks and splinters flying off the Sect's abrasive guitars. 'Rob Simmons' Fender Mustang was completely out of tune, the treble cranked up full,' he recalls. You can also hear a touch of Vic Godard in Orange Juice's lyrics: the preference for charmingly quaint, staunchly un-American language, like the chorus 'Goodness gracious/You're so audacious' Collins simpers archly on 'In a Nutshell'.

Orange Juice talked and acted in ways that broke with both rock's rebel swagger and post-punk's militant solemnity. They were literate, playful, ironic, quirky. 'Everyone used to think we were a bunch of androgynous little twits,' Collins said. This exaggerated wimpiness was a revolt against the Glasgow music scene's traditional blues–rock machismo (Frankie Miller, Nazareth, Stone the Crows), but also against the hooligan menace of Scottish punks like The Exploited. 'Simply Thrilled Honey', their third single, made sensitivity subversive. Based on a real incident, it depicted Collins as a shrinking violet – the reluctant prey of a female seducer. Collins told *Sounds*, 'I didn't want to go to bed with her. I wasn't sexually attracted to her but, above all, I didn't love her. And I think it's really important to only go to bed with someone if you love them – that's what the line "worldliness must keep apart from me" means . . . There is such a pressure on boys to be manly . . . I find going to bed with somebody you don't love . . . disorientating.'

In 'Consolation Prize', Orange Juice's loveliest song of all, Collins tries to woo a girl away from her boyfriend, a mean mistreater who has 'crumpled up' her face in tears countless times, whereas Edwyn makes her laugh with his 'so frightfully camp' Roger McGuinn fringe. Collins even contemplates buying a dress to cheer her up. 'I'll be your consolation prize,' he pleads. In the end, he's resigned to remain unrequited, but as Orange Juice's golden cascades of guitars propel the song towards a climactic slow fade, Collins almost rejoices in the fact that 'I'll never be man enough for you'. He sounds exultant rather than mournful, triumphant not defeated.

Orange Juice all came from Bearsden, a middle-class suburb of Glasgow. 'I met Edwyn on a school bus,' recalls drummer Steven Daly. 'James Kirk, our guitarist, was already my friend. On the bus Edwyn was reading *Melody Maker* – *not* the magazine to read then – and I joked, "You don't read that old shit, do you?" We were all music press slaves. The first pieces on CBGB came out in 1975. We were very interested in what was going on in New York. Television and Talking Heads had figured out more viable new ideas than most British punk bands.' Indeed, when the fledgling Orange Juice put a 'musicians wanted' advert in a local fanzine, the first line announced: 'A New York band forming in the Bearsden area'.

344

Back cover of Orange Juice's debut LP, *You Can't Hide Your Love Forever*, 1982. L to R: James Kirk, Steven Daly, David McClymont, Edwyn Collins

As much as the current CBGB bands, Orange Juice were united in a love of an earlier New York group: The Velvet Underground. Collins would place *Live 1969* on his Dansette and leave it playing on repeat for hours while he pottered around his flat. *Live 1969*'s gatefold sleeve showed Lou Reed holding a 'Country Gentleman' guitar manufactured by Gretsch, a make that took on a talismanic significance for Orange Juice. 'We avoided the two major rock guitars, the Fender and the Gibson. Playing Gretsches was about bringing back a sixties sensibility, but still having the freneticism of punk. Nobody else used them at the time.'

345

The core of Orange Juice's sound was the sparkling drive of rhythm guitar played at double time to the drum beat. The idea came half from the late-era Velvets and half from Chic. Disco was the wild card in Orange Juice's musical mix: before punk, Collins had been a regular at church-hall youth dances and the Glasgow discotheque Shuffles. 'The thing about us blending Chic and Velvets, it sounds really audacious on paper, but if you listen to *Live 69*, the double-time rhythm guitar on "Rock 'n' Roll" is not a million miles apart from Nile Rodgers' guitar playing in Chic,' says Daly. 'Very clipped. Not jangly, which is the cliché journalists always applied to Orange Juice – the strings are actually being damped, so it's more choppy than jangly.'

In 1978, a nineteen-year-old über-hipster and botany student called Alan Horne witnessed a gig by Orange Juice (then trading as the Nu-Sonics) and was struck by two things: first, their cover of 'We're Gonna Have a Real Good Time Together', an obscure Velvets song only ever captured on *Live 1969*. Cooler still, an associate of the band came onstage to chant the refrain from Chic's recent UK hit 'Dance Dance Dance (Yowsah Yowsah Yowsah)'. Daly had already met Horne through his job at a record shop called Listen. 'We got talking – Alan was an interesting, over-amped character,' recalls Daly. After checking out the band, the abrasively opinionated Horne offered them some unsolicited advice. 'He probably told us we were shit,' says Daly. 'But he could see the potential.'

In particular, Horne detected star quality in Collins. In typically prickly fashion, though, he greeted the singer – who was dressed in Levi's, motorbike boots and a plaid shirt – with 'Look at the fucking wimp – you're John Boy Walton!' For his part, Collins remembers Horne wearing 'a Harris tweed jacket and hidden under the lapel was a little Nazi badge'. A fan of provocation for its own sake, Horne liked to flirt with fascist symbols purely as a wind-up. 'He wanted to come onstage with us, wearing lederhosen, and do "Springtime for Hitler" from *The Producers*,' says Collins. 'It all came out of being a glam fan – *Cabaret*'s Berlin decadence, Lou Reed having the Iron Cross shaved in his hair on the Rock and Roll Animal tour. 1978 was when Rock Against Racism and silly things like that were going on, and Alan quipped, "I'd rather have a movement called Racism Against Rock." He also did a fanzine which featured crude little cartoons of Brian Superstar, his flatmate, in a Nazi uniform.'

Superstar and Horne both exemplify that music-scene syndrome of catalyst figures who don't necessarily contribute musically, but shape opinion and impart esoteric knowledge. Horne was a connoisseur of pre-punk music and owned boxes of classic 45s ranging from Elektra's psychedelic rock to Northern Soul. Superstar, later a member of the Scottish cult indie group The Pastels, 'would hip you to things', says Daly. 'There was so little material available in those days – you literally could not find the cool records, because record companies deleted them. But Brian would spend the extra time and money to find the exotic stuff – like Gram Parsons, say. He also had a VCR – something almost unheard of then. We'd watch certain videos over and over – like this *History of Rock* programme that showed The Byrds doing "Mr Tambourine Man". A whole golden age was brought back to life by this documentary.'

All this archival arcana and period detail informed Orange Juice's retro-eclectic approach to piecing together an identity They'd take 'jangly lead guitar lines from the more country-influenced sixties rock of Byrds and Lovin' Spoonful', says Daly, but combine that with a touch of seventies soul. Or they'd mismatch Subway Sect guitar-scratch with a disco walking bassline. 'It doesn't surprise me that Steven Daly has since become a journalist, 'cos he was the most analytical one of all of us,' says Collins. 'He used to say, "Oh, I like this sound on this record", and "Maybe we should take this sound from another record". And this was all pre-sampling.' The same applied to the way Orange Juice constructed their image. 'With Brian's videos, you could see what the groups were *wearing*,' says Daly. Scrutinizing *The History of Rock* and their favourite album covers, such as *Pet Sounds*, Orange Juice came up with a mélange look – mod-style suede jackets, hooped T-shirts redolent of Warhol's Factory, Creedence Clearwater Revival-inspired plaid shirts, raccoon hats, plastic sandals. Strikingly different from the monochrome post-punk norm, the group's appearance gave off intriguingly mixed signals – several different phases of the sixties, Americana, rock-scholarly knowingness, childhood innocence.

'Falling and Laughing' was Orange Juice's first release, jointly financed by Horne, Collins and Orange Juice's bassist David McClymont. But because Horne wasn't in the band, he gradually took on the role of manager and boss of the label, which they christened Postcard. It suited his pushy personality: 'Alan loved it when you'd jokingly call him Mr Postcard,' recalls Collins. 'He wanted to be the Svengali figure. He was a control freak. As well as running Postcard, he also sort of managed all the groups on the label. The punk managers interested him – McLaren,

Bernie Rhodes, Kay Carroll with The Fall. Alan used to say that the great thing about punk is that it's brought in an era where the manager is as important as the group –'cos in early punk interviews, the manager often assumed the same importance as the singer.'

Other punk-era managers operating in the provinces started labels purely as a way of garnering attention for their bands – the independently released single figured as a superior form of demo tape, indicating gumption and determination. Horne was more ambitious: he wanted to get Orange Juice into the pop charts without resorting to the major-label system. He intended to have hits but do it independently.

Horne was one of the very first people to sense that the independent charts had become a low horizon for bands. 'Music should always aim for the widest possible market,' he proclaimed in one of the first music-paper features on Postcard. 'The charts are there. That's where you need to be.' Borrowing a phrase from Dexy's Kevin Rowland, he mocked the 'brown rice independents' for their 'hippy attitude' of dropping out and staying pure.

To get Postcard's records distributed, though, Horne had to deal with Rough Trade, as brown rice as they came. The relationship between the motormouthed, speedy Horne and the deceptively soft-spoken but tenacious Geoff Travis was understandably frictional. 'I really loved "Falling and Laughing",' says Travis, 'but I was a little disappointed by the second single, "Blue Boy", and I wasn't particularly impressed by Alan's hustle, when they came down to London looking for a distribution deal. Then I changed my mind and realized I had made a mistake. I offered them a good deal which Alan then told everybody was a deal that would bankrupt Rough Trade. But, you know, Alan wanted to have an abrasive relationship with everybody because he thought he was Warhol.'

Horne also knew that John Peel's support was crucial for independent releases, especially those from outside London. But Peel had actually *been* a hippy once, and his Radio One show represented everything Horne despised about the new post-punk DIY ghetto. So he barged his way into the BBC and berated Peel, insulting the music the DJ played ('just a nice bore') and warning him that Postcard was 'the future and either you'll get wise to that or you'll look very stupid'. The intimidation tactic backfired. As Edwyn Collins recalled, 'That night Peel said on the air that he'd been confronted by a truculent youth from Glasgow!' Peel added that he was going to play 'Falling and Laughing' . . . but only once.

Given how peripheral Glasgow was back then in relation to the rest of the UK music scene, Postcard depended on the weekly music press. 'The papers were our only hope, really,' says Daly. 'The record industry was clueless and had to be told where to look. So who told them where to look? The music press. We thought if we send out this message in a bottle, Paul Morley at the *NME* and Dave McCullough at *Sounds* will get it.'

Morley and McCullough had been the most prominent champions of Joy Division on their respective papers. In the summer of 1980, hit hard by Ian Curtis's suicide, both writers were looking for something life-affirming – a post-punk path that led away from the literally dead end of despair represented by *Closer*. The Postcard sound arrived in the nick of time. 'Post-punk had dried up,' says Daly. 'I liked PiL's *Metal Box*, but it was pointing people in a bad direction. So Orange Juice was turning away from the dark side. And we were very influential on what ended up being called New Pop. We struck a nerve with the media-conscious people, the future tastemakers. We were very clever, meta-aware, and having fun with it.' Orange Juice's sense of humour was crucial. That was why their debut single was called 'Falling and Laughing': in the song, Collins proposed a merry sense of one's own absurdity as a salve for love's humiliations – 'What can I do but learn to laugh at myself?' Love tore you apart again, and again, but in Orange Juice's world, heartbreak always came with a side order of quips.

Orange Juice remained Postcard's priority, but Horne began filling out the label's roster with other Scottish talent, such as Glasgow's Aztec Camera and Edinburgh's Josek K, plus honorary Caledonians The Go Betweens, who hailed from Australia but had a spare, plangent sound similarly rooted in Television and early Talking Heads. 'The Sound of Young Scotland', Horne called it in a nod to Motown, whose hit-factory approach he admired. Postcard's sleeves played on tartan patterns and other clichéd Scottish imagery, as if they were a branch of the Scottish Tourist Board.

Josef K came through Daly, who'd quit Orange Juice for a while and started his own label, Absolute. In Edinburgh he'd met Malcolm Ross, guitarist in a band called TV Art. Daly convinced them the original name was terrible and they became Josef K, after the protagonist of Kafka's *The Trial*. Horne wooed Daly back into the Orange Juice fold by accompanying him on a trip to London to pick up Josef K's debut single from the pressing plant, and helped Daly take them to distributors like Small

Wonder. 'Orange Juice and Josef K formed a sort of alliance,' says Ross. 'They'd support us in Edinburgh; we'd support them in Glasgow.'

Like Orange Juice, they had a clean image (sharp monochrome suits from Oxfam) and a clean sound. They also liked a lot of the same music: the cerebral side of American punk, groups like Television, Pere Ubu, Talking Heads, the Voidoids. 'I never saw any of the New York groups as part of rock 'n' roll, all those mouldy old bands with long hair,' says frontman Paul Haig, who had been playing guitar for a while when he heard *Marquee Moon* in the record shop where he worked. 'I just thought: *That*'s how you should play guitar. I much preferred Television's crisp, clear sound to the blasting of The Clash and the Pistols. Malcolm and I went down to London to see Talking Heads. Nine hours on the long-haul coach. And then back again. Sleeping in a bus shelter. We were half asleep at the actual gig 'cos we were so tired!'

Inspired by *Talking Heads 77* and Subway Sect, Josef K tried to get their guitars to sound as 'toppy' as they could, says Ross. 'It was just a matter of avoiding distortion and turning the treble up full. We liked playing really fast rhythms, and you needed a really sharp sound for those to work – using distortion meant you'd lose the effect.' Coiled and keen, barbed and wired, Ross's and Haig's guitars careened off the fast-funk groove churned up by bassist Davy Weddell and drummer Ronnie Torrance. 'In the very early days, it was just me playing guitar with Ronnie drumming, up in his attic,' says Haig. 'Ronnie'd always follow my rhythm guitar and we carried that on into Josef K. He'd never listen to the bass, like drummers are supposed to.' The resulting 'strange chemistry' between Torrance's all-out exuberance and the scratchy guitars gave Josef K their frenetic momentum.

Josef K's disco-punk had a similar flustered quality to Orange Juice's Chic/Velvets rhythm guitar. And Haig's singing, midway between Lou Reed and Frank Sinatra, was as strikingly un-rock 'n' roll as Edwyn Collins' voice. But the overall Josef K sound was harsher and the songs came from a less poptimistic place. Haig was a literally fragile figure – 'almost anorexic, down to seven stone eleven pounds, and I'm six foot tall. I was just depressed and I didn't eat very much. I'd got obsessed with looking at calories and what I was eating . . . At that point I was fading away to nothing.' One of Josef K's best songs, 'It's Kinda Funny', was inspired by Ian Curtis's death. 'I loved Joy Division and was really freaked out that he could take his own life aged twenty-three,' recalls Haig. 'Just the thought of how easy it was to disappear through a crack in the world.' Nevertheless, he stresses that 'It's Kinda Funny', while 'not a happy song', was 'still saying you don't have to be depressed about life – you can still laugh about it'.

Throughout the Josef K songbook, Haig sounds high on anxiety, finding an odd, giddy euphoria in doubt. Nourished by an intellectual diet of Penguin Modern Classics and European existentialism, songs like 'Sorry for Laughing' ('there's too much happening') and 'Radio Drill Time' ('we can glide into trance') addressed 'man's endless struggle'. On their masterpiece, 'Endless Soul', the singer's suave croon surfs the fraught glory of Josef K's guitars, as if trying to strike the correct, flattering posture in the face of 'the absurdity of being alive in a godless, vacuous universe', as Haig puts it. Critics loved the band's literate lyrics and the music's weird mix of poise and frenzy. But, despite the rave reviews, Alan Horne was never sure about the band. 'Alan had this vision for Orange Juice all along,' says Haig, 'to turn them into a great pop band, but he found Josef K far too abrasive and dark. He wanted us on the label to add some cred and widen its output, but the cockroach became too fat on a diet of Kafka and press clippings!'

Books shaped Josef K as much as music: Kafka, obviously, but also Camus, Hesse, Dostoevsky and Knut Hamson. 'Reading gave me so many ideas for lyrics,' says Haig. 'In those days I never thought about politics for one second – I was only trying to project thoughts about the human condition. Orange Juice were into a different kind of literature – Edwyn would be reading *Catcher in the Rye* while we'd be reading *The Trial*. That explains a lot about the difference between the bands.'

Josef K quickly found themselves at the epicentre of an Edinburgh scene of post-punk bibliophiles. 'There was a certain period in Edinburgh when all the New Wave bands were into reading,' remembers Haig, laughing. 'Davey Henderson from The Fire Engines, Ross Middleton from Positive Noise, Richard Jobson from The Skids. You'd always see them with a book in their pocket.' The city's post-punk literati haunted a pub called The Tap of Lauriston, directly opposite Edinburgh's art college. Like the members of Orange Juice, though, Josef K weren't much for drinking: Ross, Haig and Weddell stuck mostly to soft drinks; only Torrance would have a pint, or several. It was as if all the band's rock 'n' rollness was concentrated in the body of their drummer. 'At gigs we'd leave the rider untouched but Ronnie would stuff all the beer in his drum bags,' recalls Haig. Torrance's appearance also stuck out like a sore thumb. 'Josef K had this band camaraderie thing and we'd all wear long grey raincoats – except for Ronnie, who'd sometimes upset us greatly by wearing yellow trousers and pointed blue suede shoes. Ron was into the whole rock 'n' roll trip. He'd even get groupies. We *never* got groupies.'

Josef K, says Ross, 'didn't like laddishness or sexism – if girls came back to the dressing room to talk, we wouldn't be trying to get off with them or anything like that'. Orange Juice were just the same. 'We were a cute band dressed in an interesting style, so we had girls following us, but I don't think we took advantage,' recalls Daly, with a hint of wistfulness. 'I remember opportunities to take advantage and not doing it. It seems absolutely ridiculous in retrospect. We were pretty naïve lads.' In an early *Sounds* feature on Postcard, Dave McCullough tagged the label's sensibility as 'New Puritan', a term borrowed from Mark E. Smith. Orange Juice, Josef K and Aztec Camera all frowned on drugs and excessive drinking. 'We *were* quite puritanical,' says Ross. 'We didn't smoke dope or believe in getting drunk. Speeding a little bit was acceptable – amphetamine related to the mod thing of being in control and alert. I wanted some kind of dignity.'

As part of their anti-rock stance, Josef K never played encores. 'I always used to find encores patronizing,' says Ross. 'The roadies would came on to pack up the guitars, but if you clapped loud enough the band would come on again. That was the kind of ritual that Postcard wanted to change.' Haig also refused to indulge the audience with banter or pleasantries. 'Instead, Paul taped intros to the songs that we'd play over the PA,' says Ross. 'We were into all these Brechtian alienation techniques.' Haig recalls being barely able to bring himself to utter the word 'gig' because it was too disgustingly rock 'n' roll: 'I preferred to say "concert", but you couldn't really say that when you were playing just a wee venue.'

When it came to anti-rockism Josef K were surpassed by The Fire Engines, another great Edinburgh group of this era, who famously played sets that lasted only fifteen minutes. 'What's the point in getting the audience bored?!' demanded singer Davey Henderson in *NME*. 'Where's the value there?! Is it the amount of time you're on or the amount of excitement you get out of it?' Yet another Scottish group triggered into existence by Subway Sect, The Fire Engines added Beefheart barbs and Contortions jolts to create a sound of prickly, itchy energy. On their archetypal tune 'Discord', high-toned beetling bass and loping drums create a nervous, hyperactive funk; the guitars throw out electric sparks like live wires that are cut and writhing, while Henderson yelps like a pixie version of James Brown at his most agitated.

Horne desperately wanted The Fire Engines for Postcard, but so did Bob Last of Fast Product, which was based in Edinburgh. Like Horne, Last believed that independent culture was in danger of becoming a ghetto, but up to this point they'd had very different ideas of how to escape from it: Horne wanted to break the major labels' stranglehold on the pop charts with Postcard; Last wanted Fast Product's acts, such as spiky-pop outfit The Scars, to sign to a major as soon as they could. Unsurprisingly, a bristling rivalry developed between the two men and their labels. It intensified when Horne, all set to release a Fire Engines live tape on his projected sub-label I Wish I Was a Postcard, was outflanked by Last, who whisked the band into the studio to record the first release for his new label, Pop:Aural. Ironically, the Pop:Aural concept was very similar to Postcard. 'I dissolved Fast and started Pop:Aural because I wanted to experiment with being more commercial,' he says. Just like Horne, he wanted to see if it was possible to break into the Top 40 while remaining independent.

The Fire Engines', *Lubricate Your Living Room*, the record that launched Pop:Aural, wasn't exactly pop music, though. For a start, it was mostly instrumental, give or take the odd stray chant or shriek of excitement from Henderson. It certainly wasn't even a single, but a deliberately unclassifiable release: nine tracks stretched across a 33 r.p.m. twelve-inch, selling at the budget price (for an album) of £2.49. Yet Henderson stressed that *Lubricate* shouldn't be taken as The Fire Engines' debut album either. Instead, it was a sort of dub remix of the debut LP before it existed: '[It's] like our songs with the words taken away and the lengths extended . . . It was Bob Last's idea and he wanted to use us and we were quite into being used in this type of way.' Echoed in the title of the track 'Get Up and Use Me', Last's governing concept was *use*ful music, as opposed to 'art' for passive contemplation. 'Background beat for active people', *Lubricate* was the hyperkinetic opposite of chill-out music or Eno's ambient soundscapes: something to vibe yourself *up* before you went out for the evening.

On its release in January 1981, *Lubricate* was a critical smash and a big independent hit. But The Fire Engines' wonderfully frangible music fell a long way short of the chart-infiltrating pop Last envisioned for Pop:Aural. 'The Fire Engines were a transitional thing because they weren't glossy,' he says. For the next single, 'Candyskin', Last hired half a dozen string players – 'not as expensive as you might imagine' – to add a hilariously incongruous symphonic patina to the group's jagged sound. 'The Fire Engines were so abrasive you could get away with using a string section without it being kitsch. But after a while, I told them they couldn't go on doing what they were doing, 'cos it'd just be less of the same. So they reinvented themselves as Win, a proper pop group.'

The Associates – Edinburgh's third and greatest group of this period – were the city's real-deal pop proposition. Unlike Josef K or Davey Henderson's mob, they would eventually 'go all the way'. Singer Billy MacKenzie had a multi-octave voice and the supernatural glow of a born star. The band's multi-instrumentalist/music director, Alan Rankine, was gorgeous, his dark, sultry looks making for perfect visual chemistry with MacKenzie's pale, vaguely aristocratic cast. 'Malcolm Ross and I went to see the first ever Associates gig in Edinburgh at the Aquarius Club,' recalls Paul Haig. 'They looked amazing – they all had on red silk shirts. We started to become friends because Josef K and The Associates played together so many times. Billy became my absolute soul-mate – off his head, but in a good way.'

Before The Associates, Rankine and MacKenzie had earned a good living as members of cabaret ensemble Mental Torture. At their hotel residencies, they performed campy remakes of showbiz standards ('Shadow of Your Smile' became 'Shadow of My Lung') and original songs like the *Rocky Horror*-like 'Not Tonight Josephine'. Shortly after they'd originally met, MacKenzie moved in with Rankine and they started writing loads of songs. 'Bill was a fizzing *mental* flatmate,' says Rankine. 'One time he absentmindedly put the plastic kettle on the gas oven and it melted.' MacKenzie buzzed with a sort of innate speediness. 'You could always tell there was something unsettled deep within him. Bill could never just switch off – unless it was watching a wildlife documentary on TV. He saw animals as pure, having this grace and nobility he admired – something he didn't see in humans. With animals, there was no agenda, no bullshit.'

Rankine and MacKenzie decided to give up entertaining middle-aged hotel patrons and have a stab at full-blown art-pop. As The Associates, they developed a sound based on their mutual appreciation for the more eccentric end of glam (Roxy Music, Sparks), disco and movie

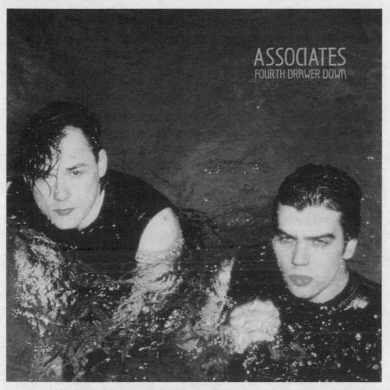

Cover of The Associates, *Fourth Drawer Down*, 1981. L to R: Billy MacKenzie, Alan Rankine

scores. 'We shared a massive love of the grandeur of film soundtracks,' says Rankine. 'We catalogued the whole thing, worked out what the composers were doing to play on people's emotions, with no lyrics. And then we put those tricks and that language into what we were doing. We threw in everything but the kitchen sink. When we recorded, we never had enough time or tracks.'

Both men shared the view that during the progressive-rock era – 1968–75 – the art of classic songcraft had died through being smothered by exhibitionistic instrumental virtuosity. And yet, ironically, Rankine was one of the post-punk era's greatest guitarists. 'There was a definite period around 1979–81 where, because of the set-up in bands – just guitar, bass, drums, vocal – it was the guitarist who virtually carried the can for all the sound textures in the group,' he says. 'I was just trying to use the most basic effects, like the Roland Space Echo turned up full, to make the biggest sounds I possibly could – just to back up the grandeur of what Bill was trying to do vocally. You've got to remember he had no backing vocals harmonizing with him. I tried to make a wall of sound without sounding like punk thrash. Post-punk was all about the creeping back in of degrees of subtlety. Giving the song a chance to breathe.'

The Associates' sound mixed post-punk modernism (the iceburn spires of Rankine's guitar) and the more postmodern traits of the New Pop. In The Associates' case that meant flashbacks to the stylized romance of bygone forms – inter-war torch songs, post-war musicals, Sinatra-style crooners, Scott Walker's orchestrated solo albums. MacKenzie's towering vocals conjured an era when the malady of love was expressed in epic proportions, when singers *luxuriated* in grief. 'There was a hell of a Germanic thing going on in our music, too,' says Rankine. 'Billy got that from Kraftwerk. He liked the starkness. A lot of Bill's vocal melodies are not rhythmic – they're stately, they've got a dignity to them. He was very conscious that he didn't want to get into things that were too obviously rhythmic, 'cos that would have been too Americanized. It's only in retrospect, when you've got a whole body of work, that you notice "Wait a minute, how come we haven't got one song that's really groovy, and with some overt sexuality to it?"'

And yet the music *was* erotic in its textured sensuousness, while MacKenzie was nothing if not a highly sexual being. 'It's the weirdest thing. I knew Bill was gay from the moment I met him in 1976, but it really didn't cross my mind again,' says Rankine. 'When we were recording, Bill would sometimes disappear from the studio for six hours at a time and I'd think maybe he's off walking around getting ideas for lyrics or just clearing his head. But for all I know he was out cruising for six hours!' MacKenzie was actually more 'omnisexual' than 'gay' in any strictly defined sense. Or, as Rankine puts it more bluntly: 'He'd shag anything with a pulse! But the serious side of that was that this was a guy who was constantly questioning himself. He was striving for the third sex.' MacKenzie himself declared: 'I'm the type of person who sees beyond genders. I don't have many emotional boundaries or hang-ups about who I like, where I like, when I like . . . I can swing with the best of them.'

For their self-released debut single, The Associates covered Bowie's 'Boys Keep Swinging'. As a way of announcing themselves to the world, it neatly combined homage to one of the biggest influences on MacKenzie's vocal style and sheer hubris (their version came out in late 1979, only months after Bowie's original had left the charts). The single caught the ear of Fiction Records, the New Wave subsidiary of Polydor. In August 1980, just as the music-press buzz about Scotland was building, Fiction released the debut Associates album, *The Affectionate Punch*: windswept never-never pop. The striking cover image showed MacKenzie and Rankine as athletes hunched together at the start of a running track – a 'clean', healthy, faintly Nietzschean image expressing the singer's belief that music, bodily movement and physical fitness were closely related. 'Bill had been a very good runner. I had been a very good tennis player,' recalls Rankine. 'So that imagery was related to trying to be . . . not superior exactly, but rising above the shit and nonsense of rock 'n' roll and the music business.'

The album's warm critical reception wasn't matched by popular success, though, and the group parted company with Fiction. MacKenzie and Rankine's masterplan for 1981 was to make their mark with six singles released in swift succession via the label Situation 2, an imprint of Beggar's Banquet. '1981 is going to be the year of singles,' MacKenzie announced. '[Singles] are a lot more fun and disposable and they've got an air of excitement about them.' The singles plan was also something of a scam. Now living in London, The Associates desperately needed income: in addition to MacKenzie and Rankine, there was also bassist Mike Dempsey and drummer John Murphy to support. They had wangled money out of a publishing company to record demos, ostensibly to send to major labels, and used the funds to book ultra-cheap graveyard-shift sessions at a studio. In a fever of chemically enhanced creativity, for ten weeks The Associates went in every Sunday night and worked until nine in the morning. The substantial difference between what the recordings cost and what Situation 2 paid for the singles enabled the group to live handsomely. 'I must stress there's *nothing illegal* about what we were doing,' says Rankine. 'It's just that we weren't telling Situation 2 we were making the singles so cheaply. So it felt like a scam to us.'

The co-producer of the Situation 2 singles, Flood – later to work with Depeche Mode and U2 – has spoken of 'the element of chaos' surrounding the sessions. Rankine and MacKenzie 'were full-on, just hyper-creative and a good laugh . . . They were pretty fuelled and go-faster on the sessions and a lot of ridiculous things went on.' Eager but naïve consumers of drugs, they once ended up in hospital after recklessly snorting seven grams of speed (they thought it was one gram of cocaine). 'We were just about dead,' MacKenzie recalled. 'It was the first time I'd taken speed and I didn't know anything about it. We just . . . seriously overdosed . . . I was a virgin, pharmaceutically . . . Freakin' out, man!' Rankine recalls the two of them being in the same hospital room on heart machines for four days. 'Bill was opposite me, so I could see his heart read-out, and when his went to 158, mine would go up in a panic attack. And when he saw my read-out, his would go up even further. It was just a vicious circle. Consequently, our balls shrank up inside our bodies and our knobs were the size of walnuts.'

The music The Associates produced during these speed-addled sessions was 'psychedelic' – not in any literal, flashback-to-1967 way, but in its pursuit of mutated sounds, saturated textures and unusual instrumentation. 'We did things like "balloon guitar", where you fill a balloon with water until it's the size of a fairly small breast, and then get feedback out of your amp and modulate it by wiggling the balloon directly on the strings,' recalls Rankine. 'We got into glockenspiels, xylophones, vibraphones, but using them in a manic way that hadn't been done before. We also did vocal treatments – "Kitchen Person" has Bill singing down the long tubing off a vacuum cleaner, while on "White Car in Germany", some of the vocals were literally sung through a greaseproof paper and a comb!'

Possibly The Associates' all-time classic, 'White Car in Germany' taps into the un-American 'Europe Endless'-ness of Bowie's Berlin trilogy: MacKenzie operatically declaims cryptic lines like 'Walk on eggs in Munich' and 'Düsseldorf's a cold place/Cold as spies can be' over a metronomic march rhythm. There was definitely something Old World about The Associates' 1981 singles, an *ancien régime* atmosphere of fading grandeur. 'Q Quarters', another immortal classic, sounds like Habsburg dub. Its furtive rhythm, broken balalaika riff, echoing footsteps, and dank electronic atmospheres evoke Cold War scenarios: *The Third Man* and *The Ipcress File*, partitioned cities, deportations, informers and double agents. 'Ooh, that's a dark song,' says Rankine. 'I've heard dogs howl to "Q Quarters", run out of the room and cover their heads with their paws! Bill just let rip with the imagery. The line "Washing down bodies seems to me a dead-end chore" comes from his grandma, who had worked in the morgue during the Second World War.'

Beginning in April 1981 and ending eight months later, the run of half a dozen singles garnered rave reviews but none got anywhere near the charts. Yet, gathered together in the compilation album *Fourth Drawer Down* (the title referred to the place the group kept the herbal sedative pills that helped them achieve a warm, pleasantly fuzzy come down after the manic Sunday night sessions), The Associates' 1981 output added up to an astonishing body of work. MacKenzie and Rankine were dissatisfied, though. 'At the beginning of last year I thought it was going to be the year of singles,' MacKenzie recollected in an early 1982 interview. 'And it was. The thing with our singles was that they got peeled off the turntable halfway through! We want to keep our singles on the turntable this year.' Their ambition wasn't going to be sated by being critical darlings and cult favourites. They wanted to be the Bowie or Roxy of the eighties. How they managed to pull this off – albeit for just a tantalizingly brief moment of pop time – is a story we'll return to later.

By mid-1981, Postcard had also reached an impasse. In many ways, the label had made astonishing strides in an incredibly short period. Orange Juice's second single, 'Blue Boy', sold nearly 20,000 copies and has been described as the Scottish 'Anarchy in the UK' for its galvanizing effect on new bands north of Hadrian's Wall. With Orange Juice, Josef K and Aztec Camera singles barraging the upper reaches of the independent chart, Postcard took Scottish pop from a buzz in 1980 to *the* sound of 1981. London's myopic A&R scouts took heed and started flying up to Glasgow and Edinburgh in their droves.

Try as they might, though, Postcard couldn't propel their groups into the pop charts. In April 1981, Orange Juice's fourth single, 'Poor Old Soul', was number 1 in the independent chart, but it reached only number 80 in the 'real' chart (penetrating the Top 75 was the industry definition of a 'hit'). Frustrated, Alan Horne began to contemplate the unthinkable: hooking up Orange Juice with a London-based major label before the momentum they'd gathered dissipated. It might even be necessary to slap a coat of gloss over the group's music – shiny and melodic compared to post-punk, Orange Juice still sounded too scruffy and scratchy in the chart-pop context.

Meanwhile, Josef K took the next logical step and recorded their debut album. What should have been a triumph turned into a debacle. *Sorry for Laughing*, as the LP was originally called, sounded too slick for the band's liking. 'The manic and abrasive edge apparent when we played live was missing,' says Haig. Josef K proceeded to rerecord the entire album (in the process jettisoning some of their best songs). Retitled *The Only Fun in Town*, it was finally released in June 1981. '*Only Fun* was all recorded in a couple of days, like a Velvet Underground record,' recalls Haig. 'We purposely drowned out the vocals with guitars in order to get a more live sound. It was an unconscious act of commercial suicide, definitely!' With the benefit of hindsight, Malcolm Ross regrets the decision: 'We should just have released the first version, *Sorry for Laughing*. It would have come out six months earlier, so we wouldn't have lost all that momentum we had.'

Josef K's critical champions, Morley at the *NME* and McCullough at *Sounds*, were horrified by *The Only Fun*, feeling the group had betrayed its pop promise and their expectations. Despite the poor reviews, the album figured high in the independent chart, and even enjoyed something of a legacy through its influence on a mid-eighties-and-beyond breed of abrasive indie guitar pop, groups like The June Brides and The Wedding Present. But in 1981 the perception was that Josef K had missed their moment. By the autumn the group had split, with Haig going on to pursue an electronic dance direction as Rhythm of Life.

In the last months of 1981, Postcard looked out of step – synths, string sections and a slickness beyond Horne's and his groups' reach were the new state of the art. Fatally, the Postcard sound was a rock scholar's idea of 'pure pop' – it played fantastically well within the circuit of the music press, John Peel and the indie charts, but, compared to the music of daytime Radio One and *TOTP*, it looked spindly and amateurish.

Postcard had played a huge role in turning hipster opinion against the dowdy seriousness of post-punk. Almost single-handedly they had made melody, fun and love songs cool again. But it was 'Love Action', The Human League's romance manifesto, that got into the Top 5, not Orange Juice's 'Simply Thrilled Honey'. 'Funk' was the big buzzword of 1981, but few remembered that Orange Juice's 'Falling and Laughing' featured a disco bassline or that the group had precociously celebrated Chic. Postcard and Orange Juice had put the concept of 'pop' back on the table. But pop, that cruel mistress, had moved too fast for them to keep up . . . Or had it?

19

PLAY TO WIN: The Pioneers of New Pop

Scritti Politti. Heaven 17. Trevor Horn. ABC.

Post-punk nearly killed Green. At least that's what it *felt* like. 'It was the whole ambulance with the sirens going to hospital deal,' the singer recalls, queasily, of that day in early 1980 when he collapsed with what seemed like a heart attack. The previous night, Scritti Politti had supported Gang of Four in Brighton. Simon Dwyer, a friend of Scritti's, recalled the gig's aftermath for a 1982 feature: 'The group and I succumbed to heavy drink and heavy conversation and slept on a friend's floor. All except for Green, who was still asking for pills of a dubious nature well into the morning. A few hours later, Green lay seriously ill in hospital.' The 'heart attack' turned out to have been a literally crippling anxiety attack, a psychosomatic paralysis that left him incapable of speech.

Although the stress of performing contributed – Green had always suffered from frightful stage nerves – the collapse really stemmed from chronic lifestyle dysfunction. 'I was living without bothering to look after myself at all,' Green recalled. 'Which seemed an appropriate thing to do at the time, but it creeps up on you without you noticing until you're in a hospital bed with people leaning over asking you what you've eaten recently and you realize that you haven't eaten anything recently. They ask you where you live and you realize it's a shithole and they ask you when you last slept and you haven't slept for ages. They asked if I had anything worrying me and EVERYTHING was worrying me.'

A post-punk excess of drinking, thinking, and speeding brought Scritti as a whole, and Green in particular, to the brink of breakdown. 'We were a sick group for some time,' Green recalled. 'I used to read and write a lot, which was the only thing I did apart from being debauched.' In addition to the group's debilitating lifestyle – 'we partied very hard, as they say nowadays,' Green admits, 'we were always pretty poorly' – there's also a sense in which Scritti's imperative to question *everything* turned toxic. 'Finding minutiae overburdened with potential significance, this can contaminate your whole life to the point where you might describe it as mental illness,' Green explains. 'Not that I was actually *bonkers*, but . . .'

When Green's estranged parents read in *NME* about his hospitalization, they set him up in a Welsh cottage to recuperate. Instead of resting his overtaxed brain, however, he embarked on a massive rethink of the Scritti project. Shortly before his collapse, there'd been tension in the collective when Green broached the idea of moving in a pop direction: he'd been listening to contemporary black dance music like Michael Jackson's *Off the Wall* and investigating the history of soul music – Aretha Franklin, Shirley Brown, Stax. He had also been absorbing the ideas of Jacques Derrida, Roland Barthes and other French post-Marxist theorists. After the disillusionment of 1968, radical French thought had undergone a kind of implosion – not exactly depoliticized but certainly channelling the lion's share of its subversive energy into academe. Here, Derrida and his confrères beaverishly gnawed at the roots of Western thought, toppling ideas of progress, reason, truth and so forth.

At some point in 1980, Green finally lost faith in Marxism as a 'science of history' that mapped the righteous path to a future society of justice and equality. Without the anchor of stable values, he found himself adrift in a world of uncertainty, where all meaning was provisional because nothing could be 'proved' correct. It was scary, but exhilarating. Derrida's corrosive influence also eroded other concepts that underpinned the old Scritti: for example, the idea of the margins versus the mainstream. Dissatisfied with the self-conscious 'quirkiness and idiosyncrasy' of early Scritti, Green was determined to extricate his trapped pop sensibility from the thorny tangles of the Scritti sound. He hadn't totally abandoned the idea of subversion, but his notions of how that might work became more oblique and subtle: a process of unsettling and undoing (deconstruction, the French theorists called it) that took place inside the very language of pop. Instead of searching for some alternative zone of authentic purity and truth that supposedly existed outside the conventional forms, it might be more productive to work *within* those structures. Rather than avoiding the love song altogether, it might be possible to locate and accentuate the internal contradictions and tautologies that already limned 'the lover's discourse', as Barthes put it.

Green felt that he couldn't simply 'announce a new direction' for Scritti. 'So I sat down for months and months and wrote screeds of justification. There was that sense of having to have it understood, approved, and thought-through by the group.' Actually, one suspects that this exercise was as much for his sake as for the others. The band came down to Wales to read the book's worth of notes and were ultimately swayed by Green's new pop vision. By the end of 1980, Scritti had worked up a new sound based around old soul, new funk and the soft, slick reggae style known as lover's rock.

The first publicly aired work by the reborn Scritti was 'The "Sweetest Girl"' – 'a perversion and an extension of lovers' rock', declared Green. Sweet was the word, to an almost diabetic coma-inducing degree. Green crooned soft and high like Gregory Isaacs blended with Al Green. Underneath pulsed a rhythm section of crisp drum machine and gentle-yet-steadfast bass. Green's hero Robert Wyatt dusted the luscious confection with ethereal flickers of reggae-style organ. To fans of the DIY-era Scritti, the new sound was at once a shocking surprise yet strangely logical. Now Scritti's anxious compulsion to avoid conventional structures at all costs was gone, Green's melodic genius was unshackled and gushed forth in a flood of pure loveliness. But there was still a lingering undertone of the old Scritti's harmonic eeriness to put a tang of bitter in the sweet.

'The "Sweetest Girl"' sounded like a hit record. And a hit was what Green had his heart set on. Lots of hits. If 'margin' was no longer a valid concept, then the mainstream was where pop meaning was made and (Derrida-style) unmade. In 1978 Green had critiqued the competitive structure of the charts and the record industry. Now he wanted to be top of the pops.

In spring 1981 'The "Sweetest Girl"' was unveiled as the opening track of *C81* – a cassette compilation pulled together by Rough Trade and the *NME* to celebrate five years of the label and by extension the first half-decade of the independent revolution. An absolute bargain at £1.50, *C81*'s line-up included such post-punk luminaries as Pere Ubu, Cabaret Voltaire, Subway Sect and The Raincoats. Thirty thousand readers sent off for it.

Yet *C81* was in many ways post-punk's swan-song. The epoch it defined was already crumbling. Many of the featured artists, like

363

Postcard's Orange Juice and Aztec Camera, had already broken ranks with independent consensus: they sounded shiny, accessible, ambitious. A few weeks before *C81* was announced, the *NME's* last issue of 1980 looked to the future with a Paul Morley feature that essentially constituted a manifesto for 'New Pop' – a shared confidence and urgency he detected among emerging groups who believed it was both possible and imperative to take on the mainstream and beat it at its own game. Of the three bands covered, Sheffield's ABC were the most stridently poptimistic. Until recently they'd been an electronic outfit in the mould of Cabaret Voltaire. Post-Numan, they'd traded in their frigid synths and oscillators for funky rhythm guitars and real drums. Guitarist Mark White talked about pursuing a 'Funk Vision' and described disco as 'an excellent vehicle'. Watching the independent charts become 'saturated with rubbish', ABC decided that the mainstream was where the action was. Morley's piece pinpointed a common drive among the *post*-post-punk groups 'towards an overground brightness, fighting for the right to bring life back to the radio, to make the single count, to be let through to their natural audience . . . No longer is there an acceptance of that cob-webbed corner they're shoved in . . . They want a big display in the supermarkets, not to be stuck on a high shelf in the corner shop.'

If Morley coined the term 'New Pop', the concept itself had several co-authors – Bob Last and The Human League, Alan Horne and Orange Juice could certainly claim roles in hatching the idea. Liverpool's Zoo label also talked of aiming for the charts and touted a bunch of bright, tuneful groups, like The Teardrop Explodes, as an antidote to monochrome post-punk. Teardrop singer Julian Cope complained in the *NME* about the re-emergence of a split between a joylessly cerebral underground and a vapid pop mainstream: 'Things seem to have come full circle . . . It's getting to be like the early seventies again where you had the hippies into all their weird music.' Wah! Heat, also from Liverpool, pitched into the fray with the derogatory description 'rockist', a word that referred less to rock as music (Wah! used guitars and could sound pretty epic) than to schlerotic attitudes and predictable rituals.

As the sensibility took hold, New Pop defined itself through a set of overlapping values: health, cleanliness, mobility, ambition. Decrying the 'unhealthy' state of independent rock in countless interviews, Green seemed to map his own physical ill-being during the squatland Scritti days on to post-punk as a whole. ABC's singer Martin Fry talked of 'cleaning up the whole idea of pop music'. As for mobility, post-punk

A Collective item

A WHOLLY self-produced and self-financed LP is released this month by the Manchester Musicians' Collective. A compilation with a track apiece by 15 new Mancurian bands, 'Unzipping The Abstract' is the first release on the MMC label.

Unlike the majority of collectives, Manchester's caring, sharing co-op — formed as recently as 1977 — has always orientated itself towards post-punk activity rather than improvised 'free' music.

The 15 groups unzipping their talents on the album are The (Manchester) Mekon,

Bathroom Renovations, Cajun Cutie, Dislocation Dance, The Enigma, God's Gift, The Hoax, If Only, The Liggers, Outer Edge, Performance, The Spurtz, The Still, Undercovermen and Vibrant Thigh. The compilation is available through the collective at 102 Burton Road, Withington, Manchester 20.

GARAGELAND

FROM PORTSMOUTH, another regional compilation, 'South Specific, is due out on August 22 on the **Brian Booster** label (13 Dover Road, Copnor, Portsmouth, Hants). Eight local bands are featured — **The Frames, Attic, Anna Blume, Dance Attack, The Nice Boys, Renaldo And The Loaf, The Chimes** and **Toxicomane**.

Nine new bands are also heard on another compilation, 'Household Shocks', released by Scunthorpe's **Stark Products** and available on mail order for £3.75 from 298 Messingham Road, Bottesford, South Humberside. Just under an hour's worth of sounds from pop to synthesiser bands, it includes tracks by **Product Of Reason, Thunderboys, One Gang Logic, Sinking Ships, The Juveniles, Mystery Girls, The Defectors, Fault 151** and **Urbantech**.

Hectic singles and EP activity continues with news of 20 new seven-inchers having arrived at NME Central within the last seven days . . .

■ **Smack**: Edward Fox (**Pinnacle**). This highly-acclaimed Manchester band have now signed to independent distributors Pinnacle for two singles and an LP.

■ **Glass**: New Colours (**Glass Records**), 97 Judd Street, London WC1. First of a set of two singles from a new London band! Produced by former Magazine/part-time Banshee guitarist John McGeoch

■ **Prefex**: Promises Promises (**Legless Records**), Westbridge, Buildwas, Shropshire).

■ **Astronauts**: Pranksters In Revolt (**Bugle Records**, 59 Heath Road, Little Heath, Potters Bar, Herts).

■ **Folk Music EP**: (**Tuzmadoner Records**, Clitterhouse Crescent, London NW2). A 12-inch/33 rpm EP containing tracks from **The Infra Red Ice Cubes, Different I's, Chancellor Of The Exchequer, Mark O'Brien**.

■ **And The Native Hipsters**: There Goes Concorde Again (**Heater Volume Records**, 79 Lower Marsh, Waterloo, London SE1).

■ **The Chefs**: Sweetie EP (**Attrix Records**, 3 Sydney Street, Brighton).

■ **The Notsensibles**: I Thought You Were Dead (**Notsensibles**, 17 Burnley Road, Walk Mill, Burnley, Lancs).

■ **X-S Discharge**: Life's A Wank (**Groucho Marxist**, Paisley, Scotland).

■ **The Dangerous Brothers**: False Noco (**Sheep Worrying Records**, 34 Alfoxton Road, Bridgewater, Somerset).

■ **Steve Hooker Band**: How Did You Know (**Wax Records**, Southend).

■ **Weekend**: Tina's Party (**DP Music**, 9 Holly Bank, Sale, Cheshire).

■ **Zounds**: War (**Cross**).

■ **Last Words**: Top Secret Single (**Armageddon Records**, 56 Standard Road, London NW10).

■ **The Observers**: This Age (**ST Records**, 28 Gospall Street, Highfields, Leicester).

■ **Eddie Stanton**: Lucifer Wants Me For a Sunbeam (**Black Eye**).

■ **Sparta**: Fighting To Be Free (**Suspect**, 42 Portland Crescent, Meden Vale, Mansfield, Notts).

■ **Felt**: Index (**Shanghai Records**, 3 Albion Cottages, Birmingham Road, Water Orton, Birmingham B46).

INDEPENDENT cassettes released this week include the extravagantly-packaged C60 'Example Of The Species' by **The Loved One**, a tape which comes with posters, a booklet and even a set of calling cards for £2.25 from 7 George Street, Bicester, Oxfordshire.

■ A C60 of 'psychedelic chamber music' by **International Cod** is available for £1 from Desmond Chin, 67 Arodene Road, Brixton, London Sw2.

■ **The Zimbabwe Brothers**' first cassette package can be obtained for £1 from Paul Drew, 32 Charles Street, Barnstaple, North Devon.

■ A quid or a blank C60 and an SAE is all it takes to secure a copy of **Karl's Empty Body**'s debut tape on **Neon Records**, 8 Elms Grove, Etwall, Derby).

■ **Snatch Tapes** (The Basement Flat, 25 Westbourne Terrace, London W2) are producing an information sheet detailing plans for their cassette fanzine, an attempt to "establish the cassette as a form in its own right, rather than a substitute record of self-indulgent meandering." Among the bands features on Snatch Tapes 1 and 2 are **The Stormbugs, N4's, Lemon Kittens, David Jackman, The Vote Police** and **Beach Surgeon**.

DIY culture runs rife. The *NME*'s Garageland column (this one from 16 August 1980) documents the self-released cassette underground

culture was increasingly characterized by critics and musicians alike in terms of stagnation, inertia, wallowing in mud. Writing about 1981's third Futurama festival, Morley recoiled aghast from groups that 'twitched in the slime', while Green lamented the independent sector's degeneration into a 'a boggy ground, a wilderness'.

Scritti Politti started out championing do-it-yourself, but now Green renounced the movement as a 'lost cause'. He pointed to the home-made cassette network as particularly pernicious and risible. 'Many people tried to sell ridiculous music, filled with irritating noises and failed attempts at music,' he declared. It was time for a return to quality control, the hierarchy of the gifted over the talentless. In August 1980 the *NME* had started a regular news column, Garageland, to cover the cassette scene along with vinyl releases so small scale they didn't have independent distribution but were sold through mail order. But only ten months later Garageland was closed down. Across the board, critics abruptly lost patience with the sonic mannerisms that only recently had indicated charming eccentricity or scrappy but honourable amateurism. Now they signified just lamentable lack of ambition.

Scritti didn't immediately embrace the 'entryist' logic of signing to a major label in order better to infiltrate the mainstream, though. They stayed on Rough Trade. However, they moved to distance themselves from DIY's 'squattage industry' (as Green put it), not just sonically but through the way they presented their music. Scritti's early DIY releases came wrapped in hand-folded sleeves, smudged photocopies of litter. The new Scritti's singles copied the stylish packaging of deluxe commodities: Dunhill cigarettes with 'The "Sweetest Girl"', Dior Eau Sauvage fragrance with 'Faithless', Courvoisier brandy with 'Asylums in Jerusalem'. Green talked of admiring their 'cheap classiness' – the non-elitist elegance of commonly available consumer disposables. 'Our covers are now made in Turin by robots!' he boasted in *Sounds*. This remark left an odd aftertaste, given Green's once keen interest in Italian post-Communist politics: were these perhaps the same sort of robots then replacing the FIAT assembly-line workers of northern Italy?

That's the sort of grim irony that would once have tortured Green and probably inspired a song. But as a lapsed Marxist, he'd shed the anxiety and guilt that fuelled the early Scritti. 'You grow up as a good, almost Catholic-leftist boy, and you learn to be scared of your sexuality, to be scared of your power,' Green explained. Now he talked about developing an improvised form of 'post-political politics', based not on overar-

The sleeve for Scritti Politti's 1982 single 'Faithless', modelled on the 'classy' commodity Eau Sauvage, contrasts with . . .

. . . the discarded consumer detritus photocopied on the inner sleeve of Scritti's *Peel Sessions* EP, 1979

179   *Scritto's Republic*

that Marxism may be of use about the world, but it is not the truth about the world. The group had come to think that the 'guarantee' of (a) political knowledge beyond its use was unrealisable. 'Theory' could not ultimately justify a particular political theory/ideology above any other, and there could be no theory, no body of ideas, which had a, or *the*, claim to being 'concrete reality' reflected or apprehended in thought.

The axioms of Marxism were not objects of science but those of discourse and were developed, established and used according to specific conditions. The point was not so much to find the 'true' guarantees of Knowledge which would then enable us to proceed with certainty of moral conviction, political theory and work and relations were bound up in a heterogenous ideological totality. The 'laws' and morality of traditional left theory had no a priori place, no given, within this. Marxism was not a value free scientific knowledge and the values had no objective status outside of the specific material conditions (needs, demands, desires, interests) of subjects.

The conception of Knowledge as produced by/geared to interest was strengthened and the starting point as desires of class struggle finally displaced. In 'common-sense' terms it meant a politics geared first and foremost to a specific contemporary anti-repression and immediately against their current lived repression — as opposed to an overbearing but weak Left evangelism and as opposed to a strategy, whose priorities were ordered along 'inexorable historical laws', i.e. a metaphysics.

The nexus and operative of much of this repression was understood to be Language. It was argued that in order for society to function, stay stable and reproduce itself — stable, functional 'communication' is a priority. Thus language needs to be regular, simple and clearly designate and predicate identities and relation, it needs to be the lowest-common denominator. It must not have ruptures or censures or inconsistencies. The rules of a society are embodied in the rules of its language. It is through common sense speech that we are approached and directed. The rules of grammar and society assert the individual as 'I', a distinct entity who

ching ideology but the pragmatic realization 'that what you've got is needs, demands, and desires, and you go out and you fight for them'.

'Desire' was a big buzzword in 1981. Drifting into popular culture from the world of critical theory, it retained an electric tinge of subversion. By the late seventies, French thinkers of the sort Green had been devouring were flirting with the once unthinkable (for the left) notion that American capitalism, despite its faults, offered a lot of spaces for doing-it-yourself and bending the law. Could it be that 'desire' had a better time of it in pluralistic free-market societies than in bureaucratic Euro-socialist states? This notion of America as more free than the Old World was naturally blasphemous within the British socialist tradition (to which Rough Trade and the independent scene broadly belonged), but then British socialism had always had a puritanical streak, a disdainful suspicion of vulgar materialism and stylistic excess. Running against the grain of both independent culture and the British left, Scritti's celebration of consumer desire and commercial design was flagrantly heretical.

In 'Jacques Derrida', Green personifies Desire as an insatiable she-monster: 'Rap-acious, rap-acious,' he chants in a fey attempt at rapping, 'Desire is so voracious/I want her to eat your nation state'. The exaltation of desire as an unstoppable force that refuses to recognize any boundaries fits the tenor of the hip crit of the day – journals like *Semiotexte* and *Tel Quel* – but it also sounds a lot like how globalization works: flows of capital, goods and culture that make a nonsense of national borders.

Green, though, recognised that utopian yearnings – for perfection, purity, the absolute – were encoded in consumerism. These same longings also expressed themselves in that form of secular mysticism known as L.O.V.E. When he put scare quotes around the words 'sweetest girl', Green wanted to make it clear that he knew this dream was a mythic construct, an unrealistic hope – even as he was unable to stop himself wanting it; or prevent himself being seduced by songs hymning this heaven on earth. Green wanted to operate like pop's deconstructionist, the Derrida of the Top 40, unravelling the lore of the love song even as he revelled in the beauty generated by its dream-lies. 'The weakest link in every chain/I always want to find it,' he crooned in 'The "Sweetest Girl"' 'The strongest words in each belief/To find out what's behind it'. The one mysticism he permitted himself was music itself – the endless mystery of melodic beauty. 'Faithless now, just got soul,' he simultaneously lamented and rejoiced on 'Faithless', a gorgeous song about the impossibility of belief, couched in the deep, testifying certainty of gospel.

Heady stuff for pop music, and Green's frequent nods in his songs to his favourite philosophers like Wittgenstein, while cute, certainly decreased the likelihood of Scritti's lyrics ever being reprinted in *Smash Hits*, the magazine of the new teenybop. 'Asylums in Jerusalem', the third single from the new Scritti, was uptempo reggae with a cloying, caramel-sweet melody. It was catchy enough to get to the edge of the Top 40, but despite Rough Trade's strongest push to date and heavy radio support, it proved to be Scritti's third not-quite-a-hit in a row. Perhaps the Nietzsche-inspired lyrics were to blame – they lacked the common touch and didn't exactly resonate unless you were a student of continental philosophy.

Although *Songs to Remember*, the debut LP, reached number 12 in the mainstream album chart in the autumn of 1982, Scritti hadn't escaped the ghetto of being a cult group. In radio terms, they were still a Peel band; they hadn't made it on to the daytime playlists yet. Like Orange Juice a year earlier, Green underwent the public humiliation of having talked loudly about 'pop' but not having become it. The problem lay partly with the music, which sounded underproduced, but mainly with the lyrics. 'Sex', for instance, wasn't really about sex: Green described it as a 'gentle parody of me and my relationship with pop music'. And, on close examination, almost every song turned out be a narcissistic account of Green's loss of faith and devotion to pop. The results were seductive – Bolan meets Barthes – but lacked emotional resonance to anyone who wasn't named Green Gartside.

'What has meaning is what sells, and what sells is what has meaning,' Green had declared after his return from the Welsh wilderness. But not enough people were buying Scritti Mark II, and for someone with a healthy ego like Green, this was crushing. In interviews, he lashed out at Rough Trade, accusing them of frittering their money on 'silly groups with silly music' – meaning Pere Ubu and The Red Crayola – instead of focusing their efforts on launching Scritti into the charts. Eventually, Green made a final break with the independent ideal and started talking to major labels. 'We were a bit sad about him wanting to leave Rough Trade but we didn't have the structure or finances to do the pop thing properly,' says Geoff Travis. 'It seemed irresponsible to hold him back.'

Green also streamlined Scritti into a solo vehicle in all but name. The old collectivist Scritti had been in decline ever since Green had returned from Wales in late 1980. In interviews, he nonchalantly renounced Scritti's 'pseudo-collectivism', ridiculing 'the very early days . . . [When] we posed for a photograph, 40 people standing in a kitchen making tea – in retrospect a lot of it was . . . hot air.' Soon he claimed to have written not just the songs but all the music, even the basslines, from day one. 'We were absolutely shocked when it was suddenly announced that Green was going to be the leader of Scritti Politti,' recalls Gina Birch of The Raincoats. 'That it was no longer a democracy.' Bassist Niall Jinks was the first to chafe against the new regime and quit; organizer Matthew Kay followed suit in mid-1982. Although increasingly superseded by the use of drum machines, Tom Morley hung on until November of that year, a few months after *Songs to Remember* came out.

Having paid off his old comrades-in-amps for the rights to the Scritti Politti brand, Green and his new manager Bob Last secured a lucrative deal with Virgin Records and set up a publishing company for Green's songs called Jouissance. Scritti was no longer a band but 'a kind of production company', said Green, with the singer as pivotal constant surrounded by a floating pool of collaborators and producers. After too many false starts, Green was determined to make good on his manifest destiny: stardom.

This 'production company' model was the in-vogue notion of 1982. After Josef K, Paul Haig set up one called Rhythm of Life. He didn't want to be in a traditional band or play live any more, just produce records aimed for the dance floor. In interviews, he dreamily imagined Rhythm of Life diversifying into 'art and prints and video, just different things . . . RoL canned peaches . . . Who knows?' The first New Pop folk to talk about rejecting the staid strictures of the band in favour of the dynamic and flexible 'production company', though, were British Electric Foundation. Formed by ex-Human League members Martyn Ware and Ian Craig Marsh, BEF went one step beyond the entryist strategy of signing to a major label and instead styled itself as a mini-corporation that negotiated with record companies as an equal. In a further innovation, BEF included one non-musical partner – their manager Bob Last.

It was actually Last who had engineered the break-up of The Human League, perceiving that the group was deadlocked and would be better off as two separate outfits. Shortly after the split, Last invited the devastated Ware to come up for a weekend in Scotland, and pitched the idea of the production company. PiL was an obvious precursor, along with Robert Fripp's talk of 'small, mobile, independent, intelligent units' replacing the unwieldy prog-era megabands like King Crimson. With their permanent members on a steady wage, bands were expensive; even if they grew successful enough to pay off their record-company debts, the profit pie ended up divided into many pieces. But a production company could hire (and fire) session musicians and vocalists on a flat-fee, no-royalty basis. Increasingly, they could work with endlessly compliant, unpaid machines.

Fripp's streamlined model made economic sense in leaner times for the record business, while Ware, Marsh and Last added a patina of parody and polemic to his pragmatic ideas. 'We liked the idea of setting up this complicated corporate structure before a note had been played,' says Last. 'It seemed like an amusing gesture. So there was literally a partnership of shareholdings, and I didn't play a note on anything but I had a share in it. My role was strategy. I was what corporations today would call "strategy director".'

Other contemporary inspirations for BEF included black disco production company the Chic Organization and George Clinton's Parliament–Funkadelic empire, where endless recombinations of the same pool of musicians were separately signed to different record companies. 'Bob was totally in awe of the way Clinton juggled these different deals,' recalls Marsh. Although Ware and Marsh were still in debt to Virgin for their part in the two unsuccessful League albums, Last negotiated a new contract with that company for BEF. 'It was a really unusual deal,' recalls Marsh. 'We had to deliver one major act to Virgin every year, and each year we had to provide albums for every act signed in previous years.' Heaven 17, BEF's first major 'act', featured Ware, Marsh and their old Meatwhistle friend Glenn Gregory as lead singer. But, along with the major releases, BEF were free to deliver up to twelve minor album projects every year, which Virgin was obliged to distribute. 'These were essentially art projects – instrumental works, like Eno's ambient series,' says Marsh.

The first BEF art-e-fact was a cassette-only mini-album of instrumentals called *Music for Stowaways*. A more animated version of ambient, the peppy synthmuzik was designed for Sony's portable cassette-players (then called Stowaways; later renamed Walkman) that had only recently come on the market. *Stowaways* bore the clear imprint of Last, being essentially an electronic remake of The Fire Engines' *Lubricate Your*

Living Room. According to Marsh, the idea was also inspired by 'moving around London on the tube, going to meetings, working all over the place, and listening to music on these Stowaways. It made you feel like you were in a film all the time. Everyone takes that for granted now, but you can't imagine how big an impact it had – almost on the level of something like virtual reality. So our concept for *Stowaways* was "a soundtrack for your life". We mixed it on headphones not speakers, so that it would sound good on portable players. And it was a limited edition, ten thousand copies, cassette only.'

Styling themselves as a corporation was part of BEF's anti-rockist polemic: they talked of abandoning the idea of music as a world-changing force and accepting it as 'just a medium for enjoyment', as Ware put it – something that enhanced your everyday life, like *Stowaways*. 'That's one of the biggest myths ever, that pop music changes the world,' Ware declared. 'It's just a confection.' Ironic, then, that the first release from Heaven 17 was a full-blown protest song, '(We Don't Need This) Fascist Groove Thang', written in the gap between Reagan's election in November 1980 and his inauguration early in 1981. 'Fascist Groove Thang' received a huge amount of press attention, and its catchy-as-hell electronic ersatz of disco-funk looked set to chart big. But the BBC grew nervous that lines like 'Reagan's President Elect/Fascist guard in motion' were slanderous and an unofficial Radio One ban effectively halted the single's rise just short of the Top 40. Heaven 17's next single, the brilliant 'I'm Your Money', was also something of a consciousness-raiser, transposing the language of business on to love and marriage ('I'm offering you the post of wife') *à la* Gang of Four's 'Contract'. If the group saw music as 'just entertainment', they equally seemed unable to refrain from slyly slipping some *Entertainment!*-like element of subversion into their glossy-surfaced pop.

And Heaven 17's pop was superlatively shiny – almost intimidating in its precision-tooled panache. To differentiate themselves from The Human League and put distance between Heaven 17 and the overdone synthpop sound, Ware and Marsh developed a pop-funk that merged state-of-the-art electronics with real bass and guitar. For 'Fascist Groove Thang' they wanted a jazzy, syncopated bassline similar to the bass break in Chic's 'I Want Your Love'. 'We found this local Sheffield musician, John Wilson, a black guy who was only seventeen,' recalls Marsh. 'We told him what we were after and he did it on the spot, almost first take.' Wilson's bass and rhythm guitar ended up all over the 'funky' side one of *Penthouse and Pavement*, Heaven 17's debut album.

Penthouse's other secret weapon was the Linn drum machine – as used by Martin Rushent to make The Human League competitive. 'Literally within a fortnight of that technology coming into the country, it was all over our album,' says Ware, who did the rhythm programming. 'I didn't know how to play conventional drums, so I did whatever I liked the sound of.' The result was amazingly funky beats that didn't resemble a drummer playing on a 'real' drum kit. Also crucial to *Penthouse*'s crisp, in-your-face sound was the 'dry' production – the technical term for the absence of reverb. Without the 'wetness' of sound reflections, you don't get an aural picture of a band playing in a real acoustic space. But Marsh and Ware didn't believe in rock's pseudo-naturalism: they liked the pop artifice of constructing records in the studio. So they mixed *Penthouse* to sound good through the two-dimensional mono speaker of a cheap transistor radio. The first, 'funky' side of *Penthouse* 'sounded fantastic on the radio', says Ware. 'It just punched out amongst everything else.'

Behind *Penthouse*'s sonic attack lay genuine aggression: after being kicked out of The Human League by his old friend Oakey, Martyn Ware was on fire with a combination of anger and creative energy. *Stowaways* and the bulk of *Penthouse* were recorded in a single burst in the weeks immediately after the split. The second side of *Penthouse* – more electronic, an extension of the original Human League – was done in just one week. 'I was incandescent with anger,' says Ware. 'And sometimes it just pours out of you, the ideas.'

Along with competitive sparring with Oakey's League – 'Let's see who'll get into the charts first' – songs like 'Play to Win' were also driven by an urge to throw off the shackles of Northern working-class inverted snobbery: Sheffield's traditional 'begrudgery', as Ware puts it, towards those who move to London to become big shots. 'Aspiration is the thread running through the entire album,' says Ware. 'At its deepest psychological level, *Penthouse* is about breaking free from home, breaking free from the constrictions of a society and going out into the big wide world. Coming from the background that Ian, Glenn and I did, it wasn't a given that we'd ever get the opportunity. We could all have ended up working in a steelworks or some grim office job.' The album's title track concerns the paradoxes of middle-class people trying to be 'street-credible' and the working classes wanting to rise to the top. 'That song is about social inequality, but also about the excitement of actually trying to make it. Not necessarily becoming rich, which is how it was interpreted – wrongly – by many people. I still get these ex-City traders telling me, "Oh yeah, that song really inspired me when I was in the City."' For these sons of Socialist Sheffield (a Tony Benn fan, Ware even believed in nationalizing the banks), the ambivalence of their aspirational imagery was obvious. But to others, the distinction between what Heaven 17 were celebrating and Thatcherite values was not at all clear.

These ambiguities came to the fore with *Penthouse*'s witty cover image – a painting depicting the group as tie-wearing executives discussing business plans and negotiating deals, based on a corporate advertisement Marsh found in *Newsweek*. On the front, the BEF logo appeared above the slogan 'The New Partnership – That's opening doors all over the world', while the words 'Sheffield. Edinburgh. London' were placed directly under the Heaven 17 brand name.

Heaven 17 as high-flying corporate executives, on the cover of *Penthouse and Pavement*, 1981. In the centre of the montage, L to R: Ian Craig Marsh, Martyn Ware, Glenn Gregory

Posing as a multinational was simultaneously a send-up, wish fulfilment and an act of rock criticism. 'We were debunking the mythology of the musician as this wandering minstrel who gets ripped off by the record company and gets paid to take drugs all the time,' says Ware. 'A reality check – Bob Dylan may *think* he's a rebel, but he's actually a multinational asset. Anybody who signs to a major label is part of a huge business machine. The idea was: "Let's get rid of all this hypocrisy of 'We're artists, we don't care about the money.' Let's strip the façade bare and have a look at what's underneath – handshakes, signing contracts, *busy*-ness."' BEF aimed to demolish other rock myths, too. They had no interest in performing live ('to me, a live show is what you do 'cos you can't get on TV', Ware had quipped, back when he was still in The Human League). They limited the promotion of *Penthouse* to PAs in discotheques, where they mimed to tapes. Says Marsh, 'That whole set of ideas to do with artistic and emotional expression, authenticity, contact with the audience, community . . . I was against that right off the bat.'

Penthouse and Pavement 'sold over a hundred thousand copies, roughly ten times more than either *Reproduction* or *Travelogue*', says Marsh. There were no hit singles, which pained Ware and Marsh as they watched The Human League's runaway success. Still, earning 1 per cent off *Dare*'s five million sales salved that wound a little. And in the critical and hipster sense, *Penthouse* was a massive success. 'That record was absolutely ubiquitous in a way that went far beyond its actual chart profile,' recalls Bob Last.

Still rolling off their initial burst of activity, Ware and Marsh launched straight into the next BEF project, *Music of Quality and Distinction, Volume One*. Like *Penthouse*, it continued Ware's mission to show that it was possible to make 'synthetic music with soul'. But this time BEF put themselves in the role of producers and arrangers. The *Quality and Distinction* concept was twofold: it consisted entirely of pop classics remade by BEF; and most of the songs were collaborations with famous singers. You could see the whole project as an essay about pop, celebrating the Tin Pan Alley/Motown/Nashville tendency to operate with a strict separation between songwriter, singer and producer. Ware and Marsh rejected rock's raw expression and aligned themselves with pop classicism: music designed with the calm deliberation of a draughtsman. 'We were fans of the genius producer, people like Phil Spector,' says Ware: 'the idea of assembling something of great beauty, almost like sonic architecture.' Beneath *Quality and Distinction* lurked a deeper psychological subtext: by elevating the producer's role as auteur, Marsh and Ware slyly implied that Martin Rushent was *the* crucial element in the success of Oakey's new League.

Quality and Distinction played some neat pop-critical games. Sandie Shaw covered 'Anyone who Had a Heart', a tune generally associated with her sixties rival Cilla Black; Billy MacKenzie attempted to outdo his idol/prototype Bowie on a remake of 'The Secret Life of Arabia' from *'Heroes'*. But, apart from Tina Turner's *tour de force* take on The Temptations' 'Ball of Confusion', the new versions failed to surpass the originals. As a unified listening experience, *Quality and Distinction* felt flat and motley; and the plan to release a series of five double-A-sided singles off the album was abandoned after the first couple got nowhere near the charts.

BEF celebrated 'dry', radio-ready production, but another, potentially fatal, kind of aridity also seemed to permeate their work. Not fatal to the records themselves (which were superb, at least in the case of Heaven 17) but to their pop prospects. Some lingering post-punk spirit of anti-mystique meant they weren't a group that everyday fans took to their hearts. 'We don't think it's healthy for people to hold up fairly ordinary people as some kind of demi-god,' Marsh declared, rejecting the very forces of identification and projection that animate pop culture. At the end of 1982, BEF found themselves in an embarrassing position – when you style yourself as a corporation, a hit factory churning out perfect consumer product, what do you do when hardly anyone's consuming your products?

Despite its deficiencies as a listening experience, *Quality and Distinction* could claim to be a seminal exercise in postmodern pop. At the end of the seventies, postmodernist concepts had started filtering down from academia to the music press via magazines like *Harper's & Queens*, where style analyst Peter York wrote a trailblazing essay elucidating its ideas. Translated into rock, the opposition between modernism and postmodernism neatly paralleled the difference between the post-punk vanguard of PiL, The Pop Group *et al.* (all striving strenuously for total innovation) and the retro-eclectic approach shared by 2-Tone, Postcard and Adam Ant (rifling through the archives, mixing and mismatching sonic and cultural elements). As a sensibility, postmodernism also eroded the certainties and assumptions of a certain kind of 'rock-think': binary oppositions like depth versus surface and authentic versus false, stodgy notions of artistic substance and durability, ailing fictions of community and resistance.

Post-punk's struggle to avoid escapism and superficiality had led to either hair-shirt propaganda (The Pop Group) or the existential abyss (Joy Division). Giddy with relief at jettisoning these twin burdens of guilt and despair, journalists like Paul Morley celebrated 'the transient thrill' of disposable pop. They trashed meaningfulness and well-meaning in favour of hedonistic paeans to consumption and polished product. And they challenged the implicitly masculine critical hierarchies that despised the synthetic and mass produced.

This gender-coded shift from 'rock' to 'pop' sensibility was in many ways a flashback to glam. In the early seventies David Bowie and Roxy Music had managed to bridge the ever-widening gap between singles-focused dance pop and album-oriented art-rock. They made 'serious' music that was also playful and image-conscious. Roxy's output especially wove together futuristic elements and period evocations, while Bowie (with *Pin-ups*) and Ferry (with his solo albums) explored the creative possibilities of the cover version to the hilt. Glam, in fact, had been postmodernist long before the term had currency outside art academia.

New Pop involved a renaissance of glam's interest in artifice and androgyny, all the delicious games you could play with pop idolatry. Perhaps the climax of all these tendencies was the bizarre critical apotheosis of Dollar, a schlocky male–female duo who had broken away from the middle-of-the-road vocal troupe Guys and Dolls. Dollar had already garnered a smidgen of campy admiration from hipsters for their sheer plasticness, but when they teamed up with superproducer Trevor Horn, the duo's fabricated fakeness took on an almost conceptual extremity, as if they were a work of Pop Art.

Horn began 1981 as a has-been, despite having scored a number 1 hit in sixteen countries with The Buggles' 'Video Killed the Radio Star' just two years earlier. After two unsuccessful Buggles albums Horn and partner Geoff Downes joined Yes for one album and a tour. Dollar were his ticket back from the brink of irrelevance. An accomplished musician who'd been in a youth orchestra and could sight-read from a score, the producer hated punk rock: for him, the true sonic revolutionaries of the late seventies were Kraftwerk, Donna Summer and Abba. Accordingly, Horn's concept for Dollar was to Moroderize the group's MOR. The first two singles he co-wrote and produced for Dollar, 'Hand Held in Black and White' and 'Mirror Mirror' dazzled the ears with their futuristic hypergloss. Dollar became hugely hip. And so did Horn.

ABC loved the Dollar singles, and they were looking for a producer to help realize their sonic dream: the fusion of symphonic disco, nouveau Roxy and piercingly intelligent lyrics. At the end of 1981, a year after Morley's New Pop feature had introduced them to the world, the Sheffield group had managed to secure a deal with Phonogram, but their music fell short of their aspirations. Their October 1981 debut single 'Tears Are Not Enough' rode music-paper buzz to get to number 19 in the charts, but the recording sounded like a scrawny demo for the spectacular sound they wanted. On *Top of the Pops*, singer Martin Fry wore a gold lamé suit, but it didn't sit right on his hulking frame; his dancing was awkward; his presence lacked authority. From sound to visuals, ABC were not yet walking it like they talked it. So they turned to Horn.

'Steve Singleton from ABC said to me, "If you produce us, you'll be the most fashionable producer in the world,"' says Horn. 'I was really taken with that – the arrogance of it.' ABC told him they wanted to make 'superhuman' records, and Horn agreed to produce the second single, 'Poison Arrow'. It took him a while to grasp what the band wanted to achieve: the orchestral disco splendour of Gloria Gaynor's 'I Will Survive' fused with the word-twisting lyrical depths of an Elvis Costello. 'It dawned on me as I was working on the record – and this is what I'd tell people at the time – "It's like Dylan, except it's disco music instead of an acoustic guitar. The guy's writing about what he really feels, but it's gonna be played in a dance club so it's gotta have the functional quality of disco."'

A lavish tempest of melodramatic grand piano chords, thunderous drums, and synth parts simulating string-sweeps and horn fanfares, 'Poison Arrow' sounded like a million bucks had been spent on it, and, yes, it sounded superhuman. Yet at its core lay the DIY principle – not so much 'anyone can do it' but 'anyone can be a star'. And ABC *did* become stars. 'Poison Arrow' reached number 6. The next single, the even more magnificently appointed 'The Look of Love' – featuring *real* strings, angelic backing vocals, timpani and trumpets – peaked at number 4 in June 1982.

To help him create the majestic sound ABC desired – James Brown meets Nelson Riddle's Sinatra – Horn assembled a crack squad that included engineer Gary Langan and Anne Dudley, a classically trained keyboard player and arranger. Both had worked on his Dollar records. ABC themselves were capable musicians, and the core of the product remained the tunes they'd written, but Horn, Langan and Dudley were given carte blanche by the group to embellish and expand upon these kernels. 'ABC weren't the least bit precious about their songs,' recalls Dudley. 'They were eager to embrace everything, totally open to making it as exciting and epic as possible. Another big reason why the album sounds so lush and bright is Gary Langan's engineering and mixing – nobody could work the studio gear like him.'

Not for nothing was the album called *The Lexicon of Love*. Fry revelled in wordplay like a Cole Porter chronically addicted to puns and alliteration, mixed metaphors and perilously extended tropes. But what, underneath the fizzy lyrical surface, were ABC *about*? 'Tears Are Not Enough' sounded almost like a New Pop manifesto (no time for wallowing or whining, strive and take pride) disguised as a song about heartbreak. Other ABC songs were more like meta-pop, playing games with pop's cliché-encrusted lore of love. 'Poison Arrow' twisted the Cupid myth; 'The Look of Love' echoed Bacharach & David; 'Many Happy Returns' quoted The Zombies' 'She's Not There'; and 'Show Me' sampled a Smokey Robinson song title and transformed it into an unrequited lover's plea for reciprocation – 'second that emotion'. 'Valentine's Day' harked back even further to 1930s Hollywood with its climactic lines about how 'If you gave me a pound for all the moments I missed/And I got dancing lessons for all the lips I shoulda kissed/I'd be a millionaire/I'd be a Fred Astaire'.

The echoes of pre-rock showbiz carried through to the look of ABC's records. Each single featured a sleevenote penned by Fry – a homage to the period (roughly pre-1967) when all long-playing records had them. To complete the atmosphere of bygone elegance, ABC added cute period touches, like the little box informing the purchaser how to get the best out of the record ('Don't use a faulty or worn stylus. Keep it clean by wiping it with an anti-static cloth'). Next to the logo for Neutron Records, ABC's imprint through Phonogram, they stamped the slogan 'Purveyors of Fine Product'.

Like BEF, ABC aimed to make music of quality and distinction. *Lexicon* was cunningly crafted to sound like no expense had been spared – it was widely assumed to be fully orchestrated, but in fact strings were used on only four tracks. ABC brought in appropriately deluxe sartorial signifiers, too: dinner jackets and bow-ties, along with those gold lamé suits. 'We wanted to look like we came from Vegas, so we went to Carnaby Street and hired this very camp tailor who used to make clothes for Marc Bolan,' recalls Fry. 'It's 1982, so he probably hadn't been asked to make a gold lamé suit for nearly a decade.' For the cover photographs, ABC wanted the rich tones of 'a Powell and Pressburger movie, where the colour red is *very* red. Steve [Singleton] and Mark [White – along with Fry, the band's principal creative force] had decided that I should be like a character – "the album's a movie and you're the star".'

Modelled on the theatre rather than cinema, *Lexicon*'s front cover depicted Martin Fry as the dashing hero of a crime melodrama, brandishing a revolver, a fainting damsel clasped in his other arm. Flip to the back of the record, and the *mise en scène* is revealed as literally *staged*. We see the backroom people behind the theatrical spectacle, as played by the other members of ABC: the prompter reading from a script, a fatigued stagehand with a greasy quiff and cigarette tucked behind the ear, a flunky with a bouquet ready for the leading lady. It was all decidedly Brechtian.

Indeed, for all the resurrection of romance and Hollywood glamour, ABC deep down retained that post-punk wariness about love and the unrealistic dreams propagated by pop. In a weird way, they resembled Gang of Four. (ABC's manager Rob Warr was not only Bob Last's partner but had previously managed Gang of Four during the *Entertainment!* era.) 'Date Stamp', at once the wittiest and most poignant song on *Lexicon*, recalled the imagery of 'Damaged Goods' – broken-hearted Fry is 'looking for a girl that meets supply with demand'. In a world where 'love has no guarantee', he's a discarded commodity whose sell-by date has expired. 'It was also a bit of a meta thing,' he says, 'about transience and ephemerality in pop.' 'All of My Heart', ABC's third Top 10 single in a row, sounded chocolate-box but its sentiments rivalled 'Love Like Anthrax' for bracing unsentimentality. 'It surprises me when people pin a Valentino tag on the group when a lot of the songs were out to demolish the power of love,' Fry told *The Face*. '"All of My Heart" for me was saying skip the hearts and flowers and wash your hands of the whole sentimental glop, you know?'

Yet for all the clever-clever cynicism, at the core of the record was the real pain of Martin Fry, disillusioned lover. His genuine bitterness was the reason why *Lexicon* worked. 'We wanted the songs to be romantic in the traditional sense, but there's also a sinister edge,' says Fry. '"Poison Arrow" is about falling in love but also how it kicks you in the teeth.' And Fry *had* been kicked in the teeth. '*Lexicon* is all about Martin getting dumped by this specific girl,' says Horn. 'All of the songs are about that

Romance and glamour resurrected on the front cover of ABC's *The Lexicon of Love* ...

... only to be revealed as stage-managed illusion, on the Brechtian back cover

381

anger and outrage he felt. And on "The Look of Love", when Martin sings, "When the girl has left you out on the table" and then there's a girl going, "Goodbye!", well, *that's the girl*. It was my suggestion – "Why don't we get the *actual girl* that you've wrote these songs for in to do the vocal?" It was very funny!'

The triumph of *Lexicon* lay in the slight gap between Fry's aspirations and his ability. Like Kevin Rowland, he wasn't quite a natural singer – his range was limited, the falsetto slightly strained. Nor did Fry have the innate panache to pull off the debonair role he'd cast himself: as on that first *TOTP* appearance, the moves still weren't slick; you could see the acne scars through the make-up. But he *willed* himself to be a star. 'I am a punk, I always have been and I always will be,' he once said. Paul Morley, ABC's fiercest champion, adds, 'What Fry took from punk was the zeal. ABC couldn't have happened without punk 'cos that gave people the possibility of creating their own masterplans and manifestos.'

ABC were also a brilliant example of music as 'active criticism'. Fry began as a music writer: he went to interview Vice Versa for his fanzine *Modern Drugs* and was offered a position in the band. ABC's rhetoric massively influenced the music press's shift to New Pop ideas. In a sense, they helped create the critical climate that would embrace them. And they repaid the compliments: they took the title *The Lexicon of Love* from the headline of Ian Penman's *NME* review of an ABC show; they gave Morley a cameo role in the Edwardian fantasia video for 'The Look of Love'.

At the end of 1982, ABC could look back on a year of grand achievements. The record of the summer, *Lexicon* was number 1 for a month and went platinum in the UK. There had been a huge showbiz-styled tour, they were working on the first ABC movie, *Mantrap*, and 'The Look of Love' had even cracked America's Top 20. ABC had talked big, but – unlike New Pop fellow travellers BEF and Scritti – they'd *surpassed* their own hype. In the process, they had set the bar impossibly high for their peers.

20

MUTANT DISCO AND PUNK-FUNK: Crosstown Traffic in Early Eighties New York (and Beyond . . .)

The B-52's. Pylon. Club 57. Mudd Club. Jean-Michel Basquiat. ZE Records. Kid Creole & The Coconuts. Was (Not Was). Material. 99 Records. Bush Tetras. ESG. Liquid Liquid. A Certain Ratio. New Order.

The B-52's Take Manhattan

MAUREEN MCGINLEY (former B-52's manager): The first time The B-52's played in New York they opened for Teenage Jesus and the Jerks. And the B's were so afraid of them, they wouldn't leave their dressing room . . . It was a Monday night at Max's and nobody was there. But six weeks later they played a second night at Max's and when we got there, everybody was there: all the Patti Smith Group, Chris and Debbie from Blondie, Gene Simmons from Kiss was there, Cheap Trick. Weird!

STEVE MAAS (owner of the Mudd Club): The B-52's were the first band I ever put on at the Mudd. Their manager Maureen was from Georgia, where I was from, so they all stayed in my apartment.

ANIMAL X (Mudd Club scenester): The band came out dressed in girdles from the 50s. On the first song they held a laugh box to the mike after every chorus. They were the only band around with a sense of humour. (Quoted in Steven Hager, *Art after Midnight*)

CINDY WILSON (The B-52's singer): I'm sick and tired of negative. (*Melody Maker*, 13 January 1979)

FRED SCHNEIDER (The B-52's singer): We came at a time when the New Wave thing was really coming on strong. I guess there was a need for a different kind of dance music, 'cause when we started there were no dance groups in New York. We'd get up in Max's Kansas City and say, OK, this is a dance song, and everybody'd be up there in their black leather coats just watching. They were enjoying it, but it wasn't cool to dance. Lord knows, we didn't look too cool. (*East Village Eye*, December 1984)

TOM CARSON (journalist): The best new music to have come out of the CBGB–Max's Kansas City circuit in months if not years is being made by a self-described 'thrift-store' rock band called The B-52's. On stage, they look like a cubist version of *Beach Blanket Bingo*: two girls – one a guitarist–organist, the other playing bongos – doing the frug in beehive hairdos and PTA matron clothes, a drummer wearing a sun visor and a Lacoste shirt, a guitarist who plays riffs straight out of *Ventures A Go-Go*, and a lead vocalist who sings like a police squawk-box and strikes poses like an Egyptian bas-relief come to life. (*Village Voice*, 12 June 1978)

MAUREEN MCGINLEY: The person who got everyone in Athens [Georgia] thrift shopping was John Martin Taylor, now a cookbook writer. He would go to thrift stores and yard sales and find the most outrageous clothes . . . He bought a lot of stuff for the B's in the early days. But we all did – you could go to the thrift store and buy a shirt for 25 cents. What a lot of guys did is buy a week's worth of shirts, all clean and pressed, on hangers. They'd wear 'em for a week, and then take them back to the thrift store, and get more shirts. It was cheaper than doing laundry. There were people collecting records and magazines and crazy books, lots of little statues and vases, and whole sets of Fiestaware and china. The thrift store, that's where Fred Schneider's first toy piano came from. But the wigs were brand new – they came from Lee Wigs in downtown Athens.

RANDY BEWLEY (Pylon guitarist): Back in '77 you'd go around to some art shows in Athens and see these guys with purple wigs and really weird clothes. Everyone in the B's wore wigs in those days. It was mainly Keith who had the purple hair. (*NME*, 6 December 1980)

MAUREEN MCGINLEY: I had known Keith Strickland, the B's drummer, and Ricky Wilson, their guitarist, since they were in high school. I vividly remember seeing them walking to school with lipstick on and their hair all done, holding hands. I'm just like, "Oh these boys, they are not gonna make it." So our house was kind of a refuge . . . In Georgia back then it was not at all cool to be gay. Keith and Ricky got harassed a lot. So we kind of all stayed together – because if you looked a little bit different, you know . . . We were such a tightly knit group. That was part of not being accepted by the larger community. We were in and out of each other's houses all the time.

VANESSA ELLISON (Pylon singer): The B-52's debut gig was Valentine's Day 1977 at an Athens house party. I wasn't there but I heard about it at the university art department. They appeared and were just instantly popular.

MAUREEN MCGINLEY: Athens, Georgia, is a university town. Very sleepy. At night we used to ride our bicycles down the middle of the main street downtown, because after six o'clock everything was closed up, there was nothing going on there. So that made everybody have parties: we had to make our own entertainment . . . I would hide my good pots and pans, because anything that was left out was going to be used as a drum before the night was over! I have a theory, I feel like there is this creative energy that settles over a place for a time, and Athens was one of those places. Because it wasn't just people making music. Music was the least of it. It all started with art. There were people painting, there were people writing, there were people doing all kinds of different things. And when people came to the music they came to the music usually through some other medium. Fred was a poet. Kate Pierson never wanted to do anything but sing, which her parents frowned upon, so after her degree she was working as a paste-up artist at a newspaper. That's what she was doing when the B's started. Keith and Ricky, their *life* was their art. Cindy Wilson was sixteen and didn't really do anything; she was Ricky's sister and so that's how she got involved in The B-52's.

MICHAEL LACHOWSKI (Pylon bassist): We all knew each other through art school for the most part and the whole party scene came out of there . . . Our interest in music was very keen – buying seven inches by groups like The Normal, The Mekons and whatever else, mostly from Britain. (*Perfect Sound Forever*, 1998)

VANESSA ELLISON: Randy Bewley and Michael Lachowski thought it would be fun to start a band, get written up in *New York Rocker*, then break up – sort of a temporary art idea. Glenn O'Brien reviewed our first single in *Interview* and said, 'They sound like they eat dub for breakfast.'

MAUREEN MCGINLEY: When The B-52's got signed to Warner Bros, one of the first things they did was open for Paul Simon in Central Park. And Pylon was the B's opening act in those days, so in Central Park, it was Pylon, The B-52's and Paul Simon. And, later, REM opened for Pylon.

VANESSA ELLISON: During the summer, we were lining up shows in New York thanks to the wild success of The B-52's that year with 'Rock Lobster'. They were an instant sensation in New York. They played at this big club, Hurrah's. When they were getting booked there, Fred Schneider gave them our tape and suggested that we should play there too. (*Perfect Sound Forever*, 1998)

MICHAEL STIPE (REM singer): Pylon had gone on tour opening for Gang of Four and had come back to Athens talking about this band that nobody in New York had even heard of. *Entertainment!* was the soundtrack to every party in Athens before New York and LA found out about it. In some weird turn of events, we were ahead of the curve. (*Spin*, 2004)

MAUREEN MCGINLEY: The Athens party thing was all about dancing. People didn't stand around talking and making snide remarks. If an Athens band played and nobody danced, they never played again.

JAMES CHANCE: Around 1979, there were all these new clubs opening up all over the city. The whole scene kind of exploded . . . People weren't into dancing so much but then me and The B-52's really got a lot of people dancing again.

Club 57 versus the Mudd Club

ARTO LINDSAY (DNA guitarist): There was this kind of Americana thing going on, poking fun at suburbia – The B-52's, Club 57, Kenny Scharf painting cartoony doodles. It was about this whole kitsch aspect of the United States.

KATE PIERSON (The B-52's singer): Without being too pretentious, you can look at a K-Mart shopping centre as a modern cultural museum and learn something from what's there and what that means. (*NME*, 3 January 1981)

KENNY SCHARF (artist): We went to all [The B-52's] shows and gave the band presents. Keith [Haring] gave them plastic fruit once and they *loved* it. (*East Village Eye*, September 1982)

MICHAEL HOLMAN (artist/musician in Gray): Club 57 was a club on St Mark's Place – it was a let's-put-on-a-show-in-the-backyard kind of thing. They did wild and crazy theme parties all the time. It was Keith Haring and Ann Magnuson's crowd.

ANN MAGNUSON (performer): I really saw Club 57 as an exorcism of Americana, all this television stuff . . . Because there were only three channels at that time, you watched these old movies, and you'd pick up the sensibilities of vaudeville, the Marx Brothers, the Smothers Brothers Comedy Hour, horror films. All that stuff informed the art.

MERLE GINSBERG (journalist): Out of what can now be referred to as the Dada doings at Club 57 grew the Ladies Auxiliary of the Lower East Side. Out of the Ladies grew Pulsallama ... They didn't know how to play, but that hadn't prevented anyone else on the circuit from doing it. So, in an act of girl defiance, they chose to hit things: beer bottles, toy machine-guns, plastic bags, cowbells ... Their lyrics, always a variation on 'Pulsallama', were exuberantly chanted in Greek choral style. (*NME*, 2 October 1982)

ANN MAGNUSON: The thing about Pulsallama was that it was just an anti-band. A parody of Bow Wow Wow and all those tribal rhythms that people were getting into. It was just 12 or 13 girls screaming and beating on pots and pans and it was very funny the first couple of times. (*East Village Eye*, August 1983)

RICHARD MCGUIRE (Liquid Liquid guitarist): What a sight. All those women. It was like a Fellini movie! Real performance art.

GLENN O'BRIEN (journalist/Mudd Club DJ): Club 57 had a camp sensibility. It was very much an artists' bar.

ANN MAGNUSON: I would create a set, a soundtrack, and a framework for people to come in and be their own characters. They'd costume themselves and we'd make a play. Once we started doing theme nights, you just had to think of new things. I'd go to thrift stores almost every day, and get my costumes and my props and get inspired by creating things from what was available. Also there was a lot of stuff on the street you could pick up. There were all these refrigerator boxes. So we'd drag all this stuff back to the club and create, say, a Jamaican shanty town and make a putt-putt miniature golf course through it and play reggae. It was a conceptual-art piece that you could be involved in. We had an Elvis Memorial Night, where we showed an Elvis movie, played Elvis music, held an Elvis lookalike contest, and had Elvis memorials.

JEAN-MICHEL BASQUIAT (artist/musician in Gray): Esthetically I really hated Club 57. I thought it was silly. All this old and bad shit. I'd rather see something old and good. (Quoted in Steven Hager, *Art after Midnight*)

ANN MAGNUSON: In one of those books Jean-Michel said he hated Club 57. I think he had a rivalry with Kenny [Scharf] and Keith

[Haring] and he associated the club with them. Jean-Michel was pretty cantankerous and could be a nasty piece of work when he wanted to be, which was a lot of the time . . . That movie *Basquiat* made it seem like there were only two or three people that were central players. But the fact is, if you had an art gallery opening in those days, you could take the camera and zoom in on any person in that gallery and have a story that was just as compelling as Jean-Michel's. That was what downtown was like at that time.

MICHAEL HOLMAN: Club 57, they were more about acid and poppers, whereas the Mudd Club was more into heroin and cigarettes. 57 was more the high-school glee club. At the Mudd Club we were more into a heavy bohemian trip. But Club 57 put on great shows, too. It was like mods and rockers, but people did hang out at both clubs. I went to Club 57 a lot but I think they would make fun of us and say how serious we were.

GLENN O'BRIEN: The first time I heard of the Mudd Club, somebody said: 'Eno's got a new bar below Canal Street, let's go.' Actually Eno had nothing to do with it, except he was living in Steve Maas's house and I think he consulted on the sound system. The club was just a ground-floor loft, decorated very minimally, but it had a good DJ and a good vibe. The Mudd was very odd and unpredictable. You would go one night and Bo Diddley would be playing, the next night Was (Not Was) and the one after, Eric Bogosian.

STEVE MAAS: In the rock business, you have to have a very strong brand identity. The Mudd Club was the complete opposite of that. In fact, Robert Christgau said it was the 'citadel of dilettantism'. We had this incredibly diversified programme – one day we'd do some avant garde composer and the next day would be The Plasmatics. And then we'd do an art show featuring all these new artists who nowadays have shows in the National Gallery.

GLENN O'BRIEN: There was a long tradition of NY art bars. Max's was the most famous. There was the Mercer Arts Center. These were bars where bohemian people would hang out. The Mudd was conceived as something like that, but with a performance aspect. When it took off, Steve started getting more and more complicated ideas. He would redecorate the club after a theme, like the pimp theme.

MICHAEL HOLMAN: I did the Soul Party, a massive installation that Steve spent ten grand on. Upstairs we had a soul kitchen with all this food from Sylvia's Kitchen – black-eyed peas and candied yams. In the back was this pimp's bedroom with plastic love beads, mirrored ceilings and a giant pimp bed with orange fur pile. We had a beauty parlour with these hairdryer chairs from a Brooklyn parlour. Downstairs I was DJ-ing, playing all this late sixties/early seventies funk music that most people at the Mudd Club had never heard. That event was the main one I did. Tina L'Hotsky did the Dead Rock Stars theme – all these shrines to different dead rock stars.

GARY INDIANA (writer/performer): I was one of the people who organized themed events at the Mudd – like the Rock 'n' Roll Funeral. That was me and Tina L'Hotsky. Tina was the goddess of the Mudd. In a postmodern way, she was like Breton's Nadja. She was almost a somnambulist: she floated through life on this cloud of ravishing beauty and something like naïvety that was also close to insanity.

STEVE MAAS: I'd studied cultural anthropology. That gave me an interest in bringing all of these diverse cultural influences together. So if we had a big theme party, like the Rock 'n' Roll Funeral Ball, there'd be mock voodoo ceremony, calling the dead. It was a way of making statements against Middle America which was kind of this monoculture – American small-town values.

MICHAEL HOLMAN: Mudd Club was this anti-Midtown, anti-disco, anti-Studio 54 thing. The paradigm was that the rich, the squares, the bridge-and-tunnel people would pay to get in, but us hip kids got in for free and got drink tickets. So the squares would subsidize the hipsters.

GARY INDIANA: I'm not sure Steve made that much money in the end because he would spend more on parties than he could ever make back. Everybody got free drinks and free everything. The fun part of the Mudd was watching the most famous people in the world trying to get in the club and being excluded. Anyone from Studio 54 couldn't get in.

Dowtown Art Meets Graffiti and Hip Hop

STEVE MAAS: Afrika Bambaataa, the first time he ever DJ-ed in a white club was at the Mudd.

GLENN O'BRIEN: A lot of the early hip hop groups came down and played at the Mudd, probably because of Fab Five Freddy.

FAB FIVE FREDDY (graffiti artist/rapper): What inspired me about what was going on was that you would wake up tomorrow morning and say 'I'm an actor,' and you'd be an actor, or 'I'm a musician' and you'd be a musician, and everyone would accept you as that. It was kind of like playing house. (*New York Times*, 2000)

MICHAEL HOLMAN: Fab Five Freddy and I became friends and we decided to throw a big party that would feature all these early players in the graffiti world. I'll never forget people saying, 'There's this guy Jean-Michel Basquiat who really wants to come.' By that time, everyone downtown had already been seeing his SAMO tags. He insisted on being part of the show. The Canal Zone party was 29 April 1979. It was the first downtown graffiti party, when all the elements of hip hop rubbed shoulders with downtown art. I was interviewing people with a video camera at the party, asking questions and pulling the mike away before they could answer – it was very silly. I did it to Jean and he gave me *this look*. Later, I went to him and tried to apologize and he said: 'That's OK. Do you want to start a band?' Later that night we started Gray.

Jean-Michel Basquiat, the renaissance man of downtown New York. From the movie *Downtown 81*, a Zeitgeist Films release

RICHARD MCGUIRE: When Jean formed Gray I thought it seemed like he wanted to do something cool like The Lounge Lizards. We played with them at some loft parties. I thought Jean was famous already because he'd been doing SAMO graffiti and there was an article about him and Al Diaz in *Village Voice*. Gray's music was like jazz-noise: Jean used to play a fucked-up little toy synth with coloured keys through some effects boxes.

GLENN O'BRIEN: Gray were experimental but in a way that was pleasing to the ear. I guess maybe they were influenced by electric-era

Miles Davis, elevator music, easy listening jazz. Jean-Michel wasn't a trained musician but he had a very good ear. They had the cheapest portable synthesizer you could get. They just took junk and made music out of it in an interesting way.

MICHAEL HOLMAN: We started with the idea of deconstructing music. It eventually became a sound-noise thing, like you were in a factory and the machines would turn themselves on and try to make music when the humans went home.

JEAN-MICHEL BASQUIAT: I was inspired by John Cage at the time – music that isn't really music. We were trying to be incomplete, abrasive, oddly beautiful. (*New York Times* magazine, date unknown)

MICHAEL HOLMAN: The members of the band were officially me, Jean, Nick Taylor and Wayne Clifford. Vincent Gallo was in the band for a minute – he did a couple of gigs. Our last gig at the Mudd, I decided I wanted to do this crazy geodesic dome. I went to the Bronx and rented $100 worth of scaffolding. On top of the stage we built this 'ignorant' geodesic dome – 'ignorant' being Jean's fave word to describe something innocently, carelessly done . . . I had Vince and Wayne four feet off the ground, strapped in at forty-five-degree angles with their keyboards. My head popped up from the surface of the stage, and Nick was so high up in the scaffolding that through the whole set all you could see were his feet. Jean walked in right on time for his sound check with his mini-Wasp synth. He doesn't say a word, just turns around and leaves. I'm thinking: Oh my God, is he coming back? Jean comes back in under five minutes with this crate he found in the garbage and throws it onstage. And then, like a mummy in an urn-like sarcophagus, he scrunches his body into this three-foot cube thing and stuffs the Wasp synth in with him. And he looks at me and smiles. It was like, you could spend for ever making something happen and he'd blow it away with one gesture . . . Jean was the ultimate arbiter of style and aesthetics on our scene. He was the king of the scene. Everybody loved him.

GARY INDIANA: I had mixed feelings about Jean-Michel, as everyone who knew him did, because he was a brat. When you saw Jean out in public, you knew he wanted to get somewhere. But how can you hold that against anybody in New York?

VINCENT GALLO (actor/director/Gray musician): The minute Jean-Michel Basquiat had a chance to move into the place he really wanted to be – the art world – he quit the band in a second. (*BB Gun* vol. 6, 2003)

ADELE BERTEI (Contortions/The Bloods): The art scene exploded in the eighties on the Lower East Side. All these galleries started opening up where the art was much more non-traditional.

RICHARD MCGUIRE: There were a lot of these *big* art shows happening that included tons of people: 1980's *Times Square Show* took place in an abandoned porn palace; all these graffiti artists were showing together with downtown people. Then, in 1981, there was a big show at PS1 in Queens, one subway stop out of Manhattan – a big museum-like alternative gallery space in an old school building. They put on a huge show called *New York/New Wave*. All sorts of downtown people were involved: David Byrne showed photos of overturned chairs; Basquiat and Haring were launched; DNA played; there were Mapplethorpe photos and lots of photos of rock stars.

ZE Records and 99 Records

IAN PENMAN (journalist): As yet in the UK there's precious little to compare with Manhattan's ZE organization. Some things – Factory, Rough Trade – have twisted around what we've come to expect of a record label and its relationship with those who release and rely on it. (Sleevenotes to ZE Records' compilation, *Mutant Disco*)

ADELE BERTEI: Michael Zilkha, the co-founder of ZE, was a smart entrepreneur. He was quite a funny character – like the Malcolm McLaren of the scene.

LYDIA LUNCH: Zilkha was very excited about the music and the New York scene at the time. No one had ever approached me who was so enthusiastic – he seemed to get where it was coming from and didn't want to manipulate it; he just wanted you to do what you did, which was fantastic. That didn't stop me from threatening to throw him from his seventeenth-floor office if he didn't pay me on the spot what he owed me – and he did.

MICHAEL ZILKHA: The artists didn't always realize how much I'd contributed to making the records. I did provide a discipline and I did mix the records – a lot of them. I wanted the records to make it clear what was happening, to be very pop and bright – but Pop *Art* pop, not pop music pop . . . I would always try to take people further out.

IAN PENMAN: Most music you'll likely find turning around a ZE label will either be edging towards an idiom of its own – if it isn't already there – or in the process of wrecking the one you might be tempted to wrap it up in. (Sleevenotes to *Mutant Disco*)

MICHAEL ZILKHA: I first met August Darnell in a recording studio, when I was still trying to figure out what records to make. August had made that incredible Dr Buzzard's Original Savannah Band record, but it all imploded when his brother Stony Browder Jr. went off into a drug-induced haze.

AUGUST DARNELL (singer/leader of Kid Creole & The Coconuts): Stony had this bizarre idea that we Mulattos had been in the closet for too long . . . the race that was ashamed to speak its name. Blacks had their Say It Loud, I'm Black and I'm Proud, whites had their movement of the superior race, so Stony said Mulattos should be proud of being half-breeds. They should stand on a pedestal and say, hey, I'm the best of both worlds. I have the black rhythm and the white intelligence. That's how far out he was. (*NME*, 4 July 1981)

GLENN O'BRIEN: August had this vision that was very exotic. He thought that was the future of music – this exotic blend, sort of world music. To me, their stuff seems so modern, especially that 'Que Pasa/Me No Pop I' record that Andy Hernandez from the Coconuts made as Coati Mundi.

MICHAEL ZILKHA: Kid Creole & The Coconuts were fantastic – so good live. What we always tried for was really tough lyrics with really happy music, and it would be the tension between the two. I do think my records were subversive – in that respect, they *were* punk. Kid Creole & The Coconuts were not a manufactured group, but the record came before the group. Same with Was (Not Was) – they were put together around the records. Don and David came to me from Detroit 'cos they'd heard the Contortions record. I just didn't have enough money to buy 'Wheel Me Out' but then they said, "We'll give it to you." Then I found the money to do an album with them.

DAVID WAS (Was (Not Was) lyricist): I think you can hear Detroit in what we do. If it sounds like we're not slaves to a certain style, it's because Detroit is such a style salad. We grew up on the best of black and white, you could get it any which way you liked. I think that's why we really can't settle on a style . . . I think we've always set ourselves up as these prankster artificieurs who try to always put the glitch in . . . So we couldn't just make a formula record, what fun would that be? (*NME*, 22 October 1983).

MICHAEL ZILKHA: When I first heard 'Wheel Me Out' I thought that was much more than merely 'clever'. David was really out there. But they're *clever*. All of my bands were *too* clever, and it took me ages to understand that 'clever' isn't necessarily it. Truly great rock music is not clever. Factory were not as 'clever' as ZE, because with Joy Division, there was something elemental there. Don't get me wrong, I love all my records, but they're not visceral like Neil Young or Prince and the record sales bear that out. I could create the illusion of elementalness, with very loud guitars, but it *was* ultimately an illusion. With Material's 'Bustin' Out', I wanted them to make a record with a disco beat and be as strange as they wanted on top. I wanted lots of heavy-metal guitar – this is way before Michael Jackson's 'Beat It'. They used George Jackson's prison letters as the text and got Nona Hendryx to sing it. And they delivered exactly what I'd wanted. It was a cynical, manufactured record. But not really – I believed that was what we *should* be making.

IAN PENMAN: Anchored in conceptual amorphousness . . . at any given point any number of nameless or famous people could be involved in a Material or Was (Not Was) song – projects then proliferate, players interchange, passions get weird, everything *moves*. (Sleevenotes to *Mutant Disco*)

MICHAEL ZILKHA: It was really Rob Partridge at Island who packaged the ZE compilation. I don't know who came up with the title *Mutant Disco*. I just came up with the subtitle: *A Subtle Discolation of the Norm*.

PAT PLACE (Contortions/Bush Tetras guitarist): I got into the funk groove through working with James Chance.

RICHARD MCGUIRE: The Bush Tetras were funky. It was Pat Place, she was the show. She had the credibility because she'd put the funk into The Contortions. 'Too Many Creeps' was a club hit. You heard it all the time.

PAT PLACE: I was sitting at my job at Bleecker Street Cinema when I jotted down those lyrics for 'Too Many Creeps'. The people on the streets were bugging me. It hasn't changed that much!

LAURA KENNEDY (Bush Tetras bassist): We're a rhythm and paranoia band. (*NME*, 8 November 1980)

RICHARD MCGUIRE: The Bush Tetras made 99 Records cool. Before it was a label, 99 Records was a small store below street level, half records and half clothes. It had a nice atmosphere. Ed Bahlman loved the music he carried, you just felt that. He had records you didn't see anywhere else. He ran the store with his girlfriend Gina, who was British. She would go back and forth to London bringing boxes of records.

GINA FRANKLYN: One day I said, 'I have to go on a [clothes] buying trip to England. Why don't you come with me?' and I used to know Geoff Travis at Rough Trade and so I introduced Ed to Geoff and they hit it off. And then I said, 'Gee, why don't you bring in all this so-called alternative music?' The stuff that Rough Trade was putting out. No one was bringing it in then. So that's what we used to do: stuff suitcases and bring them back and drag boxes of stuff back over. I remember bringing huge cartons of *Metal Box* back with me . . . so that we [would be] the first to get *Metal Box*, since that was such a big deal. (*Tuba Frenzy* vol. 4, 1998)

VIVIEN GOLDMAN (journalist/musician): I was friends with PiL and recorded the single 'Launderette' in down time at the Manor studio when they were doing *Flowers of Romance*. When I took my record to 99, it was like a cargo cult – the song hadn't even finished and they were like, 'Yes! We'll have it. We're signing you!' It seemed, for that brief moment, that London did have the high ground. You came over as an emissary from that scene and they were really keen to partake of that volcanic wellspring of energy.

RICHARD MCGUIRE: Ed wanted to develop a real exchange with England. He formed a bit of a deal with Factory Records with ESG.

ADRIAN THRILLS (journalist): Any group who are touted as a cross between Public Image and Tamla Motown deserve to be heard. A group who actually live up to such a lofty billing are something special indeed. (Review of ESG's 'You're No Good' b/w 'Moody' single on 99 Records/Factory, in the *NME*, 18 April 1981)

RENEE SCROGGINS (ESG vocalist): I don't feel like a disco group, I don't feel like a punk group, I feel like a funk group, maybe like Rick James says, punk-funk. I feel we're right here, in between, we've got something for everybody. (*Collusion*, February–April 1983)

RICHARD MCGUIRE: It was mindblowing when I first heard ESG. I think it was at Hurrah's. They opened for Young Marble Giants – what a double bill! Aretha Franklin was all I was thinking. And the songs were held together by nothing! A couple of clacking sticks and a simple bassline.

RENEE SCROGGINS: I grew up listening to James Brown and it was the funkiest music I could ever hear, especially when he would go to the bridge and let the funk rip. So I felt that he would always make that little funky space too short. You know, the part that made you want to really dance and get down? I wanted to hear something like that but let that funky space ride! (*Tuba Frenzy* vol. 4, 1998)

CAROL COOPER (journalist): I was one of the many journalists who assumed by the band's affection for Latin percussion, South Bronx origins, and mestizo looks that they were Puerto Rican. But a white father and a black mother made ESG . . . what stars like Prince and August Darnell only pretended to be . . . legitimate mulattos. (*Dance Music Report*, September 1990)

RENEE SCROGGINS: We met this guy Ed Bahlman who had a record label, 99 Records. He was one of the judges at [a] talent show . . . He became our unofficial manager and he started booking us in punk rock clubs. (source unknown)

RICHARD MCGUIRE: Ed was a tall, gangly guy: very gentle but could be very strong in his tastes, what he thought was good or bad musically. I don't know why there weren't more indie labels in New York. 99 had more of a chance to survive because of the store. Ed's brother was a DJ in some clubs and I think that helped position the records as well.

RENEE SCROGGINS: We played Hurrah's. We played Rock Lounge, Peppermint Lounge, Irving Plaza . . . We opened for Gang of Four. We opened for PiL . . . we didn't know who they was . . . We opened for The Clash. (*Venus*, date unknown)

RICHARD MCGUIRE: ESG were from a different planet. I always felt that they didn't know what they had gotten themselves into. They were all so young, playing these clubs and they couldn't even drink. Liquid Liquid played many shows with them. It was like the mini-Motown, that's how it felt: 'the 99 show'. In some ways 99 Records was family like. I remember driving down to do a show in Washington, DC, with ESG, the girls' mom coming along. She made sandwiches for everyone and it was like a family outing.

RENEE SCROGGINS: My mum didn't want us hanging out on the street, so she bought us some instruments. I was thirteen, Deborah had to be . . . seven or eight years old, and she was playing the bass . . . The Bronx can give you a lot of musical feeling because there's so much stuff going on out there. It has a lot of savage drive, with the drum beats and all. The whole summer long all you hear from sunrise to sunset is congas in the park back there. It can drive you crazy. (*Collusion*, February–April 1983)

RICHARD MCGUIRE: Mostly at the time we were absorbing what was all around us – the Lower East Side of Manhattan was very

Hispanic and you heard this Latin stuff all the time coming out of every bodega. All of our cowbell and conga sounds were coming from being exposed to that . . . I had picked up this Fela Kuti record, *Zombie*, from a friend. It made a big impression with us; he was the African James Brown. At this point I really wanted to change the name: Liquid Idiot sounded too punk. But we were already playing out under that name so I thought we shouldn't change it that much, so I just repeated the Liquid part, which seemed more rhythmic. It implied a slippery grooviness.

PAT PLACE: In New York in those days, Bush Tetras could play probably two or three times a month. For a crowd at Danceteria or Peppermint Lounge or Irving Plaza, maybe it would be 1,000, 1,500, at its most packed maybe even 2,000. Back then in our prime in New York we sometimes got paid from $6,000 to $10,000 a night. That was in the eighties, when that was a lot of money. But, well, drugs were expensive!

RICHARD MCGUIRE: Hurrah's was a former disco, all mirrored and disco balls. You can see it in Bowie's 'Fashion' video. This was the place where all the English bands would play, like Gang of Four. I remember it was a big deal for us to play there. Paradise Garage, we played there a few times – but that was later, 1983. I remember bringing the second Liquid Liquid EP over with Ed to give to Larry Levan, the big DJ guru there. The Garage was an insane place. It really was a big parking garage that was turned into a disco. I remember metal detectors. There was none of that in any club I had been to before. It was very gay, very Hispanic/black. And dancing! This was not like those rock clubs with people shuffling around; this was throbbing *disco*. When we played, they had us do three songs and then get off. This was typical for all these big dance places we played, like the Funhouse, or the Roxy. It was so much more about the DJ. By the time 'Cavern' was getting airplay on black stations we were getting all these new offers to play shows in these dance clubs.

TERRY TOLKIN (99 Records): They were playing . . . the Liquid Liquid track 'Cavern' on BLS, the biggest black station in new York . . . We were selling tons, couldn't keep it in the store. (*Tuba Frenzy* vol. 4, 1998)

RICHARD MCGUIRE: I read that Bambaataa was playing 'Cavern' at the Roxy which is where [Grandmaster Flash] apparently heard it . . . When Flash appropriated 'Cavern' for 'White Lines' it was a mixed bag. Here's somebody you're in awe of, so it's a compliment. (*Wire*, August 1997)

The Manhattan/Manchester Connection

RENEE SCROGGINS: We were playing . . . with a band called A Certain Ratio and that's where we met Tony Wilson who had Factory Records and he said to us at the club, 'Would you like to do a record?' . . . Next thing I know, 2 days later we're in the studio with Martin Hannett and we didn't even know who he was! . . . This is where we did 'Moody', 'UFO', and 'You're No Good', which are now the 'classic' ESG songs. (*Venus*, date unknown)

MARTIN MOSCROP (A Certain Ratio guitarist): Tony Wilson had been to Manhattan just before we came out there to record our first album, *To Each* . . . in 1980. Tony rented a loft in Tribeca and he bought six mattresses, six sheets and six pillows – one for each of us. And we just lived in the loft for six weeks and went to East Orange studio in New Jersey to record the album. One of the problems with that album is that Hannett took a lot of the funkiness out – he made Donald record every part of the drum kit separately. But we finished the LP early! There were three days of studio time free, already paid for, so we asked ESG if they wanted to come and record. So that was us taking a bit of New York back to the UK. And it's the same with New Order: when they came to New York, they were still sort of in the rocky phase, but they started getting more dance-oriented. We were both taking New York back to Manchester.

STEVEN MORRIS (New Order drummer): We used to check out the clubs in New York. Hurrah's was one of them, and Danceteria. Ruth Polsky, our American tour manager, was involved in both clubs. The other thing we used to do in New York was just listen to Kiss FM, those Shep Pettibone mastermix shows: Sharon Redd, Peech Boys, all that lot. Half the time we used to just stay in the hotel listening to the radio. We didn't dance, though, *didn't* dance! It takes Ecstasy to make a white man dance.

PETER HOOK (New Order bassist): As New Order, we had made a good start with the single 'Ceremony', but that was really the end of Joy Division rather than the start of something new . . . When we got to *Movement*, it was a real low point, for us and for Martin [Hannett] . . . We were confused, musically . . . in a mess . . .

depressed. (Quoted in Mick Middles, *From Joy Division to New Order*)

STEVEN MORRIS: Our Berlin friend Mark Reeder would send us tapes of electronic Italian disco that was incredibly cheerful. 'Everything's Gone Green', that was when New Order found a direction again. That was the beginning of bringing the drum machine in and pressing the start button.

PETER HOOK: We'd done 'Everything's Gone Green', 'Temptation' and *Power, Corruption and Lies* and [Factory's New York representative] Michael Shamberg suggested that we work with Arthur Baker because Arthur was really happening with [Rockers Revenge's] 'Walking on Sunshine' and [Freeez's] 'I.O.U.' . . . We thought that Arthur Baker was going to be this technological genius creating these dance records and really he was just a punk let loose in a recording studio who didn't know what the fucking hell he was doing – he was just pushing sliders up and down. We were terrified of going over there to meet him but when we got there we realized he was just like us. (www.neworderonline.com)

BARNEY SUMNER (New Order vocalist): We went into [Baker's] studio in New York with no song whatsoever. We've never done that before so it was in fact a completely experimental thing with a producer we didn't know. He was working on Freeez at the same time which is probably why ['Confusion'] sounds similar. (*Sounds*, July 1983)

ARTHUR BAKER (producer): 'Confusion' was a Funhouse record . . . I'd tell [New Order], 'We'll do it, we'll finish it and we'll go to the Funhouse so Jellybean [Benitez] can play it right away. (www.djhistory.com, 1999)

RICHARD GRABEL (journalist): Jellybean hits a button and switches from his turntables to a reel-to-reel tape deck mounted on the wall. He then turns around towards Arthur Baker, who's standing in the booth, and gestures towards the tape. He's trying out one of Baker's works-in-progress, an instrumental version of a new New Order track called 'Confusion' . . . The kids don't know what this new track is, but they're moving to it. It works. But it's hard to read Baker's expressionless face. Perhaps what he's seeing is dollars jumping into frantic motion. (*NME*, 12 May 1983)

MARTIN MOSCROP: The Hacienda was built because of Danceteria and Funhouse and the Roxy. New Order were coming to

New York and going to these fantastic clubs, thinking, Why haven't we got this in Manchester?

Mutant Disco versus No Wave Redux

MICHAEL HOLMAN: A lot of English kids were coming over at that time. They knew that New York was really the place.

JEFFREY LEE PIERCE (The Gun Club singer): Synthesizer bands from England . . . are taking over the world. I think generally most English music of this period is some of the worst stuff I've ever heard . . . It's like muzak . . . A lot of 'em sound like Genesis. (*East Village Eye*, July 1982)

LYDIA LUNCH: The Human League – vomitorium!

THURSTON MOORE (Sonic Youth guitarist/Noise Fest organizer): I think we rebel against hi-tech in the sense that it represents itself as a utopia. (*NME*, 24 November 1984)

LYDIA LUNCH: All the No Wave bands just self-destructed . . . Most people had no tolerance for it until it was over . . . Swans and Sonic Youth are the end of this particular breed of music, and from that end will sprout something else. (*NME*, 24 November 1984)

LUC SANTE (writer): I'm looking at the poster for the Noise Fest that occupied White Columns, on far west Spring Street, for nine evenings in June 1981 . . . Not all the names are dissolved in the mists of time (Glenn Branca, Elliot Sharp) or should be (Ut, Y Pants), but the only group that is still a going concern after 19 years . . . is Sonic Youth. (*Village Voice*, 28 June 2000)

THURSTON MOORE: [Noise Fest] was a watermark event because it took place at a time when the No Wave was gone and nobody knew each other. There had been no incestuousness at all. Nobody played together. (*Forced Exposure*, Summer 1985)

LUC SANTE: I didn't think of it as an epochal event, and I don't think my friends did, either. For several reasons: it was heavily identified with a certain strain that had to do with Rhys Chatham and Glenn Branca, came out of the Kitchen – very arty, sort of academic, and definitely not funky . . . The hot thing for us was the concurrent jazz–post-punk interface. We were friends with sundry Lounge Lizards, also went to see – and dance to! – Luther Thomas's Dizazz, Oliver Lake's Jump Up, Joe Bowie's group Defunkt, the great James Blood Ulmer, and bubbling along at a pre-fame simmer, Jean-Michel Basquiat's Gray. This was the future, as far as I was concerned then. It was angular and weird and spiky, and it gave up the funk, and of course it was racially mixed – not something you could say about the Noise Fest. What now gets called 'mutant disco' was a potent formula: *anything at all* plus disco bottom. Much of the Noise Fest stuff, by contrast, seemed arid and theoretical and unsexy.

MICHAEL GIRA (Swans singer): The best rock 'n' roll for me is like a big enema . . . Our music should be as physical and unavoidable as possible . . . I like anything that seems to nullify the sense of being . . . Or nullify consciousness. (*East Village Eye*, March 1983)

End of an Era

JAMES CHANCE: The whole scene in the early eighties really revolved around live music – everybody went to see bands – and somewhere around 1984 that whole era of the mega nightclub started up, where music was just one minor element.

RENEE SCROGGINS: Between word-of-mouth, and coverage by publications like the *Soho Weekly News*, *NY Rocker*, *East Village Eye*, and the European press in the early '80s, it was relatively easy to develop a local audience and a reputation for your work. But little by little all these things started to disappear . . . For a long time in the mid-'80s, only Danceteria and the Roxy were still offering live dance-funk now and then. (*Dance Music Report*, September 1990)

STEVE MAAS: I went into it as a fantasy, never expected it to make money. When the Mudd did become successful I didn't have the restaurateur's skills that are essential to running any kind of operation . . . My fantasy went out the window. (*East Village Eye*, November 1983)

JAMES CHANCE: The whole club scene became controlled by people who had a very different sensibility – much more mainstream. And it also started atomizing into little scenes based around one style of music.

ANN MAGNUSON: It was a really exciting time . . . before the big money popped in. Jean-Michel did a show in Italy and got an Armani suit and all this money falling out of his pockets. Then Keith Haring started getting really successful, and Andy Warhol started sniffing around. Madonna showed up a few years later.

GARY INDIANA: There was an incredible mix of film-makers, musicians, poets, all this crossbreeding of creative practices, but at a certain moment people began specializing. They began narrowing their field of interest to a specific thing they were going to make a career with. Reagan came in and everyone had to make money. You had to focus, you couldn't be all over the map any more.

ANN MAGNUSON: If you look back at it just as a series of parties, it does seem rather frivolous. But if you see it as people who loved each other, who were sharing their life energies, it was a celebration. They just wanted to live to the max, every second. There were some people who got into heavy drugs, but it was not about being a junkie and acting supercool. It was about joy. And when AIDS started picking everybody off one by one, it became obvious to me that it was about life. Keith Haring's paintings in particular really exemplify that energy – that radiant baby image of his. This was not that *Bright Lights Big City* version of New York in the eighties: stockbrokers running around doing cocaine and chasing models. This was about people who had to leave where they came from originally to come to New York . . . or die. Who had to create art or die.

21

NEW GOLD DREAMS 81–82–83–84: The Peak and Fall of New Pop

The Associates. Altered Images. Simple Minds. Haircut 100. Orange Juice.
Duran Duran. The Eurythmics. The Thompson Twins. Wham!. Culture Club. ABC.
The Human League. Scritti Politti.

The true sign that you're living through a golden age is the feeling that it's never going to end. There seems to be no earthly reason why it should stop. It's an illusion, of course, like the first swoony rush of falling in love. But that's how it felt to be young and British and besotted with pop music in the early eighties.

No longer wishful thinking on the part of overexcited journalists, New Pop was reality, rampaging over the surfaces of everyday life in a way that had been unthinkable only a year earlier. At some point between the winter of 1980, when Adam & The Ants rose unexpectedly from the cult netherworld, and Christmas 1981, when The Human League's 'Don't You Want Me' was number 1 for five full weeks, it felt as if an invisible switch had been pulled and the floodgates opened to irrigate the charts with a rejuvenating gush of colour, exuberance and optimism. By early 1982, it looked like the old guard of stodgy seventies leftovers and stale MOR had been decisively ousted, as a horde of fresh-faced pretenders took possession of the mainstream: Altered Images, Haircut 100, The Associates, Soft Cell, Depeche Mode, ABC, Bow Wow Wow, The Teardrop Explodes, Japan, Funboy Three, New Order . . .

To varying degrees, all these groups grasped the importance of image, its power to seduce and motivate. And they all coated their music in a patina of commercial gloss, some of them pursuing a strategy of entry-ism (a.k.a. 'the sugared pill'), while others simply revelled in sonic luxury for the sheer glam thrill of it. For some observers at the time, New

Pop's absence of blatant, punk-style gestures of threat or protest, its 'retreat' from post-punk's overt experimentalism and agit-prop, made it merely escapist. But it's simply inaccurate to characterize New Pop, as some histories of the period have done, as a 'like-punk-never-happened' scenario. Almost all of the groups mentioned above had some kind of connection to punk. Most believed they were honouring or furthering some of punk's original mission, albeit in a much transformed context. New Pop was about making the best of what was inevitable – synths and drum machines, video, the return of glamour. Colour, dance, fun and style were sanctioned as both strategically necessary (the terms of entry into pop) and pleasurable (now acceptable with the rejection of post-punk's guilt-racked puritanism).

If I had to pick one group that fulfilled the New Pop dream of a chart-busting music that combined pop's flash with post-punk's perplexity, it would be The Associates. Fittingly, their all-too-brief reign as chart stars – just nine months, February to September 1982 – coincided with New Pop's zenith. At the start of 1982, they surely seemed like unlikely contenders. The gambit of releasing six singles in swift succession during 1981 had earned them some positive critical attention but not one of their indie releases dented the charts. Still, Billy MacKenzie and Alan Rankine had several aces up their sleeves, most notably an old song called 'Party Fears Two', which became their first single after signing a new deal with a major label, WEA.

A measure of The Associates' low profile was that when they appeared to mime 'Party Fears Two' on *Top of the Pops* in February 1982 they were totally unknown to most viewers. This was the first time I even *heard* The Associates' music, and consequently was one of the four or five true pop epiphanies of my life. The sunshafts-peeking-through-clouds intro; the blithe, bittersweet piano refrain; the cold smoulder of Billy's voice; the mysterious lyrics (fractured snapshots of a break-up in progress?); the celestial cloisters of double-tracked MacKenzie harmonies at the end . . . But what really brought me to the brink of a swoon was the way Billy *moved* (at one point he sashayed *backwards*!); the impossible panache of the man. It was one of those moments when you exhale sheer awe.

That *TOTP* appearance transfixed many other people, too: 'Party Fears' shot straight to number 9 the following week. It lingered in the Top 10 long enough to occasion another delicious TV performance, with the group resurrecting the absurdist spirit of their heroes Roxy Music and Sparks. 'I came on in a white fencing suit, playing a banjo, done up like a Samurai, chopsticks stuck in my hair,' chuckles Rankine.

All zinging Nordic Chic guitar and nervous, scurrying disco bass, The Associates' second hit, 'Club Country', featured Billy's singing at its most soaring and searing. The lyrics offered a blistering rebuke to the poseurs of New Romanticism, homing right in on the hollow heart of the in-crowd: 'If we stick around/We're sure to be looked down upon'. 'Bill and I had been down to Blitz and Billy's and the Beat Route, all those places,' recalls Rankine. In one sense, MacKenzie felt at home there, because of the dandy neo-glam vibe of androgyny and ambiguity. 'But by the same token Bill could see the complete falsehood of a lot of it.' The *TOTP* appearance for 'Club Country' was even more playfully subversive than 'Party Fears Two' – Rankine strummed a chocolate guitar (specially made by Harrods for £600) which he fed to the studio audience during the song's second verse.

A similar lunatic spirit of largesse and luxury suffused *Sulk*, The Associates' second 'proper' album. Saturated with textures, overdubbed to the hilt, obsessively mixed, overwrought in both the emotional and metalwork senses, *Sulk* sounds sumptuous. 'When I was younger I went into my mother's sewing box, and beneath the balls of ordinary red or black or white thread, there'd be this thick, luxuriant embroidery thread,' says Rankine. 'Purples, turquoises, lapis lazuli colours. That's what I wanted sound-wise for *Sulk* – that vibrancy, that luxuriance of colour.'

After the perversely slight opening instrumental 'Arrogance Gave Him Up', *Sulk* really starts with 'No' – a tormented ballad with a stately Russian melody and helium-high backing vocals oozing like ghostly mist. Another peak is the second side's 'Skipping'. All frisky stealth, anxious euphoria and other unclassifiable emotions, the song contains MacKenzie's most out-there vocal performance, along with some of the duo's daftest lyrics – like prize couplet 'Ripping ropes from the Belgian Wharf's/Breathless beauxillous griffin once removed seemed dwarfed'. The words, mostly penned by MacKenzie, are absurd and portentous throughout *Sulk*, yet utterly right, with a cinematic vividness that burns into your mind's eye: 'Tear a strip from your dress/Wrap my arms in it' ('No'); 'Even a slight remark makes no sense and turns to shark' ('Party Fears Two').

Released in May 1982, *Sulk* was fruity as fuck – overripe, bruised, a headswirl of intoxicating sensations. The Associates injected all the voluptuous disorientation of psychedelic experience into pop. MacKenzie described the *Sulk* sound as 'Abba on acid'. Says Rankine, 'Bill was always out on a limb, telling the producer Mike Hedges to "make it sound like Egypt", "make it sound like it's inside a sarcophagus", "make it sound like grass".' Like The Beatles *circa* 'I Am the Walrus' or Brian Wilson with *Smile*, the group used all kinds of found sounds and scrap-metal percussion. The snap-crackle-pop of John Murphy's firework drums threaded the album. 'On a lot of *Sulk* we removed the tom-toms and remade John's kit entirely out of snare drums,' recalls Rankine. 'It made the whole record sound really explosive.'

Throughout the recording process, Mackenzie implored Hedges to 'make it sound expensive'. The imagery carried through to the third Associates hit of 1982, '18 Carat Love Affair', from its title to the picture on the sleeve: Billy, naked, lies face down on a marble floor, while pearls and precious stones are poured over his body by a beautiful girl clad in headscarf and Burberry raincoat. With a gloriously over-the-top cover of Diana Ross's 'Love Hangover' as its other A-side, it was a surprise when '18 Carat Love Affair' reached only number 21 in the charts. Already it felt like the window of opportunity that had briefly allowed freaks like MacKenzie and Rankine into the mainstream was starting to close.

At this point, a perverse self-destructive instinct seemed to grip MacKenzie, as though he subconsciously sensed that Pop was turning against them. On the eve of a major tour, he bailed out – a combination of stage-fright, perfectionism (the band weren't rehearsed enough, he felt), and terror of being sucked into the rockbiz machine. Rankine, eager to consolidate their UK success and break America (where huge sums were being offered by labels like Sire), was furious, and quit the band in October 1982. Thereafter, The Associates, effectively a solo Billy Mackenzie vehicle, continued fitfully, but without Rankine (not so much the Eno to Billy's Ferry as the entire Roxy band) the chemistry was gone. Snatching defeat from the jaws of triumph, The Associates joined the pantheon of great should-have-beens of British pop.

Two other Scottish groups, Altered Images and Simple Minds, played large roles in New Pop's wonder year. In the winter of 1981, Altered Images' 'Happy Birthday' sold like bottled sunshine, bouncing and frisking its way to number 2. From its sparkly guitars, shimmering xylophone pulse and tumbly drums, to Clare Grogan's giddy yelping glee and the sleek sheen of Martin Rushent's production, Altered Images' pop was fizzy and irresistible like lemonade. Already known for her role as a Scottish schoolgirl in the cult movie *Gregory's Girl*, Grogan captivated the nation with her odd blend of coquette and naïf. Or half the nation, at least – others found her irritating, the incarnation of everything they found frivolous and flimsy about New Pop.

Before Rushent sprinkled his stardust over their records, though, Altered Images had been a bona fide post-punk band – sort of Banshees-lite. Indeed Siouxsie & Co. took the group under their wing: Altered Images supported them on tour, and Steve Severin produced most of their debut album, including the single 'Dead Pop Stars' – a sinister tune about cruelly fickle teenyboppers tearing down the posters of last year's idols. Even with the Rushent-produced hits, if you listen deeper than the chrome surface, you'll find that the inner mechanisms of the music, its moving parts, are organized similarly to groups like Wire, Josef K, even Joy Division. The scratchy guitar figure on 'I Could Be Happy' and the twinkle-drone bassline of 'See Those Eyes' sound remarkably close to Barney Sumner's and Peter Hook's playing. Both songs are candygirl cousins to 'Ceremony' and 'Temptation', the contemporaneous hits by New Order. More sugary than the Manchester band, for sure, but the sweetness of the Altered Images singles came alloyed with a poignant fragility.

As different from Grogan and her boys as is imaginable, Simple Minds seemed at first glance to be unlikely participants in the New Pop explosion. In their early days, they came across as an art-rock throwback thinly disguised as New Wave. Simple Minds' sound was further confused by its incongruous rhythmic base, rooted in Eurodisco. This strange mixture produced one outright masterpiece, 1980's panoramic/cinematic *Empires and Dance*. Later singles, like 'Love Song' and 'Sweat in Bullet', were propulsive and almost funky, but the epic bluster of their music – all crashing drums and strident vocals that gazed into the far distance – seemed destined for arenas rather than discotheques.

And then something changed. 'Promised You a Miracle' was the first time Simple Minds intentionally made a single, as opposed to an album track that was later selected as a single. And this shifted their whole mindset from prog to pop. Simple Minds caught a lighter tone; guitars took a backseat to glinting synths; the music seemed to open up and breathe. As singer Jim Kerr noted at the time, for the first time Simple Minds sounded 'right' on the radio. 'Promised You a Miracle' reached number 13 in the late spring of 1982. During the song's slow fade – nearly two minutes in length, it's like the glorious sunset to a perfect day – Kerr's repeated rejoicing cries that 'everything is possible' capture the all-gates-open, anything-can-happen feeling of the New Pop moment. As did the album's title: *New Gold Dream (81–82–83–84)*. Even more ardent and exultant, 'Glittering Prize' was another big hit. For a brief moment, Simple Minds hovered in shimmering equipoise between pop and rock.

Meanwhile, Orange Juice seethed on the sidelines as their Scottish contemporaries made the charts their home. By the end of 1981, they had made the major-label plunge. Their Polydor debut album, *You Can't Hide Your Love Forever*, offered a polished version of their classic Postcard sound, but was already behind the pop times by its February 1982 release. Meanwhile, an English group called Haircut 100 had become huge stars with a sound/look suspiciously close to Orange Juice's. 'I *know* that Haircut 100 got a lot of their image ideas from us,' says Edwyn Collins, still aggrieved after all these years. 'I've got pictures of James Kirk, our guitarist, wearing Aran sweaters like Haircut wore on their album cover.' Haircut 100 had the choppy pop-funk sound, the clean-cut image, the fresh-faced aura. His chipmunk smile peeking out between rosy cheeks, Nick Heyward exuded innocuousness with just a twinkle of sauciness in the eyes. He even sang like a slightly more sure-of-pitch version of Collins, while song titles like 'Favourite Shirts', 'Lemon Firebrigade' and 'Love's Got Me in Triangles' had something of Orange Juice's arch faux-naïvety. But Haircut 100's high-calibre musicianship was far slicker. Listening to the snazzy-jazzy horns and rippling congas all over their *Pelican West* album, you could tell the band had grown up on Steely Dan and Average White Band, not *Live 1969* and Subway Sect.

Orange Juice could feel their momentum ebbing; their peers were leaving them behind. It was time to get serious, to go for pop's jugular. Edwyn Collins instigated a purge of 'unprofessional elements' – undermotivated dreamer James Kirk, plus Steven Daly (who was fired for siding with Kirk). A new, 'tight' Orange Juice was formulated, with Zimbabwean Zeke Manyika as drummer and ex-Josef K guitarist Malcolm Ross recruited. The new hardheaded approached produced three gorgeous singles: a cover of Al Green's 'L.O.V.E.' (sheer vocal hubris on Collins' part); the squelchy jangle-funk of 'Rip It Up'; and the

Philly-flavoured 'Flesh of My Flesh'. 'Rip It Up' was the only one that made the charts, but it hit really big: number 8 in the spring of 1983. Orange Juice were finally where they wanted to be.

The song was the perfect expression of Collins' new ideal for Orange Juice: 'a sophisticated amateurism' that wasn't 'sloppy' but also didn't 'place slickness as the ultimate virtue'. The 'sophisticated' part of the equation came through with the record's state-of-the-art eighties dance groove, which pivoted around a slippery bassline created using the Roland 303 – a recently invented machine that later became synonymous with the signature sound of acid house. The 'amateurism' survived in Collins' charmingly fallible vocals and the song's witty homage to the original DIY catalyst, *Spiral Scratch*: Collins followed the couplet 'You know the scene it's very hum-drum/And my favourite song's entitled "Boredom"' with a two-note guitar riff that copied Pete Shelley's solo on that very song.

Beyond its Buzzcocks tribute, 'Rip It Up' was classic Orange Juice meta-pop – the title echoed the fifties rock 'n' roll classic, while the chorus, 'Rip it up and start again', and reference to the scene having become 'hum-drum' obliquely indicted the state of pop. In early 1983, when Orange Juice finally joined the chart party, there was already a dawning sense that New Pop had gone wrong. The bright sparks who had pioneered the whole thing, like The Associates and Soft Cell, were being gradually displaced by opportunists who weren't as ideas or ideals driven, who had only the most tenuous connections to punk. Latching on to the surface elements of New Pop – the glossy, inventive videos, the deluxe production, the gender-bending and dressing up – the clones and careerists began to take over. This was especially the case internationally. In the States, 1983 was the year New Pop broke: ABC, The Human League and Soft Cell had all scored hits early on, but it was the second wave of New Pop – Duran Duran, The Eurythmics, Culture Club, The Thompson Twins, Wham! – who hit the American jackpot.

At the height of their success, Duran Duran were exactly the sort of group who made veterans of 1977 complain, 'It's like punk never happened.' But in fact they had come up through the same Birmingham scene as Swell Maps, and their initial musical concept was about as postpunk as could be imagined: Sex Pistols meets Chic. Soon they became the key figures in Birmingham's New Romantic scene, centred on the club Barbarella's. Like their London contemporaries Visage, they made their mark by harnessing the power of video: first with 'Girls on Film' (semi-naked fashion models cavorting in a wrestling ring) and then with a series of glitzy promos for the singles off their second album *Rio*. Persuading their record company to cough up funds for a working holiday in Sri Lanka, Duran flew out with director Russell Mulcahy in August 1982 and shot three videos full of tropical backdrops and more scantily clad girls. The blend of vapid exoticism and Pirelli calendar eroticism propelled 'Hungry Like a Wolf', 'Rio' and 'Save a Prayer' into heavy rotation on the fledgling MTV. The video for 'Rio' especially defined Duran's new, brazenly aspirational image: the band posing on a yacht, surrounded by models who could have come straight from the covers of the first five classic Roxy Music albums. By this point, Duran had traded their flouncy New Romantic look for a more Bryan Ferry-like jet-set image – jackets by Anthony Price, rolled at the sleeves. By 1983, they were global megastars. Musically, they shed any lingering synthpop Futurist trappings in favour of straightforward catchiness (as on their first number 1, 'Is There Something I Should Know') and a stiff-jointed funk-rock. They still entertained some higher ambitions, though, which leaked out in the ripe gibberish of Simon Le Bon's lyrics, the increasingly overblown videos, and the artistic affectations of keyboardist Nick Rhodes, who idolized Japan's David Sylvian and followed the dandy dilettante's lead by dabbling in Polaroid art.

Even more than Duran, The Thompson Twins were a classic example of a group who went through a drastic remodelling process to emerge as shiny New Popsters. In 1981 they were post-punk johnny-come-latelys located somewhere between Scritti and Pigbag: a seven-strong collective heavily into percussion and personal politics. At one gig that year, singer Tom Bailey informed the audience that the group had been forced to cover up some sexist murals in the venue because The Thompson Twins 'could never perform where such materials were on show'. Something of that earnest vibe endured even after the group contracted to a pop-oriented trio and Bailey started talking about how they were into the idea of making disposable music. The gender/racial balance was impeccable: one white male (Bailey), one black male (Joe Leeway), one white female (Alannah Currie, who had originally been inspired to buy a sax after seeing The Pop Group). In their cartoony videos, the threesome's oddly asexual charisma put you in mind of the dungaree-clad presenters on seventies TV-for-toddlers. Tunes like 'Hold Me Now' and 'Love on Your Side' lingered in the brain like tapeworms. By 1984's *Into the Gap*, The

Thompson Twins' 'monstrously big turnover internationally' made them the Burger King of pop: 'A multinational corporation is exactly what we are . . . bigger than a lot of the companies that are quoted on the Stock Exchange,' said Bailey. What BEF had parodied with a knowing socialist wink, The Thompson Twins became for real.

The Eurythmics weren't post-punks turned popsters, but industry veterans who had paid their dues and built their skills the old-fashioned way. Annie Lennox and Dave Stewart's dogged slog to the top of the charts long predated punk. An accomplished guitarist and former acid casualty, Stewart had joined a band called Longdancer in 1969 (they eventually signed to Elton John's Rocket label). Lennox's commanding vocals had more in common with Scottish blues-rocker Maggie Bell than New Popsters like Clare Grogan. Before forming The Eurythmics, the pair had briefly tasted chart success in 1979 in a sixties-styled guitar-pop band called The Tourists. When that petered out, they remade themselves into an electronic duo. After briefly flirting with the experimental vanguard (the debut Eurythmics album, *In the Garden*, featured Can's Holger Czukay and DAF's Robert Gorl), they quickly latched on to New Pop. On massive hits like 'Sweet Dreams (Are Made of This)', the sound and image were a canny composite: Grace Jones (the domineering vocals, the cropped haircut, the mannish build) meets Kraftwerk (the icy electronics, the cyborg aura). The video for 'Who's That Girl?' cleverly turned Bowie's gender-bent 'Boys Keep Swinging' inside out, with Lennox playing both male and female roles (at one point, her male and female personae kiss) while the song's reference to 'the language of love' dimly echoed Scritti's own echoes of Barthes' *A Lover's Discourse*.

Underneath the modish veneer of borrowed cool, though, The Eurythmics' success depended on thoroughly traditional strengths: Stewart's songcraft and the soul-power of Lennox's voice. The *Sweet Dreams* album even featured a cover of the Sam & Dave tune 'Wrap It Up'. 'The music's timeless, you see,' Stewart told *Rolling Stone*. 'That's why we don't say we're part of this new English pop invasion. We just say we're in a continuum of what we've been doin' for ages. That's why on *The Whistle Test* . . . they couldn't really call us a synthpop duo, when we're standin' there with eight gospel singers, a grand piano and an acoustic guitar. That could have been in 1971 – or it could be 1986.' In this respect, The Eurythmics resembled Paul Young, another music-biz veteran (he'd toiled for years in the retro-soul troupe Q-Tips) who passed for New Pop by singing songs with Scritti-esque titles like 'Sex' and daubing Japan-style fretless bass all over recordings like his number I smash version of Marvin Gaye's 'Wherever I Lay My Hat (That's My Home)'. Young, Lennox and Stewart (and subsequent horrors such as Howard Jones) reduced New Pop to reformism – pop that was improved and improving, *all grown up*.

The success of blue-eyed Brit soulsters like Young and Lennox made sense in a way, because the back story to New Pop was actually a black story. African-American innovations in rhythm, production and arrangement (Chic, P-Funk, the Michael Jackson/Quincy Jones sound, the New York electro and synth-funk of the early eighties) had been assimilated by the perennially quicker-off-the-mark Brits and then exported back to white America. That's why the American press heralded the 1983 breakthrough of what they called 'New Music' as the 'Second British Invasion' – a repeat of what had happened in the sixties, when The Beatles, the Stones, The Kinks *et al.* sold their version of rhythm and blues to white American teenagers. Confusing the analogy slightly, though, was the fact that many of the Second British Invasion groups didn't just borrow from contemporary black music; they also ransacked soul from the sixties and seventies. Wham! and Culture Club were the classic examples of this merger of retro and modern.

Of all the New Pop groups, Wham! had the least investment in punk: George Michael and Andrew Ridgely were basically soul-boys. After two brashly likeable hit singles, 'Wham Rap' and 'Young Guns (Go For It)', they dominated the summer of 1983 with *Make It Big!* and the massive UK hits 'Bad Boys' and 'Club Tropicana' – anthems of guilt-free hedonism for the aspirational youth of Southern England and the perfect soundtrack to inaugurate Margaret Thatcher's second term (she was re-elected that June). Wham! then cleaned up in America with a series of Motown-recycling singles like 'Wake Me up before You Go Go' and 'I'm Your Man'.

At least Culture Club were eclectic in their derivativeness, mashing together Motown, the Philly sound and lovers' rock. 'Plagiarism is one of my favourite words,' boasted Boy George. 'Culture Club is the most sincere form of plagiarism in modern music – we just do it better than most.' In another interview, he described himself as 'not a great singer: I'm a vocalist and a copyist . . . I can copy and adapt.' And so 'Church of the Poisoned Mind' rehashed the sixties soul stomp-beat; 'Time' harked back to Curtis Mayfield and The Detroit Spinners; and the light reggae of 'Do You Really Want to Hurt Me' was Sugar Minott with one or two extra spoonfuls. What made such dilute fare so massively successful was Boy George's charm and wit, plus the novelty factor of his appearance – a cannily desexualized version of drag that mixed a hint of edge with a heap of innocuousness. Chubby and cuddly, androgynous George was an object of affection rather than desire. If he was subversive, George claimed, it wasn't because he was gay (usually coy about his leanings back then, at his most candid he admitted to being 'bisexual') but because he was effeminate.

Taking that teenybop tradition of pretty-boy idols one step further, Boy George was irresistibly telegenic. Like the original British Invasion bands, the New Pop groups were attuned to style: many had been to art college; even those who hadn't usually possessed a glam-assimilated visual literacy that simply wasn't the norm in America. Along with clothes, stage presentation and record packaging, they now had the still relatively virgin form of the music video in which to express this image flair. New Pop conveniently coincided with the launch of MTV. American rock 'n' pop videos were both far less plentiful and markedly inferior to the British efforts; few domestic groups had yet grasped either the artistic or promotional potential of the format. So in 1983 MTV's 'treasonous' role in the Second British Invasion was to open the floodgates for 'English haircut bands' (the dismissive term used by American heartland rockers). As radio followed MTV's lead and switched to a 'New Music' format, the nativists and synthphobes began to feel utterly swamped by all this newfangled, foreign music. In 1983 British groups grabbed a 35 per cent share of the *Billboard* singles and albums charts; at one point in the summer, six of the Top 10 singles were of UK origin. Not everybody responded with horror, of course. Media commentators excited by the commotion, record-biz figures overjoyed at rising sales after several years of industry slump, and – not least – the millions of young American who bought the records and watched MTV for hours on end, all praised the Second British Invasion for bringing colour and energy back to pop music. *Rolling Stone* did an 'England Swings' special issue, hailing 1983 as 'the greatest year for rock since 1977', and *Newsweek* put gender-benders Annie Lennox and Boy George on its front cover in January 1984.

However, while the Durans and Wham!s were doing wonders for Britain's balance of trade, the original instigators of New Pop all seemed

'Never Cry Wolf' · Greider on George McGovern · Sci-Fi Classic

Rolli*ne*

SPECIAL ISSUE!

ENGLAND SWINGS

Great Britain invades America's music and style. Again.

Culture Club's Boy George

Boy George represents the Second British Invasion, a.k.a. New Pop, on the cover of *Rolling Stone*, 10 November 1983

to be losing their way. The victory of Thatcher in the June 1983 General Election was a turning point, especially for bands from the North, where mass unemployment had the most devastating effect. For many, the first Conservative term of office had seemed like a fluke. But when Thatcher was resoundingly re-elected, it became clear that the old post-war consensus about the Welfare State and interventionist government (propping up ailing industries in order to preserve jobs) had evaporated. A hefty portion of the population – enough to secure Thatcher her election win – clearly didn't give a shit about the unemployed.

After touring the world as a sixteen-piece band, ABC returned home to find Sheffield decimated by unemployment and heroin. Suddenly the aspirational imagery they'd been using (the ad for the single 'All of My Heart' depicted the group as country squires in tweed jackets and waistcoats, half-cocked shotguns in the crooks of their arms) seemed in questionable taste. The sonic opulence that only a year before had been a striking gesture was now the norm: Spandau Ballet aped 'All of My Heart' with the slick schlock of 'True' and topped the charts. 'The record company wanted us to make five more *Lexicon of Love*s, but everywhere we looked there were bands copying moves we'd done,' recalls Martin Fry. Pangs of social conscience, unwillingness to repeat a successful formula, a desire to leave their imitators for dust: all these combined to convince ABC to make a total career swerve. Instead of *Lexicon Part 2*, they made *Beauty Stab*: a hard, stripped-down sound with electric guitar at its centre, along with overtly political lyrics. 'With *Beauty Stab*, we probably wanted to make a record like Gang of Four, really,' says Fry. 'It's a protest album. You've had the Technicolor widescreen with *Lexicon*, now it's back to Sheffield black-and-white documentary style.' (Ironically, at this very moment, Gang of Four were desperately trying to gloss *their* sound ABC-style with the disastrous *Hard*.)

Being incurably meta, ABC trumpeted their new direction with the single 'That Was Then, This Is Now'. It reached number 18, then plummeted; the album fared no better. Fans were confused by the new 'raw' and 'live' sound. *Beauty Stab*'s ugly oil painting cover of a matador fighting a bull gave the impression of a band that didn't really know what it was doing. Inside, unwieldy protest songs like 'King Money' and 'United Kingdom' sounded glib and phoney because Fry overdid the *Lexicon*-style wordplay: 'This busted, rusted, upper-crusted, bankrupted, done and dusted, no-man-to-be-trusted United Kingdom'. The group that had once hired Trevor Horn to make their records sound exorbitant now declared, 'If your king is money, then I feel sorry for you.' In interviews Fry did some pretty undignified backsliding, telling *NME* that 'the way I see the world is very different from that quasi-Las Vegas/tuxedo period before', and claiming to have hung up his gold lamé suit. 'There is too much gloss, too much technique in record making now,' he declared.

'The idea of wanting to sound like you were produced by Quincy Jones is defunct.'

ABC's Sheffield neighbours Heaven 17 and The Human League were also hit hard by what happened to their once-prosperous home town. Heaven 17's mini-*Beauty Stab* was 'Crushed by the Wheels of Industry', an exciting slice of electro-Constructivist dance pop and by far the best thing on their second album, *The Luxury Gap*. They'd finally become pop stars, but at a terrible cost: their breakthrough single, 'Temptation', owed too much of its impact to the hired firepower of soul singer Carole Kenyon (1983 was the year of the obligatory black backing singer), and ultimately just seemed part of the lavish bombast of the times. By this point, the grand plans for BEF had largely faded away, with most of Ware and Marsh's energy going into sustaining Heaven 17 as a conventionally successful pop group.

The Human League, meanwhile, were doubly tormented – first by the challenge of how to follow up a mega-success without repeating yourself, and second by the sudden pricking of conscience and consciousness. As early as the end of 1982, Phil Oakey talked about how the New Poptimism was out of step with political reality. Perversely, or perhaps perceptively, he now wanted to go in the opposite direction, to make The Human League less like Abba and more like . . . Pink Floyd: a band of substance, dealing with serious issues, not silly love songs. 'I'd like to represent the world and point out in simple sentences what's right and what's wrong,' Oakey declared earnestly. The spur for this 'rockist' attitude shift wasn't so much Thatcher-induced economic blight, though, as the massacres of Palestinian refugees in the Lebanon. 'I was baffled,' Oakey says now. 'They came on TV and told you something really incredible and horrible, and they didn't say what you could do about it. Here are these people, in these camps, and the Israelis just stood there while the Christian militia, who are supposed to be Christian, went in and shot women and children. Next news item. And you sit there and think, Do we vote for somebody? Do we send money?' The song spawned by Oakey's sense of paralysis, 'The Lebanon', finally appeared as a single in May 1984 – an advance herald for *Hysteria*, the group's disappointing (and Rushent-free) sequel to *Dare*. Like ABC's 'That Was Then', the single broke with The Human League's classic sound and 'no standard instrumentation' mission statement – it featured electric guitar prominently. And just like ABC's single, it didn't even make the Top 10.

416

Aesthetic and commercial failures, maybe, but 'The Lebanon' and *Beauty Stab* were prophetic gestures. Those whose senses were acute (like Fry and Oakey) could smell it on the breeze: the return of rock. Down in the various indie undergrounds, you could see the early stirrings of a resurgence taking shape. All those discredited, pensioned-off concepts (authenticity, rebellion, community, transgression, resistance), all those outmoded, laughable sounds (distorted electric guitar, the raw-throated snarl), were biding their time, lurking and waiting to mount a comeback.

Just about the first post-punk musician to start talking about pop as the way forward, Green Gartside was just about the last to become a genuine pop star. By 1983, though, he was making concerted moves in the right direction: he'd signed to Virgin and severed the last links to the old squatland Scritti. His new cohorts were drummer Fred Maher and keyboardist/programmer David Gamson, New York musicians with the technical skills to help Green build the chart-competitive music he desired.

Inspired by New York's synth-funk and electro, Green and his dream team forged precision-tooled dance pop, all bright, chattering sequencer-riffs and ultra-crisp Linn beats. Relying heavily on the Fairlight and Synclavier samplers, the production was pointillist, a mosaic of hyper-syncopations and micro-rhythmic intricacies. 'We used to talk about it being like a Swiss watch,' Green recalled. 'Wood Beez (Pray Like Aretha Franklin)', the first single from this third Scritti Politti, was released in early 1984 and became the UK Top 10 hit Green had craved for so long.

'Wood Beez' and its even more stunning follow up 'Absolute' (another substantial hit) were still haunted by the old Scritti's melodic strangeness, still audibly relatives of 'PAs' and 'Skank Bloc Bologna'. But the sound of the records was slick, tough and absolutely contemporary. Green had also finally worked out a way of writing lyrics that could pass for a normal love song. On closer inspection, though, they turned out to be pretzels of contradiction, with an aporia (the post-structuralist term for voids in the fabric of meaning) lurking in the centre of every twist of language – sweet nothings that could wreck your heart.

'A Little Knowledge', for instance, was a love song about the impossibility of love: 'Now I know to love you is not to know you'. 'Wood Beez' reprised the 'Faithless' idea of losing belief but gaining soul: 'Each time I go to bed/I pray like Aretha Franklin'. For the secular Green, 'soul' signified the sweet ache of an emptiness that was paradoxically also a fullness. In interviews he described his pop songs as 'hymns for agnostics, for the disillusioned like myself'; they were also paeans to the quasireligious power of pop music, tributes that put into practice what they preached. Scritti's biggest UK single, the number 6 hit 'The Word Girl', remade 'The "Sweetest Girl"' as Lacanian lovers' rock (a page fragment from the French psychoanalyst's *Ecrits* was reproduced on the twelve-inch single's cover). The chorus, 'How your flesh and blood became the word', was both a question and an expression of wonder. Green, as always, was fascinated by the process in which an ordinary, everyday woman with flaws became idealized into a figment of the male romantic imagination ('a name for what you lose when it was never yours'), a de-realized fetish object.

The new Scritti sound – all those dazzling surfaces – paralleled the way Green's oddly depthless lyrics worked: the lover's discourse as a lexical maze, a chain of foolishness along which desire traverses endlessly, looking to heal the primal wound of lack at the heart of being. Inspired by Michael Jackson, Green developed an eerie falsetto that sounded freakishly ethereal, beyond gender. This high, almost varispeeded voice suited the hall-of-mirrors sound of songs like 'Absolute' and 'Hypnotize': perfect reflective surfaces for Green's narcissism. It's no coincidence that the inner sleeve to the album *Cupid & Psyche 85* shows the immaculately groomed Green, Gamson and Maher in a deluxe men's bathroom, staring into a mirror; Gamson and Maher are looking at Green's reflection, but the singer has admiring eyes only for himself.

Cupid & Psyche 85 finally fulfilled Green's tall talk of the past several years. Not only was it immensely successful, but it was true pop deconstruction to bring a smile to Jacques Derrida's *visage*. 'When I met Derrida, he told me what I was doing was part of the same project of undoing and unsettling that he's engaged in,' Green recalled in a 1988 interview with me, referring to a dinner with the philosopher arranged by French radio. And yet one has to wonder to what extent the casual pop consumers who bought *Cupid* actually picked up on the subtle subversions woven inside the songs.

In America, the big hit was the brashly euphoric 'Perfect Way', which peaked at number 11 in Billboard. Manager Bob Last recalls the exhilaration of that point in 1985 when Scritti finally 'achieved this high-gloss sound that could penetrate mainstream American radio'. Indeed, the *Cupid* sound was so far ahead of the game that it influenced the next wave of mid-eighties black pop – records like Janet Jackson's *Control*. Yet the vast majority of Scritti's American audience – who weren't familiar with the back story of the band's tortuous journey towards pop – most likely looked at the video for 'Perfect Way' and saw Green as just another fey, fair-haired pretty-boy from the UK. On American radio stations, surrounded by what Green called 'the bright, brittle, endless barrage' of mid-eighties pop-funk, it was hard to distinguish 'Perfect Way' from any of the other cosmetically perfected, ultra-commercial records of that era. Outside the context of indieland's frugal means, the expensiveness of the sound didn't carry any real resonance. Green angrily dismissed 'any attempts to tie it to Thatcherism' as 'nonsense', but it was hard to see how it could be read in any other terms than straightforward 'upward mobility', especially when you were faced with the beautiful models used in 'The Word Girl' video and the fact that Green himself did a modelling assignment for *Vogue*. Buying in or selling out? Was there really any difference in the end?

22

DARK THINGS: Goth and the Return of Rock

Bauhaus. Batcave. Siouxsie & The Banshees. The Cure. The Birthday Party. Killing Joke. The Virgin Prunes. Theatre of Hate. Sisters of Mercy. Southern Death Cult.

The word 'Gothic' brings to mind medieval churches, all tenebrous vaults and cold, echoing naves. Or Gothic literature and art, with their themes of death and the uncanny. Not forgetting the original Goths, those Germanic barbarians who swarmed over the dying Roman Empire and established kingdoms in Italy and Spain.

As a rock genre and youth subculture, Goth has explored and lived out all of these different evocations. In the beginning, though, 'Gothic' was a neutral adjective for a certain doomy ambience in post-punk music. In 1979, for instance, Martin Hannett described Joy Division as 'dancing music with Gothic overtones'. Quite rapidly, though, it became a critical term of abuse applied to newer bands such as Bauhaus who had emerged in the wake of Joy Division and Siouxsie & The Banshees. Finally, the word was reclaimed as a positive identity, a tribal rallying cry. This shift took place in 1982, when ideas of darkness, (sexual) dirt and a new underground started to appeal as an alternative to New Pop's squeaky-clean overground brightness.

And yet Goth and New Pop had something in common: roots in glam. ABC and The Human League loved Roxy and Bowie, but so did Bauhaus and Sex Gang Children. New Pop and Goth both represented a return to glamour and stardom – a backlash against post-punk's anti-mystique. Writing about Gang of Four and Delta 5, Greil Marcus celebrated their 'overwhelming sobriety: a sobriety that excludes not laughter but romanticism'. Whether it was The Human League's celebration of romance or Goth's patchouli-scented Romanticism, 1982 saw the return of that old (black) magic again.

The intersection point between Goth and New Pop was Adam Ant. The original Antz were proto-Goth: the songs tweaked taboos and unveiled kinky desires; the 'sex music for antpeople' concept was overtly tribal. Adam was also the first in a long line of hunky Goth singers that included Bauhaus's Peter Murphy and Southern Death Cult's Ian Astbury. Goth put a high premium on physical beauty – whether natural or aided by self-adornment and make-up. The other Goth hallmark possessed by Adam was the charismatic aura of the cult leader, which mingled various aspects of warrior chieftain, shaman and saviour.

But when Adam, impatient to become a big star, 'sold out' and went pop with *Kings of the Wild Frontier*, his original fanbase defected. 'Bauhaus picked up a lot of disaffected Ants fans,' says Goth historian Mick Mercer. *Kings* came out on 6 November 1980, the day after Bauhaus's debut *In a Flat Field*. Antz fans who didn't care for Adam's new children's storybook imagery of pirates and Red Indians turned instead to Bauhaus's hammy glam theatre of blasphemy and idolatry. Ambitious Adam declared that 'cult' was just a euphemism for 'failure'. The Goth groups, in contrast, cultivated cultishness, understanding that their audience wanted bands they could cling on to as private property.

Curiously it was Malcolm McLaren, the person who'd given Adam the image makeover that took him into the mainstream, who best understood this impulse. In a *Sounds* interview, McLaren celebrated the diehard loyalty of metal fans: 'The great example of all this is . . . Led Zeppelin. They never appeared on television or radio, yet they sold more records at that time than any other group! They *made sure* their music was outside the area of manufactured pop product . . . I wouldn't say Led Zep are a revolutionary group, but the atmosphere they created and the people who followed them had ultimately not a thing to do with CBS, Warners, selling product.' McLaren predicted the return of rock's underground spirit as a backlash against New Pop: for him, the pure triumph of marketing and media, and therefore 'the killer of danger and subversion'.

The big Goth band when McLaren spoke these words (December 1982) uncannily resembled a cross between Bow Wow Wow and Led Zeppelin. Southern Death Cult had the tribal tom-tom rhythms, while singer Ian Astbury wore a Mohican just like Annabella's, along with feather and chicken-bone necklaces (a jewellery collection that expanded with each visit to KFC). But Astbury's obsession with Native American culture went slightly deeper than Adam Ant's, with his skimmed library books and cosmetic appropriation of the Navajo nose-stripe. Astbury had spent five years in Canada as a youth, during which time he'd visited American Indian reservations and cultural centres. Returning to the UK just in time for punk, he became deeply involved in 1977's revolution. When punk died, Astbury felt bereft and rudderless, and turned to Native American culture for spiritual sustenance. The name Southern Death Cult itself came from a Mississippi Valley tribe who maintained burial mounds and shrines.

The winter of 1982–3, when New Pop grew fat and bland, was the crucial moment for Goth's emergence. All around London, a graffiti slogan started to appear: 'KILL UGLY POP'. Virtually unknown outside the gigging circuit, Southern Death Cult appeared on *NME*'s front cover in October 1982. Early in the New Year, another *NME* cover story proclaimed the arrival of 'positive punk' – journalist Richard North's bold but unsuccessful attempt to christen the new scene. Loosely tied to two rising groups – Brigandage, and Blood and Roses – the piece was essentially the Goth articles of faith, celebrating the victory of imagination and individuality against a vaguely conjured mediocrity. 'Don't dream it, be it' was the article's epigram, stolen from *The Rocky Horror Show*'s Dr Frank-N-Furter. By spring 1983 Southern Death Cult's debut single, 'Fatman', reigned at number 1 in the independent singles chart, while Sex Gang Children's *Song and Legend* topped the indie albums chart.

The vortex of the early Goth scene was the Batcave, a Soho nightclub that started in July 1982 as an alternative to the New Romantic or imported black dance fare offered by most other London nightspots. 'Absolutely no funk,' Batcave flyers vowed. Instead, the soundtrack ranged from classic glam and rockabilly to the more danceable Goth product by outfits like Alien Sex Fiend. Founded by the campy group Specimen, the Batcave favoured a leather-and-lace décor and thirties monster-movie references. 'It was a light bulb for all the freaks and people like myself who were from the sticks and wanted a bit more from life,' Specimen's Johnny Melton told Mick Mercer for his book *Gothic Rock*. 'Freaks, weirdos, sexual deviants . . .' As the club took off, it went on tour to the provinces and inspired imitators and franchise versions across the land – Batcave nights in Liverpool, at Leicester's Belfry club, at Manchester's Hacienda. It even did a one-off night at Danceteria in New York.

In 1983 Goth was legion. Young bands like Danse Society, The March Violets, Flesh for Lulu, Play Dead, Rubella Ballet, Gene Loves Jezebel, Ausgang and scores more swarmed across the live circuit and the independent charts. Indie label 4AD cornered the market for Goth-lite with Cocteau Twins, Dead Can Dance and Xmal Deutschland. But at this point almost every independent label had a 'poz punk' band on its roster. It was a movement with international reach, too: Goth's tentacles stretched from the Los Angeles 'death-rock' scene centred on Christian Death and 45 Grave to Iceland's Kukl (the name translates as 'sorcery') who sang about the country's pagan mythology and whose line-up included Björk and other future Sugarcubes.

Successful subcultures allow for diversity within uniformity: their style is loose enough for you to express your individuality yet sufficiently coherent to enable instant identification of fellow tribesfolk. Goth's palette of sonic and sartorial hallmarks meant you could recognize a Goth group within seconds and spot a Goth fan at a hundred paces. Standard musical fixtures included: scything guitar patterns and high-pitched post-Joy Division basslines that usurped the melodic role; beats either hypnotically dirge-like or tom-tom heavy and 'tribal' in some ethnically indeterminate Burundi-meets-Apache way; vocals either near operatic, harrowed, or deep, droning alloys of Jim Morrison and Ian Curtis. As for the image, you'd see some combination of deathly pallor, backcombed or ratted black hair, ruffled Regency shirts, stovepipe hats, leather garments, spiked dog collars, the ensemble accessorized with religious, magical or macabre jewellery (bone earrings, rosaries, pentacles, anks, skulls), typically made from silver.

Goth bands combined kitsch horror-movie leanings with genuine interest in the 'dark side'. Blood and Roses, for instance, took their name from a Roger Vadim vampire flick, but singer Lisa Kirby was interested in 'magic, witchcraft, anything unknown', while guitarist Bob was a bona fide student of the black arts. Death was a universal obsession: Sex Gang Children's logo was the Grim Reaper; UK Decay had songs like 'Necrophilia' and 'Rising from the Dead'. The clothing colour-scheme was funereal, the sense of glamour literally sepulchral. Connecting everything was the romance of old things. The original Gothic movement in literature had been anti-modernist. It represented the return of the repressed: all the medieval superstitions and primordial longings allegedly banished by the Industrial Revolution, all those shadowy regions of the soul supposedly illuminated by the Enlightenment. It was only when the dark, satanic mills appeared that ruined abbeys came to be considered picturesque and alluring. Goth was based on the idea that the most profound emotions you'll ever feel are the same ones felt by people thousands of years ago: the fundamental, eternal experiences of love, death, despair, awe and dread.

Goth's interest in the timeless could be seen as precisely that – a refusal of the time*ly*, the topical, the urgent issues of the day. You could certainly critique its investment in the fantastical and otherworldly (or *under*worldly) as an apolitical evasion of 'the real'. Indeed, in its early days, Goth was shaped in reaction to the two other strands that came directly out of punk – Oi! and anarcho-punk – both of which engaged with exploitation and injustice. From 1980 onwards, there had been a 'punk's not dead' resurgence, the independent charts overrun by new names like Vice Squad, Discharge, Anti-Pasti, Flux of Pink Indians, Zounds, GBH, Chron-Gen, Rudimentary Peni and countless others. The Oi! or 'real punk' contingent defined punk as rabble-rousing protest grounded in working-class experience. Focused on Crass, a band/label based in a communal farmhouse, the anarcho-punk movement was more ideological and idealistic, spewing out vinyl tracts denouncing the unholy trinity of state/church/military, while extolling pacifism and self-rule.

Up to a point, the proto-Goths enjoyed the energy at Oi! and anarcho-punk gigs, but ultimately they didn't really care for either option: lumpen Oi! wallowed in its own oppression, they felt, while anarcho-punk seemed dourly didactic and sexless. 'A lot of the people who became Goths wanted the excitement of punk but not the mundane element,' says Mercer, then documenting the nascent scene in his *Panache* fanzine. Redefining punk as inversion of values and deviance from norms, these proto-Goths proposed a flight from the crushing ordinariness of everyday English life, into a common wildness of ritual and ceremony, magic and mystery. And they fastened on any artists, says Mercer, 'who offered something a bit more intelligent and twisted, Romantic and tortured': The Banshees, Toyah, The Virgin Prunes, The Birthday Party. This new breed of punk began to recognize each other at gigs: they looked more stylish than the Oi! or anarcho-punks, showed more imagination and overt sexuality in the way they dressed. The unifying attitude was 'Stand Up, Stand Out', as Specimen titled their big anthem.

These soon-to-be-Goths started following particular bands – Theatre of Hate, UK Decay, Bauhaus – around the country, gig after gig. Other gathering places for the emergent tribe were the Futurama festivals. Significantly, they were based in Leeds: Yorkshire would become a Goth heartland, home to Danse Society (Barnsley), Southern Death Cult (Bradford), and The March Violets and Sisters of Mercy (both Leeds). At 1980's Futurama, The Banshees headlined one of the two nights. The *NME* reviewer, Paul Morley, noted that Siouxsie was 'modelling her newest outfit, the one that will influence how all the girls dress over the next few months. About half the girls at Leeds had used Sioux as a basis for their appearance, hair to ankle.'

Siouxsie Sioux, the original
Gothic ice queen, 1978.
Photo by Janette Beckman

The mother of forty thousand Gothettes, Siouxsie crystallized the movement's spirit when she declared her intention to be 'a thorn in the side of mediocrity'. At the very beginning, though, The Banshees were exemplary post-punk vanguardists, spouting the rock-is-dead rhetoric of the time. Bassist Steve Severin, co-founder with Siouxsie, saw rock as 'flaccid and perverted', and in interviews cited similar influences – Velvets, Roxy, Can, Beefheart – as their contemporaries. The Banshees' sound took shape through a process of reduction and rejection. 'It was a case of us knowing what we *didn't* want, throwing out every cliché,' says Severin. 'Never having a guitar solo, never ending a song with a loud drum smash. At one point, Siouxsie just took away the high-hat from Kenny Morris's drum kit.'

Heard on their 1978 debut, *The Scream*, the result was stark and serrated – a mortification of rock: a new, cruel geometry achieved *within* and *against* the orthodox guitar/bass/drums format. Siouxsie wanted a guitar sound like 'a cross between The Velvet Underground and the shower scene in *Psycho*', says Severin. Played by self-taught musicians operating at the very limits of their ability, it's a very physical-sounding music: 'When you listen to *The Scream*, you can hear the fingers on the strings, the effort that's actually going into it,' says Severin. 'You get to the end of a track and you can hear Kenny breathing.'

Early on, The Banshees were often lumped in with Wire, kindred spirits in angularity and emaciated minimalism. Both groups were big fans of flange – a guitar effect that doubles the musical signal and then puts the 'shadow' guitar slightly out of phase with the main signal. Unlike the blissful psychedelic phasing on sixties records, flanging is a harsh sound, glassy and brittle. The Banshees used its cold swirl to draw a sharp line of separation between what they were doing and seventies rock.

Siouxsie's ice-queen voice was equally forbidding, piercing the listener's flesh like a lance. The singing suited the songs. Jagged and jarring, Banshees tunes could be catchy ('Hong Kong Garden', their debut single, reached number 7) but they didn't *feel* melodic. The lyrics, alternately penned by Severin and Sioux, espoused a brutally unsentimental view of the world ('Love in a void/It's so numb/Avoid in love/It's so dumb'), relieved only by macabre humour: 'Carcass', for instance, concerned a butcher's assistant who falls in love with a lump of meat and amputates his own limbs on the meat grinder to more closely resemble his beloved. Siouxsie defined punk not in political terms but as 'disrupting yourself, questioning yourself', which generally translated into a morbid preoccupation with the dark side of human nature: obsession, unreason, extreme mental states. Severin's 'Jigsaw Feeling' imagined what it felt like to be autistic, while Siouxsie's 'Suburban Relapse' is a darkly witty portrait of a housewife who has a breakdown: 'Whilst finishing a chore/I asked myself "What for?"/Then something snapped'. Siouxsie told me in 1989, 'You look at these homes and realize how many of the women are out of their minds within these pruned rose gardens. There's something about the containment of emotion within suburbia.'

Severin and Siouxsie knew suburbia intimately – they grew up in Bromley and its immediate neighbour Chislehurst, on the southernmost fringe of London. But they met on the other side of the city – at a Wembley Arena Roxy Music concert in 1974. Glam fans, they had no truck with punk's do-it-yourself egalitarianism. 'Anyone *can't* do it,' quips Severin. The Banshees believed in maintaining an enigmatic distance from the audience – both offstage ('That whole concept of The Clash letting their fans stay in their hotel rooms . . .' chuckles Severin, 'I mean, *no*! We'd let them stay out in the rain') and in performance. 'There's something magical about a stage,' muses Severin. 'You think of all your favourite people, like The Doors, and you can't imagine them being the blokes next door. The stage is their church. That's what appealed about the intelligent side of glam – the fact that there was some kind of theatre going on, a drama was being presented.'

This side of The Banshees emerged on 1979's *Join Hands* with 'Icon' and the protracted 'cover version' of 'The Lords Prayer' – songs that etched the template for Goth as a modern pagan cult tapping into atavistic pre-Christian urges. 'With "Icon", we were trying to create music that you could get lost in – an intensity of sound that was hypnotic, ritualistic,' says Severin. 'That goes back to our love of things like Can, who'd play for thirty minutes, and you'd be completely lost in the same revolving patterns of sound.' The song is loosely inspired by the story of a Polish priest who set himself on fire, but it sounds more like a hymn to Siouxsie, an 'icon in the fire' of Goth desire. Fusing sacrilege and heathen exultation, 'The Lords Prayer' features the chant 'You do-gooders will never get to heaven'. You get the impression that at least one reason why Siouxsie loathes organized monotheism is because, in her universe, there's only one true goddess: Siouxsie Sioux. An object of worship, she'll countenance no rival idols.

After an early personnel upheaval – the defection of drummer Morris and guitarist John McKay – The Banshees recruited the more conventionally skilled John McGeoch (formerly guitarist with Magazine) and

427

drummer Budgie, and recorded 1980's *Kaleidoscope*, a transitional record that, as the title suggests, shifted from the monochrome severity of the first two albums to a more vivid palette of textures, even sounding pretty on the hit singles 'Happy House' and 'Christine'. *Juju*, from 1981, is the Banshee's most perfect statement: every song feels like a chip off the same darkly lustrous block. Combine *Join Hands* and *Juju*, and you have roughly 70 per cent of Goth's sound and lyrical themes. 'Sin in My Heart', 'Voodoo Dolly', 'Halloween', 'Spellbound', 'Night Shift' – for the first time in their oeuvre The Banshees flirted with ideas of magic and the supernatural. And they did so in quite a brash, cartoony way. 'Those more schlocky things we employed around *Juju*, those were influences from The Cramps,' says Severin, referring to the American ghouls who mated back-from-the-grave rockabilly with B-movie horror.

In 1982 The Banshees recorded two songs that were virtual manifestos for Goth. On their Top 30 hit 'Fireworks', Siouxsie chanted 'We are fireworks' – an exultant image of self-beautification as a glam gesture flashing against the murk of mundanity. 'Painted Bird', on *A Kiss in the Dreamhouse*, paid homage to The Banshees' audience: 'Confound that dowdy flock with a sharp-honed nerve/Because we're painted birds by our own design'. Its inspiration was Jerzy Kozinki's novel of the same title, whose protagonist collects birds. 'When he was feeling really aggressive, or frustrated,' Siouxsie explained, 'he'd paint this bird with different colours, and then throw it to its flock. And it would recognize its flock, but because it was a different colour, they would attack it.'

From its bejewelled, Klimt-inspired cover imagery to its sensuous textures, 1982's *Dreamhouse* marked The Banshees' plunge into full-on modern psychedelia. The reference points were quintessentially English: The Beatles, Syd Barrett, Traffic, the eerie, bucolic Donovan of 'Hurdy Gurdy Man' and 'Season of the Witch'. On 'Green Fingers', Siouxsie played earth mother while a childlike recorder frolicked like a butterfly in a sun-dappled glade. '*Dreamhouse* really started with the words for "Cascade",' says Severin. The imagery of 'liquid falling' seemed to demand the melting of the ice queen and the unveiling of a hitherto suppressed side to The Banshees: deliquescent, lapidary, and, on 'Melt!' (their first ever ballad), languorous and erotic. 'Slowdive', a dizzy plunge into graphic carnality, sounded like Can-gone-disco-gone-porno, with cello and violin providing a rhythm-guitar-like propulsion. *Circa The Scream*, The Banshees' music was 'sexy' in the same way as J. G. Ballard's *Crash*. But now, inspired partly by Severin's reading of Ballard's latest book *The Unlimited Dream Company* – 'where the imagery is very lush, sensual, exotic', he says – The Banshees were making make-out music. If you put *Dreamhouse* on as a seduction soundtrack, you might even get results; before then, that ruse would have worked only if your date was a psychopath or a vampire.

Their most adventurous and varied album, *Dreamhouse* loudly signalled that The Banshees had outgrown the Goth audience they'd helped create. The following year saw their cover of 'Dear Prudence' – from The Beatles' White Album – reach number 3. They closed out 1983 with a live double album, *Nocturne*, recorded at the Albert Hall. The Banshees had become too popular in a mainstream sense to remain the focus of cult love – the essence of Goth.

Around this point, John McGeoch left the group and Robert Smith replaced him as guitarist, while still fronting his own group The Cure. Although Goths liked The Cure, their music was closer to Goth-lite: a softcore version of Joy Division steeped in similar existentialist sources (the early 'Killing an Arab' was inspired by Camus's *The Stranger*), but replacing Ian Curtis's barely disguised death-wish with Smith's wan despondency and doubt. Attractive on 1979's translucent-sounding *Seventeen Seconds* (with its shades of *Another Green World* Eno, Durutti Column and Young Marble Giants), The Cure's sound became a dolorous fog on *Faith* and *Pornography*. Smith's forlornly withdrawn vocals, the listless beat and the grey-haze guitars made for some of the most neurasthenic rock music ever committed to vinyl. Yet these oppressively dispirited albums cemented The Cure's Goth stature and laid the foundation for their abiding mega-cult following – a vast legion of the unaffiliated and disillusioned, suburbia's lost dreamers.

At the furthest extreme from The Cure's mild version of Gothic gloom lay the Dionysian conflagration of The Birthday Party. *Prayers on Fire*, from 1981, opened with the tribal bedlam of 'Zoo-Music Girl'. This punk-funk love song oscillates violently between devotion and devouring, sacred and profane, and offers a vision of 'romance' that is less Nelson Riddle and more Antonin Artaud: 'I murder her dress till it hurts . . . Oh! God! Please let me die beneath her fists'.

The Birthday Party originally moved to London from Melbourne, Australia, expecting the UK to be ablaze with bands like The Pop Group, only to be bitterly disappointed by the cooler direction post-punk had taken. Shelving their well-thumbed copies of Rimbaud and Baudelaire, they veered in a deliberately American direction. When singer Nick Cave and guitarist Rowland S. Howard listed their 'consumer faves' in *NME*, the touchstone list included *Wiseblood*, Johnny Cash, Evel Knievel, Robert Mitchum in *Night of the Hunter*, Caroline Jones (a.k.a. Morticia from *The Addams Family*), Lee Hazelwood and Raymond Chandler. *Junkyard* (1982) teemed with American Gothic imagery – kewpie dolls, an evangelist's murdered daughter. Hamlet was rewritten as a gun-totin', Cadillac-drivin' cartoon psycho. Comic artist Ed Roth did the album cover, a drooling monster at the wheel of a fire-spewing dragster. Howard later said they liked Roth's work because it 'conjures sort of an inarticulacy, a certain dumbness, and that's one of the great things about rock music . . . You don't have to be thrusting your intelligence into people's faces all the time . . . If you're really smart you know when it's appropriate to be dumb.'

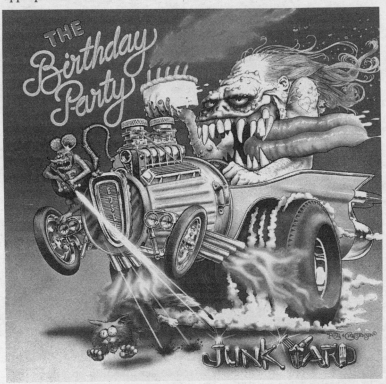

Cover of The Birthday Party's *Junkyard*, 1982

The decrepit blues of 'She's Hit', the death rattle 'n' roll of 'Big Jesus Trashcan', the roiling quagmire of the title track – *Junkyard*, in 1982, sounded like the living end of rock music, a final statement that couldn't be surpassed. Amazingly, The Birthday Party retched up two more brilliant EPs, *The Bad Seed* and *Mutiny*. High points included the Disney *noir* talking trees of 'Deep in the Woods', the Faulkner-meets-*Deliverance* horror of 'Swampland', and 'Mutiny in Heaven'. Blasphemy worthy of Lautréamont, the lyrics of 'Mutiny' conjured a corrupt and derelict heaven, riddled with trash and rats. The band matched Cave's fantastical vision with their most three-dimensionally vivid and visual music, a verminous inferno of leering gargoyles and bubbling putrescence. Cave was one of the first songwriters to reject post-punk's ultrarational, anti-religious tenor and start using Old Testament imagery – sin, retribution, curses, bad seed, damnation. In Goth terms, though, The Birthday Party's single most influential song was the 1981 single 'Release the Bats', a campy, Crampsy stampede of vampire sex that was number 1 in the independent charts for three weeks. The advert for the single declared, 'Dirtiness is next to antigodliness'.

'Release the Bats' was produced by Nick Launay, who had worked on PiL's tribal-sounding 'Flowers of Romance' and later produced another Goth dance-floor smash: 'Pagan Lovesong' by Dublin's The Virgin Prunes. The Prunes started out as Bowie boys stranded in the Republic of Ireland, then became obsessed with post-punk and regularly made pilgrimages by ferry to Liverpool to pick up the latest records and see favourite bands such as Wire and Cabaret Voltaire. But their Bowie-fan core surfaced in their 'glam savage' appearance – a poke in the eye to staid Dublin folk. Dressed in a skirt and make-up, singer Gavin Friday would saunter provocatively down Grafton Street, Dublin's upmarket shopping area. 'But we weren't Boy George types,' he says. 'I looked more like Rasputin. I loved the idea of walking down the road and you wouldn't know if I was going to kick you or kiss you.' Live, the Prunes were closer to primitivist performance art than a rock band. At Futurama in 1980, they wore loincloths with pigs' heads attached to their crotches; the first part of their set consisted of a long period of silence interrupted occasionally by a big pole being banged on the stage. Touring Europe as support to The Birthday Party, they simulated oral sex onstage.

The most Gothic element of The Virgin Prunes drew on their Irish experience: the friction between Catholic repression and Celtic pagan spirituality. 'The Virgin Prunes were one of the few people at that time who had the guts to say, "Fuck the Catholic Church",' says Friday. 'At the same time I liked a lot of religious imagery. And if religions were bands, Roman Catholicism would have the best show in the world, 'cos it's got that element of ceremony.' The Virgin Prunes invoked a primordial sublime, 'a terrible beauty'. And their keening vocals drew on 'this old Irish way of singing called *Sean nós,* basically the blues goes Celtic', says Friday. 'It was a real subliminal thing we had in our music. You can also hear it in John Lydon, in Sinead O'Connor, in country music.' The Virgin Prunes were also into 'primeval stuff' – violent and abstract vocal-noise improvisation not so far from Yoko Ono, but actually inspired by eavesdropping on the occupants of a home for mentally retarded adults.

Friday shrugs off the Goth tag, preferring to align The Virgin Prunes with the post-punk vanguard. In addition to guitar-based songs, they had a nice line in eerie ambient collages constructed from tape loops. Their 'New Form of Beauty' project began as a series of EPs for Rough Trade and culminated in the Prunes taking over a Dublin art gallery for a Vienna Aktionist-style installation whose highlights included 'an abortion piece done with a vagina of meat' and a table around which fresh turds and piss had been deposited by each member of the group. 'I turned up the heating, so the smell was *outrageous,*' giggles Friday. Still, he concedes that Prunes fans included a hefty Goth contingent. 'Because of our Bowie-esque sense of image and visuality, we did attract the white faces.'

The white faces' principal Bowie-surrogate, though, was Peter Murphy of Bauhaus. Their 1979 single 'Bela Lugosi's Dead' – generally identified as the ground zero of Goth proper – appeared in Bowie's vampire flick *The Hunger*; Bauhaus performed the song in a nightclub scene, with Murphy writhing in a cage. The Bowie-clone tag, based largely on Murphy's mannered vocals, proved impossible to shake off, and in the end Bauhaus tried to exorcize it through the sardonic gesture of covering 'Ziggy Stardust' with exacting fidelity. When they appeared on *Top of the Pops* to mime 'Ziggy' in 1982, Murphy and guitarist Daniel Ash even replicated the saucy homoerotic interplay between Bowie and Mick Ronson.

Murphy's striking looks – teeteringly tall, gaunt, with a bruised pout and perfect cheekbones – made him a Goth pin-up, the ultimate erotic enigma. But what came out of those luscious lips was portentous and preposterous, an overblown farrago of sex and death, religion and blasphemy. Raised Catholic, Murphy kicked back against his upbringing with sacrilegious ditties like 'Stigmata Martyr', which featured him reciting, 'In the name of the Father and the Son and the Holy Spirit' in Latin, and was accompanied live by simulated crucifixion postures.

With their shock-rock gestures and Guignol grotesquerie, Bauhaus were actually far closer to Alice Cooper than David Bowie: exciting, but difficult to take seriously. They had a superb grasp of rock-as-theatre, using stark white lighting to cast dramatic shadows. 'It's important to go to the theatre and escape from the street, use the space, find another element,' Murphy declared. Like Cooper, they made flashy, thrilling singles – the dark, twisted art-funk of 'A Kick in the Eye', the swirling, vaporous mystery of 'Spirit'. Ash's guitar bore comparison with Gang of Four or Joy Division at their most harsh and hacking, especially on Bauhaus's early post-punk-aligned efforts like 'Terror Couple Kill Colonel' and 'Bela Lugosi's Dead', with its fret-scraping guitar-scree and metallic dub effects. But the albums sagged under the weight of ponderous pretensions.

Bauhaus, The Banshees, The Birthday Party – these were the crucial proto-Goth groups. The fourth cornerstone of the Goth sound and sensibility was Killing Joke. Like the other three groups, they began as postpunk experimentalists – in their case, following in PiL's footsteps. In 1980 singer/keyboardist Jaz Coleman talked of wanting to keep the funk but strip away disco's 'sugarshit' sheen, replacing it 'with mangled, distorted, searing noise'. This was supplied courtesy of guitarist Geordie, who transformed the Keith Levene sound into something sulphuric, inhumane, practically inhuman. Coleman added jabs of atonal synth and electronic hums, along with the barked menace of his vocals, which sounded like he was choking on his own fury. 'Tension music', the group called it.

Initially, Killing Joke seemed vaguely political. Their striking seven-inch sleeves and a series of micro-ads in the music press grabbed your eye: the Pope receiving a Nazi salute from German troops and blessing them in return; a top-hatted Fred Astaire tap-dancing over a trench full of First World War corpses. The name Killing Joke, explained Coleman, condensed their worldview into a single phrase: 'the feeling of a guy in the First World War who's just about to run out the trenches . . . and he knows his life is going to be gone in ten minutes and he thinks of that fucker back in Westminster who put him in that position. That's the feeling that we're trying to project . . . the Killing Joke.'

KILLING JOKE
WARDANCE
PSSYCHE

Fred Astaire dancing on the mass grave of a First World War battlefield – the cover of Killing Joke's 1980 single 'Wardance'

There was much more to Jaz Coleman than a protest singer, though. He was quite an unlikely pop figure in many respects: a high-caste Brahmin Indian on his mother's side, wealthy, well educated and musically trained (after Killing Joke he became a classical composer). In almost pointed contrast to Coleman's accomplishment, Killing Joke was conceived as a barbarian entity. Seemingly deranged by a volatile mixture of Nietzsche and Nostradamus, Coleman saw their music as 'warning sounds for an age of self-destruction'. The end was nigh ('I'll give it eighteen months,' he said in 1981), but Coleman was glad, not sad. The aftermath was 'the period of time I'm looking towards at the moment', he said – because this was when a new, brutally instinct-attuned *un*civilization would emerge phoenix-like from the smoking ruins.

Starting with their second album, *What's THIS For . . .!* and reaching fruition on 1982's awesome *Revelations*, Killing Joke stripped away the modish *Metal Box*-era elements and stood proudly exposed as what they truly were: a post-punk version of heavy metal, a death-disco Black Sabbath. Like Budgie's drumming in The Banshees, Paul Ferguson's beats were tribal and turbulent, all tom-toms with hardly any high-hat. 'We try to paint a picture of a new world,' Coleman declared. 'I see a more *savage* world ahead, right? . . . It's music that inflames the heart.' Fire was Killing Joke's favourite of the four elements. They even recruited a fire-eater, Dave the Wizard, to do his act onstage with the band. 'Fire to me is symbolic of the *will power*,' declared Coleman. 'I think the power of the individual is really underestimated . . . We like to kindle the will power within them.' Yet it seemed more the case that Killing Joke's music exalted the power of the mob, the swarm. A dark, tribal energy swirled around the group. 'Our music may seem almost infernal to some', Coleman told *Sounds*. 'But to us it's sacred.'

Goth's appeal to the irrational and primal could sometimes stray into unwholesome territory. Killing Joke exemplified this. Coleman's rhetoric – exalting male energy, describing war as the natural state of the world, regarding civilization as enfeebled – and his impatience for Armageddon veered unnervingly close to that dodgy interzone between Nietzsche and Nazism. 'The violence that Killing Joke is about is not violence on the immediate level but the *mass* violence, the violence bubbling underneath your feet, the violence of nature throwing up,' Coleman solemnly explained. 'And we *become* that violence.' Even some Goths felt there was a faintly fascistic aura to the vibe catalysed by Killing Joke at their gigs.

Latent Nazi tendencies were an abiding source of anxiety in the Goth scene, something magazines regularly exorcized by asking certain bands tricky questions. You could trace the flirtation with fascist imagery back to sources like Joy Division and Siouxsie (who in her early days wore a swastika and sang the unforgivable line 'too many Jews for my liking'). Not content with imitating Joy Division sonically, The March Violets picked an even more dubious name. When Hitler pressured the Reichstag to vote German democracy out of existence and vest supreme authority in himself as Führer, there was a stampede of people trying to join the Nazi Party in the spring of 1934. The original Nazis dubbed these opportunists 'March violets'.

435

Nazi innuendoes dogged the early career of Kirk Brandon of Theatre of Hate. It didn't help that blonde Brandon looked like a poster boy for Aryan supremacy, or that early Hate releases came out on the SS label (swiftly changed to Burning Rome), or that the band's gigs were often preceded by a tape of 'The Ride of the Valkyries' (penned by Hitler's favourite composer, Wagner). Brandon's shrill, soaring voice had more than a touch of the Wagnerian about it, too. Allegory-anthems like 'Do You Believe in the Westworld?' and 'Nero' strove to make epic political statements, but were fatally garbled, their sympathies open to conjecture. Anti-American? Pro-communist? Militaristic? Pacifist? Or just hopelessly confused? 'Brave New Soldiers', a song originally written for Brandon's pre-Hate group The Pack, imagined the possibility of a European military youth crusade. All that really came through loud and unclear was Brandon's desire to push himself forward as a messianic leader. Theatre of Hate, the singer declared, wasn't just a band; it was a movement. Mixing tribal drums, spaghetti-Western guitar, histrionic sax, and Brandon's heroic singing, the music evoked vague sensations of mission, momentousness, mass rally, purpose, destiny, destination, a 'journey to glory'. After Theatre of Hate combusted, Brandon formed Spear of Destiny. The name came from the weapon with which the kind-hearted Roman centurion Longinus put Christ out of his crucifixion agony. According to Brandon, the spear passed through various hands over the centuries: whoever held it controlled the destiny of the world. The occultists in the Nazi Party were obsessed with it, and supposedly managed to gain possession of it. After VE Day, the Americans found it in a vault beneath Nuremberg Castle.

Any suspect totalitarian leanings were mostly held in check by Goth's opposing attraction to Aleister Crowley's libertine Law of Thelema 'Do what thou wilt shall be the whole of the law'. Curiously, given Goth's attraction to all things forbidden, drugs weren't especially important on the scene. But the lyrical vibe of debauchery and sexual weirdness was mirrored in clothing that incorporated fetish-wear elements with the plain vampy: fishnet stockings, black leather thigh boots, witchy eye make-up. Its emphasis on self-beautification made Goth particularly popular with women. 'To this day, it's got a bigger involvement of females than any other subculture,' claims Mick Mercer. Yet most girls in Goth bands fell into the traditional role of attractive singer. Nor did the hefty presence of women in the audience prevent Goth's rapid degeneration into a sort of post-punk version of heavy metal, that most macho of genres.

The major impetus behind this shift – from early Goth to what historians of the scene call 'Gothic rock' – came from The Sisters of Mercy and Southern Death Cult. The early Goths tended to share the post-punk mindset of The Banshees: 'rock 'n' roll' was something to be discarded, left for dead. But The Sisters of Mercy were defiantly rockist. Fans of The Birthday Party, they followed that group's lead in embracing American imagery and rejecting the Europeanism of New Pop. 'There's an awful lot of dreadful bands coming out of England, especially London,' the Sisters' singer/conceptualist Andrew Eldritch declared in 1983. 'A lot of them come onstage with this "We are not a rock band" rubbish. So we go the other way – one step forward. We say "We *are* a rock band." Very loudly.'

This was fighting talk indeed at a time when much of the London-based cool music media – from style bibles like *The Face* and *iD* to David Toop and Steve Beresford's *Collusion* magazine – had seemingly dedicated themselves to celebrating anything and everything as long as it *wasn't* rock. Whether from overseas (Washington DC go-go, New York electro, African music) or home grown (the *faux*-jazz of Working Week and Sade, the *faux*-soul of Carmel and Animal Nightlife, the *faux*-salsa of zoot-suited buffoons Blue Rondo à la Turk, the *faux*-everything of Paul Weller's Style Council), all that this disparate mélange of hipster fare had in common was the absence of power chords and fuzztone. Aghast at this brave new world where Nina Simone was a hallowed icon but Iggy was a forgotten boy, The Sisters of Mercy declared war on pop.

An Oxford-educated intellectual, Eldritch admired heavy metal's stupidity and 'relentlessness'. He thought the best way to resurrect rock was through an 'irreverent love' that accepted and affirmed its inherent ridiculousness. The result was an ultra-stylized approach that treated rock less as an evolving musical form than a gestural repertoire of mannerisms and imagery: sunglasses after dark, speed-emaciated bodies encased in black. Although Eldritch's avowed role models and benchmarks were The Stooges and Motorhead, he didn't appear to grasp how crucial having a real drummer is if you want to make music that *rocks*. Instead, the Sisters used a drum machine, nicknamed Doktor Avalanche. The guitar was atmospheric but insubstantial, the aural counterpart to the dry ice in which they shrouded themselves when onstage (a knowingly corny gesture at mystery), while the bass droned pleasantly in sub-Joy Division, standard-Goth style. But alongside the inflexible programmed beat, The Sisters of Mercy's true problem was Eldritch's hollow, dirge-drone vocals, a mannered meld of Iggy *circa The Idiot*, Alan Vega and Leonard Cohen.

The Sisters of Mercy's failings were instantly audible in their cover of The Rolling Stones' 'Gimme Shelter'. The original is one of the most physically powerful and dynamic pieces of rock ever recorded, but in the Sisters' hands it became listless and wispy. No matter: the real point of their recording 'Gimme Shelter' was to make a meta-pop gesture, Eldritch explained, an allusion to Altamont, the 1969 free festival thrown by the Rolling Stones during which a gang of Hell's Angels, hired as security, brutalized the audience and then murdered a fan while the Stones were actually playing onstage. Like the Manson murders, Altamont became a heavy symbol of the end of the sixties dream. 'If there's a part of history where rock music stopped for a second and we began . . . a point where the seeds of what we do were sown, it's probably Altamont . . . It's when the trip turned sour and it's when the best music was.'

The Sisters of Mercy's 'Temple of Love' was *the* Goth anthem of 1983, guaranteed to get the chicken-dancers out on the floor. Its closest rival was 'Fatman' by Southern Death Cult, which reached number 1 in the indie charts that spring and seemed to stay there for months. Even by Goth's declining standards, it was a poor excuse for rock: Ian Astbury's bellowed vocals, the twangy Morricone guitar and the pounding tribal drums seemed barely integrated.

In some sense, though, the music was almost irrelevant: Southern Death Cult had become a focus for the disaffected and directionless. Through touring first as support to Theatre of Hate and then with Bauhaus, SDC picked up the slack left by those groups, and by others like Killing Joke and The Banshees, when they'd split, or changed direction, or gone mainstream. But midway through 1983, SDC themselves disintegrated. Astbury formed a new band, Death Cult, with guitarist Billy Duffy of Theatre of Hate. The name soon contracted again, to The Cult, and with the jettisoning of 'Death' went the group's remaining Gothic vestiges. With amazing speed, and stunning lack of shame, The Cult devolved into a straightforward long-haired cock-rock band. The reference points were of late sixties and early seventies vintage: The Doors, Steppenwolf, Led Zeppelin, Free. A vague aura of adventure and quest clung to songs like 'Revolution' and 'Spiritwalker', to album titles like *Dreamtime* and *Love*. But essentially The Cult, by 1985, became everything The Sex Pistols and punk had aimed to destroy.

23

GLORY BOYS: Liverpool, New Psychedelia and the Big Music

Echo & The Bunnymen. Zoo. Wahl Heat. The Teardrop Explodes. The Blue Orchids.
The Waterboys. Big Country. Simple Minds. U2.

If Goth took one route from post-punk back to loud-and-proud rock,
Echo & The Bunnymen followed another path: not descent into darkness, but soaring into the light. The celestial drive of their crystal guitars
and the seeking, beseeching vocals conjured a sense of quest for a vague
grail or glory. The Bunnymen pioneered a style of purified eighties rock
– post-punk in its minimalism, yet sixties-invoking in its feeling of transcendence – that came to be known as the 'big music'. Yet it would be
The Bunnymen's rivals, U2, who ultimately took that sound and made it
really big.

In the beginning, Echo & The Bunnymen were tagged 'the new psychedelia'. In one sense, this didn't really fit, because in those days the
Liverpool group never ingested anything more deranging than pints of
mild and bitter. Then again, you could hear a touch of Jim Morrison in
Ian McCulloch's voice. And the template for The Bunnymen's sound was
Television, who were either the last sixties group or the first to make
eighties rock. Bypassing R&B influences in favour of West Coast electric
folk and acid rock, Television created a blues-less blueprint for a
cleansed, reborn rock. Yet, for all their transcendental song titles like
'Elevation', 'Glory' and 'The Dream's Dream', there was nothing retro-
psychedelic or wispily hippy-dippy about the New York group's sound –
it was diamond hard, a music of fierce purity.

Television had a much bigger impact in Britain than in America. *NME*
hailed their 1977 debut *Marquee Moon* as a peerless masterpiece and
predicted singer/guitarist Tom Verlaine would dominate the coming

decade like Dylan had the previous one. Television even scored a couple of hit singles in the UK. In a weird way, Verlaine and Television's second guitarist Richard Lloyd showed British bands the path to a *non*-American future for electric guitar, in so far as their playing owed little to Chuck Berry or the blues greats. Hearing *Marquee Moon* 'was just such a throw-down to me', U2's The Edge revealed. 'The electric guitar had really become such an unoriginal-sounding instrument.' You can hear the reverberations of Television's plangent sound right across eighties British music, but nowhere more richly than on Echo & The Bunnymen's first two albums, *Crocodiles* and *Heaven Up Here*.

Listening to 1980's *Crocodiles*, the first thing you notice is how pared and sparse the sound is: Les Pattinson's granite basslines carry the melody; Will Sergeant's jagged-quartz guitar leaves acres of empty space and avoids anything resembling a solo, apart from the odd flinty peal of lead playing; Pete DeFreitas's minimal drumming is all surging urgency. Then you marvel at the precocious authority of Ian McCulloch's voice – tapping into the Sinatra-esque poise and majesty that Jim Morrison possessed, but with a pure-hearted adolescent quality The Doors singer quickly lost through self-abuse and self-aggrandizement. Many of The Bunnymen's songs are rooted in doubt, anguish, despair – 'Is this the blues I'm singing?' wonders McCulloch on 'Rescue' – but the tightness and brightness of their sound transmits contradictory sensations of confidence, vigour and euphoria.

On 1981's *Heaven Up Here*, The Bunnymen filled out their sound with guitar overdubs, keyboard glints, vocal multitracking and atmospheric vapours. The grandeur of their music deepened, but there's also a sense of portent that occasionally ('Over the Wall') becomes portentous. Echo & The Bunnymen's audience overlapped with Joy Division's – those overcoat-clad young men with the weight of the world on their shoulders – and in some ways *Heaven Up Here* feels like an answer record to the previous year's *Closer*. It's harrowed by the same things as Joy Division: hypocrisy, distrust, betrayal, lost or frozen potential. In 'The Disease', McCulloch sings about how his life could change 'just given a chance', then pleads, 'If you get yours from heaven/Don't waste it'. 'All My Colours' is a numb trance of despondency gyrating around the vicious cycle of DeFreitas's 'drum mantra'. But whereas *Closer* shows Ian Curtis fatally mesmerized by his own dread visions, *Heaven Up Here* ultimately turns its face towards the light. 'No Dark Things' renounces death-wishful thinking and the album goes out with 'All I Want', a blasting celebration of desire for desire's sake. Stripping riff and rhythm to their barest essences, 'All I Want' is like a diagram of rock dynamics, a thrilling demonstration of the possibilities of structure, energy and tension – pure intransitive exhilaration.

Early in 1982, *Heaven Up Here* was voted the best album of 1981 by the readership of the *NME*: this was essentially an anti-New Pop protest vote by post-punk's silent majority, who'd chafed during the past year when it seemed that anything and everything was hip except what *they* liked – made-in-Britain, all-male guitar bands. Voted number 2 group in the country, Echo & The Bunnymen were effectively picking up the slack left by the demise of Joy Division. But they weren't alone: U2 also placed well in various readers' charts.

Heaven Up Here put Liverpool back on rock's map in a way it hadn't been since The Beatles. From the outside, Merseyside looked like it hadn't really responded to punk, compared with other British cities. But the upheaval of 1976 *did* galvanize Liverpool's live music scene, which had been stagnant during the early seventies. However, 'the city never produced a classic punk group or anything like Oi!,' says Paul Du Noyer, *NME*'s Liverpool correspondent at that time. Nor did post-punk flourish there – or at least not the kind of experimental sounds that emerged out of London, Sheffield and Leeds: industrial synth-noise, avant-funk, apocalyptic dub.

'All that post-punk vanguard stuff, we'd just think that was completely *stupid*,' says Bill Drummond, who managed Echo & The Bunnymen and co-founded pioneering Liverpool indie label Zoo. 'You could never have a Gang of Four, say, coming out of Liverpool.' Drummond says that it's not so much that Liverpool music has to be tuneful (although the city loves melody; always has and always will) as much as 'it had to be a *celebration*. McCulloch's lyrics were often angst-laden, but there was a gloriousness to the music.' And you could say exactly the same about the two other leading post-punk groups to come from the city during this period: Wah! Heat, with their ringing clangour and endless crescendos; and neo-psychedelic outfit The Teardrop Explodes, whose singer Julian Cope described the band's songs as 'just cries of joy . . . whatever form the songs come in, they're always some kind of rejoicing'.

Cope, McCulloch and Wah! frontman Pete Wylie were originally in a 'band' together. But The Crucial Three existed mostly as a figment of bragging and gossip: they wrote only a couple of songs, and never played a gig. This sort of phantom group – The Mystery Girls, The Nova Mob, A Shallow Madness – was a peculiar hallmark of Liverpool. Almost every significant person on the incestuous scene was involved in a band with every other significant figure at one point. 'People enjoyed the role-playing aspect,' says Du Noyer. 'They liked the process of naming groups and conceptualizing around groups more than the grind of getting equipment together and rehearsing.' So The English Opium Eaters, for instance, boasted Wylie, Paul Rutherford (later of Frankie Goes to Hollywood), Budgie (later of The Banshees) and Ian Broudie (later of The Lightning Seeds), all of whom had been in earlier groups and all of whom went on to join other phantom bands, before becoming famous later in their careers. In the book *Liverpool Explodes*, Julian Cope described a typical 'rehearsal' for The Nova Mob. 'We decided to have a group that didn't make music at all but just got on other people's nerves. We used to rehearse in this horrible trendy café called Kirklands. We'd get here at ten in the morning with enough money for one coffee each and spend the whole morning spilling sugar and rehearsing. I had this song called "Passchendale", a big heroic love song, and I'd describe it to Wylie and Griff and they'd discuss it and then we'd talk about another song or something else. That was rehearsing.'

Another key hang-out was the tea shop O'Hallaghan's, later renamed the Armadillo Tea Rooms. 'Although it was only open till six o'clock and sold just tea and biscuits, it became the meeting place for that whole generation of bands,' says Bill Drummond. The café was part of an arts complex-cum-market called the Liverpool School of Language, Music, Dream and Pun – 'a kind of free-thinking space', says Drummond. 'O'Hallaghan, the guy who rented the building, was of the generation of Liverpool Beats, all those early sixties people like Adrian Henri.' Jack Kerouac was an enduring icon in Liverpool – a revealing contrast with Ballard-obsessed Manchester and Sheffield. Self-styled 'poet ruffian' Pete Wylie 'would walk around with his copy of *On the Road* in his back pocket, sit down and read it out to people,' recalls Drummond.

The entire Liverpool scene clustered around Mathew St, where the old Cavern was. In close proximity you'd find the Liverpool School of Language, Music, Dream and Pun; Probe, the hip record store; the punk club Eric's, started by DJ/promoter Roger Eagle and a home for the city's misfits. Eric's was the laboratory for Liverpool's future stars. With most fledgling groups spending more time boasting than writing songs or playing, the leading Eric's band *circa* 1977–8 was Big in Japan. Formed by Drummond, its ranks included the charismatic glam-punkette Jayne Casey, along with Budgie, Broudie, future-Frankie singer Holly Johnson, and future Zoo co-founder/Teardrops keyboardist/music-biz mogul Dave Balfe. 'They really were like the billion-dollar quintet in terms of how rich every member of that group became,' says Du Noyer. 'Well, Jayne never became a big star, but she did become an important figure in Liverpool's club scene and instrumental in the beginnings of Cream – one of the big global brands of dance culture.'

Romping somewhere at the intersection of Roxy Music, *Rocky Horror* and The Rezillos, Big in Japan were 'an explosion of colour', says Drummond. 'We totally went for it onstage. And were totally embarrassing.' The semi-serious rivalry between Big in Japan and The Crucial Three prompted Julian Cope to start a petition asking for Big in Japan to disband. 'It was up in Probe Records, and of course we went in to sign it,' laughs Drummond. Du Noyer adds, 'It was an *incredibly* bitchy scene. The insults they heaped upon rivals was what defined them, and that got amplified when they actually all became successful. Maybe it comes from the Irish composition of the population, but there's a strong Liverpool tradition of everybody believing they're entertainers. Anyone who performed in Liverpool faced an audience full of people who reckoned they could do better.'

Unlike the Leeds groups – Gang of Four's ambivalence about entertainment, The Mekons' cultivated anonymity and ordinariness – the Liverpool post-punks felt no embarrassment about their desire to be famous. 'Stars are stars and they shine so hard,' McCulloch sang on *Crocodiles*: it's typical Bunnymen widescreen elemental imagery, but he could equally be singing about his feelings about rock's firmament – a mixture of awe and absolute confidence that he'd be joining them, and sooner rather than later. Obsessed with Bowie (for a period he insisted on being called Duke, as in Thin White Duke), McCulloch spent his teenage years feeling like 'there was this big movie camera in the sky', he told me in 1989. 'The first line in "Going Up" on *Crocodiles* – and it's a terrible line – is "Ain't thou watching my film"! It was meant to be tongue in cheek, but that was what spurred me on.' Julian Cope was the same, confessing: 'I always live as if I'm in a film.'

Neither particularly seemed like star material in the early days. Appallingly myopic, McCulloch wore 'aviator blue-tinted glasses, really crap, and often with tape at the corner 'cos they were also falling to bits', recalls Drummond. Cope, originally from the Midlands, looked every bit the teacher-training-college student he'd come to Liverpool to be: 'An extremely dowdy "long raincoat" sort of boy, with a self-effacing floppy fringe and a very introverted manner,' recalls Du Noyer. 'Initially he had an utter lack of stage presence.' Gradually, though, Cope 'just seemed to grow into glamour as if by an act of willpower'. As for McCulloch, behind his spectacles and shyness, he was a natural. Luminously pretty, big lipped and tousled, he'd also been perfecting the art of presence and projection through many narcissistic hours of self-contemplation. 'He was a tall bedroom dreamer, which is the best thing, I've learned since,' says Drummond. 'He'd spent a lot of time in his bedroom, staring into the mirror. That's where it's learned, how to put it over.' McCulloch was so certain of his destiny that he skipped the opportunity to go to university and spent two years on the dole just waiting for the absolutely perfect group to coalesce around him. And it did.

Echo & The Bunnymen, 1981. L to R: Will Sergeant, Ian McCulloch, Les Pattinson, Pete DeFreitas
Photo by Marcia Resnick

Drummond and Balfe started Zoo to put out a posthumous Big in Japan EP, then found themselves releasing singles by The Bunnymen and The Teardrop Explodes. Initially, this was just a pure exercise in DIY, but Zoo soon developed real ambition and a sort of pro-pop ideology. 'Bill and I weren't happy to be a cult,' Balfe has said. 'We wanted our groups to have hits, which was heresy in those post-punk times.' Bound up with this poptimistic stance was Zoo's guiding conviction 'that *Sgt Pepper's* was the death of pop', says Drummond. 'Because that was the beginning of album-oriented rock. Zoo's whole thing was we'd never do any albums. Only singles. And we stuck to that, apart from the Zoo compilation, *To the Shores of Lake Placid*.'

Although Drummond's personal fixation on the classic 45 stemmed mainly from his love of American soul, the Liverpool scene's idea of 'perfect pop' owed more to the sixties: Love, Pink Floyd and above all *Nuggets*, Lenny Kaye's epochal 1972 compilation of mid-sixties American garage punk. This double album was a feat of creative archiving that deposed the post-Beatles aristocracy and installed its own canon of one-hit wonders: Count Five, The Seeds, Shadows of Knight, Chocolate Watchband. Copying Brit Invasion bands like the Stones, these American teenagers hyped up the machismo and misogyny while piling on the wah-wah and fuzztone to an exhilaratingly overstated degree. When the LSD kicked in, the music went 'punkadelic' with equally thrilling effect. But when *Sgt Pepper's* ushered in the era of concept albums, and Cream invented both blues-bore purism and 'heavy' rock, the classic garage band era ended.

The Teardrop Explodes were the flagship of the Zoo aesthetic. Their music was pure gospel according to *Nuggets*, freezing pop time *circa* 1967, just before everything went wrong. They played neo-psychedelia inspired by the early Pink Floyd singles (when Syd Barrett was in the band), keyboard-driven garage bands like The Seeds (Cope owned all their records) along with New Wave groups like The Stranglers and The Fall who also used keyboards. Cope's ideal was the bittersweet aura of classic psychedelia, where the idyllic vibe is haunted by hints of madness and the uncanny. 'The whole idea of the Teardrops to me is nice, nice melodies and lyrics that, while always sung hopefully, have dark secrets in them,' he said. 'I have this theory that we're the "lurking doubt" . . . whispering in people's ears.' The terrific early Teardrops singles for Zoo nearly live up to Cope's ideal. Bass driven and organ laced, 'Sleeping Gas' is hypnotic like The Seeds or ? and the Mysterians, while 'Camera

Camera' throbs and twitches like The Doors' 'Hello I Love You'. You can hear Love's *Forever Changes* in the gauzy wistfulness of 'Treason', which sold an amazing 25,000 copies on its original Zoo release.

All the LSD evocations in the Teardrops sound and Cope's lyrics came from drug music, though, not drug experiences: it was second-hand, entirely derived from records. 'Acid didn't feature in these people's lives until long after they'd been acclaimed as psychedelic acts,' says Paul Du Noyer. Bill Drummond goes further: 'Oh, we used to *loathe* drug-taking, see it as this Southern, sleazy thing. Smoking pot was just absolutely naff and even taking speed was considered uncool. The Liverpool groups did drink alcohol, but it wasn't like a big thing. The drug thing, that really came with touring and the later success Echo and Teardrops enjoyed.' Like other Merseyside groups – Echo & The Bunnymen, obviously, Orchestral Manoeuvres in the Dark – The Teardrop Explodes chose a deliberately trippy-Technicolor, 'far-fucking-out' name primarily as a backlash against post-punk's cold, grey, dispassionate imagery. 'I hated all this I-have-no-heart, and "metal",' Cope explained. 'You don't write songs about no emotions . . . because they're the most important things.'

Cope was both the Teardrops' main attraction and their Achilles heel: unlike McCulloch, he was not a natural singer, his rather thin and inflexible voice falling inevitably into blithe, perky-sounding melodies. Reviewing Cope's 1984 debut solo album *World Shut Your Mouth*, *NME*'s Barney Hoskyns pinpointed the problem as the singer's reliance on major chords, 'so that there's never the cancer-in-the-sugar sensation he demands of music. All is delivered with the same orotund enthusiasm . . . To this day, Cope is singing "Baa-baa-baa" and meaning it.' This forced melodic brightness and an overly clean production meant that the Teardrops' 1980 debut *Kilimanjaro* ended up closer to the bubblegum psychedelia of Strawberry Alarm Clock than Cope's beloved Seeds and Thirteenth Floor Elevators. Decked with dinky keyboards and watery horns, driven by military-Motown beats, *Kilimanjaro* lost the 'balance between triteness and greatness' that was Cope's goal. The Teardrop Explodes went from the next big thing to has-been with incredible speed, even by the accelerated standards of the post-punk era.

Then the trumpet-driven, almost militantly optimistic single 'Reward' unexpectedly became a massive hit in early 1981, boosted by Cope's LSD-enhanced rendition of it on *Top of the Pops*. 'Treason', rereleased and with major-label muscle behind it, followed 'Reward' into the charts. Cope was suddenly a bona fide pop star. And a teenybop idol:

charming, frothing with enthusiasm, and blessed with a mane of shaggy blond hair, he was perfect *Smash Hits* material.

As if subconsciously defying his new pin-up status, though, Cope immediately embarked on what he later called 'the white male fuck-up' trip, a systematic derangement of the senses inspired by such genius-as-madness icons as Syd Barrett and Roky Erikson. 'I used to do outlandish, extreme things because that's what my heroes would have done,' a reformed and cleaned-up Cope told me in 1991. 'The idea was that the accumulation of all my heroes would be one hell of a god to be!' Throughout 1981–2, he gobbled hallucinogens and his erratic behaviour (at one point he cut off all his cute hair and renamed himself Kevin Stapleton) gradually alienated the band's teen following.

Possibly the most curious thing about The Teardrop Explodes is the fact that their music was far more psychedelic *before* they started tripping. The group's second album, *Wilder*, could be Exhibit A in the case to disprove the notion that drugs are creative tools. The album was a flop, and an attempt to record a third LP was abandoned. By this point, Bill Drummond had bailed out: 'It became Julian Cope and a backing band, all about hired London musicians, and I hated dealing with all that.' The Teardrop Explodes finally disintegrated in November 1982.

Although he'd benefited from the New Pop boom, Cope was one of its first discontents. In *NME*'s Christmas 1982 issue, he penned a diatribe against 'the listless, vacuous malaise' of saccharine, overproduced New Pop. In a later interview for the same paper, he railed against the irony and detachment of meta-pop: 'The most annoying thing, I found, were those apostrophes around "Sweetest" in "The 'Sweetest' Girl" by Scritti Politti. That's *such* a clever-clever thing, that's one of the biggest cop-outs I've ever seen.' Early in 1983, Cope reaffirmed his psychedelic creed with the brilliant, manifesto-like essay 'Tales from the Drug Attic'. Published in *NME*, this eulogy to sixties garage punk was loosely tied to a retro explosion of *Nuggets*-style compilations like *Pebbles* and *Mindrocker*. The piece showed such superb taste it was a shame that *World Shut Your Mouth* was so utterly devoid of the mania and magic Cope celebrated.

If Cope was really serious about kickstarting a psychedelic resurgence in the UK, he should have forgotten about making music himself and humbly applied for the job of drugs gofer in The Blue Orchids – the group formed by Fall founder-members Martin Bramah and Una Baines. That original incarnation of The Fall was Cope's favourite band in

1978–9, an obsession shared by Ian McCulloch and Will Sergeant. Cope once calculated that he saw The Fall play twenty-eight times in that period alone (you had to go to the gigs because the group didn't have any records out then). Cope and McCulloch hung around the band, with Cope even earning a lyrical namecheck from Mark E. Smith in 'Two-Steps Back'. 'McCull and I were in awe of Mark,' Cope wrote in his memoir *Head On*. 'With hindsight, I'll say that the main reason anything started to happen was because of Mark. He had very shamanistic properties, a particular ability to draw the best out of people.'

The Blue Orchids were essentially a continuation of the original Fall but slanted further towards the psychedelic. A hypno-swirl of Baines's incense-and-belladonna organ and Bramah's sky-kissing guitar over gluey bass and tumultuous drums, their sound was ramshackle but transcendent. Unlike the neophyte Cope and the still booze-oriented Bunnymen, Bramah and Baines were veterans when it came to hallucinogens. Both tracks on their double-A-sided debut single for Rough Trade, 'The Flood' and 'Disney Boys', were drug inspired. 'The Flood' was the group's mission statement, says Bramah, 'about handling the rush of all these psychedelic drugs, the flood of emotions and impressions, the rush of paradox'. Written by Baines, 'Disney Boys' was a glimpse into her 'lost year' between The Fall and The Blue Orchids, a twelve-month vacation from reality during which she claims not to have slept *at all*.

The single was recorded with The Blue Orchids high on mushrooms throughout the studio process. 'There was an element of chaos surrounding us that was really disturbing to people who tried to turn up and do a day's work – like Mayo Thompson, our producer,' laughs Bramah. 'When we did the final mix, Mayo was actually weeping – partly 'cos he'd managed to capture our thing for posterity against the odds, but also from the trauma of being with us for a couple of days!'

Psilocybin mushrooms, says Bramah, 'put us in touch with our ancestors – a lost voice, a pagan Celtic strangeness. I'd stolen a copy of *The White Goddess* by Robert Graves from the local library when I was a teenager, a treatise on the lost lore of the Druidic poets. The idea of shape-shifting fascinated us. The traumatic experiences we were going through on mushrooms and LSD made us feel like misfits. It was a shamanic thing and Mark E. Smith was the catalyst initially, but Blue Orchids tried to perpetuate this vision.' On the group's 1982 debut album, *The Greatest Hit (Money Mountain)*, Bramah's and Baines's lyrics teem with pagan and pantheistic poetry. 'Woke up one day/Threw

my name in the bin . . . Ate the fruit of surrender/Surrender to no one,'
sings Bramah in 'A Year with No Head'. 'Mad as the Mist and Snow'
took a Yeats poem as its lyric, while 'Sun Connection' reels with 'visions
of splendour' and imagery of 'hearts that burst when we salute heaven'.
One of the Orchids' most awe-struck songs, it was inspired by Bramah's
tripped-out perception of 'the sun as a living sentient being that was
aware of me on a profound level'.

Unlike the other neo-psychedelic bands of the early eighties, though,
The Blue Orchids gave their mysticism a political edge. Punning on pop
charts versus drug highs, the album title *The Greatest Hit* questioned
what true success really was, in life and in music; the *Money Mountain*
subtitle hinted at the spiritual fortune to be won if you opted out of the
rat race. Quietly refusing to 'climb the money mountain', The Blue
Orchids rejected Thatcherite values and the disenchanted worldview that
defined ambition only in material terms. 'Dumb Magician' was a
dreamer's critique of schemers ('See behind the scenes/The strings
attached to all things/"This gets me that"/Try so hard to get your foot in
the door/Get what you ask for and nothing more') that could also be read
as a dig at the New Pop careerism of their Rough Trade labelmates Scritti
Politti. The song ends with the defiant call to transcendence – 'the only
way out is UP' – as the band incandesce into a mystic blaze of keyboards
and guitar. 'Low Profile', a colossal, head-sundering deluge of sound,
served as The Blue Orchids' turn on/tune in/drop out anthem: 'No compromise in the name of truth/Keep a low profile/Serene inspiration'.

Some of the most visionary music of its era, *The Greatest Hit* topped
the independent album chart in the early summer of 1982. The Blue
Orchids seemed destined for greatness, but by then they'd fallen in with
Nico, who was living in Manchester. 'She was part of the holy trinity for
us,' says Bramah. 'It was Velvets, Bowie, Iggy.' But touring as both
Nico's backing band and support group, 'darker drugs came into play',
says Bramah. 'Heroin got thrown at us for free.' On their EP from later
that year, *Agents of Change*, 'The Long Night Out' describes Bramah's
dalliance with the poppy, while the beatific ballad 'Release' expresses the
more open-hearted side of drug use: 'Just touch the flesh of the
breeze/And feel release'. The Blue Orchids wore their inspirations on
their record sleeve with the confession: 'this extended player has been
completed under extraneous influences working upon the psyche'. In the
end, though, narcotics laid waste to their potential.

*

The Blue Orchids had been the support band on Echo & The Bunnymen's first national tour in 1981, and in some ways the two groups were like underground and mainstream versions of the same quest for 'a glory beyond all glories' (as Bill Drummond put it). You could see the affinity in the groups' record covers: *The Greatest Hit* showed the setting sun glinting over a silhouetted mountainscape, while *Heaven Up Here* pictured the four Bunnymen staring into a navy-blue sea while standing on an ebb-tide beach whose wet sand reflects the dark turquoise sky. Bill Drummond saw the group as representing 'cold, dampness, darkness', and organized The Bunnymen's triumphant Northern Hemispheres tour of 1983 to start with gigs on the isles of Skye and Lewis. The cover of their third album, *Porcupine*, and the video for their first Top 10 hit, 'The Cutter', made spectacular use of Iceland's glaciers.

This sort of elemental imagery of natural grandeur was all over British music in 1983–4: U2, with the Alpine purity of their 'New Year's Day' video and their live album *Under a Blood-Red Sky*, and The Waterboys, with songs like 'The Big Music', 'A Pagan Place' and 'The Whole of the Moon'. Big Country were in the Top 10 with 'Fields of Fire (400 Miles)' and 'In a Big Country', featuring Stuart Adamson's skirling, bagpipe-like guitar (invariably described as 'rousing' or 'stirring') and lyrics that endlessly recycled words like 'rain', 'sea', 'sun' and 'fire'. After briefly intersecting with New Pop, Simple Minds reverted to their true calling, stadium-ready art-rock, and produced an increasingly bombastic series of hits such as 'Waterfront'. Jim Kerr's panoramic lyrics, teeming with lofty intangibles, invoked wanderlust and wonderment. 'It's size, I think,' Kerr said of his band's music. 'And it's space. And subconsciously there must be some connection between sound and sight.'

All of these groups had a Celtic connection: they were all from Scotland, Ireland or Irish-tinged Liverpool. And they often gave the quest for 'indefinable glory' a vaguely military or messianic colouring. The Bunnymen tapped into this spirit with their 1980 shows that used camouflage, netting, dry ice and inventive lighting to create an *Apocalypse Now* atmosphere. Big Country's music exuded a playing-soldiers vibe that dated back to Adamson's first group, The Skids, and such songs as 'Vanguard's Crusade' and 'Dulce et Decorum Est (Pro Patria Mori)' (which translates as 'It is sweet and proper to die for one's fatherland'). U2 turned pacifism itself into a crusade on their album *War*. Bono described himself as an 'aggressive pacifist' and marched about on stage clasping a white flag.

Ian McCulloch waspishly described U2's anthems as 'music for plumbers and bricklayers', while boasting that The Bunnymen were 'an oceans and mountains band'. Behind the bitching lay an astute perception of threat: U2 were The Bunnymen's nearest rivals when it came to capturing that post-Joy Division audience left bereft after the saviour Curtis's death. True, some of the abandoned flock had veered away from the dark depths and joined in New Pop's celebration of shiny surface pleasures. 'What's been called the "new pop mentality" is a *resignation* . . . [it's] a direct inheritance of Joy Division,' OMD's singer Andy McCluskey noted perceptively. 'I think Joy Division were the very last band who could come along and *look* for something.' Those who didn't buy into the New Pop dream, though, still pined for a band that represented some sort of quest; a band worth being devout about.

U2 stepped forward to fill that role. Their first truly successful single, 'I Will Follow', made it clear that they were in the market for converts. Prior to that, they'd recorded their debut single '11 O'Clock Tick Tock' with Martin Hannett, and then done another, 'A Day Without Me' that was actually inspired by Ian Curtis (Bono sang as the departed Curtis looking back on 'a world I left behind'). If it seemed that Bono was consciously preparing to take on the role vacated by Curtis, then – according to Tony Wilson – that's pretty much the case. 'Two months after Ian died, U2 were brought round to my office at Granada TV by this plugger looking to break them, and I remember Bono sitting on my desk saying how incredibly sorry he was about Ian's death, how it had really hurt him . . . how Ian was the number-one singer of his generation, and he, Bono, knew he was always only ever going to be number two,' says Wilson. 'And he said something else, something like, "Now he's gone, I promise you I'll do it for him." Not quite that silly, but along those lines.'

The expanse in Joy Division's music always seemed destined for big spaces, maybe even arenas. U2 had the same attitude. 'If we stay in small clubs, we'll develop small minds, and then we'll start making small music,' Bono told *Trouser Press* in 1983. Everything about U2 was big: the lyrical themes, Bono's voice, the sheer size of their sound, their ambition (U2 always obviously wanted to be the biggest band in the world) and sense of purpose. Unlike Echo & The Bunnymen, who kept the nature of their quest deliberately nebulous, U2's fervour had an unmistakable moral charge. This was the real positive punk, finally an attempt to do something constructive with rock's energies.

Three members of U2 – Bono, The Edge and drummer Larry Mullen – were converts to a nonsectarian Christian group called Shalom. 'I loved the idea of being reborn,' Bono recalled. 'I think people should be reborn every day, man!' At twenty years old, this idea of 'surrender every day' and self-sacrifice to some greater good thrilled Bono and his brethren to the core. Belief infused every particle of U2's early sound, from the cold flame of The Edge's guitar to what NME's Richard Cook described as 'the beckoning ecstasy' of Bono's voice. 'We're playing rock 'n' roll and we're a change within rock 'n' roll,' declared Bono, but the change was really a restoration: the return of the old confidence and certainty that rock could make a difference. 'It would be wrong for me to say, yes, we can change the world with a song,' Bono said. 'But every time I try writing that's where I'm at!' The band's role models were Bob Marley (who fused religious faith and political ire) and The Clash (except that U2 chose more universal, liberal–humanist touchstones – Martin Luther King rather than the Sandinistas).

Bono sounded pious in one early interview when he described The Sex Pistols as 'just a con . . . Can't you see we're really rebelling against the idea of rebelling?' What saved U2 from sanctimony was the sheer exhilaration of their post-Television sound. 'I Will Follow' is like a Dublin cousin to PiL's 'Public Image': The Edge's radiant, tingling chords and Bono's ardent vocals create the classic U2 sensation, a 'chesty surge' that elevates the spirit by neglecting the body. Crucial to U2's resolutely antidance urgency was the unsyncopated, martial drumming of Larry Mullen, who'd been fired from his school's boys' marching band for having long hair!

'Boy' is the key word when it comes to understanding U2, from the soldier-boy rhythms to Bono's choirboy vocals to the beautiful blond six-year-old on the cover of their debut album, Boy. Inside were songs like 'Stories for Boys' and 'Into the Heart', in which Bono sang about retreating 'into the heart of a child', finding the naïve purity of spirit lost with adulthood. Around this time, Bono talked about aiming for a kind of baptismal atmosphere at their shows, wanting the audience to feel 'washed' – spiritually cleansed and renewed. This kind of talk naturally drew a fair amount of flak. Reviewing 1981's October for NME, Barney Hoskyns complained about the 'excessive plaintiveness of Bono's voice' and 'forced power' of songs like 'Gloria' and 'Rejoice', and critiqued the way the band flew Icarus-like over the dark, swampy regions of the human soul, evading the adult complexities of desire. But for every person alienated by Bono's messianic aura, another felt the call of his soaring, imploring voice.

In 1983 *War* propelled U2 into the big league. The single 'New Year's Day' – inspired by the struggles of Solidarity in Poland; not that you could tell that from the mercifully vague lyrics – was their first big UK hit. The American tour that followed was documented on the live album and film *Under a Blood Red Sky* – recorded at Colorado's Red Rocks open-air stadium – and left U2 on the threshold of megastardom. In 1984 'Pride (In the Name of Love)' smashed down the door. The accompanying album, *The Unforgettable Fire*, was surprisingly understated, largely shunning anthems for atmospherics. Co-producer Brian Eno encouraged the band to create sonic landscapes that turned your ears into eyes, gazing into the far distance – literally *vision*ary music. The Edge also made a conscious decision to side-step his burgeoning guitar-hero status and poured his creative energies into keyboards and 'general atmospheric work'. But this was the logical destination for his guitar-playing, which always had a curiously disembodied, synth-like quality: swirling texture-strands rather than riffs or power chords. Avoiding solos and shunning the grittiness of distortion, The Edge instead used effects like echo, slide, harmonics and extremely prolonged sustain, which blurred the link between the physicality of his playing and the amorphous sounds that emerged from the speakers. As Marcello Carlin observes, 'The Edge sometimes sounds as though he is playing guitar with no hands'. On *The Unforgettable Fire*, he blossomed into a guitarist-as-cinematographer: the title track, released as a single and another huge hit, resembles a first-class sunset or the Milky Way on the clearest of nights. The self-effacing majesty of the sound matched the selflessness of U2's creed.

The ascension of U2 to megaband status further polarized the pop world into those who recoiled from them as righteous bombast and those who hailed them as true redeemers of rock. Their old rivals Echo & The Bunnymen, meanwhile, deftly maintained a balance between taking on the BIG gestures and BIG language while remaining detached from it, taking the piss out of themselves (and everybody else, naturally). 'There was a crossover between the audiences for Echo and U2,' McCulloch recalled. 'But I think U2's audience liked the rally call, and our following liked the sarcasm.' McCulloch obsessively used words like 'heaven' as vague signifiers for some kind of beyond or unimaginable perfection, but kept the religiosity undefined and deflated any grandiosity with wisecracks.

The other big difference between U2 and Echo & The Bunnymen was sex appeal: Bono and his fellow pilgrims had none while McCulloch oozed it. In 1983, he decided it was time to work his mojo. Performing 'The Cutter' on *Top of the Pops*, he did something so embarrassingly calculated and contrived that it became cool: he blatantly, brazenly, flicked his shirt off his shoulders to expose his nipples. 'I was out of my head, totally out of my head, probably as out of my head as I've ever been. And I thought, We're at number twenty-seven, do we wanna go up the charts or not? Got to get the nipples out. All three of them. And, sure enough, we jumped sixteen places up the chart the following week!'

Ocean Rain, their fourth album, was lush, orchestrated and, with the orgasmic moans of 'Thorn of Crowns', overtly erotic for the first time. The Bunnymen's music had always been gloriously grey, but now they went Technicolor and swoony with string-laden songs like 'The Killing Moon', which showcased McCulloch's sonorous Sinatra-via-Morrison croon like never before. Deliberately distancing The Bunnymen from the other 'big music' bands of 1984 like U2 and Simple Minds, *Ocean Rain* veered away from rock towards pop. 'Kissing music' is how McCulloch described the record – a phrase that drew attention to The Bunnymen's primary teenybop sales draw: the singer's magnificent lips. The strategy worked: by a strange twist, Echo & The Bunnymen, the group who'd helped bring back 'rock' during the era of New Pop, became proper pop stars; 'pop' in the sense that Zoo originally cherished – the early sixties groups who had elicited teenage screams, rather than the post-1967 beardy art-rockers whose profundities pleased critics and grown-ups.

'Missing the point of our mission/Will we become misshapen?' McCulloch had sung on 1983's painfully art-rocky *Porcupine*, the awkwardly transitional predecessor to *Ocean Rain*. But unlike U2, for all the camouflage gear and abstract urgency, ultimately Echo & The Bunnymen didn't really have a mission beyond banishing the darkness and celebrating the glory.

24

THE BLASTING CONCEPT: Progressive Punk from SST Records to Mission of Burma

Black Flag. The Minutemen. Hüsker Dü. Mission of Burma. Meat Puppets.

Los Angeles punk matched New York and San Francisco for intensity. Curiously, though, when its original burst of energy burned out, LA didn't 'go post-punk', but instead turned its face to the past. Some ex-punks embraced 'power pop': a return to the tight, melodic, high-energy sounds of the mid-sixties (with The Knack and then The Go-Go's taking the style into the charts). A slightly 'cooler' variation on this back-to-the-sixties move came a few years later in the form of 'The Paisley Underground' – neo-psychedelic groups like The Dream Syndicate and The Rain Parade. Others embarked on a rediscovery of American roots music – rockabilly, country, blues – a vogue spearheaded by The Blasters with their 1980 debut *American Music*. SoCal's retro-roots flavours ranged from the hoodoobilly of The Gun Club and The Flesh Eaters (both influenced by The Cramps, who'd migrated from New York to LA) to the craze for 'cowpunk' (Tex & The Horseheads, Blood on the Saddle, The Beat Farmers and many more).

While the ex-punk hipsters started rifling through rock's back pages, punk itself reached Los Angeles' sprawling suburbs and turned into hardcore. On the face of it, hardcore was just as retrogressive as the nouveau Americana. Like Oi! in Britain, hardcore's 'punk will never die' stance translated into a diehard fundamentalism, freezing any impulses towards musical progress and restricting the emotional palette to snarling rage and fratboy rowdiness. That didn't matter at first: hardcore's aggression and visceral impact made it invigorating. The early records by SoCal outfits The Descendents, Angry Samoans and Circle

Jerks, along with non-LA bands like Negative Approach and Scream, were among the most thrilling music of the era.

In the early days, hardcore also served as a home for mavericks. San Francisco's Flipper, as we saw earlier, played noise-drenched dirges in defiance of hardcore's 'Loud–fast rules!' strictures; Bad Brains, from Washington, DC, could play faster than almost anybody, but their tempest had an exquisite fluency that revealed the all-black band's roots in jazz fusion. (Once called Mind Power, they'd been born again as punks and then as Rastafarians!) Most crucially, there was the SST label, founded by Black Flag and based in the Los Angeles suburb of Hermosa Beach.

Formed in 1977, Black Flag started from the most pared-down of existential stances – self as cell, body as cage – and then tried to blast their way to freedom. Greg Ginn, the group's guitarist and leader, described what they did as modern blues; Spot, SST's house producer, claimed Black Flag's music was 'as comforting as the screams that relieve pain'. Glimmers of humour like 'TV Party' relieved the darkness, but for the most part Black Flag's vision ranged from the embattled defiance of 'Rise Above' to the wallowing trauma of 'Damaged I', a slow-grind as drawn out as the death throes of a wounded animal.

After hearing the group's 1982 debut album *Damaged*, *NME*'s Barney Hoskyns hailed Black Flag as 'the only progressively retarded group on earth'. The album was such a definitive hardcore statement that it served simultaneously to codify the genre and render it nearly obsolete. As Black Flag copyists swarmed across America, the group wrestled with the same dilemma that British post-punk groups had confronted a few years earlier: progression versus stasis, challenging their audience versus pandering to it. Black Flag began to push their music in a more expansive direction. And they transformed SST into hardcore's vanguard label, drawing on local oddballs like The Minutemen and Saccharine Trust, along with out-of-town kinsmen like Meat Puppets and Hüsker Dü.

You couldn't really call this music 'post-punk', not when that term referred to bands like PiL or Cabaret Voltaire. The SST bands were too rooted in the hard riffs and heavy rhythms of *pre*-punk rock. The term 'progressive punk' fits better. As they developed, the SST bands wriggled out of hardcore's stylistic straitjacket through exploring hybrid genres, writing longer songs, introducing elements of freeform jamming and extended solos, recording instrumentals and even concept albums.

Unlike the UK post-punk groups, though, the SST acts had almost no interest in using the studio as an instrument; their innovations all took place within the context of the band as performing unit. Essentially live-in-the-studio documents, the records were made with staggering speed and cheapness – songs were typically captured in a single take, without overdubs or embellishments. Another SST hallmark was its groups' un-punk belief in virtuosity. Black Flag set the tone here: Ginn was a sort of guitar anti-hero, hacking out stunted and mutilated solos. Impelled by a monstrous work ethic, Ginn drove Black Flag 'like Patton on steroids', singer Henry Rollins said, enforcing a punishing regime of daily practice sessions. 'New redneck' is the term Joe Carducci, the label's head of marketing and promotion, invented to describe the SST sweat-hog ethos.

The SST groups had the same 'no pain no gain' attitude to touring, embarking on marathon treks that took in parts of the country no other bands visited. 'The first-wave Hollywood punk bands, none of them thought about touring,' says Mike Watt of The Minutemen. 'Only The Dils had a van, I think. I guess they all thought they'd get signed to majors and be stars. But Black Flag's idea was to build this tour circuit across the country from scratch. For kids in places like Shreveport or Boise, the only punk show all year round was when Black Flag rolled into town.' The band travelled in the most rudimentary conditions. Because most of the venues would pay only $100 tops, the band had to sleep in the van, says Carducci, 'and mooch off the people who came to the shows'.

Carducci joined SST because Black Flag were so busy touring that the label had a backlog of material in the can but unreleased, including records by The Minutemen and Saccharine Trust. SST was simply too cash-poor and too short of time to put anything out, so Carducci became one of the label's four partners and helped to fund the releases. Drawing on his experience from working at the Portland-based distributor Systematic and running his own small label, Thermidor, on the side, Carducci was able to put SST on a proper footing. ('When I joined,' he says, 'they were doing business from a phone booth!') With his help, SST became America's nearest equivalent to Rough Trade – operating with a similar mix of idealism and pragmatism, and driven by a missionary zeal to get their records to every corner of the country that earlier US inde-pendent labels had generally lacked. To be fair, these early American indies were probably defeated by the sheer geographical enormity of the country and the patchy nature of independent distribution in those days. 'There was no map for this thing at all then,' says Carducci, recalling having 'to go to the public library and look up record stores in every Yellow Pages across the country', trying to work out if the store sold unusual material, and then sending them Systematic's mail-order catalogue.

SST also shared with Rough Trade not just heroic ambition but a collectivist ethos, although in their case the vibe was more like a military unit than a post-hippy wholefood store. SST's headquarters, a one-room apartment, also served as a rough-and-ready barracks for seven people, who slept on the floor and in makeshift bunk beds created by stacking desks on top of each other. In addition to rehearsing, writing, recording and gigging, the musicians in Black Flag and other SST bands helped with the daily operations of the label, making phone calls to record stores and going on flyer-posting missions around town. At some deep psychological level, the privations of the lifestyle – cramped living quarters, little money, bad food, second-hand charity-shop clothing, endless work – were *attractive*: SST's recruits were people looking for a purpose, a mission.

If there was a political slant to SST, it wasn't socialistic, like Rough Trade's, but a brand of autonomy leaning towards the libertarian anarchist in which a distrust of all forms of authority was balanced by an equally powerful impulse towards self-discipline and hard work. Ginn had been a teenage entrepreneur, running his own ham radio equipment business, Solid State Tuners (hence the name SST). Still, SST did put the interests of its artists first: all their contracts were for one record at a time, because, Ginn said, 'We don't want to work with anyone who doesn't want to be here.' Chuck Dukowski, who switched from being Black Flag's bassist to being the label's chief organizer declared: 'Our politique is our catalogue – diversity, self-expression, the individual being allowed to develop at his own pace and in his own direction.'

Contributing to SST's strong identity was the artwork of Ginn's brother Raymond Pettibon, which appeared on many of the label's releases as well as flyers and T-shirts. Rollins' biographer James Parker wrote of how 'Pettibon's eerie, mocking artwork' seemed to offer 'some kind of uncrackable code to [Black Flag's] attitude and style'. Pettibon's ink drawings were, to put it bluntly, creepy: sometimes gallows humour, sometimes pure horror, and often tinged with an apocalyptic, mystical dread (the cover of the SST compilation *The Blasting Concept* shows a woman being strangled and raped in the foreground with a mushroom cloud on the horizon).

One of Pettibon's most famous pieces depicted Charles Manson as the fifth Beatle. Manson figured as a kind of patron anti-saint for the SST crew (Rollins even struck up a correspondence with the jailed psychopath). The year of the Sharon Tate murders and Altamont, 1969, was the foundation of Black Flag's dark worldview. Musically, too, it was ignition point for the group's two biggest influences, Black Sabbath and The Stooges (whose '1969' seemed to take perverse glee in 'war across the USA'). The germ of punk can be traced to that year – the final death of the hippy dream. But, unlike the other punk bands, Black Flag and its SST cohorts didn't give up on hippy music (Ginn was a Grateful Dead diehard) or its musical concerns (progression, artistic growth, fusion, instrumental chops). They kept those pre-punk values and combined them with punk's negativity, which they rooted in the heavy, despair-laden vision of Black Sabbath songs like 'War Pigs' as much as The Stooges' 'No Fun'. 'Our musicians were studying seventies and sixties rock; they didn't study punk rock records,' says Carducci. Former Black Flag vocalist Dez Cadena even started a band called DC3, dedicated to the classic rock sounds of his youth, like Mountain and Deep Purple.

After *Damaged*, Ginn himself started to listen closely to King Crimson and Mahavishnu Orchestra, says Carducci, while coffee – the group's previous narcotic of choice – was gradually ousted by pot. Building on the deliciously turgid grind of 'Damaged I', Ginn decided that slow tempos were the way ahead. He taught the group's new drummer Bill Stevenson how to let the rhythm 'ooze out'. The result was the trudging sludge of Black Flag's 1983 album *My War*. Side two's trio of protracted dirges, 'Nothing Left Inside', 'Three Nights' and 'Scream', appalled hardcore youth, who craved a high-velocity soundtrack for slamdancing. At Black Flag gigs, the shaven-headed kids were equally aghast when they saw the group's hair, which had followed the music's early seventies trajectory and grown long and lank.

In the gap between *Damaged* and *My War*, the hardcore scene had degenerated: by 1983 tribal identity had eclipsed artistic expression as a priority. Music was little more than a delivery system for the content, which varied only slightly. There was basic apolitical hardcore, such as Orange County's TSOL – typically affluent suburban youth, bored and looking for *Fight Club*-style release through violence, and whose anti-authoritarianism was instinctual, non-ideological and basically selfish. TSOL's Jack Grisham described their vibe as '*Clockwork* fuckin' *Orange* County'. But this brand of delinquent hardcore was increasingly being superseded by politically conscious puritans like Millions of Dead Cops and Minor Threat. The latter pioneered the Straight Edge movement – agit-prop-spouting skinhead outfits opposed to mind-dulling distractions like drink, drugs and, in some cases, even sex.

By the time *My War* appeared, the most powerful force in hardcore was the magazine *MaximumRockNRoll*, founded in 1982 by a veteran Berkeley politico called Tim Yohannon. Hardcore's elevation of content-over-form was reflected in *MRR*'s spurning of glossy paper stock: it was printed on paper so low grade and ink smutted that you'd hesitate to wipe your bum with it. '*MaximumRockNRoll* had identified what they were interested in – which was imitations of Black Flag *circa Damaged*, Minor Threat and The Dead Kennedys – and they didn't pay attention to anything else,' says Carducci. *MRR*, naturally, gave *My War* a terrible review.

The musical symbol for hardcore's homogeneity was the rapid-fire but regimented polka-like beat that virtually every band used. Ginn, in contrast, wanted Black Flag's music to *swing*. When the group embarked on a massive spate of touring in 1984, the scenario became Black Flag versus samecore. 'We've been preparing for a couple of years and now we're ready to go into an attack phase,' Ginn told a radio interviewer. 'Kill Everything Now' was the motto of their first big tour of 1984 (a year during which they would play some 200 gigs!). Hardcore responded to Black Flag's hostility in kind, with straggly-haired frontman Rollins receiving the brunt of audience abuse.

The Minutemen often encountered the same kind of resistance. 'When you get situations like hardcore where the bent is egalitarian, their idea of being *equal* is everybody being *the same*,' muses Mike Watt, the group's bassist. 'So if you're trying to experiment, like we were, that's rocking the boat – because it's taken as elitist. Hardcore's attitude got to be "Why experiment? All we want is a fast beat so we can dance." Or not even dance – just beat the shit out of each other, with the slamdancing. The big enemy is becoming generic – because that's when people stop listening and the music becomes a background sound. But we never saw punk as a style of music particularly. Early on, it was so all over the map. It seemed more like a state of mind than a genre of music.'

The Minutemen's way of going against the grain was totally different from Black Flag's: not heavy, ponderous dirge-riffs but songs like electro-convulsive jolts, over almost as soon as they had begun. *Paranoid Time*, their debut EP and SST's second release, crammed seven songs into six minutes and forty-one seconds. The Minutemen's nimble punk-funk was closer to Gang of Four than Minor Threat. 'Paranoid Chant', the stand-out tune on the EP, was a bit like Gang of Four's nuclear Armageddon satire 'In the Ditch', except funnier and much more pithy: singer/guitarist D. Boon plays the poor flustered schmuck who tries to 'talk to girls' but keeps 'thinking of World War Three'.

Unlike Black Flag, who disdained the post-punk coming out of England, The Minutemen loved Wire's compression ('really small songs, no solos', enthuses Watt), The Pop Group's mesh of 'Beefheart and Funkadelic', The Fall's half-sung/half-spoken rants. In classic post-punk fashion, the group conceived of their sound as a democracy: bass and drums on equal footing with the guitar, which definitely wasn't the lead instrument. 'D. Boon saw music in terms of economy,' says Watt. 'He said, "If you really want the bass up there, I gotta make room for it." That was the idea of him having a thin sound, playing really trebly – to leave all the lower mid-frequencies and the bottom end for me. It was very generous of him.'

On The Minutemen's classic 1981–3 albums *The Punch Line*, *What Makes a Man Starts Fires* and *Buzz or Howl Under the Influence of Heat*, Watt's bass lunges, darts, churns and pulsates like a sackful of randy hamsters; Boon's guitar, all splintered chords and spindly microsolos, is as flab-free as his pudgy physique wasn't; drummer George Hurley is a human breakbeat machine, scattering syncopations and tom-rolls like funky shrapnel. The paradox of The Minutemen is that they're a groove band but the songs are so short and delivered so fast that the effect isn't exactly groovy: it's more haywire – an uncontainable explosion of ideas, musical and lyrical.

'El Salvador is Spanish for Vietnam': badge printed by CISPES, the activist organization that protested the Reagan administration's support for the brutally repressive junta in El Salvador. D. Boon joined CISPES and proselytized for the cause at Minutemen shows.

The Minutemen were overtly political: Boon was a member of CIS-PES, the Coordinating Committee in Solidarity with the People of El Salvador, and would often leave the stage, soaked in sweat, and immediately start working the room, handing out leaflets to gig-goers. Their general worldview was anti-capitalist and pro-worker, informed by Boon and Watt's backgrounds growing up in San Pedro, a harbour town and US Navy base to the south of Los Angeles, and feeling their average-guy dads (a car worker and navy sailor, respectively) got a raw deal. In the early years of The Minutemen, Boon put out a fanzine called *Prole* that covered music, politics and art.

'The Minutemen thought of themselves in terms of the history of port labour battles, the longshoremen and unions,' says Carducci. 'They and Black Flag and other SST bands came from areas of Los Angeles where there's a certain amount of inherited bohemianism, with all the beach towns, but there's also a big blue-collar population. If you drive out on the freeways, beyond all the obvious famous places in LA, you see the true scale of the place and realize there's this whole population who aren't just pushing paper at the movie studios; they're actually *making* things.' The mix of light industry and sun-baked post-hippy bohemia in areas like Hermosa Beach and San Pedro created a distinct and unusual sensibility that fused artiness and unpretentiousness; dilettante tendencies got inoculated by the heavy-duty work ethic. 'What I loved about that area of Los Angeles was the fearlessness,' says Carducci. 'The not worrying about being cool.'

'We were kind of products of the sixties, me and D. Boon, but not adults in the sixties,' says Watt. 'We were all primed with this rebellion-minded worldview, but we missed the train.' As much as The Pop Group, they saw what they did as part of a continuum with Bob Dylan and especially Creedence Clearwater Revival. They admired the populist class-consciousness of songs like 'Fortunate Son'; Watt wore flannel in homage to Creedence singer John Fogerty. The name The Minutemen itself is a sixties allusion. Although it originally dates back to the revolutionary militias of the American War of Independence, Watt and Boon chose it as an ironic reference to a sixties group of paranoid right-wing terrorists, who called themselves The Minutemen because they felt they were defending the republic from its *internal* enemies, ranging from crypto-communist summer camps to Red infiltrators in the Justice Dept.

Along with defending the worker, The Minutemen believed in hard work. Not content with churning out records and gigging tirelessly, they ran their own indie label, New Alliance, and put out early releases by a number of artists who later wound up on SST, like Hüsker Dü and The Descendents. The Minutemen toured as hard as Black Flag did (fifty gigs in as many days was typical) and with the same low-budget, no-roadies/no-driver approach: booking their own shows, unloading their gear and setting it up themselves, sleeping in the van or on fans' floors. Singing in 'The Politics of Time' about life on the road, Boon declared 'We jam econo/It makes us stench'. 'Econo' was the band's private slang term for their ultra-frugal approach to touring and recording. Songs were rehearsed to perfection before entering the studio and then knocked out in a single take. Keeping costs down was all part of the quest for autonomy. 'Being small, you build a sense of self-reliance that you can't learn if you become a big rock band,' says Watt.

The Minutemen's down-to-earth aura allowed them to get away with being pretty avant. The lyrics were condensed into telegraphic blurts that sometimes resembled a demagogue's slogans. 'Games', from 1981's *The Punch Line*, shouts down a manipulative person, or perhaps manipulation in the abstract, with one-word cries of accusation: 'Contradictions! Lies, lies! . . . Unreal!' At other times, the words come across like opaque fragments of modernist poetry. On 'The Glory of Man', Boon sings, 'I live sweat but I dream light years/I am the tide, the rise and the fall/The reality soldier, the laugh child'. The Minutemen had a great way with a title – 'Roar of the Masses Could Be Farts', 'If Reagan Played Disco' and the self-demystifying 'Shit from an Old Notebook'. The more abstract lyrics usually came from Watt; the more straightforwardly denunciatory stuff from Boon. When the latter complained, 'Your words are too spacey, man, you gotta get more clear,' a piqued Watt took his landlady's note about the bathtub leaking and turned it into the song 'Take 5, D': 'Hope we can rely on you not to use shower/You're not keeping tub caulked.' Says Watt, 'I was, like, "This real enough for you, D.?"'

'Take 5, D' appeared on 1984's *Double Nickels on the Dime*, The Minutemen's most accomplished and conventionally pleasant record to date. The double album's forty-five songs seem like an attempt to imagine what post-punk would sound like if it were rooted in American music rather than founded on a rejection of it. '"Mr Narrator!"/This is Bob Dylan to me . . . I'm his soldier child,' Boon sang on the bittersweet and almost mellow 'History Lesson (Part II)' – a reverie about childhood friends Watt and Boon having their lives changed by punk rock. 'Coming up from Pedro, me and Boon were kind of hicks as far as the Hollywood punks were considered, provincials or something,' recalls Watt, explaining the song's description of the pair as 'fuckin' corndogs'. He adds, 'But we didn't care; it was just so liberating for us, that scene.'

They got the idea of doing a double album from Hüsker Dü, who had recorded their own (and a concept album, to boot) in a lightning-fast three-day session in late 1983. Impelled by friendly rivalry, The Minutemen set to recording *Double Nickels*. SST cunningly delayed putting out Hüsker Dü's *Zen Arcade* until July 1984 so it could be released on exactly the same day as The Minutemen's opus – to intensify the impact and the sense of SST's brand of post-hardcore reaching a peak of aesthetic maturity.

Just over three years earlier, Hüsker Dü had released their debut single 'Statues' on their own, tiny Minneapolis-based label, Reflex. Punk, the group's initial inspiration, was over; British post-punk seemed like the way ahead. 'That single sounds like Public Image; it's got that Keith Levene sound,' says Carducci, claiming that Hüsker Dü later dismissed that period in the band's life 'as a dark time . . . a weak moment of doubt'. After hearing the early hardcore of Black Flag and The Dead Kennedys, Hüsker Dü were galvanized with renewed purpose and threw themselves unreservedly into the 'loud–fast' maelstrom. The result was *Land Speed Record* – seventeen songs in twenty-six minutes, the contours of the vocal melodies almost completely disappearing in the dust-cloud of distortion the band left in its amphetamine-fuelled slipstream. Gradually, though, the love of sixties pop shared by guitarist/vocalist Bob Mould and drummer/vocalist Grant Hart re-emerged, reaching fruition with *Zen Arcade*: Beatles-like melodies, Byrdsy folk-rock harmonies, piano interludes and even some trippy backwards guitar.

What made Hüsker Dü classic SST prog-punkers was the virtuosity inside the mayhem. Hart's fleet-footed drumming sometimes recalled jazz-schooled players like Billy Cobham or Mitch Mitchell. His intricate high-hat patterns and cymbal splashes generated a spray of top-end sound, merging with the snow-flurry tempest of Mould's open-tuned guitar. Hüsker Dü's music was furious, just like punk, yet its blast achieved an abstraction to rival that of free jazz. As if to signpost the fact that this effect wasn't merely an accidental by-product of playing hard and fast, but intentional, *Zen Arcade* closed with a fourteen-minute instrumental of full-on improvisation. A devastating foray at the intersection of thrash metal, jazz-rock and raga, 'Reoccurring Dreams' fills your mind's eye with images of tornado spouts, napalm horizons, boiling seas, and gas plumes blistering from the surface of the sun.

At the time when they were making these records, Hüsker Dü's torrential noise was often compared to Mission of Burma. Some say the Boston band influenced Hüsker Dü's shift away from PiL-copyism. (Mission of Burma certainly played Minneapolis in the winter of 1980 . . . and Hüsker Dü were their support group.) They never recorded for SST – although drummer Pete Prescott, with Volcano Suns, and guitarist Roger Miller did both separately sign to SST much later – but Mission of Burma had a lot in common with the label's hardcore-but-maverick approach, its uneasy combination of raw power and experimental impulse.

And if anybody fitted the progressive-punk concept, it was Mission of Burma. 'I think we're just a closet prog-rock act that happened during punk,' says bassist and singer Clint Conley. 'We were attracted to the velocity and volume of punk. But at the same time Roger and I were both really attracted to composition.' Miller had even started a composition major at Cal Arts, writing 'very complex piano scores and pieces for percussion trios', only to quit because 'academia didn't suit me'. Then punk rock came along. 'I was just blown away by these people who could barely play guitar,' he says. 'And I could play complex pieces by Schoenberg. But things like The Sex Pistols meant more to me than complexity.'

And yet when Mission of Burma formed in Boston in 1979, the complexity crept back in. MoB loved the early post-punk emerging out of England, especially Gang of Four and Wire, who played games with song structure. As punk developed away from raw, blasting power into odd alliances of minimalism and sophistication, Miller's training suddenly became relevant. The result was 'avant-garde music you could shake your fist to', as one journalist famously put it.

Where Conley tended to write the more melodic, shout-along MoB tunes like 'Academy Fight Song' (their debut single) and 'That's When I Reach for My Revolver', Miller's tunes were more like dismantled anthems. The sheer noise assault and aggression of the MoB live experience seemed to signify 'rock', but mostly their songs frustrated the simple rock-out impulse. This combination of visceral and cerebral, pain-threshold volume and crypto-prog structural weirdness, meant that Mission of Burma were 'sort of an acquired taste', as Conley put it. 'We heard it over and over again throughout our career that people would see us the first time and it just wouldn't make any sense at all. Listening to our live tapes, I know what they're talking about. Sometimes it's just like chewing gravel or a visit to the dentist's.' Miller recalls playing Danceteria in New York 'with four hundred people in the room and by the third song there'd be six left!' Conley adds, 'I always felt like we were just interrupting people. They'd be dancing to the latest sounds from England, and we'd come on and make a big mess, and then they'd go back to their fun.'

Mission of Burma had their own Anglophile streak, but it went back well before post-punk, to sixties psychedelia. As a teenager at the end of the sixties, Miller had performed with his brother in Sproton Layer, a band heavily influenced by Syd Barrett-era Pink Floyd. In the early seventies, he explored free jazz, and then drummed in the post-psychedelic experimental noise band Destroy All Monsters. The collision of all these freak-rock influences with the more 'dry' post-punk sensibility explains the conflicted quality of the Mission of Burma experience. The music invites you to lose yourself in its head-fuck noise, but this flip-your-wig impulse is checked by the Gang of Four/Wire-like qualities of tension and rigour.

Another simultaneously conceptual and trippy element to the Mission of Burma sound came from their invisible fourth member, Martin Swope, who never appeared onstage but contributed tape treatments and phantom sound-effects at the venue's soundboard. 'What Martin did', Pete Prescott explained, 'was tape something that was going on live, manipulate it, and send it back [into the sound system] as a sort of new instrument. You couldn't predict exactly how it would sound, and that got to be the really fun thing.' Audience members would hear eerie sounds within the group's onslaught of noise and be unable to work out which member of the visible trio was responsible. But similar sound-mirages were being generated without Swope's input, too, by the sheer volume the group played at, plus Miller's and Conley's fondness for open-tuned strings. 'Just between the way Clint played bass, the wash of Pete's cymbals, and my harmonics, you could hear new melodies in there,' says Miller.

MoB's six-song EP *Signals, Calls and Marches*, released in 1981, didn't really capture the Rorschach rush of the band's live fury. Thanks to its typically post-punk production – like Gang of Four's *Entertainment!*, dry and clean – *Signals* came out 'kind of arid. It just didn't have the blood and guts of when we played live,' says Conley. The artwork exhibited significant post-punk damage, too. The cover was originally intended to be raw cardboard – the ultimate in minimalism – but for technical reasons they used a *photograph* of cardboard, which made it even more conceptual. And the lyric sheet took all the words used in the songs and arranged them in alphabetical order.

Mission of Burma made good on *Signals'* sonic deficits with their first album, *Vs.* Like Hüsker Dü's records, it was recorded live in the studio. 'We'd do, like, short sets, five songs in a row, over and over, and gradually weeded out the best takes,' recalls Miller. It captured the overwhelming quality of MoB onstage, the clangour and barely controlled chaos. But although the album was critically acclaimed, MoB still had problems expanding their audience. Their noise deluge was mindblowing, but the group didn't traffic in the sort of period trappings (sonic or sartorial) that would make them fit the neo-psychedelic scene. Their earlier singles had been well-enough produced to become college radio favourites, but *Vs.* was too much of an assault for that audience. Yet the emotionally oblique lyrics and off-kilter structures made them too avant for the hardcore scene. MoB's occasional brushes with that world (like their 1981 Hollywood date with The Dead Kennedys and The Circle Jerks) left audiences baffled. 'I loved a lot of the hardcore bands, but that scene closed off after a while,' says Conley. 'It became pretty narrow-minded, this lockstep, angry, bald-headed white-boy scene that was so intolerant of anyone outside its circle.' Still, if they never quite clicked with hardcore, MoB found an enduring cult audience of brainiac post-punkers.

In his classic *Rock and the Pop Narcotic* (which contains, alongside a wholly original theory of rock music, an insider's take on the SST story) Joe Carducci writes about how he 'never felt MoB were truly a contemporary band' – that underneath the post-punk trappings, they were a throwback to psychedelia. The same could be said of Meat Puppets, the most idiosyncratic of SST's bands, and my personal favourite. This trio of sunstruck visionaries from Phoenix, Arizona, were at heart hippies. From affluent, liberal backgrounds, the band – the brothers Curt and Cris Kirkwood on guitar and bass, plus drummer Derrick Bostrom – were able to spend their teenage years 'exploring our minds', as Bostrom euphemizes it: in other words, getting wasted and listening to music.

Meat Puppets talked about how the two biggest influences on their music were the desert and 'smoke' – meaning marijuana. Indeed, Bostrom and the Kirkwoods originally met through a shared pot dealer. 'The desert around Phoenix was where we'd go to get high,' recalls Bostrom. 'We'd cross the edge of town, find a stretch of desert, light up a joint, or trip.'

The brothers were hippies in terms of their musical taste, too, worshipping what Cris called 'the tasty fuckin' lick-meisters' of jazz-rock and prog: Gong, Mahavishnu Orchestra, Al DiMeola, Gentle Giant, ECM guitarists Ralph Towner and John Abercrombie. Learning to play their instruments, the Kirkwoods hurled themselves into developing serious instrumental chops – something you can detect even in the excruciated racket of Meat Puppets' first EP *In a Car*, where there's a discernible intricacy to the cacophony.

Although he liked to get high, Bostrom wasn't a hippy but a hipster: it was he who turned the Kirkwoods on to punk rock, playing them records by The Damned and Television. A manic Phoenix gig by Devo also rearranged the brothers' sensibilities, and they dived avidly into the modern loud–fast sound. In many ways, though, it was almost by chance that Meat Puppets ended up at SST. When they first started to visit Los Angeles, the group gravitated towards SoCal's deep-underground post-punk scene, which was centred on obscure performance spaces like the Brave Dog and the Anticlub, and shows in unusual settings, such as art galleries. 'At the start of the band, in 1980, we were hanging out with all these groups associated with the Los Angeles Free Music Society,' recalls Bostrom. 'Bands like B People, Monitor, Human Hands. On the fringe of the LAFMS, there were people like Savage Republic and 100 Flowers. One thing we all had in common was a love of Beefheart.'

A determinedly anti-rock outfit led by UCLA art student Bruce Licher, Savage Republic were something like a West Coast Einstürzende Neubauten – they used scrap metal as percussion, made music in the utility tunnels under UCLA, and staged events in the Mojave Desert. Gradually, they evolved into a trance-rock outfit with drone-tone inputs from Arabic music. As for the LAFMS, it was SoCal's nearest equivalent to The Residents or the London Musicians Collective – a coalition of post-psychedelic misfits and improvisers. Founded in 1975, it was motivated by a similar kind of boredom with mid-seventies music culture to that which sparked punk, but its response was absurdist and whimsical, based on a love of the esoteric and out-there: exotica, field recordings, soundtracks, cartoon music, Krautrock, *musique concrete*. With its base in a Pasadena record store called Poobah's, the LAFMS's sensibility was record-collector at heart: music made by and for people who knew about Sun Ra, Harry Partch, John Cage and The Shaggs. Often the same few people using different names, the LAFMS groups – The DooDooettes, Le Forte Four, Airway, Smegma – put out records throughout the late seventies and early eighties, but in very small pressings – anywhere from a few hundred copies to a thousand. At a time when punk had opened up the possibility for weird shit to sell in substantial amounts (The Residents' *Eskimo* shifted 100,000 copies, for instance), this indicated a striking lack of ambition when compared with SST's will to power.

Meat Puppets could easily have ended up happily idling in this sub-cultural backwater. Two of the group's earliest recordings were their contributions to a compilation on 100 Flowers' Happy Squid label and the LAFMS cassette *Light Bulb*. But through the LAFMS-associated band Monitor, they met Carducci just as he was joining SST, and he suggested Meat Puppets follow him. Their first three albums for SST constitute a staggering body of work: each record saw the group make a dizzying quantum leap (or perplexing leap sideways), inventing and then abandoning a unique sound upon which a shrewder band could have based an entire career.

An exquisitely lacerated snarl of thrash-punk, acid rock and country, the debut, *Meat Puppets*, makes you imagine what bluegrass would have sounded like if peyote cactus were indigenous to the Appalachians. Bostrom's drums accelerate what he calls 'the country shuffle two-step' to hardcore tempo. And the album contains two C&W covers: the Doc Watson tune 'Walking Boss' and an unravelled version of 'Tumblin' Tumbleweeds', which was originally done in the 1940s by an anodyne vocal group called Sons of the Pioneers. Curt Kirkwood doesn't sound like he'll be gracing the stage at the Grand Ole Opry any time soon, though. Gnashing the dreamily wistful words into an indecipherably mangled yowl, he sounds like a Venezuelan shaman flipping out on hallucinogenic tree-bark – you can almost see the long strings of drool dangling from his chin. According to Bostrom, the Kirkwoods were pretty close to this state when they recorded the album: 'Curt and Cris were on mushrooms. That's why there's this weird feedback that Curt couldn't squelch, and slightly off tunings – he couldn't quite get his guitar in tune because he was tripping. And we recorded the record live, with the guitar sound bleeding through the drum microphones.'

Meat Puppets at this stage made a din that was loud and frantic and extreme enough just about to pass for hardcore. But their surreal humour irritated the close-cropped fraternity. At a gig in San Francisco, opening for The Dead Kennedys, Meat Puppets kicked off with the theme from *The King and I*. 'God, it was like there was a dumpster above the stage tipping a whole load of beer cans on top of us!' Cris recalled.

By the time they came to record *Meat Puppets II* in the spring of 1983, the group 'were so sick of the hardcore thing', says Bostrom. 'We were really into pissing off the crowd.' Hence the band's swerve into psyche-delic country-rock, with Curt ditching the foaming-at-the-mouth deliv-ery in favour of a frayed country croon, plaintive and fragile. Bostrom had written all the lyrics on the debut; now that Curt was singing his own words, he had more commitment to communicating emotion. *Meat Puppets II* starts as shit-kicking and ferocious as anything on the first record, with 'Split Myself in Two'. Its sandstorm of guitar fuzz flickers with fleeting, silvery melody-swirls that suddenly billow into an ecstatic solo. But the heart of the record resides in the slower songs, like 'Aurora Borealis' and 'We're Here': Curt cleaves the sky with plangent echoplex peals or twinkles in the far distance with a needling stellar beauty.

As titles like 'Plateau', 'Climbing' and 'New Gods' hint, the album is unabashedly mystical: all about bewilderment in the wilderness, the derangement caused by the unrelenting glare of the Sonoran Desert around Phoenix. And drugs too, of course. 'Oh, Me' declares, 'I can't see the end of me/My whole expanse I cannot see'. An instrumental driven by iridescent fingerpicking, 'I'm a Mindless Idiot' is a spiritual boast – empty-headedness as state of grace. 'The BIG experiences I've had have been in the great canyons, or at the beach,' Curt testified. 'For us, the desert is such a great place to go open up your senses, get drunk, spend the night out. Thousands of miles of nothing at all. I mean, anyone who could see the Grand Canyon and *not* want to write a song . . .' Stoned out of their collective gourd, the Puppets loved to contemplate land-scapes whose changeless majesty seemed to open on to infinity and eter-nity. 'We're not into any kind of topical or political referencing in the lyrics because it's gonna be outdated, in ten years, fifty years, five hun-dred years for sure, and in fifty billion trillion years . . .' Cris explained. 'All that stuff about the System, should we eat McDonald's or not,' he continued, perhaps making a dig at the *MaximumRockNRoll* world of politicized hardcore, 'it's so trifling and fleeting . . . Why are people so attached to the idea that spirituality is unchanging, the one constant, the Universal Oneness? Why shouldn't there be a Universal Fiveness!'

But *Meat Puppets II* isn't totally blissed out. It also resurrected a certain tone of desolation that dates back to that early seventies moment of post-hippy burn-out and disillusion – the Neil Young of *Everybody Knows This Is Nowhere*, *After the Goldrush* and *Zuma*; and movies like *Two Lane Blacktop* – and found it eerily applicable to the Reagan eighties. On 'Lost', Curt sings of being 'lost on the freeways again', of having 'grown tired of living Nixon's mess', of wounds 'I know will never mend'.

Wiping the floor with the cowpunk and retro-Americana competition, *Meat Puppets II* brought the group a huge amount of critical praise on its release in April 1984. Bostrom believes it would have had even more impact if it had been released shortly after being recorded in spring 1983 – 'It would really have blown the scene apart; it would have been a huge gauntlet thrown down' – but for reasons not entirely clear, SST delayed its release for almost a year. Meat Puppets then embarked on a massive SST tour, sandwiched on the bill between the outrageously offensive Nig-Heist and the headlining Black Flag. Needless to say, the Puppets' hippy locks and long, improvisatory jams weren't warmly embraced by the hardcore community.

'We are a progressive band . . . a high-energy, post-punk, psychedelic kind of band,' Bostrom once declared. The mixture sounds like an identity crisis, a recipe for disaster, but the group's divided impulses meshed even more sublimely on the third album, *Up on the Sun*, in the form of a radiant fast funk that's something like a cross between Talking Heads and Grateful Dead. 'We came to really relate to the Dead,' admits Bostrom. Many people spotted the Jerry Garcia element in Curt's playing, but nobody noticed what Bostrom calls 'the sad and bitter truth – the band Curt was really listening to on that album was Duran Duran! He'd always pick up on some mainstream artist, and try to see what he could learn from them.'

The other, equally embarrassing, secret behind *Up on the Sun* is Curt's reliance on the Rockman – a guitar device, invented by Tom Scholz of arena rockers Boston, that created a really 'clean' distortion. As Bostrom notes, it's the sort of sterilizing technology that ruined eighties mainstream rock, but in Kirkwood's hands it became a magical tool, enabling the dragonfly glisten of 'Away' and 'Animal Kingdom', the almost brutal brightness of 'Hot Pink', the scintillating gladfoot hurtle of 'Swimming

Ground'. Throughout the album, the music gives off a strange shimmer, as if it's reaching you through the heat-haze rising off a noon-baked highway. Bostrom's buoyant drums and Cris Kirkwood's jazzy, chiming bass sustain a wonderful mood somewhere between urgent and serene. After a couple of slightly quirky warp-funk ditties on side two (one of them titled 'Buckethead'), the final stretch of *Up on the Sun* turns wholly holy: 'Seal Whales', 'Two Rivers' and 'Creator' are pantheistic hymns to what Curt once called 'the wild wonder of being' – and some of the most glorious music of the eighties.

By the time *Up on the Sun* was released in 1985, SST had crested. The previous year – with *Double Nickels*, *Zen Arcade*, *Meat Puppets II* and a slew of Black Flag records – had witnessed all the label's leading groups reach a synchronized peak. Over the next few years, Hüsker Dü maintained a high standard, with two more albums for SST and two after they left for the major-label league, but nothing quite matched their towering *Zen Arcade*. The Minutemen slackened with a desultory stab at crossover (*Project: Mersh*) and the sapped-sounding *3-Way Tie for Last*. The latter I reluctantly had to pan – as 'hardcore's *Sandinista*' (a reference to The Clash's much-derided 1980 triple album) – for one of my first assignments as a cub reviewer at *Melody Maker*. The reluctance stemmed mostly from the fact that D. Boon had recently died in a car rollover.

After *Up on the Sun*, Meat Puppets also tried to go mersh (Minutemen-slang for commercial) with the overproduced *Mirage* and the ZZ Top-style neo-boogie of *Huevos*. They eventually became a successful mainstream band in the early nineties, thanks in large part to their fan Kurt Cobain, who covered no fewer than three songs from *Meat Puppets II* for a Nirvana *Unplugged* show on MTV, and invited the Kirkwoods to sit in on the session.

By the time of 1987's *Huevos*, SST itself had gone full-on progressive and pretty much forgotten the punk part of the equation. Greg Ginn started a sideline group, Gone, an instrumental trio whose stop–start seizures of jagged bombast resembled a thrash-metal King Crimson. The SST roster became scrofulous with trippy jam bands, instrumental combos, retro-metal and Zappa-damaged buffoons. A few were great (awesome Sabbath-clones Saint Vitus), some were interesting (Always August, Paper Bag, Blind Idiot God), most were onanistic drivel. Sometimes releasing as many as seven albums a month, SST's approach weirdly degenerated into an underground parallel to the mainstream major labels' strategy of 'throw shit at the wall and hope some of it sticks'.

More than anything else, the mid-eighties output of Black Flag itself exemplified where SST went wrong. The label defined itself in opposition to hardcore, which it believed had degenerated from a music-driven scene into something determined by social considerations – solidarities based on fashion or political beliefs. SST's ethos was 'it's all about the music, man, and *only* the music'. In their refusal to pander to their audience with more of the same, Black Flag went too far in the opposite direction: an auteur trip, a monologue that ignored the existence of listeners altogether. They ended up producing the kind of Jeff Beck-style jack-off that punk originally set out to abolish, such as the *Family Man* EP (one side instrumentals, the other spoken word) and the all-instrumental *The Process of Weeding Out* – a pun on pot-damaged music-making but also a statement of Black Flag's intent to sift out the lightweights from its audience and leave just the 'real' music fans. The irony is that while some of Black Flag's late-period releases have their moments, almost everyone would agree that the band's greatest work remains their most hardcore-like and pure punk rocky: *Damaged*.

25

CONFORM TO DEFORM: The Second-Wave Industrial Infiltrators

Psychic TV. Some Bizzare. Cabaret Voltaire. Coil. Foetus. Einstürzende Neubauten. Test Dept. Swans. Depeche Mode.

New Pop was not a happy time for Genesis P-Orridge. After Throbbing Gristle disintegrated in June 1981, he found himself cast adrift in a drastically transformed musical landscape – one in which his confrontational and ultra-conceptual approach had no place. 'Groups are all . . . desperate to seem fun, superficial and groovy,' P-Orridge railed to *NME*. 'There's been a very successful smear campaign on thought in music, which I think is a shame . . . Given the options of triviality and pedantry, I'd choose pedantry.'

For all his complaints, though, P-Orridge was prepared to bend with the changing times. Psychic TV, the group he co-founded with Peter 'Sleazy' Christopherson, embraced two New Pop strategies: subversion from within and the 'sugared pill'. Psychic TV hooked up with WEA, one of the biggest major labels in the world, to release their 1982 debut *Force the Hand of Chance*. The most startling aspect of the music on *Force* was that it was, well, *musical*: full of jangly guitars, orchestral embellishments, and sweet melody.

Dropping the stylus on to side one, diehard TG fans were gobsmacked to hear 'Just Driftin'', a reverie laced with idyllic acoustic guitars and heart-tugging strings. Crooning lines like 'You surround me and cover me/Protect me and caress me/With that special simple love' in a surprisingly pleasant voice, P-Orridge revealed his secret cuddly side. From the creator of 'Slugbait' and 'Subhuman', this was quite a swerve. The equally beguiling 'Stolen Kisses' came in three parts: the first resembled Terry Jacks' 'Seasons in the Sun', the second sounded like a Postcard group doing their best late-period Velvets imitation, and the third was a strings-only coda redolent of ABC's orchestral-reprise version of 'The Look of Love'. For the first time ever, a P-Orridge project involved conventionally skilled musicians: guitarist Alex Fergusson (formerly of Alternative TV, now a full-blown Psychic TV member) plus hired hands Andrew Poppy (a classically trained arranger) and brass players Kennie Wellington and Claude Deppa.

Although P-Orridge admitted that he and Sleazy wept with laughter after recording 'Driftin'' and 'Stolen Kisses', because they sounded so 'not industrial', these were neither jokes nor perverse pranks. 'Corny as it is, Sleazy and I have both fallen in love,' he confessed. Not with each other, he hastened to add. P-Orridge had recently got married and fathered a baby daughter, Caresse (whose crying could be heard at the end of side one of *Force*). Sleazy had hooked up with a young TG devotee called Geff Rushton, who became a member of Psychic TV and eventually renamed himself John Balance. P-Orridge insisted the two tender songs were genuinely heartfelt. 'There are moments when love songs, expressed in your own words, are still very special. They shouldn't be avoided just to keep some false fantasy idea of yourself in other people.'

P-Orridge's and Sleazy's new open-heartedness also expressed itself in a change of attitude – a new, constructive approach that again oddly paralleled New Pop's positivity. If Throbbing Gristle had contemplated horror to the point of paralysis, Psychic TV was more about finding practical solutions; not just surviving but *enriching* your existence. P-Orridge and Sleazy turned to magic as something midway between art and science, something that could *change* reality. The penultimate song on *Force*, 'Ov Power', features P-Orridge chanting lines about 'dark power' over a hard-funk backdrop – it's like Aleister Crowley channelled through the body of James Brown. And the album ends with the string-swept sermon 'Message from the Temple'. A husky, hypnotic baritone intones what sounds like a motivational therapy tape: 'The Temple strives to end personal laziness and engender discipline, to focus the will on one's true desires'. Calm and medical-sounding, the voice counsels the listener to 'discard all irrelevancies': socially implanted anxieties, false needs, crutch-like friendships. 'Once you are focused on yourself internally, the external aspects of your life will fall into place. *They have to*. Sceptics will say they simply don't believe this psychic process works. But it *does*. It is the key to the Temple.' If 'Ov Power' was a disco translation of Crowley's Law of Thelema, 'Message from the Temple' suggested that through learning to direct your will, you could actually make your wishes come true – force the hand of chance, as the album title put it.

'Message from the Temple' also served as an advert, a recruiting device, for Thee Temple ov Psychick Youth. On the back sleeve of the album P-Orridge appeared wearing a priest's dog collar and a vaguely ecclesiastical-looking shirt; at the bottom in small print were the words 'File under: Fund-Raising Activities'. In the later days of Throbbing Gristle, P-Orridge had noticed that the group was a magnet for freaks, misfits and lost souls. He decided to foster and channel this cult energy by forming an organization somewhere between a fan club, a religious sect and a secret society. Although Thee Temple ov Psychick Youth had initiates and dedicated itself to rediscovering and reinventing the primordial power of ritual, it had no creed or dogma as such. Rather, it was an information exchange. TOPY acolytes unearthed and shared all kinds of esoteric knowledge, mix-and-matching elements from occultism, hermetica, geomancy, scrying, tribal shamanism and body-art. Sigils were a TOPY favourite: sex-magic spells originally developed by Austin Osman Spare, a late nineteenth-century occultist, which involved ritually focusing the energy of orgasm to make your wishes come true. Temple initiates also explored altered states using drugs and technological/neurological devices – like Brion Gysin's Dream Machine with its flickering-light patterns.

The possibilities of another flickering-light machine also caught Psychic TV's imagination. Just as the New Pop artists had seized on both the expressive potential and selling power of the promo video, P-Orridge and Sleazy realized that television was the supreme media of the modern era, and therefore the crucial battleground. Psychic TV's ultimate pipedream was to broadcast a sort of counter-MTV (Sleazy eventually went on to become a successful video director). But in the meantime, Psychic TV began making and selling videotapes of their 'truly surrealist television': ambient brain-food full of cut-up imagery, designed to be played during those 'eerie' 1 to 7 a.m. hours when the brain is at its most receptive and suggestible. *Force the Hand of Chance* came with a free bonus LP containing eight Psychic TV themes: unsettling mood-music woven from Satie-esque piano motifs and the marrow-curdling screech-drone of the thigh-bone trumpet. The latter, a grisly instrument used by Tibetan shamans to invoke the most shadowy aspects of the human soul, were supposedly fashioned from thigh bones that had belonged either to young virgins who had been raped and killed or to the murderer himself. Which sounds much closer in spirit to the old TG of 'We Hate You Little Girls' than *Force*'s honey-dripping love songs.

Psychic TV infiltrated the major-label system thanks to a character called Stevo – Throbbing Gristle fan, manager of Soft Cell, and a budding Svengali-cum-mogul. It was Soft Cell's 'darkness' as much as their pop potential that originally attracted Stevo, who signed them to his management company/record label, Some Bizzare. The group's massive worldwide success enabled him to turn Some Bizzare into a power base for dark, twisted music, operating on the very threshold of the pop mainstream. Brokering deals between Some Bizzare artists and various major labels, Stevo was able to give some of the most extreme musicians of the eighties – like the apocalyptic metal-bashing outfits Einsturzende Neubauten and Test Dept – a shot at success. He also relished redirecting the careers of his old industrial heroes – P-Orridge and Sleazy with Psychic TV, and Cabaret Voltaire.

Stevo's slogans were 'use the industry before it uses you' and 'conform to deform'. After signing the groups to Some Bizzare, he would finance the making of an album and then hawk it to the major labels. The record was then released as jointly attributed to Some Bizzare/CBS or Some Bizzare/Virgin, and so forth. 'We used the majors' distribution muscle,' says Stevo. 'That way you had the record company working for the artist, rather than the other way round.' Some Bizzare and the artist both made more money per record sold as well, although artistic control was the primary concern. Soft Cell's David Ball recalled Some Bizzare's five-year prime in the mid-eighties as 'an exciting time because it was like an independent label but it wasn't . . . It was like having the independent control but using the power of a major, which was quite new at the time.'

Raised in Suffolk, but often mistaken for a working-class east London boy, Stevo was a fan of all kinds of weird music. Dismissing punk as 'just rock 'n' roll played badly . . . not that revolutionary', he looked to more avant-garde or electronic outfits – TG, Cabaret Voltaire, The Residents, Chrome, Metaboliste. He started out as a DJ, playing exactly this kind of non-crowd-pleasing material. 'I was more interested in terrorizing the dance floor. I used to go out just to fuck the audience's heads,' he says. Amazingly, his career as a 'Futurist' DJ prospered. Soon Stevo had two DJ charts published in different music papers. Increasingly, he filled these charts not with twelve-inch singles but demo tapes that bands had sent him. The best of them, along with a few debut studio recordings financed on a barebones budget, were pulled together as *The Some Bizzare Album*. Three of the artists on the compilation – Soft Cell, The The and Depeche Mode – went on to be massive. Stevo took the first two under his management wing, but ultimately passed on Depeche, finding them 'a bit too commercial and poppy'.

Stevo soon turned to revitalizing the stalled careers of his old favourites, such as Cabaret Voltaire. He started courting them in 1981. 'Stevo invited us down to *Top of the Pops* when Soft Cell's "Tainted Love" got to number one,' recalls Richard H. Kirk. 'It was a great experience for us visiting this nerve centre of the British pop establishment. We started to think, Maybe this isn't a bad way of getting through to people.' The seed of the conform-to-deform idea was planted, but it took a while to germinate. In 1982 the Cabs reached a kind of impasse. Their early sound had been taken as far as it could go, while their audience had stabilized into a cosy cult. 'The Cabs were at a point where they could predict their sales,' says Stevo. 'I wanted to take 'em to the next level.' He approached Kirk and Stephen Mallinder and proposed that Some Bizzare fund the next Cabaret Voltaire album and tout the finished record to the majors; in return, the group would make their sound more pop-accessible by pushing Mallinder's vocals higher in the mix. To win their trust, Stevo gave the Cabs £5,000 to buy a duplication machine for their newly launched video company Doublevision. 'That meant we were totally autonomous, we could run off small numbers of copies for mail order,' says Kirk. 'So we decided to go along with Stevo's idea.'

For *The Crackdown*, their first album in a deal brokered between Some Bizzare and Virgin, Cabaret Voltaire worked with a producer in a professional recording studio for the first time. The aim was to streamline the group's sound and make their tracks work on the modern dance floor. New Order's recent success with tracks like 'Everything's Gone Green' and 'Temptation' provided the model – those singles brilliantly merged post-punk and New York electro, white angst and black groove, and they'd both made the pop charts.

New Order and Cabaret Voltaire were good friends, a relationship that dated back to Joy Division days, when the groups had played shows together. 'Ian Curtis was a big Cabs fan and always wanted to record at our Western Works studio,' says Kirk. 'Maybe out of respect, New Order did come to Sheffield and tried some stuff at the studio – some of which ended up on *Movement*. We were influenced by them and I dare say New Order were influenced by us a bit.' Cabaret Voltaire were also the first group to play at the Hacienda, the club masterminded by New Order and their manager Rob Gretton (the true dance fanatic at Factory). 'One drunken night at the Hacienda, Gretton pointed out to me this track playing on the club system,' recalls Kirk. 'It was Bambaataa's "Planet Rock". I scribbled the name down in this notebook I always carried with me. When I bought the record I was, like, "Fuckin' hell – this is like Kraftwerk, only funkier."'

Not long after, John Robie – New York electronic keyboardist and co-creator of 'Planet Rock' – approached Cabaret Voltaire about remixing 'Yashar', a track from their *2X45* album. 'He wanted to remix it to make it work for that New York electro scene,' says Kirk. 'They took quarter-inch tapes of his "Yashar" mixes down to the Funhouse, to test on the crowd. What he did with "Yashar" was a big catalyst in terms of us real-izing, "Well, we can strip this down, get rid of some of the clutter, tweak a few rhythmic elements, and it's actually going to work in a club."'

If Cabaret Voltaire never quite pulled off a 'Blue Monday', they got close with 'Just Fascination' and 'Crackdown', released together as a double-A-sided twelve-inch in 1983. Working with co-producer Flood and guest keyboard player David Ball, Kirk and Mallinder embraced the era's state-of-the-art tools – sequencers, digital delays, drum machines, harmonizers. The old Cabs sound emerged spruce and spring-heeled: chattering sequencers, pert, chugging basslines and robotic claps lent an ultra-modern sheen to the classic Voltaire vibe of twitchy tension. The transition wasn't perfect – the Cabs had exchanged their unique, if slightly shaky, take on funk for a more standardized palette of timbres and beats – but when it worked ('Animation' on *The Crackdown*; 'Sensoria' on the second Virgin album *Micro-Phonies*) the results con-firmed that Cabaret Voltaire had been right to embrace Stevo's conform-to-deform strategy. What held the Cabs back from pop crossover was their subdued vocal melodies. Songcraft wasn't really their strong suit; rhythm, texture and sinister atmosphere were.

'Stevo was only twenty-one when he got Some Bizzare going,' marvels Kirk. 'Through Soft Cell, he'd got record companies in the palm of his hand.' Stevo used his larger-and-louder-than-life persona and surreal mind games to throw industry executives off-balance. He became noto-rious for his eccentric negotiation techniques. In one deal, he peremptor-ily summoned Maurice Oberstein, the supremo of CBS, to Trafalgar

Square for the final contract signing; in another, he insisted the deluxe office chair used by WEA's managing director be included as a bonus gift. When 'wooing' the major labels for a Psychic TV deal, he sent nine-inch brass dildo statuettes to all of the big companies, etched with the slogan 'Psychic TV Fuck The Record Industry'.

For all his abrasive manner and daft stunts, though, Stevo proved to be a shrewd player of the industry game. When Psychic TV parted company with WEA after just one album, he soon managed to secure them a bigger contract with one of WEA's major competitors, CBS. The 'rolling option' deal was potentially worth a million pounds. In the event, the initial advance was much more modest, and was entirely swallowed up by the ambitious *Dreams Less Sweet* album.

Most of the £30,000 went on the expensive 'Zuccarelli Holophonic' recording process, a surround-sound technology invented by an Argentinian physicist. Instead of using microphones, the sound signal was absorbed through a simulacrum of the human body, complete with skull, ears, hairs, internal cavities and body fluids. 'It was based on how lizards hear, which is through their stomachs, 'cos they have no ears,' says Stevo. Which sort of begs the question: so why wasn't the device shaped like a giant lizard? At any rate, the mannequin-shaped microphone was subjected to all kinds of indignities by P-Orridge – dragged into deep underground caverns used by seventeenth-century occultists for sacrilegious ceremonies, surrounded by flaming petrol, even placed in a coffin and buried. Heard on headphones, some of these surround-sound effects – the telephone ringing, the ominous growl of an attack dog – do have an unnerving three-dimensional quality, as though they are right there in the room with you, or circling your head. But overall the Holophonic sound didn't quite live up to the hype.

Dreams Less Sweet was much less of a sugared pill than *Force*. The Mapplethorpe-like cover image of a gorgeous orchid on close inspection turned out to have a piercing through its stamen (presumably this was less problematic than using a photo of Genesis's perforated genitals). Laced with wistful oboe and cor anglais, 'The Orchids' reprised the winsome melodiousness of 'Just Driftin'', but most of the album shunned songs in favour of sound-collage, spoken-word recitation and abstract noisescapes. 'In the Nursery', the most perturbing track, evoked the dark Bacchanalian activities at a building in the East End where Temple ov Psychick Youth acolytes gathered for anything-goes orgies of ritualistic sex. 'Time is not time in the Nursery . . . No guilt, no retribution in the

Nursery,' intones P-Orridge. The flagellating cacophony behind him makes the Nursery sound less like a boudoir than an abattoir.

Partly motivated by worries that P-Orridge was falling into a cult-leader power-trip, Sleazy decided to leave Psychic TV in 1983. He joined up with his boyfriend John Balance in the latter's fledgling outfit Coil. Balance had been a boarder at Lord Williams's School in Thame when he started corresponding with Throbbing Gristle. 'I'd be in prep and the phone would ring and they would go, "It's Genesis P-Orridge for you . . ."' he recalled. 'I was his corrupted little schoolboy.' Balance produced the industrial 'zine *Stabmental*, developed what his headmaster called 'an unhealthy interest in the occult', and experienced shamanic visions while munching magic mushrooms on the school playing fields. Coil took Psychic TV's interest in arcana even further, developing a patchwork cosmology of ideas from shamanism, Kabbala, alchemy and Austin Osman Spare's magical philosophy Zos Kia Cultus. Unlike P-Orridge, though, their quest was private: Coil weren't looking for followers. Even more than Psychic TV, Coil's music was densely laden with reference points and symbolism. Sleazy talked about being archivists, 'librarians almost'; each content-heavy song could easily have come with footnotes and a bibliography.

The first fruit of Sleazy and Balance's union was the 1984 EP *How to Destroy Angels*: 'ritual music for accumulation of male sexual energy', according to a sleevenote, with a rhythmic structure precisely calculated in accordance with Kabbalistic numerology. The duo generated sounds by striking huge iron gongs and whirling 'bullroarers' (a stick used during male-only initiation rites) around their heads. After this 'conjuration of Martian energy . . . homosexual energy', Coil recorded a cover version of 'Tainted Love' – the Northern Soul classic recently made famous by their close friend Marc Almond. In Coil's lugubrious and poisoned rendition, though, it became the accusatory lament of someone infected with AIDS. All profits from the single went to the Terrence Higgins Trust, an AIDS charity. *Scatology*, the album, confronted taboos in the abrasive tradition of gay modernists like Burroughs, Genet and Mishima. The cover depicted a male butt-crack framed like a Greek Orthodox religious icon; the title referenced both shit-obsession and the more general dictionary definition – a morbid interest in all base instincts and forms of obscenity. Songs ranged from 'Clap' (about the action *and* the affliction) to 'The Sewage-Workers Birthday Party', inspired by a Swedish S&M magazine and concerning 'the dubious pleasures of being lashed to a toilet bowl', according to Sleazy.

Coil's music sounded vaguely ceremonial and portentous, all clumpy drum beats and bombastic fanfares. They used the Fairlight sampler heavily, seeing it as a literally alchemical instrument. Far more studio-oriented than Psychic TV, Coil filled their recordings with skewed sounds – 'the musical equivalent of catching a glimpse of something peripheral in your vision'. Like a great deal of second-wave industrial music, their records were made in a state of 'amphetamania' (Balance's term): speed amplified the music's apocalyptic atmosphere and its creators' sense of themselves as visionaries who knew the cosmic score. One of Coil's friends, Current 93's David Tibet, took so much amphetamine and LSD that he saw Enid Blyton's Noddy being crucified in the sky, decided he was a Gnostic icon, and recorded the album *Swastikas for Noddy*.

Coil's co-producer on *Scatology* was Jim 'Foetus' Thirlwell, the great collaborator of the Some Bizzare milieu. Throughout the eighties, he seemed to have a finger in every pie, making connections between industrial music, No Wave, Goth and pop. Thirlwell was tight with Soft Cell, appearing onstage with them for a crazed cover of Suicide's 'Ghost Rider', and he co-wrote 'A Million Manias' for Almond's *Torment and Toreros* (a torrid 'I'm no squeaky-clean pop star' gesture released under the name Marc and The Mambas). He formed a romantic/creative partnership with Lydia Lunch, and worked with Nurse with Wound, The Virgin Prunes, The The and even Orange Juice. He was also a member of the earliest incarnation of The Bad Seeds, the group formed by Nick Cave after The Birthday Party split.

Like The Birthday Party, Thirlwell was originally from Melbourne, Australia. Arriving in London at the end of 1978, he lived in squats, hung out with Scritti and DAF, and played with pragVEC. Thanks to self-neglect and amphetamine use, Thirlwell's lung collapsed (halfway through a This Heat show). During his convalescence, he saved the sick pay from his day job at the Virgin Megastore (where he DJ-ed and worked as a buyer) to launch his own label, Self Immolation. The resulting series of frenetic, densely arranged singles became favourites of John Peel and his listeners. You couldn't avoid being curious, what with band names like Foetus on Your Breath, Scraping Foetus off the Wheel and Foetus in Your Bed.

Exuberant gallows humour pervaded every particle of the various

Foetuses' music – from the lyrics' demolition derby of puns and mixed metaphors to the exaggerated cartoon quality of Thirlwell's vocals, as sung by alter-egos like Clint Ruin and Frank Want. 'Today I Started Slogging Again' featured the Marquis de Sade as a rapper, while 'I'll Meet You in Poland Baby' transposed the Nazi–Soviet Non-Aggression Pact on to one of Thirlwell's troubled romances. The music *sounded* comic, too – like Madness if they'd been an industrial band. Foetus's arrangements threw in elements from lounge music, experimental noise, soundtracks, systems music and burlesque. 'The showbizzy, big-band thing I really came to from the corny variety shows of the sixties, like Tom Jones,' says Thirlwell. 'I always loved that sort of real extreme screaming brass, the high notes and big stabs. Jazz I came to through the back door – through film *noir*. I hear things cinematically.' Thirlwell meticulously planned his intricate arrangements before entering the studio – partly because he played every instrument himself. 'I was composer, arranger, performer, producer, lyricist and vocalist. That was unusual back then – there was just me and Todd Rundgren!'

Alongside his labour-intensive output and prolific collaborations, Thirlwell tirelessly championed other talents. For instance, he helped bring Einstürzende Neubauten to the attention of the non-German world having seen the metal-bashing ensemble in Berlin (where The Birthday Party, fed up with London, had exiled themselves). 'It was amazing – really dramatic and exciting to watch. The guys would be running from one instrument to another. But I also dug the sheer musicality involved – these were real compositions, structured and dynamic, the instruments playing off each other.' After Thirlwell returned to London, Stevo approached him about Foetus signing to Some Bizzare. He agreed, but only on condition that Neubauten were also offered a deal. He also pulled together *80–83 Strategen Gegen Architekturen* (*Strategies Against Architecture*), a compilation of Neubauten's early singles, which Mute ultimately released.

Spiritually, if not so much sonically, Foetus and Neubauten had plenty in common. Thirlwell's notions of 'positive negativism' (purging your soul of spiritual toxins, destruction as the precondition to creativity) and 'aesthetic terrorism' applied to both bands. Foetus and Neubauten were equally impelled by a maniacal hunger for apocalypse: 'Einstürzende Neubauten' translates as 'collapsing new buildings'. Singer/conceptualist-in-chief Blixa Bargeld talked of his lust for 'a state of collapse . . . a final implosion . . . That is my *Sehnsucht*, my longing.' Taking its title

483

from the German expression for black holes, their 1981 anthem 'Kalte Sterne' declares, 'After us comes nothing/We're cold stars'.

Thirlwell and Bargeld were also prone to messianic mission statements in interviews. The latter particularly admired the Dadaist and Futurists for 'turning the manifesto into an art form in its own right'. In this spirit, he launched an artistic movement called Die Geniale Dilettanten (Genius Dilettantes) and was a prime mover in Berlin's Atonal Festivals of the early eighties. For all his Romantic belief in madness and chaos, he was a public-relations natural, with a genius for slogans and eye-catching concepts, like a tour of West Germany undertaken by Neubauten and various like-minds under the banner Die Berliner Krankheit, which translates as the Berlin Sickness.

Emaciated and rotten-toothed, Bargeld certainly looked like a man with a seriously unhealthy lifestyle. 'Amphetamines had an influence on my life and that had an influence on my music, but amphetamines aren't psychedelic,' he says. 'What makes them psychedelic is that you can't sleep. I attended studio mixing sessions that went on for seventy-two hours nonstop. But we got a perfect mix, 'cos we were able to concentrate on something really stupid for ages, like a particular drum sound.' In addition to allowing you to ignore the body's needs (sleep, food, sex) and focus on work, amphetamine has another advantage for artists: it bolsters self-belief. Neubauten celebrated the cheap 'n' nasty powder in 'Yu-Gung (Feed My Ego)'. 'On the record you can hear the sound of a blade on a mirror going "clack clack clack",' laughs Bargeld. 'Can you be any more clear than that?'

A devotee of Artaud, Bargeld believed in sacrificing everything for art: he was ready to 'squeeze my body like a lemon' and put his 'whole life forward as an experimental case'. Neubauten's music was all about physicality, from the strenuous pounding of metal to the use of the human body itself as a sound source – the noise of blood captured with a foetal heartbeat detector; Bargeld's ribcage hammered with blows from bandmate Mufti. (Neubauten also tried to record the gristly sound of a saw shredding a carcass, but couldn't capture it adequately.) Bargeld's singing seemed like the product of duress: his vocal trademark was a hissing scream like steam escaping from the cracked boiler of a locomotive. 'Very often at that time, Neubauten live shows were life threatening,' he says. 'Not to the audience, but to the members of the band, our physical and mental stability.' Neubauten were literally shedding blood for their art – Mufti, for instance, was always injuring himself with power tools.

Neubauten weren't the only metal-bashing outfit, or even the first. At the dawn of the eighties, the idea occurred independently and near simultaneously to several bands around the world: Z'ev in San Francisco, Test Dept in south London, SPK in Australia. Even in Germany, Neubauten had rivals for the metal-music concept: Die Krupps, whose music incorporated a self-invented instrument called the Stahlophon (a xylophone constructed from strips of industrial steel). The Düsseldorf group recorded the album *Stahwerksinfonie* (*Steelworks Symphony*) and the brilliant metal-bashing Krautdisko single 'Wahre Arbeit – Wahrer Lohn'. Unlike Neubauten, they were attracted to the idea of discipline not dissolution: their imagery of exertion and endurance drifted into that ambiguous, musclebound area where Constructivism overlaps with fascist aesthetics. Indeed, even the band's name contained a submerged allusion to Hitler's image of the German warrior-male as unyielding, like Krupps steel.

While Die Krupps co-founded Electronic Body Music (industrial music goes disco, basically), Neubauten's version of metal machine music was much more avant-garde. Investigating the sound-generating potential of found instruments, adapted machines and the physical environment, Neubauten's 'organized noise' constantly pushed at the boundaries between music and non-music. Bargeld's father was a carpenter: as a child he'd spent a lot of time on building sites, and grown up in a household where there were no musical instruments but plenty of power tools.

In the beginning, though, lack of money played as big a role as any experimental impulses or the urge to shock audiences. 'How do you become a musician with nothing?' says Bargeld. 'I got an electric guitar from a second-hand shop, but no amp, so we plugged the guitar into a transistor radio. Everything else, we had to make do – electric drills, whatever else we could find. Andrew Unruh sold his drum kit after our first show in 1980, then made a new one out of building materials.' Says Stevo, 'Neubauten, to me, were the definitive anarchy band. When they toured, they'd turn up to a city with no instrumentation whatsoever and just go straight out and pick stuff up from scrap heaps.'

They also drew indirect inspiration from ethnological field recordings: not specific musical or rhythmic ideas so much as the sheer percussive tribalism. 'I started buying records in the "Obscurity Department" of record stores. This was before the term "world music" was coined,' recalls Bargeld. 'One record was these Ethiopian desert nomads, mostly just singing and hand-clapping. That's when I started thinking, What is my authentic background? In West Berlin there was a lot of debris, broken things and secret places. So I thought, Let's make an ethnic record.' Neubauten discovered a strange cavity inside the foundations of a highway flyover and wormed their way inside with some equipment – a transistor radio, a tape-recorder, an electric guitar, a glockenspiel, pieces of metal. They held a four-hour, candlelit recording session, which lasted until the batteries ran out, producing tracks like 'Eisenmolekul', which appeared on the 1980 cassette-only release *Stahl Musik*.

Neubauten quickly jettisoned the guitar along with any remaining residues of rock musicality and recorded the album *Kollaps*, based entirely on the human voice and metal percussion: girders, crowbars, a large metal spring that produced a thrumming, bass-like pulse. The goal was to go beyond tonality, beyond even *notes*, and reach the point where everything and nothing could be perceived as music. Despite Bargeld's confessed intention to produce something completely unlistenable, *Kollaps* garnered Neubauten their first real attention. Soon Foetus, then Some Bizzare, entered the picture. '*Kollaps* sold maybe two thousand copies,' says Stevo. 'Any shrewd businessman would have thought, Maybe we could get them up to ten thousand. But me, I spent forty thousand pounds on the recording of their first album for Some Bizzare, *Drawings of Patient O.T.* Where's the business logic in that?' Amazingly, Stevo then managed to license the record (beautifully recorded, but totally uncommercial) to Virgin Records.

In January 1984 members of Neubauten staged a performance called *Concerto for Voice and Machinery* at London's ICA, where Throbbing Gristle had made their debut performance on the occasion of COUM's *Prostitution* exhibition. 'We got the invite and I said, "Well, we should do something very special,"' recalls Bargeld. They hired cement mixers and pneumatic drills, and brought in guest singers, like Frank Tovey from Fad Gadget. On the night, chainsaws ripped through raw materials and a piano provided by the ICA, showering the audience with sawdust; microphones and milk bottles were lobbed into the spinning cement mixers, which hurled out shards of glass and metal; one of the performers leapt offstage and began drilling through the auditorium floor. When the performance ended after only twenty-five minutes, the audience – mistakenly believing it had been cut short by ICA officials – 'went berserk, totally mad, tearing down the wooden panels', says Bargeld. 'The place had to be shut down for renovation, and we made front-page news in all the English papers.' Accompanied by Genesis P-Orridge,

Stevo had clambered onstage to participate in the mayhem, and in the aftermath hyped the event as 'an artistic cry of disgust', an attempt to test the radical-chic limits of the ICA. Says Bargeld, 'Stevo started creating rumours around the *Concerto*, that we were drilling through the stage to get to a secret bunker under the building.' According to the Some Bizzare supremo, beneath this temple of modern art liberalism lay a nuclear shelter reserved for the British establishment – the House of Lords and top military leaders.

Towards the end of 1983, the focal point for the new 'sick noise' – having drifted from London to Berlin and back again – shifted decisively to New York. Here the ideas of No Wave were being reactivated by groups like Sonic Youth and Swans, partly as an anti-dance reaction to the mutant disco era. In November 1983, Immaculate Consumptives – a collaborative project involving Jim Thirlwell, Lydia Lunch, Marc Almond and Nick Cave – staged a couple of performances in Manhattan. A sort of abject variety revue, the night's entertainment included a number of one-page plays written by Lunch and Cave, and climaxed with the Thirlwell/Almond composition 'Body Unknown', featuring Cave's primal scream, Lunch's Teenage Jesus-style guitar, Thirlwell's flailing drums, and Almond holding down the vocal melody. Soon, disenchanted with London, Thirlwell relocated to New York. 'There was this energy, this twenty-four-hour feeling, in the Lower East Side,' he recalls. 'You could go out to bars until four in the morning and then walk home. And I already knew about the new stuff coming out of New York – Glenn Branca, Sonic Youth, that first Swans EP.'

Swans shared Neubauten's aura of ordeal and endurance, but the group's instrumentation was rock's standard format: guitar, bass, drums, voice. Percussive bass fused with the drum as a single thudding instrument. No melodies, no real riffs even: just single motifs pounded out at tortuous tempos, an agony of abrasive and debasing repetition. Michael Gira's voice, a loop of sonic scar tissue, barked stripped-down lyrics that delineated relationships as vectors of domination, dependency, parasitism. Songs like 'A Screw' or 'Time Is Money (Bastard)' could be taken as political or existential, howls of protest ('REGURGITATING ACQUIRED SOCIAL FILTH' was one Swans slogan) or primal catharsis. The pleasures of Swans were frankly sadomasochistic, with Gira as much victim as violator. If he could, he would '*completely erase* my body with the music', he recalled. 'I just couldn't stand my physical presence.'

487

'Swans, to me, were like a slaveship,' says Stevo, who signed the band to Some Bizzare and released *Cop*. 'The beats are like the rows of slaves. Their music, it's like different variations of grind. It grinds you to the ground, walks straight over your face.'

Instead of a slaveship, Test Dept's metal music sounded like a Soviet factory. Or at least the idealized propaganda version: comrades interlocking like cogs in a 'single engine . . . an absolutely perfect machine', disciplined members of the revolutionary proletariat patriotically exceeding their productivity quotas. Test Dept's early performances, held at unusual, often derelict spaces, like Cannon Street tube station, 'were awesome, just a bombardment of energy and percussion', says Stevo. 'Test Dept had a totally different vibe from Neubauten's thing, which was much more highbrow, artsy and dark.'

Like Neubauten, though, Test Dept turned to scrap metal because they couldn't afford real instruments: living near the desolate, defunct docks in Deptford, south London, they found 'instruments' amid the rubble. They also shared Neubauten's notion of an *industrielle Volksmusik*, describing their primitive rhythms as ethnically English but fulfilling 'the same function within our culture as African drumming fulfils in theirs'. But there any similarities ended. Instead of Neubauten's Dionysian lust for an end to Western civilization, Test Dept's energy was constructive. Or Constructivist: they were obsessed with that brief epoch of Soviet modernism shortly after the revolution – Malevich's graphics, Shostakovich (whose music they played before going onstage). Like the Constructivists, they glorified the strength of the worker – the muscular labour power at that very moment being rendered obsolete by Thatcher's assault on traditional heavy industry. 'The old industrial thing is already dead, so what we're doing is taking its remnants and turning them into something else, something creative,' the group collectively told the *NME*.

At a time when the trade unions were being crushed by Thatcher, Test Dept 'fought back' by creating an aesthetic sensation of solidarity and communicating it to their audience as a visceral rush: 'When the music hits its peak there's a feeling amongst all four of us linking and coming to an absolutely perfect single dynamic union.' Anonymous in their skinhead crops, bleached denim, and Doc Marten boots, they strove to revive the positive sense of the word 'mass' (purposeful, forward-looking, a movement) as opposed to the weak, passive sense (mass media, mass communications). Test Dept staged large-scale events midway between spectacles and rallies, like *Beating the Retreat* (a protest against the Falklands Victory celebration), and in the autumn of 1984 undertook a national tour in support of the Miners' Strike, accompanied by a Welsh male-voice choir, with all proceeds going to the National Union of Mineworkers.

'There was a snapshot there in time where Some Bizzare had Test Dept, Foetus, Psychic TV, Cabaret Voltaire, Marc and the Mambas, Neubauten, Coil, Swans, The The,' says Jim Thirlwell, talking about 1982–6. 'That's a significant roster, and you've got to think: What happened?' Why didn't Some Bizzare endure and prosper as a bastion of left-field un-rock, like its closest counterpart, Mute Records? One reason is that, although Stevo was successful in getting most of his groups – even those as uncommercial as Neubauten – hooked up with major labels, none of them (with the exception of the poppiest, singer–songwriter Matt Johnson of The The) got within sniffing distance of the charts. Also, Stevo fell out with many of his bands. Coil, for instance, emblazoned, 'Stevo, Pay Us What You Owe Us!' on the front cover of the CD reissue of *Scatology*.

Ironically, the one outfit who pulled off Stevo's subversion-from-within strategy was Depeche Mode, the group he let slip through his fingers at the very start of Some Bizzare. True, their early hit singles seemed like synthpop at its most dinky-sounding and innocuous. Gradually, though, over the course of eighteen months or so, the music made by these Basildon pretty boys started to become more haunting. Martin Gore, the main songwriter, took to wearing a leather skirt and displayed a keen interest in all things transgressive. The band had signed to Mute partly because they admired the label's more avant-electronic acts, like The Normal and Fad Gadget. Depeche Mode also had a burgeoning political consciousness close in spirit to that of Test Dept.

The first sign of the newly committed Depeche came with 'Everything Counts', a number 6 hit in July 1983, which combined hard electro beats, wisps of bleak woodwind melody (which sound as sorrowful as a Labour voter the day after the June general election), and clumsy, if heartfelt, anti-capitalist sentiments: 'The grabbing hands grab all they can . . . it's a competitive world'. It was their biggest chart success to date. The accompanying album, *Construction Time Again*, was Test Dept-goes-pop, from its title to its cover image of a hammer, symbolic of workers' power.

Over the next year, Depeche Mode almost methodically worked their way through the 'big issues'. 'Love in Itself' was a Gang of Four-style critique of romantic love as distraction/consolation for life in an unjust world: 'There was a time when all of my mind was love/Now I find that most of the time/Love's not enough, in itself.' 'People Are People', another huge UK hit, dealt with racism, homophobia and every other kind of bigotry and intolerance. Genuinely pained perplexity seared through the painful doggerel of 'People are people so why should it be/You and I should get along so awfully?' 'Blasphemous Rumours' lugubriously accused God of having 'a sick sense of humour', while the bondage-inspired 'Master and Servant' was the pervy pop smash that Coil could only dream of. Gore had been spending time in Berlin, living wild after breaking up with his prudish Christian girlfriend, exploring the city's seedy demimonde of S&M clubs. But sly lines like 'Forget all about equality' had a personal/political reversibility to make Michael Gira smile in approval.

Musically, too, the band's 1984 singles trilogy of 'People', 'Blasphemous' and 'Master' (all from *Some Great Reward*) represented the pop translation of Some Bizzare's ideas. 'People' and 'Master' were full of crashing metal percussion and *musique concrete* sounds. 'We have nicked a few of Neubauten's ideas,' Gore confessed. 'What we're doing, though, is using [them] in a different context, in the context of pop.' Bandmate Andy Fletcher added, 'It's not just metal, anyway: when we first started sampling for the Synclavier, we went out and hit cars, we threw bricks.' Stevo could whinge about Depeche Mode 'hijacking images' off his bands all he liked. The boys from Basildon, 1981's least likely candidates when it came to subversion or shock, took the conform-to-deform concept and ran with it.

26

RAIDING THE TWENTIETH CENTURY: ZTT and Frankiemania

Malcolm McLaren. Trevor Horn. The Art of Noise. Frankie Goes To Hollywood. Propaganda. Grace Jones.

Trevor Horn ruled 1982. Everybody clamoured for his Midas touch after ABC's *The Lexicon of Love*. Horn found himself facing the choice of working with either Spandau Ballet or Malcolm McLaren. Spandau wanted the deluxe *Lexicon* production, and the conservative side of Horn saw the logic of repeating a winning formula. But McLaren appealed to his sense of adventure. 'I fancied Malcolm; he seemed like a hoot,' recalls Horn. It was a turning point for his career and for British pop.

Having given up on Bow Wow Wow, McLaren now looked to become a star in his own right. But he needed a producer who could turn his latest ragbag of subversive concepts – hip hop's scratching 'n' rapping meets ethnic rhythms from around the world – into coherent music. The ex-Svengali and the super-producer could not have been a more chalk-and-cheese pair. McLaren saw Horn as a key architect of New Pop, which he despised as edgeless and sexless. For his part, Horn had always thought The Sex Pistols fraudulent – his producer's ear could tell how *Never Mind the Bollocks* was clearly a skilfully concocted studio creation. But, despite their differences, the pair gelled. 'It's impossible not to be charmed by Malcolm,' says Horn. McLaren, meanwhile, became taken with the idea of expanding Horn's horizons by dragging him across the planet for the project, whose working title was *Folk Dances of the World*.

McLaren was convinced that a massive rediscovery of the earthy and ethnic was imminent. South African township pop, Appalachian hillbilly music, Dominican merengue, Cajun, Cuban rhythms – anything 'raw' would be embraced as a backlash against 'cooked' pop (i.e. exactly the sort of ultra-glossy product with which Horn was synonymous). Unfortunately, budget limitations meant that McLaren's planned around-the-world-of-music trek was reduced to a stint in South Africa and a longer sojourn in cosmopolitan New York, whose vast range of ethnic music meant it was easy to simulate the panglobal vibe. In Soweto, McLaren found musicians on the streets and Horn recorded them playing popular and traditional tunes (some of which McLaren later registered as his own copyright compositions). One of these reworked township tunes became the basis for 'Double Dutch', a huge hit in the summer of 1983.

McLaren was already a chart veteran by then, though, having scored a Top 10 single in the winter of 1982 with 'Buffalo Gals' – a bizarre fusion of hip hop and Appalachian square dancing which sold half a million copies, despite McLaren's tone-deaf and rhythmically challenged vocals. In New York, he had met Afrika Bambaataa and made a sort of ethno-musicological field trip to the Bronx to witness breakdancing, scratching and rapping *in situ*. He came away convinced that hip hop was black punk. The way DJs used old records to make new music was just the sort of cultural piracy to warm the cockles of his magpie heart. In this larcenous spirit, 'Buffalo Gals' nicked its main melody and title from a traditional square dance. McLaren recited lines like 'Four buffalo gals go round the outside/And do-si-doh with your pardners' in a shaky amalgam of hillbilly dancemaster and hip hop MC. DJ/rapper crew The World Famous Supreme Team contributed scratching (the first appearance of this technique in the pop mainstream), and cryptic soundbites like 'She's looking like a hobo' jutted out of the mix. In UK dance culture 'Buffalo Gals' is regarded as an old skool hip hop anthem, its collage of beats, bass and samples making it a foundational track for genres like jungle and trip hop.

To weld together this delightfully daft composite, Horn used a crack squad of musicians and technicians: engineer Gary Langan and arranger/keyboardist Anne Dudley (who'd both worked on *Lexicon of Love*) plus programmer/computer whiz J. J. Jeczalik. A non-musician, McLaren generated a surfeit of inspired ideas but no real material. For 'Buffalo Gals' and the album (now retitled *Duck Rock*), Horn's team therefore had to piece together everything and fill in the considerable gaps. 'Anne was the music department, J. J. was the rhythm department,' says Horn. During these volatile McLaren sessions, a creative *corps d'esprit* coalesced among Langan, Jeczalik and Dudley, and this became the kernel of The Art of Noise – Horn's next and most audacious production project. '*Duck Rock* proved you could make a record out of very disparate material,' says Dudley, whose crucial role earned her one-third songwriting credits. 'In that sense it was a prototype Art of Noise album.'

McLaren was so creatively scatty that even before *Duck Rock* was completed, his mind was on his next nutty notion – combining pop and opera. He would score another hit with the Puccini rip-off 'Madame Butterfly', but by then Horn had moved on. Working with McLaren had been chaotic and wearing, but ultimately the whole experience had left the producer with a massively enlarged sense of possibilities. 'I got more from that one album with Malcolm than from working with any other artist,' admits Horn. McLaren's love of concepts and provocations had rubbed off. It was going to be hard for Horn to go back to glitzing up dull pop groups.

For super-producers, one alternative to turning sows' ears into silk purses is starting your own label: there's much more control that way . . . and more money. Horn's wife/manager Jill Sinclair had the business skills and ruthless streak to make this idea work, and Horn had the spectacular sound. But he also wanted the label to have a strong identity, and knew that wasn't his forte. The Buggles, the group he'd fronted, enjoyed a worldwide number 1 with 'Video Killed the Radio Star' but became one-hit wonders largely because of their lack of image. What Horn needed was a McLaren-like figure – a magus of rhetoric and presentation who knew how to work the media. One person came to mind: Paul Morley, *NME*'s hot-headed prophet of New Pop.

'I'd spent a whole year wanting to *belt* Paul,' laughs Horn. Morley had interviewed The Buggles and headlined the feature 'Dirty Old Men with Modern Mannerisms' – meaning that they were just prog-rock session hacks disguising themselves as New Wave. 'He wasn't wrong in a way,' concedes Horn. 'It was one of The Buggles' failings that we didn't have a manifesto. When I was working with ABC, I watched Martin Fry and saw how well he had the music-paper thing worked out.' Morley and Horn both had cameo roles in 'The Look of Love' video, and on the set, Dollar-fan Morley tried to kiss Horn. ('I was taken by surprise and pushed him away!') Then Morley profiled Horn for *NME*, hailing him as the hippest producer of 1982. 'In the interview he took all the things I said and presented my ideas so much better than I did,' recalls Horn. 'I was impressed.'

Morley, meanwhile, found himself at the end of 1982 in a similar quandary to Horn. After six years of crusading for post-punk and New Pop, he was exhausted with music journalism and quit his staff-writer job at *NME*. In the age of glossy, glammy mags like *Smash Hits* and *The Face*, the drab, ink-smutted weeklies were no longer at the centre of pop culture. The blander Wham/Duran types were ousting the brighter minds that Morley had championed, and it felt like the music business, for so long thrown off-balance by punk, was now back in control. 'By 1983, both Trevor and me were questioning the value of what we did, from our different positions,' says Morley. 'I was going through a period of guilt, feeling that all I did was comment and carp from the sidelines. As a critic, I'd *tried* to make things happen. But ultimately I felt parasitical. I had this romantic idealism that I should contribute.' Then Horn called up Morley and said, 'Let's have an adventure.'

Creating an identity for Horn's label – christened Zang Tuum Tumb – came naturally for Morley. He'd always celebrated those independent labels who managed to shed the dowdy-shopkeeper aura that often clung to all things 'indie' and instead cultivated a mystique, through seductive packaging and witty allusions. Fast Product was a favourite for its design sense, as was Factory, for its gorgeous, enigmatic artwork and Dadaist japes – like giving catalogue numbers to things that weren't even records. 'Even moods and sneezes got catalogued,' claims Morley. 'And a cat!' In ZTT you can also see the influence of European labels like Sordide Sentimentale and Les Disques du Crépuscule, the latter run by a clutch of Factory-worshipping Belgian aesthetes who released esoteric compilations like *The Fruit of the Original Sin*. Other Morley faves included ZE and Fetish, who had groups like 23 Skidoo and covers designed by Neville Brody.

Although often described as ZTT's marketing director, Morley never had an official title. 'I worked like a fucking demon, to be honest. I did about five jobs – A&R, helping design sleeves, commissioning, writing all the label copy, the sleevenotes.' Playful and pretentious (in the best sense), liberally peppered with quotations from philosophers and novelists, Morley's sleevenotes became ZTT's hallmark – and the single element that most polarized the public. Although he didn't always understand what Morley was on about in the sleevenotes, Horn says, 'I loved the idea of a manifesto, because musicians are rarely any good at romanticizing themselves. Unfortunately, those sleevenotes caused Paul to fall out majorly with most ZTT artists quite quickly.'

ZTT's output was divided into two streams: the Action Series and the Incidental Series. The latter consisted of more experimental and contemplative music. In a piece for the *NME* grandiosely titled 'Who Bridges the Gap between the Record Executive and the Genius? Me', Morley argued that a new 'blockbuster' mentality had taken over the industry and was rendering extinct cult figures like Roy Harper and John Martyn, the kind of 'mid-list' artists once allowed to make record after record with only moderate sales. The Action Series, meanwhile, was designed to compete in precisely this new brutal chart-pop realpolitik oriented around singles and videos. The word 'Action' signalled ZTT's aggressive intent. 'I was sick of the people that were getting all the attention, like Gary Kemp and Simon Le Bon, so I wanted to muscle in, push these offensive characters aside,' Morley told *Melody Maker*. 'We hate videos and all that rubbish, but unfortunately we're stuck with it now,' he told another interviewer. 'So our philosophy is to get in there and . . . do it better, to do it *richer*.' If Horn's job was to ensure that ZTT records sounded sensational, Morley's was to engineer *sensations* that convulsed their way through the media. McLaren-style, he wanted to use hype, scandal and staged confrontation to conjure instant pop myth.

Zang Tuum Tumb was a phrase Morley had found in Luigi Russolo's 'The Art of Noises'. In this 1913 manifesto for a Futurist music, Russolo quoted from a letter by the movement's leader, Marinetti, which poetically used onomatopoeia to describe a battle during the Balkan Wars. 'ZANG-TUMB-TUUMB', as Marinetti rendered it, evoked the sound of Bulgarian siege cannons bombarding the Ottoman Turks. The military connotations of Zang Tuum Tumb appealed to Morley's sense of the label as declaring war on a New Pop gone wrong. In this martial spirit the first Zang Tuum Tumb release was *Into Battle with The Art of Noise*.

Although the McLaren album had laid the groundwork for the group, the true trigger for The Art of Noise came from a far less cool project: Horn and his crew's nine months of laborious production work on Yes's *90125*. During one of the many recording-session hiatuses, Jeczalik and Langan grew bored and started messing around on a Fairlight CMI Series II sampler (the first keyboard-based digital sampler). They took Alan White's drum track from an aborted Yes song as raw material, but instead of sampling individual drum hits as usual, they shoved the entire drum break into the Fairlight. When Horn heard the crashing monster-funk stampede of looped rhythm, he realized that Langan and Jeczalik had unwittingly reinvented hip hop's wheel: the breakbeat. Hip hop DJs took two copies of the same record and stretched out a track's percussion-only peak by cutting back and forth between the two turntables. But when it came to making rap records, hip hop producers in those days used drum machines or live musicians, simply because the Fairlight sampler was priced out of their league. Beating the likes of Marley Marl to the punch by a couple of years, The Art of Noise pioneered one of the foundations of hip hop: the sampled and looped breakbeat.

Sampling was at the core of The Art of Noise. In the early eighties the only performers who could afford Fairlights were art-rock superstars like Peter Gabriel and Kate Bush. Horn was a fiend for state-of-the-art machinery, though, and owned one himself. And, in Jeczalik, he also had a burgeoning sampler virtuoso. Just as well: in addition to its prohibitive cost, the Fairlight was 'very difficult to operate', says Anne Dudley. 'It also sounded dreadful,' at least by today's standards. The Fairlight reproduced sampled sounds at low resolution and could capture only 1.2-second soundbites. Yet restriction proved to be the mother of invention. 'We had to be incredibly ingenious to make this thing work,' says Dudley. 'I had to think of ways of using short sounds all the time – that's why The Art of Noise's music is so stabby.' You can hear this on 'Beatbox', the track built around the Yes drum loop, and throughout the *Into Battle* EP. Everything is staccato and punchy. Clipped orchestral fanfares jab and joust; bright bursts of unidentifiable sound ambush your ears. It's like being in an audio-cartoon version of Marinetti's Balkan battlefield. Sampled vocals, stretched across the octaves of the Fairlight keyboard, are played in stuttering patterns: a baritone belch becomes a strange, oompah-like bass pulse.

The Fairlight's grainy, low-resolution samples have a particular character and charm – a 'veiled, indistinct quality', as Timothy Warner puts it. With The Art of Noise, the samples often have a faded, Pathé newsreel aura. Indeed, *Into Battle* sounds somewhat like hip hop if it had been invented in Europe in 1916. This was how Morley saw the whole ZTT aesthetic: a flashback to the 1910s and 1920s: Futurism, Surrealism and all the other great manifesto-mongering '-isms' of that era. His slogan for ZTT was 'Raiding the Twentieth Century'. As Greil Marcus would later do in *Lipstick Traces*, Morley traced punk back through Situationism to 'the great sense of play and provocation' that animated Dada. The Art of Noise's absurdist collage of beats 'n' pieces, its 'flung together' messthetic of 'inconsistencies, hyperbole, non sequitur and

INTO
BATTLE
WITH THE
ART OF
NOISE

TITLES
battle
BEAT BOX
THE ARMY NOW
DONNA
MOMENTS IN LOVE
bright noise
FLESH IN ARMOUR
COMES AND GOES
moment in love

Front cover of ZTT's
debut release, *Into
Battle with The Art of
Noise*, 1983.

Paul Morley's (in)famous
sleevenotes make their
debut on the back cover
of *Into Battle with The
Art of Noise*

HUUMMMM ALONG WITH. . . The Art of NOISE
(a zang tuum tumb fantasy)

a. The group are perfectly capable of intelligent conversation.

b. They have an almost hygienic need for complications.

c. In any given year the group will: respect everyone; die in the field of honour; vote for so and so;
   respect nature and painting; consider themselves likeable.

d. They will never accept that a whole sentence can ever come from half a man.

e. It took the most advanced electronic equipment imaginable for the group to execute this, their first
   collection of *noise*. And a strange way of breathing.

BETWEEN jest AND earnest. . . BETWEEN love AND war. . .
BETWEEN now AND then. . . HUUMMMM along with. . .

side one (45 r.p.m.)   *side two (45 r.p.m.)*

battle   MOMENTS IN LOVE
BEAT BOX   bright noise
THE ARMY NOW   FLESH IN ARMOUR
DONNA   COMES AND GOES
                          moment in love

THE NOISE was executed by THE ART OF NOISE Trevor Horn huummmmed along. "Pinch Yourself!"
The Art of Noise are organised at the bank and in the mind of ZTT Records -- but they dress themselves.
Further information about Art of Noise, and information about all other Zang Tuummmm Tumb fantasies,
is available from: The ZTT Building, 8-10 Basing Street, London W11. Enclose s.a.e.

conflicting themes' (as Dudley put it) was actually much closer to Dada than to the carnage-crazy Italian Futurists. At the same time, it anticipated the *fin de siècle* sounds of sampladelic genres like hardcore rave and big beat. By the nineties, what had made Art of Noise eccentric – instrumental dance music that relegated vocals to the level of just another texture, while turning drum sounds and effects into hooks – was commonplace.

If Dudley, Langan and Jeczalik were the musical core of The Art of Noise, and Horn was its musical director, Morley's role was the organizer of meaning and maker of mischief. 'I acted as if I was in the group,' says Morley. 'There was a lot of hi-tech jamming, so it was quite formless, and I helped Trevor edit it together. But even if I'd only thought of the name The Art of Noise, I think that was enough. I did take credit because I named all the songs.' As Dudley puts it, *Into Battle*'s stand-out track 'is not "Moments in Love" without the title. That's incredibly important, almost worth half the publishing credit!' Indeed, it's hard to imagine this gliding moonwalk of glistening idyllictronica being called anything else, so exquisitely does the title capture the music's 'wide asleep' feeling of falling head over heels.

Much later, when it all turned sour, Jeczalik would quantify Horn and Morley's combined musical contribution as slightly less than 2 per cent. But Dudley today is much more generous: 'Paul, to his credit, was the entire creator of all the titles, the artwork, the manifestos. He gave us an identity. None of us had really intended to be a band. But Paul got very excited by it and swept us along with his enthusiasm. Without him, we wouldn't have existed – we would've been a bunch of session musicians. He gave us the name and we thought we ought to live up to it because it was so good.'

Fundamental to the Art of Noise concept was anonymity. At their first group meeting in February 1983, they all agreed that no photos of the group would appear on the records or in interviews; they'd never appear in the videos; and there would be no lead singer. This was partly pragmatic, given that no one in the group was exactly pop-star material. Morley turned this facelessness into a provocation. 'All The Art of Noise is is taking the piss a little out of pop groups, which is why the first photos we sent out were of spanners and roses,' he declared. And as he later pointed out during a ZTT showcase at London's Ambassador's Theatre, 'a spanner is intrinsically more interesting than the lead singer of Tears for Fears'. The side-effect of this anonymity, though, was that Morley became The Art of Noise's spokesperson in interviews.

ART OF NOISE

The Art Of Noise as they are.

ZTT publicity shot for The Art of Noise. L to R: Anne Dudley, J. J. Jeczalik, Gary Langan, Paul Morley. (But where's Trevor Horn?)

The Art of Noise, and ZTT in general, represented Morley's fantasy of an alternate pop history: what if European culture just carried on from where it was just before the Second World War, unaffected by the arrival of rock 'n' roll, and instead generated its own, totally un-American version of popular music? *Propaganda Present the Nine Lives of Dr Mabuse*, the third ZTT release, represented the next stage in this masterplan of raiding the (European, early) twentieth century. 'The children of Fritz Lang and Giorgio Moroder' is how *NME*'s Chris Bohn tagged Düsseldorf's Propaganda. Inspired by Lang's expressionist trilogy of movies about a shadowy master criminal, 'Dr Mabuse' was epic Eurodisco: Horn and engineer Steve Lipson constructed a monumental edifice of arching synths and percussion as imposing as pillars.

Propaganda's conceptualist, Ralf Dorper, justified this 'very bombastic sound' to *ZigZag*: 'the character Mabuse was symbolizing something extraordinary, something more or less unreal, so we had to have an unreal production'. Formerly in metal-bashing pioneers Die Krupps, Dorper was a fanatical cinephile who preferred movies to music. 'Cinema is much more inspirational to me,' he declared. 'It's much more multi-levelled: you have a storyline, a setting, a soundtrack . . .' Propaganda's ambition was as grand as their sound: to be the biggest German band in the world. Released in February 1984, 'Dr Mabuse' peaked at just number 27 in the UK charts – considerably short of the target. Still, that would normally be a decent result for a new band and a young label. Except that 'Mabuse' had already been utterly eclipsed by the gargantuan impact of ZTT's second release: 'Relax', by Frankie Goes to Hollywood.

Horn first saw Frankie on Channel 4's new music show *The Tube*, where the Liverpool group had been given a small budget to do a slightly sanitized remake of their own ultra-sleazy promo video, which the group had filmed in the hope of getting a record deal. The look was striking – singer Holly Johnson and backing vocalist Paul Rutherford in leather fetish-wear – and the sound, scrappy funk-rock, had a crude but lusty energy. 'More a jingle than a song' is how Horn describes the original 'Relax', but then he had always preferred half-written tunes rather than professionally finished songs: there was potential there for him to 'fix them up', inflate them in his inimitable style. Morley, initially more doubtful, at least liked Frankie's hardcore gay element. 'I kinda thought it could be the fun I wanted to have, to invent a pop group.' Not that he had a completely blank canvas: the S&M/fetish image pre-existed Frankie's falling into ZTT's clutches, while the disco-metal sound and 'give it *loads*' attitude came from the band.

What Frankie really brought to the table was that characteristic Liverpudlian commitment to being entertaining; that belief in oneself as already a star, just waiting for the wider world to notice. Johnson and Rutherford were veterans of the glam-turned-punk milieu centred on Eric's and Mathew Street. Rutherford had formed Liverpool's single proper, London-style punk band, The Spitfire Boys, whose main claims to fame were that they were all gay, lived together in one room, read Genet and never rehearsed. 'One week if you wore make-up you were a queer, the next you were a punk,' Rutherford recalled. It didn't make much difference either way: you still got beaten up. Bowie-boy Holly Johnson fearlessly affronted the straights with his extremist coiffure: dyeing his social-security number into the side of his head, getting a mini-Mohican, shaving his scalp and painting it red and green: 'Decadence was the key word then,' he recalled. Johnson joined Big in Japan, Liverpool's glam-punk supergroup, whose members all went on to pop success of one sort or another. Greatness eluded Holly for the longest time until, after various failed ventures, he finally hooked up with Rutherford and the three hetero members of Frankie – Peter 'Ped' Gill, Mark O'Toole and Brian 'Nasher' Nash, collectively known thereafter as 'the Lads'. The name Frankie Goes to Hollywood came from a picture from an old glamour magazine stuck to the wall of their dank rehearsal cellar, which showed a young Sinatra disembarking on Los Angeles' runway and being greeted by screaming bobby-soxers. It symbolized Frankie's determination to be stars at all costs.

Unfortunately, their lust for fame was so fierce that they signed the contract dangled by ZTT (£250 advance for each of the first two singles, with a lousy royalty rate of 5 per cent) and buckled when Jill Sinclair made the deal conditional on Frankie also signing their song-publishing rights to ZTT's sister company, Perfect Songs, for a meagre advance of £5,000. 'That's the embarrassment I have really,' admits Morley today, comparing the contract to a '1950s deal', with the recording, publishing and studio (Frankie's records would be made at Horn's SARM studios, ensuring an extra stream of profit for what Morley calls 'the family') all 'locked in with the same company. You can mount a case, but it was an unfair monopoly'. And in the long run this greed would come back to bite ZTT in the ass.

Once Frankie were securely indentured, Morley immediately went into overdrive, mapping out the Frankie marketing campaign as a military assault on pop. There would be a perfect conceptual sequence of singles tackling the biggest possible themes – 'sex, war, religion' – while the videos and packaging would maximize the shock impact of Holly and Paul's hardcore homosexuality. Explicit gayness was one of pop's few remaining taboos. Boy George opened the closet door but only by the tiniest crack: ultimately, he was too cuddly, coyly masking his sexuality with statements like the famous declaration that he'd rather have a cup of tea than sex. Pop was long overdue something that was fully 'out', that carried the scent of spunk and the harsh tang of amyl. Frankie led the way, closely followed by fellow Liverpudlian Pete Burns of Dead or Alive and Bronski Beat. The latter, whom rumour had it turned down ZTT's advances, represented the responsible side of gay pride – the struggle for dignity in the face of bigotry. Frankie, by contrast, were rampantly pleasure-principled, and far more threatening than Bronski,

Frankie Goes to Hollywood, 1983. L to R: Mark O'Toole, Holly Johnson, Paul Rutherford, Peter Gill, a.k.a. Ped, Brian Nash, a.k.a. Nasher. Photo by Kevin Cummins

whose singer, Jimmy Somerville, dapper but basically ordinary-looking in his jeans and Ben Sherman shirt, communicated the idea that 'we're just like everybody else, except in bed'. Holly, and especially Rutherford with his clone moustache, transmitted something more confrontational: 'No, we are not like you. We do extreme things in the pursuit of pleasure, inhabit a strange underworld where anything goes in the quest for kicks and cocks.'

Imagine if someone had tried to recreate punk based on a single relic of 1977: the infamous T-shirt worn by Sid Vicious of two cruising cowboys in leather chaps and little else, their giant cocks hanging down and almost touching. 'Morley had his strategy all worked out. He wanted it to be like The Sex Pistols – all the outrage, controversy – but this time with all the sex,' Rutherford recalled. Crucially, though, Frankie were the *disco* Pistols – what punk would have sounded like if modelled on Donna Summer's 'I Feel Love' rather than The Stooges' 'No Fun'.

Yet the conditions under which Frankie's records were made couldn't have been further from punk's spirit. Far from 'doing it themselves', the band were eventually excluded from the recording process by their producer. 'Relax' displayed Horn's maniacal perfectionism and his willingness to disregard the musicians he was supposedly working with and for. He quickly came to see Frankie as obstacles to his vision. In the studio, overawed and intimidated by Horn's reputation, the band were too nervous to make suggestions. 'Whatever he said we went along with,' Johnson admitted in his autobiography, *A Bone in My Flute*. 'On one occasion Trevor said to me that he had considered sacking the musicians from the band, leaving just Paul and me to front the act.' After an abortive attempt to get the Lads to play to his satisfaction, Horn hired the Blockheads, the accomplished funkateers who had once backed Ian Dury. But the results did not sound sufficiently modern, and eventually a hi-tech version of 'Relax' was constructed with the rhythm-programming assistance of The Art of Noise's Jeczalik and keyboard work from session player Andy Richards. Apart from Johnson, the band were twiddling their thumbs in Liverpool when the definitive version of 'Relax' was made at Horn's west London studio. 'Look, "Relax" *had* to be a hit,' says Horn with a mixture of self-justification and guilt. In the end, the sole sonic contribution from the band, beside vocals, was in the form of samples of the group jumping into a swimming pool. Yet Horn later admitted, 'I could never have done these records in isolation. There was no actual playing by the band . . . but the whole *feeling* came from the band.'

'Relax' sounded colossal, as well it might after Horn had lavished £70,000 on studio time on it. But, according to the producer, its monumental quality owed less to his mixing-desk trickery than to its key and the instrumentation used: '"Relax" is perfect because it's in E. The most satisfying note on the bass guitar is bottom E, and that's what's running through the whole song.' Technology did play its part, though: a new device enabled Horn to lock the Fairlight-sampled bass pulse in superhumanly tight synchrony with the four-to-the-floor of the Linn drum. The pumping bass and pounding kick-drum fuse in a 'love action' of thrust and grind. In his memoir, Johnson describes how 'Relax' merged 'rock edge' with the Hi-NRG disco that ruled gay clubs in the early eighties and broke into the pop charts in 1984. DJ/producer Ian Levine, the pioneer of this UK-based sound, defined Hi-NRG as 'melodic, straightforward dance music that's not too funky'. The non-funkiness was crucial: slamming rather than swinging, Hi-NRG's white Euro feel was accentuated by butt-bumping bass twangs at the end of each bar. 'Relax' tapped into Hi-NRG's remorseless, metronomic precision and orgiastic vibe – the spasming drum roll at the end of the single feels like an amyl nitrite rush.

'As we were making "Relax", I became more and more convinced it was all about sex,' recalls Horn. 'It was like a shagging beat. Also, the more I met the guys, I thought it was about sex – they were *obsessed* with it. By the end we were thinking of giant orgasms.' Horn filled the record with 'imaginary mayhem' – synth whooshes, gasps and exhalations. The whole song is suffused with a pre-orgasmic glow. Two-thirds of the way through, 'Relax' ignores its own advice – 'Relax, don't do it/When you want to come' – and erupts with a crass but hilariously liquid simulated ejaculation. The protracted and abstract 'Sex Mix' was even more blatant, with its rubbery squelches, bath-house splashes, boystown gang chants, slurping sounds, and Holly leerily slurring stray words like 'awesome' and 'feel'. Ironically, the song's original concept was 'if you wanna get on top of a situation, you've gotta work hard to do it', Johnson later revealed. 'The sexual innuendo was put upon it later.'

Was 'Relax' even a sexy record? Perhaps only in the exhibitionist sense of the Amsterdam leather bars Holly visited, where the sex acts had an element of 'theatre and performance' he enjoyed. 'Relax' was driven by something far stronger than sensuality: an idea of sex as weapon, shock tactic, threat. 'Relax' didn't give us flesh or delight, it revelled in the word, in saying the unsayable. The specific word in question was 'come'.

If 'Relax' was *about* anything, it appeared to be the postponement of orgasm, or oral sex, or both. Strangely, though, the moral guardians at the BBC initially failed to notice the song's suggestiveness: Radio One supported 'Relax' heavily in the weeks following its October 1983 release. It slowly inched its way up the charts until the group were invited to appear on *Top of the Pops* in January 1984, whereupon 'Relax' vaulted up to number 6. Absurdly, having made it a hit, Radio One then decreed the single unfit for broadcast, after the DJ Mike Read noticed its obscene overtones and refused to play it on his show. Within two weeks of the ban, 'Relax' inevitably reached number 1, where it stayed for five weeks – its long reign at the top only bolstered when *Top of the Pops* and BBC Television followed their radio counterpart's lead.

The only surprising aspect of the ban was that it took so long to . . . well, come. Morley had courted scandal right from the start. ZTT's ad campaign for 'Relax' began with two quarter-page ads in the music press: the first featured a mustachioed and grinning Rutherford in sailor hat, shades and leather tunic; the second had Johnson as a sinister, unsmiling sex dwarf, shaven headed and wearing rubber gloves. 'ALL THE NICE BOYS LOVE SEA MEN', declared the first ad. 'Soap it up . . . rub it up . . . Frankie goes to hollywood are coming . . . making duran duran lick the shit off their shoes . . . Nineteen inches that must be taken always.' The second ad promised 'theories of bliss, a history of Liverpool from 1963 to 1983, a guide to Amsterdam bars', and a vision that would 'grip especially those who are at home in the giant cities and in the web of their numberless interconnecting relationships'. The single's artwork laid it on thicker still: a back-cover photo of a hand tugging cruelly on the ring piercing a male nipple; a cute little logo of four wriggly-tailed spermatozoa. Divided into 'chapters', the sleevenotes kicked off with the invitation 'let's go down the hall to the disciplining room' and included a scene in which the 'monster' Frankie orders his sexual vassal Peta to 'get down there and lick that shit off my shoes'. Says Morley, 'I rang up Holly and said, "Look, I'm going to put an abbreviated pornographic novel on the back of the twelve-inch. Is that OK?" And Holly went, "Yeah, all right."'

Along with the avant-porn pantheon (de Sade, Genet, Bataille, Burroughs), Morley was doubtless influenced by *Taxi Zum Klo* (*Taxi to the Toilet*), Frank Zipploh's recent movie about German gay life, which featured unprecedentedly graphic scenes of cottaging and glory holes. DAF, the leather-clad Düsseldorf duo, were also Morley favourites. In *NME* he'd praised their *Alles Ist Gut* as 'slimy, steamy sex music', a hard

The infamous porno sleevenotes on the back sleeve of 'Relax'

electrodisco evocation of 'the rubbing, juices, pounding, striving, belching, stickiness . . . the smells, the rhythms, the passions, the secretions, the darkness, the tears of S.E.X.', and framed the review with quotes from D. H. Lawrence and radical anti-psychiatrist David Cooper. The whole Frankie escapade gave off a powerful whiff of sixties-style sex radicalism (Herbert Marcuse, Norman O. Brown, *et al.*): you could see Frankie as a last spurt of that style of libertinism that viewed the libido as inherently revolutionary, before a revitalized Thanatos (in the form of AIDS) imposed limits on Eros.

Simply through demanding 'satisfaction' (orgasm), all sixties pop music possessed a powerful insurrectionary charge. But during the permissive seventies, hetero sex gradually lost its edge: the only frissons came from the glam stars' flirtations with decadence and gender-bending.

Nevertheless, pop's forays into full-on homosexuality had been tentative and veiled. But as Johnson put it in one interview, 'there's no pussy-footing with us. We are into PLEASURE and we think that what has been regarded as a sexual perversion should be brought into the open.' You didn't see fisting or water sports, but the video for 'Relax' was still orgiastic and virtually unbroadcastable. Directed by Bernard Rose, it depicts Holly Johnson as a naïf in the big city who stumbles into a gay pleasure-dome. Here, a Nero-like fatso presides over scenes of Roman-style decadence. With Rutherford as his guide, Holly's innocence is debauched and he's last seen in the sticky midst of a frotting gang-grope.

Into Battle with The Art of Noise had minimal impact in Britain, but in America 'Beatbox' became a popular track with breakdancers. Because most Americans knew nothing of ZTT's reputation, The Art of Noise were often assumed to be a black group (indeed, their music would eventually become one of the most popular sources for sampling alongside Kraftwerk, James Brown and Parliament-Funkadelic). Inspired by this B-boy reception, which proved that their cut-up aesthetic could cut it on the dance floor, The Art of Noise reworked the track as the single 'Beatbox (Diversions One)' b/w 'Beatbox (Diversions Two)'. The remakes featured a rambling rock 'n' roll bassline and dashing tremolo guitar licks redolent of Duane Eddy or The Shadows, as if to place The Art of Noise in that noble if marginal tradition of instrumental pop hit-makers. And, indeed, the unlikely group soon joined that pantheon: while 'Relax' reigned over the UK pop chart, The Art of Noise reached number 1 in the *Billboard* Dance Chart.

'Beatbox' spawned yet another single with the closely related 'Close (to the Edit)', which reached number 8 in the UK pop chart, helped by a brilliantly surreal video directed by Zbigniew Rbczynski. Its most striking image – a prepubescent punkette dismembering a piano with a chainsaw – made for a witty visual emblem for The Art of Noise's updated version of *musique concrete*'s slice-and-dice methods. 'It's not called "Close (to the Edit)" for nothing – you could more or less stitch any bit of "Close" into "Beatbox" and it would still sound like one piece,' says Anne Dudley. 'I can't actually remember where "Close (to the Edit)" ended and "Beatbox" began because at one point they were one track.' Foregrounding what Dudley calls the music's 'disjointed wondrousness', the title also twists Yes's *Close to the Edge* to make an encrypted nod to the thunderous Alan White drum break underpinning 'Beatbox'/'Close'. You can also hear

'Close' as a homage to Kraftwerk and their 'Autobahn'-era notion of the car as a musical instrument: it begins with an engine starting, and a motor revving is turned into a melodic riff that recurs throughout.

The success of The Art of Noise was another triumph for a seemingly unstoppable ZTT, but Trevor Horn was not exactly feeling relaxed. In fact, he was incredibly nervous about Frankie turning into a one-hit wonder. He spent three months fine-tuning the follow-up, 'Two Tribes', building and discarding several versions of the single. Horn inflated Frankie's energetic but emaciated funk-metal ditty into an epic surge somewhere between Chic and Rush. Over an adrenaline-pumping bass pummel, swashbuckling guitars flash like the scimitars of jihad cavalry charging an infidel city. Featuring approximately nine lines of lyric *in toto*, 'Two Tribes' is even more jingle-like than 'Relax', and as anti-war polemic goes, the chorus – 'When two tribes go to war/A point is all that you can score' – is pretty darn trite. But Horn's supercharged production makes 'Two Tribes' sound almost as momentous as its theme: nuclear doomsday.

But it was the ancillary stuff and nonsense orchestrated by Morley that turned 'Two Tribes' into an *event*. By 1984, the Cold War had entered into its final phase, just before Gorbachev's glasnost. Soviet premier Konstantin Chernenko was a Politburo hardliner, while Ronald Reagan seemed scarily sincere when he described the USSR as the 'evil empire'. For the twelve-inch 'Annihilation Mix' of 'Two Tribes', impressionist Christopher Barrie impersonated the US president uttering absurdities like 'Just think: war breaks out and nobody turns up'. ZTT also hired actor Patrick Allen, the reassuring paternal voice of *Protect and Survive* (a record made by the British government to be played on the radio just before a nuclear attack) to repeat some of his lines: chilling advice like 'If your grandmother or any other member of the family should die whilst in the shelter, put them outside, but remember to tag them first for identification purposes.'

Morley caked the record sleeves for 'Two Tribes' – which, like 'Relax', came in several mixes – in Cold War facts and figures: a sleevenote about alcoholism in the Red Army; a table contrasting the superpowers' nuclear arsenals; a chart displaying the number of deaths (in tens of millions) caused by the diverse after-effects of a 5,000-megaton war (including fallout, toxic gases, nuclear winter, epidemics, famine and psychiatric disorders). The video featured Frankie as a TV news crew on the sidelines of a no-holds-barred wrestling match between Reagan and Chernenko lookalikes, complete with knees in the groin and ear-biting.

The pièce de résistance, though, was Morley's T-shirt campaign, openly modelled on Katharine Hamnett's agit-prop T-shirts that boasted slogans like 'WORLD NUCLEAR BAN NOW' and 'CHOOSE LIFE'. The 'FRANKIE SAY . . .' series swept the nation with variations like 'FRANKIE SAY BOMB IS A FOUR-LETTER WORD' and 'FRANKIE SAY ARM THE UNEMPLOYED' (inevitably inspiring such response T-shirts as 'WHO GIVES A FUCK WHAT FRANKIE SAY?').

Combining savage satire and sheer informative clout, 'Two Tribes' ought to be the ultimate protest record. Yet that intent is undercut by the overall feel of the record, which seems to exult in the prospect of apocalypse. 'It's not political; it sounds *glorious* I think,' said Holly Johnson. The key to 'Two Tribes' is the bursting euphoria with which Johnson sings the kiss-off line: 'Are we living in a land where sex and horror are the new gods?' It's Eros versus Thanatos again: the apocalyptic notion that anything goes in the decadent Last Days, that living like there's no tomorrow is the logical response to a world where nuclear annihilation constantly hangs over our heads. Like Prince's '1999', with its 'we could all die any day' call to party, 'Two Tribes' sounds like celebration. Which is why it's nowhere near as effectively anti-war as UB40's chilling 'The Earth Dies Screaming', or Kate Bush's 'Breathing', which took the listener inside the airless claustrophobia of the cubby-hole family shelter as recommended by *Protect and Survive*.

'Two Tribes' entered the charts at number 1 on 4 June 1984 and, partly stoked by endless remixes, stayed there for nine weeks. Amazingly, 'Relax' surged back up the charts and for one week nestled at number 2 beneath 'Two Tribes'. With the fourth ('Relax') and eleventh ('Two Tribes') highest-selling singles of *all time* under their belts, in six months Frankie had become the biggest British pop group of the eighties, and stood as a total vindication of ZTT's media-manipulation strategy. 'In a stupid sense the fantasy I had as an NME journalist about New Pop came true with *me*,' says Morley. 'So there was a glorious narrative purity to it.'

When 'The Power of Love' became their third number one in a row in December 1984, the conceptual arc of the Frankie singles was complete: following sex and war, the big theme this time was religion, or possibly redemption, or maybe love as salvation – something like that, anyway. 'The Power of Love' also represented a kind of staged sell-out, as if 'narrative purity' demanded that Frankie relapse into mere showbiz, like all rebels eventually do. Holly crooned cabaret-style about 'A force from above/Cleaning my soul'; a string section soared; Anne Dudley provided flourishes on the grand piano. It was all a bit tacky really. A blatant bid for the cherished Christmas number 1, 'The Power of Love' was ousted from the top spot after just one week by Band Aid's African-famine charity record 'Do They Know It's Christmas?'

Why not end it there, a conceptual coup? 'My plan, which was the height of naïvety and yet the height of sophistication, was to do "Power of Love", then sell Frankie for five million to someone like CBS,' says Morley. But by this point Frankiemania had developed its own fatal logic. There simply had to be an album, and it had to be a double. *Welcome to the Pleasuredome* cost just under £400,000 and took Trevor Horn's Cinemascope production to new peaks of opulence. 'The world is my oyster,' gloats Johnson on the side-long title track, just before mangling Coleridge with the cry 'In Xanadu did Kublai Khan a pleasure-dome EEEEEE-RECT'. Essentially 'Relax' at a less frantic, more regal tempo, 'Welcome to the Pleasuredome' evokes a vague quest for glory, a wild life of thrill-seeking and rapacious desire. After side two (the singles) and side three (mostly cover versions), *Pleasuredome* begins to flag seriously as it arrives at the Frankie compositions. 'Krisco Kisses' took its name from Crisco, an American cooking-fat widely used as a long-lasting sexual lubricant in pre-AIDS days, but the tune sounds as ham-fisted as Iron Maiden trampling their way through the stage backdrops of *The Lexicon of Love*. By 'Black Night White Light' and 'The Only Star in Heaven', Johnson's limited lyrical range is revealed with lines like 'Live life like a diamond ring' and 'The pleasure-seekers are dying to meet ya/They need young blood'. Worse, you can hear Horn's enthusiasm for the project audibly evaporating.

Pleasuredome's packaging was sumptuous, of course, and strewn with great jokes, from the inner sleeve's ad for ZTT merchandise (Rutherford and Propaganda vocalist Claudia Brucken modelling the 'Jean Genet boxer shorts', the 'Sophisticated Virginia Woolf vest', the 'André Gide socks' and the 'Edith Sitwell bag for life's little luxuries') to the back cover's Picasso-style canvas depicting an orgy of satyr-like beasts (follow some of the long, winding tongues and they end up at some other animal's puckered anus). But as a banquet stuffed with aphrodisiac fare, Frankie's double is ultimately a turn-off: rampant hedonism never sounded so tedious. Advance orders for *Pleasuredome* were staggering – in excess of one million in the UK alone – but as word spread, the copies didn't exactly fly out of the stores.

Paul Rutherford models Frankie merchandise – the enamel badges – on the inner sleeve of *Welcome to the Pleasuredome*, 1984

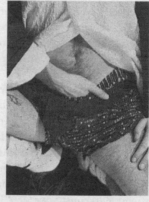

Paul Rutherford models the Jean Genet boxer shorts – more ZTT merchandise from *Pleasuredome*

Propaganda vocalist Claudia Brucken models the sophisticated Virginia Woolf vest

Rutherford and Brucken get it on with the André Gide socks

Pleasuredome almost totally eclipsed *(Who's Afraid of?)* by The Art of Noise (the two debut albums were unwisely released near simultaneously). Propaganda, likewise, never fully emerged from Frankie's shadow. ZTT spent a fortune on *A Secret Wish*, using the most costly state-of-the-art machinery and top-tier session musicians (including Yes guitarist Steve Howe). Yet the album's chart profile fell far short of expectations, as did the single 'Duel' b/w 'Jewel' – two versions of one song, the first candy-coated and catchy, the second harsh and metal-percussive, a pop Neubauten. 'Duel' dazzled in the chart context, but, for all Morley's talk of 'the private moment', Propaganda's music was too overlit to find its way into either your bedroom or your heart. ZTT, as always, were too schematic, too upfront about their designs on the listener. It isn't enough just to refer to dreams, obsession, visions, crime, to slap a Ballard quote on a Propaganda single sleeve about the Baadher-Meinhof gang and madness as 'the only freedom' in a world of bland, soul-crushing sanity. The pop song must be a spell, Marc Bolan said; the music itself has to enforce the magic. In this respect, *A Secret Wish* signally failed: the sound was characterless. Holly Johnson had the sheer lung power to impose himself on Frankie's records, to rival Trevor Horn with his own belting bombast, but there was no such presence in Propaganda, either vocally or in terms of the 'band voice' that makes any truly great rock group recognizable within a few bars. *A Secret Wish* sounded like just another ZTT record.

In 1985, it felt like ZTT developed the anti-Midas touch. Gallic chanteuse Anne Pigalle, another expression of ZTT's Europeanism, barely dented the charts. Andrew Poppy, a Glass/Nyman-style systems music composer who'd orchestrated the Psychic TV albums, fared worse. The one exception to the losing streak was ZTT's project with Grace Jones. A hit in October 1985, her single 'Slave To The Rhythm' might actually be the label's finest four minutes. As with 'Relax', Horn made a series of attempts at making the 'Slave' single, so many that Morley suggested: let's turn this into an album. You could see the *Slave To The Rhythm* LP as a prog-rock set of variations on a theme stretched over two sides, or as the harbinger of today's remix albums. Either way, it functioned as pop deconstruction, an album about the making of a single.

It's also an exercise in deconstructing an icon: Grace Jones, the fashion model turned disco diva turned performance artist turned movie star. Subtitled 'A Biography', *Slave To the Rhythm* is a concept album about the mystery of charisma. The record weaves fragments of two interviews with Jones into the music, along with text huskily intoned by actor Ian McShane and taken from *Jungle Fever* – a book about Grace written by her stylist/mentor/ex-lover Jean-Paul Goude that is a provocative and profoundly suspect meditation on Jones as art object, muse, and racial other.

In the context of Grace Jones, the words 'Slave' and 'Rhythm' are highly charged, overloaded with resonances. Tall, angular, and dark skinned, she looks African; one interview snippet on the album refers to her great-great-grandfather's tribal ancestry in Nigeria. At the same time, her imposing physique and commanding cadences give her a dominatrix-like aura. The undertones of 'Rhythm' include racial myths about black people possessing 'natural rhythm' and perennial anxieties about 'jungle rhythm' as intoxicating and addictive, a cultural contagion subjugating and stupefying Western youth. The song's lyrics play with ideas of the deadening industrial repetition of drudgery and routine versus the blissful repetition of dance-trance and sex. Another buried resonance: 'slaved' is a term in the technical jargon of MIDI, the timecode device that by 1985 was being used to synch up all the different sequencers and digital devices in the modern hi-tech recording studio, as used by Trevor Horn and partner Steve Lipson.

All these meanings were woven into the sonic fabric of 'Slave To The Rhythm', which started life sounding Germanic but veered off in a radically (or even racially) different direction when welded to the polyrhythmic chassis of go-go (a highly percussive and 'African'-sounding form of funk spawned in Washington DC). Unable to get the results they wanted from a supergroup of top go-go players, Horn and Lipson isolated a two minute sequence of the band warming up in the studio and looped the jam breakbeat-style. The new groove gave the song an eerie in-between feel – urgent yet languid – which Jones accentuated with her simultaneously imperious and fatalistic vocal. The music – in Horn's words, 'completely fabricated' in the studio – bore no relation to anything that could be performed live. As such it's perfectly aligned with the overall concept and Goude's cover photographs of Jones, which chopped up and recombined images to produce impossible versions of her body.

In Jones, the ZTT team found an artist who didn't mind being manipulated or framed one bit. 'How she presented herself suggested to me that she should be handled rather like an art object,' Trevor Horn said. At the same time it's clear that Jones was adept at using people to get where and what she wanted. At the end of the album, a fragment of an interview conducted by Morley plays up the idea of Jones as monstrously narcissistic to the point of solipsism. Jones laughs uneasily, then admits with stark candour that yes, she's the centre of her own universe. Then she turns the question on her interviewer, and the record's listeners: 'How about you?'

Slave is the ultimate distillation of ZTT's vision of producer/svengali/conceptualist driven pop. At the same time, Jones was a figure with sufficient presence and sheer despotic force of self to hold her own amidst all the aesthetic man-handling. Such instances are pretty unusual, however. Most artists aren't comfortable with being subsumed within someone else's vision. Herein lies the downfall of labels with a strong identity. The cool new groups soon start to shy away from being signed, while those already on the roster begin to chafe. Indeed, all of ZTT's original big three – first Art of Noise, then Propaganda, finally Frankie – eventually extricated themselves from their contracts, partly because they were financially invidious, but also because they didn't like being perceived as puppets.

To this day, Horn still doesn't quite get it. With surprisingly enduring bitterness, he complains that 'artists want record labels to be businessmen they can curse to give them an excuse when their own mediocrity shines through. The last thing they want is a creative record label. They want to keep the creative part all to themselves.' Morley is a little closer to grasping why the acts got frustrated. 'It comes back to this weird thing – if you're manipulated, it doesn't matter if the people manipulating you are getting you to do fantastic stuff, you still feel manipulated. You want to do it yourself.'

ZTT's fatal flaw was its adherence to the Gospel According to Malcolm. Like McLaren with the Pistols, the label saw itself as the artist and the performers as raw material, mere pigment and canvas. Like McLaren with Bow Wow Wow, ZTT believed in an ill-conceived notion of revolution catalyzed from above. And as with McLaren, this related to ZTT's self-conception as renegade capitalists outwitting the pea-brained corporate dinosaurs, as warriors pitting abstract values (imagination, verve, elegance) against the equally undefined negatives (mediocrity, sameness, dulled efficiency) that smothered the record industry.

In a curious echo of what happened to the Sex Pistols, Frankie's seemingly unstoppable ascent received a kind of reality-check when it confronted America's sheer size and impregnable imperturbability. Not only are US listeners innately more hype-resistant than the British, but the country's fragmented regional markets and vast number of radio, TV, and print outlets, actually makes it much harder to manipulate the media. Unlike in Britain, records tend to build more slowly, a process which weeds out stuff that lacks 'substance'.

Initially, Frankie's attempt to conquer America fared much better than the Pistols'. *Never Mind the Bollocks* peaked at 106 on *Billboard,* but 'Relax' reached the Top 10. However it took a toned-down repackaging of the single and a new video purged of S&M imagery to get the song onto the American charts. In a bold gesture, Frankie's first tour of America had started in Washington, DC on Election Day 1984. But in their eagerness to prove themselves a potent live band (and not just Horn's puppets), Frankie came across as bombastically rockist and ulti- mately rather conventional. Furthermore, during the tour, an already existing divide between the aesthete-diva Johnson and the boorishly het- ero Lads widened further (with Rutherford caught in no-man's land), once again recalling the fissure between Lydon and the rest of the Pistols that became unbridgeable as the band traipsed across the United States in the first weeks of 1978.

'Trevor and Jill really wanted to sell Frankie in America,' Morley rue- fully recalls. 'I said, you'll never sell them there. In America, they thought Frankie were the Village People.' One of his favourite concep- tual japes was *Pleasuredome*'s cover of 'Born To Run', Frankie bringing out a latent homoerotic element of Springsteen's appeal, along with that song's phallic imagery. According to Morley, audiences at Frankie's live shows in America responded to the cover version as sacrilege. By 1985, Springsteen was the figurehead of the New Authenticity, his 'Born in the USA' imagery striking a power chord with the Anglophobic backlash against the flouncing gender-benders who dominated MTV.

American audiences tend to set a huge premium on live performance as the benchmark of a band's authenticity and worth. Live performance is where contact between band and audience forges 'community' in that old rock(ist) sense. In Britain, though, ZTT had prevented Frankie from playing live as long as possible, fearing they couldn't come anywhere near simulating the sound of the records. Instead, they created buzz through the singles, videos and brilliantly engineered controversy. Simon Frith, one of ZTT's more acute critics, argued that this made Frankie a band without genuine fans, a marketing-driven phenomenon with no real social energy behind it.

Superficially, the Frankie escapade resembled the Sex Pistols commotion, in so far as this was pop as public gesture and media panic. But in terms of long term reverberations, Frankie couldn't compare to the Pistols, who despite their initial lack of impact in the US, ended up steadily selling over a million albums there and inspired thousands of American bands. No legion of groups formed in Frankie's image, though, not even in the UK. Nor are the Frankie Say t-shirts prized as talismanic relics of an epochal moment, like punk memorabilia still is.

On one level, you could see Frankie as punk's last blast. But on another deeper, structural level, Frankie were a taste of pop things to come – the return of the boy band. Perhaps that accounts for the curious hollowness, even at the very height of Frankiemania, to the phenomenon. In the end, both the consumers, left clutching the lavishly-appointed bombast of *Pleasuredome*, and the band, bemused by the faint trickle of royalties coming through and humiliated by the general perception of them as ZTT's creations, might justifiably feel an ancient plaint rising in their throats.

Ever get the feeling you've been cheated?

AFTERCHAPTER

The post-punk years felt like one long rush of endless surprise and inexhaustible creativity. You were constantly anticipating the next twist, the latest leap forward. By 1985, though, it seemed like almost all of that energy had dissipated, with every trajectory from punk reaching an impasse or petering out.

New Pop had plunged into decadence – something audible and visible in the overripe arrangements and bloated videos for Culture Club's 'The War Song' and Duran Duran's 'Wild Boys', both released at the end of 1984. Band Aid's 'Do They Know It's Christmas?', USA for Africa's 'We Are the World', and Live Aid in the summer of 1985 defined a new pop ruling class as sharply as 1972's Concert for Bangladesh had done with the rock royalty of its day. It was an unimpeachable cause, of course, but you couldn't help agreeing with the guy who quipped that 'Live Aid was great for Ethiopians but terrible for pop music'. That orgiastic spectacle of *noblesse oblige* fitted all too neatly with the worldview of Thatcher and Reagan (both recently re-elected), who vaunted private philanthropy rather than government intervention.

Far more than Live Aid, though, Madonna represented the true spirit of 1985. A one-woman American distillation of New Pop, she beat the Second British Invasion at their own game (repackaging ideas from black dance pop and gay culture). She had fought her way up through New York's early eighties club culture, the era of mutant disco and fashionable Anglophilia. She'd hung around the edges of Soft Cell's Manhattan milieu and taken style notes from The Slits. Ari Up once defined The Slits' anti-Babylon stance with the declaration, 'We ain't no material girls.' By pure coincidence (or was it?), Madonna used the same phrase to identify her ruthless brand of post-feminism in 'Material Girl'.

517

The really depressing thing about 1985, though, wasn't the mainstream tyranny of nouveau riche pop, so much as the lacklustre state of the alternative scene. The collective sense of purpose that had bound together the diverse initiatives of post-punk had disappeared. Everything seemed desperately disparate. John Peel hit the nail on the head when he admitted, 'I don't even like the records I like.' More than musical inspiration per se, what began to sink into a coma was the discourse *around* music. The weekly rock press was demoralized; the fanzines, mourning punk, struggled to keep faith with its lost spirit in ways that were increasingly counter-productive. Writing in the music papers and 'zines alike suffered from relentless specificity (that band, this record, that gig), shying away from a big picture overview, and instead monitoring the scattered, bitty output, whose pernicious *adequacy* kept us hanging in there – just dimly aware that the motion and meaning might be going nowhere and meaning . . . *less*.

In retrospect, you can go back to the mid-eighties and find harbingers of future revolution: rap was about to enter its most exciting phase; there were early stirrings that would evolve into house and techno. But hindsight distorts, and at the time the situation felt *grim*. Figures such as Prince and The Smiths seemed like isolated saving graces, somehow battling against the general grain. Scan the independent charts of the mid-eighties and it's a smorgasbord of the stale and second rate: past-its-prime Goth, rancid psychobilly, third-wave avant-funk, Fall copyists, trad-rock Americana, and a motley array of 'quite interesting' bands. Likewise, the leading independent labels of the time (Abstract, Illuminated, Kitchenware, 53rd and 3rd, Sweatbox, Ron Johnson) don't have the legendary aura of Rough Trade and Factory (both of which were frankly directionless by mid-decade).

The heroic phase of the independent movement was long past. By 1985, it had settled into steady but unspectacular growth. Independent culture no longer imagined it could supersede or even challenge the mainstream. The indie labels either functioned as an unofficial scouting system for the majors (as soon as their groups attained a certain level of success, a big label poached them) or maintained micro-cult artists at a level just above subsistence. Average sales of an independent single in 1985 were half what they had been in 1980. Rough Trade enjoyed a decent turnover (£2 million annually), but they couldn't propel their artists to the next level, despite having adopted the competitive practices needed to survive in the dog-eat-dog world of eighties pop: they'd abandoned the collectivist front and instituted conventional managerial structures, hired radio pluggers to push their records, and so forth. After hit-hungry acts like Scritti Politti and Aztec Camera left Rough Trade for majors, Geoff Travis found a 'solution', of sorts: while still running Rough Trade, he co-founded Blanco Y Negro, a label that gave off an 'indie' vibe but actually went through WEA.

The semantic shift from 'independent' to 'indie' contains its own story. 'Independent' had once been a neutral term indicating a record's means of production and distribution. By 1985, though, 'indie' referred to a musical genre – or rather a gaggle of subgenres – with increasingly narrow parameters. (In America the term 'college rock' also had currency, because of its links to student taste and the college-radio circuit. Later, the term 'alt-rock' took over.) 'Indie' indicated a distinct sensibility, too: a sort of resentfully impotent opposition to mainstream pop. In the mid-eighties most chart pop was glossy, guitar-free, black-influenced, soulfully strong-voiced, dance-oriented, hi-tech, ultra-modern. Indie made a fetish of the opposite characteristics: scruffy guitars, white-only sources, weak or 'pale' folk-based vocals, undanceable rhythms, lo-fi or Luddite production, and a retro (usually sixties) slant. Indie bands embraced abrasive noise as a harsh scouring force that would purge the decadent luxury of chart pop. Post-punk and New Pop had both been impure, mixing black and white, celebrating the eclectic, the hybrid, the polyglot. But by 1985, purism was back in favour. People craved 'the authentic' and found it in noise (The Jesus and Mary Chain, The Membranes), or in raw roots music: acoustic guitar-strumming protest singer Billy Bragg; the folk-punk of The Pogues and The Men They Couldn't Hang; the populist Americana of Jason & The Scorchers, Long Ryders and Los Lobos. Synths and sequencers, horns and orchestras were out: guitars, bass and drums were in.

Post-punk's essence was its vanguard mindset of constantly looking forwards. This impatience to reach the future had continued with that side of New Pop concerned with exploring the latest electronic technology and drawing inspiration from modern black dance music. Periodization is always tricky when it comes to culture (messy at the best of times; always overspilling, whatever lines you draw), but one reason why the main body of this book concludes in 1984 is that independent culture's shift from futurism to retro really hardened decisively in that year. The desire to 'rip it up and start again' that had driven first post-punk and then New Pop still existed. But for the first time that impulse took the form of looking to the past.

At the start of this book, I mentioned how I never bought old records during the post-punk era: there was too much happening in the present. From 1983, though, that changed. Like many other people, I started to buy old records in a significant number for the first time. Journalists and bands were referencing groups like Love and The Byrds, both of whom I fell for in a big way. The reissue industry, although puny by today's standards, unleashed a torrent of sixties garage-punk compilations and psychedelic anthologies. It was the beginning of the now-familiar syndrome whereby consumers use the abundance of the past to make it through the dry spell of the present.

There were obviously particular qualities about sixties music – cosmic open-heartedness, Dionysian abandon, a certain freedom in the playing – that made it attractive and refreshing to people coming out of a long period in which music had been uptight, hyper-rational and concept-driven. After post-punk's demystification and New Pop's schematics, it was liberating to listen to music rooted in mystical awe and blissed-out surrender. Post-punk had taken swaths of music off the menu – rejected for being too trippy, too excessive, too flamboyantly virtuoso. Discovering you could listen to and enjoy a guitar solo by Jimi Hendrix was a revelation and a thrill – the frisson of forbidden fruit. (I unconsciously replicated that journey while working on this book: by the time I reached '1983', I'd overdosed on dry, anally retentive post-punk and found myself compulsively listening to Byrds/Love/Hendrix as a release – anything loose, intuitive, ecstatic, rockin'!)

But it wasn't just that people started listening to sixties music again. All the new bands that were any good seemed to be name-checking that era. Jangly guitars, folk-rock harmonies and psychedelic dreaminess were everywhere. Hüsker Dü covered 'Eight Miles High' *and* 'Ticket to Ride'. And while not explicitly retro, The Smiths and REM – the two most important alt-rock bands of the day – seemed sixties-redolent because of their plangent guitar chimes and folk-styled vocals. Both bands were 'eighties groups' only in the sense of being *against* that decade. The Smiths, for instance, rejected synths and for a while vowed to make no videos. And their whole 'thing' was predicated on their audience as 'a lost generation' – exiles in their own land. Ditto REM: wistfully and abstractly, they conjured visions of new frontiers and fresh starts for America. All of the great groups of this time, like Hüsker Dü, The Replacements and The Mekons (who brilliantly reinvented themselves as a folk-and-country band), dealt in similar feelings: forlorn dreams, bewilderment, impotence, resignation. This alt-rock sensibility finally reached the mainstream in the early nineties with Nirvana, its mixed emotions crystallized in Kurt Cobain's voice: half snarl of defiance, half aching whimper of defeat.

In their struggle against the eighties, indie bands invoked the very decade that Reagan and Thatcher were attempting to discredit. Of course, there was also an element of nostalgic fascination. And fashion: revisiting the sixties was a solution to the *post*-post-punk quandary of 'Where next?' Bands could draw on the decade as a pop archive of sound and imagery. And naturally there were several 'sixties' to be picked over for period details, which increased the range of recombinant possibilities: The Jesus and Mary Chain with their Beach Boys-meets-Velvets classicism; college radio's flocks of Byrds-clones; Los Angeles' Paisley Underground of retro-psych bands like The Dream Syndicate and Rain Parade; The Sisters of Mercy with their 1969 fetish; The Cult *circa Love* with their leather tassels and Steppenwolf riffs.

Essentially sampling without possessing a sampler, The Jesus and Mary Chain pioneered 'record collection rock'. *Psychocandy*, their 1985 debut, deserves its classic status because of the thrilling manner in which they juxtaposed their always faintly *déjà vu* melodies (equal parts Ronettes, Beach Boys and Ramones) against an oddly serene wall of feedback, with the two elements of their sound – the noise and the pop – not really integrated at all. But when J&MC stripped away the torrential headrush to leave their songs exposed, you were left with pure blank homage. One song on the second album, *Darklands*, even stole the 'woo woo' backing vocals from the Stones' 'Sympathy for the Devil'. You didn't know whether to smile or weep.

The title, *Darklands*, was the first tip-off – J&MC aimed to resurrect the lineage of rock 'n' roll danger and genius-as-madness that legendary British critic Nick Kent would later canonize in his book *The Dark Stuff*. In the mid-seventies *NME* Kent had celebrated the Stones, Brian Wilson, Iggy Pop, The Velvet Underground, The New York Dolls and the more Romantic early CBGB artists like Patti Smith and Television: hard drugs, gaunt cheekbones, black leather, sunglasses after dark. If post-punk and New Pop were anti-rockist, it was precisely Kent's brand of elegantly wasted rock 'n' roll cool that they wanted to abolish.

Now, with The Jesus and Mary Chain and Creation, the indie label that released their early singles, the 'dark stuff' returned with a vengeance. Creation were virtually curators of the Kent canon. Their roster included

Nikki Sudden, whom you'll recall as frontman of DIY pioneers Swell Maps, but who by 1985 had reinvented himself as a Keith Richards-style rock 'n' roll gypsy troubadour. Creation's leading lights, though, were Primal Scream, fronted by rock scholar Bobby Gillespie (who also moon-lighted as J&MC's original drummer). Gillespie talked eloquently of music being like a library – you could pluck books off the shelf from any historical era: Dickens followed by DeLillo followed by Dostoevsky. It sounded persuasive. But that's how people *listen* to records. *Creating* music is a different issue altogether. After all, hardly anybody today writes sonnets, or fiction *à la* Flaubert. Gillespie's analogy captured an epochal shift, from post-punk groups using their influences as inspirational *fuel* to indie-rock bands increasingly deploying them as *citations*. Spotting these allusions (simultaneously ancestral homage and reflected glory) became an integral part of the listener's aesthetic response and pleasure.

Primal Scream were major players in the scene known variously as 'cutie', 'shambling bands' or 'C86'. The last epithet comes from an *NME* cassette documenting the resurgence of indie noise-pop bands that began in 1985 and peaked the following year. Although The Jesus and Mary Chain were catalysts for this scene and the sixties were a major source, the C86 groups also drew on post-punk: Postcard, Swell Maps, Buzzcocks, Subway Sect, The Fall. But it was post-punk with the most radical ele-ments (the politics, the black/white fusion, the studio experimentation) purged. For instance, the C86 shamblers left out Orange Juice's disco-funk influence but kept the sparkly guitar jangle and 'worldliness must keep apart from me' naïvety. This was the most intriguing element of the scene: its cult of innocence (reflected in the schoolkid clothes and hair-styles as much as in the chastely romantic lyrics) and androgyny-oriented sexual politics of male wimps and cute-but-tough girls (a 'wild child' image that would be the basis for Riot Grrrl a decade later). The cruel irony of the cutie movement is that its groups – The Soup Dragons, June Brides, The Pastels, The Shop Assistants – espoused an ideal of 'perfect pop' that couldn't have been more out of step with what modern main-stream pop actually was. Yet, in a way, this was the whole point of the movement: its anachronistic (anti-chronistic?) defiance of the present.

In America a parallel rediscovery of the sixties occurred as bands worked their way forward through that decade, starting with garage punk, The Byrds and early psychedelia. By 1986, the sharper bands had begun to move into the late sixties – the era of long hair, wah-wah, heavy riffs, acid rock. Sonic Youth recorded the Manson-inspired 'Death Valley 69' and sounded increasingly trippy. Butthole Surfers resembled a mobile 'acid test' with their back-projected films, naked female dancer, and occasional onstage sex acts – not forgetting the group's effects-saturated music and weird vocal treatments. Buttholes guitarist Paul Leary played full-blown, orgiastic guitar solos, as did J. Mascis of Dinosaur Jr (sounding like Hendrix meets Neil Young). Jimi, Sabbath, Blue Cheer, even the Grateful Dead, were the new hip reference points. Drugs were compulsory.

The spirit of futurism that drove post-punk and New Pop seemed to have almost completely departed from the alternative scene by the mid-eighties. You could see traces of its modernist ambition here and there: in the second- and third-wave industrial music, a.k.a. Electronic Body Music (Front 242, Skinny Puppy, Ministry and, a little later, Nine Inch Nails), or the more studio-savvy post-Goth music on labels like 4AD (Cocteau Twins, Dead Can Dance). But 'alternative' defines itself as pop's other, and this meant that the majority of independently released bands shunned synths, sequencers and samplers, and recoiled from the dance floor. The Jesus and Mary Chain took this to the extreme with their music's utter lack of rhythmic thrust: the drumming listlessly marked time, the neurasthenic noise enfolded your immobilized body in a rapt trance.

And what about the original post-punk vanguardists and New Pop futurists who had tried to unite music for the body and music for the head? Almost uniformly, they had a rough time of it. Some, like Billy MacKenzie and Marc Almond, drifted through dwindling solo careers; others, like The Human League, Heaven 17 and ABC, were ground down by the industry. Scritti's Green got lost in the studio. John Lydon went 'rock' in a big way with 1986's *Album* (Zep riffs, Ginger Baker from Cream on drums!). The Banshees and The Bunnymen lost their spark. Gang of Four gave up altogether. McLaren and ZTT should have quit at their peak, but, naturally, neither did.

ZTT's decline was particularly precipitous. In 1985, Propaganda's *A Secret Wish* and Grace Jones' *Slave To the Rhythm: A Biography* both underperformed severely. Then things got *much* worse for ZTT. The Art of Noise quit the label, pissed-off with the stingy royalty rates. Jeczalik, Langan, and Dudley decided *they* were The Art of Noise, parted company with Horn and Morley, and by the end of 1985 were signed to another label, where they scored a few more middling-sized hits with gimmicky concepts. Morley was crushed. He'd plotted out a ten-year plan of brilliant ideas for the group, but here they were, a postmodernist novelty group, tarnishing the name he'd given them and disgracing the spirit of Futurism.

Frankie Goes To Hollywood started to act up too. The first stirring of insubordination had come at the end of 1984 when they refused to cover the Velvet Underground's 'Heroin' for the B-side of 'The Power of Love', thereby thwarting Morley's project of getting ZTT bands to write a history of pop through cover versions. The following year, in a final bizarre echo of the Sex Pistols, the band resisted ZTT's plan to make a *Great Rock 'n' Roll Swindle*-style Frankie movie, which was to have been a post-apocalyptic fantasy scripted by Martin Amis and with Nic Roeg lined up to direct. Instead Frankie seemed determined to follow the conventional rock band path of consolidating their success with further recordings and touring. For the second album, Frankie insisted on playing all the music, but in order for it to sound anything like as good as *Pleasuredome*, this meant the recording process took twice as long. The second album swallowed up an astronomical 760,000 pounds. Morley came up with the title *Liverpool,* because that's where the group came from and, he knew, that's where they would soon return. Sure enough, upon its release in 1986, *Liverpool* flopped resoundingly, and before long Holly Johnson fell out with both the band and ZTT, suing to be freed from his contract.

There were exceptions to the rule of entropy: New Order cut a lustrous path through the eighties pop charts; Cabaret Voltaire kept making cool records; Mark Stewart from The Pop Group pursued a solo career that was spasmodic but compelling. Say what you like about U2, but with the aurora borealis swirl of 'With or Without You' and the crystal drive of 'Where the Streets Have No Name', they took the post-punk puritan guitar sound – massive but minimal, majestic but free of pomp – and made it hugely popular. Depeche Mode, too, became unlikely stadium stars in America, even as their music became ever more adventurous and emotionally subtle. You could also see post-punk's legacy surfacing here and there in newer bands. The Red Hot Chili Peppers' funk-metal owed a debt to Gang of Four's funk-punk (they got Andy Gill to produce their debut album) but with a fratboy rowdiness that went over better in America.

Turning its back on dance, indie rock was determinedly funkless in the mid-to-late eighties. In 1988, though, this side of post-punk re-emerged from an unexpected quarter: the Chicago house scene. The first acid house tunes seemed like the resurrection of avant-funk, half a decade after its demise, and half a world away from its birthplace in Britain and Germany. In songs like Phuture's 'Your Only Friend' and Sleezy D's 'I've Lost Control', there were uncanny echoes of PiL, A Certain Ratio, 23

Skidoo: the neurotic rhythms, the ominous basslines, the cavernous dub space. Even the imagery evoked by the track titles and stripped-down vocal chants – trance-dance as mind control – harked back to death disco.

In the UK and Europe this 'lost future' of the early Eighties came back with a bang in the form of acid mania and the rave explosion. Perhaps this explains why in UK rave culture you would find, rubbing shoulders with E'd-up teenagers and born-again clubbers, such a surprising number of post-punk and synthpop veterans. Dormant careers were instantly revitalized by the new context created by the cultural synergy of house and Ecstasy: Richard H. Kirk, for instance, scored the dance-floor success that still eluded Cabaret Voltaire as the bleep-techno outfit Sweet Exorcist.

In the mid-eighties Genesis P-Orridge had undertaken his own rediscovery of the sixties: Psychic TV dedicated itself to creating 'hyperdelia', released a tribute to Brian Jones called 'Godstar' and covered 'Good Vibrations'. In 1988 P-Orridge plunged into the acid house scene, releasing an album called *Jack the Tab*. Coil, meanwhile, gobbled E like teen ravers, saw visions of burning angels on the dance floor, and made music that for the first time moved your body. The Hacienda, once the site of Factory's unsuccessful attempt to transplant the New York club vibe to Manchester, suddenly took off as the North of England's rave Mecca.

Thanks to the mind-opening effects of Ecstasy, the hardcore electronic side of post-punk and industrial found a mass audience: at raves you heard textures and sounds that came straight out of DAF or Cabaret Voltaire. But the context (crazed collective hedonism) and the emotion (euphoria with a mystic tinge) were totally different. Acid house essentially fused post-punk futurism with sixties Dionysian frenzy. At the same time, rave culture represented an explosion of new independent labels, an epidemic of self-organizing activity. The very concept of teenagers making their own records on computers in their bedrooms, then self-releasing them, was the ultimate in do-it-yourself.

Post-punk continued to have a subliminal half-life in rave culture well into the nineties. Darkside jungle tracks sounded uncannily like This Heat, Byrne and Eno's *Bush of Ghosts* or Japan; The Chemical Brothers based the agitated bassline of their 'Block Rockin' Beats' on that in 23 Skidoo's classic 'Coup'. As the decade progressed and the clubbing industry became professionalized, however, the once chaotically creative culture degenerated into Dionysus-on-a-leash; it also gradually lost any of its lingering affinities with the post-punk spirit.

At the start of the new millennium, the next generation of hip youth emerged, and they understandably viewed club culture as totally edgeless and lacking appeal. Rather than house's ease of release or trance's nullifying ecstasy, they craved tension music. Which is one reason why, seemingly bizarrely, the early eighties came back into vogue. Cold synthpop, punk-funk, mutant disco, early industrial: for the first time in almost two decades, the angular, not-quite-fluid rhythms of post-punk dance music felt more exciting than the feel-good, go-with-the-flow fare offered by the superclubs. And it wasn't just the original early eighties music being rediscovered by fans and played by DJs; new bands emerged who were inspired by that era.

The resurgence of interest in post-punk was just a glimmer on the horizon when I first conceived this book early in 2001. In the subsequent four years there have been retro-anthologies and reissues (from Cabaret Voltaire, Throbbing Gristle, 23 Skidoo, ESG, DNA, ACR, *et al.*), clubs dedicated to playing punk-funk and electropop, and a swarm of new post-punk-influenced bands – The Rapture, Erase Errata, Liars, LCD Soundsystem, Interpol, !!!, Wolf Eyes, Franz Ferdinand. Andy Gill's guitar sound has enjoyed yet another new lease of life.

Many of these groups are just great, and it's both thrilling and enjoyably disorienting to hear the sounds of my youth resurrected. There's a sense in which today's post-punk-inspired bands treat that era as 'unfinished business', a set of sonic potentials with plenty of room for further extension and exploration. They are also responding to the aura of urgency and missionary zeal that pervades the music of the post-punk era (without necessarily knowing too much about the original context in which those bands operated). Still, it's not clear that the new post-punk (post-post-punk? neo-post-punk?) groups are fired up in the same way: vocally, they have the sound of militancy down pat; lyrically, they are rather more opaque. It's not as if they are lacking a modern equivalent of the geopolitical turmoil and right-wing shift of the late seventies that fuelled the original post-punk. As I write, Iraq is in chaos and an even more reactionary version of Ronald Reagan has just been re-elected. But perhaps overt resistance seems . . . not so much futile, as difficult to 'do' convincingly, given that the nineties sensibility of irony and disengagement has yet to relinquish its grip on popular culture. How to make 'politics in pop' work without lapsing into preaching to the converted or dour earnestness was always one of post-punk's primary quandaries. Today, most 'cool' bands deal with the problem by avoiding it altogether.

Yet the very thing that seems most worth resurrecting from post-punk is its commitment to change. This belief was expressed both in the conviction that music should keep moving forward and in the confidence that music can transform the world, even if only through altering one individual's perceptions or enlarging their sense of possibility. Which brings me right back to where I started this book: the realisation that it was punk and post-punk that originally made me believe music could matter so much. All this looking to music for answers, all this following of every twist and turn in the post-punk story, which in some ways continues to this day . . . was *all that* just a waste of energy that could and should have been spent on something 'worthwhile'? Was the idea of change – in music, and *through* music – just a diversion? I still don't know, but I'll always be grateful to this period for giving me such excessive expectations of music.

APPENDIX: MTV and the Second British Invasion

Music video was nothing new. The first examples dated back to the mid-sixties. They were typically made by bands like The Beatles and The Rolling Stones who had grown so big that making promo films was the only way they could fulfil the demands of television shows around the world. It was physically impossible for them to perform in so many places at the same time. Apart from a few 'artistic' forays, most of these early clips were rudimentary affairs depicting the band miming to their latest release. The roots of video as we understand it today lie more in the musical sequences of films like *A Hard Day's Night* and *Help!*, in which The Beatles capered around and did goofy dances instead of singing and miming with their instruments.

The Monkees TV series turned these antic interludes into a winning formula. So there's a poetic aptness to the fact that Michael Nesmith, the most serious Monkee, came up with the concept of MTV. In the seventies, pursuing his career as a solo singer–songwriter, Nesmith became enamoured with the creative possibilities of the promo video, and made a series of imaginative clips for his own singles, such as 'Rio'.

Although the videos were widely broadcast around the world, he quickly learned that there were hardly any outlets on American television. So he devised his own – a programme called *Popclips* – which was eventually shown on Nickelodeon, a channel run by a cable TV division of Warners. He also successfully pitched the idea of a video channel broadcasting pop promos around the clock. As the project developed, it began to diverge from Nesmith's more artistic conception of video, and he ultimately dropped out to make his own 'video album', *Elephant Parts*.

As well as convincing cable operators to take the station, the fledgling MTV had to sell itself to the record industry in order for them to supply the promos free of charge. In return, MTV could offer the nearest thing to a nationwide radio station, so it could be a tool for record companies to break new music – a function that radio itself had ceased to fulfil as it had lapsed into conservatism in the late seventies. Unlike Britain, with its national, state-run pop station, Radio One, American radio was a Balkanized welter of city-based and regional stations, further fragmented by formats that were precisely geared to please audience sectors defined by age, taste and race. These innumerable radio stations were incredibly competitive, yet seemed extremely similar to the naked ear. Partly this stemmed from the way in which stations increasingly contracted out their programming to radio consultancy firms, who turned playlist selection and format adjustment into a behaviourist science.

Then and now, radio in America resembles a gigantic machine designed to ensure listeners almost never encounter any music they don't already like. Radio programmers fear the fickleness of listeners above everything else, believing that the audience will instantly flip to another channel if they hear something that offends them. Hence the emergence of the classic rock format towards the end of the seventies: the play-safe selection of audience favourites spiced with a few recent hits. Over-cautious radio programming created a terrible sluggishness in the American record industry – and it was a factor in the dramatic slump in record sales that began in 1979. After all, if the radio is mostly playing records you already know and like (and therefore probably already own), you are hardly likely to rush out to the record store.

Punk/New Wave/post-punk had fared badly in America in large part because of this conservative radio programming. From the start, MTV focused on what the industry then called New Music: roughly equivalent to New Pop but slightly more expansive, the category included New Wave artists like Elvis Costello, The Psychedelic Furs and The Pretenders. Equally crucial was MTV's nationwide reach. Unlike Britain, where singles often entered the charts high (sometimes even at number 1), hits almost always gathered momentum extremely slowly in America, thanks to the uneven manner in which radio stations across the country added records to their playlists. The national impact of a record instantly breaking into heavy rotation on MTV had a dramatic effect on what Simon Frith called 'the *velocity* of sales'.

In the first year and a half after its launch in August 1981, MTV's national reach was limited – many regional cable operators didn't carry the channel and only 25 per cent of American homes were wired for cable anyway. But, wherever it was available, MTV's impact was extraordinary: unlikely Middle American towns suddenly experienced dramatic spikes in sales of New Music. Still, it was embarrassing for MTV that it was available in neither of America's two music industry capitals, New York and Los Angeles. The channel's solution was to appeal directly to the youth with the 'I Want My MTV' campaign. Broadcast on network stations in the summer of 1982, the ads featured stars like Pete Townshend, Mick Jagger, Adam Ant, Stevie Nicks and Pat Benatar instructing frustrated would-be MTV viewers to 'call your cable operator *now*' and demand they start taking the channel. The frontal assault worked: MTV debuted in Manhattan in September 1982 and appeared in Los Angeles a few months later.

Early MTV was a curious animal, almost inadvertently radical. Because videos from domestic major-label acts were scarce, the channel depended on promos from the UK and Europe, where the pop video was already well established. Artists like Queen, David Bowie, Abba and The Boomtown Rats had specialized in striking promo clips for several years. London already had the beginnings of a video industry in the late seventies, including such future auteurs of the form as Russell Mulcahy – creator of the promo for The Buggles' 'Video Killed the Radio Star', the very first clip MTV played. This pretty much set the tone for MTV's early programming: they had only a few hundred videos at their disposal, a striking 75 per cent of them from Britain. More often than not, the videos for UK New Pop acts were far more imaginative and entertaining than those made for established American rock acts like REO Speedwagon. Like the original British Invasion bands, the New Pop groups, often products of art schools, were finely attuned to style. Even if they didn't direct or storyboard their own promos, they were inherently more 'videogenic' than the Americans. Poseurs to the manner(ed) born, they simply projected better to the camera.

A few arty Americans also benefited from this early phase of MTV. Devo already had half a dozen videos in the can when the channel launched. Gerald V. Casale remembers MTV's programming director Bob Pittman and promotions director John Sykes courting the band over dinner. 'They pitched us the whole MTV concept and told us why we should give them our videos for free. And, of course, still being idealistic artists, we really thought, This is it, they understand what we've been trying to do. We were so elated and thought, Now we're going to be able to do what we want – make feature films.' Like The Residents with their aborted *Vileness Fats* movie, Devo had dreamed of making 'an anti-capitalist science-fiction movie' and wanted to be the first rock band to exploit the mixed-media potential of the laserdisc format by creating full-blown video albums.

These fantasies never quite reached fruition, but all of Devo's singles came with impressive promos, directed either by Casale on his own or in collaboration with their film-maker buddy Chuck Statler. The imagery for 'Girl U Want' matched the music's Knack-style jack-off beat with its parody of American pop TV shows: an audience of screaming teenage girls flail and jive in grotesque regimented patterns, the unlikely objects of their adoration being the spud-boys of Devo. 'Freedom of Choice' featured the heavily masked Devo as nerd-like aliens delivering the group's most straightforward and unsparing critique of America's consumer society and political system to date: 'Freedom of choice is what you've got/Freedom *from* choice is what you want'. The lead single from Devo's fourth album, *New Traditionalists*, 'Through Being Cool' was more oblique about its anti-Reaganism: it depicted the Smart Patrol, socially conscious teen misfits who scoot around their home town with laser-guns zapping brain-dead joggers and other symbols of eighties inanity.

All of Devo's early videos received heavy MTV airplay, alongside a handful of similarly video-savvy American New Wave groups – Blondie, The Cars, The Stray Cats, The Go-Go's and Talking Heads. The latter's 'Once in a Lifetime' was an MTV favourite (despite never being released in the USA as a single) thanks to its brilliant video, choreographed by Toni Basil, in which Byrne plays a kind of postmodernist televangelist preacher. Byrne remembers the early days of MTV fondly: 'You could do a vaguely experimental film thing as cheaply as you possibly could, and if it was connected to a song, MTV would play it, because they needed stuff desperately in those days. So you didn't have to tour in order to build up an audience. It was a bit like how I imagine the early days of pop singles were – you'd record something real quick, and then a month later it'd be a forty-five single in jukeboxes and it would be on the radio.'

It took most American groups longer to grasp the artistic and commercial potential of the video, though, and this interval provided the gap through which the British infiltrated the mainstream. The first hit that owed almost everything to its video and MTV's support was A Flock of Seagulls' 'I Ran (So Far Away)', which reached the *Billboard* Top 10 in the spring of 1982. This Liverpool group came to symbolize the entire British Invasion era in the minds of its enemies, on account of singer

Mike Score's impressively ludicrous hairstyle. If you managed to listen past the flying saucer-like pompadour, A Flock of Seagulls essentially played a sort of post-punk-lite: heavily effected guitar was as prominent as the synths, and the end result was really quite pleasing (not a million miles away from Alan Rankine). Back in Britain, John Peel had enthusiastically supported the band early in their career, but Score's coiffure (hairdressing was his day job) made them the ultimate image-over-content band as far as American trad rockers were concerned.

In 1983, America really was swamped by the Second British Invasion. Some of the biggest video hits of the year came from artists barely known in the UK, like synth boffin Thomas Dolby and the bland dance-rock outfit The Fixx. Even British old timers came out of the woodwork: The Kinks, veterans of the original 1960s British Invasion, scored with 'Come Dancing'; while David Bowie embraced a New Pop-oriented sound and image with 'Let's Dance', shifting from his cocaine-ravaged, decadent Berlin-era look to one of tanned health and vitality.

Commentators were quick to attribute the Anglopop hegemony entirely to MTV, but radio played a major role, too, by switching to New Music formats. Although MTV's success encouraged programmers to play more new records and fewer oldies, they were also inspired by certain pioneering radio stations, like KROQ, which became the most popular station in the Los Angeles area after it changed its focus to 'rock of the eighties' in 1981. KROQ's success was not lost on nationwide radio consultant Lee Abrams, who early in 1983 instructed the seventy album-oriented rock stations on his roster to double the amount of new music they played. 'All my favourite bands are English,' Abrams told *Rolling Stone* later that year. 'It's a more artistic place. Experimentation thrives there. Everything over here is more like McDonald's.'

Fuelled jointly by MTV and radio, this sudden surge of exposure for new music – foreign and domestic – caused record sales for the first half of 1983 to rise by 10 per cent, breaking the steady decline of the previous three years. The high turnover of unfamiliar names (to Americans, anyway) in the Top 10 – Adam Ant, Kajagoogoo, Eddy Grant, Madness – added to the sense of revolutionary turmoil. And MTV reaped the lion's share of the glory for being the saviour of the record industry. A flood of pieces in mainstream magazines celebrated the channel and the British Invasion for bringing colour and energy back to pop music. And Boy George became the poster boy (or is it a girl?) for the new, ambiguous Brits, appearing on numerous magazine covers. *Kissing to Be Clever*,

Culture Club's debut album, spawned three *Billboard* Top 10 hits; *Colour by Numbers*, their follow-up, went platinum; and the group sealed their triumphant 1983 by winning a Grammy for Best New Artist.

MTV was allowed to bask in the glory of 1983's pop boom for just a few months before the backlash against 'English haircut bands' started in earnest. Within weeks of its late 1983 'England Swings' special issue, *Rolling Stone* ran Steven Levy's 'Ad Nauseam: How MTV Sells Out Rock & Roll'. Levy's main theme – that videos were just commercials – became the media hobby horse of the season. (Its closest rival for borderline triteness was the 'videos asphyxiate your imagination' critique.) Another common accusation was that videos put power back in the hands of the record industry: even the most basic promo (concert footage) cost $15,000, and anything more creative could run up to $200,000. The real subtext of animus behind Levy's closely reasoned tirade, though, was the manner in which MTV had shifted the goal posts in ways that favoured the image-conscious, superficial Brits and made it much tougher for the home-grown acts with 'real content' to prosper.

For American trad rockers, the prevalence of synths and drum machines in British pop exacerbated their gut conviction that the video fops simply hadn't *earned* their success (synths and rhythm programming being insufficiently strenuous, white-collar work). Again, you saw that familiar Anglophobia/homophobia slippage that equated glamour and synths with effeminacy. Being the object of teenage female desire was intrinsically emasculating (and there was a psychosexual kernel underneath this prejudice, in so far as teen idols had traditionally been the protégés of gay managers, whose taste in toy boys coincided with teenage girls' ideas of cuteness). The MTV-triggered shift in radio formats from rock to pop felt like a calamitous power shift, away from young males and towards adolescent females.

Levy's *Rolling Stone* piece contrasted the eighties unfavourably with the sixties and found the Second British Invasion wanting in comparison with its precursor: 'It is easy to get lost in the fun-house environment of MTV . . . [but] behind the fun-house mirror is another story, one that makes the musical energy and optimism of the sixties seem a thousand light-years ago.' Counter-cultural rock 'n' roll had been replaced by a video channel whose business was 'to ensnare the passions of Americans who fit certain demographic or . . . "psychographic" requirements – young people who had money and the inclination to buy [certain] things'. This was a bit rich coming from *Rolling Stone*. By 1983, the magazine was hardly the vanguard of the revolution, or even cutting-edge music, and certainly was not in the least averse to making bucks from generationally focused advertising.

Still, other babyboomer critics chimed in with this theme of New Pop as all style and no substance, edgeless and (in Levy's words) 'culturally harmless'. In a Christmas 1983 *NME* piece, former *Stone* writer Greil Marcus fulminated against the invading Brits' recycled Bowie-isms and second-hand black American beats: 'Never before has a pop phenomenon appeared rooted entirely in the notion of vapidity, on the thrill of surrender.' All the Second Invasion groups, he claimed, 'will disappear and none will be remembered'. In his essay 'It's Like That: Rock & Roll on the Home Front', another sixties veteran rock critic, Dave Marsh, placed New Pop in the continuum of British imperialism: the bands 'import a raw and precious commodity – usually some form of black music – and sell it back, in "improved", processed form, to its native country. The natives then consider this "new" commodity an example of the wonders that the Empire has to offer them.'

By the time Marsh wrote his nativist counterblast in 1984, a grass-roots American *intifada* had been swelling for some time – bands like The Blasters, Violent Femmes, Blood on the Saddle, The Gun Club and Lone Justice who had mostly come up through punk but by the early eighties had rediscovered various forms of American roots music: country, blues, rockabilly, folk, Cajun. The renegade rock historian Joe Carducci – no Anglophile himself – captures this inadvertently humorous patriotic backlash against 'the limey fag-wave'. Suddenly, he writes, it was 'flag wavers vs fag-wavers . . . ex-punks and ex-new wavers were showing up in new bands trying to look like your average whiskey guzzlin', range ridin' shitkicker'. The overground version of the new Americana soon followed: John Mellencamp, the career comeback of ex-Creedence Clearwater Revival singer John Fogerty, and above all Bruce Springsteen with his stupendously successful *Born in the USA*.

At the time, this rapid resurgence of trad rock felt surprising, and dis-heartening. In hindsight, it appears inevitable. As Simon Frith writes, 'the strength of the rock and roll tradition lay in its fantasy of the streets [in the case of the new Americana, you could substitute 'the great out-doors', 'the frontier', 'the wilderness'] . . . The new pop music was, by contrast, mall music, shiny but confined. It is not surprising that the counter-sounds got louder and louder, that new myths developed of roots and region, history, authenticity. There is a limit to how long people can look as though they're having fun.' That's a little unfair to the millions who loved New Pop and weren't *pretending* to have fun (not all of them teenage girls, either). But pop culture works through a kind of oscillating internal pendulum, swinging back and forth between extremes. Some kind of return to rock values (if not inevitably to guitar music) was bound to happen. In the long run, it was hip hop that gradually took on that position formerly occupied by rock, the locus of those concerns about roots and authenticity, those fantasies of rebellion and street knowledge. And it has yet to relinquish that role.

In 1984 the British invaders were pretty much in retreat. A few hung in there – Duran, Wham!, Billy Idol – but overall it was a year in which American artists seized back *Billboard*. MTV didn't die with the New Music, though. On the contrary: it thrived like never before, because the new chart-ruling American stars – Cyndi Lauper, Prince, ZZ Top and, by the end of the year, Madonna – had all grasped the power of video and adapted well to the new pop reality. Musically, too, Americans either learned or benefited from the climate created by New Pop. The rock-funk fusions of Michael Jackson's 'Beat It' and most everything by Prince were American (and far more musically adept) versions of the kind of disco-punk dreams of British New Popsters. As well as forging a signature video style that wittily compensated for the group's lack of sex appeal, ZZ Top made their boogie more dance floor friendly by adding a metronomic sequencer-driven pulse to it. Van Halen scored their biggest hit with 'Jump', driven by a synth riff rather than Eddie's guitar. And that icon of the new back-to-the-roots backlash, Bruce Springsteen, developed a new keyboard-dominated sound on singles like 'Dancing in the Dark'. On the flipsides, you even found disco remixes from electro pioneer Arthur Baker, who had worked with New Order.

As American rockers grabbed hold of videos and synths, Devo – the original home-grown pioneers of synth-rock and video pop – found it harder to get on to MTV. 'Their playlist was suddenly based solely on what was already a radio hit. It had nothing to do with how good or innovative the video was,' says Casale. The crunch came with the single 'That's Good'. To be honest, neither the tune nor the promo was Devo's finest hour. It was one of three carbon-copy video-singles from their late 1982 *Oh, No It's Devo* album, all shot on the same unattractively carpeted sound-stage, in more or less the same outfits, with the same camera angles. The only variations were the animations on the blue-screen backdrop.

It was one of these animated sequences in 'That's Good' – a French fry 'fucking' a maple donut juxtaposed with images of a half-naked, sweaty and orgasmically frustrated porno-babe – that brought Devo's deteriorating relationship with MTV to breaking point. The programming director told the group, 'You can have the French fry, or you can have the donut, but you can't have both.' Devo protested at first, then capitulated and re-edited the video. 'By the time we got it back to them, they were looking at our "adds" [the number of radio-station playlists adding the single] and saying, "You're not getting enough,"' says Casale.

'That's Good' never made it on to the MTV playlist. Ultimately, says Casale's bandmate Mark Mothersbaugh, MTV 'became the Home Shopping Network for record companies. And instead of showing the bands with innovative videos, they pushed the bands with the expensive bloated videos.' In the mid-eighties MTV's staple became the hair-metal groups, whose long, flowing locks and heavily made-up faces surpassed even the Anglo-fops in terms of gender confusion, but whose masculinity was partially guaranteed by the phallic guitars they brandished.

BIBLIOGRAPHY

Books and Articles

Albiez, Sean. 'Senseless Acts of Beauty & Despair: Proto-Punk to Post-Punk'. Paper presented at the No Future Conference, University of Wolverhampton, 22 September 2001

Azerrad, Michael. *Our Band Could Be Your Life: Scenes from the American Indie Underground 1981–1991*. Boston: Little, Brown, 2001

Ballard, J. G. *The Drowned World*. London: Gollancz, 1963

— *The Atrocity Exhibition*. London: Jonathan Cape, 1970

— *Crash*. New York: Farrar, Straus & Giroux, 1973

— *Concrete Island*. London: Jonathan Cape, 1974

— *High Rise*. London: Jonathan Cape, 1975

— *Low-Flying Aircraft*. London: Jonathan Cape, 1976

— *The Unlimited Dream Company*. London: Jonathan Cape, 1979

— *The Best Short Stories of J. G. Ballard*. New York: Picador USA, 2001

Bangs, Lester. 'The White Noise Supremacists.' *Village Voice*, 30 April 1979 (Reprinted in Greil Marcus (ed.), *Psychotic Reactions and Carburetor Dung*. New York: Alfred A. Knopf, 1987)

Benson, Richard (ed). *Night Fever: Club Writing in* The Face *1980–1997*. London: Boxtree, 1997

Blush, Steven. *American Hardcore: A Tribal History*. Los Angeles: Feral House, 2001

Bowman, David. *This Must be the Place: The Adventures of Talking Heads in the 20th Century*. New York: HarperCollins, 2001

Bracewell, Michael. *England is Mine: Pop Life in Albion from Wilde to Goldie*. London: HarperCollins, 1997

Bradbury, Malcolm. *The History Man*. New York: Penguin, 1975

Bromberg, Craig. *The Wicked Ways of Malcolm McLaren*. New York: Harper & Row, 1989

Burchill, Julie and Parsons, Tony. *The Boy Looked at Johnny: The Obituary of Rock and Roll*. London: Pluto Press, 1980

Burgess, Anthony. *A Clockwork Orange*. London: Heinemann, 1962

Carducci, Joe. *Rock and the Pop Narcotic*. Los Angeles: 2.13.61 Press, 1994

Cavanagh, David. *The Creation Records Story: My Magpie Eyes Are Hungry for the Prize*. London: Virgin Publishing, 2000

Christgau, Robert. 'A Real New Wave Rolls Out of Ohio'. *Village Voice*, 17 April 1978

Cooper, Mark. *Liverpool Explodes!* London: Sidgwick & Jackson, 1982

Cope, Julian. 'Tales from the Drug Attic'. *New Musical Express*, 3 December 1983

— *Head-On: Memories of the Liverpool Punk Scene and the Story of Teardrop Explodes (1976–82)*. London: Thorsons, 1994

Curtis, Deborah. *Touching from a Distance: Ian Curtis and Joy Division*. London: Faber & Faber, 1995

Cutler, Chris. 'The Residents'. In *File under Popular: Theoretical and Critical Writings on Music*. London: RER Megacorp, 1991

Doyle, Tom. *The Glamour Chase: The Maverick Life of Billy MacKenzie*. London: Bloomsbury, 1998

Du Noyer, Paul. *Liverpool: Wondrous Place, Music from Cavern to Cream*. London: Virgin Books, 2002

Dwyer, Simon. 'Genesis P-Orridge and the Temple of Psychic Youth (From A to Z and Back Again)'. In Simon Dwyer (ed.), *Rapid Eye*. Brighton: R. E. Publishing, 1989

Eden, Kevin S. *Wire: Everybody Loves a History*. Wembley: SAF, 1991

Fish, M. and Hallbery, D. *Cabaret Voltaire: The Art of the Sixth Sense*. Harrow: SAF, 1989

Flowers, Claude. *New Order + Joy Division: Dreams Never End*. London: Omnibus, 1995

Ford, Simon. *Wreckers of Civilisation: The Story of COUM Transmissions & Throbbing Gristle*. London: Black Dog Publishing, 1999

Frith, Simon. 'A Different Drum'/Consuming Passions column. *Melody Maker*, 31 March 1979. (Reprinted in Simon Frith, *Music for Pleasure*. Cambridge: Polity Press, 1988)

— 'The Coventry Sound – The Specials'. *New Society*, 1980. (Reprinted in Frith, *Music for Pleasure*)

— 'Whistling in the Dark'. *Village Voice*, 1984. (Reprinted in Frith, *Music for Pleasure*)

— 'Frankie Said: But What Did They Mean?' In Alan Tomlinson (ed.), *Consumption, Identity & Style*. London: Routledge, 1990

Frith, Simon and Horne, Howard. *Art into Pop*. London: Methuen, 1987

Frith, Simon, Goodwin, Andrew and Grossberg, Lawrence (eds). *Sound & Vision: The Music Video Reader*. London: Routledge, 1993

Gans, David. *Talking Heads: The Band & Their Music*. New York: Avon, 1979

Gendron, Bernard. *Between Montmartre and the Mudd Club: Popular Music and the Avant-Garde*. Chicago: University of Chicago Press, 2002

Gill, Andy. 'This Week's Leeds – Sheffield, Yorks'. *New Musical Express*, 9 September 1978

— 'This Week's Sheffield: Sheffield'. *New Musical Express*, 8 September 1979

— 'Synthpop' (two-part special). *New Musical Express*, 5 and 12 January 1980

Gimarc, George. *Punk Diary, 1970–1979*. New York: St Martin's Press, 1994

— *Post Punk Diary 1980–1982*. New York: St Martin's Griffin, 1997

Goodwin, Andrew. *Dancing in the Distraction Factory: Music Television and Popular Culture*. Minneapolis: University of Minnesota Press, 1992

Green, Malcolm (ed.). *Brus, Muehl, Nitsch, Schwarzkogler: Writings of the Vienna Actionists*. London: Atlas Press, 1999

Gross, Axel. Brian Eno interview. *East Village Eye*, Summer 1981

Hager, Steven. *Art after Midnight: The East Village Scene*. New York: St Martin's Press, 1986

Harron, Mary. Gang of Four feature. *Melody Maker*, 26 May 1979.

Haslam, Dave. *Manchester, England: The Story of the Pop Cult City*. London: Fourth Estate, 1999

Hebdige, Dick. *Cut 'n' Mix: Culture, Identity and Caribbean Music*. London: Methuen, 1987

— *Subculture: The Meaning of Style*. London: Routledge, 1987

Henderson, Dave. 'Industrial Music survey'. *Sounds*, 7 May 1983

Heylin, Clinton. *Public Image Limited: Rise/Fall*. London: Omnibus, 1989

— (ed.). *The Penguin Book of Rock & Roll Writing*. New York: Viking, 1992

Hill, Dave. *Designer Boys & Material Girls: Manufacturing the '80s Pop Dream*. Dorset: Blandford Press, 1986

Hoberman, J. 'No Wavelength: The Para-Punk Underground'. *Village Voice*, 21 May 1979

Hoskyns, Barney. 'Birthday Party feature'. *New Musical Express*, 17 October 1981

— Feature on The Fall. *New Musical Express*, 14 November 1981

— Feature on Scritti Politti. *New Musical Express*, 31 October 1981

— Feature on Echo & The Bunnymen. *New Musical Express*, 20 February 1982

Johnson, Phil. *Straight Outta Bristol: Massive Attack, Portishead, Tricky and the Roots of Trip-Hop*. London: Hodder & Stoughton, 1996

Lydon, John. *No Irish, No Blacks, No Dogs: The Authorized Autobiography of Johnny Rotten*. London: Hodder & Stoughton, 1993

MacKinnon, Angus. Jah Wobble interview. *New Musical Express*, 9 February 1980

Marcus, Greil. *Ranters & Crowd Pleasers: Punk in Pop Music, 197—92*. New York: Doubleday, 1993

Marsh, Dave. 'It's Like That: Rock & Roll on the Home Front.' In Dave Marsh et al., *The First Rock & Roll Confidential Report: Inside the Real World of Rock & Roll*. New York: Pantheon, 1985

Marshall, George. *The Two Tone Story*. Argyll: S. T. Publishing, 1993

Marwick, Arthur. *British Society since 1945*. Harmondsworth: Penguin, 1982

McCready, John. 'On the Passage of a Few Persons through a Rather Brief Period of Time – the Real Factory Records Story'. *Dazed and Confused*, January 2002

McCullough, Dave. Specials interview. *Sounds*, 7 April 1979

McGrath, Tom. *MTV: The Making of a Revolution*. Philadelphia: Running Press, 1996

McNeil, Kirsty. 'Sound of Young Scotland'. *New Musical Express*, 9 May 1981

Mercer, Mick. *Hex Files: The Goth Bible*. New York: Overlook Press, 1996

Middles, Mick. *From Joy Division to New Order: The True Story of Anthony H. Wilson and Factory Records*. London: Virgin Books, 2002

Morley, Paul. 'New Pop UK'. In Clinton Heylin (ed.), *The Penguin Book of Rock & Roll Writing*. New York: Viking, 1992

— Feature on ABC, Essential Bop, Restricted Code/New Pop manifesto. *New Musical Express*, 20 December 1980

— 'Who Bridges the Gap between the Record Executive and the Genius? Me'. *New Musical Express*, 18 February 1984

— *Ask: The Chatter of Pop*. London: Faber & Faber, 1986

Morley, Paul and Thrills, Adrian. Feature on independent labels. *New Musical Express*, 1 September 1979

Neal, Charles. *Tape Delay*. Middlesex: SAF, 1987

Neupert, Richard. *A History of the French New Wave Cinema*. Wisconsin: University of Wisconsin Press, 2002

North, Richard. 'Positive Punk'. *New Musical Express*, 19 February 1983

Panebianco, Julie. Keith Levene interview. *New Musical Express*, 12 November 1983

Parker, James. *Turned on: A Biography of Henry Rollins*. London: Phoenix House, 1998

Parsons, Tony. 'Devo feature'. *New Musical Express*, 8 July 1978

Pearce, Kevin. *Something Beginning with O*. London: Heavenly, 1994

Penman, Ian. *Vital Signs: Music, Movies and Other Manias*. London: Serpent's Tail, 1998

Polk Museum of Art. *Mekons United*. London: Ellipsis, 1996

P-Orridge, Genesis *et al. Painful but Fabulous: The Lives & Art of Genesis P-Orridge*. New York: Soft Skull Shortwave, 2002

Pressler, Charlotte. 'Those Were Different Times: A Memoir of Cleveland Life, 1967–1973 (Part One)'. *CLE* 3A, 1978. (Available online at http://www.sca-trecords.com/eels/twdt.htm)

Rimmer, Dave. *Like Punk Never Happened: Culture Club and the New Pop*. London: Faber & Faber, 1985

Roeser, Steve. 'Meat Puppets: Swimming in a Lake of Fire'. *Goldmine*, 28 April 1995

Ross, Alaska. *The Story of a Band Called The Human League*. New York: Proteus Publishing, 1982

Ross, Tim. 'Something Like a Phenomenon: The 99 Records Story'. *Tuba Frenzy* 4, 1998.

Savage, Jon. *England's Dreaming: Anarchy, Sex Pistols, Punk Rock and Beyond*. New York: St Martin's Griffin, 2002

— *Time Travel: Pop, Media and Sexuality, 1977–96*. London: Chatto & Windus, 1996

— 'Overload and Heaven Sent: An Interview with Martin Hannett, 29 May 1989'. *Vagabond* 1, 1992

Sked, Alan and Cook, Chris. *Post-war Britain: A Political History*.
Harmondsworth: Penguin, 1984

Sontag, Susan. 'Godard'. In *Styles of Radical Will*. London: Farrar, Straus &
Giroux, 1969

Spitz, Marc and Mullen, Brendan. *We Got the Neutron Bomb: The Untold
Story of LA Punk*. New York: Three Rivers Press, 2001

Stathis, Lou. Ultravox/John Foxx (two-part feature). *Heavy Metal*, March and
April 1980

Sutcliffe, Kevin. 'Frankie, the Full Story'. *Face*, December 1984

Tamm, Eric. *Brian Eno: His Music and the Vertical Colour of Sound*. London:
Faber & Faber, 1989

Unterberger, Richie. *Unknown Legends of Rock 'n' Roll*. San Francisco: Miller
Freeman Books, 1998

Vale, V. (ed.). *Re/Search #4/5: William S. Burroughs/Throbbing Gristle/Brion
Gysin*. San Francisco: Re/Search, 1982

— (ed.). *Re/Search Industrial Culture Handbook*. San Francisco: Re/Search, 1983

— (ed.). *Search and Destroy #7–11: The Complete Reprint*. San Francisco:
Re/Search, 1997

Vale V. and Andrea Juno (eds). *Re/Search #8/9: J. G. Ballard*. San Francisco:
Re/Search, 1984.

Various (Jon Savage, Jane Suck, Vivien Goldman, Sandy Robertson, Davitt
Sigerson *et al.*). 'New Musick' (two-part feature). *Sounds*, 26 November and
3 December 1977

Various (Kurt Loder, Parke Puterbaugh, Red Saunders, Peter York, James
Henke, David Montgomery *et al.*). 'England Swings'. *Rolling Stone*, special
issue no. 408, 10 November 1983

Vermorel, Fred. *Vivienne Westwood: Fashion, Perversity, and the Sixties Laid
Bare*. New York: Overlook Press, 1996

Walsh, Steve. Subway Sect interview. *ZigZag*, September 1977

— Pop Group interview, *ZigZag*, April/May 1978

Warner, Timothy. *Pop Music – Technology and Creativity: Trevor Horn and the
Digital Revolution*. Aldershot: Ashgate Publishing, 2003

Whitehead, Phillip. *The Writing on the Wall: Britain in the Seventies*. London:
Michael Joseph, 1986

Widgery, David. *Beating Time: Riot 'n' Race 'n' Rock 'n' Roll*. London: Chatto
& Windus, 1986

Willett, John (ed. and trans.). *Brecht on Theatre*. New York: Hill & Wang,
1964

Wolcott, James. 'A Conservative Impulse in the New Rock Underground'.
Village Voice, Summer 1975. (Reprinted in Heylin (ed.), *The Penguin Book
of Rock & Roll Writing*)

Zerbib, Patrick. PiL profile. *Face*, 1983. (Reprinted in Heylin (ed.), *The
Penguin Book of Rock & Roll Writing*)

Magazines

The richest research resource is the music press of the period. In the UK that means the weekly rock papers (*New Musical Express, Sounds, Melody Maker, Record Mirror*), monthly magazines (*The Face, ZigZag*), irregular magazines (*Collusion*) and fanzines (*Jamming, Sniffin' Glue, City Fun, Vague, Ten Commandments, Gunrubber*, ad infinitum). In America, more than the national rock magazines, the most intensive contemporary coverage occurred in the music sections of city-based alternative weeklies (*East Village Eye, SoHo Weekly News, Village Voice*), and in publications located somewhere between professional and amateur (*Search and Destroy* and its successor magazine *Re/Search, Forced Exposure*). *Heavy Metal* (not ostensibly a music paper but a science-fiction magazine) had an adventurous music section for a couple of years in the early eighties thanks to columnist Lou Stathis. Eluding my search but reputedly of use: *New York Rocker, Flipside, NO*, and *Slash*.

Internet

There are too many post-punk-related sites to list them all here (and most can be found by Googling a specific artist) but one particularly notable general-music webmagazine is *Perfect Sound Forever* (http://www.furious.com/perfect/), which has built up a substantial archive of extensive interviews with post-punk figures – Keith Levene, Pylon, the list is endless and grows every month.

POST-PUNK TIMELINE

1974

April   The Residents' debut album, *Meet the Residents*.

1975

May   Cabaret Voltaire play debut gig at a Sheffield student disco. Talking Heads form.

3 September   Throbbing Gristle officially form.

December   Pere Ubu self-release their debut single, '30 Seconds over Tokyo', on own Hearthan label.

1976

February   The Residents' *The Third Reich and Roll*.

20 February   Rough Trade record shop opens in Ladbroke Grove, London W11.

March   Pere Ubu's second single, 'Final Solution'.

July   Debut issue of Mark Perry's fanzine *Sniffin' Glue*. Buzzcocks' public debut – bottom of a Sex Pistols bill at Manchester's Lesser Free Trade Hall.

August   Rock Against Racism founded.

September   Subway Sect and Siouxsie & The Banshees play their debut gigs at the 100 Club Punk Festival.

18 October   Throbbing Gristle's official live debut at the ICA in London, playing at the opening party for COUM's exhibition *Prostitution*.

November   Pere Ubu's third single, 'Street Waves'.

December   The Residents' cover version of 'Satisfaction'.

1977

January   David Bowie's *Low*.

29 January   Buzzcocks' *Spiral Scratch* – their debut single and first release for their independent label, New Hormones.

February   Howard Devoto quits Buzzcocks. Iggy Pop's *The Idiot*.

14 February   The B-52's play debut gig at an Athens, Georgia, house party.

March   Ultravox's eponymous debut album.

April   Desperate Bicycles' debut single, 'Smokescreen', self-released on their Refill Records. **Kraftwerk's** 'Trans-Europe Express' single and *Trans-Europe Express* album.

May   **Subway Sect** play Scotland and North of England as part of **The Clash's White Riot** tour; also on the bill are **The Slits**, **The Jam** and **Buzzcocks**. **Adam and the Antz** official live debut at the ICA restaurant.

June   Liverpool's **The Crucial Three** – Ian McCulloch, Julian Cope and Pete Wylie – split up without playing a single gig.

July   **Devo** make their New York debut. **Desperate Bicycles'** second DIY single, 'The Medium Was Tedium'.

23 July   **Donna Summer's** 'I Feel Love' hits number 1 in the UK and stays there for four weeks.

13 August   **Anti-Nazi League** battle **National Front** marchers (and police) in Lewisham, south London.

September   **The Slits** record four songs for a John Peel radio session, aired later that month. **Talking Heads'** debut album, *Talking Heads 77*.

November   **The Sex Pistols'** *Never Mind the Bollocks*. **Suicide's** eponymous debut album. **Wire** debut LP, *Pink Flag*. Phil Oakey joins Sheffield band **The Future**, soon renamed **The Human League**.

1978

14 January   **The Sex Pistols** end American tour at Winterland, San Francisco – band splits up shortly after.

January   **The Mekons'** first single, 'Never Been in a Riot' (also the debut release for **Fast Product**). **Warsaw** play first gig as **Joy Division**. **Swell Maps** self-release debut single, 'Read about Seymour', on **Rather**.

February   **Rough Trade** label inaugurated with **Metal Urbain's** single 'Paris Maquis'. **Throbbing Gristle's** debut album, *Second Annual Report*. **Magazine** appear on *Top of the Pops* to perform 'Shot by Both Sides'. **Devo's** single 'Jocko Homo' b/w 'Mongoloid', first issued on their Booji Boy label in late 1977, is rereleased by Stiff in the UK.

March   **Subway Sect's** debut single, 'Nobody's Scared'. **The Normal's** 'T.V.O.D' b/w 'Warm Leatherette' is the debut release for **Mute**.

April   **Pere Ubu's** debut LP, *The Modern Dance*, coincides with *Datapanik in the Year Zero*, the twelve-inch EP gathering together the first three Hearthan singles.

30 April   **Anti-Nazi League's** 80,000-strong carnival at Victoria Park, London. The bill includes **X Ray Spex**, **The Clash**, **Steel Pulse** and **The Tom Robinson Band**.

May   **No Wave** five-day festival – **Mars, Teenage Jesus & The Jerks, DNA, Contortions**, *et al.* – at Artists Space in downtown Manhattan.

Alternative TV's debut LP, *The Image is Cracked*. **Factory's** first 'release', FAC 1, is Peter Saville's poster for May/June gigs events at the Factory Club, Hulme, Manchester. One of them is **Durutti Column**'s live debut.

June **Joy Division** release their debut EP, *An Ideal for Living*, on their own label. **Devo** play England's Knebworth Festival. **Magazine**'s debut LP, *Real Life*. **The Coventry Automatics** change their name to **The Specials**. **The Human League** release their debut single, 'Being Boiled', on Fast Product.

July **Talking Heads**' second album, *More Songs about Buildings and Food.*

15 July **Rock Against Racism**'s **Northern Carnival** in Alexandra Park, Manchester. Bill includes **The Fall, Buzzcocks, John Cooper Clarke**.

August **The Fall** debut with *Bingo-Master's Break-Out* EP. **Siouxsie & The Banshees**' debut single, 'Hong Kong Garden'. **Devo**'s debut LP, *Q: Are We Not Men? A: We Are Devo!*

September **Wire**'s second album, *Chairs Missing.*

24 September **Rock Against Racism**'s massive **Brockwell Park Carnival** in London.

October **Public Image Ltd**'s debut single and Top 10 hit 'Public Image'. **Sid Vicious** arrested in New York for fatally stabbing Nancy Spungeon. **Subway Sect**'s second single, 'Ambition'. **Gang of Four**'s debut EP, *Damaged Goods*. **Cabaret Voltaire** debut EP, *Extended Play*. **Pere Ubu**'s second album, *Dub Housing.*

11 November **Throbbing Gristle** play Cryptic One Club, London; Genesis P-Orridge overdoses on pills.

November **The B-52**'s debut single, 'Rock Lobster'. **Siouxsie & The Banshees**' debut album, *The Scream*. **Scritti Politti** self-release their debut single, 'Skank Bloc Bologna', on St Pancras. **The Mekons**' second single, 'Where Were You?'

December **The Cure**'s debut single, 'Killing an Arab'. **Throbbing Gristle**'s *D.o.A: The Third and Final Report*. **Public Image Ltd**'s eponymous debut album. **Factory**'s first record release, *A Factory Sample*: a double single featuring **Joy Division, Durutti Column, Cabaret Voltaire** and **John Dowie**.

25/6 December **Public Image Ltd** make live debut with two gigs at London's Rainbow.

1979

February **Stiff Little Fingers**' debut, *Inflammable Material*, released by **Rough Trade** and goes straight in the pop album chart at number 14 – a breakthrough and triumph for the nascent independent-label movement. **The Teardrop Explodes**' debut single, 'Sleeping Gas', released by Liverpool indie label **Zoo**.

Feb–March **Animal Instincts** tour of the UK featuring **The Pop Group, Alternative TV** and **Manicured Noise**.

March **The Pop Group**'s debut single, 'She is Beyond Good and Evil'. **Alternative TV**'s *Vibing up the Senile Man*. **The Fall**'s debut LP,

Live at the Witch Trials. Contortions' *Buy* and James White & The Blacks' *Off White* released simultaneously. Echo & The Bunnymen debut with 'Pictures on My Wall' on Zoo.

25 March   A showcase at London's Lyceum Theatre with Gang of Four, The Mekons, The Human League, The Fall and Stiff Little Fingers is dubbed 'The Gig of the Century'.

April   The Human League's *The Dignity of Labour* EP. Rock Against Racism's massive Militant Entertainment tour featuring thirty bands, including Gang of Four, The Mekons, The Ruts, The Specials and Stiff Little Fingers. The Pop Group's debut album, *Y*. The Specials start their own label, 2-Tone, and release a single with their own 'Gangsters' on one side and 'The Selecter' by The Selecter on the flip. The Raincoats' debut single, 'Fairytale in the Supermarket', released on Rough Trade.

May   A Certain Ratio's debut single, 'All Night Party'.

June   Joy Division's debut LP, *Unknown Pleasures*. Cabaret Voltaire's second single, 'Nag Nag Nag'. Public Image Ltd's second single and Top 20 hit, 'Death Disco'. Swell Maps' debut LP, *A Trip to Marineville*. The B-52's eponymous debut LP.

30 June   Tubeway Army's 'Are Friends Electric?' reaches number 1 and stays there for four weeks.

July   The 2-Tone Concert at London's Electric Ballroom features The Specials, Dexys Midnight Runners, Madness and The Selecter.

August   Promoter Final Solution organizes four nights of post-punk at London's Prince of Wales conference centre – bands include Throbbing Gristle, Joy Division, Cabaret Voltaire, Clock DVA, The Teardrop Explodes, Echo & The Bunnymen, Essential Logic and Ludus. Rock Against Sexism gig at London's Electric Ballroom, featuring Delta 5 and Gang of Four. Talking Heads' third LP, *Fear of Music*. The Flying Lizards' 'Money (That's What I Want)' is a Top 5 hit.

27 August   The Zoo and Factory Label Day at Leigh – midway between Manchester and Liverpool – includes Joy Division, Orchestral Manoeuvres in the Dark, Echo & The Bunnymen and The Teardrop Explodes.

September   The Slits release debut LP, *Cut*. Sheffield's Vice Versa – later to mutate into ABC – release debut EP, *Music 4*. This Heat's eponymous debut LP. Madness's debut single, 'The Prince'. Bauhaus's debut single, 'Bela Lugosi's Dead'. Siouxsie & The Banshees' second album, *Join Hands*. The first Futurama Festival held in Leeds with Joy Division and PiL headlining the two nights. Wire's third album, *154*. Pere Ubu's third album, *New Picnic Time*. The Residents' *Eskimo*. Gang of Four's debut album, *Entertainment!* Scritti Politti's *4 A Sides* EP.

22 September   Gary Numan's 'Cars' hits number 1.

October	The Fall's second album, *Dragnet*. **The Human League**'s debut LP, *Reproduction*. **Joy Division**'s 'Transmission'. **The Specials**' eponymous debut LP. **U2**'s debut EP, *U2-Three*. **Cabaret Voltaire**'s debut LP, *Mix-Up*. **Killing Joke**'s debut EP, *Are You Receiving?* **Adam and the Antz**' debut album, *Dirk Wears White Sox*.
20 October	**The Buggles**' 'Video Killed the Radio Star' hits number 1.
November	**The Pop Group**'s 'We Are All Prostitutes'. **Scritti Politti**'s *Peel Sessions* EP. **The Beat**'s debut single and Top 10 Hit 'Tears of a Clown'. **The Mekons**' debut album, *The Quality of Mercy is Not Strnen*. **Public Image Ltd**'s *Metal Box*.
9–13 Nov	**Wire** play series of Dadaist shows at the Jeanette Cochrane Theatre, London.
December	**Delta 5**'s debut single, 'Mind Your Own Business'. **Throbbing Gristle**'s *20 Jazz Funk Greats*. **A Certain Ratio** support **Talking Heads** at London's Electric Ballroom – their performance comprises one side of **Factory**'s cassette-only release *The Graveyard and the Ballroom*. **The Raincoats**' eponymous debut LP. **Dexys Midnight Runners**' debut single, 'Dance Stance'. Rap hits the charts with **The Sugarhill Gang**'s massive 'Rapper's Delight'.

1980

January	**Durutti Column**'s debut LP, *The Return of the Durutti Column*. **Bow Wow Wow** formed by Malcolm McLaren after stealing Adam Ant's backing band.
2 February	**The Specials**' *The Special A.K.A. Live!* EP (featuring 'Too Much Too Young') hits number 1.
February	**Lydia Lunch**'s *Queen of Siam*. **Josef K**'s debut single, 'Chance Meeting'.
29 February	**Wire**'s Dadaist extravaganza at the Electric Ballroom.
March	**Orange Juice** debut with 'Falling and Laughing' on **Postcard**. **The Slits** and **The Pop Group** inaugurate **Y Records** with a joint single: 'In the Beginning There Was Rhythm' b/w 'Where There's a Will'. **DAF**'s 'Kebabtraume' released on **Mute**. **The Pop Group**'s second album, *How Much Longer Do We Tolerate Mass Murder?* **Joy Division**'s 'Atmosphere'. **Young Marble Giants**' debut album, *Colossal Youth*. **The Teardrop Explodes**' third single, 'Treason (It's Just a Story)'. **The Cure**'s 'A Forest'.
16 March	**Throbbing Gristle** and **Monte Cazazza** play gig at Oundle public school, Peterborough, whipping the boys into a frenzy.
22 March	**The Jam**'s 'Going Underground' enters the chart at number 1.
2–4 April	**Factory Records** showcase at the Moonlight in London, with **Joy Division** headlining all three nights.
April	**Delta 5**'s second single 'You'. **The Cure**'s *Seventeen Seconds*.
3 May	**Dexys Midnight Runners**' 'Geno' is number 1.
May	**The Fall**'s live album, *Totale's Turns*. **The Teardrop Explodes**' debut album, *Kilimanjaro*. **The Human League**'s second LP,

Travelogue. Pylon's debut single 'Cool' b/w 'Dub'. Einstürzende Neubauten's first single, 'Für Den Untergang'. Suicide's second album, *Alan Vega/Martin Rev.* The Birthday Party's eponymous debut album. Magazine's third album, *The Correct Use of Soap.*

18 May Ian Curtis commits suicide.

June Mission of Burma's 'Academy Fight Song'. Joy Division's 'Love Will Tear Us Apart' released and peaks at number 13. DAF's second album, *Die Kleinen und Die Bosen.* Throbbing Gristle release *Heathen Earth.*

July Joy Division's second album, *Closer.* Cabaret Voltaire's *The Voice of America.* Dexys Midnight Runners' debut album, *Searching for the Young Soul Rebels.* Echo & The Bunnymen's debut album, *Crocodiles.* Bow Wow Wow's debut single, 'C-30 C-60 C-90 Go!'. New Order make their live debut at a Manchester club.

August Jah Wobble officially announces his departure from PiL. Siouxsie & The Banshees' third album, *Kaleidoscope.* The Associates' debut album, *The Affectionate Punch.* Postcard releases Josef K's 'Radio Drill Time' and Orange Juice's 'Blue Boy'. Devo's 'Whip It' is their first US hit. The B-52's second album, *Wild Planet.*

23 August David Bowie's 'Ashes to Ashes' is number 1.

September The second Futurama Festival in Leeds – Siouxsie & The Banshees headline one night. Bush Tetras' debut single, 'Too Many Creeps', released by 99 Records. Simple Minds' third album, *Empires and Dance.* Madness's 'Baggy Trousers' and second album, *Absolutely,* both Top 3 hits. The Passage's debut album, *Pindrop.* The Specials' second album, *More Specials.*

October Soft Cell debut with the *Mutant Moments* EP. Orange Juice's third single, 'Simply Thrilled Honey'. A Certain Ratio's 'Flight'. The Residents' *The Commercial Album.* Killing Joke's eponymous debut album. Talking Heads' fourth album, *Remain in Light.* Spandau Ballet's debut single and number 5 hit, 'To Cut a Long Story Short'. *A Factory Quartet,* a double album featuring four acts: Durutti Column, Kevin Hewick, Blurt and Royal Family & The Poor. Adam & The Ants' 'Dog Eat Dog' released and soon makes the Top 5.

26 October CND rally in Trafalgar Square protests stationing of Cruise missiles in the UK. The Pop Group play their last live performance to 250,000 people.

November U2's debut LP, *Boy.* The Fall's *Grotesque (After the Gramme).* Bow Wow Wow's *Your Cassette Pet.* Adam and the Ants' *Kings of the Wild Frontier.* Bauhaus's debut LP, *In the Flat Field.* PiL's live album, *Paris au Printemps.* The Blue Orchids debut with 'The Flood' b/w 'Disney Boys'. Hüsker Dü self-release 'Statues' on Reflex.

December SST Records release The Minutemen's *Paranoid Time* EP.

January The Fire Engines' mini-LP *Lubricate Your Living Room*. **Visage** go Top 10 with 'Fade to Grey'. **The Virgin Prunes** debut with *Twenty Tens*. **Young Marble Giants** split up. **Clock DVA**'s *Thirst*. **New Order**'s debut single, 'Ceremony'. **David Byrne and Brian Eno**'s *My Life in the Bush of Ghosts*. **Duran Duran**'s 'Planet Earth' hits the Top 20. **The Teardrop Explodes**' 'Reward' becomes their first Top 10 hit. **Stevo** of **Some Bizzare** puts out the compilation *Some Bizzare Album*, featuring early tracks by **Depeche Mode** and **Soft Cell**. *NME* and **Rough Trade** announce the *C81* cassette, celebrating five years of Rough Trade and the independent-label revolution.

February **Heaven 17** debut with '(We Don't Need This) Fascist Groove Thang'.

March **Altered Images**' debut single, 'Dead Pop Stars'. **Gang of Four**'s second LP, *Solid Gold*. **Orange Juice**'s fourth single, 'Poor Old Soul'.

April **The Associates**' 'Tell Me Easter's on Friday', first of their six Situation 2 singles that year. **The Birthday Party**'s second album *Prayers on Fire*. **PiL**'s third studio album, *Flowers of Romance*. **The Fall**'s *Slates*. **The Human League** score their first Top 20 hit with 'The Sound of the Crowd'. **Madness**'s 'Grey Day'. **The Cure**'s *Faith*.

May **A Certain Ratio**'s debut album, *To Each . . . .* **The Beat**'s second album, *Wha'ppen?* **Echo & The Bunnymen**'s second album, *Heaven Up Here*. **Au Pairs**' debut LP, *Playing with a Different Sex*. **The Raincoats**' second album, *Odyshape*. **Magazine** folds as Howard Devoto quits.

29 May **Throbbing Gristle** play final gig at Kezar Pavilion, San Francisco.

June **Depeche Mode** score first hit with second single, 'New Life'. **ESG**'s 'You're No Good/UFO/Moody' released on **Factory**. **Josef K**'s debut album, *The Only Fun in Town*. **Duran Duran**'s eponymous debut album. **Siouxsie & The Banshees**' fourth album, *Juju*. **Noise Fest** at White Columns Gallery in downtown New York – nine evenings of neo-No Wave bands, including **Sonic Youth**.

23 June **Throbbing Gristle** announce that 'The Mission is Terminated' and split up.

11 July **The Specials** 'Ghost Town' hits number 1 and stays there for three weeks, during which time there are inner-city riots across the UK.

July **Mission of Burma**'s *Signals Calls and Marches*.

August **Spandau Ballet** go Top 3 with 'Chant No. 1'. **MTV** premieres on American TV. **Cabaret Voltaire**'s *Red Mecca*. **The Human League** reach number 3 with 'Love Action'.

5 September **Soft Cell**'s 'Tainted Love' reaches number 1.

September **New Order**'s 'Everything's Gone Green'. **Depeche Mode**'s 'Just Can't Get Enough' is a big UK chart hit. **Heaven 17**'s debut LP, *Penthouse and Pavement*. **Simple Minds**' *Sons and Fascination/ Sisters Feeling Call* twin-album.

19 September	Adam & The Ants' 'Prince Charming' hits number 1 and stays there for four weeks.
October	This Heat's second album, *Deceit*. Madness's third album, 7. Altered Images score first hit with the massive 'Happy Birthday', peaking at number 2. Bow Wow Wow debut LP, *See Jungle! See Jungle!*. Laurie Anderson's 'O Superman' reaches number 2. Fun Boy Three, formed by Terry Hall, Lynval Golding and Neville Staples after leaving The Specials, debuts with 'The Lunatics Have Taken Over the Asylum'. The Human League's *Dare*. Scritti Politti's 'The "Sweetest Girl"'. ABC's debut single, 'Tears Are Not Enough'. U2's second album, *October*.
November	New Order's first album, *Movement*. Haircut 100's 'Favourite Shirts (Boy Meets Girl)' is a Top 5 hit. Black Flag's debut album, *Damaged*. DAF's *Gold und Liebe*.
12 December	The Human League's 'Don't You Want Me' hits number 1, where it stays for five weeks.

1982

January	The Slits split. Meat Puppets' debut LP, *Meat Puppets I*. Orange Juice's debut album, *You Can't Hide Your Love Forever*.
February	Kraftwerk at number 1 with 'The Model'. The Associates penetrate the UK Top 10 with 'Party Fears Two'. 23 Skidoo's *Seven Songs*. Bow Wow Wow finally score a hit with 'Go Wild in the Country', which reaches number 7.
March	The Fall's *Hex Enduction Hour*. ABC's 'Poison Arrow' is a number 6 hit. Simple Minds go Top 20 with 'Promised You a Miracle'. Japan's 'Ghosts' cracks the Top 10.
April	British Electric Foundation's *Music of Quality and Distinction*. Pigbag's 'Papa's Got a Brand New Pigbag' enters the pop charts and eventually reaches number 3. Martin Hannett instigates lawsuit against Factory. Scritti Politti's 'Faithless'. The Cure's *Pornography*. Culture Club debut with 'White Boy'. Killing Joke's third album. *Revelations*. New Order's 'Temptation'.
May	The Blue Orchids' debut album, *The Greatest Hit (Money Mountain)*. Duran Duran's 'Hungry Like the Wolf' and *Rio*. The Associates' *Sulk*.
21 May	The Hacienda, a Manchester nightclub owned by Factory Records and New Order, opens.
29 May	Madness's 'House of Fun' hits number 1.
June	ABC's 'The Look of Love' reaches number 4 and *The Lexicon of Love* is released to massive acclaim. Wham!'s 'Wham Rap'. The Birthday Party's *Junkyard*.
July	Cocteau Twins' debut album, *Garlands*. The Batcave Club opened by Specimen as a dark haven for the emerging Goth nation.
7 August	Dexys Midnight Runners' 'Come on Eileen' hits number 1, where it stays for four weeks.

August	Scritti Politti's debut LP, *Songs to Remember*.
September	Simple Minds' *New Gold Dream (81–82–83–84)*. Grandmaster Flash & The Furious Five's 'The Message' is Top 10 hit.
October	The Smiths make their live debut at a Manchester club. Bauhaus score their first hit with cover of 'Ziggy Stardust'.
23 October	Culture Club's 'Do You Really Want to Hurt Me?' hits number 1 and stays there for three weeks.
November	Orange Juice's second LP, *Rip It Up*. Siouxsie & The Banshees' *A Kiss in the Dreamhouse*. Virgin Prunes' *If I Die, I Die*. The Sisters of Mercy's 'Alice'. Psychic TV, the new band formed by Throbbing Gristle's Genesis P-Orridge and Peter Christopherson, debut with *Force the Hand of Chance*. Malcolm McLaren's 'Buffalo Gals'. The Teardrop Explodes split.
December	Southern Death Cult's debut single, 'Fatman'.

1983

January	Echo & The Bunnymen's third album, *Porcupine*, and first Top 10 hit, 'The Cutter'.
February	Positive Punk is the *NME*'s cover story, with writer Richard North including Southern Death Cult, Blood & Roses, Brigandage, Specimen and Sex Gang Children as part of the genre – soon better known as Goth. U2's third album, *War*; their 'New Year's Day' goes Top 10. The Birthday Party's *The Bad Seed* EP.
5 March	Michael Jackson's 'Billie Jean' is number 1, kicking off a year of *Thriller*-mania.
March	Orange Juice finally score a Top 10 hit with 'Rip It Up'. The Eurythmics go Top 10 with 'Sweet Dreams (Are Made of This)'. New Order's 'Blue Monday'.
May	The Sisters of Mercy's *The Reptile House* EP. Heaven 17 finally score a hit single with the number 2 smash 'Temptation'.
June	Keith Levene quits PiL. The Birthday Party split.
August	Depeche Mode reach number 6 with 'Everything Counts'. New Order's 'Confusion'. Cabaret Voltaire's major-label debut, *The Crackdown*. The Art of Noise's *Into Battle with The Art of Noise* EP – the debut release for ZTT.
September	PiL's 'This Is Not a Love Song' reaches number 5.
24 September	Culture Club's 'Karma Chameleon' hits number 1 and stays there for six weeks.
October	Frankie Goes to Hollywood release 'Relax'. Cocteau Twins release *Head Over Heels* album and the *Sunburst and Snowblind* EP. The Sisters of Mercy's 'Temple of Love'.
November	The Birthday Party's final EP, *Mutiny!*. ABC's second album, *Beauty Stab*. The Immaculate Consumptives – Marc Almond, Nick Cave, Lydia Lunch and Jim Thirlwell – perform in New York. The Smiths' second single and first hit, 'This Charming Man'.

1984

January   Einstürzende Neubauten's *Concerto for Voice and Machinery* at London's ICA triggers an audience riot.

28 January   Frankie Goes to Hollywood's 'Relax' hits number 1, where it stays for five weeks.

February   Propaganda debut with 'Dr Mabuse'.

April   Scritti Politti have a Top 10 hit with major-label debut, 'Wood Beez (Pray Like Aretha Franklin)'. Echo & The Bunnymen's fourth album, *Ocean Rain*. Meat Puppets' *Meat Puppets II*.

May   The Human League's 'The Lebanon'. Bruce Springsteen's 'Dancing in the Dark' begins a year of *Born in the USA*-mania.

June   Nick Cave's solo debuts, 'In the Ghetto' and *From Her to Eternity*.

16 June   Frankie Goes to Hollywood's 'Two Tribes' hits number 1, where it stays for nine weeks.

July   Prince's 'When Doves Cry' goes Top 5.

September   U2's 'Pride (in the Name of Love)' goes Top 3. Hüsker Dü's *Zen Arcade* and The Minutemen's *Double Nickels on the Dime* released on the same day.

October   U2's *The Unforgettable Fire*.

November   Frankie Goes to Hollywood's *Welcome to the Pleasuredome*.

Nov–Dec   Madonna's 'Like a Virgin' is a massive worldwide hit.

December   Band Aid's famine-relief charity single, 'Do They Know It's Christmas?', features the aristocracy of British New Pop – Duran, Spandau, Culture Club, *et al*.

1985

March   The Sisters of Mercy's *First and Last and Always*.

April   Meat Puppets' *Up on the Sun*.

May   The Cult, formerly Southern Death Cult, score their first chart hit with 'She Sells Sanctuary'.

June   Scritti Politti's *Cupid and Psyche 85*.

7 June   Wire reform to play their first gig in five years with a show at the Museum of Modern Art, Oxford.

October   Grace Jones's 'Slave to the Rhythm'.

ACKNOWLEDGEMENTS

Massive love and gratitude to my wife Joy Press for her encouragement, advice, practical help (especially with the mutant disco oral history), patience, and, not least, discipline. Love and thanks to my little boy Kieran for *his* patience.

Very special thanks to Geeta Dayal, my research assistant, for her invaluable contributions to this project. I'm also grateful to Jon Savage for his contribution to the picture research, to my editor Lee Brackstone for his enthusiasm and guidance, to Kate Ward, Bomi Odufunade and Helen Francis at Faber, to Jason Gross for the loan of his transcription machine, and to my agent Tony Peake.

Special thanks to Jonathan O'Brien for coming up with the book's title, and to everyone else who participated in the book-naming competition at Blissblog (http://blissout.blogspot.com).

Lots of people helped with contacts, ideas, information, illustrations, making interviews happen, and providing obscure music and other historical material: Pat Blashill, Paul Kennedy, Jonathon Dale, Christian Hoeller, Matthew Ingram, Bas Van Hoof, David Stubbs, Dan Selzer, Adrian Curry, Heiko Hoffman, Hillegonda Rietveld, Vivien Goldman, Alan Licht, Paul Lester, Mike Appelstein, Mark Sinker, Liz Naylor, Graham Sanford, Simon Frith, Tony Van Dorston, Joe Carducci, Richard H. Kirk, David Toop, Paul Smith, Robert Poss, Tony Renner, Karl Blake, Jane Haughton, Marvin J. Taylor, Mike Kelly, Ian Craig Marsh, David M. Todarello, Jim Sellen, Phil Turnbull, Jason Gross, Jon Savage, James Nice, Todd Hyman, Kevin Pearce, Neil Spencer, Marcello Carlin, Stuart Argabright, Michel Esteban, Gerard Greenway, Steve Swift, Jez Reynolds. Apologies to anyone I forgot.

Thanks to the 126 people who gave interviews for this book: Mike Alway, Martin Atkins, Una Baines, Charles Ball, Blixa Bargeld, Steve Beresford, Bond Bergland, Bob Bert, Adele Bertei, Gina Birch, Karl Blake, Chris Bohn, Richard Boon, Dennis Bovell, Derrick Bostrom, Martin Bramah, Vanessa Briscoe Hay, Steve Brown, Conny Burg, Hugo Burnham, David Byrne, Joe Carducci, Gerald

555

V. Casale, Monte Cazazza, James Chance, Robert Christgau, Edwyn Collins, Clint Conley, Robin Crutchfield, Mark Cunningham, Steven Daly, Howard Devoto, Bill Drummond, Anne Dudley, Paul Du Noyer, Tony Fletcher, Gavin Friday, Tony Friel, Martin Fry, Green Gartside, Bruce Gilbert, Andy Gill (Gang of Four), Andy Gill (journalist), Vic Godard, Vivien Goldman, Robert Gotobed, Tom Greenhalgh, Gudrun Gut, Paul Haig, Dave Haslam, Charles Hayward, Michael Holman, Peter Hook, Trevor Horn, Gary Indiana, Joseph Jacobs, John Keenan, Richard H. Kirk, Scott Krauss, Bob Last, Andrew Lauder, Thomas Leer, Keith Levene, Graham Lewis, Arto Lindsay, Jeffrey Lohn, Bruce Lose, Lydia Lunch, Steve Maas, Maureen McGinley, Richard McGuire, Iain McNay, Ann Magnuson, Ian Craig Marsh, Mick Mercer, Daniel Miller, Roger Miller, Martin Moscrop, Paul Morley, Steven Morris, Mark Mothersbaugh, Stuart Moxham, Colin Newman, Adi Newton, Phil Oakey, Glenn O'Brien, Frank Owen, Cole Palme, John Peel, Ian Penman, Mark Perry, Pat Place, Robert Poss, Peter Principle, Alan Rankine, Malcolm Ross, Martin Rushent, Luc Sante, Jon Savage, Steve Severin, Bruce Smith, Neville Staple, Linder Sterling, Stevo, Mark Stewart, Nikki Sudden, Jim Thirlwell, David Thomas, Mayo Thompson, Mike Thorne, David Toop, Roy Trakin, Geoff Travis, Steve Tupper, Alex Turnbull, Johnny Turnbull, Ari Up, Fred Vermorel, Martyn Ware, Mike Watt, Tony Wilson, Dick Witts, Jah Wobble and Michael Zilkha.

All interviews conducted by the author except for Blixa Bargeld, Monte Cazazza, Clint Conley, Joseph Jacobs, Cole Palme and Mike Thorne, which were done by Geeta Dayal.

A large nod to Simon Frith and Howard Horne for *Art into Pop*, their classic analysis of the unique role of the UK art-school system in post-war British pop culture – and a significant influence on *Rip It Up and Start Again*.

RIP John Peel.

Finally, I'd like to offer a fervent salute to the journalists and editors of the weekly rock papers of the late seventies and early eighties – the *real* golden age for British music journalism, whatever you might have heard to the contrary. Alongside the original interviews conducted for the book, back issues of the three main weeklies – *NME*, *Sounds* and *Melody Maker* – served as my prime research resource. Reading the 'inkies' back in the day was what made me want to be a music writer in the first place. Rereading them for this book, I was freshly impressed by the critical insight and stylistic brilliance of the writing, the quality of the reportage, and, most of all, by the ways in which the writers made a genuine contribution to the scene of their day, by generating new ways of thinking about music. Impressed – and inspired all over again.

INDEX

THE WAKEFIELD MYSTERY PLAYS

THE
WAKEFIELD MYSTERY
PLAYS

Edited by

MARTIAL ROSE

LONDON
EVANS BROTHERS LIMITED

Drawings by HEATHER ROSE

No performance of any of the plays in this
Edition may take place, in any circumstances
whatsoever, without permission from Evans
Brothers, who also publish the Cycle in Four Parts
for the greater convenience of performers.

Unwin
Harman.

Printed in Great Britain
by W. & J. Mackay & Co Ltd, Chatham
z 5438

Author's Note

In 1954 I was asked to make a contribution to a course on Environmental Studies at Woolley Hall, near Wakefield, by producing three plays from the Wakefield cycle of mystery plays. In consequence the Bretton Hall Drama students presented *The Salutation*, *The Second Shepherds' Play*, and *The Flight into Egypt*. The plays were performed in the original language by a remarkable group of students whose own vernacular was not so very far removed from that of the original. They realized to the full both the lyricism and the buffoonery. More significant, the lyricism and the buffoonery were revealed not as independent features of the drama but as integrally related. And for once *The Second Shepherds' Play* also became integrally related to the cycle of plays from which it is so frequently torn. Even within the context of the three plays performed at Woolley it was set in a new perspective: it was not the only jewel in the Wakefield Plays; there were others, and some with as many facets.

The opportunity of presenting the major part of the cycle came in 1958, when the Principal and staff of Bretton Hall determined to focus the main work of the year on the study and production of the Wakefield Plays. An abbreviated version of twenty of the plays was made, and this formed the basis of the present edition. The production employed both mobile pageants and a stationary three-tier structure representing heaven, middle-earth and hell. The music throughout was live, sung and played from a *heavenly* tower. The running time of the twenty abbreviated plays was six and a half hours. The whole college was divided into craft groups, each group being responsible for the presentation of one or more plays. The overall production was managed by the staff.

My present endeavour to produce a complete acting version of the

Wakefield Plays has been greatly assisted by the liberal provision of the Ministry of Education, the University of Leeds, and the governors of Bretton Hall in granting me sabbatical leave in which to pursue my studies. I am especially indebted to Kay Hudson, Frances Stevens (University of Leeds) and John Stevens (University of Cambridge), and to the West Riding County Library for the more than generous supply of books. Above all, my thanks are due to the Principal, staff, and students of Bretton Hall who first gave support to the project and finally achieved, in a memorable performance, the revival after four hundred years of the most dramatic of the medieval mystery cycles.

Lastly, the enthusiasm and guidance of Lionel Hale and Peter Richards have brought this matter to print. Their conviction that this was an enterprise of some magnitude has been of the greatest encouragement, and their attention to detail has stirred me to an unwonted alertness.

MARTIAL ROSE

CONTENTS

Part Three

Part Four

An Introduction to
THE WAKEFIELD PLAYS

Why Wakefield?

The unique manuscript of the *Towneley Plays* now rests in the Huntington Library, San Marino, California. It comprises thirty-two plays all but one of which, *The Hanging of Judas,* are written in a mid-fifteenth-century hand. Five plays are in parts identical with the corresponding plays in the York cycle. The scope of the plays encompassing the creation, fall, redemption and judgement of man, approximates to that found in the other English cycles. There are, however, a few plays, *Caesar Augustus* and *The Talents* for instance, which are unique in the records of English medieval drama. It is true that the Chester *Annunciation* introduces the character of Octavian and that the other cycles include mention, if not dramatization, of the dicing for Christ's garment, but the extended treatment of this material in the Towneley Plays argues an indigenous source. The name Towneley has been given to the plays because the manuscript was for a great number of years in the possession of the Towneley family of Towneley Hall, near Burnley, Lancashire. It was sold by the family in 1814 but was returned in May, 1819, where it remained until the second sale of the Towneley library in June, 1883.

There has been so far no satisfactory explanation of how the manuscript found its way into the Towneley library. Are the plays after all a mystery cycle indigenous to Lancashire? Certainly other Lancashire names appear in the manuscript: James Blakebourn (folio 90a); Thomas Hargraves (folios 73b and 90a); moreover, against Hargraves' name (folio 90a) are the words 'of Burnley'. Associations with Lancashire are further strengthened by the 1822 introduction to the *Iudicium* (*The Judgement*), a publication for the Roxburgh Club, written by Francis Douce who attributed the original possession of the manuscript to the Abbey of Whalley from where, at the dissolution, 'it passed into the library of the neighbouring family of Towneley'.

'Wakefeld', however, is included in the heading of two of the plays.
The Creation begins with the words '*In dei nomine amen. Assit Principio,
Sancta Maria, Meo. Wakefeld*'. *Noah* is entitled '*Processus Noe cum filiis.
Wakefeld*'. This satisfactorily establishes that these two plays belong to
Wakefield, but on this evidence alone it would be rash to assume that
the whole cycle has its origin in Wakefield. Indeed Louis Wann asks
'If the entire cycle of plays was produced at Wakefield, why are these
two alone—and these not in consecutive order—designated as Wakefield plays? Does not the mention of Wakefield in the case of these
two plays establish a presumption that the others were not connected
with Wakefield?' ('A New Examination of the Manuscript of the
Towneley Plays', P.M.L.A., 1928, 151–152.) Perhaps this question
would not have arisen had 'Wakefeld' appeared at the beginning of
The Creation only. Had this been the case the whole cycle, since it is
substantially the work of one scribe, might reasonably have been
assigned to Wakefield, but the repetition in the *Noah* title complicates
the issue. The essential difference between the appearance of 'Wakefeld' in the first and the third play of the cycle is that whereas in the
third play it clearly stands as part of the title, in the first play it is the
conclusion of the scribe's invocation. In compliance with literary
convention and in anticipation of the great task that lies ahead of him,
that of copying out the whole cycle which extends to one hundred
and thirty-two leaves of vellum, the scribe asks a blessing on his work
which, as the last word signifies, will be undertaken in Wakefield.

In examining this problem, then, the first question to be asked is not
why 'Wakefeld' does not appear in the heading of all the plays, but
rather why it should have appeared as part of the heading of *Noah*. A
possible answer is that the scribe is handling a heterogeneous group of
plays, some in their pristine fourteenth-century state, some revisions
of plays from other cycles and some, five in all, brilliant new plays,
written in a vigorous nine-line stanza, this last the work of a dramatic
genius usually known as the Wakefield Master. The first play in the
cycle written in this characteristic stanza is *Noah*. The scribe copies
faithfully the text before him, and when he comes to *Noah* he copies
the author's title, who includes the word 'Wakefeld' because this is
the first of a set of plays he has written especially for the *Corpus
Christi* celebrations of the people of Wakefield.

Apart from the five completely new plays (*Noah, The First Shepherds'
Play, The Second Shepherds' Play, Herod the Great*, and *The Buffeting*)

contributed to the cycle by the Wakefield Master, he shows his hand also in a number of revisions and interpolations. *The Killing of Abel*, the second play in the Cycle, is commonly associated with the work of the Master. 'The extraordinary boldness of the play' writes A. W. Pollard in his Introduction to '*The Towneley Plays*' (O.U.P. 1897) xxii, 'and the character of its humour, make it difficult to dissociate it from the work of the author of *Shepherds' Plays*.' A. C. Cawley supports this judgement and includes *The Killing of Abel* in his edition of *The Wakefield Pageants in the Towneley Cycle* (Manchester U.P. 1958). Whoever the author, *The Killing of Abel* is indelibly stamped as a Wakefield play. Cain pleads for a Wakefield burial:

Bery me in Gudeboure at the quarell hede.   (367)

Matthew Peacock, in Anglia Vol. xii, 1901, pointed out that 'the Grammar School was built in Goodybower Close, and the stone came from the adjacent quarry. . . . Perhaps it was in the quarry that the plays were performed'. There is then consecutive evidence in the first three plays of the cycle that the Towneley Plays are concerned with Wakefield.

Other local allusions are found in *The First Shepherds' Play* (244) 'Have good ayll of Hely' (Have good ale of Healey), 'possibly a township of this name lying between Ossett and Horbury, about four miles south-west of Wakefield' (Cawley, op. cit., 101); 'the crokyd thorne' [*The Second Shepherds' Play* (403)], was most likely the outstanding landmark of the village of Thornes that lies between Horbury and Wakefield; 'Horbery shrogys' [*The Second Shepherds' Play* (455)], the bushy countryside near Horbury, a town three miles south-west of Wakefield; 'Watlyn strete' [*The Judgement* (126)], the Roman road which crossed the parish of Wakefield. This reference to Watling Street is found in one of the Wakefield Master's interpolations in *The Judgement*. Dr. Cawley argues 'Although these local allusions are confined to certain of the pageants belonging to the Wakefield Group in the Towneley cycle, it will be seen that the homogeneity of the pageants and parts of the pageants written in the Wakefield nine-line stanza allows us to infer that *all* of them have associations with the Wakefield area' (op. cit., xv.). In all this would account for thirteen plays, including all the most important plays in the Passion sequence. If we accept the first three plays of the cycle as belonging to Wakefield, the three plays of the Nativity sequence in the nine-line stanza, all the Passion plays, *The Pilgrims, The Ascension,* and *The Judgement*, we might with some justification rename the cycle the Wakefield Plays.

The references to the crafts, Tanners, Glovers, Dyers, Fishers, appearing in the manuscript on the first pages of *The Creation*, *The Killing of Abel*, *Pharaoh*, and *The Pilgrims* respectively, afford no additional evidence of Wakefield authorship. The names of the crafts are written in a sixteenth-century hand. Certainly only a wealthy town with a powerful and flourishing fraternity of guilds could have accepted responsibility for staging the plays, which in their entirety would have matched the length of the York cycle. Yet it is the very paucity of reference to the guilds that contrasts so sharply with the York and Chester plays, and in this the Wakefield cycle resembles the *Ludus Coventriae*.

THE AUTHOR?

In the notice for the 1814 sale of Towneley books and manuscripts Francis Douce wrote that the plays 'belonged to the Abbey of Wid-kirk, near Wakefield'. No explanation has been offered why eight years later he should have ascribed them to Whalley Abbey. Widkirk is generally accepted as Woodkirk, four miles north of Wakefield, where in the Middle Ages a cell was kept by Augustinian monks, dependent on Nostell Priory, and it is indeed possible that the scribe was a man in holy orders, living in or near Wakefield, and attached to the greatest monastic house in the area. The task he undertook was to copy a wide variety of manuscripts which at that time comprised the latest collection of the Wakefield Plays: some, such as *Isaac* and *Jacob*, were already nearly a hundred years old, their dramatic structure was crude and their versification gauche; some such as *The Harrowing of Hell* followed the York text closely throughout and might have been borrowed from that cycle; some, indigenous and borrowed, had been substantially altered through revision, as in the case of *The Killing of Abel*, or through interpolation (378 lines) in the case of *The Judgement*; and in the last group were the five new plays written by the Wakefield Master. The plays, then, are the work of many authors whose labours probably extended over a hundred years. These authors remain anonymous, and even the identity of the last great reviser of the cycle, who also made such a spectacular and original contribution to the drama, has escaped detection. Oscar Cargill put forward the theory ('The Authorship of the *Secunda Pastorum*',

P.M.L.A., Dec., 1926) that Gilbert Pilkington, no more of whom is known than his association with one manuscript of *The Northern Passion*, was the Wakefield Master. The main evidence was based on the colophon at the end of *The Northern Passion*:

> *Explicit Passio Domini*
> *nostri ihesu christi Quod Dominus Gilbertus*
> *Pylkyngton Amen.*

The Cambridge manuscript in which this version of *The Northern Passion* appears contains, among twenty-seven other pieces of verse, a poem entitled *The Turnament of Totenham*, a satire on chivalry written in the nine-line stanza which Cargill identifies as the Wakefield Master's. In brief, his conclusions are that Gilbert Pilkington was the author of *The Northern Passion*, *The Turnament of Totenham*, and those plays of the Wakefield cycle written in the nine-line stanza. His argument involves him in asserting that all three works were composed about 1355, an acceptable date for *The Northern Passion* but a virtually impossible date for the Wakefield Plays. Frances A. Foster has disposed of Cargill's case ('Was Gilbert Pilkington the Author of the *Secunda Pastorum*?' P.M.L.A., 1928) and Hardin Craig ('English Religious Drama', O.U.P. 1955, 234) recording Cargill's inability to substantiate his theory, writes '. . . it is rather a pity that he had no evidence'. It is strange that both Cargill and his critics have overlooked the essential difference between *The Turnament of Totenham* stanza and that of *The Second Shepherds' Play*. It is that the internal rhyme scheme of the first four lines in each stanza, the hall-mark of the Wakefield Master's verse, is nowhere to be found in *The Turnament of Totenham*.

A pity indeed, Mr. Cargill's lack of evidence! But what a fund of coincidences is revealed by an investigation of his case. Firstly, we know *The Northern Passion* exerted an influence on the formation of the fourteenth-century mystery cycles (*The Northern Passion*, vol. ii. edited by Frances A. Foster, E.E.T.S., 81–101); secondly, *The Turnament of Totenham*, although not in the identical stanza as that used by the Wakefield Master, nevertheless has many of its characteristics, and its satirical tone and mock-heroic theme calls for comparison with the Master's work, especially in view of the northern linguistic similarities; thirdly Mr. Cargill's suggestion that *The Turnament of Totenham* may once have been a satire of Tottington, the adjacent town to Pilkington in Lancashire, while no more than an outrageous guess, might nevertheless give us pause when, on examining Thomas Whitaker's *History of Whalley*, we find such frequent reference to the Manor of Tottington. Large tracts of the forest of Tottington which reached northward into the parish of Whalley were granted by thirteenth-century charters to the priory of Monk Bretton, about nine miles south-east of Wakefield, founded as a Cluniac house about 1154 and becoming a Benedictine establishment from 1281. These lands with an immense quantity of others were re-granted to John Braddyll of Whalley by letters patent of Henry VIII in 1546. In this *History of Whalley* we read that in 1469 a licence was granted to Thomas Pilkington to kernel and embattle his manor house at Bury (Towneley MSS G 13), and that a Thomas Pilkington was a generous donor to Whalley Abbey, among whose monks was one Brother John of Wakefield. Mr. Cargill had stressed that a branch of the Lancashire Pilkingtons had established themselves in Wakefield and had built there, early in the fifteenth century, Pilkington Hall. Many of the manuscripts studied by Thomas Whitaker were made accessible to him at the Towneley Hall library, and it was to Charles Towneley that he dedicated his work in 1800.

No fresh evidence for the authorship of *The Second Shepherds' Play* has been adduced, but the territorial associations between Whalley and Wakefield have been strengthened, and in both areas the Pilkington family exerted its influence. Furthermore the Pilkingtons and the Towneleys were related families: Sir John Towneley, a ward of Sir Charles Pilkington, married in 1480 Isabella, Sir Charles' daughter and heiress. The coats of arms of both families appeared in the fifteenth-century glass in the Wakefield Parish Church (J. W. Walker, *The Cathedral Church of Wakefield*, 1888, 86–88).

THE TOWNELEY POSSESSION OF THE MANUSCRIPT

In the east window of the north chancel of what was Wakefield Parish Church and is now the Cathedral appeared the Towneley coat of arms impaled by the coat of arms of the house of Nowell. This signified the marriage between the two houses of Roger Nowell and Grace Towneley in 1488. J. W. Walker in his *History of Wakefield* suggests that the plays might have found their way into the possession of the Towneley family in consequence of this marriage. Roger Nowell was an extremely affluent and influential man, founding the

Nowell Chantry in the Parish Church in 1478, and owning many acres of land in Wakefield, Stanley, Bradford, Sandal, and Wentbridge. (J. W. Walker, *The Cathedral Church of Wakefield*, 67-71). But he was also the son and heir of Alexander Nowell of Read Hall, two miles south-east of Whalley, lying in fact on the route between Towneley Hall and Whalley Abbey. The families of Nowell and Towneley were further connected by Elizabeth Kay of Rochdale marrying first John, the son of Roger Nowell, and then, after her husband's death, Charles Towneley, the heir of Towneley Hall. It is in all probability her first husband whose name appears in the records of the Wakefield Parish Church as patron of the Nowell Chantry Chaplains: 'April 8, 1511 . . . John Nowell de Whalley Armiger.' (Walker, ibid. 71.) John Towneley, the son by Elizabeth's second marriage, was a staunch Roman Catholic who suffered for his faith a life of intermittent imprisonment. By her first marriage Elizabeth had four sons, the two eldest, Alexander and Laurence, held high office in the church, the former becoming Dean of St. Paul's (1560-1602) and the latter Dean of Lichfield (1559-1576), in whose diocese Whalley lay. [R. Churton, *The Life of Alexander Nowell* (1809).]

Alexander Nowell, a life-long friend of Edmund Grindal, Archbishop of York (1570-1576) was a member of the 1576 commission to look into ecclesiastical abuses while Grindal was still Archbishop of York. Grindal's appointment to York was made on the understanding that he would root out Romish superstition in the north, and part of his campaign was waged against performances of mystery plays. In 1568 Matthew Hutton, Dean of York Minster, called in the York Creed Play for perusal, and after that date no more is heard of it. Archbishop Grindal on 30th July, 1572, asked for a copy of the York *Pater Noster* Play, after which date no record remains of it. No doubt the York Mystery Plays were similarly examined, and although their performance was discontinued, at least the manuscript has survived. 'The correction, indeed the abolition, of the plays' writes Hardin Craig (op. cit., 201), 'is attributed to the influence of Edmund Grindal, Archbishop of York, and of Matthew Hutton, the Dean of the Minster. A complete overhauling of the plays was projected for 1579, but fortunately not carried out, and we have the plays pretty much as they were written down at some time before the middle of the fifteenth century. Apparently the Dean and the Archbishop, by 1579 Edwin Sandys, took the prudent course of keeping the register in their own possession and temporizing with the citizens, who obviously still wanted the plays performed'.

That the Wakefield Plays were subject to Protestant revision there is no doubt. In *John the Baptist* (197) a passage referring to the sacraments is first altered and then the whole stanza is struck through, and in the margin is written 'corectyd and not playd'. The word 'pope' seems literally to have been dug out of the text of *Herod the Great* (263), and it is practically certain, from analogy with the other cycles, that the twelve leaves missing from the manuscript between *The Ascension* and *The Judgement* contained plays dealing with the death, assumption and coronation of the Blessed Virgin Mary, details from which are depicted over the west portal of the fourteenth-century façade of the Chantry Bridge Chapel. (This façade now graces the boat-house of Kettlethorpe Hall.) Positive evidence of the Ecclesiastical Commission suppressing the Wakefield Plays is derived from the Diocesan Court of High Commission.

> xxvij° die Maii Anno dni 1576 cora Com eccle Ebor. Cora Mrr. Matthew Hutton, John Gibson et W° Palmer Commissionarii et in pr mei Willim Fothergill notarii publici. This daie upon intelligence geven to the saide Commission that it is meant and purposed that in the towne of Wakefeld shalbe plaid this yere in Whitsonweke next or thereaboutes a plaie commonlie called *Corpus Christi* plaie which hath bene heretofore used there, wherein they are done t' understand that there be many thinges used which tende to the derogation of the Majestie and glorie of God, the prophanation of the sacramentes and the maunteynaunce of superstition and idolatrie, the said Commissioners decreed a lettre to be written and sent to the baylyffe, burgesses and other the inhabitantes of the said towne of Wakefeld that in the said playe no pageant be used or set furthe wherin the Ma^tye of God the Father, God the Sonne, or God the Holie Ghoste or the administration of either the Sacraments of baptisme or of the Lordes Supper be counterfeyted or represented, or anythinge plaied which tende to the maintenaunce of superstition and idolatrie or which be contrarie to the lawes of God (and) or of the realme.

The Commission, not content with the amendments of the Wakefield Plays on doctrinal issues, for instance the reducing of the seven sacraments to two in *John the Baptist* (197) and the subsequent deletion of the stanza and also of that stanza in *The Resurrection* (328–333) referring to transubstantiation, were obviously bent on establishing such inhibitions which made further performance of the plays impossible. Few plays were left the citizens of Wakefield to perform if no impersonations of God the Father, God the Son, and God the Holy Ghost were permitted, and if performance had been attempted of the few that remained they would, no doubt have been put down on grounds of 'superstition and idolatrie'. The York and Wakefield Cycle may well have shared the same fate as the York Creed and *Pater Noster* Plays that is, once called in by the Commission they were not released again to the civic authorities. Provided there was but one original, or register [and such from the single surviving manuscripts of the York, Wakefield, and the *Hegge Plays* (*Ludus Coventriae*) seems probable] this was as effective a method of suppression as any. After 1576 we hear of no further attempt to perform the Wakefield Plays. At Chester, however, where the manuscript of the plays remained in the hands of the citizens, despite the contrary instructions received from the Archbishop of York, in 1575 Sir John Savage, Mayor of Chester, permitted their performance. He and his successor were later arrested and taken to London to await their trial. (H. C. Gardiner, *Mysteries' End*, Yale U.P. 1946, 81.) The defiance of the Chester citizens may well have encouraged the Commission to secure in the following year the manuscript of the Wakefield Plays to reinforce their inhibition.

It is then possible that Alexander Nowell, through his association with the Ecclesiastical Commission and through his long and intimate friendship with Grindal, who by May 1576 had been elected Archbishop of Canterbury, acquired the manuscript of the Wakefield Plays and at a later date bequeathed it to his uterine brother, John Towneley, a man who had maintained his Roman Catholicism under conditions of the bitterest adversity, and for whom these plays would have been as a testament of a people's faith in that old world of a less fragmented Christendom.

THE STAGING OF THE WAKEFIELD PLAYS

The reference concerning the suppression of the Wakefield Plays in the records of the Diocesan Court of High Commission at York is one of the very few pieces of external evidence that Wakefield possessed a cycle of mystery plays. The document tells us that the plays were planned for 'Whitsonweke . . . or thereaboutes', that the bailiff and burgesses of Wakefield were responsible for their organization, and that in the plays, as we have noticed earlier as, for instance, in *John the Baptist* and *The Resurrection*, certain references were made to the sacraments which were unacceptable to the reformed church.

The only other external evidence that Wakefield had its own cycle of *Corpus Christi* plays is the Wakefield Burgess Court Rolls which, in Queen Mary's reign (1553–1558), have the following entries:

PAYNES LAYD BY THE BURGES QWEST AS FOLLOYT. IN ANNO 1554
Itm a payne is layd yt gyles Dolleffe shall brenge In or Causse to be broght ye regenall of *Corpus Xty* play before ys & wytsonday In pane. . . .
Itm a payne layde yt ye mesters of ye *Corpus Xti* playe shall Come & mayke thayre a Count before ye gentyllmen burgessus of ye toun before this & may day next. In payne of everye one not so doynge 20s.

PAYNES LAYDE BY THE BURGES ENQUESTS AT THE COURTE KEPTE AT WAKEFELDE NEXTE AFTER THE FEASTE OF SAYNTE MICHAELL THARCHAUNGELL IN THIRDE AND FOURTE YEARE OF THE REIGNES OF OUR SOVERAIGNE LORDE AND LADYE KINGE PHILYPPE AND QUENE MARYE, 1556
Itm a payne is sett that everye crafte and occupation doo bringe furthe theire pagyaunts of *Corpus Christi* daye as hathe bene heretofore used and to give furthe the speches of the same in after holydayes in payne of everye one not so doynge to forfett xls.
Itm a payne is sett that everye player be redy in his pagyaunt at setled tyme before 5 of ye clocke in ye mornynge in payne of every one not so doynge to forfett vjs. viijd.
Itm a payne is sett yt ye players playe where setled and no where els in payne of no (sic) so doynge to forfett xxs.
Itm a payne is sett yt no man goe armed to disturb ye playe or hinder ye procession in payne of everye one so doynge vjs. viijd.
Itm a payne is sett yt everye man shall leave hys weapon att hys home or at hys ynne in payne of not so doynge vjs. viijd.
Ye summe of ye expens of ye Cherche mester for ye *Corpus Christi* playe xvijs. xd.

Item payd to ye preste		xijd.
Itm payd to ye mynstrells		xxd.
Itm payd to ye mynstrells of *Corpus Christi* playe	iijs.	ivd.
Itm payde for ye *Corpus Christi* playe & wrytynge ye spechys for yt	iijs.	viijd.
Itm payd for ye Baner for ye mynstrells	vjs.	viijd.
Itm payd for ye ryngyng ye same day		vjd.
Itm payd for garlonds on *Corpus Christi* day		xijd.

It is understandable that the return to the throne of Queen Mary, a Catholic monarch, should have provided the encouragement for the re-staging of the mystery plays which in the reigns of Henry VIII and Edward VI had been discredited through the anti–papal policies of the crown. The loss of the Wakefield plays dealing with the death, assumption, and coronation of the Blessed Virgin, which were probably contained in those twelve leaves, now missing, between *The Ascension* and *The Judgement*, may have coincided with the prohibition in 1548 of the corresponding York plays. H. C. Gardiner writes '. . . the excision of the plays on the Death, Assumption, and Coronation of the Blessed Virgin in York in 1548 shows that, apart from any official decree, the spirit of Protestantism was at work'. (Op. cit., 61.)

The time of year in 1554 when the Burgess Banns (Paynes) were laid down is not clear, but from the records of Norwich and Coventry we gather that the citizens set about preparing for their *Corpus Christi* plays at Easter or soon after. In these Wakefield Banns the phrase 'before this and may day next' may indicate that their meeting took place on or just after May 1st. According to the records of the York Diocesan Court the plays were performed during 'Whitsonweke . . . or thereaboutes'. The phrasing suggests that the plays were not presented on one day only but on two or more days. The Chester cycle, though called the *Corpus Christi* plays, was performed on Monday, Tuesday and Wednesday of Whit week; a procession was held on Corpus Christi day followed by a play presented by the clergy. (Glynne Wickham, *Early English Stages*, Routledge and Kegan Paul, 1959, 346–347; E. K. Chambers, *The Mediaeval Stage*, O.U.P. 1903, ii. 138.) The shifting of the plays from *Corpus Christi* day to Whit week took place at Chester as early as 1462; at York in 1569 they were performed on Whit Tuesday, and Norwich and New Romney also record performances of the *Corpus Christi* plays in Whit week.

The 1556 Banns were prepared at the first meeting of the Burgess Court following the feast of St. Michael (29th September, 1555). The frequency of the Burgess Court meetings is unknown, but by the contents of the Banns for 1556 this particular meeting could not have been too distant from the *Corpus Christi* festivities. It seems, from the hint given in the 1554 Banns, that the 1556 meeting was probably on May Day, and that this was the occasion of the Court recording the expense accounts of those responsible for the previous year's *Corpus Christi* play; that of the churchwarden's is one such account. The churchwarden's account must refer to the festivities of the previous year (1555) because all the 1556 Banns concern the preparations for the 1556 procession and play. Surely no accounts would be submitted until after performance, and we gather from the second item in the 1554 Banns that the wardens of the *Corpus Christi* play were allowed almost a year in which to make up their accounts and submit them 'before ye gentyllmen & burgessus' of Wakefield.

The very last item in the churchwarden's account, 'payd for garlonds on *Corpus Christi* day xijd.', seems to prove that the crafts brought forth their pageants 'of *Corpus Christi* daye' *on Corpus Christi* day. But there is more than a strong suggestion in the Banns that the procession and the plays took place on separate days. The crafts are asked to bring forth their pageants on *Corpus Christi* day—and it is for this day the garlands are required—but it is 'in after holydayes' that they are 'to give furthe the speches of the same'. Does this mean that the procession took place on *Corpus Christi* day, a Thursday, and that the following Friday and Saturday were treated as holidays on which the plays were performed? Does the bringing forth of pageants then mean the joining in the *Corpus Christi* day procession which moved from the parish church through the town returning again to the church? Was there singing on the way, and did the pageants at certain stations draw back their curtains to a dumb-show representation of the drama they were to perform 'in after holydayes'? Questions abound; answers supported by circumstantial evidence are scarce. But it is clear that the Banns suggest a separation of the procession and the plays. No man may go armed lest he 'disturb ye playe or hinder ye procession'; there are two separate payments to the minstrels, one of which specifies 'ye mynstrells of *Corpus Christi* playe'; the garlands, the ringing of bells, the minstrels in procession with their very expensive banner, and the officiating priest are indications of the pro-

cession. The playbook (regenall), the rewriting of parts, the injunction
to play 'where setled and no where els' are obvious references dis-
tinguishing the plays from the procession. In York, where before
1426 the plays and the procession were undertaken on the same day,
the Proclamation of 1394 introduces a difference of phrasing in its
reference to the location of the plays which may be significant: 'And
þat men þat brynges furth pagentes þat þai play *at the places* þat is
assigned þerfore and nowere elles . . .' The Wakefield 'where setled'
is ambiguous; obviously at York there are in 1394 many stations; at
Wakefield in 1556 there may have been but one.

If the plays were not performed in Wakefield until after *Corpus
Christi* day why should the Burgesses be asking for the master copy of
the plays ('ye regenall' or original) to be returned to them before
Whit Sunday? To whom did the churchwarden pay 3s 8d. for the
Corpus Christi play and for the writing of speeches for it? And who,
anyway, was Giles Dolleffe that he should have the manuscript of the
plays in his keeping? It may be that Whit Sunday marked the beginning of the preparations for the *Corpus Christi* festival when the master
copy was called in to be, if necessary, 'corectyd', and to be the source
for the copying out of parts and, possibly, of whole plays. The
twelve days between Whit Sunday and *Corpus Christi* day might
seem too inadequate a time in which to rehearse the whole cycle, but
contemporary evidence points to very little time being spent on
rehearsal: 'these pagente shulde be played after breeffe rehearsal'
(The Banns of the Chester Plays, 60). The Coventry Smiths held their
first rehearsal in Easter week and their second in Whit week. In the
Coventry records there are seldom more than two rehearsals before
performance; the outstanding exception is the Cappers' record of five
rehearsals in 1584 for the new play *The Destruction of Jerusalem*. (Hardin
Craig, 'Two Coventry *Corpus Christi* Plays', O.U.P. 1957, 98.) It
is significant that this play was especially written for Coventry to
replace the *Corpus Christi* cycle. If the craft-guilds who undertook the
performance of this play, which from all accounts appears to have
been of a similar length to the cycle it was displacing, required only
five rehearsals,* it is reasonable to assume that two would have sufficed
for the mystery plays which had been in existence for well over a
hundred years, and which by annual performance had ingrained their

---

* Thomas Sharp asserts that 'no less than six rehearsals took place previous
to the public exhibition of this new pageant.' (H. Craig, Ibid. 90.)

contents in the mind and memory of spectators and players. It was traditional for the players to perform the same parts year after year. Only the rare change of cast would have necessitated a part being copied out. The scribe who undertook to copy parts out from the original, since he was paid by the churchwarden, was most probably one of the parish clergy. At Coventry in 1495 payment is made 'for copyyng of ij knyghts partes and demons', and in 1540 one penny is paid 'for writyng a parte for Herre Person'. (Hardin Craig, op. cit., 89, 94.) Apparently 'Herre Person' had a very small part; on the other hand the Wakefield scribe, if he earned his 3s. 8d., must have had either many parts to copy out or a new play to write. The Coventry Smiths, Cappers, and Mercers, each paid John Green five shillings for copying from the manuscript of *The Destruction of Jerusalem* the particular plays that were the responsibility of their respective companies. The 3s. 8d. in the Wakefield accounts may conceivably have been due, not only to the copying of parts but also for the writing of *The Hanging of Judas,* the only play in the manuscript which is written in a sixteenth-century hand. The scribe, it will be noticed is paid 'for ye *Corpus Christi* playe & wrytynge ye spechys for yt'. It is obvious from his payment that he was not employed to copy out the whole master copy; he may however have copied out one play which, according to Coventry rates of pay in the sixteenth century, would have earned him about five shillings. But the scribe may also have been paid for 'bearing' the book, which E. K. Chambers (op. cit., ii. 140) interprets as acting as prompter. The Coventry Smiths in 1494 record that they 'paid to John Harryes for berying of the orygynall that day vjd'.

If the Wakefield scribe then had possession of the 'original' soon after Whit Sunday, when it was handed to him through the agency first of the Burgess Court and then of the churchwarden, what was the 'original' doing in the possession of Gyles Dolleffe until Whit Sunday? The Coventry Cappers in 1584 pay one shilling 'for the kepynge the boke', but it is not clear whether payment is for prompting or for safe-keeping of the play after performance. It is more likely that Gyles Dolleffe had the plays in his safe-keeping and that he was himself one of the wardens or producers. His, too, may have been the task to prepare the text for the 1556 performance and to submit it for approval to both the Burgess Court and the ecclesiastical authorities before rehearsals commenced. We know he was a prominent citizen of Wakefield, a burgess himself, attending the Burgess Court meetings, living in Kirkgate and by trade a draper. [J. W. Walker, *Wakefield, Its History and People*, Wakefield (1934), 133, 359, 380.] His wife's death is recorded in the Archbishop's Registry at York under March 25th, 1604: 'Agnis doliffe late wife of Giles Doliffe buried xxvijth daye' [J. W. Walker, *The Cathedral Church of Wakefield*, Wakefield (1888), 293]. It would be interesting to know a good deal more about Gyles Dolleffe, for he may have been, as Thomas Colclow was for the Coventry Smiths' play (Hardin Craig, TCCCP, 83), a highly paid producer whose contract extended over a number of years.

The 1556 Banns of the Wakefield Burgess Court order every player to be ready in his pageant by 5 a.m. The 1394 York Proclamation decreed 4.30 a.m. as the time when all should assemble. A town-clerk of York, Roger Burton, made two lists of the York Plays, one undated containing fifty-seven plays, and the other dated 1415 containing fifty-one: the unique manuscript contains forty-eight (L. T. Smith, op. cit., xviii). Assuming that only forty-eight plays are to be performed in the day, we have then a drama whose total length is 13,121 lines, the average length of each play being 273 lines. The plays, as tradition has it, were performed at a number of different stations in York, the whole cycle being presented at each successive station. The number of stations varied: in 1417 there were twelve, in 1519 there were fourteen, and in 1554 sixteen (L. T. Smith, ibid. xxxii, xxxiii). The playing of 273 lines, including the music and movement, would take about fifteen minutes. At the first station, allowing five minutes for the time taken between the end of one pageant and the beginning of another, the whole cycle would last for about fifteen hours; if it started at 4.30 a.m. it would finish at 7.30 p.m. At the second station, allowing five minutes for the journey and five minutes for the combined preparation for the journey at the first station and for the playing at the second—and we have to bear in mind that these are horse-drawn pageants making their way in procession not at a gallop—performance would begin at 4.55 a.m. and the cycle would finish at 7.55 p.m. At this rate the first pageant would begin at 9.5 a.m. at the twelfth station and the last would finish just after midnight. It must be recognized that these estimates are almost impracticably conservative, and the pace at which such a schedule could be maintained would put an intolerable strain on both performers and spectators. Yet records indicate that fifty-seven plays were performed at sixteen different stations. The processional street-pageant staging of the York cycle has been too readily accepted without due consideration given to the practical problems. Why, for instance, were *all* the players asked to assemble at 4.30 a.m. if at the first station the cast of *The Judgement Day* had to wait until 7 p.m. until they performed? And were performances continued after nightfall? The records indicate provision for lanterns, cressets, torches, tapers, iron lamps for the pageants, but since an important part of both the York Proclamation and the Wakefield Banns is concerned with minimizing the possibility of rowdiness and rioting, would not the normal curfew be stringently enforced? If not, how can we account for the fact that when Queen Margaret visited Coventry in 1457 she saw at the first station a performance of the whole cycle 'save domes-day, which myght not pleyde for lak of day'? Even for the Queen of England playing could not be permitted after sun-down. If this were true also of York, what happened to the fifty-seven plays at sixteen different stations?

A study of the extant cycles reveals general similarities but individual differences, and this applies to the staging as well as to the text of the plays. In making a statement concerning the staging of the Wakefield Plays, because of the scarcity of local external evidence, recourse is had to analogy. Of those towns whose mystery cycles have survived, York is the nearest to Wakefield. Furthermore the York and Wakefield cycles have certain plays in common, and their Banns also show concern for similar problems: the necessity of an early start; the danger of armed men at the procession or the plays; the need for the players to play 'where setled'. Furthermore the Wakefield cycle is of a comparable length to the York. It contains 12,276 lines; including the lines from the missing twenty-eight leaves the total number would approach 15,000, which would make it longer than the existing York manuscript. Wakefield then shares with York the practical problem, indeed the practical impossibility, of performing the whole cycle at a number of stations in the compass of a day.

At York in 1426, for the first time, the procession and the plays were separated. The plays were performed on *Corpus Christi* day and the procession took place the day following (R. Davies, *Extracts from the Municipal Records of the City of York during the Reigns of Edward IV, Edward V, and Richard III*, 1843). At Chester the three-day performance of the plays took place in Whit week, and the *Corpus Christi* procession in the following week on the day of the festival. At Norwich the plays were performed on the Monday and Tuesday of Whit week, and, as at Chester, the procession followed on *Corpus Christi* day (O. Waterhouse, *Non Cycle Mystery Plays* xxxii). The separation of the plays from the procession arose in the first place from their divergent origins—the liturgical drama predates the *Corpus Christi* procession— and in the second from the extreme difficulty of finding time for both on the same day. In consequence the plays were generally put first and the procession followed later, either the next day, as at York, or the next week, as at Chester and Norwich. Since the York schedule shown earlier for the station-to-station playing is scarcely practicable, the stations at some stage may have been used not as acting areas for performance of the whole cycle, but rather as stopping places during the procession at which each pageant presented its scene in tableau. After 1426 the York procession took place on the day following *Corpus Christi*. If the plays performed on *Corpus Christi* day began at 4.30 a.m. they would have lasted at least until nightfall at just one station, and if the procession began the following day at 4.30 a.m. it would take the most part of the day, if combined with the religious services and the singing, to thread its way from station to station through the town. This is purely conjectural, but all the pageants moving off together does at least make sense of that reference in the Proclamation to all players being ready at 4.30 a.m. It is difficult to believe that the actors in *The Judgement Day* waited from dawn to dusk before their first line was spoken.

A similar problem attends the presentation of the Wakefield cycle. A single performance at a single station is all that is possible in a day, and this makes no allowance for the procession. The procession had to be separated from the performance, and the first item in the 1556 Banns suggests such a separation. The crafts are asked to prepare their pageants for the procession on one day and to perform the plays ('to give furthe the speches of the same in after holydayes') on the days that follow. If this interpretation is correct then Wakefield reversed the order at York, where the procession preceded the plays. From the 1576 record of the Diocesan High Court at York we may gather that under a Protestant monarch, with the prohibition of Catholic festivals, performance of the plays at Wakefield was planned for Whit week.

The thirty-two plays of the Wakefield cycle average 384 lines each.

If they were performed processionally they would have taken over fourteen hours at each station. If however they were performed at one station only, and by such an arrangement reducing the time spent in procession and in preparation before and after each performance, then the total playing time would have stretched from dawn to dusk. This playing time may at a later stage have been spread over two or more days. One possible explanation of there being two Shepherds' plays in the cycle is that *The First Shepherds' Play* was performed at the end of the first day's playing and *The Second Shepherds' Play* at the beginning of the second. It is certainly true that if the missing leaves of the manuscript are taken into account the play would be divided into three equal parts if breaks were made after *The First Shepherds' Play* and after *The Crucifixion*. (The Chester Plays which were performed on three successive days broke at *The Adoration of the Magi* and at *Christ's Descent into Hell;* the Ancient Cornish Drama, lasting also three days, broke at *The Execution of Maximilla* and *The Crucifixion*.) But whether the plays were performed on one, two, or three days, there is sufficient evidence to suggest that they were performed in the mid-fifteenth century at least, when the Wakefield Master had written his plays and made so many other revisions in the cycle, in one fixed locality, on a multiple stage, and in the round.

THE ONE FIXED LOCALITY

One particular feature of the manuscript of the Wakefield Plays, which sets it apart from the York and Chester cycles, is the sparse reference to the guilds. The names of four guilds—Barkers (Tanners), Glovers, Litsters (Dyers), and Fishers—are written on the title pages of four of the plays, but in a sixteenth-century hand. The fifteenth-century manuscript would, in its original state, have contained no reference to any of the guilds. In this the Wakefield Plays resemble the *Ludus Coventriae*. The strong case made by Hardin Craig (E.R.D. 239–280) to establish that the *Ludus Coventriae* and the Lincoln *Corpus Christi* Plays are one and the same might lead us by analogy, through what we know were the conditions under which the Lincoln Plays were produced, to the organization and staging of the Wakefield cycle.

The *Corpus Christi* plays at Lincoln were the responsibility not of the trade-guilds but of a religious guild, either the *Corpus Christi* guild or that of St. Anne. Every man and woman of Lincoln was a member of the St. Anne guild, paying annually a minimum of four pence each towards the maintenance of their guild. The *Corpus Christi* procession after about 1470 took place not on *Corpus Christi* day but on St. Anne's day (26th July). Hardin Craig maintains that on this occasion the pageants passed in procession through the city but that there was no performance until they reached the Minster. 'All the pageants would be there. It should also be remembered that all the citizens of Lincoln were, failing good excuse, obliged to be there. It may be said also that the only place in the old city of Lincoln where there could be such a concourse of people was the cathedral with its close and the vacant areas around it. It is surely no wild conjecture to suggest that the plays were acted there. One play we know was regularly performed on St. Anne's day in the nave of the cathedral church, that is, the Assumption and Coronation of the Blessed Virgin Mary. And we are not without another plausible piece of evidence that plays were to be seen at the cathedral.' (Hardin Craig, E.R.D., 275.)

One established playing site in a large area, having scaffolds specially erected for the spectators, and with the pageants moving into the spaces left between the scaffolds to complete a circle, or a horse-shoe, tallies exactly with the staging arrangements which must have prevailed for the performance of the *Ludus Coventriae*, and if these were the Lincoln *Corpus Christi* plays performed outside the cathedral church, the upper windows of The Close houses would also have provided excellent viewing.

The *Ludus Coventriae* resembles the Wakefield cycle in that it is an apparent compilation of diverse material, later than either the York or Chester cycles, but showing marked signs, particularly in the Passion sequences, of continuity of action and actors. The forty-eight York plays, both in their brevity and in their insulation, tend to become fragments rather than dramas and this, perhaps, is due to their being broken down to the requirements of the numerous guilds. On the other hand the *Ludus Coventriae* and the Wakefield Plays show an overall design which might well indicate that both the editing—if not the writing—of the plays and their preparation for performance was directed by a single organization, whether religious guild or corporation, and that responsibility for the individual plays was not assumed by the trade-guilds.

In the late fourteenth and early fifteenth century the York guilds may well have numbered over sixty. The very fact that there were at one time fifty-seven plays in the York cycle points to the flourishing guild organizations in that city. On the other hand, Wakefield in 1377, when each person over sixteen had to pay a four-penny Poll Tax, could only muster £4. 15. 8d. 'The list for the town of Wakefield shows a population of 567 over the age of sixteen years, and among the traders are found 2 mercers, 4 walkers or fullers, 5 websters or weavers, 8 tailors, 3 barkers or tanners, 3 drapers, 2 cattle-dealers, 4 wool merchants, 1 franklin or gentleman, 2 butchers, 2 wheel-wrights, 1 skinner, 2 ostlers (hotel-keepers), 4 smiths, 1 mason, 1 goldsmith, 1 glover. . . .' (J. W. Walker, *Wakefield, Its History and People*, Wakefield, 1934, 113.) We can assume then that in 1377, apart from beggars, there were approximately two hundred and eighty men living in Wakefield. But there are two hundred and forty-three different parts in the plays, and even if the population of Wakefield had doubled by 1425 it is extremely doubtful whether the plays would have been the responsibility of the guilds. For instance the Barkers would require at least eleven actors to perform *The Creation*, quite apart from the team to prepare the pageant for performance and to assist with properties and general problems of stage management. It may well have been the case that it was not until the sixteenth century that the guilds were large enough in Wakefield to undertake full production responsibilities. How then were they organized in the fifteenth century?

Performed on the trade-guild system existing in York and Chester there is the likelihood that two hundred and forty-three different actors would have been required to fill all the roles, but if the plays were performed on the basis of the *Ludus Coventriae* production, where there was one organization only to cast and direct the plays, far fewer actors would be required for, as so strongly indicated in the *Ludus Coventriae* Passion sequence, the same actors would almost certainly play the parts of the main characters throughout. In the York cycle there are twenty-seven plays in which Jesus appears. We are given to understand that in performance twenty-seven different actors played the part. Wakefield, through sheer lack of man-power, quite apart from any artistic consideration, could not support such a principle of production, at least not until well into the sixteenth century.

Where a religious guild undertook production of the plays, as at Lincoln, it was stoutly supported by the trade-guilds, without whose co-operation no progress could have been made. But the direction of the plays by a religious guild would have followed more closely the traditions laid down by the liturgical drama. The religious guild's close association with the drama still acted in the church is evident in the Lincoln example of the clergy performing *The Assumption* in the nave of the cathedral as the culmination of the St. Anne's day celebrations. Religious plays on the continent were less dependent on the trade-guilds than in England, and their staging derived more directly from liturgical drama.

'For most liturgical plays the so-called "simultaneous staging" was the rule. Thus in the Fleury *Conversion of St. Paul,* Jerusalem is on one side of the playing-space, Damascus on the other; in the Daniel plays, the *domus* of the hero to which he retires, the lions' den, and the throne occupied successively by Belshazzar and Darius, all are in view from the opening of the plays. Similarly the various St. Nicholas plays move the chief characters from one part of the playing-space to another, but always to stations visible to the audience from the beginning to the end of the performance. Only in such a highly organized spectacle as the *Presentation of the Virgin* do we find some provision for a distinct change of locale: in that *ordo* the two stages have a symbolical value, the second connoting Mary's reception into the church after her presentation. Processions were, of course, introduced at times to suggest journeys and therefore scene-shifts, but once the actors had arrived at the playing-space, the stage-setting, however far-flung the action, remained fixed.'

(Grace Frank, *Medieval French Drama,* O.U.P. 1954, 70.)

If at Wakefield the plays were produced by a religious guild, and if shortage of man-power brought about continuity of actors (that is one actor playing Jesus, or Pilate, or Caiaphas, and so on, throughout), it is more than likely that continuity of action took place in a stage-setting which 'remained fixed'.

The Norwich cycle of plays was also the responsibility of a religious guild, St. Luke's, and here, too, although they went forward in procession on *Corpus Christi* day, performance on Whit Monday and Tuesday is considered to have been stationary (O. Waterhouse, op. cit., xxxii). When in 1527 the strain of maintaining the plays became too burdensome for the St. Luke's guild, its members 'petitioned the corporation to divide the responsibility and expense among the various guilds'. A similar shedding of responsibility for certain of the plays might have taken place at Wakefield, and the appearance in the manuscript in a sixteenth-century hand of the four guilds (Tanners, Glovers, Dyers, and Fishers) tends to confirm this.

The evidence suggests that where the religious guilds assumed responsibility for the plays, although the procession remained a regular feature of the *Corpus Christi* festival, the performance was given in a fixed locality. The *Ludus Coventriae* and the *Digby Plays,* none of which was associated with trade-guilds, were also given in fixed localities. Indeed, performance by pageants in procession is the exception rather than the rule, as the stationary presentation of plays at Louth, Reading, Bassingbourne, Chelmsford, Shrewsbury, Cornwall, Aberdeen, and Edinburgh prove. (E. K. Chambers, op. cit., ii. 135.) Furthermore, the staging of the Wakefield Plays calls for a fixed locality in which heaven, paradise, earth, limbo, and hell stand always in the same relationship to each other. Also the variety of levels, the repetition of the journey motif (*Abraham,* the *Shepherds,* the *Magi,* Mary and Joseph, the road to Emmaus), and the frequent use of a messenger, crossing from one acting area to another (*Pharaoh, Caesar Augustus, Herod*), argue a complexity and spaciousness of staging which would be quite beyond the range of the processional pageant play, performed in the congestion of a medieval street. Above all, the continuity of action which informs the Passion sequence could only be realized through continuity of acting in one fixed locality.

MULTIPLE STAGING

The repeated requirement in the Wakefield Plays for staging a journey with two distinct acting areas, at the beginning and at the end, suggests the use of more than one pageant and lays considerable stress upon the acting area between the pageants. The journey motif is best exemplified in *The Second Shepherds' Play* and *The Offering of the Magi.* In the former Mak's house is opposed to the manger; the shepherds pass from one to the other and even sleep on the green (634) between the two mansions. *The Offering of the Magi* is similarly staged with Herod's palace replacing Mak's house; similarly, too, the kings sleep, but this time in a litter (590), between the two mansions. To suggest that the Wakefield Plays, which contain references to two or more mansions, could nevertheless be staged on the same pageant is to turn a blind eye to the stage directions, whether implicit in the dialogue or explicit in the rubrics, which, for instance, indicate that the three kings make separate entries from different directions on horseback, that their dialogue is continued on horseback for one hundred and forty lines, and that when they set off together to follow the star they are still mounted. On reaching Herod's palace they dismount and remount on leaving (492), but when they discover that the star they have been following is obscured—and this they attribute to Herod's malignant influence—they dismount ['here lyghtys the kyngys of thare horses' (504)] and pray. The star then appears over the mansion of the Nativity, where they go to present their gifts. This riding of horses between mansions would seem to dispose of the possibility that the mansions were placed on the same pageant. The very frequent references to characters riding horses in medieval drama suggest the use of real and not make-believe animals (The York *Flight into Egypt,* Chester *Abraham and Isaac,* the Ancient Cornish Drama, the *Ludus Coventriae Adoration of the Magi,* Caro's horse in *The Castle of Perseverance, The Conversion of St. Paul*). But horses were not the only animals used. In the Wakefield *Slaying of Abel,* for example, we have to account for Cain's plough-team of four oxen and four horses (25–43) [A. C. Cawley, *The Wakefield Pageants in the Towneley Cycle,* Manchester U.P. (1958), 91]. There are also Abraham's ass (*Abraham* 117), Pharaoh's chariots (*Pharaoh* 404), the Third Shepherd's mare (*The First Shepherds' Play,* 164), the ass on which Mary rides (*The Flight,* 151), and the Centurion's horse (*The Resurrection,* 44). It is certainly indisputable from the Norwich and Coventry records that live animals were used, at least for the drawing of the pageant, and by the extraordinary detail that was lavished on their decoration they may well have been used in the performance of the actual plays. There is a Canterbury record that 'the steeds of the Magi were made of hoops and laths and painted canvas' (E. K. Chambers, op. cit., ii. 142), but unfortunately the play is not extant. The probability is that where riding is indicated in the stage directions real horses were used. Given the acting area it would have been easier in the Middle Ages to have used a real horse rather than one made of hoops, laths, and canvas. It is interesting to note than when the animal is played by actors, as in the case of the ass in the Chester *Balaam and Balak,* it is specifically where the beast has a speaking part (Karl Young, *The Drama of the Medieval Church,* O.U.P. 1933 ii. 152).

The most weighty evidence, however, for the multiple staging of the Wakefield Plays lies in the Passion sequence, which sweeps on in continuous action from play to play and from stage to stage. For instance, *The Conspiracy*, the first play of this sequence, if divided into distinct acting areas would be represented as follows:

1. Pilate's hall (1–313)
2. Jesus and his disciples (314–333)
3. John and Peter on their way to Jerusalem, and
4. Their meeting with Paterfamilias outside his house (334–345)
5. The chamber of the Last Supper (strewn with rushes), the scene of the washing of feet (346–491)
6. The two levels of Olivet, one where Jesus prays and the other where the disciples sleep (492–599)
7. During which scene God appears in heaven's tower (528–555)
8. Pilate's hall (560–651)
9. From Olivet to the place of capture (652–707)
10. Pilate's hall (708–747)
11. Malcus and the soldiers lead Jesus to Caiaphas' hall (748–755).

This play is probably the combination of two plays, *The Conspiracy* and *The Capture*, and such a consideration underlines the unity of effect which the reviser of the Passion sequence, if not of the whole cycle, was striving to achieve. This unity could not be achieved by allowing one acting area to be used for a variety of scenes: Pilate's hall must be reserved exclusively for the scenes in which Pilate appears; God, as throughout the cycle, appears from heaven's tower; Mount Olivet is the hill on which Jesus prays, and below which his disciples sleep; the chamber strewn with rushes, set with table and benches to seat Jesus and the twelve disciples, is also most certainly a fixture throughout this play. The common area then appears to be the ground between this chamber and the other mansions, or stations; and there is every indication dramatically that the capture is staged on ground level midway between Mount Olivet and Pilate's hall.

In reconstructing the staging of *The Conspiracy* the picture that is formed is of four pageants set well apart representing heaven, Pilate's hall, Mount Olivet, and the chamber of The Last Supper, and whatever action does not take place on these pageants, such as the very first passage, in which Jesus dispatches John and Peter to find a room for the paschal feast, and the capture itself, takes place on the ground between the pageants. The pageants are placed at points on the circumference of circle so that the action between the pageants takes place in the centre of the circle. The spectators whether on raked scaffolds or thronging on the ground, fill the gaps on the circumference between the pageants.

IN THE ROUND

The manuscript of the Cornish Plays [*The Ancient Cornish Drama*, edited by Edwin Norris, O.U.P. (1859)] preserves the record of a performance in the round in which the stations in the three parts of the drama, performed on successive days, are designated as follows:

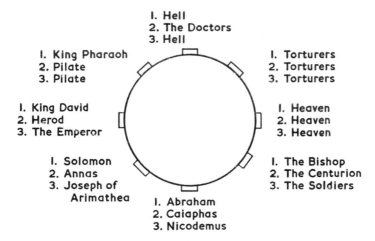

I. Hell
2. The Doctors
3. Hell

I. King Pharaoh
2. Pilate
3. Pilate

I. Torturers
2. Torturers
3. Torturers

I. King David
2. Herod
3. The Emperor

I. Heaven
2. Heaven
3. Heaven

I. Solomon
2. Annas
3. Joseph of Arimathea

I. The Bishop
2. The Centurion
3. The Soldiers

I. Abraham
2. Caiaphas
3. Nicodemus

The stage directions refer frequently to the 'platea', 'the place', the central area separating the pageants, where a great deal of the action takes place and where on occasion an additional mansion is established, as for instance the prison in *The Resurrection* in which Nicodemus and Joseph of Arimathea are confined. The plays were performed in one of the Cornish amphitheatres which accommodated the audience on the tiered seats leading down to 'the place'. The audience and the established mansions, as shown in the diagram, were placed alternately on the circumference of the amphitheatre.

Another indisputable record of medieval drama in the round is the ground plan which appears in the manuscript of *The Castle of Perseverance*, a morality play of about 1425. Richard Southern in a detailed examination of the staging of this play (*The Medieval Theatre in the Round,* Faber and Faber, 1957) reconstructs the original use of the main acting areas which were the mansions on the circumference and 'the place' in the centre. We are given to understand that *The Castle of Perseverance* was not performed in an already established amphitheatre, but that such a theatre had to be made—an obscure procedure—but the event is clear. The castle stands on stilts in the centre of 'the place' with a bed beneath its long legs; there are five mansions or scaffolds on the circumference; part of the audience have fixed seats on the embankment or hill overlooking 'the place' and a limited number move about in 'the place' following the drama from scaffold to scaffold.

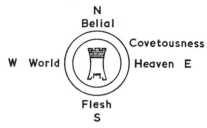

On the original plan it is the south scaffold which appears at the top but it will be more readily seen from the above diagram that the relationship of heaven to hell (east and north) corresponds exactly with that found in the Cornish Plays. Also omitted from the diagram are a great many details relative to the staging of *The Castle of Perseverance.* For example, a number of stewards (stytelerys) are required to keep the audience in order in 'the place', and to clear the way in front of the main characters when they have to cross from one scaffold to another.

Some of the plays in the Digby manuscript (*The Digby Mysteries,* edited by F. J. Furnivall, N. Trübner and Co. 1882) also provide strong evidence of their having been performed in the round. In *Herod's Killing of the Children* the knights and Watkin walking about 'the place' (232), the killing of the children in 'the place', the acting area frequently shifting to localities beyond 'the place', and the concluding dance of the virgins, suggest multiple staging in the round. 'The place' is also prominently used in *The Conversion of St. Paul,* where Saul rides with his servants 'about the place and out of the place' (140); the scaffolds of heaven (182), hell (411), Damascus (210), and Jerusalem (14) stand on the circumference of 'the place'. *Mary Magdalene,*

which in itself comprises a miniature cycle, is generally accepted as
having been played in the round, and J. Q. Adams has reconstructed
the arrangement of the pageants around 'the place' (*Chief Pre-Shake-
spearean Dramas,* Boston, 1924).

The devil makes his first entry (357) on a two-tier pageant which is
probably pushed into and around 'the place' before being established
in its stationary position for the rest of the play: 'Here xal entyr þe
prynse of dylles In a stage, and Helle ondyr-neth þat stage. . . .'
Heaven is also a two-tier pageant with a curtained upper stage (1348):
'her xall hevyne opyne and Iesus xall shew hymself'. The ship which
features so regularly in the play is extremely mobile, shaped as a
castle, and drawn or pushed about 'the place', but occupying no
fixed station.

Is there any evidence to suggest that any of the four extant English
Corpus Christi cycles were, as the Cornish Plays, *Mary Magdalene,* or
The Castle of Perseverance, also played in the round? The *Ludus
Coventriae* and *The Castle of Perseverance* have much in common:
they share the same East Midland dialect; they are both strongly
associated with Lincoln; they both contain analagous passages on an
unusual subject in English medieval drama, *The Parliament in Heaven;*
moreover the thirteen-line introductory stanzas of both plays, spoken
by the banner-bearers (*vexillatores*), leave the name of the town, where
the play is to take place, blank. This suggests that performances were
given at a variety of towns in the neighbourhood and that the appropriate town was inserted as occasion demanded. This is consistent
with the practice elsewhere. The Chelmsford *Corpus Christi* plays,
for instance, were performed in a 'pightell', or enclosure, but were also
performed at Malden and Braintree (E. K. Chambers, op. cit., ii. 122),
and of Kent Hardin Craig writes 'There was much dramatic activity
in that part of England, and the first interchange of performances
among towns suggests that these towns must have had stationary stages

and not the pageants of the *Corpus Christi* cycles'. (Hardin Craig, E.R.D., 142.)

It is the similarity of staging that brings the *Ludus Coventriae* and *The Castle of Perseverance* closest together. In the *Ludus Coventriae Adoration of the Magi* Herod, as does Caro of *The Castle of Perseverance*, enters on horseback. He retires to his pageant to dress himself more gorgeously and when he sits on his throne he commands his menials below him. His height above 'the place' is again emphasized when, after the children have been massacred, he congratulates the murderers:

> wele have ʒe wrought
> my ffo is sought
> to deth is he brought
> now come up to me.
>
> (*Ludus Coventriae, The Massacre of the Innocents,* 125–128)

All initial entries in this play appear to be mounted: Herod, his dukes, and the three kings. The riding is stressed by stage directions and dialogue:

> Heyl be ʒe kyngys tweyne
> Fferre rydyng out of ʒour regne.
>
> (*The Adoration of the Magi,* 21–22)

The kings ride along a street or across a market square:

> Sere kyng in trone
> here comyth a-none
> by strete and stone
>   kyngys thre.   (*Ibid.* 135–138)

In this play the relationship of the scaffold to 'the place' corresponds to the use of these areas in both *The Castle of Perseverance* and in the Wakefield Plays. *The Trial of Joseph and Mary* (*Ludus Coventriae*) is preceded by the Summoner who undertakes the identical task of the stewards (stytelerys) of *The Castle of Perseverance*, clearing a path in 'the place' for the more important characters:

> A-voyd Serys And lete my lorde þe buschop come
> And syt in þe courte þe lawes ffor to doo
> And I xal gon in þis place them for to somowne
> tho þat ben in my book. . . .
>
> (*Prologue of the Summoner,* 1–3)

The two Passion plays of the *Ludus Coventriae*, in so many ways resembling the Wakefield Passion sequence, abound with references to the scaffolds of Annas and Caiaphas, to the castle representing Jerusalem, and to Mount Olivet. Particularly interesting is the use of an oratory in the centre of 'the place' which serves as a counsel house for the Jews. Setting a mansion in the middle of 'the place' corresponds to the use of the bed and the castle in *The Castle of Perseverance*. When not the focus of the action the curtains round the oratory are closed; when the action returns to the oratory they are opened:

'here Crist enteryth in-to þe hous with his disciplis and ete þe paschal lomb and in þe mene tyme þe cownsel hous beforn-seyd xal sodenly onclose shewyng þe buschopys prestys and jewgys syttyng in here Astat lyche as it were A convocacyone'

(*Ludus Coventriae*, The First Passion Play, 397.)

Similarly there are curtains round the pageant on which the Last Supper is played:

'Here The Buschopys partyn in þe place and eche of hem takyn here leve be contenawns resortyng eche man to his place with here meny to make redy to take cryst and þan xal þe place þer cryst is in xal sodeynly un-close rownd Abowtyn shewyng cryst syttyng at þe table and his dyscypulys eche in ere degre . . .'

(*Ibid.* 669.)

The scene is set for the capture of Jesus. The bishops and their men have dispersed to their various pageants on the circumference of 'the place', and when Jesus and his disciples re-enter 'the place' his enemies converge on him from all sides, 'weyl be-seen in white Arneys and breganderys (body armour) and some dysgysed in odyr garmentys with swerdys gleyvys and other straunge wepone as cressettys with feyr and lanternys and torchis lyth (lit) and judas formest of Al conveyng hem to jhesu be contenawns (signs)'

(*Ibid.* 972.)

The same system of staging is maintained in *The Second Passion Play* which begins with the following stage direction:

'What tyme þat processyon is enteryd in to þe place and þe herowdys takyn his schaffalde. and pylat and annas and cayphas here schaffaldys Also þan come þer An exposytour in doctorys wede þus seyng' and goes on to clinch the case for performance in the round with that superb entry of the news-boy:

'here xal A massanger com in-to þe place rennyng and criyng Tydyngys tydyngys . and so rownd Abowth þe place . jhesus of nazareth is take . Jhesus of nazareth is take . . .'

(Ludus Coventriae, The Second Passion Play, 69.)

The *Ludus Coventriae*, then, resembles *The Castle of Perseverance* in that it was presented as a stationary performance in the round in or near Lincoln during at least the middle part of the fifteenth century. Its use of scaffolds and 'the place' tallies in every way with the staging arrangements of the morality play. An essential difference, of course, is that whereas the *Ludus Coventriae* or Lincoln cycle was organized and performed in the main by members of a religious guild to celebrate a religious festival, *The Castle of Perseverance* was performed by a touring company of professional actors. The morality play is some 3,800 lines long and, although there may have been a fair amount of doubling, the main parts, such as Humanum Genus, Belial, and Covetousness, would have been played by the same actors throughout. Would this principle of casting have been so different in the *Ludus Coventriae*? At York, where the average length of each play is 273 lines, we assume from the records that twenty-seven different actors played the part of Jesus in the twenty-seven different plays in which the part occurs. But in the *Ludus Coventriae* the two *Passion* plays, which as far as we know were never played consecutively in the same year, each exceeds 1,000 lines, and their performance by the same group of actors would obviously achieve greater unity of dramatic effect. Indeed, it is difficult to believe how the York fragmentation of the great cycle was ever tolerated. Certainly, an audience used to the continuity of playing of the *Ludus Coventriae* and of *The Castle of Perseverance* would have taken hard the York division of plays, parts, and playing space.

Despite the many affinities of the York and Wakefield cycles, fundamental disparities preclude our assuming identical staging conditions. The Wakefield Plays are fewer but on average appreciably longer; their organization and direction were by a religious guild or the town corporation at least until the sixteenth century; and there is very strong evidence, especially in the *Passion* sequence, of continuity of playing: *The Conspiracy* runs straight into *The Buffeting, The Buffeting* into *The Scourging, The Scourging* into *The Crucifixion*, and

The Crucifixion into *The Talents*. It is significant, too, that in this sequence which so clearly suggests a multiple stage, set in a circle round 'the place', none of the plays has any close association with those of York.

On the other hand, it is demonstrably on matters of staging that the Wakefield cycle reveals its affinities to the *Ludus Coventriae*. The fixed locality and the multiple stage have already been discussed as points of resemblance between the two cycles. This resemblance extends to performance in the round. Although the main setting for the *Ludus Coventriae* is stationary throughout there are two occasions on which pageants are moved into 'the place', in *Noah* (197) and in *The Trail of Joseph and Mary* (124). Such entries are not uncommon in plays performed in the round and in the Digby *Mary Magdalene* the ship on wheels and hell pageant make similar appearances. The Wakefield *Noah* also demands the drawing into 'the place' of a ship on wheels. The acting areas required are heaven for God, Noah's home, a station ('the place') beneath heaven where Noah stands to hear God's commands, and the ark itself. The producer's particular problem is that Noah has to build his ark in the full view of the audience in the course of a thirty-six line soliloquy. The ark has sail, mast, helm, and castle, a door, a window and three chambers. When Noah has finished building his ark he tries to persuade his wife to come aboard, but she persists in spinning on her hill (337). The 'hill' throughout the Wakefield Plays is referred to as the lowest level on the pageant above 'the place'. Mrs. Noah would scarcely refer to her position as 'this hill' if the ark were being constructed on the same pageant above where she was sitting. The following staging is suggested: Noah speaks to God beneath heaven's tower and God answers him giving him precise instructions for the building of the ark; Noah returns home, crossing 'the place' to his own pageant, where the first fight with his wife takes place; he then collects his tools and leaves the pageant (245) and draws into 'the place' a platform on wheels containing the ark in prefabricated sections, which Noah erects as he soliloquizes (253–288), commenting on each section of the ark as he puts it in position; he then returns home to fetch his family; Noah's wife inspects the ark; and returns to her hill in disgust; another fight ensues before all are aboard the ark, and after the waters have abated the family disembark and stand in 'the place' ('on this greyn' 534), and finally in procession lead their ark out of 'the place'.

The bringing of a pageant into 'the place' gives great flexibility to the movement of a production and echoes not only the instances quoted above from the *Ludus Coventriae* and *Mary Magdalene* but also the use of the oratory in the *Ludus Coventriae First Passion Play*. It will further be recalled that in *The Castle of Perseverance* the middle of 'the place' is occupied by the castle itself beneath which is a bed. The rubrics written on the ground plan suggest that the most important parts of the action of the play are to be seen in this area. An unusual detail in the Wakefield *Offering of the Magi* is the bed or litter in which the three kings sleep (590); its central position, between Herod's pageant and the Nativity pageant, tallies also with the placing of the bed of Ananias in the Fleury *Conversion of St. Paul* (Grace Frank, op. cit., 46) which is set in 'the place' between the main acting scaffolds.

The frequency of the journey motif is a characteristic of drama in the round, and the Wakefield Plays and the *Ludus Coventriae* share this characteristic to a high degree: *The Slaying of Abel, Abraham*, the two *Shepherds' Plays, The Offering of the Magi, The Flight, The Peregrini*, are a few of the many Wakefield Plays in which the action is dependent upon journeying. Such plays are much more satis-factorily staged in the round, and the whole Passion sequence gains greatly in dramatic power if 'the place' is used for the capture of Christ and for the procession of the cross in *The Scourging* and *The Crucifixion*, culminating in the climb (out of 'the place' and on to the pageant) to Mount Calvary.

RECONSTRUCTION

An attempt at reconstructing the staging of the Wakefield Plays, however controversial, is worth while. For the first time it takes into account the combined evidence of the Wakefield Burgess Court Banns of 1554 and 1556, the York Diocesan Court records of 1576, internal evidence from the plays themselves, and argument by analogy with other medieval plays performed in the round. The most uncertain feature of such a reconstruction is not how the plays were performed but when they were performed. Evidence points equally to either Whit week or *Corpus Christi* week. The probability is that the plays were not performed in Whit week until after Queen Mary's death in 1558, and also that they were performed not all on one day but on three.

In Wakefield then in the mid-fifteenth century, soon after dawn on *Corpus Christi* day, between twenty and thirty pageants, gaily painted and garlanded with flowers, set out on the *Corpus Christi* procession. The organization for the procession has been carried out by one of the religious guilds, that of St. Christopher or St. George. The trade guilds have given their full co-operation and now in their several liveries join the procession, each guild keeping close to the pageant with which it is most closely associated. Every citizen joins in the procession including all the clergy and the minstrels who are specially paid for their playing and singing on this occasion. The whole procession moves first to the parish church where at the service the Host of the Lord is raised and then carried out of the church, with the procession following, to various stations in the town. When the pageants reach these stations they reveal in dumb-show the climax of the play which they will perform in full on the days that follow. It is these tableaux that we see represented in all kinds of medieval iconography, in which, as for instance with the capture of Christ in the garden, so many incidents of the play are compressed within the one scene: the kiss of Judas, the soldiers seizing Christ, Peter striking off Malcus' ear, and Christ healing the wound. There are not as many pageants in the procession as there are plays in performance because many of the pageants are shared, as at Chester, by different plays. Some pageants therefore display two or more tableaux. But the whole procession winds on through the town until at last it returns to the parish church—a full day's journey.

The plays are performed on the three days that follow: the first day ends with *The First Shepherds' Play;* the second day begins with *The Second Shepherds' Play* and ends with *The Crucifixion;* the third day, which includes the (now missing) plays of Pentecost and of the death, assumption, and coronation of the Virgin, ends with *The Judgement.* The presentation takes place on the common, in the market place, or in the quarry, but each year there is only one place of performance, and here the audience gathers from far and near to secure a seat in the raked, circular auditorium that surrounds 'the place'. There are four or five gaps in the circle of the audience's scaffolds into which will be led the pageants. Heaven and hell are brought into position first and are left in place throughout the performance, heaven to the east and hell to the north. These two pageants are particularly more elaborate in design than the others. They are both two-tiered. On heaven's battlements God, the angels and the angelic choir appear. Beneath heaven's tower is paradise, and above it is the deep roof of the pageant which contains the winches, rope, and windlass, the lowering equipment required for such special effects as the ascension. It is on hell's tower that the devils set the watches on the walls [*The Deliverance* (121)] and beneath hell's tower that limbo is located. Close to limbo are the gaping jaws of hell through which the actors pass by trap-door to the ground level beneath the pageant. The hell pageant resembles that found in the *Ludus Coventriae, The Castle of Perseverance,* and *Mary Magdalene.* Access from the hell pageant to 'the place' is made through the jaws of hell; in the case of the other pageants it is made by sets of steps or ladders, such as we see in Fouquet's mid-fifteenth-century painting of the Martyrdom of St. Apollonia (*Le Livre d'heures d'Etienne Chevalier, Musée Condé, Chantilly*).

Although the pageants of heaven and hell are fixtures throughout the performance the other pageants are moved into place in the course of the cycle. For instance, the cycle begins with the pageants of *The Slaying of Abel* and *Noah* already in position, but during *Noah* the platform on which the ark is to be constructed is wheeled into the middle of 'the place', and by the time of the Nativity plays the earlier pageants have been replaced by those of the Shepherds or the Magi. During the latter play the litter for the Magi is located in the centre of 'the place'. During the Passion sequence the maximum number of pageants are in use simultaneously. Throughout a restricted number of the audience is permitted to sit or stand in 'the place'.

The players themselves are members of the religious guild which organizes and produces the play. Altogether there are about a hundred in the cast and there is a fair amount of doubling, but the main characters are played by the same actors throughout the cycle. If the itinerant professional players are available, and the funds run to it, they may take the main parts, as they do for other local religious festivals (Glynne Wickham, *Early English Stages,* Appendix C, 332–339). At the end of the third day's performance the *Te Deum* following the last words of *The Judgement* is sung by amateur and professional, by players and spectators, laymen and clergy, as a communal affirmation of faith in God and in that structured, hierarchical universe revealed in their cycle of mystery plays.

MUSIC

The liturgical roots of the mystery plays are clearly seen in the persistence of the identical church music at the various dramatic climaxes: God creates the world, and the angels sing the *Te Deum;* Gabriel hails Mary at the Annunciation; the *Gloria* is sung by the angel to the shepherds; the souls delivered from hell burst into a joyful *Salvator Mundi;* as Christ rises from the tomb the two angels sing *Christus Resurgens.* The Latin words of the liturgical music also persist into the sixteenth-century performances of the plays and the music itself, when it records a divine intervention, is played and sung by the angelic choir. The vernacular songs, such as the shepherds' 'As I rode out' or the lament of the Bethlehem mothers, 'Lully, lulla' (The Coventry Shearmen and Taylors' Play), are a later development.

A wide variety of instruments was used in liturgical drama, and records at Coventry, Lincoln, and Beverley indicate that an even greater variety was introduced for the performance of the mystery plays. The recent production by the New York Pro Musica of the thirteenth-century *The Play of Daniel* has stressed the range and effectiveness of medieval instrumentation. Noah Greenberg, the musical director of that production, has listed some of the medieval instruments and their possible modern substitutes:

straight trumpet	trumpet in C
rebec	oboe
recorders (soprano and sopranino)	soprano recorder
bowed vielle	viola
bell carillon	bell carillon or chimes
hand bells	hand bells
psaltery	zither or auto harp (without dampers)
portative organ	soprano recorder (or modern organ)
minstrel's harp	guitar

(*The Play of Daniel*, edited by Noah Greenberg, O.U.P., 1959.)

A particular feature of this production was the identification of each character with particular sounds: 'the Queen with finger cymbals, Darius with small cymbals, the envious counselors with sleigh bells. . . .'

This, in a more general way, is true of the mystery plays: God and
the angels are characterized by harmony; Satan and his rout by
cacophony. In *The Judgement*, as the trump of doom issues intermittently from heaven's battlements, Tutivillus boasts of his own
signature tune, and the mangled Latin that follows is but a verbal echo
of his discordant blast:

> Mi name is tutiuillus,
> my horne is blawen;
> ffragmina verborum tutiullus colligit horum,
> Belzabub algorum belial belium doliorum.
>
> (*The Judgement*, 249–250.)

Such a horn-blowing devil in hell's tower is included among Dr.
W. L. Hildburgh's illustrations for his 'English Alabaster Carvings as
Records of the Medieval Religious Drama' (*Archaeologia* 1949).

The main use of the instruments would be to accompany the singing,
the ceremonial processions, and the entries, such as that of Herod or
Pharaoh. In the *Ludus Coventriae Massacre of the Innocents*, for example,
even the entry of a banquet dish is the occasion for a fanfare:

> SENESCALLUS.   now blowe up mynstrall with all ʒour might þe
> servyse comyth in sone.
>
> (153–154)

And at the grand climax of this play when Herod, swollen with pride,
on the brink of an orgiastic celebration at the supposed slaughter of
Christ, is touched by the finger of Death and received with his henchmen into the jaws of hell, the fanfare sounds his last farewell:

> HEROD.   Amonges all þat grett rowthe
> he is ded I have no dowte
> þerfore menstrell rownd a-bowte
> blowe up a mery fytt.   (229–232)

> (*Hic dum buccinant mors interficiat herodem et duos milites subito et
> diabolus recipiat eos.*)

On the other hand, it is the ringing of bells that attend the Nativity
and the Resurrection.

Who were the Wakefield minstrels who were paid 3s. 4d. for their
part in the *Corpus Christi* plays in 1556? They were certainly a

trained group of musicians, singers and instrumentalists, who could
sing and play polyphonic music from memory; and since it was the
churchwarden who was responsible for paying them, there can be little
doubt of their close connection with the Wakefield Parish Church.
They would represent a range of voices, men and boys together. The
boys would have not only sung in the angel choir, but most probably
would have spoken the angels' parts. One of the grand processional
scenes in the York plays is Christ's entry into Jerusalem. A choir of
boys, walking in front of the procession, as they sing lead Christ to
the gates of the city:

FIRST BURGHER.   Go we þan with processione
                 To mete þat comely as vs awe,
                 With myghtfull songes her on a rawe,
                 Our childir schall
                 Go synge before, þat men may knawe
                 To þis graunte we all.
                 (The York Plays, *The Entry Into Jerusalem*, 260–266.)

It is evident from Roger Burton's 1415 list and synopsis of the York
cycle that the part of the angel at the Resurrection was played by a
boy:

'. . . *Juvenis sedens ad sepulcrum indutus albo, loquens mulieribus.*'
                                 ('York Plays', L. T. Smith, xxvi.)

Both angelic choir and angelic instruments are located in heaven's
tower, which, when performances of religious drama left the precincts
of the church, fulfilled largely the dramatic and ceremonial function
that had previously been allotted to the '*pulpitum*', or rood screen loft.

The Wakefield Plays are not rich in reference to the playing or
singing of music. The stage directions are appreciably less expansive
than in the other cycles. Therefore in suggesting appropriate music
for the plays recourse is had, at comparable stages of the drama, to
information derived from the other cycles. For instance, Noah's
psalm (432) is suggested by the singing included in the Chester play
of *Noah*, the shepherds' song, 'As I Rode Out', and the Bethlehem
women's lament, 'Lully lulla', are derived from the Coventry Shearmen and Taylors' Play, and the singing as Christ goes to sit in Judgement (88) is taken from York's *The Judgement Day* (216).

Play	Music	Source
The Creation	Creator of the Stars of Night	Plainsong
	Te Deum (18), Sanctus (60)	,,
Noah	Psalm (432)	,,
Abraham		
Pharaoh	Psalm 106 (431)	,,
The Prophets	David sings as he plays his harp (109–156)	,,
The Annunciation	Qui Natus Est (76)	Fayrfax Series
	Angelus ad Virginem (373)	English Gothic Music
The Salutation	Ave Regina	Fayrfax Series
The First Shepherds' Play	Gloria in excelsis (295)	Dunstable
	The Shepherds' imitation (430)	
	Nowell Sing We (502)	Medieval Carols
The Second Shepherds' Play	'As I rode Out' (189)	Coventry Play
	Gloria (637)	Dunstable
	Shepherds' imitation (664)	
	Now Make We Merthe (754)	Medieval Carols
The Adoration of the Magi	Sanctus (594)	Roy Henry
The Flight into Egypt		
Herod the Great	Lully, Lulla (324)	Oxford Carols
John the Baptist	Benedictus (200)	Plainsong
The Crucifixion	Faithful Cross (666)	,,
The Deliverance of Souls	Salvator Mundi (44)	Fauxbourdon
	Te Deum (404)	Plainsong
The Resurrection	Christus Resurgens (225)	Fauxbourdon
The Judgement	Salvator Mundi (88)	,,
	Dies Irae played line by line (531–612) on the trombone	Plainsong
	Alleluia psallat (612)	English Gothic Music
	Gloria (612)	Dunstable
	Te Deum (620)	Plainsong

This list does not contain detailed directions concerning the fanfares. Furthermore the list does not imply that in each case the whole psalm, anthem, or hymn is to be sung. This practice would impede rather than enhance the drama.

Generally speaking the music here suggested is on the one hand the elaborate polyphonic music of the fourteenth and fifteenth centuries, which is more appropriate for the angelic choir, and on the other the plainsong hymns more suitable for a crowd response. The instrumentalists, a group of woodwind and brass, might play from *Six Instrumental Pieces for Wind Instruments* by H. Isaac *c.* 1500 (*Hortus Musicus* 29). Sources for the choral music are as follows:

The plainsong hymns will be found in 'Songs of Syon', edited by G. R. Woodward. Schott 1923.

Angelus ad Virginem ⎱ English Gothic Music Series
Alleluia psallat ⎰ Schott 1943

Gloria   Musica Britannica, Vol. viii (Dunstable) edited by M. F. Bukofzer (Stainer and Bell 1953).

Old Hall MS Volume III—Plainsong and Medieval Music Society Publications 1933–1938.

Ave Regina ⎱ published in full in the Fayrfax Series of Early
Qui Natus Est ⎰ English Music. Stainer and Bell, edited A. T. Batts.

Lully, Lulla   Coventry Carol. The Oxford Book of Carols, reprinted 1956.

Nowell Sing We ⎱ Musica Britannica, Vol. iv (Medieval
                ⎬ Carols), edited by John Stevens. Stainer
Now Make We Merthe ⎰ and Bell 1952.

THE PRESENT VERSION

The order of plays in this acting edition differs from that found in the manuscript and reproduced in George England's edition of 1897. *The Prophets* follows, instead of preceding, *Pharaoh;* and *Lazarus* and *The Hanging of Judas,* instead of following *The Judgement,* are returned to their usual places in the cycle, the former, as the only play representing Christ's ministry, following *John the Baptist,* and the latter following *The Scourging.* In performance *The Hanging of Judas,* since it is an incomplete, undramatic monologue, written at a much later date than the rest of the cycle, must be omitted, and the continuity of playing maintained between *The Scourging* and *The Crucifixion.*

Two plays, *The Creation* and *Abraham,* incomplete in the manuscript, have been completed in this edition with borrowings from the York play of *Man's Disobedience and Fall from Eden* and from the Brome play of *Abraham and Isaac* respectively. *The Creation* cries out for completion, and dramatically it seemed feeble to launch this great cycle with a fragment. *Abraham*, prefiguring God's sacrifice of his Son, is strategically placed in the cycle, and requires but a few borrowed lines to make it presentable. These are the only two instances of borrowing. The other incomplete plays in the cycle are *Isaac, The Prophets, The Purification of Mary, The Doctors, The Ascension*, and *The Judgement*. *Isaac* is too fragmentary for dramatic presentation and is therefore, with *The Hanging of Judas*, printed in italics. The other plays, some without heads and others without tails, have sufficient dramatic form to warrant presentation.

This version is complete and tallies line for line with the original. The principles underlying it are that it should be directed more towards the audience than the reader, that it should be generally intelligible without making any prerequisite demands on audience or reader of a knowledge of Middle English, and that the metrical and stanzaic structure, even where there was roughness and irregularity, should be retained. The obligation of, at times, maintaining complicated rhyme schemes has resulted in certain inconsistencies: 'thou', 'ye', 'you' are sometimes, as in the original, used indiscriminately; the Second Person Singular of the verb after 'thou' mostly appears without a final 't', and such was the fifteenth-century Yorkshire practice, but 'thou has' and 'thou shall' may sound strange to southern ears. 'Ay' (as in 'say') throughout carries the meaning of 'for ever', and 'aye' (as in 'eye') means 'yes'.

The stage directions which, in the original, are written mostly in Latin are here translated and many more added.

The Notes

The Notes are primarily for the producer. Their emphasis however is not so much on how the plays might be performed today, but rather through the illustration of guild accounts, iconography, and the collateral drama, on how they were performed in the Middle Ages.

Both in the Notes and the Introduction the *Ludus Coventriae* figures prominently. This is such a misleading title that I have hesitated long before adopting it. The alternatives, the Lincoln Plays, the Hegge Plays, the N-town Plays, might still bewilder the student who, if anxious to put his hand on the text of the plays, can do so only by consulting his library catalogue under *Ludus Coventriae*, K. S. Block, O.U.P., 1922.

Part One

The First Play: The Creation

GOD	1ST GOOD ANGEL
CHERUBIM	2ND GOOD ANGEL
LUCIFER	1ST DEVIL
1ST BAD ANGEL	2ND DEVIL
2ND BAD ANGEL	ADAM
	EVE

GOD *sits upon his throne. His angels stand either side of him.*

GOD   *Ego sum alpha et omega,*
I am the first, the last also,
  One god in majesty;
Marvellous of might most,
Father, Son and Holy Ghost,
  One god in trinity.

I am without beginning,
My godhead hath no ending,
  And thus shall keep my throne;
One god in persons three,
Which may never parted be,
  For I am God alone.

All manner of things is in my thought,
Without my power there may be nought,
  All things are in my sight;
It shall be done after my will,
What I have planned I shall fulfil
  And maintain with my might.

At the beginning of our deed
Make we heaven and earth with speed,
  And fair lights for to see,
For it is good to be so;
Darkness from light we part in two,
  In time to serve and be.

Darkness we shall call the night,
And the brightness be named light,
    It shall be as I say;
After my will forth is brought,
Even and morn both are they wrought,
    And thus is made a day.

Amidst the water we assent
Now be made the firmament,
    Parted be they as is reckoned,
Be water from the land withdrawn,
Bring to pass both even and morn,
    This day which is the second.

The waters that so wide have spread,
Be gathered together in one stead,
    That dry the earth may seem;
Thereafter dry the earth shall be,
The waters shall I call the sea;
    This work well done I deem.

Herbs out of the earth shall spring,
Trees shall flourish and fruit forth bring,
    Of each kind at my word.
According to my will, so be
The even and morn at my decree
    Of this day that is third.

Sun and moon set in the heaven,
With the stars and planets seven,
    To stand in their degree.
The sun to serve the day with light,
The moon to minister at night;
    The fourth day shall this be.

The fish shall dwell within the deep,
The earth shall nourish all beasts that creep,
    That fly or stalk their way.
Multiply on earth, and be
Blessed abundantly by me;
    Thus then ends the fifth day.

CHERUBIM   Our Lord God in trinity,
62   Joy and love are due to thee,
            Our tribute before everything:
            For thou hast made at thy bidding,
            Heaven and earth and all that is,
            That joy shall never come amiss.
            Lord, thou art so full of might,
            Thou hast made Lucifer so bright;
            We love thee, Lord; bright are we
            But none of us so bright as he:
            Lucifer is that lord's name
            For he bears so bright a flame.
            He is so beauteous and so bright
            It is great joy to see that sight;
            We praise thee, Lord, with all our thought,
            That such things could make of nought.

               GOD *withdraws from his throne.*

LUCIFER   Certain it is a seemly sight,
            Since that we are all angels bright,
               And ever in bliss to be;
            If but ye behold me right,
               Worship is due to me.
            I am so fair and bright,
            From me comes all this light,
               This glamour and this glee;
            Against so great a might
               May no resistance be.

            As ye may well behold
            I am a thousandfold
               Brighter than is the sun;
            My strength may not be told,
            Know of my might may none;
               In heaven, therefore, I hold
            Myself above everyone.

            For I am lord of bliss,
            My toe the world may kiss,
               My mirth is most of all;
            Therefore, my will is this,
               Master ye shall me call.

And when I come into my own,   99
How seemly may I mount the throne
    As king of bliss;
I am so bright of blood and bone,
    My seat shall be there as was his.

LUCIFER sits in God's throne.

Say, fellows, how fits it me
To sit in seat of trinity?
I am so bright in every limb
I trust I seem as well as him.

1ST BAD
ANGEL
    In my sight thou art so fair,
Thou dost well to sit up there;
    And so it seems to me.

1ST GOOD
ANGEL
    I warn you leave your vanity,
For none may sit therein but he
    Who in his might all dooms decree.

2ND GOOD
ANGEL
    Cease your ill sport, I tell you plain,
For well I know you jest in vain;
He was never suited to that stall
So well as him that has made all.

2ND BAD
ANGEL
    Think you not Lucifer more fit,
He seems full worthy there to sit;
He is so fair without a lie,
Most worshipful to sit on high.
Therefore, fellow, hold your peace;
Prize first the sheep by its fine fleece.
He seems as worthy to sit there
As God himself if He were here.

LUCIFER
    Dear fellows, think ye not so?

1ST BAD
ANGEL
    Yea, by God, and more we know.

1ST GOOD
ANGEL
    Not us. His worship we forswear.

[4]

LUCIFER 130	Now thereof not a leek I care. Since I am myself so bright Therefore will I take a flight.

LUCIFER *tries to fly upwards above* GOD'S *throne but with the other* BAD
ANGELS *is thrust down to hell. They all shout and wail as they are driven
downwards.*

Immediately after the fall the DEVILS *emerge howling from hell-mouth.*

1ST DEVIL	Alas, alas, I wail for woe! Lucifer, why fell you so? We that were angels so fair, And sat so high above the air, Now we are made as black as coal, And ugly, tattered as a foal. What ailed thee, Lucifer, to fall? Wast thou not fairest of angels all? Brightest and best, and in the love Of God himself that sits above? Of orders ten now there are nine; That face is dark that once did shine; Fallen, who on God once leaned, From an angel to a fiend. Vile has been thy pride and vain, To rob thy bliss and bring thee pain. Alas there is nought else to say, But we are beaten, now and ay.

2ND DEVIL	Alas, the joy that we were in Is lost forever for our sin. Alas that ever came pride in thought, For it has brought us all to nought. With mirth and joy we were endowed Till Lucifer waxed over proud. Alas, we rue such wicked pride, As may ye all that stand beside. We listened to the lies he spread, And now from us our peace is fled. Our joy is lost and cannot mend, And pain our lot without an end.

[5]

The DEVILS *disappear into hell-mouth.*
GOD *sits upon his throne. The* GOOD ANGELS *stand by him.*

GOD   Creatures of earth that creep or fly,   162
      Bring forth your young and multiply;
       I see that it is good;
      Now in our likeness make we man,
      Who shall govern as he can
       All fowl and fish in flood.

GOD *stretches forth his hand.* ADAM *rises slowly until he stands beneath*
GOD'S *throne, a little lower than the* ANGELS.

      Spirit of life in thee I blow,
      Good and ill both shalt thou know;
       Rise up and stand by me.
      All that is in water or land,
      All shall bow unto thy hand,
       And sovereign shalt thou be.

      I give thee wit, I give thee strength,
      Of all thou seest, the breadth and length,
       Be wonderfully wise.
      Mirth and joy to have at will,
      And thy pleasure to fulfil,
       And dwell in paradise.

During the following lines a heaviness comes upon ADAM. *He lies down and sleeps.*

      This I make thy living place,
      Full of pleasure and solace,
       And thee I set therein.
      It is not good to be alone,
      To enjoy this treasure on thine own
       Without one of thy kin.

During what follows a GOOD ANGEL *takes a rib coloured red from*
ADAM'S *side, raises it aloft, then strikes the ground with it and* EVE *issues forth.*

      Therefore a rib from thee I take,
      And thereof a maid shall make
       To be thy helpmeet.

[6]

189   Ye both may govern what here is,
               And evermore may live in bliss
                  Close to my mercy-seat.

ADAM *and* EVE, *standing, admire each other and the world around them.*

               Ye shall have joy and bliss therein,
               While ye keep yourselves from sin,
                  And so your joy increase.
               Rise up, mine angel Cherubim,
               Take and lead them both therein,
                  And leave them there in peace.

The CHERUBIM *who has been kneeling by* GOD's *throne, stands and listens attentively to* GOD's *words but does not move towards* ADAM *and* EVE *until* GOD *has withdrawn.*

               Hear thou Adam and Eve thy wife,
               I forbid ye the tree of life,
               And my commandment must be kept,
               Take what ye will, that tree except.
               Adam, if thou scorn my breath,
               Thou shalt die a doleful death.

CHERUBIM   Our Lord, our God, thy will be done,
               To go with them I shall not shun.
               Indeed, my Lord, I shall not rest
               Till they be brought to that place blessed.
               We thank thee, Lord, with full good cheer,
               That man has made to share joy here.

GOD *withdraws.* CHERUBIM *leads* ADAM *and* EVE *to a lower level—*
paradise
               Come forth, Adam, I shall thee lead;
               Now of my counsel take good heed.
               Be mindful, man, how thou art made,
               In praise ne'er leave the Lord unpaid,
               He that made thee through his will,
               The angels' place in heaven to fill.
               Great bounty in his giving
               Thee mastery of all things living.
               He has forbad thee but a tree;

                        [7]

Look, Adam, that thou leave it be.   219
For if thou break his commandment,
No escape but punishment.
Walk here into paradise,
And warned ye be to be but wise;
And rest you well for I must go
Unto my Lord, his will is so.

CHERUBIM *withdraws into heaven.*

ADAM   Almighty Lord, thanks be to thee
            That is, and was, and ay shall be,
            For thy love and for thy grace,
            For now is here a merry place.
            Eve, my fellow, how find you this?

EVE   A garden it seems of joy and bliss,
            That God has given to thee and me;
            Blessed everlastingly be he!

ADAM   Eve, fellow, abide ye here,
            I will go visit far and near
            To see what trees have planted been;
            For more is here than we have seen:
            Grasses and other small flowers
            That smell so sweet, of many colours.

EVE   Here gladly, sir, I shall remain;
            When you have seen them, come again.

ADAM   But look well, Eve, my wife,
            You come not near the tree of life,
            For if you do we need have dread
            That we be pained as he has said.

EVE   Go forth, and wander all about;
            I shall not near it while you are out,
            For be you sure I were full loth
            To do a thing to make Him wroth.

ADAM *withdraws.*

[8]

LUCIFER, *now changed to* SATAN, *comes out of hell-mouth followed by a rout of* DEVILS.

SATAN 251	Who thought this time had ever been? We that such mirth and joy have seen, That we should suffer so much woe? Whoever would have trusted so? Ten orders in heaven have been Of angels serving as was seen Each in order of degree. The tenth part fell down with me; For they chose me as their guide, And maintained me in their pride; But hark now, fellows, what I say: The joy that we have lost for ay, God has fashioned man his friend, To have that bliss without an end, The fallen angels' place to fill, Which we have left, such is his will. And now are they in paradise, But thence they shall, if we be wise.

My content I shall contrive,
   If I might man betray,
His pleasure to deprive,
   That soon I shall assay.
In a worm's likeness will I wend,
And lead astray with subtle lying.

Moves to paradise.

Eve, Eve!

EVE	Who is there?

SATAN	I am a friend.
	For thy good I am coming,
	   And thee have sought.
	Of all the fruit that ye see hanging
	   In paradise, why eat ye nought?

EVE	We may from every one
	   Take whate'er we thought,
	But one tree we must shun,
	   Or into harm be brought.

[9]

SATAN   And why that tree? that would I know,   282
              More than others standing by?

EVE   For God forbids us near it go
              Nor eat thereof, Adam nor I,
                  We leave for fear;
              And if we did we both should die,
                  He said, and end our pleasures here.

SATAN   Ssss! Eve, now be intent
(*knowingly*)   To heed what thou shalt hear,
              What matter is here meant,
                  That he should chill your cheer.
              To eat thereof he you forbad,
                  I know it well, this was his will,
              Because he would none other had
                  The virtues this tree may instil.
              For wilt thou see,
                  Who eats the fruit, of good and ill
              Shall knowledge have as well as he.

EVE   Why what kind of thing art thou,
                  That tells this tale to me?

SATAN   A worm that knows well how
                  That ye may worshipped be.

EVE   What worship should we win thereby?
                  To eat thereof the need is nought;
              Our lordship is in mastery
                  Of all things that on earth are wrought.

SATAN   Woman, away!
              To greater state ye may be brought,
                  If ye will do as I shall say.

EVE   For no need do we long
                  That should our good dismay.

SATAN   Nay, indeed it is no wrong,
                  Safely to eat ye may.
                      [10]

315   Sure, no peril therein lies,
              But worship for the winning.
          For right as God ye shall be wise,
              And peer with him in everything.
          Aye, Gods shall ye be!
              And of good and ill have knowing,
          For to be as wise as he.

EVE   Is this true that thou say?

SATAN   Yea! why trust thou not me?
          I never would in no way
              Tell ought but truth to thee.

EVE   Thy words have won, my doubts are dashed,
              To fetch this fruit for our own food.

EVE *bites, and* SATAN *writhes in exultation.*

SATAN   Bite on boldly be not abashed,
              And take Adam to amend his mood,
                Also his bliss.

SATAN *withdraws.* ADAM *approaches.*

EVE   Adam! Have here the fruit full good.

ADAM   Alas! Woman, why took thou this?
          Our Lord commanded us both
              To shun this tree of his.
          Thy work will make him wroth,
              Alas! Thou hast done amiss.

EVE   Adam, by grief be nought beset,
              And I shall say the reason why;
          Such wisdom hissed a worm I met,
              We shall as gods be, thou and I,
          If that we ate
              Here of this tree; Adam, deny
          Not such worship for to get.
              For we shall be as wise
          As God that is so great,

[11]

> And so ourselves may prize;   346
> So eat and earn that state.

ADAM   To eat it I would not eschew,
     If certain of thy saying.

EVE   Bite on boldly, for it is true,
     As gods we shall know everything.

ADAM   To win that name
I shall it taste at thy teaching.

ADAM *bites the apple.*

>   Alas! What have I done for shame!
> Ill counsel came from thee!
>   Ah! Eve, thou art to blame,
> That thus enticed thou me;
>   My limbs against me exclaim,
> For I am naked as I think.

EVE   Alas, Adam, right so am I.

ADAM   And for sorrow why might we not sink,
     For we have grieved God almighty
That made me man,
     Broken his bidding bitterly,
Alas! That ever we it began!
     This work, Eve, thou hast wrought,
And made this bad bargain.

EVE   Nay, Adam, chide me nought.

ADAM   Alas, dear Eve, whom then?

EVE   The worm of chiding is most worthy,
     With tales untrue he me betrayed.

ADAM   Alas! I listened to thy story,
     And let with lies thou me persuade.
So may I bide,
     For that rash act I am repaid,

[12]

376   For that deed done I curse my pride.
        Our nakedness me grieves,
    Wherewith shall we it hide?

EVE   Let us take these fig-leaves
    Since they grow here beside.

ADAM   Right as thou say so shall it be,
        For we are naked and all bare.
    Full gladly now I would hide me,
        From my Lord's sight, I know not where,
    So I be not caught.

GOD   (*in his throne*) Adam! Adam!

ADAM   Lord!

GOD   Where art thou, there?

ADAM   I hear thee, Lord, but see thee nought.

GOD   Say, to whom does it belong,
        This work that thou hast wrought?

ADAM   Lord, Eve made me do wrong
    And to this plight me brought.

GOD   Say, Eve, why didst thou Adam make
    To eat the fruit that should hang still,
        Which was commanded none should take?

EVE   A worm, Lord, beguiled my will,
        So welaway!
    That ever I did that deed so ill!

GOD   Ah! Wicked worm, woe wait on thee for ay,
        For thou in this manner
    Hast caused such deep dismay;
        My malediction have thou here,
    With all the might I may.

    And on thy belly shalt thou glide

SATAN *grovels on his belly.*

                    And be ay full of enmity   405
                 To all mankind on every side,
                    And earth thy sustenance shall be
                 To eat and drink.
                    Adam and Eve, also ye
                 From work on earth ye shall not shrink,
                    But labour for your food.

ADAM   Alas! When might we sink,
                    We that had all world's good,
                 Now thrust out as I think.

GOD   Now, Cherubim, my angel bright,
                    To middle-earth quick drive these two.

CHERUBIM *descends from heaven to paradise and at the very end of the play*
drives ADAM *and* EVE *to an even lower level, that of middle-earth.*

CHERUBIM   All ready, Lord, as it is right,
                    It is thy will I seek to do,
                 To thy liking.
                    Adam and Eve, now go you two,
                 For here may ye make no dwelling.
                    Go ye forth fast to fare;
                 Of sorrow may ye sing.

ADAM   Alas! For sorrow and care,
                 Our hands now may we wring.

CHERUBIM *returns to heaven.* ADAM *and* EVE *withdraw.*

The Second Play: The Killing of Abel

BOY   ABEL
CAIN   GOD

BOY   All hail, all hail, be blithe and glad,
For here come I, a merry lad;
Have done your din, my master bad,
     Or else the devil you speed.
Know you not I come before?
And he who jangles any more
Must on my black horn blow a score,
Both behind and before,
     Till his teeth bleed.
     Fellows, look you take good heed,
Never a noise to make nor cry;
Whoever dares to do that deed,
The devil hang him up to dry!

Fellows, I am a full great man,
My master's called a good yoeman.
     Full well ye all him ken;
If with you he starts to strive,
Then certainly you'll never thrive;
But as you hope to keep alive,
     Some of you are his men.
But still your lips and study when
     Best you may speak thereon.
If my master come welcome him then.
He indicates the sort of reception that should be given to CAIN.
     Farewell, for I am gone.
The BOY *runs off.* CAIN *enters ploughing.*

CAIN   Get on, greenhorn, before I scream!
Draw on! Ill-fate may God ye deem.
Ye stand as though ye are in a dream;
     Will ye no farther fare?
Get up! Let's see how ye will draw;
Up bitch! Ye'd scarcely pull a straw.
What! Stand ye in no awe!

[15]

Ye dun nag, why stay ye there?
May God give ye sorrow and care!
Lo! Now heard she what I said;
Now art thou the worst mare
To plough that ever I bred.

CAIN calls to the BOY who appears.

How now, Pickbrain, must alone I strive?

BOY May God forbid that ever ye should thrive!

CAIN What, boy, must I both hold and drive?
   Hearst thou not how I cry?

Calling to CAIN's oxen and horses.

BOY Say, Mall and Stott, will ye not go?
   Leming, Morrell, White-horn, oh!
    Now will ye not see how they hie?

CAIN God give thee sorrow, boy; and of meat a lack.

BOY Their food, sir, therefore, I lay on their back,
   And tied the bags tight at the head,
   Within not hay but stones instead.

CAIN Your tricks one day will cost your head.

BOY Not before I have done my spite.

CAIN I am thy master, wilt thou fight?

BOY Yea, I shall measure with thee my might;
   What I borrow I shall requite.
  They fight.

CAIN Lo, now, no more! I would ere night
   That we ploughed this land.

BOY Faster Morrell, step you light—
   And let the plough stand. *(Aside.)*
  ABEL enters.

ABEL God, as he both may and can,
   Speed thee, brother, and thy man.

[16]

CAIN Come kiss my arse, God curse our clan,
60   Ye get from me no welcome hail.
     Ye should have stayed till ye were called;
     Come near and either drive or hold,
          And kiss the devil's tail.
     Go feed your sheep, man, in the dale,
     And much ill luck achieve.

ABEL Brother, why thus on me ye rail?
     Thee no one here would grieve.
     But dear brother hear my speech:
     The customs of our law us teach
     All that work should take advice
     And worship God with sacrifice.

     Our fathers bad us, and our fathers knew,
     That one tenth part to God was due.
     Come forth, brother, and let us go
     To worship God; why stay we so?
     Part of our goods to God give we
     Corn or cattle whatever it be.

     And therefore, brother, let us go;
     First cleanse us from the fiend, our foe,
          Before we sacrifice
     Then blessings forth shall flow,
          Our service shall suffice.

CAIN Now, let forth your geese the fox will preach!
     Thinkst thou me to appeach
          With thy sermoning?
     Hold still thy tongue, I say,
     As any good wife may,
     Or go the devil's way,
          With thy vain carping.

     Should I leave plough and everything
     To make with thee an offering?
     Nay, thou findst me not so mad.
     Go to the devil, and say I bad!
     What gives God thee to praise him so?
     To me he gives but sorrow and woe.

ABEL   Cain, leave this vain carping,   96
              For God gives thee thy living.

CAIN   Yet borrowed I never a farthing
              Of him, by this hand.

ABEL   Our elders have taught, and they understand,
              To offer to God, each with his hand,
              A tenth of his goods to be burnt with the brand.

CAIN   In the priest's hand lies my farthing
              Since last I offered.

ABEL   Leave, brother, let us be walking;
              I would our tithe were proffered.

CAIN   Wait! Why should I give, dear brother?
              For I am each year worse than another,
              And by my troth it is none other;
                 My making is but mean,
                 No wonder I am lean;
                 Bitter my moans to him have been,
              For, by him that has me saved,
              I doubt he'll give what I have craved.

ABEL   But all the goods you call your own,
              By God's good grace are but a loan.

CAIN   Lends he me as you thrive so?
              For he has ever been my foe;
              For had he my friend been
              Otherwise it had been seen.
              When all men's corn was fair in field,
              Not a needle would mine yield;
              When I should sow and wanted seed,
              And of corn had full great need,
              Then gave he me none of his,
              No more will I give him of this;
              Hardly hold me to blame
              If I serve him with the same.

[18]

ABEL   Dear brother, say not so,
130   But let us forth together go;
        Good brother, let us go with speed,
        To linger here we have no need.

CAIN   Yea, yea, your jangling you waste;
        The devil take me if I haste,
        As long as I may live,
        My goods to share or give
        Either to God or man;
        Keep I shall what goods I can;
        For had I given away my wealth,
        As beggar then with guile and stealth
        My lot would be to save,
        To go from door to door and crave.

ABEL   Brother, come forth in God's name,
        Afraid am I we are to blame:
        Haste we now I thee implore.

CAIN   Go! run on, in the devil's name, before!
        By God, man, I hold thee mad!
        Thinkst thou now that I would gad
        To yield of all my treasures ought?

        The devil speed him that me so taught!
        Why should I my trouble lose,
        And tear my socks while wearing shoes?

ABEL   Dear brother, it were great wonder
        That I and thou should part asunder.
        Then would our father fain ask why;
        Are we not brothers, thou and I?

CAIN   No, but prate on till your wits are dazed,
        Now, by my troth, I count thee crazed;
        Whether he be blithe or wroth,
        To give my goods I am full loth.

        Oft have I stalked a better prize,
        Whence more profit might arise.
        But well I see go must I need;

[19]

Set on before, ill might thou speed!   164
Since notwithstanding we must go.

ABEL   Dear brother, why say you so?
But go we forth both together;
Blessed be God we have fair weather.

ABEL with a sheep and CAIN with a stook of corn climb to a higher level.

CAIN   Lay down thy burden upon this hill.

ABEL   Forsooth, brother, so I will.
God of heaven, take it for good.

CAIN   Now offer first thy livelihood.

ABEL   God that made both heaven and earth,
That has delivered us from dearth,
Now take in thanks if thy will be,
My tithe I offer here to thee;
For I give with good intent
To thee, my Lord, that all has sent.
I burn it now with steadfast thought,
In praise of him that all has wrought.

CAIN   Rise, let me now, since thou hast done.
Lord, hear what boon I have begun!

The tithe that I here give to thee,
Of corn may scarce renew me;
But now begin I in my turn
Since I must needs my tithe now burn.
One sheaf, one, and this makes two,
Yet neither can I spare for you.
Two, two, now this is three,
Yea this also shall stay with me.
By saving all I spare my grief
And count it thrift to keep the sheaf.
Why, look now, four before you here!
Better grew I not this year.
In the spring I sowed fair corn,
Yet was it such when it was shorn:
Thistles and briers in great plenty,
And of weeds all kinds that could be.

[20]

199   Four sheaves, four, lo, this makes five—
The devil, I fast so long ere I thrive—
Five and six, now is this seven,
But this goes never to the God of heaven;
Nor none of these four from my right
Shall ever come within God's sight,
Seven, seven, now this is eight.

ABEL   Cain, brother, come not in God's hate.

CAIN   Therefore is it these things I say,
For I will not give my goods away.
Had I thought to give and not offend,
Then would thou say he were my friend;
But I think not, by my hood,
To forsake what does me good.
Why, eight, eight, and nine, and ten is this.
Yea, this may we best miss.
Give him that from out my store?
It goes against my heart full sore.

ABEL   Cain, tithe rightly as you mean.

CAIN   Yea, lo, twelve, fifteen sixteen.

ABEL   Cain, you offer wrong and of the worst.

CAIN   Come, hide my eyes that nothing is seen;
The waning moon is a time that's cursed;
Or else would you that I slept,
And that way I from wrong were kept?

Let me see now how it is—
Lo, I hold myself well paid,
My tithe I gave away by guess,
Even I an offering made.

ABEL   Cain, of God it seems you take no heed.

CAIN   If he get more the devil him speed!
As much in one swing one may reap
Was given to him—a bargain cheap;

[21]

Not as much great or small,   232
As he might wipe his arse withal.
For that and this that lies here
Have cost me full dear;
Ere it was shorn and made a stack,
Had I many a weary back;
Therefore ask me no more than this,
For I have given what my will is.

ABEL   Cain, I warn thee, tithe aright,
        For dread of his so powerful might.

CAIN   The way I tithe tax not your head,
        But tend thy scabby sheep instead;
        If my tithes you think not true,
        It will be the worse for you.
        Would thou I gave him this sheaf or this sheaf?
        But neither of these two will I leave;
        But take this; now has he two,
        By my soul, that's more than due,
        But it goes sore against my will,
        And he shall like this tithe but ill.

ABEL   Cain, better tithe thou, to the end
        That God of heaven rest your friend.

CAIN   My friend? Nay not unless he will!
        Reason only rules me still.
        If I need not dread him sore,
        I were a fool to give him more.

ABEL   If right thou tithed, such must thou find.

CAIN   Yea, kiss the devil's arse behind!
        The devil hang thee by the neck!
        How I may tithe never thou reck;
        Wilt thou not yet hold thy peace?
        Of this jangling I bid thee cease.
        And tithed I well or tithed I ill,
        To thee its one; keep thy tongue still.

266   But now since thou hast offered thine,
        Now will I set fire to mine.
   Choking smoke comes from the offering.
        Alas! Harrow! Help to blow!
        For me it burns no more than snow;
        Puff! This smoke does me much shame—
        Burn now in the devil's name!
        Ah, what devil of hell is it!
        Almost had my lungs been split.
        Had I blown then one blast more
        I had been choked to death full sore.
        It stank like the devil in hell,
        That longer there I might not dwell.

ABEL   Cain, this is not worth one leek;
        Such smoky offering who should seek?

CAIN   Come kiss the devil right in the arse,
        For this smoke is slow to pass;
        I would that it were in thy throat,
        Fire and sheaf, and wheat and oat.

   GOD *appears above.*

GOD   Cain, why art thou such a rebel
        Against thy brother, Abel?
        To jeer and gibe there is no need,
        If thou tithe right thou getst thy meed;
        But be thou sure if thou tithe ill,
        Repaid thou shalt be thy evil.

   GOD *withdraws.*

CAIN (*sarcastic*) Why, who is that hob-over-the wall?
        Alas, who was that that piped so small?
        Come go we hence from perils all;
          God is out of his wit.
        Come forth, Abel, and let us go;
        I find that God will be my foe,
          From here then must I flit.

   They leave the hill.

ABEL   Ah, Cain, brother, that is ill done.

[23]

CAIN   No, but fast hence let us run;   298
        And if I may, there shall I be
        Where God's eye shall not see me.

ABEL   Dear brother, I will be at hand
        In the field where our beasts stand,
        To see if they be well or sick.

CAIN   Nay, nay, abide, we have a bone to pick.
        Hark, speak with me ere thou go;
        What, thinkst thou thus to escape so?
        Nay a deep debt owe I thee by right,
        And now is time I thee requite.

ABEL   Brother, to me why show you so much spleen?

CAIN   Out, thief, why burnt thy tithe so clean,
        When mine but foully smoked
        As if it would us both have choked?

ABEL   God's will, I trust was here
        That made mine burn so clear.
        If thine smoked, am I to blame?

CAIN   Why, yea, and thou shalt smart with shame;
        With cheek-bone ere my hand I stay
        I shall have torn thy life away.
    CAIN *strikes* ABEL *with a cheek-bone.*
        So lie down there and take thy rest,
        Thus braying curs are chastised best.

ABEL   Vengeance, vengeance, Lord, I cry!
        For I am slain and not guilty.
    ABEL *dies.*

CAIN   Yea, lie thou there, wretch, lie there, lie;
    To the SPECTATORS.
        And if any of you think I did amiss,
        I shall amend it, worse than it is,
            That all men may it see:
    Menacingly.
        Much worse than it is

[24]

328   Right so shall it be.
            But now since he is brought to sleep
            Into some hole I fain would creep;
            For I fear I quake in so sore dread,
            For be I taken I be but dead;
            Here will I lie these forty days,
            And curse him who may first me raise.
      GOD *appears above.*

GOD   Cain, Cain!

CAIN   Who is that that calls me?
            Look, I am here, may thou not see?

GOD   Where is thy brother, Abel?

CAIN   Why ask of me? I think in hell,
            I trust in hell he be—
            As any there might see—
            Or somewhere fallen a-sleeping;
            When was he in my keeping?

GOD   Cain, Cain, thou art caught in a fierce flood;
            The voice of thy brother's blood
            That thou hast slain in such false wise,
            From earth to heaven vengeance cries.
            And for thou hast brought thy brother down,
            Under the flood of my fury drown.

CAIN   Yea, deal out curses, I will none,
            Or give them back when thou hast done.
            Since I have done so great a sin,
            That I may not thy mercy win,
            And thus thou thrust me from thy grace,
            I shall hide me from thy face;
            And if any man may me find,
            Let him slay me and not mind;
            Wheresoever he may me meet,
            Either by sty or in the street;
            And harshly, when that I am dead,
            Bury me in Goodybower at the Quarry Head;

                          [25]

If safe I can this place depart,   361
By all men set I not a fart.

GOD   It is not so, Cain, nay.
No man may another slay,
For he that slays thee, young or old,
He shall be punished sevenfold.

GOD *withdraws.*

CAIN   No matter, I know where I shall go;
In hell for me the fire will glow;
For mercy now to wail is vain,
For that would but increase my pain;
But this corpse I would were hid,
For suddenly might come a swain
And cry "False wretch, now God forbid,
Thou hast thy very brother slain."
If only Pickbrain, my boy, were here,
We both should bury him without a tear.
How, Pickbrain, scape-grace, Pickbrain, how!

BOY *enters.*

BOY   Master, master!

CAIN (*striking him*)   Hearest thou, boy?
There is a pudding in the pot,
Take thou that, boy, take thou that!

BOY   I'd curse thy bones for that last thud,
Though thou wert my sire of flesh and blood;
All day for you I run till I sweat,
And never once your blows withstand,
Buffets as my reward I get.

CAIN   Peace, man, I did it but to use my hand;
But hark, boy, I have counsel to thee to say:
I slew my brother this same day;
I prithee, good boy, if thou may,
To run with me away.

BOY   Alas, out upon thee, thief!
Hast thou thy brother slain?

[26]

CAIN   Peace, man, for God's pain!
394   I said it for a joke.

BOY   Yea, but fearing such another stroke
            Here I thee forsake;
            The hangman's rope will make us choke,
            If us the bailiffs take.

CAIN   Ah, sir, I cry you mercy, cease!
            And I shall give you your release.

BOY   Wilt thou cry my peace
            Throughout this land?
CAIN   Yea, I give God a vow.

BOY   What wilt thou do now?

CAIN   Stand up, my good boy, on my life.
            Peace be to them both man and wife;
            And whoso will do after me,
            Cunning in thrift then shall he be.
            But thou must be my good boy,
            And cry oyez, oyez, oy!

BOY   Broth and dumplings for thy boy.
     CAIN *begins to call out like a town-crier. The* BOY *mocks him in asides.*
CAIN   I command you in the King's name,
BOY   And in my master's too, false Cain,
CAIN   That no man find fault with them nor blame.
BOY   Yea, this cold roast from his home came.
CAIN   Neither with him nor with his boy,
BOY   My master raves now, oyez, oy!
CAIN   For they are true if all were told.
BOY   My master eats no dish but cold.
CAIN   The King writes thus unto you.
BOY   But hot or cold, I lacked my due.
CAIN   Them at least the King will save.
BOY   Yea, for a draught of drink I crave.
CAIN   At their own will let them stray.
BOY   My belly's so empty it starts to bray.
CAIN   Let no man challenge them, one or other.
BOY   This same is he that slew his brother.

[27]

CAIN   Bid them be loved the world throughout.   427
BOY   Yea, ill-spun weft ay comes foul out.
           You'll wear out your hose if you go thus about.
CAIN   Bid every man them please to pay.
BOY   Yea, do give thy horse a wisp of hay.

CAIN (*to the* BOY) Now thou hast trod the devil's way,
                May the fiend thy spirit snatch;
            For, but for Abel, my brother,
            Yet never I knew thy match.

        Speaking from the hill to the SPECTATORS.

BOY   Now old and young, before ye go,
            The same blessing may God bestow
                On all here in this place,
            That he from heaven my master gave.
            Cherish it well, your souls to save,
                Granted was it through God's grace.

CAIN   Come down yet in the devil's way,
                And anger me no more;
            And take yon plough, I say,
                And press on fast before;
            And I shall, if I may,
                Teach thee a lesson sore;
            I warn thee, lad, for ay,
                For now and evermore,
            That thou give me no gall;
                For, by God, and if you do,
                On this plough shalt thou rue,
                Hanged by this rope, lad, too,
            By him that died for all.

    The BOY *goes off pushing the plough.*
            Now farewell, fellows all,
                For now I needs must wend,
            And to the devil be thrall,
                World without end.
            There ready is my stall,
                With Satan, the foul fiend,
            Ever ill might him befall

    Shaking his fist at GOD'S *throne.*

[28]

462   That me thither did commend
                    This tide.
        Farewell great, and farewell small,
        Forever farewell, one and all,
               Accursed I needs must hide.

Exit CAIN.

The Third Play: Noah

NOAH	1ST SON	1ST SON'S WIFE
GOD	2ND SON	2ND SON'S WIFE
NOAH'S WIFE	3RD SON	3RD SON'S WIFE

NOAH   To mighty God I pray, maker of all that is,
          Three persons, no gainsay, one God in endless bliss,
          Thou made both night and day, beast, fowl, and fish,
          All creatures in thy sway, wrought thou at thy wish,
                 As well thou might;
          The sun, the moon, heaven's tent,
          Thou made; the firmament,
          The stars also full fervent,
                 To shine thou made full bright.

          Angels thou made all even, all orders to bless,
          To have the bliss in heaven, this did thou more and less,
          Now laid thereto the leaven, which fermented faithlessness,
          Marvels seven times seven than I can well express;
                 And why?
          Of all angels in brightness,
          God gave Lucifer most lightness,
          Who priding in his rightness,
                 By God himself sat high.

          He thought himself as worthy as he that him made,
          In brightness and beauty, him God had to degrade,—
          Put him in low degree, swiftly from sun to shade,
          Him and his company, howling in hell were laid,
                 For ever.
          They shall never get away
          Hence until doomsday,
          But burn in bale for ay,
                 And never dissever.

[29]

Soon after, that gracious Lord in his likeness made man,
That place to be restored, even as he began,
By the trinity in accord, Adam and Eve, that woman,
To multiply without discord he gave them space and span
    In paradise to both.
He gave in his command,   33
On the tree of life to lay no hand;
But yet the false fiend
    Made him with man wroth;

Enticed man to gluttony, stirred him to sin in pride;
But in paradise surely, may no sin abide,
And therefore man full hastily was sternly thrust outside,
In woe and wandering for to be, with all pains plied
    Without ruth;
First on earth and then in hell
Fiercely with the fiends to dwell,
But to those no harm befell
    Who trusted in his truth.

Oil of mercy through his might he promised, as is said,
To all that strove with right in peace his paths to tread,
But now before his sight all people without dread,
For most part day and night, in word and deed they spread
    Their sin full bold;
Some in pride, anger, and envy,
Some in covetousness and gluttony,
Some in sloth and lechery,
    In ways manifold.

Therefore I dread lest God on us take vengeance,
For sin escapes the rod, without repentance;
Six hundred years and odd has been my existence,
Daily on earth to plod, with great grievance
    Each way;
And now I am old
Sick, sorry and cold,
As muck upon mould,
    I wither away.

But yet I cry for mercy and call;
Noah, thy servant, am I, Lord over all!

66   Therefore me and my fry shall with me fall;
Save from villainy and bring to thy hall
    In heaven;
And keep me from sin
This world within;
Mankind's comely king,
    I pray morn and even.

GOD *appears above.*

GOD   Since I have made each thing that may live and stand,
Duke, emperor, and king with my own hand,
To live to their liking by sea and by land,
Every man to my bidding should come at command
    Full fervent;
That made man such a creature,
Fairest of favour,
Man must heed me as a lover,
    With reason and repent.

Methought I showed man love when I made him to be
All angels above, like to the trinity;
And now in great reproof full low lies he,
On earth no jot aloof from sins which displease me
    Most of all;
Vengeance will I take,
On earth for sin's sake,
My grimness thus will wake
    Both great and small.

I repent full sore that ever made I man,
By me he sets no store, and I am his sovereign;
I will destroy therefore both beast, man and woman,
All shall perish less and more that so spurned my plan,
    And ill have done.
In earth I see right nought
But sin so dearly bought;
Of those that well have wrought
    Find I but one.

Therefore shall I undo all people that are here,
With floods that shall subdue the land both far and near,
I have good cause thereto for now no men me fear,
As I say shall I do, the sword of vengeance rear,
    And make an end—

[31]

Of all that bears life,　　　　　　　　　　105
Save Noah and his wife,
They offered no strife,
　　Nor me did offend.

To him in great joy hastily will go,
Noah shall I not destroy, but warn him of his woe.
Men on earth their sin enjoy, raging to and fro,
Ever ill themselves employ, each the other's foe,
　　With evil intent;
All shall I lay low
With floodings that shall flow,
I shall work them woe,
　　That will not repent.

Noah, my friend, I tell thee, saved be thou by thy zeal,
But build a ship directly, of nail and board full well.
Thou ever showed thy loyalty to me as true as steel,
Still be obedient to me and friendship shalt thou feel
　　My power provide.
Of length thy ship shall be
Three hundred cubits, warn I thee,
Of height even thirty,
　　Of fifty cubits wide.

Anoint thy ship with pitch and tar without, also within,
The water to debar from flowing in;
Look no man it mar; three cabin rows begin,
Thou must use many a spar before this work thou win
　　To end fully.
Make in thy ship also,
Of parlours even a row
And places more to stow
　　The beasts that there must be.

One cubit in height a window shall thou make;
A side door to fit tight, fashion without mistake;
With thee shall no man fight, nor harm thee for my sake,
When all is done aright; thy wife see that thou take
　　Into the ship with thee;
Thy sons of good fame,
Ham, Japhet, and Shem,

143 On board must remain,
　　With their wives three.

For all shall be destroyed, that lives on land, but ye,
With floods that fill the void, and falling in plenty;
The heavens shall be employed to rain incessantly,
When days seven have cloyed, it shall last days forty,
　　Without fail.
Take in thy ship also
Two beasts of each kind, so,
Male and female, see they go,
　　Before thou raise thy sail.

So thou may thee avail when all these things are wrought,
Stuff thy ship with victual for hunger that ye lack nought;
For beasts, fowl, and cattle keep them in your thought
For them is my counsel, that some succour be sought,
　　Uppermost;
They must have corn and hay,
And meat enough alway;
Do now, as I thee say,
　　In the name of the holy ghost.

Noah　Ah! Benedicite! What art thou thus,
That tells before what shall be? Thou art full marvellous!
Tell me for charity thy name so gracious.
God　My name is of dignity and also full glorious
　　To know.
I am God most mighty,
One God in trinity,
Made thee and each man to be;
　　Love to me thou should show.

Noah　I thank thee, Lord, so dear, that would vouchsafe
Thus low to appear to a simple knave;
Bless us, Lord, here for charity I it crave,
The better may we steer the ship that we have,
　　Certain.

God　Noah, to thee and to thy fry
My blessing grant I;
Ye shall work and multiply,
　　And fill the earth again,
When all these floods are past and fully gone away.

NOAH   Lord, homeward will I fast in haste as that I may; (*Exit* GOD)
        My wife will I ask what she will say,   183
        And I am all aghast lest there be some fray
            Between us both;
        For she is full tetchy,
        For little oft angry,
        If anything wrong be,
            Soon is she wroth.

He goes to his wife.
        God speed thee, wife, how fare ye?

WIFE   Now, as ever might I thrive, the worse to see thee;
        Tell me, on your life, where thus long could thou be?
        To death may we drive, because of thee,
            Alack.
        When work weary we sink,
        Thou dost what thou think,
        Yet of meat and drink
            Have we great lack.

NOAH   Wife, we are hard pressed with tidings new.
WIFE   But thou ought to be dressed in stafford blue;
        For thou art always depressed, be it false or true;
        God knows I am oppressed, and that may I rue,
            Full ill;
        All I hear is thy crow,
        From even till morrow,
        Screeching ever of sorrow;
            God send thee once thy fill.

        We women may harry all ill husbands;
        I have one, by Mary! That loosed me of my bands;
        If he twits I must tarry, however so it stands,
        And seem to be full sorry, wringing both my hands
            For dread.
        But in a little while,
        What with game and guile,
        I shall smite and smile
            And pay him back instead.

NOAH   Hush! Hold thy tongue, ramshit, or I shall thee still.
WIFE   As I thrive, if thou smite, I shall pay back with skill.
NOAH   We shall see who is right, have at thee, Gill!

[34]

220   Upon the bone shall it bite!
WIFE   Ah, by Mary! Thou smitest ill!
        But I suppose
     I shall not in thy debt
     Leave this place yet!
     This strap is what you get
         To tie up thy hose!

NOAH   Ah! Wilt thou so? Mary, that is mine.
WIFE   Have thou three for two, I swear, by God divine,
NOAH   I shall requite each blow, your skin will bear my sign.
WIFE   Out upon thee, ho!
NOAH   Thou can both bite and whine
     For all thou art worth.
     For though she will strike,
     Her shrieks my ears spike,
     There is not her like
         On all this earth.

WIFE   But I will keep charity in this to-do
     Here shall no man tarry thee; I pray thee go to!
     Full well may we miss thee, as peace is our due;
     To spin will I address me.
NOAH   Farewell, then, to you;
        But wife,
     Pray for me busily,
     Till again I come to thee.
WIFE   Even as thou prayst for me,
        As ever might I thrive.

NOAH   I tarry full long, to my work I must go;
     My gear take along and watch the work grow;
     I may go all wrong, in truth, I it know;
     If God's help is not strong I may sit in sorrow,
        I ken;
     Now assay will I
     Something of carpentry,
     In nomine patris, et filii,
        Et spiritus sancti, Amen.

     To begin with this tree, my bones will I bend,
     I trust that the trinity succour will send;

The work prospers fairly to a fitting end;   255
Now blessed be he that this did commend.
    Lo, here the length,
Three hundred cubits evenly,
Of breadth lo is it fifty,
The height is even thirty
    Cubits full strength.

Now my gown will I cast and work in my coat
Make will I the mast to set in the boat,
Ah! My back breaks fast! This is a sorry note!
It is wonder that I last, so weak that I dote,
    Behold,
To begin this affair!
My bones are so bare,
No wonder they despair,
    For I am full old.

The top and the sail both will I make,
The helm and the castle also will I take,
To drive in each a nail without a mistake,
This way will never fail, that dare I undertake
    Right soon.
This was a noble plan,
These nails so swiftly ran
Through more or less the span
    Of these boards each one.

Window and door even as he said
Three cabins more, they are well made,
Pitch and tar full sure upon them have been laid,
This will ever endure, I count myself well paid;
    And why?
It is better wrought
Than I could have thought;
Him, that made all of nought,
    I thank only.

Now will I hie me despite the ill weather
My wife and my family, to bring even hither.
Listen here carefully, wife, and consider,
Hence must we flee all together
    Right fast.

[36]

WIFE   Why, sir, what ails you?
295   Who is it assails you?
           To flee it avails you,
               Yet ye be aghast.

NOAH   The yarn on the reel is otherwise, dame.
WIFE   Tell me more and less, else ye be to blame.
NOAH   He can cure our distress, blessed be his name.
           Our dole he will redress to shield us from shame
              And said,
           All this world about
           With fierce floods so stout,
           That shall run in a rout,
              Shall be overspread.

           He said all shall be slain save only we,
           Our bairns shall remain and their wives three;
           A ship he bad me ordain to save our company,
           Therefore with all our main that Lord thank we,
              Saviour of our blood;
           Get along fast, go thither.
WIFE   I know not whither,
           I daze and I dither,
              For fear of that flood.

NOAH   Be not afraid, have done, truss up our gear,
           Lest we be undone, without more fear.
1ST SON   Full soon it shall be done, brothers help me here.
2ND SON My part I shall not shun, no matter how severe,
              My brother.
3RD SON Without any yelp
           With my might shall I help.
WIFE   I've a blow for each whelp,
              If you help not your mother.

NOAH   Now are we there, as we should be;
           Go, get in our gear, cattle and company,
           Into this vessel here, my children free.
WIFE   Shut up was I never, so God save me,
              In such an oyster as this.
           In faith I cannot find
           Which is before, which is behind;

Shall we here be confined,   332
   Noah, as have thou bliss?

NOAH   Dame, peace and still, we must abide grace;
          Therefore, wife, with good will, come into this place.
WIFE   Sir, for Jack nor for Gill, will I turn my face,
          Till I have on this hill, spun a space
             On my distaff;
          Woe to him who moves me,
          Now will I down set me,
          And let no man prevent me,
             For him will I strafe.

NOAH   Behold in the heaven, the cataracts all
          That are open full even, both great and small
          And the planets seven, left have their stall,
          The thunder downdriven, and lightnings now fall
             Full stout,
          On halls and bowers,
          Castles and towers;
          Full sharp are these showers,
             That deluge about.

          Therefore, wife have done, come in the ship fast.
WIFE   Patch your shoes and run, the better they will last.
1ST WIFE Come, good mother, come, for all is overcast,
          Both the moon and the sun.
2ND WIFE   And many winds blast
             Full sharp;
          These floods may drown our kin,
          Therefore, mother, come in.
WIFE   In faith, still will I spin;
          All in vain ye carp.

3RD WIFE If ye like, ye may spin, Mother, in the ship.
NOAH   Ye be twice bidden in, dame, in all friendship.
WIFE   Whether I lose or I win, in faith, thy fellowship,
          Set I not at a pin, this spindle will I slip
             Upon this hill.
          Ere one foot I stir.
NOAH   By Peter, but ye err;
          Without further spur
            Come in if ye will.

[38]

WIFE   Yea, the water nighs so near that I sit not dry,
371   Into the ship for fear quickly will I hie
        For dread that I drown here,
NOAH   Dame, but surely,
      Paid ye have full dear, ye stayed so long by,
        Out of the ship.
WIFE   I will not at thy bidding,
      Go from door to dunghill gadding.
NOAH   In faith and for your long tarrying,
        Ye shall taste of the whip.

WIFE   Spare me not, I pray thee, do even as thou think,
      These great words shall not flay me.
NOAH   Abide dame and drink,
      For beaten shalt thou be with this staff till thou stink;
      Are these strokes good, say ye.
WIFE   What say ye? Go sink!
NOAH   Now quake!
      Cry me mercy, I say!
WIFE   To that say I nay.
NOAH   If not, by this day,
        Thy head shall I break.

WIFE   Lord, I were at ease and heartily hale
      With a pottage of pease and my widow's kale;
      For thy soul it would please me to pay penny bail,
      So would more than these I see in this dale,
        Of the wives that here stir,
      For the dance they are led,
      Wish their husbands were dead,
      For, as ever eat I bread,
        So, would I our sire were.

NOAH   Ye men that have wives, while they are young,
      If ye love your lives, chastise their tongue:
      Methinks my heart rives, both liver and lung,
      To see such a strife, wedded men among;
        But I,
      As have I bliss,
      Shall chastise this
WIFE   Yet may ye miss,
        Nichol needy!

NOAH   I shall make thee still as stone, beginner of blunder!   406
        I shall beat thee, back and bone, and break all in sunder.
    They fight.
WIFE   Out, alas, I am overthrown! Out upon thee, man's wonder!
NOAH   See how she can groan, and I lie under;
            But wife,
        Haste we, without ado,
        For my back is near in two.
WIFE   And I am beaten so blue
            And wish for no more strife.

            They enter the Ark.

1ST SON   Ah! Why fare ye thus? father and mother, both!
2ND SON   Your spite would scarce free us from such sin as wroth.
3RD SON   These scenes are so hideous, I swear on my oath.
NOAH   We will do as ye bid us, and that with no sloth.
            Sons dear!
        At the helm now I am bent
        To steer the ship as is meant.
WIFE   I see in the firmament
            The seven stars here.

NOAH   This is a great flood, wife, take heed.
WIFE   So methought as I stood we are in great need;
        That these waves be withstood.
NOAH   Now God help us, we plead!
        As thou art helmsman good, and best may succeed
            Of all;
        Rule us in this race,
        Thy word we embrace.
WIFE   This is a parlous case:
            Help God, when we call.

NOAH   To the tiller, wife, see, and I shall assay
        The deepness of the sea where we sail, if I may.
WIFE   That shall I do full wisely, now go thy way,
        For upon this flood have we fared many a day,
            In pain.
    NOAH *lowers a plummet.*
NOAH   Now the water will I sound:
        Ah! It is far to the ground;
        This labour I have found
            Brings little gain.

[40]

442   Above the hills is seen the water risen of late
Of cubits full fifteen, but in no higher state
These waves of water green will spill with former spate,
Rain forty days has been, it will therefore abate
     Its zeal.

NOAH *again lowers the plummet.*
     Again it is best,
The water to test;
Now I am impressed,
     It has waned a great deal.

Now have the storms ceased and cataracts quit,
Both the most and the least.

WIFE   Methinks, by my wit,
The sun shines in the east, lo, is not yond it?
We should have a good feast when these floods flit
     So stormy.

NOAH   We have been here, all we,
Three hundred days and fifty.

WIFE   Yea, look, now wanes the sea;
     Lord, well are we.

NOAH   The third time will I try in what depth we steer.
WIFE   Too long will you ply, lay in thy line there.
NOAH   With my hand touch I the ground even here.
WIFE   Therefore be we spry and have merry cheer;
     But husband,
What hills may there be?
NOAH   Of Armenia's country.
WIFE   Now blessed be he
     That brings us to land!

NOAH   The tops of the hills I see, many at a sight,
Nothing prevents me the sky is so bright.
WIFE   Tokens of mercy these are full right.
NOAH   Dame, now counsel me what bird best might
     Go forth,
With flight of wing
And bring without tarrying
Of mercy some tokening
     Either by south or north?

[41]

	For this is the first day of the tenth moon.	478
WIFE	The raven durst I lay will come again soon;	
	As fast as thou may, cast him forth, have done,	
	He may come back today and dispel before noon	
	Our dismay.	
NOAH	I will loose to the blue	
	Sky, doves one or two:	
	Go your way, do,	
	God send you some prey.	

Now have these fowl flown to separate countries;
Let our prayers be known, kneeling on our knees,
To him that is alone worthiest of dignities,
That he may not postpone their coming back to please
    Us with a sign.

WIFE   Land they should be gaining,
    The water so is waning.

NOAH   Thank we that God reigning,
        That made both me and mine.

It is a wondrous thing most certainly,
They are so long tarrying, the fowls that we
Cast out in the morning.

WIFE   Sir, it may be
    They bide something to bring.

NOAH   The raven is hungry
    Alway;
He is without any reason,
If he find any carrion,
No matter the season,
    He will not away.

The dove is more gentle, to her trust is due,
Like to the turtle to death she is true.

WIFE   Hence but a little she comes now, look you!
    She brings in her bill some tidings new.
        Behold!
    It is of an olive tree
    A branch, it seems to me.

NOAH   Yea sooth, verily,
        Right so is it called.

[42]

514	Dove, bird full blest, fair might thee befall,
	Thou art true to thy quest, as stone in the wall;
	Thou wert trusted as best to return to thy hall.
WIFE	A true token to attest we shall be saved all:
	For why?
	The depth, since she has come,
	Of the water by that plumb,
	Hast fallen a fathom
	And more, say I.

1ST SON	These floods are gone, father, behold.
2ND SON	There is left right none, and that be ye bold.
3RD SON	As still as a stone, our ship has firm hold,
NOAH	On land here has run; God's grace is untold;
	My children dear,
	Shem, Japhet, and Ham,
	With glee and with game,
	Go we in God's name,
	No longer abide here.

WIFE	Here have we been, Noah, long enough, now,
	With grief as is seen and full furrowed brow.
NOAH	Behold on this green, neither cart nor plough
	Is left on the scene, neither tree nor bough,
	Nor other thing,
	But all is away:
	Many castles, I say
	Great towns of array,
	Flit in this flooding.

WIFE	These floods put in fright all this world so wide,
	Which moved with great might the sea and the tide.
NOAH	But death was the plight of the proudest in pride,
	Each person in sight that ever was spied,
	With sin,
	All are they slain,
	And put to great pain.
WIFE	From thence again
	May they never win.

NOAH	Win? No, indeed, save God turn his face,
	Forgive their misdeed, and admit them to grace;

[43]

As he may hardship heed, I pray him in this space,   552
In heaven to hear our need, and put us in a place,
 That we,
With his saints in sight,
And his angels bright,
May come to his light:
 Amen for charity.

The Fourth Play: Abraham

ABRAHAM   1ST BOY
2ND BOY   GOD
ISAAC

ABRAHAM Thou very god, Adonai,
 Thou hear us when we to thee call,
As thou art he that best may,
 Most succour and help art thou to all;
Mightiful Lord, to thee I pray,
 Let once the oil of mercy fall,
I be unworthy to abide that day,
Truly yet I hope I shall.

Mercy, Lord omnipotent!
 Thou long since this world has wrought;
Say whither all our elders went!
Such matter muse I in my thought.
Since Adam gave to Eve assent,
 To eat that apple spared he nought,
For all the wisdom that he meant
 Full dear that bargain has he bought.

God's angel drove him for that wrong
 From paradise with full sad cheer,
And after lived he here full long,
 More than three hundred year,
In sorrow and in travail strong,
 And every day in doubt or fear;
His children angered him among,
 Cain slew Abel, to Adam so dear.

[44]

25 Since Noah, that was true and good,
　　He and his children three,
Were saved when all was flood:
　　That was a wonder thing to see.
And Lot from Sodom when he strode,
　　Three cities burnt, yet escaped he;
Thus, for they moved God's angry mood,
　　He smote their sin most vengefully.

When I think of our elders all,
　　And of the marvels that have been,
No gladness in my heart may fall,
　　My comfort goes away full clean.
Lord, when shall death make me his thrall?
　　A hundred years certain have I seen;
Ma foi! Soon I hope he shall,
　　For it is right high time I mean.

Yet Adam is to hell gone,
　　And there has lain many a day,
And all our elders everyone,
　　They are gone the same way,
Until God will hear their moan;
　　Now help, Lord Adonai!
For certain no surer help I own,
　　And there is none that better may.

GOD *appears above.*

GOD 　I will help Adam and his kin,
　　If any man be loyal within,
Tendering to me love and truth
　　Shunning pride and showing ruth;
My servant will I try and test,
　　Abraham, where his faith may rest;
In certain wise I will him prove,
　　If he to me be true of love.

Abraham! Abraham!

ABRAHAM Who is that? lo! Let me see!
　　I heard one name my name.

[45]

GOD   It is I, pay heed to me,   60
                That formed thy father Adam,
        And everything in its degree.

ABRAHAM   To hear thy will, ready I am,
                And to fulfil whatever it be.

GOD   Of mercy have I heard thy cry,
                My ear thy devout prayers have won;
        If thou love me, look that thou hie
                Unto the land of Vision;
        And the third day be there, bid I,
                And take with thee Isaac, thy son,
        As a beast to sacrify,
                To slay him look thou not shun.
        In offering burn him as a brand.

ABRAHAM   Ah, praised be thou, Lord, in thy throne!
                Hold over me, Lord, thy holy hand,
        Full sure thy bidding shall be done.
                Blessed be that Lord in every land
        To visit his servant thus so soon.
                Fain would I this deed were planned
        No profit is God's will to shun.

        This commandment must I needs fulfil,
                Though that my heart wax heavy as lead;
        Should I offend against his will?
                Nay, I would rather my child were dead.
        Whatso he bids me, good or ill,
                That shall be done in every stead;
        Both wife and child if he bid kill
                That should I do without a dread.

        If Isaac knew, whereso he were,
                He would be abashed now,
        How that he is in danger.
                Isaac, son, where art thou?

ISAAC *enters.*

ISAAC   Already, father, see me here;
                Now was I coming unto you;
        I love you greatly, father dear.

ABRAHAM And dost thou so? I would know how
97   Thou lovest me, son, as thou hast said.

ISAAC   Yea, father with all my heart,
             More than all that ever was made;
         May God long life to you impart!

ABRAHAM Now who would not be glad that had
             A child so loving as thou art?
         Thy loving cheer makes my heart glad,
             And loth am I that I that we must part.

         Go home, son; come soon again,

             And tell thy mother I come full fast.
    Here ISAAC *leaves his* FATHER.
             Now God bless and save him pain!
             And glad am I that he has passed!
         Alone, right here in this plain,
             Might I speak till my heart burst,
         I would that all were well, full fain,
             But it must needs be done at last.

         And it is good I nothing mar
             To be prepared full good it were;
         The land of Vision is full far,
             The third day's end must I be there,
         My ass shall with us fare,
             Our harness less and more to bear,
         No nearer Isaac gets death's scar;
             A sword must with us yet therefore.

         And I shall briskly make me yare;
             This night will I begin my way,
         Though Isaac be never so fair,
             And mine own son, the sooth to say,
         And though he be my very heir,
             And all should wield after my day,
         God's bidding shall I never spare;
             Should I that withstand? Ma foi! But nay!

         Isaac!
ISAAC   —Sir!
ABRAHAM   Be ready, son;

[47]

For certainly thyself and I,   130
   We two must now wend forth of town,
To sacrifice in far country,
   For a certain cause and reason.
Take wood and fire in haste with thee;
   By hill and dale both up and down,
Son, thou shalt ride, and by thee walk shall I.

   Look thou forget not what thou shalt need;
    Go make thee ready, my darling!
ISAAC   I am ready to do this deed,
    And ever to fulfil your bidding.

ABRAHAM My dear son, look thou have no dread,
    We shall come home with great loving;
   Both to and fro I shall us lead;
    Come now, son, with my blessing.
   To the SERVANTS.
    Ye two here with this ass abide,
    For Isaac and I will to yond hill;
    It is so high we may not ride,
    Therefore ye two shall abide here still.
1ST BOY Sir, ye shall not be denied,
    We are ready your bidding to fulfil.
2ND BOY Whatsoever to us betide
    To do your bidding ay we will.

ABRAHAM God's blessing have ye both together;
    I shall not tarry long from you.
1ST BOY Sir, we shall abide you here,
    Out of this place shall we not go.
ABRAHAM Children, ye are ay to me full dear,
    I pray God keep you ever from woe.
2ND BOY Thy bidding, sir, we keep for fear.
ABRAHAM   Isaac, now are there but we two.

We must go a full good pace,
   For it is further than I thought;
We shall make mirth and great solace,
   When this thing to end be brought.
Lo, my son, here is the place.

[48]

Isaac 167	This wood and fire my hands have sought; Tell me now, if ye have space, Why beast for burning there is naught?

ABRAHAM Now son, I may no longer lie,
    This work pierces my heart through;
Thou lived ever obediently,
    Ever to yield thy duty as due.
But certainly thou now must die,
    If my purpose hold but true.
ISAAC Now my heart as lead is heavy
    My death thus hastily to rue.

ABRAHAM Isaac!
ISAAC   Sir?
ABRAHAM   Come hither, bid I;
    Thou shalt be dead whatsoever betide.
ISAAC Ah, father, mercy! Mercy!
ABRAHAM   That I say may not be denied;
Take thy death therefore meekly.
ISAAC   Ah, good Sir, abide;
Father!
ABRAHAM   What son?
ISAAC   To do your will I am ready,
    Wheresoever ye go or ride

If I may over-take your will,
    Since I have trespassed I shall repent.
ABRAHAM Isaac!
ISAAC   What, sir?
ABRAHAM   Good son, be still.
ISAAC Father!
ABRAHAM   What, son?
ISAAC   Must my flesh be rent?
What have I done?
ABRAHAM   Truly, no ill.
ISAAC And must I be slain?
ABRAHAM   So have I meant.
ISAAC Sir, what may help?
ABRAHAM   This must I fulfil.
ISAAC I ask mercy.
ABRAHAM   Thee I must kill.

ISAAC	When I am dead and closed in clay,
	Who shall then be your son?
ABRAHAM	Ah, Lord, that I should abide this day!
ISAAC	Sir, who shall do the tasks I have done?
ABRAHAM	Speak no such words, son, I thee pray.
ISAAC	Shall ye me stay?
ABRAHAM	That shall I, son:
	Lie still! I smite!
ISAAC	Sir, let me say.
ABRAHAM	Now, my dear child, thou may not shun.

ISAAC	The shining of your bright blade,
	Makes me quake, my death to flee.
ABRAHAM	Therefore face-down thou shall be laid,
	Then when I strike thou shalt not see.
ISAAC	What have I done, father, what have I said?
ABRAHAM	Truly, nothing ill to me.
ISAAC	Then slain thus guiltless is ill-paid.
ABRAHAM	Now, good son, let such words be.

ISAAC	I love you ay.
ABRAHAM	So do I thee.
ISAAC	Father!
ABRAHAM	What, son?
ISAAC	Let now be soon
	For my mother's love.
ABRAHAM	Let be, let be!
	It would not help as thou dost mean;
	But lie still till I come to thee.
	I miss a little thing, I ween.
	(aside) He speaks so ruefully to me
	I would these tears might not be seen.

All worldly joy that I might win
    Would I give if he were unkind,
But no default I found in him;
    For him in torture I would grind;
To slay him thus I think great sin,
    So rueful words I with him find;
To part I feel such woe within
    For he will never from my mind.

[50]

225 What shall I to his mother say?
    For "Where is he?" comes quick from her;
  If I tell her, "run away",
    Swiftly answers she—"Nay, sir!"
  And I am frightened her to slay;
    I know not what I shall say to her.
  He lies full still there, as he lay
    Till I come there he dare not stir.

GOD *appears above.*

GOD Angel, hie with all thy main!
    To Abraham thou shalt be sent;
  Say, Isaac shall not be slain;
    Nor body burnt, nor his life spent.
  This deed my servant shall refrain,
    Go, put him out of his intent;
  Bid him go home again,
    I know well how he meant.

ANGELUS Gladly, Lord, I am ready
    Thy bidding shall be magnified;
  I shall speed full hastily,
    Thee to obey at evening tide;
  Thy will, thy name to glorify,
    Over all this world so wide;
  And to thy servant now haste I,
    Good, true, Abraham, will I glide.

ABRAHAM But might I yet of weeping cease,
    Till I had done this sacrifice;
  It must needs be despite his pleas,
    Though I carp thereof in this dull wise,
  The more my sorrow it will increase;
    I quake to hear his cries;
  I must rush on him my pain to ease,
    And slay him here right as he lies.

ANGEL Abraham! Abraham! (*Seizes him.*)
ABRAHAM   Who is there now?
  Alas let me go.
ANGEL   Stand up, now, stand;
  Thy good will I come to allow,

[51]

Therefore I bid thee hold thy hand.

ABRAHAM   Say, who bad so? Any but thou?
ANGEL   Yea, God; and sends this beast to thy offering brand.
ABRAHAM   But God spake lately to me how
To work this deed at his command.

ANGEL   He has perceived thy meekness
And thy goodwill also in this;
He would thou do thy son no distress,
For granted to thee is his bliss.
ABRAHAM   But know thou well that it is
As thou hast said.
ANGEL   I say thee yes.
ABRAHAM   I thank thee, Lord, well of goodness,
That all thus hast released me this.

To speak with thee have I no space,
With my dear son till I have spoken.
My good son, thou shalt have grace,
On thee now has my wrath not woken;
Rise up now, with thy comely face.
ISAAC   Sir, shall I live?
ABRAHAM   (*he kisses him*). Yea, by this token
Son, thou hast escaped a full hard grace,
Thou should have been both burnt and broken.

ISAAC   But, father, shall I not be slain?
ABRAHAM   No certain, son.
ISAAC   Then I am glad;
Good sir, put up your sword again.
ABRAHAM   Nay, hardly, but fear not my lad.
ISAAC   Is all then well?
ABRAHAM   Yea, son, certain.
ISAAC   For fear, sir, I was almost mad.

I was never so afraid before,
As I have been on yonder hill,
But, by my faith, father, I swear
I will never more come there,
Unless it be against my will.
ABRAHAM   Yea, come on with me, my own sweet son,
And homeward fast now let us be gone.

[52]

ISAAC	By my faith, father, thereto I grant,
295	I had never so good will to go home,
	And to speak with my dear mother.
ABRAHAM	Ah! Lord of heaven I thank Thee,
	For now may I lead home with me,
	Isaac, my young son so free,
	The gentlest child above all other.

Exeunt.

The Fifth Play: Isaac

ISAAC	ESAU
JACOB	REBECCA

ISAAC	Come here son and kiss me,
	That I may sense the smell of thee;
	The smell of my son is like
	To a field with flowers or honey hive.
	Where art thou, Esau, my son?
JACOB	Here, father, and ask your benison.
ISAAC	The blessing my father gave to me,
	God of heaven and I give thee;
	God thee with great plenty greet,
	Of wine, of oil, and of wheat;
	And grant thy children all
	To worship thee, both great and small;
	Whoso thee blesses, blessed be he;
	Whoso thee curses, cursed be he.
	Now hast thou my great blessing,
	Love thee shall all thine offspring;
	Go now whither thou hast to go.
JACOB	Grant mercy, sir, I will do so.

JACOB *retires.* ESAU *advances.*

ESAU	Have, eat, father, of my hunting,
	And give me then your blessing.
ISAAC	Who is that?
ESAU	I, your son
	Esau, who brings you venison.
ISAAC	Who was that was right now here,
	And brought me the broth of a deer?
	I ate well, and blessed him;
	And he is blessed, in every limb.

[53]

ESAU	Alas! I may weep and sob.
ISAAC	Thou art beguiled through Jacob,
	That is born thy very brother.
ESAU	Have ye kept me no other
	Blessing, but gave ye him each one?
ISAAC	Such another have I none;
	God grant that to thy lot may stand
	The dew of heaven and fruit of land;
	Other than this can I not say.
ESAU	Now, alas, and welaway!
	May I with that traitor meet,
	I shall repay this bitter cheat;
	My parents' grief should not away,
	For if we meet I shall him slay.

ESAU retires. REBECCA advances.

REBECCA	Isaac, my own life would slip by,
	If thus hated Jacob die.
	I will send him to Aran,
	There my brother dwells, Laban;
	And there may he serve in peace
	Till his brother's wrath will cease.
	Why should I all in a day
	Lose both my sons? Better nay.
ISAAC	Thou sayest sooth, wife; call him hither,
	And let us tell him where and whither
	That he may Esau flee
	Who vows such vengeance shall be.

JACOB advances.

REBECCA	Jacob, son! thy father and I
	Would speak with thee; come, stand us by!
	From the country must thou flee,
	So that Esau slay not thee.
JACOB	Whither should I go from here?
REBECCA	To Mesopotamia;
	With thine uncle Laban bide,
	Who dwells Jordan's stream beside;
	And there may thou with him live,
	Until Esau, my son, forgive
	And forget, and his rage be dead.
JACOB	I will go, father, as is said.
ISAAC	Yea, son, do as thy parents say;
	Come kiss us both, and wend thy way.

JACOB   Have good day, sir and dame!
            He kisses FATHER *and* MOTHER.
ISAAC   God shield thee, son, from sin and shame!
REBECCA   And give thee grace, good man to be,
70   And send me glad tidings of thee.
            JACOB *goes one way.* ISAAC *and* REBECCA *the other.*

The Sixth Play: Jacob

            JACOB   JOSEPH
            GOD   BENJAMIN
            RACHEL   ESAU
            LEAH

JACOB   Help me, Lord Adonai,
            And hold me in the right way
            To Mesopotamia;
            For I came never till now here;
            I came never to this country;
            Lord of heaven, thou help me!
            For I have gained along this street
            Sore bones and aching feet.
            The sun is down, what is best?
            Here purpose I all night to rest;
            Under my head this stone shall lie:
            A night's rest take will I.
        GOD *appears above.*
GOD   Jacob, Jacob, thy God I am;
            Of thy forefather, Abraham,
            And of thy father Isaac;
            I shall thee bless for their sake.
            This land that thou sleepest in,
            I shall thee give, and thy kin;
            I shall thy seed multiply,
            As thick as powder on earth may lie
            Thy generation shall spread wide,
            From east to west on every side,
            From the south unto the north;
            All I say I shall bring forth;
            And all the folk of thine offspring,
            Shall be blessed with thy blessing.

                    [55]

Jacob, of terror take no heed!
I shall thee clothe, I shall thee feed.
Safe and sound shall be thy state;
I shall thee help early and late;
And all in comfort shall I bring thee
Home again to thy country.
I shall not fail, be thou bold,
But I shall do as I have told.

JACOB *wakes.*

JACOB   Ah! Lord! What may this mean?
What have I heard in sleep, and seen?
That from a ladder God leaned down
And spoke to me without a frown.
And where that ladder stood but late
Is but God's house and heaven's gate.
Lord how fearful is this stead!
Where I lay down my head,
In God's praise I raise this stone,
And oil will I put thereon.
Lord of heaven, hear me now,
Here to thee I make a vow.
If thou give me meat and food
With clothes withal to be endued,
And bring me home to kith and kin,
By the way that I walk in,
Without pain in any part,
I promise to thee with steadfast heart,
As thou art my Lord and God
I shall not leave thy ways untrod.
This stone I raise in sign today
I shall hold holy kirk for ay;
And of all that comes fresh to me
Righteously shall I give to thee.

Here JACOB *leaves Aran for the country of his birth.*

God of heaven, my father dear,
That said to me with thy voice clear,
When I in Aran was dwelling,
My return should be compelling
To where I was both born and fed,
Lord, thou warned me in that stead,
As I went toward Aran
With my staff, and passed Jordan:

67 Again I come into my land,
With two hosts of men at hand.
Thou promised me, Lord, to bless me,
To multiply my seed as sand of sea;
Thou save me, Lord, through thy power
From Esau's vengeance this hour,
That he slay not, for former spite,
These mothers and children in his might.

RACHEL *enters.*

RACHEL Our anguish, sir, is manifold,
From what our messenger has told
That Esau will you slay
With four hundred men more today.

JACOB Forsooth, Rachel, I have him sent
Full many a beast and present.

LEAH *enters.*

Perchance our gifts he may yet take,
And right so shall his wrath slake.
Where are our things, are they past Jordan?

LEAH Go and look, sir, as ye can.

JACOB *wrestles with* GOD.

GOD The day springs; now let me go.

JACOB Nay, nay, I will not so,
Save thou bless me ere thou part
Thee shall I stay with all my heart.

GOD In token that thou speakest with me
On thy thigh I shall touch thee,
That limp shalt thou evermore,
But thou shalt feel no sore;
What is thy name, thou me tell?

JACOB Jacob.

GOD   Nay, but Israel;
Since thou to me such strength made known
All men on earth thy might must own.

JACOB What is thy name?

GOD   Why ask thou so?
Wonderful, if thou would know.

JACOB Ah, bless me, Lord.

GOD   I shall thee bless,
And be to thee full propitious,
And give thee my blessing for ay,
As Lord and he that all may.

[57]

I shall grace well thy going,
And ordain all thy doing:
When thou hast dread, think on me,
And thou shalt full well blessed be,
And look thou trust well what I say,
And fare thee well, now dawns the day.

JACOB   Now have I a new name, Israel,
This place shall be called Fanuel,
For I have seen in this place,
God of heaven face to face.

RACHEL   Jacob, lo, we have now word
That Esau's hosts at hand are heard.

Here JACOB *divides his hosts into three parts.*

JACOB   Rachel, with the last troop dwell,
For I would thou wert kept well;
Call Joseph and Benjamin,
And keep them close therein.

If it be so that Esau
Strike at us who go before,
Ye that are here the last
Ye may be saved if ye flee fast.

JACOB *and* ESAU *meet and kiss,* JACOB *comes and kneels in prayer to* GOD,
raises himself and runs again to ESAU *and embraces him.*

JACOB   Lord, as thou promised, I pray thee,
That thou save my kin and me.

ESAU   Welcome brother to kith and kin,
All wives and children thy host within.
How hast thou fared in that far land?
Tell tidings how things with thee stand.

JACOB   My brother Esau, well,
If no malice in your men dwell.

ESAU *speaks to his* SERVANTS.

ESAU   Look now, fellows, hold your hands,
Ye see that he and I are friends,
And friendship here will we fulfil,
Since that it is God's holy will.

JACOB   God grant it, brother, that it so is
That thou thy servant so would kiss.

ESAU   Nay, Jacob, my dear brother,
Matters stand quite other;
Thou art my lord through destiny:

[58]

140   Go we together both thou and I,
       To my father and his wife,
       Who prize thee, brother, as their life.
   They go out together.

The Seventh Play: Pharaoh

PHARAOH   2ND SOLDIER   GOD
1ST SOLDIER   MOSES   1ST BOY
                                 2ND BOY

PHARAOH   Peace, on pain that no man pass,
                   But keep the course that I command,
               And take good heed of him that has
                   Your health all wholly in his hand:
               For King Pharaoh my father was,
                   And held the lordship of this land:
               I am his heir and all surpass,
                   Ever in strength to stir or stand.

               All Egypt is my own
                   To lead after my law:
               I would my might were known
                   And held in fitting awe.
               Full low he shall be thrown,
                   And flayed till he be raw,
               If any grudge or groan,
                   Them shall I hang and draw.

               But as your King I command peace,
                   To all the people of this empire.
               Look no man thrust forth in the press,
                   But ye must do as I desire,
               And of your words look that ye cease.
                   Pay heed to me, your sovereign sire,
               That can your comfort most increase,
                   Submit to me your lives entire.

1ST SOLDIER   My lord, if any were here,
                   That would not work your will,

    If we might come them near,
      Full quick we should them kill.

PHARAOH   Throughout my Kingdom would I ken,
      And give them thanks that would me tell,
    If any were so cursed men
      That would my Kingdom fell.

2ND SOLDIER My lord, we have amongst us men
      Strong and powerful to rebel:
    The Jews that dwell in Goshen
      Called the children of Israel.

    They multiply full fast,
      And them we straight accuse
    Of plotting in the past,
      Our leadership to lose.

PHARAOH   Why, how have they such tricks begun?
    Are they of might? Ye me amaze!

1ST SOLDIER Yea, lord their numbers overrun
      As in the king, your father's days.
    They came of Joseph, Jacob's son—
      He was a prince worthy of praise—
    Rebellious deeds since have they done:
      That set your book of law ablaze.

    They will confound you clean,
      Unless you make them cease.

PHARAOH   What devil is that they mean
      That they so fast increase?

2ND SOLDIER How they increase full well we ken,
      As did our fathers understand:
    They were but sixty and ten
      When they first came unto this land:
    Since sojourning in Goshen
      Four hundred years, a crafty band:
    Now are they numbered of mighty men
      More than three hundred thousand,

    Counting no woman nor child,
      Nor cattle, a number vast.

PHARAOH   How thus might we be beguiled?
      But it shall not last:

65   For with cunning we shall them quell,
                So that they shall not further spread.
1ST SOLDIER   My lord, we have heard our fathers tell,
                And learned clerks that were well-read,
            There should a man amidst us dwell
                That should undo and strike us dead.
PHARAOH   Fie on him, to the devil of hell!
                Such destiny will we not dread:

            We shall make our midwives kill them
                When any Hebrew babes are born,
            The hopes of Hebrews, we shall spill them,
                And that race shall feel forlorn.

            For their parents hold I no awe,
                Them to such bondage I shall bind,
            To ditch and delve, and drudge and draw,
                At all the basest tasks to grind:
            So shall these lads hold to the law,
                And keep their thralldom ay in mind.

2ND SOLDIER   Such cunning shows no judgement raw,
                We soon shall fewer Hebrews find.
PHARAOH   Now help to hold them down,
                No cruelty forsake.
1ST SOLDIER   Ready, lord, true to thy crown,
                In bondage them to break.
    They go out. MOSES *enters with a rod in his hand.*
MOSES   Great God, that all this world began,
                And grounded it in good degree,
            Thou made me, Moses, unto man,
                And later saved me from the sea:
            King Pharaoh then had made a plan
                No Hebrew man-child saved should be:
            But I escaped despite his ban:
                Thus has God shown his might to me.

            Now am I set to keep
                Under this mountain side,
            Bishop Jethro's sheep,
                Till better things betide.

                    [61]

Ah, Lord, great is thy might!   101
    What may to men that marvel mean?
Yonder I see the strangest sight,
    Such in the world was never seen:
A bush I see burning full bright,
    Yet still I see the leaves are green:
If this work by man has been
    I shall discover if I might.

GOD   Moses, Moses!

Here MOSES *hastens to a bramble bush, and* GOD *speaks to him.*

Moses, come not too near,
    In that stead stay where you dwell,
And hearken unto me here:
    Take heed what I thee tell.
Unlatch thy shoes for fear,
    Tread barefoot in this dell,
The place thou stands on there
    Forsooth, is hallowed well.

I am thy Lord, and for thy sake,
    I may thy life lengthen a space:
I am the God that erstwhile spake
    To learned elders of thy race:
To Abraham and Isaac,
    And Jacob also found my grace,
A mighty multitude they make,
    Whose seed has made a populace.

But now this king, Pharaoh,
    He hurts my folk so fast,
If that I suffer him so,
    Their seed should soon be past:
Them shall I not forgo,
    If their trust in me but last
Their bondage shall I overthrow,
    Therefore as prophet thou are cast,

To bear my message, keep in mind,
    To him that would my people harass:
Thou speak to him with words full kind,
    If that he let my people pass,

138   That to the wilderness their way they find,
       To worship me as I will ask.
     If more my folk in bondage grind,
       Full soon his song shall be "alas".

MOSES   Ah, Lord! Pardon me, by thy leave,
       That lineage loves me naught:
     Gladly they would me grieve,
       Such message if I brought.
     Good Lord, to another this entrust,
       That has more force to cause folk fear.

GOD   Moses, perform this thing thou must;
       My bidding shall thou boldly bear:
     If spitefully at thee they thrust,
       Of thy safety I shall take care.

MOSES   Good Lord, me they will not trust
       For all the oaths that I can swear:

     To announce such tidings new
       To folk of wicked will,
     Without a token true,
       No good shall I fulfil.

GOD   If that he will not understand
       This token true to thee is sent,
     Before the king cast down thy wand,
       And it shall turn to a serpent:
     Then take the tail again in hand—
       To lift it boldly be intent,
     And with a rod again you stand,
       Such mastery for you is meant.

     Then in thy bosom hide thy arm,
       Straight leperous shall be its touch,
     Then whole again, no hurt nor harm:
       Lo, my tokens shall be such.

     And if he will not suffer then
       My people for to pass in peace,
     Plagues in vengeance, nine or ten,
       I shall send before I cease.

But the Hebrews, there in Goshen,
    Shall not be marked but find release:
As long as they my laws will ken
    Their comfort shall ever increase.

MOSES   Ah, Lord, we ought to love thee well,
    That makes thy folk thus free:
I shall unto them tell
    As thou has told to me.
But to the king, Lord, when I come,
    If he ask what is thy name,
And I stand still, both deaf and dumb,
    How should I escape the blame?

GOD   I tell thee thus, "*Ego sum qui sum,*"
    I am he that is the same:
If thou can neither muff nor mum,
    I shall shield thee from shame.

MOSES   I understand full well this thing,
    I go, Lord, with all the might in me.

GOD   Be bold in my blessing,
    Thy succour shall I be.

MOSES   Ah, Lord of love, I shall declare,
    And straightway all this mystery tell:
To my friends now will I fare,
    The chosen children of Israel,
To bring them comfort in their care,
    In pressing danger where they dwell.

MOSES *speaks to the* ISRAELITES.
    Patient be ye still in prayer,
    And God your griefs will surely quell.

1ST BOY   Ah, master Moses, dear!
    Our mirth is turned to mourning:
Held down harshly are we here
    As churls under the king.

2ND BOY   We may mourn for evermore,
    No man can bring us back to grace:
God may our people yet restore
    And send us comfort in this case.

MOSES   Brethren no more your dole deplore:
    God's goodness will relieve our race,
From such woe which has gone before,
    And put us in a pleasant place:
For I shall call upon the king,

215   And fast demand to make you free.
1ST BOY   God grant you good going,
                     And evermore with you be.

MOSES *goes to* PHARAOH.

MOSES   King Pharaoh, be attent.
PHARAOH   Why, boy, what tidings can you tell?
MOSES   From God himself hither am I sent
                     To fetch the children of Israel:
                 To the wilderness he would they went.
PHARAOH   Yea, go hence to the devil of hell!
                 I mind no matter he has meant,
                     In my displeasure shall thou dwell:

                 And, traitor, for thy sake,
                     In anguish they shall pine.
MOSES   Then will God vengeance take
                     On thee, and all of thine.
PHARAOH   On me? Fie on thee lad, out of my land!
                     Thinks thou thus our laws decay?

To the SOLDIERS.

                 Say, whence is yon warlock with his wand
                     That thus would whisk our folk away?
1ST SOLDIER   Yond is Moses, here at hand,
                     Against all Egypt has been ay,
                 He tried your father to withstand:
                     Now will he mar you if he may.

PHARAOH   Fie on him! Nay, nay, that dance is done:
                     Lubber, thou learnt too late.
MOSES   God bids thee not his will to shun,
                     And let me pass thy gate.
PHARAOH   Bids God me? False lubberly lies?
                     What token told he? What is sent?
MOSES   He said thou should despise
                     Both me and his commandment:
                 Therefore upon this wise,
                     My wand he bad, with thou present,
                 I should lay down, and thee advise
                     How it should turn into a serpent:

                 And in his holy name
                     Here I lay it down:

<table>
<tr><td></td><td>Lo, sir, here may thou see the same.</td><td>252</td></tr>
</table>

PHARAOH	Ah, ha, dog! The devil thee drown!
MOSES	He bad me take it by the tail,

Of his power to give proof plain:
> Then he said, surely without fail,
It should turn to a wand again.
> Lo, sir, behold!

PHARAOH   Ill luck you assail!
Certain, this is a subtle swain!
> But these boys shall abide in bale,
To them thy gadgets be no gain.
> But worse, both morn and noon,
Shall they fare, for thy sake.

MOSES   I pray God send us vengeance soon,
And on thee his wrath to wake.

1ST SOLDIER   Alas, alas! This land is torn!
> Our lives no longer can we mend:
Such mischief maimed us since morn
> Which no medicine can amend.

PHARAOH   Why cry ye so, lads? Who gives this scorn?

2ND SOLDIER   Sir King, with care we must contend
> More than knew man that e'er was born.

PHARAOH   Tell on, quickly, and make an end.

1ST SOLDIER   Sir, the waters for both man and beast
> That lately were in flood,
Through Egypt land from west to east,
> Are turned into red blood:

Full ugly and full ill is it,
> That both fresh and fair was before.

PHARAOH   Oh, ho! A wonder rare, I must admit,
> No wizard worked such heretofore!

2ND SOLDIER   More ill news, lord, I must submit,
> That sows our land with troubles sore:
For toads and frogs may no man sit,
> Their venom vexes us the more.

1ST SOLDIER   Great gnats, sir, come both day and night,
> Bite us full bitterly:
We suspect that comes this spite
> Through Moses, our great enemy.

2ND SOLDIER   My lord, unless this people leave,
> No more shall mirth to us belong.

[66]

PHARAOH 293	Go, say to him we will not grieve, Save they the speedier go along.

1ST SOLDIER	Moses, my lord you would relieve
	    By leading thy folk as you long,
	    So that at last we peace achieve.

MOSES	Full well I know, these words are wrong:

	But surely all that I have said
	    Full suddenly it shall be seen:
	Men at such marvels shall have dread
	    And King Pharaoh cry and keen.

2ND SOLDIER	Ah, lord, alas, for dole we die! We dare look out from no door.
PHARAOH	Now by the devil of hell, what ails you so to cry?

1ST SOLDIER	We fare worse than ever before:
	    Great hopping fleas over all this land they fly,
	Their bite leaves blisters big and sore,
	    And in every place our beasts dead lie.

2ND SOLDIER	Horse, ox and ass, They fall down dead, sir, suddenly.
PHARAOH	Woe! lo, there is no man that has Half as much harm as I.

1ST SOLDIER	Yes, sir, poor folk have heavy woe,
	    To see their cattle thus out-cast.
	The Jews in Goshen fare not so,
	    Their good luck seems sure to last.

PHARAOH	Then shall we give them leave to go,
	    Until this peril be just passed
	But ere too far has flit our foe,
	    In bondage bind them twice as fast.

2ND SOLDIER	Moses, my Lord gives leave That your people bid adieu.
MOSES	More mischief still ye weave Unless these tales be true.
1ST SOLDIER	Ah, lord, of no more worth is life.
PHARAOH	What, devil! Is grievance come again?

2ND SOLDIER	Yea, sir, such powder now is rife,
	    That monstrous boils bide in its train:
	It makes leprous man and wife,
	    And further hurt with hail and rain.
	Sir, mountain vines fall in this strife,
	    Such frost and thunder has them slain.

[67]

Pharaoh	Yea, but how do they in Goshen,	333

PHARAOH Yea, but how do they in Goshen, 333
    The Jews, can ye that say?
1ST SOLDIER Of all these cares nothing they ken,
    Nothing of what may us dismay.
PHARAOH No? Out harrow! The devil! Sit they in peace?
    And we every day in doubt and dread?
2ND SOLDIER My lord, our cares will ever increase,
    Till Moses away his folk has led:
    Else are we lost, our hopes here cease,
    Yet were it better that they sped.
PHARAOH That folk shall flit no more,
    His madness shall I never dread.
1ST SOLDIER Then will it soon be war:
    It were better that they sped.
2ND SOLDIER My lord, new harms have come to hand.
PHARAOH Yea, devil, will it no better be?
1ST SOLDIER Locusts are wasting all this land,
    They leave no flower nor leaf on tree.
2ND SOLDIER Against that storm may no man stand:
    And much more marvel it seems to me,
    That these three days from strand to strand
    Such mirk that no man can another see.
1ST SOLDIER Ah, my lord!
PHARAOH   Huh!
2ND SOLDIER Great pestilence comes to do us shame:
    It is like full long to last.
PHARAOH Pestilence, in the devil's name!
    Then is our pride quite past.
1ST SOLDIER My lord, this care lasts long,
    And will till Moses have his way:
    Let him go, else work we wrong,
    No shillyshallying helps today.
PHARAOH Then give them leave to go along:
    Since such I needs must say:
    Perchance we may their grief prolong
    And mar them more through this delay.
2ND SOLDIER Moses, my lord says so:
    Thou shall have passage plain.
MOSES Now have we leave to go,
    My friends, now be ye fain:
    Come forth, now shall ye wend
    To a land of ease, I say.

1ST BOY	But King Pharaoh, that false fiend,
375	Will us again betray:
	He reckons soon our race to end,
	His troops pursue in great array.
MOSES	Be not abashed, God is our friend,
	And all our foes will slay:
	Therefore come on with me,
	Have done and dread you nought.
2ND BOY	That Lord, blessed might he be,
	That us from bale has brought.
1ST BOY	Such friendship saves us in this land:
	Though dreadful perils me appal,
	The red sea is here at hand,
	We change again from free to thrall.
MOSES	I shall make way there with my wand,
	As God has said to save us all:
	On either side the sea shall stand,
	Till we be gone, right as a wall.

Leave none behind, with me keep near:
    Lo try ye now your God to please.

Here they cross the sea.

2ND BOY	Oh, Lord! The way is clear:
	Now wend we all with ease.
1ST SOLDIER	King Pharaoh! This folk is gone.
PHARAOH	Say, what annoyance new?
2ND SOLDIER	These Hebrews are gone, lord, everyone.
PHARAOH	How says thou that?
1ST SOLDIER	Lord, that tale is true.
PHARAOH	Woe! swiftly out, seize them again:
	Full readily that rout shall rue,
	We shall not cease till they be slain,
	Them to the sea we shall pursue.

With charging chariots speed,
    And fiercely follow me.

2ND SOLDIER	Already, lord, gladly indeed
	At your bidding to be.
1ST SOLDIER	Lord, we be obedient to the crown,
	For which our bodies well may bleed:
	We shall not cease, but ding all down,
	Till all be dead as is decreed.

PHARAOH   Rejoice at Mohammed's renown,   412
                    He will be near us in our need:
                  Help! The ragged devil, we drown!
                    Now must we die for our ill deed.
    The sea submerges them.
MOSES   Now are we free from all our woe,
                    And saved out of the sea:
                  Praise and love to God we owe,
                    As land we tread on safely.
IST BOY   Praise we that Lord of light,
                    And ever tell this marvel:
                  Drowned he has King Pharaoh's might,
                    Praised be that Lord Emmanuel.
MOSES   Heaven, thou attend, I say, in sight,
                    And earth my words: hear what I tell.
                  As rain or dew the earth makes bright
                    And waters herbs and trees full well.

                  Give praise unto God's majesty,
                    His deeds are done, his ways are true,
                  Honoured be he in trinity,
                    To him be honour and virtue.
                                    Amen.
    Exeunt.

The Eighth Play:
The Procession of the Prophets

MOSES	SIBYL
DAVID	DANIEL

MOSES   All ye folk of Israel
Hearken to me! I will you tell
     Tidings wondrous good;
Ye all know how it befell
Wherefore Adam was damned to hell,
     He, and all his blood.

Therefore God has mind to raise
A prophet in these evil days,
     From our brethren's kin;
All shall believe what he may say
And walk after in his way,
     From hell he shall them win.

When his time begins to dawn,
No man should turn from him in scorn,
     But greet him with great trust;
And he that will not hear in awe,
He shall be held an outlaw,
     And from his folks be thrust.

Be ready that same prophet to meet,
Who shall come hereafter, full sweet,
     And many marvels show.
Man shall fall down at his feet,
Because all ills he can defeat,
     And our bliss bestow.

All that after truth will run
Shall he save, yea everyone
     Through him the truth shall see.
A prophet everywhere is found
Where proudly men his praises sound,
     Save in his own country.

Harken all, both young and old!
God that all might may hold,
    Greets you by me;
His commandments are ten;
Behold, ye that are his men,
    Here ye may them see.

His commandments that I have brought,
Look that ye hold them nought
    For trifles, nor for fables;
For ye shall well understand
That God wrote them with his hand
    In these same tables.

Ye that these in heart will hold,
Unto heaven shall ye be called,
    The first to shun God's hate;
And ye that will not do so,
To hell's pains must ye go
    And bide a bitter fate.

Hear now, as ye hope for bliss;
The first commandment is this
    That I shall to you say;
Make no god of stick nor stone,
And trust in none but God alone,
    That made both night and day.

The second bids thou shalt not swear
For no reward nor snare,
    Falsely, in God's name;
If thou swearst unjustly,
Know thou well and wisely
    Thou deservest great blame.

The third is, that thou have in mind
The holy day, nor fail to find
    God's service in thy heart.
The fourth commandment don't neglect,
Mother and father hold in respect,
    Rich or poor to play the part.

67 The fifth commands thou shalt forsake
Fornication, and a wife take,
    And live in righteous state.
The sixth commands thou shalt not be
Manslayer for no kind of fee,
    Nor for love nor for hate.

The seventh commands thee not to steal
Nor rob, nor wrongfully to deal,
    Nor for more nor for less.
The eighth bids both old and young
That they be true of their tongue,
    And bear no false witness.

The ninth bids thee, by thy life,
Thou desire not thy neighbour's wife,
    Nor maiden that is his.
The tenth bids thee, in no case,
Covet thy neighbour's goods nor place;
    Thou come thus not amiss.

I am the same man that God chose
The ten commandments of peace to disclose
    On Mount Sinai;
This truth my speech here closes;
By name men call me Moses;
    And have now all good day. (*Exit.*)

DAVID *enters. He carries a harp.*
DAVID   Harken all that hear may,
And perceive well what I say,
    All with righteousness.
Look ye put it not away,
But think thereon both night and day,
    For it is truthfulness.

Jesse's son, ye know I am;
David is my right name,
    And I bear a crown;
If ye me doubt, ye are to blame;
Of Israel, both wild and tame,
    My rule spreads up and down.

[73]

As God of heaven has given me wit,   103
Shall I now sing you a song fit
 For my minstrelsy;
Look ye put it into writing
Mar nor mock now my reciting,
 For it is prophecy.

He plays the harp and sings.

Mirth I make for all men,
With my harp and fingers ten,
 And make them not dismayed;
God that Adam with his hand wrought
Shall send his son for our comfort,
 He earth and heaven made.

He will come down from heaven's tower,
For to be man's saviour,
 And what is lost to find;
For that I harp, and mirth make,
For on himself manhood will take,
 Of my prophecy have mind.

In heaven shall he reign again
As gracious King with might and main,
 In the highest seat;
There is neither king nor churl
Who may stain this princely pearl,
 Nor hide him from his hate.

He shall be lord and king of all,
To his feet shall kings down fall
 To offer graciously;
Blessed be that sweet flower,
That comes to be our saviour!
 Joyful may we be.

Rich gifts they shall him bring,
And to him make offering,
 Kneeling on their knee;
Well him befall that that lording,
And that dear darling,
 Might be alive to see.

[74]

139

    Men may know him by his mark
    Mirth and loving is his work,
        That shall he love most.
    Light shall be born in that time dark,
    To the unlearned and the clerk,
        Through the holy ghost.

    Both emperor and king therefore,
    Old and young, both rich and poor,
        Temper well your glee,
    Until that king descends,
    And our imprisonment ends,
        And makes us all free.

    Thou show thy mercy, Lord, to us,
    For till thou come, to hell we must,
        We have no other fate;
    Lord, if it be thy will, then give
    To us that blessed balm to live
        For thee whom we await.

    Now have I sung my song to you;
    Have it by heart lest you it rue,
        I warn with all my might;
    He through his will that made us well,
    Shield us from the pit of hell
        And grant us heaven's light. (*Exit.*)

Enter SIBYL.

SIBYL   Whoso will hear tidings glad,
    Of him that all this world made,
        Hear attentively!
    Sibyl sage is my name;
    Unless ye hear ye are to blame,
        My word is prophecy.

    All men through Adam's sin were slain,
    And without ending put to pain,
        Through the falseness of the fiend;
    A new king comes from heaven to fight
    Against the fiend to win his right,
        So is his mercy gleaned.

[75]

All the world shall he judge,   175
For those who service do not grudge
    Much mirth he shall provide;
All shall see him face to face,
Rich and poor of every race,
    From him no man may hide;

But they shall in their flesh arise,
And all shall quake to realize
    The coming of that doom,
With his saints, full many a one,
He shall be seen in flesh and bone,
    That king that is to come.

All that shall stand him before,
All shall be both less and more,
    Of one age each one.
Angels shall quake and cease from mirth,
And fire shall burn the whole of earth,
    Yea, the world and all thereon.

Nothing shall on earth be known
But burnt it be and overthrown,
    All waters and the sea.
After shall both hill and dale
Come together, great and small,
    And all shall even be.

At his coming the trump shall blow,
That all men may his coming know;
    Full sorrowful shall be that blast;
There is no man that hears it,
But he shall quake out of his wit,
    Be he never so steadfast.

Then shall hell gape and grin,
That men may know their fate therein,
    Of that high justice;
The evil doers to hell must go;
And to heaven the others also,
    That have been righteous.

[76]

211   Therefore I warn every man,
      Keep, as well as he can,
        From sin and from misdeed,
      My prophecy now have I told;
      God you save both young and old,
        And help you at your need. (*Exit.*)

DANIEL   God that made Adam and Eve,
      While they lived well, he gave them leave
        In paradise to dwell;
      But when they had that apple ate,
      They were damned, and soon beset
        By the pains of hell,

      To sorrow and suffering ever new;
      Therefore will God our great griefs rue,
        And his son down send
      Onto earth, flesh to take,
      That is all for our sake,
        Our trespass to amend.

      Flesh with flesh will be bought,
      That he lose not what he has wrought
        With his own hand;
      Of a maiden shall he be born,
      To save all that are forlorn,
        Evermore without end. (*Exit.*)

The Ninth Play: Caesar Augustus

EMPEROR
1ST COUNSELLOR

2ND COUNSELLOR
MESSENGER (LIGHTFOOT)
SIRINUS

EMPEROR   Be still, bashirs, I command you,
That no man speak a word here now
      But I myself alone;
And if ye do I make a vow,
This sword shall strike your head full low,
      Therefore be still as stone.

And look ye grieve me not,
Or bitter will be your lot,
      By Mohammed that I swear;
As ye know I reck not a jot
To slay you swiftly on the spot,
      So sit ye stone-still there.

For all is in me that up may stand,
Castles, towers, towns in every land,
      To me homage they bring;
No prince may my power withstand,
Everything bows unto my hand,
      I want no earthly thing.

I am lord and sire over all,
All bow to me both great and small,
      As lord of every land;
None is so comely on to call,
Whoso gainsays, ill shall befall,
      I set thereto my hand.

For I am he that is mighty,
And all heathendom heeding me
      Is ready at my will;
Both rich and poor, more and less,
At my liking for to redress,
      Whether I save or kill.

31 Caesar Augustus I am called,
A fairer person to behold,
　　Is not of blood and bone;
Rich nor poor, young nor old,
Such another as I am told,
　　In all this world is none.

But one thing gives me heavy care,
I fear my land will soon misfare
　　For counsel loyal I lack;
My counsellors, of wisdom rare,
Give comfort to me in my care,
　　No wise words now hold back.

As I am man of most renown
I shall your counsel richly crown,
　　If help to me ye give.

IST
COUNSELLOR

Lord we would our lives lay down
To counsel you as none in town,
　　Full gladly while we live.

Your messenger I bid ye call
For anything that may befall,
　　Bid him go hastily,
Throughout your lands over all,
Among your folk both great and small
　　Your power and peace to cry.

For to command both young and old,
None is so hardy nor so bold
　　To hold that sway but thou;
And whoso does, in bondage hold,
And look thou pain them manifold.

EMPEROR 　　I shall, I make a vow;

Good counsel in these words I see.
It shall be done full hastily,
　　Without the least respite.

2ND
COUNSELLOR

My lord, abide awhile, and why?
These words to you shall clarify.

[79]

EMPEROR   Then quickly tell me it.   66
2ND   Already, lord, without gainsay,
COUNSELLOR   This have I heard for many a day,
                    Folk in the country tell;
                A maid dwells in this land, they say
                That shall bear a child to sway
                    Greater power than you can quell.

EMPEROR   Greater power? the devil? what may this be?
                Out, harrow, full woe is me!
                    My wits fly from my head!
                Ah, fire and devil! Whence came he,
                That thus should wrest my power from me,
                    Before I see him dead?

                For certainly my strength were shorn
                If such a sneaking greenhorn
                    Should thus be my sovereign;
                If I know when that boy is born,
                Though the devil had it sworn,
                    That lad I would have slain.

1ST   Alas, my lord, grieve you not so,
COUNSELLOR   But make your messenger forth go
                    After your cousin dear,
                To speak with you a word or two,
                The best device for death to show
                    And free you of your fear.

EMPEROR   As a wise knight all men him know.
                Your counsel shall I not forgo.
                    Of wit art thou the well;
                Praise on him all men bestow,
                This lad shall not me overthrow
                    Were he the devil of hell.

                Come, Lightfoot, lad, like a hare
                With my message forth to fare,
                    To Sirinus, go quick.
                Say sorrows strike I cannot bear,
                Pray him to comfort me of care,
                    And heal him who is sick.

[80]

103   If thou come not again tonight,
           Never come within my sight,
               In no place in my land.

LIGHTFOOT   Now certain, lord, I travel light,
            Before the sun has reached his height
                You shall grasp him by the hand.
EMPEROR   Yea, boy, and as thou love me dear
            Look that thou spy, both far and near,
                Where thou come in each place;
            If any rumours there appear,
            Or any carping come to ear
                Of that lad I shall disgrace.

LIGHTFOOT   I am ready, lord, both up and down,
            To seek and spy in every town
                For talk of that young lad;
            All such whisperings I shall drown,
            And gladly crack the gossip's crown,
                Wherever I am bad.

            And therefore, lord, have now good day.
EMPEROR   Mohammed guide thee on thy way.
                That rules both wind and wave;
            And especially I thee pray,
            To speed thee as fast as thou may.
                Yea, lord, no more I crave.

LIGHTFOOT   Mohammed save Sirinus' kin!
 To SIRINUS. Caesar, my lord and your cousin,
                Greets you well by me.
SIRINUS   Thou art welcome to me and mine;
            Come near and tell me tidings thine,
                Quickly, what they be.

LIGHTFOOT   My lord prays you as you love him dear,
            Before him soon you should appear,
                To speak with him awhile.
SIRINUS   Go greet him well, thou messenger,
            Tell him I follow thee quite near,
                Behind thee not a mile.

W.M.P.—I   [81]

To CAESAR.

LIGHTFOOT	Already, lord, at your bidding,
	Mohammed magnify my King,
	And save thee by sea and sand.
EMPEROR	Welcome, bashir, tell your tiding,
	I would that hear before anything,
	What heard thou in my land?

LIGHTFOOT	I heard nothing, lord, but good;
	Sirinus in all likelihood
	Will be here this night.
EMPEROR	I thank thee, by Mohammed's blood;
	These tidings much amend my mood;
	Go rest, thou worthy knight.

SIRINUS	Mohammed unto thee I call,
	He save thee, lord of great lords all,
	Sitting in thy high degree.
EMPEROR	Welcome, Sirinus, to this hall,
	Beside myself here sit thou shall,
	Quickly come up to me.

SIRINUS	Lord, on your words I am intent.
EMPEROR	Why, sir, after thee I sent
	I shall at once recite;
	Therefore show I you the extent
	Of dangers which my land ferment.
SIRINUS	How so, by Mohammed's might?

EMPEROR	Sir, I am made to understand,
	That a loose wench in this land,
	Shall bear a child, I hear,
	Who shall be crowned a king so grand,
	That all shall bow unto his hand;
	These tidings make me fear.

He shall command both young and old,
None be so hardy nor so bold
     To give service to me;
Then would my heart grow cold
If such a beggar bold
     My crown should take from me;

[82]

175 And therefore, sir, I would thee pray,
   Give the best counsel that you may,
    To guide me as is best;
   For if my hands on him I lay
   When he be found I shall him slay,
    Either by east or west.

SIRINUS Lord, my advice is quickly said;
   I counsel you, as I eat bread,
    What therefore best may be;
   Go search in your land each homestead,
   And bid that boy be brought back dead,
    By the first who may him see;

   And also raise ye an outcry,
   To put to flight that company
    Who give this king a crown;
   Bid each man come separately
   And bring to you a penny,
    That dwells in tower or town;

   That this be done by the third day
   Then may none of his friends say,
    But he has homage given.
   If you do this your worship may
   Live in joy for now and ay,
    Your foes to fealty driven.

EMPEROR As I might thrive, sir, I thank thee,
   For these tidings that thou tell me,
    Thy counsel shall prevail;
    Lord and sire of this country,
   Without an end here make I thee,
    For thy good counsel.

   My messenger, look thou be swift,
   From town to town these rumours sift,
    And my firm will proclaim;
   I pray thee, if thou rise by thrift,
   I promise thee a precious gift,
    If thou come quick again.

Command the folk wholly each one,   211
Rich nor poor, forget thou none,
   To pay me homage truly,
And honour me as lord alone;
And slain be those who against me groan,
   This blade their bane shall be.

Both old and young bid know this thing,
That each man know me for his king,
   For dread I them dismay.
As token I am lord and king,
Bid each man a penny bring,
   And to me homage pay.

By my statutes who will not stand,
Fast they must flee out of my land,
   Bid them without mistake;
By Mohammed whom none withstand,
Thou shalt be made knight with my hand
   Speed fleetly for my sake?

LIGHTFOOT   Already, lord, it shall be done;
But I know well I come not soon,
   And therefore be not wroth;
I swear here, sir, by sun and moon,
I can't return by afternoon,
   So count it not as sloth.

But have good day, now will I wend
For longer here I may not spend,
   But soon get on my way.
EMPEROR   Mohammed his grace thee lend,
And bring thee to thy journey's end,
   With all the speed he may.

Exeunt.

Notes to the Plays (Part One)

The staging of *The Creation* demands four different levels: heaven; paradise; earth; hell. God's throne should be set well above the level on which the Angels stand. The Angels are grouped on either side of God's throne at the beginning of the play, Good and Bad interspersed. When after Lucifer's fall God creates Man, Adam should rise from near God's throne. The Cherubim then takes Adam and Eve to a slightly lower level, paradise, and later they are driven lower still, to middle-earth. The lowest level is hell-mouth which, provided the seating of the audience is suitably raked, can be played on the ground.

Existing records afford considerable guidance to the medieval manner of presentation; no two accounts indicate identical staging, but the diversity of evidence, since no one account is comprehensive in its directions, is of great value to the producer who wishes to realize the material he is handling. There are, for instance, two versions of The Fall of Man (1533 and 1565) which were performed by the Norwich Grocers. Their Account Book informs us that their pageant was 'a Howse of Waynscott paynted and buylded on a Cart with fowre whelys', painted cloths were hung about it, and it was drawn by four horses having 'headstallis of brode Inkle with knopps and tassells'. It had a square top with a large vane in the middle, another large vane at one end, and a great number of smaller ones all around. God was played in a wig and a mask (1565 Inventory 'a face and heare for ye Father'); the Serpent with a wig and crown (it; a new Heer, wt a crown for ye Serpent, 6d.) and 'a cote with hosen and a tayle steyned'; for the Angel 'An Angell's cote and overhoses of Apis Skynns'; for Adam, wig, gloves, and 'a cote and hosen steyned'; for Eve, a wig, gloves and 'two cotes and a pair of hosen steyned'. The Tree displayed a wide variety of fruit and flowers: Apples and Figs, 4d; Oranges, 10d; 3 lbs. Dates, 1s; 1 stone Almonds 3d; Paid for coloured thread to bind the flowers, 2d. Dramatically, the most interesting property is 'a Rybbe colleryd Red'.

Payment to the actors of the Grocers' Play was as Follows:

It., to Jeffrey Tybnam playeng the Father	16d.
It., to Mr. Leman's servant playing Adam	6d.
It., to Frances Fygot playing Eve	4d.
It., to Tho. Wolffe playing the Angelle	4d.
It., to Edmund Thurston playeng the Serpent	4d.

Records of the Coventry medieval guilds, although not referring specifically to *The Creation*, throw some light on the possible presentation of this play. Their pageants were strewn with rushes; in 1557 4d. was paid 'for kepyng of fyer at hell-mothe'; in 1567 'pd for makyng hell-mowth and cloth for hyt iiijs'; 1477, 'it. for mendyng the demons garment . . . it. for newe ledder to the same garment xxijd'; 1490, 'it. the devyls hede' (repairing the mask); 1494, 'it. paid to Wattis for dressyng of the devells hede viijd'; 1498, 'it. paid for peynttyng of the demones hede'; hair, 3 lbs. for the demon's coat and hose; suit for Angels—gold skins, wings for Angels; four diadems for Angels; 1578, 'it. payd for mendyng of two angelis crownes ijd'.

Eve would most probably have been played by a young apprentice, and such perhaps was 'Frances Fygot' who played the part in the Norwich Grocers' Play. All female parts were taken by men or boys. The Coventry Smiths' Company makes an entry for 1495, 'Ryngold's man Thomas that Playtt Pylatts wyff'; and in 1498, 'it. paid to Pylatts 'wyffe for his wages ijs'. The Coventry Weavers record for 1525, payd to Sodden for Ane (Anna in The Purification) xd'; and in 1450 under Fines, '(received) of Hew Heyns pleynge Anne for hys fyne vjd'. An exception to the practice of men playing women's parts is the Chester play of *The Assumption* in which *all* parts were performed by 'the wives of the town'.

There is, however, an interesting difference in the sex of the Serpent in the various versions of the Fall of Man. In the *Ludus Coventriae*, the York, and Wakefield Plays the Serpent appears uniformly masculine. In the Chester Plays Satan describes his disguise:

> A manner of an Adder is in this place,
> that wynges like a byrd she hase,
> feete as an Adder, a maydens face;
> her kinde I will take.

(The Creation 193–196)

The stage directions refer to Lucifer transforming himself to a Sphinx with feathered wings, a serpent below, a woman above. ('King Lear' IV. vi. 128–129.

> But to the girdle do the gods inherit,
> Beneath is all the fiends'.)

In the Cornish Plays Lucifer appears as 'a fyne serpen made with a virgyn face and yolowe heare upon her head'. Such a presentation is finely depicted on a misericord in Ely Cathedral. 'The snake in Paradise,' writes C. G. Jung in *The Psychology of the Unconscious*, 'is usually considered as feminine, as the seductive principle in woman, and is represented as feminine by the old artists, although properly the snake has a phallic meaning.'

The nakedness of Adam and Eve presents a problem to any producer, modern or medieval. The craft-guild that most frequently was given the responsibility for presenting *The Creation* was the Barkers or Tanners. It was the custom for Adam and Eve to be dressed in white leather skins. More practicable for modern performances are white woollen suits, made to a skin-fitting measure and dyed skin colour. The hose portion will require soles, as the Weavers of Coventry recorded in 1564, 'it. paid for solyng of Jesus hose jd'.

In the Wakefield *Creation* there are no directions for singing but, by analogy with the York Plays on this subject, the *Te Deum* would be sung shortly after the creation of the Angels (1. 30), and the *Sanctus* as God withdraws (1. 76) contrasting sharply with the discord that follows. There is no specific direction for song at the end of the play, although the Cherubim hints at it, 'Of sorrow may ye sing'. The earlier of the two Norwich versions of the Fall of Man ends:

EVA O wretches that we are, so ever we xall be inrollyd;
      Therfor ower handes we may wrynge with most dullfull song.

And so thei xall syng walkyng together about the place, wryngyng ther handes.

      Wythe dolorous sorowe, we may wayle and wepe
      Both nyght and daye in sory, sythys full depe.

N.B. These last two lines set to musick twice over and again, for a chorus of four parts.

Whereas harmony characterizes scenes in heaven, each entry or exit from hell-mouth should be marked by the most strident cacophony. In medieval times the Cooks were famed for their hell-mouth effects, to which every available culinary article contributed.

At the heading of this play appear the words '*In dei nomine amen. Assit Principio, Sancta Maria, Meo. Wakefeld*'; in the margin 'Barkers', the guild that undertook production.

The manuscript breaks off after 267 lines. The twelve leaves which

[87]

probably contained the temptation of Eve and the expulsion of Adam and Eve from paradise have been lost. The play here presented is completed by adapting the last 158 lines of the York Cowpers' Play.

The minimum number of speaking characters is listed. If the production of the whole Cycle is being attempted, and staging facilities allow, it would be preferable to increase the number both of Good and Bad Angels. Apart from the Cherubim, the Archangels Michael and Gabriel, because of the part they play in the subsequent drama, should be included. The Archangel Michael, is depicted in the cycles as bearing a flaming sword.

In the *Ludus Coventriae* and the Chester *Creation* God appears and commands Lucifer to fall. In this play (131) the Fall might be heralded by sound effects, and the Bad Angels topple down behind God's throne. If they fall down the various levels in full view of the audience, and there are only three Bad Angels to fall, the result might be an anticlimax. Immediately following the Fall it is dramatically important that two devils or more should be prepared to come scurrying out of hell-mouth to prove the swiftness of God's vengeance and the steep decline from angel to fiend. Lucifer and the Bad Angels have some 120 lines in which to transform themselves into devils.

Throughout Satan's speech (250–275), which includes the transition from the Wakefield to the York text, the devils should be clinging round hell-mouth listening gleefully to Satan's plot to corrupt man, and from their lower level watch the ensuing scene. The change from Satan to Serpent might best be accomplished through characteristic movement. The Serpent's suggestions to Eve are thick with sensuality, and his writhing and hissing reach a climax at Eve's biting of the apple, when he returns triumphant to his confederate devils. A stage direction in the Chester *Creation* (312) makes a point of the hissing: *Tunc recedet serpens, vocem serpentinam faciens.*

The creation of Adam and Eve calls for special attention in staging. If Adam has been lying supine, close to God's throne, he should not be noticed until God bids him rise (165). He certainly cannot make an entry, walking on from left or right. The Chester *Creation* has a direction 'Adam rises', and the Cornish plays show shrewd awareness of this practical problem: 'Meanwhile are got ready Adam and Eva aparlet in whytt lether in a place apoynted by the conveyour and not to be sene till they be called and thei kneel and ryse'. (O. Waterhouse, *Non Cycle Mystery Plays*, xxxiv.) The use of trapdoors for the creation of Adam and Eve is perhaps the most effective method. Failing this device, much may be concealed by the voluminous wings of the Angels. One such wing may also conceal Adam's rib (186).

[88]

In realistic terms there appears to be the necessity for at least two stage trees in paradise, one for the apple and one for the fig leaves. The Cornish play has a direction indicating that the fig-leaves were handed to Adam and Eve, as it were, from the wings: 'fig leaves redy to cover ther members'. In the Coventry Accounts there is reference to two trees, one of which no doubt carried the fig leaves. But the medieval mind would not have been in the least deterred from using the same tree for both apples and fig leaves. The stained glass representation of the Garden of Eden in the York Minster East Window shows also a wide variety of fruit on the tree. The tree used by the Norwich Grocers was decorated with oranges, figs, almonds, dates, raisins, apples, and flowers bound on by coloured thread.

The Killing of Abel

This play, as at York, was presented by the Glovers' guild. *The Killing of Abel* following *The Creation* stresses the sharpness of Man's fall. Cain is the unredeemable blasphemer: he strikes his servant, slays his brother, curses God. In the York play he even strikes an angel. The Wakefield dramatist relishes his theme and brings the outrageous destructive vigour of his main character into striking contrast with the foregoing majesty and control of *The Creation*.

A minimum of three main levels is required: (1) the ground level on which Cain enters with, as A. C. Cawley points out, 'a plough team of eight animals, comprising four oxen and four horses'; (2) the hill on which the tithe-offering is made; (3) the upper level on which God appears and speaks.

Frequently in the mystery plays characters make their entry and exit on horseback, but the boldest producer, with the most sympathetic understanding of the concrete nature of medieval thought, might blench from a literal presentation of Cain's plough team. Whatever ingenuity he may have recourse to, pretence without some material representation would be alien to the medieval dramatic tradition.

After the tithe-offering Cain and Abel descend the hill and Abel is killed at the lower level. In medieval drama the pageant itself is frequently referred to as 'the hill' and the acting area on ground level as 'the green', 'the field', or 'the place'. When in the Chester Plays Cain leads Abel from the place of sacrifice, the text itself indicates where the killing will take place:

> Come forth, brother, with me to go
> Into the field a little here fro,
> I have a thing to say.
>
> *(Chester Plays, II. The Creation* 594–6.)

A similar movement from hill to field is required in this Wakefield play (294–302). Internal evidence sometimes reveals whether the pageants stood in fields or streets. Cain in the *Ludus Coventriae,* when cursed by God, laments his fate:

> In field and town, in street and stage,
> I may never make mirth more.
>
> *(Ludus Coventriae, Cain and Abel,* 187–8.)

'street and stage' are clearly juxtaposed as alternative acting areas.

The Boy is the type of pert youth who appears elsewhere in the Wakefield Plays, for instance, as Jack Garcio in *The First Shepherds' Play.* He is the forebear of Shakespeare's Moth and Launcelot Gobbo. Cain refers to him as 'pyke-harnes' which is usually glossed as 'a stealer of armour from the slain'. 'Pickbrain' is an alternative.

The Boy enters blowing a horn and then commands silence for his master. The same formula, considerably extended, is used for the entry of the main character in the Wakefield *Herod the Great.* The Boy in his master's name gains silence for his own speech, but encourages the spectators to welcome Cain with jeers and hisses. This interpretation is consistent with his relationship to Cain throughout. Cain complains (39) that he has both to hold the plough and drive the plough team, and when it comes to a fight (52) the Boy promises to give blow for blow. He soon proves too nimble for his master who, quickly puffed, calls a truce. Cain can only enlist the Boy's support (400) by promising him his release from serfdom.

The royal proclamation (411) announces that the king extends his pardon and protection to Cain and his Boy. Human and divine judgements are deliberately and ironically confused. God has protected Cain's life by threat of seven-fold punishment on his slayer (366); in the royal proclamation spectators are asked not only to love the first murderer and his Boy (427), but also to contribute to the collection they are making on their own behalf (430).

Abel enters (54) with a sheep which he intends offering as his tithe to God. The sheep as a stage property is also needed in this cycle in *Abraham, The Second Shepherds' Play,* and *John the Baptist.*

As a medieval ploughman Cain begrudges paying to the Church tithes which stay in the pockets of the priests (103). He cheats in his tithing by miscounting the sheaves as he selects from his stook of corn one in ten to offer to God. When he sets fire to his offering and tries to blow the kindled corn into a flame (267), smoke belches out and nearly chokes him.

'The words "over the wall" (290) may refer to the balustrade of the balcony on which God made his appearance in the craft-pageants.' (A. C. Cawley, *The Wakefield Pageants in the Towneley Cycle*, 93.)

Abel being killed with a cheek-bone (318) is unbiblical but well established in medieval tradition: *Cursor Mundi* 1073; *Ludus Coventriae* 'chavyl bon' or jaw-bone (149); the York Minster East Window; a Norwich Cathedral roof boss.

Goodybower Lane (360) was the site of the present Brook Street in Wakefield. In the adjoining field was the quarry from which the stone for the parish church, the rectory, and the Chantry Bridge Chapel was obtained.

NOAH

The story of Noah was an indispensable part of the medieval mystery cycle. Versions of it are found in all the extant cycles, including the Cornish Plays, and also in the Newcastle Shipwrights' Play. The Trinity Guild of Master Mariners and Pilots of Hull records in great detail the management of their Noah Play which was performed annually on Plough Monday, the first Monday after Epiphany.

The Flood prefigures the Last Judgement. In times of local or national stress—and such times were rarely absent from medieval life—these themes maintained their homiletic and dramatic appeal. The boisterous horse-play occasioned by Noah's wife in no way militates against the essential seriousness of the playwright's intention. The characterization of Noah's wife looks back to Eve, the first disobedient wife. This is even more explicit in the Newcastle Play where the Devil tempts her to strong drink, with which in turn she plies her husband, who responds

> What the devil, what drink is it!
> By my father's soul, I have near lost my wit!

Except in the *Ludus Coventriae* version of this play, Noah's wife is depicted as the stubborn, self-willed harridan, as adept at striking as at spinning with her distaff. The domination of such a character in the plays of the Wakefield Master gives rise to biographical speculation.

For staging, three main levels are required: heaven; the hill from which Noah first speaks and on which Noah's wife persists in spinning; and the Ark. Noah builds the Ark by himself, speaking at the same time, in full view of the spectators, with forty lines (249–288) in which to complete his task. This is just enough time for him to fit together prefabricated sections lying near at hand.

In medieval times the management of this problem of stage business varied considerably. In the York Shipwrights' Play Noah in eighteen lines complains that it has taken him a hundred years to build the Ark. Lincoln accounts show that three times as much was charged for housing the Noah pageant as for the others, and the Hull Trinity Guild accounts indicate that the Ark, a considerable structure, rigged with mast and sails, costing in 1522 £5. 8s. 4d, was set upon a framework on wheels. In these two latter cases the erection of prefabricated sections within a short space of time and by one person only would have been impossible. A ship on wheels must have been used in the Digby *Mary Magdalene*, a play most probably performed in the round, in which the ship calls at different stations or pageants. In the *Ludus Coventriae*, after Noah has received his instructions to build the Ark, he withdraws with his family during the fifty-six line interlude in which Lameth kills Cain. The interpolation of the Lameth-Cain interlude, an apparent irrelevance in this context, can only be justified in its allowing Noah and his family some short space of time in which to build the Ark and return with it, which they do on Lameth's exit, singing. The Ark in the Chester Deluge is presented to full view at the beginning of the play, before even God has told Noah to build it. The first stage direction in the 1600 version reads: 'The thirde pagent of Noyes flood and first in some heigh place or in the cloudes, yf it may be, God speaketh unto Noe standing without the Arke with all his family'. It is later in this play that the family mime the building of the Ark (*Tunc faciunt signa quasi laborarent cum diversis Instrumentis*). This is indication enough that the drama is no longer truly medieval. Biblically the three cabins (129) are set one above the other: 'A window shalt thou make to the ark, and in a cubit shalt thou finish it above; and the door of the ark shalt thou set in the side thereof; with lower, second, and third stories shalt thou make it'. (Genesis 6. 16.) A stained glass representation of such an ark, with Noah leaning out of the window 'above' welcoming the dove, is to be seen in

the north aisle choir of Canterbury Cathedral. The
reference to a trap door in the Hull Trinity House
accounts (1525. Item for a band to the trape dore
vd) suggests that there, too, the cabins were constructed one above the other.

The medieval ship was frequently crenellated: an
example of such a Noah's Ark is to be found on one
of the misericords in Ely Cathedral. The Chester Noah
exhorts his wife and children to come aboard (97-98):

> Wife, in this castle we shall be kept,
> My children and thou I would in leapt.

'The hill' has hitherto in this cycle implied the lowest acting level
on the pageant—Cain and Abel offer their tithes on 'the hill'—in which
case the Ark might occupy a quite separate acting area. It is extremely
doubtful whether Noah's wife would persistently refer to her position
as 'upon this hill' if the three-storeyed Ark were towering above her
on the pageant. It is more probable that the Ark, which is mobile, is
located in another acting area. The fight certainly takes place on the
hill (407).

The sending forth of the raven and the dove (507) might be managed
by a suspension from above, as the Chester direction reads 'in some
heigh place or in the cloudes'. There is however a particular stage
direction in the Chester *Noah* which suggests how this may be done:
'Then shall Noah release a dove, and there shall be in the ship another
dove carrying a branch of olive in its mouth, which it shall drop from
the mast by means of a rope into Noah's hand'. (*Tunc emittet columbam
et erit in nave alia columba ferens olivam in ore, quam dimittet ex malo per
funem in manus Noe . . .*)

ABRAHAM AND ISAAC

Two leaves are missing in the manuscript after line 286. The version
presented here concludes with fourteen lines (287-300) adapted from
the Brome Abraham and Isaac Play.

Obedience is the theme of the plays that begin the cycle. Lucifer
and Adam fall through disobedience; Noah and Abraham are blessed
because of their obedience to God. Obedience to the deity in the
sacrifice of an innocent child is also the theme of Euripides' *Iphigenia
in Aulis*, in which Iphigenia, as Isaac, at first protests against her fate,
but finally submits to the divine will. This archetypal pattern is best
illustrated by the plays concerning Christ's Passion. The Chester

Sacrifice of Isaac ends with the Expositor underlining, rather heavily, the play's significance:

> This deed ye see done in this place,
> In example of Jesus done it was,
> That to win mankind to grace
>   Was sacrificed upon the rood.
>
> By Abraham I bring to mind
> The Father of heaven that did find
> His Son's blood needed to unbind
>   Us from the Devil, our foe.
>
> By Isaac understand I may
> Jesus that was obedient ay,
> His Father's will to work alway,
>   His death to undergo.
>   (Chester, *Sacrifice of Isaac* 465–476.)

Three acting levels are required: heaven; the hill; the ground. To begin with Abraham speaks from the lowest level, and on this level he meets Isaac, and together with the ass and the two attendants they move towards the hill, and then leaving the ass and the two attendants at ground level Abraham and Isaac climb to the hill (145–148). The hill once again may be taken as the level of the pageant stage.

In the various versions of this play there are pointed references to the characters riding:

> ABRAHAM   Get hither our horses and let us go hence,
>   Both I and Isaac and these two men.
>   (The Dublin *Abraham and Isaac* Play 128–129.)
> 'And Abraham rides towards Sara who says . . .'
>   (*Et equitat versus Saram dicit Sara.*)
>   (Stage direction following line 317,
>   Dublin Play.)
> ISAAC   Children, lead forth our Ass. . . .
>   (York. 109.)
> 'Melchisedech receiving the horse of Abraham very gladly . . .'
>   (Stage direction following line 96,
>   Chester, 1600 version.)
> 'Then Melchisadech shall ride up to Abraham. . . .'
>   (Stage direction following line 72,
>   Chester, 1592 version.)

We can assume that the animals were ridden on the ground ('upon this fair heath' Brome 407: 'Then hie thee that thou were on ground' God says as he despatches his angel to Abraham, Dublin 30). If this is so, the same station is used for hill and heaven and the riding is done in a circle to the point from which the characters started, or there are separate stations: one for heaven, one for the hill, and the dialogue between Abraham and Isaac preparatory to their journey takes place on 'the green'.

The main properties required are an altar on the hill on which Isaac is laid, a bundle of faggots, a flaming torch or the means of making fire on the altar, Abraham's sword, and the sheep for the sacrifice.

ISAAC and JACOB

The two missing leaves of the manuscript which deprived us of the ending of *Abraham and Isaac* have also deprived us of the beginning of *Isaac. Jacob*, although categorised by A. W. Pollard as a fragment (*The Towneley Plays*, Introduction xxiii) and admittedly unusually short (142 lines), nevertheless appears complete in itself, beginning, as *Noah* and *Abraham and Isaac*, with the main character calling to God, and ending with the reconciliation of Jacob and Esau. The action of *Isaac* and *Jacob* is continuous and they may be regarded as one play [Professor Ten-Brink, *History of English Literature* (English Edition), vol. ii. p. 244]. Their style, thematic treatment, and dramatic art indicate earlier work than the other plays in the cycle. They represent the only medieval dramatic version of the story of Jacob and Esau in the vernacular. We may fill in the first part of *Isaac* (excluding the allegorical passages) and learn many details of early medieval staging from Karl Young's account of the late twelfth century Latin play of *Isaac and Rebecca:*

At the opening of the first scene, as Isaac totters to his platform, a chorus sings some verses describing his decrepitude, fatigue and hunger. After he has lain down upon his bed, the choristers sing an 'allegory', in which they somewhat darkly interpret Isaac's physical weaknesses as prefigurings of Christian realities. Then Isaac querulously demands that Esau be summoned. As the messengers depart, an allegory is sung explaining that Esau symbolizes the Jews, and Jacob the Christians. When Esau is brought before Isaac, the father asks for food, and straightway sends his son off to the hunt. After another allegory has been sung, the hunting expedition of Esau is represented in dumb-show. Meanwhile Rebecca proposes to Jacob a plan whereby he shall outwit Esau and obtain Isaac's blessing. The chorus then allegorizes the two kids which Jacob kills by way of deceiving his father. Prodded and aided by his mother, Jacob clothes himself in the skins of the goats, and in garments left at home by Esau. The choral allegory explains, among other things, that the garments left behind by Esau symbolize the decalogue abandoned by the Jews. In his disguise Jacob represents himself to his blind father as Esau, and offers him food. When Isaac expresses surprise at Esau's so speedy return from hunting, Jacob attributes it to God's help. With another allegory, hardly intelligible, the fragment ends.

The play clearly undertakes to represent the biblical story of Jacob and Esau with realistic thoroughness. The playing-space is set with three main 'mansions', or *tabernacula,* one for Jacob and Rebecca, and one each for Esau and Isaac. The mansions are provided with beds and such other furnishings as can be supplied. Kitchens are arranged for both Esau and Jacob. The stage equipment includes also a roe-buck, two kids, hairy coverings for the hands and neck of Jacob, a bow and arrows, and suitable Jewish hats and other garments for all. Whether or not all this realism was effected within the church building we cannot tell.

(Karl Young, *The Drama of the Medieval Church.* O.U.P. 1933, ii. 264–265.)

For *Jacob* many non-speaking parts are required. Jacob divides his host into three parts (115), and Esau makes his entry with a band of armed followers (122). In the course of the play Jacob journeys to Mesopotamia and back again to his own country. He would take his rest on the ground or on the pageant, and on waking he would be looking at 'God's house and heaven's gate' (41), erected on the pageant. (On the opposition of heaven to hell, see Leslie Hotson's *Shakespeare's Wooden O'*, Chapter IX.) Jacob's travelling, foot-sore 'along this street', suggests a linear rather than circular movement.

According to the text an Angel wrestles with Jacob (*luctetur angelus cum eo*), but it is God who says 'The day springs; now let me go'. The biblical version is as follows: 'And Jacob was left alone; and there wrestled a man with him until the breaking of the day'. (*Genesis* 32. v 24.) Whatever spirit Jacob wrestles with must, as a ghost, glide away before dawn (108).

[96]

PHARAOH

In the manuscript *The Prophets* follows *Jacob*, and *Pharaoh* follows *The Prophets*. In the biblical order of events *Pharaoh* should precede *The Prophets*, and such is the order adopted here.

The Wakefield Dyers were responsible for the presentation of this play: 'Litsters Pagonn' (Dyers' Pageant) appears in the Manuscript margin. The play is almost identical with the York Hosiers' play. Miss Toulmin Smith sets out the parallel texts in her edition of *The York Mystery Plays* (O.U.P. 1885) and Marie C. Lyle and Grace Frank examine the interdependence of the two cycles (M. C. Lyle, *The Original Identity of the York and Towneley Cycles*, PMLA, xliv, 1929, 319–328; G. Frank, *On the Relation of the York and Towneley Plays*, PMLA, xliv, 1929, 313–319).

The cast of the York play includes two Counsellors who do not appear in the Wakefield *Pharaoh*. Their parts are almost identical with some of the speeches given to the Wakefield 1st. and 2nd. Soldiers. The reporting of the plagues is far better managed in the York version through four speakers than through the two of the Wakefield version. In a dramatic presentation of the Wakefield play it might be advisable to extend the number of Soldiers to four and to reallocate the Soldiers' parts, or to follow the York example and introduce two Counsellors who might appropriate some of the Soldiers' speeches. Left as it is, the Wakefield play demands that the two Soldiers rush on and off with news of fresh plagues with a relay-race rapidity that may too easily induce hilarity in the audience.

Both the Wakefield and York versions disregard the biblical tenth plague, the death of the first-born of Egypt, and replace it with the pestilence, the most terrible of afflictions in the Middle Ages. Pharaoh's words would be deeply felt:

> Pestilence, in the devil's name!
> Then is our pride quite past.

And, understandably, his decision to release the Israelites follows immediately. Even in the Middle Ages the Jews were frequently held responsible for the pestilence: 'in Mainz and other German-speaking towns (they) were burned in their hundreds or thousands by an infuriated mob in the belief that the plague was a malignant device of the Semitic race for the confusion of the Catholic creed' (H. A. L. Fisher, *A History of Europe*, 319). Furthermore, the massacre of the Jews at York in 1185 would not have been forgotten when the local medieval drama was written and performed.

The York play concludes very suddenly with the drowning of

Pharaoh, his Egyptians, and his horses and chariots, at which the Hebrews burst into song '*Cantemus domino,* to God a song sing we'. The Wakefield version ends less precipitously but without reference to singing. A hymn of praise or a psalm of deliverance, Psalm 46 or Psalm 106 for example, might be a fitting conclusion to the play (*Exodus* 15, v. 1–21).

The staging of the Cornish play may give some guidance here. After God has ascended to heaven (1478), Pharaoh struts about on the pageant (*Hic pompabit rex pharo . . .*). There is every possibility that Pharaoh 'pomps it' on the pageant, because in a later stage direction we learn that he descends (1584 *hic descendit pharo*) to the arena where Moses has been walking (1534 *Moyses ambulat in platea*). It is in 'the place' that Moses mounts his horse (1626 *ascendit super equum*) to lead the Israelites out of the land of Egypt. When Moses encounters the Red Sea he strikes at it (1674 *percutit mare*) and the following dialogue describes the dramatic action ensuing:

MOSES In the name of God, thou fair sea,
      I strike thee with my rod;
       Open wide a path for us,
      That we may go to the land
      Which is ordained for us perfectly,
      By the Lord of heaven, really.

2ND. SOLDIER As I say, Lord, to thee,
      Moses far is gone
      Into the sea, as it seems to me;
      Forth quickly going,
      The water striking wide
       Every moment before him.

A SQUIRE All his people, they are
      Following him every one;
       And the sea on every side, to them
      Standing like two walls.
      They are kept within the enclosure,
       And water will certainly never drown them.

(Edwin Norris' translation in his edition of *The Ancient Cornish Drama*, The Beginning of the World, 1675–1692.)

That the Red Sea is a very material stage property is emphasized by an item under Miscellaneous Entries in the Coventry Cappers' Company accounts (*Two Coventry Corpus Christi* Plays Hardin Craig, 97), 'it. pd. for halfe a yard of rede sea vjd'.

THE PROCESSION OF THE PROPHETS

The Procession of the Prophets is an unfinished play, but it may be performed as complete in itself because of its unusual lineal structure: each prophet enters in succession, says his piece and departs. Daniel's 'Evermore without end' seems an admirable line on which to close the play, although in the completed text, no doubt, more prophecies would have followed. There are, for instance, twenty-six prophets, although mostly with only four lines apiece, in the *Ludus Coventriae Procession of the Prophets*. The York and Chester cycles contain no such play. In the *Ludus Coventriae* version the prophets, in the brief speeches allotted them, illustrate how their deeds and words have prefigured Christ's coming: King David reflects on the regal power of Christ; Jonas foretells the resurrection:

> I, Jonas, say that on the third morn
> From death he shall rise: this is a true tale,
> Figured in me which long before
> Lay three days buried in the whale.

> (*Ludus Coventriae, Procession of the Prophets*, 67–70.)

The essential difference between the two extant vernacular versions of this play is that whereas the *Ludus Coventriae* play is literally processional, the Wakefield play, both in the allocation of much longer speeches to the prophets and in the severe homiletic character of their harangues, looks back directly to the common origin, which was a sermon. 'This substantial homiletic piece, found among the spurious works attributed to St. Augustine, is entitled *Contra Judaeos, Paganos, et Arianos Sermo de Symbolo*. Although the Augustinian authorship is now discredited, the attribution to the great bishop persisted throughout the Middle Ages. The sermon appears to have been written during the fifth or sixth century. . . . It opens (Chapter XI in the modern edition) with a direct arraignment of the Jews for their perverse disbelief in the Messiahship of Christ. Since the Jews stubbornly demand evidence, the preacher grimly proposes to bring testimony from their own law. He first summons Isaiah, bidding him testify concerning Christ. . . . Similarly are summoned the prophets Jeremiah, Daniel, Moses, David, and Habbakuk. . . . With a tart reminder to the Jews that the testimony already adduced should be ample, the preacher adds utterances from the Gentiles, Virgil and Nebuchadnezzar, and finally a prophetic passage in hexameters from the Erythraean Sibyl. ['These prophetic verses are quoted and interpreted by St. Augustine in his *De Civitate Dei* (lib. xviii, cap. 23, Migne, P.L., xli, 579–581). Their appearance throughout the Middle Ages is frequent.'] (Karl Young, op. cit., ii. 125–132.)

In production of this play a remarkable fact emerges. Whereas the text appears devoid of dramatic incident and interplay of characters, if presented as a succession of short sermons delivered from a pulpit on a pageant around which throng the spectators, no play in the whole Cycle is more fraught with dramatic tension. This is partly due to the variety within the play of character and homiletic material, but mainly to the astonishing power, though largely forgotten in our day, that a fiery sermon can exert on a mass of listeners. The achievements of Adolf Hitler and Billy Graham in this medium are recent reminders of such power.

Details of dress, make-up, and properties relating to the Latin plays on the same subject, originally performed on the feast of the Circumcision (1st January) at Laon and Rouen cathedrals, indicate that Moses is bearded, he carries his *tables* and a rod and is clad in a dalmatic or alb. David appears as a king; Sibyl, crowned and with hair streaming, has an expression of mad inspiration. Daniel, in a green tunic, has a youthful appearance and carries an ear of corn.

In the Wakefield play Moses would certainly carry his *tables,* which he would rest on the pulpit, referring to them as the text from which he preaches. David is crowned and carries a harp or lyre on which he accompanies himself as he sings (108–162). After Sibyl's spine-chilling forecasts, Daniel concludes with the comfort of the promised redemption.

CAESAR AUGUSTUS

The only Middle English text of a *Caesar Augustus* play is the one from the Wakefield Cycle. The Chester *Annunciation* introduces the character of Octavian, before whom Sibyl is commanded to prophesy; but although, on his first appearance, Octavian conducts himself in the conventional manner of the medieval stage despot [he struts (*pompabit*), interlards his speech with French, and swears by Mohammed], on his second appearance, when Sibyl informs him that Jesus has been born, he loses his afflatus, and in humility worships the child.

The Wakefield *Caesar Augustus* is the tyrant throughout showing, as the Herod of the Coventry Pageant of the *Shearmen and Taylors,* particular pleasure in his own beauty (14). In performance the two Counsellors might be contrasted: the first quick and incisive, the second heavy and slow. Lightfoot is the nimble lad we have met as Garcio in *The Killing of Abel* and will meet again in the *First Shepherds' Play*. The staging requires two 'mansions' set apart, possibly on the same pageant: one for Caesar Augustus and one for Sirinus.

END OF PART ONE

[100]

Part Two

The Tenth Play: The Annunciation

GOD   MARY
GABRIEL   JOSEPH

GOD

Since I have made all things of nought
And Adam with my hands have wrought,
Like to mine image, by my device,
And given him joy in paradise
To live therein as that I bad,
Until he did what I forbad;
And then I put him from that place,
But yet I mean to grant him grace,
And the oil of mercy for his gain,
And in time to ease his pain.
For he has suffered sin full sore,
For these five thousand years and more,
First on earth and then in hell;
But long therein he shall not dwell.
Beyond pain's power he shall be laid,
I will not lose what I have made.
I will make redemption,
As promised, in my person,
All with reason and with right
Both through mercy and through might.
With joy we shall be reconciled,
For he was wrongfully beguiled;
He shall out of prison pass
Because that he beguiled was
Through the serpent and his wife;
They made him touch the tree of life,
And eat the fruit that I forbad,
That doomed him to a life full sad.
Righteousness will we perform;
My son shall take on human form,
And reasons therefore shall be three,
A man, a maiden, and a tree:
Man for man, tree for tree,
Maiden for maiden; thus shall it be.

My son shall by a maid be born,   35
The fiend of hell to hold in scorn;
Without a spot, as sun through glass,
So pure a maid may none surpass.
Both God and man shall he be,
And both mother and maiden she.
To Abraham I once decreed
To save both him and all his seed;
And I intend that prophecy
Be here fulfilled by me;
For I am Lord and live anew,
My prophets shall be found most true.
As said Moses and Isaiah,
King David and Jeremiah,
Habakkuk and Daniel,
Sibyl sage, that spoke so well,
And mine other prophets all,
As they have said, it shall befall.
Rise up, Gabriel, and find

GABRIEL *appears by* GOD.

A gentle maiden, meek and kind,
In Nazareth of Galilee,
Where she dwells in that city.
To that virgin and her spouse,
To a man of David's house,
Who as Joseph known is he,
And the maiden named Mary.
Angel must to Mary go,
For to Eve the fiend was foe;
He was hateful in my sight,
But thou art angel fair and bright;
And hail that maiden, as I plan,
As graciously as thou can.
On my behalf thou shall her greet,
I have her chosen, that maiden sweet,
She shall conceive my darling,
Through thy word and her hearing.
In her body will I come,
That to me is cleanly done;
She shall of her body bear
God and man, nor harm a hair;

[2]

75   Blessed shall she be, and ever so;
            Bestir thee, Gabriel, and go.
    GABRIEL *goes to* MARY.

GABRIEL   Hail, Mary, gracious!
          Hail, maiden, and God's spouse!
            To thee I bow, devout;
          Of all virgins thou art queen,
          That ever was, or shall be seen,
            Without a doubt.

          Hail, Mary, and well thou be!
          My Lord of heaven is with thee,
            Without an end;
          Hail, woman, most of grace!
          Fear not nor feel disgrace,
            That I commend.

          For thou hast found, without a doubt,
          The grace of God that has gone out
            For Adam's plight.
          This is the grace that gives thee bloom,
          Thou shalt conceive within thy womb
            A child of might.

          When he is come, that is thy son,
          He shall take circumcision,
            Call him Jesus.
          God's son men shall him call
          Who comes to free the thrall
            Within us.

          My lord shall also give to him
          David's throne to sit therein,
            His lineage to show.
          He shall be king of Jacob's kin,
          And the crown eternal win,
            Lady, you must know.

MARY   What is thy name?
GABRIEL   Gabriel,
          God's strength and his angel,
            That comes to thee.

[3]

MARY   Wondrous words are in thy greeting,   110
        But to bear God's gentle sweeting,
            How should it be?

        I slept never by man's side,
        But in maidhood would abide
            Unshaken.
        Therefore, I know not how
        This may be, because a vow
            I have taken.

        Nevertheless, full well I know
        God may work his will below
            Thy words fulfilling.
        But, I know not the manner,
        Therefore, teach me, thou messenger,
            God's way instilling.

GABRIEL Lady, this the secret hear of me;
        The holy ghost shall come to thee,
            And in his virtue
        Thee enshroud and so infuse,
        Yet thou thy maidhood shall not lose,
            But ay be new.

        The child that thou shalt bear, madame,
        Shall God's son be called by name;
            And, Mary, understand,
        Elizabeth, thy cousin, whom barren all believed,
        A son in her old age she has conceived
            By her husband.

        And this is, for who will know,
        The sixth month since she conceived so,
            Whom barren all thought.
        No word, lady, that I thee bring,
        Is impossible to heaven's king,
            Who all has wrought.

MARY   My lord's love will I not withstand,
        I am his maiden at his hand,
            And in his fold.

[4]

146   Gabriel, I believe that God will bring
            To pass with me each several thing
              As thou hast told.

GABRIEL   Mary, gentle maid,
            Too long now have I stayed,
              My leave of you I take.
MARY   Fare to my friend,
            Who did thee send,
              For mankind's sake.
    GABRIEL *retires;* JOSEPH *advances.*

JOSEPH   Almighty God, what may this be!
            Mary, my wife, amazes me,
              Herself she has forgot.
            Her body is great, and she with child!
            By me she never was defiled,
              Mine therefore is it not.

            I am irked full sore with my life,
            That ever I wed so young a wife,
              Repent I of that plan;
            To me it was a doleful deed,
            I might have known the wench had need
              To love a younger man.

            I am old, indeed to say,
            And passed the pleasures of love's play,
              Those games from me are gone.
            Youth and age are poorly paired;
            That know I well, since ill I fared,
              Some other she dotes on.

            She is with child, I know not how;
            Who could trust any woman now?
              No man of any good;
            I know not what now I should do
            Save go to her and ask her who
              Shall own the fatherhood.

JOSEPH   Hail, Mary, and well ye be!
            Why, but woman, what cheer with thee?
MARY   The better, sir, for you.

JOSEPH   So would I, woman, that ye were;   182
          A mock now Mary you'll incur
              And your state sadly rue.

          But one thing I must ask of thee,
          This child's father, who is he?
MARY   Sir, ye, and God of heaven.
JOSEPH   Mine, Mary, leave be thy din;
          Ye know, I have no part therein,
              Swear it, by those stars seven.

          Wherefore link ye me thereto?
          I had never with thee to do,
              How should it then be mine?
          Whose is that child, so God thee speed?
MARY   Sir, God's and yours, I say indeed.
JOSEPH   Spare those words of thine.

          For none of mine it is, I know,
          And I repent thou hast done so
              Ill deed as is seen;
          And had thou thought thyself to kill,
          Though full sore against my will,
              It better might have been.

MARY   By God's will, Joseph, must it be,
          For certainly save God and ye
              I know no other man;
          Nor in flesh have been defiled.
JOSEPH   How then art thou thus with child?
              Excuse that if ye can.

          So God save me, I blame thee not
          To weaken for a woman's lot;
              But to thee I must say this,
          Well ye know, and so do I
          That thy state cannot deny
              That thou hast done amiss.

MARY   Yea, God he knows all my doing.
     MARY *retires a little.*
JOSEPH   Woe! Now this is a wondrous thing,
              I can say nought thereto;

[6]

218 But in my heart I feel full sore,
And ever longer more and more;
 For dole what shall I do?

God's and mine she says it is;
I will not father it, she says amiss;
 With shame she is beset
To excuse her villainy to me.
With her I can no longer be,
 I ruc that ever we met.

And how we met ye shall soon know:
Young children used to the temple go
 In learning's way to tread;
And so did she, till she grew more
Than other maidens wise of lore,
 Then to her the bishops said,

"Mary, it behoves thee to take
Some young man thy mate to make,
 As others have done before,
In the temple whom thou wilt name."
And she said, none, for still the same
 God of heaven she would adore.

She would none other for any saw;
They said she must, it was the law,
 She was of age thereto.
To the temple they gathered old and young,
All those from Judah's lineage sprung,
 To give the law its due.

They gave each man a white wand there,
And bad us in our hand it bear,
 To offer with good intent;
They offered their wands up at that tide,
But I was old and stood beside,
 I knew not what they meant.

They lacked one which came not nigh,
All had offered, they said, but I,
 For I ay withdrew me.

[7]

Forth with my wand they made me stand,   254
With bloom it flourished in my hand;
   Then said they all to me,

"Though thou be old, this marvel on thee
Shows God of heaven, thus ordains he,
   Thy wand shows clearly.
It flourishes so, without gainsay,
That to marry maid Mary is your way."
   A sorrier man then was I.

I was full sorry to be thus caught,
My age put marriage past my thought
   For us to share a tether;
Her youth would find my age no use,
But they would hear of no excuse,
   But wed us thus together.

When I all thus had wed her there,
We and my maidens home did fare,
   That kings' daughters were.
They all at silk worked everyone,
Mary wrought purple all alone,
   No other colour.

I left them in good peace, I thought,
And in the country where I wrought
   My craft with might and main,
I went to earn what we should need;
Of Mary I prayed them take good heed,
   Until I came again.

Nine months away from Mary mild,
When I came home she was with child;
   Alas, I said, for shame!
I asked those women who had that done,
They told me an angel had come,
   None other was to blame.

An angel spoke with Mary bright,
And no man else by day or night,
   "Sir, thereof be ye bold."
They excused her thus readily,

[8]

291   To clear her of all folly,
         And mock me that am old.

Should an angel this deed have wrought?
Such excuses help me nought,
    Nor no cunning that they can;
A heavenly thing, forsooth, is he,
And she is earthly; this may not be;
    It is some other man.

Her misdeed grieves me sore, in truth,
But yet such is the way of youth
    So wantonly to sport.
Young women ever yearn to play
With youths and turn the old away,
    Such is the world's report.

But Mary and I played never love's game,
Never together so closely we came,
    Never so near.

As clean as uncut crystal she,
And shall be while I live, for me,
    The law will have it so.
And then am I cause of her deed?
Of good counsel I am sore in need,
    Alas, who recks my woe!

And if indeed it so befall
With God's son that she be withal,
    Such grace is me denied;
I know well I am not he
Who should worthy deemed to be
That blessed body beside,

Nor yet to be in company;
To the wilderness then flee,
    And there my fate deplore;
In future never with her deal,
But secretly from her shall steal,
    That meet shall we no more.
JOSEPH *moves away from* MARY.

[9]

GABRIEL   Be warned, Joseph, and change thy thought   326
           Which to wandering thee has brought
               In the wilderness so wild;
           Turn home to thy spouse again
           Thy wife she is without a stain,
               Nor ever was defiled.

           Tax not from earth the heavenly host,
           She has conceived the holy ghost,
               And God's son she shall bear;
           Therefore with her, in thy degree,
           Meek and obedient, look thou be
               And of her take good care.

JOSEPH   Ah, Lord, I love thee above all,
           For so great boon as may befall
               That I should tend this stripling:
           I that so ungracious were
           To cast on her the slightest slur,
               Mary, my dear darling.

           Repent I now what I have said
           Against her matchless maidenhead,
               For she is pure in deed;
           Therefore to her now will I go
           And pray her be my friend not foe,
               And her forgiveness plead.

JOSEPH *returns to* MARY.

           Ah, Mary, wife, what cheer?
MARY   The better, sir, that ye are here;
               Thus long where have ye been?
JOSEPH   Fretting and walking up and down,
           And troubled how to smooth thy frown
               Against my thoughts unclean.

           But now I know and clearly see
           My trespass against God and thee;
               Forgive me, I thee pray.

MARY   Now all that ever ye said to me
           God forgives as I do thee,
               With all the might I may.

[10]

JOSEPH   Blessed be, Mary, thy good will
363   In forgiving my words ill
       When I did thee upbraid;
And blessed be he with such a wife;
Though dowerless, to share his life,
       He may count himself well paid.

Lo, I am as light as a leaf!
He that can quench all grief
       And every wrong amend,
Lend me grace, power, and might
My wife and her sweet son of light
       To keep to my life's end.

They go off together.

The Eleventh Play:
The Salutation of Elizabeth

MARY   ELIZABETH

MARY   My lord of heaven that sits on high,
And all things sees with his eye,
       Save thee Elizabeth.

ELIZABETH   Welcome, Mary, blessed bloom,
Joy I now that thou hast come
       To me from Nazareth.

MARY   How stands it with you, cousin mine?

ELIZABETH   Daughter dear, I never pine,
Though I grow fast old.

MARY   To speak with you has been my care,
For in age a child you'll bear,
       Though barren you be called.

ELIZABETH   Full long shall I the better be,
That I may speak my fill with thee,
       My dear kinswoman;

[11]

To know how thy friends afar,
Fare in the land where now they are,
    Thereof tell me thou can,
And how thou farest my dear darling.

MARY   Well, dame, thank you for your asking,
You speak with purpose fair.

ELIZABETH   And Joachim, thy father there,
And Anna, my niece, thy mother dear,
    How stands it with him and with her?

MARY   Dame, yet do they still have life,
Both Joachim and Anna his wife.

ELIZABETH   Else were my heart full sore.

MARY   Dame, God that does all,
Make good to befall,
    And bless you therefore.

ELIZABETH   Of all women be thou blest,
And the fruit that now doth rest
    Within the womb of thee.
And this time may I bless
That my Lord's mother is
    Come thus unto me.

For since that time full well I found
The trumpet voice of angel sound
    Aringing in mine ear;
A wondrous thing comes with that word
The child makes joy, as any bird,
    That I in body bear.

And now, Mary, be thou blest,
So steadfastly to rest
    In the words of heaven's king.
Therefore all things shall known be now
That unto thee were pledged in vow
    By the angel's greeting.

[12]

MARY   *Magnificat anima mea dominum,*
50   My soul doth praise my Lord above,
                 My spirit sings with love,
                     For God my hopes renew.

                 For he has been seen again
                 And saved his servant without stain
                     And kept me maiden true.
                 Lo, what now shall me betide—
                 All nations on every side,
                     Blessed shall me call;
                 For he that is full of might,
                 Has raised me in his sight;
                     His name be blessed overall.

                 And his mercy is also
                 Upon mankind that meekly go
                     The Lord's way faring.
                 Mighty in arms is he;
                 He brings to low degree
                     Proud men with high bearing.

                 Mighty men he hath put down;
                 But on those he set a crown,
                     Meek men of heart.
                 The hungry with good things he filled,
                 But left the rich without a shield,
                     Sadly to part.

                 Israel regards by law
                 His own son with great awe,
                     By means of his mercy;
                 As before by name he told
                 Abraham, our father old,
                     And seed of his body.

                 Elizabeth, mine aunt dear,
                 My leave I take of you here,
                     For I have tarried long.
ELIZABETH   If thou wilt go, then never fear,
                 Come kiss me daughter with good cheer,
                     Before you go along

Farewell now, whom God hath wooed,   86
I pray thee be of comfort good,
    For thou art full of grace.
Greet well our kin of blood;
The Lord that thee with grace endued,
    Save all within this place.

They part.

The Twelfth Play: The First Shepherds' Play

1ST SHEPHERD	JACK GARCIO
2ND SHEPHERD	ANGEL
3RD SHEPHERD	JESUS
	MARY

1ST SHEPHERD   Lord, but they are well that hence have passed,
           For nought they feel them to downcast.
           Here miseries dwell and long may they last,
           Now in heart a happy spell, now in wet now in blast
               Now in care,
           Now in comfort again,
           Now is fair, now is rain,
           Now in heart full fain,
               And after despair.

           Thus this world, as I say, fares on each side,
           For after our play cruel sorrows abide:
           For he that most may as he sits in his pride,
           When he makes his assay is cast quite aside,
               This is seen:
           When richest is he,
           Then comes poverty,
           Horseman Jack Cope
               Walks then, I mean.

           Thanks be to God, hark ye what I mean,
           For even or for odd great grief keeps me lean:
           As heavy as a sod I cry and I keen,

[14]

22   When I nap or I nod for care that has been,
            And sorrow.
        All my sheep are gone,
        I am not left one,
        All by plague undone:
            Now beg I and borrow.

        My hands may I wring and in misery quake,
        If no good will spring the country forsake:
        Rent dues are coming full more than I make,
        I have almost nothing, to pay nor to take.
            I may sing
        With purse penniless,
        What makes this heaviness,
        Woe is me this distress!
            And have no helping.

        Thus set I my mind, now by St. Stephen,
        By my wit to find what from me was riven:
        For my sheep I have pined for odd for even:
        Now if fortune be kind God from his heaven
            Send grace.
        To the fair will I hie,
        To buy sheep, perdy,
        And yet may I multiply,
            For all this hard case.

2ND SHEPHERD   Benedicite, benedicite, be us among,
        And save all that I see, here in this throng,
        He save you and me across and along,
        Who hung on a tree, I tell you no wrong:
            Christ save us
        From all mischiefs,
        From robbers and thieves,
        From those men's griefs
            That oft go against us.

        Both boasters and braggers grant God overthrow,
        That with their long daggers do us mighty woe.
        These stabbers and stranglers with fierce knives that go
        Such twisters and wranglers that bully and bellow,
            Cause us quake.

                        [15]

Who seeks to complain,   60
Were better be slain:
Both plough and wain
    Amends will not make.

He will prance as though proud as a lord that he were,
With his head in the cloud and curled all his hair:
He speaks out aloud, with grim looks that scare,
None would have allowed more gay in his gear
    Than he glides.
I know not the better,
Nor which is the greater,
The lad or the master,
    So stoutly he strides.

If he ask ought that he would we him pay,
Full dear is it bought if we say him nay:
By God that all wrought to thee now I say,
By his help be they brought to a better way
    For their soul:
And send them good mending
With a short ending,
On thy word attending
    When that thou call.

How, Gib, good morn, whither goes thou?
Thou goes over the corn, Gib, I say, how!

1st Shepherd Who is that? John Horn, I make God a vow!
I say not in scorn, then, how fares thou?

2nd Shepherd   Ha, hay!
Are ye in this town?

1st Shepherd Yea, by my crown.

2nd Shepherd I thought by your gown
    This was your array.

1st Shepherd The same to a stitch. Still the old grudge I nurse
That no shepherd is rich in this land, but fares worse.

2nd Shepherd Poor men are in the ditch and empty their purse:
This world is a bitch, but idle to curse,
    Help is none here.

1st Shepherd This from life I derive,
"A man may not wive

[16]

98   And also thrive,
                          All in a year."

2ND SHEPHERD First we must creep and afterwards go.

1ST SHEPHERD I go to buy sheep.
2ND SHEPHERD   Nay not so:
                   What, dream ye or sleep? Where should they go?
                   Here shall thou none keep.

1ST SHEPHERD   Ah, good sir, ho!
                   Who am I?
                   Their pasture shall be
                   Whereso it please me,
                   Here shall thou them see.
2ND SHEPHERD   Not so hardy!

                   Not one sheep's tail shall thou bring hither.

1ST SHEPHERD I shall bring, without fail, a hundred together.

2ND SHEPHERD What, does thou ail, long thou to go whither?

1ST SHEPHERD They shall go, though, ye wail. Go now, bell-wether!

2ND SHEPHERD   I say, turn.
1ST SHEPHERD I say, turn, now again
                   I say skip over the plain.

2ND SHEPHERD Would you were never so fain,
                       Tup, I say, turn!

1ST SHEPHERD What, will thou not yet, I say, let the sheep go?
                   Whop!

2ND SHEPHERD   Abide yet.

1ST SHEPHERD   Will ye but so?
                   Knave, hence I bid thee flit, 't were good that thou do,
                   Or I shall thee hit on thy pate, lo,
                       Shall thou reel:
                   I say give the sheep space.

2ND SHEPHERD Sir, give over your grace,   124
　　　　　　　Here comes Slow-pace
　　　　　　　From the mill-wheel.

3RD SHEPHERD What a do, what a do is this you between?
　　　　　　　A good day thou and thou.

1ST SHEPHERD   Hark what I mean
　　　　　　　You to say:
　　　　　　Of sheep bought I a store,
　　　　　　And drove them me before,
　　　　　　He says not one more
　　　　　　　Shall pass by this way:

　　　　　　If witless did what he could this way shall they go.

3RD SHEPHERD Yea, but tell me, good, where are your sheep, lo?

2ND SHEPHERD Now, sir, by my hood, neither see I nor know,
　　　　　　　Not since I here stood.

3RD SHEPHERD   God give you woe
　　　　　　　And sorrow!
　　　　　　Ye fish without net,
　　　　　　Ye fight and ye fret,
　　　　　　Such fools never I met
　　　　　　　By even or morrow.

　　　　　　It is wonder to wit, where wit should be found;
　　　　　　Here are old knaves yet standing on this ground,
　　　　　　These would by their wit make a ship be drowned;
　　　　　　He were well quit who had sold for a pound
　　　　　　　Such two.
　　　　　　They fight and they flight,
　　　　　　Though senseless their spite;
　　　　　　No need them to smite
　　　　　　　To cause such ado.

　　　　　　Sauce sooner ye need than sorrow I pray;
　　　　　　Like Moll may ye speed, that went by the way—
　　　　　　Many sheep counted she, only one had she ay—

[18]

155   To her count she took heed, while her pitcher, I say,
            Was broken.
         "Oh, God," she said,
         But one sheep instead,
         And the milk pitcher sped,
            And the pieces the token.

But since ye are bare of wisdom and lore,
Take heed how I fare and learn from me more:
Ye need not to care save my words ye ignore:
Hold ye my mare, throw this sack furthermore
        On my back,
Whilst I with my hand,
Loose the sack's band:
Come nearby and stand
        Both Gib and Jack.

Is not all shaken out and no jot left in?

1ST SHEPHERD   Yea, there is no doubt.

3RD SHEPHERD   Your wit is so thin.
When ye look well about ye gawp and ye grin,
So goes your wit out even as it comes in:
        Gather up,
And seek it again.

2ND SHEPHERD By our brawn and our brain,
He has told us full plain
        Wisdom to sup.

JACK GARCIO   Now God give you care, all fools to a man:
Saw I never none so fare but the fools of Gotham.
Your parents had better beware, your sire and your dam,
Had she brought forth a hare, a sheep, or a lamb,
        Had been well.
Of all the fools I can tell,
From heaven unto hell,
Ye three bear the bell:
        God grant your sorrows swell.

1ST SHEPHERD   Good friend, now tell me, how pasture our sheep then?

JACK GARCIO   In grass to the knee.

2ND SHEPHERD	Fair befall thee! Amen! 190
JACK GARCIO	If ye will ye may see, your beasts ye ken.

1ST SHEPHERD Sit we down all three and drink shall we men.

3RD SHEPHERD   What a turd!
I'd rather eat:
What, drink without meat?
A meal I entreat,
      And set up a board.

Then may we go dine our bellies to fill.

2ND SHEPHERD Let be thy whine.

3RD SHEPHERD   Not for thee I will!
I am worthy the wine, and ready to swill:
No service of mine ye get, I fare ill
      At your manger.

1ST SHEPHERD Pack off to our meat,
Peace kept is sweet,
Better not bleat,
      Nor stand in danger:

Thou has ever been curst since we met together.

3RD SHEPHERD Now in faith, if I durst, ye are even my brother.

2ND SHEPHERD Sirs, let us mind first for one thing or other,
That these words be pursed, and let us stuff fodder
      Within.
Lay forth all our store,
Lo, here! Brawn of a boar.

1ST SHEPHERD Set mustard before,
      Our meal now begin.

Here's a foot of a cow well sauced, I ween,
The shank of a sow that spiced has been,
Two blood-puddings, I vow, with liver between:
Let gladly, sirs, now, my brothers, be seen
      What more.
Both beef, and mutton

[20]

221   Of a ewe that was rotten,
            Good meat for a glutton.
                Eat of this store.

2ND SHEPHERD I have in my bag no kale, but boiled and roast,
            Even an ox-tail that would not be lost:
            Ha, Ha, good-hail! I stop for no cost,
            A good pie or we fail: this is good for a frost
                In the morning:
            Of two pigs the groin,
            All a hare but the loin
            No spoons we enjoin
                Here at our feasting.

3RD SHEPHERD Here is to record the leg of a goose,
            Basted for our board, pork or partridge to choose,
            A tart for a lord, how the gravy doth ooze.
            A calf's liver stored with the verjuice:
                Good sauce,
            A restorative right
            For a good appetite.

1ST SHEPHERD Is this a church rite
                You make such discourse?
            If ye could by your grammary reach us a drink,
            I should be more merry, bring me to the brink.

2ND SHEPHERD Good ale is the ferry to slumber, I think,
            If you deeply it bury, in thy pate it will sink.

1ST SHEPHERD   Ah, so:
            This is balm of our bale,
            Good wholesome ale.

3RD SHEPHERD Ye hold long the scale,
                Now for my go.
2ND SHEPHERD Now curse those lips, but leave me some part.

1ST SHEPHERD By God, he but sips, beguiled thou art:
            Behold how he nips.

2ND SHEPHERD   I cuss you so smart,

[21]

And me on my hips, death to thy heart,   254
   Abate.
Be thou wine, be thou ale,
Until my breath fail,
I shall set thee asail:
   God give me such state.

3RD SHEPHERD By my dam's soul, Alice, that was deeply drunken.

1ST SHEPHERD Now as ever I have bliss, to the bottom it is sunken.

2ND SHEPHERD Another bottle here is.

3RD SHEPHERD   That is well spoken!
   That must we kiss.

2ND SHEPHERD   That had I forgotten.
   But hark!

Whoso can best sing
Shall have the beginning.

They sing.

1ST SHEPHERD Now pray at the parting,
   I shall set you to work.

We have done our part and sung right well,
I drink for a start.

2ND SHEPHERD   Stay, let the cup still.

1ST SHEPHERD God curse thy thirsty heart, thou drinks with much zeal.

3RD SHEPHERD Thou has drunken a quart, therefore choke thee the devil.

1ST SHEPHERD   Thou raves:
For even a sow's share
There is drink to spare.

3RD SHEPHERD   A blight on ye both I swear!
    Ye be both knaves.

1ST SHEPHERD Nay! We be knaves all, thus think I it best,
So, sir, should ye call.

[22]

2ND SHEPHERD   And so let it rest:
282   We will not brawl.

1ST SHEPHERD   Then would I suggest
        This meat we shall pack in a pannier chest

3RD SHEPHERD   Hear, sirs:
        For our souls let us so,
        On poor men bestow.

1ST SHEPHERD   Gather up, lo, lo,
        Ye hungry begging friars.

2ND SHEPHERD   It draws near tonight, prepare we to rest:
        All misty my sight, I think it the best.

3RD SHEPHERD   For fear and for fright by a cross be we blest,
        Christ's cross keep us right, east and west,
        In need.
        Jesus onazorus
        Cruciefixus,
        Marcus, Andreus,
        God be our speed.
  They sleep.

"Gloria in Excelsis" is sung in heaven.

ANGEL   Hearken, shepherds, awake! Give praises ye shall.
        He is born for your sake, Lord perpetual:
        He has come to take and ransom you all,
        Your sorrows to slake, King imperial,
        Star of the east:
        That child is born
        At Bethlehem this morn,
        Ye shall find him ere dawn
        On each side a beast.

1ST SHEPHERD   By God, our dear dominus! What was that song?
        It was full curious with short notes among:
        I pray to God save us, now in this throng:
        I am frightened, by Jesus, somewhat is wrong:
        Methought,

[23]

One screamed out aloud: 310
I suppose it was a cloud
In my ears it soughed,
    By him that me bought!

2ND SHEPHERD Nay, that may not be, I tell you certain,
For he spake to us three, as he had been a man:
When he lit up this lea, my heart to shake began,
An angel was he that tell you I can,
    No doubt.
    Of a bairn he spake,
    Whom to seek we now wake,
    That star shines for his sake,
        That yonder stands out.

3RD SHEPHERD It was a marvel to see so brightly it shone,
The sky I thought truly with lightning strown,
But I saw with my eye, as I leaned on this stone:
With sound fully merry, such heard I never none,
    I record.
    As he said in a scream,
    Or else that I dream
    We should go to Bethlehem,
        To worship that lord.

1ST SHEPHERD That same child is he of whom prophets told,
Should make them free whom Adam had sold.

2ND SHEPHERD Give heed unto me this is enrolled,
In the words of Isaiah, a prince most bold
        Shall he be,
    And king with crown,
    Set on David's throne,
    Such was never known
        For us to see.

3RD SHEPHERD Also Isaiah says, our fathers us told,
That of Jesse's race a virgin that would
Bring forth by grace a flower so bold;
That virgin in this place may those words now uphold,
        As ye see.

[24]

346   Trust it now we may,
                 He is born this day,
                 Exiet virga
                    De radice Jesse.

1ST SHEPHERD Of him spake more, sage Sibyl I mean,
              And Nebuchadnezzar, to our faith unclean,
              In the furnace there were three children seen,
              The fourth stood before, who God's son must have been.

2ND SHEPHERD   That figure
                 Was given by revelation,
                 That God would have a son;
                 This is a good lesson
                    For us to consider.

3RD SHEPHERD Of him did Jeremiah testify, and Moses also,
              Where he saw him standing by a bush burning, lo!
              When he came to espy if it were so,
              Unburning was it truly when he stood close below.
                    A wonder
                 That was for all to see,
                 Her holy virginity
                 That undefiled should be;
                    On this I ponder,

              And she should have a child, such was never seen.
2ND SHEPHERD Peace, man, thou art beguiled, thou shalt see him, I mean,
              Of a maiden so mild no marvel so mighty has been;
              Yea, and she undefiled, a virgin as clean
                 Is none.

1ST SHEPHERD   Nothing is impossible,
                 Indeed, through God's will;
                 But God shall fulfil
                    What he would have done.

2ND SHEPHERD Habakkuk and Ely prophesied so,
                 Elizabeth and Zachary, and many more, you know,
                 And David as verily is witness thereto,
                 John the Baptist surely, and Daniel also.

[25]

3RD SHEPHERD	So saying,	381
	He is God's son alone,	
	Without him shall be none,	
	His seat and his throne	
	Shall ever be lasting.	

1ST SHEPHERD Virgil in his poetry said in his verse,
Even thus by grammary, as I shall rehearse;
"Iam nova progenies celo demittitur alto,
Iam rediet virgo, redeunt saturnia regna."

2ND SHEPHERD Alas! Turd! What speak ye, conjure ye or curse?
Give us no clergy, I count you with the friars
   Who preach;
  By the Latin you know
  You have learnt your Cato.

1ST SHEPHERD Hark, sirs, ere you go,
  I shall you teach.

From heaven he said his son he would send,
Through a virgin's maidenhead our ills to amend,
By her to be bred, thus make I an end;
And yet more may be read, God himself shall bend
   Unto us,
  With peace and plenty,
  With a great company,
  True love and charity
  Shall be among us.

3RD SHEPHERD And I hold it true for there should be,
When comes that King new, peace by land and sea.

2ND SHEPHERD Now brothers, adieu! Give heed unto me:
I would that we knew of this song so free
   Of the angel:
  I heard by his sound,
  From heaven he was bound.

1ST SHEPHERD It is truth ye have found,
  As his words tell.

2ND SHEPHERD Now, by God that me bought, it was a merry song:
I dare say that he brought four and twenty to a long.

3RD SHEPHERD I would it were sought to sing us among.

[26]

1ST SHEPHERD   In faith I trust nought, so many he strung
417   In a heap:
                    They were gentle and small,
                    And well toned withal.

3RD SHEPHERD   Yea, but I know them all,
                    The tune I shall keep.

1ST SHEPHERD   Sing not through your nose, let's see how ye yelp.

3RD SHEPHERD   My voice with my cold goes, save I have help.

2ND SHEPHERD   Ah, thy heart is in thy hose!

1ST SHEPHERD   Now on pain of a skelp
                    This song ere ye dose.

3RD SHEPHERD   Thou art an ill whelp
                    For anger!

2ND SHEPHERD   Begin, if you please!

1ST SHEPHERD   He will now take his ease

3RD SHEPHERD   God let us never cease:
                    List to my clangour.
   They sing.

1ST SHEPHERD   Now end we our croon of the song at this tide.
2ND SHEPHERD   Thy snout who did prune, thy voice so to hide?
3RD SHEPHERD   Then let us go soon, I will not abide.
1ST SHEPHERD   No light lends the moon, that have I espied;
                    Nevertheless
                    Let us keep our behest.
2ND SHEPHERD   That hold I best.
3RD SHEPHERD   Then must we go east,
                    After my guess.

1ST SHEPHERD   Would God that we might this young babe see!

2ND SHEPHERD   Many prophets that sight desired verily
                    To see that child bright.

[27]

3RD SHEPHERD   If God would decree   443
     To show us that mite, we could say truly,
      We had seen
     What many saints desired,
     With prophets inspired,
     When they him required
      Yet dead long have been.

2ND SHEPHERD God grant us that grace.

3RD SHEPHERD   God do so.
1ST SHEPHERD Abide sirs, a space, lo, yonder, lo!
     It comes at a race, how yon star doth glow.

2ND SHEPHERD It makes a great blaze, our way let us go,
      Here he is!
  They go to Bethlehem.

3RD SHEPHERD Aye, this be the door.
1ST SHEPHERD Who shall go in before?

2ND SHEPHERD Ye are eldest by a score
      It seems you for this.
  They enter the stable.

1ST SHEPHERD Hail, King I thee call! Hail, most of might!
     Hail, the worthiest of all! Hail, duke! Hail knight!
     Of great and small thou art Lord by right:
     Hail perpetual! Hail babe so bright!
      Here I offer
      I pray thee to take—
      If thou would, for my sake,
      Thou may game with this make,—
      This little spruce coffer.

2ND SHEPHERD Hail, little tiny mop, rewarder of meed!
     Hail, but one drop of grace at my need:
     Hail, little milk-sop! Hail, David's seed!
     Of our creed thou art top, hail, in good heed!
      This ball
      That thou would receive,—
      So little I grieve,

474   This with thee I leave,
                         To please thee withal.

3RD SHEPHERD Hail, maker of man, hail, sweeting!
                    Hail, as well as I can, pretty miting!
                    I bow to thee then in joy of this greeting:
                    Hail, Lord! in token I give at our meeting
                         This bottle—
                    It is an old by-word,
                    That a jest or bourd
                    May be had from a gourd,
                         Of two quarts or a pottle.

MARY   He that all might may sway, our heaven's King,
                    That is for to say, my son, my sweeting,
                    Reward you this day, as in seven he made all spring:
                    He grant you for ay, his grace and his blessing
                         Continuing:
                    He give you good grace,
                    Tell forth of this case,
                    He speed you apace,
                         And grant you good ending.

1ST SHEPHERD Farewell, fair Lord, with thy mother also.

2ND SHEPHERD We shall this record, wherever we go.

3RD SHEPHERD We must be restored, God grant it be so!

1ST SHEPHERD Amen, to that word, sing we thereto
                         On high:
                    Together in joy,
                    Our mirth now employ
                    To the praise of this boy
                         Sing we for ay.
     They leave singing.

[29]

The Thirteenth Play:
The Second Shepherds' Play

1ST SHEPHERD	MAK	ANGEL
2ND SHEPHERD	GILL, HIS WIFE	MARY
3RD SHEPHERD		JESUS

1ST SHEPHERD   Lord, but this weather is cold, and I am ill wrapped,
My hands in frost's hold, so long have I napped;
My legs they fold, my fingers are chapped,
It is not as of old, for I am lapped
    In sorrow.
In storms and tempest,
Now in the east, now in the west,
Woe to him who has no rest
    Now or tomorrow.

But we simple shepherds that walk on the moor,
Are soon by richer hands thrust out of door;
No wonder as it stands, if we be poor,
For the tilth of our lands lies as fallow as the floor,
    As you know.
We are so lamed,
Overtaxed and maimed,
And cruelly tamed,
    By our gentlemen foe.

Thus they rob us of our rest, may ill-luck them harry!
These proud men are our pest they make the plough
                    [tarry.
What men say is for the best, we find it contrary:
Thus are ploughmen oppressed, no hope now to carry
    Alive.
Thus hold they us under,
Thus bring us into blunder;
It were great wonder,
    If ever we should thrive.

If one gets a modish sleeve or a brooch nowadays,
Take care if you him grieve or once cross his ways!

[30]

30   Dares no man bid him leave the power that he sways,
          And yet may not believe one word that he says
               The better
          He grasps for his gain
          In his bragging vein,
          And boasts men maintain
               Him, who are far greater.

          There shall come a swain, a proud peacock you know,
          He must borrow my wain, my plough also,
          This for my gain I must grant ere he go.
          Thus live we in pain, anger and woe;
               By night and day
          He craves what comes to his head,
          And I give in great dread;
          I were better be dead,
               Than once say him nay.

          It does me good as I walk thus on my own,
          Of this world for to talk, and so make my moan.
          To my sheep will I stalk and listen anon;
          There abide on a balk or sit on a stone
               Full soon.
          For believe you me,
          True men, if they be,
          We get more company
               Ere it be noon.

2ND SHEPHERD *enters.*

2ND SHEPHERD *Benedicite dominus!* What may this mean?
          The world faring thus, how oft have we seen?
          Lord, this weather works through us, and the wind is
                                                  [so keen
          And frost will undo us, fast blind I have been,
               No lie.
          Now in dry, now in wet,
          Now in snow, now in sleet,
          When my shoes freeze to my feet,
               It's not at all easy.

          But as far as I ken or yet as I go,
          We poor wedded men suffer much woe;

[31]

We have sorrow ever again, it falls often so;   66
Old Capel, our hen, both to and fro
   She cackles;
But begin she to croak
To prod or to poke,
For our cock it is no joke
   For he is in shackles.

These men that are wed have not their own will,
When full bitter they have sped their tongue they keep
                      [still:
God knows they are led in a grim dance full ill;
In bower and in bed, but speak not their fill
   Nor chide.
My part have I found,
Learnt my lesson sound.
Woe to him who is bound
   For he must abide.

But now late in our lives a marvel to me
That I think my heart rives such wonders to see.
Where that destiny drives it should so be;
Some men will have two wives, and some men three
   In store.
Some are woe without any,
But so far as I see,
Woe is him that has many,
   For he rues it sore.

But young men a-wooing, on God be your thought,
Be well warned of wedding, and think ere you're taught,
"Had I known" is a thing too lately you're taught;
Much bitter mourning has wedding home brought:
   You achieve
With many a sharp shower,
What you may catch in an hour,
Which shall savour full sour,
   A life-time to grieve.

As I've read Paul's Epistle, my helpmeet is here,
As sharp as a thistle, as tough as a spear;
She is browed like a bristle, with a sour looking cheer;

[32]

103   If she once wets her whistle she can sing full clear
      Her paternoster.
     As great as a whale withal,
     She has a gallon of gall,
     By him that died for us all
      I would I had lost her.

1ST SHEPHERD Look over the hedgerow, are you deaf as you stand?
2ND SHEPHERD The devil take you for so long have I scanned.
     Where saw you Daw go?
1ST SHEPHERD   Here on the lea land.
     I heard his pipe blow: he comes near at hand
      Hereby;
     Stand still.
2ND SHEPHERD   Why?
1ST SHEPHERD For he comes, say I.
2ND SHEPHERD He will beguile us with a lie
      Unless we be spry.
  Enter 3RD SHEPHERD.

3RD SHEPHERD Christ's cross me speed and Saint Nicholas!
     Thereof have I need; it is worse than it was.
     Who knows should take heed, and let the world pass;
     It is doomed as decreed and brittle as glass
      And slithers.
     This world fared never so:
     As great marvels grow,
     Move us from weal to woe,
      The whole world withers.

     Was never since Noah's flood such floodings seen;
     Winds and rains so rude and storms so keen;
     Some stumbled some stood in doubt, as I ween;
     Now God turn all to good, I say as I mean,
      And ponder.
     These floods they so drown,
     Both in fields and in town,
     And bear all things down,
      And that is a wonder.

     We that walk in the nights our cattle to keep,
     We see fearful sights when other men sleep.

Now I think my eye lights on some rascals that peep;
And to put all to rights I must give my sheep   139
    A turn.
But full ill have I meant,
And amend my intent,
I may lightly repent,
    My toes if I spurn.

Ah, sir, God you save, and master mine!
A deep drink would I have and somewhat to dine.
IST SHEPHERD Christ's curse, you slave, you are a sluggish swine!
2ND SHEPHERD What! Let the boy rave; sit down and dine.
    We have had our fill
Ill luck be thy fate
Though the lad come late,
Yet he is in a state
    To sup if he will.

Such servants as I who work till we sweat
Eat our bread quite dry and that makes me fret;
We are often weak and weary when our masters sleep
    [yet;
Late home and dreary, in food and drink we get
    Less than our due.
Both our dame and our sire,
When we run in the mire
They dock us of our hire
    And pay us late too.

But hear the truth master, for what I am paid
I shall work no faster than a stubborn jade;
I shall be slacker and sport like a maid,
For never has my supper my stomach dismayed
    In fields,
Why should I weep?
With my staff can I leap;
Men say a bargain cheap
    Poorly yields.

IST SHEPHERD You were an ill lad to go a-wooing
With a master that had but little for spending.
2ND SHEPHERD Peace, I say, lad, no more of jangling,

[34]

175   Or you will rue it sad, by heaven's king!
                       Hold your tongue!
                     Where are our sheep, boy, we've shorn?
3RD SHEPHERD Sir, this same day at morn
                     I left them in the corn,
                       When matins were rung.

                     They have pasture good they cannot go wrong.
1ST SHEPHERD That is right, by the rood! These nights are long,
                     Yet ere we went I would someone gave us a song.
2ND SHEPHERD So I thought as I stood, our mirth to prolong.
3RD SHEPHERD   I grant.
1ST SHEPHERD Let me sing the tenor free.
2ND SHEPHERD And I shall sing the trebel key.
3RD SHEPHERD Then the alto falls to me.
                       Let's see how we chant.
       SHEPHERDS *sing*.
       Then MAK *enters. He wears a short mantle over his gown.*

MAK   Now Lord, in thy names seven that made both moon
                                                    [and stars,
                     More than I can count in heaven, thy will from bliss
                                                    [me bars;
                     My life is uneven with jangles and jars;
                     Now would God I were in heaven where no bairn's
                                                    [tear mars
                       The still.
1ST SHEPHERD Who is it that pipes so poorly?
MAK   Would God ye knew of me, surely!
                     Footing the moors so sorely,
                       Drudging against my will.

2ND SHEPHERD Mak, where hast thou been? Tell us thy tidings.
3RD SHEPHERD If Mak come on the scene, look well to your things.

       3RD SHEPHERD *takes away* MAK'S *mantle*.

MAK   What! I be a yeoman true and one the king's;
                     One who from no mean lord a mighty message brings.
                       No lie.
                     Fie on you go hence
                     Out of my presence!
                     I must have reverence;
                       Why? Who am I?

                               [35]

1ST SHEPHERD   Why are your quirks so quaint? Mak, you do wrong.
2ND SHEPHERD   Would you rather be a saint, Mak? Your wish is so
                                                    [strong.
3RD SHEPHERD   If the knave can paint to the devil might he belong.
MAK   I shall make complaint; beaten you'll be ere long,
                   At a word,   212
               And wracked without ruth.
1ST SHEPHERD   But, Mak, is that truth?
               Now take out that southern tooth,
                   And set in a turd.

2ND SHEPHERD   Mak, the devil's in thee, a blow you'll be getting.
3RD SHEPHERD   Mak, know ye not me? Your blood I'll be letting.
MAK   God save you all three, now why are you fretting?
               You are a fair company.
1ST SHEPHERD   What snare are you setting?
2ND SHEPHERD   Why creep
               You so late on your toes,
               What will men suppose?
               And thou hast an ill nose
                   For stealing of sheep.

MAK   That I am true as steel no men debate,
               But a sickness that I feel has brought me to this state,
               My belly lacks a meal and suffers ill fate.
3RD SHEPHERD   Seldom lies the devil dead by the gate.
MAK   Therefore
               Full sore am I and ill,
               If I stand stone still
               I've ate not a needle
                   This month and more.

1ST SHEPHERD   How fares thy wife, by my hood, how fares she?
MAK   Rolls around by the rood; by the fire she'll be,
               And a house full of brood, with the bottle she's free,
               Cares not for any good, whatever she may see;
                   But so
               Eats as fast as she can,
               And each year that comes to a man
               Adds another to our clan;
                   And some years two.

[36]

244 Now were I richer than the Pope of Rome
I would be eaten out of house and home.
So foul a wench, if close you come
You'll scarce believe; no worser one
    A man's peace stole.
Would you see what I would proffer;
I'd give all within my coffer
If tomorrow I might offer
    A prayer for her soul.

2ND SHEPHERD I have watched without nodding as none in this shire;
    I must sleep though it means taking less for my hire.
3RD SHEPHERD I am cold and ill-clad and long for a fire.
1ST SHEPHERD I am worn out with walking and covered in mire.
    Look to!
2ND SHEPHERD Nay, down I shall lie
    For I must sleep soundly.

3RD SHEPHERD As good a man's son I
    As any of you.

    But, Mak, come hither, and with us lie down.
MAK   Then your whisperings between you with snores I
        [would drown.
    Pay heed;
From my top to my toe,
Manus tuas commendo,
Pontio Pilato,
    Christ's cross me speed!
When the SHEPHERDS *are asleep* MAK *rises.*
MAK   It is time now to strike ere the iron grows cold,
And craftily creep then into the fold,
And nimbly to work, but not be too bold,
For bitter the bargain, if all were told
    At the ending;
My doubts may dispel,
But he needs good counsel
That would gladly fare well
    With but little for spending.

Put about you a circle as round as the moon,
Till I have done what I will, until it be noon.

[37]

Lie you stone still as though in a swoon,   280
While I summon my skill some magic to croon
    Over you.
Above your heads I raise my hand.
Your sight is lost on sea and land!
But I must gain much more command
    To get my due.

Lord, but they sleep hard, as you may well hear;
Never yet was I shepherd, but of that I've no fear,
If the flock be scared, then I shall nip near
Till one I've ensnared. Then will soon disappear
    Our sorrow.

MAK *seizes a sheep.*
A fat sheep I dare say,
A good fleece I dare lay,
I'll requite when I may,
    But this will I borrow.

MAK *goes home.*
How Gill, are you in? Get us some light!

MAK'S WIFE   Who makes such a din, this time of the night?
I've sat down to spin; I hope now I might
Not rise for a pin. I'll curse in my spite
    With no pause;
A housewife that has been
Fretted betwixt and between,
Has no work to be seen
    For such small chores.

MAK   Good wife, open this hatch; see you not what I bring?
MAK'S WIFE   I will let you draw the latch. Come in, my sweeting.
MAK   You care not a scratch for my long standing.
MAK'S WIFE   Now your neck may catch a rope at a hanging.
MAK   Away!
I earn what I eat,
For in a fix can I get
More than they that toil and sweat
    All the long day.

Thus it fell to my lot, Gill, you cannot gainsay.
MAK'S WIFE   It were a foul blot to be hanged, as you may.

[38]

MAK	I have escaped scot-free a far fiercer fray.
MAK'S WIFE	But so long goes the pot to the water, men say,
318	At last
	Comes it home broken.
MAK	Well know I the token,
	But let it never be spoken,
	But come and help fast.

I would he were slain, I want so to eat.
For more than a year I've dreamt of this treat.

MAK'S WIFE	They'll come ere he's slain, and hear the sheep bleat,
MAK	Then might I be ta'en; that gives me cold feet!
	Go bar
	The outer door.
MAK'S WIFE	Yes, Mak,
	For if they pounce on your back. . . .
MAK	Then might I get from the whole pack
	A jolt and a jar.

MAK'S WIFE	A fine jest have I spied, since you think of none;
	Here shall we hide him until they are gone,
	In my cradle to abide, but let me alone,
	And I shall lie beside in childbed, and groan.
MAK	Them warn
	I shall that in the night
	Was born a boy for our delight.
MAK'S WIFE	Now bless I that day bright,
	That ever I was born!

This is a cunning play and well cast;
What a woman may say can help at the last.
None will gainsay; but get you back fast.

MAK	If when they wake I'm away, there'll blow a cold blast.
	I will go sleep.

MAK *returns to the* SHEPHERDS *and resumes his place.*
Yet sleeps the whole company
So I must tread carefully,
As though it had never been I
That stole their sheep.

IST SHEPHERD	*Resurrex a mortruis!* Hold hard my hand!
	Judas carnas dominus! I scarcely can stand.

[39]

My foot sleeps, by Jesus, my belly's a brand;   352
My dream seemed to bring us quite near to England.
2ND SHEPHERD   Say ye!
Lord, but I slept well;
As fresh as an eel.
As light I do feel
    As leaf on a tree.

3RD SHEPHERD   Blessed all be within! My heart so quakes
To leap out of its skin such noise it makes.
Who makes all this din? My head sorely aches.
I must stir from within for my fellows' sakes.
    We were four.
Saw you ought of Mak now?
1ST SHEPHERD   We were up ere thou.
2ND SHEPHERD   Man, I give God a vow,
    He's still in the straw.

3RD SHEPHERD   I dreamt he was wrapped in a wolf's skin.
1ST SHEPHERD   Many such have entrapped now our poor kin.
2ND SHEPHERD   When long had we napped I dreamt of Mak's sin,
A fat sheep he had trapped by stealth with no din.
3RD SHEPHERD   Be still!
Your dream proves you mad;
Your fancy's a fad.
1ST SHEPHERD   God keep us from bad
    If it be his will.

2ND SHEPHERD   Rise, Mak, for shame! Thou liest right long.
MAK   Now Christ's holy name be us among!
What is this? By Saint James, I can't get along!
I trust I be the same. Ah! My neck has lain all wrong
    In this hole.
They help him.
Many thanks! Since yester-even,
Now by Saint Stephen,
A dream sent from heaven
    Struck fear in my soul.

I dreamt Gill in her smock cried out full sad,
Gave birth at the first cock to a young lad,
To add to our flock; then be I never glad.

[40]

389   Of cares I've a stock more than ever I had.
        Ah, my head!
    Those moans of hunger pains,
    The devil knock out their brains!
    Woe to him whose brood complains
        Of too little bread.

    I must go home, by your leave, to Gill, as I thought.
    First look up my sleeve that I've stolen nought:
    I am loth you to grieve, or from you take ought.

MAK *goes home.*

3RD SHEPHERD Go forth, ill-luck achieve! Now would I we sought
        This morn
    For the sheep in our care.
1ST SHEPHERD First I shall fare.
    Let us meet.
2ND SHEPHERD   Where?
3RD SHEPHERD   At the crooked thorn.

The SHEPHERDS *part.*

MAK   Undo this door! Who is here? How long shall I stand?
MAK'S WIFE   Who roars then out there? Be ye one or a band?
MAK   Ah, Gill, what cheer? It is I, Mak, your husband.
MAK'S WIFE   Ah, then never fear, the devil is at hand
        With guile.
    Lo, he strikes a harsh note,
    As though held by the throat,
    And cares never a groat
        My work to beguile.

MAK   Oh, the fuss that she makes when I stir her repose.
    She feigns all her aches and picks at her toes.
MAK'S WIFE   Why, who works, and who wakes, who comes and
                        [who goes?
    Who brews and who bakes? Who darns all your hose?
    And then
    It is sad to behold,
    Or e'er to be told,
    How woeful the household
        That wants a woman.

[41]

	But how have you sped with the shepherds, Mak?
MAK	The last word that they said when I turned my back,
	They would count each head of the sheep in their pack.
	Now have we no dread when they their sheep lack,
	Pardy; 426
	But howe'er the game goes,
	They'll be here, I suppose,
	Our theft to disclose,
	And cry out upon me.

Now do as you promised.

MAK'S WIFE   To that I agree,
I'll swaddle him now, in his crib he will be;
A fine trick to twist on our poor shepherds three.
To bed! Come assist. Tuck up!

MAK   Let me.
MAK'S WIFE   Behind.
Come Coll and his mate
To pry and to prate,
For help I'll cry straight
    The sheep if they find.

MAK'S WIFE   Hark now for their call; on the breeze be it blown.
Come make ready all and sing on thine own;
Sing lullay you shall, for loud I must groan,
And cry out by the wall on Mary and Joan
    Full sore.
Sing lullay quite fast
When you hear them at last;
If my part is miscast,
    Trust me no more.

3RD SHEPHERD Ah, Coll, good morn, why sleepest thou not?
1ST SHEPHERD Alas that ever I was born! A sad grief we have got.
Lost! A fat wether unshorn.
3RD SHEPHERD   By God, a foul blot.
2ND SHEPHERD Who should give us this scorn? It won't be forgot.
1ST SHEPHERD   This he shall rue.
I have searched with my dogs
All Horbury shrogs,
And of fifteen hogs,
    Found I but one ewe.

3RD SHEPHERD	Now trust me, if ye will, by St. Thomas of Kent,
459	Either Mak or Gill, had a hand in this event.
1ST SHEPHERD	Peace, man, be still! I saw when he went.
	You slander him ill, you ought to repent
	With good speed.
2ND SHEPHERD	Now as ever I might thrive,
	As I hope to keep alive,
	Only Mak could contrive
	To do that same deed.

3RD SHEPHERD	Then off to his homestead, he brisk on our feet.
	I shall never eat bread till we've proved this deceit.
1ST SHEPHERD	Nor have drink in my head till with him I meet.
2ND SHEPHERD	I will rest in no stead till him I may greet,
	My brother.
	My promise I plight
	Till I have him in sight,
	Shall I ne'er sleep one night.
	May I do no other.

They go to MAK's *house—singing within.*

3RD SHEPHERD	Do ye hear how they croak? My lord will now croon.
1ST SHEPHERD	Ne'er heard I sing folk so clean out of tune;
	Call him.
2ND SHEPHERD	Mak, may you choke! Undo your door soon!
MAK	Who is it that spoke, as if it were noon?
	Who scoffed?
	Who is that I say?
3RD SHEPHERD	Good fellows, were it day!
MAK	As far as ye may,
	Speak soft,

	Over a sick woman's head, who is not at her ease,
	I had rather be dead than she had a disease.

The SHEPHERDS *enter* MAK's *home.*

MAK's WIFE	Be off from the bed, let me breathe, if you please!
	Each step that you tread from my nose to my knees
	Goes through me.
1ST SHEPHERD	Tell us, Mak, if ye may,
	How fare ye, say?
MAK	But are ye in town today?
	Now how fare ye?

[43]

Ye have run in the mire, and now are all wet.   494
I shall make you a fire now we are met.
A nurse would I hire. Think ye on yet
My dream which entire has fulfilled its threat
    In due season.
I have bairns if ye knew,
Far more than a few,
But we must drink as we brew,
    And that is but reason.

	Would ye dined ere ye went? Ye sweat, as I think.
2ND SHEPHERD	Our feelings be vent not for meat nor for drink.
MAK	Is ought then ill meant?
3RD SHEPHERD	Yea, in a wink,
	A sheep lost we lament, borne off ere we blink.
MAK	Drink sirs.
	Had I been there
	Some had suffered full dear.
1ST SHEPHERD	In that is our fear;
	None of us errs.

2ND SHEPHERD	Against you goes the grouse, Mak, thief that ye be,
	Either you or your spouse, and so say we.
MAK	Nay, knit not your brows against my Gill or me.
	Come comb through our house, and then ye may see
	Who had her.
	If any sheep I've got,
	Alive or in the pot—
	And Gill, my wife, rose not
	Here since she laid her.

	As I am true as steel, to God here I pray,
	That this be the first meal that I shall eat this day.
1ST SHEPHERD	Mak, is such thy zeal! Then be advised, I say:
	He learns in time to steal that never could say nay.
MAK'S WIFE	I faint!
	Out thieves from my home,
	Ere I claw with my comb!
MAK	If you marked but her foam,
	You'd show some restraint.

MAK'S WIFE	Out thieves from my cot, step you soft on the floor.

MAK	If ye knew her harsh lot, your hearts would be sore.
532	Your behaviour's a blot, here to rant and to roar:
	Gill's plight ye've forgot. But I say no more.
MAK'S WIFE	Ah, my middle!
	I pray to God so mild,
	If ere I you beguiled,
	That I should eat this child
	That lies in this cradle.

MAK	Peace, woman, for God's pain, and cry not so:
	Thou'lt burst thy brain and make me full of woe.
2ND SHEPHERD	I believe our sheep be slain, and that ye know.
3RD SHEPHERD	Our search has been in vain, now let us go.
	He chatters
	His way through our mesh.
	Here's to be found no flesh,
	Soft nor hard, salt nor flesh,
	But two empty platters.

	No creature but this, tame or wild,
	As hope I for bliss, smelt so defiled.
MAK'S WIFE	No, so God me bless, and give me joy of my child!
1ST SHEPHERD	We have aimed amiss; we be but beguiled.
2ND SHEPHERD	Have done!
	Sir, our Lady him save!
	Be this a boy brave?
MAK'S WIFE	Any lord might him have.
	This child for his son.

	When he wakes he smiles that joy is to see.
3RD SHEPHERD	May now the world's wiles this bairn leave be.
	Who stood at the font that so soon were ready?
MAK	The first folk of these isles.
1ST SHEPHERD	A lie now, hark ye!
MAK	God give them thanks.
	Parkin and Gibbon Waller, I say,
	And gentle John Horn in grey.
	He made such droll display
	With his long shanks.

2ND SHEPHERD	Mak, friends will we be, for we are all one.
MAK	We? count not on me, for amends get I none.

[45]

Farewell all three! And gladly begone.   568

They leave the cottage.

3RD SHEPHERD   Fair words there may be, but love there is none
    This year.
1ST SHEPHERD   Gave ye the child anything?
2ND SHEPHERD   Not I, ne'er a farthing.
3RD SHEPHERD   I shall find an offering.
    Wait for me here.

He returns to the cottage.

3RD SHEPHERD   Mak, by your leave, your son may I see?
MAK   A mere mock I believe; his sleep you may mar.
3RD SHEPHERD   This child will not grieve, that little day star.
    Mak, by your leave, thy bairn never bar
    From sixpence.
MAK   Nay, go away, he sleeps.
3RD SHEPHERD   I think he peeps.
MAK   When he wakes he weeps;
    I pray you go hence.

The other SHEPHERDS *come back.*

3RD SHEPHERD   Give me leave him to kiss, and once lift him out.
    What the devil is this? He has a long snout!
1ST SHEPHERD   He is marked amiss. Come, best meddle nowt.
2ND SHEPHERD   The ill-spun weft is ever foully turned out.
    Quit talk!
    He is like to our sheep.
3RD SHEPHERD   How, Gib! May I peep?
1ST SHEPHERD   Aye, cunning will creep
    Where it may not walk.

2ND SHEPHERD   A ruse to record, and craftily cast.
    It was a fine fraud.
3RD SHEPHERD   And prettily passed.
    Let's burn this bawd and bind her fast.
    This shrew with a cord will be hanged at last.
    So shalt thou.
    Will you see how they swaddle
    His four feet in the middle.
    Saw I never in a cradle
    A horned lad ere now.

[46]

MAK	Peace, I say, what! Let be your blare!
604	I am he that him got, and yon woman him bare.
1ST SHEPHERD	Have you named him not, nor made him your heir?
2ND SHEPHERD	Now leave him to rot, and God give him care,
	I say.
MAK'S WIFE	A pretty child is he
	As sits on a woman's knee;
	A dillydown dilly,
	To make a man gay.

3RD SHEPHERD	I know him by the ear mark; that is a good token.
MAK	I tell you sirs, hark! His nose here was broken.
	Warned was I by a clerk what such spells did betoken.
1ST SHEPHERD	Do you hear the dog bark? Would fists first had
	[spoken!
	Let be.
MAK'S WIFE	He was witched by an elf;
	I saw it myself:
	When the clock struck twelve,
	Misshapen was he.

2ND SHEPHERD	Both be of ill-spun weft of twisted thread.
	Since they uphold their theft, let's strike them dead.
MAK	If more I thieve, bereft may I be of my head.

MAK kneels to the SHEPHERDS.

	At your mercy I am left.
1ST SHEPHERD	Sirs, hear what's said.
	For this trespass
	We will neither curse nor chide,
	No more deride,
	Nor longer bide,
	But toss him in a canvas.

They toss MAK in a canvas, after which MAK and his WIFE return home.

1ST SHEPHERD	Lord, but I am sore; to leave now were best.
	In faith I may no more, therefore must I rest.
2ND SHEPHERD	As a sheep of seven score pound he weighed on my
	[chest,
	Now to sleep out of door I'd count myself blest.
3RD SHEPHERD	Then, I pray,
	Lie down on this green.
1ST SHEPHERD	Brisk have these thieves been.

[47]

3RD SHEPHERD Never split your spleen 636
            For them, I say.
  They sleep. The ANGEL *sings "Gloria in Excelsis" then speaks.*

ANGEL   Rise, shepherds, attend! For now is he born
             Who shall fetch from the fiend what from Adam was
                                                    [torn.
             That warlock to end, this night is he born.
             God is made your friend; now at this morn—
                Leave your flocks:
             To Bethlehem go see
             Where he lies so free,
             A child in crib poorly,
                Between ass and ox.

1ST SHEPHERD This was a sweet sound as ever yet I heard;
             To tell would astound where we this averred.
2ND SHEPHERD That God's son be unbound from heaven, spoke he
                                                    [word;
             And lightning then crowned the woods as they stirred
                In their fear.
3RD SHEPHERD He came us to warn,
             In Bethlehem will be born
             A babe.
1ST SHEPHERD   Be we drawn
                By yon star there.

2ND SHEPHERD Say, what was his song? Heard ye not how it went?
             Three shorts and a long.
3RD SHEPHERD   The very accent.
             With no crochet wrong, and no breath misspent.
1ST SHEPHERD For to sing us among as he merciful meant,
                I can.
2ND SHEPHERD Let's see how ye croon.
             Can ye bark at the moon?
3RD SHEPHERD Hold your tongues full soon!
1ST SHEPHERD   Or sing after, man.
  He sings.

2ND SHEPHERD To Bethlehem he bad that we should go:
             And sure we be mad to tarry so.
3RD SHEPHERD Be merry and not sad, our mirth may overflow:

                       [48]

668   To be forever glad is the reward we shall know
               And choose.

1ST SHEPHERD   Then let us hither hie,
               Though we be wet and weary,
               To that child and that lady;
                 We have no time to lose.

2ND SHEPHERD   We find by the prophecy—let be your din—
               Of Isaiah and David, and more of their kin,
               They prophesied by clergy that in a virgin
               Should God come to lie, to atone for our sin,
                 And abate it.
               Our folk freed from woe,
               Isaiah said so.
               For a maid comes to show
                 A child that is naked.

3RD SHEPHERD   Full glad may we be and abide that day,
               That sweet sight to see who all power may sway.
               Lord so bless me, for now and for ay,
               Might I kneel on my knee some word for to say
                 To that child.

               But the angel said
               In a crib was he laid;
               He was poorly arrayed,
                 Both meek and mild.

1ST SHEPHERD   Patriarchs have been, and prophets have sworn
               They desired to have seen this child that is born,
               Past hope now to glean the gold of this corn.
               To see him we mean now ere it be morn,
                 As a token.
1ST SHEPHERD   When I see him and feel,
               Then know I full well
               It is as true as steel
                 What prophets have spoken.

               To so poor as we are that he would appear
               First, and to us declare by his messenger.
2ND SHEPHERD   Go we now, let us fare, the place is us near.

3RD SHEPHERD   I am glad to go there; set off in good cheer   704
           To that mite mild.
         Lord, if thy will be,
         We are unlearned, all three,
         Grant us thy gracious glee
           To comfort thy child.

1ST SHEPHERD   Hail, comely and clean! Hail, young child!
         Hail, maker, as I mean, of maiden so mild!
         Thou hast crushed in his spleen, the warlock so wild;
         That false traitor has been beyond doubt beguiled.
           Lo, he merry is.
         Lo, he laughs, my sweeting,
         A welcome meeting;
         Take my promised greeting:
           Have a bob of cherries.

2ND SHEPHERD   Hail, sovereign saviour, for thou hast us sought!
         Hail, joyous food and flower, that all things hast
                              [wrought!
         Hail, full of favour, that made all of nought.
         Hail, I kneel and I cower. A bird have I brought,
           Bairn that ye are.
         Hail, little tiny mop,
         Of our creed thou art top,
         At your mass I shall stop,
           Little day star.

3RD SHEPHERD   Hail, darling dear, full of godhead!
         I pray thee be near when that I have need.
         Hail, sweet is thy cheer! My heart would bleed
         To see thee sit here in so poor a stead
           With no pennies.
         Hail, hold forth thy hand small;
         I bring thee but a ball:
         Have thou and play withall,
           And go to the tennis.

MARY   The father of heaven, God omnipotent,
         Made all in days seven, his son has he sent.
         My name has he given, his light has me lent.
         Conceived I him even through his might as he meant,

741 And now is he born.
May he keep you from woe!
I shall pray him do so.
Tell of him as you go;
Have mind on this morn.

1ST SHEPHERD Farewell, lady, so fair to behold,
With child on thy knee!

2ND SHEPHERD But he lies full cold.
Lord, well is me, now back to our fold.

3RD SHEPHERD In truth already it seems to be told
Full oft.

1ST SERVANT What grace we have found.

2ND SERVANT Come, now are we unbound.

3RD SERVANT Let's make a glad sound,
And sing it not soft.

The SHEPHERDS *leave singing.*

The Fourteenth Play: The Offering of the Magi

HEROD   1ST DOCTOR OF LAW
MESSENGER   2ND DOCTOR OF LAW
1ST KING: JASPER   ANGEL
2ND KING: MELCHIOR   MARY
3RD KING: BALTHASAR   JESUS

HEROD Peace, I bid, both far and near,
Let none speak when I appear:
Who moves his lips while I am here,
I say, shall die.
Of all this world both far and near,
The lord am I.

Lord am I of every land,
Of tower and town, of sea and sand:
Against me dares no man stand,
That prizes life:
All earthly things bow to my hand,
Both man and wife.

[51]

Man and wife, pay heed my vow,   13
Who in this world are living now,
To Mohammed and me shall bow,
    Both old and young:
Homage to us must all allow,
    Both purse and tongue.

For anything it shall be so;
Lord of all wherever I go,
Who gainsays shall be laid low,
    Whereso he dwell;
The fiend, if he were my foe,
    I should him fell.

I kill all traitors to my crown,
And destroy those dogs in field and town,
Who trust not in Mohammed's renown,
    Our god so sweet;
Those false fellows I shall strike down
    Under my feet.

Under my feet they shall ill fare,
Those lads who dare my laws forswear;
My might is measured everywhere
    By such a pack;
Clean and shapely, hide and hair,
    Without a lack.

My mighty power may no man gauge,
If any cause me rant and rage,
Dinged to death will be his wage,
    And lasting woe:
His blood will flow my wrath to assauge,
    Before I go.

And therefore will I send and see
In all this land, full hastily,
To look if any dwelling be
    In tower or town,
That will not hold wholly to me,
    And Mohammed's renown.

[52]

49   If any be found under my sway,
        With bitter pain I shall them slay.
    To the MESSENGER.
            My messenger, speed on thy way
                Through this country,
            In all this land, by night and day,
                I command thee.

            And truly look thou subtly spy,—
            In every corner thou come by,—
            Who scorns Mohammed the mighty,
                Our god so free.
            And look thou bring them hastily
                Hither unto me.

            And fast I shall them strip to flay,
            Those lads that will our law gainsay:
            Therefore, boy, now I thee pray
                Speed my cause.
MESSENGER   It shall be done, lord, if I may,
                Without a pause.

            And sure, if any I may find,
            I shall not leave them there behind.
HEROD   No, but boldly thou them bind
                And with thee lead:
            Mohammed that wields water and wind,
                Thee spur and speed!

MESSENGER   All peace, lordings, and hold you still
            Till I have said what I will:
            Take good heed unto my skill,
                What news I bring:
            This command quickly fulfil
                From Herod, the King.

            He commands you everyone,
            To have no king but him alone,
            And other gods ye worship none
                But Mohammed so free:
            But if ye do ye be undone,
                Thus told he me.

    Then enters the IST KING *riding: he looks at the star and says,*

[53]

ıst King   Lord, from whom this light is lent,   85
And unto me this sight has sent,
I pray to thee, with good intent,
    From shame me stay,
That from harm's path I be bent,
    And so wild a way.

Also I pray thee specially,
Thou grant me grace of company,
That some fellowship be nigh,
    Of good avail:
Then as I fare, to live or die,
    I shall not fail.

Until to that land I have been,
To find out what this star might mean,
That has led me by its sheen
    From my country:
Go I now my meed to glean,
    The truth to see.

Then enters the 2ND KING riding.

2ND King   Ah, Lord, that is without an end!
From where could such strange light descend,
Whose bright bidding made me bend
    Out of my land,
And pointed me which way to wend,
    Till still it stand?

Sure, I saw never none so bright:
I shall ne'er rest by day nor night,
Until I learn whence comes this light,
    And from what place:
He that it sent unto my sight
    Grant me that grace!

ıst King   Ah, sir, whither are ye away?
Tell me, good sir, I you pray.
2ND King   Certainly, the truth to say,
    None knows but I:
Yon star has patterned out my way
    From Araby.

[54]

121   For I am king of that country,
               And Melchior there men call me.
1ST KING   And King, sir, was I wont to be,
                    Of Tarsus fame,
               Both of town and city,
                    Jaspar is my name.

               The light of yon star saw I thither.
2ND KING   That Lord be loved that sent me hither!
               For it will surely show us whither,
                    That we shall wend:
               We ought to love him both together,
                    That such to us would send.
Then enters the 3RD KING *riding.*

3RD KING   Ah, Lord! In land what may this mean?
               So strange a sight was never seen,
               A star shining with so great sheen,
                    Saw I never none:
               Its light is spread throughout this scene
                    By him alone.

               What it may mean, that know I nought:
               But yonder are two, methinks, in thought,
               I thank him that them here has brought
                    Thus unto me:
               I shall assay if they know ought
                    What it may be.

               Lordings, I give you greetings dear,
               I pray you tell me with good cheer
               Whither ye wend, be it far or near,
                    And where that ye have been:
               And of this star, that shines thus clear,
                    What it may mean.

1ST KING   Sir, I tell you certainly,
               From Tarsus yon star sought have I.
2ND KING   To see yon light from Araby,
                    Was my intent.
3RD KING   Now heartily to him thanks be,
                    That it has sent.

                         [55]

1ST KING	Sir, what land counts you no stranger?
3RD KING	This light has led me from Saba: And my name is Balthasar, The truth to tell.
2ND KING	And two kings, sir, we are, There where we dwell.

3RD KING	Now, sirs, since we are gathered here,
	I counsel that we ride together,
	Until we know, in what manner,
	    For good or ill,
	That it may mean, this star so clear
	    That shines there still.

1ST KING	Ah, lordings, behold the light
	Of yonder star, with beams so bright!
	Saw I never such a sight
	    In any land;
	A star thus about midnight,
	    A blazing brand!

1ST KING	It gives more light itself alone
	Than any sun that ever shone,
	Or moon, borrowed from that burning zone
	    Of light so clean:
	A stranger sight was never known
	    What e'er it mean.

2ND KING	Behold, lordings, see its speed,
	Its nearness to the earth, give heed:
	It is a token clear indeed
	    Of great portent:
	A marvel, we are all agreed,
	    From high is sent.

For such a star was never seen,
As wide in world as we have been,
Its blazing beams, shining full sheen,
    From it are sent.
Marvel I what it may mean
    In my intent.

3RD KING   Certain, sirs, the truth to say,
194   I shall unfold now if I may,
                 What it may mean so bright a ray,
                     Shining on us:
                 It has been said since many a day
                     It should be thus.

                 Yon star betokens, well know I,
                 The birth of a prince, sirs, surely,
                 As proved well in prophecy
                     That it so be:
                 Or else the laws of astronomy
                     Deceive me.

1ST KING   Certain, Balaam speaks of this thing,
                 That from Jacob a star shall spring
                 That shall overcome kaiser and king,
                     Without a strife:
                 Him shall all folk be obeying
                     That cherish life.

                 Now know I well this is the same,
                 Who every home as his may claim,
                 All bow to him who bear a name
                     In each country;
                 All unbelievers are to blame,
                     Who e'er they be.

2ND KING   Certain, lordings, full well know I,
                 Fulfilled is now the prophecy:
                 That prince shall overcome on high
                     Kaiser and king,
                 This star bears witness, surely,
                     Of his coming.

3RD KING   Now is fulfilled here in this land
                 What Balaam said, I understand;
                 Now is he born that sea and sand
                     Shall wield at will:
                 Such means this star, that blazing brand,
                     This to fulfil.

[57]

1ST KING   Lordings, go we now all three
                To worship straight that child so free,
                In token that he King shall be
                        Of everything:
                This gold now will I bear with me,
                        As my offering.

2ND KING   Go we fast, sirs, I you pray,
                To worship him if that we may:
                I bring incense, the truth to say,
                        As I intend
                By token his godhead to convey,
                        Without an end.

3RD KING   Sirs, counsel I as ye have said:
                Haste we quickly to that stead
                To worship him, as our great head,
                        With our offering:
                In token that he shall be dead,
                        This myrrh I bring.

1ST KING   Where is that king of Jews' land,
                That shall be lord of sea and sand,
                And folk shall bow unto his hand
                        Both great and small?
                Here no longer let us lingering stand,
                        But go we all.

2ND KING   We shall not rest, even nor morn,
                Until we come where he is born.
3RD KING   Surely we be not forlorn,
                        If that star guide us:
                Then press onward, I ye warn,
                        Let none outride us.

The KINGS *retire:* HEROD *and his* MESSENGER *advance.*

MESSENGER   Mohammed that is most mighty,
                My lord, sir Herod, thee save and see!
HEROD   Where hast thou been so long from me,
                        Vile stinking lad?
MESSENGER   Lord, as your herald, through this land,
                        As ye me bad.

HEROD	Thou liest, loafer, the devil thee hang!
266	Why has thou dwelt away so long?
MESSENGER	Lord, ye chide me all too wrong.
HEROD	What tidings? say!
MESSENGER	Some ill with good is mixed among.
HEROD	How? I thee pray.

	Tell me now fast how thou has fared,
	And thy reward shall not be spared.
MESSENGER	As I searched, one road I shared,
	Lord, on the way,
	With three kings, who a babe they declared
	They sought that day.

HEROD	They sought a babe? For what thing?
	What tidings of him did they bring?
MESSENGER	Why, lord, they said he should be king
	Of town and tower:
	Therefore they went with their offering,
	Him to honour.

HEROD	King! The devil! But of what empire?
	Of what land should that lad be sire?
	My tortures shall that traitor tire:
	Sore shall he rue!
MESSENGER	Lord, by a star as bright as fire
	This king they knew:

	It led them out of their country.
HEROD	Woe, fie! Fie! Devils on them all three!
	He shall never master me,
	That new born lad.
	Those whose trust in a star may be
	I hold them mad.

	Those great louts know not what they say:
	They've split my head, that dare I lay:
	No such tidings for many a day
	Caused me more rue:
	For woe my wit is all away:
	What shall I do?

Why, what the devil is in their mind?
What wisdom in the stars they find?
Such news makes me in grief to grind:
      And of this thing
The very truth shall I unwind,
      Of this new king.

King? What the devil! Who else but I!
Woe, fie on devils! Fie, fie!
This that boy shall dear abuy!
      To death downright!
Shall he be king thus hastily?
      Who the devil made him knight?

Alas, for shame! This is a scorn!
Find they no reason, night nor morn,
Why should that wretch that late is born
      Be most of main?
Nay, if the devil of hell had sworn,
      He shall again.

Alas, alas, for grief and care!
I never supped of sorrow's fare:
If this be truth, then I despair,
      I am undone:
My counsellors must now prepare
      My fate to shun.

But first yet will I send and see
The answer of those lubbers three.
Messenger, straight hasten thee,
      Be brief and bold:
Go bid those kings come speak with me,
      Of whom you told.

	Say a message I have for them still.
MESSENGER	It shall be done, lord, at your will, Your bidding shall I soon fulfil In this country.
HEROD	Mohammed thee shield from every ill, As he is mighty.

[60]

MESSENGER 338	Mohammed you save, sir Kings all three,
	I have a message for you privily,
	From Herod, king of this country,
	Who is our chief:
	And lo, sirs, if ye trust not me,
	Here is my brief.

1ST KING	Welcome be thou heartily!
	His will thou tell us fully.
MESSENGER	Certain, sir, that know not I
	But thus he said to me.
	That ye should come full hastily
	To him all three.

	For needful news, he told me so.
2ND KING	Messenger, ahead thou go,
	And tell thy lord we gladness show
	His will to do:
	Both I and my fellows two
	Will follow you.

MESSENGER	Mohammed guard my lord so dear.
HEROD	Welcome be thou, messenger!
	How has thou fared since thou was here?
	Thou quickly say.
MESSENGER	Lord, I have travelled far and near
	Without a stay.

	And done your bidding sir, truly:
	Three kings with me brought have I,
	From Saba, Tarsus, Araby,
	Thee have they sought.
HEROD	And thy repayment shall be high,
	For what is wrought:

The KINGS *dismount and greet* HEROD.

	For certainly you cure my ill.
	Welcome, sirs, renowned in skill.
3RD KING	Lord, thy bidding to fulfil
	We came with speed.
HEROD	Much thanks for your goodwill
	To meet my need.

For certain, I coveted greatly   373
To speak with you, and hear reply:
Tell me, I pray you specially
　　Above anything,
What token saw ye in the sky
　　Of this new king?

1ST KING　　　We saw his star rise in the east,
That shall be king of man and beast,
Therefore, lord, we have not ceased,
　　Since that we knew,
With our gifts, both most and least,
　　To hear his due.

2ND KING　　Lord, when shone that star as dawn,
Thereby we knew that child was born.
HEROD　　　Out, alas, I am forlorn
　　For ever more!
I would my flesh be rent and torn
　　For sorrows sore.

Alas, alas, I am full of woe!
Sir Kings, sit down, and rest you so.
From scripture, sirs, what do ye know?
To the DOCTORS.
　　　Quickly speak:
What tidings therefrom flows
　　Speedily seek.

These kings make me understand,
That born is newly in this land
A king that shall rule sea and sand:
　　They tell me so:
And therefore, sirs, I you command
　　To your books go.

And sharply look for anything
Concerning ought of such a king.
1ST DOCTOR　It shall be done at your bidding,
　　We shall report
Right soon and tidings bring
　　If we find ought.

[62]

2ND DOCTOR Soon shall I know, lord, if I may,
410   What our written law does say.
HEROD   Therefore, masters, I you pray,
                 Yourselves bestir.
1ST DOCTOR   Come forth, let us assay
                 With our books to confer.

2ND DOCTOR Certain, sir, lo, here find I
             Well written in a prophecy.
             How that prophet Isaiah,
                 That never beguiled,
             Tells that a maiden of her body
                 Shall bear a child.

1ST DOCTOR   And also, sir, to you I tell
             The most marvellous that e'er befell,
             Her maidhood still with her shall dwell,
                 And take no scorn:
             That child be called "Emmanuel"
                 When he is born.

2ND DOCTOR Lord, this truth I verify,
             So doth Isaiah prophesy.
HEROD   Out, alas, for dole I die,
                 Long ere my day!
             Shall he have more power than I?
                 Ah, welaway!

             Alas, alas, I am forlorn!
             I would my flesh be rent and torn:
             But look again, if ye may warn
                 For love of me:
             And tell me where that boy is born:
                 Make haste and see.

1ST DOCTOR   Already, lord, right as you bad.
HEROD   Have done in haste or I go mad:
             And it were better for that lad
                 To grieve me nought:
             That bairn's blood shall make me glad,
                 By him that me has bought.

[63]

2ND DOCTOR   Micah, the prophet, without gainsay,   445
               Writes, as I shall tell you, if I may:
               In Bethlehem of Judea, yea,
                  Now bear in mind,
               Shall spring a duke, I say:
                  Now thus we find.

1ST DOCTOR   Sir, thus we find in prophecy:
               Therefore we tell you surely,
               In Bethlehem, most certainly,
                  Born is that king.
HEROD   The devil hang you high to dry,
               Such news you bring!

               And certainly ye lie! It cannot be!
2ND DOCTOR   Lord, we witness to it truly:
               Here the truth yourself may see,
                  If ye can read.
HEROD   Ah, welaway! full woe is me!
                  The devil you speed!

1ST DOCTOR   Lord, it is truth, all that we say,
               Read it in our law, we pray.
HEROD   Go hence, harlots, in twenty devils' way,
                  If ye would survive!
               Mighty Mohammed, as well he may,
                  Let you never thrive!

               Alas, why wear I a crown?
               Or am called of great renown?
               I am the foulest born in town
                  Of any man:
               And foulest scamp both up and down,
                  That no good can.

               Alas, that ever I should be knight,
               Or held a man of such great might,
               If a lad should rob me of my right,
                  So young a foe.
               Sooner death I would invite
                  Ere this were so.

481
    Ye noble kings, be kind and hear!
    Ye have safe conduct, never fear:
    But again to me appear
        Before ye go:
    I shall prove your friend sincere
        If ye do so.

    If it be truth, this new tiding,
    Some homage would I pay that king,
    Therefore I pray you that ye bring
        Me tidings soon.

1ST KING   Already, lord, at your bidding
        It shall be done

The KINGS mount their horses.

2ND KING   Alas, in world how have we sped!
    Where is the light that has us led?
    Some cloud about that star has spread
        And hidden away:
    In sad straits we are stead:
        What may we say?

3RD KING   Woe work on Herod, cursed wight!
    Woe to that tyrant day and night!
    For through him have we lost that sight,
        And through his guile,
    That shone to us with beams so bright
        For that short while.

Here the KINGS dismount.

1ST KING   Lordings, let us pray all three
    To that Lord, whose nativity
    That star betokened we did see,
        As was his will:
    Pray we specially that he
        Would show it to us still.

Here all three KINGS kneel down.

2ND KING   Thou child, whose might no tongue may tell,
    As thou art Lord of heaven and hell,
    Thy noble star, Emmanuel,
        Send for our prayer:

That we may know by firth and fell   515
Which way to fare.

3RD KING   Ah, to that child be ever honour,
That our grief has stemmed this hour,
And lent us light as our succour
Our fears to free:
We love thee, Lord of town and tower,
Wholly, all three.

Here they all rise up.

We ought to love him above everything,
That thus has sent us our asking:
Behold, yon star aloft is staying,
Sirs, surely:
Of this child shall we have knowing,
Speedily.

2ND KING   Lordings dear, dread need we nought,
Our great travel to an end is brought:
Yond is the place that we have sought
From far country:
Yond is the child that all has wrought,
Behold and see!

3RD KING   Let us make offering, all three,
Unto this child most mighty,
And worship him with gifts freely
That we have brought:
Our balm of bale ay will he be,
Well have we sought.

1ST KING   Hail to thee, maker of everything!
That balm of our bale may bring!
In token that thou art our King,
And shall be ay,
Receive this gold as my offering,
Prince, I thee pray.

2ND KING   Hail, conqueror of king and knight!
That formed fish and fowl in flight!

[66]

549   For thou art God's son, most of might,
            And all ruling,
        I bring thee incense, as is right,
            As my offering.

3RD KING   Hail, King by kind, cowering on my knee!
        Hail, one-fold God in persons three!
        In token that thou dead shall be,
            Without gainsay,
        For thy grave this myrrh of me
            Receive, I pray.

MARY   Sir kings, be comfort you between,
        And marvel not what it may mean:
        This child, that from me born has been,
            All strife may win:
        I am his mother, and maiden clean
            Without a sin.

        Therefore, lordings, where so ye fare,
        Boldly tell ye everywhere
        How I this blessed child did bear,
            That best shall be:
        Yet kept my maidhood, clean and fair,
            Through his glory.

        And truly, sirs, how may ye know
        Such other Lord is none below:
        Both man and beast shall worship show
            In town and field:
        My blessing, sirs, take as ye go,
            With comfort shield.

1ST KING   Ah, lordings dear! The truth to say,
        That star did not our wits betray:
        We love this Lord, that shall last ay
            Without an end:
        He is our comfort, night and day,
            Where'er we wend.

2ND KING   Lordings, we have travelled long,
        With little rest our road along:

[67]

To make us for our journey strong   585
    As we go home,
Sleep we a spell, nor count it wrong
    Before we roam.

For in great stress have we been stead.
Lo, here is a litter ready spread.
3RD KING   I love my Lord! We have well sped,
    To rest herein:
Lordings, since we shall go to bed,
    Ye shall begin.

ANGEL   Sir courteous kings, of me take heed,
    And turn in time, ill-fate to flee:
God himself bad me thus speed
    As faithful friend to warn all three
How Herod's fears on malice feed,
    He means your murderer to be:
To be so from his fury freed,
    Another way God will guide ye
    Into your own country:
And if ye ask him any boon,
God shall grant it to you soon,
    Your comfort will he be.

1ST KING   Awake, awake, lordings dear!
We must dwell no longer here:
An angel spake close to my ear,
    And bad us all,
We should not go, for mortal fear,
    Home by Herod's hall.

2ND KING   Almighty God in trinity,
With heart entirely thank I thee,
That thine angel sent to us three,
    Such words to say:
Our false foe swiftly for to flee,
    That would us slay.

3RD KING   We must love him great and small,
The comely King of mankind all:

[68]

Play

Anthony   Angel Sandra
is wife ~~Kristy~~ Jane   Mary   ~~Mrs~~ Jenny
Peter   Jean.

r
—

ph Nic   Mary

Williams is the Black Flatcoat. Bramble Dene
Amber my brother-in-law's Mole Hall have
Golden Retriever. BDbladeshore
I'm afraid that both our Williams Sheffield
and Amber passed away last 536 351.
year. They were both lovely dogs! Sopran.

Dear Mrs Poins's.
Just to tell you that there's been
a delay printing our new novelets.
I'm sorry about this, and will send
your order off ASAP, when I get
the novelets.
Thanks for your order.
Mavis Rowson

sability Living Allowance

ies, lack their own protest voice and are in
their local Council and the public at large.

e. I can only give you the example of my

rm future well-being, safety and happiness lay
e still found it easy to adapt her way of life.

asingly uncertain.

ents where she lives
financial viability of her community uncertain
lead towards supported living - which would

to pull out of supported housing projects
pany my daughter when she would like to use

1. Noah top 77 – top 92

2. The Salutation of Elizabeth
Middle p 159 – top of 162

3. <u>Next</u> The Second Shepherds' Play
P178 – middle P. 199

4. <u>Next</u> The Flight into Egypt.
Bottom P217 – top P. 222

621   It grieves me we apart must fall
                In such a way:
          For we gladly came at the star's call
                From afar to obey.
The KINGS *mount.*

1ST KING   We must part, sirs, without delay,
               And each fare on his several way:
               This will me lead, the truth to say,
                    To my country:
               Therefore, lordings, now have good day!
                    God with you be!

2ND KING   Now I must pass by sea and sand:
               This is the gate, I understand,
               That will lead me unto my land
                    The right way:
               May God of heaven your guardian stand,
                    And have good day!

3RD KING   This is the way that I must wend:
               Now God to us his succour send,
               And he that is without an end
                    And ay shall be,
               Save us from falseness of the fiend,
                    Lord, almighty.
The KINGS *go their several ways.*

The Fifteenth Play: The Flight into Egypt

ANGEL   JOSEPH   MARY

ANGEL   Awake, Joseph, and take good heed!
               Arise and sleep no more!
               If thou wilt save thyself indeed
               Fast flee to foreign shore.
               I am an angel at your need
               Sent to shield you as decreed
               And save from evils sore.
               If not hence soon thou speed

[69]

	For pity thou wilt plead 9
	And mourn thy fate the more.
JOSEPH	God on his throne!
	What wondrous deed
	Yields so sweet tone?
ANGEL	No, Joseph, it is I,
	An angel sent to thee.
JOSEPH	Alas! I pray thee why?
	What is thy will with me?
ANGEL	Fast from here now hie,
	And take with thee Mary,
	And also her child so free;
	For Herod deems must die
	All boys born, surely,
	But yet of age that be
	Not two.
JOSEPH	Alas, full woe is me!
	What shall we do?
ANGEL	To Egypt shall thou fare
	With all the speed you may;
	And Joseph, bide you there
	Till otherwise I say.
JOSEPH	This is a sad affair
	For a man so old to bear,
	To feel such fear to stay.
	My bones are bruised and bare,
	Unfit to fare. Would it were
	My life's last day
	Come to an end.
	I know not which is the way;
	How shall we wend?
ANGEL	Thereof have thou no dread;
	Go forth and cease thy din;
	The Lord, where thou wilt tread,
	Will guide thy steps from sin.
JOSEPH	God guard us where we're led
	Or we shall be ill sped
	Before we can begin;
	Therefore my wits are fled,
	I that am almost dead,
	In age how should I win
	My way.

[70]

51   I am full bare and thin,
      My strength—decay

      Now fails my strength, I fear,
      And sight that I should see,
      Mary, my darling dear,
      I am full woe for thee!
MARY Sweet Joseph now, what cheer?
      To see you shed a tear
      It truly troubles me.
JOSEPH Our cares are coming near
      If we dwell longer here;
      Therefore we have to flee
      Unseen.
MARY Alas! How may this be?
      Whatever may this mean?
JOSEPH It means of sorrows a blight.
MARY Ah, Joseph dear, how so?
JOSEPH As I dreamt in the night
      As I turned to and fro,
      An angel full of light
      As on bough is blossom bright
      Warned me of our woe:
      How Herod in his spite
      All boys born would affright
      With death: he would also,
      That fiend,
      Thy son's life in his might
      Most shamefully end.

MARY My son? Alas, my care!
      Who may my sorrows still?
      Ill may false Herod fare.
      My son why should he kill?
      Alas! Let's seek a lair,
      This bairn I bore to snare
      What worldly wretch had will?
      His heart should feel the tear
      Which he will have to bear
      That never yet did ill.
      Nor't thought.
JOSEPH Now Mary dear, be still;
      This helps us nought.

                [71]

It is not well to weep
When weeping is in vain;
Our cares we still must keep,
And this makes more our pain.

MARY The sorrows that I reap
That my sweet son asleep,
Is sought for to be slain.
Should I to Herod creep
I'd show my hatred deep.
Sweet Joseph speak words plain
To me.

JOSEPH Swift swaddle your son again,
And his death flee.

MARY His death would I not see
For all the world to win;
Alas, full woe were me,
Our bane should so begin;
My sweet child on my knee,
To slay him were pity,
And a foul heinous sin.
Dear Joseph, what say ye?

JOSEPH To Egypt wend shall we;
Therefore let be thy din
And cry.

MARY The way how shall we win?

JOSEPH Full well know I.

As quickly as we may
Now haste we out of here;
There is nought else to say
But quick pack up our gear.
For fear of future fray
Let us wend hence away
While danger lurks so near.

MARY Great God, as he well may,
That made both night and day
Shield us, we have great fear
To roam.
My child how should I bear
So far from home.

Alas I am full woe!

132
JOSEPH

Our plight's beyond my skill
God knows I may say so,
That burden bear I still;
For barely can I go
And lead from land such two;
No wonder I feel ill
And face now such a foe.
Will no death lay me low?
My life I like it ill.
Now hear,
He that all hurts may heal,
Keep me from care.

So riled a wretch as I,
In world was never man;
Household and husbandry,
Man's bane since he began;
That bargain dear I buy.
Young men beware, say I:
My wedding makes me wan.
Take hold thy bridle, Mary,
Look to that lad lively,
With all the care you can;
And may
He that this world began,
Show us the way.

MARY

Alas, full woe is me!
None is so sad as I!
My heart will break in three,
My son to see him die.

JOSEPH

Ah, Mary love, let be,
And nothing dread for thee.
In haste hence let us hie;
To save thy lad so free,
Fast forth now let us flee,
Dear wife—
To meet his enemy
It were to lose our life.

And that will I not hear.
Away then we must be,
My heart would be full drear

You two apart to see.   172
To Egypt let us fare;
This pack till I come there
Thou leave me to carry.
Therefore have thou no care
My help I shall not spare
Thou wilt find no fault in me,
I say.
God bless this company,
And have now all good day!

They go out.

The Sixteenth Play: Herod the Great

MESSENGER	1ST COUNSELLOR
HEROD	2ND COUNSELLOR
1ST SOLDIER	1ST WOMAN
2ND SOLDIER	2ND WOMAN
3RD SOLDIER	3RD WOMAN

CHILDREN

MESSENGER   Mohammed of mighty renown, make for you mirth!
Both of borough and town, by fell and by firth,
Both king with crown, and barons of birth;
Rumours up and down tell of peace on earth
        That shall come.
Give ear and attend
What our words portend;
Lest ill be your end,
        Listen, but be dumb.

Herod, the good King, by Mohammed's renown,
In Jewry and Jourmonting, sternly with crown,
All life that is living in tower and in town,
With grace gives you greeting, commands you bow
down
        At his bidding;
Love him with loyalty,
Dread him that is doughty!
He charges you be ready
        To run at his ruling.

[74]

HEROD THE GREAT

What man dare unfold a grievance or pain,
His grief shall be told, knight, squire, or swain;
Be he never so bold, buys he that bargain
Twelve thousandfold, when his hopes in vain
    Are dashed.
Herod in his hurry,
Is heavy with worry,
For a babe, in this flurry,
    Has him abashed.

A king they him call, and that we deny;
How should it so fall great marvel have I;
Therefore over all shall I make a cry,
That ye'd better not brawl nor gossip nor lie
    This tide;
Carp of no king
But Herod, that lording,
Or beware of a whipping
    Your heads for to hide.

He is king of kings whom all must adore
Chief lord of lordings, chief leader of law,
Knights waft on his wings to the heights they may soar,
Great dukes he down flings, in his great awe,
    Makes humble.
Tuscany and Turkey,
All India and Italy,
Syria and Sicily,
    At his feet tumble.

From paradise to Padua to Mount Flascon;
From Egypt to Mantua into Kemp Town;
From Saraceny to Susa to Greece it may abound;
Both Normandy and Norway bow to his crown;
    How spread
His fame no tongue can tell,
From heaven to hell,
Of him none speak so well
    As his cousin Mohammed.

He is the worthiest of all boys that are born;
Free men are his thrall and in his rage torn;

[75]

Begin he to brawl men must suffer his scorn;   57
Obey must we all or straight be forlorn
        And moan.
Drop down on your knees
All that him sees,
If him you displease,
        He will break every bone.

Here he comes now, I cry, of that lord I spake;
Fast before will I hie, me swiftly betake
To welcome him worshipfully, his mirth for to make,
As he is most worthy, and kneel for his sake
        So low;
Down demurely to fall,
Most royal prince to call;
Hail, the worthiest of all!
        My service to show.

HEROD *enters with* COUNSELLORS *and* SOLDIERS.

Hail, lovely lord, anew; thy laws most firm are laid;
I have done what I could do, and peace these people
                                        [prayed;
And much more thereto, openly displayed;
But rumours rush through their mind till is made
        A vain boast.
They carp of a king,
They cease not such chattering.
HEROD   But I shall tame their talking,
        Though some of them roast.

Leave, loafers, your din, to all be it known!
Till I have gone in make not a moan,
For if I begin I shall break every bone,
Till carcass from skin lie scattered and strown,
        By my decree!
Cease all this wonder,
And make you no blunder,
Lest I rip you in sunder,
        Be ye foolhardy.

Peace both young and old, at my bidding I have said,
For princely power I hold to have you alive or dead;

93   Who that is so bold I shall brain him through the head;
Speak not before I have told what I wish in this stead;
     Ye know not
How you I shall grieve;
Stir not till ye have leave,
If ye do I shall cleave
     You small as meat in pot.

My mirth is turned to pain, my meekness into ire,
This boy burns my brain, within I feel a fire,
If I see this young swain, I shall give him his hire;
Unless my will I gain, I were a simple sire
     Upon throne.
Had I that lad in hand,
As I am king in land
I should with this steel brand
     Break every bone.

My name spreads far and near the doughtiest, men me
                                                  [call,
That ever ran with spear, a lord and king royal;
What joy for me to hear, a lad will seize my stall!
If I this crown may bear that boy shall pay for all.
     Stronger
My anger, what devil me ails,
To torment me with tales,
That by God's dear nails,
     I'll stand it no longer!

What the devil! How I blast for anger and spleen!
I fear those kings have passed that here with me have
     been;
They promised me full fast before now to be seen,
Or else I should have cast another sleight, I mean.
     I tell you,
A boy they said they sought,
With offering that they brought;
It moves my heart right nought
     To break his neck in two.

But if they passed me by, by Mohammed in heaven,
Then in haste shall I set all at six and seven,

[77]

Think ye a king as I will suffer them even   129
To have any mastery but what to me is given?
    Nay, friend.
The devil me hang and draw,
If once that boy I saw
And then let slip my law
    Before his life I rend.

These perils foretold increase if they be gone;
If so ye hear it told I pray tell me anon,
For if they be so bold by God that sits on throne,
Tortures untold they shall suffer each one,
    For ire.
Such pains heard never man tell,
Both furious and fell
That Lucifer in hell,
    Their bones shall break entire.

1ST SOLDIER	Lord, think not ill if I tell you how they are passed;

My tongue lies not truly: since they came here last,
Another road hereby they tread and that full fast.

HEROD   Why and have they passed me by? Woe! Out! The
                                        [devil them blast!
    Woe! Fie!
Fie on the devil! Where may I abide?
But fight in my fury and at these cheats chide!
Thieves, I say, ye should full better have spied
    And told when they went by.

Knights I trusted most! Nay, wretches and thieves!
I could yield up my ghost, so sore my heart grieves.

2ND SOLDIER   Be not abashed, I dare boast these are no great mischiefs;
You may play yet the host.

3RD SOLDIER   Why give us these griefs
    Without cause?
Thus should ye not chide us,
Ungainly deride us,
And not abide us,
    Without better pause.

HEROD   Lazy lubbers and liars! Loafers each one!
Traitors to my fears! Knaves, but knights none!

165   Had ye been worth your ears, hence had they not run;
Come those kings near my spears, I'll break every bone;
   First vengeance
Shall I see on their bones;
If ye cluster like crones
I shall strike you with stones,
    Such addled attendants.

I know not where to sit for anger and spleen;
My crown I've not quit, as clearly is seen;
Fie! Devil! Now how is it? None comes in between.
I have no cause to flit, but be king as I mean
   For ever.
To safeguard my part,
I tell you my heart,
I shall make them start,
   Or else trust me never.

1ST SOLDIER   Sir, they went suddenly, before any knew,
Else had met us, trust me, in a meeting to rue.
2ND SOLDIER   So bold nor so hardy, to counter our crew,
Was none of that company; none saw my fist
   But feared.
3RD SOLDIER   They dared not abide,
But ran home to hide;
Might I them have spied,
   Elsewhere had they steered.

   What could we more do to save your honour?
1ST SOLDIER   We were ready thereto, and shall be each hour.
HEROD: Now since it is so, ye shall have favour;
Whither ye will, go, by town and by tower,
   Go hence!
SOLDIERS *withdraw.*
   I have tidings to tell
To my privy council;
Clerks, bear ye the bell,
   Burn for me incense.

One spoke in my ear, a wonderful talking,
Said a maiden should bear another to be king;
Sirs, I pray you find where, in all writing,

[79]

In Virgil, in Homer, in each other thing   202
  But legend;
They look at their books.
 In Boethius, in tales;
 Where church work prevails,
 Mass scarcely avails,
  So elsewhere attend.

 I pray you tell truly, now what ye find.

1ST   Truly, sir, prophecy, it is not blind;
COUNSELLOR Isaiah writes plainly, he shall be so kind,
 That a maiden meekly, most pure of mind,
  Shall him bear;
 "Virgo concipiet,
 Natumque pariet."
 Emmanuel is yet
  His name to declare.

2ND   "God is with us," that is for to say.
COUNSELLOR And others say thus, trust me ye may:
 "From Bethlehem a gracious lord shall hold sway,
 That of Jewry spacious King shall be ay,
  Lord mighty;
 And him shall honour
 Both king and emperor."

HEROD Why, and should I to him cower?
  Your lies I take lightly.

 Fie the devil thee speed and me, hear my moan!
 This has thou done indeed to make me grieve and groan;
 And thou, knave, thy meed shall have, by cock's bone!
 Ye know not half your creed! Out thieves from my
           throne!
  Fie, knaves!
 Fie, dotty polls, with your books!
 Go cast them in the brooks!
 With your wiles and sly looks
  Whereat my wit raves!

 Heard I never quirk so quaint that a knave so slight
 Should come like a saint and rob me of my right;
 Nay without restraint, I shall kill him downright;

238   Woe! For fury I faint; now strive I to fight
           The stronger;
       My guts will burst out
       If I hang not this lout;
       If my vengeance he flout,
           I may live no longer.

       Should a cub in cave but of one year of age,
       Thus make me to rave.

1ST COUNSELLOR   Sir, cease this outrage!
COUNSELLOR Away let ye wave all such language,
           Your worship to save; is he ought but a page
               Of a year?
       We two shall between
       Plot in our spleen,
       That if ye do as I mean,
           He shall die on a spear.

2ND   For fear that he reign, do as is said;
COUNSELLOR Through Bethlehem proclaim, and each other stead,
       That knights must ordain, and ding down dead
       All boys to their bane that be two, and dread
           No more.
       This child may ye kill,
       Thus at your own will.
HEROD   These noble words fill
           Me with joy evermore.

       If I live in this land a long life as I hope,
       By this shall I stand to make thee Pope.
       How my heart may expand, surprising its scope!
       For this news at your hand, you shall not long grope
           Without gain;
       Pence, shillings, and pounds,
       Great castles and grounds.
       Booty beyond bounds
           Be yours to retain.

       Now will I proceed and take vengeance;
       The flower of knighthood call to allegiance;
       Bashir, I thee bid it may advance.

MESSENGER   Lord, I shall me speed and bring, perchance,   274
                To thy sight.

HEROD *retires.* KNIGHTS *advance.*

                Hark knights, I you bring
                Here new tiding;
                Unto Herod King.
                    Haste with all your might!

                In all the haste that ye may in armour full bright,
                In your best array to seem a gay sight.
1ST SOLDIER   What should we say?
2ND SOLDIER   This is not all right.
3RD SOLDIER   Sirs, without a delay I fear that we fight.
MESSENGER   I pray you,
                As fast as ye may,
                Come to him this day.
1ST SOLDIER   What, in our best array?
MESSENGER   Yea, sirs, I say you.

2ND SOLDIER   Somewhat is in hand, whatever it mean.
3RD SOLDIER   Tarry not for to stand before we have been.

    HEROD *advances.*

MESSENGER   Herod, king of this land, well be ye seen!
                Your knights to command, in armour full sheen,
                    At your will.
1ST SOLDIER   Hail, doughtiest of all!
                We have come at your call,
                So trust to us all
                    Your wish to fulfil.

HEROD   Welcome, lords, in bliss, both great and small!
                The cause now is this, that I sent for you all;
                A lad, a knave, born is that should be king royal;
                Unless I kill him and his I burst, I guess, my gall;
                    Therefore, sirs,
                Vengeance shall ye take,
                All for that lad's sake,
                And honour shall it make
                    For you evermore, sirs.

                To Bethlehem take your way, and all the coast about,
                All male children ye slay, and, lords, ye shall be stout,

                    [82]

309   That be but two this day, and leave of all that rout
          No child me to dismay that lies in swaddling clout,
                I warn you.
          Spare no one's blood,
          Let all run in flood,
          The mothers ye thud,
                If mad of mood they scorn you.

          Hence! Now go your way, make haste, I implore.
2ND SOLDIER   I fear there'll be a fray, but I will go before.
3RD SOLDIER   Ah, think, sirs, I say, I shall hunt like a boar.
1ST SOLDIER   Let me make assay, I shall kill by the score;
                Herod all hail!
          We shall for your sake
          This massacre make.
HEROD   If my vengeance ye take
                Seek favour without fail.

    HEROD *withdraws.*

2ND SOLDIER   Play our parts now by rote, and handle them well.
3RD SOLDIER   I shall pay them on the coat, begin I to revel.
    1ST WOMAN *and* CHILD *advance.*
1ST SOLDIER   Hark, fellows, ye dote, do the work of the devil;
          I hold here a groat, she views me as evil,
                And would part;
    To the WOMAN.

          Dame, think it not ill,
          Thy knave if I kill.
1ST WOMAN   What thief! Against my will?
                Lord, save his sweet heart.

1ST SOLDIER   Abide, now, abide, no farther he goes.
1ST WOMAN   Peace, thief! Shall I chide and make here a noise?
1ST SOLDIER   I shall rob thee of pride: Kill we these boys!
1ST WOMAN   Ill thee betide; keep well thy nose,
                False thief!
          Have then at thy hood.
1ST SOLDIER   How whore! What hardihood!
    Kills the CHILD.

1ST WOMAN   Out, alas my child should
                Bleed, for grief.

                [83]

Alas for shame and sin! Alas that I was born!   343
My weeping must begin to see my child forlorn?
My comfort and my kin, my son thus cruelly torn!
Vengeance for this sin, I cry, both even and morn.

2ND SOLDIER   Well done!

2ND WOMAN and CHILD advance.

Come hither hag, and why?
That lad of thine shall die.

2ND WOMAN   Mercy, lord, I cry!
It is mine own dear son.

2ND SOLDIER   No mercy receive you for your moans, Maud!

2ND WOMAN   Then thy scalp shall I cleave! Do you wish to be clawed?
Leave, I bid thee leave!

2ND SOLDIER   Peace, bid I, bawd!

2ND WOMAN   Fie, fie, for reprieve! Fie, full of fraud!
No man!
Have at thy tabard,
A guy for a guard!
Now shall it go hard!
I curse as I can!

He kills the CHILD.

Out! Murder! Man, I say, cruel traitor and thief!
Out! Alas! And welaway! My boy's life was so brief!
My love, my blood, my play, that gave man no grief!
Alas, alas, this day! Break heart beyond belief
In sunder!
Vengeance I cry and call,
On Herod and his knights all!
Vengeance, Lord, upon them fall,
That wicked men may wonder!

3RD SOLDIER   This is well wrought gear that ever may be;

3RD WOMAN and CHILD advance.

Come ye hither here! Ye need not to flee!

3RD WOMAN   Will ye harm no hair of my child or me?

3RD SOLDIER   He shall die, I thee swear, his heart blood shall thou see.

3RD WOMAN   God forbid!
Thief! Thou sheds my child's blood!

He kills the BOY.

Of my body the bud!

[84]

377   Alas my heart is all in flood,
               To see my child thus bleed.

         By God, thou shall abuy this deed that thou has done.
3RD SOLDIER   Hag, nought reck I, by moon and sun.
3RD WOMAN   Have at thee, say I! Take thee there a foin!
         Out on thee I cry! Have at thy groin
               Another!
         This keep I in store.
3RD SOLDIER   Peace now, no more!
3RD WOMAN   I cry and I roar,
             Out on thee, man's murderer!

         Alas! My babe, mine innocent! Begot of my flesh! For
                                 [sorrow
         That God grievously sent, who of my bales would
                               [borrow?
         Thy body is sadly rent; I cry both even and morrow,
         Vengeance for thy blood thus spent! Out! I cry, and
                              [harrow!
1ST SOLDIER   Go quickly!
         Get out of this place!
         And, trotts, leave no trace,
         Or by cock's bone's apace
             I shall shift you slickly.
   The MOTHERS *retire.*

         Let them go and rot, they fear to abide.
2ND SOLDIER   Let us run foot hot, now would I we hide,
         And tell of this lot, that these boys have died.
3RD SOLDIER   You can quit this spot, that do I decide;
             Go forth now,
         Tell thou Herod our tale!
         For all our avail,
         I tell you without fail,
             He reward will allow.

1ST SOLDIER   I am best of you all and ever have been;
         The devil have my soul, but I be first seen;
         It fits me to call him my lord as I mean.
2ND SOLDIER   What need now to brawl? Be not so keen
                          In this anger;

I shall say thou did best,   411
Save myself, as I guessed. (*Aside.*)

1ST SOLDIER   Now that is most honest.
3RD SOLDIER   Go, tarry no longer.
They approach HEROD.

1ST SOLDIER   Hail Herod, our king, full glad may ye be!
Good tidings we bring, hark now unto me;
We have roved in our riding throughout Jewry:
And know ye one thing, that murdered have we
Many thousands.
2ND SOLDIER   I held them full hot
And paid them on the dot;
Their dames now cannot
Ever bind them in bands.

3RD SOLDIER   Had ye seen how I fared, when I came among them!
There was none that I spared, but laid on and dang them.
When they were so scared began I to bang them.
I stood and I stared, no pity to hang them
Had I.
HEROD   By Mohammed's renown,
That spreads up and down,
As I swear this crown
Ye shall have a lady,

For each one a maid to wed at his will.
1ST SOLDIER   So long have ye said, but unpaid is the bill!
2ND SOLDIER   And I was never flayed, for good nor for ill.
3RD SOLDIER   Ye can count it well-paid our wish to fulfil,
It strikes me,
With treasure untold,
Before us to unfold,
Both silver and gold
To give us great plenty.

HEROD   As I am king crowned I think it but right!
There goes none on ground as ye by this light;
A hundred thousand pound is good wage for a knight,
Of pennies good and round to enjoy day and night
Such store;
And ye knights of ours

[86]

448   Shall have castles and towers,
        Both for you and yours,
         For now and evermore.

1ST SOLDIER   Was never none born by down nor by dale,
        Before us, be it sworn, that could so prevail.
2ND SOLDIER   We have castles and corn, of much gold to avail.
3RD SOLDIER   It will never be worn without any tail;
         All hail!
        Hail lord! Hail king!
        Forth are we faring!
HEROD   Now Mohammed you bring
         To his faith without fail.

       Now in peace may I stand, through Mohammed's re-
                [nown!
       And give of my land that belongs to my crown;
       And bring to my hand both fortress and town;
       Marks for each a thousand, shortly paid down,
         Shall ye hold.
       I shall give for your gain,
       My word was not vain,
       Watch when I come again,
         Then to beg be ye bold.
HEROD *dismisses the* SOLDIERS.

       I set by no good now my heart is at ease,
       That I shed so much blood, I reign as I please!
       For to see this flood from the feet to the knees
       Moves nothing my mood, I laugh that I wheeze;
         As down,
       So light is my soul,
       That all of sugar is my gall;
       I may now do withal
         What I wish with my crown.

       I was cast into care so fearful afraid,
       Now I need not despair for low is he laid
       As these knights declare who so have him flayed;
       Else great wonder, where that so many strayed
         In the way,
       That one should escape

        [87]

Without hurt this scrape;   484
Too many mothers gape
        Childless, their wrongs to abate.

A hundred thousand, I know, and forty are slain,
And four thousand; also passed is my pain;
Such murder and woe shall never be again.
Had I but one blow at that poor swain
        So young,
It should have been seen
What my vengeance had been
And the spate of my spleen
        Told by many a tongue.

Thus knaves shall I teach example to take,
In their wits that screech, such masters to make;
In vain ye may preach and in babel out break!
Saved by no sovereign's speech your necks shall I shake
        In sunder;
No king on to call
But on Herod the royal,
Else many a thrall
        Shall pay for that blunder.

For if I hear it spoken when I come again,
Your brains shall be broken, so pay heed to pain;
The sleeping shall be woken, it shall be so plain;
Now by this token my nose may disdain
        Such a stench.
Sirs, this is my counsel,
Be not too cruel,
But adieu—to the devil!
        I know no more French!

Exit HEROD *followed by his* MESSENGER.

The Seventeenth Play: The Purification of Mary

SYMEON	JOSEPH
1ST ANGEL	MARY
2ND ANGEL	JESUS

SYMEON

Mighty God, that us to aid
Heaven and earth and all has made;
Bring us to bliss that never shall fade,
*   As thou well may;*
And think on me that am unwell—
Lo, I so limp and hobble,
Sadly my years begin to tell—
*   Now help, Lord, Adonai!*

But yet I marvel, both even and morn,
Of elders long before me born,
If they be safe or quite forlorn,
*   Where they may be;*
Abel, Noah, and Abraham,
David, Daniel, and Balaam,
And many more by name,
*   In their degree.*

I thank thee, Lord, with good intent,
For all the guidance thou has sent,
That thus long time my life has lent,
*   Now many a year;*
For all are past now but only I;
I thank thee, Lord God almighty!
For none is old as I, truly,
*   Now living here.*

For I am old Symeon;
So old in life know I none,
That is made of flesh and bone,
*   On middle-earth today.*
No wonder if my woes I tell;
Fever and flux keep me unwell;
So thin my arms and legs as well,
*   And all my beard is grey.*

[89]

My eyes are worn both dim and blind;   33
My breath is short, and I want wind;
Thus has age destroyed my kind,
    And me bereft of all;
But shortly must I wend away;
What time and when, I cannot say,
For it has gone full many a day
    Since death began to call.

There is no task that I may work,
But scarcely crawl I to the kirk;
When I come home I feel such irk
    That further may I nought;
But sit me down with grunts and groans,
And lie and rest my weary bones,
And yawn all night amidst my moans,
    Till I to sleep be brought.

But, nevertheless, the truth to say,
If I may neither night nor day
For age neither stir nor play,
    Nor make no cheer,
Yet if I be never so old,
I mind full well what prophets told,
That now are dead and laid full cold,
    Gone since many a year.

They said that God, full of might,
Should send his son from heaven bright,
In a maiden for to alight,
    Come of David's kin;
Flesh and blood in her to take,
And become man for our sake,
Our redemption for to make,
    That lost has been through sin.

Lord, grant us thy promised grace aright,
Send me thy word both day and night,
Grant me that grace of heaven's light,
    And let me never die,
Until such grace to me thou send,
That I may touch him as my friend,
Who shall come our ills to amend,
    And see him with my eye.

1ST ANGEL 74	*Thou, Symeon, dread thou nought!* *My Lord, that thou has long besought,* *For thou has righteous been,* *Thine asking has he granted thee,* *Without death in life to be,* *Till thou thy Christ has seen.*
2ND ANGEL	*Then Symeon, hearken a space!* *I bring thee tidings of solace;* *Therefore, rise up and go* *To the temple; there shall he be* *God's son before thee,* *Whom thou yearned for so.*
SYMEON	*Praised be my Lord in will and thought,* *That forgets his servant nought,* *When that he sees time!* *Well is me I shall not die* *Till I have seen him with my eye,* *That child sublime.*

Praised be my Lord in heaven above,
That by his angel showed such love,
And warned me of his coming!
Therefore will I with intent
Put on me my vestment,
In worship of that king.

He shall be welcome unto me;
That Lord shall make us all free,
Of all mankind the king;
For with his blood he shall us save
Both from hell and from the grave,
That were slain through sin.

The bells ring out.

Ah, dear God! what may this be?
Our bells ring so solemnly,
For whomsoever it is;
I cannot understand this ringing,
Unless my Lord God be bringing
Our saviour and our bliss.

[91]

This noise gives my old heart cheer,
I shall never rest if I stay here,
Though I must go alone.
Now blessed am I, I dare avow,
For such noise heard I never ere now;
Our bells ring on their own.

JOSEPH *with two doves, and* MARY *with her baby advance.*

JOSEPH

Mary, it begins to pass,
Forty days since that thou was
Delivered of thy son;
To the temple I say we draw,
To cleanse thee and fulfil the law,
Our elders' wont be done.

Therefore Mary, maid and friend,
Take thy child and let us wend
Unto the temple;
And we shall with us bring
These turtles two as our offering,
The law will we fulfil.

MARY

Joseph, that will I with a cheerful heart,
That the law in every part
Be fulfilled in me.
Lord, that all things may,
Give us grace to do this day
What is pleasing unto thee!

The ANGELS *sing.*

1ST ANGEL

Thou, Symeon, righteous and true,
Thou has desired both old and new,
To have a sight of Christ Jesu,
As prophecy has told!
Oft has thou prayed to have a sight
Of him that did in maid alight;
Here is that child of so great might,
Now that thou would, behold!

2ND ANGEL

Thou has desired it most of all.

[Incomplete]

[92]

The Eighteenth Play: The Play of the Doctors

1st Doctor	Jesus
2nd Doctor	Mary
3rd Doctor	Joseph

[The beginning of this play is missing.]

2ND DOCTOR   *That a maiden a bairn should bear;*
    And his name thus did they tell,
From the time that he born were,
    He shall be called Emmanuel;

    Counsellor and God of Strength,
      And Wonderful also
Shall he be called, of breadth and length,
      As far as man may go.

3RD DOCTOR   *Masters, your reasons are right good,*
    And wonderful to name,
Yet find I more by Habakkuk;
    Sirs, listen while I quote the same.

    Bliss of our bale shall be the fruit
      Hereafterward some day;
A wand shall spring from Jesse's root,—
      The certain truth, thus did he say,—

    And from that wand shall spring a flower,
      That shall rise to a great height:
Thereof shall come full sweet odour,
      And thereupon shall rest and light

    The holy ghost, full of such might;
      The ghost of wisdom and of wit,
Shall build his nest with power and right,
      And in it breed and sit.

1ST DOCTOR   *But when, think ye, this prophecy*
    Shall be fulfilled in deed,
That here is told so openly,
    As we in scriptures read?

[93]

2ND DOCTOR   *A great marvel it is decreed,*
               For us to hear such mastery;
             A maid to bear a child, indeed,
               Without man's seed is mystery.

3RD DOCTOR   *The holy ghost shall in her light,*
               And keep her maidenhead full clean;
             Whoso may bide to see that sight,
               They need not dread, I ween.

1ST DOCTOR   *Of all these prophets wise of lore*
               That knew the prophecy, more and less,
             Was none that told the time before,
               When he should come to us in peace?

2ND DOCTOR   *Whether he be come or not,*
               No knowledge have we for certain;
             But he shall come, that doubt we not;
               The prophets have preached it full plain.

3RD DOCTOR   *Prophets foretelling this event*
               Owe thanks to God that is on high,
             Who gave them knowledge of his intent,
               His will to tell and glorify.
JESUS *enters.*
JESUS   *Masters, love be to you sent,*
               And comfort all this company!
1ST DOCTOR   *Son, hence away I would thou went,*
               For other things in hand have we.

2ND DOCTOR   *Son, whoever thrust thee near,*
               They were not wise, thus tell I thee;
             For we have other tales to hear,
               Than playing now with bairns to be.

3RD DOCTOR   *Son, if thou list ought to learn to live by Moses' law,*
             Come, we shall not spurn thee, but hear and then withdraw.

             For in some mind it may thee bring
               To hear our sayings read in rows.
JESUS   *To learn of you need I nothing,*
               Your deeds and sayings, know I those.

[94]

1st Doctor *Hark to yon bairn and his bragging!*
64   *He thinks he kens more than he knows;*
          Now, son, thou art but a fledgeling,
                Not clergy knowing how law goes.

Jesus   *I know as well as ye how that your law was wrought.*
2nd Doctor *Come sit, son, we shall see, for certain seems it nought.*

3rd Doctor *It were wonder if any wight*
                Unto our reasons right should reach;
          And thou says thou has in sight
                Our laws truly to tell and teach.
Jesus   *The holy ghost did in me alight,*
                And anoint me like a leech,
          And gave to me both power and might
                The kingdom of heaven to preach.

2nd Doctor *Whence ever this bairn may be*
                Who tells these tidings new?
Jesus   *Certain, sirs, I was ere ye,*
                And shall be after you.

1st Doctor *Son, thy sayings soothe and heal,*
                And thy wit is a wondrous thing;
          But, nevertheless, full well I feel
                That it may fail in working;
          For David deems of such to deal,
                And thus he says of children young:

          "Ex ore infantium et lactentium, perfecisti laudem."

          Out of their mouths, said David well,
                Our Lord has brought forth praising.

          Nevertheless, son, stint thou should yet,
                Here for to speak at large;
          For where masters are met,
                Children's words must not take charge.

          For certain if thou would never so fain
                Give all thou could to learn the law,
          Thou art neither of might nor main
                To know as clerk without a flaw.

[95]

JESUS

Sirs, I tell you for certain,
   That truth alone shall be my saw;
And power have I full and plain,
   That ye my speaking hold in awe.

1ST DOCTOR

Masters, what may this mean?
   Marvel, methinks, do I
Wherever this bairn has been,
   That speaks thus knowingly.

2ND DOCTOR

In world as wide as ever we went,
   Found we none such ever before;
Certain, I think this bairn be sent
   From heaven to heal our sore.

JESUS

Sirs, I shall prove with you present,
   All the saws I said before.

3RD DOCTOR

How say you the first commandment
   And the greatest in Moses' law?

JESUS

Sirs, since ye sit in a row,
   And to your books you can give heed,
Let us see, sirs, if it is so,
   How correctly you can read.

1ST DOCTOR

I read that this is the first bidding
   That Moses in us did instil;
Honour thy God above everything,
   With all thy wit and all thy will;
And all thy heart to him shall cling,
   Early and late, both loud and still.

JESUS

Ye need no other books to bring,
   But strive first this to fulfil.

The second may men prove,
   And clergy know thereby;
Your neighbours shall ye love
   Right as yourself truly.

This commanded Moses to all men,
   In his commandments clear;
On these two biddings, shall ye ken,
   Hang all the laws we need to hear.

[96]

133   *Whoso fulfils these two, then*
    With might and main, holding them dear,
He fulfils truly all ten,
    Which follow altogether.

Then we should God honour
    With all our might and main,
And love well every neighbour,
    Right as ourself certain.

1ST DOCTOR   *Now, son, since thou has told us two,*
    Which are the eight, can thou ought say?
JESUS   *The third bids, whereso ye go,*
    That ye shall hallow the holy day;
From bodily work ye take your rest;
    Your household, too, look they do so,
Both wife, child, servant, and beast.
    The fourth is then, in weal and woe,

Thy father and mother, thou shall honour,
    Not only with thy reverence,
But in their need thou them succour,
    And keep ay good obedience.

The fifth bids thee no man slay,
    Nor harm him never in word nor deed,
Nor suffer him in woe to stay,
    If thou may help him in his need.

The sixth bids thee thy wife to take
    But none other lawfully;
Lust of lechery thou flee and fast forsake,
    And fear God whereso thou be.

The seventh bids thee be no thief,
    Nor nothing win through treachery;
Usury and simony will bring you grief,
    But conscience clear keep truly.

The eighth bids thee be true in deed,
    And no false witness look thou bear;
Lie not for friend, it is decreed,
    Lest thy soul's weal thou might impair.

The ninth bids thee not desire
 Thy neighbour's wife nor his women,
But as holy kirk would thee inspire,
 Set thy purpose right therein.

The tenth bids thee for nothing
 Thy neighbour's goods to yearn for;
His house, his rent, nor his having,
 And the Christian faith hold evermore.

Thus in tables, shall ye ken,
 Our Lord to Moses wrote;
These are the commandments ten,
 For true men to take note.

2ND DOCTOR *Behold, our laws how he displays,*
 And learnt he never on book to read!
Full subtle saws, methinks, he says,
 And also true, if we take heed.
3RD DOCTOR *Yet let him forth on his ways,*
 For if he stay, well we may dread
The people will full soon him praise
 Well more than us for all our deed.

1ST DOCTOR *Nay, nay, then work we wrong!*
 Such speaking we deplore;
As he came, go along,
 And move us now no more.
 JOSEPH *and* MARY *enter.*

MARY *Ah, dear Joseph! How ill have we sped!*
 No comfort in our loss find we;
My heart is heavy as any lead,
 Until my comely son I see.
Now have we sought in every stead,
 Both up and down, for these days three;
But whether he be quick or dead
 Yet know we not, so woe is me!

JOSEPH *Sorrow had never man more!*
 But mourning, Mary, may not amend;

[98]

203   *Let us go on before,*
        Till God some succour send.

    About the temple if he be ought,
        That would I know ere it be night.

MARY   *For certain I see what we have sought!*
        In world was never so seemly a sight;
    Lo, where he sits, see ye him nought
        Among yon masters of so great might?

JOSEPH   *Bless God who us hither brought.*
        In land now lives there none so light.

MARY   *Now, dear Joseph, for all our sake,*
        Go forth and fetch your son and mine;
    Now far is it past day-break,
        And homeward we must start in time.

JOSEPH   *With men of might I never spake,*
        Such bidding I must needs decline;
    I cannot with them meddle or make,
        They are so gay in their furs fine.

MARY   *To them you must your errand say,*
        Sure to that no dread you feel!
    They will take heed to you alway,
        Because of age, I know it well.

JOSEPH   *When I get there what shall I say?*
        For I know not how I should deal,
    But thou would have me shamed for ay,
        For I can neither crook nor kneel.

MARY   *Go we together, I hold it best,*
        To yon men dressed so fine indeed;
    And if I see, as I have rest,
        That ye will not, then I must need.

JOSEPH   *Go thou and tell thy tale first,*
        Thy son to see will take good heed;
    Wend forth, Mary, and do thy best,
        I come behind, as God me speed.

MARY   *Ah, dear son, Jesus!*
        Since we love thee alone,
    Why does thou this to us,
        Thus to make us moan?

Thy father and I between us two,
Son, for thy love, have fared but ill,
We have thee sought both to and fro,
Weeping sorely as parents will.

JESUS   *Wherefore, mother, should ye seek me so?*
My life, you know how I must fill,
My father's works for weal or woe,
Thus am I sent for to fulfil.

MARY   *These sayings on them I dwell,*
And truly understand,
I shall think on them well,
And what follows take in hand.

JOSEPH   *Now truly, son, the sight of thee*
Has comforted us of all our care;
Come forth now with thy mother and me!
At Nazareth I would we were.

JESUS   *Believe then, ye lordings free!*
For with my friends now will I fare.

1ST DOCTOR *Son, whereso thou shall abide or be,*
God make thee good man evermore.

2ND DOCTOR *No wonder if thou, wife,*
At his finding be fain;
He shall, if he have life,
Prove a worthy swain.

3RD DOCTOR *Son, look thou mind, for good or ill,*
The matters that we have named but now;
And if thou like to abide here still,
And with us dwell, welcome art thou.

JESUS   *Grammercy, sirs, for your good will!*
No longer must I bide with you,
My friends' wish will I fulfil,
And to their bidding meekly bow.

MARY   *Full well is me this tide,*
Now may we make good cheer.

JOSEPH   *No longer will we bide;*
Now farewell all folk here.

MARY, JOSEPH *and* JESUS *go off together.*

[100]

Notes to the Plays (Part Two)

THE ANNUNCIATION

The action of the play is located in three different places: heaven, the house of Joseph and Mary, and the wilderness. Gabriel descends from heaven's tower to greet Mary. When they part (154) Gabriel retires beneath heaven's tower and Mary withdraws to her mansion opposite. The manuscript does not identify the Angel who addresses Joseph (326) with Gabriel, but such an identification is adopted here as a staging convenience. Joseph's first words refer to Mary's pregnancy (158), and if she is going to appear pregnant she will need to prepare herself in her mansion before her dialogue with Joseph begins. All medieval texts on this theme stress Mary's physical appearance and the stress would have been as apparent in medieval drama. A direction in the thirteenth-century play of The Prophets performed in Laon cathedral, refers to Elizabeth as 'dressed as a woman and pregnant'. It is highly probable that such a detail found in a cathedral production would have been carried over to the more secular management of the mystery plays.

God, having dispatched Gabriel, looks on during the subsequent action (77–154). His concern in Mary's conception is depicted in The Annunciation by the Master of the *Heures de Rohan* (fifteenth century), in which as the angel kneels to Mary, who is seated, God looks down and sends his blessing from above. The centre panel of the Altarpiece of *Aix-en-Provence, Église de la Madeleine*, represents the Annunciation as taking place within a church with Mary kneeling at a lectern and Gabriel fully robed and winged kneeling facing her. God and his angels look down from the triforium casting beams of golden light upon the Virgin. A regular feature of paintings of the Annunciation is a flowering plant, sometimes held by the angel, sometimes in a vase, as for instance it occurs in The Annunciation of the Master of St. Sebastian, in which Gabriel appears suspended between heaven and earth.

Karl Young describes the early treatment of this theme in medieval churches: 'At Salisbury and at Bayeux, when the deacon read the gospel in Matins on Wednesday of Ember Days in December, he held a branch of palm in his hand, as an angelic symbol. At Parma, in the Mass, artificial figures of the Angel Gabriel and Mary were used at the pulpit where the gospel was read. The figure of Gabriel was lowered from an opening in the roof. . . . From Tournai we have a full description of this ceremony as arranged there by Pierre Cotrel in the sixteenth century (a ceremony established at Tournai as early as 1231). This was performed on Ember Wednesday in December. During Matins two boys are to be costumed as Mary and the angel, and after the seventh lesson they are to mount their respective curtained platforms. At the beginning of Mass, which follows Matins, the curtains of Mary's 'sedes' are opened, showing her in a kneeling posture. Gabriel is not disclosed until the singing of the *Gloria in excelsis*. When the deacon sings the gospel, Mary and Gabriel themselves utter the words assigned to them in the text. In singing the words *Ave, gratia plena*, Gabriel bows to Mary thrice. At the words *Spiritus Sanctus superveniet in te*, the image of a dove is made to descend to a position before the platform of Mary, and there it remains until after the *Agnus Dei*, when it is drawn aloft again. After the *Ite, missa est*, Mary and Gabriel leave their platforms, and with lights preceding them, go to the vesting-room.'

(op. cit., ii. 245, 246.)

The Holy Ghost appears as a speaking character in the *Ludus Coventriae* play of *The Parliament of Heaven*. The stage direction at the moment of conception reads: 'Here the holy ghost descends with three beams to our lady, the son of the godhead next with three beams to the holy ghost, the father godly with three beams to the son. And so enter all three to her bosom . . .' The liturgical plays, the cycle plays, and pictorial representations of the Annunciation, in which frequently are depicted the three beams that occasion the divine conception, stress the material interpretation given to this theme in the Middle Ages. No doubt somewhere in the accounts for the properties of the *Ludus Coventriae* play was to be found an item concerning nine beams, three for the Holy Ghost, three for the Son, and three for God. This medieval approach to the subject is reinforced by records of performances in the churches at Besançon and Padua. 'At Besançon the part of Mary was taken by a young girl ten or twelve years of age; and in the gallery from which the dove descended was stationed an elderly man to represent God (1452). . . . In an "ordo" of the fourteenth century from the cathedral of Padua . . . at Gabriel's words *Spiritus Sanctus superveniet in te*, a dove is let down over Mary, and as she says *Ecce ancilla Domini*, she receives it under her cloak, thus symbolizing her conception.' (Karl Young, op. cit., ii. 246, 248, 250.)

Mary's vow of chastity (117/118) and the manner of her marriage with Joseph derive from non-biblical sources and are fully dramatized in the *Ludus Coventriae*, in which the three maidens (270) that attend on Mary are given names, and they defend Mary's innocence against Joseph's accusations. In the Chester play of *The Annunciation* Joseph lists the tools of his trade that he carries with him:

> With this axe that I bear,
> This gimlet and this auger,
> Axe, hammer, together
> I have won my meat.

> (Chester Plays, *The Annunciation*, 409–412.)

The play is an obvious occasion for the introduction of music. There are no directions for music in the Wakefield Annunciation, but the York, Chester and Coventry Annunciation plays include references to the *Ave Maria* and the *Magnificat*. The *Magnificat* is, however, contained in the following play in the Wakefield Cycle, *The Salutation of Elizabeth*. A hymn of praise might be sung by the angels before God speaks at the beginning of the play; the angels might also sing the *Ave Maria* as Gabriel descends from Heaven to Mary (76), or the example in the *Ludus Coventriae Conception of Mary* might be followed: 'here the Angel descends, the heaven singing *Exultet celum laudibus resultet terra gaudiis Archangelorum gloria sacra canunt solemnia*'. The York *Annunciation* includes Gabriel singing *Ne timeas Maria* following his salutation of the Virgin. This Wakefield play might end with the angel choir singing *Angelus ad Virginem*.

THE SALUTATION

This is the shortest, simplest and most harmonious play in the Cycle. There is no problem of staging: the two characters meet, speak, and part on the same pageant or stage. *The Visit of Elizabeth* in the *Ludus Coventriae*, on the other hand, represents Mary and Joseph travelling fifty-two miles (*et sic transient circa placeam*) to meet Elizabeth. And in this *Ludus Coventriae* play the *Magnificat* is spoken alternately by Mary and Elizabeth, each taking two lines at a time, Mary the Latin and Elizabeth the English equivalent. Mary concludes this section on a didactic note:

> This psalm of prophecy said between us two,
> In heaven it is written with angel's hand,
> Ever to be sung and also to be said
> Every day among us at evensong.

> (*Ludus Coventriae*, *The Visit to Elizabeth*, 105–108.)

[103]

In the Wakefield play the *Magnificat* is spoken by Mary alone. If these words are delivered slowly against an angel-choir singing the *Magnificat*, perhaps in Latin, some of the antiphonal character of the *Ludus Coventriae Magnificat* may be recreated, and the significance of the scene itself will be enriched and deepened. A suggestion for the music at the beginning and the end of the play comes also from the *Ludus Coventriae*:

> With Ave we began, and Ave is our conclusion,
> *Ave regina celorum* to our lady we sing.

(*Ludus Coventriae, Epilogue of Contemplacio to The Visit to Elizabeth,* 35/36.)

The First Shepherds' Play

At the beginning of the play it is necessary for the initial speeches of the First and Second Shepherd, which are addressed to the audience, to be delivered from two distinct acting areas. At the end of his first speech the First Shepherd moves off 'to the fair' (42) and he comes near to where the Second Shepherd has been speaking after forty lines (82). In its simplest form the play can be performed with only two stations or main acting areas: the one for the entry of the Second Shepherd, the main dialogue of the three Shepherds, the feasting, and the appearance of the Angel; the other for heaven—the lodging of the heavenly choir— and beneath heaven the mansion which later reveals the Holy Family, and it is in front of this mansion that the First Shepherd opens the play. On the other hand a multiple stage might make production even more flexible, whereby journeys could be made from station to station, incorporating the ground between as part of the acting area—the Third Shepherd enters riding a mare (164). Some support is given to this presentation of the Shepherds' plays by references to lea, valley, and hill as stage areas (Wakefield 316, York 51, Coventry Shearmen and Taylors' 214, 218). Different levels for the Shepherds' action are stressed in the Chester version:

> THIRD SHEPHERD   Hankin, hold up thy hand and have me,
> That I were on high there by thee.

(Chester, *Adoration of the Shepherds,* 93–94.)

[104]

When in this play the Shepherds reach the manger, they hesitate before the door (454), arguing who shall go in first. It is probable then that there is either a door or a curtain representing a door which, when opened, reveals the Holy Family. A Chartres stained glass representation of the Nativity is framed in a curtained setting, and in the earlier liturgical form of the play as performed at Rouen in the thirteenth century, when the Shepherds come to Bethlehem they approach the altar, beyond which is set the crib, on either side clergy as midwives, and when the curtain over the crib is drawn aside, the artificial figures of the Virgin Mary and the child are revealed.

The actual orientation of heaven's tower and Mary's mansion to the east of the pageant or acting area, perhaps another vestige of the liturgical drama, is strongly suggested in plays on this theme. Reference occurs in this Wakefield play (438) to the Shepherds moving towards the east, and the following from York, when the Shepherds look towards the angel choir:

> Lo! Hud! behold unto the east!
> A wondrous sight there shall you see
> Up in the sky.
>
> (York, *The Angels and Shepherds*, 46–48.)

The heritage of liturgical drama may also account for the laconic parts in this play allotted to Mary and Joseph. As artificial plastic figures they traditionally left the main part of the drama to be conducted by the Shepherds and Midwives. In the mystery plays on this theme Joseph says very little or nothing at all, as in this Wakefield play; indeed it is debatable whether he should even appear. Medieval iconography frequently omits him from this scene, and when he does appear he is often depicted as either bored or asleep, as in the Chartres example. The First Shepherd's description of Joseph in the Chester play might interest the make-up artist:

> Whatever this old man that here is,
> Take heed his head is hoar,
> His beard like bush of briers,
> With a pound of hair about his mouth and more.
>
> (Chester, *Adoration of the Shepherds*, 507–510.)

It is traditional in this scene for the Holy Family to be revealed only when the Shepherds arrive at Bethlehem and are ready to present their gifts.

[105]

The part of Jack Garcio may well be absorbed into that of the Third Shepherd. It is obviously unsatisfactory as it stands. His abuse of the First and Second Shepherds is in the same tone as that administered by the Third Shepherd. Like the Third Shepherd in the following play, Jack Garcio appears to be the youngest and responsible to the others for finding pasture for the sheep. The main difficulty in giving Jack Garcio's lines to the Third Shepherd lies in the following section of his part:

> Of all the fools I can tell,
> From heaven unto hell,
> Ye three bear the bell.   (185–187.)

Either the last line is changed to 'Ye two bear the bell', or the Third Shepherd, as the jester of the group, thrusts a coxcomb with a bell into one of the other Shepherds' hands (the Chester First Shepherd offers the baby Jesus a bell). It is barely plausible that the jest may be of the kind Feste in *Twelfth Night* makes at the expense of Sir Toby Belch and Sir Andrew Aguecheek: 'Did you never see the picture of "we three"?'

The persistence of satire, at times little more than tomfoolery, at times trenchant social criticism, in the Shepherds' plays of the mystery cycles, relates them to the ceremonies of the Boy Bishop, the Feast of Fools, and the pagan Kalends, all festivities falling in the same Christmas season. Accepted order is reversed, revered tradition is discarded, and the young mock their elders and betters. This last point is admirably illustrated by the Garcio of the Chester play wrestling with, and throwing, each of the three Shepherds in turn. In the Wakefield play the hallowed *Gloria in excelsis* is hilariously muffed (430), the lordly fare of the aristocrats is lumped with the blood-puddings of the peasants (217), and Latin, the language of religion, is hooted at (390) or reduced to gibberish (292).

The folk-lore which informs these mid-winter festivities is clearly pre-Christian. In a time of desperate need great plenty appears. The First Shepherd, having lost all, imagines that he has regained a hundred sheep (110). The groans of poverty and oppression give way to orgiastic delight in the Shepherds' gargantuan feast. The sky which one moment is gloomy and foreboding (434) is the next ablaze with light (452). Such details suggest that a spring festival has been moved back to mid-winter, and although the rebirth themes associated with spring are everywhere apparent, the original performances of the liturgical Shepherds' plays in the mid-winter season is amply evinced by the repeated references to the cold weather. The Wakefield Cycle was performed on *Corpus Christi* Day or, in the late sixteenth century, during Whitsun week, but in both of the Shepherds' plays we hear of the suffering caused by a bitter winter. The cold itself is turned to exquisite dramatic purpose in the Coventry Pageant of the *Shearmen and Taylors:*

MARY   Ah! Joseph, husband, my child grows cold,
          And we have no fire to warm him with.

JOSEPH   Now in my arms I shall him fold,
          King of kings by field and frith;
          He might have had better, if truth were told,
          Than the breathing of beasts to warm him with.
                                  (287–292.)

In one of the Six Scenes From the Life of Christ in the Psalter of Robert, Baron de Lisle (before 1339), we see the Shepherds well wrapped up and one of them wearing mittens.

The section of the play (341–403) which contains the Shepherds' learned references to the prophets and even the First Shepherd's quotation from Virgil, might in production be omitted, especially if *The Procession of the Prophets* has already been performed. The passage, however, is of particular interest in illustrating the 'type and antitype' which medieval dramatist and artist were equally fond of juxtaposing. There is, for instance, a stained glass window at Canterbury cathedral, down the centre of which are scenes from the life of Christ, while either side are 'types' from the Old Testament, which illustrate or prefigure these scenes. In this play the story of the burning bush is a 'type' to the 'antitype' of the Virgin birth (360–367). This association is most vividly depicted in Nicholas Froment's The Virgin in the Burning Bush—The Vision of Moses (1476), in Saint-Sauveur Cathedral, Aix-en-Provence.

The Angels in heaven sing the *Gloria in excelsis* (295) and the Shepherds give their discordant version of it (431). The season and the play call for song. After feeding and drinking the Shepherds sing (266), and they sing again at the very end of the play (502). No song is extant in the Wakefield text, but the Pageant of the *Shearmen and Taylors* of Coventry presents us with the following Shepherds' songs, appropriate to the above occasions:

        As I rode out this other night,
        Of three jolly shepherds I saw a sight,
        And all about their fold a star shone bright;

They sang terli terlow;
So merrily the shepherds their pipes did blow.

and

Down from heaven, from heaven so high
Of angels there came a great company,
With mirth and joy and great solemnity,
They sang terli terlow;
So merrily the shepherds their pipes did blow.

THE SECOND SHEPHERDS' PLAY

Two mansions are required, one for Mary and the child, and one for Mak's home. Above Mary's mansion is heaven from where the Angel speaks to the Shepherds (638). In the original text (649) the Second Shepherd suggests to us the direction from which the Angel appeared: 'he spak upward'. The part of the stage or pageant between the two mansions can be used for the rest of the action, although it may be preferable, and indeed more true to the original production, to use the ground space in front of the pageant. Daw, the Third Shepherd, comes over the lea land (111), the Shepherds sleep out of door (632) on the 'green' (634), and their journey to Bethlehem is more convincing if they have in fact farther to travel and another level to climb. The tossing of Mak in a canvas or blanket—a popular medieval method of accelerating childbirth—is more conveniently and safely carried out on ground level. The curtains around the mansions conceal the actors within until the action of the play is transferred to the mansions. On the occasions when Mak returns home (295 and 404), although a curtain representing a door might divide Mak from his wife, to enjoy the dialogue fully, the audience should be able to see both characters simultaneously. The meeting of the three Shepherds at the Crooked Thorn, if staged below the level of the pageant, might lend greater dramatic effect to their threatening move towards Mak's house (475).

Reference is made to the pranked-up dress of the swaggering retainers. Their 'modish sleeve' (28) displayed their livery, and as some nobleman's henchmen they oppressed the peasantry. On his first entry Mak pretends to wield such authority (201), but his short cloak, beneath which he might have concealed his 'pickings', is wrenched from his shoulders by the Third Shepherd (200); and after he has already stolen the sheep Mak ostentatiously invites the three Shepherds to examine his capacious sleeves to make sure that he is innocent of any theft (396).

[108]

In his endeavour to impress the three Shepherds with his superiority Mak apes the speech of the south, but they know him too well to be taken in (216). His Latin likewise is false (267), and shortly after having called a doubtful blessing on the sleepers in the name of Pontius Pilate, he proceeds to cast over them a magic spell which will enable him to steal their sheep with impunity. The First Shepherd's Latin (350–351) is no more accurate than Mak's, but at least without pious affectation.

Daw, the Third Shepherd's name, is a diminutive for David, but more probably has here the connotation of 'fool'. In which case it corresponds to 'Slow-pace', the Third Shepherd in *The First Shepherds'* Play. John Horn and Gibbon (Gib), asserted by Mak as the godparents of his child, are also the names of the First and Second Shepherd in the earlier play.

The Shepherds' painful attempts to reproduce in song the Angel's *Gloria* extend intermittently from l. 665 to l. 674. The Second Shepherd's threatening 'let be your din' brings such an attempt to an end. The two Shepherds' songs from the Coventry Pageant of the *Shearmen and Taylors* might be used here: the first, 'As I rode out', as the part song (189), the second, 'Down from heaven, from heaven so high', in conclusion.

THE OFFERING OF THE MAGI

The structure and staging of this play is, in many ways, similar to that of *The Second Shepherds' Play*. The liturgical plays of the Magi were very much more popular than those of the Shepherds, and the latter may have derived many of their characteristics from the former. That the Magi should be three in number, and by analogy the Shepherds also, is probably due to the number of gifts ascribed to them in the Bible (*Matthew* 2. 11). The symbolism of these gifts becomes a feature also of *The Second Shepherds' Play*: the bird representing, as the dove in the Annunciation and the Baptism, the Holy Ghost; the tennis ball, the orb, the symbol of royalty; the bob of cherries, the mid-winter miracle, the symbol of death and resurrection. The Magi in medieval iconography, like the Shepherds in the plays, are depicted as one old, one middle-aged, and one young (*L'Art Religieux du XIIIe Siecle en France* by

Emile Male, 228–230). The tradition that the 'wise men' were kings arose during the sixth century, if not before, and the names they bear in this play were assigned to them during the twelfth century. The tradition of representing one of the Magi as a Moor may go back to the early Middle Ages. 'According to the information available from Besançon it appears that before the singing of the gospel three of the clergy costume themselves with crowns and differently coloured regal garments. They are accompanied by attendants carrying gifts in gold vases, and by other clerics bearing silver staffs, lighted candles, and thuribles. The attendants are dressed as Persians, and one of them is blacked to represent a Moor.' (Karl Young, op. cit., ii. 41.)

In this Wakefield play the Magi enter on horseback and conduct their initial soliloquies and subsequent dialogue from the saddle (85–258). They dismount for their meeting with Herod and again for the adoration. They ride away, as they came, in different directions, the Second King referring to the gate through which he must pass (632). It is possible that the original staging of this play took place in an area resembling an amphitheatre with two mansions placed opposite each other on the raised part of the circumference. This would allow for the separate mounted entries of the Kings, for their continuing their journey following the star round the amphitheatre while the main attention of the audience is given to Herod, and for their resting in the litter (590) placed either in another mansion on the circumference of the amphitheatre or, as the bed in *The Castle of Perseverance*, in the very centre. This use of the litter is unique in the English versions of this play, although a stone carving at Chartres shows the three Kings in one bed, while beyond a partitioning door a servant holds their three horses by the bridle.

The Magi plays from other Cycles, with the exception of York, suggest presentation in the round. The Kings are mounted, and in *Ludus Coventriae* Herod himself enters on horseback and asks the audience to excuse him while he retires to his chamber to dress more splendidly. In the Coventry Pageant of the *Shearmen and Taylors* the three Kings ride towards each other on horseback and speak in the street together (539, 570, 582), and later in the play 'Herod rages in the pageant and in the street also'. The *Ludus Coventriae* Magi ride towards Herod over 'street and stone' (137), they dismount and kneel before Herod, and on their way towards Bethlehem lie down on a bank beneath the bright star, and it is on 'this hill' (291) that the Angel warns them of the danger of returning to Herod's court. The Chester Magi leave their horses while they climb a hill to pray (48), and there the star appears to them. The stage direction following line 112 in this Chester version stresses the arena form of presentation (*Descendunt et circumamblant bis et tunc ad Equos*).

The star in liturgical drama was frequently drawn by a string over the Magi's heads. At Rouen two stars were used, one over the action which occurred at the main altar, and one over the altar in the nave where the Kings present their gifts. The Magi in the Coventry Pageant see a child in the star (588), and the Chester Magi see in the star the Virgin carrying the child, a plastic representation apparently, for the stage direction following line 89 suggests that the Angel carried the star (*Tunc Reges iterum genua flectunt, et Angelus Stellam portans dicat*).

The opposition of Herod's mansion to the manger is paralleled in *The Second Shepherds' Play* by the opposition of Mak's house to the manger. The Shepherds and Kings treat the space between as neutral territory, but it is clear that Herod's hall and Mak's house, where is found 'the horned lad', have close affinities with hell.

THE FLIGHT INTO EGYPT

In the Wakefield and York cycles *The Flight into Egypt* stands as a separate play; in the *Ludus Coventriae* and Chester cycles and in the Coventry Pageant of the *Shearmen and Taylors* it is absorbed into the larger structure of *The Massacre of the Innocents*. The York and Wakefield versions resemble each other in many ways, but whereas in the York play a humorous situation is developed out of Joseph's predicament at being faced with yet another hazardous long journey—he complains with some bitterness that he does not even know the way to Egypt—the Wakefield playwright develops a more sympathetic and harmonious relationship between Joseph and Mary. The lyricism of the shorter line and the ambitious rhyme scheme contribute to this effect.

[111]

The acting area used by Joseph and Mary can be the same for the sequence of plays from *The Second Shepherds'* to *Herod the Great*. Their manger is visited by both Shepherds and Kings, and the ass that has warmed Jesus at his nativity now bears his mother to Egypt. The ass is a feature introduced into all the other cycle plays on this theme and, mostly, with specific reference to riding (York, 199, *Ludus Coventriae*, 83, Chester 273). E. K. Chambers, quoting the Ducange Glossary, and Karl Young, referring to a thirteenth-century service-book of Padua cathedral, show how, in liturgical representations of the Flight into Egypt, Mary, seated on the ass would be led through the church. The association of this ceremony with those of the Boy Bishop and the Feast of Fools recalls the buffoonery of Herod's part in the preceding play *The Adoration of the Magi*, and in the following play, *Herod the Great*.

In the Chester play of *The Slaying of the Innocents*, the Angel appears to Joseph, warns him of Herod's plans and accompanies the holy family to Egypt, singing as they go. The stage direction suggests that, if possible, as the Angel sings, idols and statues should come crashing down:

ANGEL   For Mohammeds, both one and all,
        That men of Egypt gods do call,
        At your coming down shall fall,
           When I begin to sing.

(*Tunc ibunt, et Angelus cantabit 'Ecce dominus super nubem levem, et ingredietur Egiptum, et movebuntur simulacra Egipti a facie Domini Exercituum', et si fieri poterit, cadet aliqua statua sive imago.*)

The same Angel appears after Herod's death in this play to lead Mary and Joseph back to Judah, again offering to sing:

ANGEL   Forsooth I will not from you go
        But ever help you from your foe.
        And I will make a melody,
        And sing here in your company.
        A word was said in prophecy
        A thousand years ago.

(*Ex Egipto vocavi filium meum, ut Salvum faciet populum meum.*)
(Chester *Slaying of the Innocents*, 491–496.)

The performance of the Wakefield *Flight into Egypt* might be enhanced by the angel-choir making such a melody.

HEROD THE GREAT

 Two main acting areas are required, one for Herod's court and one for the killing of the children. Herod is traditionally seated on a high throne. In his raging he may descend, as indicated by the stage direction in the Coventry Pageant of the *Shearmen and Taylors* (Herod rages in the pageant and in the street also), but in general the plays stress the proud height at which Herod sits. In the *Ludus Coventriae* Herod greets the soldiers returning from their killing of the children:

> Well have ye wrought,
> My foe is sought,
> To death is he brought;
>   Now come up to me.

(*Ludus Coventriae, The Massacre of the Innocents*, 125–128.)

The staging of the Wakefield play necessitates that the killing should take place well away from Herod's court. Internal evidence from the Coventry Pageant suggests that it took place in the street or in the arena area. The avenging mothers are at some disadvantage in striking at the mounted soldiers:

3RD WOMAN Sit he never so high in saddle,
> But I shall his brain-pan addle,
> And here with my pot-ladle
>   With him will I fight.

(Coventry Pageant of the *Shearmen and Taylors*, 862–865.)

A similar area may have been used for the Wakefield play, but there is no indication that the Soldiers are mounted, indeed they are much more assailable: the Women strike at hood, tabard, and groin (339, 357, 382).

Such references to tabard and hood are interesting pointers to costume. Herod's soldiers, the sort of retainers, about whom the Shepherds are so bitter, wear on their tabards Herod's coat-of-arms. Cowards that they are, they would also wear helmets for the fray:

2ND WOMAN Their basinets be big and broad;
> Beat on now! let's see!

(Chester, *Slaying of the Innocents*, 319–320.)

[113]

The killing of the children in their mothers' arms is most effectively done with short knives rather than with spears, the method suggested by the First Counsellor (252). The *Ludus Coventriae* Women probably carried dolls with readily detachable heads:

> 1ST WOMAN   Long lulling have I lorn,
> Alas, why was my bairn born,
> With swiping sword now is he shorn,
> The head right from the neck . . .

(*Ludus Coventriae*, *The Massacre of the Innocents*, 89–92).

The Women's defence rests in boots and distaff (Chester) and the pot-ladle (Coventry). The Wakefield Women attack with no less venom and might add to the above weapons their bodkins (337) and their nails (353).

In the Chester *Slaughter of the Innocents*, Herod's Son, himself a victim of the massacre, is described as dressed in gold 'painted wondrous gay'. The Goldsmiths presented this pageant and they would certainly have made Herod a truly resplendent sight. His headwear, since he claims kinship with Mohammed, might well be a large crown fitting over a turban. It is apparent from the following account taken from the Coventry Smiths' Company records that Herod's headpiece was the most vulnerable of stage articles:

'1477, it. to a peynter for peyntyng the fauchon and Herods face xd. It. for assadyn, silver papur and gold paper, gold foyle and green foyle ij s j d, it. for redd wax ij d, it. payd to Thomas Suker for makyng the crests xxij d; 1478, it. for assaden for the harnes x d; 1480, expense for a slop for Herod (inter alia), pd for peyntyng and dressyng Heruds stuf ij d; 1487, it. for mendyng of Arrodes crast xij d; 1489, it. paid for a gowen to Arrode vij s iiij d, it. paid for peyntyng and steynyng ther-off vjs iiij d, it. payd for Arroddes garment peynttyng that he went a prossasyon in xx d; 1490, a fawchon, a septur, and a creste for Heroude repaired; 1494, it. payd for iij platis to Heroddis crest of iron vj d, it. payd for a paper of aresdyke xij d, it. payd to Hatfield for dressyng of Herods creste xiiij d: 1499, it. payd to John Hatfielde for colours and gold foyle and sylver foyle for the crest and for the fawchem (inter alia); 1501, it. for vj yards satten iij quarters xvj s x d, it. for v yardus of blowe bokeram ij s xj d, it. pd for makyng of Herodus gone xv d; 1516, it payd to a peynter for peyntyng and mendyng of Herodes heed iiij d; 1547, pd to John Croo for mendyng of Herrods hed and a myter and other thyngs ij s; 1554, payd to John Hewet payntter for dressyng of Erod hed and the faychon ij s.'

(Hardin Craig, *Two Coventry Corpus Christi Plays*, 86.)

[114]

Apart from the headdress it will be seen that the falchion, a broad curved sword, calls for constant attention. This is obviously much used by the tyrant upon his menials. He might also use his sceptre which could be made of flexible material, similar to those inflated bladders originally used in the thirteenth-century celebrations of Innocents' Day in the cathedral at Padua:

'At Padua, it appears, in the absence of a decorous play of the Magi, Herod takes a lawless part in the concluding parts of Matins itself. After the eighth lesson he and his chaplain come from the sacristy, clad in untidy tunics, and carrying wooden spears. Before he mounts the platform, Herod angrily hurls his spear towards the chorus, and then proceeds, *cum tanto furore*, to read the ninth lesson. Meanwhile his attendants dash about the choir belabouring bishop, canons and choristers with an inflated bladder. At the conclusion of his reading, Herod joins in these antics *cum supradicto furore*—presumably whilst the chorus is attempting to sing the last responsory.'

(Karl Young, op. cit., ii 100.)

The regularity with which all the tyrants of the mystery plays, on making their first entry, call for silence indicates that they were invariably greeted with a storm of jeers and cat-calls. But, like the devils, Herod could be both ridiculous and terrifying. His mansion is adjacent to hell-mouth; in the Chester version he sees the fiends swarming out of hell to seize him:

> I bequeath here in this place
> My soul to be with Satan.
> (Chester, *The Slaying of the Innocents*, 429–430.)

The entry of Death in the *Ludus Coventriae* play (167) at the moment of Herod's triumphant feasting is superb drama. As the minstrels blow 'a merry fit' death strikes Herod and the Devil receives him exultantly:

> All ours, all ours, this castle is mine.

Herod's castle is opposed to heaven's tower. Although the Wakefield Herod remains triumphant at the end, fanfares of trumpets heralding his coming and going would be appropriate throughout. This cowardly, ignorant, mean and malicious monster makes a characteristic final exit holding a nosegay to his face as he inveighs against the stench of the multitude.

The Soldiers ape the bragging cowardly conduct of their master and add a touch of their own gallows' humour (331). Their parts are grotesque but never farcical. The response of the Women to the killing of their children should be deeply felt, and this would be impossible if the Soldiers were played farcically. To dispel any suspicion of the farcical element the Women might make their entry singing the Coventry Carol:

Lully, lullay, thou little tiny child,
By by, lully lullay, thou little tiny child,
    By by, lully lullay!

O sisters two,
How may we do
    For to preserve this day
This poor youngling
For whom we do sing
    By by, lully lullay?

Herod, the king,
In his raging,
    Charged he hath this day
His men of might
In his own sight
    All young children to slay,—

That woe is me,
Poor child for thee,
    And ever mourn and may
For thy parting
Neither say nor sing,
    By by, lully lullay.

THE PURIFICATION OF MARY AND THE PLAY OF THE DOCTORS

Two leaves of the manuscript are missing between the end of *The Purification of Mary* and the beginning of *The Play of the Doctors*. The *Ludus Coventriae* and the Coventry Pageant of the Weavers preserve complete plays of *The Purification of Mary*, and *The Play of the Doctors* is included in the York Cycle and the Coventry *Pageant of the Weavers;* the York version from line 73 until the end is a very close parallel of the Wakefield play.

END OF PART TWO

Part Three

The Nineteenth Play: John the Baptist

JOHN   2ND ANGEL
1ST ANGEL   JESUS

JOHN

God, that made both more and less,
Heaven and earth, at his own will,
And marked man to his likeness,
As one who would his wish fulfil,
Upon the earth he sent lightness,
Both sun and moon to shine there still,
He save you all from sinfulness,
And keep you clean from every ill.

Among prophets then am I one
That God has sent to teach his law,
And man to amend, that wrong has done,
Both with example and with saw.
My name, forsooth, is baptized John;
My father's faith contained a flaw
For which the angel thereupon
Dumb, till my birth, kept him in awe.

Elizabeth my mother was,
Aunt unto Mary, maiden mild;
And as the sun shines through the glass,
Within her womb so did her child.
The Jews yet ask me as I pass
If I be Christ; they are beguiled,
Jesus shall amend man's trespass,
Whose faith through frailty is defiled.

I am sent but a messenger
From him who may all sins amend;
I go before, such words to bear,
As a forerunner to my friend.
His law to teach, his way to fare,
To all mankind that may offend.
Of buffets full bitter his share,
Before he brings all things to end.

These Jews shall hang him on a cross,   33
He grieves so for man's unbelief,
That of his life he suffers loss,
As he were traitor or a thief,
Dying, to cleanse us of our dross,
And save us from our own mischief;
Thus gladly away his life will toss,
And rise again for our relief.

In water clear then baptize I
The people living on this coast;
But he shall do more mightily,
And baptize in the holy ghost;
And with the blood of his body
Wash our sins both least and most,
Therefore, it fits, both ye and me
Against the fiend to join God's host.

I am not worthy to unloose
The least thong that ties up his shoe,
But God almighty us may use
On earth indeed his will to do.
I thank thee, Lord, that did diffuse
Among mankind thy seed; it grew.
Now every day earth doth produce
For each man food as is his due.

We are, Lord, duty bound to thee,
To love thee here both day and night.
For thou hast sent thy son so free
To save man's soul from perilous plight.
Through Adam's sin and Eve's folly,
Our parents fell through the fiend's might;
But, Lord, on man now have pity,
And bless thy bairns in heaven so bright.
Enter two ANGELS, JESUS *follows at a distance.*

1ST ANGEL   John the Baptist hearken to me!
The father of heaven he greets thee well,
For true and trusty finds he thee,
Doing thy devoir where thou dost dwell;
Welcome his will in this decree,

[2]

70 Since thou standst firm though faced with hell,
 Baptized by thee Christ Jesus be
 In Jordan's river, man's care to quell.

JOHN Ah! Dear God! What may this be?
 I heard a voice but nought I saw.
1ST ANGEL John, it is I that spake to thee;
 To do this deed stand not in awe.
JOHN Should I abide till he come to me?
 That should not be, I thee implore;
 I shall go meet that Lord so free,
 Fall at his feet him to adore.

2ND ANGEL Nay, John, that is not well fitting;
 His father's will thou needs must work.
1ST ANGEL John, be thou here abiding,
 But when he comes feel thou no irk.
JOHN This tells my understanding
 That children should be brought to kirk,
 In every land for baptizing;
 This law to keep man must not shirk.

2ND ANGEL John, this place it is pleasing,
 And is called the river Jordan;
 Here is no kirk, nor no building
 But where the father will ordain,
 It is God's will and his bidding.
JOHN By this, forsooth, it seems clear then
 This work shall be to his liking;
 And so please the Lord should all men.

 Since I must needs his wish fulfil
 He shall be welcome unto me;
 I yield me wholly to his will,
 Wheresoever I abide or be.
 I am his servant, to be still
 Messenger to that Lord free;
 Whether he will cure or kill
 I shall not grudge in no degree.

JESUS John, God's servant and prophet,
 My father, that to thee is dear,

[3]

Has sent me to thee, well thou wit,
To be baptized in water clear;
To reprieve man's fall, as is writ,
The law I will fulfil right here;
My father's ordinance, thus is it,
And thus my will is, never fear.

I come to thee baptism to take,
To whom my father has me sent,
With oil and cream that thou shalt make
Unto that worthy sacrament.
And therefore, John, it not forsake,
But come to me in this present,
No further shall myself betake
Till I have done his commandment.

JOHN   Ah, Lord! I love thee for thy coming!
I am ready to do his will,
In word in work in every thing,
Whatsoever I must fulfil;
This beauteous Lord himself to bring
To his own servant humble still
A knight to baptize his Lord King,
This task may be beyond my skill.

And if I were worthy
For to fulfil this sacrament,
I have no cunning, surely,
To do it for thee as is meant;
And therefore, Lord, I ask mercy;
Hold me excused if I dissent;
I dare not touch this blessed body,
My heart will never to it assent.

JESUS   Of thy cunning, John, dread thou nought,
My father himself he will thee teach;
He that all this world has wrought,
He sent thee plainly for to preach;
He knows man's heart, his deed, his thought;
He knows how far man's might may reach,
Therefore hither have I sought;
My father's wish none may impeach.

[4]

145　　　　　Behold he sends his angels two,
　　　　　　In token I am both God and man;
　　　　　　Give me baptism before I go,
　　　　　　And dip me in river Jordan.
　　　　　　Since he will thus, I would know who
　　　　　　Durst him gainsay? John, come on then,
　　　　　　And baptize me for friend or foe,
　　　　　　And do it, John, right as thou can.

1ST ANGEL　Obedience, John, do not disdain,
　　　　　　And be not grudging in no thing,
　　　　　　Gladly you ought to count it gain
　　　　　　For to fulfil my Lord's bidding.
　　　　　　Early and late, with might and main,
　　　　　　Therefore to thee this word I bring,
　　　　　　My Lord has given thee power plain,
　　　　　　And dread thee nought of thy cunning.

2ND ANGEL　He sends thee here his own dear child,
　　　　　　Thou welcome him with right good cheer,
　　　　　　Born of a maiden meek and mild,
　　　　　　That he may now to thee appear;
　　　　　　With sin was never his mother defiled,
　　　　　　There was never man who came her near,
　　　　　　In word nor work she was never wild,
　　　　　　Therefore her son thou baptize here.

1ST ANGEL　This reason for you I will draw
　　　　　　Why that he comes thus unto thee;
　　　　　　He comes now to fulfil the law,
　　　　　　From peerless principality;
　　　　　　And therefore, John, hold thee in awe,
　　　　　　Fail no function in no degree—
　　　　　　To baptize him that thou here saw
　　　　　　For wit thou well this same is he.

JOHN　　　　I am not worthy to do this deed;
　　　　　　Yet I shall meet God's great demand;
　　　　　　But yet, dear Lord, look on my need,
　　　　　　As act I must at thy command.
　　　　　　I tremble and I quake for dread!

[5]

I dare not touch thee with my hand,   182
But to my gain I will give heed;
Abide, my Lord, and by me stand.

He baptizes JESUS.

I baptize thee, Jesus, on high,
In the name of thy father free,
In nomine patris et filii,
Since he wills that it so be,
Et spiritus altissimi,
And of the holy ghost on high;
I ask thee, Lord, of thy mercy,
Hereafter that thou would bless me.

Here I thee anoint also
With oil and cream, with this intent,
That men may know, where so they go,
This is a worthy sacrament.
There are six others, no more so,
The which thyself to earth hath sent,
And in true token here below,
The first on thee now is it spent.

Thou guide me Lord if I go wrong;
My will is bent to do but well;
My part I fear I may prolong,
If I did right I should down kneel.
Bless me before thou go along,
So that I may thy friendship feel;
I have desired this sight so long,
Now death would come as no ordeal.

JESUS   This beast, John, thou bear with thee,
             It is a beast full blessed;
Here he gives him the lamb of God.
             John, I give this lamb to thee,
             None such among the rest;
             To keep thee from adversity,
             So guard it as the best;
             By this beast known shalt thou be,
             That thou art John Baptist.

[6]

JOHN
218

For I have seen the lamb of God
Who washes away the sin of this world,
And touched him, for even or odd,
My heart before was ever hard.
To show me truth's way lay untrod
An angel had me almost marred,
But he that rules all with his rod
He bless me when I draw homeward.

JESUS

I grant thee, John, for thy travail,
Ay lasting joy in bliss to abide;
And to all those that trust this tale,
And saw me not yet glorified.
I shall bring comfort to their bale,
And send them succour from every side;
My father and I may them avail,
Men and women that leave their pride.

But, John, go thou forth and preach
Against the folk that do amiss;
And to the people the truth thou teach;
To righteousness turn those remiss,
And as far as thy wit may reach
Bid them be there to bide my bliss;
For at doomsday I shall impeach
All who scorn thee nor trust not this.

Bid them leave sin, for I it hate;
For it I must die on a tree,
By prophecy I know my fate;
Indeed my mother that sight must see,
That sorrow shall her joys abate
For I was born of her body.
Farewell, John, I go my gait;
I bless thee with the trinity.

JESUS *withdraws slowly. The two* ANGELS *precede him.*

JOHN

Almighty God in persons three,
All in one substance ay engrossed,
I thank thee, Lord, in majesty,
Father, son, and holy ghost!

[7]

From heaven thou sent thy son so free,   253
To Mary mild, unto this coast,
And now thou sends him unto me.
For to be baptized in this host.

Farewell! The favour that none shall forget!
Farewell! Flower more fresh than flower de luce!
Farewell! Steersman for them so beset
In storms, by sickness and distress!
Thy mother wed but was maiden yet;
Farewell! Pearl of price peerless!
Farewell! The loveliest that on earth was set!
Thy mother is of hell empress.

Farewell! Blessed both blood and bone!
Farewell! The seemliest that ever was seen!
To thee, Jesu, I make my moan;
Farewell! Comely, of body so clean!
Farewell! Gracious Lord so close to God's throne,
Much grace through thee we now may glean;
Leave us thy living way on loan,
Mending our ways more than we mean.

I will go preach both to more and less,
As I am charged most surely;
Sirs, forsake your wickedness,
Pride, envy, sloth, wrath and lechery.
Hear God's service as ye guess,
Please God with praying, thus say I;
Beware when death comes with distress,
So that ye die not suddenly.

Death spares none that life has borne,
Therefore think on what I say;
Beseech your God both even and morn
You for to save from sin that day.
Think how in baptism ye are sworn
To be God's servant, without a nay;
Let never his love from you be lorn,
God bring you to his bliss for ay.

Goes out.

[8]

The Twentieth Play: Lazarus

JESUS	THOMAS
PETER	MARTHA
JOHN	MARY
	LAZARUS

JESUS
> Come now, brethren, and go with me;
> We will pass forth unto Judea;
> To Bethany will we wend,
> To visit Lazarus our friend.
> Gladly would I with him speak
> For he is sick that we should seek.

PETER
> I counsel ye not thither go,
> Where the Jews hold you for their foe;
> I counsel ye near not that stead,
> For if ye do then ye be dead.

JOHN
> Master, trust thou not one Jew,
> Since many a day now thou them knew,
> And last time that we were there,
> We kept our lives in dreadful care.

THOMAS
> When we were last in that country
> This other day, both thou and we,
> We thought thou there should have been slain;
> Will thou now go thither again?

JESUS
> Hearken, brethren, this counsel keep;
> Lazarus our friend has fallen asleep;
> The way to him now will we take,
> To stir that knight and bid him wake.

PETER
> Sir, methinks it were the best
> To let him sleep and take his rest;
> And watch that no man come him near,
> If he sleep he will mend his cheer.

JESUS
> I tell you truly without fail,
> No watching may to him avail,

[9]

No sleep may stand him in good stead,   29
I tell you surely, he is dead;
Therefore I say to you at last
Leave this speech and go we fast.

THOMAS   Sir, whatsoever ye bid us do
Willingly we assent thereto;
I hope to God ye shall not find
None of us shall lag behind;
For any peril that may befall,
Wend we with our master all.

They go to MARTHA'S *house.*

MARTHA   Help me, Lord, my rest is fled!
Lazarus, my brother, now is dead,
That was to thee beloved and dear;
He had not died had thou been here.

JESUS   Martha, Martha, peace to your pain,
Thy brother shall rise and live again.
MARTHA   Lord, I know that he shall rise
And come before the good justice;
For at the dreadful day of doom
There must ye keep him when he come,
To look what doom ye will him give;
Then must he rise, then must he live.

JESUS   I warn you, both man and wife,
I am the rising, and I am the life;
And whoso truly trusts in me,
That I was ever and ay shall be,
One thing I shall him give,
Though he be dead yet shall he live,
Say thou, woman, trust thou this?

MARTHA   Yea, forsooth, my Lord of bliss,
Else were I worthy to be chid,
For from thee no truth is hid.

JESUS   Go tell thy sister, Magdalene,
That I come ye may be fain.

[10]

MARTHA Sister, leave this sorrowful band,
64   Our Lord comes close by here at hand,
        And his apostles with him also.

MARY   Ah, for God's love let me go!
        Blessed be he that sends me grace,
        That I may see thee in this place.
        Lord, much sorrow may men see
        Befall my sister here and me;
        We are as heavy as any lead,
        For our brother that thus is dead.
        Had thou been here and him first seen,
        Dead forsooth had he not been.

JESUS   Hither to you now we fare,
        To bring you comfort for your care,
        But look no faintness nor no sloth
        Bring you from the steadfast truth,
        Then shall I grant you both my aid,
        Lo, where have ye his body laid?

MARTHA Lord, if it be thy will,
        I doubt by this he savours ill,
        For it is now the fourth day gone
        Since he was laid under yon stone.

JESUS   I told thee right now as thou stood
        That thy truth should ay be good,
        And if thou may that fulfil
        All shall be done right as thou will.

JESUS *prays to the Father.*

        Father, I pray thee that thou raise
        Lazarus that was thine,
        And bring him out of hell's fierce blaze
        That he no more need pine.

        When I thee pray thou says always
        Thy will is such as mine,
        Therefore we shall increase his days
        If thou to me incline.

[11]

Come forth, Lazarus, and stand us by,   97
In earth shall thou no longer lie;
Take and loose him foot and hand,
And from his throat take the band,
To one side that napkin throw,
And all that gear and let him go.

LAZARUS   Lord, that all things made of nought,
All praise be to thee,
That such wonder here has wrought,
Greater may none be.
When I was dead hell's gate I sought,
And thou, almighty,
Raised me up and thence me brought,
Behold and ye may see.

There is none so bold decreed,
Nor none so proud to greet,
Nor none so doughty in his deed,
Nor none for daïs more meet,
Nor king, nor knight, nor bondman freed,
Death's destiny could defeat,
Nor flesh where he was wont to feed,
But it shall be worms' meat.

Your death is worm's cook,
Your mirror here ye look,
And let me be your book,
    Example take from me;
Though charms for death ye took,
    Such shall ye all be.

Each one in such array, death shall him suddenly smite,
And close him in cold clay, whether he be king or knight
For all his garments gay that were a seemly sight,
His flesh shall fall away, as for many in this plight.
    On them a worm delights
    To gnaw at these gay knights,
    At their lungs and at their lights,
        Their hearts eaten asunder;
    These masters held the heights,
        Thus shall they be brought under.

[12]

135 Under the earth ye shall thus full of care then couch;
The roof of your hall your naked nose shall touch;
Neither great nor small to you will kneel nor crouch;
A sheet shall be your pall, toads for jewels will vouch;
　　The slime of toads shall smear,
　　The fiends fill you with fear,
　　Your flesh that fair was here
　　　　Thus ruefully shall rot;
　　Instead of a gay collar
　　　　Such bands shall bind your throat.

Your cheer that was so red, your looks the lily like,
Then shall be wan as lead and stink as dog in dyke;
And worms be in you bred as bees breed in a hive,
The eyes out of your head shall spotted toads thus rive;
　　To pick you are pressed
　　Many a loathsome beast,
　　Thus they shall make a feast
　　　　Of your flesh and of your blood.
　　Your sorrows then are least
　　When greatest seems your good.

Your goods ye shall forsake though ye be never so loth,
And nothing with you take but such a winding cloth;
Your wife's sorrow shall slake, also your children's both,
Your memory all shall forsake though ye be never so wroth;
　　They mind you as nothing
　　That may be to your helping,
　　Neither in mass singing
　　　　Nor even with alms deed;
　　Therefore in your leaving,
　　　　Be wise and take good heed.

Take heed then how you deal while ye still have life,
To frail friends never appeal, trust not child nor wife,
Executors do but steal; and for your goods will strive;
Where lies your soul's weal may no man there them shrive.
　　To shrive no man them may,
　　After your ending day,
　　　　Your soul for to glad;
　　Your executors will swear nay,
　　And say ye owed more than ye had.

[13]

Amend thee, man, whilst thou may,   174
    Let never no mirth undo thy mind;
Think thou on that dreadful day
    When God shall judge all mankind.
Think thou fares as doth the wind;
    This world is wasted clean away;
Man, have this in thy mind,
    And amend thee whilst that thou may.

Amend thee, man, whilst thou art here,
    Lest thou abide a bitter fate;
When thou art dead and laid on bier,
    Wit thou well thou art too late;
For if all thy goods however great
    Were given for thee after thy day,
In heaven it would not mend thy state,
    Therefore amend thee whilst thou may.

Though thou be right royal in rent,
    As is the steed standing in stall,
In thy heart know and think
    That they are God's goods all.
He might have made thee poor and small
    As he that begs from day to day;
But a true account give thou shall,
    Therefore amend thee whilst thou may.

And if I might with you dwell
    To tell you what I mean,
A long tale could I tell
    What I have heard and seen,
Of many a great marvel,
    Of many a sight unclean,
In the halls of hell,
    There where I have been.

Been have I in woe,
    Therefore fear ye may show;
Whilst ye live do so,
    If ye will dwell with him
That can make you thus go,
    And heal you joint and limb.

[14]

212   He is a Lord of grace,
            Bethink you in this case,
                  And pray him full of might,
            He keep you in this place
                  And have you in his sight.
All withdraw.

The Twenty-first Play: The Conspiracy

PILATE	JUDAS	ANDREW
CAIAPHAS	ST. JOHN	SIMEON
ANNAS	PETER	THADEUS
1ST SOLDIER	PATERFAMILIAS	MALCUS
2ND SOLDIER	JESUS	GOD

PILATE   Peace, curs, I command, uncouth churls I call you;
            I say stop and stand, or foul might befall you.
            Not this burnished brand, now when I behold you,
            I warn you withstand, or else the devil scold you
                  To moans.
            All men hold me in awe,
            As leader of law;
            Wise men, heed every saw
                  Lest I break all your bones.

            Ye know well what I mean, what great king has come
                                                    [to town,
            So comely clad and clean, a ruler of great renown;
            In sight if I were seen, Mohammed's my grandson,
            My name Pilate has been, was never king with crown
                  More worthy;
            My wisdom and my wit,
            In seat here as I sit,
            Was never more like it,
                  My deeds to descry.

[15]

For I am he that may make or mar a man;   19
Myself if I it say as men of court now can;
Support a man today, tomorrow against him plan,
On both parts thus I play, and, feigning, fight in the van
          Of right;
But all false indictors,
Courtmongers and jurors,
And all these false outriders,
          Are welcome to my sight.

More need had I never of such servants now, I say you,
If I did well consider the truth I must displease you,
And therefore come I hither; so peace therefore I pray
                                        [you;
There is a lazy lubber, I would not should dismay you,
          About;
As prophet is he praised,
And a great rout has raised,
But if my bans be blazed,
          His death is due, no doubt.

Preaches to the people here, that false fellow Jesus,
That if he live a year our law shall fall with us;
And yet I stand in fear, so wide his works and virtuous,
No fault in him is clear, that many come to tell us;
          But sleight
Against him shall be sought,
That all this woe has wrought;
A bitter bargain shall be bought,
          In vengeance for our right.

That fellow says that three should ever dwell in one
                                        [godhead,
That ever was and shall be, a truth for men to heed;
He says of a maiden born was he, that never took man's
                                        [seed,
And that himself shall die on tree, and man's soul out of
                                        [prison lead;
          Let him alone,
If this be true indeed,
His power shall spread with speed,
          And overcome our own.

          [16]

CAIAPHAS   Sir Pilate, prince of princes, prize,
55   Proved in power without a peer,
                    And lords that our words legalize,
                    To the law now must we adhere,
                    And in our works we must be wise,
                    For else we lose our wealth, I fear,
                    Therefore say now what you advise
                    For hideous harms that we have here,

                    Touching that traitor strong,
                    That brings us this belief,
                    For if thus he goes along,
                    It will be to our grief.

ANNAS   Sir, our folk are so afraid,
                    His lies our laws outweigh;
                    Amendment must be made,
                    That he wend not away.
PILATE   Now certain, sirs, this was well said,
                    And I assent, right as ye say,
                    Some privy point to be purveyed,
                    To mar his might if that we may;

                    And therefore, sirs, in this present,
                    Which point most we may praise,
                    Let all be in assent,
                    Let's see what each man says.

CAIAPHAS   Sir, before I said must not be borne
                    His subtleties and sleights so sore;
                    He turns our folk both even and morn,
                    And ay makes marvels more and more.
ANNAS   Sir, if he escape it were great scorn;
                    So kill him quickly we implore,
                    For if our laws are thus outworn,
                    Men would our foolishness deplore.

PILATE   For certain, sirs, ye speak right well.
                       And wittily, say I;
                    But yet some fault in him now tell
                    Wherefore that he should die;

And therefore, sirs, think ye not so?   90
For what thing we should him slay?

CAIAPHAS   Sir, I can reckon you a row
Of thousand wonders, more some say,
Of many maimed men we well know,
Who sound in limb he sent away,
Our law he would have laid full low,
From us he tempts our folk to stray.

ANNAS   Lord, deaf and dumb in our presence
Delivers he, by down and dale;
Whatever hurt or harm they sense,
Full hastily he makes them hale.
When for such work he needeth pence
Of each man's wealth he may avail,
But unto us he gives offence,
For all men trust well in his tale.

PILATE   Yea, devil! And does he thus
As ye well bear witness?
Such fault falls to us,
By our rule for to redress.

CAIAPHAS   And also, sir, I have heard say,
Another annoyance comes us near,
He will not keep our sabbath day,
That holy should be held ay here,
But forbids men far and near
To work as we demand.

PILATE   By Mohammed's blood so dear,
He shall cower at my command.

The devil will he be there?
I have so great a hating.

ANNAS   Nay, nay, well more is there;
He calls himself heaven's king,
And says that he is so mighty
To teach the righteous where to tread.

PILATE   By Mohammed's blood, that shall he abuy
With bitter bales ere I eat bread!

1ST SOLDIER   Lord, Lazarus of Bethany
That lay stinking in one stead,

[18]

128   Quick he raised up bodily
                      The fourth day after he was dead.
2ND SOLDIER   And for that he him raised,
                      That had lain dead so long a space,
                      The people him profusely praised
                      Over all in every place.

ANNAS   Amongst the folk he has the name
                      That he is God's son and none else,
                      And himself says the same,
                      That his father in heaven dwells;
                      That he shall rule both wild and tame;
                      In all such matters he excels.
PILATE   This is the devil's game!
                      Would any trust such tales he tells?

CAIAPHAS   Yes, lord, have here my hand,
                      And each man holds him as his brother;
                      Such quaint tricks doth he understand,
                      Lord, ye never knew such another.
PILATE   Why, and knows he not that I have
                      Bold men to be his bane?
                      I command both knight and knave
                      Cease not till that lad be slain.

1ST SOLDIER   Sir Pilate, calm you now your care,
                      But soothe your heart and mend your mood;
                      For if that sneak-thief learn our snare,
                      And leave his tricks, he were as good;
                      For in our temple we will not spare
                      To take this madcap as we should.
PILATE   In our temple? The devil! What did he there?
                      That shall he abuy, by Mohammed's blood!

2ND SOLDIER   Lord, we knew not your will;
                      With wrong ye us scold;
                      Had ye told us to kill,
                      We should have been more bold.

PILATE   The devil, he hang you high to dry!
                      Know ye not what our laws say?
                      Go, bring him hither hastily.

[19]

	So that he wend not thus away.	165
CAIAPHAS	Sir Pilate, be not too hasty.	
	But suffer to pass our sabbath day;	
	In the meantime to seek and spy	
	More of his marvels, if men may.	

ANNAS   Yea, sir, and when his feast is done
           Then shall his knacks be known.
PILATE   With you, sirs, I am one
           For to abide as ye have shown.

Then JUDAS *enters.*

JUDAS   Masters, mirth be to this gang,
           And grace this noble company!
CAIAPHAS   Go back again from whence thou sprang
           With sorrow; who sent after thee?
JUDAS   Sirs, if I hindered your harangue,
           At your own bidding will I be.
PILATE   Go hence, harlot, high might thou hang!
           Whence, in the devil's name, had we thee?

JUDAS   Good sir, I mean not you to grieve;
           My venture then might not avail.
ANNAS   Look, lad, thou should ask leave
           To come amid such counsel.

JUDAS   Sir, all your counsel well I ken;
           Ye mean my master for to take.
ANNAS   Ah ha! Here is one of his men.
           That thus unwitting makes us wake.
PILATE   Lay hands on him, and hurl him then
           Among you for his master's sake;
           For we have matters more than ten,
           More troublesome far to undertake.

CAIAPHAS   Set on him buffets sad,
           His master to disgrace,
           And teach ye such a lad
           Better to know his place.
JUDAS   Sir, my presence may both please and pay
           To all the lords that gather here.
PILATE   Out! Go hence in the devil's way!
           We have no leisure time, I fear.

[20]

JUDAS 203	The prophet that doth your power dismay With wondrous works where he draws near, If ye will crush him as ye say, His sale to you I will make clear.
PILATE	Ah, sir, hark! What say you? Let's see, and show thy skill.
JUDAS	Sir, a bargain, I pray you Buy it if ye will.
ANNAS	What is thy name? Tell quick, no lie, That we may know if you do wrong.
JUDAS	Judas Iscariot, called am I, That with the prophet have dwelled long.
PILATE	Sir, thou art a welcome ally! Your purpose here now we would know.
JUDAS	Nought else but if ye will him buy; Now tell me truly ere I go.
CAIAPHAS	Yes, friend, in faith will we, Naught else; but heartily say How that bargain may be, And prompt we shall thee pay.
ANNAS	Judas, for to hold thee hale, And for to ward off foul defame, Look that thou vouchsafe this sale; Then may thou be without a blame.
JUDAS	Sir, of my grief give ye no heed, If once you bring him here to shame; Following him I found no meed, He certainly shall find the same.
CAIAPHAS	Sir Pilate, hear your fill, Listen and lose nought, Then may ye do your will On him that ye have bought.
ANNAS	Yea, and then may we be bold From all the folk to hold him free;

[21]

But keep him hard within our hold.　　236
Right as one of your company.

PILATE　　　Now Judas, since he shall be sold,
　　　　　　How prize thou him? That say to me.
JUDAS　　　For thirty pennies truly told,
　　　　　　Or else may not that bargain be.
　　　　　　So much he made me lose
　　　　　　Maliciously and ill;
　　　　　　Therefore ye may now choose,
　　　　　　To buy or let be still.

ANNAS　　　Made he thee lose? I pray thee, why?
　　　　　　Tell us now promptly ere thou pass.
JUDAS　　　I shall straight tell without a lie,
　　　　　　Every word right as it was.
　　　　　　In Simon's house with him sat I
　　　　　　With other company that he has;
　　　　　　A woman came that fellow nigh,
　　　　　　Calling him "Lord", saying "alas!"

　　　　　　She wept that she had wrought
　　　　　　Always such sin and vice,
　　　　　　And an ointment she brought,
　　　　　　That precious was of price.

　　　　　　With tears she washed him in his seat,
　　　　　　And then dried him with her hair;
　　　　　　This ointment her dole to defeat,
　　　　　　Upon his head she put it there,
　　　　　　That it ran all about his feet;
　　　　　　It was a wonderful affair,
　　　　　　The house was full of odour sweet;
　　　　　　Then to speak might I not spare,

　　　　　　For certainly I had not seen
　　　　　　No ointment half as fine;
　　　　　　Thereat I split my spleen
　　　　　　To waste what was so fine.
　　　　　　I said it was worthy to sell
　　　　　　For three hundred pence as a present,
　　　　　　Which parted between us were well;

[22]

273   But would ye see what there I meant?
           The tenth part, truly to tell,
           To keep by me was my intent;
           For of the treasure that to us fell,
           The tenth part ever with me went;

           And if three hundred be right told,
           The tenth part is just thirty;
           Right so he shall be sold;
           Say if ye will him buy.

PILATE   Now certain, sir, thou sayst right well,
           Since he tricked you with such a sleight,
           Repay your wrong, your hurt now heal,
           And for his fury have no fright.

ANNAS   Sir, as you ask so shall we deal,
           Here shall thou have what is your right;
           But look that we no falsehood feel.

JUDAS   Sir, my promise here I plight.
           What I have spoken in my spite
           I shall fulfil in deed,
           And well more with my might,
           In time when I see need.

PILATE   Judas, of speaking thou must spare,
           And chatter never, night nor day;
           What we know make no man aware,
           For fear of a far fiercer fray.
CAIAPHAS   Meet us no more then, take good care;
           We are well pleased, take there thy pay.
    Giving him money.
JUDAS   He made me lose what was my share;
           Now are we even for once and ay.

ANNAS   This promise will not fail,
           Thereof we may be glad;
           Now were the best counsel,
           In haste that we him had.

PILATE   We shall him have, and so hie ye,
           Full hastily here in this hall.

Sir knights that are of deeds doughty,   308
Stay never in stead nor stall,
But look ye bring him hastily,
That fellow false whate'er befall.

1ST SOLDIER   Sir, be not abashed thereby,
For as ye bid, work shall we all.
All retire, then JESUS *and his* DISCIPLES *advance.*
ST. JOHN   The Passover, Sir, where will ye eat?
Tell us that we may dress your meat.

JESUS   Go forth, John and Peter, to yon city;
When ye come there ye shall then see
Straightway in the street a man
Bearing water in a can;
The house he goes to greet,
Follow that ye may him meet;
The lord of that house ye shall find,
A simple man both meek and kind,
To him ye shall speak and say
That I come here by the way;
Say, I pray him, if his will be,
A little while to ease me,
That I and my disciples all
Might rest awhile within his hall,
Our Passover we may eat there.

PETER   Lord, we shall hasten in our care,
Till that we come to that city;
Your Passover shall ordered be.
Then JOHN *and* PETER *go to the city and meet a man.*
Sir, our master, the prophet,
Comes behind in the street;
A large room would he have, if you please,
To eat and drink therein with ease.

PATERFAMILIAS Sirs, he is welcome unto me,
And so is all his company;
With all my heart and all my will
Is he welcome to stay his fill.
Lo, a chamber lies close here,
Wherein to keep your feasting cheer,

[24]

344   With rushes strewn, although well swept;
      You shall see it neatly kept.

Then JOHN *and* PETER *prepare the table.* JESUS *enters.*

JOHN   Sir, your meat is ready with good cheer,
      Will ye wash and sit down here?

JESUS   Hand me the water, be content
      To take the grace that God has sent;
      Come forth each one with another,
      If I be master I will be brother.

They eat together and JUDAS *thrusts his hand into* JESUS' *dish.*

      Judas, by this what mean you?

JUDAS   Nothing, Lord, but to eat with you.

JESUS   Eat on, brothers, I you pray,
      For one of you shall me betray.

PETER   Lord, whoever that be may,
      Lord, I shall never thee betray.
      Say, dear master, is it I?

JESUS   Not thou, Peter, certainly.

JOHN   Master, can I be he then?

JESUS   Nay, not thou John, of all men.

ANDREW   Master, is it I, that shrew?

JESUS   Not thou, forsooth, Andrew.

SIMON   Master, then can it be I?

JESUS   Nay, not Simon, surely.

PHILIP   Is it then I should do that deed?

JESUS   Nay Philip thou hast no need.

THADEUS   Should I, Thadeus, betray thee?

JAMES   Or we two James?

JESUS   Nay, none of you is he;
      But he that eats from my own dish,
      My body's betrayal is his wish.

JUDAS   What then, think ye me to name?

JESUS   Thou sayst true, thou bearst the blame;
      Each one of you shall this night
      Forsake me, and well he might.

JOHN   Now God forbid and take good heed
      That never should we do that deed.

PETER   If all, master, forsake thee,
      Shall I never from thee flee.

JESUS   Peter, thrice shalt thou deny me so,
      And forsake me ere cock crow,

[25]

Take up this cloth, I go with you,   382
For we have other things to do.

Here he washes the DISCIPLES' *feet.*

Sit all down here at your ease
I wash your feet upon my knees.

And taking water in a bowl he comes to PETER.

PETER   Lord, should thou kneel and wash my feet?
          My service, Lord, would be more meet.

JESUS   Ye know not yet why I do so,
          Peter, hereafter thou shalt know.

PETER   Nay, master, now I thee implore
          That thou wash our feet no more.

JESUS   Unless I wash thee thou must miss
          Part of me in heaven's bliss.

PETER   Nay, Lord, before I that forgo,
          Wash head, hands and feet also.

JESUS   Ye are clean, but not all;
          That shall be seen when time shall fall;
          Who shall be washed as I mean,
          He dare not wash his feet clean;
          And forsooth clean are ye,
          But not all as ye should be.
          I shall tell you take good heed
          Why that I have done this deed;
          Ye call me master and Lord by name;
          Ye say full well for so I am;
          As doth your Lord and master kneel
          To wash your feet, so ye must deal.
          Now know ye well what I have done;
          Example have I given you;
          Look ye do the like, each one;
          Each other's feet may ye wash too.

          For he that servant is
          In truth, I tell you,
          Not more than his lord he is,
          To whom service is due.

          Before this night be gone,
          Alone will ye leave me;
          For in this night each one
          From me away shall flee;

[26]

420   The shepherd when he is smitten,
        The sheep shall flee away,
        Be scattered wide and bitten;
        Thus do the prophets say.

PETER   Lord, if that I should die,
        Forsake thee shall I nought.
JESUS   Forsooth, Peter, to thee say I,
        In so great dread thou shalt be brought

        That ere the cock can have crowed twice,
        Thrice shalt thou me deny.
PETER   Never shall I, Lord, for no price;
        Rather shall I with thee die.

JESUS   Now look your heart be grieved nought,
        Neither in dread nor woe;
        But trust in God who hath you wrought,
        And trust in me also;

        In my father's house, indeed,
        Is many a meet homestead
        That hereafter as their meed
        Men shall have when they are dead.

        And here may I no longer bide
        But I shall go before,
        That your going I may guide
        And bring you to that shore;

        I shall come to you again,
        And take you to me;
        That wherever I remain,
        Ye shall with me be.

        I am the way, the path of truth,
        The life that ever shall be;
        And to my father comes none, forsooth,
        Except they come through me.

        I will not leave you all helpless,
        As men without a friend,

[27]

As fatherless and motherless,   454
Though from you I must wend;

I shall come once to you again;
This world shall me not see,
But ye shall see me well certain,
And living shall I be.

And ye shall live in heaven;
Then shall ye know all this,
That I am in my father even,
And my father in me is.

And I in you, and ye in me,
And each man like thereto,
My commandment that keeps truly
And after it will do.

Now have ye heard what I have said;
I go and come again;
Be pleased this news to spread;
Your joy is not in vain.

For to my father I wend;
For more than I is he;
I let you know, as faithful friend,
Before that it shall be.

That ye may trust when it is done;
For indeed I may not now
Say certain things to anyone
Nor break that silence vow.

For the prince of this world comes herein,
But no power has he in me,
But as that all the world within
May both hear and see.

My love is to my father due,
Since he me hither sent,
And all things that I do
After his commandment.

[28]

488   Rise ye up each one,
       And wend we on our way,
       The path we may not shun,
       To Olivet to pray.

       Peter, James, and thou, John,
       Rise up and follow me!

They go to Olivet.
       My time now comes anon;
       Abide still here, ye three.

       Pray here while ye have breath,
       From the tempter God you save;
       My soul is heavy unto death
       To go down to the grave.

Then he shall pray, saying:
       Father, let this great pain be still,
       And pass away from me;
       But, father, not that my will,
       But thine fulfilled may be.

He turns to the DISCIPLES.

       Simon, I say, sleepst thou?
       Awake, I tell you all!
       Satan assails you now
       Into despair to fall.

       But I shall pray my father too
       That he may keep you clear
       My spirit is depressed thereto,
       My flesh is sick for fear.

He prays again.

       Father, thy son I was,
       Of thee I ask this boon;
       If this pain may not pass,
       Father, at thy will soon.

He returns to the DISCIPLES.

       Ye sleep, brothers, still, I see,
       It is for sorrow that ye do so;

                [29]

Ye have so long wept for me   518
That ye are dazed and lapped in woe.

The third time he prays.

Dear father, thou hear my will!
This passion thou put from me away;
And if my life I must needs spill,
I shall fulfil thy will today;

Therefore this bitter passion
If I may not put by,
My doom in humble fashion
I meet, for comfort sure is nigh.

GOD   My comfort, son, I shall thee tell,
And give therefore the reason;
As Lucifer, for sin that fell,
Betrayed Eve with his false treason,
And Adam weakened to Eve's will;
The wicked spirit asked a boon
Which has irked mankind full ill;
These were the words he uttered soon:

All that came of Adam's stock
With the fiend should find their fate,
With him to dwell, a mirthless flock,
In pain that never shall abate.

Until a child might be born
Of a maiden whom none surpass,
As pure as petal in the morn,
As clean as silver or shining glass:
But soon when death dimmed that child's sight
Himself he raised on the third day,
And entered heaven through his own might.
To do this none but God may.

Since thou art man, and needs must die,
And as others go to hell;
But that were wrong without a lie.
That God's son there should dwell—

[30]

552   In pain with that unruly rout;
                Ponder well, it must be plain,
                When one is ransomed all shall out,
                And saved be from their pain.

JESUS returns to pray; the DISCIPLES sleep.

JESUS   Sleep ye now and take your rest!
                My time is near at hand;
                And I am near the traitor's nest,
                Betrayed into the sinners' band.

PILATE   Peace! I command you curs remain
                And stand as still as any stone!
                In dungeon deep he shall find pain,
                If any move or make a moan;

                For I am governor of the law;
                My name it is Pilate!
                You I may happily hang or draw,
                I stand in such estate,

                To do what so I will,
                And therefore peace I bid you all!
                And look ye hold you still,
                And with no beggars brawl.
                Till we have done our deed,
                Who so makes noise or cry,
                His neck I shall make bleed,
                With this I bear on high.

Showing his sword.

                For this traitor let us make,
                That would destroy our law,
                Judas, thou may it not forsake,
                But my word keep in awe.

                Think what thou hast done,
                That hath thy master sold;
                Time now this bargain were begun;
                Thou hast thy money in thy hold.

[31]

JUDAS   Name ye knights to come with me,   584
Richly arrayed, sturdy and stout;
Then my pledge fulfilled shall be,
If such fellows be about.

PILATE   Whereby, Judas, should we him know,
If we work wisely, not amiss?
Some know him not for friend or foe.

JUDAS   Lay hands on him that I shall kiss.

PILATE   Have done, sir knights, make known your strength,
And nimbly strike when you see need;
Seek over all both breadth and length!
Spare ye not but spur with speed!

We have sought him less and more,
His lodging could not learn;
Malcus, thou shalt go before,
And bear with thee a lantern.

MALCUS   Sir, this journey I undertake
With all my might and main,
If I should, for Mohammed's sake,
Here in this place be slain,
Christ that prophet for to take,
It shall be for our gain.
Our weapons look ye ready make,
To seize this strutting swain
      This night.
Go we now on our way,
Our power for to sway;
Take what lanterns that we may,
      And look they be alight.

2ND SOLDIER   Sir Pilate, prince peerless of all,
Made from most mighty men's mould,
We are ever more ready to come at thy call,
And bow to thy bidding as bachelors bold.

But that prince of apostles hold we in scorn,
Men call him Christ, come down from David's kin,

[32]

619　His life full soon shall be forlorn,
　　　And easy victory we shall win,
　　　　　And soon!
　　　For, as ever I eat bread
　　　Ere I stir from this stead,
　　　I would strike off his head;
　　　　　Lord, I ask that boon.

1ST SOLDIER　That boon grant to our need,
　　　And vengeance on him soon shall fall;
　　　For we shall snare him with all speed;
　　　God's son himself he shall not call.
　　　We shall give him his true meed;
　　　By Mohammed, god of all,
　　　Such three knights boldly might succeed
　　　To bind the devil as our thrall,
　　　　　Indeed;
　　　For a thousand were too few,
　　　Prophets and apostles too,
　　　Such before these two hands slew,
　　　And bravely made them bleed.

PILATE　Now courteous kaisers of Cain's kin,
　　　Most gentle Jews that I may find,
　　　My comfort from care may ye soon win,
　　　That prophet if ye bring and bind.

　　　But go ye hence speedily, spare not I implore;
　　　My friendship, my furtherance, shall still with you be;
　　　And Mohammed most mighty be gracious evermore!
　　　Come you safe and sound with that beggar to me!
　　　　　What place
　　　Wherever ye wend,
　　　Noble knights, your friend,
　　　Sir Lucifer, the fiend,
　　　　　May cheer you in the chase.
All retire, JESUS *and his* DISCIPLES *advance.*

JESUS　Rise up, Peter, and go with me,
　　　And follow me without a strife
　　　Judas wakes, and sleeps not he;
　　　He comes to betray me of my life.

Woe be to him that works such wrong!   656
He were better far his life forsake;
But come forth, Peter, you bide too long.
Lo, where they come that will me take!

JUDAS   Rest well, master, Jesus free!
               That thou wouldst kiss me once, I pray;
               I have come to succour thee;
               Thou art espied, make no delay.

JESUS   Judas, thy part is overplayed!
               Thinkst thou not I know thy will?
               With kissing hast thou me betrayed:
               That sometime shalt thou rue full ill.

   To the KNIGHTS.

               Whom seek ye, sirs, by name?
2ND SOLDIER   We seek Jesus the Nazarene.
JESUS   I have not hid myself in shame;
               Lo, I am here, the same ye mean;
               Whom would ye with these weapons maim?
1ST SOLDIER   To tell thee truth and not to lie,
               We seek Jesus the Nazarene.
JESUS   I told you once that it was I.
MALCUS   Dare no man on him lay a hand?
               I shall catch him if I may;
               A flattering fool whom none withstand,
               But now has come thy ending day.
PETER   I would be dead within short space
               Ere I should see this sight!

   Strikes MALCUS.

               Go, groan unto Sir Caiaphas,
               And bid him do thee right!

MALCUS   Alas, the time that I was born!
               That ever I took breath!
               My right ear I have forlorn!
               Help, alas, I bleed to death!

JESUS   Thou man, that moans thy hurt so sore,
               Come hither, let me thy wound see;
               Take thy ear that be off shore;
               In nomine patris whole thou be!

[34]

MALCUS 693	Now am I whole, healed is my ear, My hurt is never the worse; Therefore, fellows, draw me near! Who spares him may the devil curse!
JESUS	Therefore, Peter, I tell thee this, In my book it must be written: Put up thy sword nor do amiss, For he that smites, he shall be smitten.

Ye knights that now are coming here,
Thus assembled in a rout,
As if a band of thieves ye fear,
With weapons circle me about;

Methinks, forsooth, ye do full ill
Thus for to seek me in the night:
But work on me your evil will,
Let not my fellows share my plight.

2ND SOLDIER	Lead him forth fast by the gate! Hanged be he that spares him ought!

JESUS *is led to* PILATE.

1ST SOLDIER	How think ye, sir Pilate, About this wretch that we have brought?
PILATE	Is he the self same prophet, say, That has caused us this care? It has been told now many a day, His works all men declare. It gave us a great woe That Lazarus thou raised to life; On sea men saw thee stalking go; The maimed you heal both man and wife. Thy deeds pass Caesar's by, Or sir Herod, our King.
2ND SOLDIER	Let's doom him fast to die, And stop now for nothing.
1ST SOLDIER	Since he against our law has spoke, Let us hang him high up here.
PILATE	I will not grant so swift a stroke, A wiser course I shall make clear.
MALCUS	A wiser course? The devil! How so? And strengthen our grievance the more? Should he in freedom thus forth go, He would destroy our law.

[35]

	Would ye all assent to me,
	This bargain shall be quickly done;
	Dead by night-time should he be,
	For such a course votes everyone.
PILATE	Peace, harlots, the devil you speed!
	Would you thus privily murder a man?
MALCUS	If every man to that agreed,
	Let's hear spoken a better plan.
PILATE	To Caiaphas' hall look fast ye work,
	And thither right he shall be led;
	He has the rule of holy kirk,
	To doom him downright quick or dead;
	For he has wrought against our law,
	Sir Caiaphas has most craft thereon.
2ND SOLDIER	Your order, sir, we hold in awe;
	Come forth, good sirs, let us be gone.
MALCUS	Step forth, thou art in our hand! (*To* JESUS.)
	Thinkest thou ay to stand still?
	Nay, lurking lubber, laws of the land
	Shall fail, but we shall have our will;
	Out of my hands shalt thou not pass
	For all the craft thou can;
	Till thou come to Sir Caiaphas,
	Save thee shall no man.

All withdraw.

The Twenty-second Play: The Buffeting

1ST TORTURER	ANNAS
2ND TORTURER	JESUS
CAIAPHAS	FROWARD

1ST TORTURER	Go forth there, ho! And trot on apace!
	To Annas will we go and sir Caiaphas;
	Know thou well of them two thou getst not grace,
	But everlasting woe for thy wilful trespass
	So great.
	Thy fate is to fare
	Far worse in cruel care;
	Thou hast been everywhere
	False and fickle to the state.

[36]

2ND TORTURER It is a marvel to me thus to be going;
11   We have had for thee such a sharp stinging;
           But at last shall we be eased of our hearts' longing;
           By thee shall two or three heads be worth the hanging;
               No wonder!
           Such mischief can thou make
           Force the people forsake
           Our laws, and thine take;
               Thus art thou brought in blunder.

1ST TORTURER Gainsay this thou mayn't, if thou be true;
           Some men hold thee a saint, and that shalt thou rue;
           Fair words can thou paint, and lay down laws new.
2ND TORTURER Now be ye attaint, for we will pursue
               This matter.
           Many words hast thou said,
           Many men hast misled,
           As good had thou instead
               Left off thy clatter.

1ST TORTURER Better to sit still than rise up and fall;
           Thou has long had thy will and made many a brawl;
           At the last would thou kill and ruin us all,
           If we did never ill.
2ND TORTURER   I trust not, he shall
               Endure it:
           For if other men abuse him,
           We shall accuse him,
           Himself shall not excuse him;
               To you I assure it,

           With my allegiance.
1ST TORTURER   He would sleep in a twink,
           By the cast of his countenance, I say as I think.
2ND TORTURER He has done us grievance, therefore shall he drink;
           And come to much mischance; we sweat till we stink,
               For walking,
           That scarce may I more.
1ST TORTURER Peace, here is the door!
           I shall walk in before,
               And tell of his talking.
       They come to CAIAPHAS *and* ANNAS.

[37]

Hail, sirs, as ye sit, on those worthy thrones!   46
Why ask ye not yet how fared have your crones?

2ND TORTURER   Sir, bitterly we admit all weary are our bones;
Our quest we did not quit, though with great groans
    We tarried.

CAIAPHAS   Say, were ye put in dread?
Were ye ought misled?
In such a strait, ye said?
    Sirs, which of you miscarried?

ANNAS   Say, were ye ought in doubt for lack of light
As ye there watched out?

1ST TORTURER   Sir, as I am true knight,
Since as babe I learnt to shout, had I never such a night;
My eyes were kept throughout watching right
    Since morn,
But yet it was well spent,
This traitor to present
To you, sir, as we meant,
    Who gave so great scorn.

CAIAPHAS   Can ye him now impeach? Fled his men for fear?
2ND TORTURER   He has been used to preach for full many a year;
And to the people teach a new law.

1ST TORTURER   Sirs, hear!
So far as his wit may reach many lend an ear;
    When we took him,
In a garden we him found,
My sword I swung around,
His disciples to confound,
    And soon they forsook him.

2ND TORTURER   Sir, he said he could destroy too our temple so gay,
And once more build anew on the third day.

CAIAPHAS   How might that be true? It took much to array,
The masons I knew that built it, I say,
    So wise,
That hewed every stone.

1ST TORTURER   Good sir, let him alone;
He lies for the whetstone,
    I give him the prize.

[38]

2ND TORTURER The halt runs, the blind sees, through his false wiles;
83   Thus gets he many fees of them he beguiles.
1ST TORTURER Dead men he raised with ease; folk come from many
                                                    [miles;
            And ever through his sorceries our Sabbath day defiles
            Evermore, sir.
2ND TORTURER This is his wont and custom,
            To heal the deaf and dumb,
            Wheresoever he come;
                I told you before, sir.

1ST TORTURER Men call him prophet, king, and God's son, the same;
            Down gladly would he bring our laws to ill fame.
2ND TORTURER Yet is there another thing that I heard him declaim;
            He sets not a flea's wing, by sir Caesar's great name;
                He says thus;
            Sir, this same is he
            That excused with his subtlety
            A woman in adultery;
                Full well may ye trust us.

1ST TORTURER Sir Lazarus he could raise, back his breath he gave,
            When he had lain four days dead in his grave,
            All men him praise, both master and knave,
            Such his witchcraft ways.
2ND TORTURER   If us he brave
                Much longer,
            Curse him we can,
            For turning many a man;
            Since the time he began,
                Our hate is the stronger.

1ST TORTURER He will not believe it though he be culpable;
            Men call him a prophet, a lord most notable,
            Sir Caiaphas, by my wit, he should be damnable,
            But would ye two, as ye sit, make it firm and stable
                Together;
            For ye two held in awe,
            May defend all our law;
            To you therefore we draw,
                And bring this wretch hither.

[39]

2ND TORTURER Sir, I can tell you before, as might I be married,   118
              If he reign any more our laws be miscarried.
IST TORTURER Sir, his works we deplore, his power should be parried;
              We may not ignore where he has long tarried
                    And walked.
              His cheer is misbegotten
              There is something forgotten,
              I shall thrust out what's rotten,
                    Before we have talked.

CAIAPHAS   Now fair you befall for your talking!
              For certain I myself shall make an examining.
              Hearest thou, harlot, of all? For care mayst thou sing!
To JESUS.
              How durst thou thee call either emperor or king?
                    I defy thee!
              What the devil dost thou hear?
              That claim will cause thee fear;
              Come whisper in my ear,
                    Or I shall decry thee.

              An ill hour wast thou born! Hark! Says he nought
                                                      [still?
              Thou shalt before morn be glad to say thy fill.
              This is a great scorn your tricks to fulfil;
              Wolf's-head I thee warn we have thee at will
                    Vile traitor!
              Thou might say something with ease,
              It might our rage appease,
              Et omnis qui tacet
                    Hic consentire videtur.

              Speak but one word, now in the devil's name!
              Was thy sire abroad when he met with thy dame?
              What neither booted nor spurred and a lord of some
                                                      [fame!
              Speak on for a turd, the devil give thee shame,
                    Sir Sibree!
              Indeed, if thou wert King,
              Yet might thou be riding;
              Fie on thee, foundling!
                    Thou livest but by bribery.

[40]

154

Lad, I am a prelate, a lord of degree,
I sit in great state as thou may see,
Knights may on me wait of divers degree;
Thy pride shall abate, thou shalt kneel on thy knee
      In my presence;
As ever sing I mass,
Whoso keeps the law has
By profession a mass
      More than his land's rents.

The devil give thee shame that ever I knew thee!
Neither blind nor lame will none pursue thee;
Therefore I shall thee name that ever shall rue thee,
King Coppin in our game, thus shall I indue thee,
      Impostor.
Say, to speak art thou afeared?
I will not be thus fleered,
Alack! The devil's dirt in thy beard,
      Vile false traitor!

Whatso thy quirks betoken, yet still thou might say,
                                                [mum;
Great words hast thou spoken, then wast thou not
                                                [dumb;
Be it whole word or broken, come, out with some,
Lest my rage be awoken, or thy death the outcome
      Of all.
Either thou hast no wit,
Or stopped your ears to it;
Why but hear you not yet,
      So I cry and bawl?

ANNAS

Ah, sir, be not ill-paid, though he answer not;
He is inwardly afraid, his reason may rot.

CAIAPHAS

But the words he has said make me fear a plot.

ANNAS

At his trial none will him aid.

CAIAPHAS

                                 That shall not be forgot.

ANNAS

      May this ease you.

CAIAPHAS

Now foul might him befall!

ANNAS

Sir, ye are vexed at all,
And peradventure he shall
      Hereafter please you.

[41]

        By law we may though examine him first.   190

CAIAPHAS   Unless I give him a blow, my beart will burst.

ANNAS   Abide till ye his purpose know.

CAIAPHAS   But thrust out I durst
        Both his eyes in a row.

ANNAS   Sir, be not athirst
        For vengeance.
        But let me oppose him.

CAIAPHAS   Yea, with death to depose him.

ANNAS   Sir, we may not dispose him,
        But be damned for mischance.

CAIAPHAS   He deserves to be dead, a king himself called;
        Out! Let me strike off his head!

ANNAS   No! Be ye forestalled;
        Sir, heed what is said, be not so galled.

CAIAPHAS   Shall I never eat bread till he be installed
        In the stocks.

ANNAS   Sir, speak soft and still;
        Let us do as the law will

CAIAPHAS   Nay, I myself shall him kill,
        And murder with knocks.

ANNAS   Sir, think ye that ye are a man of holy kirk,
        Ye should be our teacher meekness to work.

CAIAPHAS   Yea, but he sticks like a burr on my heart it to irk.

ANNAS   Softly to go is farthest to stir, our laws are not murk,
        I mean;
        Your words are rambusteous,
        Et hoc nos volumus
        Quod de jure possumus:
        What comes will be seen.

        It is best that we treat him with fairness.

CAIAPHAS   But, nay!

ANNAS   And so we might get him some word for to say.

CAIAPHAS   Alack! Let me beat him!

ANNAS   Come, sir, away!
        For if thus ye meet him, he speaks not this day;
           But hear:
        If he cease and abide,
        I shall take him aside

224   And inquire of his pride,
          How he brings folk cheer.

CAIAPHAS   He has robbed over long with all his false lies,
       And done us great wrong, sir Caesar he defies;
       To hang him I long before I arise.

ANNAS   Sir, the law is so strong, his fate he can no wise
         Avert.
       But first would I hear
       What he would answer;
       Except his crimes be clear
         How can we do him hurt?

       And therefore examining first will I make,
       Since he calls himself a king.

CAIAPHAS   Save he that forsake,
       I shall give him a wring that his neck shall break.

ANNAS   Sir, ye may not him ding, no word yet he spake,
         That I know.
       Hark, fellow, stand there!

To JESUS.

       Hast thou never a care?
       I marvel that thou dare
         Thyself endanger so.

       But I shall do as the law will if the people abuse thee;
       Say, did thou do this ill? Can thou ought excuse thee?
       Why standest thou so still, when men thus accuse thee?
       For to hang on a hill hark how they use thee
         To damn.
       Say, the God of heaven's son art thou,
       As thou art wont to avow?

JESUS   So thou sayest even now,
         And right so I am;

       For after this shalt thou see when that I come down
       From heaven shining brightly in the clouds that form
                        [my gown.

CAIAPHAS   Ah, ill might the feet be that brought thee to town!
       To die thou art worthy! Say, thief, where is thy
                         [crown?

[43]

ANNAS	Abide sir,	257

Let us lawfully redress.

CAIAPHAS We need no witness,
If thus he express;
   Why should I not chide, sir?

ANNAS Was there never man so wicked but he might amend.
When it comes to the prick it is better to bend.

CAIAPHAS Nay, sir, but I shall him stick even with my own hand:
For if he rob and stay quick we are at an end,
   And damned!
Therefore while I have breath,
Let me put him to death.

ANNAS *Sed nobis non licet*
   Interficere quemquam.

Sir ye know better than I, we should slay no man.

CAIAPHAS His deeds I defy, curse his works we can
And that he shall abuy.

ANNAS   Nay, but by another plan,
And do it lawfully.

CAIAPHAS   As how?

ANNAS   Tell you I can.

CAIAPHAS   Let's see.

ANNAS Sir, take heed of my saws;
Men of temporal laws
They may judge such a cause,
   But so may not we.

CAIAPHAS My heart is full cold, yet I almost melt;
For the tales that are told, I burst out of my belt,
It scarcely can hold my body, if ye it felt;
Yet would I give my gold yon traitor to pelt
   For ever.

ANNAS Sir, do as ye said to me.

CAIAPHAS What if he overthrew me?
Sir Annas, if ye undo me
   Forgive I you never.

ANNAS Sir, ye are a prelate.

CAIAPHAS   So may I well seem,

290 Myself if I say it.
ANNAS   It does not beseem
Such men of estate so fierce to have been;
But send him to Pilate in temporal law supreme
    Is he;
He may best greet him,
Rebuff and ill-treat him;
You need not to beat him
    Therefore, sir, let be.

CAIAPHAS Fie on him, beware! I am out of my gate;
Say why stands he so far.
ANNAS   Sir, he came but late.
CAIAPHAS No, but I have knights that dare rap him on the pate.
ANNAS Ye need but to scare, be calm and abate,
    Good sir.
Why spend you your spite?
What need you to fight?
If yon man you smite,
    You are irregular.

CAIAPHAS He that first made me clerk and taught me of prayer
To browse in books dark, the devil give him care!
ANNAS Ah, good sir, hark! Such words might ye spare.

CAIAPHAS Else had I left my mark on yon noisome nightmare,
    Perdy!
But ere he go I would
This were done for my good,
That some knights knock his hood
    With knocks two or three.

For since he has trespassed and broken our law,
Let us make him aghast and set him in awe.

ANNAS Sir, as ye have asked, so I you assure.
Come make ready fast, ye knights now draw
    Your armament;
And that king to you take,
And with knocks make him wake.
CAIAPHAS Yea, sirs, and for my sake
    Give him good payment.

[45]

	For if I joined your ring as I would that I might,
	I should vow by the king that once before midnight
	I should make his head sing where that I hit right.
1st Torturer	Sir, fear you nothing, nor at him take affright
	Today, 329
	For we shall so rock him
	And with buffets knock him.
Caiaphas	Then look that ye lock him
	That he run not away.

Bide for no benefit if that lad be fled.

2nd Torturer	Sir, on us be it, but we'll clout well his head.
Caiaphas	If ye beat as ye boast it would soon ding him dead.
1st Torturer	See, see ye and sit, how our blows have sped.
	Hold fast,
	But ere we do this thing,
	Bless us, lord, with thy ring.
Caiaphas	Now they shall have blessing
	Who best buffets cast.

2nd Torturer	Go we now to our trade with this fond fool.
1st Torturer	He shall learn how is played a new play for Yule.
	And find himself flayed. Froward, a stool
	Go fetch us!
Froward	Ye jade! Let me overrule;
	Let him rough it.
	For the woe that he shall see
	Let him kneel on his knee.
2nd Torturer	And so shall he for me;
	Go fetch us a light buffet.

Froward	Why must he sit soft who made such mischance
	That has vexed us so oft?
1st Torturer	Sir, at this prank we prance;
	If he stood up aloft, we must hop and dance
	As cocks in a croft.
Froward	Now a vengeance
	Come on him!
	Good skill do ye show,
	As I by my blow;
	Take this, bear it, so!
	Soon all fall upon him.

[46]

2ND TORTURER Come, sir, and sit down, must ye be prayed?
362   Like a lord of renown; your seat is arrayed.
1ST TORTURER We shall prove on his crown the words he has said.
2ND TORTURER There is none in this town, I trust, be ill-paid
                 For his sorrow,
               But the father that him got.
1ST TORTURER Now truly I know not
               But his kin have forgot
                 His body to borrow.

2ND TORTURER I would we got onward.
1ST TORTURER   But his eyes must be hid.
2ND TORTURER But if they be well sparred we lost what we did;
               Step forth thou, Froward!
FROWARD   Now what would you bid?
1ST TORTURER Thou art ever in the rearward.
FROWARD   Must none be chid
               But me?
               My ill luck I bewail.
2ND TORTURER Thou must get us a veil.
FROWARD   It is ever the old tale.
1ST TORTURER   Ill luck light on thee!

               Well had thou thy name for thou wast ever curst.
FROWARD   Sir, I might say the same to you if I durst;
               Yet my hire may I claim, no penny I pursed;
               I have had great shame, hunger and thirst,
                 In your service.
1ST TORTURER Not one word so bold!
FROWARD   Why, it is true that I told!
               The proof I still hold.
2ND TORTURER   At the church porch tell this.

FROWARD   Here a veil have I found, I trust it will last.
1ST TORTURER Good son, hand it round, it is just what I asked.
FROWARD   How should it be bound?
2ND TORTURER   About his head cast.
1ST TORTURER Yea, and when it is well wound, knit a knot fast,
                 As I said.
FROWARD   Is it well?
2ND TORTURER   Yea, knave.
FROWARD   What, think ye that I rave?

[47]

Christ's curse might he have   395
    That last bound his head!

1ST TORTURER   Now since he is blindfold I must begin,
    And thus was I counselled the mastery to win.
2ND TORTURER   Nay, wrong hast thou told thus should thou come in!
FROWARD   I stand and behold, ye touch not the skin,
    I feel.
1ST TORTURER   How will thou I do?
2ND TORTURER   In this manner too!
FROWARD   Yea, ye give him his due,
    There starts up a weal.

1ST TORTURER   Thus we him bereave of all his fond tales.
2ND TORTURER   Thy fist fails to grieve or else thy heart fails.
FROWARD   I can my hand upheave and upset the scales.
1ST TORTURER   God forbid then ye leave but set in your nails
    As you thrust.
    Sit up and prophesy.
FROWARD   But tell us no lie.
2ND TORTURER   Who smote thee last?
1ST TORTURER   Was it I?
FROWARD   He knows not, I trust.

1ST TORTURER   Fast to Sir Caiaphas go we together.
2ND TORTURER   Rise up with ill grace so come thou hither.
FROWARD   It seems by his pace he grudges to go thither.
1ST TORTURER   We have given him a glaze that, ye may consider,
    Will keep.
2ND TORTURER   Sir, for his great boast,
    He looks more like a ghost.
FROWARD   In faith, sir, we had almost
    Knocked him to sleep.

CAIAPHAS   Now since he is well beat, pass through the gate,
    And tell of this cheat to sir Pilate;
    He sits in the judge's seat among men of state,
    Make haste I entreat.
1ST TORTURER   Come forth, old crate,
    Look alive!
    We shall lead thee a trot.
2ND TORTURER   Lift thy feet mayst thou not,

[48]

FROWARD   Then no task I have got
432   But come after and drive.

CAIAPHAS: Alas, now take I heed!
ANNAS   Why mourn ye so?
CAIAPHAS   In fear I proceed, in wonder and woe,
              Lest Pilate for meed, let Jesus go;
              But had I slain him indeed with my hands at a blow,
                 At once,
              All then had been quit;
              But gifts many men admit,
              If he dare him acquit,
                 The devil have his bones!

              Sir Annas, thou art to blame, for had ye not been,
              I had made him full tame, yea struck him I mean,
              To the heart so to maim, with this dagger so keen.
ANNAS   Sir, feel you no shame to use words so unclean
              To men?
CAIAPIIAS   I will not stay in this stead,
              But spy how they him led,
              And pursue till he is dead.
                 Farewell! We go, then.

The Twenty-third Play: The Scourging

PILATE	JESUS
1ST TORTURER	JOHN
2ND TORTURER	MARY
3RD TORTURER	MARY MAGDALENE
1ST COUNSELLOR	MARY JACOBI
2ND COUNSELLOR	SIMON

PILATE   Peace at my bidding, be tame as ye are told!
              Look none be so hardy to speak word but I,
              Or by Mohammed most mighty, my force shall un-
                                             [fold,
              With this brand that I bear ye shall bitterly abuy.
              Say, know ye not I am Pilate, peerless to behold?
              Most doughty in deeds of all dukes of Jewry;

At beguiling in battles I am the most bold,   7
Therefore my name is not, surely,
   Amiss.
I am full of subtlety,
Falsehood, guile, and treachery;
Therefore I am named by clergy
   As *mali actoris.*

For like as on both sides of iron the hammer makes it
                              [plane,
So do I that have here the law in my keeping,
The right side to succour certain I am full fain,
If I may get thereby advantage or winning;
Then to the false part I turn me again,
For I see the bribes I'm offered are surprising;
Thus every man should fear I cause him pain,
And all faint-hearted fellows be me obeying,
   Truly.
All false indictors,
Inquesters and jurors,
All such outriders
   Are welcome to me.

Now this prophet, that has preached and published so
                              [plain
Christian law, Christ they call him in our country;
But our princes full proudly this night have him ta'en,
Full soon to be damned he shall be hurled before me;
I shall seem him to favour as friend, most certain,
And show him fair countenance and words of vanity,
But ere this very night on cross shall he be slain,
Thus against him in my heart I bear great enmity
   Full sore.
Ye men that use back-bitings,
And seethe with slanderings,
Ye are my dear darlings,
   And Mohammed's for evermore.

For nothing in this world does me more grieve
Than to hear of Christ and of his new laws;
To know he were God's son my heart would crack and
                              [cleave,

43   Though he be true in deed and word, that thought me
                                      [awes;
            Therefore shall he suffer of me much mischief,
            And every disciple that unto him draws;
            For above any solace it lightens my grief
            Christian blood to be shedding, that Jewry adores,
                I avow.
            My knights now so strong,
            Will their strength show ere long,
            If they tarry they do wrong;
                Lo, where they come now!

1ST TORTURER   I have run till I sweat from sir Herod our King
            With this man that will let our laws come to nothing;
            Our mercy must be forfeit, of care may he sing:
            He is doomed by sir Pilate to get an ill ending
                And sore;
            The great works he has wrought
            Shall serve him as nought,
            But they be dearly bought
                Believe me no more.

            But make room in this pass and lest there be strife,
            Your noise ye now cease, both man and wife;
            To sir Pilate on daïs this man will we drive,
            His death gives us peace, so we rob him of life
                This day;
            Go draw him forward!
            Why stand ye so backward?
            Come on, sir, hitherward,
                As fast as ye may!

2ND TORTURER   Go, pull him apace while we are going;
            I shall spit in his face though it be fair shining;
            Of us three getst thou no grace, thou art so annoying,
            The more thy disgrace our mirth is increasing,
                No lack.
            Fellows, with a quick cast,
            With this band that will last
             Let us bind him fast,
                Both hands behind his back.

3RD TORTURER   I shall lead thee a dance unto sir Pilate's hall;   80
                Thou fell on ill chance to come among us all.
                Sir Pilate, with your chieftains, to you we cry and call
                That ye make some ordinance for this wretched thrall,
                    With skill;
                This man we have led
                On cross ye kill him dead.

PILATE   What! Without more said?
                    That is not my will;

                But ye, wisest of law, attend as ye stand;
                This man without awe which ye lead in a band,
                In word or deed I saw no wrong to reprimand,
                Why here ye should him draw or bear falsely in hand
                    With ill.
                Ye say he turns our people,
                Ye call him false and fickle.
                To see his life-blood trickle
                    With shame should you fill.

                Of all causes ye have shown which ye put on him;
                Herod, true as any stone, could find no fault in him;
                Nothing was known that signified a sin;
                Why should I then be prone further to pry therein?
                    Therefore
                This is my counsel,
                I will not with him meddle;
                Let him go where he will
                    For now and evermore.

1ST   Sir, I tell thee one thing, and not amiss,
COUNSELLOR   He calls himself a king when none he is
                Thus down would he bring our laws by this,
                With his false lying, we cannot dismiss
                    This rebel.
PILATE   Hark, fellow, come near!
                Thou knowest I have power
                To excuse or damn thee here,
                    And house thee ay in hell.

[52]

JESUS   Such power hast thou nought to work thy will thus
                                                              [with me,

117   But from my father that is brought, one-fold God in
                                                              [persons three.

PILATE   Certain, it comes well into my thought, at this time as
                                                              [well know ye,

                  A thief that any felony has wrought, him let we escape
                                                              [or go free

                      Away;
                  Therefore ye let him pass.
1ST TORTURER   Nay, nay, but Barabbas!
                  And Jesus in this case
                      To death ye damn this day.

PILATE   Sirs, look ye take good heed, strip his dress without
                                                              [ado,

                  His body make ye bleed, and beat him black and blue.
2ND TORTURER   This man, as might I speed, that brought us bane anew,
                  Now "judicare" comes in the creed, that lesson he
                                                              [shall rue,

                      And his cause.
                  Bind him to this pillar.
3RD TORTURER   Why standest thou so far?
1ST TORTURER   To beat his body bare,
                      Without a pause.

2ND TORTURER   Now fall I the first to flap on his hide.
3RD TORTURER   My heart would near burst till his body I chide.
1ST TORTURER   A glad swipe, if I durst, would I lend thee this tide.
2ND TORTURER   No, I am athirst to see the blood down glide
                      So quick.
3RD TORTURER   Have at!
1ST TORTURER   Take thou that!
2ND TORTURER   I shall knock thee flat,
                      So strong is my trick.

3RD TORTURER   Where now serves thy prophecy, thou tell us in this
                                                              [case,

                  And all thy works of great mastery thou showed in
                                                              [divers place?

                              [53]

1ST TORTURER Thy apostles full readily ran swiftly from the race, 145
              Thou art here in our custody without a hope of grace
                   Or escape.
2ND TORTURER Go, thrash him!
3RD TORTURER And slash him!
1ST TORTURER Nay, I myself should smash him
                   But for Sir Pilate.

              Sirs, at the feast of Architreclyn this prophet had a place,
              There turned he water into wine, that day he had such
                                                            [grace,
              That made to him some men incline, and others sought
                                                          [his face;
              The sea he lived by as a sign it let him walk thereon
                                                          [apace
                   At will;
              The elements were seen,
              The winds that are so keen
              And the firmament I mean,
                   His bidding to fulfil.

2ND TORTURER A leper came full fast to this man that here stands,
              And prayed him in all haste from bale to loose his
                                                          [bands,
              His trouble was not waste though he came from far
                                                          [lands;
              This prophet to him passed and healed him with his
                                                          [hands,
                   Full glad.
              The son of the centurion,
              For whom his father made great moan,
              Of the palsy he healed anon,
                   For that much praise he had.

3RD TORTURER Sirs, as he came from Jericho, a blind man sat by the
                                                          [way;
              To this wretch amid the rout thus crying did he say,
              "Thou son of David ere thou go of blindness heal thou
                                                          [me this day."
              There was he healed of all his woe, such wonders can
                                                          [he work alway
                   At will;

[54]

175   He raises men from death to life,
                      And casts out devils that stir up strife;
                      He soothes the sickness that is rife,
                          He heals them all of ill.

1ST TORTURER   For all these deeds of great loving, four things have I
                                                      [found, certainly
                      For which he is worthy to hang: one is our king that
                                                      [he would be;
                      Our Sabbath day finds him working, not resting to heal
                                                      [the sick, truly;
                      He says our temple he shall down bring, and in three
                                                      [days build it on high
                          All whole again;
                      Sir Pilate, as ye sit,
                      Look wisely to your wit,
                      Damn Jesus ere ye flit,
                          On cross to suffer pain.

PILATE   Thou man that suffers all this ill, why will thou us no
                                                      [mercy cry?
                      Humble thy heart and thy high will whilst that we have
                                                      [mastery!
                      In such great works show us thy skill; men call thee
                                                      [king, thou tell us why;
                      Wherefore the Jews seek thee to kill, the cause I would
                                                      [know certainly,
                          Inform me.
                      Say what is thy name,
                      Feel thou no shame?
                      They put on thee great blame,
                          Else might thou escape from me.

2ND TORTURER   Sir Pilate, prince peerless, hear what is said,
                      That he escape not harmless but ye doom him dead:
                      He calls himself king in every place, thus has he misled
                      Our people for a space, and might our laws down tread
                          In all.
                      Sir, your knights count it loss
                      Save to the people you him toss
                      To hang him high upon a cross,
                          For that they cry and call.

                              [55]

PILATE   Now, sure this is a wondrous thing that ye would
                     [bring to nought
        Him that is your liege lording; in faith, this was far
                     [sought;
        But say, why be ye not obeying him whom all has
                     wrought?

3RD TORTURER Sir Caesar is our chief lording, sitting in his Roman
                     [court
        So bold.   210
        Pilate, do after us,
        And damn to death Jesus,
        Or to sir Caesar we'll shift us,
          And make thy friendship cold.

PILATE   Now that I am blameless of this blood shall ye see;
        Both my hands expressly washed now shall be;
        This blood is dear bought, I guess, that ye spill so free.

1ST TORTURER We pray it fall endless on us and our company
        For ever.
PILATE   Now your desire I give you all
        Away you may him haul,
        On cross to put that thrall,
          His life there to sever.

1ST TORTURER Come on! Trip on thy toes, without any feigning;
        Fulsome lying arose from thy false talking.
2ND TORTURER Much praise be to those that thus have brought a king
        From sir Pilate and other foes thus into our ring
          Without delay.
        Sirs, he calls himself king,
        So a crown is the thing.
3RD TORTURER I swear by everything
        I shall make one this day.

1ST TORTURER Lo! here a crown of thorn to burn his brain within,
        Put on his head with scorn and spear it through the
                     [skin.
2ND TORTURER Hail King! Where wast thou born, such worship for
                     [to win?
        We kneel night and morn our service to begin,
        That be thou bold;

238   Now by Mohammed's blood!
No meat will do me good
Till he be hanged on rood,
    And his bones be cold.

1ST TORTURER Sirs, we may be fain for I have found a tree,
I tell you for certain it is of great beauty,
On which he shall suffer pain, fastened by nails three,
There shall he nothing gain thereon till dead he be,
    Surely, say I.
Go bring him hence.
2ND TORTURER Then heave our gear thence.
3RD TORTURER I would spend all my pence
    To see him hang high.

1ST TORTURER This cross up thou take though it break every bone,
Without grudging betake thee through the town on
        [thy own;
Mary, thy mother, I know will make great mourning
        [and moan,
But for thy false deeds' sake shalt thou be slain alone,
    No nay;
The people of Bedlem,
And gentles of Jerusalem,
All the commoners of this realm,
    Shall wonder on this day.

JOHN *and the* HOLY WOMEN *appear in another part.*

JOHN THE   Alas! For my master most of might,
APOSTLE   That yester-even with lantern bright
    Before Caiaphas was brought;
Both Peter and I saw that sight,
And after we fled away in fright,
    When the cruel Jews him caught;
At morn among them was said false witness should be
        [sought,
Who might condemn him dead that no wrong had
        [wrought.

Alas! For his mother that this must know,
My mother and her sister also,

[57]

Sat together sighing sore;   270
They knew nothing of all this woe,
Therefore to tell them will I go,
Since I may mend no more.
If he should die thus soon and they not know before,
They may me then impugn; I will go fast therefore.

Goes to the WOMEN.

God save you, sisters together!
Dear lady, if thy will were,
I must tell tidings plain.

MARY
Welcome, John, my cousin dear!
How fares my son since thou wast here?
What peace to ease my pain?

JOHN
Ah, dear lady, with your leave the truth must still
[remain,
At God's will never grieve.

MARY
Why, John, is my son slain?

JOHN
Nay, lady, I said not so,
But bear in mind he told us two
And them that with us were,
How he in pain from us should go,
And again should come to us so
To amend our signing sore;
Avails it not instead for you to weep therefore.

MARY
MAGDALENE
Alas! This day for dread! Good John, name this no
[more!

Speak privily I thee pray,
I fear if she be told this fray,
That she will run and rave.

JOHN
The truth behoves I needs must say,
He is doomed to death this day,
No sorrow may him save.

MARY JACOBI
Good John, tell unto us two what thou of her will
[crave,
And We will gladly go and help what thou wouldst
[have.

JOHN
Sisters, your mourning may not this amend;
If once ye would before his end,
Speak with my master free,

[58]

303	Then must ye rise and with me wend
	To find him who has been your friend,
	Beyond this same city;
	With me if ye draw near, come fast and follow me.
MARY	Ah, help me, sisters dear! That I my son may see.
MARY	Lady, we would ease your pain,
MAGDALENE	Heartily, with might and main,
	Your comfort to compose.
MARY	Go, John, before and ascertain.
JOHN	Lo, where he comes to us again
	And round him flock his foes!
	Weeping is in vain, no tear may give him now repose.
MARY	Alas, for my son dear, that me as mother chose!

They meet JESUS.

	Alas dear son for care, I see thy body bleed;
	My life for thee I'd spare or for thy pardon plead,
	This cross on my shoulder bear to help thee in thy need,
	Though it bring me deep despair, whither they will
	[thee lead.
JESUS	This cross is large in length and rough to hold withal;
	If thou put to thy strength, to the earth thou must
	[down fall.
MARY	Ah, dear son, thou let me help thee in this case!

And he shall incline the cross to his MOTHER.

JESUS	Lo, mother, I tell it thee, thou might not for one pace.
MARY	I pray thee, dear son, it may so be, to man thou givest
	[thy grace,
	On thyself thou have pity, and now thy foes outface.
JESUS	Mother, there is no other way but death upon the tree,
	And from death rise on the third day, thus prophets say
	[of me;
	Man's soul that I loved ay, I shall redeem surely,
	Unto bliss of heaven for ay, I shall bring it to me.
MARY	It is to all a sorrowful sight Jesus with these Jews to see,
MAGDALENE	Here set in such a painful plight, my wailing will I not
	[let be.
MARY JACOBI	This lord that is of might, did never ill truly,
	These Jews they do not right if condemned to die is he.
MARY	Alas! What shall we say! Jesus our so dear chief,
MAGDALENE	To death these Jews this day lead him in unbelief.
MARY JACOBI	He was full true I say, though they damn him as a thief,
	Mankind he loved alway; my heart will crack for grief.

[59]

JESUS   Ye daughters of Jerusalem, I bid you weep no more for
                                               [me,
         But for yourselves and your children, behold I tell you
                                               [surely,
         With pains this realm shall teem in days hereafter for
                                               [to be;
         Your mirth to misery shall stream in every place of this
                                               [city.

         Children, blessed be they indeed, women that no
                                               [children bear,
         And the breasts that gave no suck, so heavy their heart
                                               [with care;
         The mountains high and these great hills shall fall upon
                                               [them there,
         For my blood that guiltless spills will bring my foes
                                               [despair.

2ND TORTURER   Walk on, and leave thy vain carping, it will not save
                                               [thee from thy death,
                Whether these women cry or sing, for saving thee they
                                               [waste their breath.
3RD TORTURER   Say why do we hang thus here about,   348
                And hear these harlots scream and shout?
                Will no man change their cheer?
1ST TORTURER   Get home and howl whore, with that clout!
                Or, by the Lord I'll lay about,
                Thou shalt abuy it dear.
MARY   This deed shall vengeance call on you all together.
MAGDALENE
2ND TORTURER   Go, hurry hence withal, or bide a beating here!
3RD TORTURER   Let all this bickering be, since our toils are before;
                This traitor and this tree I would we were fain there.
2ND TORTURER   No further can he fetch this cross that gives him care,
                But yonder comes a wretch shall help him it to bear.
    Enter SIMON *of Cyrene.*

                Thereof shall we soon make assay.
                Hark, good man, whither lies thy way?
                Thy striding shows no sloth.
SIMON   Sirs, I have a great journey
                That must be done this same day,

[60]

365   Or harm comes, by my troth.
3RD TORTURER Thou may with little pain ease him and thyself both.
SIMON   Good sirs, I gladly would remain, but to tarry I am
                                                    [loth.

1ST TORTURER Nay, nay! Thou shalt full soon be sped;
             Lo here's a lad that must be led
                    For his ill deeds to die,
             And he is bruised and long has bled,
             Such are our straits as I have said;
                    So, sir, do not deny,
             That thou wilt take this tree to bear to Calvary.
SIMON   Good sirs, that may not be, for full great haste have I,

             Though I would grant your boon.
2ND TORTURER In faith, thou shalt not go so soon
                    For nought that thou can say
             This may not be eschewn,
             And this churl dead by noon,
             And now is near midday;
             Help therefore in our need and make no more delay.
SIMON   I pray you do your deed and let me go my way;

             And I shall come full soon again,
             To help this man with might and main,
                    At your own will.
2ND TORTURER Once gone thou comest not again!
             Nay, fellow, thou shalt be fain,
                    Our bidding to fulfil;
             Or by Mohammed's renown thou shalt find it ill.
1ST TORTURER Quick, ding this dastard down, if stubborn he be still.

SIMON   Indeed it were unwisely wrought,
             To beat me save I trespassed ought
                    Either in word or deed.
2ND TORTURER Upon thy back it shall be brought,
             Bear it whether thou will or nought!
                    The devil! Whom should we heed?
             Take it therefore, on thy life, and bear it with good
                                                    [speed.
SIMON   Now here avails no strife, to bear it then I need;

[61]

And therefore, sirs, I lend my aid;   400
As ye have said, I am well paid,
This man his pain to spare.

3RD TORTURER Ah, ha! Now are we right arrayed,
But look our gear be ready laid,
For work when we come there.

1ST TORTURER I warrant all ready, of our tools there's no loss.
Now sir Simon truly, bear before us the cross.

By Mohammed, our heaven's king,
I would that we were in that stead
Where on the cross we might him bring
Step on before, let him be led
Apace.
Come on, thou!

2ND TORTURER Step forth, thou!

3RD TORTURER I come fast now,
And follow in the chase.

The procession goes off.

The Twenty-fourth Play:
The Hanging of Judas

JUDAS   *Alas, alas, and welaway!*
Accursed caitiff I have been ay;
I slew my father, and after lay
With my mother;
And later, falsely, did betray
My own master.

My father's name was Reuben, right;
Sibaria my mother bright;
He knew her once upon a night
In fleshly wise,
In her sleep she saw a sight
Beyond surmise.

[62]

13

She thought there lay her side within
A loathly lump of fleshly sin,
Of the which destruction should begin
        Of all Jewry;
That cursed clot of Cain's kin,
        Forsooth was I.

Dread of that sight made her awake,
And all her body did tremble and quake;
She thought her heart would well-nigh break—
        No wonder was—
The first word my mother spake
        Was alas, alas!

Alas, alas! She cried full fast,
With weeping she was deep downcast:
My father stirred himself at last,
        And asked her why;
She told him how she was aghast,
        No word of lie.

My father bad "let be thy woe!
My counsel is, if it be so,
A child begotten betwixt us two,
        Daughter or son,
Let it never on earth once go,
        But be undone.

"Better it is undone to be
Than it should slay both thee and me,
For in a while then shall we see,
        And know forsooth
Whether that dream was vanity
        Or held some truth."

The time was come that I was born,
And from my mother's body torn;
Alas that I had been forlorn
        Within her side!
For there then sprang a cursed thorn
        That spread full wide.

For I was born without a grace,
They me named and called Judas;
The father of the child ay has
　　Great pity;
He would not suffer before his face
　　My death to see.

My death to see then might be nought;
A basket small he bad be wrought;
A-bed within there I was brought
　　And bound full fast;
And then the deep salt sea they sought,
　　And in me cast.

The waves rose, the wind blew;
That I was cursed full well they knew;
The storm me on an island threw,
　　In that cot;
And from that land my name I drew,
　　Judas Iscariot.

There, as wrecked in sand I lay,
The queen came passing by that way,
With her maidens to sport and play;
　　And privily
A child she found in such array,
　　Most strangely.

Nevertheless she was well paid,
And gently on her lap me laid;
She me kissed and with me played,
　　For I was fair;
"A child God has me sent" she said,
　　"To be my heir."

She had me nursed, and all was done
To foster me as her own son,
And told the king that she had gone
　　All year with child;
And with fair words his ear she won,
　　And him beguiled.

[64]

85 *Then the king had made a feast*
For all the land, right of the best,
For begotten was a guest
    A sweet small thing,
When he was dead and brought to rest,
    That might be king.

Soon afterwards, within years two,
In the land it befel so,
The queen herself with child did go;
    A son she bore;
No fairer child from top to toe
    Was seen before.

(Incomplete)

The Twenty-fifth Play: The Crucifixion

PILATE	JESUS
1ST TORTURER	MARY
2ND TORTURER	JOHN
3RD TORTURER	LONGEUS
4TH TORTURER	JOSEPH OF ARIMATHEA
	NICODEMUS

PILATE

Peace I bid you one and all!
Stand as still as stone in wall,
Whilst ye are present in my sight;
That none of you chatter nor call;
Then I shall be to you a blight,
I warn each one both great and small,
With this brand burnished so bright,
Therefore in peace look ye be all.

What! Peace in the devil's name!
Ye dastards and dolts, I mean!
Or the gallows shall make you tame,
Thieves and cut-purses keen!
Will ye not peace when I bid you?
By Mohammed's blood, my spleen

W.M.P.–X   [65]

Will split, save I devise for you, 15
Such pains as never were seen,
Soon to be shown!
Be ye so bold beggars, I warn you,
Full boldly shall I beat you,
To hell the devil shall draw you,
Body, back, and bone.

I am a lord, magnificent in might,
Prince of all Jewry, sir Pilate, by right,
Next to King Herod, greatest of all;
Bow at my bidding both great and small,
Or else be destroyed;
Therefore steer your tongues, I warn you all,
That I be not annoyed.

1ST TORTURER All peace, all peace, among you all!
And hearken now what shall befall
To this false fellow here;
That with his dark devices,
As none but God suffices
Among us to appear.
He calls himself a prophet,
Says the sick he can make fit,
And bring comfort to all lands;
But ere long it shall be plain
Whether he heals his own pain,
Or escapes out of our hands.

Was not this a wondrous thing,
That he durst call himself a king,
And make so great a lie?
But by Mohammed, whilst I live,
Such proud words shall I never forgive,
Till he be hanged on high.

2ND TORTURER His pride, fie, we set at nought,
But each man now cast in his thought,
That of nothing we be scant,
For I shall try, if that I may,
By the order of knighthood, today
To cause his heart to pant.

[66]

3RD TORTURER And so shall I with all my might,
54   Abate his pride this very night,
                          And amend his creed;
                      He let on he could do no ill,
                      But he can surely, when he will,
                          Do a full foul deed.

4TH TORTURER Yea, fellows, yea, as I have rest!
                      Now is time as I have guessed
                          To bring this thief to death;
                      Look that we have what we should need,
                      To fasten this fellow firm, give heed.
1ST TORTURER Thou speakst with noble breath!

                      Lo, here I have the bands,
                      If need be to bind his hands,
                          This thong, I trust, will last.

2ND TORTURER And this one for the other side,
                      That shall abate his pride,
                          So be it first drawn fast.

3RD TORTURER Lo, here's a hammer and nails also,
                      For to fasten down our foe
                          To this tree, soon now.

4TH TORTURER Ye are wise to take this heed
                      Of those things that we shall need,
                          And so for them allow.

1ST TORTURER Now dare I say hardly
                      Shall he with his idolatry
                          Find it serve him well.

2ND TORTURER Since Pilate sent him to us again
                      Have done quick and make it plain
                          At what tortures we excel.

3RD TORTURER Now are we at the Mount of Calvary;
                      Have done fellows and let's now see
                          That we no sport may lack.

4TH TORTURER Yea, for as proud as he may appear,   86
Yet he would have changed his cheer,
If he had had the rack.

1ST TORTURER In faith, sir, since ye call yourself a king,
You must prove a worthy thing
That wends thus to the war;
You must joust in tournament;
Unless ye sit fast ye may repent,
By me thrust down before.

2ND TORTURER If thou be God's son, as thou tell,
Thou can surely keep thee well?
Else a mystery most complete.
And if thou can we will not own
What thou hast said, but make our moan
When thou sittst in yon seat.

3RD TORTURER Thank us when thy steed thou straddle
For we shall set thee in thy saddle,
Fear no fall, be thou bold.
I promise no lance will shift thee,
Unless thou sit well thou had better let be
The tales that thou hast told.

4TH TORTURER Stand near, fellows, and let us see
How we can horse our king so free,
By any chance;
Stand thou yonder on that side,
And we shall see how he can ride,
And how well wield a lance.

1ST TORTURER Sir, come hither and have done,
Your palfrey would it were begun,
He is ready, I can tell.
That ye be bound on be not wroth,
To mount you unfirm we are loth,
Lest ever ye down fell.

2ND TORTURER Knit thou a knot with all thy strength,
Out to draw this arm in length,
Till it come to the bore.

[68]

3RD TORTURER Thou madest man, by this light!
123   It lacks to each man's sight,
               Half a span and more.

4TH TORTURER Yet draw out this arm and fix it fast,
              With this rope that well will last,
               And each man lay hand to.

1ST TORTURER Yea, and bind thou fast that band;
              We shall go to that other hand
              And look what we can do.

2ND TORTURER Drive a nail right here throughout,
              And then we need us nothing doubt
               That home it comes to rest.

3RD TORTURER That shall I do, as might I thrive!
              For to clench and for to drive,
               Of all I am the best.
              So let it stay for it is well.

4TH TORTURER As have I bliss, the truth you tell!
              Move it no man might.

1ST TORTURER Hold down his knees.
2ND TORTURER   That shall I do,
              Your nurse no better help gave you;
               Pull his legs down tight.

3RD TORTURER Draw out his limbs much further yet.

4TH TORTURER That was well drawn and cost much sweat;
              Fair befall him that pulled so!
              For to have brought him to the mark
              Unlettered churl nor clerk
               More skill could show.

1ST TORTURER Hold it now fast therefore,
              And one of you take the bore,
               And then it may not fail.
2ND TORTURER That shall I do with good heed,
              As ever hope I well to speed,
               And cause him bitter bale.

3RD TORTURER So that is well, it stood the test,   155
             But now let's see who does the best
             With any sleight of hand.

4TH TORTURER Go we now to the other end;
             Your hands, fellows, look you lend
             To pull well at this band.

1ST TORTURER I tell thee fellows, by this weather,
             That we draw now altogether,
             And look how it will fare.

2ND TORTURER Let's now see, and leave your din!
             His sinews now to snap within;
             For nothing let us spare.

3RD TORTURER Nay, fellows, this is no game!
             All of us pull not the same,
             Some slacking have I spied.

4TH TORTURER Yea, for as I hope for bliss,
             Some tug while some twitch this,
             Not straining at our side.

1ST TORTURER It is better, as I hope,
             Each by himself to draw this rope,
             And then may we see
             Who it was that erstwhile
             Thought his fellows to beguile,
             In this company.
2ND TORTURER Since thou wilt have it so, here's for me!
             Draw I not hard, as thou might see?
3RD TORTURER   Thou drew right well;
             Have here for me half a foot!
4TH TORTURER Why, man! Not an inch more you put!
             It budged not, I can tell.
             But have from me here what I may!
1ST TORTURER Well drawn, son, by this day!
             In thy work there's a spark!
2ND TORTURER Yet again, while thy hand is in,
             Pull thereat like an engine.
3RD TORTURER   Yea, and bring it to the mark.

[70]

4TH TORTURER	Pull, pull!
1ST TORTURER	Have now!
2ND TORTURER	Let's see!
3RD TORTURER	Ah, ha!
4TH TORTURER	Heave, ho!
1ST TORTURER	Now we have not far.
2ND TORTURER	Hold still, I implore!
3RD TORTURER	So fellows! Now look alive,

195
    Which of you now best can drive,
        And I shall take the bore.

4TH TORTURER Now to try my turn let me;
    Best farrier I hope to be
        For to clench it right.
    Do rouse him up now when we may,
    For I hope he and his palfrey
        Shall not part this night.

1ST TORTURER Come hither, fellows, and lend hand!
    And make this tree to stand
        Aloft with all your might.

2ND TORTURER Yet let us work awhile,
    And none the other beguile,
        Till it stand to its height.

3RD TORTURER Fellows, your hands now you lend,
    For to raise this tree on end,
        And let's see who is last.

4TH TORTURER It is best to do as he says;
    Set we the tree in the mortice,
        And there will it stand fast.

1ST TORTURER Up with the timber.
2ND TORTURER   Ah, it holds!
    For him that all this world upholds
        Thrust from thee with thy hand!

3RD TORTURER Hold even amongst us all.
4TH TORTURER Yea, and let it in the mortice fall,
        For then will it best stand.

1ST TORTURER Go we to it and be we strong,
    And raise it, be it never so long,
        Since firmly we have done.

2ND TORTURER Up with the timber fast on end!
3RD TORTURER Fellows, your full force now lend!
4TH TORTURER So sir, gape against the sun!
1ST TORTURER Now fellow, wear thy crown!

[71]

2ND TORTURER Trust thou this timber will fall down?   228
3RD TORTURER   Yet help that it were fast.
4TH TORTURER Shake him well and let us lift.
1ST TORTURER Full short shall be his shrift.
2ND TORTURER   Ah, it stands up like a mast.

JESUS   I pray you people that pass me by,
                   That lead your life so pleasantly,
                        Heave up your hearts on high!
                   Behold if ever ye saw body
                   Buffeted and beaten bloody,
                        Or thus dolefully to die;
                   In world no wretch as I
                        That suffered half so sore,
                   In mind and mood I sigh
                   For sorrow comes me nigh,
                        And comfort comes no more.

                   My folk, what have I done to thee,
                   That thou all thus shall torment me
                        That for thy sin I suffer?
                   How have I grieved thee? answer me,
                   That thou thus nails me to a tree,
                        And all for thine error;
                        Where shalt thou seek succour?
                   This mistake how shalt thou mend?
                        When that thou thy saviour
                        Drives to this dishonour,
                   His feet and hands to rend!

                   All creatures have a home to rest
                   Beasts and birds, all have their nest,
                        When they are woe-begone;
                   But God's son that should be best,
                   Has not whereon his head to rest,
                        But on his shoulder bone.
                   To whom now may I make my moan?
                        When they thus martyr me,
                   And guiltless make me groan,
                   And beat me, blood and bone,
                        That should my brothers be

                              [72]

266 What kindness further could I do?
Have I not done what I ought to,
　　Made thee in my likeness?
Robbed of all rest that is man's due,
Thus mocked by all men who me view!
　　Such is thy wickedness.
I have shown you kindness, unkindly ye requite;
See thus thy wickedness! Behold your deep despite!

To guiltless death ye me consign,
Not, man, for my sins, but for thine,
　　Thus rent on rood am I,
I would not lose that treasure fine,
That I marked and made for mine,
　　Thus Adam's blood I buy,

That sunken was in sin,
　　Within no earthly good,
　　But with my flesh and blood
That loth was to win.

My brothers that I came to buy,
Have hanged me here thus hideously,
　　And friends find I few;
Thus have they done most dreadfully,
Spat at me most spitefully,
　　And heaved me up to view.
Father in heaven I pray to you,
Forgive them thou this guilt,
Grant but this boon:
They know not what they do,
Nor whose blood they have spilt.

1ST TORTURER Yes, what we do full well we know.
2ND TORTURER We pay back fully what we owe.
3RD TORTURER Now the plague take his corpse, say I.
　　　　　　Thinks he that we should care or cry,
　　　　　　　　What the devil, that he should ail?
4TH TORTURER He would hold us here all day,
　　　　　　Of his death to make delay,
　　　　　　　　I tell you, without fail.
1ST TORTURER Lift up this tree among us all.

[73]

2ND TORTURER Yea, and let it in the mortice fall,   304
          And that should give him a jar.
3RD TORTURER Yea, this should rend him limb from limb.
4TH TORTURER Breaking every joint within,
          He may not our sport mar.

MARY *advances.*

MARY   Alas! For care I cry, and stagger in my need!
          Why hangst thou, son, so high? My ills begin to breed.
          All blemished is thy beauty, I see thy body bleed!
          In world, son, had we never such ill fate decreed.

          My flesh that I have fed,
          In life lovingly led,
          Full straitly art thou stead
              Among thy foemen fell;
          Such sorrow for to see,
          My dearest child on thee,
          Is more pain to me
          Than any tongue can tell.

          Alas, thy holy head
          Without rest is revealed;
          Thy face, with blood now red,
              Was fair as flower in field;
          Who may not stand in dread
          To see her bairn thus bled,
          Beaten blue as lead,
              And have no limb to wield!

          Fastened by hands and feet
          With nails that his flesh eat,
          With wounds his foes him greet,
              Alas, my child for care!
          Thy flesh is open wide
          I see on either side
          Tears of blood down glide
              Over all thy body bare.
          Alas that I should bide
          To see my son thus fare!

JOHN *advances.*

[74]

JOHN
340

Alas, for woe, my lady dear!
Quite changed now is thy cheer,
To see this prince without a peer
     Thus lapped all in woe;
He was thy child, thy fairest one,
Thy hope thy joy, thy lovely son,
That high on tree thus hangs alone
     Beaten by many a blow;
Alas!
     Him, many of us know
     No master could surpass.
But lady, since it is his will
The prophecy to fulfil,
That mankind should know their ill,
     For them he suffers pain;
He with his death shall ransom make,
As before the prophets spake,
Thy sorrow therefore thou forsake,
     Weeping may nothing gain;
He now in sorrow takes our stain,
That we live clean tomorrow.

MARY

Alas! Thine eyes as crystal clear, that shone as sun in sight,
That lent thy countenance such cheer, lost they have
                                        [their light,
And faded fast I fear, all dim and dark as night!
In pain hast thou no peer, none suffered such a plight.

Sweet son, tell me thy thought,
What wonders hast thou wrought
To be in pain thus brought
     Thy span of life to end?
Ah, son, think on my woe!
Wilt thou thus from me go?
On earth no man I know
     Who may my mirth amend.

JOHN

Comely lady, kind and true, gladly would I comfort
                                        [thee;
My master spoke these words unto all within his
                                        [company,
That he should suffer so sore pain and die upon a tree,

[75]

And then to life rise up again the third day should it be
    Full right!   378
Therefore, my lady sweet,
Thy weeping is not meet!
Our dole he shall defeat
    In his risen might.

MARY   My sorrow it is so sad, no solace may me save,
My mourning makes me mad, no hope of help I have;
Such woe I never had, I fear that I may rave,
Nought now may make me glad till I be in my grave.

To death my dear is driven,
His robe is rent and riven,
That him by me was given,
    And fashioned by my hands;
These Jews with him have striven, their evil he with-
                 [stands.

Alas, my lamb so mild, why wilt thou leave me so?
Among these wolves so wild, that work thee all this
                   [woe?
From shame who may thee shield, if friends thus from
                   [thee go,
Alas, my comely child, why wilt thou leave me so?

Maidens, make your moan!
And weep ye wives, each one,
With me who grieve alone
    For the babe that was born best!
My heart is stiff as stone that breaks not in my breast.

JOHN   Ah, lady, well know I, thy heart is full of care
When thou thus openly seest thy child thus fare;
Love drives him forcibly, himself he will not spare,
To redeem all faithfully, us who have sinned our share
    And more,
My dear lady, truly, your mourning cease, therefore.

MARY   Alas! May ever be my song, whilst I my life may lead;
Methinks now that I live too long, to see my bairn thus
                   [bleed.

408

The Jews have done to him great wrong, but why did
         [they this deed?
Lo, so high they have him hung, with shameless spite
         [and speed:
   Why so
Is he his foes among? His friends are few below.
I see this fair flower from me go; what shall become of
         [me?
Thou art so wrapped in woe and spread out on this
         [tree
   So high.
I grieve, but none may know, the pain seen in thine
         [eye.

JOHN

Dear lady, well were me
If I might comfort thee;
For the sorrow that I see
   Shears my heart asunder;
When that I see my master hang
In pain both bitter and strong,
Was never wretch with wrong
   Wrought to so great wonder.

MARY

Alas, death thy delay is long! Why art thou hid from
         [me?
Who made thee to my child belong to enshroud him
         [on the tree;
Now wickedly thou workst all wrong, the more shall
         [I chide thee,
My life thou need no more prolong but make me with
         [him free
   To abide;
Sore sighing is my song, for his wounds gape wide.

Ah, death, what hast thou done? With thee would I
         [were soon,
Since of children I had but one, the best under sun and
         [moon;
Friends few had I won, that makes me weep and swoon
   Full sore.
Good Lord, grant me my boon, and let me live no
         [more!

[77]

Gabriel, so good, that one time did me greet,   435
And then I understood thy words that were so sweet;
But now they change my mood, that promised grace
[replete,
To bear of my body and blood a child our bale to
[defeat
  Through right;
Now hangs he here on rood. Is this the promised sight?

All that thou of bliss promised me in that stead,
From mirth has fared amiss, yet trust I what thou said;
Thy counsel now in this, how should my life be led,
When from me gone is he that was my head,
    So soon?
My death now come it is. Dear Son, grant mercy's
[boon!

JESUS   My mother mild, change thou thy cheer!
Cease with sorrow thy soul to sear,
    It weighs my heart with heavy care;
The sorrow is sharp I suffer here,
That pain thee pierces, mother dear.
    My martyrdom none share.
  To do my father's will I dare
From bonds to loose mankind;
    His son will he not spare,
    To save them that despair
That in the fiend's grasp grind.

The first cause, mother, of my coming
Was for mankind's miscarrying,
    To save their souls I sought;
Mother make now no more mourning,
Since mankind through my dying
    May thus to bliss be brought.
    Woman weep thou right nought!
Take there John unto thy child!
    Mankind must needs be bought,
    And thou cast, cousin, in thy thought;
John, lo there thy mother mild!

Blue and bloody sorely beset,
Wickedly whipped till with blood I sweat,

[78]

471   Mankind, for thy misdeed!
Would thou for me thy lust regret
When thy heart is sadly set,
        Since thus for thee I bleed?
        Such life, forsooth, I lead,
That scarcely may I more;
        This suffer I for thy need,
        For thy grace I do this deed;
Now thirst I wonder sore.

1ST TORTURER   Nought but hold thy peace!
Thou shall have drink to give thee ease,
        Myself shall be thy slave;
Have here a draught to cool thy heat,
I doubt if you will find it sweet,
        I give but what you crave.

2ND TORTURER   So sir, say now all your will!
For if your tongue you had kept still
        Ye had not here been led.
3RD TORTURER   Thou would of all the Jews be King,
But now, I trust, rue everything,
        All that thou hast said.
4TH TORTURER   He has boasted of great prophecies,
That he should make our temple,
        Clean to the earth down fall;
And yet he said he should it raise
As once it stood, within three days!
        He lies, that know we all;

And for his lies, in our great hate
We will divide his clothing straight,
        Unless he works his art.
1ST TORTURER   Yea, as I hope my fortunes mend,
Soon will we this mantle rend,
        And each man take his part.
2ND TORTURER   How would thou we share his clothes?
3RD TORTURER   If his garment this way goes,
        In sections it is spoiled;
But let my word be law,
And each of us lots draw,
        Then none of us is foiled.

[79]

How so befalls now will I draw!   510
This is mine by common law,
 That may none gainsay.
Now since it may no better be,
Bargain thou for it with me,
 My groats may make you gay.

2ND TORTURER How fellows, see ye not yon scrawl?
Written in that time withal
 When our lots we drew.
3RD TORTURER Indeed, there is no man alive,
But for Pilate, as might I thrive,
 That dare write in our view.

4TH TORTURER Go we fast and let us look
What is written in yon book,
 Whatever it may mean.
1ST TORTURER Ah, the more I look thereon,
The less I think upon;
 All is not worth a bean.

2ND TORTURER Yes, forsooth, methinks I see
Languages written thereon three,
 Hebrew and Latin.
And Greek, methinks is written thereon,
Full hard it is to expound upon.
3RD TORTURER Say on, by Appolyon!

4TH TORTURER Yea, as I am a knight most true,
I am better at Latin than you
 Of this company;
I will go without delay
And tell you what it has to say;
 Listen, sirs, carefully.

Yonder is written "Jesus of Nazareth
He is King of Jews" it saith.
1ST TORTURER Ah, that is written wrong.
2ND TORTURER He names himself, but none him own.
3RD TORTURER Go we to Pilate and make our moan;
 Have done, and dwell not long.
They approach PILATE.

[80]

546   Pilate, yond are lies upon that label,
           Thereon is written nought but fable;
              Of Jews he is not King!
           Himself says so, but none is he;
           It is therefore written falsely,
              A much mistaken thing.

PILATE   Boys, I say, what tell ye me?
           As it is written so shall it be,
              For certain;
           Quod scriptum scripsi,
           Such I decree,
              Which fellow fears not to complain?

4TH TORTURER Since that he is a man of law, he must needs have his
                                         [will;
           I trust he had not written that saw without some proper
                                         [skill.

4TH TORTURER Yea, let it hang above his head,
           It shall avail him little dead,
              Nor ought that he can write.
2ND TORTURER Now ill the day that he was born.
3RD TORTURER His life and hope both are forlorn,
              His death will slake our spite.

           If thou be Christ as men thee call,
           Come down among us all,
              And endure not this dismay.
4TH TORTURER Yea, and help thyself that we may see,
           And all of us shall trust in thee,
              Whatsoever thou say.

1ST TORTURER He calls himself a god of might,
           I would gladly see that sleight
              Performed for such a deed.
           Lazarus, from the grave he raised,
           To help himself he is too dazed
              Now in his great need.

JESUS   Eloi, Eloi, lamasabacthany!
           My God, my God, wherefore and why
              Hast thou forsaken me?

2ND TORTURER How, hear ye not as well as I,   581
How he did on Eloi cry?
For his ill teaching?

3RD TORTURER Yea, there is no god in this country
Shall deliver him from our company
For all his preaching.

4TH TORTURER I warrant it is time almost
That he shall soon yield up the ghost,
For torture takes it toll.

JESUS My flesh no more this pain withstands!
Father of heaven, into thy hands
I commend my soul!

1ST TORTURER Let one prick him with a spear,
If he flinch not, never fear,
Then is his life quite past.

2ND TORTURER This blind knight may that best do.
LONGEUS Force not on me what I shold rue.
3RD TORTURER   No, but thrust up fast.

LONGEUS Ah, Lord, what may this be?
Blind was I quite, now may I see;
God's son, hear me, Jesu!
Forgive what I most sorely rue
Lord, men made me play this part
That I struck thee to the heart;
Thou hangst on high I see
And die to fulfil the prophecy.

4TH TORTURER Go we hence and leave him here,
For plainly now it doth appear
He feels no more pain;
Through neither god nor man,
Do whatever good they can,
Gets he his life again.

Exeunt TORTURERS. JOSEPH OF ARIMATHEA *and* NICODEMUS *advance.*

JOSEPH Alas, alas, and welaway!
That ever I should live this day,
To see my master dead;
So fiercely has his flesh been rent,

[82]

617   With so bitter torment,
              Through what the Jews have said.

              Nicodemus, we have need
              That to sir Pilate we might speed,
                  His body for to crave;
              I will make haste with all my might,
              For his body to ask that knight,
                  To grant it but a grave.
      They go to PILATE.
NICODEMUS   Joseph, I will wend with thee
              To do all that is in me,
                  For that body to pray;
              For our good will and our travail
              I hope that it may us avail
                  Hereafterward some day.

JOSEPH   Sir Pilate, God thee save!
              Grant me what I crave,
                  If that it be thy will.
PILATE   Welcome, Joseph, might thou be!
              Whatso thou asks I grant it thee,
                  If it I may fulfil.

JOSEPH   For my long service I thee pray
              Grant me the body—say me not nay—
                  Of Jesu, dead on rood.
PILATE   I grant well if dead he be,
              Good leave shalt thou have of me,
                  Do with him what thou thinkest good.

JOSEPH   Grammercy, sir, for your good grace,
              So freely granted in this place;
                  Go we on before:
      They return to Calvary.
              Nicodemus come forthwith,
              For I myself shall be the smith
                  The nails out for to draw.

NICODEMUS   Joseph I am ready here
              To go with thee with full good cheer,
                  To help with all my might;
                      [83]

Pull forth the nails on either side,   652
And I shall hold him here beside;
   Ah, Lord, such is thy plight!

JOSEPH   Help now, fellow, with all thy might,
Till he be bound and dressed aright,
   And lay him in this bier;
Bear we him forth unto the kirk
To the tomb that has been my work
   Since full many a year.

NICODEMUS   It shall be so without a nay.
He that died on Good Friday
   And crownéd was with thorn,
Save you all that now here be!
That Lord that died for thee
   And rose on paschal morn.

Notes to the Plays (Part Three)

JOHN THE BAPTIST

John throughout plays on an acting area distinct from the Angels, and here Jesus joins him. It is feasible that this is the arena area below the pageant, on which most probably the Angels are ensconced in heaven's tower. The Second Angel refers pointedly to the area where the baptism will take place as being without a building of any sort (91), and when the First Angel speaks John hears but does not see him (73).

An alternative presentation suggested by the York and *Ludus Coventriae* plays might take place on the pageant with provision for the heavens to open and for the Holy Spirit to descend while God speaks from above (*Ludus Coventriae*, stage direction following 91, *Spiritus sanctus hic descendat super ipsum et deus pater celestis dicet in celo*). The York direction is contained in the words of the Second Angel to John (63–68):

> But in his baptism, John, take tent,
> The heavens shall be open seen,
> The holy ghost shall down be sent
> To see in sight,
> The father's voice with great talent
> Be heard full right. . . .

Pictorial representations of the baptism frequently depict God leaning through a cloud, holding in his hand the dove of the Holy Ghost above Jesus' head. The York *Transfiguration* suggests the use of lowering machinery for clouds and characters (stage direction following 168, *Hic descendunt nubes, Pater in nube*). In the York version, following the baptism, the two Angels sing (stage direction following 154, *Tunc cantabunt duo angeli 'Veni creator spiritus'*).

Tradition has John thinly clad, possibly half-naked, bearded, and bearing a staff. In this play he carries oil and cream as well with which to anoint Jesus. Jesus carries, or at least should have easy access to, the lamb which he hands to John after the baptism (210).

Of particular interest is line 197 referring to the sacraments of the Roman Church ('There are six others, no more so'). In the manuscript six, represented in Roman numerals, has the 'v' erased, and the whole stanza has been crossed through and in the margin, in what must be a post-Reformation hand, are the words 'correctyd & not playd'.

LAZARUS

Two acting areas are required, one for the dialogue between Jesus and his disciples (1–38) and one for Martha's house. Lazarus' tomb, with what appears to be a stone over the top, should be placed a little way from the house. Both the Chester play and the *Ludus Coventriae* indicate that Lazarus is buried in clay, but most versions agree that a heavy stone rests on top. The play is clearly a prefiguration of the resurrection. It can be simply staged on a pageant using one mansion.

At his resurrection we see Lazarus completely bandaged and Jesus, having raised him, directly orders his bands to be loosed from foot, hand and throat. Each of the Cycle plays on this theme emphasizes the dreadful stink of corrupted flesh which all fear at the opening of the tomb, and this is reflected too in medieval art. 'The Raising of Lazarus' by Gerard de Saint-Jean of the Dutch School, painted in the second half of the fifteenth century, shows, among the many by-standers looking on as Lazarus sits up in his tomb, one holding his nose and grimacing painfully, and another with his cloak pressed to his nose and mouth.

The structure of the play presents a staging problem. It proceeds in normal dialogue up to the raising of Lazarus, but following this event no other character but Lazarus speaks, and he indulges in a long homiletic harangue on the terrors of carnal corruption. The difficulty of the situation is aggravated by Jesus being among the other characters who, with the audience, are exhorted to heed the sermon. It may be more satisfactory if Lazarus and Jesus take deliberate and ceremonial leave of each other at line 110, allowing Lazarus to continue his blood-chilling account of mortality after Jesus has withdrawn.

In the manuscript *Lazarus* appears after *The Judgement,* and although as a play it is complete in itself, its structure is so unusual and its verse forms so extraordinarily divergent that it is manifestly the result of much revision. It is, however, included in this edition within the main body of the Mystery Cycle because of its importance as a prefiguration play, and because of the terrifying power of its homily which, as Professor Owst has observed, bears such close resemblance to a sermon preached by the Dominican, John Bromyard. This power is most apparent when the verse form approximates to that used by the Wakefield Master (125–173).

The Conspiracy

The action of this play covers both the conspiracy against Jesus and his capture, and within this framework contains *The Entry into Jerusalem*, *The Last Supper*, and *The Agony and Betrayal*, each of which is represented by a separate play in the York Cycle. The play is therefore composite and a great number of different acting areas are required; moreover it would be particularly difficult to use the same acting area for different groups of actors because each area has its marked characteristic: Pilate's hall; the room of the Last Supper; Mount Olivet; God in heaven (528); the Garden of Gethsemane. There are altogether seven different localities in the play, and there is also a stress on the movement of groups of actors: Jesus and his disciples meet (313), John and Peter are dispatched to the city, and they are later followed there by Jesus and the other disciples, all of whom sit down to the Last Supper. This scene alone requires considerable acting space. Allowance must be made for the table and benches, and sufficient space left for Jesus to move round the table washing the disciples' feet. Here are obvious reasons why in production this area should be used exclusively for this scene. But the movement of groups continues: Jesus goes with his three disciples to Mount Olivet. When Jesus reaches the Mount he leaves his disciples at a lower level and climbs up to pray, and it is from an even higher level that God speaks (528–555). This arrangement of levels immediately suggests the disciples at the foot of the pageant, Jesus standing or kneeling in prayer on the pageant itself, and God speaking from heaven, the castle-like structure erected on the pageant.

If the Last Supper and the Mount Olivet scenes point to distinct acting areas, it is also apparent that Pilate in his three scenes is to be located in his own acting area, although his soldiers pass freely from his hall to the Garden of Gethsemane and back again. The soldiers at the end of the play lead Jesus to the hall of Sir Caiaphas (740, 754), and the next play, *The Buffeting*, begins as this has left off with the soldiers, who are now called Torturers, dragging their victim towards the unscrupulous priest.

Practical staging considerations suggest that Pilate's hall, Caiaphas' hall, the scene of the Last Supper, and Mount Olivet are located on different scaffolds or pageants, and that it is in 'the place', 'green', or arena that the first dialogue between Jesus and his disciples is conducted and also the scene in the Garden of Gethsemane. A similar arrangement of the playing area is indicated in the *Ludus Coventriae*, in which Annas, Caiaphas and Pilate each have separate scaffolds. The interior of the house in which the Last Supper takes place can be, probably through the use of a curtain, quickly concealed or revealed ('and þan xal þe place þer cryst is in xal sodenly unclose rownd Abowtyn shewyng cryst syttyng at þe table and his dyscypulys eche in ere degre . . .' *Ludus Coventriae*, Passion Play 1, stage direction following 669). The same contrivance for concealing or revealing an interior scene is used for the oratory erected in the very middle of 'the place' ('here þe buschopys with here clerkys and þe pharaseus mett in þe myd place and þer xal be a lytil oratory with stolys and cusshonys cleynly be-seyn lych as it were a cownsel hous . . .'; '. . . and in þe mene tyme þe cownsel hous beforn-seyd xal sodenly onclose shewyng þe buschopys prestys and jewgys syttyng in here Astat lyche as it were A convocacyone.' (*Ludus Coventriae*, Passion Play 1, stage directions following 124 and 397.) In *The Conspiracy* of the Wakefield Cycle scenes are similarly concealed and revealed thus enabling action to pass swiftly from, say, Pilate's hall to the Last Supper. At (559) where the action turns from Mount Olivet to Pilate's hall, there is no need for the drawing of a curtain to conceal Jesus and the three disciples; when Pilate is sending out his soldiers to apprehend Jesus, there is a tableau on Mount Olivet of Jesus praying and below him his three disciples sleeping, and this tableau is held until the action returns to Mount Olivet on (652).

The medieval dress worn by the actors in the mystery cycles is exemplified by the references to costume in the following stage directions from the *Ludus Coventriae*:

'Here xal annas shewyn hym-self in his stage be-seyn after a busshop of þe hoold lawe in a skarlet gowne and over þat a blew tabbard furryd with whyte and a mytere on his hed after þe hoold lawe. ij doctorys stondyng by hym in furryd hodys and on be-forn hem with his staff of A-stat and eche of hem on here hedys a furryd cappe with a gret knop in þe crowne and on stondyng be-forn as a sarazyn þe wich xal be his masangere . . .'

(*The Passion Play* 1, following John the Baptist's Prologue.)

'here goth þe masangere forth and in þe mene tyme cayphas shewyth him-self in his skafhald Arayd lych to Annas savyng his tabbard xal be red furryd with white ij doctorys with hym arayd

with pellys aftyr þe old gyse and furryd cappys on here hedys . . .'
(*The Passion Play* I, following (44).)

'here jhesus with his dyscipulis goth in-to þe place and þer xal come
in A x personys weyl be-seen in white Arneys and breganderys
(body armour) and some dysgysed in odyr garmentys with swerdys
gleyvys (spears) and other straunge wepone as cressettys with feyr
and lanternys and torchis lyth. . . .'
(*The Passion Play* I, following 972.)

Annas and Caiaphas of the Wakefield Cycle would also be dressed
as medieval bishops. The last extract referring to the lighted torches
corresponds to a similar stage effect in the Wakefield play (599, 611,
612). Medieval iconographic representations of the capture of
Jesus almost invariably depict weapons and lanterns or torches held
aloft.

Apart from these torches and a variety of weapons, essential properties are also the thirty silver pennies, perhaps most conveniently
contained in a glove, as in the *Ludus Coventriae Conspiracy* (625, 626),
and also the bowl and towel for the washing of feet, Pilate's sword
(575), Peter's sword (681), and the cord with which Jesus is bound and
by which he is dragged away at the end of the play. Pilate, who, like
the other tyrants in the Cycle, is given to laying about him in his
frequent fits of fury, might be allotted, as in the Coventry *Corpus
Christi* Plays, a club and balls, stuffed with wool and covered with
leather (Hardin Craig, *Two Coventry Corpus Christi Plays*, p. 96).

THE BUFFETING

The action of this play is continuous with the
last, and indeed this is so of the whole Passion
sequence of plays. One play flows directly into
another. At the end of *The Conspiracy* the action
is swept from Pilate's hall to Caiaphas' hall where
The Buffeting takes place. At the end of *The
Buffeting* the action returns to Pilate's hall, and the
dialogue appears deliberately included to cover
these journeys. For instance in *The Buffeting* the
Torturers drive Jesus for forty-five lines, bitterly
complaining of the distance they have to cover to
Caiaphas' hall (40–41), and their return journey to Pilate's hall is
covered at the beginning of *The Scourging* by Pilate's fifty-two line
prologue.

[89]

The medieval practice of having completely different casts for each play, while serving admirably for a production staged on pageants moving from station to station through a city, might be less satisfactory for performances given in a single area, employing 'the place' and a series of fixed pageants set in a circle or semi-circle on the periphery of 'the place'. Continuity of action, which is strongly suggested here by the sequence of the Passion plays, is surely strengthened by continuity of actors.

In *The Buffeting* the references to the Torturers leading Jesus from Pilate's to Caiaphas' hall suggest movement in 'the place'. Such stage movement is explicit in the *Ludus Coventriae* direction, 'here þei ledyn jhesu A-bowt þe place tyl þei come to þe halle' (*Passion Play* II, following 244). When the procession reaches Caiaphas' hall the two priests are seated on thrones (46). Acting as false witnesses the Torturers stand on the pageant by the priests' thrones and, when given the word, they drag Jesus back into 'the place' just below the pageant, so that the priests may enjoy the ensuing action (337) and, making a ring round Jesus (325), administer the buffeting. Following this, not needing to mount the pageant, they lead Jesus to its edge (415) and receive their orders from Caiaphas to take their victim to Pilate (425). It is for Pilate's hall, too, that Annas and Caiaphas leave at the end of the play.

The Torturers play with Jesus the game of Hot Cockles. They sit him on a foot-stool or 'light buffet' (351), an obvious pun; Froward begins to blindfold him but leaves the final touch, and consequently 'Christ's curse', to the Second Torturer. The bandage is taken off by Froward on (412) 'But tell us no lie', which coincides with the culmination of the Torturers' brutality. Their weapons for the buffeting may well have been leather casings, stuffed with wool, set on wooden handles.

Caiaphas is infuriated that Jesus stands beyond the range of his blows (299) but he has access to other weapons that will reach. He carries a dagger in his belt (281, 444) and it is only the strongest persuasion from Annas that prevents him using it. Both he and Annas wear on their fingers bishops' rings. Caiaphas will not bless the torturers with his ring (340) until he has discovered which of them delivers the harshest blows.

Jesus' description of how he shall return to earth (253, 254) may be interpreted as a stage direction relevant to both *The Ascension* and *The Judgement*. A wooden miniature in the museum at Chartres shows Jesus attached to a blue cloud which can be raised or lowered.

The Scourging

All the other English mystery cycles contain at this stage the scene of *Christ's Trial Before Herod*. There are signs that at one time such a play had its place in the Wakefield Cycle also: the First Torturer makes his entry with the words 'I have run till I sweat from sir Herod our king' (53), and Pilate himself says 'Herod, true as any stone, could find no fault in him' (99). In the manuscript, however, there is no obvious omission between *The Buffeting* and *The Scourging*, and if such a Herod play did exist, then on some subsequent revision of the Cycle it was deliberately omitted. As mentioned before in reference to the previous play, the dramatic action from *The Buffeting* to *The Scourging* may be treated as continuous.

The Torturers' initial dialogue extends over thirty lines (53–82) before they reach Pilate's hall. Their path probably lies through 'the place', where they have to ask for room to be made for them to pass (62) before they can confront Pilate sitting on his dais (82, 184). On the pageant level Jesus is bound to a pillar (130) and beaten, the Torturers making, as they did in *The Buffeting*, a ring round their victim (227). When Jesus is unbound he is thrust again into 'the place' where he moves slowly and painfully with the cross over his shoulder.

The scene between John and the Marys may be played on a pageant or in another part of 'the place'. The meeting between this group and Jesus' procession is best staged in 'the place', from where both groups move towards that most important pageant which is to represent Calvary.

A bowl, water and towel will be required for the washing of Pilate's hands (216). An even more refined touch is introduced in the York *Judgement of Jesus* (443), when Pilate's Beadle says 'Will ye wash while the water is hot?' Other cycles specify that a white garment is put on Jesus after the buffeting and a purple one after the scourging, but no such indication exists in the Wakefield Cycle. The cross itself is the major property of the whole cycle. It is required to be strong enough and large enough to support the body of a man, and yet not too heavy for a man to carry, or at least drag, with some ease. The scourges themselves may be made of long strips of felt set on short wooden stocks.

Maximum dramatic effect might be gained from the Torturers'

persuasion of Simon of Cyrene to take up the cross, if they adopt an unwonted politeness in their preliminary overtures to him (361–390) which explodes into violence and compulsion (391). The force of

> As ye have said, I am well paid,
> This man his pain to spare.   (401–402.)

is brought home when Simon, having shouldered the cross, looks for the first time into Jesus' face.

THE HANGING OF JUDAS

This play, which is incomplete, appears at the very end of the manuscript and is written in a sixteenth-century hand. It is a poem rather than a drama, and even in its complete form it seems probable that the monologue would have been sustained throughout. Classical, biblical, and romantic elements meet together in what must be one of the strangest fragments in the Mystery Cycles. Judas looks into his past for, as it were, a psychological justification of his actions, and he sees there not only the 'Oedipus complex' but Oedipus himself.

The more usual interpretation of this theme as, for instance, in the York Cycle and the *Ludus Coventriae*, is centred on the action which stems from Judas' remorse at his betrayal of Christ, his return to the high priests, offering back the money and pleading for Jesus' release, and their contemptuous rejection. The biblical conclusion comes in the *Ludus Coventriae* stage direction (*Passion Play* II, following 236) 'þan judas castyth down þe mony and goth and hangyth hymself.'

THE CRUCIFIXION

The play begins with a prologue spoken by Pilate in his own pageant. The procession to Calvary, as at the end of *The Scourging* continues on its way. By approximately line forty-seven the procession establishes itself on or near the pageant which is to represent Mount Calvary. The nailing of Jesus to the cross calls for considerable space, and it might be advisable to group the majority of the onlookers, while this action is taking place, at the foot of the pageant. Indeed it would be extremely difficult and even dangerous for any other action to be taking place on the pageant until the cross is raised (232).

[92]

It is evident that Pilate is located initially in an entirely different area from Calvary, because each time there is communication between him and a group from Calvary a journey appears necessary (544 and 619–620). It appears that Pilate crosses from his pageant and places the superscription on the cross while the torturers are haggling over Jesus' clothing (498–515). How Pilate manages to place what he has written on the cross above Christ's head is a staging problem on which the Wakefield text is completely unhelpful. In the Chester *Christ's Passion* (stage direction following l. 600), Pilate orders a soldier to fix the superscription before the cross is raised, a device not easily transferred to the Wakefield play. The *Ludus Coventriae,* however, faces the staging difficulty squarely and deals with it in a way that may be of help to the producer of the Wakefield text:

'here xal pylat Askyn penne and inke and A tabyl xal be take hym wretyn Afore hic est jhesus nazarenus rex judeorum. and he xal make hym to wryte and þan gon up on A leddere and settyn þe tabyl abovyn crystys hed. . . .'

(*Ludus Coventriae, Passion Play* II, following l. 853.)

The Torturers who cross from Calvary to Pilate's pageant (545) in a violently querulous mood are quelled by Pilate's own aggression and return (560–562) to their vicious taunting of Jesus.

All the cycles include Longeus being cured of his blindness. The detail of the miracle, obscure in the Wakefield play, is explicit elsewhere. Longeus, his spear-hand guided, thrusts at Jesus' heart. The blood falls from the wound on to Longeus' hands which he puts to his eyes and is so healed of his affliction.

Joseph of Arimathea and Nicodemus, witnesses of the crucifixion, approach the cross when the Torturers withdraw (612). They go together from Calvary to Pilate's pageant at the end of or during Nicodemus' speech (625–630). On their return to Calvary they take Jesus down from the cross, Joseph using long pincers to extract the nails (648). In this they may be glad of assistance from Simon of Cyrene and John the Evangelist. The detail of the deposition is most graphically described in the *Ludus Coventriae,* Passion Play II, stage directions following l. 1131 and l. 1139:

'an joseph doth set up þe lederys and nychodemus comyth to help hym.'

'here joseph and nychodemus takyn cryst of þe cros on on o ledyr and þe tother on An-other leddyr and qwan is had down joseph leyth hym in oure ladys lappe. . . .'

[93]

Joseph and Nicodemus carry Jesus out of the acting area. The burial is not enacted in full view of the audience. Indeed, if at some stage the action and the actors of this cycle were continuous, the playwright seems here to have shown as much concern for resting his main character, after what is in effect a most severe physical ordeal, as Shakespeare in relaxing the burden on his tragic protagonist in the fourth act. Jesus does not appear in *The Talents*, the play following *The Crucifixion*. On the other hand any producer of this cycle must concern himself with placing the intervals in relationship to the development of the drama. The end of *The Crucifixion* is a possible choice. The Cornish Plays which extended over three days, brought their second day to an end with *The Crucifixion*.

> The blessing of Jesus on ye ever,
> And that always I pray.
> Go ye all on the side of home,
> The Play is ended;
> And come early
> To-morrow, I pray you,
> To see how Christ rose
> Out of the tomb, bright and gentle.

(*The Ancient Cornish Drama*, Volume 1, p. 477, translated by Edwin Norris.)

The complicated business of nailing Jesus to the cross might be managed as follows: Jesus lies down on the cross with the First, Second, and Third Torturers at his right hand and the Fourth Torturer at his left hand (118); the Second and Third Torturers tie a cord to his right hand, which they stretch out along the cross and nail down (134); the First Torturer goes to help the Fourth Torturer with the left hand at (129); at (140) the Second Torturer goes to the knees and the Third Torturer goes to help the Second Torturer with stretching out the knees at (143); the Fourth Torturer leaves the left hand and goes to Jesus' feet at (143); the Third Torturer hammers the nail into the feet at (157), after which all pull at the left hand, which the Fourth Torturer hammers down (202).

The four of them raise the cross vertically between (202) and (215) and on (224), with it still vertical, lift it towards the mortice and place it in (225). On (230) they shake the cross, lift it out of the mortice slightly and let it fall back into position. By (232) it should be firmly established and, if necessary, wedged. The horseplay of (308) can be mere pretence of lifting, shaking, and letting the cross fall once more.

Jesus is supported on the cross by the ropes round his arms and feet. A small ledge should support his feet, and wooden pegs in the cross between thumb and finger help to distribute the strain. If some nails are already half sunk into the cross, the Torturers at the appropriate time can give a very much more realistic impression of zestful hammering.

END OF PART THREE

Part Four

The Twenty-sixth Play: The Talents

PILATE   2ND TORTURER (SPELL PAIN)
1ST TORTURER   3RD TORTURER
                         COUNSELLOR

PILATE
Cernite qui statis quod mire sim probitatis,
Hec cognoscatis vos cedam ni taceatis,
Cuncti discatis quasi sistam vir deitatis
Et maiestatis michi fando ne neceatis,
    Hoc modo mando;
  Neve loquaces,
  Sive dicaces,
  Poscite paces,
    Dum fero fando.

Stint, I say! Men give place, *quia sum dominus domi-*
                                [norum!
He that dares me outface *rapietur lux ocvlorum;*
Therefore give ye me space *ne tendam vim brachiorum,*
And then get ye no grace, *contestor Iura polorum,*
    Caveatis;
  Rule I in Jewry,
  Maxime pure,
  Town *quoque rure,*
    Me paveatis.

Stemate regali, King Atus begat me of Pila;
Tramite legali, I am ordained to reign in Judah,
Nomine vulgari, Pontius Pilate who holds you in awe,
Qui bene vult fari should call me founder of all law.
    Iudeorum
  Iura guberno,
  Please me and say so,
  Omnia firmo
    Sorte deorum.

Mighty lord of all, *me Caesar magnificavit;*   28
Down on your knees ye fall, great God *me sanctificavit,*
Me to obey over all, *regi reliquo quasi* David,
Hanged high be the thrall *hoc iussum qui reprobavit,*
    I swear now;
    And be your head
    Bare in this stead,
    Lest my sword turn red;
    Beware now!

Atrox armipotens I grant men peace by my good grace,
Atrox armipotens, most mighty called in every place,
Vir quasi cunctipotens, I grant men peace by my good
    [grace,
Tota refert huic gens, that none is worthier in the face,
Quin eciam bona mens, truth and right my true laws
    [trace,

    Silete!
    In generali,
    Sic speciali,
    Yet again bid I
    Iura tenete.

Look that no boy be boisterous, no blast here to blow,
But truly to my talking hear my harangue;
If here be any boy that will not our law follow,
By mighty Mohammed, high shall he hang;
    South, north, east and west,
In all this world in breadth and length,
    Is none so doughty as I, the best,
On foot or horse who strikes with strength.

    Therefore I say,
Look ye incline to my liking,
Or a clout ye will get for your grieving,
Diligently comply to my pleasing,
    As prince most mighty me pay.

    Say nought, by this sword;
For who stirs or any din makes
The ash of my anger he rakes,
If as sovereign me he not takes
    And as his own lord.

[2]

65   He is master of his night's rest that naps not at noon-
                                                             [tide!
            Boy, lay me down softly and wrap me well from cold;
            Look that no lads annoy me with crying nor crooning,
            Nor in my sight none grieve me so bold.
            If there be any boys that make any cry,
            Or else that will not obey me,
            They were better be hanged up high,
            Than in my sight once move me.

1ST TORTURER Look to! For now come I,
            The most curst in this country;
            Full fast in haste here run have I,
                Hither to this town;
            To this town now come have I
            From the mount of Calvary:
            There Christ hung, and that full high,
                I swear here by my crown.

            At Calvary when he hanged was,
            I spued and spat right in his face,
            When that it shone as any glass
                So seemly to my sight;
            But yet for all that fair thing
            I laughed at him in hating,
            Robbed him of his clothing,
                To me it was but right.

            And when his clothes were off together,
            Lord, we so laughed, and made good cheer,
            And crowned that churl with a briar,
                As he had been a king;
            And yet I did full properly,
            I clapped his corpse by and by,
            I thought I did full curiously
                In faith him for to hang.

            But to Mohammed I make a vow,
            Hither have I brought his clothing now,
            To try the truth before you,
                Even this same night;
            Of me and of my fellows two

                        [3]

To whom these garments ought to go;   102
But sir Pilate must cast lot too,
   I tell you by this light.

For whosoever may get these clothes,
Need reck never where he goes,
To him good fortune flows,
   If so that he them wear.

But now, good fellows of renown,
Because the devil comes to town,
Let us rumour up and down,
   Of our most gracious gear.

2ND TORTURER Make way, before I knock you down!
For I must meet my mates in town,
And I shall clout him on the crown
   That dares stand in my way;
By leaps and bounds I needs must flit,
As though I now had lost my wit;
My breeches I had almost shit,
   So great was my delay.

But, by Mohammed! Now am I here!
The most accursed, that dare I swear,
That ye shall find anywhere,
   Spell pain my name, a knight
That was at Calvary this same day,
Where the King of Jews lay,
And there I taught him a new play,
   Truly I thought it right.

The play we lately had in town,
That he should lay his head low down,
And straight I bobbed him on the crown,
   That game methought was good.
When we had played with him our fill,
Then led we him unto a hill,
And there we wrought with him our will,
   And hung him on a rood.

No more now of this talking,
But the cause of my coming,

[4]

139   As token meet for promising
        This coat I would I had;
    For if I might this coat entreat,
    Then my joy would be complete,
    I would even fast from drink and meat,
        In faith as I were mad.

3RD TORTURER   Out, alas! how do ye crones,
    Haste have I made to break my bones!
    I have burst both my bollock stones,
        So fast I hurried hither;
    Nothing gives me such relief
    As murder a cut-purse or hang a thief;
    If here be any that cause me grief
        I shall thrash them altogether;

    For I swear in any sin
    I am the worst of all my kin,
    That is from this town unto Lynn,
        Here my two fellows, lo!
    Now have we three come in
    A new game for to begin,
    This same coat for to win,
        Before we further go.

    Now to sir Pilate, I guess, that we go before,
    And give him the cause why hither we gad;
    But this gown that is here, I tell you therefore,
    By mighty Mohammed I would not he had.
1ST TORTURER   I assent to those words by Mohammed's renown!
    Let us go to sir Pilate and tell him no fable;
    But, sirs, on my oath, he gets not this gown;
    Among us three we count it profitable;
        Spell pain what sayst thou?

2ND TORTURER   Your cunning counsel I assent to now.
1ST TORTURER   Then will I straightway in this place,
    Speak to Pilate, if he allow,
    For I am seemly and fair of face;
    And we shall profit, that I vow.
3RD TORTURER   Sir, tell me, by my loyalty,
    Where that prince, sir Pilate, is?

[5]

COUNSELLOR	Sir, as might I thrive, I tell thee,	177
	He lies here in the devil's service.	
1ST TORTURER	With that prince—foul him befall—	
	Must we have to do.	
COUNSELLOR	I shall go to him and call,	
	What ye would say to him, look to.	

My lord, my lord!

PILATE	What boy, let once suffice!
	Call no more, thou hast called twice.
COUNSELLOR	My lord!
PILATE	What mite of grievance moves me in my mind?
COUNSELLOR	I, lord, your counsellor, come to entreat you go.
PILATE	Are there any traitors, or plots of any kind?
COUNSELLOR	Nay, lord, none that I know.
PILATE	Annoy us no more with this noise;
	You careless curs, who bad you call me?
	By your mad mothers you are but boys,
	That ye shall abuy, else foul befall me.
	I shall not die in your debt!
	Come sir, I bid that up thou take me,
	And in my seat me softly set.

Now shall we know and that right now,
If that be true what thou did say;
If lies be told, pay for it shalt thou,
For meddling in matters of law today.

COUNSELLOR	Nay sir, not so, without delay,
	The cause of my calling is of that boy bold,
	For it is said forsooth now this same day,
	That he should die in doleful pain;
	For certain
	Then may your cares grow cold
	If guiltless he be slain.
PILATE	Fair and softly, sir, and say not too much;
	Seem to be sorry, then truth shows the less,
	The law look thou study, show deference to such,
	Lest I grieve thee greatly with buffets express;
	False fellow, in faith I shall slay thee!

[6]

214   Thy reasons so reckless thou had better redress,
Or meddle no more with these matters, I pray thee.

COUNSELLOR   Why should I not mention what I have you taught?
Though ye be prince Pilate without any peer,
Were it not for my wisdom, your wits come to
[nought;
As is seen expressly and plainly right here,
Else be ye misled.

PILATE   Why, boy, but has thou said?
COUNSELLOR   Yea, lord.
PILATE   Therefore, the devil thee speed, thou churl, thou thing!
Tales of such fellows are laughed at abroad!
The behaviour ye know not that belongs to a king.

1ST TORTURER   Mohammed most mighty, make glad your reign,
Sir Pilate, peerless prince, all your days,
And save you sir, sitting, so seemly a sovereign!
We have come to your hall along hazardous ways,
But this must be said:
Ye know whom he doomed this day upon dais,
We fear not his doing for now is he dead.

PILATE   Ye are welcome indeed, right worthy ye are;
If that traitor be dead, that deed makes for my gain.
2ND TORTURER   We have done for that dotard, no more shall he mar;
We prayed you, sir Pilate, to put him to pain,
And we thought it well wrought.

PILATE   Leave sirs, from such words look ye refrain;
For the part I played name ye it nought.
3RD TORTURER   Make mirth of that meddler as much as we may,
And love more our lives for loss of that lad;
But, sir Pilate peerless, one point I thee pray;
Have ye hope in your heart that harness he had
To hold that was his?
PILATE   That belongs unto me, by my faith! Art thou mad?
I meant in no manner you men to have this.

1ST TORTURER   Move thee not, master, though more he may ask,
Nor part from our pilfering however he plead.

[7]

PILATE   Start not so aback nor be so aghast;   249
                This gown as a gift I would you decreed;
                It may make profit for you.
2ND TORTURER Wherefore this flattery? You have made known your
                                                           [need,
                But it falls first to us four before you.

PILATE   My needs are no man's business but mine.
3RD TORTURER   Yea, lord, let us tear it in shreds.
PILATE   Now to that I agree, take thou this, and thou that,
                And this shall be thine,

                And by warrant of law this is left still.
1ST TORTURER   Oh, lording! We do this all wrong,
                In good time I took it, if we follow thy will,
                   The fairest parts to thee, the foulest to us belong.

PILATE   And thou art paid for thy part full truly I trust.
1ST TORTURER   It is shame for to see, I am left but a shred.
2ND TORTURER That the whole of this harness be yours is unjust,
                   If I am left but a scrap with scarcely a thread,
                      So tattered and torn.
3RD TORTURER   By mighty Mohammed, of our faith the head,
                      If he escape with this coat it would give us
                                                           [great scorn.

PILATE   Now since ye fret so at this, take it to you
                   With all my spite and that of Mohammed's re-
                                                           [nown!
1ST TORTURER Dread ye not doubtless, for so will we do;
                   Grieve ye not greatly, ye get not this gown,
                      But in four as it falls.
2ND TORTURER For a falchion to cut it despite Pilate's frown!
3RD TORTURER   Lo, one is here for whoever calls.

                It is sharp to cut with, shear if thou may.
2ND TORTURER   Even in the middle to mark the mastery for me.
1ST TORTURER Most seemly it is for certain the seam to assay.
2ND TORTURER I have sought all this side and none can I see,
                      Great or small.
PILATE   Bashirs, abide you, I bid you let be!
                   I command not to cut it, but keep it whole all.

[8]

THE TALENTS 369

1ST TORTURER	Now are we bound, because ye bad, to do as ye tell?
PILATE	Out! Harlots! Go hang you, for whole shall it be.
3RD TORTURER	Grieve you not greatly, he meant it but well.
PILATE	Had I thought that he spoke then in scorn of me,
287	Swift had I struck then to kill him.
2ND TORTURER	That would grieve him, my lord, on my loyalty,
	Therefore grant him your grace.
PILATE	No grievance I will him.

1ST TORTURER	Grammercy thy goodness!
PILATE	But grieve me no more, look to!
	Full dear is it bought
	In faith, if ye do.

1ST TORTURER	Shall I then save it?
PILATE	Yea, so say I, but to draw lots is best,
	And lo, who gets the long cut shall win.
3RD TORTURER	We agree to your saying and put it to test;
	Let one now assay, but who shall begin?

PILATE	Ye follow after, the first falls to me.
2ND TORTURER	Nay, dread you not doubtless, for that do ye nought
	O, he seeks to deceive us that plainly we see.
3RD TORTURER	Good fellows, give ear, I have here brought
	Three fine dice along.
1ST TORTURER	That is of all games the best, by him that me bought,
	For at dicing he does us no wrong.

PILATE	And I am glad of that game; one assay, who shall
	[begin?
1ST TORTURER	First shall ye, and then after we all.
	Have the dice and have done,
	And leave all your din,
	For whoso throws most this garment may call
	His own and the dice.
PILATE	I assent to your saying, assay now I shall,
	As I would at one throw win all in a trice.
PILATE *throws.*	
2ND TORTURER	Ah! Ha! How now! Here are a heap.
PILATE	Have mind then among you how many there are.
3RD TORTURER	Thirteen among three, that score ye may keep.
PILATE	Then shall I win or many men mar.

[9]

1ST TORTURER   Truly, lord, so may it befall;   319
                But grieve you not greatly, your joy I may jar,
                If fortune attend me, have here for all!
He throws.
PILATE   And I have seen as great a knight of his promise failed.
                I count but eight for all your groans.
1ST TORTURER   Eight? by his arms, that is all! Whatever me ailed!
                I was falsely beguiled with these bitched bones;
                    There cursed they be!
2ND TORTURER   He gets not the garment who these dice disowns,
                I fain would this fortune might fall unto me.

PILATE   An ill affair, in faith, if thou won.
2ND TORTURER   No, but stand out of my way.
He throws.
3RD TORTURER   By Mohammed's bones, this is ill done!
                Seven is but the second, the sooth for to say.
2ND TORTURER   Woe, fie! That is short.
3RD TORTURER   Go shoot at thy hood! Now I should be first,
                If I have luck for this gown, and goes all good;
                    Bitched bones be as I bid ye or be curst!
He throws.
                Fellows, as I forecast here have I fifteen!
                As ye know I am worthy this gown for to win.
PILATE   What, whistle ye and the moon waning! Where have
                                                        [ye been?
                Thou shalt abuy that throw, have done your din!
3RD TORTURER   Here be men in this throng,
                Loyal to our law, not scared of their skin,
                And witness they may if I wrought any wrong.
1ST TORTURER   Thou wrought no deceit, forsooth, that we know,
                Therefore thou art worthy and gained the gown at thy
                                                        [own will.
PILATE   Yea, but I play not the game with a puff or a blow;
                I reck not nor reason if right be his skill,
                    I grudge it him nought.
3RD TORTURER   Have good day, sir, and grieve you not ill,
                For if it were double full dear is it bought.
PILATE   Sir, since thou hast won this gown, wilt thou vouch-
                                                        [safe, say,
                To give of thy goodness this garment to me?
3RD TORTURER   Sir, this shall ye not have, I say thee nay.

[10]

PILATE   Thou shalt repent with no delay,
355   Fie, what art thou free?
                Accursed then remain!
3RD TORTURER   For your threats go through me,
                Were there such three
                I'd give them you truly.
     Gives the garment to PILATE.
PILATE   Now, grammercy, again!
                Many thanks, and have mind of a payment.
1ST TORTURER   But I had not left it so lightly if play my way went.
PILATE   No, but he is faithful and free, as truly I meant,
                And more if I may,
                If of me he have need,
                To him shall I heed.
3RD TORTURER   I vouchsafe it be so, the sooth for to say.

1ST TORTURER   Now these dice are unworthy for the loss of this good,
                Here I forswear heartily, by Mohammed's blood;
                For I was never so happy in mind or in mood,
                To win with such subtlety my very life's food,
                     As ye ken;
                These dicers and these drabbers,
                These boozers and these brawlers,
                And all purse-cutters,
                     Be well warned of these men.

2ND TORTURER   Fie, fie, on these dice, may the devil them take!
                Unwitty, unwise, to set all on a stake;
                As may fortune devise to mar or to make;
                Men she can make rise, or downhill them take;
                     The rich
                She turns upside-down,
                The poor gain a crown,
                Most chief in renown
                     She casts in the ditch.

                By her means she makes dicers to sell,
                As they play at their stakes, their corn and their cattle;
                Then with cries and with crakes they are ready for
                                                            [battle,
                His oven then bakes no simnel
                     As it used.

                          [11]

But farewell, thrift!   391
Is there none other shift
But a sweet lady's gift?
    These dicers are confused.

3RD TORTURER   What comes of dicing I pray you hark after,
    But loss of goods in playing and often men's slaughter!
    Thus sorrow is at parting, if at meeting there be
                  [laughter;
    Better leave such vain thing and serve God hereafter,
      For heaven's bliss;
    That Lord is most mighty,
    And gentlest of Jewry,
    We hold him as holy;
      How think ye of this?

PILATE   Well worthy all three, most doughty indeed!
    Of all scholars I know, most cunning ye be,
    Your sayings of subtlety, your laws kept dutifully;
    I grant you full power and friendship freely,
      I say;
    Dieu vous garde, monseigneurs!
    Mohammed most mighty in castles and towers
    He keep you, lordings, and all yours,
      And have all good day.

The Twenty-seventh Play:
The Deliverance of Souls

JESUS	MOSES
ADAM	RIBALD
EVE	BEELZEBUB
SYMEON	DAVID
JOHN THE BAPTIST	SATAN
	ISAIAH

JESUS   My father me from bliss did send
    To earth for mankind's sake,
Adam's misdeed to amend,
    My death I needs must take.

[12]

5   I dwelt there thirty years and two
                And something more, the truth to say:
           In anguish, pain, and bitter woe,
                I died on cross this day.

           Therefore to hell now will I go,
                To challenge what is mine;
           Adam and Eve and more to show,
                That there no longer need they pine.

           The fiend beguiled them with a lie,
                Through fraud of earthly food,
           Redeemed I have them truly,
                By the shedding of my blood.

           And now I will that place restore,
                Which the fiend fell from for sin;
           Some token will I send before,
                With mirth they may their games begin.

           A light I would they saw,
                To know that soon I come;
           My body in death's maw
                Lies till this be done.

ADAM   My brothers, hearken to me here!
                More hope of health never we had;
           Four thousand and six hundred year
                Have suffered we this darkness sad;
           See signs of solace now appear,
           A glorious gleam to make us glad,
           Whereby I hope that help is near,
                That soon shall slake our sorrows sad.

EVE   Adam, my husband kind,
                This means solace certain;
           Such light did we find
                In paradise full plain.

ISAIAH   Adam, through thy sin
                Here were we put to dwell,
           This wicked place within;
                The name of it is hell;

[13]

Pain's wheel ay shall spin
For those wicked and fell,
To love that Lord begin,
Whose life for us would sell.

And all shall sing "The Saviour of the World", the first verse.

Adam, thou well understand
I am Isaiah, as God me sent.
I spake of folk in a dark land,
And said a light should them be lent;
This light now comes at Christ's command,
Which he to us has hither sent,
Thus my point is proved in hand,
As prophet preached I this event.

SYMEON So might I marvels more reveal,
For in the temple I saw him stand,
And grew in grace with him to deal,
And clasped him homely with my hand;
I said, Lord, let thy servant loyal
Pass in peace to life's far strand;
Thy salvation now I feel,
No longer long to live in land.

This light thou hast purveyed
For them that live in need;
What I before of thee have said
I see it is fulfilled indeed.

JOHN THE My crying voice did recommend
BAPTIST The ways of Christ for men to scan;
I baptized him as my dear friend
In water of river Jordan;
The holy ghost did then descend
As white as dove's down on me then;
The father's voice, our mirth to amend,
Was made for me like as a man;

"Yond is my son", he said,
"Who pleases me full well."
His light is on us laid,
He comes our cares to quell.

[14]

Moses   Now this same night great news have I,
78   To me, Moses, he showed his might,
                   And to another prophet truly,
                   Where on a hill we stood at height;
                   As white as snow was his body,
                   His face was like the sun so bright,
                   No man on earth was so mighty
                   Who dared look against that light;

                   And that same light here see I now
                   Shining on us, certain,
                   Whereby truly I avow
                   That we shall soon pass from this pain.

Ribald   Since first that hell was made, and I was put therein,
                   Such sorrow never I had, nor heard I such a din;
                   My joys begin to fade, my wit waxes thin,
                   No longer be we glad, these souls we cannot win.
                   How Beelzebub! Bind these boys, such harrow was never
                                                    [heard in hell!
Beelzebub Out Ribald! Thou roars, what is betid? Can thou ought
                                                    [tell?
Ribald   Why, hearest thou not this ugly noise?
                   These lubbers that in limbo dwell,
                   They make meaning of many joys,
                        And mirth makes them to swell.

Beelzebub Mirth? Nay, nay! That point is past,
                   More hope of health shall they never have.
Ribald   They cry on Christ full fast,
                   And says he shall them save.

Beelzebub Yea, though he do not, I shall,
                        For they are sparred in special space;
                   Whilst I am prince and principal,
                        They shall never pass out of this place.
                   Call up Astaroth and Anabal,
                        To give us counsel in this case;
                   Bell, Berith, and Belial,
                        These men their mastery to outface.

[15]

Say to sir Satan, our sire,   III
    And bid him stir also
Sir Lucifer's ire.

RIBALD   All ready lord I go.

JESUS   *Attollite portas, principes, vestras et elevamini portae aeternales,*
et introibit rex gloriae.

RIBALD   Out, harrow, out! What devil is he
    That calls him king over us all?
Hark Beelzebub, with me,
    For hideously I heard him call.

BEELZEBUB   Go, spar the gates, ill might thou be!
    And set the watches on the wall;
If once that wretch we see
    Fight we till we fall.

And if he more call or cry,
    To make us more debate,
Lay on him lustily,
    And drive him from the gate.

DANIEL   Nay, with him may ye not fight,
    For he is king and conqueror,
And of so great a might
    Doughty in deeds and dour;
From him comes all this light
    That shines now in this bower;
He is full fierce in fight,
    Worthy to win honour.

BEELZEBUB   Honour! Hearest, thou harlot, for what deed?
    All earthly men to me are thrall;
That lad that thou calls Lord, indeed,
    Had never harbour, house, nor hall.

How, sir Satan, come thou near
    And hearken to this cursed rout!

SATAN   The devil, what is this I hear!
    What ails thee so to shout?
And me, if I come near,
    Thy brainpan shall I clout!

[16]

BEELZEBUB   Help bar the gate up here,
147   We are besieged about.
SATAN   Besieged about! Why, who durst be so bold
                    For fear to give us such a fray?
BEELZEBUB   It is the Jew that Judas sold
                    That died on cross this other day.

SATAN   How! In time that tale was told,
                    That traitor treats us ill each way;
                He shall be here full hard in hold,
                    But look he pass not, I thee pray.

BEELZEBUB   Pass, nay, nay, he will not void
                    From hence without a war;
                Nor pause till is destroyed
                    All hell in this uproar.

SATAN   Fie, fellows! Thereof shall he fail,
                    For all his fame I him defy;
                I know his tricks from top to tail,
                    He gloats on gauds and glory.
                Thereby he brought forth from our bale
                    The loathed Lazarus of Bethany,
                But to the Jews I gave counsel
                    That they should cause him die;

                I entered there into Judas,
                    That fortune to fulfil,
                Therefore his hire he has,
                    Always to live here still.

RIBALD   Sir Satan, since we hear thee say
                    Thou and the Jews came to assent,
                And knew that Lazarus he won away
                    That in our care was surely sent,
                Hopest thou the least him mar thou may
                    To mend the malice that he has meant?
                For if he rob us of our prey
                    We will chide ye ere he went.

SATAN   Be not at all dismayed
                    But boldly seek renown,

Call cunning to your aid,   182
    And ding that dastard down.

JESUS   *Attollite portas, principes, vestras et elevamini portae aeternales,*
                                                           [*et introibit rex gloriae.*

RIBALD   Out, harrow! What harlot is he
    That says such kingdom lies ahead?

DAVID   That may thou in psalter see,
    For of this prince thus ere I said;

    I said that he should break
        Your bars and bonds by name,
    On your works vengeance take;
        Now shalt thou see the same.

JESUS   Princes of hell open your gate,
        And let my folk forth go;
    The prince of peace comes in his state
        Whether ye will or no.

RIBALD   What art thou that speakest so?
JESUS   A king of bliss called Jesus.
RIBALD   Yea, hence fast I guess thou go,
    And meddle thou not with us.

BEELZEBUB Our gates I trust will last,
        Though strongly he assail;
    If but our bars hold fast
        They surely shall prevail.

JESUS   This place shall be no longer barred;
        Open up, and let my people pass.
RIBALD   Out harrow, our mirth is marred,
    And burst are all our bonds of brass!

BEELZEBUB Harrow! Our gates begin to quake!
        In sunder, I see them go,
    All hell I fear to shreds will shake.
        Alas, I wail with woe!

RIBALD   Limbo is lost, alas!
    Sir Satan see our loss;

[18]

215   This work is worse than ever it was.
SATAN   Yea, hanged be thou on a cross!

          Thieves, I bad ye show renown,
               If he made mastery more,
          To ding that dastard down,
               And beset him sad and sore.

BEELZEBUB Beset him sore, that is soon said!
               Come thou thyself and serve him so;
          This bitter battle we may dread,
               To more than us he would bring woe.

SATAN   Fie, fellow, wherefore have ye fled?
               Be bold to bandy blow for blow.
          Give me my gear, time now I sped,
               Myself shall to that gelding go.

          Now, thou hell-breaker, abide,
               For all thy champion's cheer!
          And tell me at this tide
               What mastery makest thou here?

JESUS   I make no mastery but for mine,
               I will them save, whom held hast thou;
          Thou hast no power to make them pine,
               In my prison I did allow
          Them to sojourn, nought as thine,
               But thy curst cunning knows just how.
SATAN   Where hast thou been that thy design
               Was not to come near them ere now?

JESUS   Now is the time certain
               My father ordained therefore,
          That they should pass from pain,
               In bliss to dwell for evermore.

SATAN   Thy father knew I well by sight,
               Carpentry he traded in;
          Mary, thy mother, named aright,
               The utmost end of all thy kin;
          Say who made thee wield such might?

[19]

JESUS   Thou wicked fiend, let be thy din!   250
My father lives in heaven's light,
And bides in endless bliss therein.

I am his only son, his promise to fulfil,
To confound thee I come, to sunder at my will.

SATAN   God's son! Nay, then might thou be glad,
For nothing need thou crave;
But thou hast lived ay like a lad,
In sorrow, as a simple knave.

JESUS   Ah, that was for the love I had
For man's soul, it for to save,
And thee to make amazed and mad,
And ruefully at these tidings rave.

My godhead was not shown
Save to that mother mine,
Whence never was it known
To thee nor none of thine.

SATAN   How now? Would this were told in town;
Thou says God is thy sire;
I shall prove by my renown
Thou moves astray as man in mire.
To break thy bidding these full soon
Had wrought most readily my desire;
From paradise thou put them down,
In hell here to have their hire;

And thou thyself by day and night,
Among men taught full long,
To follow reason and the right
But here thou workest all wrong.

JESUS   I work no wrong nor I teach it,
If I my men from woe will win;
My prophets plainly preach it,
All this business I begin;
Of hell they said I would breach it,
When that I should enter in,

[20]

285   To save my servants from that pit
        Where damnéd souls sit for their sin.

    And each true prophet's tale
        Shall be fulfilled in me;
    Redeemed now from their bale,
        In bliss now shall they be.

SATAN   Now since thou please to pass the laws,
        And boast ye be above all sin,
    For those that thou as witness draws
        Full plain against thee shall begin;
    As Solomon said in his saws,
        Who that once comes hell within
    Never shall escape its claws,
        Therefore, fellow, let be thy din.

    Job thy servant also
        In his time did tell
    That neither friend nor foe
        Shall find release from hell.

JESUS   He said full sooth, that shalt thou see,
        In hell shall be no more release,
    But of that place then meant he
        Where sinful care shall ay increase,
    In that bale ay shalt thou be,
        Where sundry sorrows never cease,
    And my folk that were most free
        Shall pass unto the place of peace;

    For they were here with my will,
        And so they shall forth wend;
    Thou shalt thyself full fill
        The cup of sorrow without end.

SATAN   Wilt thou then make me all forgo?
        Methinks thou art indeed unkind;
    Nay, I pray thee do not so;
        Bethink thee better in thy mind;
    Or else then let me with thee go,
        I pray thee leave me not behind!

[21]

JESUS   Nay, traitor, thou shalt live in woe,   321
        And to a stake I shall thee bind.

SATAN   Now hear I how thou meanst among
        Us all with malice to meddle;
    But since thou says it shall be long,
        Yet some let always with us dwell.

JESUS   Yes, know thou well, else were great wrong;
        Thou shalt have Cain that slew Abel,
    And all that hastes themselves to hang,
        As did Judas and Achitophel;

And Dathan and Abaron, and all of their assent,
Cursed tyrants every one, that me and mine torment.

And all that will not heed my law,
    That I have left in land as new,
That they may hold my name in awe,
    And all my sacraments pursue.

My death, my rising, hold in awe,
    Who believes them not they are untrue;
Under my doom I shall them draw,
    And judge them worse than any Jew.

And they that list to hear my law and live thereby,
Shall never have harm here, but wealth as is worthy.

SATAN   Have here my hand, I am well paid,
        This points to profit I avow.
    If this be true that thou hast said,
        We shall have more than we have now.
    These laws that late thou hast down laid,
        I shall them teach not to allow;
    If they believe they are betrayed,
        I quickly shall them trick somehow.

I shall walk east, I shall walk west,
    And work them fiercely, never fear.

JESUS   Nay fiend, fast in arrest,
        Thou stay, nor shall thou flit from here.

[22]

SATAN 356	Fast? Fie! That were a wicked treason! Fellow, I thee fiercely hit.
JESUS	Devil, I command thee down Into thy seat where thou shalt sit.
SATAN	Alas, for dole and care! I sink into hell pit!
RIBALD	Sir Satan, so said I ere, Now shalt thou have a fit.

JESUS

    Come now forth, my children all,
        Forgiven now what was amiss;
    With me now go ye shall
        To joy and endless bliss.

ADAM

    Lord, thou art full strong in might,
        So meek to come in this manner,
    To help us all the fiend to fight,
        When we had paid that forfeit dear;
    Here have we dwelt without a light
        Four thousand and six hundred year;
    Now see we by this solemn sight
        What means thy mercy to us here.

EVE

    Lord, we are worthy more torments to taste;
    But now, Lord, thy mercy will not lay us waste.

JOHN

    Lord, I love thee inwardly,
        Who me would make thy messenger,
    Thy coming on earth to cry,
        And teach thy faith both far and near;
    Since before thee I was to die,
        To bring them tidings that be here,
    How they should have God's help from high,
        Now see I all those points appear.

MOSES

    David, thy prophet true,
        Oft-times told unto us,
    Of thy coming he knew,
        And said it should be thus.

DAVID

    As I said ere yet say I so,
    "Ne derelinquas, domine,

[23]

Animam meam in inferno;"　　　　　　　　391
"Leave never my soul, Lord, after thee,
In deep hell where the damned shall go;
Suffer thou never thy saints to see
The sorrow of such as live in woe,
Ay full of fear, and may not flee."

MOSES　　Make mirth both more and less,
　　　　　And love our Lord we may,
　　　　That has brought us from bitterness
　　　　　In bliss to abide for ay.

ISAIAH　　Therefore now let us sing
　　　　　In love of Lord Jesus;
　　　　Unto his bliss he will us bring,
　　　　　Te deum laudamus.

They process out of hell-mouth.

The Twenty-eighth Play: The Resurrection

PILATE	4TH SOLDIER
CAIAPHAS	1ST ANGEL
CENTURION	2ND ANGEL
ANNAS	JESUS
1ST SOLDIER	MARY MAGDALENE
2ND SOLDIER	MARY JACOBI
3RD SOLDIER	MARY SALOME

Enter PILATE, ANNAS, CAIAPHAS, *and* SOLDIERS.

PILATE　　Peace, I warn you, if you have wit!
　　　　And stand aside or else go sit,
　　　　For here are men that go not yet,
　　　　　And lords of so great might;
　　　　We think to abide and not to flit,
　　　　　I tell you all in sight.

　　　　Spare your speech, ye bondmen bold,
　　　　And cease your cry till I have told

[24]

9   How my fame I shall unfold
        Here in this place;
      Who dares my due withhold,
        Hanged high be his bones apace.

      Know ye not that I am Pilate,
      That sat as Justice but of late,
      At Calvary where I was at
        This day at morn?
      I am he of so great state,
        Who saw that lad all torn.

      Now since that loathed lubber is dead,
      A great joy round me has spread,
      Therefore I would in every stead
        All should take heed,
      Lest any fellows his ways should tread,
        Or dare follow his lead.

      For if I knew it, cruelly
      His life is lost and that shortly,
      That he were better hung full high
        On gallows tree;
      Therefore ye prelates should espy
        If any such be.

      As I am man of might the most,
      If there be any that blow such boast,
      In keenest torments shall he roast
        For evermore;
      The devil to hell shall harry his ghost,
        But I say no more.

CAIAPHAS   Sir, ye need be nothing adread,
      The centurion in that stead,
      Guards as he has said
        To see that none offend;
      We left him there as man most wise,
      If any ribalds dare to rise,
      To seize them for the next assize,
        And then to make an end.

The CENTURION *enters on horseback.*   45

CENTURION   Ah, blessed Lord Adonai,
             What may this marvel signify
             That here was shown so openly
                 Unto our sight
             When did the righteous Jesus die
                 In our despite.

             All heaven seemed to swoon,
             Then ceased to shine both sun and moon,
             And dead men also rose up soon,
                 Out of their grave;
             Stones lay splintered and strewn
                 From wall and architrave.

             There was seen many a fearful sight,
             Our princes indeed, did nothing right,
             And so I said to stop their spite;
                 As it is true,
             That he was most of might,
                 The son of God, Jesu.

             Fowls in the air and fish in flood,
             That day changed their mood,
             When that he was rent on rood,
                 Lord Adonai;
             Full well they understood
                 That he was slain that day.
             Therefore right as I mean to them fast will I ride,
             And straight from them all glean what they will say this
                                                              [tide

                 Of this affray;
             I will no longer bide,
                 But fast ride on my way.

             God save you, sirs, on every side!
             Worship and wealth in world so wide!
PILATE   Centurion, welcome this tide,
                 Our comely knight!
CENTURION   God grant you grace well for to guide,
                 And rule you right.

                     [26]

PILATE 81	Centurion, welcome, draw near at hand! Tell tidings now for which we long, For ye have gone throughout our land, Ye know all still.
CENTURION	Sir, I fear me ye have done great wrong And wondrous ill.
CAIAPHAS	Wondrous ill? I pray thee why? Declare that to this company.

CENTURION	So shall I, sir, full surely,
	    With all my main;
	A righteous man is he, say I,
	    That ye have slain.

PILATE	Centurion, thy wit is raw;
	Ye are a great man of our law,
	And should we any witness draw,
	    Us to excuse,
	Ye should not now withdraw
	    And us refuse.

CENTURION	To maintain truth is well worthy;
	I said when I saw him die,
	That it was God's son almighty,
	    That hung there,
	So say I still and abide thereby,
	    Now and for ever.

ANNAS	Yea, sir, such reasons may ye rue, Thou should not name this thing anew But thou know some tokens true, Unto us tell.
CENTURION	Such sights of wonder never ye knew As then befell.
CAIAPHAS	We pray thee, tell us, of what thing?

CENTURION	The elements did themselves down fling,
	And in a manner made great mourning,
	    With strident breath;
	They knew by countenance that their king
	    Was done to death.

[27]

The sun for woe waxed all wan,   116
The moon and stars ceased shining on
The earth that trembled thereupon
    As though it spake;
Stones that never stirred, anon
    In sunder burst and brake.

        And dead men rose up bodily, both great and small.
PILATE   Centurion, beware withal!
The scholars the eclipse it call
    Such sudden sight;
That sun and moon a season shall
    Lack of their light.

CAIAPHAS   Sir, if dead men rise up bodily,
That may be done through sorcery,
Therefore we nothing set thereby,
    And nothing grieve.

CENTURION   Sir, that saw I truly,
    What I shall evermore believe.

Not that for each deed ye did work,
Not only that the sun grew murk,
But how the veil rent in the kirk,
    I gladly would know.

PILATE   Ah, such tales full soon would us irk,
    If they were told so.

Harlot, what the hole from where thou sprang
Amongst us with thy damned harangue?
Wend forth! High might thou hang,
    Vile traitor!
CAIAPHAS   Be off, before thou feel a bang,
    And hold still thy chatter!

CENTURION   Since your faith in me I must forgo, have now good
God lend you grace to know the truth alway.   [day!

ANNAS   Withdraw thee fast, if fear thou heed,
For we shall well maintain our deed.

[28]

CENTURION *withdraws.*

PILATE   Such wonderful reasons were never to read,
151   Now or before.
CAIAPHAS   To say such things, even or morn, we need
                  Never no more.

              But of more trouble to beware,
              That afterwards might cause us care,
              Therefore, sir, while ye are here
                    Among us all,
              Let us no counsel spare
                    What may befall.

CAIAPHAS   Now Jesus said full openly
              Unto the men that stood him by,
              A thing that grieves all Jewry,
                    And right so may,
              That he should rise up bodily
                    Within the third day.

              If it be so, as might I speed,
              Dread we then the latter deed
              More than the first, if we take heed
                    And tend thereto;
              Advise you, sir, for you have need,
                    What best to do.

ANNAS   Sir, nevertheless if he said so,
              He has no might to rise and go,
              Save his disciples steal also
                    His corpse away;
              That were for us a bitter blow,
                    A fearful fray.

              Then would the people say each one
              That he had raised himself alone;
              Give orders then to guard that stone
                    Which knights defend
              Till these three days be come and gone
                    And brought to end.

                        [29]

PILATE Now, certain, sir, full well ye say,   184
    And for this same point to purvey
    I shall, if that I may;
     He shall not rise,
    Nor none shall win him thence away
     In no wise.

    Sir knights, that are of deeds doughty,
    And chosen chief of chivalry,
    As I may herewith notify,
     By day and night
    Go ye and guard Jesu's body
     With all your might.

    And for what happen may,
    Guard him well until the third day,
    That no traitor steal his corpse away,
     Out of that stead;
    For if they do, truly I say,
     Ye shall be dead.

1ST SOLDIER Yes, sir Pilate, for certain,
    We shall guard with might and main;
    No traitor tricks us, that is plain,
     To steal him so;
    Get we what gear is for our gain,
     And let us go.

  They go to the tomb.

2ND SOLDIER No doubt we are the best in town
    To guard him for your great renown;
    Upon each side let us sit down,
     Altogether;
    And straightway I shall crack his crown
     Whoso comes hither.

1ST SOLDIER Who should be where, that would I know?
2ND SOLDIER Even on this side will I go.
3RD SOLDIER And at his feet I sit me so.
4TH SOLDIER And I shall stay quite near!
    Now by Mohammed, who dares to show
     Themselves in here

220   This corpse in treason for to take,
        Though dragon from a burning lake,
        Yet would I strike, make no mistake;
            Have here my hand;
        This corpse, though for three days we wake,
            Bides with our band.

Then the ANGELS *sing "Christus resurgens" and then* JESUS *speaks.*

JESUS   Earthly man, that I have wrought,
        Lightly wake, and sleep thou nought!
        With bitter bale I have thee bought,
            To make thee free;
        To this dungeon deep I am brought,
            And all for love of thee.

        Behold how dear I would thee buy!
        My wounds are wet and all bloody;
        Thee sinful man full dear bought I
            With cares most keen;
        Defile not now but fortify,
            Now thou art clean.

        Clean have I made thee, sinful man,
        With woe and wandering I thee won,
        From heart and side the blood out ran,
            Such pain was mine;
        Thou must love me that my life's span
            Gave for thine.

        Thou sinful man past me ye pace,
        Swiftly to me thou turn thy face,
        Behold my body, in each place,
            How sore a sight;
        Torn in this deep disgrace
            Man, for thy plight.

        With cords enough and coarse ropes tough
        My limbs outdrawn by fell Jews rough,
        For that I was not size enough
            Unto the bore;
        These deep wounds, man, and thy rebuff
            Suffered I therefore.

[31]

A crown of thorn, that is so keen,   256
On me they set, me to demean,
Two thieves hung they me between,
    For spite of old;
For this and these wounds here now seen
    May I thee scold.

Behold my shanks and my knees,
My arms and thighs and these;
He holds out his hands.
    Behold me well, look what each sees,
        But sorrow and pain;
    This death I met to do thee ease
        And for thy gain.

And yet more understand thou shall;
Instead of drink they gave me gall,
Mixed it with vinegar withal,
    Those Jews fell;
Through my death may the fiend enthrall
    No soul in hell.

Behold my body, how the Jews did it wrong
With knots of whips and scourges strong;
My bright blood sprang out for long
    On every side;
Knots where they hit, well may thou wit,
    Made wounds so wide.

And therefore thou shall understand
In body, head, feet, and hand,
Five hundred wounds and five thousand
    Here may thou see;
And thereto nine were dealt full even
    For love of thee.

Behold in me nought else is left,
Before thou were from me bereft,
I should again bear each blow deft,
    And for thee die;
Here may thou see that I love thee,
    Man, faithfully.

[32]

292
Since I for love, man, bought thee dear.
As thou thyself the sooth sees here,
I pray thee heartily, with good cheer,
    Love me again;
That it pleased me that I for thee
    Suffered this pain.

If thou thy life in sin have led,
Mercy to ask be not adread;
The least drop I for thee bled
    Might cleanse thee now,
All the sin the world within
    Though done had thou.

I was more enangered with Judas
For that he would not ask me grace,
Than I was for his trespass
    That he me sold;
I was ready to show mercy,
    Of none would he be told.

Lo, how I stretch my arms out wide,
For thee safely to provide,
For thee my love shall ay abide,
    Well may thou know!
Some love again I would full fain
    Thou would me show.

Save love nought else ask I of thee,
And that thou try all sin to flee;
Strive thou to live in charity
    Both night and day;
Then in my bliss that never shall miss
    Thou shall dwell ay.

For I am very prince of peace,
From all sins I may thee release,
And whoso will from their sins cease
    And mercy cry,
Through mass I grant them ease
    By bread, of my body.

That very bread of life   328
Becomes my flesh in these words five;
Who it receives in sin or strife
    Is dead for ever;
Whoso it takes in righteous life
    Die shall he never.

Jesus retires and the three Marys *advance.*

MARY   Alas! Death only may relieve my plight!
MAGDALENE   In woe I long for endless night,
I droop and daze to see that sight
    That I did see;
My Lord, magnificent in might,
    Is dead for me.

Alas! That I should see his pain,
Him never shall I see again,
For every ill he could obtain
    The cure for all;
Hope and help would all men gain
    Who on him call.

MARY JACOBI   Alas! How stand I on my feet
When I think of his wounds wet!
Jesus, that was in life so sweet,
    And never did ill,
Is dead and buried, his defeat
    Is with us still.

MARY   Without reason these Jews each one
SALOME   That lovely Lord they have undone,
And trespass did he never none,
    Nor ever said;
To whom now may we, mourning, run,
    Since our Lord is dead?

MARY   Since he is dead, my sisters dear,
MAGDALENE   Wend we will with full good cheer
With our anointments fair and clear
    That we have brought,
For to anoint his wounds severe,
    Which Jews on him wrought.

[34]

MARY JACOBI 365 Go we then, my sisters free,
For sore I long his corpse to see,
But I know not how best it be;
We are alone,
And which shall of us sisters three
Remove the stone?

MARY SALOME Without more help we do not so,
For it is high and heavy also.

MARY MAGDALENE Sisters, no further need we go
Nor make mourning;
I see two sit where we should go
In white clothing.

MARY JACOBI Certain, the truth we may not hide,
The grave stone here is put aside.

MARY SALOME Certain for what thing that may betide
Now will we wend.
To seek his love, and with him bide,
That was our friend.

1ST ANGEL Ye mourning women in your thought,
Here in this place whom have ye sought?

MARY MAGDALENE Jesu that unto death was brought,
Our Lord so free.

2ND ANGEL Indeed, women, here is he nought;
Come near and see.

1ST ANGEL He is not here, the sooth to say,
The place is void wherein he lay;
The clothing for his grave ye may
Clearly behold;
He is risen and gone his way,
As he you told.

2ND ANGEL Even as he told so done has he,
And risen up most powerfully;

[35]

He shall be found in Galilee,
   In flesh and fell;
To his disciples now wend ye,
   And thus them tell.

ANGELS *withdraw*.

MARY   My sisters free, since it is so,
MAGDALENE He has defied death's final blow,
          And risen as said these angels two,
             Such must we teach;
          As ye have heard, where'er ye go
             Look that ye preach.

MARY JACOBI As we have heard, so shall we say;
          Mary, our sister, have good day!
MARY   Now very God, as he well may,
MAGDALENE   Man most of might,
          He guide you, sisters, well in your way,
             And rule you right.

          Alas, what now shall become of me?
          My caitiff heart will break in three,
          When that I think on that same body
             How it was spilt;
          Through feet and both hands nailed was he
             Though free from guilt.

          Though free from guilt yet was he ta'en,
          That lovely Lord, they have him slain,
          From sin he was without a stain,
             Nor yet did amiss;
          For my guilt he suffered pain,
             And not for his.

          How might I, as I loved him sweet,
          Who suffered for me such defeat,
          Since he is buried beneath my feet,
             Such kindness tell?
          There is no way till that we meet
             Can make all well.

The WOMEN *retire and the* SOLDIERS *wake*.

[36]

1ST SOLDIER	Out, alas! What shall I say?
431	Where is the corpse that herein lay?
2ND SOLDIER	What ails thee man? He is away
	Whom we should guard!
1ST SOLDIER	Rise up and see.
2ND SOLDIER	Harrow! Thieves, for ay
	Our lives are marred.

3RD SOLDIER	What devil ails you two
	To make so loud to-do?
2ND SOLDIER	Why, he is gone
3RD SOLDIER	Alas, but who?
2ND SOLDIER	He that here lay.
3RD SOLDIER	Harrow! Devil, how got he away?

4TH SOLDIER	What, could he so from us escape,
	False traitor, make this tomb so gape,
	And those clothes there neatly drape?
	We are undone!
	Our heads will roll, each from the nape
	Wholly each one.

1ST SOLDIER	Alas, what shall I do this day,
	Since this traitor has won a way?
	And safely, sirs, I dare well say
	He rose alone.
2ND SOLDIER	If sir Pilate hears this fray
	Be we dead as stone.

4TH SOLDIER	Believe ye well he rose indeed?
2ND SOLDIER	I saw myself from hence him speed.
1ST SOLDIER	When that he stirred we gave no need
	None could it ken.
4TH SOLDIER	Alas, full hard shall be my need
	Among all men.

3RD SOLDIER	Yea, but knows Sir Pilate he is fled,
	That we were sleeping when he sped,
	We must forfeit, without dread,
	All that we have.
4TH SOLDIER	We must tell lies, each for his head,
	That he may save.

[37]

1ST SOLDIER	I count that well, so might I go.	466
2ND SOLDIER	And I assent thereto also.	
3RD SOLDIER	A thousand numbered all our foe	

              Well armed each one,
Forced us his corpse then to forgo,
              Almost undone.

4TH SOLDIER   Nay, certain, I hold nought so good
As say the sooth right as it stood,
How that he rose with main and mood,
              And went his way;
Though slay us sir Pilate should,
              Thus dare I say.

1ST SOLDIER   Why, and dare thou to sir Pilate go
With these tidings and tell him so?

2ND SOLDIER   So say I that we do also
              We die but once.

ALL SOLDIERS Now he that worked us all this woe
              Curse all his bones.

4TH SOLDIER   Together may our fortunes mend,
Since we must to sir Pilate wend,
I trust that each remain a friend
              Ere that we pass.

They come to PILATE.

1ST SOLDIER   Now I shall tell our tale to the end,
              Right as it was.

              Sir Pilate, prince without a peer,
Sir Caiaphas and Annas there,
And all the lords about you here,
              To call by name,
Mohammed save and keep you clear
              From sin and shame.

PILATE   Ye are welcome, our knights so keen,
Much mirth for you we mean,
But tell your story us between,
              How ye have wrought.

1ST SOLDIER   Our watching, lord, as we have seen,
              Has come to nought.

[38]

CAIPHAS	To nought? Alas, say you not so.
2ND SOLDIER	The prophet Jesu, that ye well know,
504	Is risen and gone some time ago,
	With main and might.
PILATE	Therefore the devil death thee show,
	Vile, recreant knight!

What! Cowardly curs I you call!
Ye let him pass among you all?

3RD SOLDIER	Sir, what could we do withal
	When forth he sped?
4TH SOLDIER	Such fear we felt we down did fall,
	And quake for dread.

1ST SOLDIER	We were so dazed, each one,
	When that he put aside the stone,
	We quaked for fear, and durst stir none,
	And could do no more.
PILATE	Why, but rose he by himself alone?
2ND SOLDIER	Yea, lord, of that be ye sure.

We heard never such, even or morn,
Nor yet our fathers, I'll be sworn,
Such melody, midday nor morn,
    Was made before.

PILATE	Alas, then are our laws forlorn
	For evermore!

Ah, devil! what shall happen now?
By wisdom fares the world, I vow;
I pray you, Caiaphas, tell us how
    To foil this fray.

CAIAPHAS	Sir, if my book-learning would allow,
	Fain would I say.

ANNAS	To say the best forsooth I shall;
	It shall be profit for us all,
	Yon knights' words let us recall,
	How he is missed;
	We would not, for what might befall,
	That any wist.

[39]

And therefore, by your courtesy,
Reward them generously.

PILATE   Of this counsel well paid am I,
    It shall be thus.
Sir knights, that are of deeds doughty,
    Pay heed to us.

Hearken now how ye shall say,
Whereso ye go by night and day;
Ten thousand men of good array
    Came you to kill,
And stole from you his corpse away
    Against your will.

Look ye say this in every land,
And if ye keep to my command
Ten thousand pounds you have in hand
    As your reward;
And my friendship, ye understand,
    I shall spare not as your lord.

But look ye say as I intend.

1ST SOLDIER   Yea, sir, as Mohammed me amend,
In every country where we wend
    By night or day,
Whereso we go, whereso we wend,
    This shall we say.

PILATE   Mohammed bless you night and day!

PILATE *and the* SOLDIERS *retire.* MARY *and* JESUS *advance.*

MARY   Tell me gardener, I thee pray,
MAGDALENE   If thou bore ought my Lord away;
Tell me the truth, say me not nay
    Where that he lies,
I shall remove him if I may,
    In any wise.

JESUS   Woman, why weepest thou? Be still!
Whom seekest thou? Tell me thy will,
    Deny me not with nay.
MARY   For my Lord I pine full ill;
MAGDALENE   The place his body now may fill
    Tell me I pray;

[40]

575   And I shall, if I may, his body bear with me,
        Unto my dying day the better should I be.

JESUS   Woman, woman, turn thy thought!
        Know thou well I hid him nought,
            Then bore him nowhere with me;
        Go seek, look if thou find him ought.
MARY   In faith I have him sought,
MAGDALENE   But nowhere him may see.

JESUS   Why, what was he to thee, in all truth now to say?
MARY   Ah! Dear he was to me that no longer dwell I may.
MAGDALENE
JESUS   Mary, thou seeks thy God, and that am I.

MARY   Raboni, my Lord so dear!
MAGDALENE Now am I whole that thou art here,
        Suffer me to nigh thee near,
            And kiss thy feet;
        Might I do so, no more I fear,
            For thou art sweet.

JESUS   Nay, Mary, touch not thou me,
        For to my father, tell I thee,
            Ascended have I nought;
        Tell my brethren I shall be
        Before them all in trinity
        Whose will that I have wrought.
        To peace now are they brought, that imprisoned were in
                                                    [pain.
        Wherefore rejoice in thought, that God has come again.

        Mary, thou must from me go,
        Mine errand shalt thou surely show,
            In no temptation fall;
        To my disciples say thou so,
        That wretched are and lapped in woe,
            That I them succour shall.
        By name Peter thou call, and say I shall be
        Before him and them all, myself in Galilee.

MARY   Lord, I shall make my voyage
MAGDALENE   To tell them hastily;

When they hear that message,   610
They will be all merry.
This Lord was slain, certainly,
Falsely killed, no man knew why,
    He did nought amiss;
But with him spake I bodily
    Thereof comes my bliss.

My bliss has come, my care is gone,
My lovely Lord I met alone;
I be as blithe in blood and bone
    As ever I might;
Our Lord has thrust aside death's stone.
    My heart is light.

I am as light as leaf on tree,
For joyful sight that I did see,
For well I know that it was he
    My Lord Jesu;
Lord, he that betrayed thee
    Sorely may rue.

To Galilee now will I fare,
Call his disciples from their care;
With joy the risen Lord declare
    That makes their bliss begin;
That worthy child that Mary bare,
    He save you all from sin.

The Twenty-ninth Play: The Pilgrims

CLEOPHAS   LUKE   JESUS

CLEOPHAS   Almighty God, Jesu,
               That born was of a maiden free,
           Thou was a lord and prophet true,
               Whilst thou had life and sought to be
                   Amongst us men:
           Ill was thy death, and woe is me
               That I it ken!

[42]

8   I ken it well that thou was slain
            Wholly for me and all mankind:
        The Jews readily caused that pain
            Alas, why was thou man so blind
                Thy Lord to slay?
        On him why would thou have no mind
                But him betray?

        Blue thou beat him bare, his breast thou made all black,
        His wounds all wet they were: of pain there was no lack!
LUKE   As physician none could teach our Lord so meek and mild,
        Who so well could preach, by sin stayed undefiled:
        Readily he taught each to leave ways rough and wild,
        His death has made a breach, for they him so beguiled
                This day,
        Alas why did they so
        To tug him to and fro?
        From him they would not go
                Till his life ebbed away.
CLEOPHAS These cursed Jews, on them cry woe!
        They made our Lord his life forgo,
        In innocence he was brought low
                Upon the cross,
        To beat his body blue, his foe
                Thought it no loss.

LUKE   Thou says the truth, they caused him pain,
        And at that were they glad and fain.
        They would not leave till he was slain
             And done to death:
        Therefore we mourn with might and main
             With pain-drawn breath.

CLEOPHAS Yea, wretchedly we may it rue,
        For him that was so good and true
        That through the falsehood of a Jew
            Was thus betrayed:
        Therefore our sorrow comes anew,
            Our joys must fade.

LUKE   Certain it is a wondrous thing
        That they would for no tokening,

Nor yet for his teaching,
    Trust him as true;
They might have seen in his doing
    Full great virtue.

46

CLEOPHAS   For all that they to him did say
He answered never yea nor nay,
But as a lamb meek was he ay,
    When they did bawl;
He spake never, by night or day,
    No word at all.

LUKE   As if he were in no such plight,
But meeting death before our sight,
As though he were of little might,
    He suffered all;
He stood as still and upright
    As stone in wall.

CLEOPHAS   Alas, for dole! What was their skill
That precious Lord his life to spill?
And he served never none ill
    In word or deed;
But prayed for them with all his will,
    When more was his need.

LUKE   When I think on his passion,
With tears I well nigh drown,
And his mother in compassion,
    Did for sharp sorrow shake;
Under the cross when she fell down,
    For her son's sake.

CLEOPHAS   Methinks my heart was full of woe
When I saw him to death go;
The wicked Jews such spite did show
    In rage so rough;
Blue was his body through many a blow
    With strokes enough.

LUKE   Methinks my heart dropped all in blood
When I saw him hang on the rood,

[44]

82   And ask a drink in full mild mood,
                    Right from on high;
            Vinegar and gall, that was not good,
                    They brought him then truly.

CLEOPHAS   Never no man had more need
            That suffered half so great misdeed
            As he, when death took him with speed,
                    Nor yet the care;
            Therefore on sorrow I shall feed
                    Wheresoever I fare.

LUKE   Whereso I fare he is in my mind,
            But when I think on him so kind,
            How bitterly they did him bind
                    Upon a tree,
            Scarce my wits I then can find,
                    Such misery besets me.

    Enter JESUS *dressed as a* PILGRIM.

JESUS   Pilgrims, why make ye this moan,
                    And walk so ruefully by the way?
            Scold ye every stick and stone?
                    Or what ails ye, say!

            What say ye as ye go along,
            As ye your sad path do prolong?
            To hear your grief full sore I long,
                    Your cares to know;
            It seems ye are in sorrows strong,
                    Here as ye go.

CLEOPHAS   What way, for shame, man, has thou taken
                    That thou know not of this affair?
            Has thou all company forsaken,
                    To be of such news unaware?

JESUS   I pray you, if it be your will,
            Of such things to me speak your fill;
            Ye are of heart so heavy and ill
                    Here in this way;

[45]

That you would show me now your will
    I would you pray.

LUKE   Art thou a pilgrim thyself alone,
            Walking the country on thine own,
            And know not what has come and gone
                These last few days?
            Methinks thou should make moan
                And weep here in thy ways.

JESUS   Why, what is done, can ye now say,
                In this land this very day?
            Has there befallen any fray
                In the land anywhere?
            If ye can, tell me I pray,
                Before I farther fare.

CLEOPHAS   Why, know you not who met his fate
            Here at Jerusalem of late,
            Whom the Jews killed in their hate,
                Not long ago?
            On the true prophet we meditate
                And on his woe.

LUKE   Yea, on Jesus, the Nazarene,
            That was a prophet true and clean,
            In word and work, full meek, I mean,
                And that we found:
            And so has he full long been
                To all around.

            To God and to the people too;
            Therefore they thought his death was due,
            And death the Jews without ado
                Contrived his plight;
            Therefore his fate so sad we rue
                By day and night.

CLEOPHAS   Him wicked Jews betrayed with guile,
            To their high priests within a while,
            And all began him to revile,
                To curse and threat:

[46]

152   Upon a cross, not hence a mile,
          His death he met.

LUKE   We hoped it was he truly
        Who his own death would defy,
        As is told in prophecy
            Of Christ's doing:
        But certainly, that will not be
            For nothing.

        From off the cross he was ta'en,
        And full soon laid low again,
        In a stone grave to remain,
            We saw him go:
        Whether he be risen again
            We do not know.

JESUS   Pilgrims your speech is sad astray,
            And I shall say directly why,
        Your trust is merely in hearsay,
            You cannot, surely, stand thereby,
                The thing you hear:
            And prophets told it openly
                In this manner.

        They said a child there should be born
            To save mankind from sin and shame,
        This same before had David sworn
            And other prophets of learned fame,
                And Daniel:
        Some said he dead should be
        And lie in earth days three,
        And then as Lord almighty,
            Rise up in flesh and fell.

CLEOPHAS Now, sir, forsooth, as God me save,
            Women have scared us in our thought:
        They said that they were at his grave,
            And that instead they found him nought,
                But said a light
            Came down with angels, and up him brought
                There in their sight.

[47]

We would not trust them for nothing,
If they were there in the morning,
We said they knew not his rising
    When it sould be:
But some of us without waiting,
    Went thither to see.

LUKE   Yea, some of us, sir, have been there,
    And found it as the women said,
Of any corpse that grave was bare,
    Aside the gravestone also laid,
      This sight we saw:
    I wept for I was so dismayed,
      My grief so raw.

JESUS   Ye fools, ye are not stable!
    Where is your wit, I say?
Both bewildered and unable
    To reckon the right way,
For believe it is no fable
    That has befallen this same day.
He knew, when at his table,
    That Judas should him soon betray.

Methinks you little faith allow,
    Nor with might and main
Heed what prophecies avow,
    Which are not vain.
Told they not what wise and how
    That Christ should suffer pain?
And so to his passion bow
    To enter to his joy again.

Take heed of Moses and more also,
That were prophets true and good;
They said Jesus to death should go,
    And be tortured on the rood;
And by the Jews be beaten so,
    His wounds running with red blood;
After should he rise and go,
    Such things the prophets understood.

[48]

226   Christ behoved to suffer this,
                    Forsooth, right as I say,
               And after enter to his bliss
                    Unto his father for ay,
               Ever to live with him and his,
                    Wherever is game and play:
               Of that mirth shall he never miss
                    When he wends hence away.

CLEOPHAS   Now, sir, we thank thee oft and well
                    For coming to us hither:
               And so kindly us to tell
                    The prophecies altogether.

JESUS   By your leave, sirs, for I must wend,
                    For I have far to journey.
LUKE   Now, sir, we pray you, as our friend,
                    All night to abide for charity
                         And take your rest:
               Then in the morning may ye be
                    For travelling best.

CLEOPHAS   Sir, we pray you, for God's sake,
               This night penance with us take,
               With such cheer as we can make,
                    And that we pray:
               We may no further walk nor wake,
                    Gone is the day.

LUKE   Dwell with us, sir, if ye might,
               For now it grows toward the night,
               The day is gone that was so bright,
                    Let rest prevail:
               Meat and drink is but your right
                    For thy good tale.

JESUS   I thank you both for this good cheer,
               At this time I may not dwell here,
               My way to walk is still severe,
                    Where I must tread:
               I cannot longer bide so near,
                    As ye have said.

CLEOPHAS   Now, as I hope no more to smart,
At this time we shall not part,
Unless you thrust us through your art
    Further away:
Unto the city with good heart,
    Now wend our way.

LUKE   Thou art a pilgrim, as we are,
This night shall thou fare as we fare,
Be it less or be it more
    Thou shall assay:
Then tomorrow thou prepare
    To wend thy way.

JESUS   Friends, for to fulfil your will
    I will abide with you awhile.
CLEOPHAS   Sir, ye are welcome, though small our skill,
    Such as we have lacks any guile.

LUKE   Now are we here at this town,
Let us now go sit us down,
Our care in supper let us drown,
    Here is our food:
We have enough, sir, by my crown,
    By God so good.

They then prepare a table.

CLEOPHAS   Lo, here a board and cloth is laid,
And bread thereon freshly arrayed:
Sit down our care is well repaid
    And make good cheer:
It is but penance, as we said
    That we have here.

Then they shall sit down and JESUS *shall sit in the midst of them: then shall* JESUS *bless the bread and break it into three pieces, and afterwards he shall vanish from their sight:*

LUKE   Lo! Of this man what has become,
    Right here that sat between us two?
He broke the bread and gave us some:
    How might he hence thus from us go—
    And leave this spot?
It was our Lord, it must be so,
    And we knew not.

CLEOPHAS When went he hence, whither, and how,
299   Such knew I not in world so wide,
          For had I known, I make a vow,
              He should have stayed, what so betide:

          But it was Jesus, that with us was,
              Strange, methinks, the truth to say,
          Thus privily from us to pass,
              I knew not when he went away.
          We were indeed full blind, alas!
              And as I think beguiled for ay,
          For speech and beauty that he has
              Man might him know this day.

LUKE   Ah, dear God, what may this be?
          Right now was he here by me:
          Again now all is empty,
              He is away:
          We are beguiled truly,
              So may we say.

CLEOPHAS Where was our heart, where was our thought,
          So far on way as he us brought,
          Knowledge of him that we had nought
              In all that time?
          He was so like methought
              To a pilgrim.

LUKE   Dear God, why could we not him know?
          So plainly seen by us below,
          His words alone himself did show
              One by one.
          And now from us so soon to go,
              Us now to shun.

CLEOPHAS I had no knowledge it was he,
          Until he broke this bread in three,
          And dealt it here to thee and me
              With his own hand;
          When he passed hence we could not see,
              Nor understand.

LUKE   We are to blame, yea, indeed.   334
That we took no better heed
When to come with us he agreed,
    Where we were bound:
We might have known when we did feed,
    Sitting on ground.

CLEOPHAS   When he took bread full well I knew,
With his own hand he broke it true,
And gave it us, us to renew,
    Right as he meant:
I knew him then as hitherto,
    With good intent.

LUKE   That we knew him, well he saw,
Therefore he did himself withdraw,
For us he would not overawe
    Should he abide:
I wonder greatly by what law
    Away that he should glide.

CLEOPHAS   Alas, we were full murk in thought
    Too prompt our own ideas to spread:
Man, for shame why did thou nought
    When he on board broke us this bread?

He told the prophecy more and less
    And spake it here with his own breath,
That to him so great distress
    Was done by Jews to bring him death,
      And more:
We will go seek that king
    That suffered such wounds sore.

LUKE   Rise, go we hence from this place,
To Jerusalem make we apace,
And tell our brethren of this case,
    Readily thus:
When he rose from death's embrace,
    He appeared to us.

[52]

CLEOPHAS In Jerusalem I understand
370 Our old friends will be at hand,
In that country and in that land
We shall them meet.
Our words none shall withstand,
Right in the street.

LUKE Let us not tarry for less nor more,
But fast on foot our way explore:
Our comfort soon he shall restore,
A sign was this:
That blessed child that Mary bore
Grant you his bliss.

They go out.

The Thirtieth Play: Thomas of India

MARY MAGDALENE   6TH APOSTLE
PAUL   7TH APOSTLE
PETER   8TH APOSTLE
3RD APOSTLE   9TH APOSTLE
4TH APOSTLE   10TH APOSTLE
5TH APOSTLE   THE APOSTLE THOMAS

MARY Hail brethren! And God be here!
I bring news to amend your cheer,
Trust ye it and know:
He is risen, the truth to say,
I met him going by the way,
He bad me tell you so.

PETER Away, woman, an idle boast!
It was some spirit, or some ghost:
Otherwise nought:
We may not trust in any wise
That dead men may to life rise:
This then is our thought.

[53]

PAUL   It may be truly for man's meed,   13
             The Jews made him grimly bleed
                 Through feet, hands, and side:
             With nails on cross they hanged him long,
             Wherefore, woman, thou says wrong,
                 As might I bliss abide.

MARY   Stop arguing and forget your loss!
             I have seen him that died on cross,
                 And spoken to him as I do now:
             Therefore to both of you, say I,
             Put away your heresy,
                 Trust steadfastly as I avow.

PETER   Away, woman! Let be thy fare,
                 For shame and also sin!
             If we mourned with heavier care
                 His life may we not win.

PAUL   And it is written in our law
             No woman's judgement hold in awe,
                 Nor too quickly show belief:
             For with their cunning and their guile
             They can laugh then weep awhile,
                 When nothing gives them grief.

             In our books thus find we written,
             All manner of men have so been bitten,
                 By women in this wise:
             Like an apple ripe is she,
             A joy, without a doubt to see,
                 On the board as it lies.

             If any take and start to chew
             It is rotten through and through
                 To the core within:
             Wherefore in woman is no law,
             For she holds nothing in awe,
                 As Christ me save from sin.

             Therefore we trust not easily,
             Unless we saw it surely,

49   And the manner how:
        In woman's word trust have we nought,
        For they are fickle in word and thought,
            To that I make my vow.

MARY   As I am freed from all my care,
        It is as true as you stand there,
            By him that is my brother.
PETER   I dare wager with my head,
        That before we go to bed,
            We shall hear some other.

PAUL   If it be truth and not hearsay,
        And if this be the third day
            Then shall we plainly see.
MARY   If no truth lies in my speech,
        And it proved, ye I beseech
            For false that ye hold me.

PETER   Out, alas! I think, my dears, as I stand in this stead,
        Such sorrow my heart shears, in a whirl is all my head:
        Since Magdalene this witness bears, that Jesus rose
                                                [from dead,
        My poor eyes have wept salt tears, on earth to see him
                                                [tread.
        But alas, that ever I awaked that dread and doleful
                                                [night,
        When I for care and cold quaked by a fire burning full
                                                [bright,
        When I my Lord Jesus forsook, for dread of woman's
                                                [might:
        To righteous judgement will I look that I lose not that
                                                [seemly sight,

        Alas for such mad hardihood, no man repented faster:
        I said, in need if he stood, to him none should be truer:
        I said I knew not that good creature my master.

        Alas! That we from thee fled, nor to thee had turned
                                                [again;
        When thou among the Jews was led, none dared thee to
                                                [sustain,

[55]

But forsook thee that us fed, for we would not be
[ta'en;
We were as prisoners sore adread by the Jews for to be
[slain.

PAUL   Now Jesu, for thy life sweet, who hath thus mastered
[thee?
That in the bread that we eat, thyself given would be:
And later through hands and feet, be nailed upon a
[tree:

Grant us grace, we entreat, thy light in man to see.

Then comes JESUS *and sings "Peace shall be to you shortly, this is the day
which the Lord has made".*

This is the day that God made, and mirth without
[alloy,
The holy ghost comes as our aid, God's most gracious
[envoy:
In apparel red arrayed he brings us bliss and joy:
Softly on earth he stayed our doldrums to destroy.

4TH APOSTLE   This deed through God is done, thus in all our sight,
Mighty God, true King on throne, who in Mary did
[alight,

Send us, Lord, this blessed boon: as thou art God of
[might,

Surely to see him soon and have of him a sight.

Again JESUS *appears and sings "Peace be shortly with you".*

5TH APOSTLE   Whoso comes in God's great name, ay blessed must
[he be!
Mighty God shield us from shame, in thy mother's
[name, Mary:
These wicked Jews will us blame: thou grant us for to
[see

Thy very body and the same that died upon the tree.

JESUS   Peace be with you everyone! It is I, dread thou nought,
That with you so much have done, and dearly with
[death you bought.
Grope and feel flesh and bone and form of man well
[wrought:
Of such things ghosts have none: look whether ye
[know me ought.

[56]

100   That dead but now alive, no man that truth may hide:
        Behold my wounds all five, through hands and feet
                                                  [and side:
        To death did love me drive, my life blood to provide.
        Of sin who will him shrive, these wounds shall be his
                                                  [guide.

        For one so sweet a thing myself so dear had wrought,
        Man's soul, my dear darling, to battle was I brought:
        For that they did me ding, to force me from my
                                                  [thought,
        Upon the cross to bring, yet love forgot I nought.

        Love makes me as ye may see, sprinkled with blood so
                                                  [red:
        Love made my heart so free, it opens in every stead:
        Love so freely condemned me, and drove me to be
                                                  [dead:
        Love raised me by power almighty, sweeter than mead
                                                  [I sped.

        Know thou, man, to thee I cry, hold my father in thy
                                                  [fear;
        Thine own soul keep cleanly, whilst thou art living
                                                  [here;
        Slay it not with thy body, beguiled by sins severe,
        On me and it have mercy, for I have bought it dear.

        My dear friends, now may ye see, in truth that it is I,
        That died upon that blessed tree and after rose up
                                                  [bodily:
        And that the steadfast truth it be, ye shall see suddenly:
        Of your meat give ye me, such as ye have ready.

A table is prepared, and the 6TH APOSTLE *offers a honeycomb filled with
honey and fish.*

6TH APOSTLE   Lord, lo here a roasted fish and a comb of honey
               Laid full fair in a dish and full honestly:
               Here is no other meat but this in all our company,
               But well are we that we have this to thy liking only.

[57]

JESUS

My father of heaven dear, that made me born to be
Of a maiden kept most dear, and after to die on tree,
From death to life to appear, raised me by power
                                    [almighty,
Speaking to allay fear, this meat thou bless through me.

In the father's name and the son and the holy ghost,
In three persons all in one glorious godhead steadfast:
I give this meat my benison, through words mightiest
                                    [most
Now will I eat as anyone again my manhood to taste
My dear friends come lay to, and eat for charity:
As my father bids me do I eat and so eat ye.
I eat that it may be true what is written of me
In Moses' law, that anew it fulfilled might be.   135

Remember ye what I you told in certain time and stead,
When I gave my power to hold to you in form of
                                    [bread,
That my body should be sold, my blood be spilt so
                                    [red:
This body buried dead and cold, the third day rise
                                    [from dead?

Your hearts were filled with woe and dread while I
                                    [have from you been:
My rising up from dead, no doubt can come between:
By truth your way be sped through steadfast words
                                    [and clean.
Dear friends, trust now the dead, that ye with eyes have
                                    [seen.

Ye have disgrace and shame for your disseverance,
I forgive you the blame, in me rest your assurance:
To folk whose sin them lame, preach them to repen-
                                    [tance,
Forgive sin in my name, enjoin them to penance.

The grace of the holy ghost within receive here from
                                    [me

At this he breathes into them.

[58]

149   The which shall never cease within. I give you power
                            [almighty
    Whom in earth ye cleanse of sin, in heaven cleansed
                            [shall be,
    And whom in earth ye bind therein, bound in heaven
                            [be he.

At this he leaves them.

7TH APOSTLE   Jesu Christ in trinity to thee I cry and call,
    That born was of a maiden free, save us sinners all!
    For us was hanged upon a tree, drank vinegar and gall,
    Thy servants save from vanity, in despair that we not
                            [fall.

8TH APOSTLE   Brethren, be we stable in thought, despair put we away,
    In unbelief that we be nought, for we may safely say,
    He that mankind on cross has bought from death rose
                          [the third day:
    We saw the wounds in him were wrought, all bloody
                          [still were they.

9TH APOSTLE   He told us first he should be ta'en and for man's sin
                          [should die,
    Be dead and buried under a stone and after rise up
                          [bodily;
    Now is he quick from grave gone, he came and stood
                          [us by,
    And let us see each one the wounds of his body.

10TH APOSTLE Death that is so keen Jesu overcome has,
    As he told us, so we glean, from death how he should
                          [pass:
    Jesu stood as witness between all with him that dwell-
                          [ing was,
    All his disciples have him seen, save only Thomas.

Enter THOMAS.

THOMAS   If that I proud as peacock go, my heart is full of care:
    If any sorrow might slay man so, apart my heart-
                          [strings tear:
    My life worries me with woe, of bliss I am full bare,
    Yet would I neither friend nor foe knew my deep
                          [despair.

[59]

Jesu, my life so good, than whom none better be,
No wiser man nor better food, nor none kinder than
[he:
The Jews have nailed him on the rood, nailed with
[nails three
And with a spear they spilt his blood, great sorrow it
[was to see.

To see the blood run down his skin well more than
[dole it was,
Such great pain for man's sin, such doleful death on
[cross:
My life has no more joy within since he to death did
[pass,
For he was fair of cheek and chin, for dole of death
[alas!

At this he goes to the DISCIPLES.

Mighty God that stays alive, that never died, nor shall,
Woe and hardship from you drive, that ye not therein
[fall.

PETER   He thee save with his wounds five, to Jesus Christ we
[call,
That rose from death to life and came before us all.

THOMAS   What, Peter! Art thou mad? Living who was him
[like?
For his death I am not glad, my heart deep sorrows
[spike,
Such torture from the Jews he had, his death stemmed
[their dislike:
Thou forsook him when most sad, for fear they might
[thee strike.

PAUL   Those words, dear Thomas, unsay, such thoughts from
[thy mind drive,
For Jesus rose the third day from death in flesh alive;
With us he made short stay, and showed us his wounds
[five,
And eaten, as man may, honey taken from hive.

[60]

THOMAS   Let be for shame! Clearly a phantom deceives thee!
193   Ye saw him not bodily, his spirit it might well be,
              To gladden hearts so sorry in your adversity:
              He loved us well and faithfully, therefore sorrow slays
                                                            [me.

3RD APOSTLE   You know, Thomas, and truth it was, and often heard
                                                            [it say.
              How a fish swallowed Jonas, three days therein he lay:
              Yet God gave him might to pass, and safely win away:
              Might not God that such might has, raise his son the
                                                            [third day?

THOMAS   Man, if thou can understand, Christ said himself to
                                                            [you and me,
              All might was in his hand, all one was God and he!
              Full dark was all the land when he died on the tree.
              I dread that none may stand his comforter to be.

4TH APOSTLE   The holy ghost to Mary came, and in her maidenhead
              God's mother she became, to manhood she him bred:
              For love he went to claim his kingdom without dread:
              Having fought, from human frame and human
                                                            [clothes he sped.

THOMAS   If he skipped out of his clothing, yet you grant his
                                                            [corpse was dead:
              It was his corpse that made showing unto you in his
                                                            [stead:
              For to trust in your carping my heart is heavy as lead:
              His death gives me great mourning, my wits whirl in
                                                            [my head.

5TH APOSTLE   His spirit went to hell a space while his body lay slain,
              And brought the souls from Satan's place, at price of
                                                            [Satan's pain:
              His way the third day he did trace unto the body again,
              God and man are raised through grace, and therefore
                                                            [are we fain.

THOMAS   It seems you all conflict as you your reasons show,
              But tell, no truth omit, each of you in a row:

[61]

When Christ came you to visit, as ye tell me this was
[so,
Whether as man or spirit, what gave ye cause to know?

6TH APOSTLE   Thomas, unto thee anon, hereto answer I will: 220
Man has both flesh and bone, hue, hair, and hide as
[well:
Such things has spirit none, Thomas, your doubts to
[still:
God's son took flesh and bone, his purpose to fulfil.

THOMAS   Thou has answered me with zeal and full skilfully,
But my heart is hard as steel to trust such mastery,
Say, bad he any of you feel the wounds of his body,
With flesh or bone to deal to assay him readily?

7TH APOSTLE   Yes, Thomas, he bad us see, and with our hands him
[touch,
To find whether it were he, Jesu, that we might clutch,
That died upon a tree, flesh and bone and such,
It was the sharpest pity his bleeding wounds to touch.

THOMAS   Out, alas! Ye are no good! Your reasons are defaced,
Ye are as women scared of blood, too easily solaced:
It was a ghost before you stood, like him in his blood
[laced,
His body that died on rood, for ever hath death
[embraced.

8TH APOSTLE   Certain, Thomas, greater care, might no sinful woman
[have
Than weeping in her sad despair, the Magdalene at his
[grave:
Wrenched for sorrow her own hair and started so to
[rave,
When Jesus stood before her there from her deep
[sorrow to save.

THOMAS   Lo, ye let your wisdom rust, wise men that should be,
That thus a woman's witness trust more than what ye
[see!

[62]

242   Your reasons are not right or just, your endeavours fail
                [ye:
     If I see Jesus, my hand's thrust, not groping should
               [decide me.

9TH APOSTLE Leave, Thomas, thy despair, and be not so misled,
     Or else tell us when and where Christ cheated in any
               [stead:
     For he told us when thou was there, when he gave him-
             [self in bread,
     That he should save us from our care, by rising from
               [the dead.

THOMAS   He was true in everything, that dare I heartily say,
     His way was righteousness to bring to each and every
               [day:
     But since he suffered death's sharp sting as on the tree
               [he lay,
     His life is brought to nothing, trust but in death I may.

10TH APOSTLE Let not thy soul be severed by thy hard heart within,
     Jesus has death conquered, and washed us all from sin.
     May neither knife nor sword victory over him win:
     God's might in him appeared, reigning evermore
               [therein.

THOMAS   God's spirit I trust full well came before your sight,
     But in body never a deal Jesus that wounded wight.
     My heart is hard as steel to trust in such a might,
     Unless that wound I feel, that him gave Longeus, the
               [knight.

PETER   That wound have we seen, Thomas, and so have more
               [than we:
     With Luke and with Cleophas he walked a day's
               [journey:
     Each heart for him was sorry, which he comforted
             [with prophecy,
     To Emmaus castle they did pass, there hostelled they
               [all three.

Jesu, God's son of heaven, at supper sat between:
And the bread he broke as even as though it cut had
[been.

THOMAS   Nothing ye say even, would for me his rising mean,
If ye told me such seven, it would but tax my spleen.

PAUL   Thomas, brother, turn thy thought, and trust what I
[tell thee:
Jesu so dear has bought our sins upon a tree,   269
Whose rising hath brought to heaven Adam and his
[company.

THOMAS   Let be your speech! Say it nought that he alive should
[be.

3RD APOSTLE   That must thou needs allow, if thou thy soul will save,
For what we saw we dare avow, the living Jesu rose
[from grave.

THOMAS   As I said once so say I now such words away I wave:
No risen Jesus saw thou, but beguiled ye rave.

4TH APOSTLE   For we say that we have seen thou doubt our wits hold
[good;
Jesus living came between, our Lord that with us stood.

THOMAS   I say ye know never what ye mean, a ghost before you
[stood;
Ye thought that it had been the corpse that died on
[rood.

4TH APOSTLE   The corpse that died on tree was buried in a stone;
Which laid aside found we, within that grave corpse
[was none:
His napkin there could we see, but he thence living
[gone.

THOMAS   No, but stolen is he by the Jews that have him slain.

6TH APOSTLE   Certain, Thomas, thou says not right, they would not
[him steal,
For they did watch him day and night, those knights
[they held most loyal:
He rose as we have seen despite what the Jews might
[feel.

THOMAS   I believe not unless I might myself with him deal.

[64]

7TH APOSTLE   He told us tidings, Thomas, that reminds me,
289   That as Jonas three days was in a fish in the sea,
               So should he be, and has been in earth for days three,
               So should he rise from death; as he said, done has he.

THOMAS   Indeed, those words I heard him say, and so heard ye
                                                      [him all,
               But for nothing trust I may that it should so befall,
               That he should rise the third day who drank vinegar and
                                                      [gall:
               Since he was God and dead lay, from death who might
                                                      [him call?

8TH APOSTLE   The father that him sent, raised him that was dead,
               He comfort in our mourning lent and counselled us in
                                                      [dread:
               He bad us trust with good intent his rising in every
                                                      [stead:
               Thine absence makes thy soul feel rent and makes thee
                                                      [heavy as lead.

THOMAS   Thou says truth, right tardy am I to trust what to me
                                                      [ye say:
               My hardness I trust wilfully, for he told us thus ay,
               That his father was ever him by, for all but one were
                                                      [they:
               That he rose up bodily, in no way trust I may.

9TH APOSTLE   Trust thou not what we do know, forsooth that it was
                                                      [he?
               Thomas, whereto should we say so? The truth we tell
                                                      [to thee.
THOMAS   I know your hearts are full of woe and hurt through
                                                      [vanity;
               Though all and more should swear this so, I trust it not
                                                      [until I see.

10TH APOSTLE   Thomas, spurn this sin, and for us change thy mood:
               He is risen from his grave within since he died upon
                                                      [the rood.

Save that place my finger win wherein the very nail
[stood,
And his side my hand put in whence shed he his heart's
[blood.

JESUS *enters.*

JESUS   Brethren all, be with you peace! Leave strife that now
[is here!
Thomas, from thine error cease, and true witness thou
[bear:
Put thy hand in my side, never fear, where Longeus put
[his spear:
And see my rising is no lie, there is no cause for your
[despair.

THOMAS   Mercy, Jesu, pity me, my hand now bears thy blood!
Mercy, Jesu, for I see thy might which I never under-
[stood!
Mercy, Jesu, I pray to thee who for sinners died on
[rood!
Mercy, Jesu, of mercy free, for thy goodness that is so
[good!

Cast away my staff will I and with no weapon go:
Mercy will I call and cry, Jesu, that suffered woe:
Pity me, king of mercy, let me not long cry so!   322
Mercy, for the villainy the Jews to you did show.

My hat will I cast away, my coat too I would shun:
Help unto the poor it may, for riches know I none.
In mercy will I dwell, and pray to thee Jesu, alone:
My sinful deed I rue for ay, to thee make I my moan.

Mercy, Jesu Lord, sweet, for thy five wounds so sore,
Thou suffered through hands and feet, thy seemly side
[a spear it tore:
Mercy, Jesu Lord, is meet for thy mother that thee bore!
Mercy, for thy tears, I entreat, thou wept Lazarus to
[restore!

My girdle gay and purse of silk, and coat away with all:
While I am wearer of such ilk, the longer mercy may
[I call.

334   Jesu, that sucked the maiden's milk, wear nought but
                                [raiment royal,
       Thy clothes which from thee they did filch, left thee
                              [bare on cross withal.

       Mercy, Jesu, honour to man, mercy, Jesu, man's
                                [succour!
       Mercy, Jesu, pity thy darling, man's soul, thou bought
                                [full sour!
       Mercy, Jesu, that may and can, forgive sins and be
                                [succour!
       Mercy, Jesu, as thou us won, forgive, and give man thy
                                [honour.

JESUS   None might bring thee to that state for ought that they
                                [might say,
       But believe that I came straight from death to life
                                [away.
       My soul and body mate in a knot that shall last ay:
       Thus shall I raise, know well thy fate, each man at
                              [doom's day.

       Whoso has not trusted right, to hell I shall them lead,
       Where evermore is dark as night, and great pains give
                                [heed:
       Those that trust in my might and love well alms' deed,
       They shall shine as sun bright, and heaven have for
                                [their meed.

       That bliss, Thomas, I promise thee, which is in heaven's
                                [city,
       For thy tears that I see, on thee I have pity:
       Thomas, thy wet tears for me, thy sin forgiven be,
       And so shall sinners pardoned be, that sore have grieved
                                [me.

       Thomas, that thou felt me and my wounds bare,
       My rising gave faith to thee, where earlier was despair;
       All that trust but never see, and of my words take care,
       Ever blessed may they be, a place in heaven to share.

JESUS *disappears from their sight, and the* APOSTLES *withdraw.*

[67]

The Thirty-first Play:
The Ascension of the Lord

THOMAS	JESUS	MARY
APOSTLE JOHN	ANDREW	MATTHEW
SIMON	JAMES	1ST ANGEL
PETER	PHILIP	2ND ANGEL

THOMAS Brethren all, as ye have been,
   Forget my Lord that may I nought:
  I know not what it may mean,
   But greater wonders will be wrought.

JOHN My Lord Jesus will work his will,
   Plead we never against his thought,
  For us he fashions by his skill,
   The handiwork that he has wrought.

SIMON Upon his words will I rest
   The which he said he would fulfil,
  Steadfastly to trust is best,
   Unbelief begets much ill.

PETER In heaven and earth his might may be,
   His wit and his will also:
  The holy ghost, brethren, meant he,
   Thus will he never from us go.

  Forty days now draw near
   Since his resurrection complete:
  And soon again he will appear,
   Thus suddenly not leave us yet.

  In Bethany here let us abide,
   We know not yet what may befall:
  Peradventure it may betide
   He shall full well comfort us all.

JESUS *appears to the* DISCIPLES.

JESUS Peace now, my dear friends!
   Peace be with you ever and ay!
  For peace all wrong amends:
   Peace, brethren, to all I say!

[68]

29   Brethren, in hearts be nothing heavy
          The time that I from you am gone,
      I must go soon and speedily,
          But nevertheless make ye no moan:

      For I shall send to you anon
          The holy ghost to comfort you,
      And guide when you are on your own,
          And I shall tell you the manner how.
      You shall profit, I avow,
          That thus for you I go:
      It has been said ere now
          My father's will is so.

      With him must I abide and dwell,
          For so it is his will:
      For your comfort thus I you tell,
          Be steadfast for good or ill.
      Wait for me here right on this hill
          Until I come to you again.
      This first command ye must fulfil,
          No longer here I will remain:
      And in obedience be ye fain,
          And also true and steadfast,
      And live your lives without a stain
          When that I am passed.

At this he departs.

PETER   Full heavy in heart now may we be
              That our master thus shall go,
          But nevertheless thus said he
              He would not long stay so.
          What wonder then if we feel woe,
              Who suddenly our master miss,
          And, masters, none of us can show
              The wisdom that may comfort this.
          He will pass forth to bliss,
              And leave us here behind,
          No marvel now it is
              If we mourn now in our mind.

ANDREW   In our mind mourn we may,
              As men that are amazed and mad,

And yet also it is no nay,   67
   We may be blithe and glad,
Because of tidings that we had,
   That himself to us did say;
He bad be blithe and nothing sad,
   For he would not be long away.
But yet both night and day
   Our hearts may be full sore,
By my faith, as I may say,
   For his words spoken before.

THOMAS   Long before he said full openly,
   That he needs from us must part,
And to his master go on high,
   To heaven's endless joy depart;
Therefore we mourn with heavy heart,
   But merry also yet may be;
He bad us all our joy impart,
   Be glad and blithe in each degree,
And said that come should he
   To comfort us kindly;
But yet heavy are we
   Till we see him truly.

JAMES   With eyes would we him see, our saviour Christ, God's
                       [son,
That died upon a tree, yet such grace may be won:
God grant to us each one, that with his blood us bought,
To see him in his throne, as he made all of nought:
His will now has he wrought and gone from us away,
And forsaken in his thought therefore mourn we may.

PHILIP   We may mourn, no marvel why, for we our master thus
                      [shall miss,
That shall go from us suddenly, and we not know what
                      [the cause is;
Nevertheless, the truth is this, he said that he should come
                      [again
To bring us all to bliss, thereof may we be fain.
That coming brings us much gain, and may our souls all
                      [save,
And puts us from that pain that we were like to have.

[70]

JESUS *again appears.*

JESUS   Hearken to me now, everyone, and hear what I will say,
102   For I must needs from you be gone, such is my father's
                                               [way,
        And therefore peace be with you ay, together and alone,
        And save you from all fray, my peace be with you blood
                                        [and bone.
        I leave it with you one by one, but not as the world here
                                        [knows;
        It shall be true as any stone to defend you from your foes.

        Let not your hearts be heavy, dread not for anything,
        Ye have heard me say full plainly I go, and to you I am
                                        [coming.
        If ye therefore love me ye should be glad of this doing,
        For I go full surely to my father, heaven's king;
        The which without lying is more mighty than I,
        Therefore be ye thus trusting, when all is ended fully.
        Ye have been full of doubt, hard of heart and also of will;
        The proof of my rising ye did flout, no credence ye gave
                                        [them still;
        Mary Magdalene spoke my will, that I was risen, ye did
                                        [but scold
        Her, trusting not for good or ill the truth as she it told.
        Such harms in hearts ye hold, unsteadfast in your prizing,
        To believe none were ye bold, who bore witness of my
                                        [rising;

        Therefore ye shall go teach in all this world so wide,
        And to all the people preach who baptism will abide,
           And believe truly
        My death and rising,
        And also my ascending,
        And also my returning,
           They shall be saved surely.

        And who believes not this
        That now repeated is,
        He shall be shut from bliss,
           Such vengeance on him wreak.
        Tokens of truth be seen
        In all believers I mean:

Devils shall they cast out clean,
And with new tongues speak.

Serpents shall they put away,
And venomous drink, by night and day,
Shall not annoy them, as I say:
And where they lay on hands
On sick men far and near,
They shall be whole and clear
Of all sickness and heavy fear,
For ever in all lands.

And therefore now I bid that ye
Bide in Jerusalem city,
But obey my father's decree
Everywhere,
As ye have heard here of me:
For John baptized to his degree,
In water forsooth he baptized me:
His task ye share:

But ye for sure on every coast
Shall baptize in the holy ghost,
Through his virtue that is the most,
Lord God of might.
Within few days now following:
And at this marvel ye nothing.
For this shall be his own working,
Shown in your sight.

He leaves them.

PETER   Wondrous ill now may we fare
In missing our master, Jesus:
Our hearts may sigh with laden care,
These Jews for wrath will seize us.

Us to betray they mean,
They are about by night and day;
For Jesus that is so seldom seen,
As mazed men mourn we may.

ANDREW   Mourning makes us mazed and mad,
As men that live in dread;
We are so comfortless and sad,
Lacking him who has us led.

JAMES 171
These Jews that follow their faithless will,
   And deemed our master to be dead,
With might and main they would him kill,
   If they knew how in town or stead.

JOHN
Let us keep from their carping keen,
   And come but little in their sight;
When least expected our Lord will be seen,
   He will us rule and govern aright.

THOMAS
Of this carping now no more,
   It draws near the time of day:
For meat I would we go before,
   He send us succour that best may.

MARY
Succour soon he will you send,
   If ye belief on him bestow:
Your moan meekly will he mend,
   My brethren dear, this may ye know.

The pledges that to me were plight,
   He has fulfilled in word and deed;
He lied never by day or night,
   Therefore, brethren, not doubt ye need.

MATTHEW
Certain, lady, thou says full well:
   He will us mend for us so he may:
We have found true, just as you tell,
   All that ever we heard him say.

JESUS
Peter, and ye my darlings dear,
   As men amazed methinks ye stare:
Wholly to you I have shown here
   That I bring your hearts from care.

In care your hearts are cast,
   And in your faith untrue;
In hardness your hearts are fast,
   As men that nothing knew.

Sent was I for your sake from my father dear,
Flesh and blood to take of a maid so dear;
Since then for me ye sought and wholly followed me,
Of wonders that I have wrought some have I let you see.

[73]

The dumb, the blind as any stone,
    I healed as I passed by,
The dead I raised anon,
    Through my might truly;

And works of wonder many more,
    I wrought wisely before you all;
My pain, my passion, I told before,
    Wholly throughout as it should fall.

My rising on the third day,
    As a token many have seen:
Your true sense had been cast away
    Had not my blessed mother been.

In her did constant faith abide,
    Your deeds should cause you bitter shame:
Here may ye see my sad wounds wide,
    How that I bought you out of blame.

But, John, think when I hung on rood,
    That I assigned thee Mary mild:
Keep her yet in stable mood,
    She is thy mother, and thou her child.

Look thou her love, and be her friend,
    And abide with her in well and woe,
For to my father now will I wend,
    Need none of you ask whither I go.

PHILIP   Lord, if it be thy will,
    Show us thy father we thee pray:
We have been with thee in good and ill,
    And saw him never, night nor day.

JESUS   Philip, that man that may see me,
    He sees my father full of might:
Trust thou not he dwells in me
    And I in him if thou trust right?

In his house is many a place,
    Which I go to prepare for you:
Ye shall all be filled with grace,
    The holy ghost I shall send you.
He shall you guide, your heart possess,
    In word and deed, just as I say:

[74]

244   With all my heart I you bless—
            My mother, my brethren, have all good day!
Then he goes to begin his Ascension.

        Father of heaven, with good intent,
           I pray thee hear me specially:
        From heaven to earth thou me sent
           Thy name to preach and glorify.
        Thy will obediently I have done,
           In earth will I no longer be:
        Open the clouds, for now I come
           In joy and bliss to dwell with thee.

And thus he ascends: while the ANGELS *sing "I ascend to my Father".*

1ST ANGEL   Ye men of Galilee,
        Wherefore marvel ye?
        Heaven behold and see
           How Jesus up did wend
        Unto his father free,
        Where he sits in majesty,
        With him ay for to be
           In bliss without an end.

        And as ye saw him nigh
        Unto heaven on high,
        In flesh and fell in his body,
           From earth now here,
        Right so shall he surely,
        Come down again truly,
        With his wounds bloody,
           To judge altogether.

2ND ANGEL   Marvel no man might,
        Nor wonder at this sight,
        For it is through his might,
           That all things may.
        Whatso he will by day or night,
        In hell, earth, or heaven's height,
        Or yet in darkness or in light,
           Without gainsay;

        For he is God most grand,
        Over heaven and hell, sea and sand,
        Wood and water, fowl, fish, and land,

According to his will;
He holds all things in his hand,
No living thing may him withstand,
Then marvel not but understand.

1ST ANGEL   And for this skill,

Right as he from you did wend,
    So come again he shall,
In the same manner at the end,
    To judge both great and small.

2ND ANGEL   Whoso his bidding will obey,
And their lives amend,
    With him shall win to bliss that day,
And dwell there without end.

And who that work amiss,
    And themselves amend will never,
Shall never come to heaven's bliss,
    But to hell be banished ever.

MARY   A wondrous sight yonder now is,
    Behold now, I you pray!
A cloud has born my child to bliss,
    My blessing bears he ever and ay!

But, son, think on thy mother dear,
    That thou has left among thy foes!
Sweet son, let me not dwell here,
    Let me go with thee where thou goes.

But John, in thee is all my trust,
    I pray thee forsake me nought.
JOHN   Mary, look up without mistrust,
    For thy will shall ay be wrought.

Here may we see and reckon so,
    That he is God, most of might;
In him is good we know,
    Wholly to serve him day and night.

PETER   A marvellous sight is yon,
    That he from us so soon was ta'en;
From his foemen he is gone
    With no other help is plain.

MATTHEW Where is Jesus, our master dear,
319   That here with us spoke right now?
JAMES   A wonderful sight, men may see here,
            My brethren dear, how think you?

THOMAS   A wonder seems it all,
            That our master should thus go;
          For his help I guess we call,
            That he might us some token show.

BARTHOLO- A greater marvel men ne'er saw
  MEW   Than now is seen among us here:
           We saw a cloud to heaven him draw
             While angels sang with mirthful cheer.

           From us, methinks, he is full long,
             Yet longer, I think, he will;
           Alas! My heart it is so strong,
             That I may not weep my fill
                 Anon.
           A wondrous sight it was to see
           When he climbed up so suddenly
           To his father in majesty,
               By himself alone.

MATTHEW   Alone, indeed, up he went, into heaven to his father,
          And no one knew what he meant, nor how he rose in
                                          [what manner,
          But on climbing up was bent, in flesh and fell from earth
                                          [up here:
          He said his father for him sent, that made us all to harbour
            This night: [fear
          Nevertheless full well know we
          As that he will so must it be,
          For he has power almighty,
            And that is right.

MARY   Almighty God, how may this be?
            A cloud has borne my child to bliss,
          Save that I know now where is he,
            My heart would break, well know I this.

          His ascension up to bliss on high,
            It is the source of all my joys;

My blessing, bairn, light on thy body!   354
  Let never thy mother be rent by the Jews.

Son so sweet, thy mother mind,
  Let me not suffer the Jews' harsh scorn;
Help, for my son's love, John so kind,
  For fear that I by the Jews be torn.

My flesh it quakes as leaf on tree,
  To shun the showers sharper than thorn:
Help me, John, if kind thou be,
  My son's missing makes me to mourn.

JOHN   Your servant, lady, he me made,
  And bad me you in comfort keep:
Blithe were I, lady, thy joy to aid,
  And serve thee gladly without sleep.

Therefore be afraid for nothing,
  For ought that the Jews would do to you;
I shall be ready at your bidding,
  As my Lord bad, your servant true.

MARY   Glad am I, John, while I have thee;
  More comfort, save Jesus, I cannot crave;
So calm thou my care, and quietly speak to me,
  Whilst I thee see I feel most safe.
Was none, save my son, more trusty to me,
  Therefore his grace shall never from thee go;
He shall thee requite, that died on a tree,
  If thou mend my mood, when I am in woe.

SIMON   Let us hasten from this hill, and to the town wend,
  For fear of the Jews, that are pitiless and proud:
To our dear lady our company lend,
  And pray to her dear son, right here aloud.
To her obediently, I say, we bend,
  Since her dear son from us is gone in a cloud,
And heartily salute our gracious friend,
  To our master is she mother, seemly in shroud.

Ah, Mary so mild; thee missed we have;
  Was never maid more gracious to behold

[78]

390   As thou art, and mother clean, but this would we crave,
       If this were Jesus, thy son, that Judas has sold,
     Show us the truth, it may us all save;
       We pray thee, dear lady, that frankly thou told,
     Excuse us our asking but else might we rave,
       But fain would we surely this mystery unfold.

MARY   Peter, Andrew, John, and James, I assent,
       Simon, Judas, and Bartholomew the bold,
     And all my brethren dear, to this now be attent,
       Give heed to what is said, until my tale be told
     Of my dear son, what I have meant,
       That hence is heaved to his own hold;
     He taught you the truth ere he to heaven went;
       He was born of my bosom as prophets foretold.

MARY   He is God and man that unto heaven rose:
       Preach thus to the people that most are of price.
     Ye Apostles eleven, look to the saving of those,
       To the Jews of Jerusalem, as your way lies,
     To the whole city these tidings disclose,
     Tell the words of my son in world most wise:
     Bid them in him their belief to repose,
       Or else be they damned as men full of vice.

(The play is unfinished: there is a gap of twelve leaves in the manuscript.)

The Thirty-second Play: The Judgement

1ST EVIL SOUL	TUTIVILLUS
2ND EVIL SOUL	JESUS
3RD EVIL SOUL	1ST GOOD SOUL
4TH EVIL SOUL	2ND GOOD SOUL
AN ANGEL	3RD GOOD SOUL
1ST DEMON	4TH GOOD SOUL
2ND DEMON	

JESUS *and the* ANGELS *in heaven, the* GOOD *and* EVIL SOULS *on earth.*

2ND EVIL SOUL   Full dark has been our deed, at his coming our care;
       This day we take our meed, for nothing may we spare.
    Trump.

[79]

Alas, I heard that horn that calls us to our doom,
All that ever were born, thither behoves them come.
May neither land nor sea us from this doom hide,
For fear fain would I flee, but I must needs abide;
Alas, I stand in awe, to see that Justice beckon,
Where no man may on law or legal quibble reckon,
Advocates ten or twelve may not help him in his need,
But each man for himself shall answer for his deed.

Alas, that I was born!   11
I see my Lord's flesh torn
    Before me with wounds five;
How may I on him look,
That falsely him forsook,
    Most sinful wretch alive?

3RD EVIL SOUL   Alas, careworn caitiffs may we rise,
Sore may we wring our hands and weep;
For being cursed and covetous,
Damned be we in hell full deep.
Gave we never to God in service,
His commandments would we not keep,
But ofttimes made we sacrifice
To Satan, when we stole from sleep.

Trump.

Alas! That clarion calls our care,
Our wicked works can we not hide,
But on our backs we must them bear,
That give us sorrow on every side.
Our deeds this day will cost us dear,
Our judgement here we must abide,
And fiends, that fill us full of fear,
Will pounce upon us in their pride.
Boldly before us be they brought,
Our deeds that damn us as unclean;
That ear that heard, or heart that thought,
Mouth that has spoken, or eye seen,
That foot that trod or hand that wrought,
At any time our lives between;
Full dear this day now be it bought;
Alas! Unborn that had I been!

Trump.

[80]

4TH EVIL SOUL Alas, I am forlorn! A bitter blast here blows!
42   I heard by yonder horn, I know whereto it goes;
              I would I were unborn! What may this day dispose!
              Now must be damned this morn we who bewail our
                                                        [woes!
              The evil that I did, alas, has left a stain
              For which I am now chid, as ye shall see full plain.
              That would I fain were hid, my sinful words and vain,
              So that I may be rid this reckoning for my gain.

              Alas, fain would I flee for deeds that I have done,
              But that may now not be, my fate I may not shun;
              My hope was never to see this dreadful day begun,
              When on his throne to me he turns, where shall I run?

              Who can his wounds withstand! This is a doleful case;
              Alas! How shall I stand, or look him in the face?
              So courteous I him found that gave me life so long a
                                                        [space;
              My care is close at hand, alas! Where is my grace?

              Alas! Caitiffs unkind, whither was our thought?
              Alas! Where was our mind, so wicked works we
                                                        [wrought?
              See his suffering for mankind, so dear our love he
                                                        [bought.
              Alas! We were full blind, now are we worse than
                                                        [nought.

              Alas! My covetize, my ill will, and mine ire!
              My neighbour to despise, most was my desire;
              Ill deeds I would devise, methought high to aspire,
              I have been too unwise, now am I quit my hire.

              Where I was wont to go and speak my words at will,
              Now am I set full low and fain to hold me still;
              I went both to and fro, methought I did never ill,
              To slay my neighbours so, or harm them through my
                                                        [skill.

              Woe be to the father that begat me to be born!
              That ever he let me stir, that now am so forlorn;

Accursed by my mother, and accursed be the morn
That I was born of her, alas, for shame and scorn!

ANGEL (*with a sword*) Stand not together, part in two!   73
Together be ye not in bliss;
Our Lord of heaven will have it so,
For many of you have done amiss,
On his right hand ye good shall go,
The way to heaven he shows you this;
Ye wicked souls wend ye below,
On his left hand as none of his.

JESUS   The time has come I shall make end,
My father in heaven wills it so be,
Therefore to earth now will I wend
Myself to sit in majesty.

To deal my doom I will descend
This body will I bear with me,
It was made man's sin to mend
All mankind there shall it see.

Trump.

1ST DEMON   Out, harrow, out, out! Hearken to this lord,
I was never in doubt ere now at this morn;
So sturdy a shout, since that I was born
Heard I never hereabout in earnest nor scorn;
        A wonder!
I was bound full fast
In irons for to last,
My bonds broke with that blast
        And shook all in sunder.

2ND DEMON   I shivered and shook and shuddered for fear,
I heard what I took for the doom of us here,
But to swear on a book, I durst not appear;
I durst not look, for all earth, either drear
        Or pale;
But grinned and grimaced,
My fear I outfaced,
But all was but waste,
        It might not avail.

[82]

1ST DEMON	It was like to a trump, it had such a sound;
108	I fell down in a lump, in a swoon I was found.
2ND DEMON	There I stood on my stump as to a stake bound,
	Though cramped by this clump yet held I my ground
	Half numb.
1ST DEMON	Make ready our gear,
	To welcome war here,
	For now dare I swear
	That doomsday has come.

	For our souls all have fled and none are in hell
	If we stay we are sped, here let us not dwell.
2ND DEMON	It behoves us instead this rising to quell,
	As Parliament peers said, whatever befell;
	It is needful
	To look to your own,
	Where the wind shall be blown;
	If the court practice be known,
	The Judge is right dreadful.

1ST DEMON	We have an empty home; our rout has been complete,
2ND DEMON	Let us go to our doom up Watling Street.
1ST DEMON	I had rather go to Rome, yea thrice, on my feet,
	Than to grieve yonder groom, or with him for to
	Wisely [meet;
	Of things may he prate,
	His power is great,
	If he threaten his hate
	He looks full grisly.

	But first take our rentals, hie, let us go hence!
	Ere on us falls the great sentence.
2ND DEMON	Here stand the thralls, we offer no defence,
	For all these damned souls, without repentance,
	As is just.
1ST DEMON	Although we be crooks,
	Examine our books
2ND DEMON	Here is a bag full of looks,
	Of pride and of lust,

Of wranglers and twisters, a bag full of briefs,
Of carpers and criers, cutpurses and thieves,

Of lubbers and liars, that no man believes,   145
Of a rout of rioters that robbed goods receives;
   These know I,
Of all estates
That go by the gates,
Their pride that God hates,
   Twenty so many.

1ST DEMON   Peace, I pray thee be still! I laugh that I kink,
Is ought ire in thy bill, for then shall thou drink.

2ND DEMON   Sir, such mighty ill-will, that they would sink
Their foes in a fire still, but nought that I think
   Dare I say,
Before him he praises him,
Behind him he abuses him,
Thus double he uses him;
   Thus do they today.

1ST DEMON   Hast thou ought written there of the feminine gender?

2ND DEMON   Yea, more than I may bear, of rolls for to render;
They are as sharp as a spear though they seem but
        [slender;
They have ever sour cheer: and if they be tender,
   Ill-fettled;
She that is most meek,
When sick she seems to peak,
She can raise a shriek
   If she be well nettled.

Trump.

1ST DEMON   Of rascals thou art best that ever came beside us.

2ND DEMON   Yea, but go we now to rest, for fain would we hide us;
That blast blown with such zest, shows they will not
        [abide us;
Let us dally not lest sorely they chide us
   Together.

1ST DEMON   Make ready our tools,
For we deal with no fools.

2ND DEMON   Sir, all the clerks of our schools
   Are ready to go thither.

2ND DEMON   But, sir, I tell you before, had doomsday ought tarried,
We must have widened hell more, the world is so
        [sullied.

1ST DEMON	Now get we double store of bodies miscarried
182	To the souls where they were together to be harried.
2ND DEMON	These rolls
	Are of backbiters,
	And false indictors,
	I had no help of writers
	To list these damned souls.

Faith and truth, ma fay, have no feet to stand;
The poor people must pay, if ought be in hand,
The dread of God is away, and law out of land
    This season.

2ND DEMON	Sir, it is said in old saws—
	Though near the dawn draws—
	"Worse people worse laws."
1ST DEMON	I laugh at thy reason.

All this was a token, doomsday to dread;
Full oft was it spoken, full few looked ahead;
Our vengeance is woken, and devours them instead,
Now the seal is so broken of deeds dark and red
    With ire;
All their sins shall be known,
Other men's and their own.

2ND DEMON	And if this blast be well blown,
	"Dick is in the mire."

Enter TUTIVILLUS.

TUTIVILLUS	Why ask ye not, sir, no questions?
	I am one of your order and one of your sons;
	I stand at my station which each of you shuns.
1ST DEMON	Now thou art my own chorister, ye live with the
	Do tell me. [nuns;
TUTIVILLUS	Tax-gatherer in chief,
	Court rollsman in brief,
	Master lollard in belief,
	As such none excel me.

I have brought to your hand of souls, I dare say,
More than ten thousand in an hour of a day;
Some at ale-houses I found and some at a fray,
Some cursed to be bound, some yea, some nay;
    So many

[85]

| | Thus brought I to hell, | 220 |
| | Thus worked I so well. |

1ST DEMON   All us ye excel
    None such heard I any.

TUTIVILLUS   Here's a roll of ragman of the round table,
Of briefs in my bag, man, of sins damnable;
Certainly I say, man, and weary of your stable,
While I set my stag, man.

2ND DEMON   Abide, ye are able
    To take wage;
Ye know the court ways
Which your service repays,
I forecast foul frays
    When ye come of age.

TUTIVILLUS   Here be I guess many to mock at,
In care and curstness whom we may knock at,
Gay gear and witless, his hood with a cocket,
As proud as penniless, his sleeve has no pocket,
    Full senseless;
His shoes are trimmed soon,
He comes home with the moon,
And is out at high noon,
    While his bairns are breadless.

A horn and a Dutch axe, his sleeve must be flecked,
His hair fair as flax, his gown must be specked,
Thus took I your tax, thus are my books blacked.

1ST DEMON   So great you may wax that what be lacked
    Be shown;
With words will thou fill us,
But now thy name tell us.

TUTIVILLUS   My name is Tutivillus
    My horn has blown;
Fragmina verborum, Tutivillus colligit horum,
Beelzebub algorum, Belial belium doliorum.

2ND DEMON   What, ye know your grammary and somewhat of art;
Had I but a penny to study I should start.

TUTIVILLUS   Of females a quantity here find I a part.

1ST DEMON   Tutivillus, let us see, God forbid we stay apart!

TUTIVILLUS   So jolly

256   Each lass in the land
            Ladylike here at hand,
            So fresh none may withstand,
                Leads men to folly.

            If she be never so foul a dowd, with her nets and her
                                                        [pins,
            The shrew herself can shroud, both her cheeks and her
                                                        [chins;
            She can caper full proud with japes and with gins,
            Her head high in a cloud, but not shamed by her sins
                Or evil;
            With this powder and paint,
            She plans to look quaint,
            She may smile like a saint,
                But at heart is a devil.

            She is horned like a cow, and full secret her sin;
            Her side gaiter hangs now, furred with a cat's skin,
            All these are for you, they have come of your kin.
2ND DEMON   Now, the best body art thou that ever came herein.
TUTIVILLUS   In fact,
            The fashion, I undertake,
            Brings wedlock to break,
            And sinful living for its sake,
                And many a broken contract.

            Yet a point not to shun, I tell you before,
            More liars shall hither come than a thousand score;
            Their swearing grieves God's son and pains him more
                                                        [and more,
            Therefore with us they are one in hell for evermore.
                I say thus,
            That raisers of false tax
            And gatherers of green wax,
            Diabolus est mendax
                Et pater eius.

            A point of the new mode yet my tale I shall spin,
            Of pranked up gowns and shoulders high set and
                                        [moss and flock sewn within;
            To have this fashion they would fret, they say it is no
                                                        [sin,

                        [87]

But on such fellows I me set and clap them cheek and
    No nay.   [chin,
David in his psaltery says thus,
That to hell they be thrust,
Cum suis adinvencionibus,
    For once and for ay.   295

Yet of these churchchatterers here is an army,
Of bargainers and usurers, and lovers of simony,
Of gossips and scandalmongers, God casts them out
                                        [truly,
From his temple all such misdoers, I catch them to me
    Full soon;
For written I know it is
In gospel without amiss,
Et eam fecistis
    Speluncam latronum.

Yet of the sins seven something special
Now quickly to reckon that runs over all;
These lads strut even as lords most royal,
To be pictured even in royal robes withal,
    As kings;
His tail may none dock it,
A codpiece like a pocket,
He scorns not to cock it
    When he his tail wrings.

His buttocks they bulge like a fulling mill clog,
His head like a stook bristles like a hog,
His blown up belly filled full like a frog,
This Jelian Jook drives he no dog
    To shelter.
But with your yellow locks,
For all your many mocks,
Ye shall climb on hell's cross
    With a halfpenny halter.

And Tess with trifles both crisp and of silk,
Look well to your quiffles about your neck as milk;
With ribands and bridals of Satan your sire,
With his knacks and his idols for her gay attire,
    This wench knave;

328

It is open behind,
Before it is pinned;
Beware of a west wind
        Your smock lest it wave.

Of ire and of envy find I more to show,
Of covetousness and gluttony, and many more also;
They call and they cry, "Go we now, go!
I die I am so dry!" and there sit they so
        All night;
They cackle and cavil,
Singing of evil,
These are hounds of hell,
        That is their right.

In sleuth then they sin, God's works they not work;
To belch they begin, and spue what may irk;
His head must be held in, there in the murk,
Then defies he with din the bells of the kirk,
        When they clatter;
The clerk he would hang
For he the bell rang,
But dares not him bang
        For fear of a halter.

And ye gatemen of the stews, ye lechers aloft,
Your bale now brews, adulterers full oft,
Your pleasures ye lose, but I shall set you soft;
Your sorrow accrues, come to my croft
        All ye;
All harlots and whores,
Each bawd that procures,
That fetches and lures,
        Welcome to my see!

Ye lubbers and liars, and all ye who thieve,
Ye foul-tempered knifers, who cause men to grieve,
Wreckers, extortioners, my welcome receive,
False jurors and usurers, that to simony cleave,
        Here dwell;
Gamesters and dicers,
False deeds forgers,
Slanderers and backbiters,
        Welcome to hell.

[89]

1ST DEMON   Many had such a trick, both furious and fell,   368
The good were few to pick, I had much marvel,
And thought it drew near the prick.

2ND DEMON   Sir, a word of counsel;
Souls came so thick of late now to hell
    As ever;
Our porter at hell-gate
Is in so sad a strait,
Up early and down late,
    Rest has he never.

1ST DEMON   Thou art peerless of those that ever yet knew I,
When I will may I go if thou be by;
Go we now, we two.

2ND DEMON   Sir, I am ready.

1ST DEMON   Take our rolls also, ye know the cause why;
    Do come
And hearken this day.

2ND DEMON   Sir, as well as I may.

1ST DEMON   *Qui vero mala*
    In ignem eternum.

Trump.

JESUS   Each creature be intent
On the message I you bring,
This wicked world is spent,
And I come crowned as king;
My father of heaven has me sent
To judge your deeds and make ending;
Come has the day of judgement,
Of sorrow may every sinner sing.

The day has come for caitiffness,
All those find care that are unclean,
The day of battle and bitterness,
Full long a-coming has it been;
The day of dread to more and less,
Of joy, of trembling pain extreme,
For each creature's wickedness
May say, alas this day is seen.

Here may ye see my wounds so wide
That I suffered for your misdeed.

[90]

404
Through heart, head, foot, hand and side,
Not for my guilt but for your need.
Behold both back, body and side,
How dearly for you I did bleed,
These bitter pains I would abide
Your bliss to buy as was decreed.

My body was scourged with ill will,
My bitter fate I had to meet;
On cross they hung me on a hill,
Blue and bloody thus was I beat;
With crown of thorn thrusting full ill,
A spear into my heart they sent;
My heart blood spared they not to spill.
Man, for thy love I was beset.

The Jews spat on me spitefully,
They spared me no more than a thief;
When they me smote I stood meekly,
To them I gave no kind of grief.
Behold, mankind, this same am I,
That for thee suffered such mischief,
Thus was I slain for thy folly,
Man, loved I thee beyond belief.

Thus was I served thy sorrow to slake;
Man, thus behoved thy pledge to be;
In all my woe no wrath did wake
My will it was for love of thee.
Man, for sorrow ought thee to quake,
This dreadful day this sight to see;
All this I suffered for thy sake;
Say, man, what suffered thou for me?

Then turning to the GOOD SOULS *he says to them:*

My blessed bairns on my right hand,
Your doom this day not dread ye need,
For all your joy is to command,
Your life in pleasure ye shall lead.
Come to that kingdom that ay shall stand,
That is prepared for your good deed,
Full blithely, there, ye understand,
Much joy in heaven is your meed.

[91]

When I was hungry ye me fed,   442
To slake my thirst ye were full free;
When I was naked ye me clad,
Ye would no sorrow on me see;
In prison when I was hard stead
On my penance ye had pity;
Full sick when I was brought to bed,
Kindly ye came to comfort me.

When I was worn and weariest,
Ye harboured me full easily,
Full glad then were ye of your guest,
And shared my poverty piteously;
Betimes ye brought me of the best
And made my bed where I should lie,
Therefore in heaven shall be your rest,
In joy and bliss to bide me by.

1ST GOOD SOUL   Lord, when had thou such great need?
Hunger or thirst, how might it be?

2ND GOOD SOUL   When was our heart free to feed?
In prison, when might we thee see?

3RD GOOD SOUL   When sick or naked had thou need?
And when helped we to harbour thee?

4TH GOOD SOUL   When had thou need of such a deed?
When did we all these things to thee?

JESUS   My blessed bairns, I shall you say
What time these deeds were to me done;
When any that need had night or day,
Asked of you help and had it soon;
Your free heart said them never nay,
Early nor late, midnight, nor noon,
As often times as they would pray,
They need but ask and have their boon.

Then shall he speak to the EVIL SOULS.

Ye cursed caitiffs of Cain's kin,
Ye gave no comfort to my care
Now ye from me apart shall spin,
And dwell for ever in despair;
Your bitter bales cease not therein,

[92]

479

That ye shall suffer once in there,
Thus be ye served for your deep sin,
For the dark deeds which ye all share.

When I had need of meat and drink,
Caitiffs, ye chased me from your gate;
When benched as sires and dressed in mink,
Weary and wet I had to wait,
Yet none of you would on me think,
To have pity on my poor estate;
Therefore to hell I shall you sink,
Well are ye worthy to go there straight.

When I was sick and sorriest
Ye came not near for I was poor;
In prison fast when I was pressed
My plight ye all chose to ignore,
When I knew never where to rest,
With blows ye drove me from your door,
Your pride ye ever did attest,
My flesh, my blood, ye oft forswore.

Clotheless when that I was cold,
Though for you I had gone naked,
My miseries saw ye manifold,
But none of you my sorrows slaked.
But ever forsook me young and old,
Therefore shall ye now be forsaken.

1ST EVIL SOUL   Lord, when had thou, that all has,
Hunger or thirst as God no less?
When was it thou in prison was?
When naked thou or harbourless?

2ND EVIL SOUL   When did we see thee sick, alas!
And showed thee such unkindness?

3RD EVIL SOUL   When did we thee helpless pass?
When did we thee this wickedness?

4TH EVIL SOUL   Alas, for dole this day!
Alas, I ever thee annoyed!
Now am I damned for ay,
Nor may this doom avoid.

[93]

JESUS
Caitiffs, alas, ye did forbid   516
The needful that asked in my name,
Ye heard them nought, your ears were hid,
All help to them ye did disdain;
Ye me with that unkindness chid,
Therefore ye bear this bitter blame,
To the least of mine when ye ought did
To me ye did the very same.

My chosen children, come to me!
With me to dwell now shall ye wend,
Where joy and bliss ever shall be,
To live in pleasure without end.

Ye cursed creatures, from me ye flee,
In hell to dwell without an end!
There shall ye nought but sorrow see,
And sit by Satan's side, the fiend.

1ST DEMON
Do now forth go, bustle and rush again!
Unto endless woe, everlasting pain;
Nay tarry not so, not here is our domain.

2ND DEMON
Hie hitherward, ho, hurry this mob amain!
    Look out!
Nibble the alto shall ye,
Then the treble falls to me,
Now to the devil go we,
    With this whole rout.

TUTIVILLUS
Your lives are forlorn, and come has your care;
Ye may curse ye were born, the bodies ye bear,
And your fathers before, so cursed ye are.

1ST DEMON
Ye may bemoan the morn and day that ye were
    Of your mother
First born for to be,
For what woe comes to thee.

2ND DEMON
Each of you may see
    Sorrow strike the other.

Where are the goods and the gold that ye gathered
                                    [together?
That merry company so bold riding hither and thither?

[94]

TUTIVILLUS   Gay girdles, dagged hoods that fold, pranked gowns,
                                              [whither?
553   Of your wits have ye hold, ye brought nought hither
                    But sorrow,
                And your sins in your necks.
1ST DEMON   Curse them that ought recks
                He comes too late that beckons,
                    Your bodies to borrow.

2ND DEMON   Sir, I would give them a scold, and make them be
                                              [known,
                They were haughty and bold, great boasts have they
                                              . [blown;
                Your proud prancing, behold, away has it flown,
                Of man's error ye told, but forgot quite your own.
TUTIVILLUS   Moreover,
                Their neighbours they grudge,
                Themselves them did judge,
                But now must they budge,
                    Their saints' days are over.

1ST DEMON   Their neighbours they rated with words full ill,
                The worst ay they stated, yet had no skill.
2ND DEMON   With pence never sated, but stole and kept still;
                As misers calculated, but had no will
                    For heart's fare;
                But rich and ill-deedy,
                Gluttonous and greedy,
                Ever nipping yet needy,
                    Your goods never spare.

TUTIVILLUS   For the wealth that ye spared and did extortion,
                For your children ye cared, you hired your son,
                All to us now has fared and your years are run,
                In hell be it shared, lame malison
                    To bind it.
                Ye set nought by cursing,
                Nor no such small thing.
1ST DEMON   Nought but praise at the parting
                    For now must ye find it.

                With sweethearts and females your wedlock ye break;
                Tell me what it avails so merry to make?

See so falsely it fails.   588

2ND DEMON   Sir, I dare undertake
They will tell no tales, but see they so quake
    Like sheep;
He that to that game goes,

TUTIVILLUS   Trots lamely on old toes.
The praise that ye grudge those,
    From mind I did sweep.

1ST DEMON   Sir, may they meet their doom which long has been
                                                    [knelling;
Will ye witness their gloom.

2ND DEMON   Thou art ay telling;
Now shall they have room in pitch and tar dwelling,
Their grief they will groom and ay be a-yelling
    In our care.

TUTIVILLUS   By your leave may we move you?
1ST DEMON   If you can I shall prove you!
2ND DEMON   Yet tonight to improve you
    See a feat of ill fare.

TUTIVILLUS   For those cursed and forsworn and each that here wends,
Blow, wolfs-head and out-horn now, namely my
                                                    [friends.

Trump.
1ST DEMON   Ill luck were ye born, your own shame you rends,
That shall ye find ere morn.

2ND DEMON   Come now with fiends
    To your anger;
Your deeds damn you hither
Come, go we together,
We have you on tether,
    Come, tarry no longer.

1ST GOOD SOUL We love, thee, Lord, in everything,
That for thine own has ordained thus,
That we may have now our dwelling
In heaven's bliss given unto us.
Therefore full boldly may we sing
As we mount up thus;
Make we all mirth and loving
With *Te Deum Laudamus*.

[96]

Notes to the Plays (Part Four)

THE TALENTS

This play is unique in medieval drama for the extended treatment of its theme which, when it appears in other cycles, is but an insignificant fragment of the drama of the crucifixion. Such a play at this stage of the Cycle might be inserted for tactical reasons. If actors and action are continuous *The Talents* certainly allows the actor playing the role of Christ a much needed rest. The play begins and ends with the familiar nine-line stanzas of the Wakefield Master and throughout it is informed with his characteristic bouncing vigour and skilful handling of dialogue. It forms the most striking contrast in tone, intensity, and subject matter to *The Crucifixion* which precedes it, and to *The Deliverance of Souls* which follows it. Its theme, its position in the cycle, and its treatment illustrate the deliberate art of an outstanding dramatist.

Tired tyrants getting into bed, leaving instructions for their menials not to disturb them, are such regular occurrences in medieval drama as to conform to a formula. However, this is the only instance in the Wakefield Plays when recourse is had to such a formula. Pilate's couch is probably positioned on the inner section of his pageant in front of which a curtain can be drawn, so that he at least seems undisturbed by the preliminary dialogue of the Torturers which is played on the fore part of his pageant (73–182).

The Third Torturer appears to yield the seamless coat too readily to Pilate, and, indeed, contrary to his previous stubbornness (353). Such a change can be made dramatically acceptable if Pilate's threats are interpreted as intending to transform the Third Torturer, who is free in the feudal sense, into a bondman (355–356).

A hint as to the manner of dicing the Torturers adopt is given by Pilate (346):

'Yea, but I play not the game with a puff or a blow.'

The Torturers hold the three dice in their cupped hands into which they puff and blow before throwing, a quirk of gaming unchanged by the centuries.

The moralizing at the end of the play (368–412), breath-taking in its sudden conversion of the seamiest villains of the cycle, nevertheless should be played straight. It is easy and superficially effective to play it tongue-in-cheek, with the Torturers leering at their own hypocritical piety ['How think ye of this?' (403)], but to treat their very last appearance in the Cycle cynically is to misrepresent the essential spirit of a great religious drama.

THE DELIVERANCE OF SOULS

The acting areas specified in this play are paradise, limbo, and hell. Dramatically it is important that Adam and Eve should be led by Jesus back to paradise; theologically the righteous souls cannot accompany Jesus to heaven until the Last Judgement. Limbo, by definition, is the region on the border of hell, the abode of the just who died before Christ's coming, and of unbaptized infants. It is therefore in limbo where Adam and Eve and the prophets are located, but a limbo which is part of hell's outer defences over which, until the Deliverance, Satan and his devils hold sway. Limbo might be represented dramatically as a fortress that guards hell-mouth. The contest between Jesus and Satan is conceived in heroic terms, and the conflict in hell with its frequent references to siege-warfare supports such a setting. That the Souls are 'sparred in a special space' (104) might indicate that they are confined by a stage portcullis. Ribald is later urged to spar the gates and 'set the watches on the wall' (120–121), which also strongly suggests siege preparations in a fortress. It is certainly these gates which crack and collapse (209), giving rise to Ribald's despairing cry 'Limbo is lost, alas!' (213). *The Last Judgement*, a painting by Stephan Lochner (c 1405–1451), depicts heaven and hell as two opposing towers. Hell's tower burns and the damned are being dragged to the lower left of the picture (stage left) to what one assumes is the pit of hell.

The main problem in Jesus leading the Souls out of a fortress rather than out of a gaping hell-mouth is that such a representation appears to be contrary to most early medieval iconography on the subject, in which Jesus holds out his hand to Adam and Eve who stand within the very jaws of hell. On the other hand, sparring the jaws of hell yet leaving sufficient room for its inmates to move, to speak, and to be seen, calls for a hell-mouth of very considerable dimensions, and even then it may fail to represent adequately the 'gates of hell' or 'the watches on the wall'. The illustration of the Valenciennes Mystery Play in K. Mantzius' *A History of Theatrical Art in Ancient and Modern Times* shows both the tower of limbo, with the Souls peering through prison-bars while a cannon engulfed in fire looms above them, and hell, stage left of limbo, with winged fiends watching from the walls above and others issuing from the jaws below. The Anglo-Norman *Resurrection* in its arrangement of mansions includes a limbo (jaiole)

placed next to hell, the former opposing the sepulchre and the latter
heaven (E. K. Chambers, *The Mediaeval Stage,* ii. 83), and in the
fifteenth-century French *Resurrection* 'the aforesaid tower of Limbo
shall be adorned all round with curtains of black cloth', which later
are 'subtly drawn aside' (Allardyce Nicoll, *Masks, Mimes, and Miracles,*
204).

Hell-mouth or hell-pit, however, must be included, for such is
certainly Satan's destination (360). That Satan speaks no more once
he has fallen into hell-pit is a factor relevant to the main staging problem. His fall from limbo's tower to hell-pit, if so staged, may aptly
recall Lucifer's fall from heaven.

The heroic element in this Wakefield play is emphasized by Jesus
alone facing the combined forces of hell. In most other versions of
The Harrowing of Hell Jesus is supported by a legion of angels, and it is
Michael's specific charge to bind Satan and to lead the Souls to paradise (York, Chester, and Cornish Plays). Satan's confrontation of
Jesus, opposing his spear or trident against Jesus' tree-cross and banner,
is the climax of the scene.

Sound effects are in this play particularly important, because on the
one hand the deafening disharmony of hell must contrast with the
defiant song of the hopeful Souls who, according to the original stage
direction, sing the first verse of *Salvator Mundi* (44), and in their procession to paradise the *Te Deum.*

THE RESURRECTION

The two main playing areas
are Pilate's Court and the sepulchre. The Centurion makes his
entry on horseback [stage direction following (44) *Tunc veniet
centurio velut miles equitans*], most
probably in 'the place' and could
pass by the sepulchre and address
his first speech to the cross, which might, with considerable dramatic
effect be left in position from *The Crucifixion* to *The Judgement.*

Pilate, Annas, Caiaphas, and the four soldiers are all located on
Pilate's pageant at the beginning of the play. The soldiers are later
dispatched (201) to the sepulchre where they take up their positions,
one on each side of a rectangular tomb. The producer has the particular problem of making sure that the actor playing Jesus can get
himself into the tomb unobserved by the audience between the end
of *The Deliverance of Souls* and the beginning of *The Resurrection.* If

in medieval times the two plays were performed by separate and mobile companies of guildsmen there would have been no great staging problem involved. If, however, it is wished to emphasize the continuity of place, action, and performer, then either a curtain must screen the tomb on the pageant, and Jesus after *The Deliverance of Souls* enters the tomb unseen, or before the dialogue of *The Resurrection* begins Joseph of Arimathea, Nicodemus, Simon of Cyrene, and John the Evangelist carry in the tomb containing Jesus and place it on the pageant. It is interesting to note that in the *Ludus Coventriae* while Jesus is still on the cross another actor plays the role of Christ's Spirit and descends into hell, and it is only subsequent to this action that Jesus is taken down from the cross and buried.

The Soldiers having propped themselves against the tomb go to sleep, but at least one of the Soldiers witnesses the resurrection (455), and evidence from art forms and other cycles representing this episode suggests that usually while two Soldiers are fast asleep two are staring, amazed and helpless, as Jesus steps from the tomb. The actual resurrection begins with the entry of two Angels singing, strongly supported by the heavenly choir, *Christus Resurgens,* they lay the stone aside and Jesus rises holding the cross-banner, the symbol of the resurrection ('With him a cross on his banner soon he displayed' *Ancient Cornish Drama, The Resurrection,* 527), and steps on to one of the Soldiers, a regular feature in the medieval iconographic treatment of this subject and specifically referred to in the Chester *Resurrection* (270–277):

> 1ST SOLDIER That time that he his way took,
> Durst I neither speak nor look,
> But for fear I lay and quook,
> And lay in a sound dream.
>
> He set his foot upon my back,
> That every limb began to crack;
> I would not abide such another shock
> For all Jerusalem.

Jesus speaks from near the tomb and then withdraws. The two Angels sit on the tomb, one at the head and one at the feet and themselves withdraw after they have spoken to the three Marys (399). The Angels may have been played by boys as suggested by the Chester *Resurrection* (425/6):

> 1ST ANGEL   Woman, why weepest thou so ay?
> MARY MAGDALENE   Son, for my lord is taken away.

[100]

A young boy's treble might equip him splendidly for the angelic choir, but it seems rather damaging to an Angel's dignity to be called 'Son'.

The soldiers on waking are still half in a trance and are slow to realize the full implications for them of the resurrection. Their first impulse is to lie to Pilate, but their later unanimous decision for truth approximates in dramatic feeling to the evangelistic zeal of the *Ludus Coventriae* Soldiers whose enthusiasm, however, is greatly moderated by Pilate's promise of meed.

The Ancient Cornish Drama and the *Ludus Coventriae* indicate that Mary Magdalene meets Jesus at a little distance from the tomb. Jesus, according to a stage direction in the Chester play (432), appears dressed in an alb and carrying a cross-staff. Certainly in this Wakefield play, as in the biblical version, Mary Magdalene mistakes Jesus for a gardener (563), and a gardener's costume together with a spade is accorded Jesus in the Lincoln misericord.

The Pilgrims

'fysher pagent' under the title in the manuscript indicates that the responsibility for staging the play was undertaken by the Wakefield Fishermen's guild, a powerful enough body in the days when the River Calder could be relied on for a rich yield.

The pilgrim's habit [*hic venit jhesus in apparatu peregrini* stage direction following (97)] might most simply be conveyed by scrip and staff. The stage directions give little help on Jesus' vanishing from the disciples' sight:

> *Tunc recumbent et sedebit ihesus in medio eorum, tunc benedicet ihesus panem et fanget in tribus partibus, et postea evanebit ab oculis eorum. . . .*
> [stage direction following (290).]

A trap-door near where Jesus is sitting might be a possible solution. There is ample evidence of there being trap-doors on the medieval pageants.

The action of the play takes place partly on the road between Jerusalem and Emmaus (1–278), and partly in the house at Emmaus (279–380). The first part, comprising the journey, is best portrayed moving in 'the place', the second part on a pageant, which in all the other Cycles is expressly referred to as the Castle of Emmaus.

Thomas of India

The play is simply staged on a single pageant with most of the characters making their entries from behind, but perhaps Thomas, because of his initial soliloquy, making his entry from 'the place'. Mary Magdalene's part in the play appears to end at (64) and, although not indicated by any stage direction in the manuscript, it is appropriate for her to make her exit at this point. She is not present when Jesus appears to the disciples (83) nor when Thomas in turn answers the arguments of the disciples. Had Mary Magdalene been present Thomas would certainly have turned his attention to her in his refutation of the evidence for Jesus' resurrection.

Jesus makes three appearances in the play (83, 91, 311). The persistent use of a trap-door for these appearances would be damaging to the effect required; curtains might be used with greater dignity. As indicated by (86) Jesus is dressed in a red garment. He sings on his first two entries [*pax vobis et non tardabit, hec est dies quam fecit dominus* (83)], and although not specified in the original text his third entry should also be attended with music (311).

Thomas' first speech (168–179) is a soliloquy with the dramatic intention of conveying to the audience that although he may appear to strut as proudly as a peacock (168) and in the subsequent scene seem to be impatient with the disciples and scornful of Christ's power, he nevertheless has been profoundly moved by the tragedy of the cross. In effect he is saying 'I am not what I am', and with this the dramatic soliloquy has undergone a startling development.

There are two matters in this play which refer specifically to the previous play *The Pilgrims*. The term Emmaus castle (263) suggests the setting for the scene in *The Pilgrims* in which Jesus breaks the bread, and that the bread is broken cleanly in three as though cut by a knife is indicated by (265) and by the *Ludus Coventriae Christ's Appearance to Cleophas and Luke* (286).

THE ASCENSION

The play is incomplete, but the four hundred and eleven lines that remain represent the average length of the plays in the Wakefield Cycle, and indeed the main action is completed in *The Ascension* as it stands. However, both verse and dramatic structure are sufficiently tedious to dissuade most modern producers from taking further interest.

The most fascinating matter raised by the play is the stage management of the actual ascension. It takes place on a hill (45) or pageant, and when Jesus is ready to ascend he calls for the clouds to open (252), and it is enclosed in these clouds that Mary and the disciples watch him rise to heaven (300, 349). The stage cloud is apparently an extremely firm structure, worked by pulleys concealed above the acting area, made probably of wood as suggested by the miniature in the Chartres museum, which opens to allow Jesus to secure himself within it, leaving, below the cloud as he ascends, the bottom of his gown and his feet still visible to those looking up from the ground. The cloud is obviously a highly organized, smoothly working piece of stage machinery. In this play the Angels sing as Jesus ascends, but in the Chester play Jesus himself sings and stays suspended in mid-air for some considerable time. Most Ascension plays refer to Jesus' return to earth at the Last Judgement as being in the same manner as his ascension (York, 219; Chester, 160; Wakefield, 262).

This form of raising and lowering characters on the medieval pageant is common to all the cycles. Although the *Ludus Coventriae Ascension* is too fragmentary to yield evidence on this score, *The Assumption of the Virgin* from the same cycle makes repeated references to this two-way vertical movement. Most memorable perhaps is Jesus' plea in the York *Ascension* (175):

Send down a cloud, father! For
I come to thee, my father dear.

THE JUDGEMENT

The beginning of this play is missing in the manuscript. The producer has the choice of presenting it as it stands or of borrowing the first 144 lines of the York play. If the latter course is adopted, the whole Cycle may be given firmer shape by God's first speech: in *The Creation* God made man, in *The Judgement* man's life on earth will be brought to an end [York, *The Judgement Day* (56)]. There may, however, be stronger reasons for staging the Wakefield fragment as a play complete in itself. The York play is solemn and uniform in tone; the Wakefield play, which appears to be a zestful revision of the York play, or the revision of a common ancestor, abounds with interpolations which are the work of the Wakefield Master who imparts those indelible characteristics which might jar against rather than complement the uniformity of the York version. Undoubtedly the play can be effectively staged with the text as we have it. If at the very beginning the trump sounds, and the scattered Souls, Good and Evil, from their several entries move slowly into 'the place', which in effect will then be filled with nearly every actor taking part in the whole Cycle, a fitting prologue to the grand finale has been found.

Heaven, earth, and hell are the critical acting areas in the play. Paradise may also be included if the passage of the righteous Souls to heaven is to be shown. Jesus, after their deliverance from limbo, set them in paradise to await the Last Judgement.

More than in any other play there needs to be a very firm means of communication between heaven and earth. The Angel descends to part the Souls (73), Jesus descends to sit in judgement (83), and at the end of the play all the Good Souls are led into heaven by Jesus and the Angels, all singing the *Te Deum*. A stout staircase is called for, built either inside or outside heaven's tower.

So many medieval works of art depicting the Last Judgement show the Angels slightly above Jesus, holding in their hands the hammer, the nails, the crown of thorns, and sometimes the cross. This may be reproduced in the staging if, when Jesus descends to sit in majesty on earth, his throne should be placed immediately beneath heaven's tower from which the angels display the instruments of torture. A Chester stage direction, while supporting this arrangement of the Angels, suggests that Jesus, instead of being enthroned on earth, is suspended in mid-air on a cloud:

> *Finitis Lamentationibus mortuorum, descendet Iesus quasi in nube, si fieri poterit; Quia secundum Doctorum Opiniones in Aere prope terram iudicabit filius Dei. Stabunt Angeli cum Cruce, Corona Spinea, lancea, aliisque Instrumentis, omnia demonstrantes.*
>
> [Chester, *The Last Judgement*, following (356).]

If presentation is linear then hell will be opposed to heaven, that is to the left of Jesus as he sits in judgement. If presentation is in the round, and the usual conventions are being observed, then heaven will be to the east and hell to the north. At the parting of souls the good shall stand at the right of the throne and the evil at the left, and when the devils garner the Evil Souls into hell (612), they drag them from the east, probably through the south and west points, to hustle them north into hell-mouth.

The devils all carry scrolls on which are inscribed the names of the damned (183, 212, 224, 380), but these should be easily disposed of, tucked in a belt or a pouch, because the devils will need both hands to harry the Evil Souls into hell. Many medieval tympana and indeed also the Chester play (376) suggest that the devils carried their victims to the everlasting bonfire.

Perhaps no play in the range of medieval drama is richer in its references to the contemporary costume. Dramatic effectiveness is gained by dressing the Evil Souls in compliance with the suggestions in the text and directing the devils' speeches to the characters wearing the corresponding costumes. The producer may wish to include an even more august hierarchy of Souls, Good and Evil, which, as at Chester, will contain popes, emperors, kings and queens.

END OF PART FOUR

Finis

[104]